More Than Just

Internet Resources

Step 1 Connect to OK Math Online glencoe.com

Step 2 Connect to online resources by using QuickPass codes. You can connect directly to the chapter you want.

OK3470c1

Enter this code with the appropriate chapter number.

For Students

Connect to the student edition ***eBook*** that contains all of the following online assets. You don't need to take your textbook home every night.

- Personal Tutor
- Extra Examples
- Self-Check Quizzes
- Multilingual eGlossary
- Concepts in Motion
- Chapter Test Practice
- Test Practice
- Study to Go
- Hotmath Math Homework Help Homework Help

For Teachers

Connect to professional development content at glencoe.com and the ***eBook AdvanceTracker*** at AdvanceTracker.com.

For Parents

Connect to glencoe.com for access to the ***eBook*** and all the resources for students and teachers that are listed above.

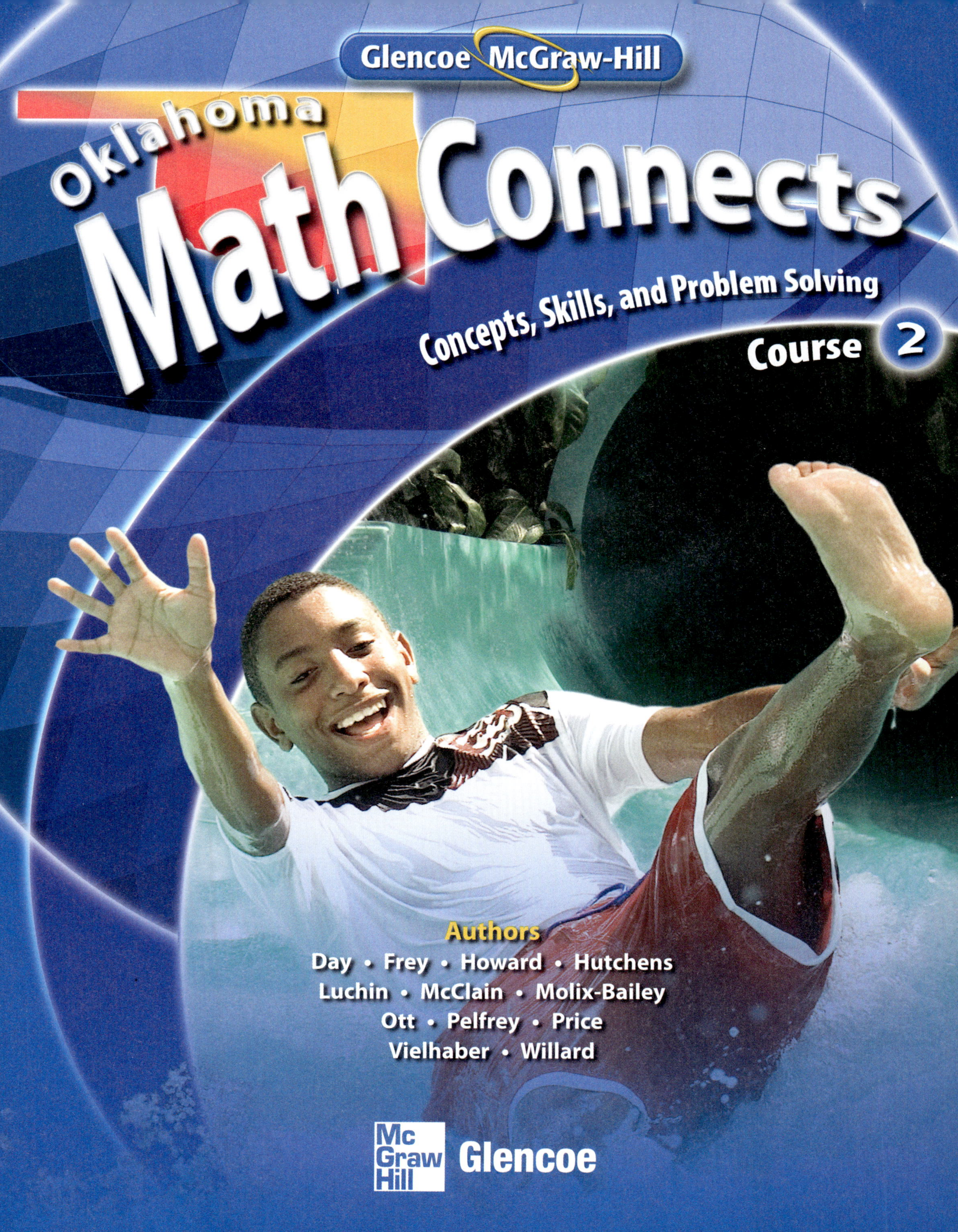
Glencoe McGraw-Hill
Oklahoma
Math Connects
Concepts, Skills, and Problem Solving
Course 2
Authors
Day • Frey • Howard • Hutchens
Luchin • McClain • Molix-Bailey
Ott • Pelfrey • Price
Vielhaber • Willard
Mc Graw Hill Glencoe

About the Cover

Nothing beats the thrill of a giant waterslide! Next time you are at a water park, think about math. The waterslide is exciting because there is a big vertical drop in a small horizontal distance. In math, that is expressed as the ratio $\frac{\text{rise}}{\text{run}}$, which is called *slope*. You'll learn more about slope in Chapter 6.

Cover image photographed on location courtesy Busch Gardens/Adventure Island, Tampa, Florida. Credit Richard Hutchings.

About the Graphics

Twisted torus. Created with *Mathematica*.
A torus with a rose-shaped cross section is constructed. Then the cross section is rotated around its center as it moves along a circle to form a twisted torus. For more information, and for programs to construct such graphics, see: www.wolfram.com/r/textbook.

Photo Credits:

vi–vii Panoramic Images/Getty Images; **OK0–OK1** National Geographic/Getty Images; **OK6** G.K. Vikki Hart/Getty Images; **OK12** G.K. Vikki Hart/Getty Images; **OK22** (tb) Adam Hart-Davis/Photo Researchers; **OK28** CMCD/Getty Images.

The McGraw-Hill Companies

Send all inquiries to:
Glencoe/McGraw-Hill
8787 Orion Place
Columbus, OH 43240-4027

ISBN: 978-0-07-892347-0
MHID: 0-07-892347-6

Printed in the United States of America.

3 4 5 6 7 8 9 10 DOW 18 17 16 15 14 13 12 11 10

Contents in Brief

Authors

Roger Day, Ph.D.
Mathematics Department Chair
Pontiac Township High School
Pontiac, Illinois

Patricia Frey, Ed.D.
Math Coordinator at Westminster Community Charter School
Buffalo, New York

Arthur C. Howard
Mathematics Teacher
Houston Christian High School
Houston, Texas

Deborah A. Hutchens, Ed.D.
Principal
Chesapeake, Virginia

Beatrice Luchin
Mathematics Consultant
League City, Texas

Kay McClain, Ed.D.
Assistant Professor
Vanderbilt University
Nashville, Tennessee

OK Math Online Meet the Authors at glencoe.com

Rhonda J. Molix-Bailey
Mathematics Consultant
Mathematics by Design
DeSoto, Texas

Jack M. Ott, Ph.D.
Distinguished Professor of Secondary Education Emeritus
University of South Carolina
Columbia, South Carolina

Ronald Pelfrey, Ed.D.
Mathematics Specialist
Appalachian Rural Systemic Initiative and Mathematics Consultant
Lexington, Kentucky

Jack Price, Ed.D.
Professor Emeritus
California State Polytechnic University
Pomona, California

Kathleen Vielhaber
Mathematics Consultant
St. Louis, Missouri

Teri Willard, Ed.D.
Assistant Professor
Department of Mathematics
Central Washington University
Ellensburg, Washington

Contributing Author

FOLDABLES™ **Dinah Zike**
Educational Consultant
Dinah-Might Activities, Inc.
San Antonio, Texas

Master Oklahoma's Priority Academic Student Skills in 3 Easy Steps

1 Practice the Standards throughout the Lessons

- The lessons address Oklahoma's Priority Academic Student Skills (PASS) for Mathematics.
- Your textbook also contains more lessons for Oklahoma. Look for the *Focus on Oklahoma* section after the Table of Contents.
- Lessons contain Test Practice questions that are aligned to Oklahoma's Priority Academic Student Skills. These questions are like those on the OCCT and they will provide you with ongoing opportunities to sharpen your test-taking skills.

Tulsa, Oklahoma Skyline

Oklahoma Reviewers

Each Oklahoma Reviewer gave feedback and suggestions for improving the effectiveness of the PreK–8 *Oklahoma Math Connects* program.

Kristi Adams
Mathematics Teacher
Owasso 6th Grade Center
Owasso, OK

Tom Dill
Math Teacher
Robert S. Kerr Elementary
Tulsa, OK

Lahonda Gardella
Mathematics Teacher
Monroney Middle School
Midwest City, OK

Robert Hanna
Mathematics Teacher
Monroney Middle School
Midwest City, OK

Teresa R. McCain
Kindergarten Teacher
Bixby North Elementary
Bixby, OK

Joe Mercier
Secondary Math Curriculum Specialist
Tulsa Public Schools
Tulsa, OK

Cathy O'Dell
Mathematics Teacher
Union High School
Tulsa, OK

Linda Scott
Mathematics Teacher
Brink Junior High School
Oklahoma City, OK

Tonya Williams
Mathematics Teacher
Edison Middle School
Tulsa, OK

2 Practice the Standards throughout the Chapter

- Every chapter contains two full pages of Test Practice. The Test Practice gives you a chance to put your math skills to use.

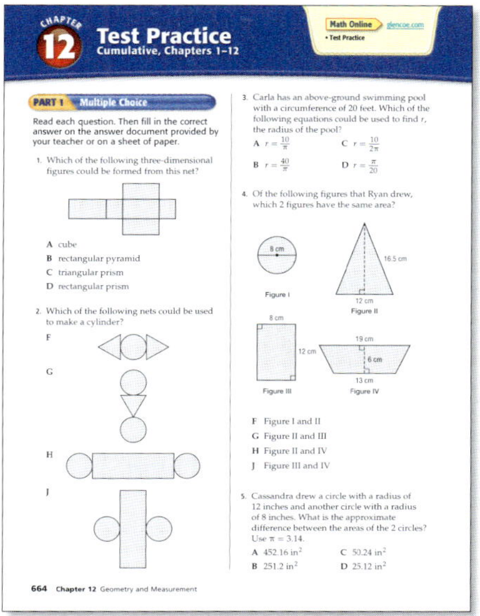
CHAPTER 12 Test Practice
Cumulative, Chapters 1–12

Math Online glencoe.com
• Test Practice

PART 1 Multiple Choice

Read each question. Then fill in the correct answer on the answer document provided by your teacher or on a sheet of paper.

1. Which of the following three-dimensional figures could be formed from this net?

A cube
B rectangular pyramid
C triangular prism
D rectangular prism

2. Which of the following nets could be used to make a cylinder?

F
G
H
J

3. Carla has an above-ground swimming pool with a circumference of 20 feet. Which of the following equations could be used to find r, the radius of the pool?

A $r = \frac{10}{\pi}$ C $r = \frac{10}{2\pi}$
B $r = \frac{40}{\pi}$ D $r = \frac{\pi}{20}$

4. Of the following figures that Ryan drew, which 2 figures have the same area?

8 cm
Figure I
16.5 cm
12 cm
Figure II
8 cm
12 cm
Figure III
19 cm
6 cm
13 cm
Figure IV

F Figure I and II
G Figure II and III
H Figure II and IV
J Figure III and IV

5. Cassandra drew a circle with a radius of 12 inches and another circle with a radius of 8 inches. What is the approximate difference between the areas of the 2 circles? Use $\pi = 3.14$.

A 452.16 in^2 C 50.24 in^2
B 251.2 in^2 D 25.12 in^2

664 Chapter 12 Geometry and Measurement

3 Practice the Standards Before the Test

- If you've followed steps 1 and 2, you should be more than ready for the OCCT test. But just in case you want to make sure, use the *Get Ready for the OCCT* section at the end of your book to practice questions that are organized by strand. Lesson references are included for you should you need a little refresher.

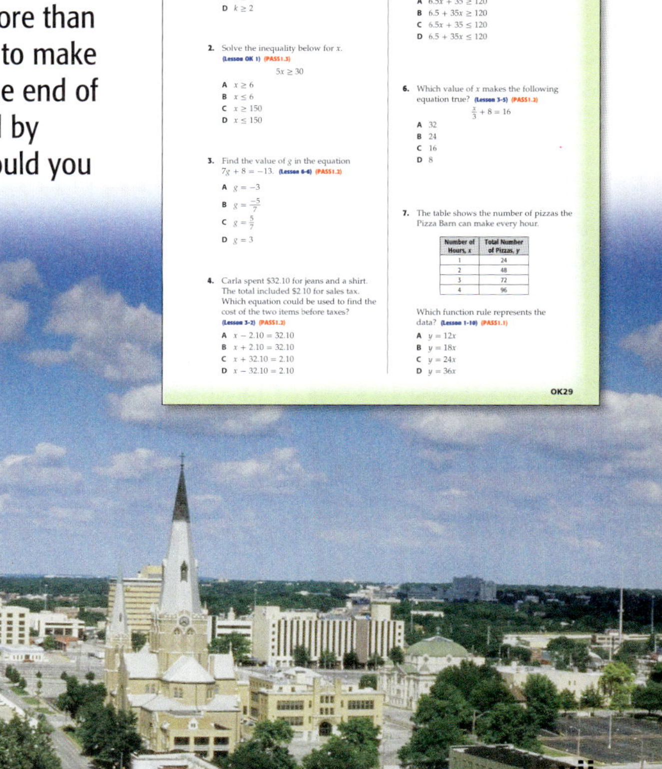
Get Ready for the OCCT

Algebraic Reasoning

1. Solve the inequality below for k. (Lesson OK 1) (PASS1.3)

$3k + 7 \geq 16$

A $k \leq 3$
B $k \leq 2$
C $k \geq 3$
D $k \geq 2$

2. Solve the inequality below for x. (Lesson OK 1) (PASS1.3)

$5x \geq 30$

A $x \geq 6$
B $x \leq 6$
C $x \geq 150$
D $x \leq 150$

3. Find the value of g in the equation $7g + 8 = -13$. (Lesson 6-4) (PASS1.2)

A $g = -3$
B $g = -\frac{5}{7}$
C $g = \frac{5}{7}$
D $g = 3$

4. Carla spent \$32.10 for jeans and a shirt. The total included \$2.10 for sales tax. Which equation could be used to find the cost of the two items before taxes? (Lesson 3-2) (PASS1.3)

A $x - 2.10 = 32.10$
B $x + 2.10 = 32.10$
C $x + 32.10 = 2.10$
D $x - 32.10 = 2.10$

5. Party House charges \$35 plus \$6.50 per person for a birthday party. Mrs. Lutz wants to spend no more than \$120 on her party. Which of the following inequalities could be used to solve this problem? (Lesson 6-6) (PASS1.3)

A $6.5x + 35 \geq 120$
B $6.5 + 35x \geq 120$
C $6.5x + 35 \leq 120$
D $6.5 + 35x \leq 120$

6. Which value of x makes the following equation true? (Lesson 3-5) (PASS1.2)

$\frac{x}{3} + 8 = 16$

A 32
B 24
C 16
D 8

7. The table shows the number of pizzas the Pizza Barn can make every hour.

Number of Hours, x	Total Number of Pizzas, y
1	24
2	48
3	72
4	96

Which function rule represents the data? (Lesson 1-10) (PASS1.1)

A $y = 12x$
B $y = 18x$
C $y = 24x$
D $y = 36x$

OK29

Consultants

Glencoe/McGraw-Hill wishes to thank the following professionals for their feedback. They were instrumental in providing valuable input toward the development of this program in these specific areas.

Mathematical Content

Viken Hovsepian
Professor of Mathematics
Rio Hondo College
Whittier, California

Grant A. Fraser, Ph.D.
Professor of Mathematics
California State University, Los Angeles
Los Angeles, California

Arthur K. Wayman, Ph.D.
Professor of Mathematics Emeritus
California State University, Long Beach
Long Beach, California

English Language Learners

Josefina V. Tinajero, Ph.D.
Dean, College of Education
The University of Texas at El Paso
El Paso, Texas

Gifted and Talented

Ed Zaccaro
Author and Consultant
Bellevue, Iowa

Graphing Calculator

Ruth M. Casey
National Mathematics Consultant
National Instructor, Teachers Teaching with Technology
Frankfort, Kentucky

Learning Disabilities

Kate Garnett, Ph.D.
Chairperson, Coordinator Learning Disabilities
School of Education
Department of Special Education
Hunter College, CUNY
New York, New York

Mathematical Fluency

Jason Mutford
Mathematics Instructor
Coxsackie-Athens Central School District
Coxsackie, New York

Pre-AP

Dixie Ross
Mathematics Teacher
Pflugerville High School
Pflugerville, Texas

Reading and Vocabulary

Douglas Fisher, Ph.D.
Professor of Language and Literacy Education
San Diego State University
San Diego, California

Lynn T. Havens
Director of Project CRISS
Kalispell, Montana

Reviewers

Each reviewer reviewed at least two chapters of the Student Edition, giving feedback and suggestions for improving the effectiveness of the mathematics instruction.

Sheila J. Allen
Mathematics Teacher
A.I. Root Middle School
Medina, Ohio

Paula Barnes
Mathematics Teacher
Minisink Valley CSD
Slate Hill, New York

Deborah Barnett
Mathematics Consultant
Lake Shore Public Schools
St. Clair Shores, Michigan

Laurel W. Blackburn
Teacher/Mathematics Department Chair
Hillcrest Middle School
Simpsonville, South Carolina

Drista Bowser
Mathematics Teacher
New Windsor Middle School
New Windsor, Maryland

Matthew Bowser
Teacher
Oil City Middle School
Oil City, Pennsylvania

Susan M. Brewer
Mathematics Teacher
Brunswick Middle School
Brunswick, Maryland

Patricia A. Bruzek
Mathematics Teacher
Glenn Westlake Middle School
Lombard, Illinois

Luanne Budd
Supervisor of Mathematics
Randolph Township
Randolph, New Jersey

Ella Violet Burch
Mathematics Teacher
Penns Grove High School
Carneys Point, New Jersey

Hailey Caldwell
7th Grade Mathematics Teacher
Greenville Middle Academy of Traditional Studies
Greenville, South Carolina

Linda K. Chandler
7th Grade Mathematics Teacher
Willard Middle School
Willard, Ohio

Debra M. Cline
7th Grade Mathematics Teacher
Thomas Jefferson Middle School
Winston-Salem, North Carolina

Randall G. Crites
Principal
Bunker R-3
Bunker, Missouri

Rose Dickinson
Science and Mathematics Teacher
Seneca Middle School
Clinton Township, Michigan

Joyce Wolfe Dodd
6th Grade Mathematics Teacher
Bryson Middle School
Simpsonville, South Carolina

John G. Doyle
Middle School Chairperson/ Mathematics Teacher
Wyoming Valley West School District
Kingston, Pennsylvania

Katie England
Secondary Mathematics Resource Teacher
Carroll County Public Schools
Westminster, Maryland

Carol A. Fincannon
6th Grade Mathematics Teacher
Southwood Middle School
Anderson, South Carolina

Sally J. Fulmer
7th Grade Mathematics Teacher/ Department Chair
C.E. Williams Middle School
Charleston, South Carolina

Marian K. Geist
Mathematics Teacher/Leadership Team
Baker Prairie Middle School
Canby, Oregon

Becky Gorniack
Middle School Mathematics Teacher
Fremont Middle School
Mundelein, Illinois

Donna Tutterow Hamilton
Curriculum Facilitator
Corriher Lipe Middle School
Landis, North Carolina

Danny Liebertz
8th Grade Mathematics Instructor
Fowler Middle School
Tigard, Oregon

Marie Merkel
Learning Support
North Pocono School District
Scranton, Pennsylvania

Tonda North
Algebra 1/8th Grade Mathematics Teacher
Indian Valley Middle School
Enon, Ohio

Natasha L.M. Nuttbrock
7th Grade Mathematics Teacher
Ferguson Middle School
Beavercreek, Ohio

Paul Penn
Curriculum Team Leader, Mathematics
Lima City Schools
Lima, Ohio

Casey Condran Plackett
7th Grade Mathematics Teacher
Kennedy Junior High School
Lisle, Illinois

E. Elaine Rafferty
Mathematics Consultant
Summerville, South Carolina

Edward M. Repko
Mathematics Teacher
Kilbourne Middle School
Worthington, Ohio

Alfreda Reynolds
Teacher
Charlotte-Mecklenburg School System
Charlotte, North Carolina

Alice Roberts
Mathematics Teacher
Oakdale Middle School
Ijamsville, Maryland

Jennifer L. Rodriguez
Mathematics Teacher
Glen Crest Middle School
Glen Ellyn, Illinois

Natalie Rohaley
6th Grade Mathematics
Riverside Middle School
Greer, South Carolina

Annika Lee Schilling
Mathematics and Science Teacher
Duniway Middle School
McMinnville, Oregon

Sherry Scott
Mathematics Teacher
E.A. Tighe School
Margate, New Jersey

Eli Shaheen
Mathematics Teacher/ Department Chair
Plum Senior High School
Pittsburgh, Pennsylvania

Kelly Eady Shaw
7th Grade Mathematics Teacher
Rawlinson Road Middle School
Rock Hill, South Carolina

Evan J. Silver
Mathematics Teacher
Walkersville Middle School
Frederick, Maryland

Charlotte A. Thore
6th/7th Grade Mathematics Teacher
Northwest School of the Arts
Charlotte, North Carolina

Gene A. Tournoux
Mathematics Department Head
Shaker Heights High School
Shaker Heights, Ohio

Pamela J. Trainer
Mathematics Teacher
Roland-Grise Middle School
Wilmington, North Carolina

David A. Trez
Mathematics Teacher
Bloomfield Middle School
Bloomfield, New Jersey

Pauline D. Von Hoffer
Mathematics Teacher
Wentzville School District
Wentzville, Missouri

Kentucky Consultants

Jenn Crase
8th Grade Mathematics Teacher/ Department Chair
South Oldham Middle School
Crestwood, Kentucky

Max DeBoer Lux
8th Grade Mathematics
Summit View Middle School
Independence, Kentucky

Jennifer Wells Phipps
Middle School Mathematics Teacher
Corbin Middle School
Corbin, Kentucky

Bea Torrence
Teacher/Mathematics Content Leader
Camp Ernst Middle School
Burlington, Kentucky

J. Ron Vanover
Advanced Placement Calculus
Boone County High School
Florence, Kentucky

Contents

Start Smart

OK PASS

***The prefix 6- on a standard reference was devised by the publisher to indicate that the lesson is a reinforcement of that particular Grade 6 standard.**

Unit 1

Algebra and Functions

Introduction to Algebra and Functions

OK PASS

TEST PRACTICE

H.O.T. Problems
Higher Order Thinking

Table of Contents

Chapter 2 Integers

OK PASS

Algebra: Linear Equations and Functions

OK PASS

TEST PRACTICE

H.O.T. Problems
Higher Order Thinking

Unit 2

Number Sense: Fractions

Fractions, Decimals, and Percents

OK PASS

ASSESSMENT

TEST PRACTICE

H.O.T. Problems

Higher Order Thinking

Applying Fractions

OK PASS

Table of Contents

Unit 3

Algebra and Number Sense: Proportions and Percents

Ratios and Proportions

OK PASS

TEST PRACTICE

H.O.T. Problems
Higher Order Thinking

Applying Percents

OK PASS

TEST PRACTICE

H.O.T. Problems
Higher Order Thinking

Unit 4

Statistics, Data Analysis, and Probability

Statistics: Analyzing Data

CHAPTER 9

Probability

OK PASS

TEST PRACTICE

H.O.T. Problems
Higher Order Thinking

Unit 5

Geometry and Measurement

Geometry: Polygons

OK PASS

TEST PRACTICE

- Extended Response 569
- Multiple Choice 513, 517, 523, 529, 537, 545, 551, 557, 5627
- Short Response/Grid In 551, 569
- Worked Out Example 527

H.O.T. Problems
Higher Order Thinking

- Challenge 513, 517, 523, 529, 537, 545, 550, 556, 562
- Collect the Data 523
- Find the Error 537
- Open Ended 529, 550, 562
- Reasoning 529, 537, 550, 556
- Which One Doesn't Belong? 552

CHAPTER 11

Measurement: Two- and Three-Dimensional Figures

**The prefix 8- on a standard reference was devised by the publisher to indicate that the lesson is a preparation for that particular Grade 8 standard.

TEST PRACTICE

H.O.T. Problems

Higher Order Thinking

Geometry and Measurement

OK PASS

TEST PRACTICE

H.O.T. Problems
Higher Order Thinking

DO NOT
GET
ON/OFF
RIDE
WHILE RIDE
IS IN
MOTION

Wichita Mountains Wildlife Refuge, Oklahoma

Contents

OK PASS

Linear Inequalities

MAIN IDEA

Write and solve one-step linear inequalities in one variable.

OK PASS

1.3 Inequalities: Model, write, solve, and graph one-step linear inequalities with one variable. *Also addresses 7M1.1, 7M4.2.*

OK Math Online

glencoe.com

GET READY for the Lesson

POPULATION The table at the right gives the estimated population for three cities in Oklahoma for a recent year. The population of Edmond is less than the population of Lawton.

Estimated Population	
Bartlesville	34,885
Edmond	76,644
Lawton	87,540

Source: U.S. Census Bureau

1. The inequality 76,644 < 87,540 represents this situation. If the population increases by 1,000 people in both cities, will this still be true?
2. Add 1,000 to each side of the inequality 76,644 < 87,540. Write the resulting inequality.

The population of Edmond is greater than the population of Bartlesville. The inequality 76,644 > 34,885 represents this situation.

3. If the population decreases by 100 in both cities, will this still be true?
4. Subtract 100 from each side of the inequality 76,664 > 34,885. Write the resulting inequality.

The examples above demonstrate the Addition and Subtraction Properties of Inequality. These properties are similar to the Addition and Subtraction Properties of Equality and are true for $<$, $>$, $\leq$, and $\geq$.

Properties of Inequality

Key Concept

Addition Property of Inequality

Words	Example
If you add the same number to each side of an inequality, the inequality remains true.	$2 > -5$ $2 + 4 > -5 + 4$ $6 > -1$ ✓

Subtraction Property of Inequality

Words	Example
If you subtract the same number from each side of an inequality, the inequality remains true.	$7 \leq 11$ $7 - 3 \leq 11 - 3$ $4 \leq 8$ ✓

Solving an inequality means finding the values of the variable that make the inequality true. You can use the Addition and Subtraction Properties of Inequality to solve simple inequalities involving addition and subtraction.

EXAMPLE Solving a Subtraction Inequality

1 **Solve $n - 8 < 15$. Check your solution.**

$n - 8 < 15$	Write the inequality.
$+8 \quad +8$	Add 8 to each side.
$n < 23$	Simplify.

The solution is $n < 23$. You can check this solution by substituting a number less than 23 into the inequality.

Check	$n - 8 < 15$	Write the inequality.
	$22 - 8 \stackrel{?}{<} 15$	Replace n with a number less than 23, such as 22.
	$14 < 15$ ✔	This statement is true.

Study Tip

Equivalent Inequalities
If 23 is greater than n, then n is less than 23.

When you solved the inequality in Example 1, the variable was on the left side of the inequality. Sometimes, the variable will be on the right side of the inequality. It is often easier to read the inequality when the variable is on the left. You can rewrite an inequality so that the variable is on the left. The examples below illustrate this concept.

$3 < 5$	Write an inequality. Three is less than 5. This means that 5 is greater than three.
$5 > 3$	Rewrite the inequality. Reverse the inequality symbol.
$9 > x$	The number 9 is greater than the variable x. This means that the variable x is less than the number 9.
$x < 9$	The variable is now on the left side of the inequality. Reverse the inequality symbol.

EXAMPLE Solving an Addition Inequality

2 **Solve $-4 \geq a + 7$. Check your solution.**

$-4 \geq a + 7$	Write the inequality.
$-4 - 7 \geq a + 7 - 7$	Subtract 7 from each side.
$-11 \geq a$ or $a \leq -11$	Simplify.

The solution is $a \leq -11$. Graph the solution.

Place a closed dot at -11. Then draw a line and arrow to the left. All numbers less than or equal to -11 make the sentence true.

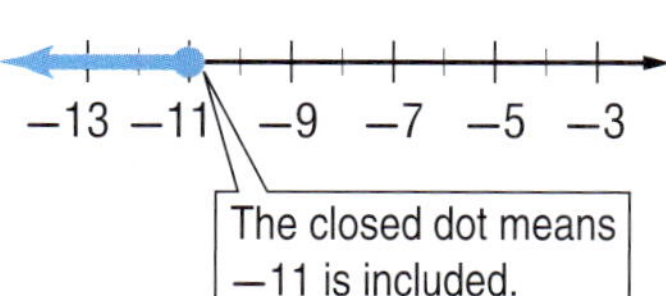

Study Tip

Graphing Inequalities
When inequalities are graphed, an open dot means the number is not included (< or >) and a closed dot means it is included (≤ or ≥).

You can also solve simple inequalities using multiplication and division. The rules for inequalities involving multiplication and division by a positive number are similar to the rules for inequalities involving addition and subtraction.

Properties of Inequality

Key Concept

Multiplication and Division by a Positive Number

Words

If you multiply or divide each side of an inequality by a positive number, the inequality remains true.

Examples

$$9 > 2 \qquad\qquad -10 \leq 15$$

$$4(9) > 4(2) \qquad\qquad \frac{-10}{5} \leq \frac{15}{5}$$

$$36 > 8 \checkmark \qquad\qquad -2 \leq 3 \checkmark$$

You can use these rules to solve one-step inequalities involving multiplication or division by a positive number.

Study Tip

Checking Solutions You can check the solution in Example 3 by substituting numbers greater than −6 into the inequality and testing it to verify that it holds true.

EXAMPLE Solve Inequalities by Dividing

3 **Solve $7y > -42$. Check your solution.**

$7y > -42$ Write the inequality.

$\frac{7y}{7} > \frac{-42}{7}$ Divide each side by 7.

$y > -6$ Simplify.

The solution is $y > -6$. You can check this solution by substituting a number greater than −6 into the inequality.

Check $7y > -42$ Write the inequality.

$7(-4) > -42$ Replace y with a number greater than −6, such as −4.

$-28 > -42$ ✓ This statement is true.

EXAMPLE Solve Inequalities by Multiplying

Solve $\frac{1}{3}x \leq 8$. Check your solution.

$\frac{1}{3}x \leq 8$ Write the inequality.

$3\left(\frac{1}{3}x\right) \leq 3(8)$ Multiply each side by 3.

$x \leq 24$ Simplify.

The solution is $x \leq 24$. You can check this solution by substituting a number less than or equal to 24 into the inequality.

Check $\frac{1}{3}x \leq 8$ Write the inequality.

$\frac{1}{3}(21) \leq 8$ Replace x with a number less than or equal to 24, such as 21.

$7 \leq 8$ ✓ This statement is true.

What happens when each side of an inequality is multiplied or divided by a negative number?

Graph 3 and 5 on a number line.

–5–4–3–2–1 0 1 2 3 4 5

Since 3 is to the left of 5, $3 < 5$.

Multiply each number by -1.

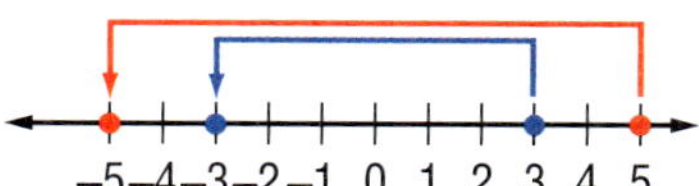

Since -3 is to the right of -5, $-3 > -5$.

Notice that the numbers being compared switched positions as a result of being multiplied by a negative number. In other words, their order reversed.

The example above demonstrates the following properties of inequality for multiplication and division. These properties hold true for $<$, $>$, $\leq$, and $\geq$.

Properties of Inequality

Key Concept

Multiplication and Division by a Negative Number

Words

If you multiply or divide each side of an inequality by a negative number, the direction of the inequality symbol must be reversed for the inequality to remain true.

Examples

$8 > 3$		$-3 \leq 12$
$-2(8) < -2(3)$	Reverse the inequality symbols.	$\frac{-3}{-3} \geq \frac{12}{-3}$
$-16 < -6$ ✓		$1 \geq -4$ ✓

EXAMPLES Multiply or Divide by a Negative Number

5 **Solve $\frac{a}{-2} \geq 8$. Check your solution.**

$\frac{a}{-2} \geq 8$	Write the inequality.
$-2\left(\frac{a}{-2}\right) \leq -2(8)$	Multiply each side by -2 and reverse the inequality symbol.
$a \leq -16$	Check this result.

6 **Solve $-24 > -6n$. Check your solution.**

$-24 > -6n$	Write the inequality.
$\frac{-24}{-6} < \frac{-6n}{-6}$	Divide each side by -6 and reverse the inequality symbol.
$4 < n$ or $n > 4$	Check this result.

CHECK Your Understanding

Examples 1, 2 (p. OK3)

Solve each inequality. Check your solution. Then graph on a number line.

1. $5 + x \leq 18$
2. $10 + n \geq -2$
3. $y + 4 < 15$
4. $m - 1 > 7$
5. $p - 9 \leq 20$
6. $-2 + b < 14$
7. $3a \geq 45$
8. $81 \leq -9w$
9. $6k > -6$

Examples 3–6 (pp. OK4, OK5)

10. $\frac{h}{3} > 9$
11. $\frac{g}{-2} \leq -6$
12. $5 \leq \frac{s}{-5}$
13. **ANIMALS** An adult male elephant can weigh as much as 13,000 pounds. Write and solve an inequality that describes how much weight w a young male elephant is likely to gain if its current weight is 2,200 pounds.

Practice and Problem Solving

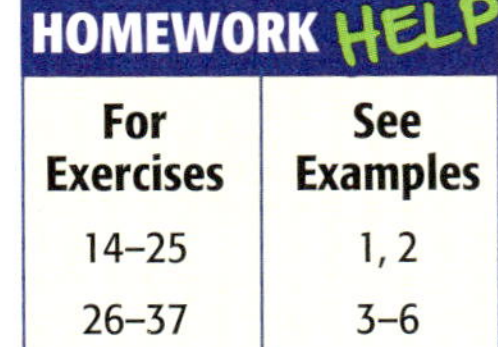

HOMEWORK HELP

For Exercises	See Examples
14–25	1, 2
26–37	3–6

Solve each inequality. Check your solution. Then graph on a number line.

14. $3 + k \leq 9$
15. $4 + x \leq 5$
16. $1 + c \leq 9$
17. $2 + m \leq 11$
18. $12 + b \leq 48$
19. $13 + s \leq 20$
20. $n - 3 > 12$
21. $-7 + a < 22$
22. $d - 8 > 31$
23. $-14 + q < 3$
24. $f - 6 > 1$
25. $h - 15 > 35$
26. $6a \geq 42$
27. $4 \leq -p$
28. $-2w \geq 12$
29. $7y \geq -21$
30. $12g \geq 144$
31. $-40 \leq -5z$
32. $-2 \geq \frac{v}{-3}$
33. $12 \geq \frac{h}{-4}$
34. $\frac{j}{6} > -10$
35. $\frac{m}{4} > 13$
36. $\frac{t}{21} > 3$
37. $41 \geq \frac{r}{-1}$

38. **JOBS** Mark earns $6.25 an hour to mow lawns. He wants to earn enough money to buy a skateboard that costs $175. Write and solve an inequality to find how many hours h Mark must work to earn at least enough money to buy the skateboard.

39. **CATS** A healthy weight for an adult cat is 10 pounds. Elisa's kitten currently weighs $3\frac{1}{4}$ pounds. Write and solve an inequality to find the number of pounds that Elisa's kitten could gain and be considered a healthy adult cat.

40. **TEXT MESSAGING** Lawrence is charged $0.10 per text message that he sends. He wants to spend less than $5.00 a month on text messages. Write and solve an inequality to find the number of text messages t Lawrence can send on his cell phone.

41. **JETS** A certain passenger jet can seat up to 150 passengers. There are currently 78 passengers on board the airplane. Write and solve an inequality to find how many more people p are able to board the airplane.

Write and solve an inequality that can be used to find each number described below.

42. Five more than a number is at least 13.
43. The difference between a number and 11 is less than 8.
44. Nine less than a number is more than 4.
45. The sum of a number and 17 is no more than 6.
46. Three times a number is less than -66.
47. The quotient of a number and -5 is at most 7.
48. The product of -1 and a number is at least 12.
49. A number divided by 4 is greater than -20.

H.O.T. Problems

50. **OPEN ENDED** Write two different inequalities that each have the solution $x \geq 20$. One inequality should be solved using the Addition Property of Inequality and the other inequality should be solved using the Subtraction Property of Inequality.

51. **CHALLENGE** In five games, you score 16, 12, 15, 13, and 17 points. The inequality $\frac{73 + p}{6} \geq 15$ represents the number of points p you must score in the sixth game to have an average of at least 15 points. Use your understanding of solving two-step equations to solve this two-step inequality for p. Explain how you solved the inequality.

REASONING Determine whether each equation or inequality has *no* solution, *one* solution, or *more than one* solution. Justify your response.

52. $x - x = 0$
53. $h + 3 = 11$
54. $5y \geq 30$
55. $m > m + 1$

56. **WRITING IN MATH** Explain when you should reverse the inequality symbol when solving an inequality.

OCCT Practice PASS1.3

57. Diego is planning a party at an ice skating rink. The party room at the rink can hold no more than 40. Diego has already invited 12 friends. Which of the following inequalities can be used to find the number of friends n he is still able to invite?

   A $12 + n \geq 40$
   B $12 + n \leq 40$
   C $12n \leq 40$
   D $12n \geq 40$

58. If $y - 11 < 30$, then y could be all of the following values except for which one?

   A 11
   B 30
   C 40
   D 41

Nonlinear Functions

MAIN IDEA

Determine whether a function is linear or nonlinear.

OK PASS

1.1 Identify, describe, and analyze functional relationships (linear and nonlinear) between two variables (e.g., as the value of x increases on a table, do the values of y increase or decrease, identify a positive rate of change on a graph and compare it to a negative rate of change). *Also addresses 7M1.6, 7M2.1, 7M2.3.*

Key Vocabulary

nonlinear functions

OK Math Online

glencoe.com

GET READY for the Lesson

TRAVEL The table shows the number of miles per hour a family drove on their spring break.

Time (h)	Distance (mi)
1	60
3	180
5	300

1. What was the family's average speed in miles per hour?
2. Were the miles traveled proportional to the number of hours? Explain.

Linear functions represent relationships that have a constant rate of change. This occurs when the rate of change between any two data points is proportional. **Nonlinear functions** are functions that do not have a constant rate of change.

EXAMPLES Identify Linear or Nonlinear Functions

Determine whether each table represents a *linear* or *nonlinear* function.

1

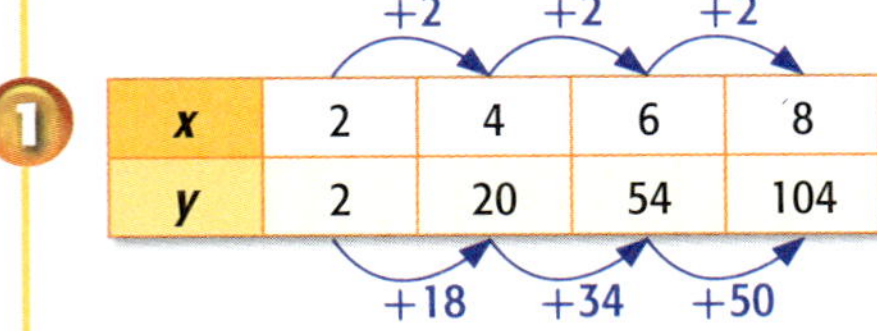

x	2	4	6	8
y	2	20	54	104

As x increases by 2, y increases by a greater amount each time. The rate of change is not constant, so this function is nonlinear.

2

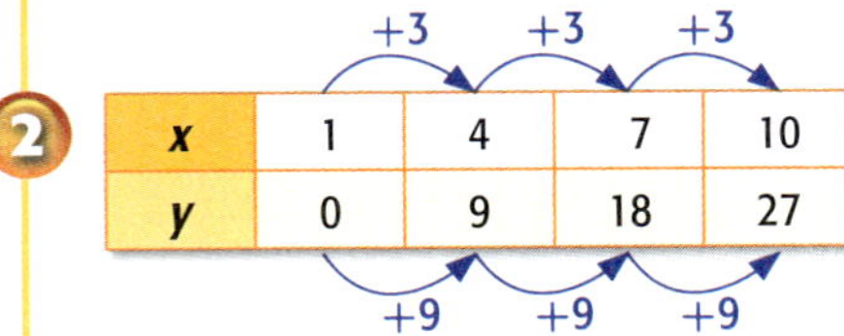

x	1	4	7	10
y	0	9	18	27

As x increases by 3, y increases by 9 each time. The rate of change is constant, so this function is linear.

3

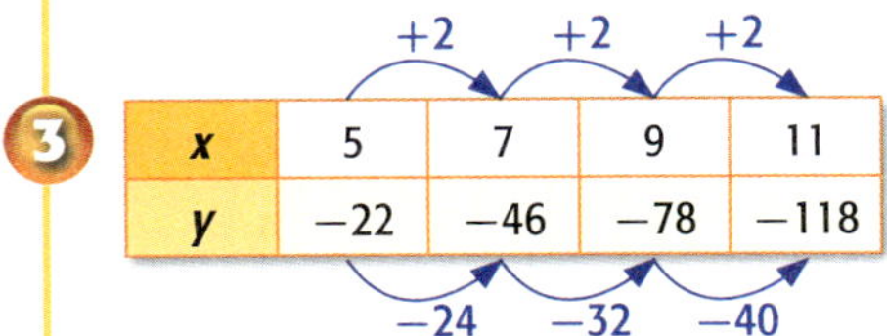

x	5	7	9	11
y	−22	−46	−78	−118

As x increases by 2, y increases by a greater amount each time. The rate of change is not constant, so this function is nonlinear.

You can also identify linear and nonlinear functions using graphs. The graph of a linear function is a straight line. A straight line has a constant rate of change. The graph of a nonlinear function is not a straight line.

EXAMPLES Identify Linear or Nonlinear Functions

Determine whether each graph represents a *linear* or *nonlinear* function. Explain.

4

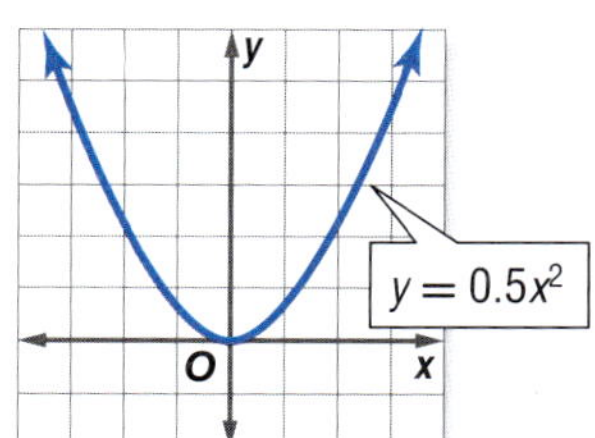

The graph is a curve, not a straight line. So, it represents a nonlinear function.

5

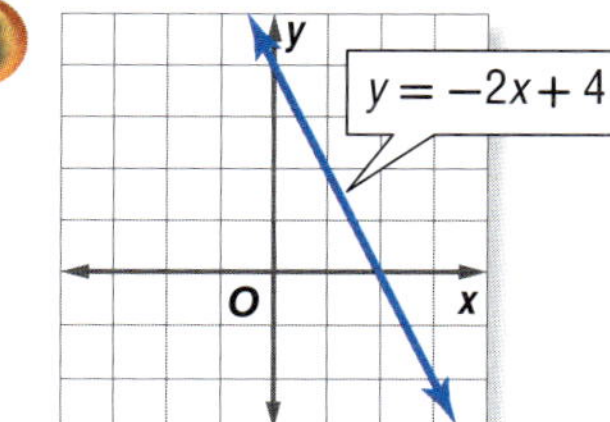

This graph is a straight line. So, it represents a linear function.

Real-World EXAMPLE

6 **TICKETS The cost of each student ticket for the championship basketball game is $5. Are ticket sales a linear function of the number of tickets sold? Explain.**

Tickets Sold	1	2	3
Ticket Sales ($)	5	10	15

Examine the relationship between the number of tickets sold and ticket sales.

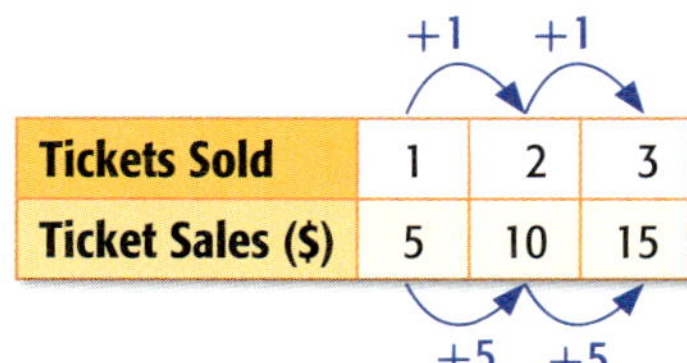

Tickets Sold	1	2	3
Ticket Sales ($)	5	10	15

The rate of change is $5 per 1 ticket.

The rate of change is constant. As the number of tickets sold increases by 1, the total ticket sales increases by $5. Therefore, the ticket sales represent a linear function of the number of tickets sold.

Check Graph the data to verify that the ordered pairs form a straight line.

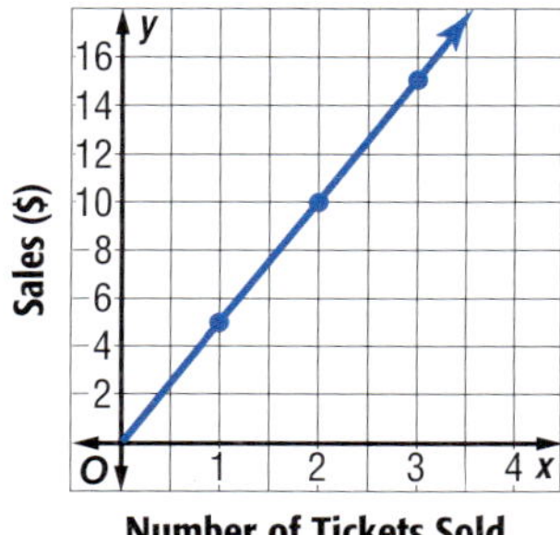

Since the graph that represents the ordered pairs forms a straight line, the function is linear.

CHECK Your Understanding

Examples 1–5 (pp. OK8–OK9)

Determine whether each table or graph represents a *linear* or *nonlinear* function. Explain.

1.

x	0	5	10	15
y	20	16	12	8

2.

x	0	2	4	6
y	0	2	8	18

3. 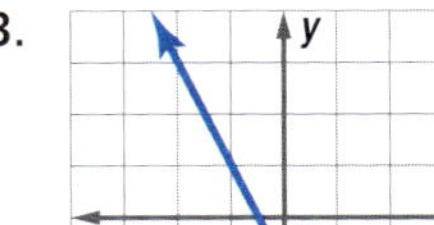

4. 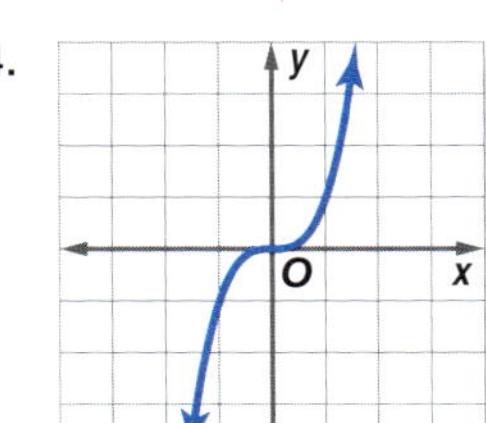

Example 6 (p. OK9)

5. **TIME** The table at the right shows the number of revolutions per hour that the minute hand on a clock makes. Determine if the revolutions per hour are a linear function of the number of hours that pass. Explain your reasoning.

Hour	Minute Hand Revolutions
1	60
2	120
3	180
4	240
5	300

Practice and Problem Solving

HOMEWORK HELP

For Exercises	See Examples
6–14	1–4
15–23	5

Determine whether each table or graph represents a *linear* or *nonlinear* function. Explain.

6.

x	1	2	3	4
y	1	4	9	16

7. 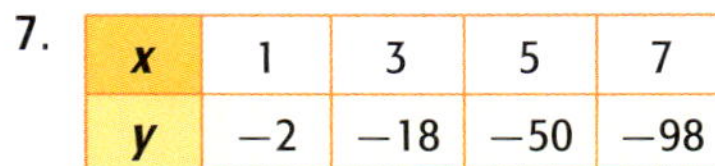

x	1	3	5	7
y	−2	−18	−50	−98

8.

x	−2	0	2	4
y	4	0	4	16

9. 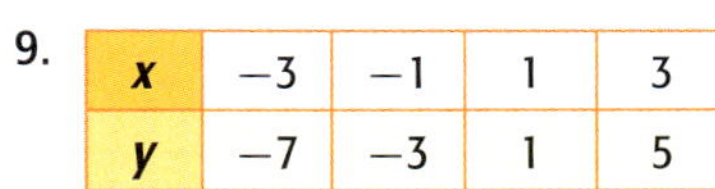

x	−3	−1	1	3
y	−7	−3	1	5

10. 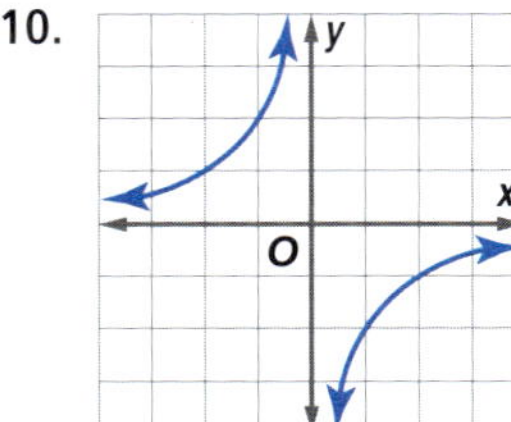

11. 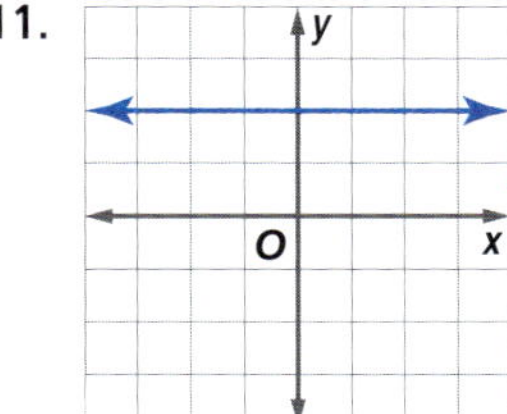

12. 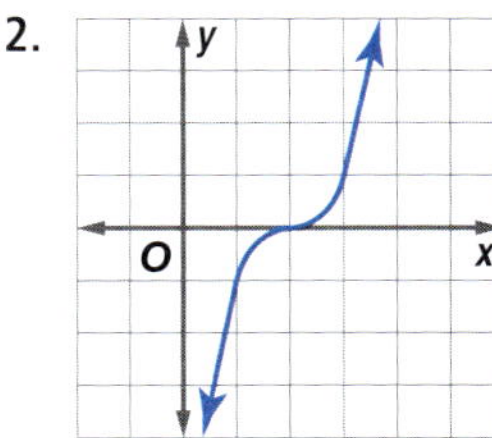

13. 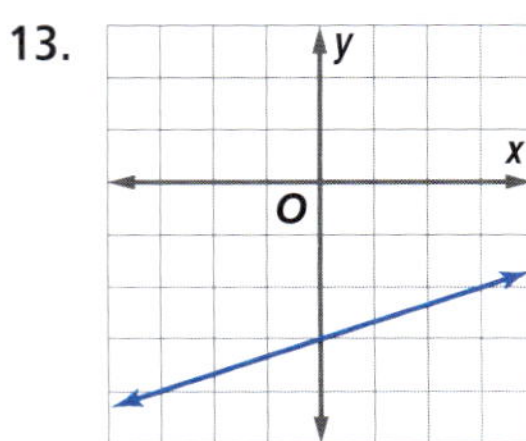

14. 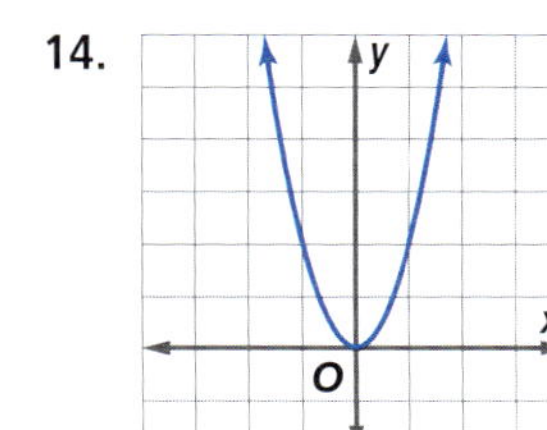

15. 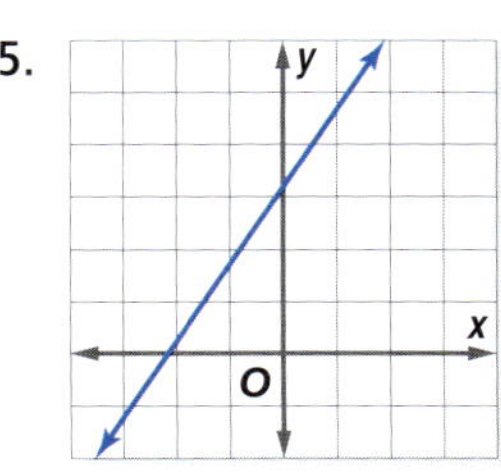

16. **CAMELS** The table shows the number of liters of water a camel drinks over a certain number of minutes. Use the table to determine whether the number of liters is a linear function of time. Explain your reasoning.

Time (minutes)	Number of Liters
3	30
5	50
7	70

ALGEBRA For Exercises 17–19, use the following information.
The equation of a linear function can be written in *slope-intercept form*, $y = mx + b$, where m is the slope, or rate of change, and b is the y-intercept. State whether the following functions are linear.

17. $y = \frac{1}{2}x - 5$

18. $y = x^2$

19. $y = x^3 + 11$

MEASUREMENT For Exercises 20 and 21, use the following information.
Recall that the circumference of a circle is equal to π times its diameter and that the area of a circle is equal to π times the square of its radius.

20. Is the circumference of a circle a linear or nonlinear function of its diameter? Explain your reasoning.

21. Is the area of a circle a linear or nonlinear function of its radius? Explain your reasoning.

H.O.T. Problems

22. **OPEN ENDED** Make a graph showing the area of a square as a function of its perimeter. Explain whether or not the function is linear.

23. **CHALLENGE** Does the graph of $x = 5$ represent a linear function? Explain your reasoning.

24. **WRITING IN MATH** Describe a method for determining whether or not a function is linear given its equation.

OCCT Practice PASS1.1

25. Which of the following is true concerning the graph shown below?

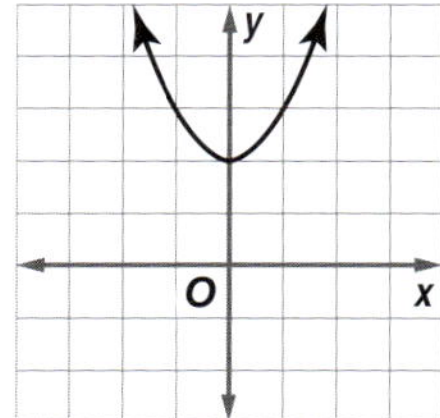

A It represents a linear function.

B It represents a nonlinear function.

C As the value of x increases, the value of y increases by the same amount.

D It has a constant rate of change.

26. Which of the following tables shows a nonlinear function?

A

x	4	8	12	16
y	3	0	−3	−6

B

x	5	10	15	20
y	13	28	43	58

C

x	2	4	6	8
y	10	12	16	24

D

x	3	6	9	12
y	12	10	8	6

Negative Rate of Change

MAIN IDEA

Identify and analyze positive and negative rates of change.

OK PASS

1.1 Identify, describe, and analyze functional relationships (linear and nonlinear) **between two variables (e.g., as the value of *x* increases on a table, do the values of *y* increase or decrease, identify a positive rate of change on a graph and compare it to a negative rate of change).** *Also addresses 7M1.6.*

OK Math Online

glencoe.com

GET READY for the Lesson

The average weight of a fully grown border collie is 50 pounds. As a puppy, it will gain about 2 ounces per day until it is fully grown. Lilly's border collie currently weighs 10 pounds 12 ounces.

1. Make a table to find the border collie's weight 2, 4, 6, and 8 days from now.
2. Write an equation to represent y, the border collie's total weight, x days from now.
3. Use your equation to find in how many days the border collie will be fully grown.

Recall that a *rate of change* is a rate that describes how one quantity changes in relation to another. In the above example, the border collie's weight increases as the number of days increases.

Recall in Lesson 6-3 you found the rate of change and graphed the values from a table. Rate of change can be positive or negative. *Positive rates of change* are shown when the value of y increases as the value of x increases. *Negative rates of change* are shown when the value of y decreases as the value of x increases, or vice versa.

EXAMPLE Find Positive Rate of Change

1 **The table at the right shows the sum of the angles of several polygons based on the number of sides. Use the information to find the rate of change in degrees per side.**

Sum of Angles of Polygons	
Number of Sides	Sum of Angles
3	180°
4	360°
5	540°
6	720°

(Number of Sides: +1, +1, +1; Sum of Angles: +180°, +180°, +180°)

Find the unit rate to determine the rate of change.

$$\frac{\text{change in sum}}{\text{change in number of sides}} = \frac{180^\circ}{1\text{ side}}$$

So, the sum of the angles of various polygons increases by 180° for each increase in one side. Since the value of y increases as x increases, this shows a positive rate of change.

EXAMPLE Find Negative Rate of Change

2 **The graph at the right shows the number of gallons of gas y remaining in a vehicle along with the miles traveled x. Find the rate of change in gallons of gas remaining per mile traveled.**

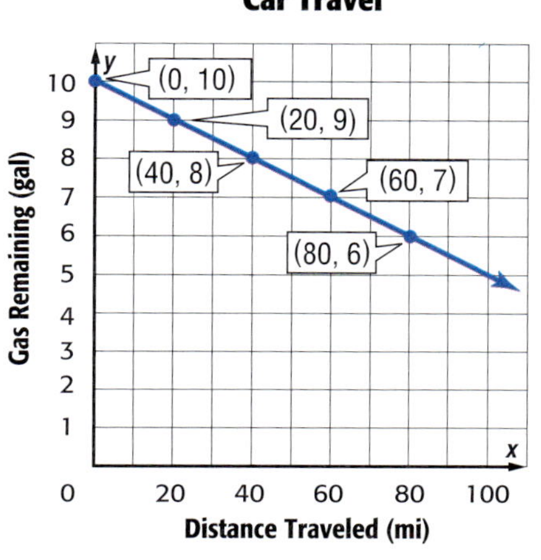

Choose any two points on the line.

(60, 7) → 60 miles, 7 gallons

(80, 6) → 80 miles, 6 gallons

$$\frac{\text{change in gallons of gas}}{\text{change in miles}} = \frac{6 - 7}{80 - 60}$$

$$= \frac{-1 \text{ gallon}}{20 \text{ miles}}$$

So, the number of gallons of gasoline decreases by 1 for every 20 miles traveled. This shows a negative rate of change.

To show that the rate of change is constant, you can find the rate of change between other pairs of points on the line.

(0, 10) and (20, 9) → $\frac{9 - 10}{20 - 0}$ or $\frac{-1}{20}$ (40, 8) and (60, 7) → $\frac{7 - 8}{60 - 40}$ or $\frac{-1}{20}$

So, the rate of change, $\frac{-1}{20}$, is constant.

CHECK Your Understanding

Examples 1, 2 (pp. OK12, OK13)

1. **MUSIC** The table at the right shows the length of time it takes to burn a song onto a CD based on the total number of songs. Use the information to find the rate of change in seconds per song. Does the relationship represent a positive or negative rate of change? Explain your answer.

Number of Songs	Time (seconds)
2	32
3	48
4	64
5	80

2. **HIKING** The line graph at the right shows the altitude of a group of hikers during a hike. Find the rate of change of the altitude based on the length in minutes of the hike. Does the relationship represent a positive or negative rate of change? Explain your answer.

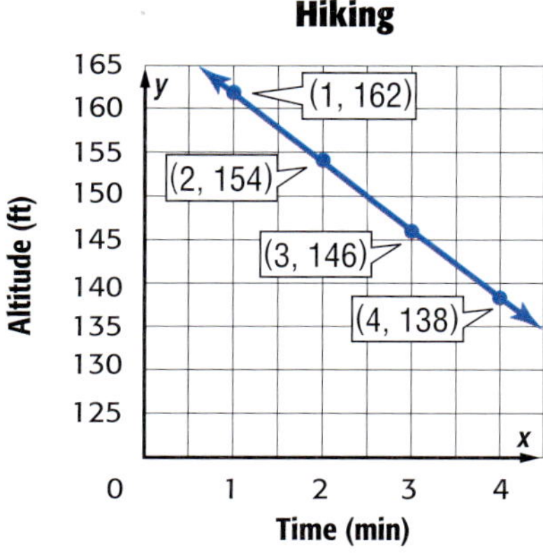

Practice and Problem Solving

HOMEWORK HELP	
For Exercises	See Examples
3–13	1, 2

For Exercises 3–8, determine whether the relationship represents a positive or negative rate of change. Then find the rate of change.

3.

Time (h)	Wages ($)
0	20
1	30
2	40

4.

Time (min)	Calls
5	30
10	20
15	10

5.

Speed (mph)	Time (min)
9	16
10	14
11	12

6.

Length (ft)	Cost ($)
1	7
3	14
5	21

7.

Shirts	Cost ($)
2	10
4	15
6	20

8.

Temperature (°F)	Snow (in.)
12	7
16	5
20	3

For Exercises 9–12, determine whether the relationship represents a positive or negative rate of change. Then find the rate of change.

9.

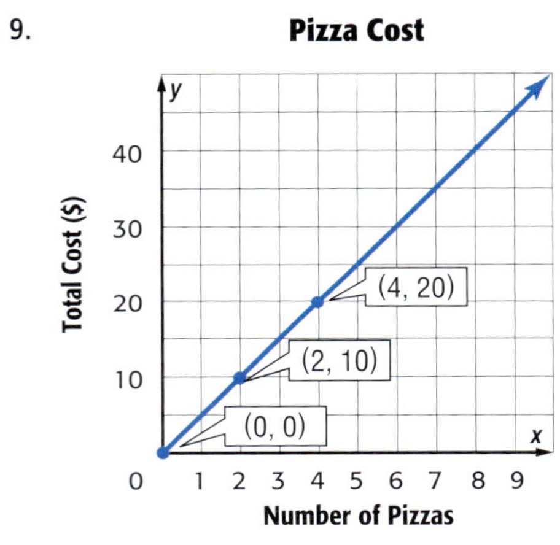

10.

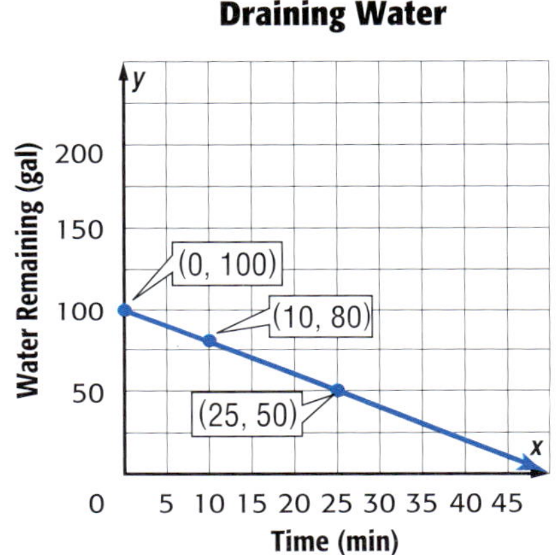

11.

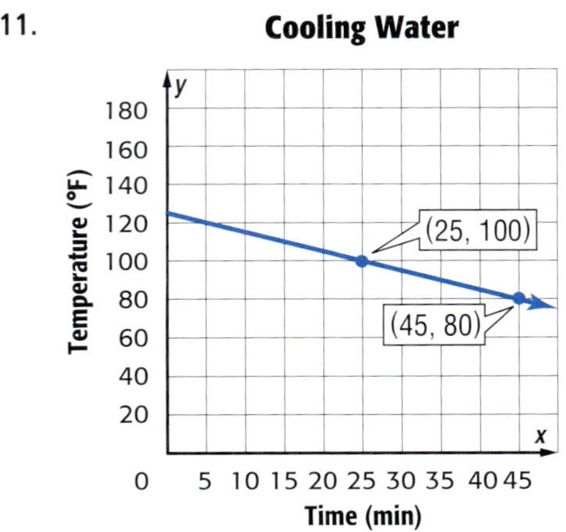

12.

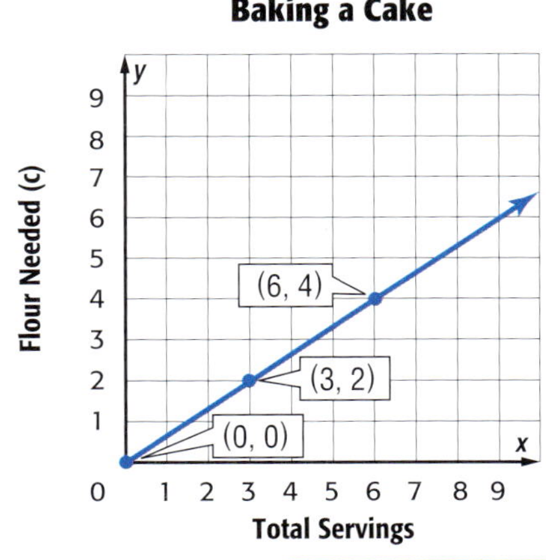

13. **BOOKS** Miguel is reading a novel. The table shows the number of pages remaining in the novel after each day he reads. Identify the relationship as having a positive or negative rate of change.

Day	Pages Remaining
1	117
2	71
3	25

H.O.T. Problems

14. **OPEN ENDED** Describe a real-world relationship between two quantities that involves a negative rate of change.

15. **OPEN ENDED** The graph of a line passes through the point (3, −2). Give three different points on the line if the line has a positive rate of change. Then give three different points on the line if the line has a negative rate of change.

16. **CHALLENGE** Could a rate of change be zero? Explain why or why not.

17. **REASONING** Determine whether the following statement is true or false. Explain your reasoning.

    A negative rate of change cannot be constant.

18. **WRITING IN MATH** Explain how you can determine whether the relationship between two variables represents a positive or negative rate of change.

OCCT Practice

PASS1.1

19. Which of the following graphs represents a constant negative rate of change?

A

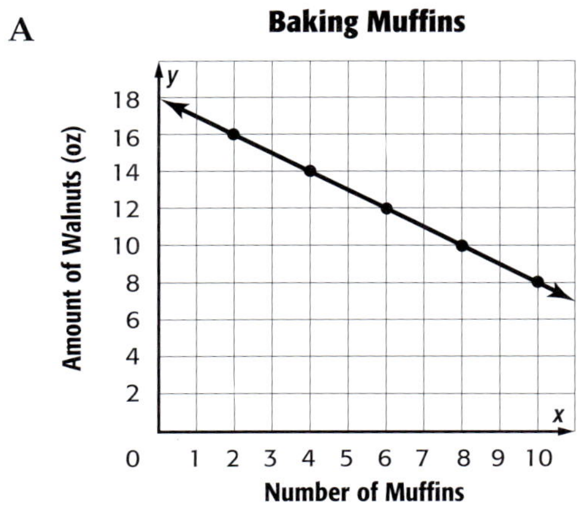

C

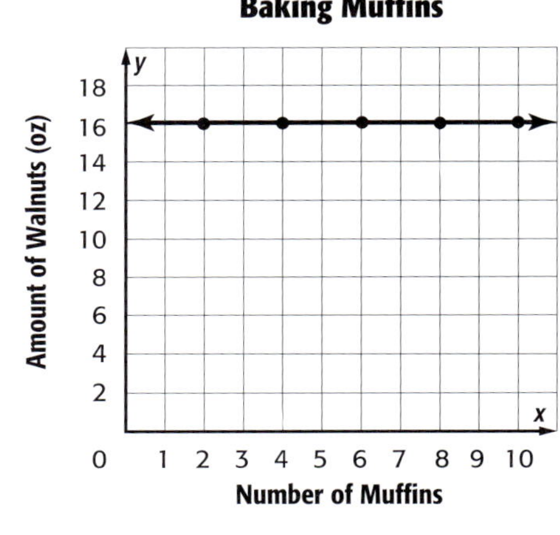

B

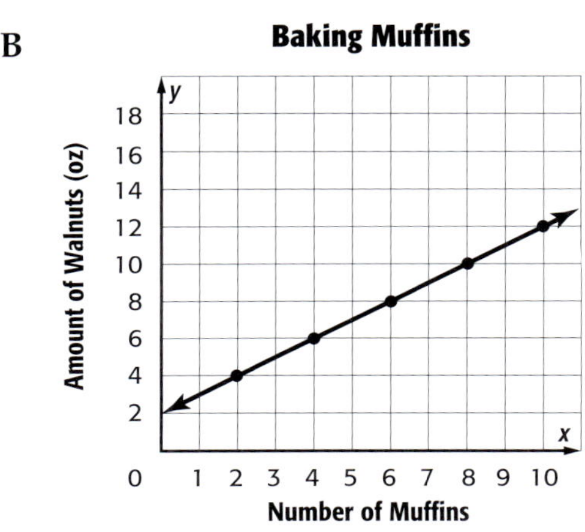

D

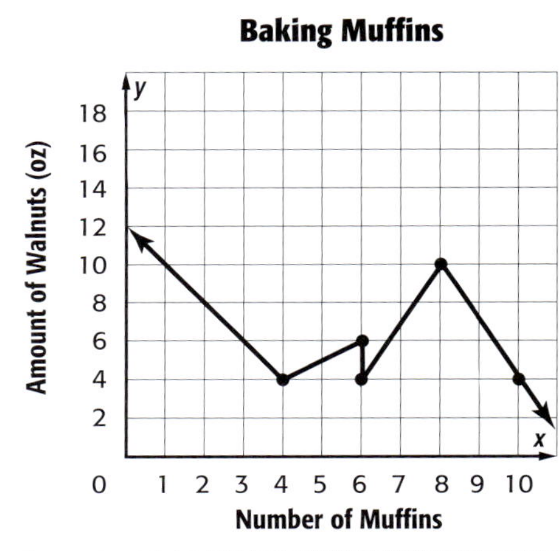

4 Rotations

MAIN IDEA

Identify and graph rotations on a coordinate plane.

OK PASS

3.3 Construct geometric figures and identify geometric transformations on the rectangular coordinate plane (e. g., **rotations,** translations, reflections, magnifications). *Also addresses 7M5.2.*

New Vocabulary

rotation
rotational symmetry
angle of rotation

OK Math Online

glencoe.com

MINI Lab

STEP 1 Draw and label triangle ABC with vertices $A(-4, 1)$, $B(-4, 5)$, and $C(-1, 1)$.

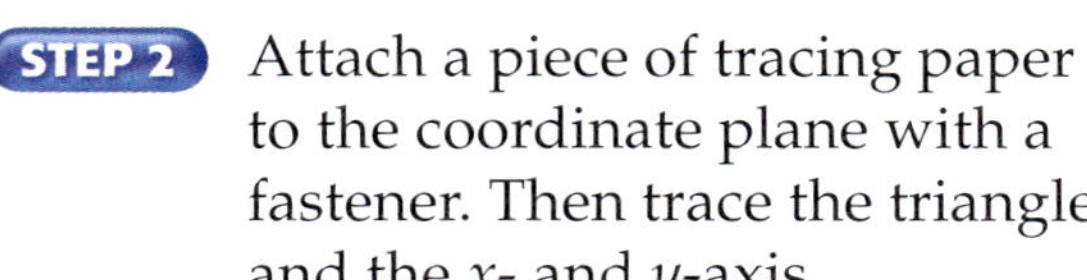

STEP 2 Attach a piece of tracing paper to the coordinate plane with a fastener. Then trace the triangle and the x- and y-axis.

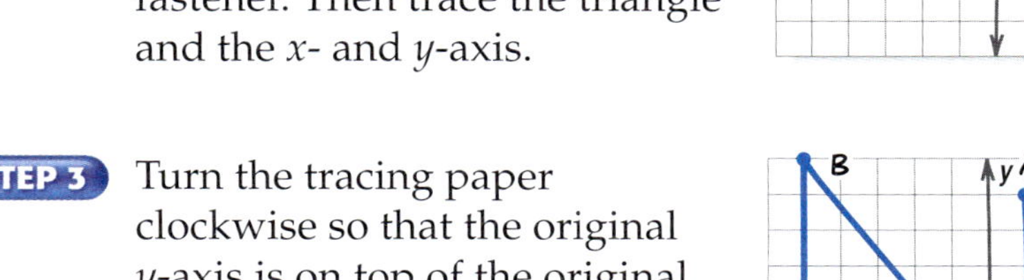

STEP 3 Turn the tracing paper clockwise so that the original y-axis is on top of the original x-axis.

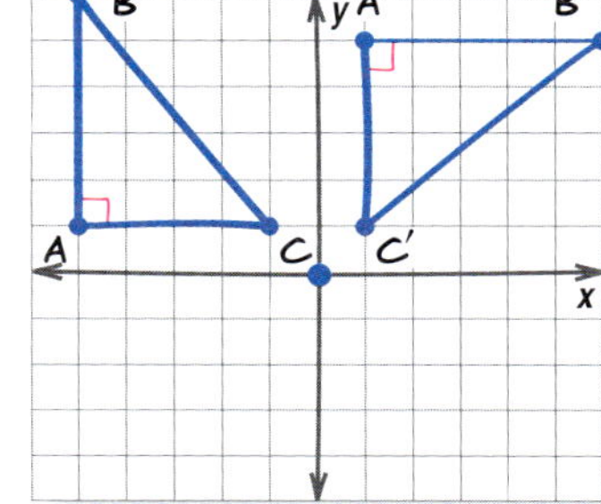

1. Describe the transformation that occurred from triangle ABC to triangle $A'B'C'$.
2. What are the coordinates of triangle $A'B'C'$?
3. Measure the line segment connecting point C and the origin. Then measure the segment connecting point C' and the origin. What do you notice?
4. Measure the angle formed by the segments in Exercise 3. What is this angle measure?

A **rotation** occurs when a figure is rotated around a point, such as the origin. A rotation does not change the size or shape of the figure. The three different rotations shown below are clockwise around the origin.

90° Rotation

180° Rotation

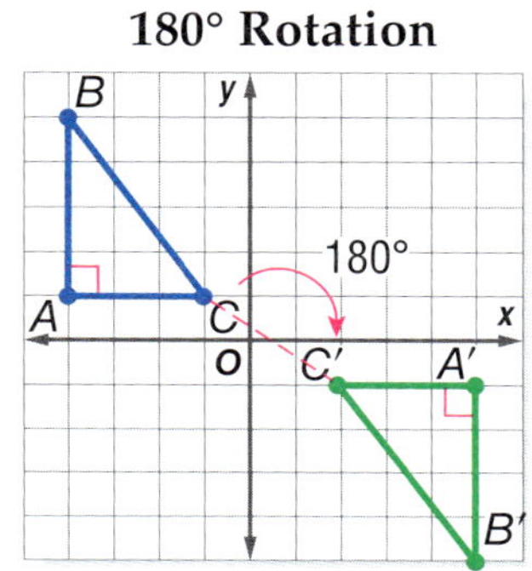

270° Rotation

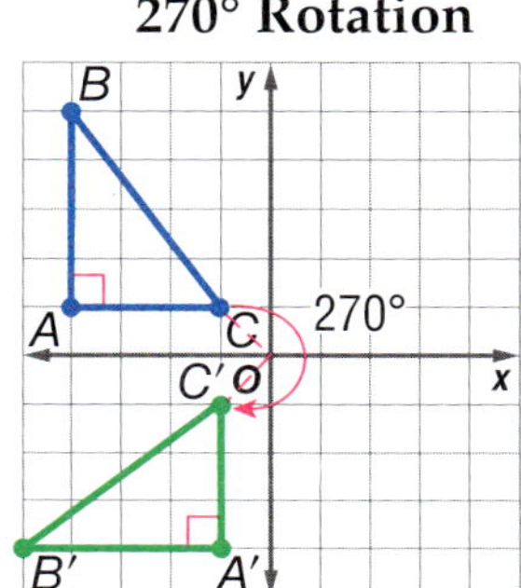

EXAMPLE Rotate a Figure About the Origin

1 **Triangle ABC has vertices $A(-4, 4)$, $B(-1, 2)$, and $C(-3, 1)$. Graph the figure and its rotated image after a clockwise rotation of 90° about the origin. Then give the coordinates of the vertices for $\triangle A'B'C'$.**

STEP 1 Graph $\triangle ABC$ on a coordinate plane.

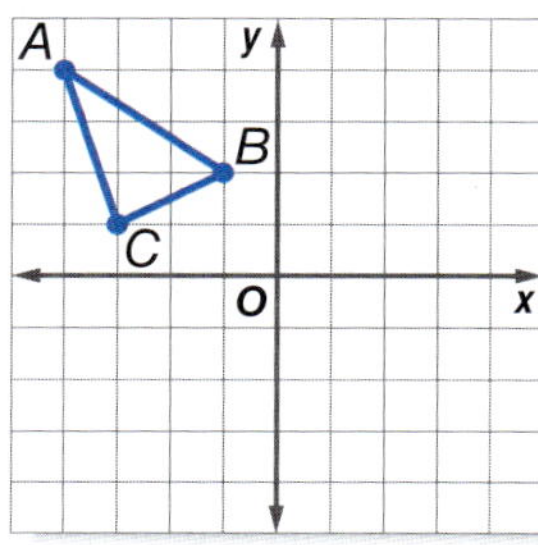

Reading Math

Segment Notation $\overline{BO}$ means the line segment connecting points B and O.

STEP 2 Sketch segment $\overline{BO}$ connecting point B to the origin. Sketch another segment, $\overline{B'O}$, so that the angle between point B, O, and B' measures 90° and the segment is congruent to $\overline{BO}$.

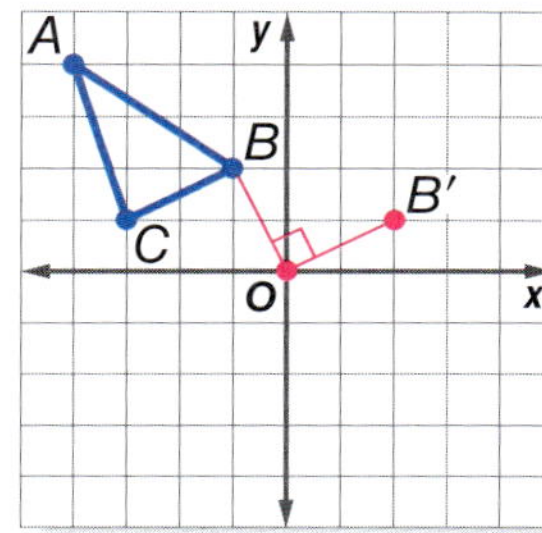

STEP 3 Repeat Step 2 for points A and C. Then connect the vertices to form $\triangle A'B'C'$.

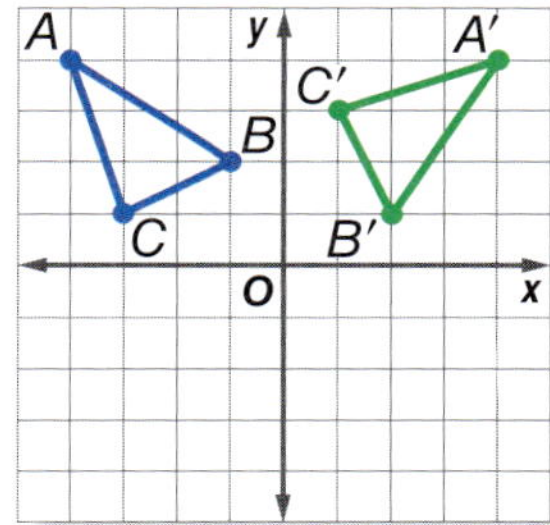

So, the coordinates of the vertices of $\triangle A'B'C'$ are $A'(4, 4)$, $B'(2, 1)$, and $C'(1, 3)$.

EXAMPLE Rotate a Figure About a Point

2 **Triangle LMN has vertices $L(5, 4)$, $M(5, 7)$, and $N(8, 7)$. Graph the figure and its rotated image after a counterclockwise rotation of 180° about vertex L. Then give the coordinates of the vertices for $\triangle L'M'N'$.**

STEP 1 Graph the original triangle.

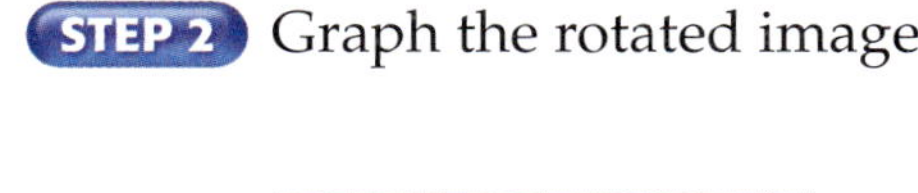

STEP 2 Graph the rotated image.

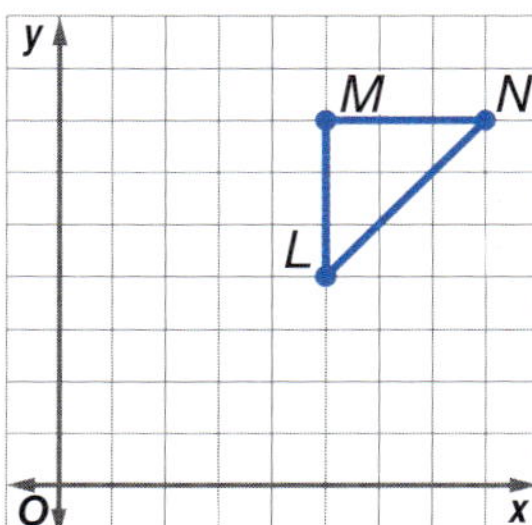

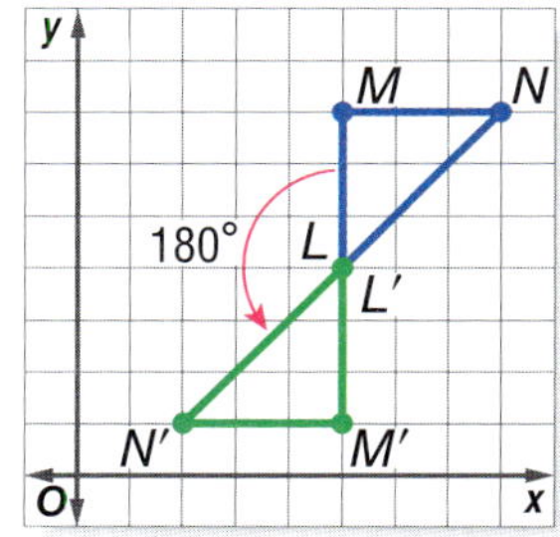

So, the coordinates of the vertices of $\triangle L'M'N'$ are $L'(5, 4)$, $M'(5, 1)$, and $N'(2, 1)$.

A figure can have **rotational symmetry** if it can be rotated a certain number of degrees about its center and still look like the original. The **angle of rotation** is the degree measure of the angle through which the figure is rotated.

Real-World EXAMPLE Determine Rotational Symmetry

3 **SNOW Determine whether the snowflake has rotational symmetry. Write *yes* or *no*. If *yes*, name its angle(s) of rotation.**

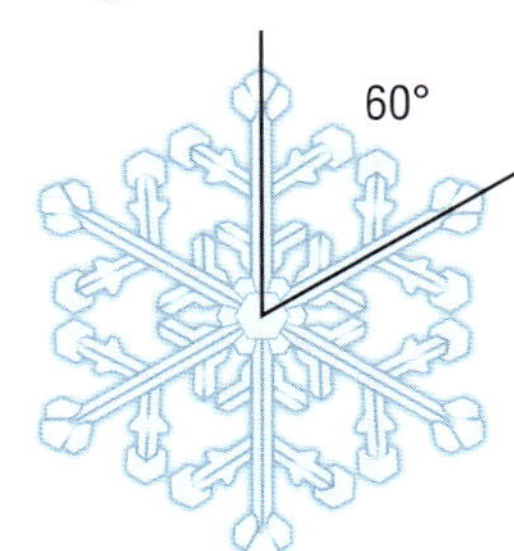

Since the snowflake can be rotated and still look like it does in its original position, the snowflake has rotational symmetry. The snowflake will match itself after being rotated 60°, 120°, 180°, 240°, 300°, and 360°.

CHECK Your Understanding

Examples 1–2 (p. OK17)

Graph $\triangle XYZ$ and its rotated image after each rotation. Then give the coordinates of the vertices for $\triangle X'Y'Z'$.

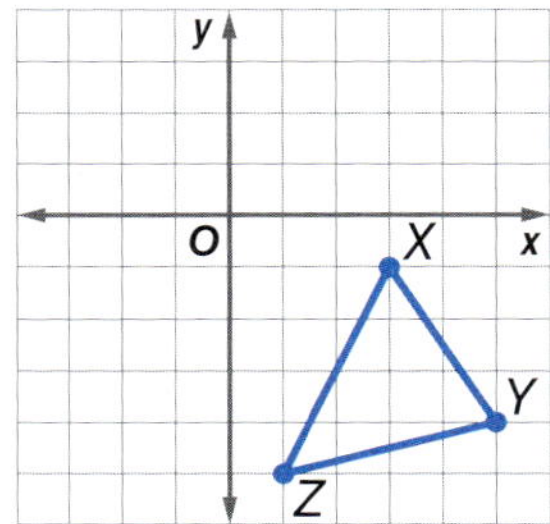

1. 180° clockwise about the origin
2. 270° counterclockwise about vertex X
3. 90° counterclockwise about the origin
4. 270° clockwise about vertex Y
5. 180° counterclockwise about vertex Z
6. 90° clockwise about the origin

Example 3 (p. OK18)

Determine whether each figure has rotational symmetry. Write *yes* or *no*. If *yes*, name its angle(s) of rotation.

7.

8.

Practice and Problem Solving

HOMEWORK HELP

For Exercises	See Examples
9–14	1–2
15–18	3

Graph quadrilateral $ABCD$ and its rotated image after each rotation. Then give the coordinates of the vertices for quadrilateral $A'B'C'D'$.

9. 90° counterclockwise about the origin
10. 90° clockwise about vertex A
11. 180° counterclockwise about vertex D
12. 270° clockwise about the origin
13. 90° clockwise about the origin
14. 180° clockwise about vertex B

Determine whether each figure has rotational symmetry. Write *yes* or *no*. If *yes*, name its angle(s) of rotation.

15. 

16. 

17. 

18. 

H.O.T. Problems

19. **OPEN ENDED** Sketch a figure that has rotational symmetry. Describe the angle(s) of rotation.

20. **WRITING IN MATH** Describe what information is needed to rotate a figure.

OCCT Practice PASS3.3

21. Which figure shows the letter F after a rotation of 270° clockwise?

A 
C 
B 
D 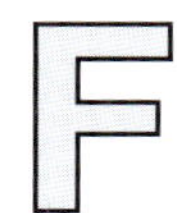

22. Triangle XYZ has vertices $X(2, -2)$, $Y(5, 0)$, and $Z(3, -4)$. What are the coordinates of point Z after a rotation of 180° about point Y?

A (4, 7) C (0, 5)
B (8, 2) D (7, 4)

Magnifications

MAIN IDEA

Construct and identify transformations such as magnifications on the coordinate plane.

OK PASS

3.3 Construct geometric figures and identify geometric transformations on the rectangular coordinate plane (e.g., rotations, translations, reflections, **magnifications**).

New Vocabulary

dilation
magnification
center

OK Math Online

glencoe.com

GET READY for the Lesson

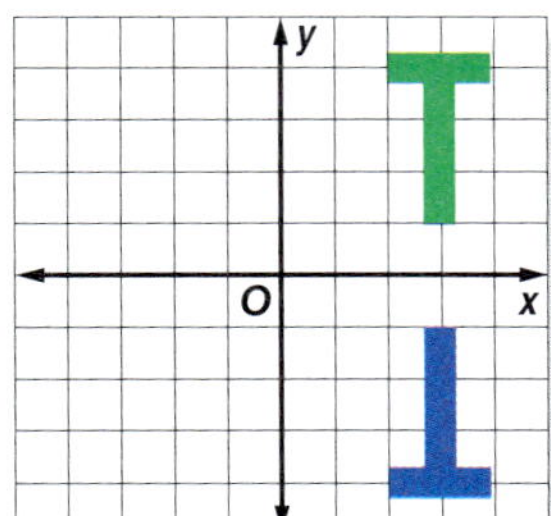

Refer to the coordinate plane shown at the right. The original figure is shown in blue. The *image*, or the transformed figure, is shown in green.

1. Identify the transformation.
2. Describe the size and shape of the image related to the original figure.

The image produced by enlarging or reducing a figure is called a **dilation**. A dilation with a scale factor greater than 1 produces a **magnification**, or an image that is larger than the original figure.

An image produced by a magnification is similar to the original figure. This means that corresponding lengths on the two figures are proportional.

The **center** of the magnification is a fixed point used for measurement when altering the size of the figure. The ratio of a length on the image to a length on the original figure is the scale factor of the magnification.

EXAMPLE Draw a Magnification

1 **Copy polygon *ABCD* as shown on graph paper. Then draw the image of the figure after a magnification with center *A* by a scale factor of 2.**

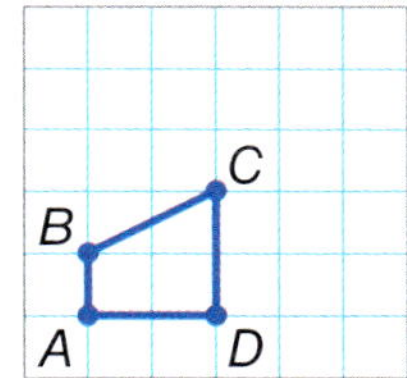

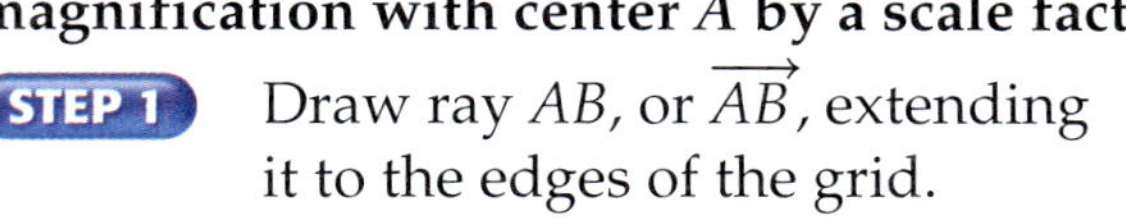

STEP 1 Draw ray *AB*, or $\overrightarrow{AB}$, extending it to the edges of the grid.

STEP 2 Use a ruler to locate point B' on $\overrightarrow{AB}$ such that $AB' = 2(AB)$.

Since the side length of $\overline{AB}$ is 1 unit, the side length of $\overline{AB}$ should be 2(1), or 2 units.

The side length of $\overline{AD'}$ should be 2(2), or 4 units.

The side length of $\overline{D'C'}$ should be 2(2), or 4 units.

Connect points B' and C' to from $\overline{B'C'}$.

STEP 3 Repeat Steps 1 and 2 for points C' and D'. Then draw polygon $A'B'C'D'$ where $A = A'$.

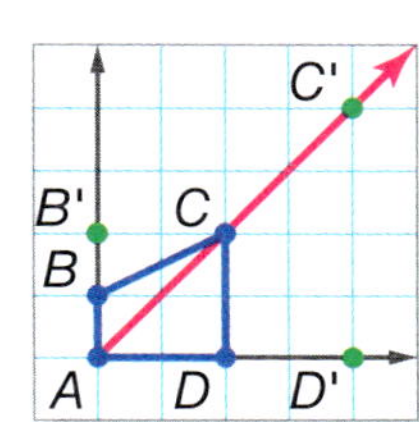

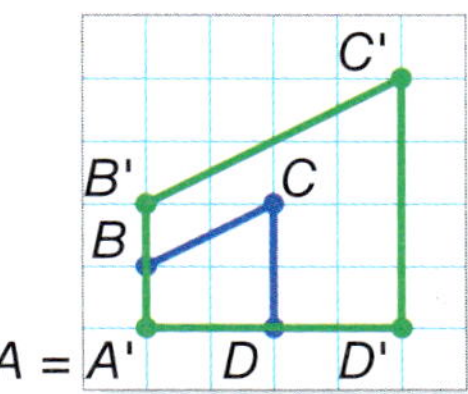

Refer to Example 1. If point A has coordinates (0, 0), then the table below lists the coordinates of corresponding points on the original figure and its image. Notice that the coordinates of the image are (ax, ay), where a is the scale factor, 2.

Original Coordinates	Scale Factor	Image Coordinates
$D(2, 0)$	$(2 \cdot 2, 0 \cdot 2)$	$D'(4, 0)$
$C(2, 2)$	$(2 \cdot 2, 2 \cdot 2)$	$C'(4, 4)$
$B(0, 1)$	$(0 \cdot 2, 1 \cdot 2)$	$B'(0, 2)$
$A(0, 0)$	$(0 \cdot 2, 0 \cdot 2)$	$A'(0, 0)$

To find the coordinates of the vertices of an image after a magnification with center (0, 0), multiply the x- and y-coordinates by the scale factor.

Study Tip

Magnifications
A magnification by a scale factor of 2 results in an image whose side lengths are twice as long as the original figure.

EXAMPLE Graph Magnifications

2 Graph $\triangle JKL$ with vertices $J\left(\frac{3}{2}, 4\right)$, $K(5, 3)$, and $L(4, 1)$ on the coordinate plane. Then graph the image $\triangle J'K'L'$ after a magnification with a scale factor of 2.

To find the vertices of the magnification, multiply each coordinate in each of the ordered pairs by 2.

Original Coordinates	Scale Factor	Image Coordinates
$J\left(\frac{3}{2}, 4\right)$	$\left(\frac{3}{2} \cdot 2, 4 \cdot 2\right)$	$J'(3, 8)$
$K(5, 3)$	$(5 \cdot 2, 3 \cdot 2)$	$K'(10, 6)$
$L(4, 1)$	$(4 \cdot 2, 1 \cdot 2)$	$L'(8, 2)$

Graph both the original figure and its image on the same coordinate plane.

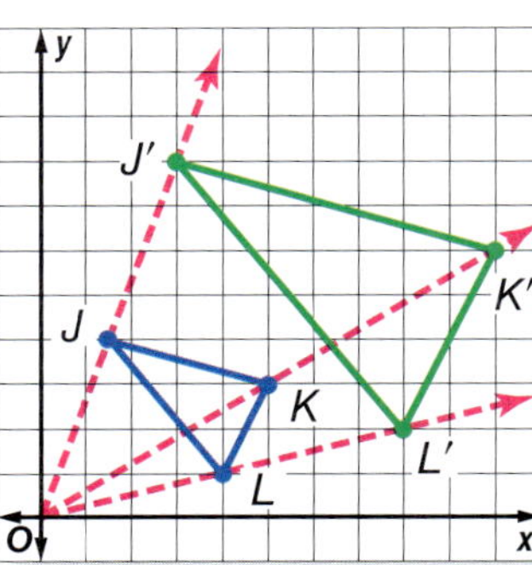

Check for Reasonableness

Draw three dotted lines through the origin and each of the vertices of the original figure as shown at the right. The vertices of the magnification should lie on those same three lines.

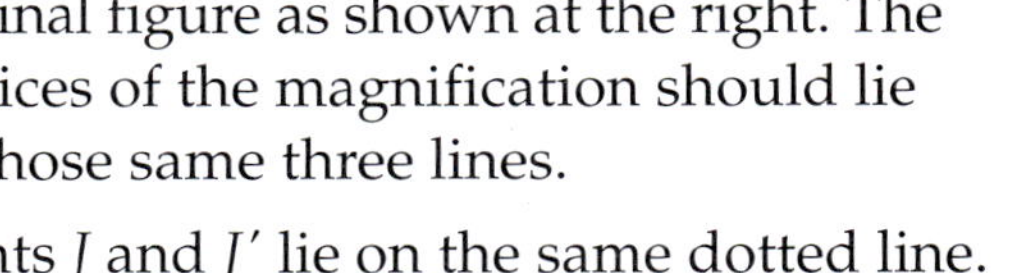

Points J and J' lie on the same dotted line.

Points K and K' lie on the same dotted line.

Points L and L' lie on the same dotted line.

So, the answer is reasonable.

CHECK Your Understanding

Examples 1–2 (pp. OK20–OK21)

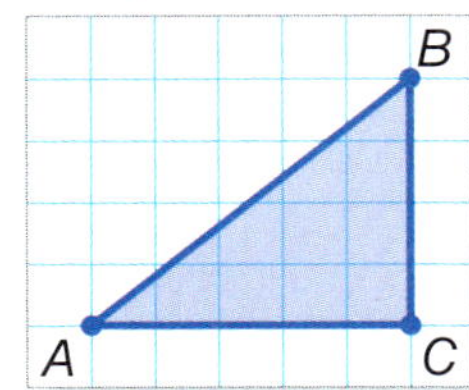

1. **GEOMETRY** Copy $\triangle ABC$ on graph paper. Then draw the image of the figure after a magnification with the center C and scale factor of $\frac{3}{2}$.

2. **GEOMETRY** Triangle JKL has vertices $J(-4, 2)$, $K(-2, -4)$, and $L(3, 6)$. Find the vertices of $\triangle J'K'L'$ after a magnification about the origin with a scale factor of 3. Then graph $\triangle JKL$ and $\triangle J'K'L'$ on the coordinate plane.

Practice and Problem Solving

HOMEWORK HELP	
For Exercises	See Examples
3–13	1, 2

Copy each figure on graph paper. Then draw the image of the figure after a magnification with the given center and scale factor.

3. center: X, scale factor: 2

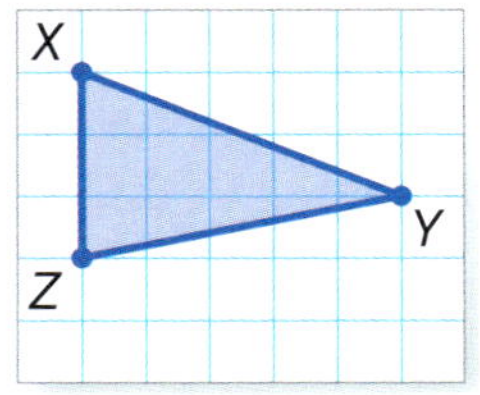

4. center: N, scale factor: 2

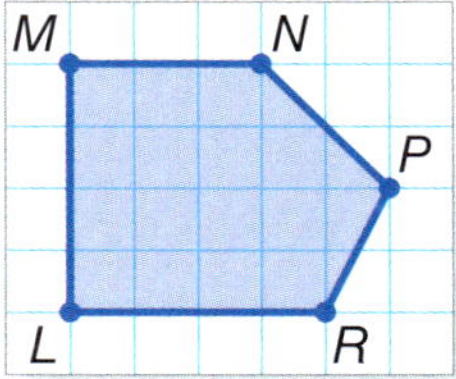

Find the vertices of polygon $H'J'K'L'$ after polygon $HJKL$ is magnified using the given scale factor. Then graph polygon $HJKL$ and polygon $H'J'K'L'$ on the same coordinate plane.

5. $H(-1, 3)$, $J(3, 2)$, $K(2, -3)$, $L(-2, -2)$; scale factor: 2

6. $H(0, 2)$, $J(3, 1)$, $K(0, -4)$, $L(-2, -3)$; scale factor: 3

7. **EYES** An optometrist dilates a patient's pupils by a factor of $\frac{5}{3}$. If the pupil had a diameter of 5 millimeters before dilation, find the new diameter after dilation.

Before Dilation

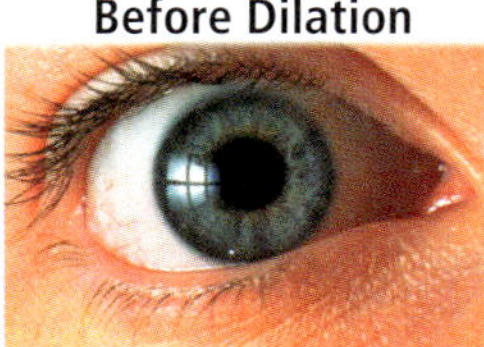

After Dilation

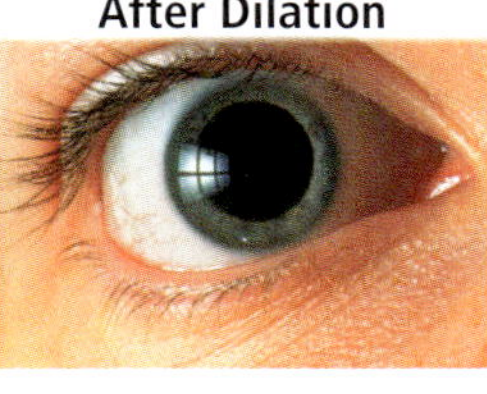

8. **COMPUTERS** Dante uses an image of his dog as the wallpaper on his computer desktop. The original image is 5 inches high and 7 inches wide. If his computer scales the image by a factor of $\frac{5}{4}$, what are the dimensions of the magnified image?

9. **GEOMETRY** The coordinates of a polygon after a magnification with a scale factor of $\frac{7}{2}$ are $M'(0, 0)$, $N'\left(3\frac{1}{2}, 10\frac{1}{2}\right)$, $O'\left(-7, 17\frac{1}{2}\right)$, and $P'\left(10\frac{1}{2}, -14\right)$. Find the coordinates of the original polygon.

On each graph below, one figure is a magnification of the other. Find the scale factor of each magnification.

10. 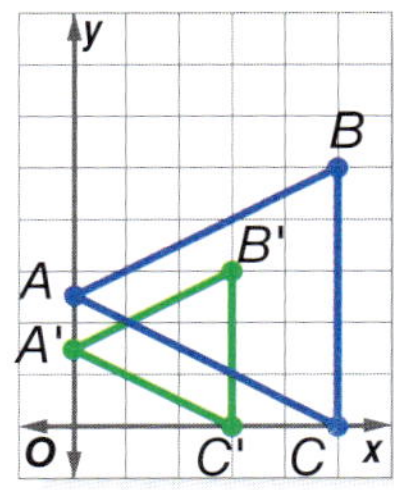

11. 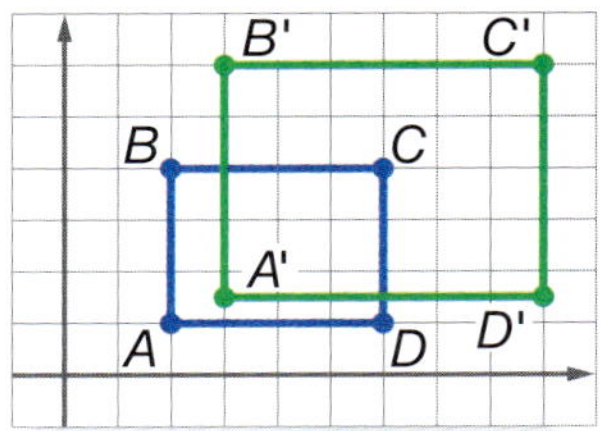

12. 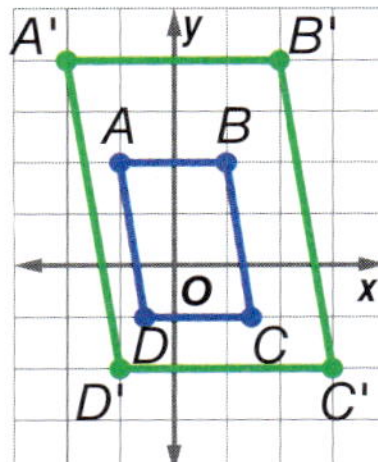

13. 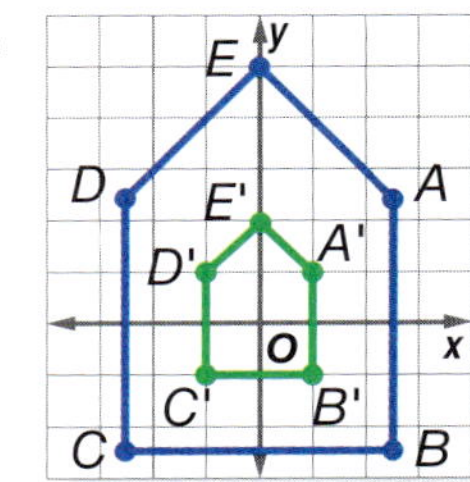

H.O.T. Problems

14. **OPEN ENDED** Graph a triangle and its image after a magnification with a scale factor of $\frac{4}{3}$.

15. **REASONING** Three figures are each dilated. Figure 1 is dilated by a scale factor of $\frac{3}{2}$. Figure 2 is dilated by a scale factor of $\frac{7}{8}$. Figure 3 is dilated by a scale factor of 4.25. Each dilation is a magnification except for which one? Explain your reasoning.

16. **CHALLENGE** Write a general rule for finding the new coordinates of any ordered pair (x, y) after a magnification with a scale factor of k.

17. **WRITING IN MATH** Four figures A, B, C, and D each undergo a different transformation. Figure A is translated. Figure B is reflected. Figure C is rotated. Figure D is magnified. Write a few sentences describing the effects on the shape and size of each of the original figures after each kind of transformation.

OCCT Practice PASS3.3

18. Identify the transformation shown on the coordinate plane at the right.

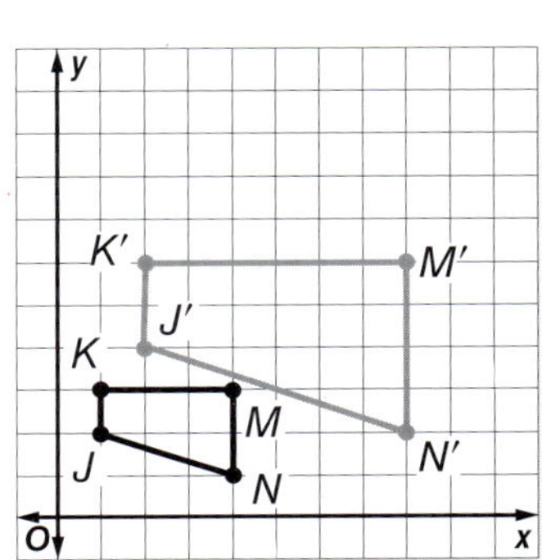

A rotated 90° clockwise around point K

B translated up 4 units and to the right 1 unit

C magnified by a scale factor of 2

D rotated 270° counterclockwise around the origin

Perimeter of Composite Figures

MAIN IDEA

Find the perimeter of composite figures to solve real-world problems.

OK PASS

4.3 Find the area and **perimeter of composite figures to solve application problems.** *Also addresses 7M4.1.*

OK Math Online

glencoe.com

GET READY for the Lesson

SWIMMING POOLS The Perez family is installing a swimming pool in their backyard like the one shown at the right.

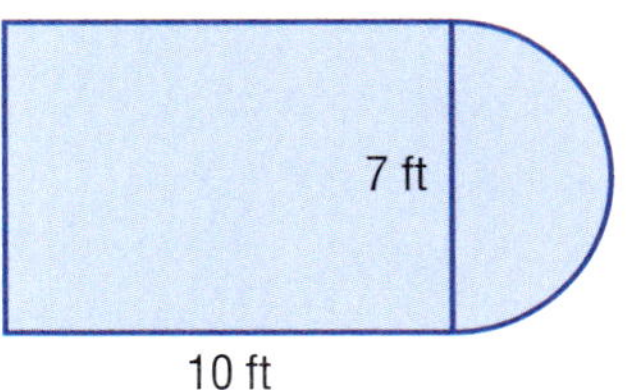

1. What shapes make up the swimming pool?
2. If the family wants to find the distance around the swimming pool, how can they determine this distance?
3. Find the perimeter of the rectangle.
4. Find the circumference of the semicircle.
5. Do the rectangle and the semicircle share a common interior edge? If so, what is its length?
6. Add the lengths from Exercises 3 and 4. Then subtract the length from Exercise 5. What is the result?

The swimming pool above is a real-world example of a composite two-dimensional figure. Recall that the perimeter is the distance around any closed geometric figure. So, the perimeter of a composite figure is the sum of the lengths of its outside edges. Look at the figure shown below.

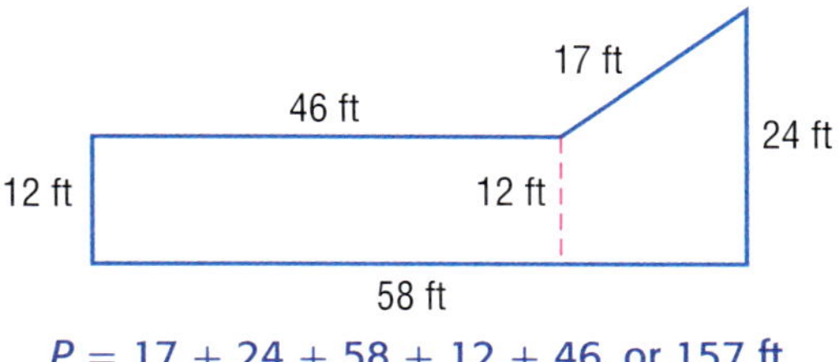

$P = 17 + 24 + 58 + 12 + 46$, or 157 ft

Note that the length represented by the dotted lines is not counted in the perimeter of the composite figure because it does not represent an outside edge.

Recall that circumference and perimeter both describe the distance around a figure. So, if a composite figure includes a semicircle, then the perimeter of the composite figure includes the circumference of the semicircle.

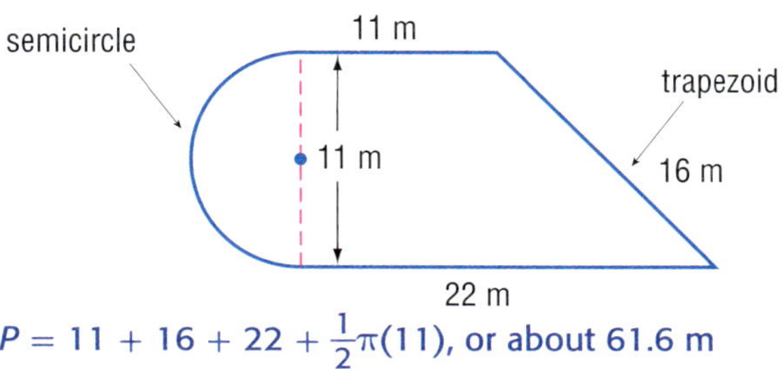

$P = 11 + 16 + 22 + \frac{1}{2}\pi(11)$, or about 61.6 m

Read Math

Composite Figures Composite figures are also sometimes called *complex figures* or *irregular figures.*

EXAMPLE Perimeter of a Composite Figure

Calculate the perimeter of the composite figure shown at the right.

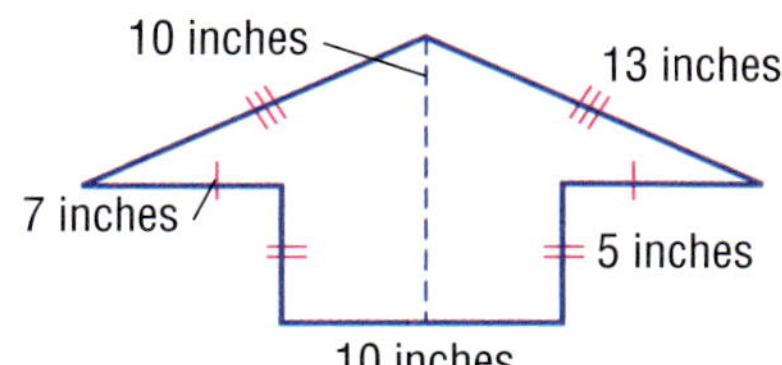

Start at the top vertex of the figure and add clockwise to find the perimeter of the figure. Do not include the length represented by the dotted line as this is not an outside edge.

The perimeter is 13 + 7 + 5 + 10 + 5 + 7 + 13, or 60 inches.

Real-World EXAMPLE

PATIOS Mrs. Thorne wants to plant flowers around her patio as shown by the figure at the right. What is the perimeter of her patio?

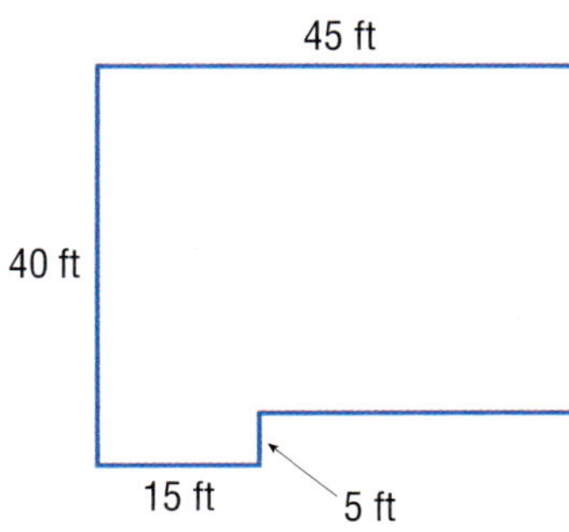

There are two unknown lengths. Label those lengths as x and y as shown below.

Find the unknown lengths by breaking the figure into two shapes.

Find x. You know that $x + 5$ must equal 40. So, $x = 35$ feet.

Find y. You know that $y + 15$ must equal 45. So, $y = 30$ feet.

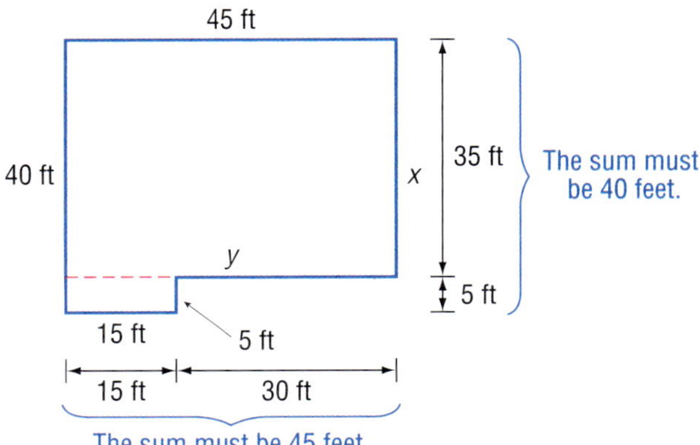

Find the perimeter of the composite figure.

The perimeter of the patio is 45 + 40 + 15 + 5 + 30 + 35, or 170 feet.

Check for Reasonableness Since each side is about 45 feet, find 45×4. $45 \times 4 = 180$. So, $180 \approx 170$. ✔

CHECK Your Understanding

Calculate the perimeter of each composite figure.

Example 1 (p. OK25)

1. 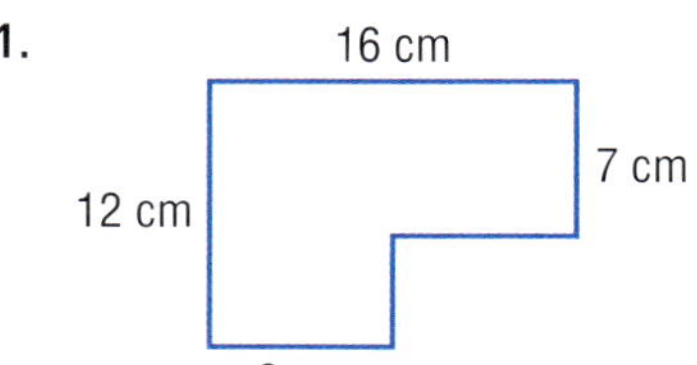

2. 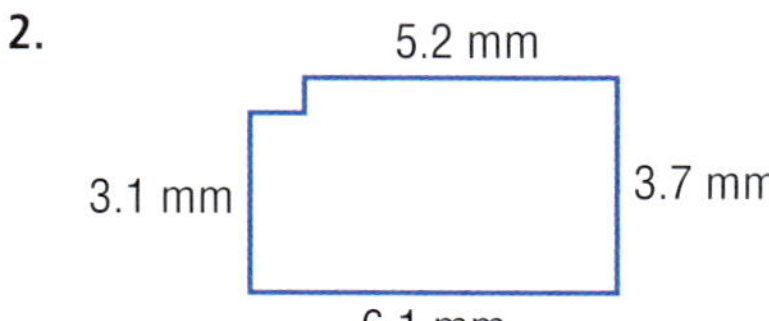

Example 2 (p. OK25)

3. **WINDOWS** A builder wants to place a wooden border around a window as shown. What is the perimeter of the window? Use 3.14 for π.

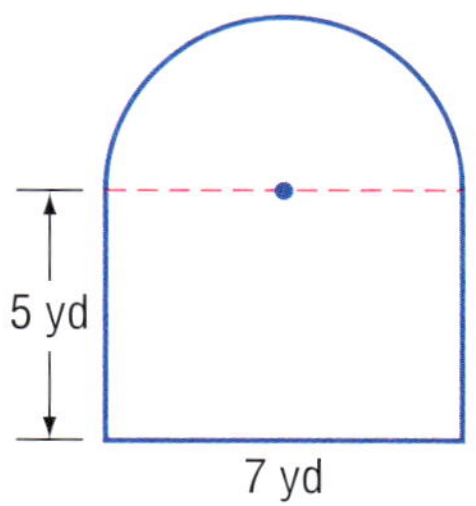

Practice and Problem Solving

HOMEWORK HELP	
For Exercises	See Examples
4–11	1, 2

Calculate the perimeter of each composite figure.

4. 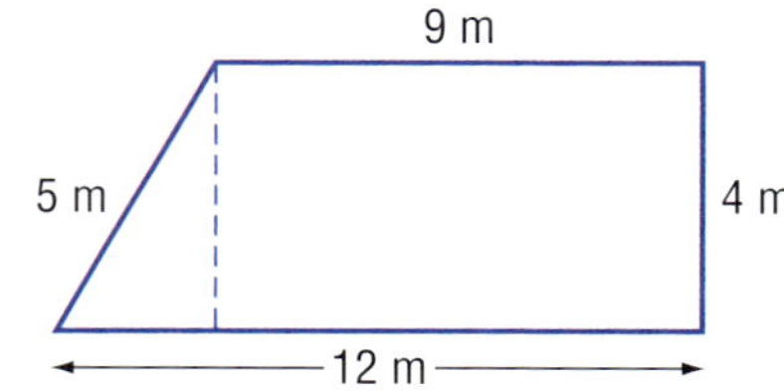

5. 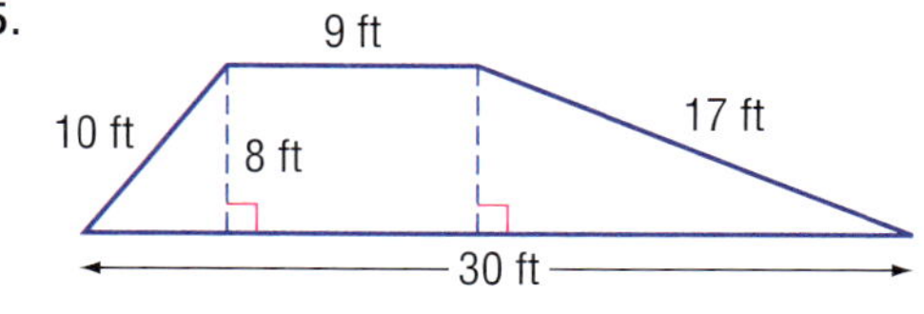

6. 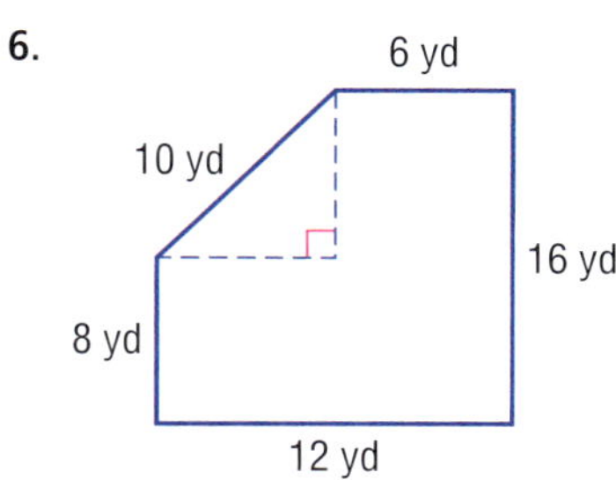

7. 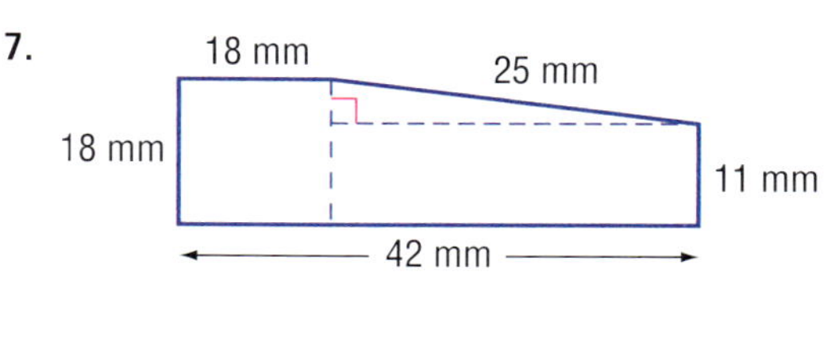

8. **BORDERS** Sophia wants to install a border around the ceiling of her kitchen. The dimensions of her kitchen are shown at the right. Calculate the perimeter of the kitchen.

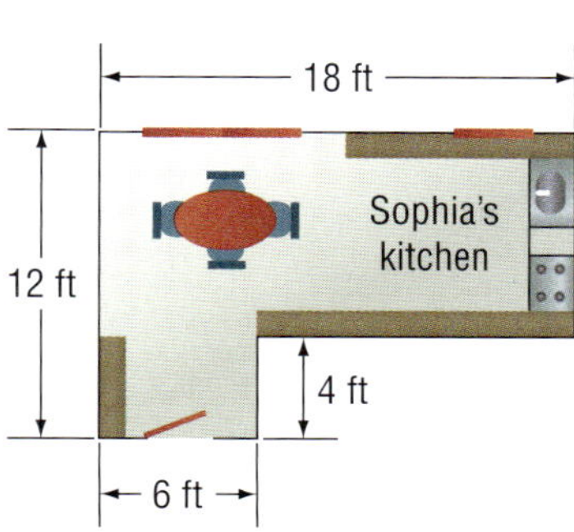

9. **GEOMETRY** Refer to Exercise 5. The height of the composite figure is 8 feet. Is this information needed to find the perimeter of the figure? the area? Explain your reasoning.

10. **MEASUREMENT** Refer to the composite figure at the right. Each grid square has a side length of one foot. Calculate the perimeter of the composite figure.

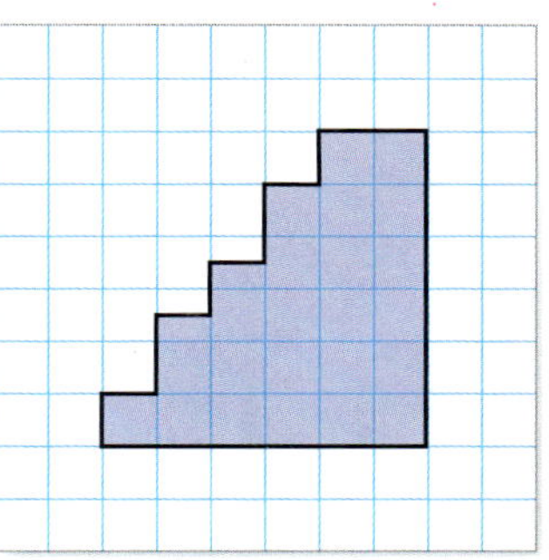

11. **GEOMETRY** A trapezoid can be thought of as a composite figure. One particular trapezoid is comprised of a rectangle and two congruent right triangles. The rectangle has a length of 24 centimeters and a width of 15 centimeters. Each triangle has a base of 8 centimeters and a height of 15 centimeters. The remaining side of each triangle is 17 centimeters. Find the perimeter of the trapezoid.

H.O.T. Problems

12. **CHALLENGE** Find the distance around the composite figure at the right.

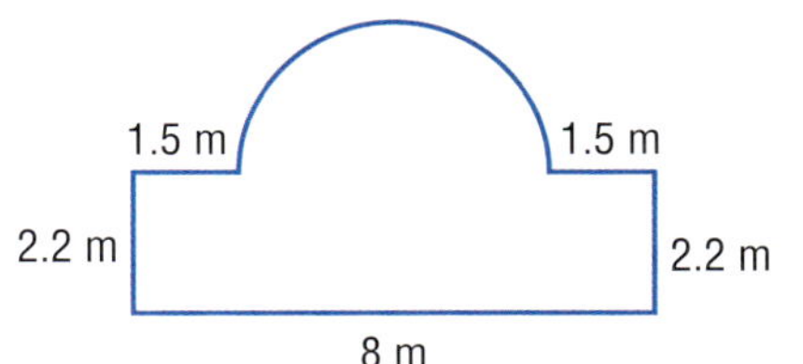

13. **OPEN ENDED** Draw a composite figure in which there is extra information given but no missing information that is required to calculate the figure's perimeter. Then calculate its perimeter.

14. **WRITING IN MATH** Describe how you would calculate the distance around the composite figure shown at the right.

1.5 m
1.5 m
2.2 m
2.2 m
8 m

OCCT Practice PASS4.3

15. The composite figure shown is made up of line segments that meet at right angles.

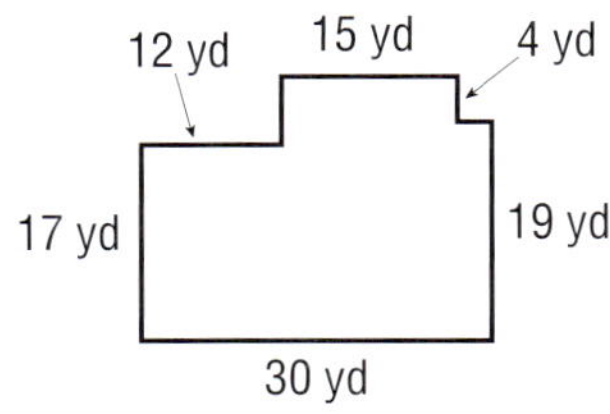

What is the perimeter of the composite figure?

A 97 yards

B 100 yards

C 103 yards

D 106 yards

16. A sandbox at the local park is in the shape shown below.

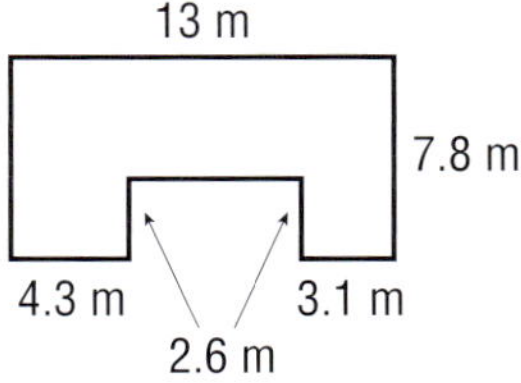

What is the perimeter of the sandbox?

A 46.8 meters

B 41.6 meters

C 41.2 meters

D 33.4 meters

GET READY FOR THE OCCT

This spring, you will take your Grade 7 OCCT test. OCCT stands for Oklahoma Core Curriculum Tests. You will apply the concepts and skills that you have learned throughout the year in order to answer multiple-choice questions.

Multiple-Choice Items

You will select the correct response from four answer choices. Your teacher will provide you with an answer sheet to fill in your answer choices.

How Can I Get Ready?

The OCCT covers Oklahoma's Priority Academic Student Skills (PASS) for Mathematics, Grade 7. The following pages give you practice questions similar to those found on the test. You can use these practice pages in the weeks before the test to determine if you are ready. If you are struggling with any of the items, lesson references are provided so you can go back and review from the pages in your textbook.

Algebraic Reasoning

1. Solve the inequality below for k. **(Lesson OK 1)** **(PASS1.3)**

$$3k + 7 \geq 16$$

A $k \leq 3$
B $k \leq 2$
C $k \geq 3$
D $k \geq 2$

2. Solve the inequality below for x. **(Lesson OK 1)** **(PASS1.3)**

$$5x \geq 30$$

A $x \geq 6$
B $x \leq 6$
C $x \geq 150$
D $x \leq 150$

3. Find the value of g in the equation $7g + 8 = -13$. **(Lesson 6-6)** **(PASS1.2)**

A $g = -3$
B $g = \frac{-5}{7}$
C $g = \frac{5}{7}$
D $g = 3$

4. Carla spent \$32.10 for jeans and a shirt. The total included \$2.10 for sales tax. Which equation could be used to find the cost of the two items before taxes? **(Lesson 3-2)** **(PASS1.2)**

A $x - 2.10 = 32.10$
B $x + 2.10 = 32.10$
C $x + 32.10 = 2.10$
D $x - 32.10 = 2.10$

5. Party House charges \$35 plus \$6.50 per person for a birthday party. Mrs. Lutz wants to spend no more than \$120 on her party. Which of the following inequalities could be used to solve this problem? **(Lesson 6-6)** **(PASS1.3)**

A $6.5x + 35 \geq 120$
B $6.5 + 35x \geq 120$
C $6.5x + 35 \leq 120$
D $6.5 + 35x \leq 120$

6. Which value of x makes the following equation true? **(Lesson 3-5)** **(PASS1.2)**

$$\frac{x}{3} + 8 = 16$$

A 32
B 24
C 16
D 8

7. The table shows the number of pizzas the Pizza Barn can make every hour.

Number of Hours, x	Total Number of Pizzas, y
1	24
2	48
3	72
4	96

Which function rule represents the data? **(Lesson 1-10)** **(PASS1.1)**

A $y = 12x$
B $y = 18x$
C $y = 24x$
D $y = 36x$

Get Ready for the OCCT

8. Which of the following tables displays a negative rate of change? **(Lesson OK 3)** **(PASS1.1)**

A

x	1	3	5	7
y	2	3	4	5

B

x	0	3	6	9
y	1	3	5	7

C

x	1	2	3	4
y	8	6	4	2

D

x	2	3	4	5
y	6	7	8	9

9. All of the following statements are false concerning a linear relationship except for which one? **(Lesson OK 2)** **(PASS1.1)**

A A linear function always has a constant rate of change.

B A linear function always passes through the origin.

C A linear function always has a positive rate of change.

D A linear function always has a negative rate of change.

10. Brittany needs \$35 to go to the water park. She has \$11. She earns \$6 per hour working at her job. The equation $6h + 11 = 35$ shows this relationship. How many hours does Brittany need to work to earn enough money to go to the water park? **(Lesson 3-5)** **(PASS1.2)**

A 7 hours

B 6 hours

C 5 hours

D 4 hours

11. Twice a number increased by 10 is equal to 30. What is the number? **(Lesson 3-5)** **(PASS1.2)**

A 2

B 5

C 8

D 10

12. Find the slope of the line below that shows the cost of T-shirts and the number of T-shirts sold. **(Lesson 6-3)** **(PASS1.1)**

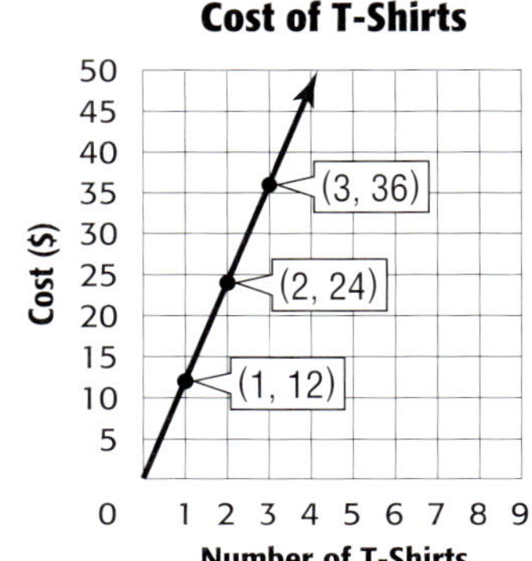

A 6

B 12

C 18

D 24

13. Which of the following graphs has a y-intercept of 3 and a rate of change that is equal to -2? **(Lesson OK 3)** **(PASS1.1)**

A

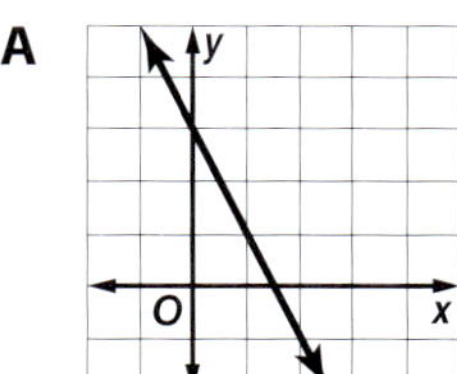

C

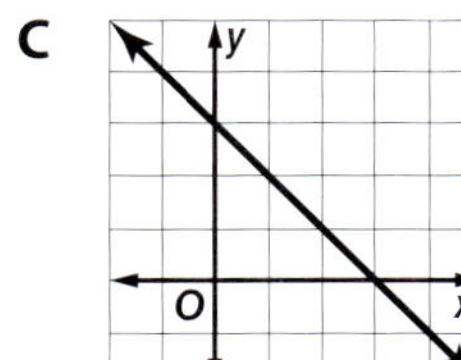

B

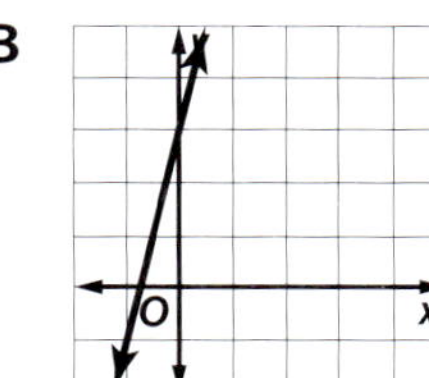

D

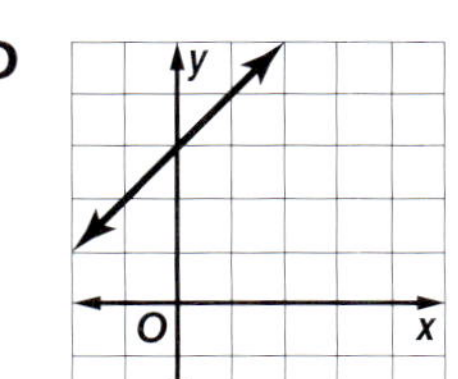

14. Which of the following best describes the positive rate of change between the variables x and y shown in the table below? **(Lesson OK 3)** **(PASS1.1)**

x	y
0	0
1	5
2	10
3	15

A As the values of x increase, the values of y also increase.

B Each value of x is five times the corresponding value of y.

C As the values of x decrease, the values of y increase.

D Each value of y is the square root of each corresponding value of x.

15. Which graph below shows a negative rate of change? **(Lesson OK 3)** **(PASS1.1)**

A

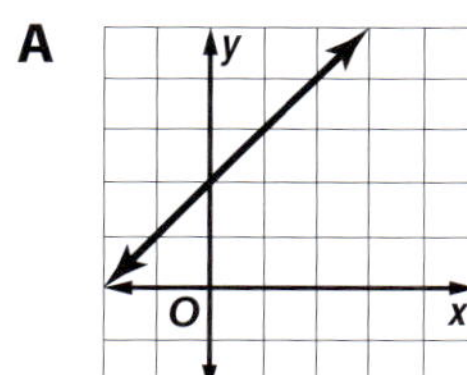

C

y
O
x

B

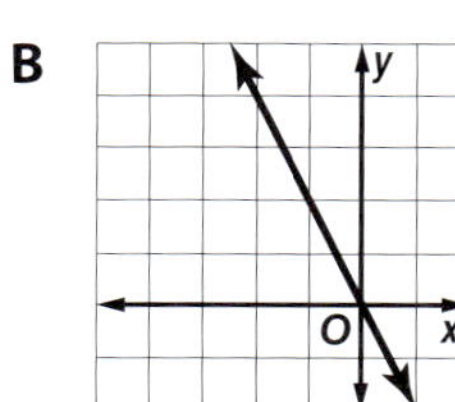

D

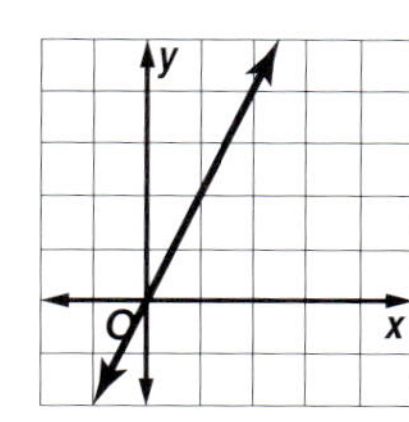

16. What is the value of b if $-5b - 6 = -21$? **(Lesson 3-5)** **(PASS1.2)**

A -3

B -2

C 3

D 4

17. Anna wrote the equation $3m - 1 = 14$ in her notebook. What should be her first step to solve this equation correctly? **(Lesson 3-5)** **(PASS1.2)**

A Subtract 1 from each side of the equal sign.

B Divide both sides of the equation by 3.

C Add 1 to each side of the equal sign.

D Multiply both sides of the equation by 3.

18. Which number line below represents the solution to the inequality $x + 16 \leq 25$? **(Lesson OK 1)** **(PASS1.3)**

A

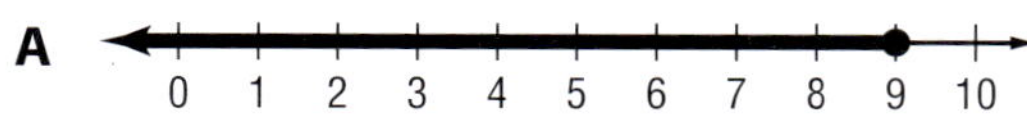

B

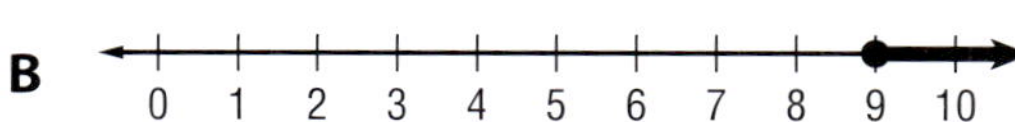

C

0 1 2 3 4 5 6 7 8 9 10

D

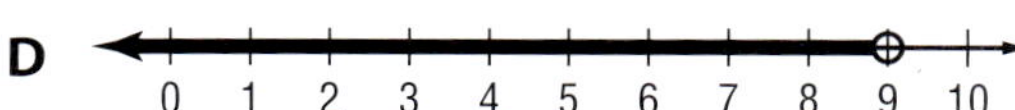

19. Kareem has already read 95 pages of a novel. He continues to read 25 pages each day. Which equation represents the number of days d it will take Kareem to read 350 pages? **(Lesson 3-5)** **(PASS1.2)**

A $95d + 25 = 350$

B $95 + 25d = 350$

C $95 - 25d = 350$

D $95d - 25 = 350$

20. Which of the following graphs has a y-intercept of 4 and a rate of change that is equal to 1? **(Lesson OK 3)** **(PASS1.1)**

A

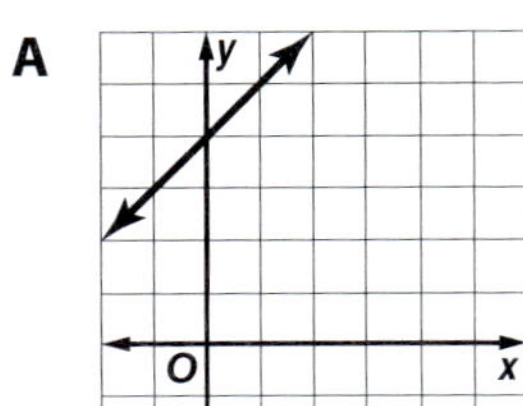

B

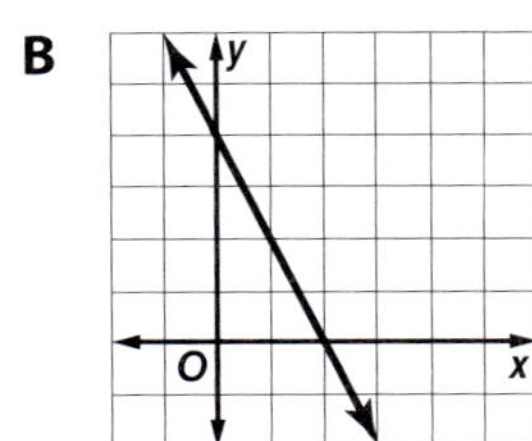

C

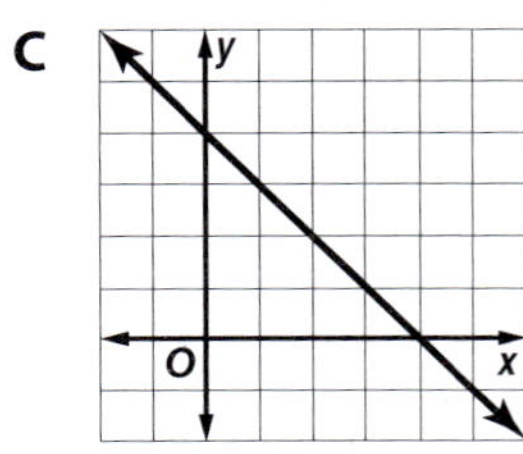

D

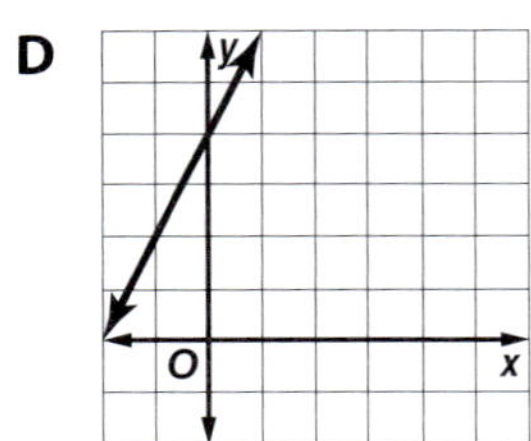

21. Monica has $21 to spend at the movies. She knows that her ticket will cost at least $8. Which inequality below represents the amount of money m in dollars she will have left over after she buys her ticket? **(Lesson OK 1)** **(PASS1.3)**

A $m < 29$

B $m > 29$

C $m < 13$

D $m > 13$

22. All of the following statements are true concerning the graph below except for which one? **(Lesson OK 3)** **(PASS1.1)**

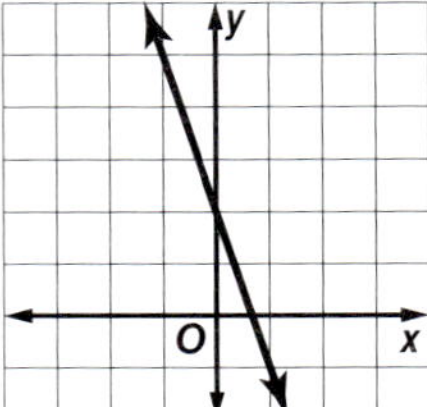

A The graph is linear.

B The graph displays a positive rate of change.

C The y-intercept of the graph is 2.

D The slope of the graph is –3.

23. Which statement is true concerning the graph below? **(Lesson OK 2)** **(PASS1.1)**

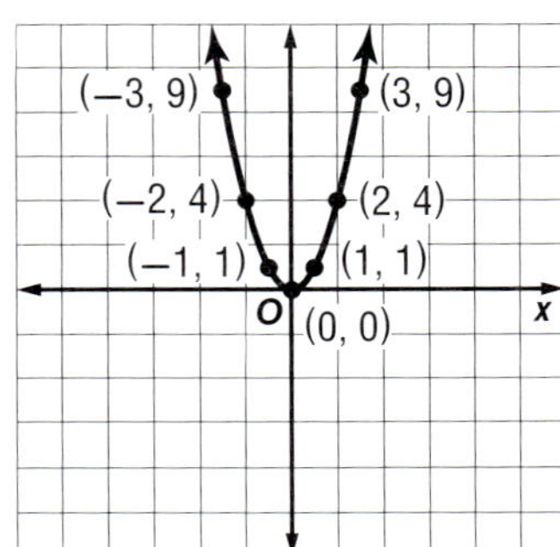

A The graph is linear.

B The graph is nonlinear.

C The graph has a constant rate of change.

D The slope of the graph is $\frac{2}{3}$.

24. Aida is 4 years older than Brad. Together their ages total 22 years. Which of the following equations could be used to find Brad's age b? **(Lesson 6-6)** **(PASS1.2)**

A $4b = 22$

B $4b + b = 22$

C $b + 4 = 22$

D $2b + 4 = 22$

Number Sense and Operation

1. Shenequa took her friends out to dinner at a nice restaurant. The bill came to a total of \$39.90. Shenequa decided to leave a 20% tip. Which of the following represents the amount of the tip? **(Lesson 7-6)** **(PASS2.2.b)**

A \$7.98
B \$6.50
C \$4.77
D \$3.99

2. Which of the following statements is true? **(Lesson 12-1)** **(PASS2.1.b)**

A $3^3 = \sqrt{3}$
B $(\sqrt{3})^2 = 3$
C $(\sqrt{3})^3 = 3$
D $3^2 = \sqrt{3}$

3. Which of the following represents the numbers -8, 8.5, $-7\frac{4}{5}$, and -8.5 in order from least to greatest? **(Lesson 4-9)** **(PASS2.1.a)**

A $8.5, -7\frac{4}{5}, -8, -8.5$
B $8.5, -8, -7\frac{4}{5}, -8.5$
C $-8.5, -7\frac{4}{5}, -8, 8.5$
D $-8.5, -8, -7\frac{4}{5}, 8.5$

4. Jackson needs to show the correct relationship between 25% and $\frac{1}{3}$. Which statement should he write? **(Lesson 4-9)** **(PASS2.1.a)**

A $25\% < \frac{1}{3}$
B $25\% > \frac{1}{3}$
C $\frac{1}{3} < 25\%$
D $\frac{1}{3} = 25\%$

5. A square dog pen has an area of 16 square feet. The length in feet of each side can be found by evaluating $\sqrt{16}$. Which of the following points shows the location of $\sqrt{16}$ on the number line? **(Lesson 1-3)** **(PASS2.1.b)**

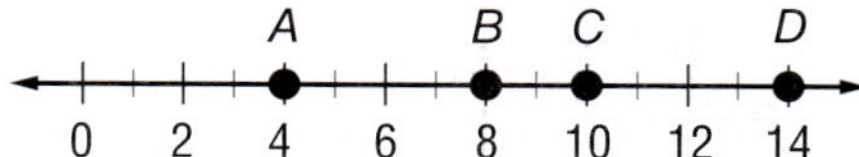

A point A
B point B
C point C
D point D

6. Which of the following expressions has the same value as $7^2 \cdot 8^3$? **(Lesson 1-2)** **(PASS2.2.c)**

A $7 \cdot 2 \cdot 8 \cdot 3$
B $7 \cdot 7 \cdot 8 \cdot 8 \cdot 8$
C $7 \cdot 2 + 8 \cdot 3$
D 56^6

7. How many square feet are in a square yard? **(Lesson 6-3)** **(PASS2.2.a)**

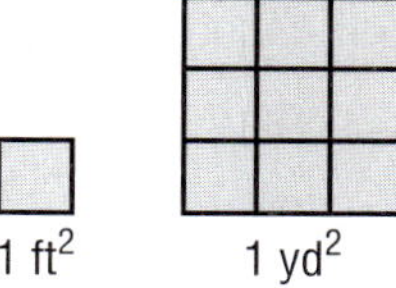

A 3
B 6
C 9
D 12

8. Figures 1 and 2 below are similar. The side lengths of Figure 2 are $1\frac{2}{3}$ times as long as the side lengths of Figure 1. Find the value of x. **(Lesson 10-7)** **(PASS2.1.c)**

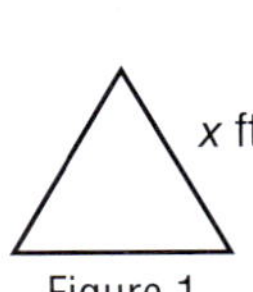

Figure 1

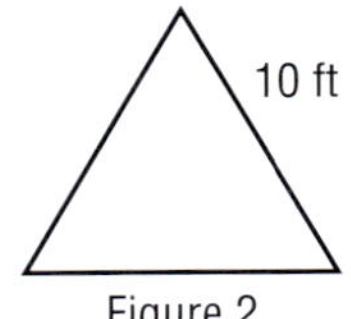

Figure 2

A 15 ft
B 9 ft
C 8 ft
D 6 ft

9. Liseli created a scale drawing of her bedroom. One centimeter on her drawing represents 3 feet in the actual dimensions of her bedroom. If her bedroom measures 12 feet by 15 feet, what are the dimensions of her scale drawing? **(Lesson 6-8)** **(PASS2.1.b)**

A 3 cm by 4 cm
B 3 cm by 5 cm
C 4 cm by 5 cm
D 5 cm by 6 cm

10. Mei-Ling bought a sweater for $28. The original price of the sweater was $36. Which proportion can be used to find p, the percent of discount? **(Lesson 7-7)** **(PASS2.2.b)**

A $\frac{p}{100} = \frac{8}{36}$
B $\frac{p}{36} = \frac{28}{100}$
C $\frac{p}{28} = \frac{36}{100}$
D $\frac{p}{100} = \frac{28}{36}$

11. A number is squared. The result is 100. Which operation would you perform to find the original number? **(Lesson 12-1)** **(PASS2.1.b)**

A $100 \div 2$
B $100 - 50$
C 100×100
D $\sqrt{100}$

12. The area of the model below is 49 square units. Which of the following expressions represents the length of one side of the model? **(Lesson 1-3)** **(PASS2.1.b)**

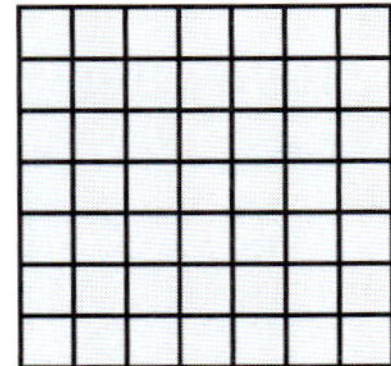

A $\sqrt{25}$
B $\sqrt{36}$
C $\sqrt{49}$
D $\sqrt{64}$

13. Canned soup is on sale at the grocery store for a price of $5 for 4 cans of soup. How much will it cost to buy 10 cans of soup at this price? **(Lesson 6-6)** **(PASS2.2.a)**

A $10.00
B $12.50
C $17.50
D $20.00

14. The square root of 50 is between which two whole numbers? **(Lesson 1-3)** **(PASS2.1.b)**

A 4 and 5
B 5 and 6
C 6 and 7
D 7 and 8

15. Which one of the following statements is true? **(Lesson 4-9)** **(PASS2.1.a)**

A $\frac{2}{3} < \frac{3}{5}$

B $3.14 \leq 3.41$

C $2.35 \geq 2.53$

D $1\frac{1}{4} > 1\frac{1}{3}$

16. Kirima is buying a new coat. The original price of the coat she would like to buy is $53.00. The sign below is displayed in the store window.

Find the sale price of the coat after the discount is applied. **(Lesson 7-7)** **(PASS2.1.b)**

A $37.10 **C** $26.50

B $35.00 **D** $15.90

17. Which model below demonstrates that the square root of 16 is 4? **(Lesson 1-3)** **(PASS1.1.b)**

A

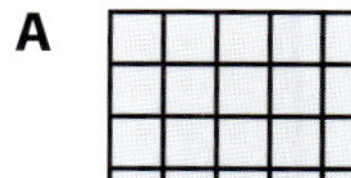

C

B

D

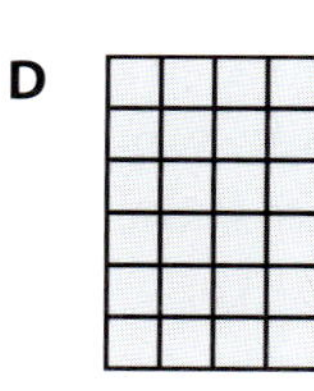

18. Simplify the expression $6^8 \times 6^4$. **(Lesson 1-2)** **(PASS2.2.c)**

A 6^4 **C** 6^{32}

B 6^{12} **D** 36^{12}

19. The number line below correctly demonstrates which one of the following statements? **(Lesson 1-3)** **(PASS2.1.b)**

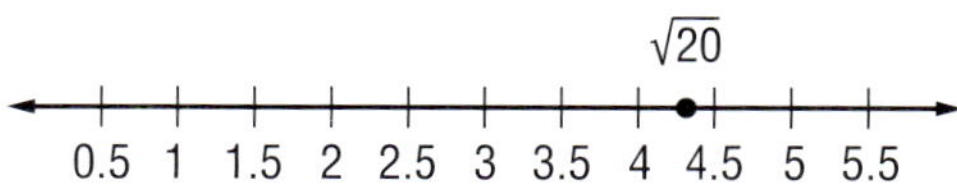

A The square root of 20 is between 4 and 5.

B The square root of 20 is greater than 5.

C The square root of 20 is about 4.8.

D The square root of 20 is less than 4.

20. A scale drawing of an apartment is shown below. If 1 inch on the drawing is equivalent to 3 feet, what are the actual dimensions of the living room? **(Lesson 6-8)** **(PASS2.1.c)**

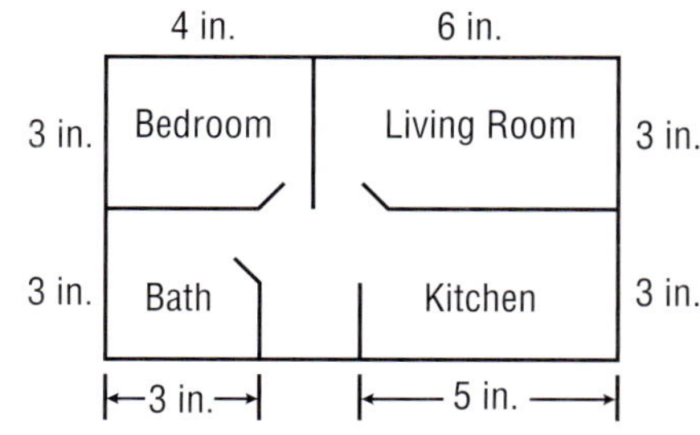

A 3 ft by 6 ft **C** 9 ft by 18 ft

B 3 ft by 9 ft **D** 18 ft by 27 ft

21. Simplify the expression $9^2 \div 3 + 4 \cdot 5$. **(Lesson 1-4)** **(PASS2.2.c)**

A 144 **C** 47

B 81 **D** 36

22. The Jeffers family went to a restaurant for lunch. The bill came to $27. If they want to leave a 15% tip, how much should they leave? **(Lesson 7-2)** **(PASS2.2.b)**

A $405 **C** $4.05
B $40.50 **D** $0.45

23. House cats sleep for about 65% of each day. Which proportion can be used to find the total number of hours h that a typical house cat will sleep over a period of 5 days? **(Lesson 7-2)** **(PASS2.2.b)**

A $\frac{65}{100} = \frac{h}{5}$ **C** $\frac{65}{100} = \frac{120}{h}$
B $\frac{h}{100} = \frac{65}{120}$ **D** $\frac{65}{100} = \frac{h}{120}$

24. Which one of the following number lines represents the square root of 12? **(Lesson 1-3)** **(PASS2.1.b)**

A −0.5 0 0.5 1 1.5 2 2.5 3 3.5 4 4.5

B −0.5 0 0.5 1 1.5 2 2.5 3 3.5 4 4.5

C −0.5 0 0.5 1 1.5 2 2.5 3 3.5 4 4.5

D −0.5 0 0.5 1 1.5 2 2.5 3 3.5 4 4.5

25. Pedro created a scale drawing of his room. One inch on his drawing represents 2.5 feet in the actual dimensions of the room. If the room measures 36 feet by 40 feet, what are the dimensions of the drawing? **(Lesson 6-8)** **(PASS2.1.b)**

A 3.6 in. by 4 in. **C** 14.4 in. by 16 in.
B 6 in. by 5 in. **D** 18 in. by 20 in.

26. Martin is buying an MP3 player. The original price of the MP3 player is $75.00 and it is discounted by 15%. What is the amount of the discount? **(Lesson 7-7)** **(PASS2.1.b)**

A $7.50 **C** $15.00
B $11.25 **D** $63.75

27. Brent wants to compare the two numbers below. Which symbol makes the statement true? **(Lesson 4-9)** **(PASS2.1.a)**

$$2\frac{1}{4} \bullet 2.14$$

A $<$ **C** $=$
B $>$ **D** $\geq$

28. The area of the model below is 81 square units. Which of the following expressions represents the length of one side of the model? **(Lesson 1-3)** **(PASS2.1.b)**

A $\sqrt{81}$ **C** $\sqrt{64}$
B $\sqrt{49}$ **D** $\sqrt{9}$

29. If the area of a square is 196 square inches, what is the length in inches of the sides of the square? **(Lesson 12-1)** **(PASS2.1.b)**

A 11 **C** 13
B 12 **D** 14

30. Figures 1 and 2 below are similar. The side lengths of Figure 2 are $4\frac{1}{2}$ times as long as the side lengths of Figure 1. Find the value of x. **(Lesson 10-7)** **(PASS2.1.c)**

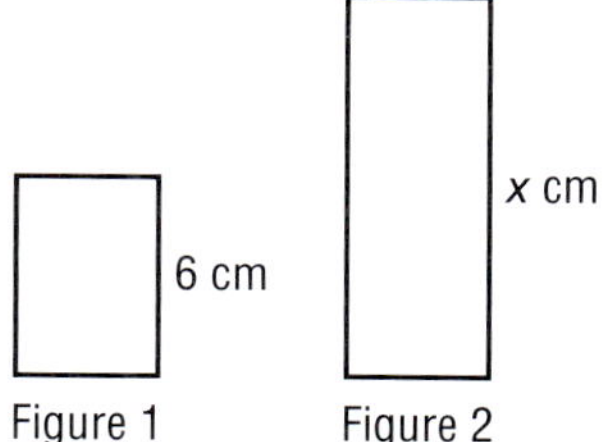

A 10.5 cm
B 24 cm
C 27 cm
D 30 cm

31. If each dimension of the rectangle below is doubled, what is the percent of increase in the area? **(Lesson 7-6)** **(PASS2.2.b)**

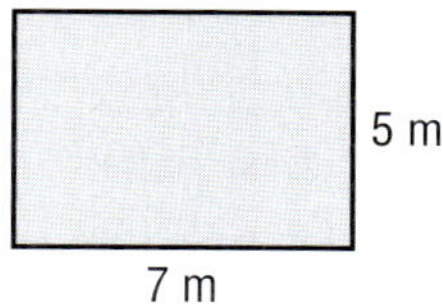

A 100%
B 200%
C 300%
D 400%

32. Hannah spent \$11.75 at the bakery. She bought 3 donuts at \$0.75 each and 6 bagels for \$1.25 each. How much money did she leave for a tip? **(Lesson 7-6)** **(PASS2.2.b)**

A \$1.25
B \$1.50
C \$1.75
D \$2.00

33. Simplify the expression below. **(Lesson 1-4)** **(PASS2.2.c)**

$$(4^2 - 2^3) + (3 \times 4 \div 2)$$

A 38
B 28
C 14
D 6

34. The number line below correctly demonstrates which one of the following statements? **(Lesson 1-3)** **(PASS2.1.b)**

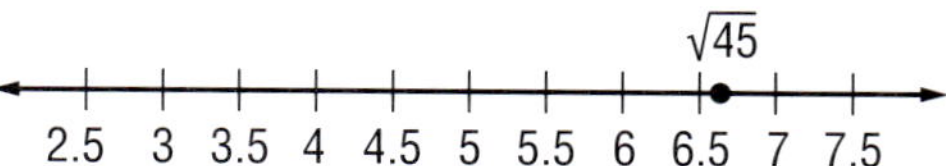

A The square root of 45 is about 6.25.
B The square root of 45 is greater than 7.
C The square root of 45 is less than 6.
D The square root of 45 is between 6 and 7.

35. Simplify the expression below. **(Lesson 1-4)** **(PASS2.2.c)**

$$6 + 4^3 \cdot 2 - 15 \div 3$$

A 345
B 135
C 129
D 36

36. Which model represents the square of 3? **(Lesson 1-3)** **(PASS2.1.b)**

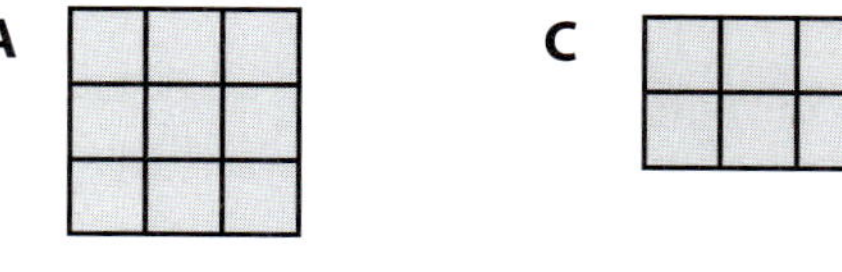

37. What is the value of $2(5^2 + 3^2 \cdot 7)$? **(Lesson 1-4)** **(PASS2.2.c)**

A 88
B 176
C 238
D 476

Geometry

1. All of the following statements are true concerning the triangle below except for which one? **(Lesson 10-4)** **(PASS3.1)**

A The triangle is an equilateral triangle.
B The triangle is an isosceles triangle.
C The triangle is an acute triangle.
D The triangle is a polygon.

2. Candace wants to write a true statement comparing squares and rectangles. Which of the following statements could she write? **(Lesson 10-6)** **(PASS3.1)**

A Squares have four right angles while rectangles have only one right angle.
B All squares are rectangles.
C All rectangles are squares.
D Rectangles have four congruent sides, while squares only have one pair of opposite and congruent sides.

3. Find the value of x in the figure below. Lines m and n are parallel. **(Lesson LA 3)** **(PASS3.2)**

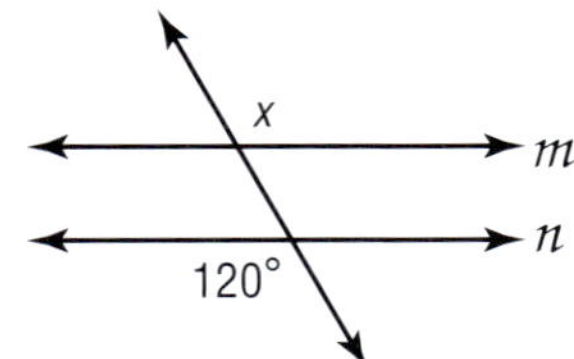

A 40° **C** 100°
B 60° **D** 120°

4. Which graph shows triangle ABC with vertices at $A(3, 6)$, $B(4, 9)$, and $C(7, 6)$ after a translation of 3 units left? **(Lesson 10-9)** **(PASS3.3)**

A

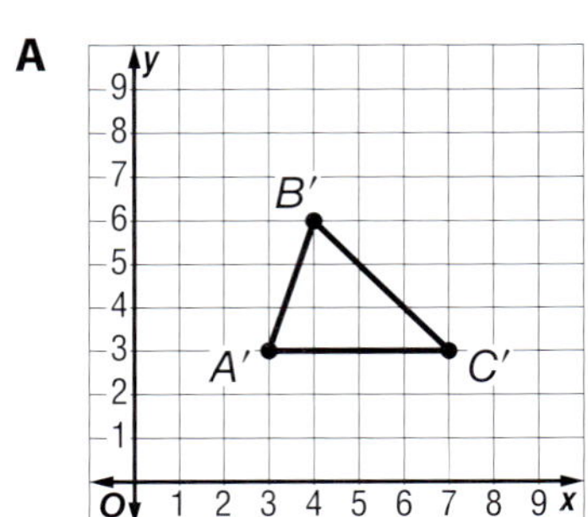

B

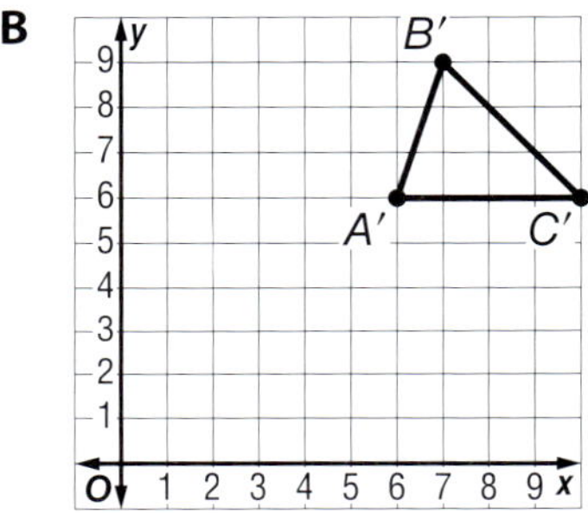

C

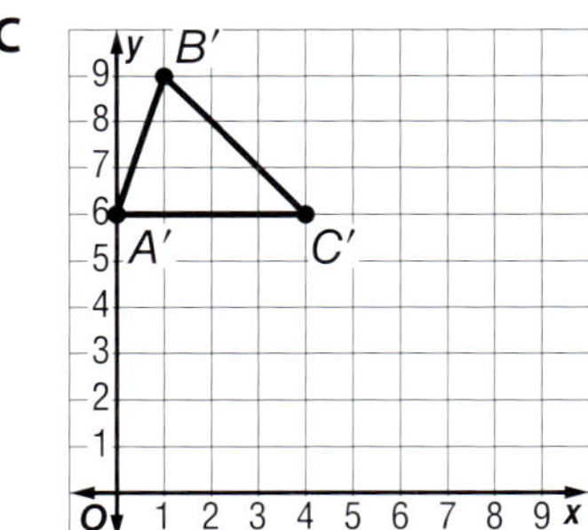

D

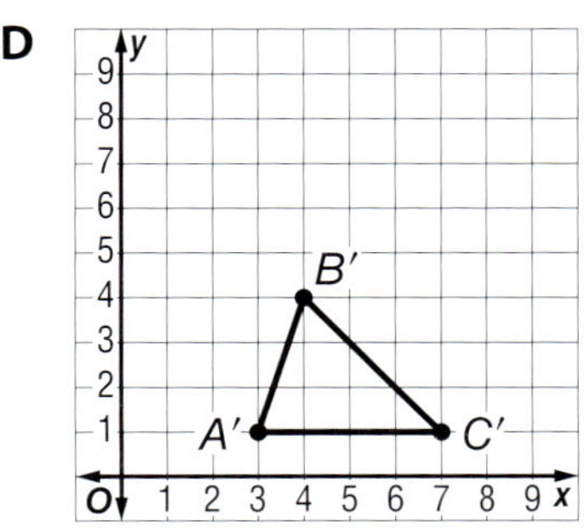

5. Which of the following is the best classification for the figure below? **(Lesson 10-6)** **(PASS3.1)**

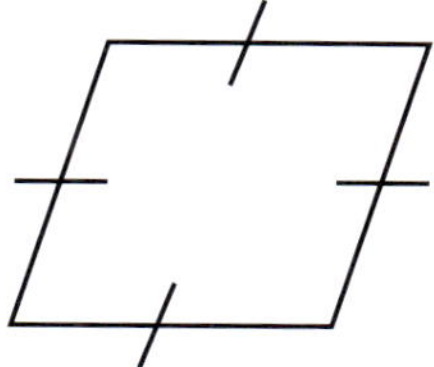

A square

B rhombus

C rectangle

D trapezoid

6. Which one of the following figures shows that $\angle 1$ and $\angle 2$ are alternate exterior angles? **(Lesson LA 3)** **(PASS3.2)**

A

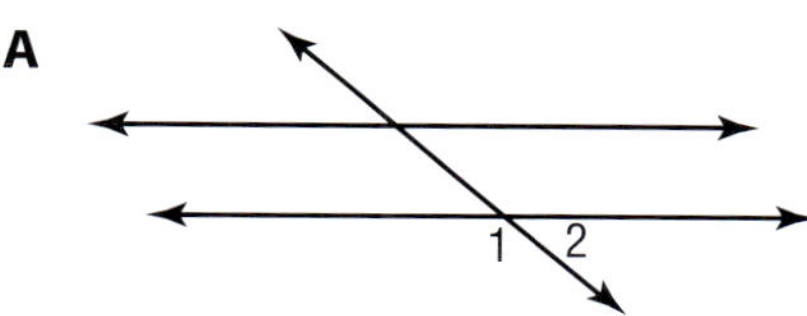

B

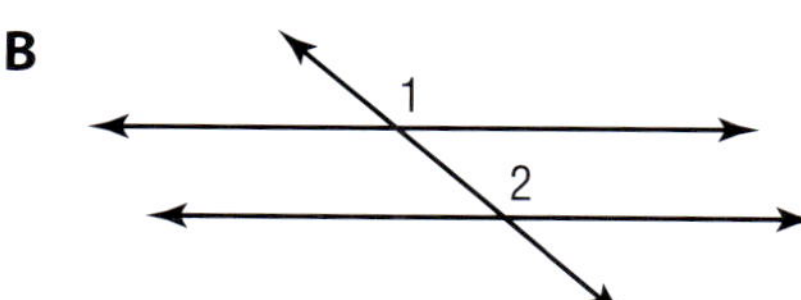

C

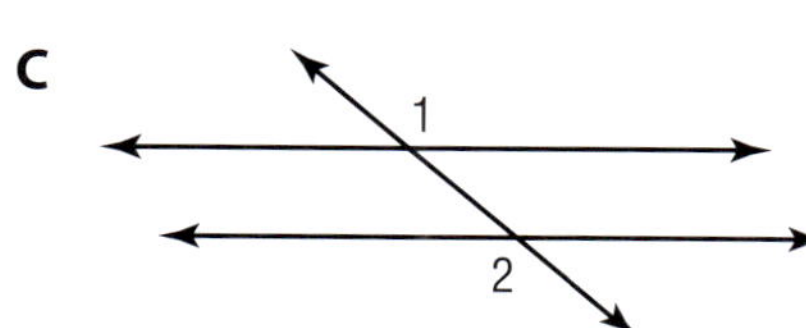

D

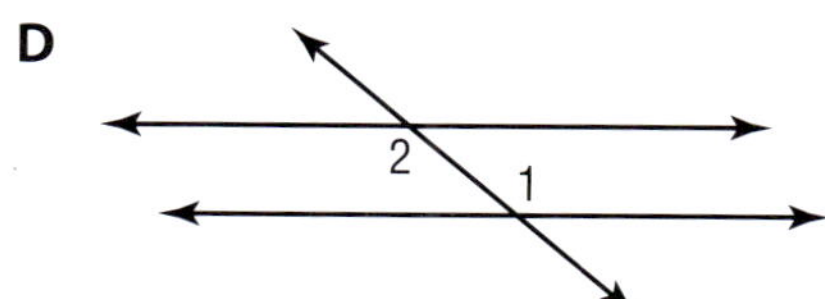

7. Which transformation is shown below? **(Lesson 10-9)** **(PASS3.3)**

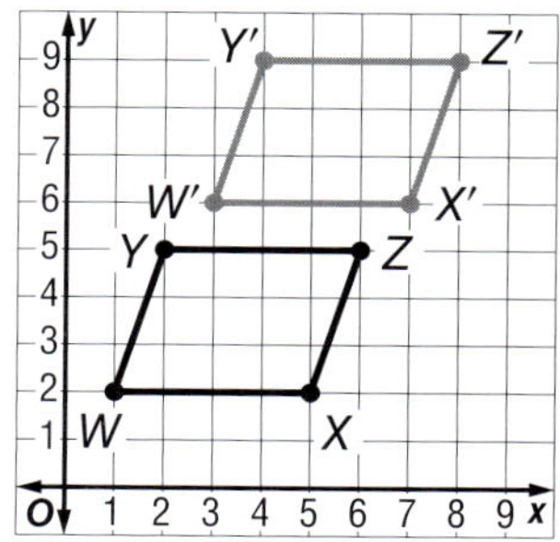

A rotation

B reflection across the y-axis

C translation up four units and right two units

D translation up two units and right four units

8. Which of the following figures is a regular polygon? **(Lesson 10-8)** **(PASS3.1)**

A **C**

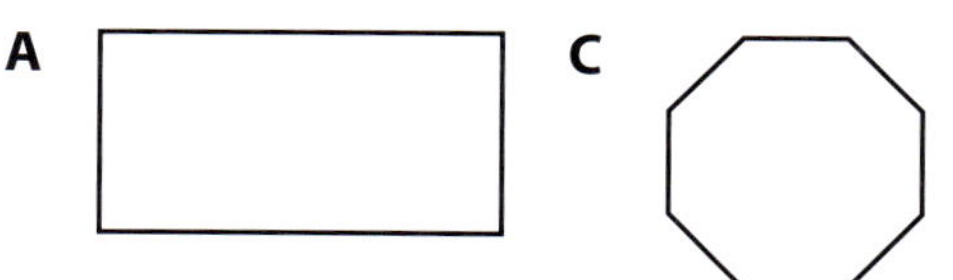

B

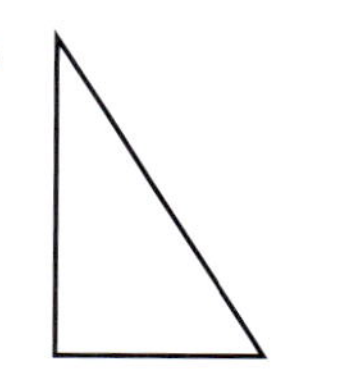

D

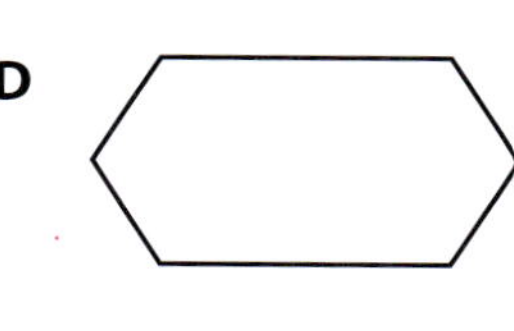

9. Lines k and g are parallel and line h is a transversal. Find the value of x. **(Lesson LA 3)** **(PASS3.2)**

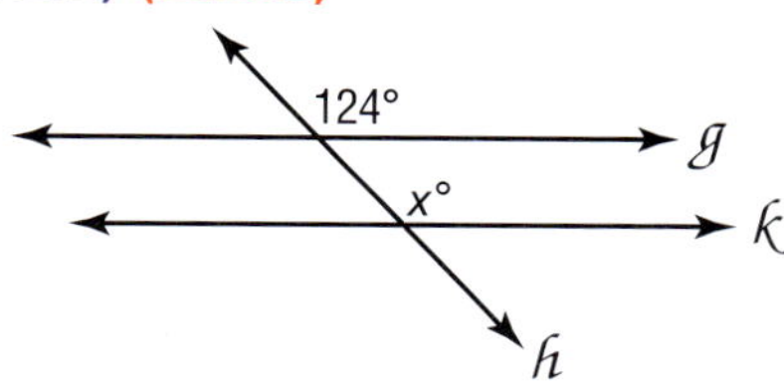

A 180

B 124

C 80

D 56

Get Ready for the OCCT

10. Which graph shows only a rotation of the figure about the point (5, 2)? **(Lesson OK 4)** **(PASS3.3)**

A

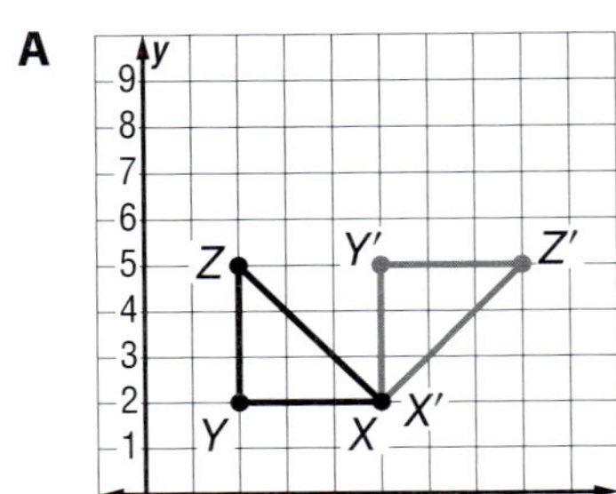

B

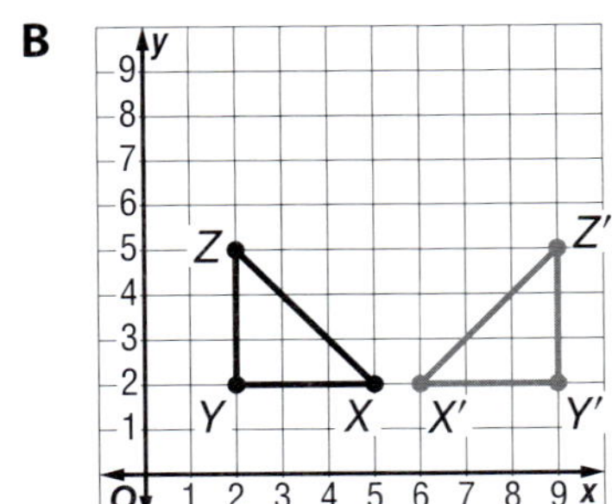

C

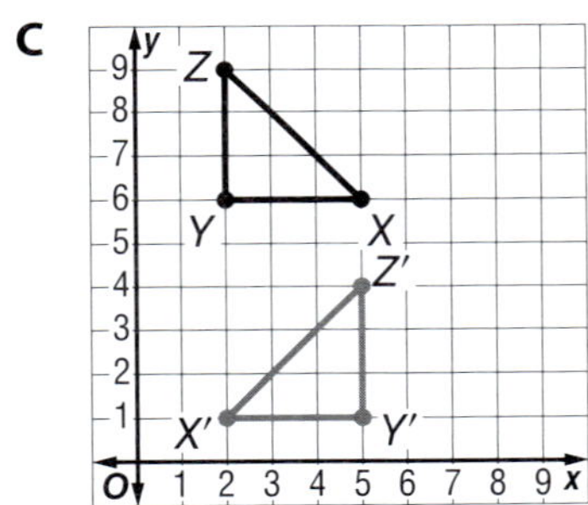

D

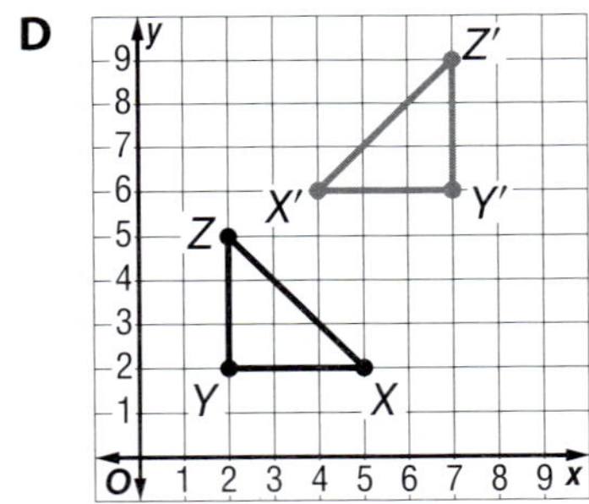

11. The point (−3, 5) is translated down 2 units and to the right 4 units. What are the resulting coordinates? **(Lesson 10-9)** **(PASS3.3)**

A (−5, 9)

B (1, 3)

C (−1, 9)

D (−5, 1)

12. All of the following statements are true regarding the figure below except for which one? **(Lesson 10-8)** **(PASS3.1)**

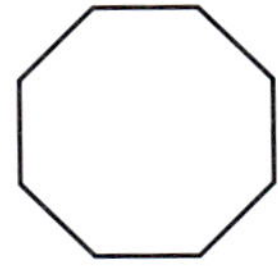

A The figure is regular.

B The figure is a polygon.

C The figure is irregular.

D The figure is an octagon.

13. Lines p and q are parallel and line t is a transversal. Classify the special relationship between $\angle 1$ and $\angle 2$. **(Lesson LA 3)** **(PASS3.2)**

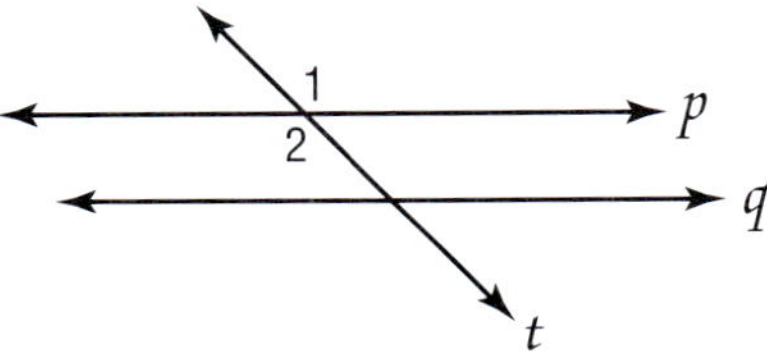

A They are vertical angles.

B They are alternate interior angles.

C They are alternate exterior angles.

D They are adjacent angles.

14. Which of the following is the best classification for the figure below? **(Lesson 10-4)** **(PASS3.1)**

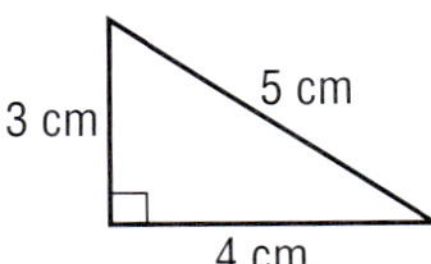

A scalene acute triangle

B isosceles right triangle

C equilateral triangle

D scalene right triangle

15. The point (9, −4) was translated n units up and m units to the right. Then it was reflected across the y-axis. The resulting coordinates were (−12, −2). Which of the following is true regarding the values of m and n? **(Lesson 10-10)** **(PASS3.3)**

A The value of m is positive and the value of n is negative.

B The value of m is negative and the value of n is positive.

C They are both positive.

D They are both negative.

16. Find the value of y in the figure below. Lines g and h are parallel. **(Lesson LA 3)** **(PASS3.2)**

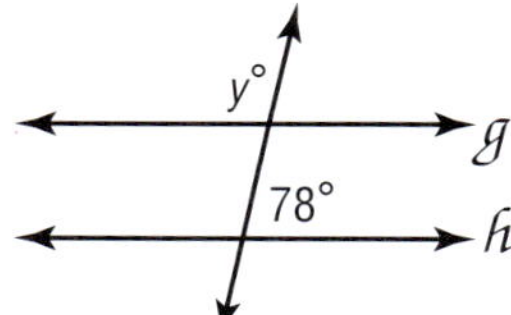

A 78 **C** 110
B 102 **D** 180

17. Which transformation is represented by the figure and its image? **(Lesson 10-10)** **(PASS3.3)**

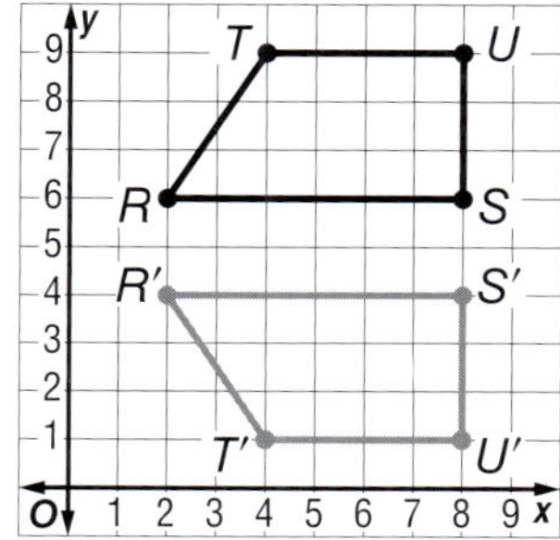

A rotation of 180° about the origin

B reflection across a horizontal line

C translation up two units

D translation up nine units

18. A triangle with vertices $A(3, 4)$, $B(2, -5)$ and $C(-1, 6)$ is reflected across the x-axis. Then it is translated up three units and to the right four units. What are the resulting coordinates of the triangle after both transformations? **(Lesson 10-10)** **(PASS3.3)**

A $A'(3, -1)$, $B'(2, 8)$ and $C'(-1, -3)$

B $A'(3, -4)$, $B'(2, 5)$ and $C'(-1, -6)$

C $A'(7, 7)$, $B'(6, -2)$ and $C'(3, 9)$

D $A'(7, -1)$, $B'(6, 8)$ and $C'(3, -3)$

19. Lines p and q are parallel. Which statement is true concerning ∠1 and ∠2 below? **(Lesson LA 3)** **(PASS3.2)**

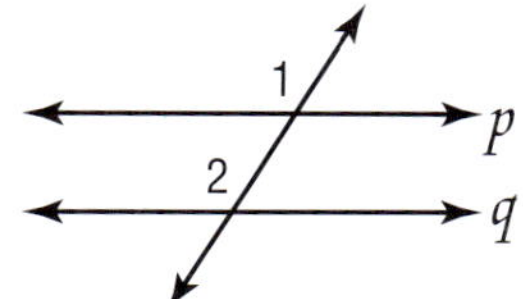

A They are complementary.

B They are congruent.

C They are supplementary.

D They are vertical.

20. All of the following statements are true regarding the figure below except for which one? **(Lesson 10-8)** **(PASS3.1)**

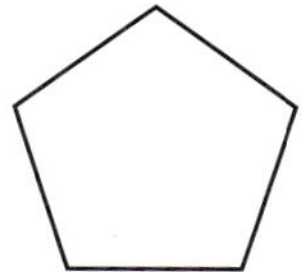

A The figure is regular.

B The figure is a polygon.

C The figure is irregular.

D The figure is a pentagon.

Measurement

1. Caitlin's parents bought a house with an attic that has the dimensions shown below. They are carpeting it and need to determine the number of square meters that make up the attic's floor. Find the area. **(Lesson 11-2)** **(PASS4.1)**

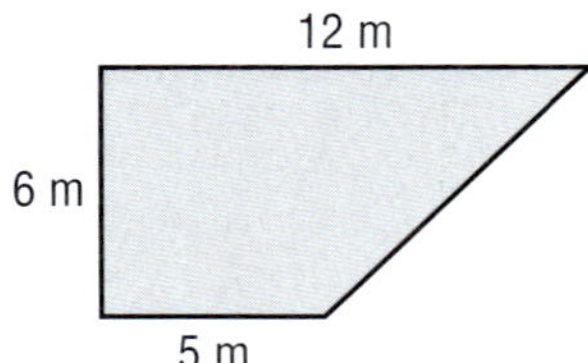

A 23 m^2 **C** 51 m^2
B 30 m^2 **D** 72 m^2

2. How is the area of a triangle related to the area of a parallelogram with the same base and height? **(Explore 11-2)** **(PASS4.1)**

A The area of a triangle is twice the area of a parallelogram with the same base and height.

B The area of a triangle is one-third the area of a parallelogram with the same base and height.

C The area of a triangle is three times the area of a parallelogram with the same base and height.

D The area of a triangle is half the area of a parallelogram with the same base and height.

3. What is the circumference of a circle with a radius of 5 meters? **(Lesson 11-3)** **(PASS4.2)**

A 5π **C** 15π
B 10π **D** 20π

4. Mr. Wong is mulching the flower bed shown below. If one bag of mulch covers 32 square feet, how many bags of mulch does Mr. Wong need? **(Lesson 11-1)** **(PASS4.1)**

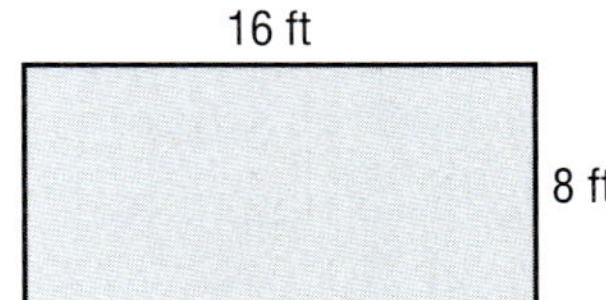

A 3 bags **C** 5 bags
B 4 bags **D** 6 bags

5. Find the area of the circle shown. Use 3.14 for π. **(Lesson 11-4)** **(PASS4.2)**

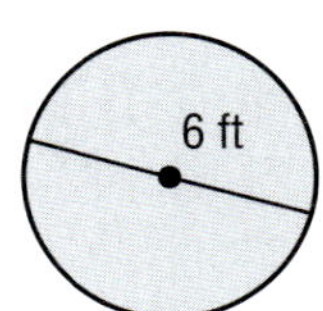

A 18.84 ft^2 **C** 56.52 ft^2
B 28.26 ft^2 **D** 113.04 ft^2

6. Which of the following expressions gives the area of a trapezoid with bases of 15 inches and 18 inches and a height of 4 inches? **(Lesson 11-2)** **(PASS4.1)**

A $\frac{1}{2}(18)(15 + 4)$

B $2(4)(15 + 18)$

C $\frac{1}{2}(4)(15 + 18)$

D $\frac{1}{2}(15)(4 + 18)$

7. Find the area of the figure shown below. **(Lesson OK 6)** **(PASS4.3)**

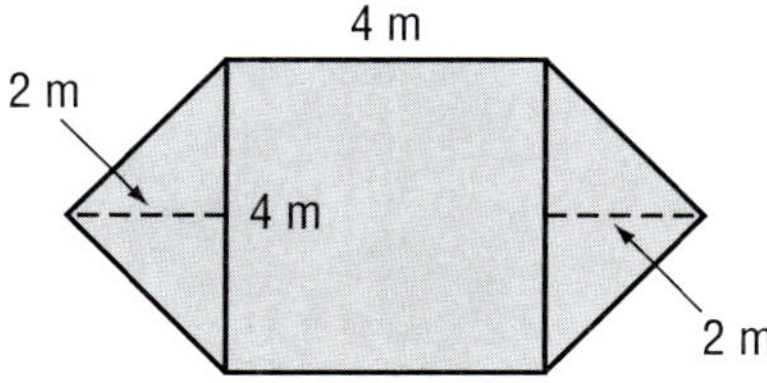

A 24 m^2
B 32 m^2
C 48 m^2
D 64 m^2

8. Mr. Yoshitaka is installing a concrete patio in his backyard with the dimensions shown. About how many square feet of concrete will he need? **(Lesson 3-7)** **(PASS4.1)**

A 16.75 ft^2
B 33.5 ft^2
C 65.63 ft^2
D 656.25 ft^2

9. Find the circumference of the circle shown. Use 3.14 for π. **(Lesson 11-3)** **(PASS4.2)**

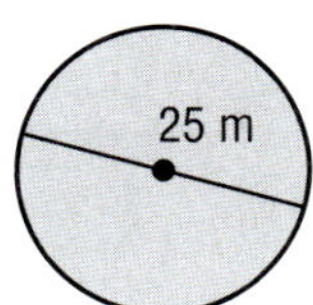

A 246.49 m **C** 157 m
B 175 m **D** 78.5 m

10. The dimensions of Mrs. Wallace's backyard are shown below. She wants to enclose her yard with a fence. Find the perimeter of her backyard. **(Lesson 11-1)** **(PASS4.1)**

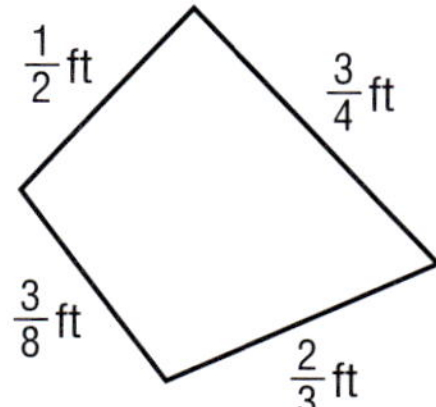

A $\frac{9}{17}$ ft **C** $2\frac{7}{24}$ ft
B $\frac{18}{24}$ ft **D** $1\frac{23}{24}$ ft

11. Marcia's parents are building a circular swimming pool in their backyard. They need to know how much area the pool will cover. The diagram below shows the pool they would like to build. Which expression gives the area of the pool in square feet? **(Lesson 11-3)** **(PASS4.2)**

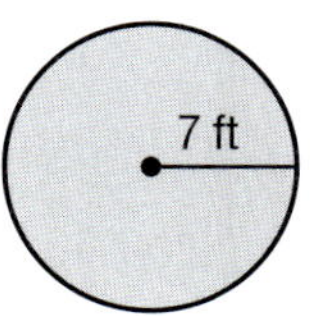

A 49π **C** 14π
B 28π **D** 7π

12. Find the perimeter of the figure shown below. **(Lesson OK 6)** **(PASS4.3)**

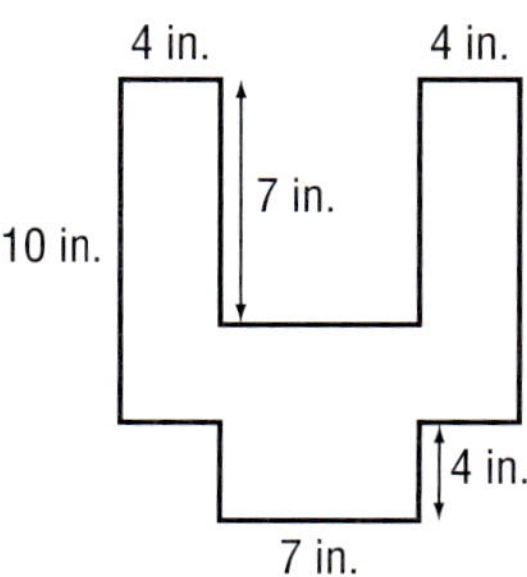

A 34 in. **C** 60 in.
B 48 in. **D** 72 in.

Get Ready for the OCCT

13. The circumference of a circle is 12π. Which figure below best represents a circle with a circumference of 12π? **(Lesson 11-3)** **(PASS4.2)**

A

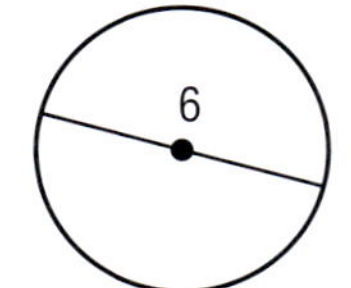

B

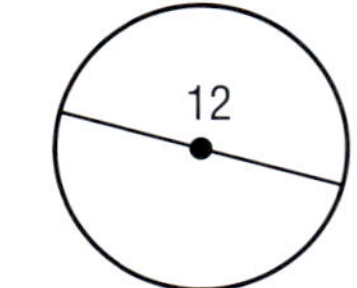

C

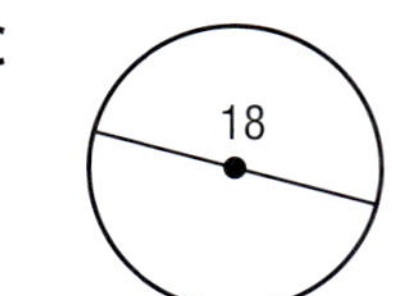

D

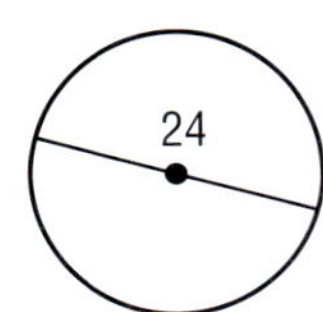

14. Which of the following formulas gives the area of a triangle in square yards with a height of 9 yards and a base of 12 yards? **(Lesson 11-2)** **(PASS4.1)**

A $\frac{1}{2}(9 \cdot 12)$ **C** $4.5 \cdot 6$

B $9 \cdot 12$ **D** 12π

15. Find the circumference of the circle shown. Use 3.14 for π. **(Lesson 11-3)** **(PASS4.2)**

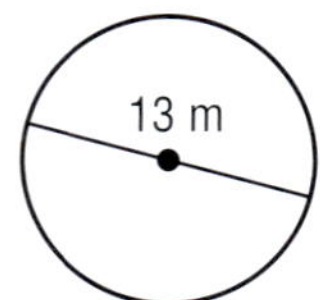

A 20.42 m **C** 132.72 m

B 40.82 m **D** 530.72 m

16. Meghan's deck is in the shape below. Find the area of the deck. **(Lesson OK 6)** **(PASS4.3)**

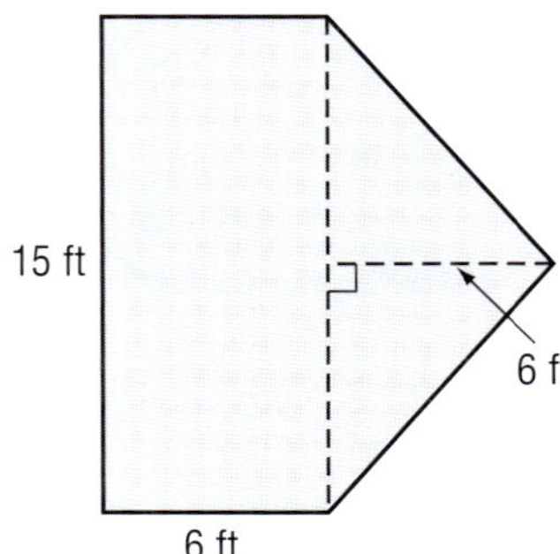

A 270 ft^2 **C** 155 ft^2

B 180 ft^2 **D** 135 ft^2

17. Find the area of the circle shown. Use 3.14 for π. **(Lesson 11-4)** **(PASS4.2)**

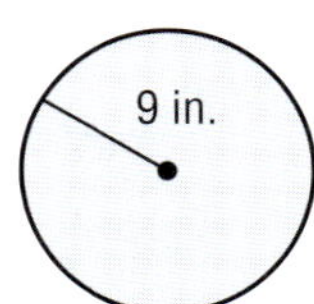

A 254.34 in^2 **C** 56.52 in^2

B 88.74 in^2 **D** 28.26 in^2

18. What is the perimeter of the equilateral triangle below? **(Lesson 11-2)** **(PASS4.1)**

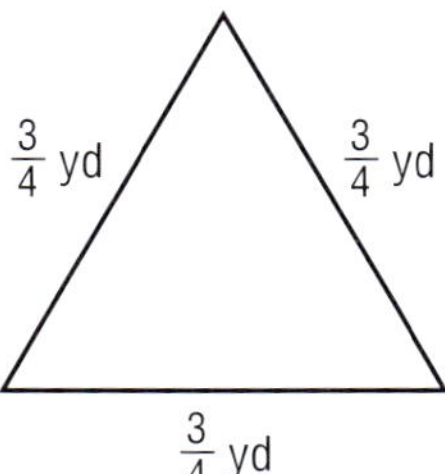

A $2\frac{1}{3}$ yd **C** $2\frac{2}{3}$ yd

B $2\frac{1}{4}$ yd **D** $2\frac{3}{4}$ yd

Data Analysis

1. When Mrs. Hollern entered a department store, she was given a scratch-off game card with this statement:

1 out of 16 cards is a winner!

What is the probability that Mrs. Hollern did not receive a winning game card? **(Lesson 9-1)** **(PASS5.2)**

A 6.25%
B 12.5%
C 87.5%
D 93.75%

2. Sabino randomly selects one letter from the word *piano*. What is the probability that he selects the letter *p* or the letter *o*? **(Lesson 9-8)** **(PASS5.2)**

A $\frac{1}{5}$
B $\frac{2}{5}$
C $\frac{3}{5}$
D $\frac{4}{5}$

3. A prize wheel at a fair is divided into 5 sections of equal size. The sections are labeled A through E. If the arrow is spun once, what is the probability that it will stop on a section labeled A or B? **(Lesson 9-1)** **(PASS5.2)**

A $\frac{1}{6}$
B $\frac{2}{5}$
C $\frac{2}{3}$
D $\frac{5}{6}$

4. Ernesto is playing basketball. The graph shows how many total points he has after each basket he makes. For every two baskets, by how many points does his score increase? **(Lesson 8-6)** **(PASS5.1)**

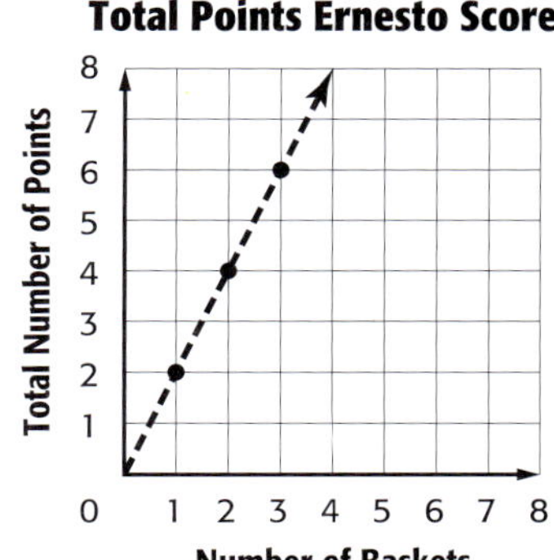

A 1
B 2
C 4
D 8

5. As part of a probability experiment, Brent rolled two fair number cubes, one after the other. One cube is numbered 1 through 6. The other cube is numbered 7 through 12. What is the probability that the first cube landed on 3 and the second cube landed on 12? **(Lesson 9-4)** **(PASS5.2)**

A $\frac{1}{36}$
B $\frac{1}{20}$
C $\frac{1}{12}$
D $\frac{1}{6}$

6. If Kohana rolls a 6-sided number cube and flips a coin, what is the chance that he will roll a 3 and the coin will land on tails? **(Lesson 9-8)** **(PASS5.2)**

A $\frac{1}{12}$
B $\frac{1}{6}$
C $\frac{1}{4}$
D $\frac{1}{2}$

7. If a coin is tossed and a number cube labeled 1 through 6 is rolled, what is the probability of tossing heads <u>and</u> rolling a 3? **(Lesson 9-1)** **(PASS5.2)**

A $\frac{1}{12}$ **C** $\frac{1}{4}$

B $\frac{1}{6}$ **D** $\frac{1}{2}$

8. Jeremy will randomly select one letter from the word *giraffe*. What is the probability that he will <u>not</u> select the letter *f*? **(Lesson 9-1)** **(PASS5.2)**

A $\frac{2}{7}$

B $\frac{3}{7}$

C $\frac{5}{7}$

D $\frac{6}{7}$

9. Wakim saw the graph shown below in a magazine article about dog ownership. He spends about $240 a year on dog food. Which of the following represents the approximate annual cost to own his dog? **(Lesson 8-7)** **(PASS5.1)**

Cost of Owning a Dog

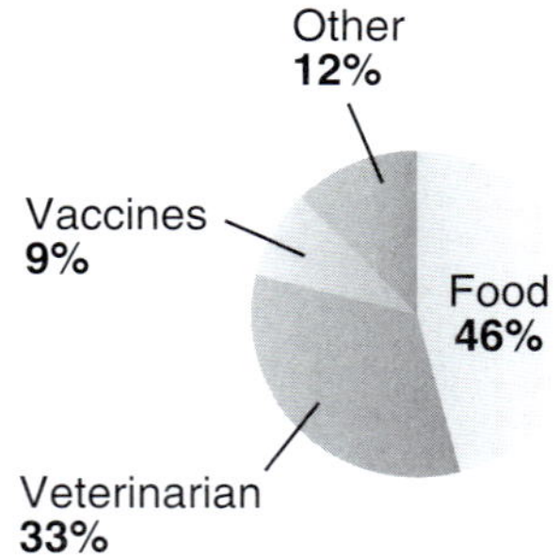

A $110

B $260

C $520

D $680

10. If Danielle spins a spinner like the one shown below 400 times, how many times should she expect the spinner to land on the circle <u>or</u> the square? **(Lesson 9-7)** **(PASS5.2)**

A 300

B 200

C 100

D 75

11. Which statement is true concerning the data set below? **(Lesson 8-2)** **(PASS5.3)**

{100, 110, 109, 25, 105, 107, 100}

A The mean is most affected by the outlier.

B The median is most affected by the outlier.

C The mode is most affected by the outlier.

D None of the measures of central tendency are affected by the outlier.

12. A spinner has 8 equal sections labeled A through H. The spinner is spun once. What is the probability that it will <u>not</u> land on a vowel? **(Lesson 9-1)** **(PASS5.2)**

A $\frac{1}{8}$

B $\frac{1}{4}$

C $\frac{1}{2}$

D $\frac{3}{4}$

13. The graph shows the number of people that attended Rochester's Fourth of July celebration each year. How many people should be expected to attend the celebration in 2010? **(Lesson 8-6)** **(PASS5.1)**

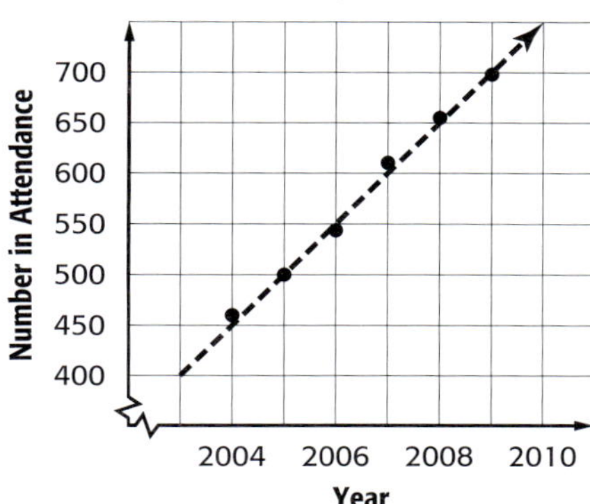

A 600
B 650
C 700
D 750

14. What is the best reason for why the following graph is misleading? **(Lesson 8-9)** **(PASS5.1)**

A The vertical axis is not labeled.
B The vertical axis has no scale.
C Since the length and width are both doubled, the area is 4 times as large, so it appears as if the new pesticide is 4 times as effective.
D The graph only compares two types of pesticides.

15. A popular board game uses letter tiles to form words. The vowel distribution is shown in the table below.

Letter	A	E	I	O	U
Number of Tiles	9	12	9	8	4

If Anna randomly chooses a tile and replaces it 50 times, about how many times should she expect to choose a tile that is not "O"? **(Lesson 9-7)** **(PASS5.2)**

A 4
B 6
C 15
D 41

16. The number of siblings each student on the tennis team has is listed below. What is the mean number of siblings? **(Lesson 8-2)** **(PASS5.3)**

0, 3, 0, 1, 2, 7, 0, 1, 3, 2

A 0
B 1.5
C 1.9
D 7

17. What makes the following graph misleading? **(Lesson 8-9)** **(PASS5.1)**

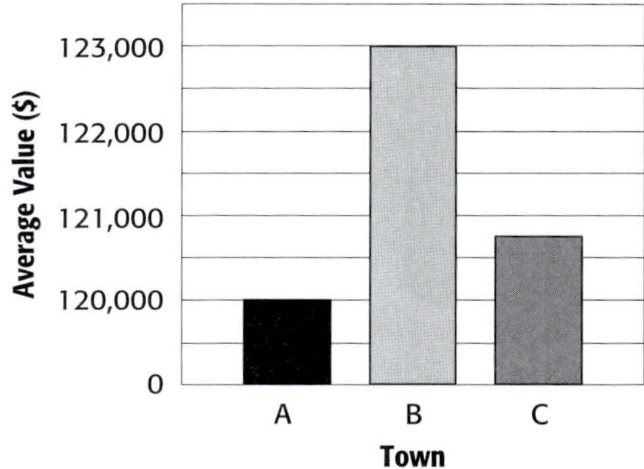

A The intervals on the vertical axis make it appear that the averages are far apart when they are fairly close.
B The average house value should be listed on the horizontal axis.
C The graph compares only three towns.
D A bar graph is not an appropriate type of display for this information.

18. The circle graph shows the results of a poll to which 500 students at Rosalinda's school responded.

Do You Own a Cell Phone?

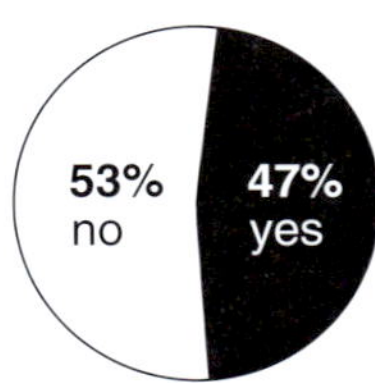

If there are 25 students in Rosalinda's homeroom, how many would you predict own cell phones? **(Lesson 8-6) (PASS5.1)**

A 12 **C** 47
B 13 **D** 53

19. Mrs. Everly teaches 60 students. The Venn diagram shows the sports that some of her students play.

Sports

Baseball 22
6
Tennis 11
3
3
2
Volleyball 9
4

If Mrs. Everly chooses a student at random, what is the probability that the student plays tennis <u>or</u> volleyball? **(Lesson 9-1) (PASS5.2)**

A $\frac{1}{30}$ **C** $\frac{17}{30}$
B $\frac{1}{2}$ **D** $\frac{2}{3}$

20. Rochelle's French test scores are shown below.

86, 84, 80, 65, 90, 75, 88

Her teacher will drop the lowest score. By about how much will Rochelle's average change? **(Lesson 8-2) (PASS5.3)**

A −3 points **C** +5 points
B +3 points **D** +7 points

21. Which of the following types of displays is most appropriate to show how Jaclyn's height has changed over time? **(Lesson 8-6) (PASS5.1)**

A histogram **C** line graph
B stem-and-leaf plot **D** line plot

22. The manager of a fast food restaurant made the graph below showing what percent of the daily sales were from each type of food. If he expects 250 customers today, how many hot dogs should he prepare? **(Lesson 8-6) (PASS5.1)**

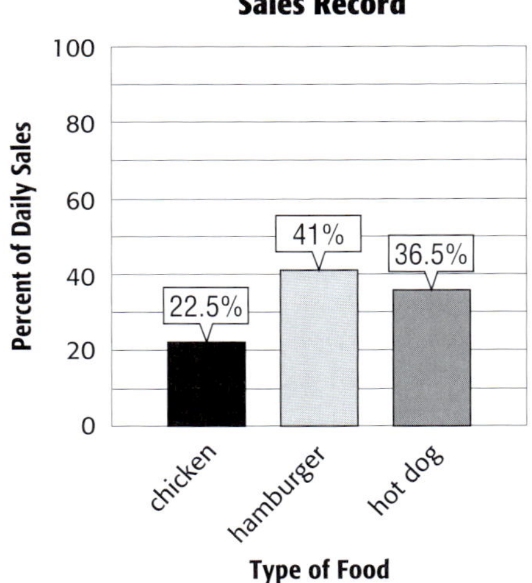

A 56 **C** 103
B 91 **D** 250

23. A deli offers customers a side choice of soup or salad with the purchase of a sandwich. Customers can choose from a ham, turkey, or tuna sandwich. The tree diagram below shows the possible outcomes.

Sandwich	Side	Outcome
Ham	Soup	Ham, Soup
	Salad	Ham, Salad
Turkey	Soup	Turkey, Soup
	Salad	Turkey, Salad
Tuna	Soup	Tuna, Soup
	Salad	Tuna, Salad

What is the probability that a customer will randomly select a ham or turkey sandwich? **(Lesson 9-2)** **(PASS5.2)**

A $\frac{1}{6}$

B $\frac{1}{2}$

C $\frac{2}{3}$

D $\frac{3}{4}$

24. If Della randomly selects one marble out of a hat containing 2 yellow marbles, 3 red marbles, and 2 white marbles, what is the probability she does not choose a white marble? **(Lesson 9-8)** **(PASS5.2)**

A $\frac{2}{7}$

B $\frac{5}{7}$

C $\frac{2}{3}$

D $\frac{3}{5}$

25. If you randomly draw 2 cards from the cards shown below, one after the other without replacing the first, what is the probability that you draw a star first and then a square? **(Lesson 9-8)** **(PASS5.2)**

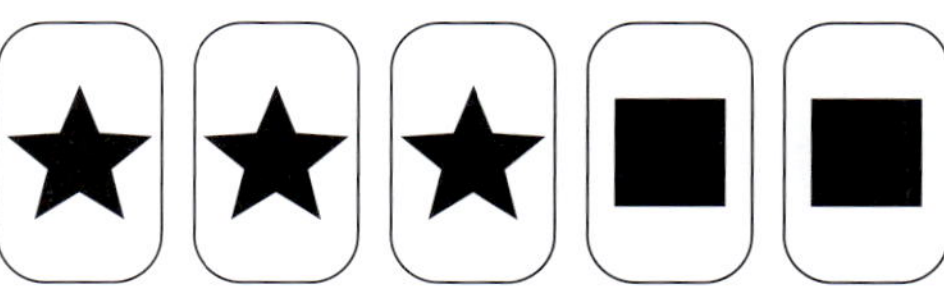

A $\frac{6}{25}$

B $\frac{1}{4}$

C $\frac{3}{10}$

D $\frac{1}{2}$

26. John makes $5 for every hour of work. Below is a graph that shows how much he gets paid compared to how long he works. If Fatima makes $8 each hour, how would her graph compare to John's? **(Lesson 8-6)** **(PASS5.1)**

A It would be steeper.

B It would be less steep.

C The lines would have the same slope.

D The lines would have different y-intercepts.

27. A number cube is rolled once. Find the probability that a multiple of 2 does not turn up. **(Lesson 9-1)** **(PASS5.2)**

A $\frac{2}{3}$

B $\frac{1}{2}$

C $\frac{1}{3}$

D $\frac{1}{6}$

To the Student

As you gear up to study mathematics, you are probably wondering, "What will I learn this year?" You will focus on these three areas.

- **Number and Operations, Algebra, and Geometry:** Develop and apply an understanding of proportions, including similarity.
- **Measurement and Geometry:** Find surface areas and volumes of three-dimensional shapes.
- **Number and Operations and Algebra:** Solve linear equations and deepen an understanding of operations on all rational numbers.

Along the way, you'll learn more about problem solving, how to use the tools and language of mathematics, and how to THINK mathematically.

How to Use Your Math Book

Have you ever been in class and not understood all of what was being presented? Or, you understood everything in class, but got stuck on how to solve some of the homework problems? Don't worry. You can find answers in your math book!

- **Read** the **MAIN IDEA** at the beginning of the lesson.
- **Find** the **New Vocabulary** words, **highlighted in yellow**, and read their definitions.
- **Review** the **EXAMPLE** problems, solved step-by-step, to remind you of the day's material.
- **Refer** to the **HOMEWORK HELP** boxes that show you which examples may help with your homework problems.
- **Go** to **OK Math Online** where you can find extra examples to coach you through difficult problems.
- **Review** the notes you've taken on your **FOLDABLES™**.
- **Find** the answers to odd-numbered problems in the back of the book. Use them to see if you are solving the problems correctly.

Scavenger Hunt

Let's Get Started

Use the Scavenger Hunt below to learn where things are located in each chapter.

1. What is the title of Chapter 1?
2. How can you tell what you'll learn in Lesson 1-1?
3. Sometimes you may ask, "When am I ever going to use this?" Name a situation that uses the concepts from Lesson 1-2.
4. In the margin of Lesson 1-2, there is a Vocabulary Link. What can you learn from that feature?
5. What is the key concept presented in Lesson 1-3?
6. How many examples are presented in Lesson 1-3?
7. What is the title of the feature in Lesson 1-3 that tells you how to read square roots?
8. What is the Web address where you could find extra examples?
9. Suppose you're doing your homework on page 40 and you get stuck on Exercise 18. Where could you find help?
10. What problem-solving strategy is presented in the Problem-Solving Investigation in Lesson 1-5?
11. List the new vocabulary words that are presented in Lesson 1-7.
12. What is the web address that would allow you to take a self-check quiz to be sure you understand the lesson?
13. There is a Real-World Career mentioned in Lesson 1-10. What is it?
14. On what pages will you find the Study Guide and Review for Chapter 1?
15. Suppose you can't figure out how to do Exercise 25 in the Study Guide and Review on page 72. Where could you find help?

MATH SYMBOLS

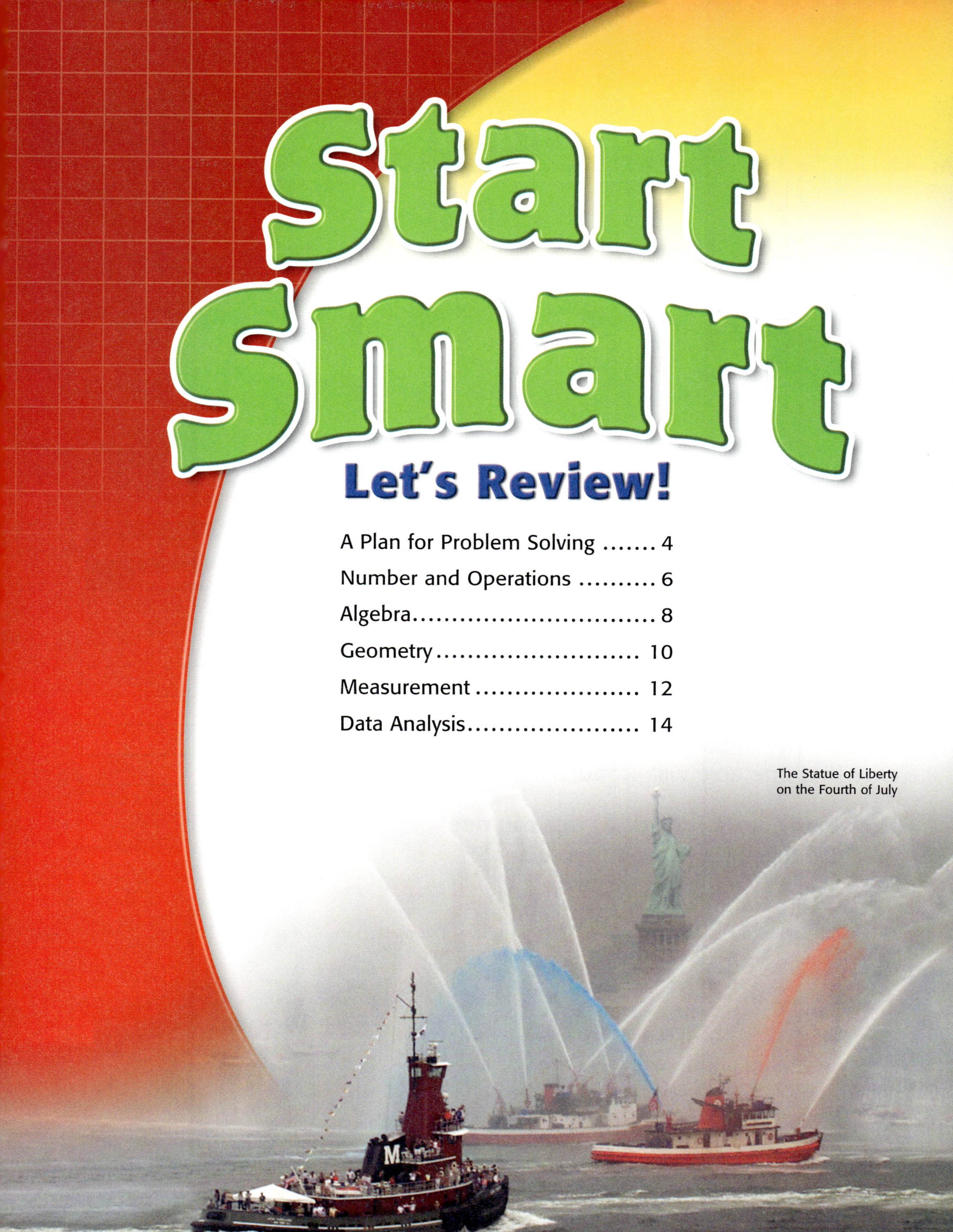

Start Smart

Let's Review!

The Statue of Liberty on the Fourth of July

A Plan for Problem Solving

Amber Waves of Grain

There are about 2.13 million farms in the United States. The average size of each farm is about 440 acres. One acre is about the size of a football field, without the end zones. The table shows the number of pounds of each crop that one acre will produce in a season.

How many more pounds of rice can one acre produce in a season than wheat?

Production from One Acre

Crop	Amount (lb)
Cotton	725
Lettuce	35,000
Potatoes	36,700
Rice	5,500
Strawberries	42,800
Sweet Corn	11,600
Wheat	2,880

Source: American Farm Bureau

You can use the four-step problem-solving plan to solve many kinds of problems. The four steps are Understand, Plan, Solve, and Check.

Understand

- **Read the problem carefully.**
- **What facts do you know?**
- **What do you need to find?**

You know the number of pounds of rice and wheat produced by each acre. You need to find how many more pounds of rice the average farm produces in a season than wheat.

Plan

- **How do the facts relate to each other?**
- **Plan a strategy to solve the problem.**

One acre produces 5,500 pounds of rice or 2,880 pounds of wheat. Subtract 2,880 from 5,500.

Solve

- **Use your plan to solve the problem.**

$$\begin{array}{r} \overset{4}{\cancel{5}},\overset{14}{\cancel{5}}\overset{10}{\cancel{0}}0 \\ -2,880 \\ \hline 2,620 \end{array}$$

In one season, one acre can produce 2,620 more pounds of rice than wheat.

Check

- **Look back at the problem.**
- **Does your answer make sense?**
- **If not, solve the problem another way.**

Estimate. Round 5,500 to 6,000 and 2,880 to 3,000.
6,000 – 3,000 = 3,000

Since 3,000 is close to 2,620, the answer is reasonable.

CHECK Your Understanding

1. One pound of wheat can make 0.98 pound of whole-wheat flour but only 0.74 pound of refined flour. How many more pounds of whole wheat flour could one acre of wheat make than refined flour?

2. **WRITING IN MATH** How many more pounds of rice can the average-size farm in the United States produce in one season than wheat? Explain.

The Indianapolis 500 consists of 200 laps covering a total distance of 500 miles. Each lap covers 2.5 miles. The table shows the winners of the Indianapolis 500 and their average speeds in miles per hour from 2000 to 2007.

Winners of the Indianapolis 500 2000–2007

Year	Winner	Average Speed (mph)
2000	Juan Montoya	167.607
2001	Helio Castroneves	153.601
2002	Helio Castroneves	166.499
2003	Gil de Ferran	156.291
2004	Buddy Rice	138.518
2005	Dan Wheldon	157.603
2006	Sam Hornish, Jr.	157.085
2007	Dario Franchitti	151.774

Source: ESPN

Compare and Order Decimals

When comparing and ordering decimals, first line up the decimal points. Then compare the digits in each place to order the amounts.

Use the information in the table on page 6 to answer each question.

1. Which of the Indianapolis 500 winners listed in the table had the greatest average speed? the least?
2. Between Dan Wheldon and Gil de Ferran, who had the lower average speed?
3. List the Indianapolis 500 winners in order from least to greatest average speed.

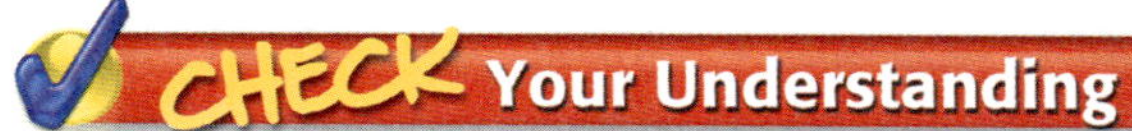

Subtract Decimals

When subtracting decimals, first line up the decimal points. Then subtract as with whole numbers and place the decimal point in the answer.

Use the table on page 6 to answer each question.

4. How much greater was the average speed in 2000 than in 2007?
5. How much greater was the average speed in 2007 than in 2004?
6. How much greater was the average speed in 2006 than in 2007?
7. **WRITING IN MATH** The table shows the fastest lap speeds on record for the Indianapolis 500 from 2002 to 2007. Use the information to write and solve a real-world problem about the fastest lap speeds.

Year	Fastest Lap Speed (mph)
2002	226.499
2003	229.188
2004	218.401
2005	228.102
2006	221.251
2007	223.420

Algebra

Lcdr Anthony Walley

The Sky's the Limit

Since 1946, the Blue Angels have represented the United States Navy in flight demonstrations around the country. There are six jets in the formation during each demonstration. The pilots perform approximately 30 maneuvers during a demonstration that lasts for approximately 1 hour 15 minutes. The table shows several speeds of the Boeing F/A-18 Hornet jets used in the demonstration.

Boeing F/A-18 Hornet	Speed (mph)
Slowest Cruising Speed	120
Sneak Pass Maneuver	700
Top Speed	1,400

Variables and Equations

Use the table on page 8 to answer the following questions.

1. The average speed of the Boeing F/A-18 Hornet Jet is 200 miles per hour less than its top speed. If s represents its top speed, write an expression that represents its average speed.

2. Evaluate the expression you wrote in Exercise 1. What is the average speed of the Boeing F/A-18 Hornet jet?

3. The equation $d = rt$ represents the distance d in miles that the jet can travel at its average speed of r miles per hour in h hours. Use your answer from Exercise 2 to find the distance the jet can travel in 2 hours.

4. The jets are transported by the C-130 Hercules aircraft *Fat Albert* which has an average speed 230 more miles per hour than the jet's slowest cruising speed. Write an equation that could be used to represent *Fat Albert's* average speed s.

5. Evaluate the expression you wrote in Exercise 4. What is *Fat Albert's* average speed?

For Exercises 6 and 7, use the table and the information below.

The table shows the heights of two of the most famous maneuvers of the Blue Angels.

6. The maximum rate of climb for the Boeing F/A-18 Hornet jet is 30,000 feet per minute. How long would it take the jet to climb 15,000 feet?

7. **WRITING IN MATH** Write a real-world problem to represent the relationship between the heights of a Sneak Pass and a Vertical Roll. Then solve the equation.

Maneuver	Height (ft)
Sneak Pass	50
Vertical Roll	15,000

Geometry

What's Your Angle?

Geometric angles are used in architectural design. The Seattle Central Library in Seattle, Washington, has many different geometric angles in its design. Several of those angles are outlined in different colors in the photo above.

Estimate Angle Measures

Use the photo of the Seattle Central Library to estimate the measure of each of the following angles.

1. the angle outlined in red

2. the angle outlined in green

3. the angle outlined in yellow

4. the angle outlined in purple

Measure Angles

The photo below is of the interior of the Denver Art Museum in Denver, Colorado. Use a protractor to measure each of the following angles.

5. the angle outlined in blue

6. the measure of the angle outlined in yellow

7. the angle outlined in green

8. the angle outlined in red

9. Use the Internet or another source to find a photo that uses geometric angles in art or architecture. Estimate the measure of several angles in the photo. Then use a protractor to measure the angles. Compare to your estimates.

10. **WRITING IN MATH** Write a few sentences explaining how to use a protractor to find the measure of an angle.

Measurement

Dynamite Dimensions!

Mount Rushmore, located in the Black Hills of South Dakota, is a tribute to four American presidents: George Washington, Thomas Jefferson, Theodore Roosevelt, and Abraham Lincoln. More than 90% of the monument was carved by dynamite! The table gives the measurements of several of the facial features for one of the presidents.

Feature	Measurement (ft)
head	60 (height)
nose	20 (height)
mouth	18 (length)
eye	11 (length)

Source: Mount Rushmore National Monument

Standard units of measurement are most commonly used in the United States. They include *inch*, *foot*, *yard*, and *mile*.

Check Your Understanding

Use Appropriate Units

1. How many inches are in one foot? How many feet are in one yard?
2. Which is a more reasonable estimate for the height in yards of each president's head on Mount Rushmore: 20 yards or 180 yards? Justify your response.
3. How tall or long is each presidential feature in yards? Round to the nearest tenth if necessary.
4. Which is a more reasonable estimate for the length in inches of each president's eye on Mount Rushmore: 1 inch or 120 inches? Justify your response.
5. How tall or long is each presidential feature in inches? Round to the nearest tenth if necessary.
6. Mount Rushmore is about 6,000 feet above sea level. Which is a more reasonable estimate for this height: about 2,000 yards or about 18,000 yards? Justify your response.
7. **WRITING IN MATH** The photo below shows the Stone Mountain Confederate Memorial Carving in Atlanta, Georgia. The carving measures 90 feet by 190 feet. Explain how to find the carving's dimensions in yards. Then find the carving's dimensions in yards, rounding to the nearest tenth if necessary.

Data Analysis

Do You Hear What I Hear?

Bats have a much greater range of hearing than humans. They use this sense to locate food and prey. Many other animals also have a greater hearing range than humans. The frequency of a dog whistle is about 22,000 Hertz (Hz) which is greater than the maximum hearing frequency for humans. The table shows the minimum and maximum frequencies for hearing of ten animal species, including humans.

Hearing Ranges of Animal Species

Species	Minimum Frequency (Hz)	Maximum Frequency (Hz)
bat	2,000	110,000
Beluga whale	1,000	123,000
cat	45	64,000
dog	67	45,000
elephant	16	12,000
goldfish	20	3,000
horse	55	33,500
human	64	20,000
mouse	1,000	91,000
owl	200	12,000

Source: Louisiana State University

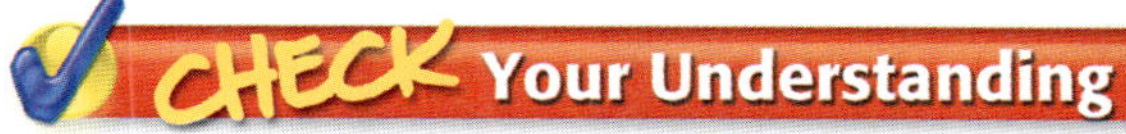

Pictographs

1. Copy and complete the pictograph below using the data of the maximum hearing frequencies in the table on page 14.

Maximum Hearing Frequencies (Hz) of Different Animal Species

Animal	Frequency
bat	
Beluga whale	👂👂👂👂👂👂👂👂👂👂👂👂 (partial ear)
cat	
dog	👂👂👂👂 (partial ear)
elephant	👂 (partial ear)
goldfish	(partial ear)
horse	👂👂👂 (partial ear)
human	
mouse	👂👂👂👂👂👂👂👂👂 (partial ear)
owl	

👂 = 10,000 Hz

2. Name two animals whose maximum hearing frequencies are about the same.

3. About how many times greater is a Beluga whale's maximum hearing frequency than a cat's?

4. The table gives the loudness of different sounds measured in decibels (dB). Construct a pictograph of the information.

Sound	Decibels (dB)
jet engine	140
chainsaw	120
lawn mower	100
alarm clock	80
normal speech	60
whisper	40

5. **WRITING IN MATH** Refer to pictograph you created in Exercise 4. Write one or two sentences describing the data.

Data File

The following pages contain data that you'll use throughout the book.

Temperature

Record Temperatures in New York State					
Record	°F	°C	Date	Location	Elevation (feet)
High	108	42.2	July 22, 1976	Troy	35
Low	−52	−46.7	February 18, 1979	Old Forge	1,720

Source: National Climatic Data Center

Vertical Velocity Roller Coaster

Amusement Park: Six Flags Great America, Illinois
Length: 2,700 feet
Height: 185 feet
Speed: 65 miles per hour
Duration: 1 minute
Vehicles: 1
Riders per vehicle: 28

Source: Coaster Buzz

Kentucky Stadiums

Stadium	Location	Capacity
Churchill Downs	Louisville	120,000
Commonwealth Stadium	Lexington	67,530
Kentucky Speedway	Sparta	66,089
Papa John's Cardinal Stadium	Louisville	42,000
Rupp Arena	Lexington	23,000
Roy Kidd Stadium	Richmond	20,000

Source: World Stadiums

Harker's Island, North Carolina

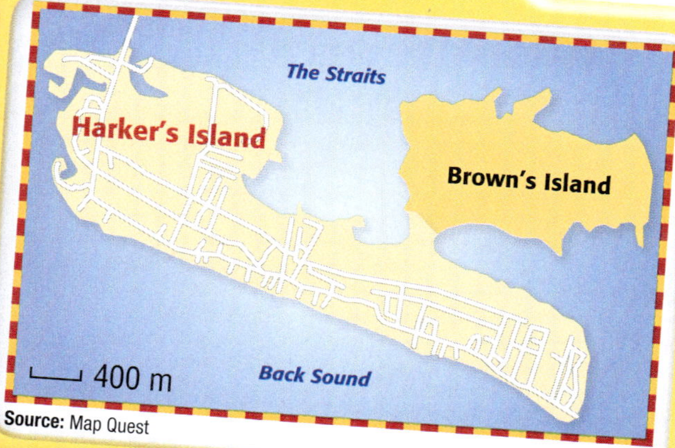

Source: Map Quest

Museum of Glass, Tacoma

WASHINGTON

Regular Ticket Prices

- $10 Adults
- $8 Seniors (age 62+), Military, and Students (age 13+)
- $4 Children (age 6–12)
- $30 Families (two adults and up to four children under age 18)
- Free: Museum of Glass Members, Children under age 6, and Third Thursday of each month (5-8 P.M.)

Golden Eagle

Source: National Geographic

Height: about 3 feet (91 cm)

Wingspan: 7 feet (213 cm)

Habitat: Usually found in high altitudes throughout the mountains of Arizona and along the Colorado River.

U.S. Bank Center, Milwaukee

WISCONSIN

Height: 183 meters

Floors: 42

Exterior: 66% glass

Windows: 5,000

Foundation: 500 steel H-piles capable of holding 640 tons each

Source: Emporis

Delicate Arch, Arches National Park

Source: Climb-Utah

UTAH Delicate Arch, located in Arches National Park, is found along a hiking trail that is 1.5 miles each way. The average time to hike the trail is $1\frac{1}{4}$ hours each way. The elevation of the arch is 4,800 feet, and the arch towers 80 feet above the average hiker. It is recommended that each person carries 2 liters of water for the hike.

Riverbanks Zoo and Garden, Columbia

SOUTH CAROLINA

Number of Animals: more than 2,000
Number of Animal Species: 350
Number of Plant Species: 4,200
Annual Attendance: about 900,000
Hours: 9 A.M.–5 P.M.
Admission: $9.75 for adults
$7.25 ages 3–12
Sea Lion Feedings: 10:30 A.M. and 3 P.M.
Penguin Feedings: 11 A.M. and 3:30 P.M.
Elephant Training: 11:30 A.M.

Source: Riverbanks Zoo and Garden

George S. Mickelson Trail

SOUTH DAKOTA Bicyclists of all ages and abilities can enjoy the George S. Mickelson Trail, in the Black Hills of South Dakota, which runs for a total of 114 miles. It tops out at 6,100 feet but never exceeds a 4% grade.

Source: Travel South Dakota

Boston Baked Beans

Boston Baked Beans

Ingredients

2 cups navy beans
$\frac{1}{2}$ cup brown sugar
$\frac{1}{4}$ cup molasses
1 cup bean liquid
1 teaspoon salt

Rock City

KANSAS Rock City is a tiny park, located 3.5 miles from Minneapolis, Kansas. It contains about 200 huge sandstone concretions. The rocks are up to 27 feet in diameter. There is no other place in the world where there are so many rocks of such giant size.

Source: Kansas Travel and Tourism

Montana Rivers

The longest and shortest rivers in the United States can be found in Montana. The Roe River is exclusively located in Montana and is also the shortest river in the world.

Source: Montana Kids

River	Total Length	Length in Montana
Missouri	2,540 mi (13,411,200 ft)	1,029 mi (5,433,120 ft)
Roe	$\frac{5}{132}$ mi (200 ft)	$\frac{5}{132}$ mi (200 ft)

Mackinac Island

MICHIGAN Mackinac Island is an island covering 3.8 square miles. There are 61 miles of roads and trails within Mackinac Island State Park, most of which are wooded inland trails for hikers, bikers, and horseback riders in spring, summer, and fall. Fort Holmes is at the island's highest point, 320 feet above lake level.

Source: Mackinac State Historic Parks

Baltimore Oriole

Habitat: Usually found in Maryland during the summer months and in the southern states during winter months. Male orioles have a bright orange color on their shoulders and underbelly. Females are light orange.

Size: 7 to $8\frac{1}{4}$ inches

Weight: $1\frac{1}{5}$ ounces

Source: National Geographic

Philadelphia 76ers

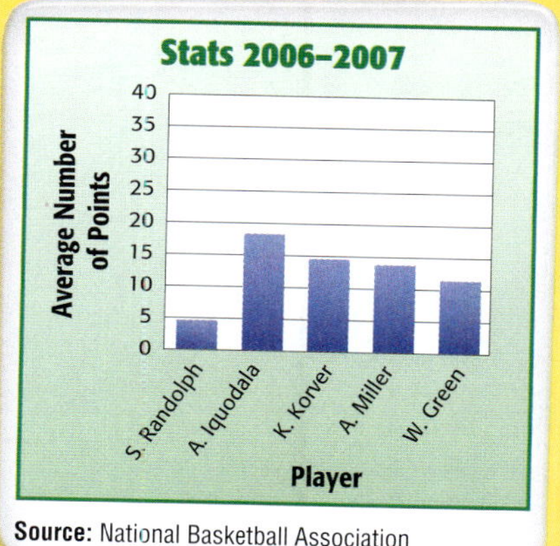

Source: National Basketball Association

Denver International Airport

COLORADO

Opening Date: February 28, 1995

Size: 34,000 acres, 53 square miles

Runways: 6 (five are 12,000 feet long, and the sixth is 16,000 feet long)

Concourses: 3

Gates: 89

Passenger Airlines: 23

Source: Denver International Airport

Flight and baggage information display monitors: 1,500

Accommodation: 50 million passengers per year

Unit 1

Algebra and Functions

Focus

Use appropriate operations to solve problems and linear equations.

CHAPTER 1
Introduction to Algebra and Functions

BIG Idea Represent relationships in numerical, verbal, geometric and symbolic form.

CHAPTER 2
Integers

BIG Idea Know the properties of, and compute with, integers.

CHAPTER 3
Algebra: Linear Equations and Functions

BIG Idea Solve linear equations in one variable.

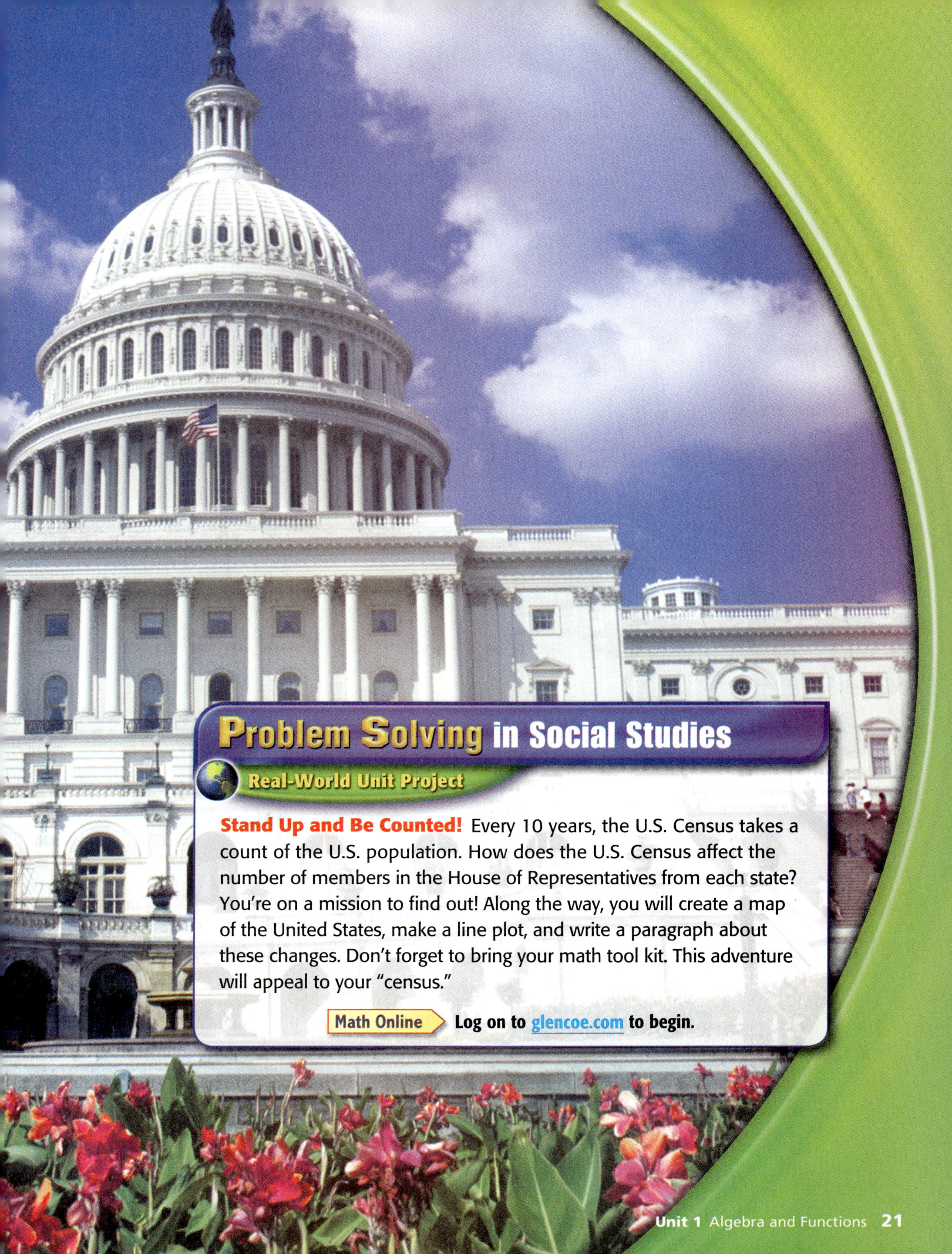

Problem Solving in Social Studies

Real-World Unit Project

Stand Up and Be Counted! Every 10 years, the U.S. Census takes a count of the U.S. population. How does the U.S. Census affect the number of members in the House of Representatives from each state? You're on a mission to find out! Along the way, you will create a map of the United States, make a line plot, and write a paragraph about these changes. Don't forget to bring your math tool kit. This adventure will appeal to your "census."

Math Online **Log on to glencoe.com to begin.**

Introduction to Algebra and Functions

BIG Idea

- Represent relationships in numerical, verbal, geometric, and symbolic form.

Key Vocabulary

algebra (p. 44)
defining the variable (p. 50)
evaluate (p. 31)
numerical expression (p. 38)

Real-World Link

PARKS Admission to the Kentucky Horse Park in Lexington, Kentucky, costs $15 for each adult and $8 for each child. You can use the four-step problem-solving plan to determine the cost of admission for a family of 2 adults and 3 children.

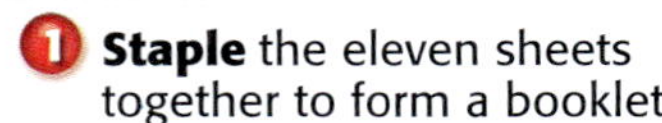

Introduction to Algebra and Functions Make this Foldable to help you organize your notes. Begin with eleven sheets of notebook paper.

1. **Staple** the eleven sheets together to form a booklet.

2. **Cut** tabs. Make each one 2 lines longer than the one before it.

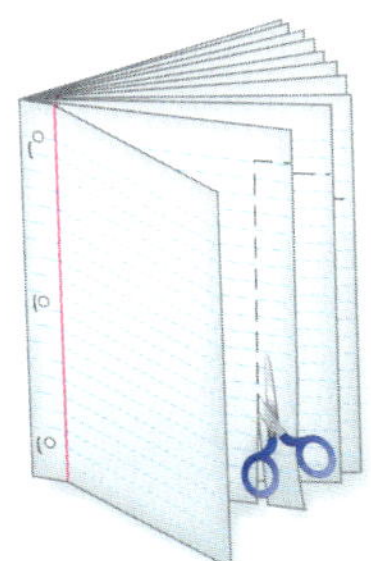

3. **Write** the chapter title on the cover and label each tab with the lesson number.

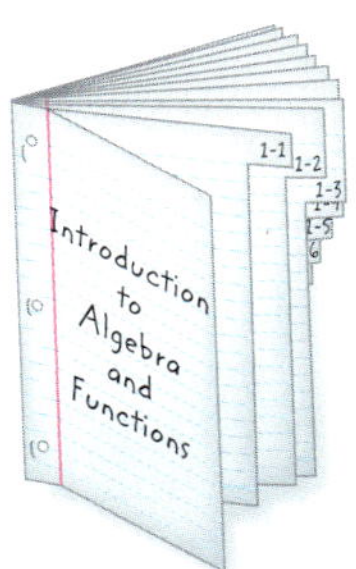

GET READY for Chapter 1

Diagnose Readiness You have two options for checking Prerequisite Skills.

Option 2

Math Online Take the Online Readiness Quiz at glencoe.com.

Option 1

Take the Quick Quiz below. Refer to the Quick Review for help.

QUICK Quiz	QUICK Review
Add. (Prior Grade) 1. 89.3 + 16.5 2. 7.9 + 32.45 3. 54.25 + 6.39 4. 10.8 + 2.6 5. **TECHNOLOGY** Patrick bought a personal electronic organizer for \$59.99 and a carrying case for \$12.95. What was his total cost, not including tax? (Prior Grade)	**Example 1** Find 17.89 + 43.2. 17.89 Line up the decimal points. + 43.20 Annex a zero. 61.09
Subtract. (Prior Grade) 6. 24.6 − 13.3 7. 9.1 − 6.6 8. 30.55 − 2.86 9. 17.4 − 11.2	**Example 2** Find 37.45 − 8.52. 37.45 Line up the decimal points. − 8.52 28.93
Multiply. (Prior Grade) 10. 4 × 7.7 11. 9.8 × 3 12. 2.7 × 6.3 13. 8.5 × 1.2	**Example 3** Find 1.7 × 3.5. 1.7 ← 1 decimal place × 3.5 ← + 1 decimal place 5.95 ← 2 decimal places
Divide. (Prior Grade) 14. 37.49 ÷ 4.6 15. 14.31 ÷ 2.7 16. 6.16 ÷ 5.6 17. 11.15 ÷ 2.5 18. **PIZZA** Four friends decided to split the cost of a pizza evenly. The total cost was \$25.48. How much does each friend need to pay? (Prior Grade)	**Example 4** Find 24.6 ÷ 2.5. 2.5)24.6 → 25.)246. Multiply both numbers by the same power of 10. 9.84 25)246.00 Annex zeros. −225 210 Divide as with whole numbers. −200 100 −100 0

READING to SOLVE PROBLEMS

Making Sense

When you solve a word problem, the first thing to do is to read the problem carefully. The last thing to do is to see whether your answer makes sense. Sometimes a picture or diagram can help.

> Kelly lives 5 miles from school. This is 4 times as far as Miguel lives from school. How far does Miguel live from school?

If you look just at the key words in the problem, it might seem that 4 *times* 5 would give the solution.

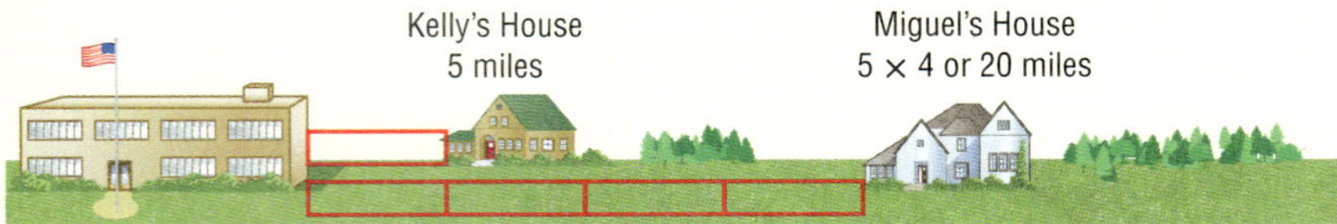

But the important question is, "Does this solution make sense?" In this case, the solution does *not* make sense because Kelly lives farther away. This problem is solved by dividing.

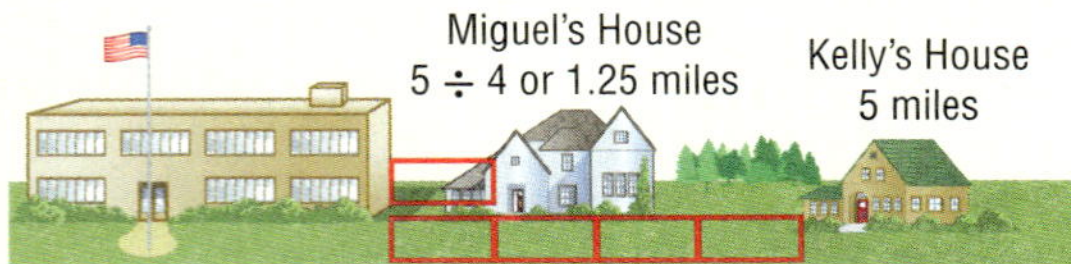

So, Miguel lives 1.25 miles away from school.

PRACTICE

For Exercises 1 and 2, choose the model that illustrates each problem. Explain your reasoning. Then solve.

1. Jennifer has saved \$210 to purchase an MP3 player. She needs \$299 to buy it. How much more money does she need?

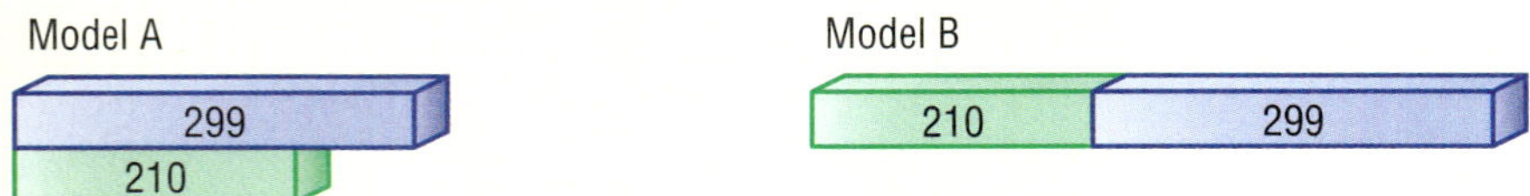

2. The school cafeteria sold 465 lunches on Thursday. They expect to sell 75 more lunches on Friday because they serve pizza that day. How many lunches do they expect to sell on Friday?

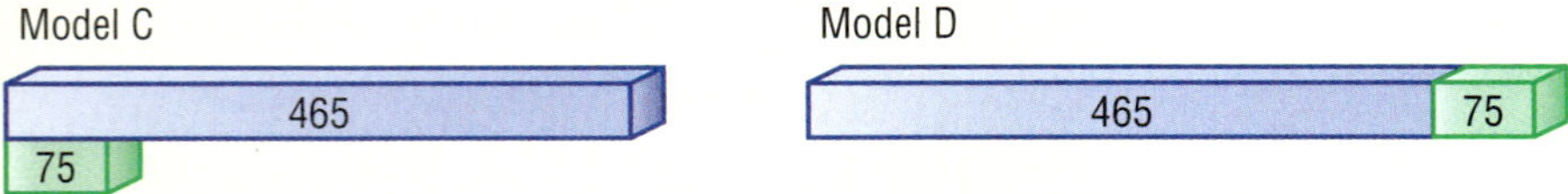

A Plan for Problem Solving

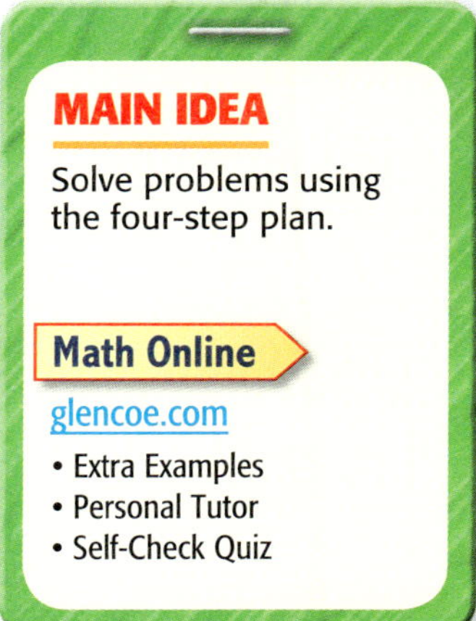

GET READY for the Lesson

ANALYZE GRAPHS The graph shows the countries with the most world championship motocross wins. What is the total number of wins for these five countries?

1. Do you have all of the information necessary to solve this problem?
2. Explain how you would solve this problem. Then solve it.
3. Does your answer make sense? Explain.
4. What can you do if your first attempt at solving the problem does not work?

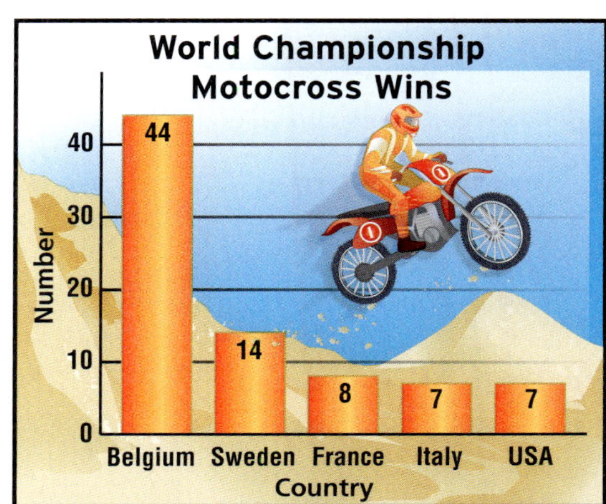

In mathematics, there is a *four-step plan* you can use to help you solve any problem.

Understand
- Read the problem carefully.
- What information is given?
- What do you need to find out?
- Is enough information given?
- Is there any extra information?

Plan
- How do the facts relate to each other?
- Select a strategy for solving the problem. There may be several that you can use.
- Estimate the answer.

Solve
- Use your plan to solve the problem.
- If your plan does not work, revise it or make a new plan.
- What is the solution?

Check
- Does your answer fit the facts given in the problem?
- Is your answer reasonable compared to your estimate?
- If not, make a new plan and start again.

Real-World Link In a recent year, worldwide consumers purchased 8.8 million LCD (Liquid Crystal Display) TVs.
Source: DisplaySearch

EXAMPLE Use the Four-Step Plan

1 **TELEVISION There were about 268 million TVs in the U.S. in 2007. This amount increases by 4 million each year after 2007. In what year will there be at least 300 million TVs?**

Understand *What are you trying to find?*
In what year will there be at least 300 million TVs in the U.S.?

What information do you need to solve the problem?
You know how many TVs there were in 2007. Also, the number increases by 4 million each year.

Plan Find the number of TVs needed to reach 300 million. Then divide this number by 4 to find the number of years that will pass before the total reaches 300 million TVs.

Solve The change in the number of TVs from 268 million to 300 million is 300 − 268 or 32 million TVs. Dividing the difference by 4, you get 32 ÷ 4 or 8.

You can also use the *make a table* strategy.

Year	'07	'08	'09	'10	'11	'12	'13	'14	'15
Number (millions)	268	272	276	280	284	288	292	296	300
	+4	+4	+4	+4	+4	+4	+4	+4	

So, there will be at least 300 million TVs in the U.S. in the year 2015.

Check $8 \text{ years} \times 4 \text{ million} = 32 \text{ million}$
$268 \text{ million} + 32 \text{ million} = 300 \text{ million}$  ✓

CHECK Your Progress

a. **WHALES** A baby blue whale gains about 200 pounds each day. About how many pounds does a baby blue whale gain per hour?

Problems can be solved using different operations or strategies.

Problem-Solving Strategies — Concept Summary

guess and check	use a graph
look for a pattern	work backward
make an organized list	eliminate possibilities
draw a diagram	estimate reasonable answers
act it out	use logical reasoning
solve a simpler problem	make a model

EXAMPLE Use a Strategy in the Four-Step Plan

2 **GEOMETRY** A *diagonal* connects two nonconsecutive vertices in a figure, as shown at the right. Find how many diagonals a figure with 7 sides would have.

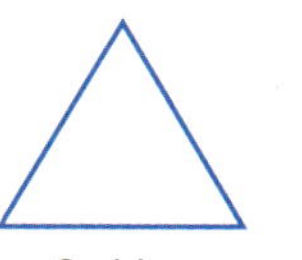
3 sides
0 diagonals

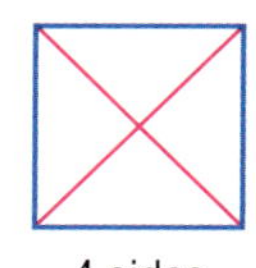
4 sides
2 diagonals

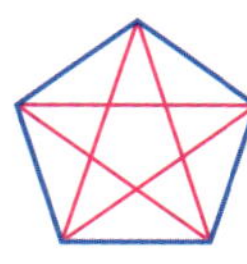
5 sides
5 diagonals

Understand You know the number of diagonals for figures with three, four, and five sides.

Plan You can look for a pattern by organizing the information in a table. Then continue the pattern until you find the diagonals for an object with 7 sides.

Solve

Sides	3	4	5	6	7
Diagonals	0	2	5	9	14

+2 +3 +4 +5

So, a 7-sided figure would have 14 diagonals.

Check Check your answer by making a drawing.

CHECK Your Progress

b. **GEOMETRY** Numbers that can be represented by a triangular arrangement of dots are called *triangular numbers*. The first five triangular numbers are shown below. Write a sequence formed by the first eight triangular numbers. Write a rule for generating the sequence.

1

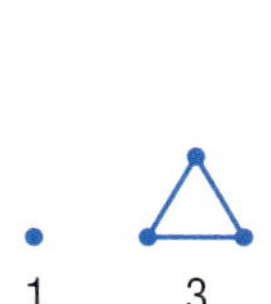
3

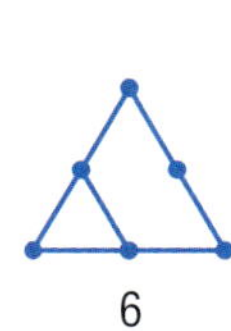
6

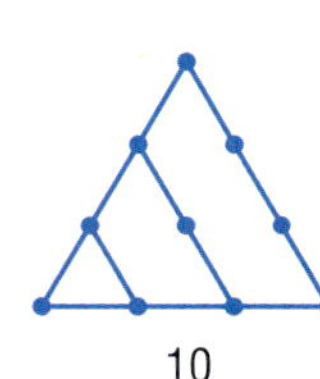
10

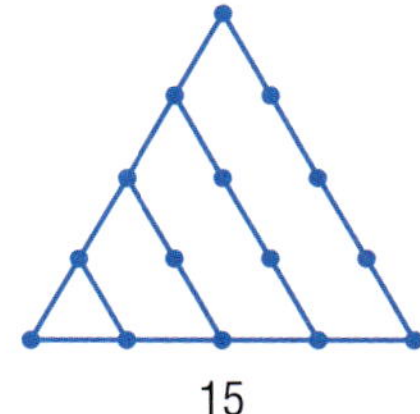
15

CHECK Your Understanding

Use the four-step plan to solve each problem.

Example 1 (p. 26)

1. **ANALYZE TABLES** The table lists the sizes of six of the largest lakes in North Carolina. About how many times as large is High Rock Lake than Hyco Lake?

Lake	Size (acres)
Lake Mattamuskeet	40,000
Falls Lake	12,000
Hyco Lake	3,750
Lake Gaston	20,000
Lake James	6,500
High Rock Lake	15,000

Example 2 (p. 27)

2. **ALGEBRA** What are the next two numbers in the pattern below?

1, 1, 2, 6, 24, ■, ■

Practice and Problem Solving

HOMEWORK HELP	
For Exercises	See Examples
3–6	1
7–10	2

Use the four-step plan to solve each problem.

3. **BIRDS** Most hummingbirds flap their wings about 50 times a second. How many times can a hummingbird flap its wings in one minute?

4. **PLANETS** Jupiter is about 3 times the size of Neptune. If the diameter of Jupiter is 88,736 miles, estimate the diameter of Neptune.

5. **FIELD TRIPS** To attend a field trip to a museum, each student will have to pay $6.00 for transportation and $5.75 for admission. If there are 65 students attending the field trip, how much money will their teacher need to collect?

6. **CANOE RENTALS** A state park took in $12,000 in canoe rentals during March. June rentals are expected to double that amount. If canoes rent for $40, how many canoe rentals are expected in June?

7. **GEOMETRY** What are the next two figures in the pattern?

8. **ALGEBRA** What are the next two numbers in the pattern below?

9, 27, 81, 243, 729, ■, ■

ANALYZE TABLES For Exercises 9 and 10, use the commuter train schedule shown.

A commuter train departs from a train station and travels to the city each day. The schedule shows the first five departure and arrival times.

Commuter Train Schedule	
Departure	Arrival
6:30 A.M.	6:50 A.M.
7:15 A.M.	7:35 A.M.
8:00 A.M.	8:20 A.M.
8:45 A.M.	9:05 A.M.
9:30 A.M.	9:50 A.M.

9. How often does the commuter train arrive in the city?

10. What is the latest time that passengers can depart from the train station if they need to arrive in the city no later than noon?

11. **HOMEWORK** Angel has guitar practice at 7:00 P.M. He has homework in math, science, and history that will take him 30 minutes each to complete. He also has to allow 20 minutes for dinner. What is the latest time Angel can start his homework?

12. **ESTIMATION** Terry opened a savings account in December with $132 and saved $27 each month beginning in January. Estimate the value of Terry's account in July. Then calculate the amount and evaluate the reasonableness of your estimate.

13. **FIND THE DATA** Refer to the Data File on pages 16–19 of your book. Choose some data and write a real-world problem in which you would use the four-step plan to solve the problem.

14. **ANALYZE TABLES** The sizes of Earth's oceans in millions of square kilometers are shown in the table. If the combined size of Earth's oceans is 367 million square kilometers, what is the size of the Pacific Ocean?

Earth's Oceans	
Ocean	Size (million km^2)
Arctic	45
Atlantic	77
Indian	69
Pacific	■
Southern	20

Source: *The World Factbook*

15. **MONEY** Meli wants to buy a pair of rollerblades that cost $140.75. So far, she has saved $56.25. If she saves $6.50 every week, in how many weeks will she be able to purchase the rollerblades?

See pages 668, 704.

H.O.T. Problems

16. **CHALLENGE** Use the digits 5, 6, 7, and 8 to form two 2-digit numbers so that their product is as great as possible. Use each digit only once.

17. **OPEN ENDED** Create a real-world problem that can be solved by adding 79 and 42 and then multiplying the result by 3.

18. **WRITING IN MATH** Explain why it is important to plan before solving a problem.

TEST PRACTICE

19. Sheryl has $2 to spend at the school store. Based on the choices below, which three items from the table could Sheryl purchase?

Item	Cost
Folder	$1.50
Pencil	$0.20
Pen	$0.50
Ruler	$1.75
Highlighter	$0.40

A folder, pencil, pen

B folder, highlighter, pencil

C pencil, pen, highlighter

D ruler, highlighter, pencil

20. Mr. Brooks went on a business trip. The trip was 380 miles, and the average price of gasoline was $3.15 per gallon. What information is needed to find the amount Mr. Brooks spent on gasoline for the trip?

F Number of times Mr. Brooks stopped to fill his tank with gasoline

G Number of miles the car can travel using one gallon of gasoline

H Number of hours the trip took

J Average number of miles Mr. Brooks drove per day

GET READY for the Next Lesson

PREREQUISITE SKILL Multiply.

21. 10×10 22. $3 \times 3 \times 3$ 23. $5 \times 5 \times 5 \times 5$ 24. $2 \times 2 \times 2 \times 2 \times 2$

1-2 Powers and Exponents

MAIN IDEA

Use powers and exponents.

New Vocabulary

- factors
- exponent
- base
- powers
- squared
- cubed
- evaluate
- standard form
- exponential form

Math Online

glencoe.com

- Extra Examples
- Personal Tutor
- Self-Check Quiz

GET READY for the Lesson

TEXT MESSAGING Suppose you text message one of your friends. That friend then text messages two friends after one minute. The pattern continues.

Minutes	Number of Text Messages	
0	1	= 1
1	1 × 2	= 2
2	2 × 2	= 4
3	2 × 2 × 2	= 8

1. How is doubling shown in the table?
2. How many text messages will be sent after 4 minutes?
3. What is the relationship between the number of 2s and the number of minutes?

Two or more numbers that are multiplied together to form a product are called **factors**. When the same factor is used, you may use an exponent to simplify the notation. The **exponent** tells how many times the base is used as a factor. The common factor is called the **base**.

$$16 = 2 \cdot 2 \cdot 2 \cdot 2 = 2^4$$

(4 ← exponent; 2 ↑ base)

Numbers expressed using exponents are called **powers**.

Powers	Words
5^2	five to the second power or five **squared**
4^3	four to the third power or four **cubed**
2^4	two to the fourth power

EXAMPLES Write Powers as Products

Write each power as a product of the same factor.

1 7^5

Seven is used as a factor five times.

$7^5 = 7 \cdot 7 \cdot 7 \cdot 7 \cdot 7$

2 3^2

Three is used as a factor twice.

$3^2 = 3 \cdot 3$

CHECK Your Progress

Write each power as a product of the same factor.

a. 6^4 **b.** 1^3 **c.** 9^5

You can **evaluate**, or find the value of, powers by multiplying the factors. Numbers written without exponents are in **standard form**.

EXAMPLES Write Powers in Standard Form

Evaluate

Everyday Use to find what something is worth

Math Use find the value of

Evaluate each expression.

3 2^5

$2^5 = 2 \cdot 2 \cdot 2 \cdot 2 \cdot 2$ — 2 is used as a factor 5 times.

$= 32$ — Multiply.

4 4^3

$4^3 = 4 \cdot 4 \cdot 4$ — 4 is used as a factor 3 times.

$= 64$ — Multiply.

Evaluate each expression.

d. 10^2 e. 7^3 f. 5^4

Numbers written with exponents are in **exponential form**.

EXAMPLE Write Numbers in Exponential Form

5 **Write 3 • 3 • 3 • 3 in exponential form.**

3 is the base. It is used as a factor 4 times. So, the exponent is 4.

$3 \cdot 3 \cdot 3 \cdot 3 = 3^4$

Write each product in exponential form.

g. $5 \cdot 5 \cdot 5$ h. $12 \cdot 12 \cdot 12 \cdot 12 \cdot 12 \cdot 12$

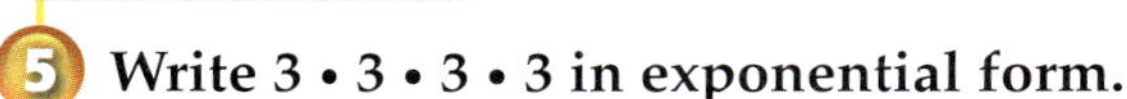

CHECK Your Understanding

Examples 1, 2 (p. 30)

Write each power as a product of the same factor.

1. 9^3
2. 3^4
3. 8^5

Examples 3, 4 (p. 31)

Evaluate each expression.

4. 2^4
5. 7^2
6. 10^3
7. **POPULATION** There are approximately 5^{10} people living in North Carolina. About how many people is this?

Example 5 (p. 31)

Write each product in exponential form.

8. $5 \cdot 5 \cdot 5 \cdot 5 \cdot 5 \cdot 5$
9. $1 \cdot 1 \cdot 1 \cdot 1$
10. $4 \cdot 4 \cdot 4 \cdot 4 \cdot 4$

Practice and Problem Solving

HOMEWORK HELP	
For Exercises	See Examples
11–16	1, 2
17–24	3, 4
25–28	5

Write each power as a product of the same factor.

11. 1^5
12. 4^2
13. 3^8
14. 8^6
15. 9^3
16. 10^4

Evaluate each expression.

17. 2^6
18. 4^3
19. 7^4
20. 4^6
21. 1^{10}
22. 10^1

23. **BIKING** In a recent year, the number of 12- to 17-year-olds that went off-road biking was 10^6. Write this number in standard form.

24. **TRAINS** The Maglev train in China is the fastest passenger train in the world. Its average speed is 3^5 miles per hour. Write this speed in standard form.

Write each product in exponential form.

25. $3 \cdot 3$
26. $7 \cdot 7 \cdot 7 \cdot 7$
27. $1 \cdot 1 \cdot 1 \cdot 1 \cdot 1 \cdot 1 \cdot 1 \cdot 1$
28. $6 \cdot 6 \cdot 6 \cdot 6 \cdot 6$

Write each power as a product of the same factor.

29. *four to the fifth power*
30. *nine squared*

Evaluate each expression.

31. *six to the fourth power*
32. *6 cubed*

GEOMETRY For Exercises 33 and 34, use the puzzle cube below.

33. Suppose the puzzle cube is made entirely of unit cubes. Find the number of unit cubes in the puzzle. Write your answer using exponents.

34. Why do you think the expression 3^3 is sometimes read as *3 cubed*?

35. **NUMBERS** Write $5 \cdot 5 \cdot 5 \cdot 5 \cdot 4 \cdot 4 \cdot 4$ in exponential form.

36. **COMPUTERS** A gigabyte is a measure of computer data storage capacity. One gigabyte stores 2^{30} bytes of data. Use a calculator to find the number in standard form that represents two gigabytes.

Order the following powers from least to greatest.

37. $6^5, 1^{14}, 4^{10}, 17^3$
38. $2^8, 15^2, 6^3, 3^5$
39. $5^3, 4^6, 2^{11}, 7^2$

EXTRA PRACTICE
See pages 668, 704.

40. **OPEN ENDED** Select a number between 1,000 and 2,000 that can be expressed as a power.

H.O.T. Problems

41. **CHALLENGE** Write two different powers that have the same value.

42. **Which One Doesn't Belong?** Identify the number that does not belong with the other three. Explain your reasoning.

121	361	576	1,000

43. **WRITING IN MATH** Analyze the number pattern shown at the right. Then write a convincing argument as to the value of 2^0. Based on your argument, what do you think will be the value of 2^{-1}?

$2^4 = 16$
$2^3 = 8$
$2^2 = 4$
$2^1 = 2$
$2^0 = ?$

TEST PRACTICE

44. Which model represents 6^3?

A

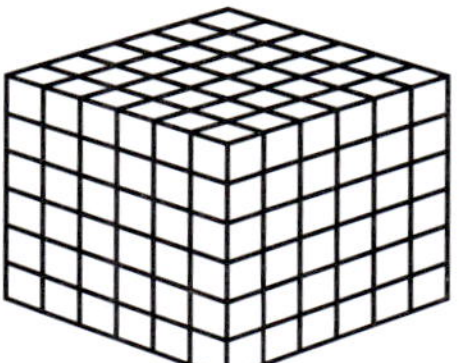

B

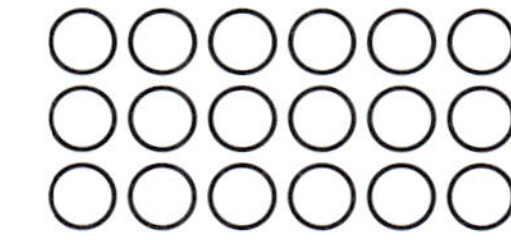

C

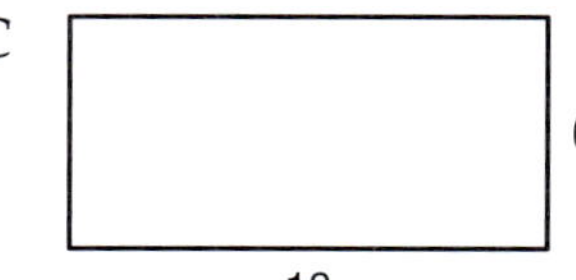

D

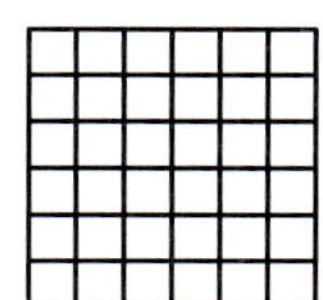

Spiral Review

45. **FOOTBALL** The graph shows the number of wins the Pittsburgh Steelers had from 2003–2006. How many more wins did the Steelers have in 2004 than 2006? (Lesson 1-1)

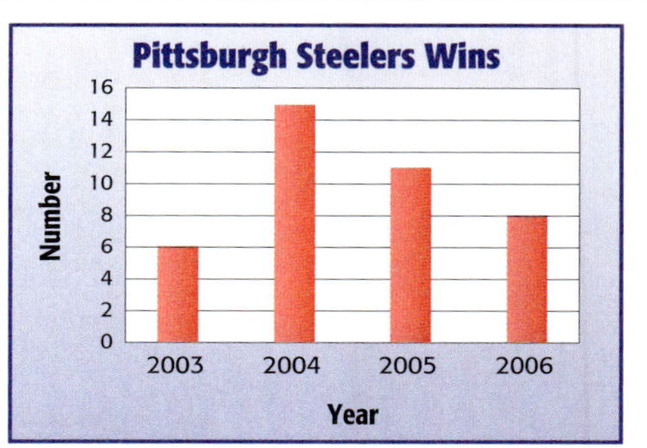

Source: National Football League

46. **COOKING** Ms. Jackson is serving fried turkey at 5:00 P.M. The 12-pound turkey has to cook 3 minutes for every pound, and then cool for at least 45 minutes. What is the latest time she can start frying? (Lesson 1-1)

GET READY for the Next Lesson

PREREQUISITE SKILL Multiply.

47. $2 \cdot 2$
48. $3 \cdot 3$
49. $5 \cdot 5$
50. $7 \cdot 7$

1-3 Squares and Square Roots

MAIN IDEA

Find squares of numbers and square roots of perfect squares.

New Vocabulary

square
perfect squares
square root
radical sign

Math Online

glencoe.com

- Extra Examples
- Personal Tutor
- Self-Check Quiz

MINI Lab

A square with an area of 36 square units is shown.

1. Using tiles, try to construct squares with areas of 4, 9, and 16 square units.
2. Try to construct squares with areas 12, 18, and 20 square units.
3. Which of the areas form squares?
4. What is the relationship between the lengths of the sides and the areas of these squares?
5. Using your square tiles, create a square that has an area of 49 square units. What are the lengths of the sides of the square?

The area of the square at the right is 5 • 5 or 25 square units. The product of a number and itself is the **square** of that number. So, the square of 5 is 25.

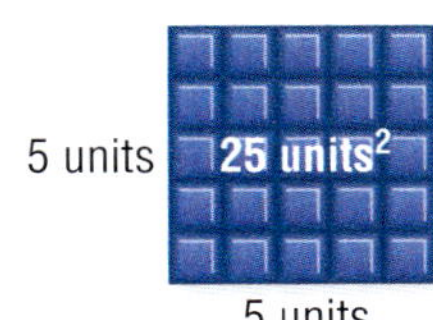

EXAMPLES Find Squares of Numbers

1 **Find the square of 3.**

$3 \cdot 3 = 9$ Multiply 3 by itself.

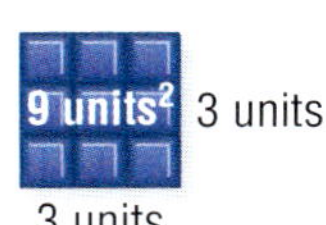

2 **Find the square of 28.**

METHOD 1 **Use paper and pencil.**

$$\begin{array}{r} 28 \\ \times\ 28 \\ \hline 224 \\ +\ 560 \\ \hline 784 \end{array}$$

Multiply 28 by itself.

Annex a zero.

METHOD 2 **Use a calculator.**

28 [x^2] [ENTER] 784

CHECK Your Progress

Find the square of each number.

a. 8 b. 12 c. 23

Numbers like 9, 16, and 225 are called square numbers or **perfect squares** because they are squares of whole numbers.

The factors multiplied to form perfect squares are called **square roots**. A **radical sign**, $\sqrt{\ }$, is the symbol used to indicate a square root of a number.

Reading Math

Square Roots Read $\sqrt{16} = 4$ as *the square root of 16 is 4.*

Square Root — Key Concept

Words A square root of a number is one of its two equal factors.

Examples

Numbers	Algebra
$4 \cdot 4 = 16$, so $\sqrt{16} = 4$.	If $x \cdot x$ or $x^2 = y$, then $\sqrt{y} = x$.

EXAMPLES Find Square Roots

3 Find $\sqrt{81}$.

$9 \cdot 9 = 81$, so $\sqrt{81} = 9$. What number times itself is 81?

4 Find $\sqrt{225}$.

2nd [$\sqrt{\ }$] 225 ENTER 15

So, $\sqrt{225} = 15$.

CHECK Your Progress

Find each square root.

d. $\sqrt{64}$

e. $\sqrt{289}$

Real-World EXAMPLE

Real-World Link The average lifespan of a major league baseball is 7 pitches.
Source: SuperKids

5 SPORTS The infield of a baseball field is a square with an area of 8,100 square feet. What are the dimensions of the infield?

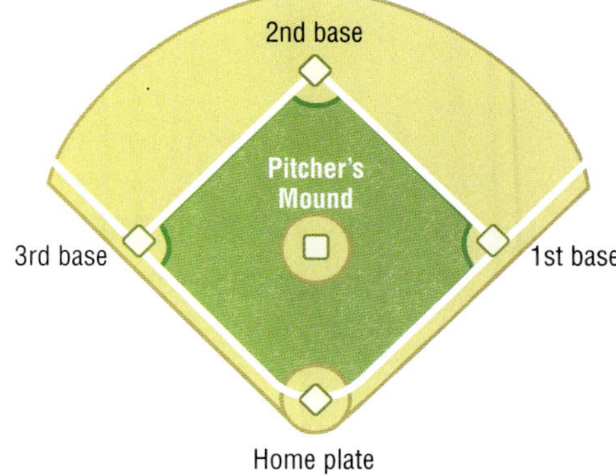

The infield is a square. By finding the square root of the area, 8,100, you find the length of one side of the infield.

$90 \cdot 90 = 8{,}100$, so $\sqrt{8{,}100} = 90$.

The length of one side of the infield is 90 feet. So, the dimensions of the infield are 90 feet by 90 feet.

CHECK Your Progress

f. **SPORTS** The largest ring in amateur boxing is a square with an area of 400 square feet. What are the dimensions of the ring?

CHECK Your Understanding

Examples 1, 2 (p. 34)

Find the square of each number.

1. 6
2. 10
3. 17
4. 30

Examples 3, 4 (p. 35)

Find each square root.

5. $\sqrt{9}$
6. $\sqrt{36}$
7. $\sqrt{121}$
8. $\sqrt{169}$

Example 5 (p. 35)

9. **ROAD SIGNS** Historic Route 66 from Chicago to Los Angeles is known as the Main Street of America. If the area of a Route 66 sign measures 576 square inches and the sign is a square, what are the dimensions of the sign?

Practice and Problem Solving

HOMEWORK HELP

For Exercises	See Examples
10–17	1, 2
18–25	3, 4
26–27	5

Find the square of each number.

10. 4
11. 1
12. 7
13. 11
14. 16
15. 20
16. 18
17. 34

Find each square root.

18. $\sqrt{4}$
19. $\sqrt{16}$
20. $\sqrt{49}$
21. $\sqrt{100}$
22. $\sqrt{144}$
23. $\sqrt{256}$
24. $\sqrt{529}$
25. $\sqrt{625}$

26. **MEASUREMENT** Emma's bedroom is shaped like a square. What are the dimensions of the room if the area of the floor is 196 square feet?

27. **SPORTS** For the floor exercise, gymnasts perform their tumbling skills on a mat that has an area of 1,600 square feet. How much room does a gymnast have to run along one side of the mat?

28. What is the square of 12?

29. Find the square of 19.

30. **GARDENING** A square garden has an area of 225 square feet. How much fencing will a gardener need to buy in order to place fencing around the garden?

GEOGRAPHY For Exercises 31–33, refer to the squares in the diagram. They represent the approximate areas of Florida, North Carolina, and Pennsylvania.

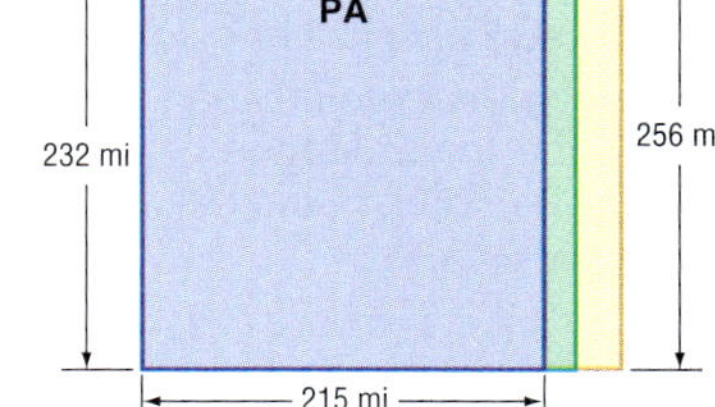

31. What is the area of North Carolina in square miles?

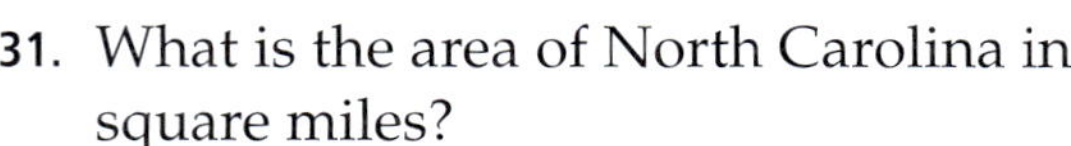

32. How much larger is Florida than Pennsylvania?

33. The water areas of Florida, North Carolina, and Pennsylvania are 11,881 square miles; 5,041 square miles; and 1,225 square miles, respectively. Make a similar diagram comparing the water areas of these states.

EXTRA PRACTICE
See pages 668, 704.

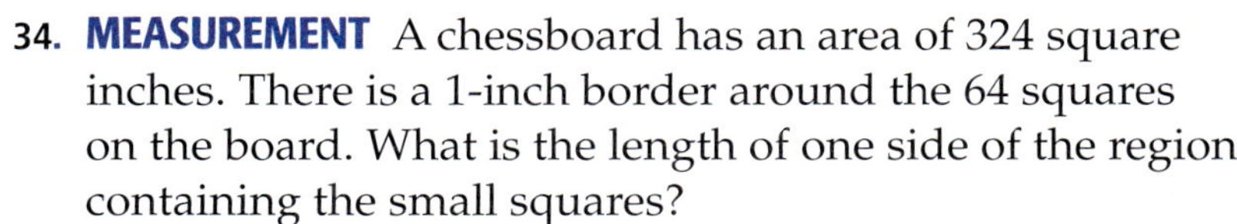

34. **MEASUREMENT** A chessboard has an area of 324 square inches. There is a 1-inch border around the 64 squares on the board. What is the length of one side of the region containing the small squares?

35. **MEASUREMENT** The area of a square that is 7 meters by 7 meters is how much greater than the area of a square containing 8 square meters? Explain.

H.O.T. Problems

36. **OPEN ENDED** Write a number whose square is between 100 and 150.

CHALLENGE For Exercises 37 and 38, use the diagram shown.

37. Could the area of the dog's pen be made larger using the same amount of fencing? Explain.

38. Describe the largest pen area possible using the same amount of fencing. How do the perimeter and area compare to the original pen?

39. **WRITING IN MATH** Explain why raising a number to the second power is called *squaring* the number.

TEST PRACTICE

40. Which model represents the square of 4?

A

B

C 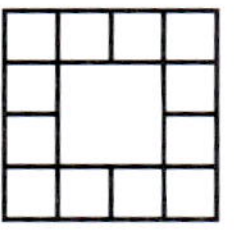

D 

41. Which measure can be the area of a square if the measure of the side length is a whole number?

F 836 sq ft

G 949 sq ft

H 1,100 sq ft

J 1,225 sq ft

Spiral Review

Write each power as a product of the same factor. (Lesson 1-2)

42. 3^4 43. 8^5 44. 7^2 45. 2^6

46. **SHIPPING** Jocelyn spent a total of $24 to ship 4 packages. If the packages are equal in size and weight, how much did it cost to ship each package? (Lesson 1-1)

GET READY for the Next Lesson

PREREQUISITE SKILL Add, subtract, multiply, or divide.

47. $13 + 8$ 48. $10 - 6$ 49. 5×6 50. $36 \div 4$

1-4 Order of Operations

MAIN IDEA

Evaluate expressions using the order of operations.

New Vocabulary

numerical expression
order of operations

Math Online

glencoe.com

- Extra Examples
- Personal Tutor
- Self-Check Quiz
- Reading in the Content Area

GET READY for the Lesson

SPORTS The Kent City football team made one 6-point touchdown and four 3-point field goals in its last game. Megan and Dexter each use an expression to find the total number of points the team scored.

Megan	Dexter
$6 + 4 \cdot 3 = 6 + 12$ $= 18$	$(6 + 4) \cdot 3 = 10 \cdot 3$ $= 30$
The team scored 18 points.	The team scored 30 points.

1. List the differences between their calculations.
2. Whose calculations are correct?
3. Make a conjecture about what should be the first step in simplifying $6 + 4 \cdot 3$.

The expression $6 + 4 \cdot 3$ is a **numerical expression**. To evaluate expressions, use the **order of operations**. These rules ensure that numerical expressions have only one value.

Order of Operations — Key Concept

1. Evaluate the expressions inside grouping symbols.
2. Evaluate all powers.
3. Multiply and divide in order from left to right.
4. Add and subtract in order from left to right.

EXAMPLES Use Order of Operations

1 Evaluate 5 + (12 − 3). Justify each step.

$5 + (12 - 3) = 5 + 9$ — Subtract first, since 12 − 3 is in parentheses.
$= 14$ — Add 5 and 9.

2 Evaluate 8 − 3 • 2 + 7. Justify each step.

$8 - 3 \cdot 2 + 7 = 8 - 6 + 7$ — Multiply 3 and 2.
$= 2 + 7$ — Subtract 6 from 8.
$= 9$ — Add 2 and 7.

CHECK Your Progress

Evaluate each expression. Justify each step.

a. $39 \div (9 + 4)$

b. $10 + 8 \div 2 - 6$

Study Tip

Scientific Calculators If you have a scientific calculator, you can enter numbers and operations in order from left to right. The scientific calculator follows the order of operations.

EXAMPLE Use Order of Operations

3 **Evaluate $5 \cdot 3^2 - 7$. Justify each step.**

$5 \cdot 3^2 - 7 = 5 \cdot 9 - 7$	Find the value of 3^2.
$= 45 - 7$	Multiply 5 and 9.
$= 38$	Subtract 7 from 45.

CHECK Your Progress

c. 3×10^4

d. $(5 - 1)^3 \div 4$

In addition to using the symbols × and •, multiplication can be indicated by using parentheses. For example, $2(3 + 5)$ means $2 \times (3 + 5)$.

EXAMPLE Use Order of Operations

4 **Evaluate $14 + 3(7 - 2)$. Justify each step.**

$14 + 3(7 - 2) = 14 + 3(5)$	Subtract 2 from 7.
$= 14 + 15$	Multiply 3 and 5.
$= 29$	Add 14 and 15.

CHECK Your Progress

e. $20 - 2(4 - 1) \cdot 3$

f. $6 + 8 \div 2 + 2(3 - 1)$

Real-World EXAMPLE

5 **MONEY** **Julian orders 3 rolls of crepe paper, 4 boxes of balloons, and 2 boxes of favors for the school dance. What is the total cost?**

Item	Unit Cost
crepe paper	$2
favors	$7
balloons	$5

Words	cost of 3 rolls of crepe paper	+	cost of 4 boxes of balloons	+	cost of 2 boxes of favors
Expression	3 × 2	+	4 × 5	+	2 × 7

$3 \times 2 + 4 \times 5 + 2 \times 7 = 6 + 20 + 14$	Multiply from left to right.
$= 40$	Add.

The total cost is $40.

CHECK Your Progress

g. What is the total cost of twelve rolls of crepe paper, three boxes of balloons, and three boxes of favors?

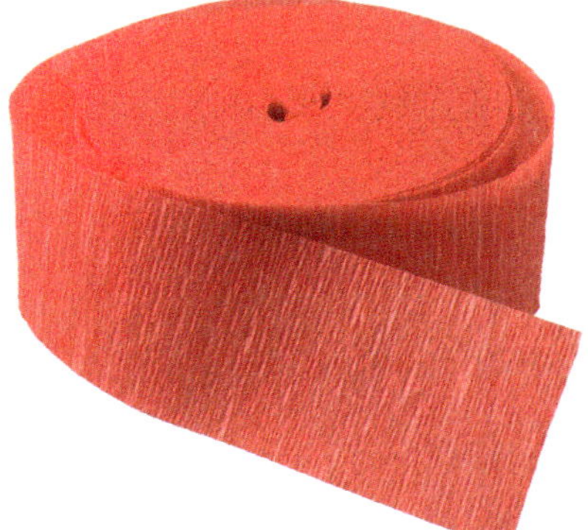

Real-World Link Crepe paper originated in the late 1700s. It was critical to the invention of masking tape! The texture allows the tape to partially adhere to the surface, making it easily removable.

Source: Wilsonart International

CHECK Your Understanding

Evaluate each expression. Justify each step.

Examples 1, 2 (p. 38)

1. $8 + (5 - 2)$
2. $25 \div (9 - 4)$
3. $14 - 2 \cdot 6 + 9$
4. $8 \cdot 5 - 4 \cdot 3$

Examples 3, 4 (p. 39)

5. 4×10^2
6. $45 \div (4 - 1)^2$
7. $17 + 2(6 - 3) - 3 \times 4$
8. $22 - 3(8 - 2) + 12 \div 4$

Example 5 (p. 39)

9. **COINS** Isabelle has 3 nickels, 2 quarters, 2 dimes, and 7 pennies. Write an expression that can be used to find how much money Isabelle has altogether. How much money does Isabelle have?

Practice and Problem Solving

HOMEWORK HELP

For Exercises	See Examples
10–17	1, 2
18–23	3
24–27	4
28, 29	5

Evaluate each expression. Justify each step.

10. $(1 + 8) \times 3$
11. $10 - (3 + 4)$
12. $(25 \div 5) + 8$
13. $(11 - 2) \div 9$
14. $3 \cdot 2 + 14 \div 7$
15. $4 \div 2 - 1 + 7$
16. $12 + 6 \div 3 - 4$
17. $18 - 3 \cdot 6 + 5$
18. 6×10^2
19. 3×10^4
20. $5 \times 4^3 + 2$
21. $8 \times 7^2 - 6$
22. $8 \div 2 \times 6 + 6^2$
23. $9^2 - 14 \div 7 \cdot 3$
24. $(17 + 3) \div (4 + 1)$
25. $(6 + 5) \cdot (8 - 6)$
26. $6 + 2(4 - 1) + 4 \times 9$
27. $3(4 + 7) - 5 \cdot 4 \div 2$

For Exercises 28 and 29, write an expression for each situation. Then evaluate to find the solution.

28. **MP3 PLAYERS** Reina is buying an MP3 player, a case, three packs of batteries, and six songs. What is the total cost?

Item	Quantity	Unit Cost
MP3 player	1	$200
case	1	$30
pack of batteries	3	$4
songs	6	$2

29. **BOOKS** Ian goes to the library's used book sale. Paperback books are $0.25, and hardback books are $0.50. If Ian buys 3 paperback books and 5 hardback books, how much does he spend?

Evaluate each expression. Justify each step.

30. $(2 + 10)^2 \div 4$
31. $(3^3 + 8) - (10 - 6)^2$
32. $3 \cdot 4(5.2 + 3.8) + 2.7$
33. $7 \times 9 - (4 - 3.2) + 1.8$

34. **MONEY** Suppose that your family orders 2 pizzas, 2 orders of garlic bread, and 1 order of BBQ wings from Mario's Pizza Shop. Write an expression to find the amount of change you would receive from $30. Then evaluate the expression.

Mario's Pizza Shop	
Item	**Cost**
14″ pizza	$8
garlic bread	$2
BBQ wings	$4

EXTRA PRACTICE
See pages 669, 704.

H.O.T. Problems

35. **FIND THE ERROR** Phoung and Peggy are evaluating $16 - 24 \div 6 \cdot 2$. Who is correct? Explain your reasoning.

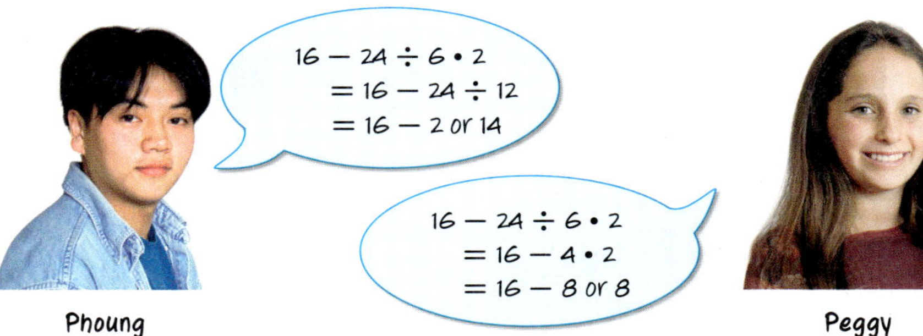

36. **CHALLENGE** Insert parentheses to make $72 \div 9 + 27 - 2 = 0$ a true statement.

37. **WRITING IN MATH** Write a real-world problem in which you would need to use the order of operations or a scientific calculator to solve it.

TEST PRACTICE

38. Simplify $3^2 + 9 \div 3 + 3$.

A 3 **C** 15

B 9 **D** 18

39. Grace has 2 boxes that contain 24 straws each and 3 boxes that contain 15 cups each. Which expression *cannot* be used to find the total number of items she has?

F $2(24) + 3(15)$

G $3 \times 15 + 2 \times 24$

H $5 \times (24 + 15)$

J $15 + 15 + 15 + 24 + 24$

40. The steps Alana took to evaluate the expression $4y + 4 \div 4$ when $y = 7$ are shown below.

$4y + 4 \div 4$ when $y = 7$
$4 \times 7 = 28$
$28 + 4 = 32$
$32 \div 4 = 8$

What should Alana have done differently in order to evaluate the expression correctly?

A divided $(28 + 4)$ by (28×4)

B divided $(28 + 4)$ by $(28 + 4)$

C added $(4 \div 4)$ to 28

D added 4 to $(28 \div 4)$

Spiral Review

Find each square root. (Lesson 1-3)

41. $\sqrt{64}$ 42. $\sqrt{2{,}025}$ 43. $\sqrt{784}$

44. **INTERNET** Each day, Internet users perform 2^5 million searches using a popular search engine. How many searches is this? (Lesson 1-2)

GET READY for the Next Lesson

45. **PREREQUISITE SKILL** A Chinese checkerboard has 121 holes. How many holes can be found on eight Chinese checkerboards? (Lesson 1-1)

1-5 Problem-Solving Investigation

MAIN IDEA: Solve problems using the guess and check strategy.

P.S.I. TEAM +

e-Mail: GUESS AND CHECK

TREVOR: My soccer team held a car wash to help pay for a trip to a tournament. We charged \$5 for a car and \$7 for an SUV. During the first hour, we washed 10 vehicles and earned \$58.

YOUR MISSION: Use guess and check to find how many of each type of vehicle were washed.

Understand	You know car washes are \$5 for cars and \$7 for SUVs. Ten vehicles were washed for \$58.
Plan	Make a guess and check it. Adjust the guess until you get the correct answer.
Solve	Make a guess. 5 cars and 5 SUVs $5(5) + 7(5) = \$60$ too high Adjust the number of SUVs downward. 5 cars and 4 SUVs $5(5) + 7(4) = \$53$ too low Adjust the number of cars upward. 6 cars and 4 SUVs $5(6) + 7(4) = \$58$ correct ✓ So, 6 cars and 4 SUVs were washed.
Check	Six cars cost \$30, and four SUVs cost \$28. Since $\$30 + \$28 = \$58$, the guess is correct.

Analyze The Strategy

1. Explain why you should keep a careful record of each of your guesses.
2. **WRITING IN MATH** Write a problem that could be solved by guess and check. Then write the steps you would take to find the solution to your problem.

Mixed Problem Solving

Use the *guess and check* strategy to solve Exercises 3–6.

3. **TICKET SALES** The total ticket sales for the school basketball game were $1,625. Adult tickets were $7, and student tickets were $3. Twice as many students bought tickets as adults. How many adult and student tickets were sold?

4. **NUMBERS** A number is multiplied by 6. Then 4 is added to the product. The result is 82. What is the number?

5. **ANALYZE TABLES** Camila is transferring her home videos onto a DVD. Suppose the DVD holds 60 minutes. Which videos should Camila select to have the maximum time on the DVD without going over?

Video	Time
birthday	25 min 15 s
family picnic	18 min 10 s
holiday	15 min 20 s
vacation	19 min 20 s

6. **MONEY** Susan has $1.60 in change in her purse. If she has an equal number of nickels, dimes, and quarters, how many of each does she have?

Use any strategy to solve Exercises 7–13. Some strategies are shown below.

7. **BRIDGES** The total length of wire used in the cables supporting the Golden Gate Bridge in San Francisco is about 80,000 miles. This is 5,300 miles longer than three times the distance around Earth at the Equator. What is the distance around Earth at the Equator?

8. **GEOMETRY** What are the next two figures in the pattern?

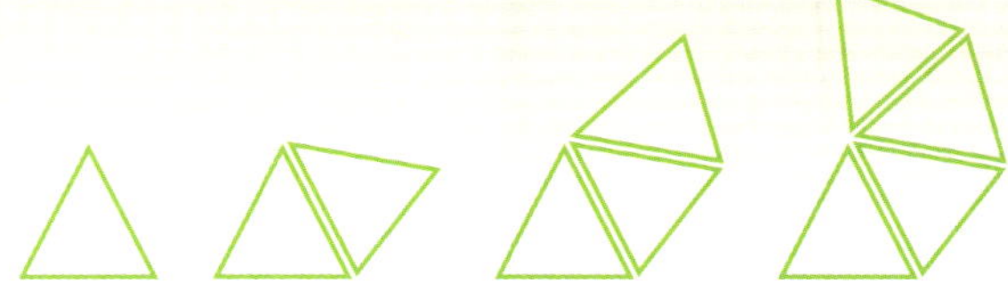

9. **ALGEBRA** What are the next two numbers in the pattern?

16, 32, 64, 128, 256, ■, ■

10. **FRUIT** Mason places 4 apples and 3 oranges into each fruit basket he makes. If he has used 24 apples and 18 oranges, how many fruit baskets has he made?

11. **ANALYZE TABLES** The table gives the average snowfall, in inches, for Valdez, Alaska, for the months of October through April.

Month	Snowfall
October	11.6
November	40.3
December	73.0
January	65.8
February	59.4
March	52.0
April	22.7

Source: National Climatic Data Center

How many inches total of snowfall could a resident of Valdez expect to receive from October to April?

12. **ROLLER COASTERS** The Jackrabbit roller coaster can handle 1,056 passengers per hour. The coaster has 8 vehicles. If each vehicle carries 4 passengers, how many runs are made in one hour?

13. **NUMBERS** Della is thinking of 3 numbers from 1 through 9 with a product of 36. Find the numbers.

1-6 Algebra: Variables and Expressions

MAIN IDEA

Evaluate simple algebraic expressions.

New Vocabulary

variable
algebra
algebraic expression
coefficient

Math Online

glencoe.com

- Concepts In Motion
- Extra Examples
- Personal Tutor
- Self-Check Quiz

MINI Lab

A pattern of squares is shown.

1. Draw the next three figures in the pattern.
2. Find the number of squares in each figure and record your data in a table like the one shown below. The first three are completed for you.

Figure	1	2	3	4	5	6
Number of Squares	3	4	5	■	■	■

3. Without drawing the figure, determine how many squares would be in the 10th figure. Check by making a drawing.
4. Find a relationship between the figure and its number of squares.

In the Mini Lab, you found that the number of squares in the figure is two more than the figure number. You can use a placeholder, or variable, to represent the number of squares. A **variable** is a symbol that represents an unknown quantity.

figure number ⟶ $n + 2$
⟶ number of squares

The branch of mathematics that involves expressions with variables is called **algebra**. The expression $n + 2$ is called an **algebraic expression** because it contains variables, numbers, and at least one operation.

EXAMPLE Evaluate an Algebraic Expression

1 **Evaluate $n + 3$ if $n = 4$.**

$n + 3 = 4 + 3$ Replace n with 4.

$= 7$ Add 4 and 3.

CHECK Your Progress

Evaluate each expression if $c = 8$ and $d = 5$.

a. $c - 3$ b. $15 - c$ c. $c + d$

In algebra, the multiplication sign is often omitted.

The numerical factor of a multiplication expression that contains a variable is called a **coefficient**. So, 6 is the coefficient of $6d$.

EXAMPLES Evaluate Expressions

2 **Evaluate $8w - 2v$ if $w = 5$ and $v = 3$.**

$8w - 2v = 8(5) - 2(3)$ Replace w with 5 and v with 3.

$= 40 - 6$ Do all multiplications first.

$= 34$ Subtract 6 from 40.

3 **Evaluate $4y^2 + 2$ if $y = 3$.**

$4y^2 + 2 = 4(3)^2 + 2$ Replace y with 3.

$= 4(9) + 2$ Evaluate the power.

$= 38$ Multiply, then add.

CHECK Your Progress

Evaluate each expression if $a = 4$ and $b = 3$.

d. $9a - 6b$ e. $\frac{ab}{2}$ f. $2a^2 + 5$

The fraction bar is a grouping symbol. Evaluate the expressions in the numerator and denominator separately before dividing.

Real-World EXAMPLE

4 **HEALTH** **Use the formula at the left to find Latrina's minimum training heart rate if she is 15 years old.**

$\frac{3(220 - a)}{5} = \frac{3(220 - 15)}{5}$ Replace a with 15.

$= \frac{3(205)}{5}$ Subtract 15 from 220.

$= \frac{615}{5}$ Multiply 3 and 205.

$= 123$ Divide 615 by 5.

Latrina's minimum training heart rate is 123 beats per minute.

Real-World Link Athletic trainers use the formula $\frac{3(220 - a)}{5}$, where a is a person's age, to find their minimum training heart rate.
Source: CMPMedica Ltd.

CHECK Your Progress

g. **MEASUREMENT** To find the area of a triangle, you can use the formula $\frac{bh}{2}$, where h is the height and b is the base. What is the area in square inches of a triangle with a height of 6 inches and base of 8 inches?

CHECK Your Understanding

Example 1 (p. 44)

Evaluate each expression if $a = 3$ and $b = 5$.

1. $a + 7$
2. $8 - b$
3. $b - a$

4. **HEALTH** The standard formula for finding your maximum heart rate is $220 - a$, where a represents a person's age in years. What is your maximum heart rate?

Examples 2–4 (p. 45)

Evaluate each expression if $m = 2$, $n = 6$, and $p = 4$.

5. $6n - p$
6. $7m - 2n$
7. $3m + 4p$
8. $n^2 + 5$
9. $15 - m^3$
10. $3p^2 - n$
11. $\frac{mn}{4}$
12. $\frac{3n}{9}$
13. $\frac{5n + m}{8}$

Practice and Problem Solving

HOMEWORK HELP

For Exercises	See Examples
14–29	1–3
30–31	4

Evaluate each expression if $d = 8$, $e = 3$, $f = 4$, and $g = 1$.

14. $d + 9$
15. $10 - e$
16. $4f + 1$
17. $8g - 3$
18. $f - e$
19. $d + f$
20. $10g - 6$
21. $8 + 5d$
22. $\frac{d}{5}$
23. $\frac{16}{f}$
24. $\frac{5d - 25}{5}$
25. $\frac{(5 + g)^2}{2}$
26. $6f^2$
27. $4e^2$
28. $d^2 + 7$
29. $e^2 - 4$

30. **BOWLING** The expression $5n + 2$ can be used to find the total cost in dollars of bowling where n is the number of games bowled. How much will it cost Vincent to bowl 3 games?

31. **HEALTH** The expression $\frac{w}{30}$, where w is a person's weight in pounds, is used to find the approximate number of quarts of blood in the person's body. How many quarts of blood does a 120-pound person have?

Evaluate each expression if $x = 3.2$, $y = 6.1$, and $z = 0.2$.

32. $x + y - z$
33. $14.6 - (x + y + z)$
34. $xz + y^2$

35. **CAR RENTAL** A car rental company charges \$19.99 per day and \$0.17 per mile to rent a car. Write an expression that gives the total cost in dollars to rent a car for d days and m miles.

36. **MUSIC** A Web site charges \$0.99 to download a song onto an MP3 player and \$12.49 to download an entire album. Write an expression that gives the total cost in dollars to download a albums and s songs.

37. **SCIENCE** The expression $\frac{32t^2}{2}$ gives the falling distance of an object in feet after t seconds. How far would a bungee jumper fall 2 seconds after jumping?

38. **GEOMETRY** To find the total number of diagonals for any given polygon, you can use the expression $\frac{n(n-3)}{2}$, where n is the number of sides of the polygon. What is the total number of diagonals for a 10-sided polygon?

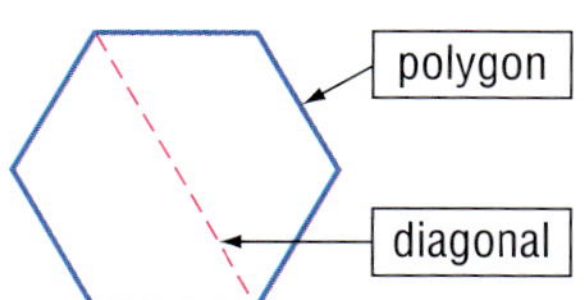

See pages 669, 704.

H.O.T. Problems

39. **OPEN ENDED** Write an algebraic expression with the variable x that has a value of 3 when evaluated.

40. **CHALLENGE** Name values of x and y so that the value of $5x + 3$ is greater than the value of $2y + 14$.

41. **WRITING IN MATH** Tell whether the statement below is *sometimes*, *always*, or *never* true. Justify your reasoning.

The expressions $x - 3$ and $y - 3$ represent the same value.

TEST PRACTICE

42. Which expression could be used to find the cost of buying b books at $7.95 each and m magazines at $4.95 each?

A $7.95b + 4.95m$

B $7.95b - 4.95m$

C $12.9(b + m)$

D $12.9(bm)$

43. Tonya has x quarters, y dimes, and z nickels in her pocket. Which of the following expressions gives the total amount of change she has in her pocket?

F $\$0.25x + \$0.05y + \$0.10z$

G $\$0.25x + \$0.10y + \$0.05z$

H $\$0.05x + \$0.25y + \$0.10z$

J $\$0.10x + \$0.05y + \$0.25z$

Spiral Review

44. **SHOPPING** A grocery store sells hot dog buns in packages of 8 and 12. How many 8-packs and 12-packs could you buy if you needed 44 hot dog buns? Use the *guess and check* strategy. (Lesson 1-5)

Evaluate each expression. (Lesson 1-4)

45. $6(5) - 2$

46. $9 + 9 \div 3$

47. $4 \cdot 2(8 - 1)$

48. $(17 + 3) \div 5$

49. Find $\sqrt{361}$. (Lesson 1-3)

GET READY for the Next Lesson

PREREQUISITE SKILL **Determine whether each sentence is *true* or *false*.** (Lesson 1-4)

50. $15 - 2(3) = 9$

51. $20 \div 5 \times 4 = 1$

52. $4^2 + 6 \cdot 7 = 154$

Mid-Chapter Quiz

Lessons 1-1 through 1-6

1. **MULTIPLE CHOICE** A cycling club is planning an 1,800-mile trip. The cyclers average 15 miles per hour. What additional information is needed to determine the number of days it will take them to complete the trip? (Lesson 1-1)

   A The number of cyclists in the club

   B The number of miles of rough terrain

   C The number of hours they plan to cycle each day

   D Their average speed per minute

Write each power as a product of the same factor. (Lesson 1-2)

2. 4^5

3. 9^6

4. **OCEANS** The world's largest ocean, the Pacific Ocean, covers approximately 4^3 million square miles. Write this area in standard form. (Lesson 1-2)

5. **ZOOS** The Lincoln Park Zoo in Illinois is $2 \cdot 2 \cdot 2 \cdot 2 \cdot 2 \cdot 2 \cdot 2$ years old. Write this age in exponential form. (Lesson 1-2)

6. **MULTIPLE CHOICE** The model below represents $\sqrt{49} = 7$.

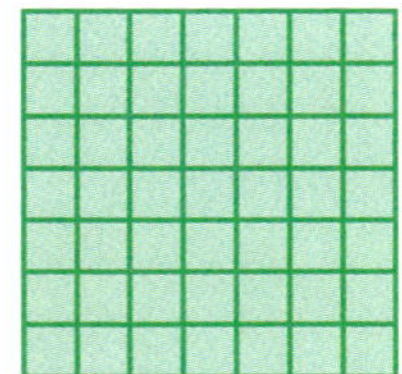

   Which arrangement of small squares can be used to model a large square that represents $\sqrt{324}$? (Lesson 1-3)

   F 9 rows of 36 squares

   G 18 rows of 18 squares

   H 12 rows of 27 squares

   J 6 rows of 54 squares

Find the square of each number. (Lesson 1-3)

7. 4

8. 12

Find each square root. (Lesson 1-3)

9. $\sqrt{64}$

10. $\sqrt{289}$

11. **LANDSCAPING** A bag of lawn fertilizer covers 2,500 square feet. Describe the largest square that one bag of fertilizer could cover. (Lesson 1-3)

Evaluate each expression. (Lesson 1-4)

12. $25 - (3^2 + 2 \times 5)$

13. $\dfrac{2(7-3)}{2^2}$

14. **MEASUREMENT** The perimeter of a rectangle is 42 inches, and its area is 104 square inches. Find the dimensions of the rectangle. Use the *guess and check* strategy. (Lesson 1-5)

15. **MULTIPLE CHOICE** Ana buys some baseball bats at \$35 each and some baseball gloves at \$48 each. Which expression could be used to find the total cost of the sports items? (Lesson 1-6)

   A $35b \cdot 48g$

   B $\dfrac{35b}{48g}$

   C $35b + 48g$

   D $48g - 35b$

Evaluate each expression if $x = 12$, $y = 4$, and $z = 8$. (Lesson 1-6)

16. $x - 5$

17. $3y + 10z$

18. $\dfrac{yz}{2}$

19. $\dfrac{(y+8)^2}{x}$

20. **HEALTH** A nurse can use the expression $110 + \dfrac{A}{2}$, where A is a person's age, to estimate a person's normal systolic blood pressure. Estimate the normal systolic blood pressure for a 16-year-old. (Lesson 1-6)

1-7 Algebra: Equations

MAIN IDEA

Write and solve equations using mental math.

New Vocabulary

equation
solution
solving an equation
defining the variable

Math Online

glencoe.com

- Extra Examples
- Personal Tutor
- Self-Check Quiz

GET READY for the Lesson

VOLLEYBALL The table shows the number of wins for six women's college volleyball teams.

1. Suppose each team played 34 games. How many losses did each team have?
2. Write a rule to describe how you found the number of losses.
3. Let w represent the number of wins and ℓ represent the number of losses. Rewrite your rule using numbers, variables, and an equals sign.

Women's College Volleyball

Team	Wins	Losses
Bowling Green State University	28	■
Kent State University	13	■
Ohio University	28	■
University of Akron	7	■
University at Buffalo	14	■
Miami University	13	■

Source: Mid-American Conference

An **equation** is a sentence that contains two expressions separated by an equals sign, =. The equals sign tells you that the expression on the left is equivalent to the expression on the right.

$$7 = 8 - 1 \qquad 3(4) = 12 \qquad 17 = 13 + 2 + 2$$

An equation that contains a variable is neither true nor false until the variable is replaced with a number. A **solution** of an equation is a numerical value for the variable that makes the sentence true.

The process of finding a solution is called **solving an equation**. Some equations can be solved using mental math.

EXAMPLE Solve an Equation Mentally

1 **Solve $18 = 14 + t$ mentally.**

$18 = 14 + t$ Write the equation.

$18 = 14 + 4$ You know that 14 + 4 is 18.

$18 = 18$ Simplify.

So, $t = 4$. The solution is 4.

CHECK Your Progress

Solve each equation mentally.

a. $p - 5 = 20$ b. $8 = y \div 3$ c. $7h = 56$

TEST EXAMPLE

Test-Taking Tip

Backsolving To find which answer choice is the solution, you can also substitute each value for x to see which answer choice makes the left side of the equation equal to the right side.

2 **Each day, Sierra cycles 3 miles on a bicycle trail. The equation $3d = 36$ represents how many days it will take her to cycle 36 miles. How many days d will it take her to cycle 36 miles?**

A 10 **B** 12 **C** 15 **D** 20

Read the Item

Solve $3d = 36$ to find how many days it will take to cycle 36 miles.

Solve the Item

$3d = 36$ Write the equation.

$3 \cdot 12 = 36$ You know that $3 \cdot 12$ is 36.

Therefore, $d = 12$. The answer is B.

CHECK Your Progress

d. Jordan has 16 video games. This is 3 less than the number Casey has. To find how many video games Casey has, the equation $v - 3 = 16$ can be used. How many video games v does Casey have?

F 13 **G** 15 **H** 18 **J** 19

Choosing a variable to represent an unknown quantity is called **defining the variable**.

Real-World EXAMPLE

Study Tip

Defining the Variable Although any symbol can be used, it is a good idea to use the first letter of the word you are defining as a variable. For example, m stands for the number of miles.

3 **WHALES** **Each winter, Humpback whales migrate 1,500 miles to the Indian Ocean. However, one whale migrated 5,000 miles in one season. How many miles farther than normal did this whale travel?**

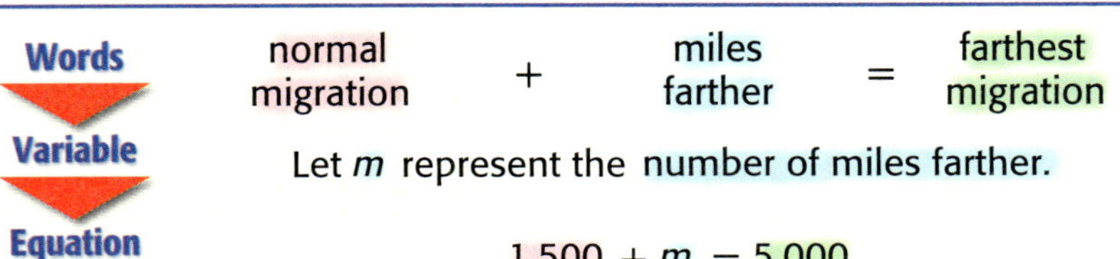

$1{,}500 + m = 5{,}000$ Write the equation.

$1{,}500 + 3{,}500 = 5{,}000$ Replace m with 3,500 to make the equation true.

So, $m = 3{,}500$. The whale went 3,500 miles farther than normal.

e. Aaron buys a movie rental, popcorn, and a soft drink for a total cost of \$6.25. What is the cost of the popcorn if the movie rental and soft drink cost \$4.70 together?

CHECK Your Understanding

Example 1 (p. 49)

Solve each equation mentally.

1. $75 = w + 72$
2. $y - 18 = 20$
3. $\frac{r}{9} = 6$

Example 2 (p. 50)

4. **MULTIPLE CHOICE** Daniel scored 7 points in a football game. Together, he and Judah scored 28 points. Solve the equation $7 + p = 28$ to find how many points p Judah scored.

   A 14 **B** 21 **C** 23 **D** 35

Example 3 (p. 50)

5. **MONEY** Jessica buys a notebook and a pack of pencils for a total of \$3.50. What is the cost of the notebook if the pack of pencils costs \$1.25?

Practice and Problem Solving

HOMEWORK HELP

For Exercises	See Examples
6–17	1
18–19, 33–34	2
20–21	3

Solve each equation mentally.

6. $b + 7 = 13$
7. $8 + x = 15$
8. $y - 14 = 20$
9. $a - 18 = 10$
10. $25 - n = 19$
11. $x + 17 = 63$
12. $77 = 7t$
13. $3d = 99$
14. $n = \frac{30}{6}$
15. $16 = \frac{u}{4}$
16. $20 = y \div 5$
17. $84 \div z = 12$
18. **MONEY** Rosa charges \$9 per hour of baby-sitting. Solve the equation $9h = 63$ to find how many hours h Rosa needs to baby-sit to earn \$63.
19. **SNACKS** A box initially contained 25 snack bars. There are 14 snack bars remaining. Solve the equation $25 - x = 14$ to find how many snack bars x were eaten.

For Exercises 20 and 21, define a variable. Then write and solve an equation.

20. **BASKETBALL** During one game of his rookie year, LeBron James scored 41 of the Cleveland Cavaliers' 107 points. How many points did the rest of the team score?
21. **EXERCISE** On Monday and Tuesday, Derrick walked a total of 6.3 miles. If he walked 2.5 miles on Tuesday, how many miles did he walk on Monday?

Solve each equation mentally.

22. $1.5 + j = 10.0$
23. $1.2 = m - 4.2$
24. $n - 1.4 = 3.5$
25. $13.4 - h = 9.0$
26. $9.9 + r = 24.2$
27. $w + 15.8 = 17.0$
28. **CATS** The table shows the average weight of lions. Write and solve an addition equation to find how much more male lions weigh than female lions.

Lions	Weight (lb)
Female	275
Male	372

EXTRA PRACTICE
See pages 670, 704.

29. **FOOD** The total cost of a chicken sandwich and a drink is \$6.25. The drink costs \$1.75. Write and solve an equation that can be used to find how much the chicken sandwich is alone.

H.O.T. Problems

30. **CHALLENGE** Find the values of a and b if $0 \cdot a = b$. Explain your reasoning.

31. **FIND THE ERROR** Justin and Antonio each solved $w - 35 = 70$. Whose solution is correct? Explain your reasoning.

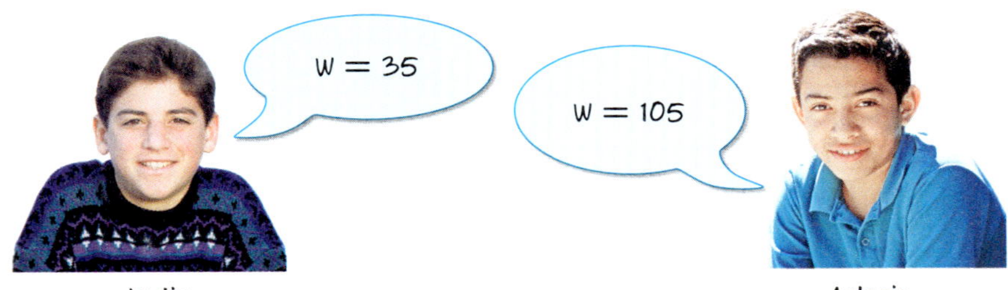

32. **WRITING IN MATH** Explain what it means to solve an equation.

TEST PRACTICE

33. The diagram shows the distance from Madison to Hudson and from Lawrence to Hudson. Which equation can be used to find how many more miles x Lawrence is from Madison?

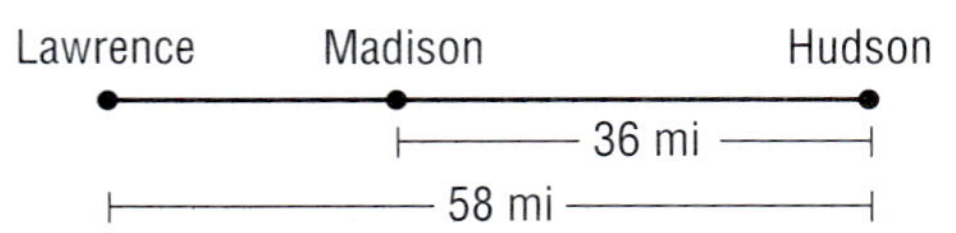

A $58 = x + 36$
B $58 = \frac{x}{36}$
C $36 \cdot 58 = x$
D $x - 36 = 58$

34. **SHORT RESPONSE** What value of h makes the following equation true?

$$h \div 4 = 32$$

35. Solve $u + 8 = 15$.

F 23
G 22
H 8
J 7

Spiral Review

36. **ALGEBRA** Evaluate $3a + b^2$ if $a = 2$ and $b = 3$. (Lesson 1-6)

Evaluate each expression. (Lesson 1-4)

37. $11 \cdot 6 \div 3 + 9$

38. $5 \cdot 13 - 6^2$

39. $1 + 2(8 - 5)^2$

40. **FARMING** A farmer planted 389 acres of land with 78,967 corn plants. How many plants were planted per acre? (Lesson 1-1)

GET READY for the Next Lesson

PREREQUISITE SKILL **Multiply.** (Lesson 1-4)

41. $2 \cdot (4 + 10)$

42. $(9 \cdot 1) \cdot 8$

43. $(5 \cdot 3)(5 \cdot 2)$

44. $(6 + 8) \cdot 12$

1-8 Algebra: Properties

MAIN IDEA

Use Commutative, Associative, Identity, and Distributive properties to solve problems.

New Vocabulary

equivalent expressions
properties

Math Online

glencoe.com
- Extra Examples
- Personal Tutor
- Self-Check Quiz

GET READY for the Lesson

MUSEUMS The admission costs for the Louisville Science Center are shown.

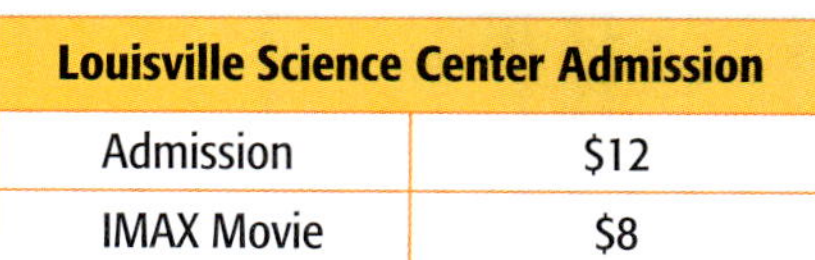

Louisville Science Center Admission	
Admission	$12
IMAX Movie	$8

Source: Louisville Science Center

1. Find the total cost of admission and a movie ticket for a 4-person family.
2. Describe the method you used to find the total cost.

Here are two ways to find the total cost.

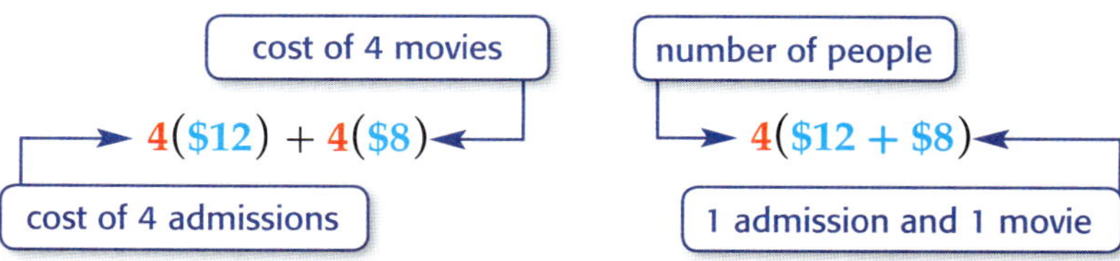

The expressions 4($12) + 4($8) and 4($12 + $8) are **equivalent expressions** because they have the same value, $80. This shows how the **Distributive Property** combines addition and multiplication.

Distributive Property — Key Concept

Words To multiply a sum by a number, multiply each addend of the sum by the number outside the parentheses.

Examples

Numbers	Algebra
$3(4 + 6) = 3(4) + 3(6)$	$a(b + c) = a(b) + a(c)$
$5(7) + 5(3) = 5(7 + 3)$	$a(b) + a(c) = a(b + c)$

EXAMPLES Write Sentences as Equations

Use the Distributive Property to rewrite each expression. Then evaluate it.

1 $5(3 + 2)$

$5(3 + 2) = 5(3) + 5(2)$
$= 15 + 10$ Multiply.
$= 25$ Add.

2 $3(7) + 3(4)$

$3(7) + 3(4) = 3(7 + 4)$
$= 3(11)$ Add.
$= 33$ Multiply.

CHECK Your Progress

a. $6(1 + 4)$

b. $6(9) + 6(3)$

Real-World Link American Lance Armstrong won the Tour de France seven times in a row from 1999 through 2005.

Source: Capital Sports Entertainment

Real-World EXAMPLE

3 **TOUR DE FRANCE** **The Tour de France is a cycling race through France that lasts 22 days. If a cyclist averages 90 miles per day, about how far does he travel?**

Use the Distributive Property to multiply 90×22 mentally.

$90(22) = 90(20 + 2)$	Rewrite 22 as 20 + 2.
$= 90(20) + 90(2)$	Distributive Property
$= 1{,}800 + 180$	Multiply.
$= 1{,}980$	Add.

The cyclist travels about 1,980 miles.

CHECK Your Progress

c. Jennifer saved $120 each month for five months. How much did she save in all? Explain your reasoning.

Properties are statements that are true for all numbers.

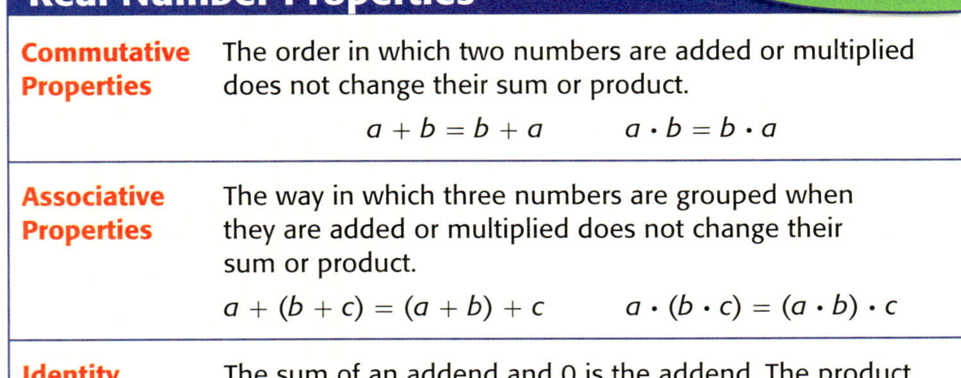

Real Number Properties — Concept Summary

Commutative Properties	The order in which two numbers are added or multiplied does not change their sum or product. $a + b = b + a$ $\quad a \cdot b = b \cdot a$
Associative Properties	The way in which three numbers are grouped when they are added or multiplied does not change their sum or product. $a + (b + c) = (a + b) + c$ $\quad a \cdot (b \cdot c) = (a \cdot b) \cdot c$
Identity Properties	The sum of an addend and 0 is the addend. The product of a factor and 1 is the factor. $a + 0 = a$ $\quad a \cdot 1 = a$

EXAMPLE Use Properties to Evaluate Expressions

Study Tip

Mental Math Look for sums or products that end in zero. They are easy to compute mentally.

4 **Find $4 \cdot 12 \cdot 25$ mentally. Justify each step.**

$4 \cdot 12 \cdot 25 = 4 \cdot 25 \cdot 12$	Commutative Property of Multiplication
$= (4 \cdot 25) \cdot 12$	Associative Property of Multiplication
$= 100 \cdot 12$ or $1{,}200$	Multiply 100 and 12 mentally.

CHECK Your Progress

Find each of the following. Justify each step.

d. $40 \cdot (7 \cdot 5)$

e. $(89 + 15) + 1$

CHECK Your Understanding

Examples 1, 2 (p. 53)

Use the Distributive Property to rewrite each expression. Then evaluate it.

1. $7(4 + 3)$
2. $5(6 + 2)$
3. $3(9) + 3(6)$
4. $6(17) + 6(3)$

Example 3 (p. 54)

5. **MENTAL MATH** Admission to a baseball game is \$12, and a hot dog costs \$5. Use the Distributive Property to mentally find the total cost for 4 tickets and 4 hot dogs. Explain your reasoning.

6. **MENTAL MATH** A cheetah can run 65 miles per hour at maximum speed. At this rate, how far could a cheetah run in 2 hours? Use the Distributive Property to multiply mentally. Explain your reasoning.

Example 4 (p. 54)

Find each expression mentally. Justify each step.

7. $44 + (23 + 16)$
8. $50 \cdot (33 \cdot 2)$

Practice and Problem Solving

HOMEWORK HELP

For Exercises	See Examples
9–12	1, 2
13–22	4
23, 24	3

Use the Distributive Property to rewrite each expression. Then evaluate it.

9. $2(6 + 7)$
10. $5(8 + 9)$
11. $4(3) + 4(8)$
12. $7(3) + 7(6)$

Find each expression mentally. Justify each step.

13. $(8 + 27) + 52$
14. $(13 + 31) + 17$
15. $91 + (15 + 9)$
16. $85 + (46 + 15)$
17. $(4 \cdot 18) \cdot 25$
18. $(5 \cdot 3) \cdot 8$
19. $15 \cdot (8 \cdot 2)$
20. $2 \cdot (16 \cdot 50)$
21. $5 \cdot (30 \cdot 12)$
22. $20 \cdot (48 \cdot 5)$

MENTAL MATH For Exercises 23 and 24, use the Distributive Property to multiply mentally. Explain your reasoning.

23. **TRAVEL** Each year about 27 million people visit Paris, France. About how many people will visit Paris over a five-year period?

24. **ROLLER COASTERS** One ride on a roller coaster lasts 108 seconds. How long will it take to ride this coaster three times?

The Distributive Property also can be applied to subtraction. Use the Distributive Property to rewrite each expression. Then evaluate it.

25. $7(9) - 7(3)$
26. $12(8) - 12(6)$
27. $9(7) - 9(3)$
28. $6(12) - 6(5)$

ALGEBRA Use one or more properties to rewrite each expression as an equivalent expression that does not use parentheses.

29. $(y + 1) + 4$
30. $2 + (x + 4)$
31. $4(8b)$
32. $(3a)2$
33. $2(x + 3)$
34. $4(2 + b)$
35. $6(c + 1)$
36. $3(f + 4) + 2f$

MILEAGE **For Exercises 37 and 38, use the table that shows the driving distance between certain cities in Pennsylvania.**

From	To	Driving Distance (mi)
Pittsburgh	Johnstown	55
Johnstown	Allentown	184

37. Write a sentence that compares the mileage from Pittsburgh to Johnstown to Allentown, and the mileage from Allentown to Johnstown to Pittsburgh.

See pages 670, 704.

38. Name the property that is illustrated by this sentence.

H.O.T. Problems

39. **OPEN ENDED** Write an equation that illustrates the Associative Property of Addition.

40. **NUMBER SENSE** Analyze the statement $(18 + 35) \times 4 = 18 + 35 \times 4$. Then tell whether the statement is *true* or *false*. Explain your reasoning.

41. **CHALLENGE** A *counterexample* is an example showing that a statement is not true. Provide a counterexample to the following statement.

Division of whole numbers is associative.

42. **WRITING IN MATH** Write about a real-world situation that can be solved using the Distributive Property. Then use it to solve the problem.

43. Which expression can be written as $6(9 + 8)$?

A $8 \cdot 6 + 8 \cdot 9$

B $6 \cdot 9 + 6 \cdot 8$

C $6 \cdot 9 \cdot 6 \cdot 8$

D $6 + 9 \cdot 6 + 8$

44. Jared deposited $5 into his savings account. Six months later, his account balance had doubled. If his old balance was b dollars, which of the following would be equivalent to his new balance of $2(b + 5)$ dollars?

F $2b + 5$

G $2b + 7$

H $b + 10$

J $2b + 10$

Spiral Review

Name the number that is the solution of the given equation. (Lesson 1-7)

45. $7.3 = t - 4$; 10.3, 11.3, 12.3

46. $35.5 = 5n$; 5.1, 7.1, 9.1

47. **CATS** It is believed that a cat ages 5 human years for every calendar year. This situation can be represented by the expression $5y$ where y is the age of the cat in calendar years. Find the human age of a cat that has lived for 15 calendar years. (Lesson 1-6)

48. Evaluate $(14 - 9)^4$. (Lesson 1-4)

PREREQUISITE SKILL **Find the next number in each pattern.**

49. 2, 4, 6, 8, ▒

50. 10, 21, 32, 43, ▒

51. 1.4, 2.2, 3.0, 3.8, ▒

Algebra: Arithmetic Sequences

MAIN IDEA

Describe the relationships and extend terms in arithmetic sequences.

New Vocabulary

sequence
term
arithmetic sequence

Math Online

glencoe.com

- Concepts In Motion
- Extra Examples
- Personal Tutor
- Self-Check Quiz

MINI Lab

Use centimeter cubes to make the three figures shown.

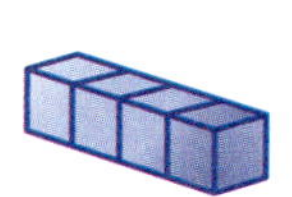
Figure 1

Figure 2

Figure 3

1. How many centimeter cubes are used to make each figure?
2. What pattern do you see? Describe it in words.
3. Suppose this pattern continues. Copy and complete the table to find the number of cubes needed to make each figure.

Figure	1	2	3	4	5	6	7	8
Cubes Needed	4	8	12					

4. How many cubes would you need to make the 10th figure? Explain your reasoning.

A **sequence** is an ordered list of numbers. Each number in a sequence is called a **term**. In an **arithmetic sequence**, each term is found by adding the same number to the previous term. An example of an arithmetic sequence is shown.

8, 11, 14, 17, 20, ...
+3 +3 +3 +3

Each term is found by adding 3 to the previous term.

EXAMPLE Describe and Extend Sequences

1 **Describe the relationship between the terms in the arithmetic sequence 8, 13, 18, 23, ... Then write the next three terms in the sequence.**

8, 13, 18, 23, ...
+5 +5 +5

Each term is found by adding 5 to the previous term. Continue the pattern to find the next three terms.

$23 + 5 = 28$ $\quad$ $28 + 5 = 33$ $\quad$ $33 + 5 = 38$

The next three terms are 28, 33, and 38.

CHECK Your Progress

Describe the relationship between the terms in each arithmetic sequence. Then write the next three terms in the sequence.

a. 0, 13, 26, 39, ...

b. 4, 7, 10, 13 ...

Arithmetic sequences can also involve decimals.

EXAMPLE Describe and Extend Sequences

2 Describe the relationship between the terms in the arithmetic sequence 0.4, 0.6, 0.8, 1.0, ... Then write the next three terms in the sequence.

0.4, 0.6, 0.8, 1.0, ...

+0.2 +0.2 +0.2

Each term is found by adding 0.2 to the previous term. Continue the pattern to find the next three terms.

$1.0 + 0.2 = 1.2$ $1.2 + 0.2 = 1.4$ $1.4 + 0.2 = 1.6$

The next three terms are 1.2, 1.4, and 1.6.

CHECK Your Progress

Describe the relationship between the terms in each arithmetic sequence. Then write the next three terms in the sequence.

c. 1.0, 1.3, 1.6, 1.9, ...

d. 2.5, 3.0, 3.5, 4.0, ...

In a sequence, each term has a specific position within the sequence. Consider the sequence 2, 4, 6, 8, 10, ...

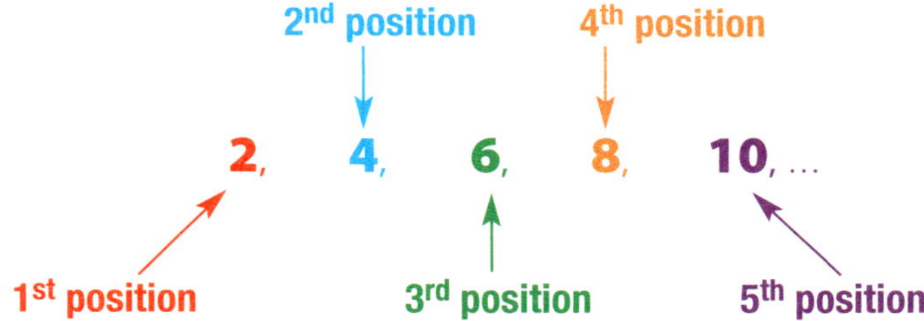

The table below shows the position of each term in this sequence. Notice that as the position number increases by 1, the value of the term increases by 2.

Position	Operation	Value of Term
1	$1 \cdot 2 = 2$	2
2	$2 \cdot 2 = 4$	4
3	$3 \cdot 2 = 6$	6
4	$4 \cdot 2 = 8$	8
5	$5 \cdot 2 = 10$	10

(Position: +1, +1, +1, +1; Value of Term: +2, +2, +2, +2)

You can also write an algebraic expression to represent the relationship between any term in a sequence and its position in the sequence. In this case, if n represents the position in the sequence, the value of the term is $2n$.

Real-World EXAMPLE

3 **GREETING CARDS** **The homemade greeting cards that Meredith makes are sold in boxes at a local gift store. Each week, the store sells five more boxes.**

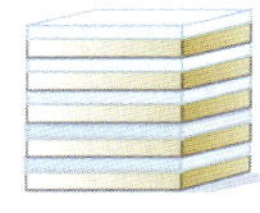
Week 1

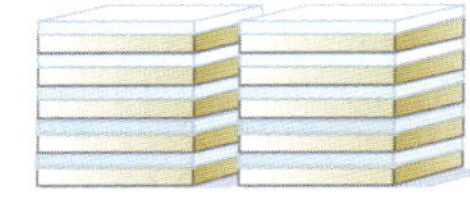
Week 2

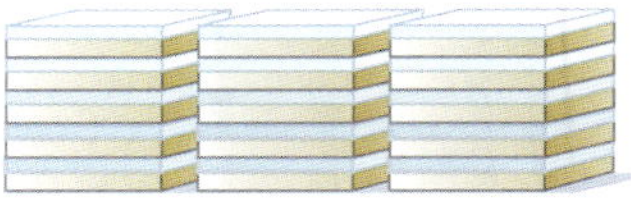
Week 3

If this pattern continues, what algebraic expression can be used to help her find the total number of boxes sold at the end of the 100th week? Use the expression to find the total.

Make a table to display the sequence.

Position	Operation	Value of Term
1	1 • 5	5
2	2 • 5	10
3	3 • 5	15
n	n • 5	$5n$

Each term is 5 times its position number. So, the expression is $5n$.

$5n$ — Write the expression.

$5(100) = 500$ — Replace n with 100.

So, at the end of 100 weeks, 500 boxes will have been sold.

Study Tip

Arithmetic Sequences When looking for a pattern between the position number and each term in the sequence, it is often helpful to make a table.

CHECK Your Progress

e. **GEOMETRY** If the pattern continues, what algebraic expression can be used to find the number of circles used in the 50th figure? How many circles will be in the 50th figure?

Figure 1

Figure 2

Figure 3

CHECK Your Understanding

Examples 1, 2 (pp. 57–58)

Describe the relationship between the terms in each arithmetic sequence. Then write the next three terms in each sequence.

1. 0, 9, 18, 27, …
2. 4, 9, 14, 19, …
3. 1, 1.1, 1.2, 1.3, …
4. 5, 5.4, 5.8, 6.2, …

Example 3 (p. 59)

5. **PLANTS** The table shows the height of a certain plant each month after being planted. If this pattern continues, what algebraic expression can be used to find the height of the plant at the end of twelve months? Find the plant's height after 12 months.

Month	Height (in.)
1	3
2	6
3	9
4	12

Practice and Problem Solving

HOMEWORK HELP

For Exercises	See Examples
6–11	1
12–17	2
18, 19	3

Describe the relationship between the terms in each arithmetic sequence. Then write the next three terms in each sequence.

6. 0, 7, 14, 21, …
7. 1, 7, 13, 19, …
8. 26, 34, 42, 50, …
9. 19, 31, 43, 55, …
10. 6, 16, 26, 36, …
11. 33, 38, 43, 48, …
12. 0.1, 0.4, 0.7, 1.0, …
13. 2.4, 3.2, 4.0, 4.8, …
14. 2.0, 3.1, 4.2, 5.3, …
15. 4.5, 6.0, 7.5, 9.0, …
16. 1.2, 3.2, 5.2, 7.2, …
17. 4.6, 8.6, 12.6, 16.6, …

18. **COLLECTIONS** Hannah is starting a doll collection. Each year, she buys 6 dolls. Suppose she continues this pattern. What algebraic expression can be used to find the number of dolls in her collection after any number of years? How many dolls will Hannah have after 25 years?

19. **EXERCISE** The table shows the number of laps that Jorge swims each week. Jorge's goal is to continue this pace. What algebraic expression can be used to find the total number of laps he will swim after any given number of weeks? How many laps will Jorge swim after 6 weeks?

Week	Number of Laps
1	7
2	14
3	21
4	28

Describe the relationship between the terms in each arithmetic sequence. Then write the next three terms in each sequence.

20. 18, 33, 48, 63, …
21. 20, 45, 70, 95, …
22. 38, 61, 84, 107, …

In a *geometric sequence*, each term is found by multiplying the previous term by the same number. Write the next three terms of each geometric sequence.

23. 1, 4, 16, 64, …
24. 2, 6, 18, 54, …
25. 4, 12, 36, 108, …

26. **GEOMETRY** Kendra is stacking boxes of tissues for a store display. Each minute, she stacks another layer of boxes. If the pattern continues, how many boxes will be displayed after 45 minutes?

1 Minute

2 Minutes

3 Minutes

NUMBER SENSE **Find the 100th number in each sequence.**

27. 12, 24, 36, 48, …
28. 14, 28, 42, 56, …
29. 0, 50, 100, 150, …
30. 0, 75, 150, 225, …

31. **RESEARCH** The Fibonacci sequence is one of the most well-known sequences in mathematics. Use the Internet or another source to write a paragraph about the Fibonacci sequence.

H.O.T. Problems

CHALLENGE **Not all sequences are arithmetic. But, there is still a pattern. Describe the relationship between the terms in each sequence. Then write the next three terms in the sequence.**

32. 1, 2, 4, 7, 11, …

33. 0, 2, 6, 12, 20, …

34. **OPEN ENDED** Write five terms of an arithmetic sequence and describe the rule for finding the terms.

35. **SELECT A TOOL** Suppose you want to begin saving \$15 each month. Which of the following tools would you use to determine the amount you will have saved after 2 years? Justify your selection(s). Then use the tool(s) to solve the problem.

paper/pencil	real object	technology

36. **WRITING IN MATH** Janice earns \$6.50 per hour running errands for her neighbor. Explain how the hourly earnings form an arithmetic sequence.

TEST PRACTICE

37. Which sequence follows the rule $3n - 2$, where n represents the position of a term in the sequence?

A 21, 18, 15, 12, 9, …

B 3, 6, 9, 12, 15, …

C 1, 7, 10, 13, 16, …

D 1, 4, 7, 10, 13, …

38. Which expression can be used to find the nth term in this sequence?

Position	1	2	3	4	5	n^{th}
Value of Term	2	5	10	17	26	

F $n^2 + 1$

G $2n + 1$

H $n + 1$

J $2n^2 + 2$

Spiral Review

Find each expression mentally. Justify each step. (Lesson 1-8)

39. $(23 + 18) + 7$

40. $5 \cdot (12 \cdot 20)$

Solve each equation mentally. (Lesson 1-7)

41. $f - 26 = 3$

42. $\frac{a}{4} = 8$

43. $30 + y = 50$

44. **SCIENCE** At normal temperatures, sound travels through water at a rate of $5 \cdot 10^3$ feet per second. Write this rate in standard form. (Lesson 1-2)

GET READY for the Next Lesson

PREREQUISITE SKILL **Find the value of each expression.** (Lesson 1-6)

45. $2x$ if $x = 4$

46. $d - 5$ if $d = 8$

47. $3m - 3$ if $m = 2$

Extend 1-9

Algebra Lab
Exploring Sequences

MAIN IDEA

Explore patterns in sequences of geometric figures.

ACTIVITY

STEP 1 Use toothpicks to build the figures below.

Figure 1 Figure 2 Figure 3

STEP 2 Make a table like the one shown and record the figure number and number of toothpicks used in each figure.

Figure Number	Number of Toothpicks
1	4
2	
3	

STEP 3 Construct the next figure in this pattern. Record your results.

STEP 4 Repeat Step 3 until you have found the next four figures in the pattern.

ANALYZE THE RESULTS

1. How many additional toothpicks were used each time to form the next figure in the pattern? Where is this pattern found in the table?
2. Based on your answer to Exercise 1, how many toothpicks would be in Figure 0 of this pattern?
3. Remove one toothpick from your pattern so that Figure 1 is made up of just three toothpicks as shown. Then create a table showing the number of toothpicks that would be in the first 7 figures by continuing the same pattern as above.

Figure 1

4. How many toothpicks would there be in Figure n of this new pattern?
5. How could you adapt the expression you wrote in Exercise 4 to find the number of toothpicks in Figure n of the original pattern?
6. **MAKE A PREDICTION** How many toothpicks would there be in Figure 10 of the original pattern? Explain your reasoning. Then check your answer by constructing the figure.
7. Find the number of toothpicks in Figure n of the pattern below, and predict the number of toothpicks in Figure 12. Justify your answer.

Figure 1 Figure 2 Figure 3

Algebra: Equations and Functions

MAIN IDEA

Make function tables and write equations.

New Vocabulary

function
function rule
function table
domain
range

Math Online

glencoe.com

- Concepts In Motion
- Extra Examples
- Personal Tutor
- Self-Check Quiz

GET READY for the Lesson

MAGAZINES Suppose you can buy magazines for $4 each.

1. Copy and complete the table to find the cost of 2, 3, and 4 magazines.
2. Describe the pattern in the table between the cost and the number of magazines.

Number	Multiply by 4	Cost ($)
1	4×1	4
2		
3		
4		

A relationship that assigns exactly one *output* value for each *input* value is called a **function**. In a function, you start with an input number, perform one or more operations on it, and get an output number. The operation performed on the input is given by the **function rule**.

You can organize the input numbers, output numbers, and the function rule in a **function table**. The set of input values is called the **domain**, and the set of output values is called the **range**.

EXAMPLE Make a Function Table

1 **MONEY Javier saves $20 each month. Make a function table to show his savings after 1, 2, 3, and 4 months. Then identify the domain and range.**

Input	Function Rule	Output
Number of Months	Multiply by 20	Total Savings ($)
1	20×1	20
2	20×2	40
3	20×3	60
4	20×4	80

The domain is {1, 2, 3, 4}, and the range is {20, 40, 60, 80}.

CHECK Your Progress

a. Suppose a student movie ticket costs $3. Make a function table that shows the total cost for 1, 2, 3, and 4 tickets. Then identify the domain and range.

Study Tip

Input and Output When x and y are used in an equation, x usually represents the input, and y usually represents the output.

Functions are often written as equations with two variables—one to represent the input and one to represent the output. Here's an equation for the situation in Example 1.

$$20x = y$$

Function rule: multiply by 20

Input: number of months

Output: total savings

Real-World EXAMPLES

2 **ANIMALS** **An armadillo sleeps 19 hours each day. Write an equation using two variables to show the relationship between the number of hours h an armadillo sleeps in d days.**

Input	Function Rule	Output
Number of Days (d)	Multiply by 19	Number of Hours Slept (h)
1	1×19	19
2	2×19	38
3	3×19	57
d	$d \times 19$	$19d$

Words	Number of hours slept	equals	number of days	times	19 hours each day.
Variable	Let d represent the number of days. Let h represent the number of hours.				
Equation	$h = 19d$				

3 **How many hours does an armadillo sleep in 4 days?**

$h = 19d$ Write the equation.

$h = 19(4)$ Replace d with 4.

$h = 76$ Multiply.

An armadillo sleeps 76 hours in 4 days.

Real-World Career

How Does a Botanist Use Math? A botanist gathers and studies plant statistics to solve problems and draw conclusions about various plants.

Math Online

For more information, go to glencoe.com.

CHECK Your Progress

BOTANIST **A botanist discovers that a certain species of bamboo grows 4 inches each hour.**

b. Write an equation using two variables to show the relationship between the growth g in inches of this bamboo plant in h hours.

c. Use your equation to explain how to find the growth in inches of this species of bamboo after 6 hours.

CHECK Your Understanding

Example 1 (p. 63)

Copy and complete each function table. Then identify the domain and range.

1. $y = 3x$

x	3x	y
1	3 • 1	3
2	3 • 2	
3	3 • 3	
4		

2. $y = 4x$

x	4x	y
0	4 • 0	
1	4 • 1	
2		
3		

3. **MUSIC** Jonas downloads 8 songs each month onto his digital music player. Make a function table that shows the total number of songs downloaded after 1, 2, 3, and 4 months. Then identify the domain and range.

Examples 2, 3 (p. 64)

SPORTS For Exercises 4 and 5, use the following information.

The top speed reached by a race car is 231 miles per hour.

4. Write an equation using two variables to show the relationship between the number of miles m that a race car can travel in h hours.
5. Use your equation to explain how to find the distance in miles the race car will travel in 3 hours.

Practice and Problem Solving

HOMEWORK HELP

For Exercises	See Examples
6–10	1
11–14	2, 3

Copy and complete each function table. Then identify the domain and range.

6. $y = 2x$

x	2x	y
0	2 • 0	0
1	2 • 1	
2		
3		

7. $y = 6x$

x	6x	y
1		
2		
3		
4		

8. $y = 9x$

x	9x	y
1		
2		
3		
4		

Make a function table for each situation. Then identify the domain and range.

9. **PIZZA** A pizza shops sells 25 pizzas each hour. Find the number of pizzas sold after 1, 2, 3, and 4 hours.
10. **TYPING** Suppose you can type 60 words per minute. What is the total number of words typed after 5, 10, 15, and 20 minutes?

CELL PHONES For Exercises 11 and 12, use the following information.

A cell phone provider charges a customer $40 for each month of service.

11. Write an equation using two variables to show the relationship between the total amount charged c, after m months of cell phone service.
12. Use your equation to explain how to find the total cost for 6 months of cell phone service.

Real-World Link Crickets are among the 800,000 different types of insects in the world.

INSECTS **For Exercises 13 and 14, use the following information.**

A cricket will chirp approximately 35 times per minute when the outside temperature is 72°F.

13. Write an equation using two variables to show the relationship between the total number of times a cricket will chirp t, after m minutes at this temperature.

14. Use your equation to explain how to find the number of times a cricket will have chirped after 15 minutes at this temperature.

Copy and complete each function table. Then identify the domain and range.

15. $y = x - 1$

x	$x - 1$	y
1		
2		
3		
4		

16. $y = x + 5$

x	$x + 5$	y
1		
2		
3		
4		

17. $y = x + 0.25$

x	$x + 0.25$	y
0		
1		
2		
3		

18. $y = x - 1.5$

x	$x - 1.5$	y
2		
3		
4		
5		

MEASUREMENT **For Exercises 19 and 20, use the following information.**

The formula for the area of a rectangle with length 6 units is $A = 6w$.

19. Make a function table that shows the area in square units of a rectangle with a width of 2, 3, 4, and 5 units.

20. Study the pattern in your table. Explain how the area of a rectangle with a length of 6 units changes when the width is increased by 1 unit.

ANALYZE TABLES **For Exercises 21–23, use the table that shows the approximate velocity of certain planets as they orbit the Sun.**

Orbital Velocity Around Sun

Planet	Velocity (mi/s)
Mercury	30
Earth	19
Jupiter	8
Saturn	6
Neptune	5

21. Write an equation to show the relationship between the total number of miles m Jupiter travels in s seconds as it orbits the Sun.

22. What equation can be used to show the total number of miles Earth travels?

23. Use your equation to explain how to find the number of miles Jupiter and Earth each travel in 1 minute.

See pages 671, 704.

H.O.T. Problems

CHALLENGE **Write an equation for the function shown in each table.**

24.

x	y
1	3
2	4
3	5
4	6

25.

x	y
2	6
4	12
6	18
8	24

26.

x	y
1	3
2	5
3	7
4	9

27. **OPEN ENDED** Write about a real-world situation that can be represented by the equation $y = 3x$.

28. **WRITING IN MATH** Explain the relationship among an *input*, an *output*, and a *function rule.*

TEST PRACTICE

29. The table shows the number of hand-painted T-shirts Mi-Ling can make after a given number of days.

Number of Days (x)	Total Number of T-Shirts (y)
1	6
2	12
3	18
4	24

Which function rule represents the data?

A $y = 4x$

B $y = 5x$

C $y = 6x$

D $y = 12x$

30. Cristina needs to have 50 posters printed to advertise a community book fair. The printing company charges $3 to print each poster. Which table represents this situation?

F

Posters	Cost ($)
3	3
6	6
9	9
p	p

H

Posters	Cost ($)
1	3
2	6
3	9
p	$3 + p$

G

Posters	Cost ($)
1	3
2	6
3	9
p	$3p$

J

Posters	Cost ($)
3	1
6	2
9	3
p	$p \div 3$

Spiral Review

31. **ALGEBRA** Write the next three terms of the sequence 27, 36, 45, 54, … (Lesson 1-9)

Use the Distributive Property to rewrite each expression. Then evaluate it. (Lesson 1-8)

32. $5(9 + 7)$

33. $(12 + 4)4$

34. $8(7) - 8(2)$

35. $10(6) - 10(5)$

36. **ALLOWANCE** If Karen receives a weekly allowance of $8, about how much money in all will she receive in two years? (Lesson 1-1)

Extend 1-10

Graphing Calculator Lab
Functions and Tables

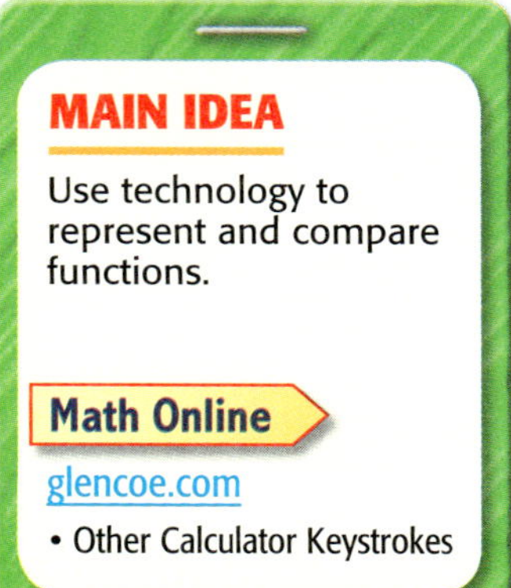

You can use a graphing calculator to represent functions.

ACTIVITY

1 **GROCERIES** **A grocery store has 12-ounce bottles of sports drink on sale for \$1.80 each, with no limit on how many you can buy. In addition, you can use a coupon for \$1 off one bottle. Make a table showing the cost for 3, 4, 5, 6, and 7 bottles of this drink.**

STEP 1 Write an equation to show the relationship between the number of bottles purchased x and their cost y.

Cost is \$1.80 per bottle less \$1.

$$y = 1.80x - 1$$

STEP 2 Press [Y=] on your calculator. Then enter the function into Y_1 by pressing 1.80 [X,T,θ,n] [−] 1 [ENTER].

STEP 3 Next, set up a table of x- and y-values. Press [2nd] [TBLSET] to display the table setup screen. Then press [⇩] [⇩] [⇨] [ENTER] to highlight Indpnt: Ask.

STEP 4 Access the table by pressing [2nd] [TABLE]. Then key in each number of bottles, pressing [ENTER] after each entry.

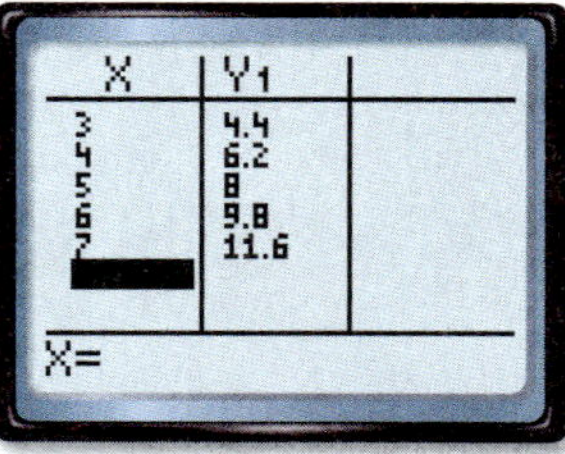

Analyze the Results

1. Analyze the table to determine how many bottles you can buy for \$10. Explain your reasoning.

2. **MAKE A CONJECTURE** Notice that you can purchase 5 bottles for the whole dollar amount of \$8. How many bottles will you be able to purchase for \$9, the next whole dollar amount? Use the calculator to test your conjecture.

ACTIVITY

2 **CAMPING** **Out-There Campground charges each group a camping fee of $20 plus $4.25 per person per night. Roughing-It Campground charges $6.25 per person per night. Make a table showing the one-night fee for 2, 3, 4, 5, and 6 people to camp at each campground.**

STEP 1 Write an equation to show the relationship between the number of people x and the one-night fee y for them to camp at each campground.

Out-There Campground

Fee is $20 plus $4.25 per person.

$$y = 20 + 4.25x$$

Roughing-It Campground

Fee is $6.25 per person.

$$y = 6.25x$$

STEP 2 Enter the function for the Out-There Campground into Y_1 and the function for the Roughing-It Campground into Y_2.

```
Plot1 Plot2 Plot3
\Y1=20+4.25X
\Y2=6.25X
\Y3=
\Y4=
\Y5=
\Y6=
\Y7=
```

STEP 3 Next, set up a table of x- and y-values as in Activity 1.

STEP 4 Then access the table and key in each number of people. Notice that the calculator follows the order of operations multiplying each x-value by 4.25 first and then adding 20.

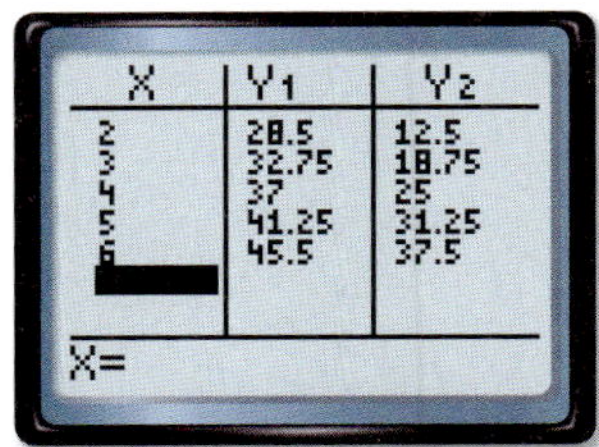

X	Y1	Y2
2	28.5	12.5
3	32.75	18.75
4	37	25
5	41.25	31.25
6	45.5	37.5

X=

Reading Math

The phrase *$4.25 per person* means *$4.25 for each person.*

Analyze the Results

3. For 2, 3, 4, 5, and 6 people, which campground charges the greater total nightly cost to camp?
4. **MAKE A CONJECTURE** Will the total nightly cost to camp at each campground ever be the same? If so, for what number of people?
5. Use the graphing calculator to test your conjecture from Exercise 4. Were you correct? If not, use the graphing calculator to guess and check until you find the correct number of people.
6. If all other aspects of these two campgrounds are equal, write a recommendation as to which campground a group of n people should choose based on your cost analysis.

CHAPTER 1 Study Guide and Review

Math Online glencoe.com
- STUDY TO GO
- Vocabulary Review

GET READY to Study

Be sure the following Big Ideas are noted in your Foldable.

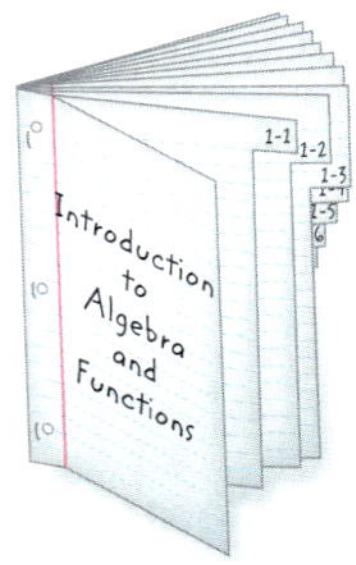

BIG Ideas

Squares and Square Roots (Lesson 1-3)
- The square of a number is the product of a number and itself.
- A square root of a number is one of its two equal factors.

Order of Operations (Lesson 1-4)
- Do all operations within grouping symbols first. Evaluate all powers before other operations. Multiply and divide in order from left to right. Add and subtract in order from left to right.

Properties (Lesson 1-8)
- Distributive Property
  $5(2 + 4) = 5 \cdot 2 + 5 \cdot 4$
  $(3 + 2)4 = 3 \cdot 4 + 2 \cdot 4$
- Commutative Property
  $3 + 2 = 2 + 3$
  $7 \cdot 4 = 4 \cdot 7$
- Associative Property
  $6 + (3 + 8) = (6 + 3) + 8$
  $5 \cdot (2 \cdot 3) = (5 \cdot 2) \cdot 3$
- Identity Property
  $4 + 0 = 4$
  $4 \cdot 1 = 4$

Functions (Lesson 1-10)
- A function is a relationship that assigns exactly one *output* value for each *input* value.
- In a function, the function rule gives the operation to perform on the input.

Key Vocabulary

algebra (p. 44)
algebraic expression (p. 44)
arithmetic sequence (p. 57)
base (p. 30)
coefficient (p. 45)
defining the variable (p. 50)
domain (p. 63)
equation (p. 49)
equivalent expressions (p. 53)
evaluate (p. 31)
exponent (p. 30)
factors (p. 30)
function (p. 63)
function rule (p. 63)
numerical expression (p. 38)
order of operations (p. 38)
perfect square (p. 34)
powers (p. 30)
radical sign (p. 35)
range (p. 63)
sequence (p. 57)
solution (p. 49)
square (p. 34)
square root (p. 35)
term (p. 57)
variable (p. 44)

Vocabulary Check

State whether each sentence is *true* or *false*. If *false*, replace the underlined word or number to make a true sentence.

1. Numerical expressions have the same value.
2. Two or more numbers that are multiplied together are called powers.
3. The range of a function is the set of input values.
4. A function assigns exactly two *output* values for each *input* value.
5. An equation is a sentence that contains an equals sign.
6. A sequence is an ordered list of numbers.
7. The product of a number and itself is the square root of the number.

Lesson-by-Lesson Review

1-1 A Plan for Problem Solving (pp. 25–29)

Use the four-step plan to solve each problem.

8. **PHONE CALLS** When Tamik calls home from college, she talks ten minutes per call for 3 calls each week. How many minutes does she use in a 15-week semester?

9. **RUNNING** Darren runs at a rate of 6 feet per second, and Kim runs at a rate of 7 feet per second. If they both start a race at the same time, how far apart are they after one minute?

10. **WORK** Alan was paid \$9 per hour and earned \$128.25. How many hours did he work?

Example 1 **One quart of paint covers 40 square feet of wall space. Brock uses 5 quarts of paint to cover his walls. How many square feet did Brock paint?**

Understand	Brock uses 5 quarts of paint, each covering 40 square feet.
Plan	Multiply 40 by 5.
Solve	$40 \cdot 5 = 200$ Brock painted 200 square feet.
Check	$200 \div 5 = 40$, so the answer is reasonable.

1-2 Powers and Exponents (pp. 30–33)

Write each power as a product of the same factor.

11. 3^4
12. 9^6
13. 5^1
14. 7^5
15. Write *5 to the fourth power* as a product of the same factor.

Evaluate each expression.

16. 3^5
17. 7^9
18. 2^8
19. 18^2
20. 10^4
21. 100^1
22. Write $15 \cdot 15 \cdot 15$ in exponential form.
23. **PATHS** At the edge of a forest, there are two paths. At the end of each path, there are two additional paths. If at the end of each of those paths there are two more paths, how many paths are there at the end?

Example 2 **Write 2^3 as a product of the same factor.**

The base is 2. The exponent 3 means that 2 is used as a factor 3 times.

$2^3 = 2 \cdot 2 \cdot 2$

Example 3 **Evaluate 4^5.**

The base is 4. The exponent 5 means that 4 is used as a factor 5 times.

$$4^5 = 4 \cdot 4 \cdot 4 \cdot 4 \cdot 4$$
$$= 1{,}024$$

CHAPTER 1 Study Guide and Review

1-3 Squares and Square Roots (pp. 34–37)

Find the square of each number.

24. 4 **25.** 13

Find each square root.

26. $\sqrt{81}$ **27.** $\sqrt{324}$

28. MEASUREMENT The area of a certain kind of ceramic tile is 25 square inches. What is the length of one side?

Example 4 Find the square of 15.

$15 \cdot 15 = 225$ Multiply 15 by itself.

Example 5 Find the square root of 441.

$21 \cdot 21 = 441$, so $\sqrt{441} = 21$.

1-4 Order of Operations (pp. 38–41)

Evaluate each expression.

29. $24 - 8 + 3^2$ **30.** $48 \div 6 + 2 \cdot 5$

31. $9 + 3(7 - 5)^3$ **32.** $15 + 9 \div 3 - 7$

33. SEATING In planning for a ceremony, 36 guests need to be seated with 4 guests per table. An additional 12 guests need to be seated with 3 guests per table. Write an expression to determine how many tables are needed. Then evaluate the expression.

Example 6 Evaluate $24 - (8 \div 4)^4$.

$24 - (8 \div 4)^4 = 24 - 2^4$ Divide 8 by 4.

$= 24 - 16$ Find the value of 2^4.

$= 8$ Subtract.

1-5 PSI: Guess and Check (pp. 42–43)

Solve. Use the *guess and check* strategy.

34. TRAVEL Lucinda is driving away from Redding at 50 miles per hour. When she is 100 miles away, Tom leaves Redding, driving at 60 miles per hour in the same direction. After how many hours will Tom pass Lucinda?

35. FARMING A farmer sells a bushel of soybeans for \$5 and a bushel of corn for \$3. If he hopes to earn \$164 and plans to sell 40 bushels in all, how many bushels of soybeans does he need to sell?

Example 7 Find two numbers with a product of 30 and a difference of 13.

Make a guess, and check to see if it is correct. Then adjust the guess until it is correct.

5 and 6 — $5 \cdot 6 = 30$ and $6 - 5 = 1$ incorrect

3 and 10 — $3 \cdot 10 = 30$ and $10 - 3 = 7$ incorrect

2 and 15 — $2 \cdot 15 = 30$ and $15 - 2 = 13$ correct

The two numbers are 2 and 15.

Mixed Problem Solving
For mixed problem-solving practice, see page 704.

1-6 Algebra: Variables and Expressions (pp. 44–47)

Evaluate each expression if $a = 10$, $b = 4$, and $c = 8$.

36. $(a - b)^2$

37. $ab \div c$

38. $3b^2 + c$

39. $\frac{(b + c)^2}{3}$

40. **CLOTHING** The cost of buying h hats and s shirts is given by the expression $\$5.75h + \$8.95s$. Find the cost of purchasing 3 hats and 5 shirts.

Example 8 Evaluate $2m^2 - 5n$ if $m = 4$ and $n = 3$.

$2m^2 - 5n = 2(4)^2 - 5(3)$ Replace m with 4 and n with 3.

$= 2(16) - 5(3)$ Find the value of 4^2.

$= 32 - 15$ Multiply.

$= 17$ Subtract.

1-7 Algebra: Equations (pp. 49–52)

Solve each equation mentally.

41. $h + 9 = 17$

42. $31 - y = 8$

43. $\frac{t}{9} = 12$

44. $100 = 20g$

45. **COUNTY FAIRS** Five friends wish to ride the Ferris wheel, which requires 3 tickets per person. The group has a total of 9 tickets. Write and solve an equation to find the number of additional tickets needed for everyone to ride the Ferris wheel.

Example 9 Solve $14 = 5 + x$ mentally.

$14 = 5 + x$ Write the equation.

$14 = 5 + 9$ You know that $5 + 9 = 14$.

$14 = 14$ Simplify.

The solution is 9.

1-8 Algebra: Properties (pp. 53–56)

Find each expression mentally. Justify each step.

46. $(25 \cdot 15) \cdot 4$

47. $14 + (38 + 16)$

48. $8 \cdot (11 \cdot 5)$

49. **ROSES** Wesley sold roses in his neighborhood for \$2 a rose. He sold 15 roses on Monday and 12 roses on Tuesday. Use the Distributive Property to mentally find the total amount Wesley earned. Explain your reasoning.

Example 10 Find $8 + (17 + 22)$ mentally. Justify each step.

$8 + (17 + 22)$

$= 8 + (22 + 17)$ Commutative Property of Addition

$= (8 + 22) + 17$ Associative Property of Addition

$= 30 + 17$ or 47 Add 30 and 17 mentally.

1-9 Algebra: Arithmetic Sequences (pp. 57–61)

Describe the relationship between the terms in each arithmetic sequence. Then find the next three terms in each sequence.

50. 3, 9, 15, 21, 27, ...
51. 2.6, 3.4, 4.2, 5, 5.8, ...
52. 0, 7, 14, 21, 28, ...

MONEY For Exercises 53 and 54, use the following information.

Tanya collected $4.50 for the first car washed at a band fund-raiser. After the second and third cars were washed, the donations totaled $9 and $13.50, respectively.

53. If this donation pattern continues, what algebraic expression can be used to find the amount of money earned for any number of cars washed?
54. How much money will be collected after a total of 8 cars have been washed?

Example 11 **At the end of day 1, Sierra read 25 pages of a novel. By the end of days 2 and 3, she read a total of 50 and 75 pages, respectively. If the pattern continues, what expression will give the total number of pages read after any number of days?**

Make a table to display the sequence.

Position	Operation	Value of Term
1	$1 \cdot 25$	25
2	$2 \cdot 25$	50
3	$3 \cdot 25$	75
n	$n \cdot 25$	$25n$

Each term is 25 times its position number. So, the expression is $25n$.

1-10 Algebra: Equations and Functions (pp. 63–67)

Copy and complete the function table. Then identify the domain and range.

55. $y = 4x$

x	$4x$	y
5		
6		
7		
8		

56. **NAME TAGS** Charmaine can make 32 name tags per hour. Make a function table that shows the number of name tags she can make in 3, 4, 5, and 6 hours.

Example 12 **Create and complete a function table for $y = 3x$. Then identify the domain and range.**

Select any four values for the input x.

x	$3x$	y
3	3(3)	9
4	3(4)	12
5	3(5)	15
6	3(6)	18

The domain is {3, 4, 5, 6}.
The range is {9, 12, 15, 18}.

CHAPTER 1 Practice Test

Math Online glencoe.com
• Chapter Test

1. **PIZZA** Ms. Carter manages a pizza parlor. The average daily cost is \$40, plus \$52 to pay each employee. It also costs \$2 to make each pizza. If 42 pizzas were made one day, requiring the work of 7 employees, what was her total cost that day?

Write each power as a product of the same factor. Then evaluate the expression.

2. 3^5
3. 15^4

4. **MEASUREMENT** Gregory wants to stain the 15-foot-by-15-foot deck in his backyard. One can of stain covers 200 square feet of surface. Is one can of stain enough to cover his entire deck? Explain your reasoning.

Find each square root.

5. $\sqrt{121}$
6. $\sqrt{900}$

7. **MULTIPLE CHOICE** What is the value of $8 + (12 \div 3)^3 - 5 \times 9$?

   A 603
   B 135
   C 27
   D 19

8. **ANIMALS** Sally has 6 pets, some dogs and some birds. Her animals have a total of 16 legs. How many of each pet does Sally have?

Evaluate each expression if $x = 12$, $y = 5$, and $z = 3$.

9. $x - 9$
10. $8y$
11. $(y - z)^3$
12. $\frac{xz}{y + 13}$

Solve each equation mentally.

13. $9 + m = 16$
14. $d - 14 = 37$
15. $32 = \frac{96}{t}$
16. $6x = 126$

17. **SAVINGS** Deb is saving \$54 per month to buy a new camera. Use the Distributive Property to mentally find how much she has saved after 7 months. Explain.

Find each expression mentally. Justify each step.

18. $13 + (34 + 17)$
19. $50 \cdot (17 \cdot 2)$

20. **MULTIPLE CHOICE** The table shows the number of hours Teodoro spent studying for his biology test over four days. If the pattern continues, how many hours will Teodoro study on Sunday?

Day	Study Time (hours)
Monday	0.5
Tuesday	0.75
Wednesday	1.0
Thursday	1.25

   F 1.5 hours
   G 1.75 hours
   H 2.0 hours
   J 2.5 hours

Describe the relationship between the terms in each arithmetic sequence. Then write the next three terms in the sequence.

21. 7, 16, 25, 34, …
22. 59, 72, 85, 98, …

23. **TRAVEL** Beth drove at the rate of 65 miles per hour for several hours. Make a function table that shows her distance traveled after 2, 3, 4, and 5 hours. Then identify the domain and range.

MONEY For Exercises 24 and 25, use the following information.

Anthony earns extra money after school doing yard work for his neighbors. He charges \$12 for each lawn he mows.

24. Write an equation using two variables to show the relationship between the number of lawns mowed m and number of dollars earned d.
25. Then find the number of dollars earned if he mows 14 lawns.

CHAPTER 1 Test Practice
Cumulative, Chapter 1

Math Online glencoe.com
- Test Practice

PART 1 Multiple Choice

Read each question. Then fill in the correct answer on the answer document provided by your teacher or on a sheet of paper.

1. A store owner bought some paperback books and then sold them for \$4.50 each. He sold 35 books on Monday and 52 books on Tuesday. What piece of information is needed to find the amount of profit made from sales on Monday and Tuesday?

   A Number of books sold on Wednesday

   B Number of hardback books sold on Monday and Tuesday

   C Total number of paperback books sold

   D How much the owner paid for each of the paperback books

2. The table shows the number of milkshakes sold at an ice cream shop each day last week.

Day of Week	Number of Milkshakes
Sunday	31
Monday	9
Tuesday	11
Wednesday	15
Thursday	18
Friday	24
Saturday	28

Which statement does *not* support the data?

   F There were almost three times as many milkshakes sold on Sunday as on Tuesday.

   G There were half as many milkshakes sold on Monday as on Thursday.

   H There were 11 more milkshakes sold on Tuesday than on Saturday.

   J The total number of milkshakes sold during the week was 136.

3. Which description shows the relationship between the value of a term and n, its position in the sequence?

Position	1	2	3	4	5	n
Value of Term	3	6	9	12	15	

   A Add 2 to n.

   B Divide n by 3.

   C Multiply n by 3.

   D Subtract n from 2.

TEST-TAKING TIP

Question 3 Have students eliminate unlikely answer choices. Since the value of each term is greater than its position, eliminate answer choices B and D.

4. Andrew spent $\frac{1}{2}$ of his Saturday earnings on a pair of jeans and $\frac{1}{2}$ of the remaining amount on a DVD. After he spent \$7.40 on lunch, he had \$6.10 left. How much did Andrew earn on Saturday?

   F \$13.50

   G \$27

   H \$54

   J \$108

5. Lemisha drove an average of 50 miles per hour on Sunday, 55 miles per hour on Monday, and 53 miles per hour on Tuesday. If s represents the number of hours she drove on Sunday, m represents the number of hours she drove on Monday, and t represents the number of hours she drove on Tuesday, which of the following expressions gives the total distance Lemisha traveled?

   A $50s + 53m + 55t$

   B $55s + 50m + 53t$

   C $50s + 55m + 53t$

   D $53s + 55m + 50t$

Preparing for Standardized Tests

For test-taking strategies and practice, see pages 716–733.

6. Mrs. Albert drove 850 miles and the average price of gasoline was $2.50 per gallon. What information is needed to find the amount Mrs. Albert spent on gasoline for the trip?

   F Number of hours the trip took

   G Number of miles per hour traveled

   H Average number of miles the car traveled per gallon of gasoline

   J Average number of miles Mrs. Albert drove per day

7. Mr. Thompson wants to estimate the total amount he spends on insurance and fuel for his car each month. Insurance costs about $300 per month, and he expects to drive an average of 150 miles per week. What else does he need to estimate his monthly expenses?

   A The cost of fuel and the one-way distance to work

   B The cost of fuel and the number of miles per gallon his car gets

   C The cost of fuel and his weekly pay

   D The gallons of fuel needed per week

8. Jeremy bought 3 hamburgers at $1.99 each, 2 orders of onion rings at $0.89 each, and 4 soft drinks at $1.25 each. He paid 6.75% tax on the whole order. What other information is necessary to find Jeremy's correct change?

   F Total cost of the order

   G Amount he paid in tax

   H Reason for buying the food

   J Amount he gave the cashier

PART 2 Short Response/Grid In

Record your answers on the answer sheet provided by your teacher or on a sheet of paper.

9. Emily bought 2.5 pounds of salami for $1.99 per pound. About how much did she pay?

10. How do you correctly evaluate the expression $4 \times (5 + 4) - 27$?

11. What value of t makes the following equation true?

$$t \div 6 = 48$$

12. Use the Distributive Property to rewrite $4(3 + 5)$.

PART 3 Extended Response

Record your answers on the answer sheet provided by your teacher or on a sheet of paper. Show your work.

13. **GEOMETRY** The first and fifth terms of a toothpick sequence are shown below.

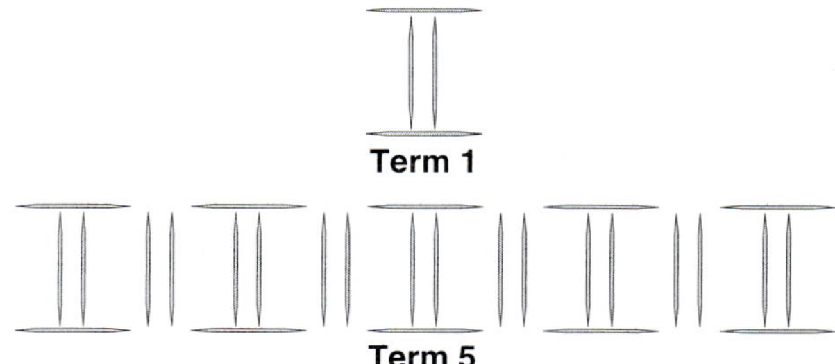

   a. What might the third term look like?

   b. Write a rule that connects the term number and the number of toothpicks in your sequence.

NEED EXTRA HELP?													
If You Missed Question...	1	2	3	4	5	6	7	8	9	10	11	12	13
Go to Lesson...	1-1	1-1	1-9	1-1	1-6	1-1	1-1	1-1	1-1	1-4	1-6	1-8	1-9

Integers

BIG Idea

- Add, subtract, multiply, or divide integers to solve problems and justify solutions.

Key Vocabulary

graph (p. 80)
integer (p. 80)
negative integer (p. 80)
positive integer (p. 80)

Real-World Link

Sports In miniature golf, a score above par can be written as a positive integer and a score below par can be written as a negative integer.

FOLDABLES® Study Organizer

Integers Make this Foldable to help you organize your notes. Begin with two sheets of $8\frac{1}{2}$" by 11" paper.

1. **Fold** one sheet in half from top to bottom. Cut along fold from edges to margin.

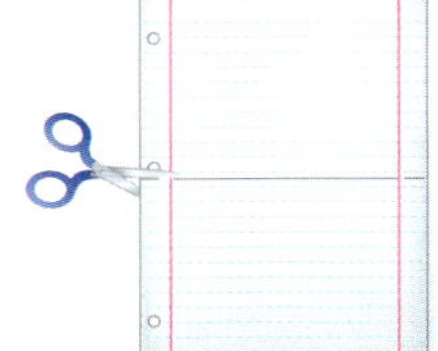

2. **Fold** the other sheet in half from top to bottom. Cut along fold between margins.

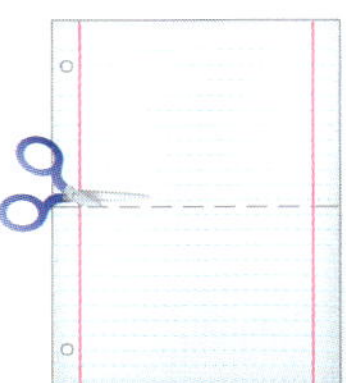

3. **Insert** first sheet through second sheet and align folds.

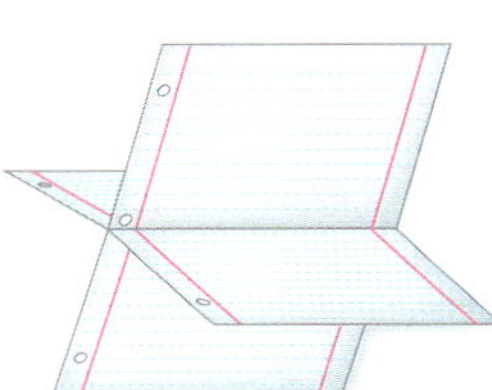

4. **Label** each inside page with a lesson number and title.

2-1
Integers and
Absolute Value

GET READY for Chapter 2

Diagnose Readiness You have two options for checking Prerequisite Skills.

Option 2

Math Online Take the Online Readiness Quiz at glencoe.com.

Option 1

Take the Quick Check below. Refer to the Quick Review for help.

QUICK Quiz

Replace each ● with < or > to make a true sentence. (Prior Grade)

1. 1,458 ● 1,548
2. 36 ● 34
3. 1.02 ● 1.20
4. 76.7 ● 77.6
5. **COINS** Philippe has \$5.17 in coins and Garrett has \$5.71 in coins. Who has the greater amount? (Prior Grade)

Evaluate each expression if $a = 7$, $b = 2$, and $c = 11$. (Prior Grade)

6. $a + 8$
7. $a + b + c$
8. $c - b$
9. $a - b + 4$
10. **TEMPERATURE** At 8 A.M., it was 63°F. By noon, the temperature had risen 9 degrees Fahrenheit. What was the temperature at noon? (Prior Grade)

Evaluate each expression if $m = 9$ and $n = 4$. (Prior Grade)

11. $6mn$
12. $n \div 2 - 1$
13. $m + 5 \times n$
14. $m^2 \div (n + 5)$
15. **PLANES** The distance in miles that an airplane travels is given by rt where r is the rate of travel and t is the time. Find the distance an airplane traveled if $t = 4$ hours and $r = 475$ miles per hour. (Prior Grade)

QUICK Review

Example 1

Replace the ● with < or > to make a true sentence.

3.14 ● 3.41

3.14
3.41
↑

Line up the decimal points. Starting at the left, compare the digits in each place-value position.

The digits in the tenths place are not the same. Since 1 tenth < 4 tenths, 3.14 < 3.41.

Example 2

Evaluate the expression $11 - a + b$ if $a = 2$ and $b = 8$.

$11 - a + b = 11 - 2 + 8$	Replace a with 2 and b with 8.
$= 9 + 8$	Subtract 2 from 11.
$= 17$	Add 9 and 8.

Example 3

Evaluate the expression $n^2 \div 16 + m$ if $m = 3$ and $n = 8$.

$n^2 \div 16 + m = 8^2 \div 16 + 3$	Replace m with 3 and n with 8.
$= 64 \div 16 + 3$	Evaluate 8^2.
$= 4 + 3$	Divide 64 by 16.
$= 7$	Add 4 and 3.

2-1 Integers and Absolute Value

MAIN IDEA

Read and write integers, and find the absolute value of a number.

New Vocabulary

integer
negative integer
positive integer
graph
absolute value

Math Online

glencoe.com

- Extra Examples
- Personal Tutor
- Self-Check Quiz

GET READY for the Lesson

SKATEBOARDING The bottom of a skateboarding ramp is 8 feet below streetlevel. A value of −8 represents 8 feet *below* street level.

1. What does a value of −10 represent?
2. The top deck of the ramp is 5 feet *above* street level. How can you represent 5 feet *above* street level?

Numbers like 5 and −8 are called integers. An **integer** is any number from the set {…, −4, −3, −2, −1, 0, 1, 2, 3, 4, …} where … means *continues without end*.

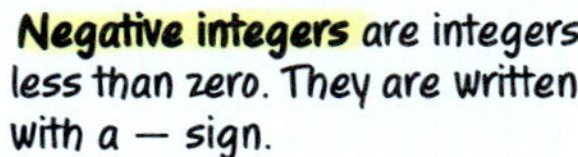

Positive integers are integers greater than zero. They can be written with or without a + sign.

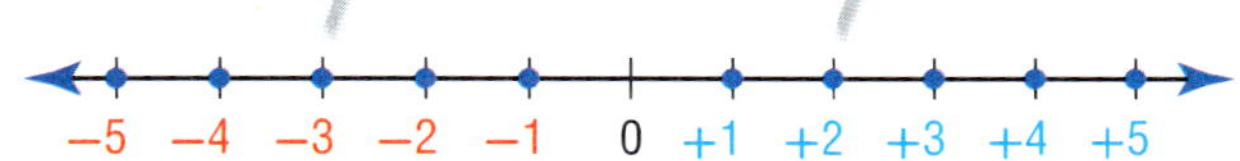

Zero is neither negative nor positive.

Real-World EXAMPLES

WEATHER **Write an integer for each situation.**

1 **an average temperature of 5 degrees below normal**

Because it represents *below* normal, the integer is −5.

2 **an average rainfall of 5 inches above normal**

Because it represents *above* normal, the integer is +5 or 5.

CHECK Your Progress

Write an integer for each situation.

a. 6 degrees above normal
b. 2 inches below normal

Integers can be graphed on a number line. To **graph** a point on the number line, draw a point on the line at its location.

EXAMPLE Graph Integers

3 **Graph the set of integers {4, −6, 0} on a number line.**

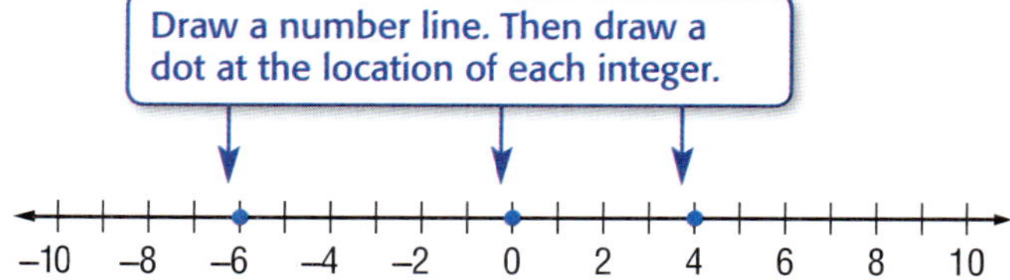

CHECK Your Progress

Graph each set of integers on a number line.

c. {−2, 8, −7}

d. {−4, 10, −3, 7}

On the number line below, notice that −5 and 5 are each 5 units from 0, even though they are on opposite sides of 0. Numbers that are the same distance from zero on a number line have the same **absolute value**.

Absolute Value — Key Concept

Words The absolute value of a number is the distance between the number and zero on a number line.

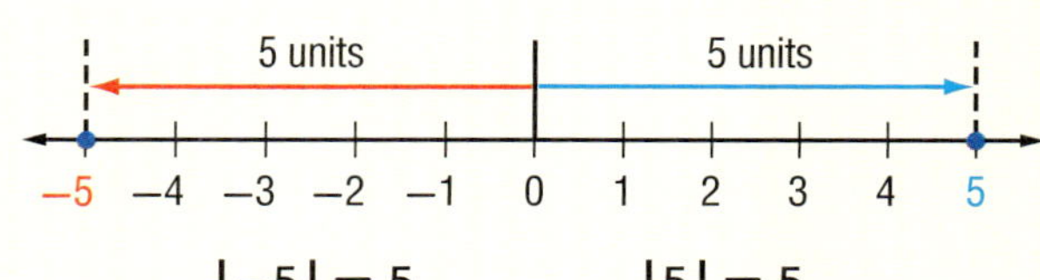

Examples $|-5| = 5$ $|5| = 5$

Reading Math

Absolute Value

$|-5|$ *absolute value of negative five*

EXAMPLES Evaluate Expressions

Evaluate each expression.

4 $|-4|$

On the number line, the point −4 is 4 units from 0.

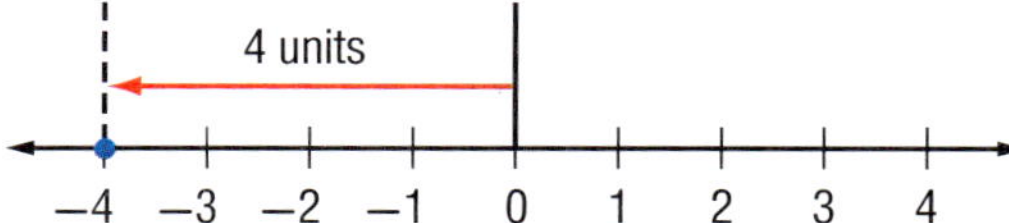

So, $|-4| = 4$.

5 $|-5| - |2|$

$|-5| - |2| = 5 - 2$ $|-5| = 5, |2| = 2$

So, $|-5| - |2| = 3$.

Order of Operations The absolute value bars are considered to be a grouping symbol. When evaluating $|-5| - |2|$, evaluate the absolute values before subtracting.

CHECK Your Progress

Evaluate each expression.

e. $|8|$

f. $2 + |-3|$

g. $|-6| - 5$

CHECK Your Understanding

Examples 1, 2 (p. 80)

Write an integer for each situation.

1. a loss of 11 yards
2. 6°F below zero
3. a deposit of $16
4. 250 meters above sea level
5. **FOOTBALL** The quarterback lost 15 yards on one play. Write an integer to represent the number of yards lost.

Example 3 (p. 81)

Graph each set of integers on a number line.

6. $\{11, -5, -8\}$
7. $\{2, -1, -9, 1\}$

Examples 4, 5 (p. 81)

Evaluate each expression.

8. $|-9|$
9. $1 + |7|$
10. $|-1| - |-6|$

Practice and Problem Solving

HOMEWORK HELP

For Exercises	See Examples
11–20	1, 2
21–24	3
25–30	4, 5

Write an integer for each situation.

11. a profit of $9
12. a bank withdrawal of $50
13. 53°C below zero
14. 7 inches more than normal
15. 2 feet below flood level
16. 160 feet above sea level
17. an elevator goes up 12 floors
18. no gains or losses on first down
19. **GOLF** In golf, scores are often written in relationship to *par,* the average score for a round at a certain course. Write an integer to represent a score that is 7 under par.
20. **PETS** Javier's pet guinea pig gained 8 ounces in one month. Write an integer to describe the amount of weight his pet gained.

Graph each set of integers on a number line.

21. $\{0, 1, -3\}$
22. $\{3, -7, 6\}$
23. $\{-5, -1, 10, -9\}$
24. $\{-2, -4, -6, -8\}$

Evaluate each expression.

25. $|10|$
26. $|-12|$
27. $|-7| - 5$
28. $7 + |4|$
29. $|-9| + |-5|$
30. $|8| - |-10|$
31. $|-10| \div 2 \times |5|$
32. $12 - |-8| + 7$
33. $|27| \div 3 - |-4|$
34. **SCUBA DIVING** One diver descended 10 feet, and another ascended 8 feet. Which situation has the greater absolute value? Explain.

35. **SCIENCE** If you rub a balloon through your hair, you can make the balloon stick to a wall. Suppose there are 17 positive charges on the wall and 25 negative charges on the balloon. Write an integer for each charge.

H.O.T. Problems

36. **REASONING** If $|x| = 3$, what is the value of x?

37. **CHALLENGE** Determine whether the following statement is *true* or *false*. If *false*, give a counterexample.

The absolute value of every integer is positive.

38. **WRITING IN MATH** Write a real-world situation that uses negative integers. Explain what the negative integer means in that situation.

TEST PRACTICE

39. Which point has a coordinate with the greatest absolute value?

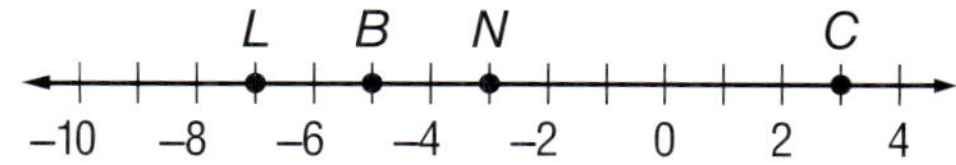

A Point *B*

B Point *C*

C Point *L*

D Point *N*

40. Which statement about these real-world situations is *not* true?

F A $100 check deposited in a bank can be represented by +100.

G A loss of 15 yards in a football game can be represented by −15.

H A temperature of 20 below zero can be represented by −20.

J A submarine diving 300 feet under water can be represented by +300.

Spiral Review

Copy and complete each function table. Identify the domain and range. (Lesson 1-10)

41. $y = x - 4$

x	$x - 4$	y
4		
5		
6		
7		

42. $y = 9x$

x	$9x$	y
0		
1		
2		
3		

43. $y = 5x + 1$

x	$5x + 1$	y
1		
2		
3		
4		

44. **GEOMETRY** The table shows the side length and perimeter of several equilateral triangles. Write an expression that describes the perimeter if x represents the side length. (Lesson 1-9)

Side Length (in.)	2	3	4	5	6
Perimeter (in.)	6	9	12	15	18

GET READY for the Next Lesson

PREREQUISITE SKILL **Replace each ● with < or > to make a true sentence.**

45. 16 ● 6

46. 101 ● 111

47. 87.3 ● 83.7

48. 1,051 ● 1,015

Comparing and Ordering Integers

MAIN IDEA

Compare and order integers.

Math Online

glencoe.com

- Concepts In Motion
- Extra Examples
- Personal Tutor
- Self-Check Quiz
- Reading in the Content Area

GET READY for the Lesson

TOYS The timeline shows when some toys were invented.

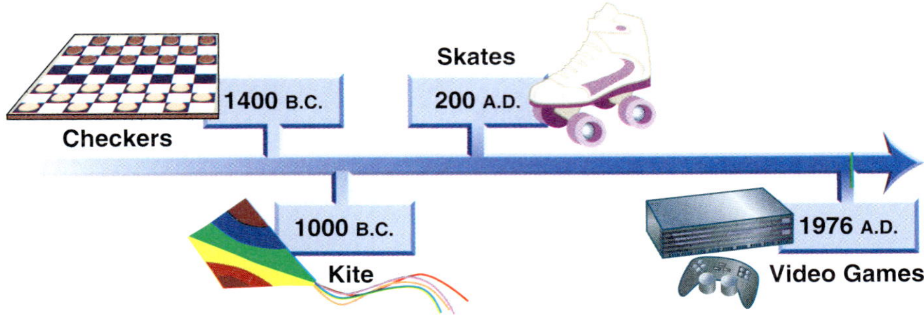

1. The yo-yo was invented around 500 B.C. Was it invented before or after the kite?
2. Modern chess was invented around 600 A.D. Between which two toys was this invented?

When two numbers are graphed on a number line, the number to the left is always less than the number to the right. The number to the right is always greater than the number to the left.

Compare Integers — Key Concept

Model

(number line from −5 to 1 with points at −4 and −2)

Words	−4 is less than −2.	−2 is greater than −4.
Examples	$-4 < -2$	$-2 > -4$

EXAMPLE Compare Two Integers

1 **Replace the ● with < or > to make −5 ● −3 a true sentence.**

Graph each integer on a number line.

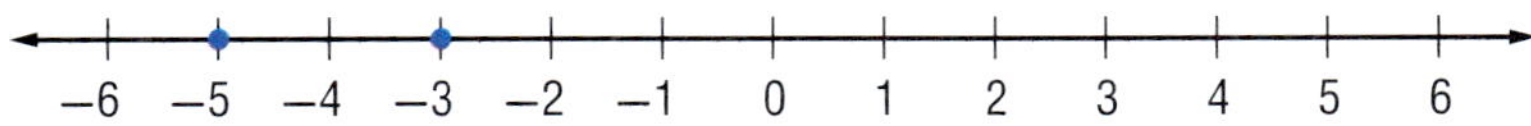

Since −5 is to the left of −3, $-5 < -3$.

CHECK Your Progress

Replace each ● with < or > to make a true sentence.

a. −8 ● −4 b. 5 ● −1 c. −10 ● −13

TEST EXAMPLE

2 **The elevations, in feet, for the lowest points in California, Oklahoma, Louisiana, and Kentucky are listed. Which list shows the elevation in order from highest to lowest?**

State	Elevation (ft)
California	−282
Oklahoma	289
Louisiana	−8
Kentucky	257

A 289, −282, 257, −8

B −8, 257, −282, 289

C −282, −8, 257, 289

D 289, 257, −8, −282

Test-Taking Tip

Eliminating Answer Choices
If you are unsure of the correct answer, eliminate the choices you know are incorrect. Then consider the remaining choices. You can eliminate choices B and C since those lists begin with a negative number.

Read the Item

To order the integers, graph them on a number line.

Solve the Item

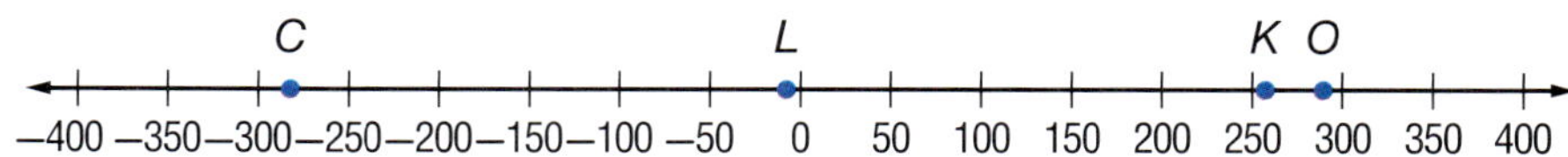

Order the integers by reading from right to left:
289, 257, −8, −282. So, the answer is D.

CHECK Your Progress

d. A newspaper reporter lists the third round scores of the top five finishers in a golf tournament. Which list shows these scores from least to greatest?

F 5, 2, 0, −1, −3
G −1, −3, 0, 2, 5
H −3, −1, 0, 2, 5
J 0, −1, 2, −3, 5

CHECK Your Understanding

Example 1 (p. 84)

Replace each ● with < or > to make a true sentence.

1. −4 ● −6
2. −2 ● 8
3. 0 ● −10

Example 2 (p. 85)

Order the integers in each set from least to greatest.

4. {−13, 9, −2, 0, 4}
5. {12, −16, −10, 19, −18}

6. **MULTIPLE CHOICE** The lowest temperatures in Hawaii, Illinois, Minnesota, and South Carolina are listed. Which list shows these temperatures in order from coldest to warmest?

A −19, −36, −60, 12
B 12, −19, −36, −60
C −60, −36, −19, 12
D −60, −19, 12, −36

Practice and Problem Solving

HOMEWORK HELP

For Exercises	See Examples
7–14	1
15–20	2
35–36	2

Replace each ● with $<$ or $>$ to make a true sentence.

7. -7 ● -3
8. -21 ● -12
9. -6 ● -11
10. -15 ● -33
11. 17 ● -20
12. 4 ● -4
13. -5 ● 17
14. -12 ● 8

Order the integers in each set from least to greatest.

15. $\{-8, 11, 6, -5, -3\}$
16. $\{7, -2, 14, -9, 2\}$
17. $\{5, -6, -7, -4, 1, 3\}$
18. $\{-12, 15, 8, -15, -23, 10\}$

19. **ANALYZE TABLES** The ocean floor is divided into five zones according to how deep sunlight penetrates. Order the zones from closest to the surface to nearest to the ocean floor.

Zone	Beginning Ocean Depth
Abyssal	−4,000 m
Hadal	−6,000 m
Midnight	−1,000 m
Sunlight	0 m
Twilight	−200 m

20. **STOCK MARKET** Kevin's dad owns stock in five companies. The change in the stock value for each company was as follows: Company A, +12; Company B, −5; Company C, −25; Company D, +18; Company E, −10. Order the companies from the worst performing to best performing.

Replace each ● with $<$, $>$, or $=$ to make a true sentence.

21. -13 ● $|-14|$
22. $|36|$ ● -37
23. -12 ● $|12|$
24. $|-29|$ ● $|92|$

FOOTBALL For Exercises 25 and 26, use the information at the right. It shows the yardage gained each play for five plays.

Play	1	2	3	4	5
Yardage	10	−2	5	−5	20

25. Order the yardage from least to greatest.
26. Which run is the middle, or *median*, yardage?

27. **WEATHER** The wind chill index was invented in 1939 by Paul Siple, a polar explorer and authority on Antarctica. Wind chill causes the air to feel colder on human skin. Which feels colder: a temperature of 10° with a 15-mile-per-hour wind or a temperature of 5° with a 10 mile per hour wind?

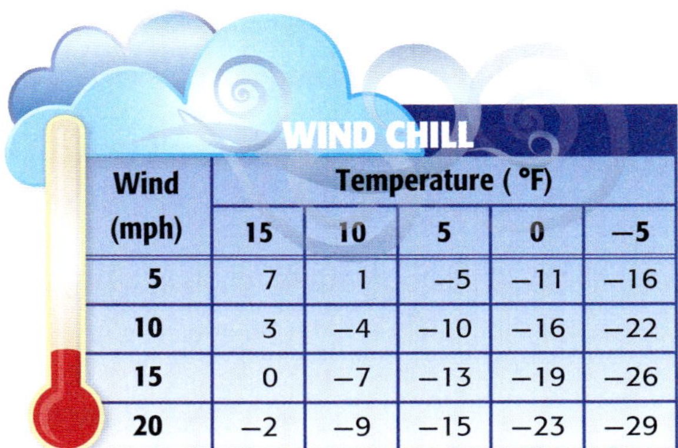
WIND CHILL

Wind (mph)	Temperature (°F)				
	15	10	5	0	−5
5	7	1	−5	−11	−16
10	3	−4	−10	−16	−22
15	0	−7	−13	−19	−26
20	−2	−9	−15	−23	−29

Determine whether each sentence is *true* or *false*. If *false*, change one number to make the sentence true.

28. $-8 > 5$
29. $-7 < 0$
30. $|5| < -6$
31. $10 > |-8|$

EXTRA PRACTICE
See pages 671, 705.

H.O.T. Problems

32. **NUMBER SENSE** If 0 is the greatest integer in a set of five integers, what can you conclude about the other four integers?

33. **CHALLENGE** What is the greatest integer value of n such that $n < 0$?

34. **WRITING IN MATH** Develop a method for ordering a set of negative integers from least to greatest without the aid of a number line. Explain your method and use it to order the set $\{-5, -8, -1, -3\}$.

TEST PRACTICE

35. On a certain game show, contestants receive positive numbers of points for correct responses and negative numbers of points for incorrect responses. Which list gives the points a contestant received during one round of the game in order from highest to lowest?

A −200, −400, −1000, 200, 600

B 600, −1000, −400, −200, 200

C 600, 200, −200, −400, −1000

D −1000, −400, −200, 600, 200

36. Which statement about the values shown is *not* true?

State	Low Temperature (°F)
AR	−29
GA	−17
MS	−19
VA	−30
TX	−23

Source: *The World Almanac*

F Virginia's record low is less than the record low for Arkansas.

G Arkansas' record low is less than the record low for Georgia.

H Mississippi's record low is greater than the record low for Texas.

J Texas' record low is less than the record low for Arkansas.

Spiral Review

Write an integer for each situation. (Lesson 2-1)

37. 9°C below zero

38. a gain of 20 feet

HOBBIES For Exercises 39 and 40, use the following information. (Lesson 1-10)

Sophia estimates that she knits 6 rows of an afghan each hour.

39. Write an equation using two variables to represent the total number of rows r completed by Sophia after time t.

40. How many rows will Sophia have completed after 4 hours?

GET READY for the Next Lesson

PREREQUISITE SKILL Graph each point on a vertical number line that goes from −10 on the bottom to 10 at the top. (Lesson 2-1)

41. −3

42. 0

43. 4

44. −7

2-3 The Coordinate Plane

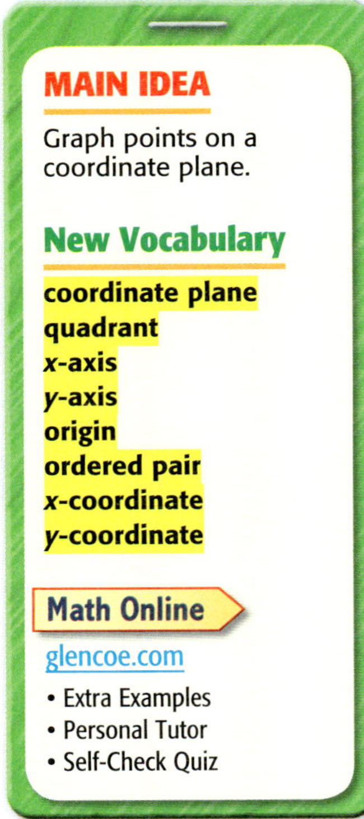

GET READY for the Lesson

GPS A GPS, or global positioning system, is a satellite based navigation system. A GPS map of Raleigh, North Carolina, is shown.

1. Suppose Mr. Diaz starts at Shaw University and drives 2 blocks north. Name the street he will cross.
2. Using the words *north*, *south*, *east*, and *west*, write directions to go from Chavis Park to Moore Square.

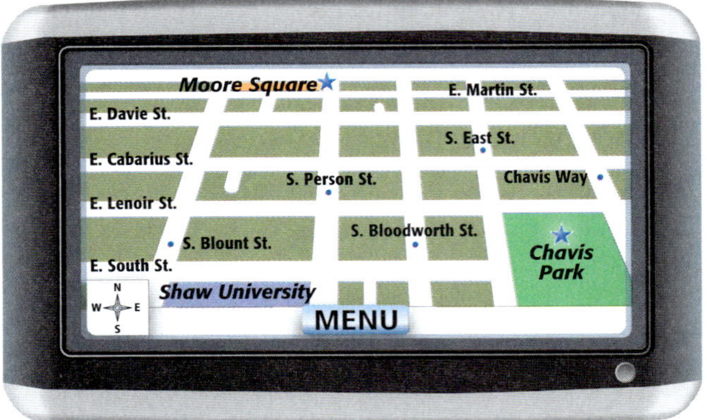

On a GPS, towns and streets are often located on a grid. In mathematics, we use a grid called a coordinate plane, to locate points. A **coordinate plane** is formed when two number lines intersect. The number lines separate the coordinate plane into four regions called **quadrants**.

Coordinate Plane

Key Concept

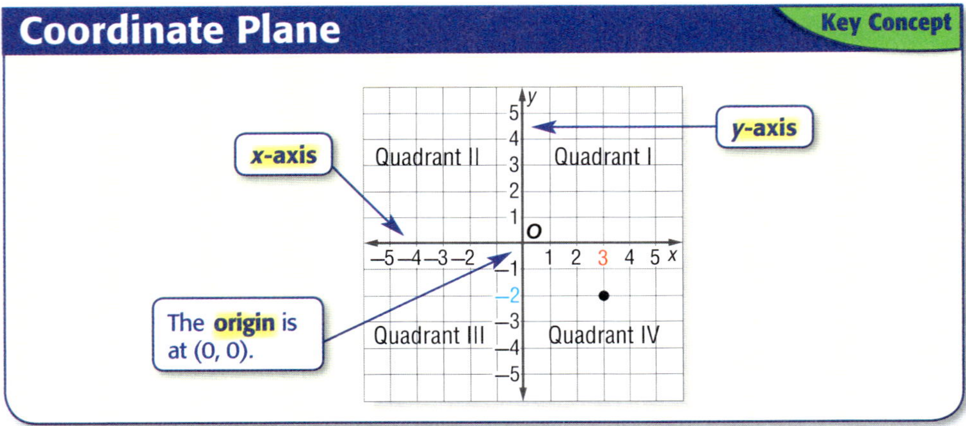

An **ordered pair** is a pair of numbers, such as (3, −2), used to locate a point in the coordinate plane.

x-coordinate corresponds to a number on the *x*-axis. (3, −2) *y*-coordinate corresponds to a number on the *y*-axis.

When locating an ordered pair, moving *right* or *up* on a coordinate plane is in the *positive* direction. Moving *left* or *down* is in the *negative* direction.

EXAMPLE Naming Points Using Ordered Pairs

1 **Write the ordered pair that corresponds to point D. Then state the quadrant in which the point is located.**

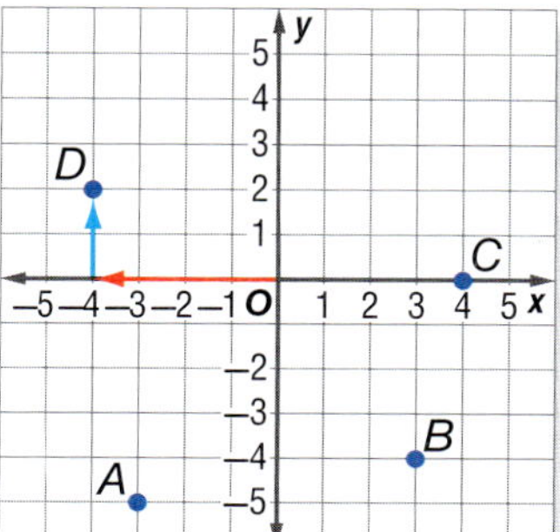

- Start at the origin.
- Move left on the x-axis to find the x-coordinate of point D, which is -4.
- Move up to find the y-coordinate, which is 2.

So, point D corresponds to the ordered pair $(-4, 2)$. Point D is located in Quadrant II.

CHECK Your Progress

Write the ordered pair that corresponds to each point. Then state the quadrant or axis on which the point is located.

a. A **b.** B **c.** C

EXAMPLE Graph an Ordered Pair

2 **Graph and label point K at $(2, -5)$.**

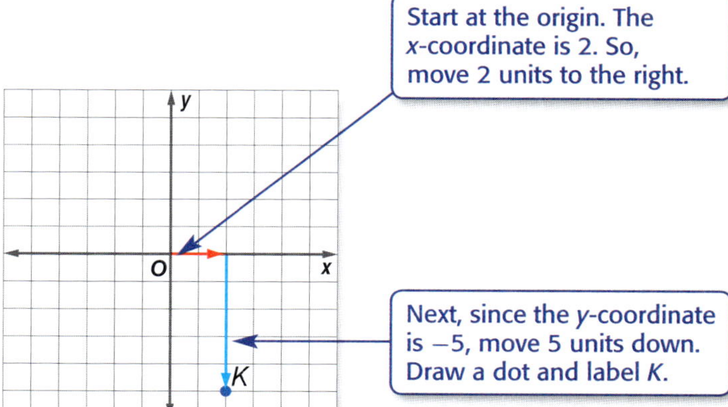

Reading Math

Scale When no numbers are shown on the x- or y-axis, you can assume that each square is 1 unit long on each side.

CHECK Your Progress

On graph paper, draw a coordinate plane. Then graph and label each point.

d. $L(-4, 2)$ **e.** $M(-5, -3)$ **f.** $N(0, 1)$

New York Aquarium has a marine mammal exhibit that includes sea otters. Large male sea otters can grow to be over 4 feet in length.

Real-World EXAMPLES

3 **AQUARIUMS** **A map can be divided into a coordinate plane where the x-coordinate represents how far to move right or left and the y-coordinate represents how far to move up or down. What exhibit is located at (6, 5)?**

Real-World Link

New York Aquarium, Bronx, NY

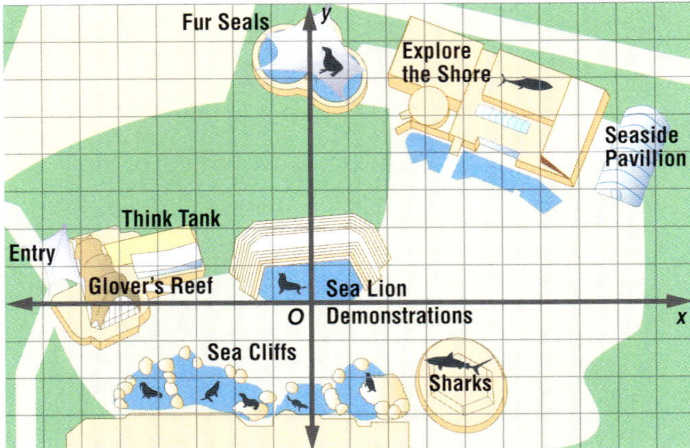

Start at the origin. Move 6 units to the right and then 5 units up. Explore the Shore is located at (6, 5).

4 **In which quadrant is the Shark Exhibit located?**

The Shark Exhibit is located in Quadrant IV.

CHECK Your Progress

For Exercises g and h, use the map above.

g. Find the ordered pair that represents the location of the Think Tank.

h. What is located at the origin?

CHECK Your Understanding

Example 1 (p. 89)

Write the ordered pair corresponding to each point graphed at the right. Then state the quadrant or axis on which each point is located.

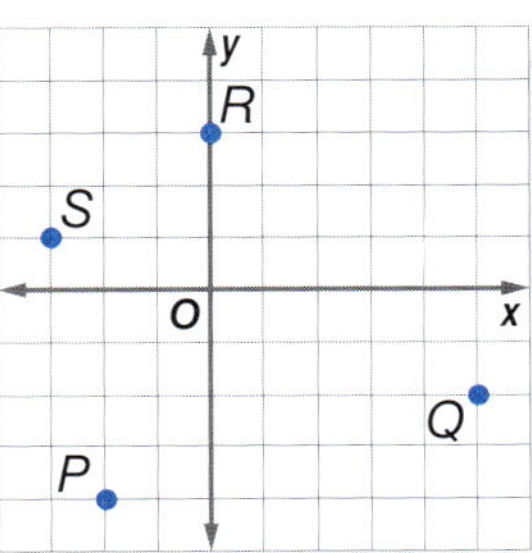

1. P
2. Q
3. R
4. S

Example 2 (p. 89)

On graph paper, draw a coordinate plane. Then graph and label each point.

5. $T(2, 3)$
6. $U(-4, 6)$
7. $V(-5, 0)$
8. $W(1, -2)$

Examples 3, 4 (p. 90)

GEOGRAPHY **For Exercises 9 and 10, use the map in Example 3 above.**

9. What exhibit is located at $(0, -3)$?
10. In which quadrant is the Seaside Pavillion located?

Practice and Problem Solving

HOMEWORK HELP

For Exercises	See Examples
11–22, 37	1
23–34, 38	2
35–36	3

Write the ordered pair corresponding to each point graphed at the right. Then state the quadrant or axis on which each point is located.

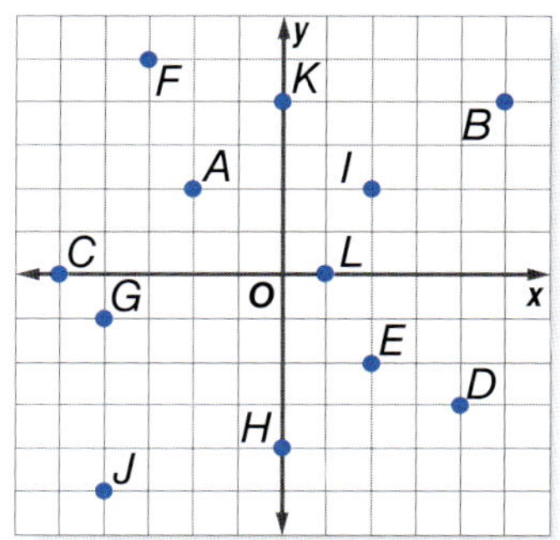

11. A	**12.** B	**13.** C
14. D	**15.** E	**16.** F
17. G	**18.** H	**19.** I
20. J	**21.** K	**22.** L

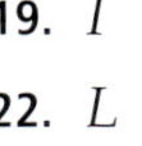

On graph paper, draw a coordinate plane. Then graph and label each point.

23. $M(5, 6)$	**24.** $N(-2, 10)$	**25.** $P(7, -8)$	**26.** $Q(3, 0)$
27. $R(-1, -7)$	**28.** $S(8, 1)$	**29.** $T(-3, 7)$	**30.** $U(5, -2)$
31. $V(0, 6)$	**32.** $W(-5, -7)$	**33.** $X(-4, 0)$	**34.** $Y(0, -5)$

GEOGRAPHY **For Exercises 35–38, use the world map.**

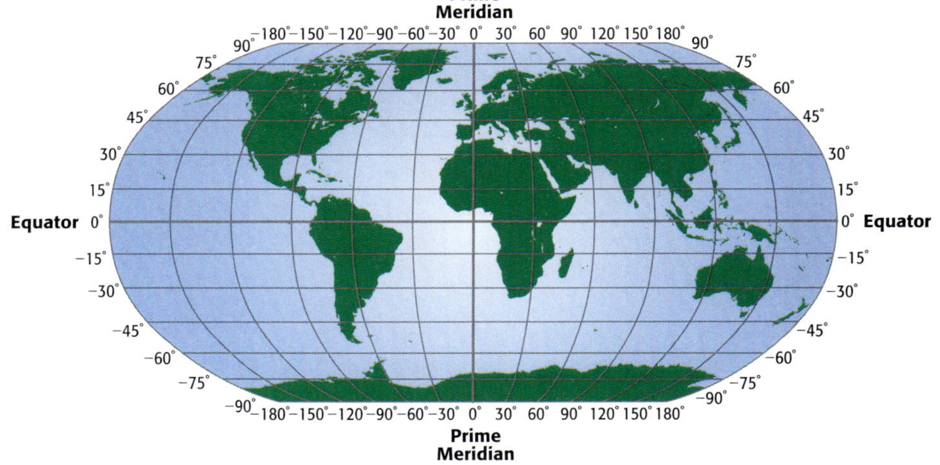

35. The world map can be divided into a coordinate plane where (x, y) represents (degrees longitude, degrees latitude). In what continent is the point (30° longitude, −15° latitude) located?

36. Which of the continents is located entirely in Quadrant II?

37. In what continent is the point (−90° longitude, 0° latitude) located?

38. Name a continent on the map that is located entirely in Quadrant I.

On graph paper, draw a coordinate plane. Then graph and label each point.

39. $X(1.5, 3.5)$	**40.** $Y\left(3\frac{1}{4}, 2\frac{1}{2}\right)$	**41.** $Z\left(2, 1\frac{2}{3}\right)$

42. **GEOMETRY** Graph four points on a coordinate plane so that they form a square when connected. Identify the ordered pairs.

43. **RESEARCH** Use the Internet or other resources to explain why the coordinate plane is sometimes called the Cartesian plane.

Determine whether each statement is *sometimes*, *always*, or *never* true. Explain or give a counterexample to support your answer.

44. Both x- and y-coordinates of a point in Quadrant III are negative.

45. The y-coordinate of a point that lies on the y-axis is negative.

46. The y-coordinate of a point in Quadrant II is negative.

H.O.T. Problems

47. **OPEN ENDED** Create a display that shows how to determine in what quadrant a point is located without graphing. Then provide an example that demonstrates how your graphic is used.

48. **CHALLENGE** Find the possible locations for any ordered pair with x- and y-coordinates always having the same sign. Explain.

49. **WRITING IN MATH** Explain why the location of point $A(1, -2)$ is different than the location of point $B(-2, 1)$.

50. Which of the following points lie within the triangle graphed at the right?

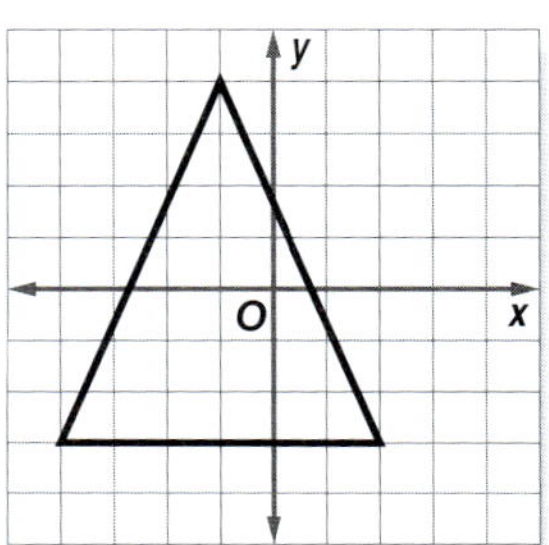

A $A(-4, -1)$

B $B(1, 3)$

C $C(-1, 2)$

D $D(2, -2)$

51. What are the coordinates of the point that shows the location of the lunch room on the map?

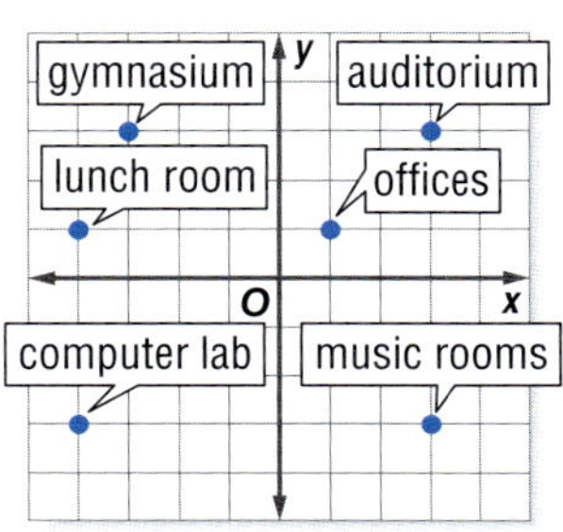

F $(4, -1)$

G $(-4, 1)$

H $(1, 4)$

J $(1, -4)$

Spiral Review

Replace each ● with $<$, $>$, or $=$ to make a true sentence. (Lesson 2-2)

52. -8 ● -3

53. 26 ● -30

54. 14 ● $|-15|$

55. -40 ● $|40|$

56. Find the absolute value of -101. (Lesson 2-1)

57. **RUNNING** Salvador is training for a marathon. He runs 5 miles each day on weekdays and 8 miles each day on the weekends. How many miles does Salvador run in one week? (Lesson 1-1)

GET READY for the Next Lesson

PREREQUISITE SKILL **Add.**

58. 138 + 246

59. 814 + 512

60. 2,653 + 4,817

61. 6,003 + 5,734

Explore 2-4

Algebra Lab
Adding Integers

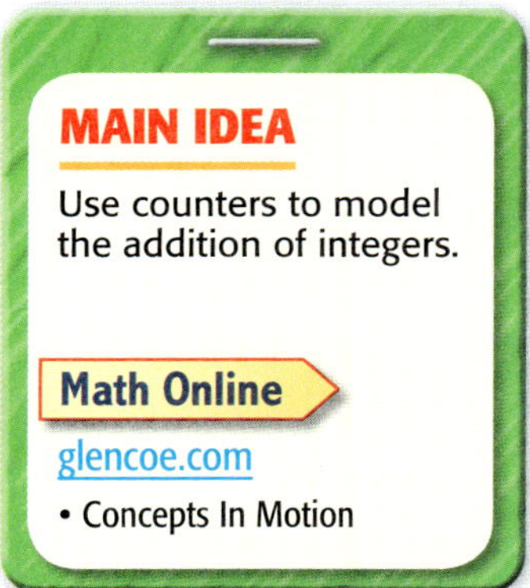

You can use positive and negative counters to model the addition of integers. The counter ⊕ represents 1, and the counter ⊖ represents −1. Remember that addition means *combining* two sets.

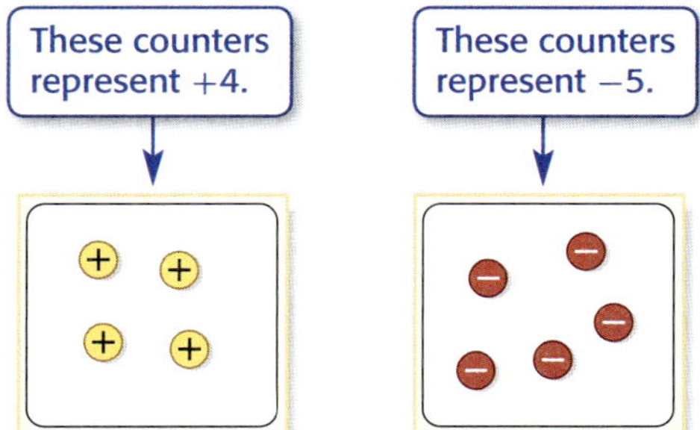

ACTIVITY

1 **Use counters to find −3 + (−6).**

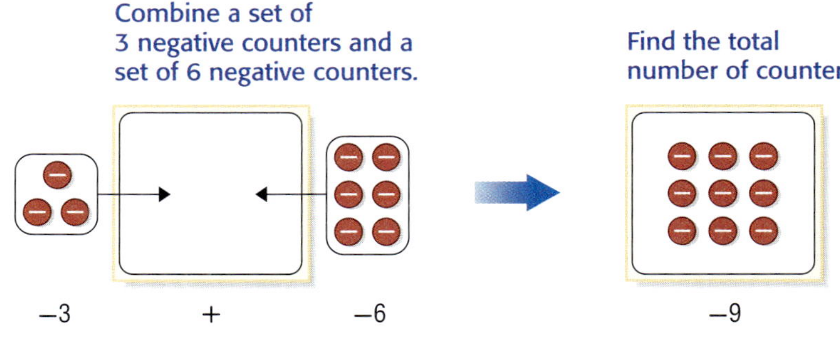

So, $-3 + (-6) = -9$.

CHECK Your Progress

Use counters or a drawing to find each sum.

a. $5 + 6$ **b.** $-3 + (-5)$ **c.** $-5 + (-4)$

d. $7 + 3$ **e.** $-2 + (-5)$ **f.** $-8 + (-6)$

The following two properties are important when modeling operations with integers.

- When one positive counter is paired with one negative counter, the result is called a **zero pair.** The value of a zero pair is 0.
- You can add or remove zero pairs from a mat because adding or removing zero does not change the value of the counters on the mat.

ACTIVITIES

Study Tip

Adding Integers
If there are more negatives than positives, the sum is negative.

Use counters to find each sum.

2 $-4 + 2$

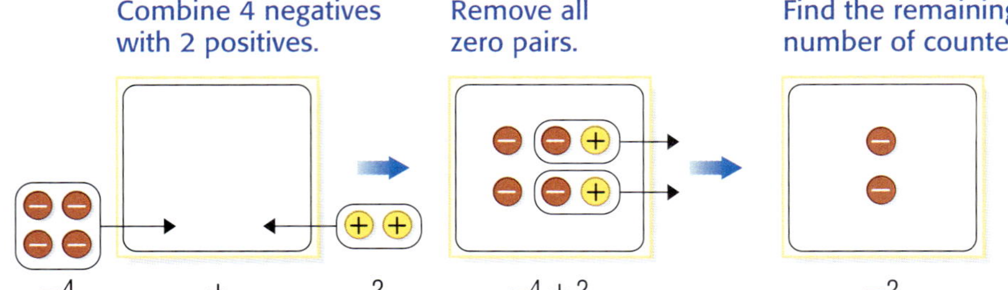

So, $-4 + 2 = -2$.

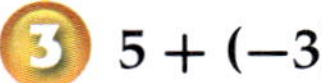

3 $5 + (-3)$

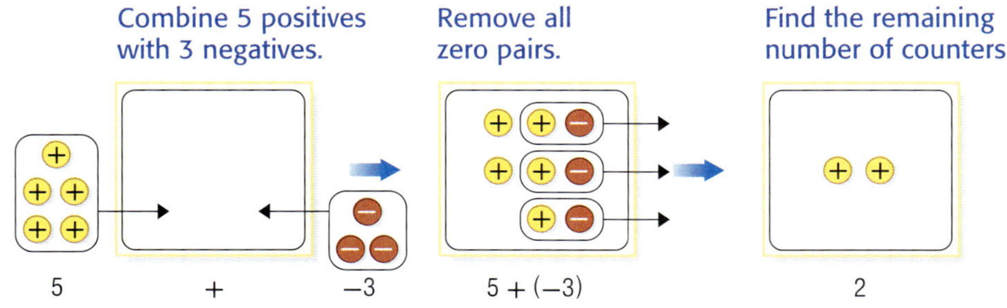

So, $5 + (-3) = 2$.

CHECK Your Progress

Use counters or a drawing to find each sum.

g. $-6 + 5$ h. $3 + (-6)$ i. $-2 + 7$

j. $8 + (-3)$ k. $-9 + 1$ l. $-4 + 10$

Analyze the Results

1. Write two addition sentences where the sum is positive. In each sentence, one addend should be positive and the other negative.

2. Write two addition sentences where the sum is negative. In each sentence, one addend should be positive and the other negative.

3. **MAKE A CONJECTURE** What is a rule you can use to determine how to find the sum of two integers with the same sign? two integers with different signs?

2-4 Adding Integers

MAIN IDEA

Add integers.

New Vocabulary

opposites
additive inverse

Math Online

glencoe.com

- Extra Examples
- Personal Tutor
- Self-Check Quiz

GET READY for the Lesson

SCIENCE Atoms are made of negative charges (electrons) and positive charges (protons). The helium atom shown has a total of 2 electrons and 2 protons.

1. Represent the electrons in an atom of helium with an integer.
2. Represent the protons in an atom of helium with an integer.
3. Each proton-electron pair has a value of 0. What is the total charge of an atom of helium?

Combining protons and electrons in an atom is similar to adding integers.

EXAMPLE Add Integers with the Same Sign

1 Find $-3 + (-2)$.

Use a number line.

- Start at 0.
- Move 3 units left to show -3.
- From there, move 2 units left to show -2.

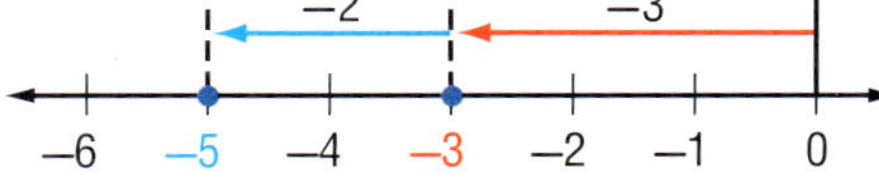

So, $-3 + (-2) = -5$.

CHECK Your Progress

a. $-5 + (-7)$

b. $-10 + (-4)$

These and other examples suggest the following rule.

Add Integers with the Same Sign — Key Concept

Words To add integers with the same sign, add their absolute values. The sum is:

- positive if both integers are positive.
- negative if both integers are negative.

Examples $7 + 4 = 11$ $\quad -7 + (-4) = -11$

EXAMPLE Add Integers with the Same Sign

2 **Find −26 + (−17).**

$-26 + (-17) = -43$ Both integers are negative, so the sum is negative.

c. $-14 + (-16)$

d. $23 + 38$

Vocabulary Link
Opposite
Everyday Use something that is across from or is facing the other way, as in running the opposite way

Math Use two numbers that are the same distance from 0, but on opposite sides of 0 on the number line

The integers 5 and −5 are called **opposites** because they are the same distance from 0, but on opposite sides of 0. Two integers that are opposites are also called **additive inverses**.

Additive Inverse Property — Key Concept

Words The sum of any number and its additive inverse is 0.

Examples $5 + (-5) = 0$

Number lines can also help you add integers with different signs.

EXAMPLES Add Integers with Different Signs

3 **Find 5 + (−3).**

Use a number line.

- Start at zero.
- Move 5 units right.
- Then move 3 units left.

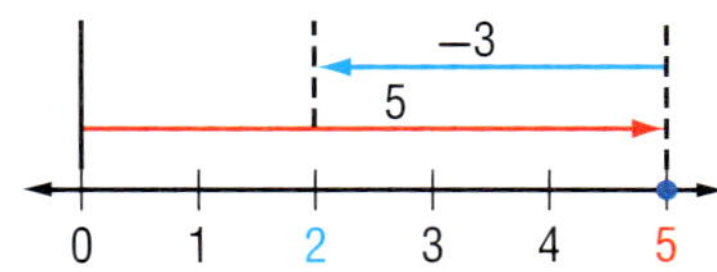

So, $5 + (-3) = 2$.

4 **Find −3 + 2.**

Use a number line.

- Start at zero.
- Move 3 units left.
- Then move 2 units right.

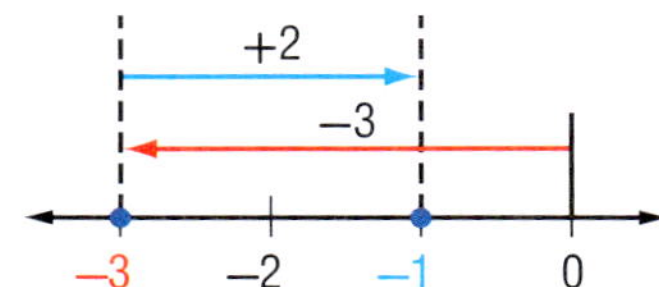

So, $-3 + 2 = -1$.

e. $6 + (-7)$

f. $-15 + 19$

Study Tip
Look Back You can review **absolute value** in Lesson 2-1.

Add Integers with Different Signs — Key Concept

Words To add integers with different signs, subtract their absolute values. The sum is:

- positive if the positive integer's absolute value is greater.
- negative if the negative integer's absolute value is greater.

Examples $9 + (-4) = 5$ $-9 + 4 = -5$

EXAMPLES Add Integers with Different Signs

5 **Find $7 + (-1)$.**

$7 + (-1) = 6$ Subtract absolute values; $7 - 1 = 6$. Since 7 has the greater absolute value, the sum is positive.

6 **Find $-8 + 3$.**

$-8 + 3 = -5$ Subtract absolute values; $8 - 3 = 5$. Since -8 has the greater absolute value, the sum is negative.

Study Tip

Properties Using the Commutative, Associative, and Additive Inverse Properties allows the calculation to be as simple as possible.

7 **Find $2 + (-15) + (-2)$.**

$2 + (-15) + (-2) = 2 + (-2) + (-15)$ Commutative Property (+)

$= [2 + (-2)] + (-15)$ Associative Property (+)

$= 0 + (-15)$ Additive Inverse Property

$= -15$ Additive Identity Property

CHECK Your Progress

g. $10 + (-12)$ h. $-13 + 18$ i. $(-14) + (-6) + 6$

Real-World EXAMPLE

8 **ROLLER COASTERS The graphic shows the change in height at several points on a roller coaster. Write an addition sentence to find the height at point D in relation to point A.**

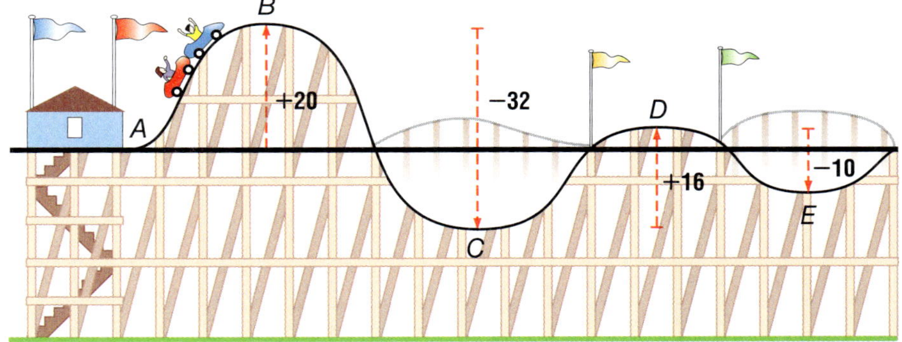

$20 + (-32) + 16 = 20 + 16 + (-32)$ Commutative Property (+)

$= 36 + (-32)$ $20 + 16 = 36$

$= 4$ Subtract absolute values. Since 36 has the greater absolute value, the sum is positive.

The result is a positive integer. So, point D is 4 feet higher than point A.

CHECK Your Progress

j. **WEATHER** The temperature is −3°F. An hour later, it drops 6° and 2 hours later, it rises 4°. Write an addition sentence to describe this situation. Then find the sum and explain its meaning.

CHECK Your Understanding

Examples 1–6 (pp. 95–97)

Add.

1. $-6 + (-8)$
2. $4 + 5$
3. $-3 + 10$
4. $-15 + 8$
5. $7 + (-11)$
6. $14 + (-6)$

Example 7 (p. 97)

7. $-17 + 20 + (-3)$
8. $15 + 9 + (-9)$

Example 8 (p. 97)

9. **MONEY** Camilia owes her brother \$25, so she gives her brother the \$18 she earned dog-sitting for the neighbors. Write an addition sentence to describe this situation. Then find the sum and explain its meaning.

Practice and Problem Solving

HOMEWORK HELP

For Exercises	See Examples
10–13	1, 2
14–21	3–6
22–27	7
28–31	8

Add.

10. $-22 + (-16)$
11. $-10 + (-15)$
12. $6 + 10$
13. $17 + 11$
14. $18 + (-5)$
15. $13 + (-19)$
16. $13 + (-7)$
17. $7 + (-20)$
18. $-19 + 24$
19. $-12 + 10$
20. $-30 + 16$
21. $-9 + 11$
22. $21 + (-21) + (-4)$
23. $-8 + (-4) + 12$
24. $-34 + 25 + (-25)$
25. $-16 + 16 + 22$
26. $25 + 3 + (-25)$
27. $7 + (-19) + (-7)$

Write an addition expression to describe each situation. Then find each sum and explain its meaning.

28. **SCUBA DIVING** Lena was scuba diving 14 meters below the surface of the water. She saw a nurse shark 3 meters above her.

29. **PELICANS** A pelican starts at 60 feet above sea level. It descends 60 feet to catch a fish.

30. **BANKING** Stephanie has \$152 in the bank. She withdraws \$20. Then she deposits \$84.

31. **FOOTBALL** A quarterback is sacked for a loss of 5 yards. On the next play, his team receives a penalty and loses 15 more yards. Then the team gains 12 yards on the third play.

32. **MONEY** Josephine is saving money for a new bike and has already saved \$17. Write the integers she should use to represent each entry.

Deposit	Withdrawal	Balance
\$15		■
	\$13	■
\$10		■
	\$4	■
\$13		■

ALGEBRA **Evaluate each expression if $x = -10$, $y = 7$, and $z = -8$.**

33. $x + 14$
34. $z + (-5)$
35. $x + y$
36. $x + z$

37. **FIND THE DATA** Refer to the Data File on pages 16–19 of your book. Choose some data and write a real-world problem in which you would add a positive and a negative integer. Then find the sum and explain its meaning.

H.O.T. Problems

38. **FIND THE ERROR** Beth and Jordan are finding $-12 + 15$. Who is correct? Explain your reasoning.

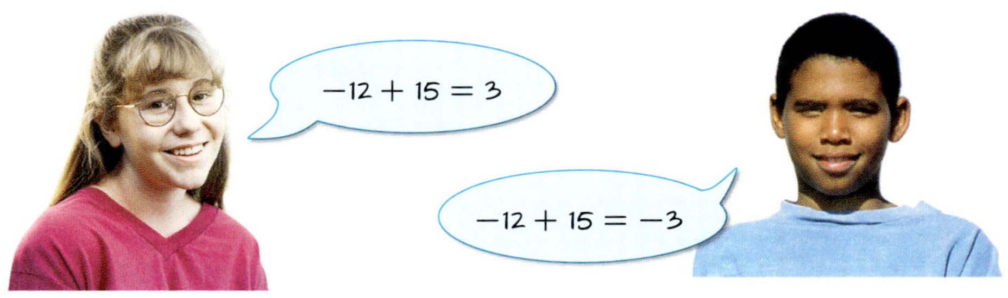

CHALLENGE **Simplify.**

39. $8 + (-8) + a$ 40. $x + (-5) + 1$ 41. $-9 + m + (-6)$ 42. $-1 + n + 7$

43. **WRITING IN MATH** Explain how you know whether a sum is positive, negative, or zero without actually adding.

TEST PRACTICE

44. **SHORT RESPONSE** Find $-8 + (-11)$.

45. Find $-8 + 7 + (-3)$.

A -18 C 2

B -4 D 18

46. At 8 A.M., the temperature was 3°F below zero. By 1 P.M., the temperature rose 14°F and by 10 P.M. dropped 12°F. What was the temperature at 10 P.M.?

F 5°F above zero

G 5°F below zero

H 1°F above zero

J 1°F below zero

Spiral Review

Write the ordered pair for each point graphed at the right. Then name the quadrant or axis on which each point is located. (Lesson 2-3)

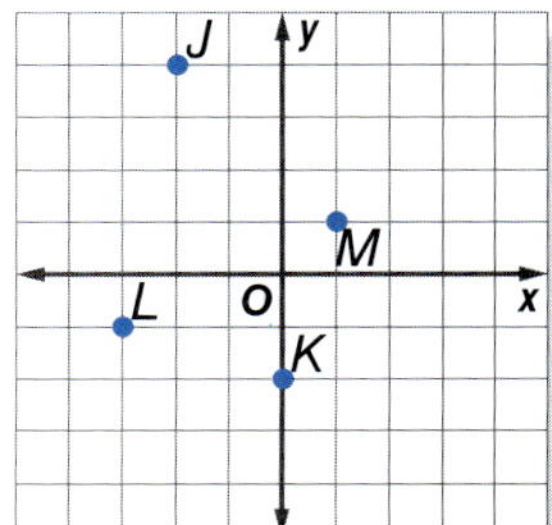

47. J 48. K 49. L 50. M

51. Order 6, −3, 0, 4, −8, 1, and −4 from least to greatest. (Lesson 2-2)

GET READY for the Next Lesson

PREREQUISITE SKILL **Subtract.**

52. 287 − 125 53. 420 − 317 54. 5,684 − 2,419 55. 7,000 − 3,891

CHAPTER 2

Mid-Chapter Quiz

Lessons 2-1 through 2-4

Write an integer for each situation. (Lesson 2-1)

1. dropped 45 feet
2. a bank deposit of \$100
3. gained 8 pounds
4. lost a \$5 bill

5. **OCEANS** The deepest point in the world is the Mariana Trench in the Western Pacific Ocean at a depth of 35,840 feet below sea level. Write this depth as an integer. (Lesson 2-1)

Evaluate each expression. (Lesson 2-1)

6. $|-16|$
7. $|24|$
8. $|-9| - |3|$
9. $|-13| + |-1|$

10. **ANALYZE TABLES** The table shows the record low temperatures for January and February in Lincoln, Nebraska.

Month	Temperature (°F)
January	−33
February	−27

Source: University of Nebraska, Lincoln

Which month had the coldest temperature? (Lesson 2-2)

11. **MULTIPLE CHOICE** The local news records the following changes in average daily temperature for the past week: 4°, −7°, −3°, 2°, 9°, −8°, 1°. Which list shows the temperatures from least to greatest? (Lesson 2-2)

A 9°, 4°, 2°, 1°, −3°, −7°, −8°
B −7°, −8°, 1°, −3°, 2°, 4°, 9°
C −8°, −7°, −3°, 1°, 2°, 4°, 9°
D −8°, −7°, 1°, 2°, 3°, 4°, 9°

Replace each ● with <, >, or = to make a true sentence. (Lesson 2-2)

12. −4 ● 4
13. −8 ● −11
14. $|-14|$ ● $|3|$
15. $|-12|$ ● $|12|$

On graph paper, draw a coordinate plane. Then graph and label each point. (Lesson 2-3)

16. $D(4, -3)$
17. $E(-1, 2)$
18. $F(0, -5)$
19. $G(-3, 0)$

20. **MULTIPLE CHOICE** Which line contains the ordered pair (−1, 4)? (Lesson 2-3)

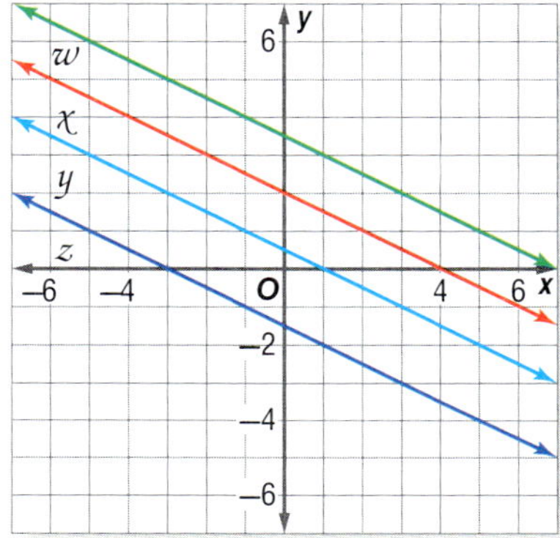

F line w
G line x
H line y
J line z

Add. (Lesson 2-4)

21. $3 + 4 + (-3)$
22. $7 + (-11)$
23. $-5 + (-6)$
24. $8 + (-1) + 1$

25. **MULTIPLE CHOICE** Kendra deposited \$78 into her savings account. Two weeks later, she deposited a check for \$50 into her account and withdrew \$27. Which of the following expressions represents the amount of money left in her account? (Lesson 2-4)

A \$78 + (−\$50) + (−\$27)
B \$78 + (−\$50) + \$27
C \$78 + \$50 + (−\$27)
D \$78 + \$50 + \$27

Explore 2-5

Algebra Lab
Subtracting Integers

MAIN IDEA

Use counters to model the subtraction of integers.

You can also use counters to model subtraction of integers. Remember one meaning of subtraction is to *take away*.

ACTIVITY

Use counters to find each difference.

1 **5 − 2**

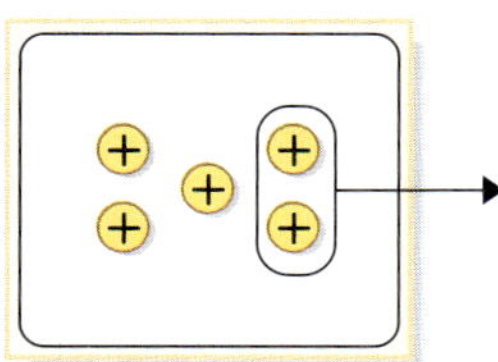

Place 5 positive counters on the mat. Remove 2 positive counters.

So, $5 - 2 = 3$.

2 **4 − (−3)**

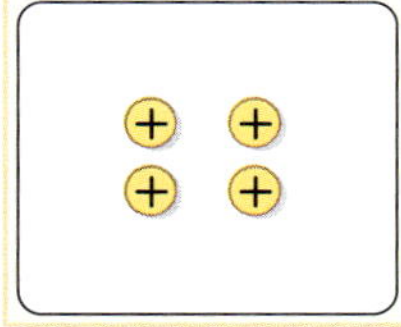

Place 4 positive counters on the mat. Remove 3 negative counters. However, there are 0 negative counters.

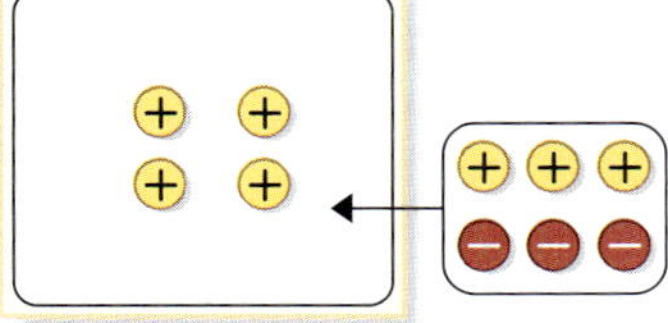

Add 3 zero pairs to the set.

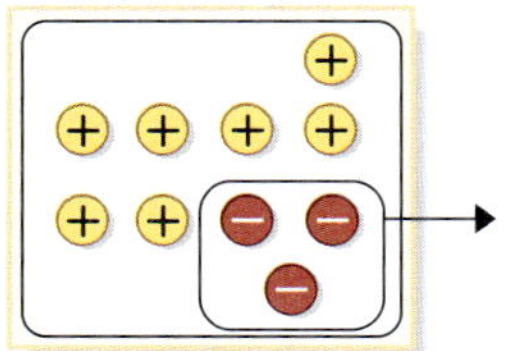

Now you can remove 3 negative counters. Find the remaining number of counters.

So, $4 - (-3) = 7$.

CHECK Your Progress

Use counters or a drawing to find each difference.

a. $7 - 6$ **b.** $5 - (-3)$ **c.** $6 - (-3)$ **d.** $5 - 8$

ACTIVITY

Use counters to find each difference.

3 $-6 - (-3)$

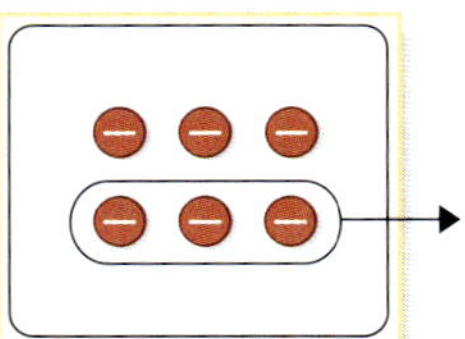

Place 6 negative counters on the mat. Remove 3 negative counters.

So, $-6 - (-3) = -3$.

4 $-5 - 1$

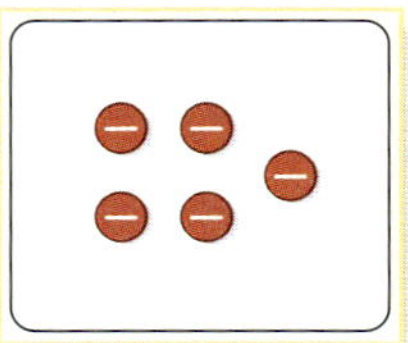

Place 5 negative counters on the mat. Remove 1 positive counter. However, there are 0 positive counters.

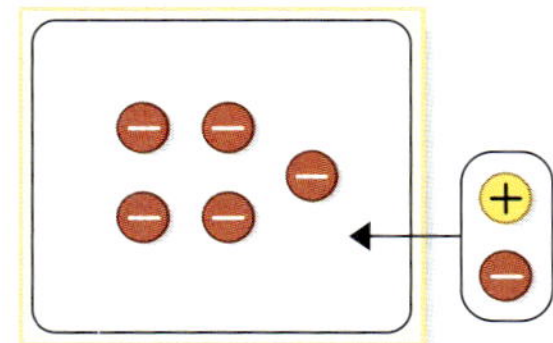

Add 1 zero pair to the set.

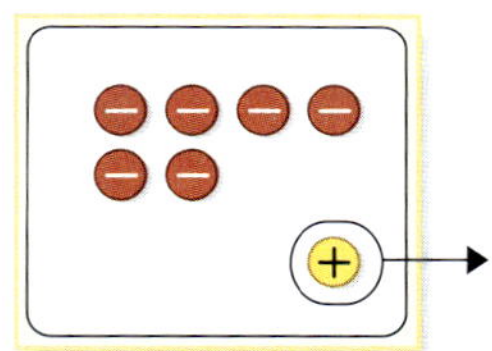

Now you can remove 1 positive counter. Find the remaining number of counters.

So, $-5 - 1 = -6$.

CHECK Your Progress

Use counters or a drawing to find each difference.

e. $-6 - (-2)$ f. $-7 - 3$ g. $-5 - (-7)$

Reading Math

Minuends, Subtrahends, and Differences In the subtraction sentence $-5 - 1 = -6$, -5 is the *minuend*, 1 is the *subtrahend*, and -6 is the *difference*.

ANALYZE THE RESULTS

1. Write two subtraction sentences where the difference is positive. Use a combination of positive and negative integers.
2. Write two subtraction sentences where the difference is negative. Use a combination of positive and negative integers.
3. **MAKE A CONJECTURE** Write a rule that will help you determine the sign of the difference of two integers.

2-5 Subtracting Integers

MAIN IDEA

Subtract integers.

Math Online

glencoe.com

- Concepts In Motion
- Extra Examples
- Personal Tutor
- Self-Check Quiz

MINI Lab

You can use a number line to model a subtraction problem.

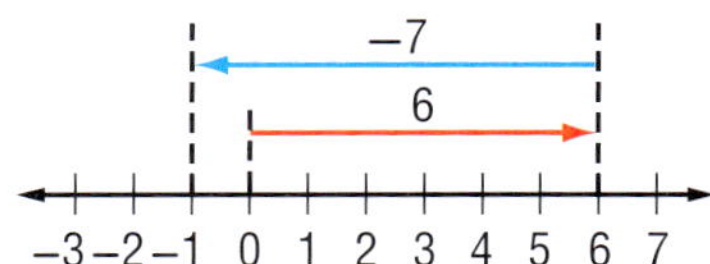

1. Write a related addition sentence for the subtraction sentence.

Use a number line to find each difference. Write an equivalent addition sentence for each.

2. $1 - 5$
3. $-2 - 1$
4. $-3 - 4$
5. $0 - 5$

When you subtract 7, the result is the same as adding its opposite, −7.

opposite

$$6 - 7 = -1 \qquad 6 + (-7) = -1$$

same result

This and other examples suggest the following rule.

Subtract Integers — Key Concept

Words	To subtract an integer, add its opposite.
Examples	$4 - 9 = 4 + (-9) = -5$ $\quad$ $7 - (-10) = 7 + (10) = 17$

EXAMPLES Subtract Positive Integers

1 **Find $8 - 13$.**

$8 - 13 = 8 + (-13)$ To subtract 13, add −13.

$= -5$ Simplify.

2 **Find $-10 - 7$.**

$-10 - 7 = -10 + (-7)$ To subtract 7, add −7.

$= -17$ Simplify.

CHECK Your Progress

a. $6 - 12$
b. $-20 - 15$
c. $-22 - 26$

EXAMPLES Subtract Negative Integers

3 **Find $1 - (-2)$.**

$1 - (-2) = 1 + 2$ To subtract −2, add 2.

$= 3$ Simplify.

4 **Find $-10 - (-7)$.**

$-10 - (-7) = -10 + 7$ To subtract −7, add 7.

$= -3$ Simplify.

CHECK Your Progress

d. $4 - (-12)$ e. $-15 - (-5)$ f. $18 - (-6)$

EXAMPLE Evaluate an Expression

5 **ALGEBRA** **Evaluate $x - y$ if $x = -6$ and $y = -5$.**

$x - y = -6 - (-5)$ Replace x with −6 and y with −5.

$= -6 + (5)$ To subtract −5, add 5.

$= -1$ Simplify.

CHECK Your Progress

Evaluate each expression if $a = 5$, $b = -8$, and $c = -9$.

g. $b - 10$ h. $a - b$ i. $c - a$

Real-World Link
The mean surface temperature on the Moon during the day is 107°C.
Source: Views of the Solar System

Real-World EXAMPLE

6 **SPACE** **The temperatures on the Moon vary from −173°C to 127°C. Find the difference between the maximum and minimum temperatures.**

To find the difference in temperatures, subtract the lower temperature from the higher temperature.

Estimate $100 + 200 = 300$

$127 - (-173) = 127 + 173$ To subtract −173, add 173.

$= 300$ Simplify.

So, the difference between the temperatures is 300°C.

CHECK Your Progress

j. **GEOGRAPHY** The Dead Sea's deepest part is 799 meters below sea level. A plateau to the east of the Dead Sea rises to about 1,340 meters above sea level. What is the difference between the top of the plateau and the deepest part of the Dead Sea?

CHECK Your Understanding

Examples 1, 2 (p. 103)

Subtract.

1. $14 - 17$
2. $10 - 30$
3. $-4 - 8$
4. $-2 - 23$

Examples 3, 4 (p. 104)

5. $14 - (-10)$
6. $5 - (-16)$
7. $-3 - (-1)$
8. $-11 - (-9)$

Example 5 (p. 104)

ALGEBRA **Evaluate each expression if $p = 8$, $q = -14$, and $r = -6$.**

9. $r - 15$
10. $q - r$
11. $p - q$

Example 6 (p. 104)

12. **EARTH SCIENCE** The sea-surface temperatures range from -2°C to 31°C. Find the difference between the maximum and minimum temperatures.

Practice and Problem Solving

HOMEWORK HELP

For Exercises	See Examples
13–16, 21–24	1, 2
17–20, 25–28	3, 4
29–36	5
37–40	6

Subtract.

13. $0 - 10$
14. $13 - 17$
15. $-9 - 5$
16. $-8 - 9$
17. $4 - (-19)$
18. $27 - (-8)$
19. $-11 - (-42)$
20. $-27 - (-19)$
21. $12 - 26$
22. $31 - 48$
23. $-25 - 5$
24. $-44 - 41$
25. $52 - (-52)$
26. $15 - (-14)$
27. $-27 - (-33)$
28. $-18 - (-20)$

ALGEBRA **Evaluate each expression if $f = -6$, $g = 7$, and $h = 9$.**

29. $g - 7$
30. $f - 6$
31. $-h - (-9)$
32. $f - g$
33. $h - f$
34. $g - h$
35. $5 - f$
36. $4 - (-g)$

ANALYZE TABLES **For Exercises 37–40, use the information below.**

State	California	Georgia	Louisiana	New Mexico	Texas
Lowest Elevation (ft)	−282	0	−8	2,842	0
Highest Elevation (ft)	14,494	4,784	535	13,161	8,749

37. What is the difference between the highest elevation in Texas and the lowest elevation in Louisiana?
38. Find the difference between the lowest elevation in New Mexico and the lowest elevation in California.
39. Find the difference between the highest elevation in Georgia and the lowest elevation in California.
40. What is the difference between the lowest elevations in Texas and Louisiana?

See pages 672, 705.

ALGEBRA **Evaluate each expression if $h = -12$, $j = 4$, and $k = 15$.**

41. $-j + h - k$
42. $|h - j|$
43. $k - j - h$

H.O.T. Problems

44. **OPEN ENDED** Write a subtraction sentence using integers. Then, write the equivalent addition sentence, and explain how to find the sum.

45. **FIND THE ERROR** Alicia and Mei are finding $-15 - (-18)$. Who is correct? Explain your reasoning.

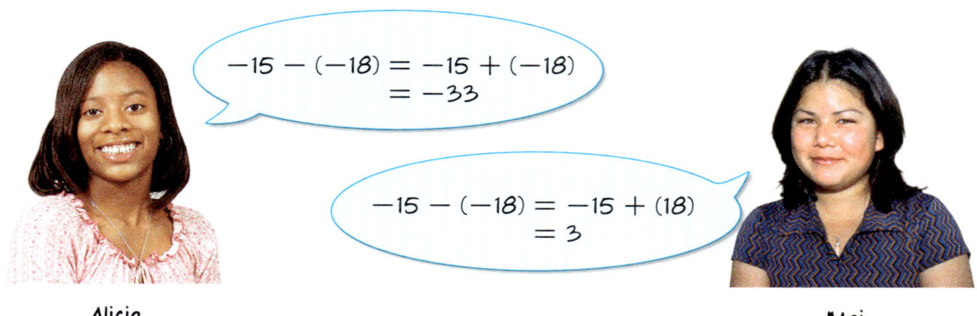

46. **CHALLENGE** *True* or *False*? When n is a negative integer, $n - n = 0$.

47. **WRITING IN MATH** Explain how additive inverses are used in subtraction.

TEST PRACTICE

48. Which sentence about integers is *not* always true?

   A positive − positive = positive

   B positive + positive = positive

   C negative + negative = negative

   D positive − negative = positive

49. Morgan drove from Los Angeles (elevation 330 feet) to Death Valley (elevation −282 feet). What is the difference in elevation between Los Angeles and Death Valley?

   F 48 feet

   G 148 feet

   H 582 feet

   J 612 feet

Spiral Review

Add. (Lesson 2-4)

50. $10 + (-3)$

51. $-2 + (-9)$

52. $-7 + (-6)$

53. $-18 + 4$

54. In which quadrant does the ordered pair $(5, -6)$ lie? (Lesson 2-3)

55. **NUMBERS** A number times 2 is added to 7. The result is 23. What is the number? Use the *guess and check* strategy. (Lesson 1-5)

GET READY for the Next Lesson

Add. (Lesson 2-4)

56. $-6 + (-6) + (-6) + (-6)$

57. $-11 + (-11) + (-11)$

58. $-2 + (-2) + (-2) + (-2)$

59. $-8 + (-8) + (-8)$

2-6 Multiplying Integers

MAIN IDEA

Multiply integers.

Math Online

glencoe.com

- Extra Examples
- Personal Tutor
- Self-Check Quiz

MINI Lab

Counters can be used to multiply integers.

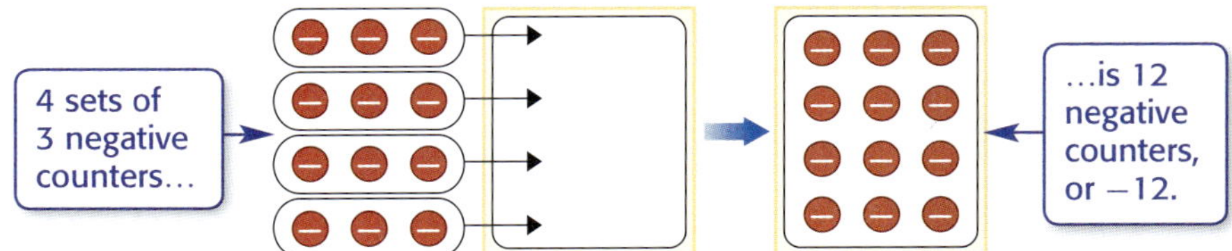

1. Write a multiplication sentence that describes the model above.

Find each product using counters or a drawing.

2. 3(−2)
3. 4(−3)
4. 1(−7)
5. 5(−2)

Remember that multiplication is the same as repeated addition.

$4(-3) = (-3) + (-3) + (-3) + (-3)$ −3 is used as an addend four times.

$= -12$

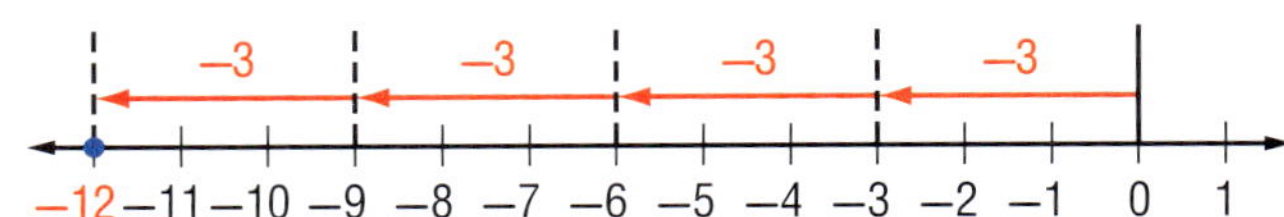

By the Commutative Property of Multiplication, $4(-3) = -3(4)$.

Multiply Integers with Different Signs — Key Concept

Words The product of two integers with different signs is negative.

Examples $6(-4) = -24$ $-5(7) = -35$

EXAMPLES Multiply Integers with Different Signs

1 **Find 3(−5).**

$3(-5) = -15$ The integers have different signs. The product is negative.

2 **Find −6(8).**

$-6(8) = -48$ The integers have different signs. The product is negative.

CHECK Your Progress

a. 9 (−2)

b. −7(4)

The product of two positive integers is positive. You can use a pattern to find the sign of the product of two negative integers.

Study Tip

Multiplying by Zero The Multiplicative Property of Zero states that when any number is multiplied by zero, the product is zero.

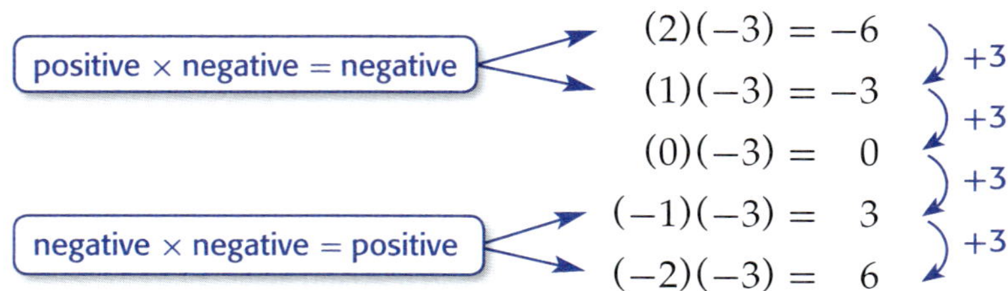

Each product is 3 more than the previous product. This pattern can also be shown on a number line.

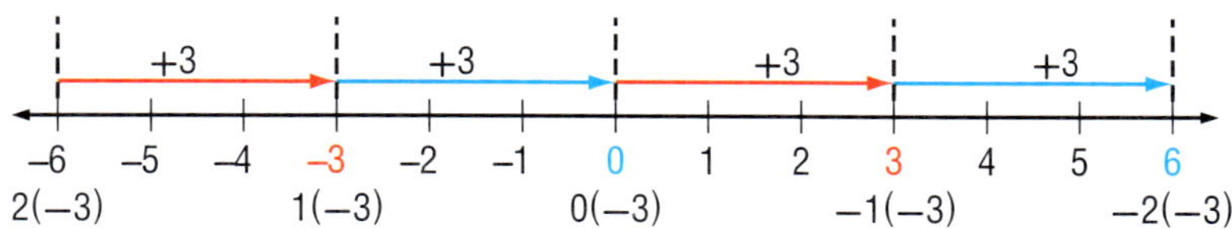

These and other examples suggest the following rule.

Multiply Integers with Same Sign

Key Concept

Words The product of two integers with the same sign is positive.

Examples $2(6) = 12$ $-10(-6) = 60$

EXAMPLES Multiply Integers with the Same Sign

3 **Find $-11(-9)$.**

$-11(-9) = 99$ The integers have the same sign. The product is positive.

Study Tip

Look Back You can review **exponents** in Lesson 1-2.

4 **Find $(-4)^2$.**

$(-4)^2 = (-4)(-4)$ There are two factors of −4.

$= 16$ The product is positive.

5 **Find $-3(-4)(-2)$.**

$-3(-4)(-2) = [-3(-4)](-2)$ Associative Property

$= 12(-2)$ $-3(-4) = 12$

$= -24$ $12(-2) = -24$

CHECK Your Progress

c. $-12(-4)$ d. $(-5)^2$ e. $-7(-5)(-3)$

Real-World Link
The MIR submersible that explored the Titanic shipwreck was able to descend to −20,000 feet.
Source: Space Adventures

Real-World EXAMPLE

6 **SUBMERSIBLES** **A submersible is diving from the surface of the water at a rate of 90 feet per minute. What is the depth of the submersible after 7 minutes?**

If the submersible descends 90 feet per minute, then after 7 minutes, the vessel will be at $7(-90)$ or -630 feet. Thus, the submersible will descend to 630 feet below the surface.

CHECK Your Progress

f. **MONEY** Mr. Simon's bank automatically deducts a $4 monthly maintenance fee from his savings account. What integer represents a change in his savings account from one year of fees?

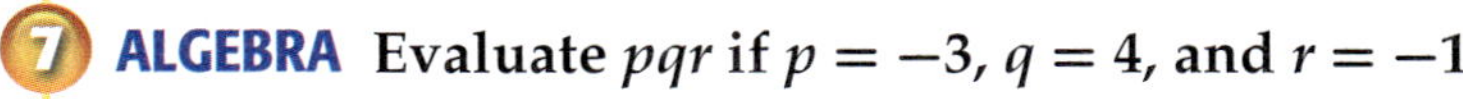

Negative numbers are often used when evaluating algebraic expressions.

EXAMPLE Evaluate Expressions

7 **ALGEBRA** **Evaluate pqr if $p = -3$, $q = 4$, and $r = -1$.**

$pqr = -3(4)(-1)$	Replace p with -3, q with 4, and r with -1.
$= (-12)(-1)$	Multiply -3 and 4.
$= 12$	Multiply -12 and -1.

CHECK Your Progress

g. Evaluate xyz if $x = -7$, $y = -4$, and $z = 2$.

CHECK Your Understanding

Examples 1, 2 (p. 107)

Multiply.

1. $6(-10)$
2. $11(-4)$
3. $-2(14)$
4. $-8(5)$

Examples 3–5 (p. 108)

Multiply.

5. $-15(-3)$
6. $-7(-9)$
7. $(-8)^2$
8. $(-3)^3$
9. $-1(-3)(-4)$
10. $2(4)(5)$

Example 6 (p. 109)

11. **MONEY** Tamera owns 100 shares of a certain stock. Suppose the price of the stock drops by $3 per share. Write a multiplication expression to find the change in Tamera's investment. Explain the answer.

Example 7 (p. 109)

ALGEBRA **Evaluate each expression if $f = -1$, $g = 7$, and $h = -10$.**

12. $5f$
13. fgh

Practice and Problem Solving

HOMEWORK HELP

For Exercises	See Examples
14–19, 28	1, 2
20–27, 29	3–5
30–37	7
38–39	6

Multiply.

14. $8(-12)$
15. $11(-20)$
16. $-15(4)$
17. $-7(10)$
18. $-7(11)$
19. $25(-2)$
20. $-20(-8)$
21. $-16(-5)$
22. $(-6)^2$
23. $(-5)^3$
24. $(-4)^3$
25. $(-9)^2$
26. $-4(-2)(-8)$
27. $-9(-1)(-5)$
28. Find the product of 10 and -10.
29. Find -7 squared.

ALGEBRA Evaluate each expression if $w = 4$, $x = -8$, $y = 5$, and $z = -3$.

30. $-4w$
31. $3x$
32. xy
33. xz
34. $7wz$
35. $-2wx$
36. xyz
37. wyx

Write a multiplication expression to represent each situation. Then find each product and explain its meaning.

38. **ECOLOGY** Wave erosion causes a certain coastline to recede at a rate of 3 centimeters each year. This occurs uninterrupted for a period of 8 years.

39. **EXERCISE** Ethan burns 650 Calories when he runs for 1 hour. Suppose he runs 5 hours in one week.

ALGEBRA Evaluate each expression if $a = -6$, $b = -4$, $c = 3$, and $d = 9$.

40. $-3a^2$
41. $-cd^2$
42. $-2a + b$
43. $b^2 - 4ac$

44. **BANKING** Tamika's aunt writes a check for $150 each month for her car loan. She writes another check for $300 twice a year to pay for car insurance. Write an expression involving multiplication and addition to describe how these expenses affect her checking account balance on a yearly basis. Then evaluate the expression and explain its meaning.

45. **FIND THE DATA** Refer to the Data File on pages 16–19 of your book. Choose some data and write a real-world problem in which you would multiply integers.

GEOMETRY For Exercises 46–48, use the graph at the right.

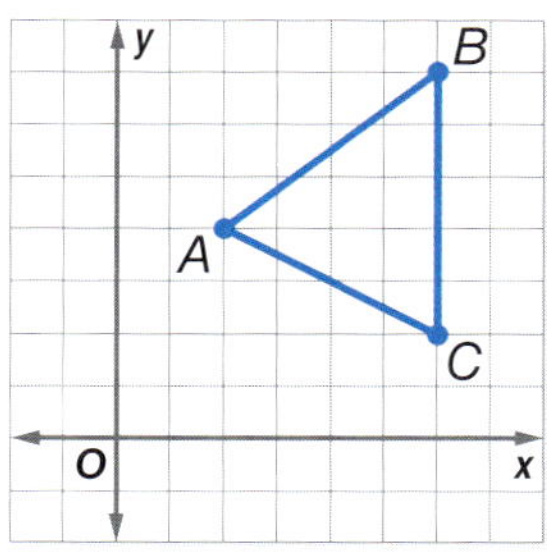

46. Name the ordered pairs for A, B, and C. Multiply each x- and y-coordinate by -1 to get three new ordered pairs.

47. Graph the ordered pairs and connect them to form a new triangle. Describe its position with respect to the original triangle.

48. In which quadrant would a new triangle lie if only the y-coordinates of the original triangle are multiplied by -1?

EXTRA PRACTICE

See pages 673, 705.

H.O.T. Problems

49. **OPEN ENDED** Write a multiplication sentence with a product of -18.

50. **NUMBER SENSE** Explain how to evaluate each expression as simply as possible.

    a. $(-9)(-6)(15)(-7 + 7)$ b. $(-15)(-26) + (-15)(25)$

51. **CHALLENGE** Evaluate $(-1)^{50}$. Explain your reasoning.

52. **SELECT A TECHNIQUE** Luis is trying to determine whether the product of three negative integers is negative or positive. Which of the following techniques might he use to determine the answer? Justify your selections. Then provide an example that illustrates the answer.

mental math	number sense	estimation

53. **WRITING IN MATH** Explain when the product of three integers is positive.

TEST PRACTICE

54. The temperature drops 2 degrees per hour for 3 hours. Which expression does *not* describe the change in temperature?

    A $-2(3)$

    B $-2 + (-2) + (-2)$

    C $-2 - 2 - 2$

    D $2(3)$

55. Which of the following numbers is the 7th number in the sequence shown?

    $1, -2, 4, -8, 16, \ldots$

    F -64

    G -32

    H 32

    J 64

Spiral Review

56. **TEMPERATURE** The highest and lowest recorded temperatures in Europe are 122°F and −67°F. Find the difference in these temperatures. (Lesson 2-5)

Subtract. (Lesson 2-5)

57. $-25 - (-33)$
58. $-6 - 14$
59. $9 - 30$
60. $13 - (-12)$

ALGEBRA Evaluate each expression if $x = -4$, $y = 6$, and $z = 1$. (Lesson 2-4)

61. $x + (-2)$
62. $-1 + z$
63. $-15 + y$
64. $x + y$

65. **PENGUINS** The Emperor penguin's average height is 51 inches, and the Adelie's average height is 18 inches. Write and solve an addition equation to find how much taller Emperor penguins are than Adelie penguins. (Lesson 1-7)

GET READY for the Next Lesson

66. **NUMBERS** A number is multiplied by −4. Then 15 is added to the product, and the result is 3. What is the number? Use the *guess and check* strategy. (Lesson 1-5)

Problem-Solving Investigation

MAIN IDEA: Solve problems by looking for a pattern.

P.S.I. TEAM +

e-Mail: LOOK FOR A PATTERN

LAURA: I've been practicing free throws every day after school to get ready for basketball tryouts. Now, I can make 3 free throws out of every 5 attempts I make.

YOUR MISSION: Look for a pattern to find the number of free throws Laura can make after 30 attempts.

Understand	Laura can make an average of 3 free throws out of every 5 attempts. You need to find the number of free throws she can make after 30 attempts.
Plan	Look for a pattern. Then extend the pattern to find the solution.
Solve	Laura can make 3 free throws out of every 5 she attempts. Extend the pattern.
Check	She makes free throws a little more than half the time. Since 18 is a little more than 15, the answer is reasonable. ✓

+3 +3 +3 +3 +3

Free throws	3	6	9	12	15	18
Attempts	5	10	15	20	25	30

+5 +5 +5 +5 +5

She can make 18 free throws out of 30 attempts.

Analyze The Strategy

1. Explain when you would use the *look for a pattern* strategy to solve a problem.
2. Describe how to solve a problem using the *look for a pattern* strategy.
3. WRITING IN MATH Write a problem that could be solved by looking for a pattern.

Mixed Problem Solving

EXTRA PRACTICE
See pages 673, 705.

Use the *look for a pattern* strategy to solve Exercises 4–6.

4. **DISPLAYS** A display of cereal boxes is stacked as shown below.

If the display contains 7 rows of boxes and the top three rows are shown, how many boxes are in the display?

5. **MONEY** Peter is saving money to buy an MP3 player. After one month, he has \$50. After 2 months, he has \$85. After 3 months, he has \$120. After 4 months, he has \$155. He plans to keep saving at the same rate. How long will it take Peter to save enough money to buy an MP3 player that costs \$295?

6. **INSECTS** The table shows how many times a cricket chirps at different temperatures. About how many times will a cricket chirp when the temperature is 60°F?

Outside Temperature (°F)	Chirps per Minute
85°F	180
80°F	160
75°F	140
70°F	120

Use any strategy to solve Exercises 7–14. Some strategies are shown below.

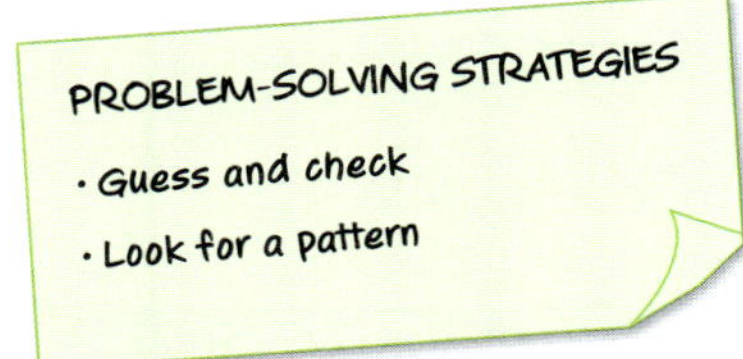

7. **COINS** Adelina has six coins that total \$0.86. What are the coins?

8. **ELEVATION** The lowest point in Mexico is Laguna Salada with an elevation of −10 meters. The highest point in Mexico is Volcan Pico de Orizaba with an elevation of 5,700 meters. What is the difference in these elevations?

9. **MONEY** While on vacation, Edmundo sent postcards and letters to his friends. He spent \$3.42 on postage. A stamp for a letter costs 41¢, and a stamp for a postcard costs 26¢. How many postcards and letters did he send?

10. **GEOMETRY** What is the next figure in the pattern shown?

11. **POPULATION** The total land area of North Carolina is about 48,711 square miles. If an average of 183 persons were living in each square mile of North Carolina in 2007, what was the population of North Carolina in 2007?

12. **GOLF** Allie's golf scores for the first five holes are given in the table. What is her total score after the first five holes?

Hole	Score
1	0
2	1
3	−1
4	−2
5	3

13. **FLOWERS** A sunflower grows to be about 252 centimeters tall in 3 months. What is the average rate of growth per month?

14. **NUMBERS** Determine the next three numbers in the pattern below.

48, 42, 36, 30, 24, …

2-8 Dividing Integers

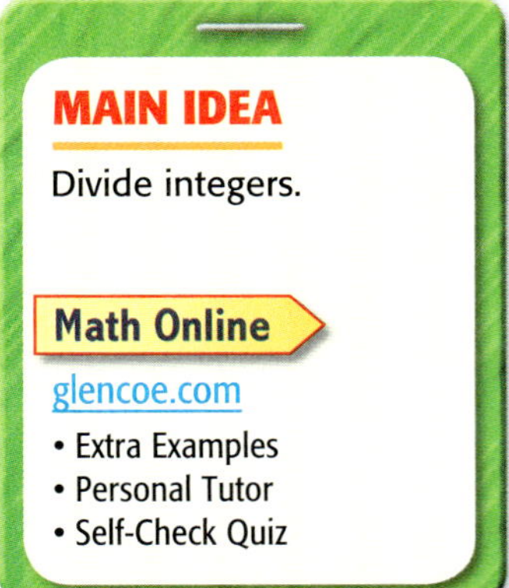

MINI Lab

You can use counters to model division of integers. Follow these steps to find $-8 \div 2$.

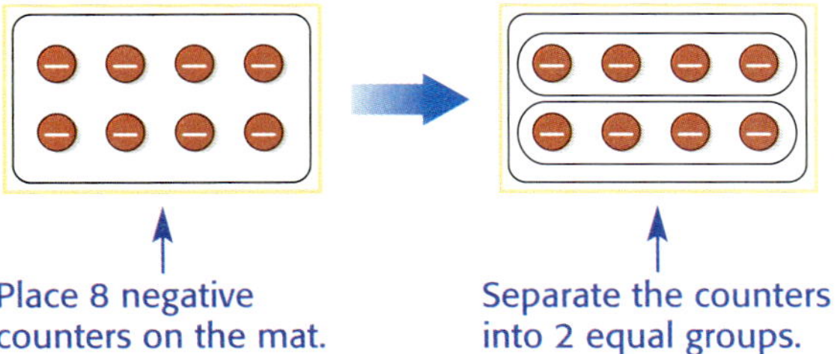

Place 8 negative counters on the mat.

Separate the counters into 2 equal groups.

There are 4 negative counters in each group. So, $-8 \div 2 = -4$.

Find each quotient using counters or a drawing.

1. $-6 \div 2$
2. $-12 \div 3$

Division of numbers is related to multiplication. When finding the quotient of two integers, you can use a related multiplication sentence.

The factor in the multiplication sentence ...

$2(6) = 12 \rightarrow 12 \div 2 = 6$

$4(5) = 20 \rightarrow 20 \div 4 = 5$

... is the quotient in the division sentence.

Since multiplication and division sentences are related, you can use them to find the quotient of integers with different signs.

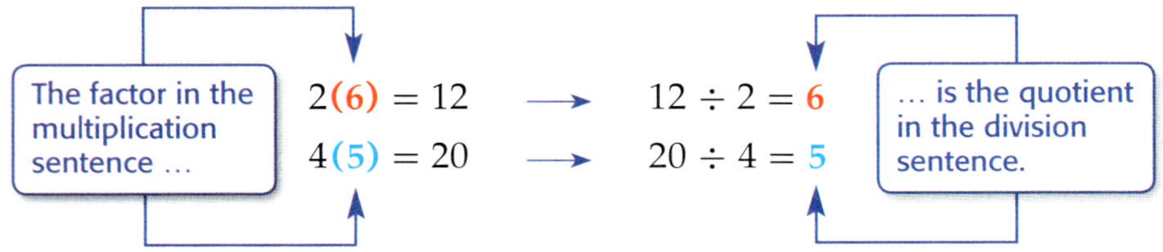

These related sentences lead to the following rule.

Dividing Integers with Different Signs — Key Concept

Words The quotient of two integers with different signs is negative.

Examples $33 \div (-11) = -3$ $\quad -64 \div 8 = -8$

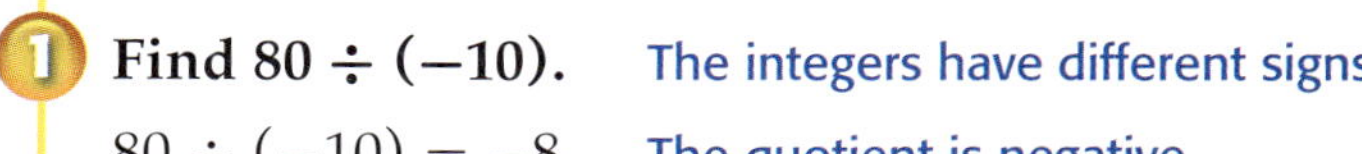

1 **Find $80 \div (-10)$.** The integers have different signs.

$80 \div (-10) = -8$ The quotient is negative.

2 **Find $\frac{-55}{11}$.** The integers have different signs.

$\frac{-55}{11} = -5$ The quotient is negative.

CHECK Your Progress

a. $20 \div (-4)$ b. $\frac{-81}{9}$ c. $-45 \div 9$

Study Tip

Dividing Integers Dividing integers with same or different signs follow the same rules as the ones for multiplication.

You can also use multiplication and division sentences to find the quotient of integers with the same sign.

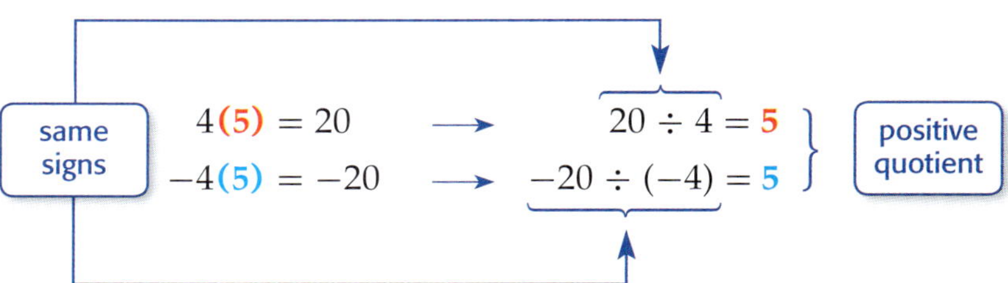

These related sentences lead to the following rule.

Divide Integers with the Same Sign

Key Concept

Words	The quotient of two integers with the same sign is positive.	
Examples	$15 \div 5 = 3$	$-64 \div (-8) = 8$

EXAMPLES Dividing Integers with the Same Sign

3 **Find $-14 \div (-7)$.** The integers have the same sign.

$-14 \div (-7) = 2$ The quotient is positive.

4 **ALGEBRA** **Evaluate $-16 \div x$ if $x = -4$.**

$-16 \div x = -16 \div (-4)$ Replace x with -4.

$= 4$ Divide. The quotient is positive.

CHECK Your Progress

d. $-24 \div (-4)$ e. $-9 \div (-3)$ f. $\frac{-28}{-7}$

g. **ALGEBRA** Evaluate $a \div b$ if $a = -9$ and $b = -3$.

Real-World Link
An adult koala is 25–30 inches long and weighs 15–30 pounds.
Source: Koala Express

Real-World EXAMPLE

5 **ANIMALS** **Ten years ago, the estimated Australian koala population was 1,000,000. Today there are about 100,000 koalas. Use the expression $\frac{N-P}{10}$, where N represents the new population and P the previous population to find the average change in the koala population per year for the 10-year period.**

$$\frac{N-P}{10} = \frac{100{,}000 - 1{,}000{,}000}{10}$$ Replace N with 100,000 and P with 1,000,000.

$$= \frac{-900{,}000}{10} \text{ or } -90{,}000$$ Divide.

The koala population has changed by $-90{,}000$ per year.

CHECK Your Progress

h. **WEATHER** The average temperature in January for North Pole, Alaska, is -24.4°C. Use the expression $\frac{9C + 160}{5}$, where C represents the number of degrees Celsius, to find this temperature in degrees Fahrenheit.

Operations with Integers

Concept Summary

Operation	Rule
Add	**Same Sign:** Add absolute values. The sum has the same sign as the integers. **Different Signs:** Subtract absolute values. The sum has the sign of the integer with greater absolute value.
Subtract	To subtract an integer, add its opposite.
Multiply and Divide	**Same Signs:** The product or quotient is positive. **Different Signs:** The product or quotient is negative.

CHECK Your Understanding

Examples 1–3 (p. 115)

Divide.

1. $32 \div (-8)$
2. $-16 \div 2$
3. $\frac{42}{-7}$
4. $-30 \div (-5)$
5. $55 \div 11$
6. $\frac{-16}{-4}$

Example 4 (p. 115)

ALGEBRA **Evaluate each expression if $x = 8$ and $y = -5$.**

7. $15 \div y$
8. $xy \div (-10)$

Example 5 (p. 116)

9. **TEMPERATURE** The lowest recorded temperature in Wisconsin is -55°F on February 4, 1996. Use the expression $\frac{5(F-32)}{9}$ to find this temperature in degrees Celsius. Round to the nearest tenth.

Practice and Problem Solving

HOMEWORK HELP	
For Exercises	See Examples
10–13, 16–19	1, 2
14–15, 20–23	3
24–31	4
32–33	5

Divide.

10. $50 \div (-5)$
11. $56 \div (-8)$
12. $-18 \div 9$
13. $-36 \div 4$
14. $-15 \div (-3)$
15. $-100 \div (-10)$
16. $\frac{22}{-2}$
17. $\frac{84}{-12}$
18. $\frac{-26}{13}$
19. $\frac{-27}{3}$
20. $\frac{-21}{-7}$
21. $\frac{-54}{-6}$
22. Divide -200 by -100.
23. Find the quotient of -65 and -13.

ALGEBRA **Evaluate each expression if $r = 12$, $s = -4$, and $t = -6$.**

24. $-12 \div r$
25. $72 \div t$
26. $r \div s$
27. $rs \div 16$
28. $\frac{t - r}{3}$
29. $\frac{8 - r}{-2}$
30. $\frac{s + t}{5}$
31. $\frac{t + 9}{-3}$

32. **MONEY** Last year, Mr. Engle's total income was \$52,000, while his total expenses were \$53,800. Use the expression $\frac{I - E}{12}$, where I represents total income and E represents total expenses, to find the average difference between his income and expenses each month.

33. **SCIENCE** The boiling point of water is affected by changes in elevation. Use the expression $\frac{-2A}{1,000}$, where A represents the altitude in feet, to find the number of degrees Fahrenheit the boiling point of water changes at an altitude of 5,000 feet.

ALGEBRA **Evaluate each expression if $d = -9$, $f = 36$, and $g = -6$.**

34. $\frac{-f}{d}$
35. $\frac{12 - (-f)}{-g}$
36. $\frac{f^2}{d^2}$
37. $g^2 \div f$

38. **PLANETS** The temperature on Mars ranges widely from -207°F at the winter pole to almost 80°F on the dayside during the summer. Use the expression $\frac{-207 + 80}{2}$ to find the average of the temperature extremes on Mars.

39. **ANALYZE GRAPHS** The *mean* of a set of data is the sum of the data divided by the number of items in the data set. The graph shows the approximate depths where certain fish are found in the Caribbean. What is the mean depth of the fish shown?

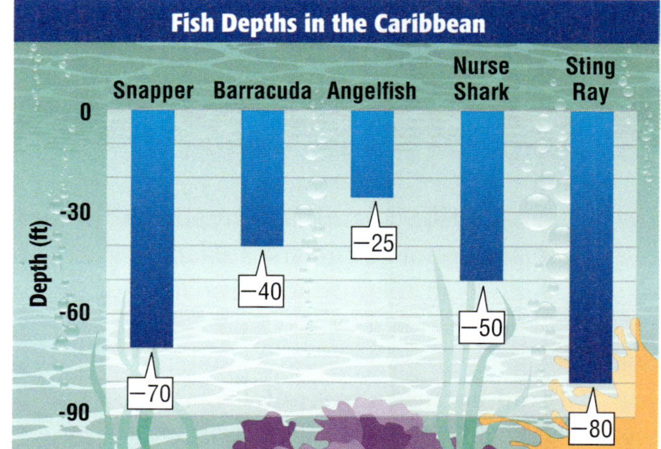

EXTRA PRACTICE
See pages 673, 705.

H.O.T. Problems

40. **OPEN ENDED** Write a division sentence with a quotient of -12.

41. **Which One Doesn't Belong?** Identify the expression that does not belong with the other three. Explain your reasoning.

$-66 \div 11$	$-32 \div (-4)$	$16 \div (-4)$	$-48 \div 4$

42. **PATTERNS** Find the next two numbers in the pattern 729, -243, 81, -27, 9, … . Explain your reasoning.

43. **CHALLENGE** Order from least to greatest all of the numbers by which -20 is divisible.

44. **WRITING IN MATH** Evaluate $-2 \cdot (2^2 + 2) \div 2^2$. Justify each step in the process.

TEST PRACTICE

45. Find $18 \div (-3)$.

A -6

B $\frac{-1}{6}$

C 6

D 15

46. On December 24, 1924, the temperature in Fairfield, Montana, fell from 63°F at noon to -21°F at midnight. What was the average temperature change per hour?

F -3.5°F

G -7°F

H -42°F

J -84°F

Spiral Review

47. **GEOMETRY** What is the next figure in the pattern shown at the right? (Lesson 2-7)

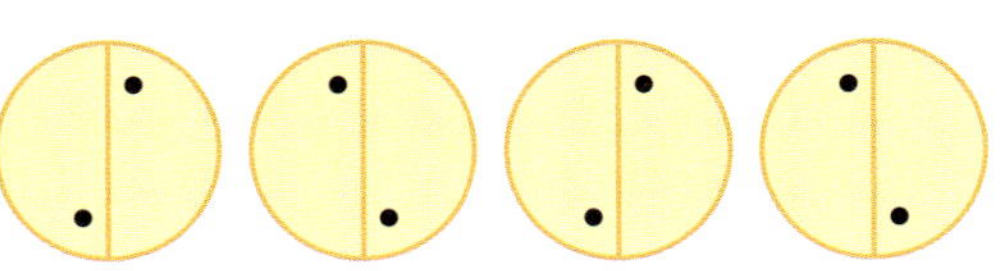

Multiply. (Lesson 2-6)

48. $14(-2)$

49. $-20(-3)$

50. $-5(7)$

51. $(-9)^2$

52. Find $6 - (-12)$. (Lesson 2-5)

53. **DIVING** Valentina jumped into 10 feet of water and touched the bottom of the pool before she surfaced. Write an integer to describe where Valentina was in relation to the surface of the water when she touched the bottom of the pool. (Lesson 2-1)

Find each square root. (Lesson 1-3)

54. $\sqrt{324}$

55. $\sqrt{900}$

56. $\sqrt{196}$

CHAPTER 2

Study Guide and Review

Math Online glencoe.com

- STUDY TO GO
- Vocabulary Review

FOLDABLES® Study Organizer

GET READY to Study

Be sure the following Big Ideas are noted in your Foldable.

BIG Ideas

Absolute Value (Lesson 2-1)

- The absolute value of a number is the distance the number is from zero on a number line.

Comparing and Ordering Integers (Lesson 2-2)

- When two numbers are graphed on a number line, the number to the left is always less than the number to the right.

Graphing Points (Lesson 2-3)

- On a coordinate plane, the horizontal number line is the x-axis and the vertical number line is the y-axis. The origin is at (0, 0) and is the point where the number lines intersect. The x-axis and y-axis separate the plane into four quadrants.

Integer Operations (Lessons 2-4, 2-5, 2-6, 2-8)

- To add integers with the same sign, add their absolute value. The sum is positive if both integers are positive and negative if both integers are negative.
- The sum of any number and its additive inverse is 0.
- To add integers with different signs, subtract their absolute values. The sum is positive if the positive integer's absolute value is greater and negative if the negative integer's absolute value is greater.
- To subtract an integer, add its opposite.
- The product or quotient of two integers with different signs is negative.
- The product or quotient of two integers with the same sign is positive.

Key Vocabulary

absolute value (p. 81)
additive inverse (p. 96)
coordinate plane (p. 88)
graph (p. 80)
integer (p. 80)
negative integer (p. 80)
opposites (p. 96)
ordered pair (p. 88)
origin (p. 88)
positive integer (p. 80)
quadrant (p. 88)
x-axis (p. 88)
x-coordinate (p. 88)
y-axis (p. 88)
y-coordinate (p. 88)

Vocabulary Check

State whether each sentence is *true* or *false*. If *false*, replace the underlined word or number to make a true sentence.

1. Integers less than zero are positive integers.
2. The origin is the point where the x-axis and y-axis intersect.
3. The absolute value of 7 is −7.
4. The sum of two negative integers is positive.
5. The x-coordinate of the ordered pair (2, −3) is −3.
6. Two integers that are opposites are also called additive inverses.
7. The product of a positive and a negative integer is negative.
8. The x-axis and the y-axis separate the plane into four coordinates.
9. The quotient of two negative integers is negative.

Study Guide and Review

Lesson-by-Lesson Review

2-1 Integers and Absolute Value (pp. 80–83)

Write an integer for each situation.

10. a loss of \$150
11. 350 feet above sea level
12. a gain of 8 yards
13. 12°F below 0

Evaluate each expression.

14. $|100|$
15. $|-32|$
16. $|-16| + |9|$
17. **JUICE** Mavis drank 48 milliliters of apple juice before replacing the carton in the refrigerator. Write an integer that shows the change in the volume of juice in the carton.

Example 1 **Write an integer for 8 feet below sea level.**

Since this situation represents an elevation *below* sea level, −8 represents the situation.

Example 2 **Evaluate $|-10|$.**

On the number line, the graph of −10 is 10 units from 0.

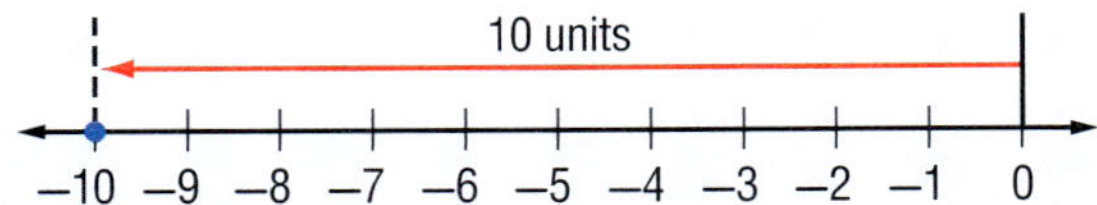

So, $|-10| = 10$.

2-2 Comparing and Ordering Integers (pp. 84–87)

Replace each ● with $<$ or $>$ to make a true sentence.

18. −3 ● −9
19. 8 ● −12
20. −3 ● 3
21. $|-10|$ ● $|-13|$
22. 25 ● $|8|$
23. 0 ● $|-4|$

Order each set of integers from least to greatest.

24. $\{-3, 8, -10, 0, 5, -12, 9\}$
25. $\{-21, 19, -23, 14, -32, 25\}$
26. $\{-17, -18, 18, 15, -16, 16\}$
27. **WEATHER** The high temperatures in degrees Celsius for ten cities were 0, 10, −5, 12, 25, −6, 20, −10, 5 and 2. Order these temperatures from least to greatest.

Example 3 **Replace ● with $<$ or $>$ to make −4 ● −7 a true sentence.**

Graph each integer on a number line.

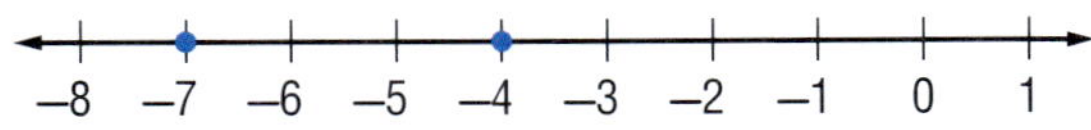

Since −4 is to the right of −7, $-4 > -7$.

Example 4 **Order the integers −4, −3, 5, 3, 0, −2 from least to greatest.**

Graph the integers on a number line.

Order the integers by reading from left to right: −4, −3, −2, 0, 3, 5.

Mixed Problem Solving
For mixed problem-solving practice, see page 705.

2-3 The Coordinate Plane (pp. 88–92)

On graph paper, draw a coordinate plane. Then graph and label each point.

28. $E(1, -4)$
29. $F(-4, 2)$
30. $G(-2, -3)$
31. $H(4, 0)$

32. **ROUTES** Starting at the school, Pilar walked 1 block east and 3 blocks south. From there, she walked 5 blocks west and 4 blocks north to the park. If the school represents the origin, what is the ordered pair for the park?

Example 5 Graph and label the point $S(3, -1)$.

Draw a coordinate plane. Move 3 units to the right. Then move 1 unit down. Draw a dot and label it $S(3, -1)$.

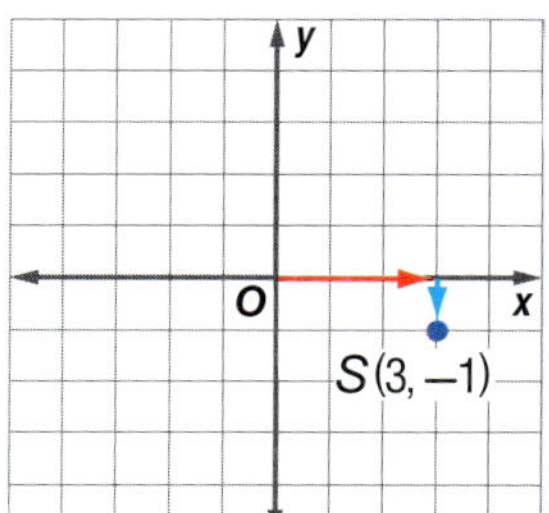

2-4 Adding Integers (pp. 95–99)

Add.

33. $-6 + 8$
34. $-4 + (-9)$
35. $7 + (-12)$
36. $-18 + 18$

37. **HIKING** Samuel hiked 75 feet up a mountain. He then hiked 22 feet higher. Then, he descended 8 feet, and finally climbed up another 34 feet. What is Samuel's final elevation?

Example 6 Find $-4 + 3$.

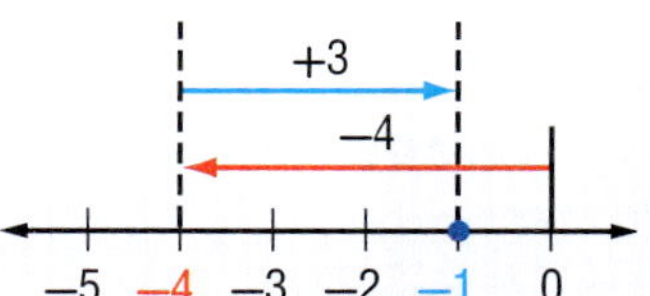

So, $-4 + 3 = -1$.

2-5 Subtracting Integers (pp. 103–106)

Subtract.

38. $-5 - 8$
39. $3 - 6$
40. $5 - (-2)$
41. $-4 - (-8)$

42. **GOLF** Owen shot 2 under par while his friend Nathan shot 3 above par. By how many shots was Owen's score better than Nathan's?

Example 7 Find $-3 - 9$.

$-3 - 9 = -3 + (-9)$ To subtract 9, add -9.

$= -12$ Simplify.

CHAPTER 2 Study Guide and Review

2-6 Multiplying Integers (pp. 107–111)

Multiply.

43. $-4(3)$
44. $8(-6)$
45. $-5(-7)$
46. $-2(40)$

ALGEBRA Evaluate each expression if $a = -4$, $b = -7$, and $c = 5$.

47. ab
48. $-3c$
49. bc
50. abc

Example 8 Find $-5(3)$.

$-5(3) = -15$ The integers have different signs. The product is negative.

Example 9 Evaluate xyz if $x = -6$, $y = 11$, and $z = -10$.

xyz

$= (-6)(11)(-10)$ $x = -6, y = 11, z = -10.$

$= (-66)(-10)$ Multiply -6 and 11.

$= 660$ Multiply -66 and -10.

2-7 PSI: Look for a Pattern (pp. 112–113)

Solve. Look for a pattern.

51. **HEALTH** The average person blinks 12 times per minute. At this rate, how many times does the average person blink in one day?

52. **SALARY** Suki gets a job that pays \$31,000 per year. She is promised a \$2,200 raise each year. At this rate, what will her salary be in 7 years?

53. **DOGS** A kennel determined that they need 144 feet of fencing to board 2 dogs, 216 feet to board 3 dogs, and 288 feet to board 4 dogs. If this pattern continues, how many feet of fencing is needed to board 8 dogs?

Example 10 **A theater has 18 seats in the first row, 24 seats in the second row, 30 seats in the third row, and so on. If this pattern continues, how many seats are in the sixth row?**

Begin with 18 seats and add 6 seats for each additional row.

So, there are 48 seats in the sixth row.

Row	Number of Seats
1	18
2	24
3	30
4	36
5	42
6	48

2-8 Dividing Integers (pp. 114–118)

Divide.

54. $-45 \div (-9)$
55. $36 \div (-12)$
56. $-12 \div 6$
57. $-81 \div (-9)$

Example 11 Find $-72 \div (-9)$.

$-72 \div (-9) = 8$ The integers have the same sign. The quotient is positive.

Chapter 2 Practice Test

Math Online glencoe.com
• Chapter Test

1. **WEATHER** Adam is recording the change in the outside air temperature for a science project. At 8:00 A.M., the high temperature was 42°F. By noon, the outside temperature had fallen 11°F. By mid-afternoon, the outside air temperature had fallen 12°F and by evening, it had fallen an additional 5°F. Write an integer that describes the final change in temperature.

Evaluate each expression.

2. $|-3|$
3. $|-18| - |6|$

Replace each ● with <, >, or = to make a true sentence.

4. -3 ● -9
5. $|9|$ ● $|-12|$
6. The Iowa Hawkeyes recorded the following yardage in six plays: 9, –2, 5, 0, 12, and –7. Order these integers from least to greatest.

7. **MULTIPLE CHOICE** Which of the following coordinates lie within the rectangle graphed below?

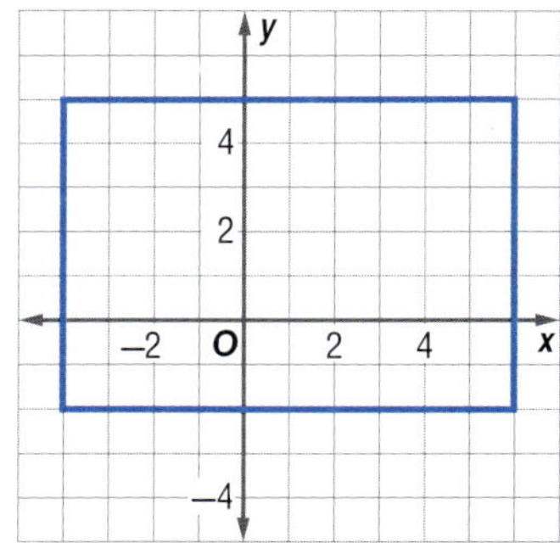

A (5, 6) C (–5, 1)
B (0, –3) D (–3, 0)

8. **DEBT** Amanda owes her brother \$24. If she plans to pay him back an equal amount from her piggy bank each day for six days, describe the change in the amount of money in her piggy bank each day.

Write the ordered pair for each point graphed. Then name the quadrant in which each point is located.

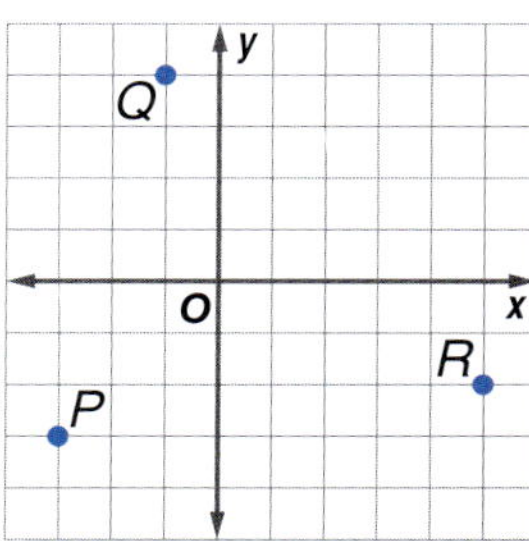

9. P
10. Q
11. R

Add, subtract, multiply, or divide.

12. $12 + (-9)$
13. $-3 - 4$
14. $-7 - (-20)$
15. $-7(-3)$
16. $5(-11)$
17. $-36 \div (-9)$
18. $-15 + (-7)$
19. $8 + (-6) + (-4)$
20. $-9 - 7$
21. $-13 + 7$

22. **MULTIPLE CHOICE** Kendrick created a 6-week schedule for practicing the piano. If the pattern continues, how many hours will he practice during the sixth week?

The table shows the number of hours he practiced in the first three weeks.

Week	1	2	3
Hours	4	7	10

F 15 hours H 19 hours
G 18 hours J 22 hours

Evaluate each expression if $a = -5$, $b = 4$, and $c = -12$.

23. $ac \div b$
24. $\frac{a - b}{3}$

25. **STOCKS** The value of a stock decreased \$4 each week for a period of six weeks. Describe the change in the value of the stock at the end of the six-week period.

CHAPTER 2

Test Practice
Cumulative, Chapters 1–2

Math Online glencoe.com

• Test Practice

PART 1 Multiple Choice

Read each question. Then fill in the correct answer on the answer document provided by your teacher or on a sheet of paper.

1. The daily low temperatures for Cleveland, Ohio, over the last five days were 15°F, −2°F, 8°F, −6°F, and 5°F. Which expression can be used to find the average daily low temperature during the last five days?

   A $(15 + 2 + 8 + 6 + 5) \div 5$

   B $15 + 2 + 8 + 6 + 5 \div 5$

   C $[15 + (-2) + 8 + (-6) + 5] \div 5$

   D $15 + (-2) + 8 + (-6) + 5 \div 5$

TEST-TAKING TIP

Question 1 Check every answer choice of a multiple-choice question. Each time you find an incorrect answer, cross it off so you remember that you've eliminated it.

2. Marcia runs r miles on Mondays, Tuesdays, and Thursdays. She bicycles for b miles on Wednesday and Saturdays. If she rests on Fridays and Sundays, which equation represents the total number of miles M she exercises each week?

   F $M = 3r + 2b$

   G $M = r + b$

   H $M = 2r + 3b$

   J $M = 5(r + b)$

3. Simplify the expression below.

$$3 + 6(10 - 7) - 3^2$$

   A 0

   B 12

   C 18

   D 74

4. At 8 A.M., the temperature was 13°F below zero. By 1 P.M., the temperature rose 22°F and by 6 P.M. dropped 14°F. What was the temperature at 6 P.M.?

   F 5°F above zero

   G 5°F below zero

   H 21°F above zero

   J 21°F below zero

5. Sue typically spends between $175 and $250 each month on clothes. Which of the following is the best estimate for the amount she spends in 6 months?

   A From $600 to $1,200

   B From $900 to $1,300

   C From $1,050 to $1,500

   D From $1,200 to $1,500

6. On their first play, a football team gained 17 yards. On their next play, they lost 22 yards. On their third play, they gained 14 yards. Which expression represents the total number of yards gained after the third play?

   F $17 + (-22) + 14$

   G $17 + 22 + (-14)$

   H $-17 + (-22) + (-14)$

   J $-17 + 22 + 14$

7. The top four runners of a race were Alicia, Kyle, Drew, and Juanita. Drew finished before Juanita. Alicia finished after both boys, but before Juanita. What information is needed to determine the order of the runners from first to fourth?

   A Did Kyle finish before or after Drew?

   B Did Alicia finish before or after Juanita?

   C Did Drew finish before or after Alicia?

   D Did Kyle finish before or after Alicia?

Preparing for Standardized Tests

For test-taking strategies and practice, see pages 716–733.

8. The lowest point in Japan is Hachiro-gata (elevation −4 meters), and the highest point is Mount Fuji (elevation 3,776 meters). What is the difference in elevation between Mount Fuji and Hachiro-gata?

   F 3,780 meters

   G 3,772 meters

   H 3,080 meters

   J 944 meters

9. Which of the following relationships is best represented by the data in the table?

x	y
1	36
2	72
3	108
4	144
5	180

   A Conversion of feet to inches

   B Conversion of inches to yards

   C Conversion of feet to yards

   D Conversion of yards to inches

10. A storeowner has n employees and pays each employee \$440 per week. If the owner also pays \$$d$ weekly to rent the building and \$$w$ for utilities, which equation below represents the total E of these weekly expenses?

   F $E = 440w + n + w$

   G $E = 440n + dw$

   H $E = 440n + d + w$

   J $E = 440(n + d + w)$

PART 2 Short Response/Grid In

Record your answers on the answer sheet provided by your teacher or on a sheet of paper.

11. Nick spends a total of 75 hours per week at work and at the gym. He goes to the gym from 6:45 A.M. to 8:45 A.M., Monday through Friday. Write an equation that can be used to find t, the maximum number of hours Nick works at his job each week.

12. Find $-8 - 17$.

PART 3 Extended Response

Record your answers on the answer sheet provided by your teacher or a sheet of paper. Show your work.

13. A rectangle and a square are graphed on a coordinate plane. Use the graph below to answer the questions.

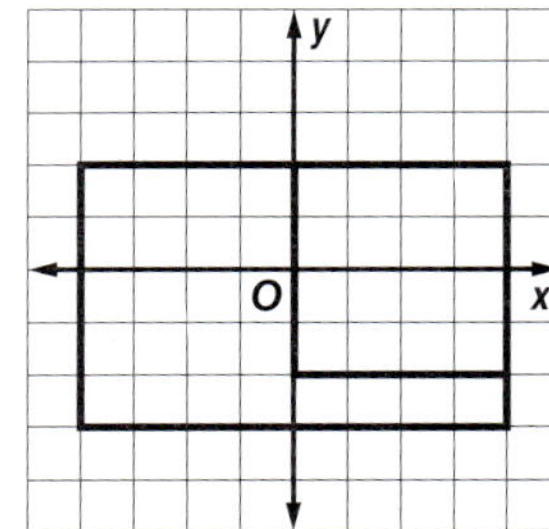

   a. Pick an ordered pair both objects have in common.

   b. Find an ordered pair that is inside the rectangle, but not the square.

   c. How could you increase the size of the square so that it still lies within the rectangle? What are the four coordinates?

   d. Draw a graph with the new square inside the rectangle.

NEED EXTRA HELP?													
If You Missed Question...	1	2	3	4	5	6	7	8	9	10	11	12	13
Go to Lesson...	1-6	1-7	1-4	2-4	1-1	2-4	1-1	2-5	2-7	1-6	1-7	2-5	2-3

Algebra: Linear Equations and Functions

BIG Idea

- Solve linear equations in one variable.

Key Vocabulary

formula (p. 144)
linear equation (p. 164)
two-step equation (p. 151)
work backward strategy (p. 148)

Segways The Segway's top speed is 12.5 miles per hour–two to three times faster than walking. You can use the equation $d = 12.5t$ to find the distance d you can travel in t hours.

FOLDABLES® Study Organizer

Algebra: Linear Equations and Functions Make this Foldable to help you organize your notes. Begin with a sheet of 11″ by 17″ paper.

1. **Fold** the short sides toward the middle.

2. **Fold** the top to the bottom.

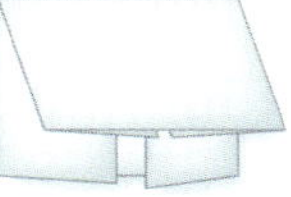

3. **Open.** Cut along the second fold to make four tabs.

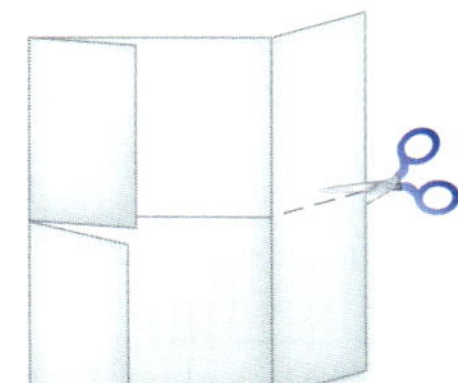

4. **Label** each of the tabs as shown.

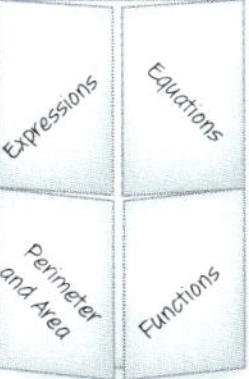

GET READY for Chapter 3

Diagnose Readiness You have two options for checking Prerequisite Skills.

Option 2

Math Online Take the Online Readiness Quiz at glencoe.com.

Option 1

Take the Quick Quiz below. Refer to the Quick Review for help.

QUICK Quiz

Name the number that is the solution of the given equation. (Lesson 1-6)

1. $a + 15 = 19$; 4, 5, 6
2. $11k = 77$; 6, 7, 8
3. $x + 9 = -2$; 7, −11, 11

Graph each point on a coordinate plane. (Lesson 2-3)

4. $(-4, 3)$
5. $(-2, -1)$
6. **HIKING** Keith hiked 4 miles north and 2 miles west from the campground before he rested. If the origin represents the campground, graph Keith's resting point. (Lesson 2-3)

Add. (Lesson 2-4)

7. $-3 + (-5)$
8. $-8 + 3$
9. $9 + (-5)$
10. $-10 + 15$

Subtract. (Lesson 2-5)

11. $-5 - 6$
12. $8 - 10$
13. $8 - (-6)$
14. $-3 - (-1)$

Divide. (Lesson 2-8)

15. $-6 \div (-3)$
16. $-12 \div 3$
17. $10 \div (-5)$
18. $-24 \div (-4)$

QUICK Review

Example 1 Name the number that is the solution of $24 \div a = 3$; 7, 8, or 9.

$24 \div a = 3$ Write the equation.
$24 \div 7 = 3$? No. Substitute $a = 7$.
$24 \div 8 = 3$? Yes. Substitute $a = 8$.
$24 \div 9 = 3$? No. Substitute $a = 9$.

Example 2 Graph the point $(-1, 3)$ on a coordinate plane.

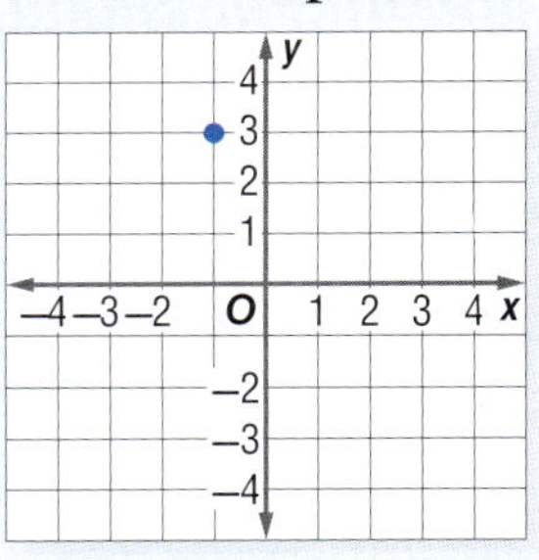

The first number in an ordered pair tells you to move left or right from the origin. The second number tells you to move up or down.

Example 3 Find $-4 + (-2)$.

$-4 + (-2) = -6$ Since −4 and −2 are both negative, add their absolute values. The sum is negative also.

Example 4 Find $9 - (-7)$.

$9 - (-7) = 9 + (7)$ Subtracting −7 is the same as adding 7.
$= 16$ Add.

Example 5 Find $-16 \div 2$.

$-16 \div 2 = -8$ Since −16 and 2 have opposite signs, their quotient is negative.

3-1 Writing Expressions and Equations

MAIN IDEA

Write verbal phrases and sentences as simple algebraic expressions and equations.

Math Online

glencoe.com

- Extra Examples
- Personal Tutor
- Self-Check Quiz

GET READY for the Lesson

PLANETS Earth has only one moon, but other planets have many moons. For example, Uranus has 21 moons, and Saturn has 10 more moons than Uranus.

1. What operation would you use to find how many moons Saturn has? Explain.
2. Jupiter has about three times as many moons as Uranus. What operation would you use to find how many moons Jupiter has?

Words and phrases in problems often suggest addition, subtraction, multiplication, and division. Here are some examples.

Addition and Subtraction		Multiplication and Division	
sum	difference	each	divide
more than	less than	product	quotient
increased by	less	multiplied	per
in all	decreased by	twice	separate

EXAMPLE Write a Phrase as an Expression

1 **Write the phrase *five dollars more than Jennifer earned* as an algebraic expression.**

Words	five dollars more than Jennifer earned.
Variable	Let d represent the number of dollars Jennifer earned.
Expression	$d + 5$

CHECK Your Progress

Write the phrase as an algebraic expression.

a. 3 more runs than the Pirates scored

Remember, an equation is a sentence in mathematics that contains an equals sign. When you write a verbal sentence as an equation, you can use the equals sign (=) for the words *equals* or *is*.

EXAMPLES Write Sentences as Equations

Write each sentence as an algebraic equation.

2 Six less than a number is 20.

Six less than a number is 20.

Let n represent the number.

$n - 6 = 20$

3 Three times Jack's age equals 12.

Three times Jack's age equals 12.

Let a represent Jack's age.

$3a = 12$

Reading Math

Less Than You can write *six more than a number* as either $6 + n$ or $n + 6$. But *six less than a number* can only be written as $n - 6$.

CHECK Your Progress

Write each sentence as an algebraic equation.

b. Seven more than a number is 15.

c. Five times the number of students is 250.

Real-World Link

The tallest waterfall in South Carolina is Raven Cliff Falls, located in Caesars Head State Park.

Source: South Carolina Department of Parks, Recreation, and Tourism

Real-World EXAMPLE

4 WATERFALLS The tallest waterfall in the United States is Yosemite Falls in California with a height of about 739 meters. This height is 617 meters taller than Raven Cliff Falls. What is the height of Raven Cliff Falls? Write an equation that models this situation.

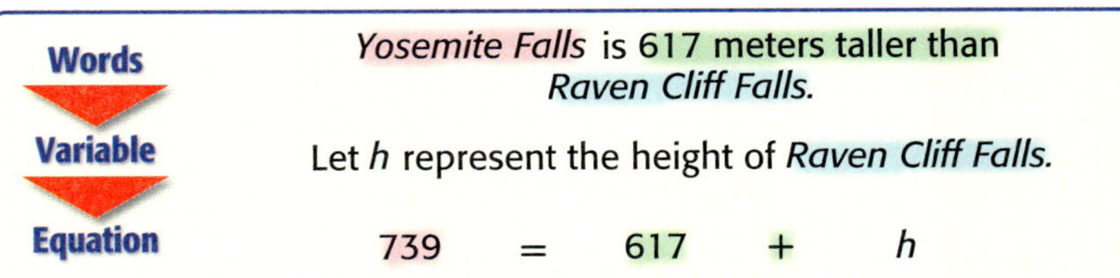

Words	*Yosemite Falls* is 617 meters taller than *Raven Cliff Falls.*
Variable	Let h represent the height of *Raven Cliff Falls.*
Equation	$739 \quad = \quad 617 \quad + \quad h$

The equation is $739 = 617 + h$.

CHECK Your Progress

d. **ANIMALS** North American cougars are about 1.5 times as long as cougars found in the tropical jungles of Central America. If North American cougars are about 75 inches long, how long is the tropical cougar? Write an equation that models this situation.

TEST EXAMPLE

5 Which problem situation matches the equation $x - 5.83 = 3.17$?

A Tyler ran 3.17 kilometers. His friend ran the same distance 5.83 seconds faster than Tyler. What is x, the time in seconds that Tyler ran?

B Lynn and Heather measured the length of worms in science class. Lynn's worm was 5.83 centimeters long, and Heather's worm was 3.17 centimeters long. What is x, the average length of the worms?

C Keisha's lunch cost \$5.83. She received \$3.17 in change when she paid the bill. What is x, the amount of money she gave the cashier?

D Mr. Carlos paid \$3.17 for a notebook that originally cost \$5.83. What is x, the amount of money that Mr. Carlos saved?

Test-Taking Tip

Vocabulary Terms Before taking a standardized test, review the meaning of vocabulary terms such as *average*.

Read the Item

You need to find which problem situation matches the equation $x - 5.83 = 3.17$.

Solve the Item

- You can eliminate A because you cannot add or subtract different units of measure.
- You can eliminate B because to find an average you add and then divide.
- Act out C. If you gave the cashier x dollars and your lunch cost \$5.83, you would subtract to find your change, \$3.17. This is the correct answer.
- Check D, just to be sure. To find the amount Mr. Carlos saved, you would calculate $5.83 - 3.17$, not $x - 5.83$.

The solution is C.

CHECK Your Progress

e. **Which problem situation matches the equation $4y = 6.76$?**

F Mrs. Thomas bought 4 gallons of gas. Her total cost was \$6.76. What is y, the cost of one gallon of gas?

G Jordan bought 4 CDs that were on sale for \$6.76 each. What is y, the total cost of the CDs?

H The width of a rectangle is 4 meters. The length is 6.76 meters more than the width. What is y, the length of the rectangle?

J The average yearly rainfall is 6.76 inches. What is y, the amount of rainfall you might expect in 4 years?

Example 1 (p. 128)

Write each phrase as an algebraic expression.

1. a number increased by eight
2. ten dollars more than Grace has

Examples 2, 3 (p. 129)

Write each sentence as an algebraic equation.

3. Nine less than a number equals 24.
4. Two points less than his score is 4.
5. Twice the number of miles is 18.
6. One half the regular price is $13.

Example 4 (p. 129)

7. **ALGEBRA** The median age of people living in Arizona is 1 year younger than the median age of people living in the United States. Use this information and the information at the right to write an equation to find the median age in the United States.

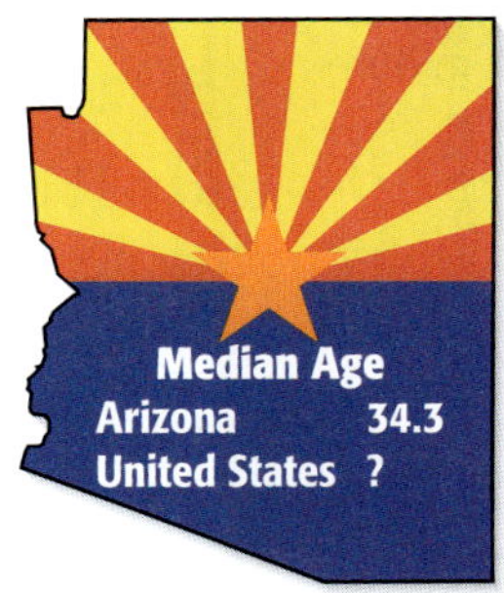

Example 5 (p. 130)

8. **MULTIPLE CHOICE** Which problem situation matches the equation $x - 15 = 46$?

   A The original price of a jacket is $46. The sale price is $15 less. What is x, the sale price of the jacket?

   B Mark had several baseball cards. He sold 15 of the cards and had 46 left. What is x, the amount of cards Mark had to start with?

   C Sonja scored 46 points in last week's basketball game. Talisa scored 15 points less. What is x, the amount of points Talisa scored?

   D Katie earned $15 babysitting this week. Last week she earned $46. What is x, her average earnings for the two weeks?

Practice and Problem Solving

HOMEWORK HELP

For Exercises	See Examples
9–16	1
17–22	2, 3
23–24	4
41	5

Write each phrase as an algebraic expression.

9. fifteen increased by t
10. five years older than Luis
11. a number decreased by ten
12. three feet less than the length
13. the product of r and 8
14. twice as many oranges
15. Emily's age divided by 3
16. the quotient of a number and -12

Write each sentence as an algebraic equation.

17. The sum of a number and four is equal to -8.
18. Two more than the number of frogs is 4.
19. The product of a number and five is -20.
20. Ten times the number of students is 280.
21. Ten inches less than her height is 26.
22. Five less than a number is 31.

Real-World Link A giraffe's heart can pump 16 gallons of blood in one minute.
Source: Woodland Park Zoo

For Exercises 23 and 24, write an equation that models each situation.

23. **ANIMALS** A giraffe is 3.5 meters taller than a camel. If a giraffe is 5.5 meters tall, how tall is a camel?

24. **FOOTBALL** Carson Palmer led the National Football League with 32 touchdown passes in a season. This was twice as many touchdown passes as Donovan McNabb had. Find the number of touchdown passes for McNabb.

MEASUREMENT For Exercises 25–28, describe the relationship that exists between the length and width of each rectangle.

25. The width is x, and the length is $4x$.
26. The length is $x + 3$, and the width is x.
27. The length is x, and the width is $x - 5$.
28. The length is x, and the width is $0.5x$.

Write each phrase as an algebraic expression.

29. 2 more than twice as many bikes
30. nine CDs less than three times the number of CDs Margaret owns
31. 43 dollars off the price of each admission, which is then multiplied by 3 admissions
32. the quotient of a number w and (-8), which is then increased by 7
33. the square of a number k which is then multiplied by 13
34. the sum of a number p and 0.4 which is then decreased by the fifth power of the same number

ANALYZE TABLES For Exercises 35 and 36, use the table.

The table shows the average lifespan of several types of pets. Let y represent the average lifespan of a gerbil.

35. Which lifespan can be represented by $3y$?
36. Write an expression to represent the lifespan of a cat.

Pets	
Type	**Lifespan (years)**
American toad	15
cat	25
dog	22
gerbil	5
rabbit	9

See pages 674, 706.

H.O.T. Problems

37. **OPEN ENDED** Write a verbal sentence for the equation $n - 3 = 6$.

38. **FIND THE ERROR** Sancho and Candace are writing an algebraic expression for the phrase *5 less than a number*. Who is correct? Explain.

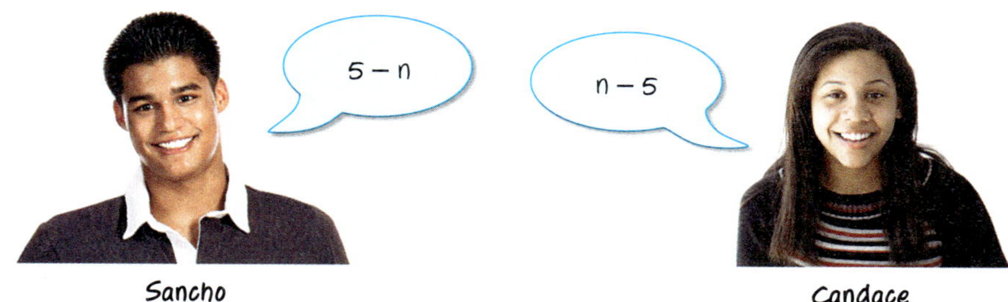

39. **CHALLENGE** If x is an odd number, how would you represent the odd number immediately following it? preceding it?

40. **WRITING IN MATH** Analyze the meaning of the expressions $a + 5$, $a - 3$, $2a$, and $\frac{a}{2}$ if a represents someone's age.

TEST PRACTICE

41. Asha had some change in her purse. After her brother gave her \$0.79, Asha had \$2.24 altogether. Which equation can she use to find the original amount of money m she had in her purse?

A $2.24 = m - 0.79$

B $m = 2.24 \times 0.79$

C $m + 0.79 = 2.24$

D $m + 2.24 = 0.79$

42. Which algebraic equation best describes the total distance D traveled in miles after a 6-hour period, if r represents the rate of travel in miles per hour?

F $D = 6 + r$

G $D = \frac{r}{6}$

H $D = 6r$

J $D = \frac{6}{r}$

Spiral Review

Divide (Lesson 2-8)

43. $-42 \div 6$

44. $36 \div (-3)$

45. $-45 \div (-3)$

46. **MONEY** Jordan withdraws \$14 per week from his savings account for a period of 7 weeks. Write a multiplication expression to represent this situation. Then find the product and explain its meaning. (Lesson 2-7)

Evaluate each expression. (Lesson 1-4)

47. $3 + 7 \cdot 4 - 6$

48. $8(16 - 5) - 6$

49. $75 \div 3 + 6(5 - 1)$

ANALYZE DATA **For Exercises 50–52, use the table that shows the cost of two different plans for downloading music.** (Lesson 1-1)

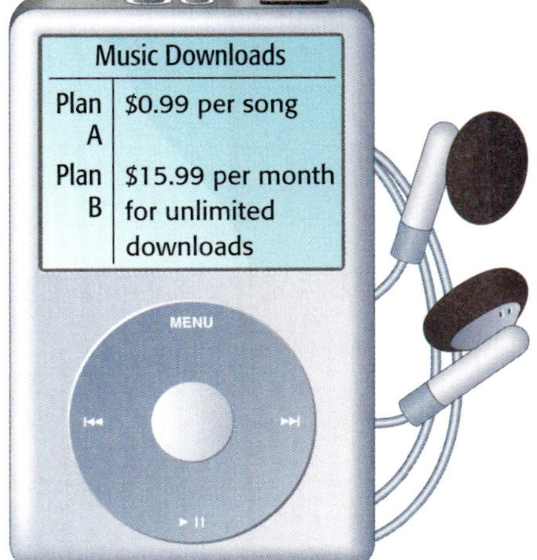

Music Downloads	
Plan A	\$0.99 per song
Plan B	\$15.99 per month for unlimited downloads

50. Suppose you download 12 songs in one month. Find the cost per song using Plan B.

51. Which plan is less expensive for downloading 9 songs in one month?

52. When is it less expensive to use Plan B instead of Plan A?

GET READY for the Next Lesson

PREREQUISITE SKILL **Find each sum.** (Lesson 2-4)

53. $-8 + (-3)$

54. $-10 + 9$

55. $12 + (-20)$

56. $-15 + 15$

Algebra Lab
Solving Equations Using Models

MAIN IDEA

Solve equations using models.

In Chapter 2, you used counters to add, subtract, multiply, and divide integers. Integers can also be modeled using algebra tiles. The table shows how these two types of models are related.

Type of Model	Variable x	Integer 1	Integer −1
Cups and Counters	(cup)	(+)	(−)
Algebra Tiles	x	1	−1

You can use either type of model to solve equations.

ACTIVITY

1 Solve $x + 2 = 5$ using cups and counters or a drawing.

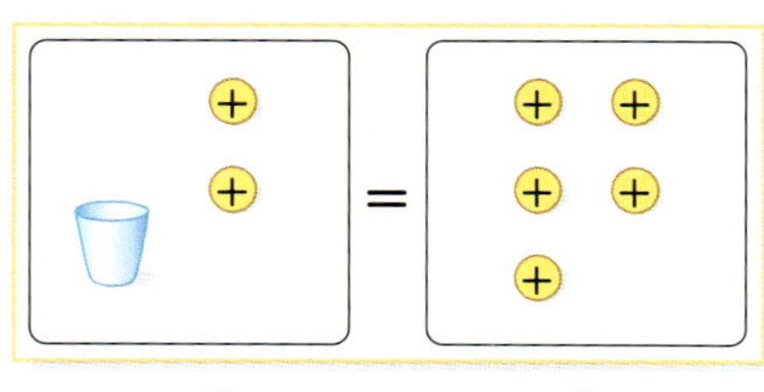

$x + 2 = 5$

Model the equation.

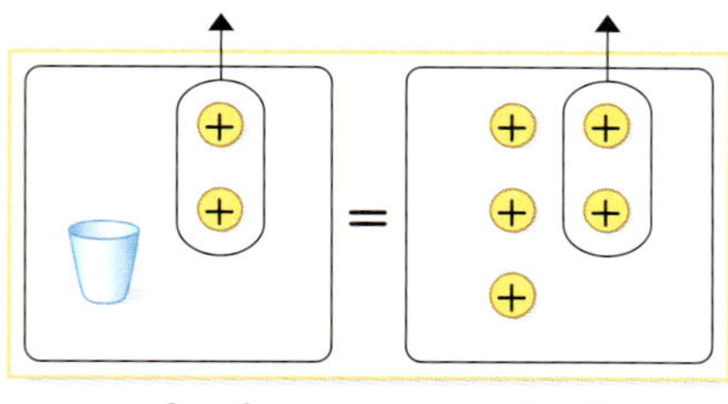

$x + 2 - 2 = 5 - 2$

Remove the same number of counters from each side of the mat until the cup is by itself on one side.

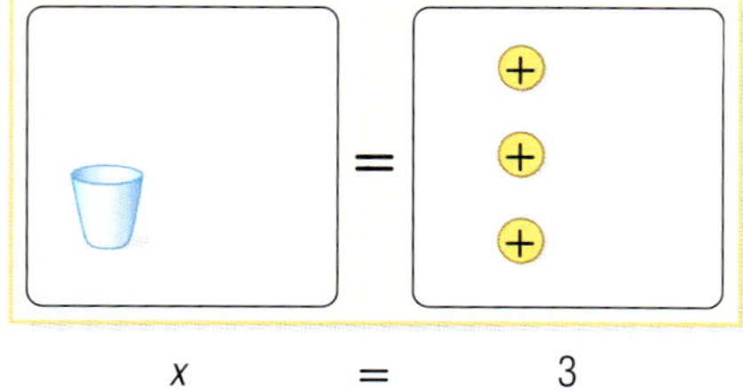

$x = 3$

The number of counters remaining on the right side of the mat represents the value of x.

Therefore, $x = 3$. Since $3 + 2 = 5$, the solution is correct.

CHECK Your Progress

Solve each equation using cups and counters or a drawing.

a. $x + 4 = 4$ b. $5 = x + 4$ c. $4 = 1 + x$ d. $2 = 2 + x$

Review Vocabulary

zero pair a number paired with its opposite; Example: 2 and −2. (Explore 2-4)

You can add or subtract a zero pair from either side of an equation without changing its value, because the value of a zero pair is zero.

ACTIVITY

2 **Solve $x + 2 = -1$ using models.**

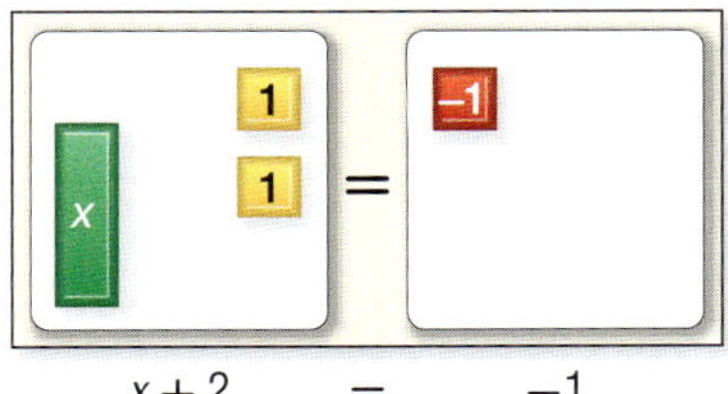

Model the equation.

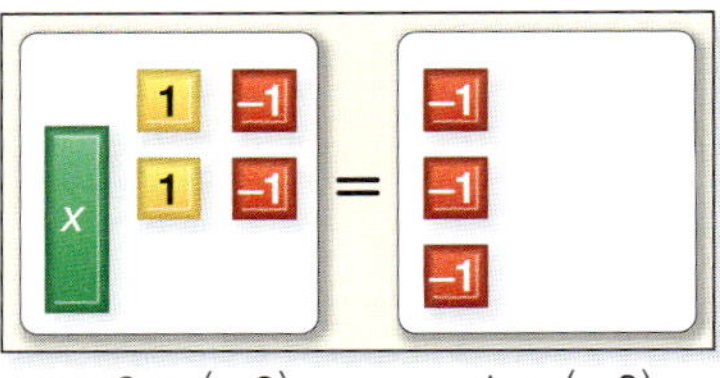

Add 2 negative tiles to the left side of the mat and add 2 negative tiles to the right side of the mat.

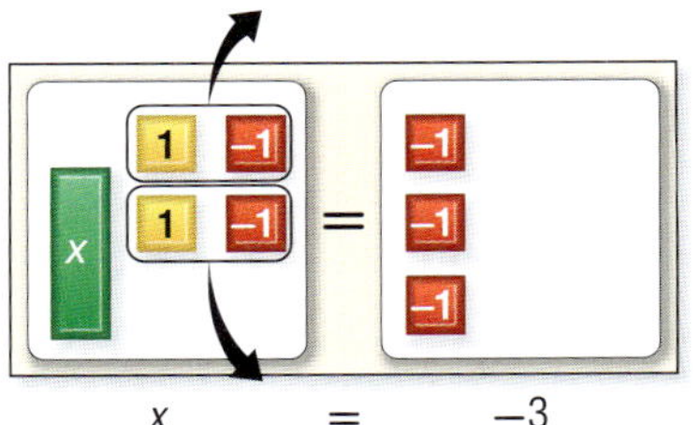

Remove all of the zero pairs from the left side. There are 3 negative tiles on the right side of the mat.

Therefore, $x = -3$. Since $-3 + 2 = -1$, the solution is correct.

CHECK Your Progress

Solve each equation using models or a drawing.

e. $-2 = x + 1$ f. $x - 3 = -2$ g. $x - 1 = -3$ h. $4 = x - 2$

Analyze the Results

Explain how to solve each equation using models or a drawing.

1. 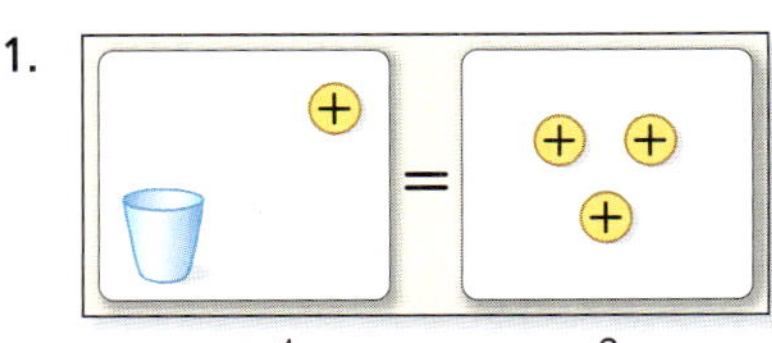

2. 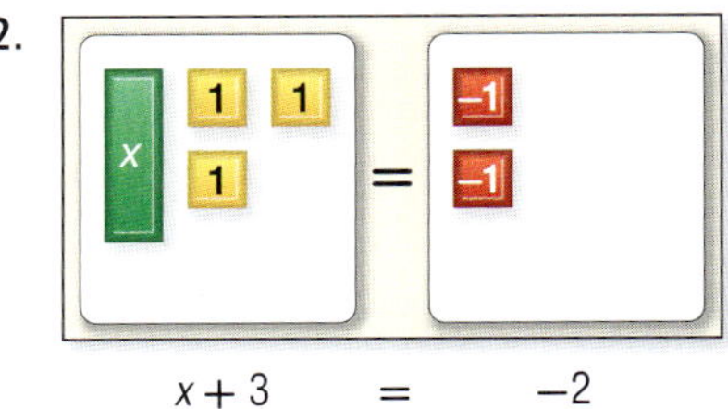

3. **MAKE A CONJECTURE** Write a rule that you can use to solve an equation like $x + 3 = 2$ without using models or a drawing.

Solving Addition and Subtraction Equations

MAIN IDEA

Solve addition and subtraction equations.

Math Online

glencoe.com

- Extra Examples
- Personal Tutor
- Self-Check Quiz
- Reading in the Content Area

GET READY for the Lesson

VIDEO GAMES Max had some video games, and then he bought two more games. Now he has six games.

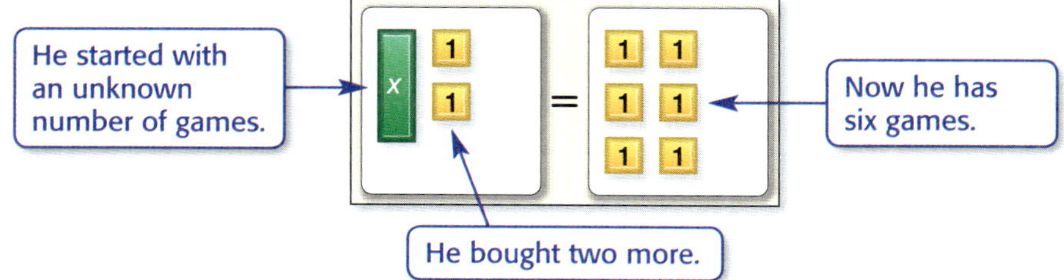

1. What does x represent in the figure?
2. What addition equation is shown in the figure?
3. Explain how to solve the equation.
4. How many games did Max have in the beginning?

You can solve the equation $x + 2 = 6$ by *removing*, or subtracting, the same number of positive tiles from each side of the mat. You can also subtract 2 from each side of the equation. The variable is now by itself on one side of the equation.

Use Models

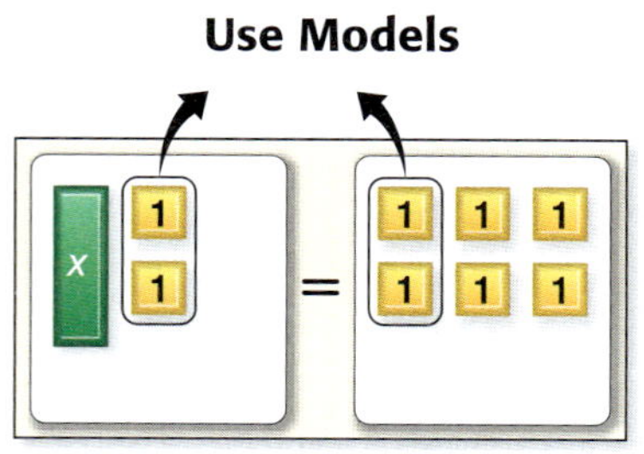

Use Symbols

$$\begin{aligned} x + 2 &= 6 \\ -2 &= -2 \\ \hline x &= 4 \end{aligned}$$

Subtracting 2 from each side of an equation illustrates the Subtraction Property of Equality.

Subtraction Property of Equality (Key Concept)

Words If you subtract the same number from each side of an equation, the two sides remain equal.

Symbols If $a = b$, then $a - c = b - c$.

Examples

Numbers	Algebra
$6 = 6$	$x + 2 = 6$
$-2 = -2$	$-2 = -2$
$4 = 4$	$x = 4$

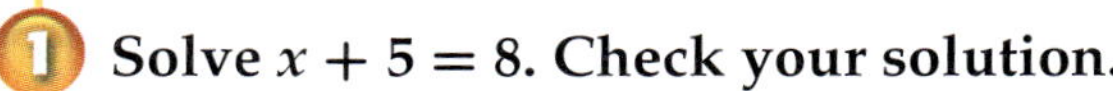

EXAMPLES Solve Addition Equations

1 **Solve $x + 5 = 8$. Check your solution.**

$$\begin{aligned} x + 5 &= 8 && \text{Write the equation.} \\ -5 &= -5 && \text{Subtract 5 from each side.} \\ x &= 3 && \text{Simplify.} \end{aligned}$$

Check $x + 5 = 8$ — Write the original equation.

$3 + 5 \stackrel{?}{=} 8$ — Replace x with 3.

$8 = 8$ ✓ — The sentence is true.

The solution is 3.

Study Tip

Solutions Notice that your new equation, $x = 3$, has the same solution as the original equation, $x + 5 = 8$.

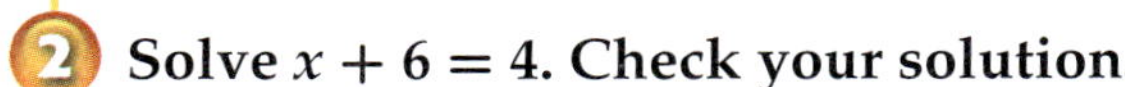

2 **Solve $x + 6 = 4$. Check your solution.**

$$\begin{aligned} x + 6 &= 4 && \text{Write the equation.} \\ -6 &= -6 && \text{Subtract 6 from each side.} \\ x &= -2 && \text{Simplify.} \end{aligned}$$

The solution is -2. — Check the solution.

CHECK Your Progress

Solve each equation. Check your solution.

a. $y + 6 = 9$ b. $x + 3 = 1$ c. $-3 = a + 4$

Real-World EXAMPLE

3 **MARINE BIOLOGY** **Clownfish and angelfish are popular tropical fish. An angelfish can grow to be 12 inches long. If an angelfish is 8.5 inches longer than a clownfish, how long is a clownfish?**

Words	An angelfish	is	8.5 inches longer than	a clownfish.
Variable	Let c represent the length of the clownfish.			
Equation	12	=	8.5 +	c

$$\begin{aligned} 12 &= 8.5 + c && \text{Write the equation.} \\ -8.5 &= -8.5 && \text{Subtract 8.5 from each side.} \\ 3.5 &= c && \text{Simplify.} \end{aligned}$$

A clownfish is 3.5 inches long.

Real-World Career . . .
How Does a Marine Biologist Use Math?
A marine biologist uses math to analyze data about marine plants, animals, and organisms.

Math Online
For more information, go to: glencoe.com.

CHECK Your Progress

d. **WEATHER** The highest recorded temperature in Warsaw, Missouri, is 118°F. This is 158° greater than the lowest recorded temperature. Write and solve an equation to find the lowest recorded temperature.

Vocabulary Link

Inverse

Everyday Use something that is opposite

Math Use undo

Similarly, you can use inverse operations and the Addition Property of Equality to solve equations like $x - 2 = 1$.

Addition Property of Equality

Key Concept

Words If you add the same number to each side of an equation, the two sides remain equal.

Symbols If $a = b$, then $a + c = b + c$.

Examples

Numbers	Algebra
$5 = 5$	$x - 2 = 4$
$+3 = +3$	$+2 = +2$
$8 = 8$	$x = 6$

EXAMPLE Solve a Subtraction Equation

4 **Solve $x - 2 = 1$. Check your solution.**

$x - 2 = 1$ Write the equation.

$+2 = +2$ Add 2 to each side.

$x = 3$ Simplify.

Check the solution. Since $3 - 2 = 1$, the solution is 3.

CHECK Your Progress

e. $y - 3 = 4$ f. $r - 4 = -2$ g. $q - 8 = -9$

5 **SHOPPING** **A pair of shoes costs \$25. This is \$14 less than the cost of a pair of jeans. Find the cost of the jeans.**

Words	Shoes	are	\$14 less than		jeans
Variable	Let j represent the cost of jeans.				
Equation	25	=	j	−	14

$25 = j - 14$ Write the equation.

$+14 = +14$ Add 14 to each side.

$39 = j$ Simplify.

The jeans cost \$39.

Study Tip

Check for Reasonableness Ask yourself which costs more: the shoes or the jeans. Then check your answer. Does it show that the jeans cost more than the shoes?

CHECK Your Progress

h. **ANIMALS** The average lifespan of a tiger is 22 years. This is 13 years less than a lion. Write and solve an equation to find the lifespan of a lion.

CHECK Your Understanding

Examples 1, 2 (p. 137)

Solve each equation. Check your solution.

1. $n + 6 = 8$
2. $7 = y + 2$
3. $m + 5 = 3$
4. $-2 = a + 6$

Example 3 (p. 137)

5. **FLYING** Orville and Wilbur Wright made the first airplane flights in 1903. Wilbur's flight was 364 feet. This was 120 feet longer than Orville's flight. Write and solve an equation to find the length of Orville's flight.

Example 4 (p. 138)

Solve each equation. Check your solution.

6. $x - 5 = 6$
7. $-1 = c - 6$

Example 5 (p. 138)

8. **PRESIDENTS** John F. Kennedy was the youngest president to be inaugurated. He was 43 years old. This was 26 years younger than the oldest president to be inaugurated—Ronald Reagan. Write and solve an equation to find how old Reagan was when he was inaugurated.

Practice and Problem Solving

HOMEWORK HELP

For Exercises	See Examples
9–12	1
13–16	2
17–20	4
21–24	3, 5

Solve each equation. Check your solution.

9. $a + 3 = 10$
10. $y + 5 = 11$
11. $9 = r + 2$
12. $14 = s + 7$
13. $x + 8 = 5$
14. $y + 15 = 11$
15. $r + 6 = -3$
16. $k + 3 = -9$
17. $s - 8 = 9$
18. $w - 7 = 11$
19. $-1 = q - 8$
20. $-2 = p - 13$

For Exercises 21–24, write an equation. Then solve the equation.

21. **MUSIC** Last week Tiffany practiced her bassoon a total of 7 hours. This was 2 hours more than she practiced the previous week. How many hours did Tiffany practice the previous week?

22. **CIVICS** In the 2004 presidential election, Ohio had 20 electoral votes. This is 14 votes less than Texas had. How many electoral votes did Texas have in 2004?

23. **AGES** Zack is 15 years old. This is 3 years younger than his brother Tyler. How old is Tyler?

24. **BASKETBALL** The Miami Heat scored 79 points in a recent game. This was 13 points less than the Chicago Bulls score. How many points did the Chicago Bulls score?

Solve each equation. Check your solution.

25. $34 + r = 95$
26. $64 + y = 84$
27. $-23 = x - 18$
28. $-59 = m - 11$
29. $-18 + c = -30$
30. $-34 = t + 9$
31. $a - 3.5 = 14.9$
32. $x - 2.8 = 9.5$
33. $r - 8.5 = -2.1$
34. $z - 9.4 = -3.6$
35. $n + 1.4 = 0.72$
36. $b + 2.25 = 1$

For Exercises 37–42, write an equation. Then solve the equation.

37. **MONEY** Suppose you have d dollars. After you pay your sister the $5 you owe her, you have $18 left. How much money did you have at the beginning?

38. **MONEY** Suppose you have saved $38. How much more do you need to save to buy a small television that costs $65?

39. **GEOMETRY** The sum of the measures of the angles of a triangle is 180°. Find the missing measure.

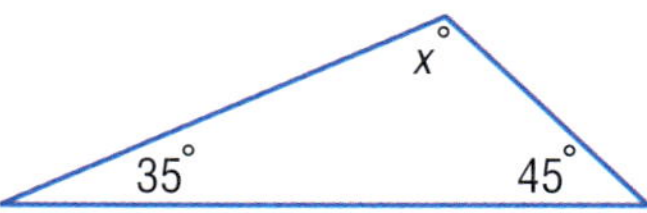

40. **VOLCANOES** Alaska, Hawaii, and Washington have active volcanoes. Alaska has 43, Hawaii has 5, and Washington has v. If they have 52 active volcanoes in all, how many volcanoes does Washington have?

41. **GOLF** The table shows Cristie Kerr's scores for four rounds of the 2007 U.S. Women's Open. Her total score was −5 (5 under par). What was her score for the third round?

Round	Score
First	0
Second	+1
Third	s
Fourth	−1

42. **BUSINESS** At the end of the day, the closing price of XYZ Stock was $62.87 per share. This was $0.62 less than the opening price. Find the opening price.

Real-World Link Cristie Kerr donates $50.00 to breast cancer research for every birdie she makes.
Source: Birdies for Breast Cancer

ANALYZE TABLES **For Exercises 43–45, use the table.**

Tallest Wooden Roller Coasters	Height (feet)	Drop (feet)	Speed (mph)
Son of Beast	218	214	s
El Toro	181	176	70
The Rattler	180	d	65
Colossos	h	159	75
Voyage	163	154	67

Source: Coaster Grotto

43. The difference in speeds of Son of Beast and The Rattler is 13 miles per hour. If Son of Beast has the greater speed, write and solve a subtraction equation to find its speed.

44. The Rattler has a drop that is 52 feet less than El Toro. Write and solve an addition equation to find the height of The Rattler.

45. Colossos is 13 feet taller than Voyage. Write and solve a subtraction equation to find the height of Colossos.

EXTRA PRACTICE
See pages 674, 706.

H.O.T. Problems

46. **Which One Doesn't Belong?** Identify the equation that does not have the same solution as the other three. Explain your reasoning.

$x - 1 = -4$	$b + 5 = -8$	$11 + y = 8$	$-6 + a = -9$

47. **CHALLENGE** Suppose $x + y = 11$ and the value of x increases by 2. If their sum remains the same, what must happen to the value of y?

48. **WRITING IN MATH** Write a problem about a real-world situation that can be represented by the equation $p - 25 = 50$.

TEST PRACTICE

49. The Oriental Pearl Tower in Shanghai, China, is 1,535 feet tall. It is 280 feet shorter than the Canadian National Tower in Toronto, Canada. Which equation can be used to find the height of the Canadian National Tower?

A $1{,}535 + h = 280$

B $h = 1{,}535 - 280$

C $1{,}535 = h - 280$

D $280 - h = 1{,}535$

50. Which of the following statements is true concerning the equation $x + 3 = 7$?

F To find the value of x, add 3 to each side.

G To find the value of x, add 7 to each side.

H To find the value of x, find the sum of 3 and 7.

J To find the value of x, subtract 3 from each side.

Spiral Review

51. **SCIENCE** The boiling point of water is 180° higher than its freezing point. If p represents the freezing point, write an expression that represents the boiling point of water. (Lesson 3-1)

52. **ALGEBRA** Evaluate the expression $xy \div (-4)$ if $x = 12$ and $y = -2$. (Lesson 2-8)

53. **ALGEBRA** The table shows the number of pages of a novel Ferguson read each hour. If the pattern continues, how many pages will Ferguson read during the 8th hour? (Lesson 2-7)

Hour	Number of Pages Read
1	11
2	13
3	16
4	20
5	25

GET READY for the Next Lesson

PREREQUISITE SKILL **Find each quotient.**

54. $15.6 \div 13$

55. $8.84 \div 3.4$

56. $75.25 \div 0.25$

57. $0.76 \div 0.5$

Solving Multiplication Equations

MAIN IDEA

Solve multiplication equations.

New Vocabulary

formula

Math Online

glencoe.com

- Concepts In Motion
- Extra Examples
- Personal Tutor
- Self-Check Quiz

MINI Lab

MONEY Suppose three friends order an appetizer of nachos that costs \$6. They agree to split the cost equally. The figure below illustrates the multiplication equation $3x = 6$, where x represents the amount each friend pays.

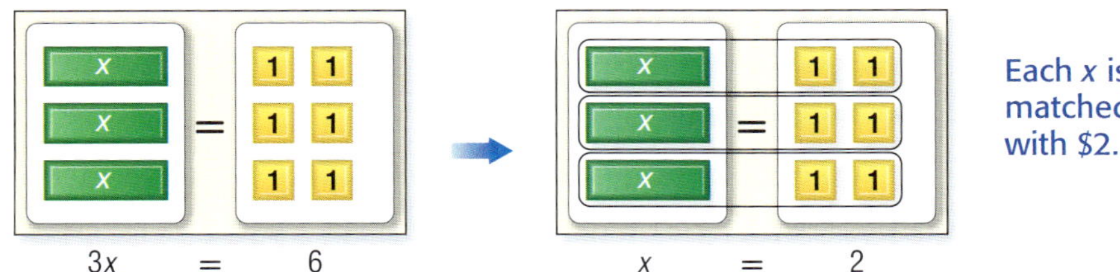

Each friend pays \$2. The solution of $3x = 6$ is 2.

Solve each equation using models or a drawing.

1.

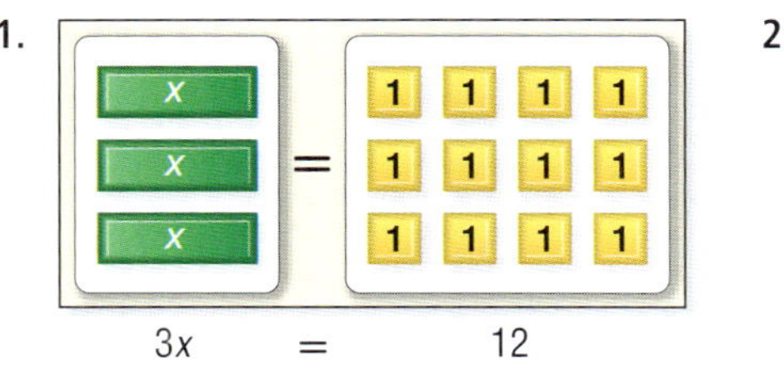

2.

$2x = -8$

3. $4x = 20$
4. $8 = 2x$
5. $3x = -9$
6. What operation did you use to find each solution?
7. How can you use the coefficient of x to solve $8x = 40$?

Equations like $3x = 6$ are called multiplication equations because the expression $3x$ means 3 *times the value of* x. So, you can use the Division Property of Equality to solve multiplication equations.

Division Property of Equality

Key Concept

Words If you divide each side of an equation by the same nonzero number, the two sides remain equal.

Symbols If $a = b$ and $c \neq 0$, then $\frac{a}{c} = \frac{b}{c}$.

Examples

Numbers	Algebra
$8 = 8$	$2x = -6$
$\frac{8}{2} = \frac{8}{2}$	$\frac{2x}{2} = \frac{-6}{2}$
$4 = 4$	$x = -3$

Review Vocabulary

coefficient the numerical factor for a multiplication expression; Example: the coefficient of x in the expression $4x$ is 4. (Lesson 1-4)

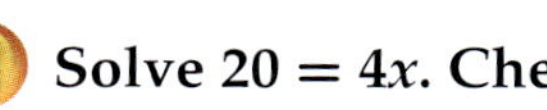

Solve Multiplication Equations

1 **Solve $20 = 4x$. Check your solution.**

$20 = 4x$	Write the equation.
$\frac{20}{4} = \frac{4x}{4}$	Divide each side of the equation by 4.
$5 = x$	$20 \div 4 = 5$
The solution is 5.	Check the solution.

2 **Solve $-8y = 24$. Check your solution.**

$-8y = 24$	Write the equation.
$\frac{-8y}{-8} = \frac{24}{-8}$	Divide each side by -8.
$y = -3$	$24 \div (-8) = -3$
The solution is -3.	Check the solution.

Solve each equation. Check your solution.

a. $30 = 6x$ b. $-6a = 36$ c. $-9d = -72$

Many real-world situations increase at a constant rate. These can be represented by multiplication equations.

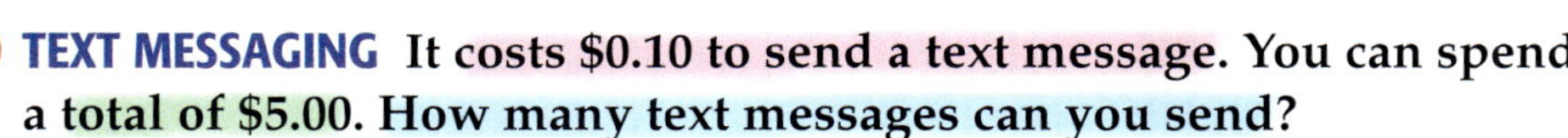

3 **TEXT MESSAGING** **It costs \$0.10 to send a text message. You can spend a total of \$5.00. How many text messages can you send?**

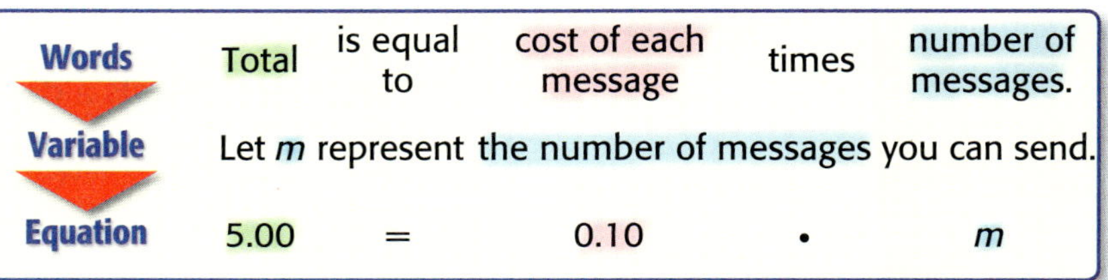

Words	Total	is equal to	cost of each message	times	number of messages.
Variable	Let m represent the number of messages you can send.				
Equation	5.00	=	0.10	•	m

$5.00 = 0.10m$	Write the equation.
$\frac{5.00}{0.10} = \frac{0.10m}{0.10}$	Divide each side by 0.10.
$50 = m$	$5.00 \div 0.10 = 50$

At \$0.10 per message, you can send 50 text messages for \$5.00.

Real-World Link

Over 60% of teenagers' text messages are sent from their homes—even when a landline is available.

Source: Xerox

CHECK Your Progress

d. **TRAVEL** Mrs. Acosta's car can travel an average of 24 miles on each gallon of gasoline. Write and solve an equation to find how many gallons of gasoline she will need for a trip of 348 miles.

A **formula** is an equation that shows the relationship among certain quantities. One of the most common formulas is the equation $d = rt$, which gives the relationship among distance d, rate r, and time t.

Real-World EXAMPLE

Reading Math

Speed Another name for *rate* is *speed*.

4 ANIMALS The tortoise is one of the slowest land animals, reaching an average top speed of about 0.25 mile per hour. At this speed, how long will it take a tortoise to travel 1.5 miles?

You are asked to find the time t it will take to travel a distance d of 1.5 miles at a rate r of 0.25 mile per hour.

METHOD 1 **Substitute, then solve.**

$d = rt$	Write the equation.
$1.5 = 0.25t$	Replace d with 1.5 and r with 0.25.
$\frac{1.5}{0.25} = \frac{0.25t}{0.25}$	Divide each side by 0.25.
$6 = t$	$1.5 \div 0.25 = 6$

METHOD 2 **Solve, then substitute.**

$d = rt$	Write the equation.
$\frac{d}{r} = \frac{rt}{r}$	Divide each side by r to solve the equation for t.
$\frac{d}{r} = t$	Simplify.
$\frac{1.5}{0.25} = t$	Replace d with 1.5 and r with 0.25.
$6 = t$	$1.5 \div 0.25 = 6$

It would take a tortoise 6 hours to travel 1.5 miles.

CHOOSE Your Method

e. **SCIENCE** A sound wave travels a distance of 700 meters in 2.5 seconds. Find the average speed of the sound wave.

CHECK Your Understanding

Examples 1, 2 (p. 143)

Solve each equation. Check your solution.

1. $6c = 18$
2. $15 = 3z$
3. $-8x = 24$
4. $-9r = -36$

Example 3 (p. 143)

5. **WORKING** Antonia earns $6 per hour helping her grandmother. How many hours does she need to work to earn $48?

Example 4 (p. 144)

6. **SWIMMING** A shark can swim at an average speed of about 25 miles per hour. At this rate, how long will it take a shark to swim 60 miles?

Practice and Problem Solving

HOMEWORK HELP	
For Exercises	See Examples
7–12	1
13–18	2
19–20	3
21–22	4

Solve each equation. Check your solution.

7. $7a = 49$
8. $9e = 27$
9. $2x = -6$
10. $3y = -21$
11. $35 = 5v$
12. $72 = 12r$
13. $-4j = 36$
14. $-12y = 60$
15. $-4s = -16$
16. $-6z = -36$
17. $48 = -6r$
18. $-28 = -7f$

For Exercises 19–22, write an equation. Then solve the equation.

19. **MONEY** Brandy wants to buy a digital camera that costs \$300. If she saves \$15 each week, in how many weeks will she have enough money for the camera?

20. **COMPUTERS** The width of a computer monitor is 1.25 times as long as its height. Find the height of the computer monitor at the right.

21. **SPEED** A racecar can travel at a rate of 205 miles per hour. At this rate, how long would it take to travel 615 miles?

22. **INSECTS** A dragonfly, the fastest insect, can fly a distance of 50 feet in about 2 seconds. Find a dragonfly's average speed in feet per second.

Solve each equation. Check your solution.

23. $0.4x = 9.2$
24. $0.9y = 13.5$
25. $5.4 = 0.3p$
26. $9.72 = 1.8a$
27. $3.9y = 18.33$
28. $2.6b = 2.08$

ANALYZE TABLES For Exercises 29 and 30, use the following information. The table shows women's championship record holders for several track events.

29. Without calculating explain whether Evelyn Ashford or Sanya Richards has the faster average speed.

30. Find the average speed of each athlete in meters per second. Round to the nearest hundredth.

Name	Race (m)	Time (s)
Evelyn Ashford	200	21.88
Sanya Richards	400	49.27

Source: USA Outdoor Track & Field

31. **HURRICANES** A category 3 hurricane reaches speeds up to 20.88 kilometers per hour. The distance from Cuba to Key West is 145 kilometers. Write and solve a multiplication equation to find how long it would take a category 3 hurricane to travel from Cuba to Key West.

EXTRA PRACTICE
See pages 674, 706.

32. **WATER** A case of water bottles costs \$9.48. If there are 12 water bottles in the case, find the cost per bottle. Then find the decrease in cost per bottle if the cost of a case is reduced to \$8.64.

H.O.T. Problems

33. **FIND THE ERROR** Steve and Becky are solving $-6x = 72$. Who is correct? Explain.

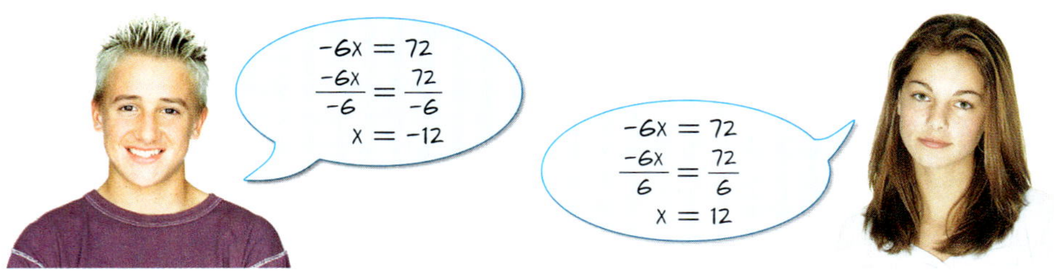

34. **CHALLENGE** Solve $3|x| = 12$. Explain your reasoning.

WRITING IN MATH Write a real-world problem that could be represented by each equation.

35. $2x = 16$

36. $3x = 75$

37. $4x = -8$

TEST PRACTICE

38. A football player can run 20 yards in 3.4 seconds. Which equation could be used to find y, the number of yards the football player can run in a second?

A $20y = 3.4$

B $3.4 - y = 20$

C $3.4y = 20$

D $20 + y = 3.4$

39. **SHORT RESPONSE** Use the formula $A = bh$ to find the base in inches of a rhombus with a height of 7 inches and an area of 56 square inches.

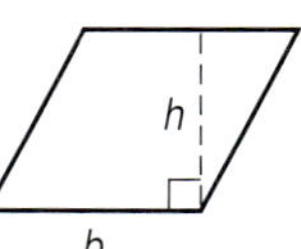

Spiral Review

ALGEBRA Solve each equation. Check your solution. (Lesson 3-2)

40. $y + 8 = -2$

41. $x - 7 = -2$

42. $20 = z + 23$

43. **ALGEBRA** Write an algebraic expression for the phrase *the product of −3 and y*. (Lesson 3-1)

44. **MONTHS** A lunar month, the time from one new moon to the next, is 29.5 days. How many days longer is our calendar year of 365 days than 12 lunar months? (Lesson 1-1)

GET READY for the Next Lesson

PREREQUISITE SKILL Draw the next two figures in the pattern. (Lesson 2-7)

45.

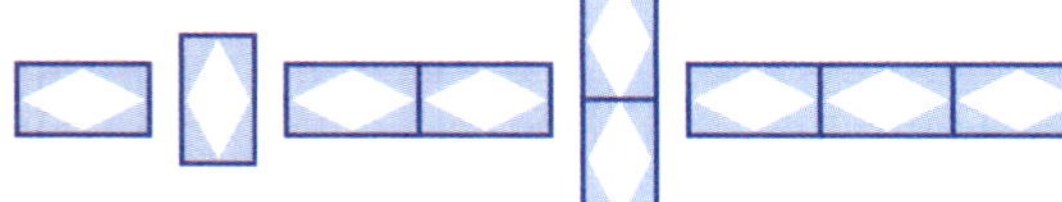

Chapter 3 Mid-Chapter Quiz

Lessons 3-1 through 3-3

Write each sentence as an algebraic equation. (Lesson 3-1)

1. The product of a number and 3 is -16.
2. 10 less than a number is 45.

3. **CLIMBING** A rock climber is at an altitude of a feet before she climbs up another 80 feet. Write an expression for her new altitude. (Lesson 3-1)

4. **MULTIPLE CHOICE** Stephanie has 5 dollars more than Necie. If Necie has d dollars, which expression represents the number of dollars Stephanie has? (Lesson 3-1)

   A $d - 5$ C $5 - d$

   B $d + 5$ D $5d$

Solve each equation. Check your solution. (Lesson 3-2)

5. $21 + m = 33$
6. $a - 5 = -12$
7. $p + 1.7 = -9.8$
8. $56 = k - (-33)$

9. **GEOMETRY** The sum of the measures of the angles of a triangle is 180°. Write and solve an equation to find the missing measure m. (Lesson 3-2)

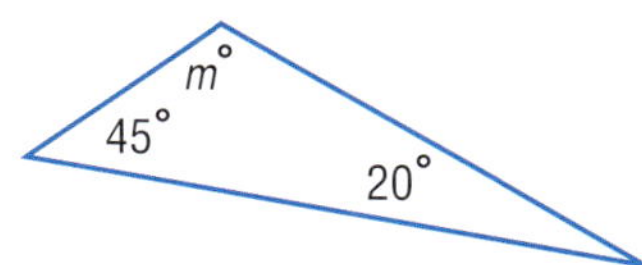

10. **MULTIPLE CHOICE** Trevor's test score was 5 points lower than Ursalina's test score. If Ursalina scored 85 on the test, which equation would give Trevor's score d when solved? (Lesson 3-2)

    F $85 = d + 5$

    G $d - 5 = 85$

    H $80 = d + 5$

    J $d - 5 = 80$

11. **PETS** Cameron has 11 adult Fantail goldfish. This is 7 fewer Fantail goldfish than his friend Julia has. Write and solve a subtraction equation to determine the number of Fantail goldfish g that Julia has. (Lesson 3-2)

12. **MEASUREMENT** The Grand Canyon has a maximum depth of almost 5,280 feet. An average four-story apartment building has a height of 66 feet. Write and solve a multiplication equation to determine the number of apartment buildings b, stacked on top of each other, that would fill the depth of the Grand Canyon. (Lesson 3-3)

Solve each equation. Check your solution. (Lesson 3-3)

13. $5f = -75$
14. $-1.6w = 4.8$
15. $63 = 7y$
16. $-28 = -2d$
17. $3.7g = -4.44$
18. $2.25 = 1.5b$

19. **MULTIPLE CHOICE** Michelann drove 44 miles per hour and covered a distance of 154 miles. Which equation accurately describes this situation if h represents the number of hours Michelann drove? (Lesson 3-3)

    A $154 = 44 + h$

    B $44h = 154$

    C $154 = 44 \div h$

    D $h - 44 = 154$

20. **LAWN SERVICE** Trey estimates he will earn $470 next summer cutting lawns in his neighborhood. This amount is 2.5 times the amount a he earned this summer. Write and solve a multiplication equation to find how much Trey earned this summer. (Lesson 3-3)

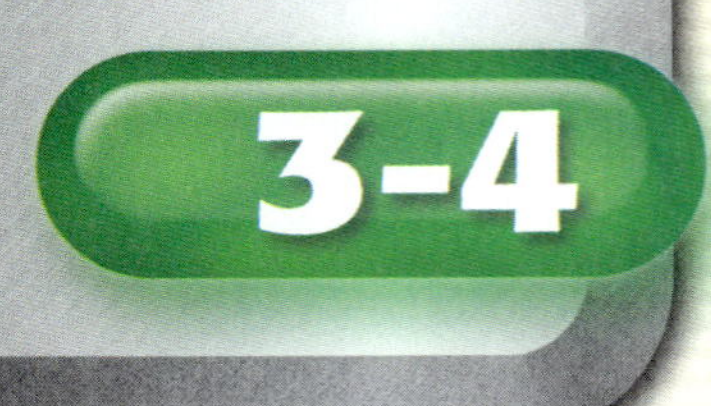

Problem-Solving Investigation

MAIN IDEA: Solve problems using the work backward strategy.

P.S.I. TEAM +

e-Mail: WORK BACKWARD

MIGUEL: Yesterday, I earned extra money by doing yardwork for my neighbor. Then I spent $5.50 at the convenience store and four times that amount at the bookstore. Now I have $7.75 left.

YOUR MISSION: Work backward to find how much money Miguel had before he went to the convenience store and the bookstore.

Understand	You know he has $7.75 left. You need to find the amount he started with.	
Plan	Start with the end result and work backward.	
Solve	He has $7.75 left. **Undo** the four times $5.50 spent at the bookstore. Since $5.50 × 4 is $22, add $7.75 and $22. **Undo** the $5.50 spent at the convenience store. Add $5.50 and $29.75. So, Miguel had $35.25 to start with.	$7.75 + 22.00 $29.75 + $5.50 $35.25
Check	Assume Miguel started with $35.25. After going to the convenience store, he had $35.25 − $5.50 or $29.75. He spent four times the amount he spent at the convenience store at the bookstore. So, he had $29.75 − 4($5.50) or $7.75 left. So, $35.25 is correct. ✓	

Analyze The Strategy

1. Explain when you would use the work backward strategy to solve a problem.
2. Describe how to solve a problem by working backward.
3. WRITING IN MATH Write a problem that could be solved by working backward. Then write the steps you would take to find the solution to your problem.

Mixed Problem Solving

Use the *work backward* strategy to solve Exercises 4–7.

4. **MONEY** Marisa spent \$8 on a movie ticket. Then she spent \$5 on popcorn and one half of what was left on a drink. She has \$2 left. How much did she have initially?

5. **NUMBER THEORY** A number is multiplied by -3. Then 6 is subtracted from the product. After adding -7, the result is -25. What is the number?

6. **TIME** Timothy's morning schedule is shown. At what time does Timothy wake up?

Timothy's Schedule	
Activity	**Time**
Wakes up	■
Get ready for school – 45 min	■
Walk to school – 25 min	9:00 A.M.

7. **LOGIC** A small box has 4 tennis balls inside it. There are 6 of these small boxes inside a medium box. There are 8 medium boxes inside each large box, and there are 100 large boxes shipped in a large truck. How many tennis balls are on the truck?

Use any strategy to solve Exercises 8–15. Some strategies are shown below.

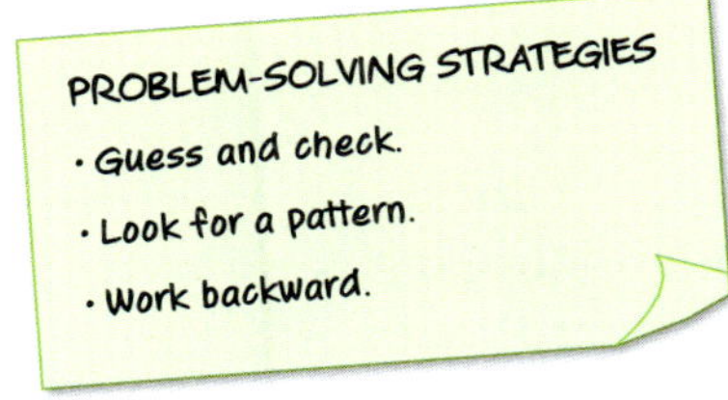

8. **GEOGRAPHY** The land area of North Dakota is 68,976 square miles. This is about 7 times the land area of Vermont. Estimate the land area of Vermont.

9. **AGE** Brie is two years older than her sister Kiana. Kiana is 4 years older than their brother Jeron, who is 8 years younger than their brother Trey. Trey is 16 years old. How old is Brie?

10. **ELEVATION** New Orleans, Lousiana, has an elevation of -8 feet related to sea level. Death Valley, California, is 274 feet lower than New Orleans. What is the elevation of Death Valley?

11. **GEOMETRY** Draw the sixth figure in the pattern shown.

12. **WATERFALLS** Angel Falls in Venezuela, the highest waterfall in the world, is 3,212 feet high. It is 87 feet higher than 2.5 times the height of the Empire State Building. Find the height of the Empire State Building.

13. **AIRCRAFT** An aircraft carrier travels about 6 inches per gallon of fuel. Raquel's car travels about 28 miles per gallon of fuel. If there are 5,280 feet in one mile, how many more inches per gallon would Raquel's car get than an aircraft carrier?

14. **SCHOOL SUPPLIES** Alexandra wishes to buy 5 pens, 1 ruler, and 7 folders to start the school year. The prices are shown in the table.

Item	Cost
Pens	\$2.09
Ruler	\$0.99
Folder	\$1.19

If there is no tax, is \$20 enough to pay for Alexandra's school supplies? Explain your reasoning.

15. **MONEY** Antonio has saved \$25 in cash to spend at the arcade. If he has 10 bills, how many of each kind of bill does he have?

READING to SOLVE PROBLEMS

Simplify the Problem

Have you ever tried to solve a long word problem and didn't know where to start? Try to rewrite the problem using only the most important words. Here's an example.

STEP 1 Read the problem and identify the important words and numbers.

CELL PHONES There is a wide range of cell phone plans available for students. With Janelle's plan, she pays $15 per month for 200 minutes, plus $0.10 per minute once she talks for more than 200 minutes. Suppose Janelle can spend $20 each month for her cell phone. How many minutes can she talk?

STEP 2 Simplify the problem. Keep all of the important words and numbers, but use fewer of them.

The total monthly cost is the $15 for 200 minutes plus $0.10 times the number of minutes over 200. How many minutes can she talk for $20?

STEP 3 Simplify it again. Use a variable for the unknown.

The cost of m minutes at $0.10 per minute plus $15 is $20.

PRACTICE

Use the method above to simplify each problem.

1. **MONEY** Akira is saving money to buy a scooter that costs $125. He has already saved $80 and plans to save an additional $5 each week. In how many weeks will he have enough money for the scooter?

2. **SHOPPING** Online shopping is a popular way to buy books. Cheryl wants to order several books that cost $7 each. In addition, she will pay a shipping fee of $8. How many books can she order with $43?

3. **TEMPERATURE** The current temperature is 40°. It is expected to rise 5° each hour for the next several hours. In how many hours will the temperature be 60°?

4. **MONEY** Joaquin wants to buy some DVDs that are each on sale for $10 plus a CD that costs $15. How many DVDs can he buy if he has $75 to spend?

3-5 Solving Two-Step Equations

MAIN IDEA

Solve two-step equations.

New Vocabulary

two-step equation

Math Online

glencoe.com

- Concepts In Motion
- Extra Examples
- Personal Tutor
- Self-Check Quiz

MINI Lab

MONEY A florist charges $2 for each balloon in an arrangement and a $3 delivery fee. You have $9 to spend. The model illustrates the equation $2x + 3 = 9$, where x represents the number of balloons.

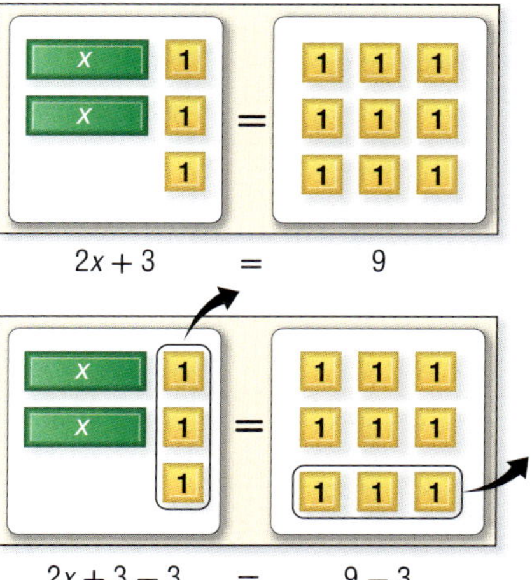

To solve $2x + 3 = 9$, remove three 1-tiles from each side of the mat. Then divide the remaining tiles into two equal groups. The solution of $2x + 3 = 9$ is 3.

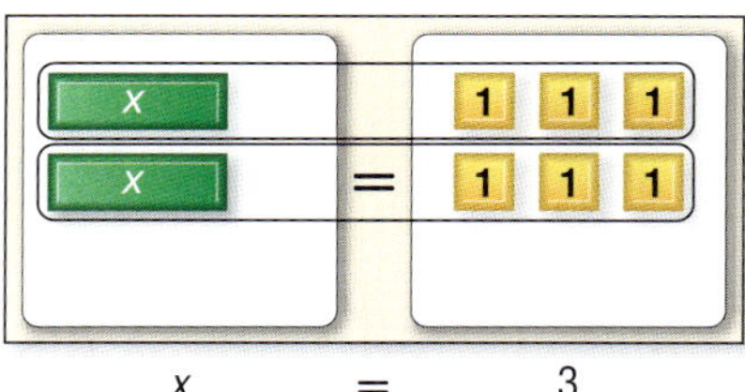

Solve each equation by using models or a drawing.

1. $2x + 1 = 5$
2. $3x + 2 = 8$
3. $2 = 5x + 2$

A **two-step equation** has two different operations. To solve a two-step equation, undo the operations in reverse order of the order of operations. You can review the order of operations in Lesson 1-4.

EXAMPLE Solve a Two-Step Equation

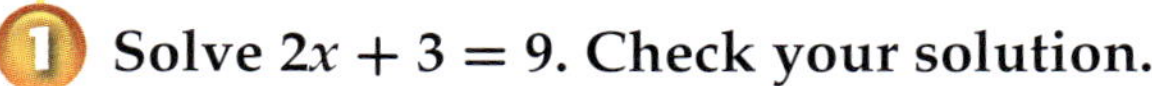

1 **Solve $2x + 3 = 9$. Check your solution.**

$$2x + 3 = 9 \quad \text{Write the equation.}$$
$$-3 = -3 \quad \text{Undo the addition first by subtracting 3 from each side.}$$
$$2x = 6$$
$$\frac{2x}{2} = \frac{6}{2} \quad \text{Next, undo the multiplication by dividing each side by 2.}$$
$$x = 3 \quad \text{Simplify.}$$

Check the solution. Since $2(3) + 3 = 9$, the solution is 3.

CHECK Your Progress

Solve each equation. Check your solution.

a. $2x + 4 = 10$ b. $3x + 1 = 7$ c. $5 = 2 + 3x$

Study Tip

Order of Operations Multiplication comes before addition in the order of operations. To undo these operations, reverse the order. So, undo the addition first by subtracting. Then, undo the multiplication by dividing.

EXAMPLES Solve Two-Step Equations

2 **Solve $3x + 2 = 23$. Check your solution.**

$3x + 2 = 23$	Write the equation.
$\underline{\quad -2 = -2}$	Undo the addition first by subtracting 2 from each side.
$3x = 21$	
$\frac{3x}{3} = \frac{21}{3}$	Divide each side by 3.
$x = 7$	Simplify.

Check	$3x + 2 = 23$	Write the original equation.
	$3(7) + 2 \stackrel{?}{=} 23$	Replace x with 7.
	$21 + 2 \stackrel{?}{=} 23$	Simplify.
	$23 = 23$ ✓	The sentence is true.

The solution is 7.

3 **Solve $-2y - 7 = 3$. Check your solution.**

$-2y - 7 = 3$	Write the equation.
$\underline{\quad +7 = +7}$	Undo the subtraction first by adding 7 to each side.
$-2y = 10$	
$\frac{-2y}{-2} = \frac{10}{-2}$	Divide each side by -2.
$y = -5$	Simplify.
The solution is -5.	Check the solution.

Study Tip

Equations Remember, solutions of the new equation are also solutions of the original equation.

4 **Solve $4 + 5r = -11$. Check your solution.**

$4 + 5r = -11$	Write the equation.
$\underline{-4 \quad = -4}$	Undo the addition of 4 first by subtracting 4 from each side.
$5r = -15$	
$\frac{5r}{5} = -\frac{15}{5}$	Divide each side by 5.
$r = -3$	Simplify.
The solution is -3.	Check the solution.

CHECK Your Progress

Solve each equation. Check your solution.

d. $4x + 5 = 13$ **e.** $8y + 15 = 71$ **f.** $-3n - 8 = 7$

g. $-5s + 8 = -2$ **h.** $1 + 2y = -3$ **i.** $-2 + 6w = 10$

Solving Two-Step Equations — Key Concept

To solve a two-step equation like $3x + 4 = 16$ or $2x - 1 = -3$:

Step 1 Undo the addition or subtraction first.

Step 2 Then undo the multiplication or division.

Some real-world situations start with a given amount and increase at a certain rate.

Real-World EXAMPLE

5 **MOVIES** **Aisha wants to have her birthday party at the movies. It costs \$27 for pizza and \$8.50 per friend for the movie tickets. Since it is Aisha's birthday, she does not have to pay for her movie ticket. How many friends can Aisha have at her party if she has \$78 to spend?**

Real-World Link Most teenagers see more than 7 movies a year.
Source: Gallup News Service

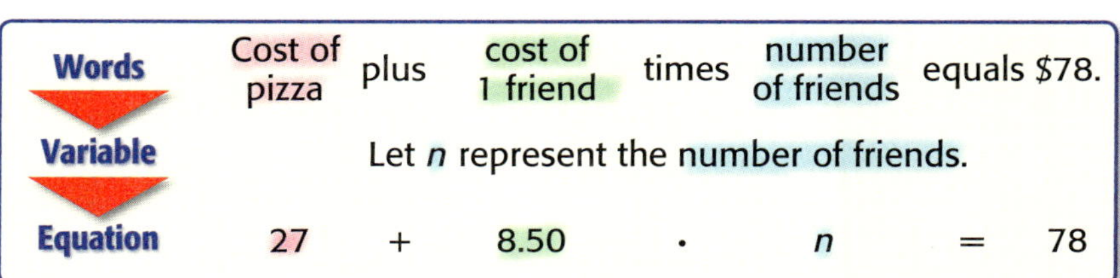

Words	Cost of pizza	plus	cost of 1 friend	times	number of friends	equals \$78.
Variable	Let n represent the number of friends.					
Equation	27	+	8.50	·	n	= 78

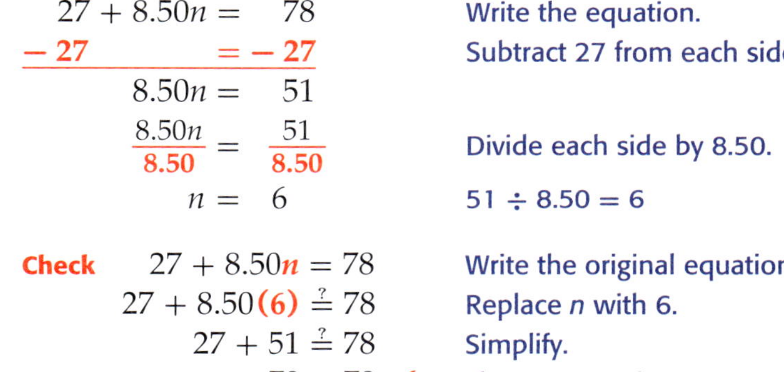

$27 + 8.50n = 78$	Write the equation.
$-27 \quad = -27$	Subtract 27 from each side.
$8.50n = 51$	
$\frac{8.50n}{8.50} = \frac{51}{8.50}$	Divide each side by 8.50.
$n = 6$	$51 \div 8.50 = 6$

Check	
$27 + 8.50n = 78$	Write the original equation.
$27 + 8.50(6) \stackrel{?}{=} 78$	Replace n with 6.
$27 + 51 \stackrel{?}{=} 78$	Simplify.
$78 = 78$ ✓	The sentence is true.

Aisha can have 6 friends at her party.

CHECK Your Progress

j. **FITNESS** A fitness club is having a special offer where you pay \$22 to join plus a \$16 monthly fee. You have \$150 to spend. Write and solve an equation to find how many months you can use the fitness club.

CHECK Your Understanding

Examples 1–4 (pp. 151–152)

Solve each equation. Check your solution.

1. $3x + 1 = 7$
2. $4h - 6 = 22$
3. $-6r + 1 = -17$
4. $-3y - 5 = 10$
5. $13 = 1 + 4s$
6. $-7 = 1 + 2n$

Example 5 (p. 153)

7. **MONEY** Syreeta wants to buy some CDs, each costing \$14, and a DVD that cost \$23. She has \$65 to spend. Write and solve an equation to find how many CDs she can buy.

Practice and Problem Solving

HOMEWORK HELP

For Exercises	See Examples
8–11	1, 2
12–15	3
16–19	4
20–21	5

Solve each equation. Check your solution.

8. $3x + 1 = 10$
9. $5x + 4 = 19$
10. $2t + 7 = -1$
11. $6m + 1 = -23$
12. $-4w - 4 = 8$
13. $-7y + 3 = -25$
14. $-8s + 1 = 33$
15. $-2x + 5 = -13$
16. $3 + 8n = -5$
17. $5 + 4d = 37$
18. $14 + 2p = 8$
19. $25 + 2y = 47$

For Exercises 20 and 21, write an equation. Then solve the equation.

20. **BICYCLES** Cristiano is saving money to buy a new bike that costs \$189. He has saved \$99 so far. He plans on saving \$10 each week. In how many weeks will Cristiano have enough money to buy a new bike?

21. **PETTING ZOOS** It cost \$10 to enter a petting zoo. Each cup of food to feed the animals is \$2. If you have \$14, how many cups of food can you buy?

Solve each equation. Check your solution.

22. $2r - 3.1 = 1.7$
23. $4t + 3.5 = 12.5$
24. $16b - 6.5 = 9.5$
25. $5w + 9.2 = 19.7$
26. $16 = 0.5r - 8$
27. $0.2n + 3 = 8.6$

For Exercises 28 and 29, write an equation. Then solve the equation.

28. **CELL PHONES** A cell phone company charges a monthly fee of \$39.99 for unlimited *off-peak* minutes on the nights and weekends but \$0.45 for each *peak* minute during the weekday. If Brad's monthly cell phone bill was \$62.49, for how many *peak* minutes did he get charged?

29. **PLANTS** In ideal conditions, bamboo can grow 47.6 inches each day. At this rate, how many days will it take a bamboo shoot that is 8 inches tall to reach a height of 80 feet?

TEMPERATURE For Exercises 30 and 31, use the following information and the table.

Temperature is usually measured on the Fahrenheit scale (°F) or the Celsius scale (°C). Use the formula $F = 1.8C + 32$ to convert from one scale to the other.

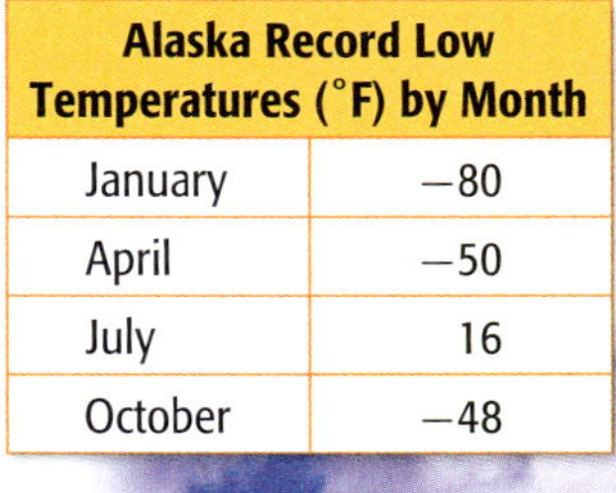

Alaska Record Low Temperatures (°F) by Month	
January	−80
April	−50
July	16
October	−48

30. Convert the temperature for Alaska's record low in July to Celsius. Round to the nearest degree.

31. Hawaii's record low temperature is −11°C. Find the difference in degrees Fahrenheit between Hawaii's record low temperature and the record low temperature for Alaska in January.

EXTRA PRACTICE
See pages 675, 706.

H.O.T. Problems

32. **CHALLENGE** Refer to Exercises 30 and 31. Is there a temperature at which the number of Celsius degrees is the same as the number of Fahrenheit degrees? If so, find it. If not, explain why not.

33. **CHALLENGE** Suppose your school is selling magazine subscriptions. Each subscription costs \$20. The company pays the school half of the total sales in dollars. The school must also pay a one-time fee of \$18. What is the fewest number of subscriptions that can be sold to earn a profit of \$200?

34. **SELECT A TECHNIQUE** Bianca rented a car for a flat fee of \$19.99 plus \$0.26 per mile. Which of the following techniques might she use to determine the approximate number of miles she can drive for \$50? Justify your selection(s). Then use the technique(s) to solve the problem.

Mental Math	Number Sense	Estimation

35. **WRITING IN MATH** Write a real-world problem that would be represented by the equation $2x + 5 = 15$.

TEST PRACTICE

36. A rental car company charges \$30 a day plus \$0.05 a mile. Which expression could be used to find the cost of renting a car for m miles?

    A $30.05m$

    B $30m + 0.05m$

    C $30 + 0.05m$

    D $30m + 0.05$

37. The Rodriguez family went on a vacation. They started with \$1,875. If they spent \$140 each day, which expression represents how much money they had after d days?

    F $1{,}735d$

    G $1{,}875 - 140d$

    H $140d$

    J $1{,}875 + 140d$

Spiral Review

38. **SCHEDULES** Jaime needs to be at the bus stop by 7:10 A.M. If it takes her 7 minutes to walk to the bus stop and 40 minutes to get ready in the morning, what is the latest time that she can set her alarm in order to be at the bus stop 5 minutes earlier than she needs to be? (Lesson 3-4)

ALGEBRA **Solve each equation. Check your solution.** (Lessons 3-2 and 3-3)

39. $4f = 28$
40. $-3y = -15$
41. $p - 14 = 27$
42. $-11 = n + 2$

43. **HIKING** Two people are hiking in the Grand Canyon. One is 987 feet below the rim and the other is 1,200 feet below the rim. Find the vertical distance between them (Lesson 2-5)

GET READY for the Next Lesson

PREREQUISITE SKILL **Multiply or divide.**

44. 2.5×20
45. 3.5×4
46. $4{,}200 \div 2.1$
47. $104 \div 6.5$

3-6

Measurement: Perimeter and Area

MAIN IDEA

Find the perimeters and areas of figures.

New Vocabulary

perimeter
area

Math Online

glencoe.com

- Extra Examples
- Personal Tutor
- Self-Check Quiz

GET READY for the Lesson

MEASUREMENT At the end of gym class, Mrs. Dalton has the students run around the perimeter of the gym.

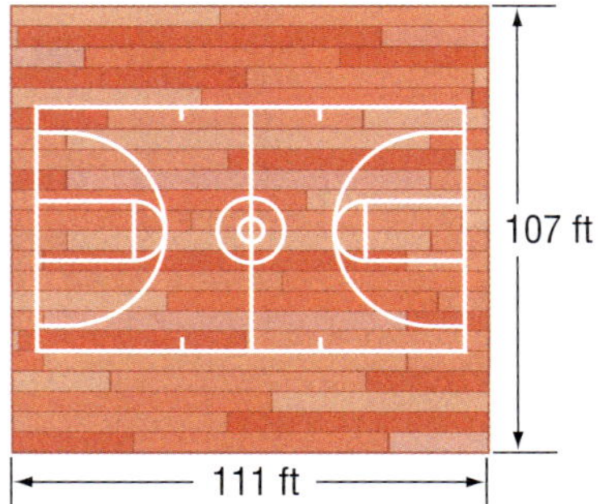

1. If the students run around the gym 5 times, how far would they run?
2. Explain how you can use both multiplication and addition to find the distance.

The distance around a geometric figure is called the **perimeter**. To find the perimeter of a rectangle, you can use these formulas.

Perimeter of a Rectangle — Key Concept

Words The perimeter P of a rectangle is twice the sum of the length ℓ and width w.

Symbols $P = \ell + \ell + w + w$

$P = 2\ell + 2w$ or $2(\ell + w)$

Model (rectangle with sides ℓ and w)

EXAMPLE Find the Perimeter of a Rectangle

1 **Find the perimeter of the rectangle shown at the right.**

(rectangle: 4 cm by 15 cm)

$P = 2\ell + 2w$	Perimeter of a rectangle
$P = 2(15) + 2(4)$	Replace ℓ with 15 and w with 4.
$P = 30 + 8$	Multiply.
$P = 38$	Add.

The perimeter is 38 centimeters.

CHECK Your Progress

a. Find the perimeter of a rectangle whose length is 14.5 inches and width is 12.5 inches.

 Real-World EXAMPLE

Find a Missing Side

2 **GARDENS** **Elan is designing a rectangular garden. He wants the width to be 8 feet. He also wants to put a fence around the garden. If he has 40 feet of fencing, what is the greatest length the garden can be?**

$P = 2\ell + 2w$	Perimeter of a rectangle
$40 = 2\ell + 2(8)$	Replace *P* with 40 and *w* with 8.
$40 = 2\ell + 16$	Multiply.
$-16 = \quad -16$	Subtract 16 from each side.
$24 = 2\ell$	Simplify.
$12 = \ell$	Divide each side by 2.

The greatest length the garden can be is 12 feet.

 CHECK Your Progress

b. **FRAMES** Angela bought a frame for a photo of her friends. The width of the frame is 8 inches. If the distance around the frame is 36 inches, what is the length of the frame?

The distance *around* a rectangle is its perimeter. The measure of the surface *enclosed* by a rectangle is its **area**.

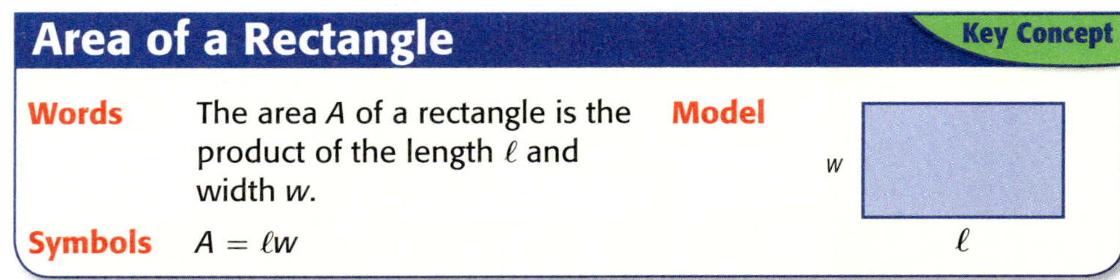

Area of a Rectangle — Key Concept

Words The area *A* of a rectangle is the product of the length ℓ and width *w*.

Symbols $A = \ell w$

Model

EXAMPLE

Find the Area of a Rectangle

Study Tip

Area Units
When finding area, the units are also multiplied. So, area is given in *square units*. Consider a rectangle 2 ft by 3 ft.

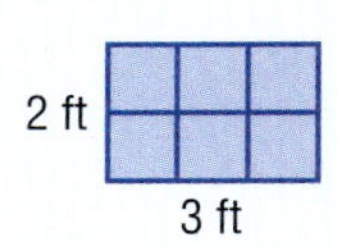

$A = 2 \text{ ft} \cdot 3 \text{ ft}$

$A = (2 \cdot 3)(\text{ft} \cdot \text{ft})$

$A = 6 \text{ ft}^2$

3 **TOYS** **Find the area of the top of the wooden train table shown at the right.**

$A = \ell w$	Area of a rectangle
$A = 49 \cdot 35$	Replace ℓ with 49 and *w* with 35.
$A = 1{,}715$	Multiply.

The area is 1,715 square inches.

 CHECK Your Progress

c. **VIDEO GAMES** Find the perimeter and area of the top of a video game console that measures 18 inches long and 15 inches wide.

EXAMPLE Use Area to Find a Missing Side

4 **The area of a rectangle is 53.94 square feet. If the width is 8.7 feet, find the length.**

METHOD 1 **Substitute, then solve.**

$A = \ell w$	Write the equation.
$53.94 = \ell(8.7)$	Replace *A* with 53.94 and *w* with 8.7.
$\frac{53.94}{8.7} = \frac{\ell(8.7)}{8.7}$	Divide each side by 8.7.
$\ell = 6.2$	Simplify.

METHOD 2 **Solve, then substitute.**

$A = \ell w$	Write the equation.
$\frac{A}{w} = \frac{\ell w}{w}$	Divide each side by *w*.
$\frac{A}{w} = \ell$	Simplify.
$\frac{53.94}{8.7} = \ell$	Replace *A* with 53.94 and *w* with 8.7.
$\ell = 6.2$	Simplify.

So, the length of the rectangle is 6.2 feet.

Study Tip

Check for Reasonableness You know that $53.94 \approx 54$ and that $8.77 \approx 9$. Since $54 \div 9 = 6$, the answer is reasonable.

CHOOSE Your Method

d. What is the width of a rectangle that has an area of 135 square meters and a length of 9 meters?

CHECK Your Understanding

Example 1 (p. 156)

Find the perimeter of each rectangle.

1.

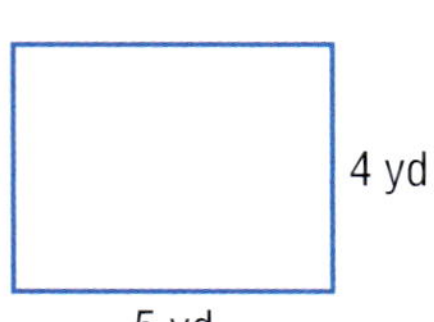

2.

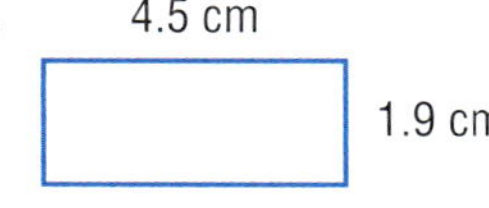

Example 2 (p. 157)

3. **PHOTOGRAPHY** A photograph is 5 inches wide. The perimeter of the photograph is 24 inches. What is the length of the photograph?

Example 3 (p. 157)

Find the area of each rectangle.

4.

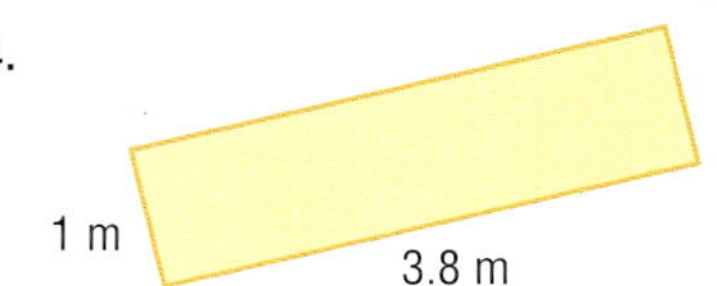

5.

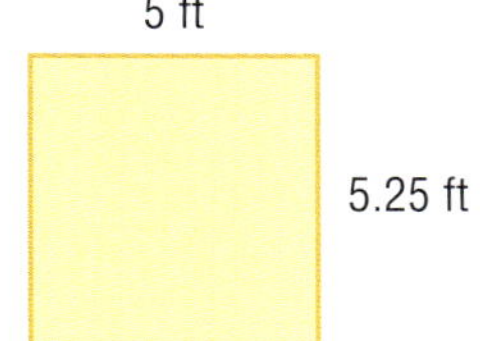

Example 4 (p. 158)

6. **MEASUREMENT** The area and length of a rectangle are 30 square feet and 6 feet, respectively. What is the width of the rectangle?

Practice and Problem Solving

HOMEWORK HELP

For Exercises	See Examples
7–12	1
13–14	2
15–20	3
21–22	4

Find the perimeter of each rectangle.

7.
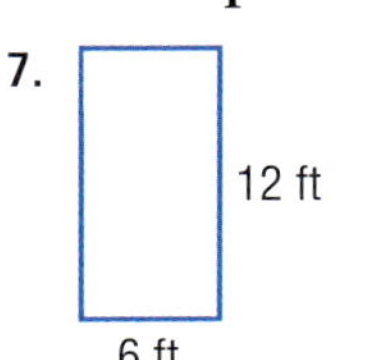

8. 18 in.
23 in.

9.
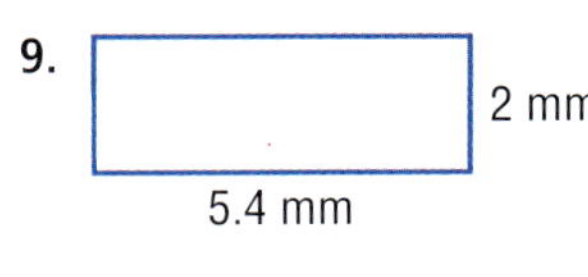

10. 3.8 cm
2.4 cm

11. $\ell = 1.5$ ft, $w = 4$ ft

12. $\ell = 5.75$ ft, $w = 8$ ft

13. **SEWING** The fringe used to outline a placemat is 60 inches. If the width of the placemat is 12 inches, what is the measure of its length?

14. **GAMES** Orlando marks off a rectangular section of grass to use as a playing field. He knows that he needs to mark off 111 feet around the border of the playing field. If the field is 25.5 feet long, what is its width?

Find the area of each rectangle.

15. 13 ft
6 ft

16. 3 yd
11 yd

17.
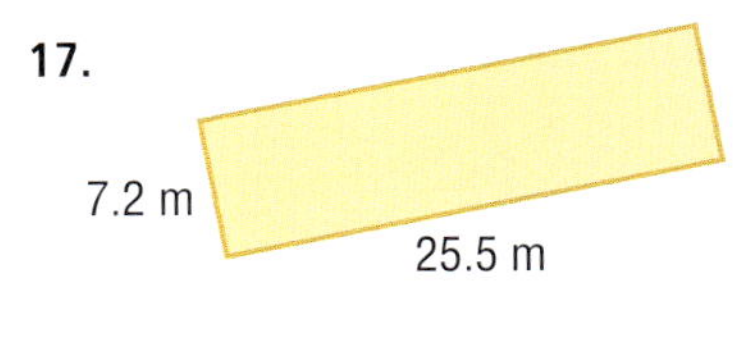

18. 16.5 cm
8.4 cm

19. $\ell = 3.25$ in., $w = 2$ in.

20. $\ell = 4.5$ ft, $w = 10.6$ ft

21. **QUILTING** Daniela's grandmother is making a quilt that is 7 squares wide. If she needs 35 squares total, how many squares long is the length?

22. **PAINTING** A rectangular mural is painted on a wall. If the mural is 12 feet wide and covers 86.4 square feet, what is the height of the mural?

Find the missing measure.

23. $P = 115.6$ ft, $w = 24.8$ ft

24. $A = 189.28 \text{ cm}^2$, $w = 16.9$ cm

ANALYZE TABLES **For Exercises 25 and 26, use the table shown.**

Youth Soccer Fields

Age (years)	Length (yards)	Width (yards)
10	70	40
12	80	50
14	100	60

25. How much greater is the area of a soccer field for a 14-year-old than for a 10-year-old?

26. An *acre* equals 4,840 square yards. How many acres are there in a field for a 12-year-old? Round to the nearest hundredth.

For Exercises 27–30, determine whether the problem involves perimeter, area, or both. Then solve.

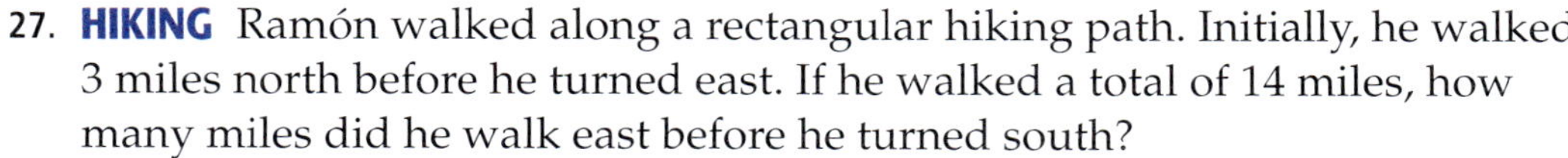

27. **HIKING** Ramón walked along a rectangular hiking path. Initially, he walked 3 miles north before he turned east. If he walked a total of 14 miles, how many miles did he walk east before he turned south?

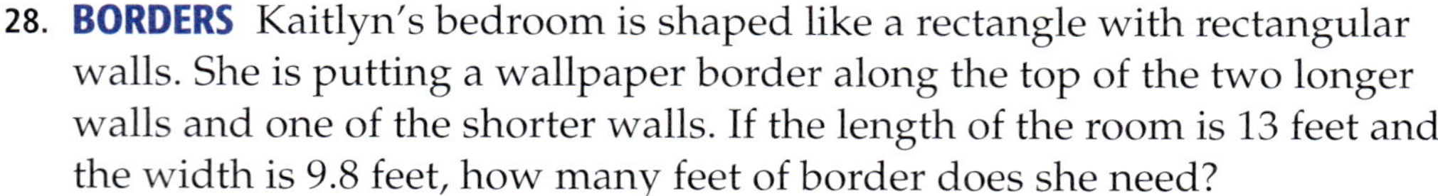

28. **BORDERS** Kaitlyn's bedroom is shaped like a rectangle with rectangular walls. She is putting a wallpaper border along the top of the two longer walls and one of the shorter walls. If the length of the room is 13 feet and the width is 9.8 feet, how many feet of border does she need?

29. **DECKS** Armando built a rectangular deck in his backyard. The deck takes up 168.75 square feet of space. If the deck's width is 12.8 feet, what is its approximate length?

30. **FENCING** Kina plans to fence her rectangular backyard on three sides. Her backyard measures 48 feet in length. She will not fence one of the shorter sides. If the area of her backyard is 1,752 square feet, how many feet of fencing is required?

Real-World Link
Regulation volleyball courts are 18 meters long by 9 meters wide, not including the free zone.
Source: USA Volleyball

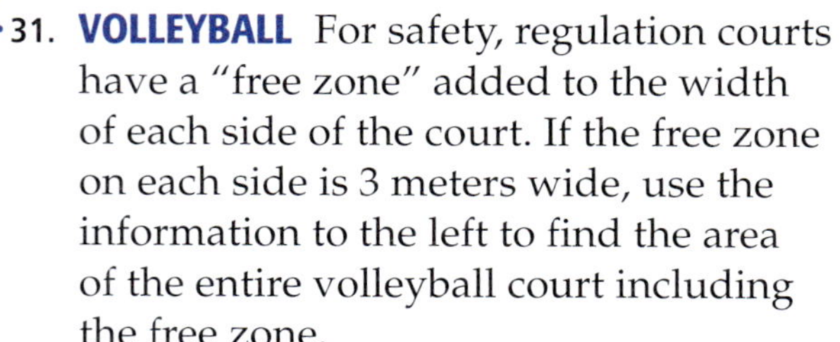

31. **VOLLEYBALL** For safety, regulation courts have a "free zone" added to the width of each side of the court. If the free zone on each side is 3 meters wide, use the information to the left to find the area of the entire volleyball court including the free zone.

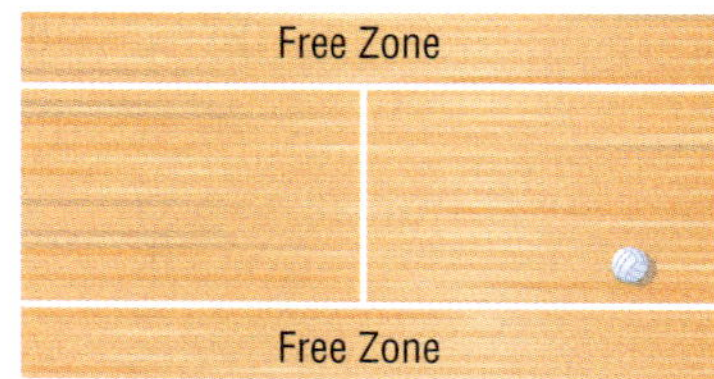

32. **GEOMETRY** Use the diagram at the right to write formulas for the perimeter P and area A of a square.

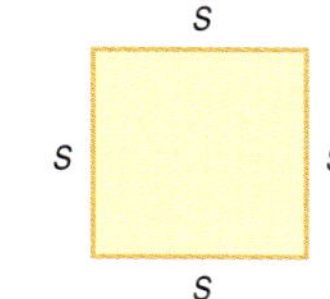

33. **FIND THE DATA** Refer to the Data File on pages 16–19. Choose some data and write a real-world problem in which you would find the perimeter and area of a rectangle.

EXTRA PRACTICE
See pages 675, 706.

H.O.T. Problems

34. **OPEN ENDED** Draw and label three different rectangles that have an area of 24 square centimeters.

CHALLENGE For Exercises 35–38, find each equivalent measurement. Provide a diagram to justify your answers. The diagram for Exercise 35 is shown.

35. $1 \text{ yd}^2 = \blacksquare \text{ ft}^2$
36. $4 \text{ yd}^2 = \blacksquare \text{ ft}^2$
37. $1 \text{ ft}^2 = \blacksquare \text{ in}^2$
38. $2 \text{ ft}^2 = \blacksquare \text{ in}^2$

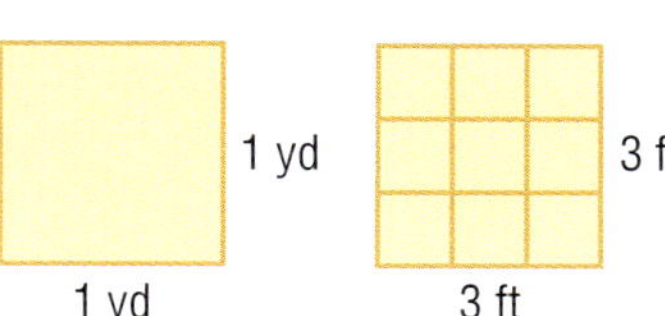

NUMBER SENSE For Exercises 39 and 40, describe the effect on the perimeter and area in each of the following situations.

39. The width of a rectangle is doubled.
40. The length of a side of a square is doubled.

41. **CHALLENGE** A rectangle has width w. Its length is one unit more than 3 times its width. Write an expression that represents the perimeter of the rectangle.

42. **WRITING IN MATH** Decide whether the statement is *true* or *false*. Explain your reasoning and provide examples.

Of all rectangles with a perimeter of 24 square inches, the one with the greatest area is a square.

TEST PRACTICE

43. Oakland Garden Center created a design plan for the Nelson family's rock garden. The shaded areas will hold flowers and the rest of the garden will be rock.

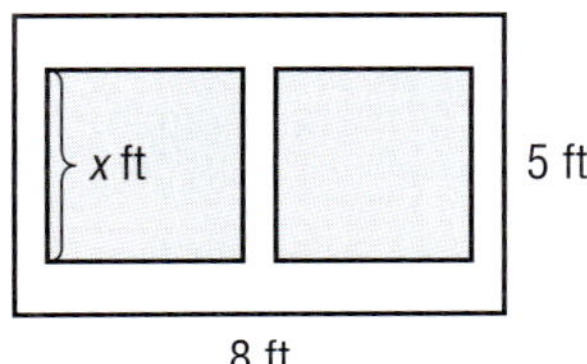

If each shaded area is a square, which expression represents the area of the garden that will be rock?

A $(40 - 2x^2)$ ft^2 **C** $(40 + x)$ ft^2

B $(40 - x)$ ft^2 **D** $(40 + x^2)$ ft^2

44. The rectangle below has width 4.75 feet and perimeter P feet.

4.75 ft

ℓ ft

Which of the following could be used to find the length of the rectangle?

F $P = 4.75 + \frac{\ell}{2}$

G $P = 4.75 - \ell$

H $P = 9.5 + 2\ell$

J $P = 9.5 - 2\ell$

Spiral Review

Solve each equation. Check your solution. (Lesson 3-5)

45. $5d + 12 = 2$ 46. $13 - f = 7$ 47. $10 = 2g + 3$ 48. $6 = 3 - 3h$

49. **ALGEBRA** Anna was charged \$11.25 for returning a DVD 5 days late. Write and solve an equation to find how much the video store charges per day for late fees. (Lesson 3-3)

Multiply. (Lesson 2-6)

50. $14(-5)$ 51. $(-3)^3$ 52. $-10(2)(-8)$

53. **AGE** The sum of Denise's and Javier's ages is 26 years. If Denise is 4 years older than Javier, find Javier's age. Use the *guess and check* strategy. (Lesson 1-5)

GET READY for the Next Lesson

PREREQUISITE SKILL **Graph and label each point on a coordinate plane.** (Lesson 2-3)

54. $(-4, 2)$ 55. $(3, -1)$ 56. $(-3, -4)$ 57. $(2, 0)$

Explore
3-7

Measurement Lab
Representing Relationships

MAIN IDEA

Graph data to demonstrate the relationship between the dimensions and the perimeter of a rectangle.

In this lab, you will investigate the relationships between the dimensions and the perimeter of a rectangle.

ACTIVITY

STEP 1 Use 10 chenille stems, 24 centimeters in length, to form 10 rectangles with different dimensions.

STEP 2 Measure and record the width and length of each rectangle to the nearest centimeter in a table like the one at the right.

Width (cm)	Length (cm)

Analyze the Results

1. What rectangle measure does 24 centimeters represent?
2. Find the sum of the width and length for each of your rectangles. Write a sentence that describes the relationship between this sum and the measure of the length of the stem for each rectangle. Then write a rule that describes this relationship for a rectangle with a width w and length ℓ.
3. In this activity, if a rectangle has a length of 4.5 centimeters, what is its width? Explain your reasoning. Write a rule that can be used to find w when ℓ is known for any rectangle in this Activity.

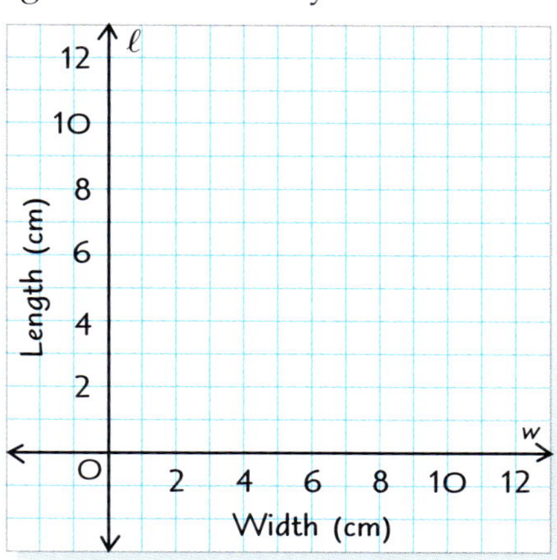

4. **GRAPH THE DATA** Graph the data in your table on a coordinate plane like the one at the right.
5. Describe what the ordered pair (w, ℓ) represents. Describe how these points appear on the graph.
6. Use your graph to find the width of a rectangle with a length of 7 centimeters. Explain your method.
7. **MAKE A CONJECTURE** If the length of each chenille stem was 20 centimeters, how would this affect the data in your table? the rule you wrote in Exercise 3? the appearance of your graph?

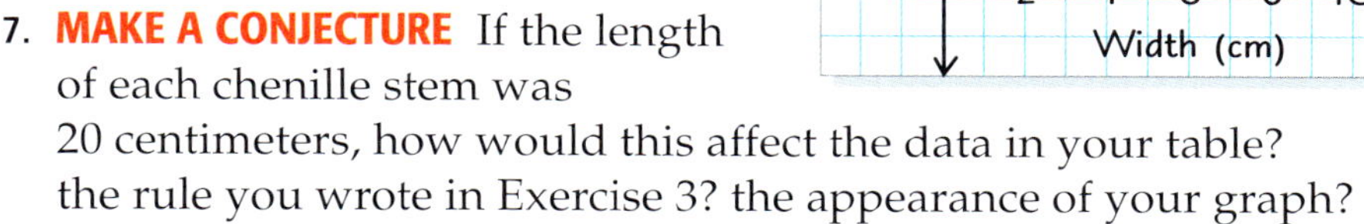

3-7 Functions and Graphs

MAIN IDEA

Graph data to demonstrate relationships.

New Vocabulary

linear equation

Math Online

glencoe.com

- Extra Examples
- Personal Tutor
- Self-Check Quiz

GET READY for the Lesson

MONEY The Westerville Marching Band is going on a year-end trip to an amusement park. Each band member must pay an admission price of \$15. In the table, this is represented by $15m$.

Total Cost of Admission

Number of Members	$15m$	Total Cost (\$)
1	15(1)	15
2	15(2)	30
3	15(3)	
4		
5		
6		

1. Copy and complete the function table for the total cost of admission.
2. Graph the ordered pairs (number of members, total cost).
3. Describe how the points appear on the graph.

If you are given a function, ordered pairs in the form (input, output), or (x, y), provide useful information about that function. These ordered pairs can then be graphed on a coordinate plane and form part of the graph of the function. The graph of the function consists of the points in the coordinate plane that correspond to *all* the ordered pairs of the form (input, output).

Real-World EXAMPLE

1 **TEMPERATURE** **The table shows temperatures in Celsius and the corresponding temperatures in Fahrenheit. Make a graph of the data to show the relationship between Celsius and Fahrenheit.**

Celsius (input)	Fahrenheit (output)
5	41
10	50
15	59
20	68
25	77
30	86

The ordered pairs (5, 41), (10, 50), (15, 59), (20, 68), (25, 77), and (30, 86) represent this function. Graph the ordered pairs.

Celsius to Fahrenheit

Review Vocabulary

function a relation in which each element of the input is paired with exactly one element of the output according to a specified rule (Lesson 1-10)

CHECK Your Progress

a. **MUSIC** The table shows the money remaining on a \$75 gift certificate after a certain number of CDs are bought. Make a graph to show how the number of CDs bought and the remaining balance are related.

$75 Music Gift Certificate	
Number of CDs	**Balance ($)**
1	63
2	51
3	39
4	27
5	15

The solution of an equation with two variables consists of two numbers, one for each variable, that make the equation true. The solution is usually written as an ordered pair (x, y).

EXAMPLE Graph Solutions of Linear Equations

Graph $y = 2x + 1$.

Select any four values for the input x. We chose 2, 1, 0, and -1. Substitute these values for x to find the output y.

x	$2x + 1$	y	(x, y)
2	$2(2) + 1$	5	(2, 5)
1	$2(1) + 1$	3	(1, 3)
0	$2(0) + 1$	1	(0, 1)
-1	$2(-1) + 1$	-1	$(-1, -1)$

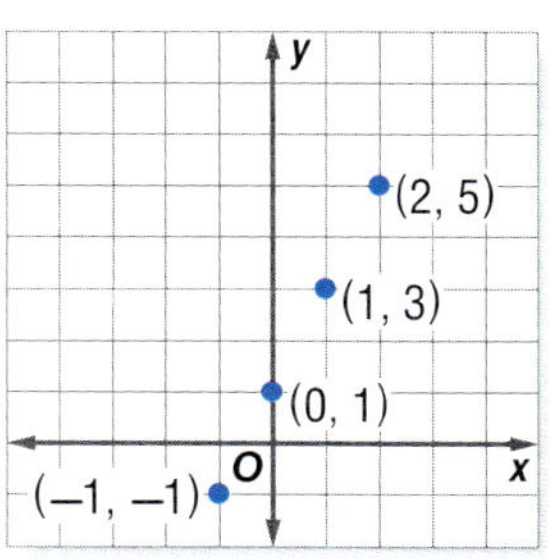

The four inputs correspond to the solutions (2, 5), (1, 3), (0, 1), and $(-1, -1)$. By graphing these ordered pairs, you can create the graph of $y = 2x + 1$.

CHECK Your Progress **Graph each equation.**

b. $y = x - 3$ c. $y = -3x$ d. $y = -3x + 2$

Study Tip

Graphing Equations Only two points are needed to graph the line. However, graph more points to check accuracy.

Notice that all four points in the graph lie on the same straight line. Draw a line through the points to graph *all* solutions of the equation $y = 2x + 1$. Note that the point (3, 7) is also on this line.

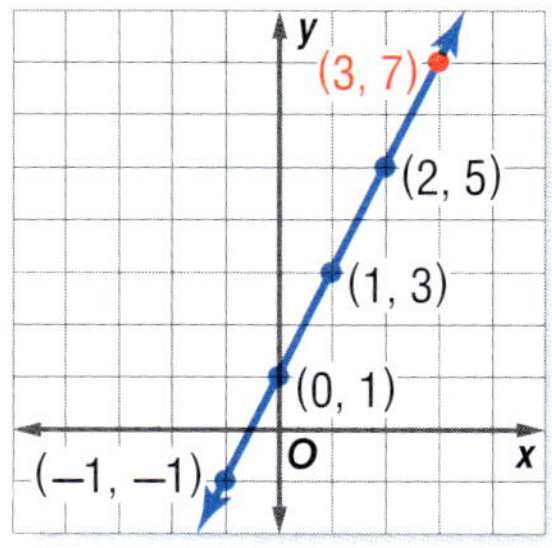

$y = 2x + 1$ Write the equation.

$7 \stackrel{?}{=} 2(3) + 1$ Replace x with 3 and y with 7.

$7 = 7$ ✓ This sentence is true.

So, (3, 7) is also a solution of $y = 2x + 1$. An equation like $y = 2x + 1$ is called a **linear equation** because its graph is a straight line.

Real-World EXAMPLE

3 **SWIMMING** **Michael Phelps swims the 400-meter individual medley at an average speed of 100 meters per minute. The equation $d = 100t$ describes the distance d that he can swim in t minutes at this speed. Represent the function by a graph.**

Step 1 Select any four values for t. Select only positive numbers because t represents time. Make a function table.

t	$100t$	d	(t, d)
1	100(1)	100	(1, 100)
2	100(2)	200	(2, 200)
3	100(3)	300	(3, 300)
4	100(4)	400	(4, 400)

Step 2 Graph the ordered pairs and draw a line through the points.

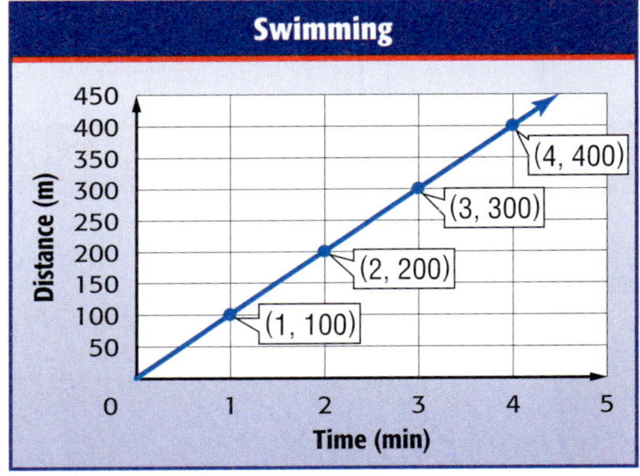

CHECK Your Progress

e. **JOBS** Sandi makes $6 an hour babysitting. The equation $m = 6h$ describes how much money m she earns babysitting for h hours. Represent this function by a graph.

Representing Functions

Key Concept

Words There are 12 inches in one foot.

Table

Feet	Inches
1	12
2	24
3	36
4	48

Graph

Convert Feet to Inches

Inches: 10, 20, 30, 40, 50, 60

Feet: 0, 1, 2, 3, 4

Equation $f = 12n$, where f represents the number of feet and n represents the number of inches.

CHECK Your Understanding

Example 1 (p. 163)

Graph the function represented by each table.

1.

Total Cost of Baseballs	
Baseball	**Total Cost ($)**
1	4
2	8
3	12
4	16

2.

Convert Minutes to Seconds	
Minutes	**Seconds**
1	60
2	120
3	180
4	240

Example 2 (p. 164)

Graph each equation.

3. $y = x - 1$
4. $y = -1x$
5. $y = -2x + 3$

Example 3 (p. 165)

6. **MEASUREMENT** The perimeter of a square is 4 times greater than the length of one of its sides. The equation $p = 4s$ describes the perimeter p of a square with sides s units long. Represent this function by a graph.

Practice and Problem Solving

HOMEWORK HELP

For Exercises	See Examples
7–8	1
9–14	2
15–16	3

Graph the function represented by each table.

7.

Total Phone Bill	
Time (min)	**Total (¢)**
1	8
2	16
3	24
4	32

8.

Calories in Fruit Cups	
Servings	**Total Calories**
1	70
3	210
5	350
7	490

Graph each equation.

9. $y = x + 1$
10. $y = x + 3$
11. $y = x$
12. $y = -2x$
13. $y = 2x + 3$
14. $y = 3x - 1$

For Exercises 15 and 16, represent each function by a graph.

15. **CARS** A car averages 36 miles per gallon of gasoline. The function $m = 36g$ represents the miles m driven using g gallons of gasoline.

16. **FITNESS** A health club charges $35 a month for membership fees. The equation $c = 35m$ describes the total charge c for m months of membership.

Graph each equation.

17. $y = 0.25x$
18. $y = x + 0.5$
19. $y = 0.5x - 1$

See pages 676, 706.

20. **SHOPPING** You buy a DVD for $14 and CDs for $9 each. The equation $t = 14 + 9c$ represents the total amount t that you spend if you buy 1 DVD and c CDs. Represent this function by a graph.

H.O.T. Problems

21. **OPEN ENDED** Draw the graph of a linear function. Name three ordered pairs in the function.

CHALLENGE For Exercises 22 and 23, let x represent the first number and let y represent the second number. Draw a graph of each function.

22. The second number is three more than the first number.

23. The second number is the product of -3 and the first number.

24. **WRITING IN MATH** Describe how you use a function table to create the graph of a function.

TEST PRACTICE

25. The graph shows the relationship between the number of hours Jennifer spent jogging and the total number of miles she jogged. Which table best represents the data in the graph?

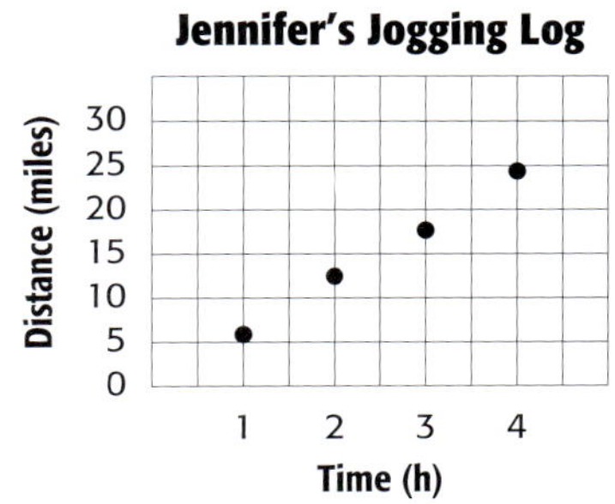

A

Time (h)	Distance (mi)
6	4
12	3
18	2
24	1

B

Time (h)	Distance (mi)
2	6
3	12
4	18
5	24

C

Time (h)	Distance (mi)
1	6
2	12
3	18
4	24

D

Time (h)	Distance (mi)
4	6
3	6
2	6
1	6

Spiral Review

26. **MEASUREMENT** The area and width of a rug are 323 square inches and 17 inches respectively. What is the perimeter of the rug? (Lesson 3-6)

Solve each equation. Check your solution. (Lesson 3-5)

27. $4y + 19 = 7$

28. $10x + 2 = 32$

29. $48 - 8j = 16$

30. $14 = 2 - 6d$

31. Evaluate $|5| + |-10|$. (Lesson 2-1)

Problem Solving in Social Studies

Real-World Unit Project

Stand Up and Be Counted! It's time to complete your project. Use the data you have gathered about how the U.S. Census affects the House of Representatives to prepare a poster. Be sure to include a map, frequency table, and paragraph discussing the changes in the House of Representatives.

Math Online **Unit Project at** glencoe.com

Extend 3-7

Graphing Calculator Lab
Graphing Relationships

MAIN IDEA

Use technology to graph relationships involving conversions of measurement.

You can use a graphing calculator to graph relationships.

ACTIVITY

1 **MEASUREMENT** **Use the table at the right to write a function that relates the number of yards x to the number of feet y. Then graph your function.**

Yards (x)	Feet (y)
1	3
2	6
3	9
4	12

STEP 1 By examining the table, you can see that the number of feet is 3 times the number of yards. Write a function.

The number of feet — is — 3 times — the number of yards.

$y = 3x$

STEP 2 Press [Y=] and enter the function $y = 3x$ into Y_1.

STEP 3 Adjust your viewing window. Press [WINDOW] and change the values to reflect the range of values in the table.

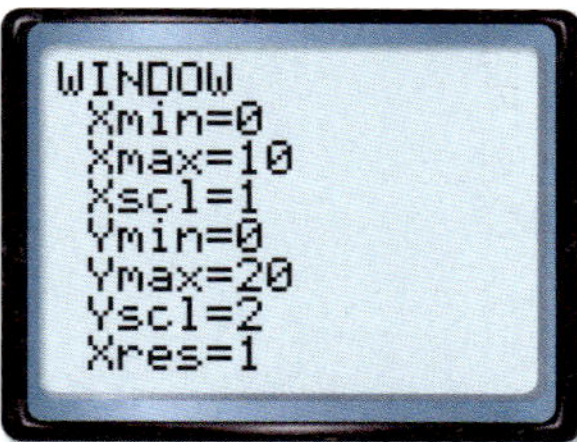

STEP 4 Finally, graph the function by pressing [Graph].

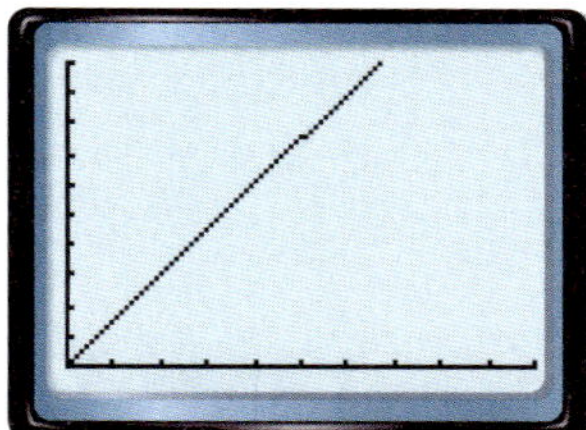

Analyze the Results

1. Test the function above using one of the values from the table and the CALC feature on your calculator. Press [2nd] [CALC] 1 and then enter an x-value of 3. What y-value is displayed? What do each of these values represent and how are they represented on the graph?
2. Use your graph to convert 7 yards into feet. Explain your method.
3. **MAKE A CONJECTURE** Write a function that could be used to convert feet into yards. What is an appropriate window for a graph of this function? Graph and test your function.
4. Use your function from Exercise 3 to convert 16 feet into yards.
5. Write a function that could be used to convert 36 ounces to pounds. Indicate an appropriate window, then use a graph of the function to convert 36 ounces to pounds. (*Hint*: 1 pound = 16 ounces)

Chapter 3 Study Guide and Review

Math Online glencoe.com
• STUDY TO GO
• Vocabulary Review

GET READY to Study

Be sure the following Big Ideas are noted in your Foldable.

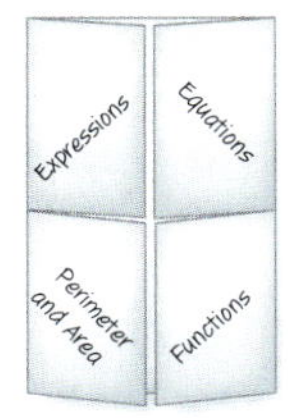

BIG Ideas

Solving Equations (Lessons 3-2, 3-3, and 3-5)

- If you add or subtract the same number from each side of an equation, the two sides remain equal.
- If you divide each side of an equation by the same nonzero number, the two sides remain equal.
- To solve a two-step equation like $3x + 4 = 19$ or $2x - 1 = -5$:
  - Step 1 Undo the addition or subtraction first.
  - Step 2 Then undo the multiplication or division.

Perimeter and Area Formulas (Lesson 3-6)

- The perimeter P of a rectangle is twice the sum of the length ℓ and width w.
- The area A of a rectangle is the product of the length ℓ and width w.

Linear Functions (Lesson 3-7)

- The graph of a linear function is a straight line. Ordered pairs in the form (x, y) can be used to represent a function and graphed on the coordinate plane as part of the graph of the function.

Key Vocabulary

formula (p. 144)
linear equation (p. 164)
two-step equation (p. 151)
work backward strategy (p. 148)

Vocabulary Check

State whether each sentence is *true* or *false*. If *false*, replace the underlined word or number to make a true sentence.

1. The expression $\frac{1}{3}y$ means <u>one third of y</u>.
2. The words *more than* sometimes suggest the operation of <u>multiplication</u>.
3. The formula <u>$d = rt$</u> gives the distance d traveled at a rate of r for t units of time.
4. The algebraic expression representing the words *six less than m* is <u>$6 - m$</u>.
5. Use the <u>work backward</u> strategy when you are given a final result and asked to find an earlier amount.
6. The word *each* sometimes suggests the operation of <u>division</u>.
7. In solving the equation $4x + 3 = 15$, first <u>divide each side by 4</u>.
8. The solution to the equation $p + 4.4 = 11.6$ is <u>7.2</u>.
9. The process of solving a <u>two-step equation</u> uses the work backward strategy.
10. The expression $5x$ means <u>5 more than x</u>.
11. To find the distance around a rectangle, use the formula for its <u>area</u>.
12. The word *per* sometimes suggests the operation of <u>subtraction</u>.

CHAPTER 3

Study Guide and Review

Lesson-by-Lesson Review

3-1 Writing Expressions and Equations (pp. 128–133)

Write each phrase as an algebraic expression.

13. the sum of a number and 5
14. six inches less than her height
15. twice as many apples

Write each sentence as an algebraic equation.

16. Ten years older than Theresa's age is 23.
17. Four less than a number is 19.
18. The quotient of 56 and a number is 14.

19. **AMUSEMENT PARKS** This year, admission to a popular amusement park is $8.75 more than the previous year's admission fee. Write an expression describing the cost of this year's admission.

Example 1 **Write the phrase as an algebraic expression.**

four times the price

Let p represent the price.

The algebraic expression is $4p$.

Example 2 **Write the sentence as an algebraic equation.**

Six less than the number of cookies is 24.

Let c represent the number of cookies.

The equation is $c - 6 = 24$.

3-2 Solving Addition and Subtraction Equations (pp. 136–141)

Solve each equation. Check your solution.

20. $x + 5 = 8$
21. $r + 8 = 2$
22. $p + 9 = -4$
23. $s - 8 = 15$
24. $n - 1 = -3$
25. $w - 9 = 28$
26. **COOKIES** Marjorie baked some chocolate chip cookies for her and her sister. Her sister ate 6 of these cookies. If there were 18 cookies left, write and solve an equation to find how many cookies c Marjorie baked.

Example 3 **Solve $x + 6 = 4$.**

$$\begin{aligned} x + 6 &= 4 \\ -6 &= -6 \quad \text{Subtract 6 from each side.} \\ x &= -2 \end{aligned}$$

Example 4 **Solve $y - 3 = -2$.**

$$\begin{aligned} y - 3 &= -2 \\ +3 &= +3 \quad \text{Add 3 to each side.} \\ y &= 1 \end{aligned}$$

Mixed Problem Solving
For mixed problem-solving practice, see page 706.

3-3 Solving Multiplication Equations (pp. 142–146)

Solve each equation. Check your solution.

27. $7c = 28$
28. $-8w = 72$
29. $10y = -90$
30. $-12r = -36$
31. **MONEY** Matt borrowed \$98 from his father. He plans to repay his father at \$14 per week. Write and solve an equation to find the number of weeks w required to pay back his father.

Example 5 **Solve $-4b = 32$.**

$-4b = 32$

$\frac{-4b}{-4} = \frac{32}{-4}$ Divide each side by −4.

$b = -8$

3-4 PSI: Work Backward (pp. 148–149)

Solve. Use the *work backward* strategy.

32. **BASEBALL** Last baseball season, Nelson had four less than twice the number of hits Marcus had. Nelson had 48 hits. How many hits did Marcus have last season?
33. **CREDIT CARDS** Alicia paid off \$119 of her credit card balance and made an additional \$62.75 in purchases. If she now owes \$90.45, what was her starting balance?

Example 6 **A number is divided by 2. Then 4 is added to the quotient. After subtracting 3, the result is 18. What is the number?**

Start with the final value and work backward with each resulting value until you arrive at the starting value.

$18 + 3 = 21$ Undo subtracting 3.

$21 - 4 = 17$ Undo adding 4.

$17 \cdot 2 = 34$ Undo dividing by 2.

The number is 34.

3-5 Solving Two-Step Equations (pp. 151–155)

Solve each equation. Check your solution.

34. $3y - 12 = 6$
35. $6x - 4 = 20$
36. $2x + 5 = 3$
37. $5m + 6 = -4$
38. $10c - 8 = 90$
39. $3r - 20 = -5$
40. **ALGEBRA** Ten more than five times a number is 25. Find the number.

Example 7 **Solve $3p - 4 = 8$.**

$3p - 4 = 8$

$\underline{+4 = +4}$ Add 4 to each side.

$3p = 12$

$\frac{3p}{3} = \frac{12}{3}$ Divide each side by 3.

$p = 4$

CHAPTER 3

Study Guide and Review

3-6 Measurement: Perimeter and Area (pp. 156–161)

Find the perimeter and area of each rectangle.

41. **42.**

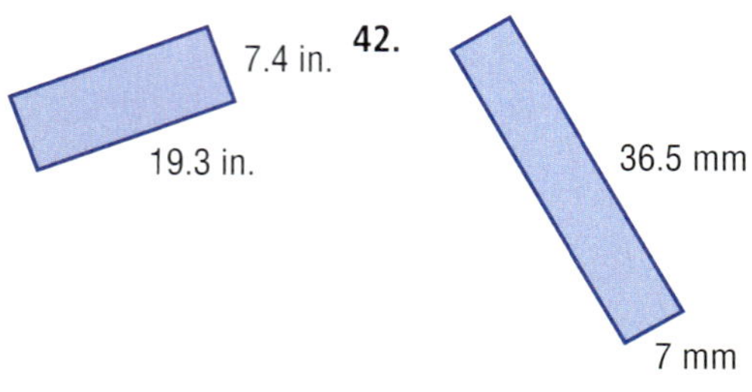

Find the missing measure.

43. $P = 56$ mi, $\ell = 21$ mi

44. $A = 10.26$ ft^2, $w = 2.7$ ft

45. $A = 272$ yd^2, $\ell = 17$ yd

46. $P = 14.2$ cm, $w = 2.6$ cm

47. **CARPET** In order to carpet her rectangular living room, Flora needs 192 square feet of carpet. If the length of her living room is 16 feet, find the width.

Example 8 **The perimeter of a rectangle is 38 meters. If the length is 7 meters, find the width.**

$P = 2\ell + 2w$ Perimeter formula

$38 = 2(7) + 2w$ Replace P with 38 and ℓ with 7.

$38 = 14 + 2w$ Simplify.

$24 = 2w$ Subtract 14 from each side.

$\frac{24}{2} = \frac{2w}{2}$ Divide each side by 2.

$12 = w$ Simplify.

The width is 12 meters.

Example 9 **The area of a rectangle is 285 square inches. If the width is 15 inches, find the length.**

$A = \ell w$ Area formula

$285 = \ell(15)$ Replace A with 285 and w with 15.

$\frac{285}{15} = \frac{15\ell}{15}$ Divide each side by 15.

$19 = \ell$ Simplify.

The length is 19 inches.

3-7 Functions and Graphs (pp. 163–167)

Graph each equation.

48. $y = x + 5$

49. $y = x - 4$

50. $y = 2x$

51. $y = -1x$

52. $y = 3x + 2$

53. $y = -2x + 3$

MONEY **For Exercises 54–56, use the following information.**

Clara earns \$9 per hour mowing lawns.

54. Make a table that shows her total earnings for 2, 4, 6, and 8 hours.

55. Write an equation in which x represents the number of hours and y represents Clara's total earnings.

56. Graph the equation.

Example 10 Graph $y = x + 3$.

Select four values for x. Substitute these values for x to find values for y.

x	$x + 3$	y
−1	−1 + 3	2
0	0 + 3	3
1	1 + 3	4
2	2 + 3	5

Four solutions are (−1, 2), (0, 3), (1, 4), and (2, 5). The graph is shown below.

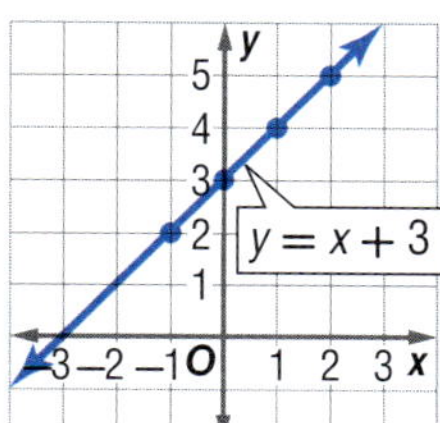

CHAPTER 3

Practice Test

Math Online glencoe.com

• Chapter Test

Write each phrase as an algebraic expression or equation.

1. $5 less than Tomasita has
2. 4 years older than Hana
3. 56 inches is 9 inches shorter than Jacob's height.
4. Twice the distance from the park to the post office is 5 miles.

5. **FLOWERS** The number of tulips in Paula's garden is 8 less than the number of marigolds. If there are 16 tulips, write and solve an equation to determine the number of marigolds m.

6. **MULTIPLE CHOICE** If you divide a number by 8 and subtract 11 from the result, the answer is 4. Which equation matches this relationship?

   A $\frac{n-11}{8} = 4$

   B $4 = \frac{n}{8} - 11$

   C $\frac{n}{8} = 11 - 4$

   D $4 = 11 - \frac{n}{8}$

ANALYZE TABLES **For Exercises 7–9, use the table below. It shows how Jared's age and his sister Emily's are related.**

Jared's age (yr)	1	2	3	4	5
Emily's age (yr)	7	8	9	10	11

7. Write an equation in which x represents Jared's age, and y represents Emily's age.
8. Graph the equation.
9. Predict how old Emily will be when Jared is 10 years old.

10. **TOURISM** The Statue of Liberty is 151 feet tall. It is 835 feet shorter than the Eiffel Tower. Write and solve an equation to find the height of the Eiffel Tower.

Solve each equation. Check your solution.

11. $x + 5 = -8$
12. $y - 11 = 15$
13. $9z = -81$
14. $-6k + 4 = -38$
15. $3z - 7 = 17$
16. $2g - 9 = -5$

17. **PIZZA** Chris and Joe shared a pizza. Chris ate two more than twice as many pieces as Joe, who ate 3 pieces. If there were 3 pieces left, how many pieces were there initially? Use the *work backward* strategy.

18. **MULTIPLE CHOICE** A giant cake in the shape of and decorated as an American flag was 60 feet in length. If it took A square feet of icing to cover the top of the cake, which of the following would represent the cake's perimeter?

   F $P = 120 + 2 \cdot \frac{A}{60}$

   G $P = 120 + 2A$

   H $P = 60 + \frac{A}{60}$

   J $P = 60 + 2A$

Find the perimeter and area of each rectangle.

19. 20.

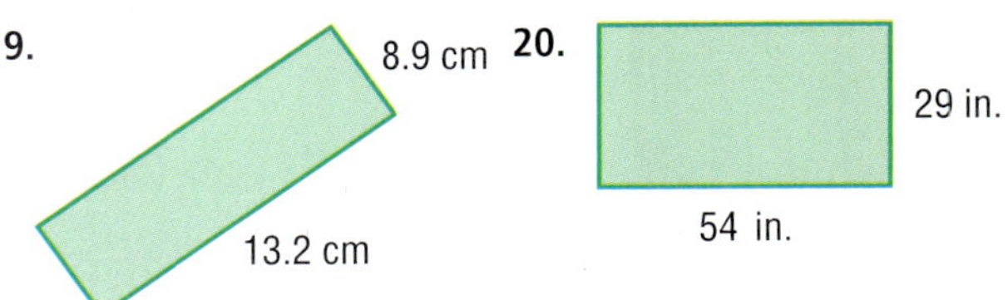

Graph each equation.

21. $y = x + 1$
22. $y = 2x$
23. $y = 2x - 3$
24. $y = -x + 1$

25. **MOVIES** A student ticket to the movies costs \$6. The equation $c = 6t$ describes the total cost c for t tickets. Make a function table that shows the total cost for 1, 2, 3, and 4 tickets and then graph the equation.

Chapter 3 Test Practice
Cumulative, Chapters 1–3

Math Online glencoe.com
• Test Practice

PART 1 Multiple Choice

Read each question. Then fill in the correct answer on the answer sheet provided by your teacher or on a sheet of paper.

1. During a bike-a-thon, Shalonda cycled at a constant rate. The table shows the distance she covered in half-hour intervals.

Time (h)	Distance (mi)
$\frac{1}{2}$	6
1	12
$1\frac{1}{2}$	18
2	24

Which of the following equations represents the distance d Shalonda covered after h hours?

A $d = 6 + h$

B $d = 6h$

C $d = 12 + h$

D $d = 12h$

2. Which line contains the ordered pair $(-2, 4)$?

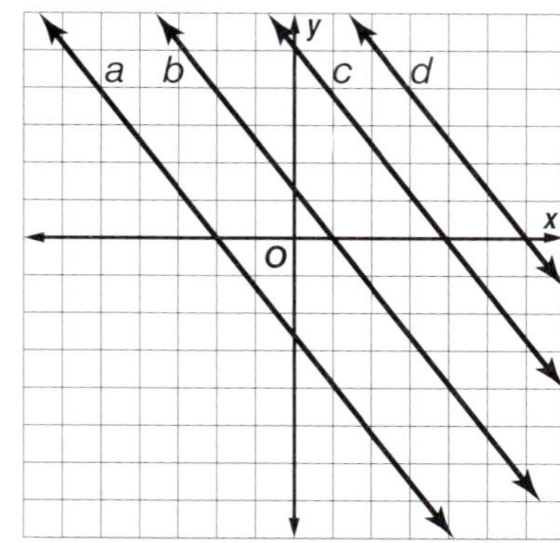

F line a
H line b
G line c
J line d

3. The table gives the value of several terms and their positions in a sequence.

Position	3	4	5	6	7	n
Value of Term	13	17	21	25	29	

Which description shows the relationship between a term and n, its position in the sequence?

A Add 4 to n.

B Multiply n by 5 and add 1.

C Multiply n by 3 and add 2.

D Multiply n by 4 and add 1.

4. Mr. McDowell owes \$1,750 on his car loan and pays off \$185 each month towards the loan balance. Which expression represents how much money in dollars he still owes after x months?

F $1{,}750x$

G $1{,}750x + 185$

H $1{,}750x - 185$

J $1{,}750 - 185x$

5. Which of the following problems can be solved by solving the equation $x - 9 = 15$?

A Allison is nine years younger than her sister Pam. Allison is 15 years old. What is x, Pam's age?

B David's portion of the bill is \$9 more than Sam's portion of the bill. If Sam pays \$9, find x, the amount in dollars that David pays.

C The sum of two numbers is 15. If one of the numbers is 9, what is x, the other number?

D Pedro owns 15 CDs. If he gave 9 of them to a friend, what is x, the number of CDs he has left?

Preparing for Standardized Tests

For test-taking strategies and practice, see pages 716–733.

6. The table below shows values for x and corresponding values for y.

x	y
18	2
27	3
9	1
36	4

Which of the following represents the relationship between x and y?

F $y = x + 16$

G $y = 9x$

H $y = \frac{1}{9}x$

J $y = x + 9$

TEST-TAKING TIP

Question 7 Read the question carefully to check that you answered the question that was asked. In question 7, you are asked to pick which coordinates lie within the triangle, not to identify a vertex.

7. Which of the following coordinates lies within the triangle graphed below?

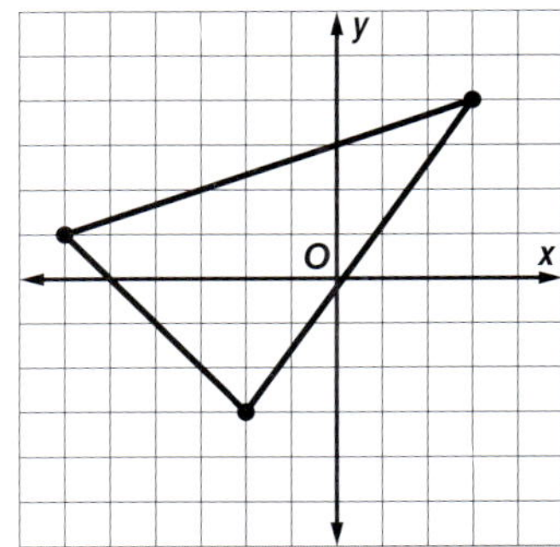

A (3, 4)

B (2, 0)

C (−3, 6)

D (−1, −1)

PART 2 Short Response/Grid In

Record your answers on the answer sheet provided by your teacher or on a sheet of paper.

8. Write an expression that can be used to find the maximum number of 3-foot pieces of lumber than can be cut from a 12-foot length of lumber.

9. Tonya bought p pounds of sand. Each pound of sand costs \$0.40. How many pounds of sand could Tonya buy with \$3.20?

PART 3 Extended Response

Record your answers on the answer sheet provided by your teacher or on a sheet of paper. Show your work.

10. The distances traveled by cars traveling at 40 miles per hour and at 60 miles per hour are given in the table.

Time (hours)	Distance (miles) at 40 mph	Distance (miles) at 60 mph
0	0	0
1	40	60
2	80	120
3	120	180
4	160	240

a. Graph the ordered pairs (time, distance) for 40 miles per hour.

b. Graph the ordered pairs (time, distance) for 60 miles per hour.

c. Predict where the ordered pairs for 50 miles per hour would be graphed. Explain how you know.

NEED EXTRA HELP?										
If You Missed Question...	1	2	3	4	5	6	7	8	9	10
Go to Lesson...	3-7	3-7	1-9	3-1	3-1	3-7	3-7	2-8	1-7	3-7

Unit 2

Number Sense: Fractions

Focus

Represent and use numbers in a variety of equivalent forms and apply addition, subtraction, multiplication, and division of fractions.

CHAPTER 4
Fractions, Decimals, and Percents

BIG Idea Represent and use numbers in a variety of forms.

CHAPTER 5
Applying Fractions

BIG Idea Extend understandings of operations. Add, subtract, multiply, and divide to solve fraction problems.

Problem Solving in Geography

Real-World Unit Project

A Traveling We Will Go You're about to embark on a journey to your favorite vacation spot in the United States. In your role as a travel agent, you will plan a vacation for you and your family. You will calculate the total cost including transportation, lodging, and tourist attractions. So bring your sense of adventure and get ready to set off on your trip!

Math Online **Log on to glencoe.com to begin.**

Fractions, Decimals, and Percents

- Represent and use numbers in a variety of equivalent forms.

Key Vocabulary

equivalent fractions (p. 192)
percent (p. 202)
ratio (p. 202)
simplest form (p. 192)

Reptiles North Carolina's state reptile is the Eastern Box Turtle. Adults range in size from $4\frac{1}{2}$ inches to $5\frac{9}{10}$ inches. You can write these fractions as 4.5 and 5.9, respectively.

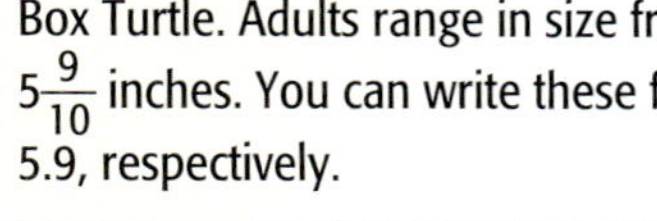

Fractions, Decimals, and Percents Make this Foldable to help you organize your notes. Begin with five sheets of $8\frac{1}{2}'' \times 11''$ paper.

1. **Stack** five sheets of paper $\frac{3}{4}$ inch apart.

2. **Roll** up bottom edges so that all tabs are the same size.

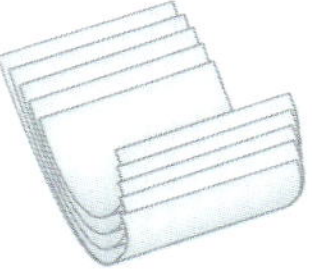

3. **Crease** and staple along the fold.

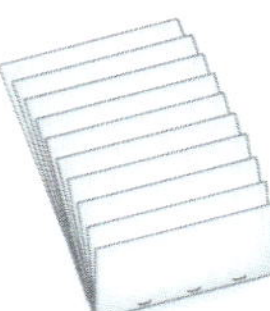

4. **Write** the chapter title on the front. Label each tab with a lesson number and title.

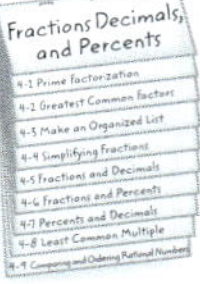

GET READY for Chapter 4

Diagnose Readiness You have two options for checking Prerequisite Skills.

Option 2

Math Online Take the Online Readiness Quiz at glencoe.com.

Option 1

Take the Quick Quiz below. Refer to the Quick Review for help.

QUICK Quiz

State which decimal is greater. (Prior Grade)

1. 0.6, 0.61
2. 1.25, 1.52
3. 0.33, 0.13
4. 1.08, 10.8
5. **LUNCH** Kirsten spent \$4.21 on lunch while Almanzo spent \$4.12. Who spent the greater amount? (Lesson 3-9)

Use divisibility rules to determine whether each number is divisible by 2, 3, 5, 6, or 10. (Prior Grade)

6. 125
7. 78
8. 37
9. **MUFFINS** Without calculating, determine whether 51 banana nut muffins can be evenly distributed among 3 persons. Explain. (Prior Grade)

Divide. (Prior Grade)

10. $12 \div 6$
11. $18 \div 3$
12. $2 \div 5$
13. $3 \div 4$

Write each power as a product of the same factor. (Lesson 1-2)

14. 2^3
15. 5^5
16. 7^2
17. 9^4

QUICK Review

Example 1

State which decimal is greater, 7.4 or 7.04.

7.4
7.04

7.4 is greater.

Line up the decimal points and compare place value. The 4 in the tenths place is greater than the 0 in the tenths place.

Example 2

Use divisibility rules to determine whether 84 is divisible by 2, 3, 5, 6, or 10.

2: Yes, the ones digit, 4, is divisible by 2.
3: Yes, the sum of the digits, 12, is divisible by 3.
5: No, the ones digit is neither 0 nor 5.
6. Yes, the number is divisible by both 2 and 3.
10: No, the ones digit is not 0.

Example 3

Find $1 \div 5$.

$$\begin{array}{r} 0.2 \\ 5\overline{)1.0} \\ \underline{-10} \\ 0 \end{array}$$

Divide 1 by 5 until there is a remainder of 0 or a repeating pattern.

Example 4

Write 4^3 as a product of the same factor.

$4^3 = 4 \times 4 \times 4$

Math Lab
Exploring Factors

The students in Mrs. Faccinto's homeroom have lockers numbered 1–30, located down a long hallway. One day the class did an experiment.

ACTIVITY

STEP 1 The first student, Student 1, walked down the hall and opened every locker.

STEP 2 Student 2 closed Locker 2 and every second locker after it.

STEP 3 Student 3 closed Locker 3 and changed the state of every third locker after it. This means that if the locker was open, Student 3 closed it; if the locker was closed, Student 3 opened it.

STEP 4 Student 4 changed the state of every fourth locker, starting with Locker 4. The student continued this pattern until all 30 students had a turn.

Analyze the Results

1. Which lockers were open after Student 30 took a turn? What do the numbers on the open lockers have in common?
2. Explain why the lockers you listed in Exercise 1 were open after Student 30 took a turn.
3. Suppose there were 100 lockers. Which lockers would be open after Student 100 took a turn?
4. **CHALLENGE** Which lockers were touched the greatest number of times?
5. What are the fewest lockers and students needed for 31 lockers to be open at the end of the experiment?

4-1 Prime Factorization

MAIN IDEA

Find the prime factorization of a composite number.

New Vocabulary

prime number
composite number
prime factorization
factor tree

Math Online

glencoe.com

- Concepts In Motion
- Extra Examples
- Personal Tutor
- Self-Check Quiz

MINI Lab

There is only one way that 2 can be expressed as the product of whole numbers. The geoboard shows that there is only one way that two squares can form a rectangle.

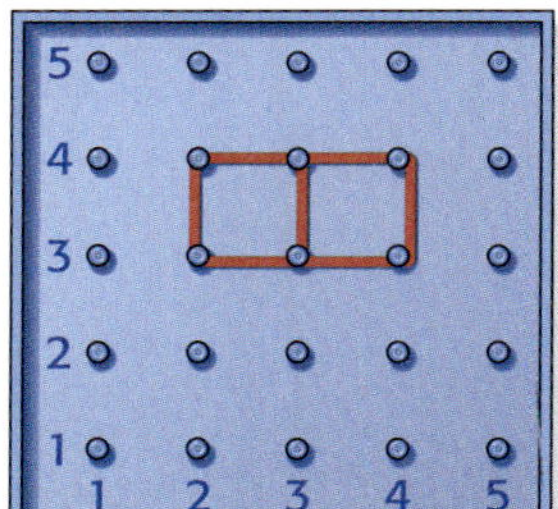

1. Using your geoboard, make as many different rectangles as possible containing 3, 4, 5, 6, 7, 8, 9, and 10 squares.
2. Which numbers of squares can be made into only one rectangle? Into more than one rectangle?

The rectangles in the Mini Lab illustrate prime and composite numbers.

A **prime number** is a whole number greater than 1 that has exactly two factors, 1 and itself.

A **composite number** is a whole number greater than 1 that has more than two factors.

Whole Numbers	Factors
2	1, 2
3	1, 3
5	1, 5
7	1, 7
4	1, 2, 4
6	1, 2, 3, 6
8	1, 2, 4, 8
9	1, 3, 9
10	1, 2, 5, 10
0	many
1	1

The numbers 0 and 1 are neither prime nor composite.

EXAMPLES Identify Numbers as Prime or Composite

Determine whether each number is *prime* or *composite*.

1 **17**

The number 17 has only two factors, 1 and 17, so it is prime.

2 **12**

The number 12 has six factors: 1, 2, 3, 4, 6, and 12. So, it is composite.

Review Vocabulary

factor two or more numbers that are multiplied together to form a product; *Example*: 2 and 3 are factors of 6. (Lesson 1-2)

CHECK Your Progress

Determine whether each number is *prime* or *composite*.

a. 11 **b.** 15 **c.** 24

Every composite number can be written as a product of prime numbers. This product is the **prime factorization** of the number. You can use a **factor tree** to find the prime factorization. The following two factor trees show the prime factorization of 60.

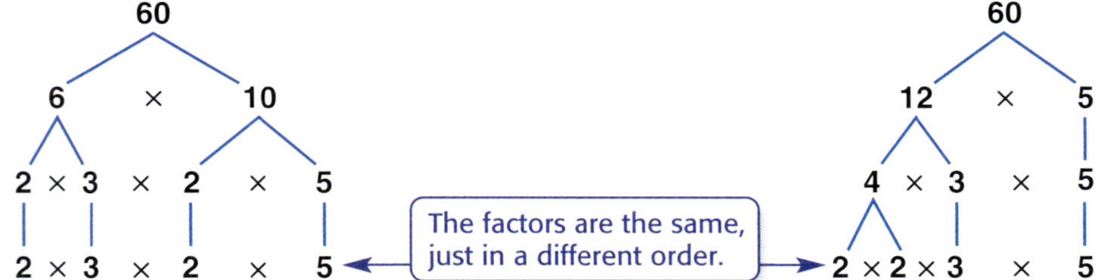

Study Tip

Factors You can also choose any other pair of whole-number factors of 60 such as 3 × 20 or 4 × 15.

The prime factorization of 60 is $2 \times 2 \times 3 \times 5$, or $2^2 \times 3 \times 5$.

EXAMPLE Find the Prime Factorization

3 **Find the prime factorization of 24.**

METHOD 1

Use a factor tree.

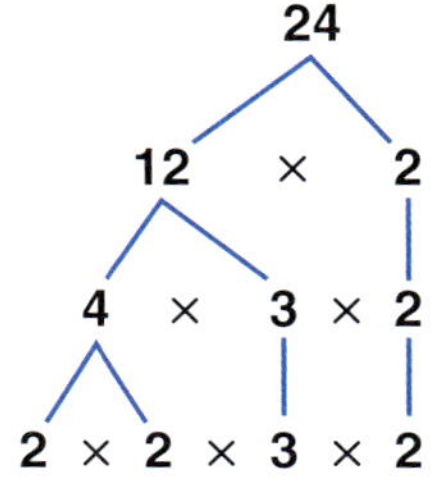

METHOD 2

Divide by prime numbers.

2)24
2)12
2) 6
3

The divisors are 2, 2, 2, and 3.

The prime factorization of 24 is $2 \times 2 \times 3 \times 2$ or $2^3 \times 3$.

CHOOSE Your Method

Find the prime factorization.

d. 18 e. 28 f. 16

Algebraic expressions like $6ab$ can also be factored as the product of prime numbers and variables.

EXAMPLE Factor an Algebraic Expression

4 **ALGEBRA** **Factor $6ab$.**

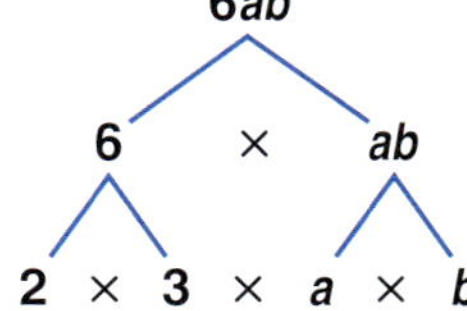

$6ab = 2 \cdot 3 \cdot a \cdot b$

CHECK Your Progress

g. **ALGEBRA** Factor $18xy$.

Examples 1, 2 (p. 181)

Determine whether each number is *prime* or *composite*.

1. 7
2. 50
3. 67
4. **GARDENING** Louisa has 72 flowers to plant in rows in a flower bed. How many different ways can she plant the flowers? Justify your answer.

Example 3 (p. 182)

Find the prime factorization of each number.

5. 34
6. 30
7. 12

Example 4 (p. 182)

ALGEBRA Factor each expression.

8. $10ac$
9. $16x^2$
10. $11g^3$

Practice and Problem Solving

HOMEWORK HELP

For Exercises	See Examples
11–18	1, 2
19–28	3
29–34	4

Determine whether each number is *prime* or *composite*.

11. 22
12. 44
13. 13
14. 39
15. 81
16. 31
17. 97
18. 43

Find the prime factorization of each number.

19. 96
20. 42
21. 99
22. 64
23. 210
24. 180
25. 126
26. 375
27. **LOBSTERS** Lobsters can live up to 50 years. What is this amount expressed as a product of primes?

28. **DOGS** Greyhounds can jump a distance of 27 feet. Write this distance as a product of primes.

ALGEBRA Factor each expression.

29. $15mn$
30. $20pq$
31. $34jkm$
32. $49y^2$
33. $52gh^2$
34. $48a^2b^2$

Replace each ▢ with prime factors to make a true sentence.

35. $2^3 \cdot$ ▢ $\cdot\ 11 = 616$
36. $2 \cdot$ ▢ $\cdot\ 5^2 = 450$
37. $3 \cdot 2^4 \cdot$ ▢ $= 1{,}200$
38. $2^2 \cdot$ ▢ $\cdot\ 3 = 1{,}500$
39. **RIVERS** The Colorado River is 1,450 miles long. Write 1,450 as a product of primes.

ALGEBRA For Exercises 40 and 41, determine whether the value of each expression is *prime* or *composite* if $a = 1$ and $b = 5$.

40. $3a + 6b$
41. $7b - 4a$

CONTESTS **For Exercises 42 and 43, use the following information.**

Sandcastle Day at Cannon Beach, Oregon, is one of the largest sandcastle contests on the west coast. Entrants from each age division are given lots measuring 81 square feet, 225 square feet, or 441 square feet, on which to build their castles.

42. Find the prime factorization of 81, 225, and 441.

43. Use the prime factors to determine two possible dimensions for each plot.

H.O.T. Problems

44. **RESEARCH** Use the Internet or another source to make a Sieve of Eratosthenes to determine the prime numbers up to 100.

45. **CHALLENGE** This whole number is between 30 and 40. It has only two prime factors whose sum is 5. What is the number?

46. **OPEN ENDED** Primes that differ by two are called *twin primes*. For example, 59 and 61 are twin primes. Give three examples of twin primes that are less than 50.

47. **WRITING IN MATH** Suppose n represents a whole number. Is $2n$ prime or composite? Explain.

TEST PRACTICE

48. Which number is a prime factor of both 63 and 140?

    A 2 **C** 5

    B 3 **D** 7

49. Which of the following numbers is *not* a prime number?

    F 2 **H** 16

    G 11 **J** 31

Spiral Review

50. **ALGEBRA** Graph $y = 3x$. (Lesson 3-7)

51. **MEASUREMENT** Find the perimeter and area of a rectangle with a length of 13 feet and width of 5 feet. (Lesson 3-6)

Add. (Lesson 2-4)

52. $6 + (-4)$

53. $-13 + 9$

54. $25 + (-26)$

55. $-5 + 5$

GET READY for the Next Lesson

PREREQUISITE SKILL **State whether each number is divisible by 2, 3, 5, 6, 9, or 10.** (Page 668)

56. 24

57. 70

58. 120

59. 99

READING to SOLVE PROBLEMS

Everyday Meaning

The key to understanding word problems is to understand the meaning of the mathematical terms in the problem. Many words used in mathematics are also used in everyday language.

For example, you will use the terms *factor* and *multiple* in this chapter. Here are two sentences that show their everyday meanings.

- Weather was a *factor* in their decision to postpone the picnic.
- The star quarterback won *multiple* post-season awards.

The table below shows how the everyday meaning is connected to the mathematical meaning.

Term	Everyday Meaning	Mathematical Meaning	Connection
factor from the Latin *factor,* meaning doer	something that actively contributes to a decision or result	2 and 3 are *factors* of 6.	A *factor* helps to make a decision, and in mathematics, factors "make up" a product.
multiple from the Latin *multi-*, meaning many, and *plex,* meaning fold	consisting of more than one or shared by many	The *multiples* of 2 are 0, 2, 4, 6, … .	*Multiple* means many, and in mathematics, a number has infinitely many multiples.

PRACTICE

1. Make a list of other words that have the prefixes *fact-* or *multi-*. Determine what the words in each list have in common.
2. **WRITING IN MATH** Write your own rule for remembering the difference between *factor* and *multiple.*

RESEARCH Use a dictionary to find the everyday meanings of *least, greatest,* and *common.* Then use the definitions to determine how to find each number. Do not solve.

3. the greatest common factor of 10 and 15
4. the least common multiple of 2 and 3.

4-2 Greatest Common Factor

MAIN IDEA

Find the greatest common factor of two or more numbers.

New Vocabulary

Venn diagram
greatest common factor (GCF)

Math Online

glencoe.com
- Extra Examples
- Personal Tutor
- Self-Check Quiz
- Reading in the Content Area

GET READY for the Lesson

VENN DIAGRAM The Venn diagram shows the prime factors of 12 and 18.

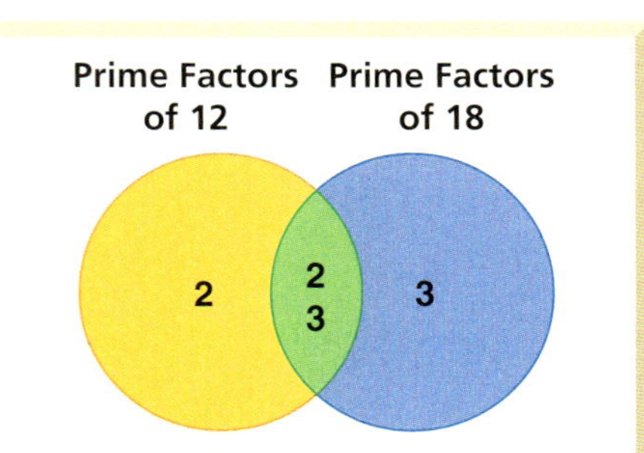

1. Which factors are in the overlapping section? What does this mean?
2. Is the product of 2 and 3 also a factor of 12 and 18?
3. Make a Venn diagram showing the prime factors of 12 and 20. Identify the common factors and find their product.

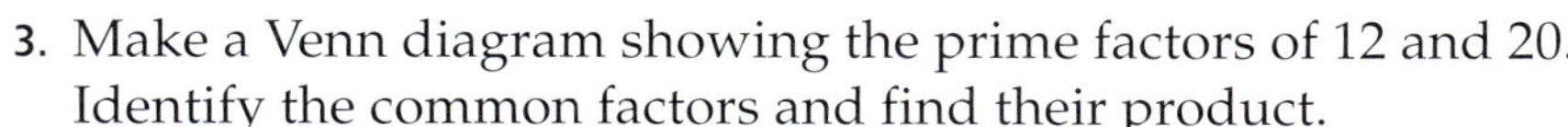

As shown above, **Venn diagrams** use overlapping circles to show how common elements among sets of numbers or objects are related. They can also show common factors. The greatest of the common factors of two or more numbers is the **greatest common factor, or GCF**.

EXAMPLE Find the Greatest Common Factor

1 Find the GCF of 18 and 48.

METHOD 1 **List the factors of the numbers.**

factors of 18: **1**, **2**, **3**, **6**, 9, 18

factors of 48: **1**, **2**, **3**, 4, **6**, 8, 12, 16, 24, 48

List the factors of 18 and 48.

The common factors of 18 and 48 are 1, 2, 3, and 6.
So, the greatest common factor or GCF is 6.

METHOD 2 **Use prime factorization.**

Write the prime factorization. Circle the common prime factors.

$18 = 2 \times 3 \times 3$

$48 = 2 \times 2 \times 2 \times 2 \times 3$

Write the prime factorizations of 18 and 48.

The greatest common factor or GCF is 2×3 or 6.

CHOOSE Your Method

Find the GCF of each pair of numbers.

a. 8, 10
b. 6, 12
c. 10, 17

Reading Math

Greatest Common Factor
The greatest common factor is also called the *greatest common divisor* because it is the greatest number that divides evenly into the given numbers.

EXAMPLE Find the GCF of Three Numbers

2 **Find the GCF of 12, 24, and 60.**

Write the prime factorization. Circle the common prime factors.

$12 = 2 \times 2 \times 3$

$24 = 2 \times 2 \times 2 \times 3$ — Write the prime factorization of 12, 24, and 60.

$60 = 2 \times 2 \times 3 \times 5$

The common prime factors are 2, 2, and 3. So, the GCF is $2 \times 2 \times 3$, or 12.

CHECK Your Progress

Find the GCF of each set of numbers.

d. 30, 45, 75

e. 42, 70, 84

Real-World EXAMPLES

3 **SCHOOL SPIRIT** **The cheerleaders are making spirit ribbons. Blue ribbon comes in a 24 inch spool, red ribbon comes in a 30 inch spool, and gold ribbon comes in a 36 inch spool. The cheerleaders want to cut strips of equal length and use the entire spool of each ribbon. What is the length of the longest piece of ribbon that can be cut from each spool?**

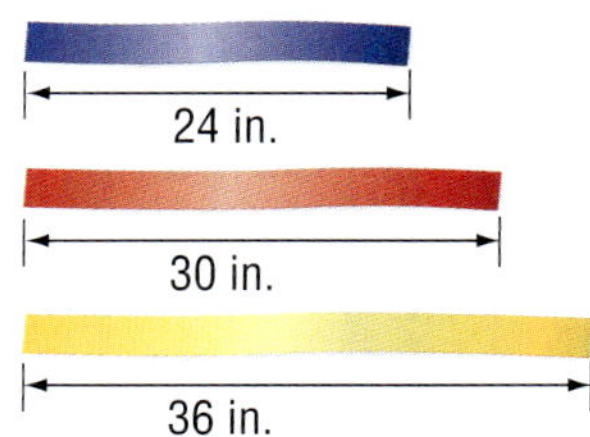

The length of the longest ribbon that can be cut from each spool is the GCF of the three lengths.

$24 = 2 \times 2 \times 2 \times 3$

$30 = 2 \times 3 \times 5$ — Write the prime factorization of 24, 30, and 36.

$36 = 2 \times 2 \times 3 \times 3$

The GCF of 24, 30, and 36 is 2×3 or 6. So, the ribbons should be 6 inches long.

4 **How many spirit ribbons can be made if the ribbons are cut into 6-inch pieces?**

There is a total of $24 + 30 + 36$, or 90 inches of ribbon. So, $90 \div 6$, or 15 spirit ribbons can be made.

Study Tip

Prime Numbers
The GCF of a group of prime numbers is 1.

CHECK Your Progress

f. **CARPENTRY** Mr. Glover wants to make shelves for his garage using an 18-foot board and a 36-foot board. He will cut the boards to make shelves of the same length and wants to use all of both boards. Find the longest possible length of each shelf. How many shelves can he make?

CHECK Your Understanding

Examples 1, 2 (pp. 186–187)

Find the GCF of each set of numbers.

1. 18, 30
2. 45, 60
3. 20, 50
4. 6, 8, 12
5. 8, 20, 40
6. 18, 42, 60

JOBS **For Exercises 7 and 8, use the following information.**
A store manager wants to display the inventory of three styles of bicycle helmets in rows with the same number of each style in each row.

Bike Helmets	
Style	**Inventory**
Sport	36
Road	72
Mountain	45

Examples 3, 4 (p. 187)

7. Find the greatest number of helmets that can be placed in each row.
8. How many rows of each helmet are there?

Practice and Problem Solving

HOMEWORK HELP	
For Exercises	**See Examples**
9–16	1
17–20	2
21–24	3, 4

Find the GCF of each set of numbers.

9. 12, 78
10. 40, 50
11. 20, 45
12. 32, 48
13. 24, 48
14. 45, 75
15. 56, 96
16. 40, 125
17. 18, 24, 30
18. 36, 60, 84
19. 35, 49, 84
20. 36, 50, 130

BANDS **For Exercises 21 and 22, use the following information.**
In a marching band, there are 64 woodwinds, 88 brass, and 16 percussion players. When they march in a parade, there is the same number of students in each row.

21. Find the greatest number of students in each row.
22. How many rows of each group are there?

COMMUNITY SERVICE **For Exercises 23 and 24, use the following information.**
You want to make care packages for a local shelter. You have 18 toothbrushes, 30 combs, and 12 bars of soap. Each package has the same number of each item.

23. What is the greatest number of care packages you can make using all the items?
24. How many of each item are in each package?

Find the GCF of each set of numbers.

25. 25¢, \$1.50, 75¢, \$3.00
26. 6 feet, 15 feet, 21 feet, 9 feet

ALGEBRA **Find the greatest common divisor of each set of expressions.**

27. $24a$, $6a$
28. $30mn$, $40mn$
29. $15xy$, $55y$

Find two numbers whose greatest common divisor is the given number.

30. 9
31. 12
32. 15
33. 30

GEOMETRY **For Exercises 34 and 35, use the following information.**

Jeremy is building rectangular prisms using one-inch cubes. He is planning to build three prisms, the first with 96 blue cubes, the second with 240 red cubes, and the third with 200 yellow cubes. All of prisms must be the same height, but not necessarily the same length and width.

EXTRA PRACTICE
See pages 676, 707.

34. What is the maximum height of each prism Jeremy can build?

35. What are the dimensions of all three prisms?

H.O.T. Problems

CHALLENGE **Determine whether each statement is *sometimes*, *always*, or *never* true.**

36. The GCF of two numbers is greater than both numbers.

37. If two numbers have no common prime factors, the GCF is 1.

38. The GCF of two numbers is one of the numbers.

39. **WRITING IN MATH** Using the words *factor* and *greatest common factor*, explain the relationship between the numbers 4, 12, and 24.

TEST PRACTICE

40. Student Council earned \$26 selling bottled water, \$32 selling oranges, and \$28 selling energy bars. If all items cost the same, what is the greatest possible price per item?

A \$2 **C** \$7

B \$4 **D** \$8

41. Which set of numbers has the greatest GCF?

F 4, 5, 20

G 18, 36

H 18, 36, 45

J 23, 29

Spiral Review

42. What is the prime factorization of 75? (Lesson 4-1)

ALGEBRA **Graph each equation.** (Lesson 3-7)

43. $y = -x$ 44. $y = x + 3$ 45. $y = 2x - 1$

46. **ALGEBRA** Solve the equation $-7y + 18 = 39$. Check your solution. (Lesson 3-5)

GET READY for the Next Lesson

47. **PREREQUISITE SKILL** Serena received a gift card to download music from the Internet. She downloaded 3 songs on Monday, 5 songs on Tuesday, and one half of what was left on Wednesday. She has 6 songs left. How many songs were initially on the gift card? Use the *work backward* strategy. (Lesson 3-4)

Problem-Solving Investigation

MAIN IDEA: Solve problems by making an organized list.

P.S.I. TEAM +

e-Mail: MAKE AN ORGANIZED LIST

NIKKI: I am ordering a pizza. The crust choices are thin or hand-tossed. The meat choices are pepperoni or sausage. The vegetable choices are olives, mushrooms, or banana peppers.

YOUR MISSION: Nikki chooses from one crust, one meat, and one vegetable choice. Make an organized list to find how many different types of pizza Nikki can order.

Understand	You know the crust, meat, and vegetable options for the pizza. You need to find all the possible pizza combinations that can be made.
Plan	Make an organized list of all the possible combinations. Use T for thin, H for hand-tossed, P for pepperoni, S for sausage, O for olives, M for mushrooms, and B for banana peppers.
Solve	(see list below) There are 12 different combinations of pizza that can be ordered.
Check	Draw a tree diagram to check the result.

Choosing thin crust:		
T P O	T P M	T P B
T S O	T S M	T S B
Choosing hand-tossed crust:		
H P O	H P M	H P B
H S O	H S M	H S B

There are 12 different combinations of pizza that can be ordered.

Analyze The Strategy

1. Explain why making an organized list was a useful strategy in solving this problem.
2. WRITING IN MATH Write a problem that can be solved by making an organized list. Then explain how to solve the problem using this strategy.

Mixed Problem Solving

For Exercises 3–6, solve each problem by making an organized list.

3. **SHOPPING** Charmaine went to the store and bought a yellow shirt, a blue shirt, and a red shirt. She also bought a pair of jeans and a pair of khaki dress pants. How many different outfits can be made using one shirt and one pair of pants?

4. **WORK** The following four numbers are used for employee identification numbers at a small company: 0, 1, 2, and 3. How many different employee identification numbers can be made using each digit once?

5. **PHOTOS** Joshua, Diego, and Audri stand side-by-side for a photo. How many different ways can the three friends stand next to each other?

6. **CELL PHONES** How many phone numbers are possible for one area code if the first three numbers are 268, in that order, and the last four numbers are 0, 9, 7, 1 in any order?

Use any strategy to solve Exercises 7–14. Some strategies are shown below.

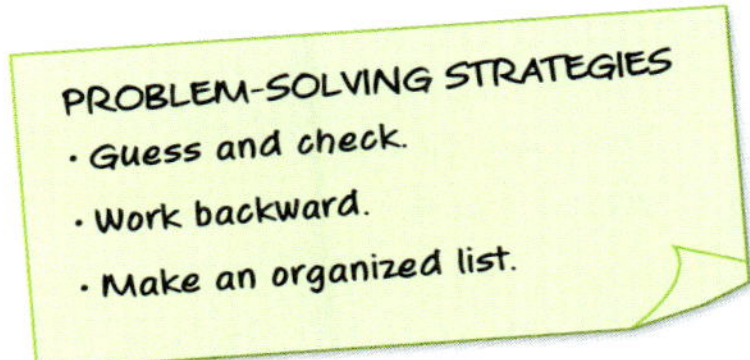

7. **ALGEBRA** Consecutive odd numbers are numbers like 1, 3, 5, and 7. Find two consecutive odd numbers whose sum is 56 and whose product is 783.

8. **FOOD** The table shows the choices for ordering a deli sandwich. How many different subs can be ordered if you choose only one kind of bread and one kind of meat?

The Sandwich Shop	
Bread	White, Wheat, Whole Grain
Meat	Ham, Turkey, Roast Beef
Cheese	American, Swiss
Dressing	Italian, Ranch

9. **DVDS** Paul rented 2 times as many DVDs as Angelina last month. Angelina rented 4 fewer than Bret, but 4 more than Jill. Bret rented 9 DVDs. How many DVDs did each person rent?

10. **CLOTHES** Jeffrey owns 3 shirts, 2 pairs of pants, and 2 pairs of shoes. How many different outfits can he create?

11. **SNOWFALL** A total of 17 inches of snow fell in a 72-hour period. In the last 24 hours, 6 inches fell, and in the previous 24 hours, 4 inches fell. How many inches fell in the first 24 hours?

12. **GAS MILEAGE** Mrs. Acosta travels 44 miles in her car and uses 2 gallons of gas. If her gas mileage continues at the same rate, how many gallons of gas would she use to travel 528 miles?

13. **SCIENCE** Hydrothermal vents are similar to geysers, but are found on the ocean floor. A hydrothermal vent chimney can grow at an average rate of 9 meters in 18 months. What is the average rate of growth per month?

14. **CRAFTS** Paul makes three different sizes of birdhouses. He can paint each style in red, brown, or yellow. How many different birdhouses can Paul make?

4-4 Simplifying Fractions

MAIN IDEA

Write fractions in simplest form.

New Vocabulary

equivalent fractions
simplest form

Math Online

glencoe.com

- Extra Examples
- Personal Tutor
- Self-Check Quiz

MINI Lab

On grid paper, draw the two figures shown. Shade 4 out of the 10 squares in one figure. Shade 2 out of the 5 rectangles in the other.

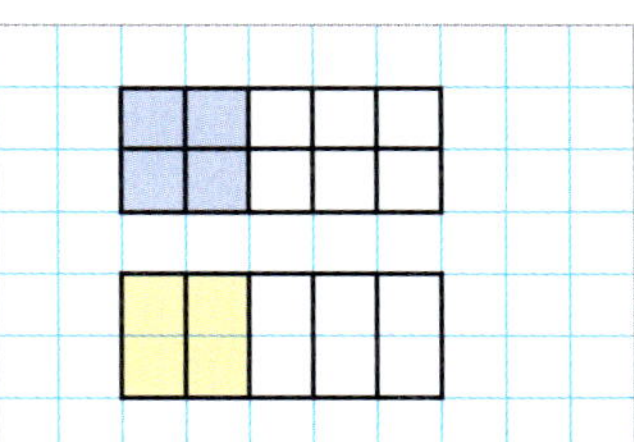

1. Write a fraction to describe each figure: $\frac{\text{number of shaded parts}}{\text{total number of parts}}$
2. Based on the figures, what can you conclude about the fractions?

Equivalent fractions have the same value. A fraction is in **simplest form** when the GCF of the numerator and denominator is 1.

EXAMPLES Write a Fraction in Simplest Form

1 **Write $\frac{6}{24}$ in simplest form.**

METHOD 1 **Divide by common factors.**

$\frac{6}{24} = \frac{6 \div 2}{24 \div 2} = \frac{3}{12}$ — 2 is a common factor of 6 and 24, so divide by 2.

$\frac{3}{12} = \frac{3 \div 3}{12 \div 3} = \frac{1}{4}$ — 3 is a common factor of 3 and 12, so divide by 3.

The fraction $\frac{1}{4}$ is in simplest form since 1 and 4 have no common factors greater than 1.

METHOD 2 **Divide by the GCF.**

First, find the GCF of the numerator and denominator.

factors of 6: 1, 2, 3, 6
factors of 24: 1, 2, 3, 4, 6, 8, 12, 24

The GCF of 6 and 24 is 6.

Then, divide the numerator and denominator by the GCF, 6.

$\frac{6}{24} = \frac{6 \div 6}{24 \div 6} = \frac{1}{4}$ — Divide the numerator and denominator by the GCF, 6.

So, $\frac{6}{24}$ written in simplest form is $\frac{1}{4}$.

2 Write $\frac{36}{45}$ in simplest form.

First, find the GCF of the numerator and denominator.

factors of 36: 1, 2, 3, 4, 6, **9**, 12, 18, 36

factors of 45: 1, 3, 5, **9**, 15, 45

The GCF of 36 and 45 is 9.

Then, divide the numerator and denominator by the GCF, 9.

$\frac{36}{45} = \frac{36 \div 9}{45 \div 9} = \frac{4}{5}$ Divide the numerator and denominator by the GCF, 9.

So, $\frac{36}{45}$ written in simplest form is $\frac{4}{5}$.

Study Tip

More Than One Way
To write in simplest form, you can also divide by common factors.

$\frac{36}{45} = \frac{36 \div 3}{45 \div 3} = \frac{12}{15}$

$\frac{12}{15} = \frac{12 \div 3}{15 \div 3} = \frac{4}{5}$

So, $\frac{36}{45} = \frac{4}{5}$.

CHOOSE Your Method

Write each fraction in simplest form.

a. $\frac{7}{28}$ b. $\frac{8}{20}$ c. $\frac{27}{36}$

Real-World EXAMPLE

3 SCIENCE **Lauren measured a grasshopper for her science project. Each line on her ruler represents $\frac{1}{16}$ inch. Find the length of the grasshopper in simplest form.**

$\frac{14}{16} = \frac{\overset{1}{\cancel{2}} \cdot 7}{\underset{1}{\cancel{2}} \cdot 2 \cdot 2 \cdot 2}$

$= \frac{7}{8}$

The slashes mean that part of the numerator and part of the denominator are both divided by the same number. For example, $2 \div 2 = 1$.

So, $\frac{14}{16}$ written in simplest form is $\frac{7}{8}$.

Real-World Career
How Does a Carpenter Use Math?
Carpenters use fractions when they measure and cut boards.

Math Online
For more information visit: glencoe.com

CHECK Your Progress

d. **CARPENTRY** A carpenter measured a shelf and found it to be $\frac{10}{16}$ inch thick. Find the simplified fraction.

e. **CARPENTRY** A carpenter measured a board to be $\frac{8}{16}$ inch thick. Find the simplified fraction.

CHECK Your Understanding

Examples 1, 2 (pp. 192–193)

Write each fraction in simplest form.

1. $\frac{3}{9}$
2. $\frac{4}{18}$
3. $\frac{10}{25}$
4. $\frac{36}{40}$

Example 3 (p. 193)

5. **ALLOWANCE** Mary received $15 for her weekly allowance. She spent $10 at the movie theater with her friends. What fraction of the money, in simplest form, was spent at the theater?

Practice and Problem Solving

HOMEWORK HELP

For Exercises	See Examples
6–17	1,2
18–19	3

Write each fraction in simplest form.

6. $\frac{9}{12}$
7. $\frac{25}{35}$
8. $\frac{16}{32}$
9. $\frac{14}{20}$
10. $\frac{10}{20}$
11. $\frac{12}{21}$
12. $\frac{15}{25}$
13. $\frac{24}{28}$
14. $\frac{48}{64}$
15. $\frac{32}{32}$
16. $\frac{20}{80}$
17. $\frac{45}{54}$

18. **PRESIDENTS** Of the 43 U.S. presidents, 15 were elected to serve two terms. What fraction of the U.S. presidents, in simplest form, was elected to serve two terms?

19. **TV SHOWS** A television station has 28 new TV shows scheduled to air this week. What fraction of the television shows, in simplest form, are 30-minute programs?

WYTB Programming	
30-minute	60-minute
20	8

Write each fraction in simplest form.

20. $\frac{45}{100}$
21. $\frac{60}{150}$
22. $\frac{16}{120}$
23. $\frac{35}{175}$

24. **TIME** Fifteen minutes is what part of one hour?

25. **MEASUREMENT** Nine inches is what part of one foot?

26. **CALENDAR** Four days is what part of the month of April?

27. **SLEEP** Marcel spends 8 hours each day sleeping. What fraction of a week, written in simplest form, does Marcel spend sleeping?

28. **MONEY** Each week, Lorenzo receives a $10 allowance. What fraction of his yearly allowance, in simplest form, does he receive each week?

29. **FIND THE DATA** Refer to the Data File on pages 16–19 of your book. Choose some data and write a real-world problem in which you would simplify fractions.

30. **OPEN ENDED** Select a fraction in simplest form. Then, write two fractions that are equivalent to it.

H.O.T. Problems

31. **CHALLENGE** Both the numerator and denominator of a fraction are even. Is the fraction in simplest form? Explain your reasoning.

32. **FIND THE ERROR** Nhu and Booker both wrote $\frac{16}{36}$ in simplest form. Who is correct? Explain.

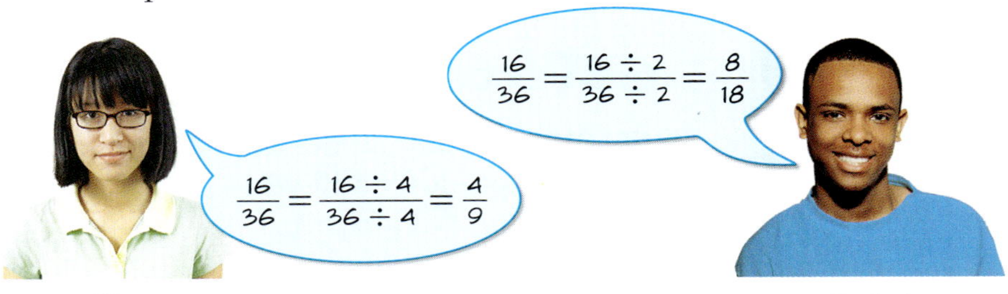

33. **WRITING IN MATH** Explain how to determine whether a fraction is in simplest form.

TEST PRACTICE

34. It takes Benito 12 minutes to walk to school. What fraction represents the part of an hour it takes Benito to walk to school?

A $\frac{12}{1}$ C $\frac{5}{30}$

B $\frac{4}{15}$ D $\frac{1}{5}$

35. What fraction of a foot is 2 inches?

F $\frac{1}{6}$ H $\frac{1}{3}$

G $\frac{1}{4}$ J $\frac{1}{2}$

Spiral Review

36. **SANDWICHES** A deli offers sandwiches with ham, turkey, or roast beef with American, provolone, Swiss, or mozzarella cheese. How many different types of sandwiches can be made if you choose one meat and one cheese? Use the *make an organized list* strategy. (Lesson 4-3)

Find the GCF of each set of numbers. (Lesson 4-2)

37. 27, 36

38. 16, 28

39. 20, 50, 65

40. **ANALYZE GRAPHS** Refer to the graph. At these rates, about how much longer would it take a blue shark to swim 280 miles than it would a sailfish? Use the formula $d = rt$. Justify your answer. (Lesson 3-3)

Source: *Top Ten of Everything*

GET READY for the Next Lesson

PREREQUISITE SKILL **Divide.** (Page 676)

41. $2\overline{)1.0}$

42. $4\overline{)1.00}$

43. $10\overline{)7.0}$

44. $8\overline{)3.000}$

4-5 Fractions and Decimals

MAIN IDEA

Write fractions as terminating or repeating decimals and write decimals as fractions.

New Vocabulary

terminating decimals
repeating decimals
bar notation

Math Online

glencoe.com

- Extra Examples
- Personal Tutor
- Self-Check Quiz

GET READY for the Lesson

NASCAR The table shows the winning speeds for a 10-year-period at the Daytona 500.

1. What fraction of the speeds are between 130 and 145 miles per hour?
2. Express this fraction using words and then as a decimal.
3. What fraction of the speeds are between 145 and 165 miles per hour? Express this fraction using words and then as a decimal.

Daytona 500		
Year	**Winner**	**Speed (mph)**
1998	D. Earnhardt	172.712
1999	J. Gordon	148.295
2000	D. Jarrett	155.669
2001	M. Waltrip	161.783
2002	W. Burton	142.971
2003	M. Waltrip	133.870
2004	D. Earnhardt Jr.	156.345
2005	J. Gordon	135.173
2006	J. Johnson	142.667
2007	K. Harvick	149.335

Source: ESPN Sports Almanac

Our decimal system is based on powers of 10. So, if the denominator of a fraction is a power of 10, you can use place value to write the fraction as a decimal. For example, to write $\frac{7}{10}$ as a decimal, place a 7 in the tenths place.

Words	Fraction	Decimal
seven tenths	$\frac{7}{10}$	0.7

If the denominator of a fraction is a *factor* of 10, 100, 1,000, or any higher power of ten, you can use mental math and place value.

EXAMPLES Use Mental Math

Write each fraction or mixed number as a decimal.

1 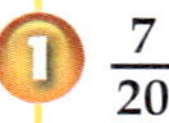 $\frac{7}{20}$

THINK $\frac{7}{20} = \frac{35}{100}$ (× 5 numerator and denominator)

So, $\frac{7}{20} = 0.35$.

2 $5\frac{3}{4}$

$5\frac{3}{4} = 5 + \frac{3}{4}$ Think of it as a sum.

$= 5 + 0.75$ You know that $\frac{3}{4} = 0.75$.

$= 5.75$ Add mentally.

So, $5\frac{3}{4} = 5.75$.

CHECK Your Progress

a. $\frac{3}{10}$ b. $\frac{3}{25}$ c. $6\frac{1}{2}$

Study Tip

Mental Math It will be helpful to memorize the following fraction-decimal equivalencies.

$\frac{1}{2} = 0.5$

$\frac{1}{3} = 0.\overline{3}$ $\frac{2}{3} = 0.\overline{6}$

$\frac{1}{4} = 0.25$ $\frac{3}{4} = 0.75$

$\frac{1}{5} = 0.2$ $\frac{1}{10} = 0.1$

$\frac{1}{8} = 0.125$

Any fraction can be written as a decimal by dividing its numerator by its denominator. Division ends when the remainder is zero.

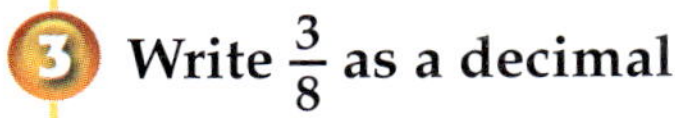

EXAMPLES Use Division

3 **Write $\frac{3}{8}$ as a decimal.**

$$\begin{array}{r} 0.375 \\ 8\overline{)3.000} \\ -24 \\ 60 \\ -56 \\ 40 \\ -40 \\ 0 \end{array}$$

Divide 3 by 8.

Division ends when the remainder is 0.

So, $\frac{3}{8} = 0.375$.

4 **Write $\frac{1}{40}$ as a decimal.**

$$\begin{array}{r} 0.025 \\ 40\overline{)1.000} \\ -80 \\ 200 \\ -200 \\ 0 \end{array}$$

Divide 1 by 40.

So, $\frac{1}{40} = 0.025$.

CHECK Your Progress

Write each fraction or mixed number as a decimal.

d. $\frac{7}{8}$ e. $2\frac{1}{8}$ f. $7\frac{9}{20}$

Vocabulary Link
Terminate

Everyday Use coming to an end, as in terminate a game

Math Use a decimal whose digits end

In Examples 1–4, the decimals 0.35, 5.75, 0.375, and 0.025 are called terminating decimals. A **terminating decimal** is a decimal whose digits end.

Repeating decimals have a pattern in their digits that repeats forever. Consider $\frac{1}{3}$.

$$\begin{array}{r} 0.333\ldots \\ 3\overline{)1.000} \\ -9 \\ 10 \\ -9 \\ 10 \\ -9 \\ 1 \end{array}$$

The number 3 repeats. The repetition of 3 is represented by three dots.

You can use **bar notation** to indicate that a number pattern repeats indefinitely. A bar is written only over the digits that repeat.

$0.33333\ldots = 0.\overline{3}$ $0.121212\ldots = 0.\overline{12}$ $11.3858585\ldots = 11.3\overline{85}$

EXAMPLE Write Fractions as Repeating Decimals

5 **Write $\frac{7}{9}$ as a decimal.**

$$\begin{array}{r} 0.777\ldots \\ 9\overline{)7.000} \\ -63 \\ \hline 70 \\ -63 \\ \hline 70 \\ -63 \\ \hline 7 \end{array}$$

Divide 7 by 9.

Notice that the remainder will never be zero. That is, the division never ends.

So, $\frac{7}{9} = 0.777\ldots$ or $0.\overline{7}$.

CHECK Your Progress

Write each fraction or mixed number as a decimal. Use bar notation if the decimal is a repeating decimal.

g. $\frac{2}{3}$

h. $\frac{3}{11}$

i. $8\frac{1}{3}$

Every terminating decimal can be written as a fraction with a denominator of 10, 100, 1,000, or a higher power of ten. Place the digits that come after the decimal point in the numerator. Use the place value of the final digit as the denominator.

Real-World Link
The recommended water temperature for goldfish is 65–72°F.
Source: Animal-World

Real-World EXAMPLE Use a Power of 10

6 **FISH** **Use the table to find what fraction of the fish in an aquarium are goldfish. Write in simplest form.**

Fish	Amount
Guppy	0.25
Angel Fish	0.4
Goldfish	0.15
Molly	0.2

$0.15 = \frac{15}{100}$ The final digit, 5, is in the hundredths place.

$= \frac{3}{20}$ Simplify.

CHECK Your Progress

Determine the fraction of the aquarium made up by each fish. Write the answer in simplest form.

j. molly

k. guppy

l. angel fish

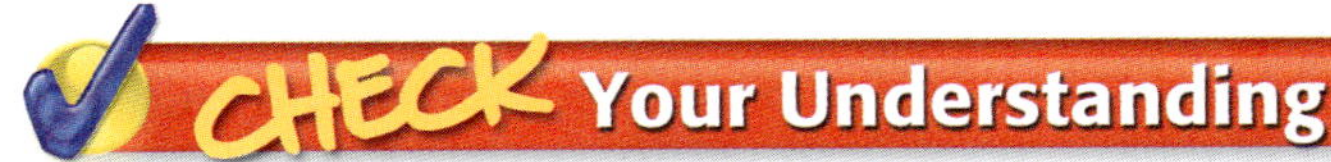

Examples 1–5 (pp. 196–198)

Write each fraction or mixed number as a decimal. Use bar notation if the decimal is a repeating decimal.

1. $\frac{2}{5}$
2. $\frac{9}{10}$
3. $7\frac{1}{2}$
4. $4\frac{3}{20}$
5. $\frac{1}{8}$
6. $3\frac{5}{8}$
7. $\frac{5}{9}$
8. $1\frac{5}{6}$

Example 6 (p. 198)

Write each decimal as a fraction or mixed number in simplest form.

9. 0.22
10. 0.1
11. 4.6
12. **HOCKEY** During a hockey game, an ice resurfacer travels 0.75 mile during each ice resurfacing. What fraction represents this distance?

Practice and Problem Solving

HOMEWORK HELP

For Exercises	See Examples
13–16	1, 2
17–22	3, 4
23–28	5
29–36	6

Write each fraction or mixed number as a decimal. Use bar notation if the decimal is a repeating decimal.

13. $\frac{4}{5}$
14. $\frac{1}{2}$
15. $4\frac{4}{25}$
16. $7\frac{1}{20}$
17. $\frac{5}{16}$
18. $\frac{3}{16}$
19. $\frac{33}{50}$
20. $\frac{17}{40}$
21. $5\frac{7}{8}$
22. $9\frac{3}{8}$
23. $\frac{4}{9}$
24. $\frac{8}{9}$
25. $\frac{1}{6}$
26. $\frac{8}{11}$
27. $5\frac{1}{3}$
28. $2\frac{6}{11}$

Write each decimal as a fraction or mixed number in simplest form.

29. 0.2
30. 0.9
31. 0.55
32. 0.34
33. 5.96
34. 2.66
35. **INSECTS** The maximum length of a praying mantis is 30.5 centimeters. What mixed number represents this length?

36. **GROCERIES** Suppose you buy a 1.25 pound package of ham for $4.99. What fraction of a pound did you buy?
37. **FIND THE DATA** Refer to the Data File on page 16–19 of your book. Choose some data and write a real-world problem in which you would write a percent as a decimal.

Write each of the following as an integer over a whole number.

38. -13
39. $7\frac{1}{3}$
40. -0.028
41. -3.2

See pages 677, 707.

42. **MUSIC** Nicolás practiced playing the cello for 2 hours and 18 minutes. Write the time Nicolás spent practicing as a decimal.

43. **SOFTBALL** The batting average of a softball player is the number of hits divided by the number of at-bats. If Felisa had 50 hits in 175 at-bats and Harmony had 42 hits in 160 at-bats, who had the better batting average? Justify your answer.

H.O.T. Problems

44. **OPEN ENDED** Write a fraction that is equivalent to a terminating decimal between 0.5 and 0.75.

45. **CHALLENGE** The value of pi (π) is 3.1415926… . The mathematician Archimedes believed that π was between $3\frac{1}{7}$ and $3\frac{10}{71}$. Was Archimedes correct? Explain your reasoning.

46. **WRITING IN MATH** Fractions with denominators of 2, 4, 8, 16, and 32 produce terminating decimals. Fractions with denominators of 6, 12, 18, and 24 produce repeating decimals. What causes the difference? Explain.

47. Which decimal represents the shaded region of the model?

A 0.666 C 0.667
B $0.\overline{6}$ D $0.66\overline{7}$

48. Based on the information given in the table, what fraction represents $0.\overline{8}$?

F $\frac{4}{5}$
G $\frac{80}{99}$
H $\frac{5}{6}$
J $\frac{8}{9}$

Decimal	Fraction
$0.\overline{3}$	$\frac{3}{9}$
$0.\overline{4}$	$\frac{4}{9}$
$0.\overline{5}$	$\frac{5}{9}$
$0.\overline{6}$	$\frac{6}{9}$

Spiral Review

Write each fraction in simplest form. (Lesson 4-4)

49. $\frac{10}{24}$ 50. $\frac{39}{81}$ 51. $\frac{28}{98}$ 52. $\frac{51}{68}$

53. **PIZZA** How many different pizzas can Alfonso order if he can choose thick, thin, or deep dish crust and one topping from either pepperoni, sausage, or mushrooms? Use the *make an organized list* strategy. (Lesson 4-3)

GET READY for the Next Lesson

PREREQUISITE SKILL **Write a fraction for the number of shaded squares to the total number of squares.**

54. 55. 56. 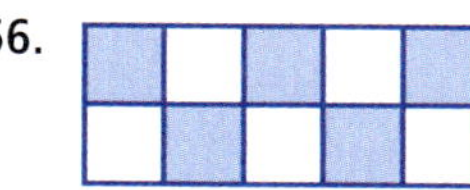 57.

CHAPTER 4

Mid-Chapter Quiz

Lessons 4-1 through 4-5

Determine whether each number is *prime* or *composite*. (Lesson 4-1)

1. 24
2. 61
3. 2

4. **AGE** Kevin just turned 13 years old. How old will he be the next time his age is a prime number? (Lesson 4-1)

Find the prime factorization of each number. (Lesson 4-1)

5. 30
6. 120

Factor each expression. (Lesson 4-1)

7. $14x^2y$
8. $50mn$

Find the GCF of each set of numbers. (Lesson 4-2)

9. 16, 40
10. 65, 100

11. **MULTIPLE CHOICE** Lakeesha wants to cut a 14-inch by 21-inch poster board into equal-size squares for an art project. She does not want to waste any of the poster board, and she wants the largest squares possible. What is the length of the side of the largest squares she can cut? (Lesson 4-2)

 A 14
 B 7
 C 6
 D 2

12. **MULTIPLE CHOICE** Lynne cannot remember her password to check the messages on her cell phone. She knows that it is a three-digit number consisting of the numbers 1, 4, and 7, but she cannot remember the order. Which list shows all the different possibilities for her password? (Lesson 4-3)

 F 147, 174, 417, 714, 741
 G 147, 174, 417, 471, 714, 741
 H 417, 471, 714, 741
 J 147, 174, 74, 417, 17, 471, 714, 741

13. **PIANO** Evelina spends 40 minutes practicing the flute each afternoon after school. What part of one hour does she spend practicing? Write as a fraction in simplest form. (Lesson 4-4)

Write each fraction in simplest form. (Lesson 4-4)

14. $\frac{20}{36}$
15. $\frac{45}{60}$
16. $\frac{63}{108}$
17. $\frac{60}{72}$

18. **VOTING** In the 2004 presidential election, Kentucky had 8 out of 538 total electoral votes. Write Kentucky's portion of the electoral votes as a fraction in simplest form. (Lesson 4-4)

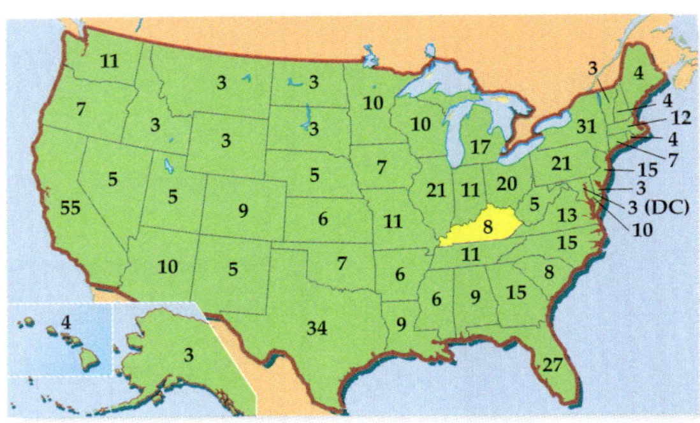

Write each fraction or mixed number as a decimal. Use bar notation if the decimal is a repeating decimal. (Lesson 4-5)

19. $\frac{7}{8}$
20. $\frac{2}{9}$
21. $3\frac{13}{20}$

Write each decimal as a fraction in simplest form. (Lesson 4-5)

22. 0.6
23. 0.48
24. 7.02

25. **ANIMALS** The maximum height of an Asian elephant is 9.8 feet. What mixed number represents this height? (Lesson 4-5)

4-6 Fractions and Percents

MAIN IDEA

Write fractions as percents and percents as fractions.

New Vocabulary

ratio
equivalent ratios

Math Online

glencoe.com

- Extra Examples
- Personal Tutor
- Self-Check Quiz

GET READY for the Lesson

In a recent survey, students were asked to choose their favorite sport to play. The results are shown in the table.

Sport	Number of Students
Basketball	3 out of 20
Football	3 out of 25
Gymnastics	1 out of 20
Swimming	9 out of 100

1. For each sport, shade a 10×10 grid that represents the number of students that chose the sport.
2. What fraction of the students chose swimming?

A **ratio** is a comparison of two quantities by division. Ratios like 9 out of 100 can also be written as 9:100 or $\frac{9}{100}$. When a ratio compares a number to 100, it can be written as a **percent**.

Percent — Key Concept

Words A percent is a part to whole ratio that compares a number to 100.

Symbols $\frac{n}{100} = n\%$

Example

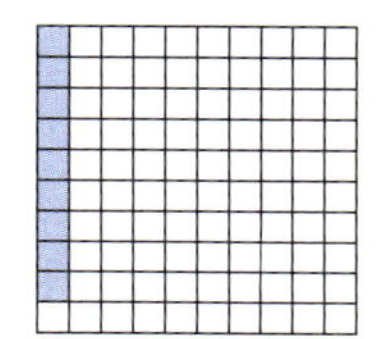

9 out of 100 = 9%

EXAMPLES Write Ratios as Percents

Write each ratio as a percent.

1 Annie answered 90 out of 100 questions correctly.

$\frac{90}{100} = 90\%$

Annie answered 90% of the questions correctly.

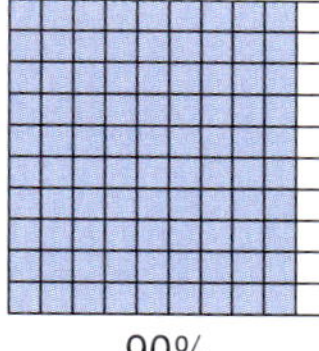

90%

2 On average, 50.5 out of 100 students own a pet.

$\frac{50.5}{100} = 50.5\%$

On average, 50.5% of the students own a pet.

Reading Math

Percent *Percent* means per *hundred* or *hundredths*. The symbol % means percent.

CHECK Your Progress

a. 45 out of 100 cars sold

b. \$3.30:\$100 spent on soft drinks

Study Tip

Percents In Chapter 6 you will learn another way to write percents that does not use equivalent fractions.

Fractions and percents are ratios that can represent the same number. You can write a fraction as a percent by finding an equivalent fraction with a denominator of 100.

EXAMPLE Write a Fraction as a Percent

3 **Write $\frac{3}{20}$ as a percent.**

First, find an equivalent fraction with a denominator of 100. Then write the fraction as a percent.

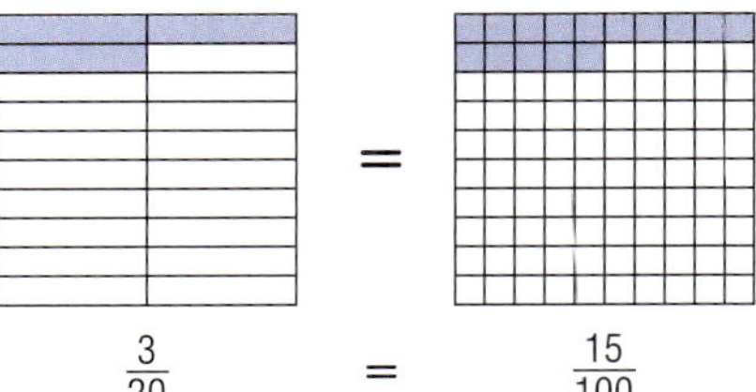

$\frac{3}{20} = \frac{3 \times 5}{20 \times 5} = \frac{15}{100}$ or 15%

So, $\frac{3}{20} = 15\%$.

CHECK Your Progress

Write each fraction as a percent.

c. $\frac{17}{20}$ d. $\frac{3}{5}$ e. $\frac{2}{25}$

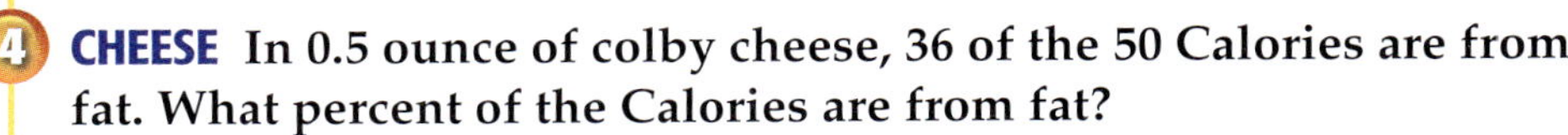

4 **CHEESE In 0.5 ounce of colby cheese, 36 of the 50 Calories are from fat. What percent of the Calories are from fat?**

$\frac{36}{50} = \frac{72}{100}$ Write an equivalent fraction with a denominator of 100.

$= 72\%$ $\frac{72}{100} = 72\%$

About 72% of the Calories are from fat.

Real-World Link Almost 90% of all cheese sold in the United States is cheddar.

Source: Food Reference

CHECK Your Progress

f. **CHEESE** In a small piece of mozzarella cheese, 17 of the 25 Calories come from fat. What percent of the Calories come from fat?

EXAMPLE Write a Percent as a Fraction

5 **Write 48% as a fraction in simplest form.**

$48\% = \frac{48}{100}$ Definition of percent

$= \frac{12}{25}$ Simplify.

CHECK Your Progress

Write each percent as a fraction in simplest form.

g. 40% h. 6% i. 24%

CHECK Your Understanding

Examples 1, 2 (p. 202)

Write each ratio as a percent.

1. 57 : 100 insects are spiders
2. \$29.20 per \$100

Example 3 (p. 203)

Write each fraction as a percent.

3. $\frac{1}{4}$
4. $\frac{6}{10}$
5. $\frac{17}{20}$

Example 4 (p. 203)

6. **TECHNOLOGY** Tansy used $\frac{2}{5}$ of the memory available on her flash drive. What percent of the memory did she use?

Example 5 (p. 203)

Write each percent as a fraction in simplest form.

7. 90%
8. 75%
9. 22%

Practice and Problem Solving

HOMEWORK HELP

For Exercises	See Examples
10–15	1, 2
16–23	3
24–25	4
26–33	5

Write each ratio as a percent.

10. 87 out of 100 books read
11. 42 per 100 teenagers
12. 12.2 out of 100 points earned
13. 99.9 : 100 miles driven
14. $11\frac{3}{4}$ out of 100 feet
15. $66\frac{2}{3}$: 100 yards run

Write each fraction as a percent.

16. $\frac{7}{10}$
17. $\frac{16}{20}$
18. $\frac{15}{25}$
19. $\frac{13}{50}$
20. $\frac{1}{5}$
21. $\frac{3}{5}$
22. $\frac{19}{20}$
23. $\frac{10}{10}$

24. **PETS** Twenty out of every 25 households own one dog. What percent of households own one dog?

25. **SPORTS** If 15 out of every 50 teens like to ski, what percent of teens like to ski?

Write each percent as a fraction in simplest form.

26. 45%
27. 30%
28. 62%
29. 88%
30. 68%
31. 13%
32. 2%
33. 300%

Replace each ● with >, <, or =.

34. $\frac{1}{4}$ ● 25%
35. $\frac{9}{20}$ ● 55%
36. 78% ● $\frac{3}{5}$
37. 38% ● $\frac{19}{50}$
38. 12% ● $1\frac{1}{5}$
39. $2\frac{2}{5}$ ● 24%

40. **VOLUNTEERING** A Girl Scouts event is expecting 40 out of 50 people to volunteer at a charity auction. So far 30 volunteers have arrived at the auction. What percent of the volunteers have not yet arrived?

H.O.T. Problems

41. **GEOMETRY** What percent of the larger rectangle shown is *not* shaded?

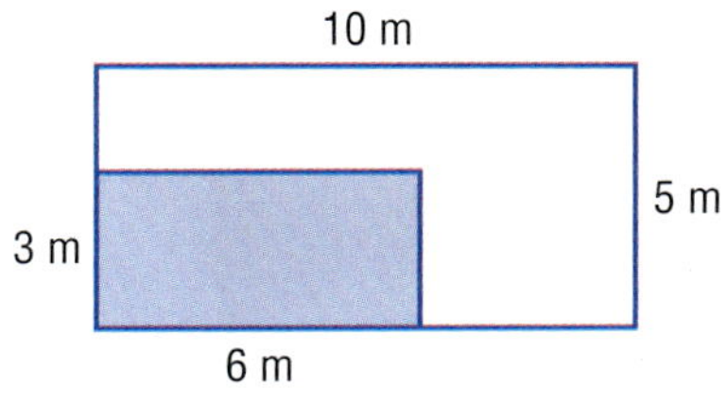

42. **CHALLENGE** Apply what you know about percents, fractions, and decimals to write $12\frac{1}{2}\%$ as a fraction. Justify your answer.

43. **Which One Doesn't Belong?** Identify the ratio that does not have the same value as the other three. Explain your reasoning.

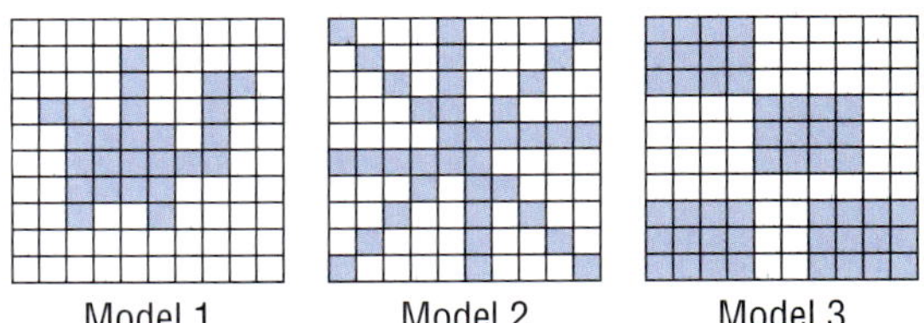

44. **WRITING IN MATH** Explain how you know which model represents 36%. Then explain why that model also represents $\frac{9}{25}$.

Model 1 Model 2 Model 3

TEST PRACTICE

45. What percent of the model is shaded?

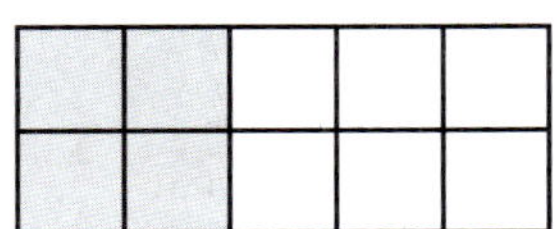

A 25% C 40%

B 30% D 60%

46. Cats spend about $\frac{3}{10}$ of their time awake grooming themselves. Which number is equivalent to $\frac{3}{10}$?

F 3% H 33.3%

G 30% J 300%

Spiral Review

Write each decimal as a fraction or mixed number in simplest form. (Lesson 4-5)

47. 0.6 48. 0.15 49. 2.8

50. **TIME** The drive to a football game took 56 minutes. Twenty-four minutes of the time was spent stopped in traffic. What fraction of the drive, in simplest form, was spent in stopped traffic? (Lesson 4-4)

Solve each equation. (Lesson 3-2)

51. $x + 7 = 10$ 52. $m - 2 = 8$ 53. $12 + a = 16$

GET READY for the Next Lesson

PREREQUISITE SKILL **Multiply or divide.** (Pages 675, 676)

54. 16.2×10 55. 0.71×100 56. $14.4 \div 100$ 57. $791 \div 1{,}000$

4-7 Percents and Decimals

MAIN IDEA

Write percents as decimals and decimals as percents.

Math Online

glencoe.com

- Concepts in Motion
- Extra Examples
- Personal Tutor
- Self-Check Quiz

GET READY for the Lesson

SCHOOL UNIFORMS The graph shows students' favorite school uniform colors.

1. Write the percent of students who chose black as a fraction.
2. Write the fraction as a decimal.
3. What do you notice about the percent and decimal form for who chose black?

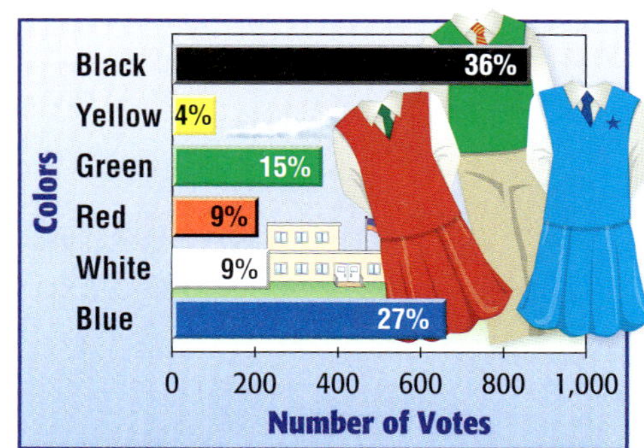

Source: *Kids USA Survey*

Any percent can be written as a fraction with the percent as the numerator and 100 as the denominator. Use this fact to help write percents as decimals.

EXAMPLE Write Percents as Decimals

1 **Write 7% as a decimal.**

METHOD 1 **Write the percent as a fraction.**

$7\% = \frac{7}{100}$ Write the percent as a fraction.

$= 0.07$ Write the fraction as a decimal.

METHOD 2 **Divide mentally.**

The % symbol means to divide by 100. So, remove the % symbol and divide by 100.

$7\% = .07$ Remove the % symbol and divide by 100. Add placeholder zero.

$= 0.07$ Add leading zero.

So, 7% = 0.07.

CHOOSE Your Method

Write each percent as a decimal.

a. 8%

b. 54%

c. 85.2%

Real-World EXAMPLE

2 **GEOGRAPHY** **Alaska is the largest state, making up about $16\frac{1}{10}\%$ of the land area of the United States. Write this amount as a decimal.**

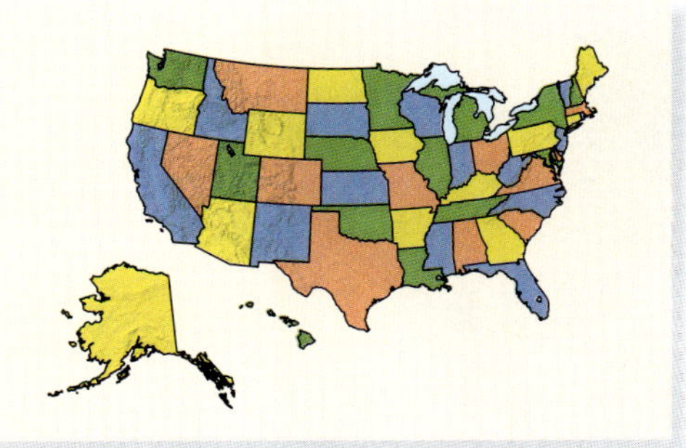

$16\frac{1}{10}\% = 16.1\%$ Write $\frac{1}{10}$ as 0.1.

$= 16.1$ Remove the % symbol and divide by 100.

$= 0.161$ Add leading zero.

So, $16\frac{1}{10}\% = 0.161$.

CHECK Your Progress

d. **GEOGRAPHY** About $6\frac{4}{5}\%$ of the total area of the United States is water. What decimal represents this amount?

e. **GEOGRAPHY** The total area of Australia is about $38\frac{11}{20}\%$ of the total area of North America. Write the amount as a decimal.

EXAMPLE Write Decimals as Percents

3 **Write 0.4 as a percent.**

METHOD 1 **Write the decimal as a fraction.**

$0.4 = \frac{4}{10}$ or $\frac{40}{100}$ Write the decimal as a fraction.

$= 40\%$ Write the fraction as a percent.

METHOD 2 **Multiply mentally.**

Multiply by 100 and add the % symbol.

$0.4 = 0.40$ Multiply by 100. Add a placeholder zero.

$= 40\%$ Add the % symbol.

So, $0.4 = 40\%$.

Study Tip

Multiplication When multiplying by 100, the decimal point moves two places right.

CHOOSE Your Method

Write each decimal as a percent.

f. 0.5

g. 0.34

h. 0.98

Real-World Link Of the world's icebergs, 93% are found surrounding the Antarctic.
Source: JPL Polar Oceanography Group

Real-World EXAMPLE

4 **SCIENCE** **About 0.875 of an iceberg's mass is underwater. What percent of an iceberg's mass is underwater?**

$0.875 = 0.875$ Multiply by 100.

$= 87.5\%$ Add the % symbol.

So, 87.5% of an iceberg's mass is underwater.

CHECK Your Progress

i. **EXERCISE** Each day, Rico and his dog walk 0.625 mile. What percent of a mile do they walk?

Percent as a Decimal (Key Concept)

To write a percent as a decimal, divide the percent by 100 and remove the percent symbol.

$25\% = .25$ or 0.25

Decimal as a Percent (Key Concept)

To write a decimal as a percent, multiply the percent by 100 and add the percent symbol.

$0.58 = 0.58 = 58\%$

CHECK Your Understanding

Example 1 (p. 206)

Write each percent as a decimal.

1. 68%
2. 5%
3. 27.6%

Example 2 (p. 207)

4. **SPENDING** A family spends about $33\frac{2}{5}\%$ of their annual income on housing. What decimal represents the amount spent on housing?

Example 3 (p. 207)

Write each decimal as a percent.

5. 0.09
6. 0.3
7. 0.73

Example 4 (p. 208)

8. **BASKETBALL** The table shows the top five WNBA players with the highest free throw averages. What percent of the time does Sue Bird make a free throw?

Player	Average
Eva Nemcova	0.897
Seimone Augustus	0.897
Elena Tornikidou	0.882
Sue Bird	0.878
Cynthia Cooper	0.871

Source: Women's National Basketball Association

Practice and Problem Solving

HOMEWORK HELP	
For Exercises	See Examples
9–20	1
21–22	2
23–34	3
35–37	4

Write each percent as a decimal.

9. 27%
10. 70%
11. 6%
12. 4%
13. 18.5%
14. 56.4%
15. 2.2%
16. 3.8%
17. $27\frac{7}{10}\%$
18. $15\frac{1}{2}\%$
19. $30\frac{1}{4}\%$
20. $46\frac{2}{5}\%$
21. **BONES** An adult human body has $68\frac{3}{5}\%$ of the number of bones it had at birth. What decimal represents this amount?
22. **VIDEO GAMES** Brian reaches the sixth level of a video game $92\frac{3}{4}\%$ of the time he plays. What decimal represents this percent?

Write each decimal as a percent.

23. 0.7
24. 0.6
25. 5.8
26. 8.2
27. 0.95
28. 0.08
29. 0.17
30. 0.78
31. 0.675
32. 0.145
33. 0.012
34. 0.7025

BASEBALL The table shows the top five Major League Baseball players with the highest batting averages in a recent year. Express each player's batting average as a percent.

Player	Average
Joe Mauer	0.347
Freddy Sanchez	0.344
Derek Jeter	0.344
Robinson Cano	0.342
Miguel Cabrera	0.339

Source: Major League Baseball

35. Joe Mauer
36. Derek Jeter
37. Miguel Cabrera

Replace each ● with >, <, or = to make a true sentence.

38. 0.25% ● 0.125
39. 0.76 ● 76.5%
40. 500% ● 50
41. 99% ● 0.985
42. 0.325 ● 30%
43. 56% ● 0.5625

44. **SPORTS** A tennis player won 0.805 of the matches she played. What percent of the matches did she lose?

ANALYZE TABLES For Exercises 45–48, use the table and the information given.

Model airplane measurements are based on a scale of the life-size original. For example, a scale of $\frac{1}{72}$ is about 1% of the size of the original. Percents are rounded to the nearest thousandth.

Scale	Percent Equivalent
$\frac{1}{72}$	1.389%
$\frac{1}{24}$	4.167%
$\frac{1}{48}$	2.083%
$\frac{1}{20}$	5%
$\frac{1}{32}$	3.125%

45. Find the decimal equivalents for each scale.
46. Which scale is the smallest?
47. About how long is a model of an actual 88.5-foot C-119 boxcar plane using a $\frac{1}{72}$ scale?
48. Which scale is used if a model of an 88.5-foot C-119 boxcar plane is about 33.1875 inches long?

EXTRA PRACTICE
See pages 678, 708.

H.O.T. Problems

49. **OPEN ENDED** Write any decimal between 0 and 1. Then write it as a fraction in simplest form and as a percent.

50. **FIND THE ERROR** Emilio and Janelle both wrote 0.992 as a percent. Who is correct? Explain.

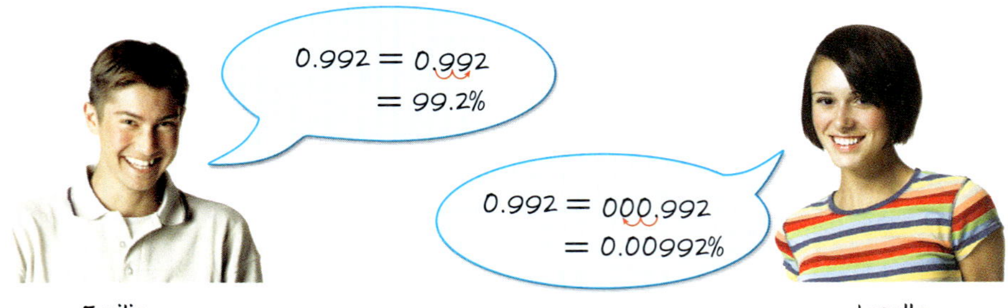

CHALLENGE **Write each fraction as a percent.**

51. $\frac{3}{8}$

52. $\frac{1}{40}$

53. $\frac{1}{32}$

54. **WRITING IN MATH** Write a word problem about a real-world situation in which you would change a decimal to a percent.

TEST PRACTICE

55. It is estimated that 13.9% of the population of Texas was born outside the United States. Which number is *not* equivalent to 13.9%?

   A $\frac{139}{1{,}000}$

   B $\frac{13.9}{100}$

   C 0.139

   D 1.39

56. Which of the following is ordered from least to greatest?

   F 0.42, $\frac{2}{5}$, 50%, $\frac{3}{4}$

   G $\frac{2}{5}$, 0.42, 50%, $\frac{3}{4}$

   H $\frac{3}{4}$, $\frac{2}{5}$, 0.42%, 50%

   J $\frac{3}{4}$, 0.42, $\frac{2}{5}$, 50%

Spiral Review

Write each ratio as a percent. (Lesson 4-6)

57. 72 out of 100 animals

58. \$9.90:\$100

59. 3.1 out of 100 households

60. Write $9\frac{3}{8}$ as a decimal. (Lesson 4-5)

61. **AIRPLANES** Write an integer that represents an airplane descending 125 feet. (Lesson 2-1)

62. **MONEY** Marina earned \$187.50 by working 30 hours. If she works 35 hours at this rate, how much will she earn? (Lesson 1-1)

GET READY for the Next Lesson

PREREQUISITE SKILL **Write the prime factorization of each number.** (Lesson 4-1)

63. 50

64. 32

65. 76

66. 105

4-8 Least Common Multiple

MAIN IDEA

Find the least common multiple of two or more numbers.

New Vocabulary

multiple
least common multiple (LCM)

Math Online

glencoe.com

- Extra Examples
- Personal Tutor
- Self-Check Quiz

MINI Lab

Use cubes to build the first row of each prism as shown.

1. Add a second row to each prism. Record the total number of cubes used in a table like the one shown below.

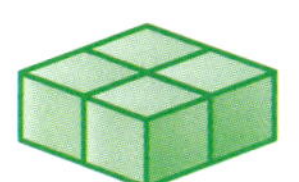
Prism A

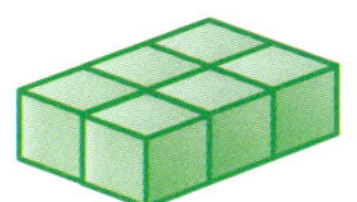
Prism B

Number of Rows	1	2	3	4
Cubes in Prism A	4	■	■	■
Cubes in Prism B	6	■	■	■

2. Add rows until each prism has four rows.
3. Describe two prisms that have the same number of cubes.
4. If you keep adding rows, will the two prisms have the same number of cubes again?

A **multiple** is the product of a number and any whole number. The **least common multiple**, or **LCM**, of two or more numbers is the least of their common multiples, excluding zero.

Vocabulary Link

Multiply
Everyday Use to find the product

Multiple
Math Use the product of a number and any whole number

EXAMPLES Find the LCM

1 **Find the LCM of 6 and 10.**

METHOD 1 **List the nonzero multiples.**

List the multiples of 6 until you come to a number that is also a multiple of 10.

multiples of 6: 6, 12, 18, 24, **30**, …

multiples of 10: 10, 20, **30**, …

Notice that 30 is also a multiple of 10. The LCM of 6 and 10 is 30.

METHOD 2 **Use prime factorization.**

$6 = 2 \cdot 3$

$10 = 2 \cdot 5$

The prime factors of 6 and 10 are 2, 3, and 5.

The LCM is the least product that contains the prime factors of each number. So, the LCM of 6 and 10 is $2 \cdot 3 \cdot 5$ or 30.

2 **Find the LCM of 45 and 75.**

Use Method 2. Find the prime factorization of each number.

$45 = 3 \cdot 3 \cdot 5$ or $3^2 \cdot 5$

$75 = 3 \cdot 5 \cdot 5$ or $3 \cdot 5^2$

The prime factors of 45 and 75 are 3 and 5. Write the prime factorization using exponents.

The LCM is the product of the prime factors 3 and 5, with each one raised to the *highest* power it occurs in *either* prime factorization. The LCM of 45 and 75 is $3^2 \cdot 5^2$, which is 225.

CHOOSE Your Method

Find the LCM of each set of numbers.

a. 3, 12 b. 10, 12 c. 25, 30

Real-World EXAMPLE

Real-World Link Each day, about 700,000 people in the U.S. celebrate their birthday.

3 **PARTY Ling needs to buy paper plates, napkins, and cups for a party. Plates come in packages of 12, napkins come in packages of 16, and cups come in packages of 8. What is the least number of packages she will have to buy if she wants to have the same number of plates, napkins, and cups?**

First find the LCM of 8, 12, and 16.

$8 = 2 \cdot 2 \cdot 2$ or 2^3

$12 = 2 \cdot 2 \cdot 3$ or $2^2 \cdot 3$

$16 = 2 \cdot 2 \cdot 2 \cdot 2$ or 2^4

The prime factors of 8, 12, and 16 are 2 and 3. Write the prime factorization using exponents.

The LCM of 8, 12, and 16 is $2^4 \cdot 3$, which is 48.

To find the number of packages of each Ling needs to buy, divide 48 by the amount in each package.

cups: $48 \div 8$ or 6 packages

plates: $48 \div 12$ or 4 packages

napkins: $48 \div 16$ or 3 packages

So, Ling will need to buy 6 packages of cups, 4 packages of plates, and 3 packages of napkins.

CHECK Your Progress

d. **VEHICLES** Mr. Hernandez changes his car's oil every 3 months, rotates the tires every 6 months, and replaces the air filter once a year. If he completed all three tasks in April, what will be the next month he again completes all three tasks?

CHECK Your Understanding

Examples 1–3 (pp. 211–212)

Find the LCM of each set of numbers.

1. 4, 14
2. 6, 7
3. 12, 15
4. 21, 35
5. 3, 5, 12
6. 6, 14, 21

Example 3 (p. 212)

7. **GOVERNMENT** The number of years per term for a U.S. President, senator, and representative is shown. Suppose a senator was elected in the presidential election year 2008. In what year will he or she campaign again during a presidential election year?

Elected Office	Term (yr)
President	4
Senator	6
Representative	2

Practice and Problem Solving

HOMEWORK HELP

For Exercises	See Examples
8–13, 20	1, 2
14–19, 21	3

Find the LCM for each set of numbers.

8. 6, 8
9. 8, 18
10. 12, 16
11. 24, 36
12. 11, 12
13. 45, 63
14. 2, 3, 5
15. 6, 8, 9
16. 8, 12, 16
17. 12, 15, 28
18. 22, 33, 44
19. 12, 16, 36

20. **CHORES** Hernando walks his dog every two days. He gives his dog a bath once a week. Today, Hernando walked his dog and then gave her a bath. How many days will pass before he does both chores on the same day?

21. **TEXT MESSAGING** Three friends use text messaging to notify their parents of their whereabouts. If all three contact their parents at 3:00 P.M., at what time will all three contact their parents again at the same time?

Find the LCM of each set.

22. \$3.00, \$14.00
23. 10¢, 25¢, 5¢
24. 9 inches, 2 feet

Write two numbers whose LCM is the given number.

25. 35
26. 56
27. 70
28. 30

29. **SNACKS** Alvin's mom needs to buy snacks for soccer practice. Juice boxes come in packages of 10. Oatmeal snack bars come in packages of 8. She wants to have the same number of juice boxes and snack bars, what is the least number of packages of each snack that she will have to buy?

EXTRA PRACTICE See pages 678, 707.

30. **REASONING** The LCM of two consecutive positive numbers is greater than 200 and is a multiple of 7. What are the least possible numbers?

H.O.T. Problems

31. **CHALLENGE** Two numbers have a GCF of $3 \cdot 5$. Their LCM is $2^2 \cdot 3 \cdot 5$. If one of the numbers is $3 \cdot 5$, what is the other number?

32. **SELECT A TECHNIQUE** The schedule for each of three trains is shown. Suppose a train from each line leaves Clark Street at 11:35 A.M. Which of the following technique(s) might you use to determine the next time all three trains will be leaving at the same time? Justify your selection(s). Then use the technique to solve the problem.

Clark Street Train Station	
Train	**Leaves Station**
Red-line	every 14 minutes
Blue-line	every 16 minutes
Brown-line	every 8 minutes

mental math | number sense | estimation

33. **OPEN ENDED** Write three numbers that have an LCM of 30.

34. **WRITING IN MATH** Describe the relationship between 4, 20, and 5 using the words *factor* and *multiple.*

35. Which rule describes the common multiples of 12 and 18, where n represents the counting numbers?

A $12n$

B $18n$

C $36n$

D $216n$

36. **SHORT RESPONSE** Wil swims every third day, runs every fourth day, and lifts weights every fifth day. If Wil does all three activities today, how many days will pass before he does all three activities on the same day again?

Spiral Review

Write each percent as a decimal. (Lesson 4-7)

37. 55% 38. 26.4% 39. $\frac{1}{4}$% 40. 2%

41. **DIAMONDS** Sixty-eight percent of engagement rings have a diamond that is round in shape. Write this percent as a fraction in simplest form. (Lesson 4-6)

42. **ALGEBRA** Solve $3x = 18$. (Lesson 3-3)

43. **ALGEBRA** Rose swam 7 laps more than twice the number of laps her sister swam. Write an algebraic expression to represent this situation. (Lesson 3-1)

PREREQUISITE SKILL **Replace each ● with <, > or = to make a true sentence.** (Page 670)

44. 6.85 ● 5.68 45. 2.34 ● 2.43 46. 6.9 ● 5.99

4-9 Comparing and Ordering Rational Numbers

MAIN IDEA

Compare and order fractions, decimals, and percents.

New Vocabulary

rational numbers
common denominator
least common denominator (LCD)

Math Online

glencoe.com

- Extra Examples
- Personal Tutor
- Self-Check Quiz

MINI Lab

In Chapter 2, you used a number line to compare integers. You can also use a number line to compare positive and negative fractions. The number line shows that $-\frac{1}{8} < \frac{3}{8}$.

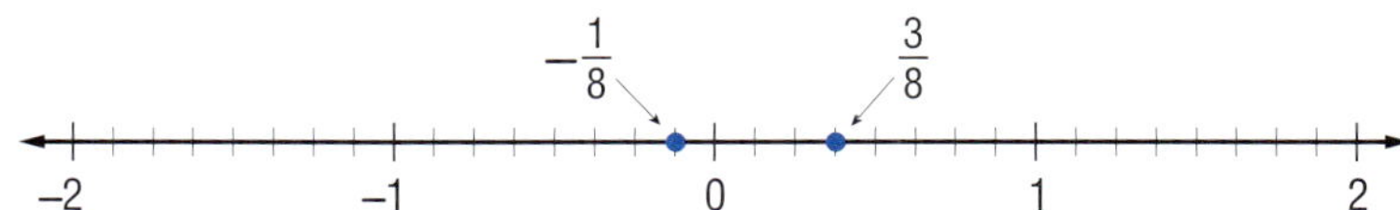

Graph each pair of numbers on a number line. Then determine which number is less.

1. $-\frac{7}{8}, -\frac{3}{8}$
2. $-\frac{5}{8}, -1\frac{1}{8}$
3. $-\frac{13}{8}, -\frac{3}{8}$
4. $-1\frac{7}{8}, -1\frac{5}{8}$
5. $-\frac{1}{2}, -\frac{3}{4}$
6. $1\frac{1}{4}, -1\frac{1}{4}$

The different types of numbers you have been using are all examples of rational numbers. A **rational number** is a number that can be expressed as a fraction. Fractions, terminating and repeating decimals, percents, and integers are all rational numbers. The points corresponding to rational numbers begin to "fill in" the number line.

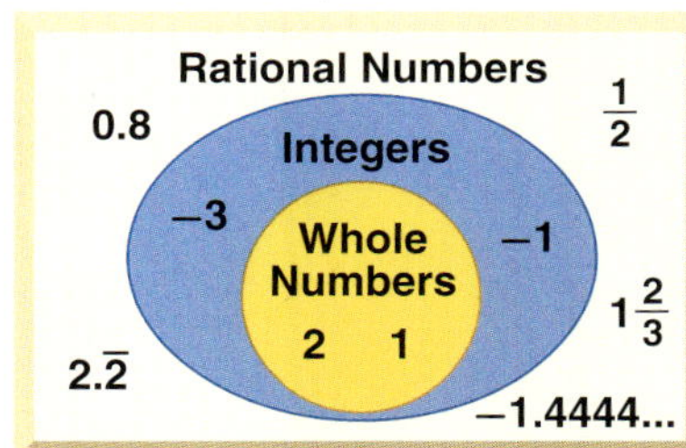

EXAMPLE Compare Rational Numbers

1 **Replace the ● with <, >, or = to make $-1\frac{5}{6}$ ● $-1\frac{1}{6}$ a true sentence.**

Graph each rational number on a number line. Mark off equal size increments of $\frac{1}{6}$ between −2 and −1.

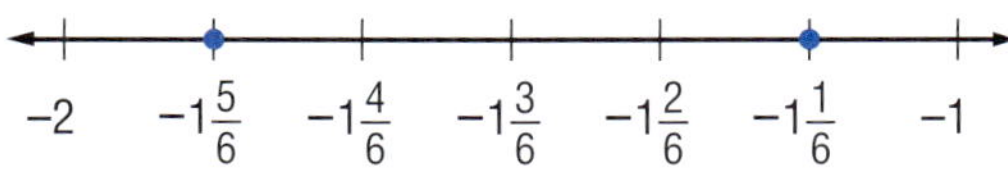

The number line shows that $-1\frac{5}{6} < -1\frac{1}{6}$.

CHECK Your Progress

a. **Replace the ● with <, >, or = to make $-5\frac{5}{9}$ ● $-5\frac{1}{9}$ a true sentence.**

A **common denominator** is a common multiple of the denominators of two or more fractions. The **least common denominator** or **LCD** is the LCM of the denominators. You can use the LCD to compare fractions.

EXAMPLE Compare Rational Numbers

2 **Replace the ● with <, >, or = to make $\frac{7}{12}$ ● $\frac{8}{18}$ a true sentence.**

$12 = 2^2 \cdot 3$ and $18 = 2 \cdot 3^2$. So, the LCM is $2^2 \cdot 3^2$ or 36. The LCD of the denominators 12 and 18 is 36.

$$\frac{7}{12} = \frac{7 \times 3}{12 \times 3} = \frac{21}{36} \qquad \frac{8}{18} = \frac{8 \times 2}{18 \times 2} = \frac{16}{36}$$

Since $\frac{21}{36} > \frac{16}{36}$, then $\frac{7}{12} > \frac{8}{18}$.

CHECK Your Progress

Replace each ● with <, >, or = to make a true sentence.

b. $\frac{5}{6}$ ● $\frac{7}{9}$

c. $\frac{1}{5}$ ● $\frac{7}{50}$

d. $-\frac{9}{16}$ ● $-\frac{7}{10}$

You can also compare fractions by writing each fraction as a decimal and then comparing the decimals.

Real-World EXAMPLE

3 **ROLLER SHOES** **In Mr. Huang's math class, 6 out of 32 students own roller shoes. In Mrs. Trevino's math class, 5 out of 29 students own roller shoes. In which class do a greater fraction of students own roller shoes?**

Since the denominators are large, write $\frac{6}{32}$ and $\frac{5}{29}$ as decimals and then compare.

$6 \div 32 = 0.1875 \qquad 5 \div 29 \approx 0.1724$ Divide.

Since $0.1875 > 0.1724$, then $\frac{6}{32} > \frac{5}{29}$.

So, a greater fraction of students in Mr. Huang's class own roller shoes.

Real-World Link The first roller shoe was introduced in 2001.

Source: Associated Content, Inc.

CHECK Your Progress

e. **BOWLING** Twelve out of 32 students in second period class like to bowl. In fifth period class, 12 out of 29 students like to bowl. In which class do a greater fraction of the students like to bowl?

These fraction-decimal-percent equivalents are used frequently.

Fractions-Decimals-Percents — Key Concept

$\frac{1}{4} = 0.25 = 25\%$	$\frac{1}{5} = 0.2 = 20\%$	$\frac{1}{8} = 0.125 = 12.5\%$	$\frac{1}{10} = 0.1 = 10\%$
$\frac{1}{2} = 0.5 = 50\%$	$\frac{2}{5} = 0.4 = 40\%$	$\frac{3}{8} = 0.375 = 37.5\%$	$\frac{3}{10} = 0.3 = 30\%$
$\frac{3}{4} = 0.75 = 75\%$	$\frac{3}{5} = 0.6 = 60\%$	$\frac{1}{3} = 0.\overline{3} = 33.\overline{3}\%$	$\frac{7}{10} = 0.7 = 70\%$
$1 = 1.00 = 100\%$	$\frac{4}{5} = 0.8 = 80\%$	$\frac{2}{3} = 0.\overline{6} = 66.\overline{6}\%$	$\frac{9}{10} = 0.9 = 90\%$

The Greek letter π (pi) represents the nonterminating and nonrepeating number whose first few digits are 3.1415926.... This number is not rational. You will learn more about *irrational numbers* in Chapter 12.

Test-Taking Tip

Reading Choices Read all answer choices carefully before deciding on the correct answer. Often two choices will look very familiar.

TEST EXAMPLE

4 Which list shows the numbers 3.44, π, 3.14, and $3.\overline{4}$ in order from least to greatest?

A π, 3.14, 3.44, $3.\overline{4}$

B π, 3.14, $3.\overline{4}$, 3.44

C 3.14, π, $3.\overline{4}$, 3.44

D 3.14, π, 3.44, $3.\overline{4}$

Read the Item

Compare the digits using place value.

Solve the Item

Line up the decimal points and compare using place value.

3.140	Annex a zero.	3.440	Annex a zero.
3.1415926...	$\pi \approx 3.1415926...$	3.444...	$3.\overline{4} = 3.444...$
Since $0 < 1$, $3.14 < \pi$.		Since $0 < 4$, $3.44 < 3.\overline{4}$.	

So, the order of the numbers from least to greatest is 3.14, π, 3.44, and $3.\overline{4}$. The answer is D.

CHECK Your Progress

f. The amount of rain received on four consecutive days was 0.3 inch, $\frac{3}{5}$ inch, 0.75 inch, and $\frac{2}{3}$ inch. Which list shows the amounts from least to greatest?

F 0.3 in., $\frac{2}{3}$ in., $\frac{3}{5}$ in., 0.75 in.

G 0.3 in., $\frac{3}{5}$ in., $\frac{2}{3}$ in., 0.75 in.

H 0.75 in., $\frac{2}{3}$ in., $\frac{3}{5}$ in., 0.3 in.

J $\frac{3}{5}$ in., $\frac{2}{3}$ in., 0.3 in., 0.75 in.

CHECK Your Understanding

Examples 1–2 (pp. 215–216)

Replace each ● with <, >, or = to make a true sentence. Use a number line if necessary.

1. $-\frac{4}{9}$ ● $-\frac{7}{9}$
2. $-1\frac{3}{4}$ ● $-1\frac{6}{8}$
3. $\frac{3}{8}$ ● $\frac{6}{15}$
4. $2\frac{4}{5}$ ● $2\frac{7}{8}$

Example 3 (p. 216)

5. **SOCCER** The table shows the average saves for two soccer goalies. Who has the better average, Elliot or Shanna? Explain.

Name	Average
Elliot	3 saves out of 4
Shanna	7 saves out of 11

6. **SCHOOL** On her first quiz in social studies, Majorie answered 23 out of 25 questions correctly. On her second quiz, she answered 27 out of 30 questions correctly. On which quiz did Majorie have the greater score?

Example 4 (p. 217)

7. **MULTIPLE CHOICE** The lengths of four insects are 0.02 inch, $\frac{1}{8}$ inch, 0.1 inch, and $\frac{2}{3}$ inch. Which list shows the lengths in inches from least to greatest?

   A 0.1, 0.02, $\frac{1}{8}$, $\frac{2}{3}$

   B $\frac{1}{8}$, 0.02, 0.1, $\frac{2}{3}$

   C 0.02, 0.1, $\frac{1}{8}$, $\frac{2}{3}$

   D $\frac{2}{3}$, 0.02, 0.1, $\frac{1}{8}$

Practice and Problem Solving

HOMEWORK HELP

For Exercises	See Examples
8–19	1, 2
20–25, 49	3
26–31, 48	4

Replace each ● with <, >, or = to make a true sentence. Use a number line if necessary.

8. $-\frac{3}{5}$ ● $-\frac{4}{5}$
9. $-\frac{5}{7}$ ● $-\frac{2}{7}$
10. $-7\frac{5}{8}$ ● $-7\frac{1}{8}$
11. $-3\frac{2}{3}$ ● $-3\frac{4}{6}$
12. $\frac{7}{10}$ ● $\frac{2}{3}$
13. $\frac{4}{7}$ ● $\frac{5}{8}$
14. $\frac{2}{3}$ ● $\frac{10}{15}$
15. $-\frac{17}{24}$ ● $-\frac{11}{12}$
16. $2\frac{3}{4}$ ● $2\frac{2}{3}$
17. $6\frac{2}{3}$ ● $6\frac{1}{2}$
18. $5\frac{5}{7}$ ● $5\frac{11}{14}$
19. $3\frac{11}{16}$ ● $3\frac{7}{8}$
20. 40% ● 112 out of 250
21. 3 out of 5 ● 59%
22. 0.82 ● 5 out of 6
23. 9 out of 20 ● 0.45

24. **MONEY** The table shows how much copper is in each type of coin. Which coin contains the greatest amount of copper?

Coin	Amount of Copper
Dime	$\frac{12}{16}$
Nickel	$\frac{3}{4}$
Penny	$\frac{1}{400}$
Quarter	$\frac{23}{25}$

25. **BASKETBALL** Gracia and Jim were shooting free throws. Gracia made 4 out of 15 free throws. Jim *missed* the free throw 6 out of 16 times. Who made the free throw a greater fraction of the time?

Order each set of numbers from least to greatest.

26. 0.23, 19%, $\frac{1}{5}$
27. $\frac{8}{10}$, 81%, 0.805
28. $-0.615, -\frac{5}{8}, -0.62$
29. $-1.4, -1\frac{1}{25}, -1.25$
30. $7.49, 7\frac{49}{50}, 7.5$
31. $3\frac{4}{7}, 3\frac{3}{5}, 3.47$

MEASUREMENT **Replace each ● with <, >, or = to make a true sentence.**

32. $\frac{5}{8}$ yard ● $\frac{1}{16}$ yard
33. 0.25 pound ● $\frac{2}{9}$ pound
34. $2\frac{5}{6}$ hours ● 2.8 hours
35. $1\frac{7}{12}$ gallons ● $1\frac{5}{8}$ gallons

MEASUREMENT **Order each of the following from least to greatest.**

36. 4.4 miles, $4\frac{3}{8}$ miles, $4\frac{5}{12}$ miles
37. 6.5 cups, $6\frac{1}{3}$ cups, 6 cups
38. 1.2 laps, 2 laps, $\frac{1}{2}$ lap
39. $\frac{1}{5}$ gram, 5 grams, 1.5 grams

Real-World Link

The Olympic gold medals are actually made out of 92.5% silver, with the gold medal covered in 6 grams of pure gold.

ANIMALS **For Exercises 40–42, use the table that shows the lengths of the smallest mammals.**

Animal	Length (ft)
Eastern Chipmunk	$\frac{1}{3}$
Kitti's Hog-Nosed Bat	$0.8\overline{3}$
European Mole	$\frac{5}{12}$
Masked Shrew	$\frac{1}{6}$
Spiny Pocket Mouse	0.25

Source: *Scholastic Book of World Records*

40. Which animal is the smallest mammal?

41. Which animal is smaller than the European mole but larger than the spiny pocket mouse?

42. Order the animals from greatest to least size.

SOFTBALL **For Exercises 43 and 44, use the following table which shows the at-bats, hits, and home run statistics for four players on the 2004 Olympics U.S. Women's softball team.**

Player	At-Bats	Hits	Home Runs
Crystal Bustos	26	9	5
Kelly Krestschman	21	7	1
Stacey Nuveman	16	5	2
Natasha Watley	30	12	0

Source: Olympic Movement

43. Write the ratio of hits to at-bats as a decimal to the nearest thousandth for each player. Who had the greatest batting average during the Olympic games?

44. Write the ratio of home runs to at-bats as a decimal for each player. Who had the greatest home run average during the Olympic games?

H.O.T. Problems

45. **Which One Doesn't Belong?** Identify the ratio that does not have the same value as the other three. Explain your reasoning.

12 out of 15	0.08	80%	$\frac{4}{5}$

46. **CHALLENGE** Explain how you know which number, $1\frac{15}{16}$, $\frac{17}{8}$, or $\frac{63}{32}$, is nearest to 2.

47. **WRITING IN MATH** Write a word problem about a real-world situation in which you would compare rational numbers. Then solve the problem.

TEST PRACTICE

48. Which point shows the location of $\frac{7}{2}$ on the number line?

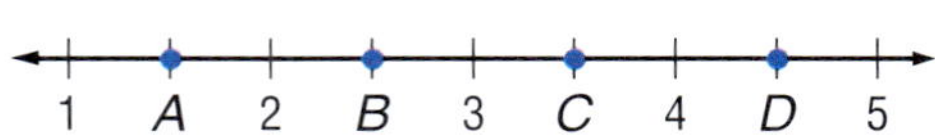

A point A

B point B

C point C

D point D

49. Which list of numbers is ordered from least to greatest?

F $\frac{1}{4}$, $4\frac{1}{4}$, 0.4, 0.04

G 0.04, 0.4, $4\frac{1}{4}$, $\frac{1}{4}$

H 0.04, $\frac{1}{4}$, 0.4, $4\frac{1}{4}$

J 0.4, $\frac{1}{4}$, 0.04, $4\frac{1}{4}$

50. Which of the following fractions is closest to 0?

A $-\frac{3}{4}$

B $-\frac{2}{3}$

C $\frac{7}{12}$

D $\frac{5}{8}$

Spiral Review

Find the LCM of each set of numbers. (Lesson 4-8)

51. 14, 21

52. 3, 13

53. 12, 16

SALES TAX The table shows the sales tax rate for the states shown. Write each sales tax rate as a decimal. (Lesson 4-7)

54. Kentucky

55. Illinois

56. North Carolina

State	Sales Tax
Illinois	6.25%
Kentucky	6%
North Carolina	4.25%
South Carolina	5%

Source: Federation of Tax Administrators

Find the GCF of each set of numbers. (Lesson 4-2)

57. 18, 72

58. 40, 12

59. 72, 20

ALGEBRA Solve each equation. (Lesson 3-5)

60. $4x + 3 = 15$

61. $2n - 5 = 19$

62. $-8 = -3d + 1$

CHAPTER 4

Study Guide and Review

Math Online glencoe.com
- STUDY TO GO
- Vocabulary Review

GET READY to Study

Be sure the following Big Ideas are noted in your Foldable.

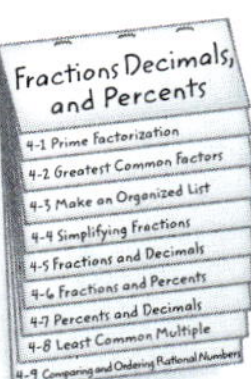

BIG Ideas

Greatest Common Factor (Lesson 4-2)

- The greatest common factor or GCF is the greatest of the common factors of two or more numbers.

Fractions, Decimals, and Percents

(Lessons 4-4 to 4-7)

- A fraction is in simplest form when the GCF of the numerator and denominator is 1.
- A terminating decimal is a decimal whose digits end. Repeating decimals have a pattern in their digits that repeats forever.
- A percent is a part to whole ratio that compares a number to 100.
- To write a percent as a decimal, divide the percent by 100 and remove the percent symbol.
- To write a decimal as a percent, multiply the percent by 100 and add the percent symbol.

Least Common Multiple (Lesson 4-8)

- The least common multiple or LCM of two or more numbers is the least of their common multiples.

Rational Numbers (Lesson 4-9)

- A rational number is one that can be expressed as a fraction.

Key Vocabulary

bar notation (p. 197)
common denominator (p. 216)
composite number (p. 181)
equivalent fractions (p. 192)
factor tree (p. 182)
greatest common factor (GCF) (p. 186)
least common denominator (p. 216)
least common multiple (LCM) (p. 211)
multiple (p. 211)
percent (p. 202)
prime factorization (p. 182)
prime number (p. 181)
ratio (p. 202)
rational number (p. 215)
repeating decimal (p. 197)
simplest form (p. 192)
terminating decimal (p. 197)
Venn diagram (p. 186)

Vocabulary Check

State whether each sentence is *true* or *false*. If *false*, replace the underlined word or number to make a true sentence.

1. A ratio is a comparison of two numbers by <u>multiplication</u>.
2. A <u>rational number</u> is a whole number greater than 1 that has exactly two factors, 1 and itself.
3. 1.875 is an example of a <u>terminating decimal</u>.
4. A common denominator for the fractions $\frac{2}{3}$ and $\frac{1}{4}$ is <u>12</u>.
5. The <u>greatest common factor</u> of 3 and 5 is 15.
6. A ratio that compares a number to <u>100</u> is a percent.
7. The fractions $\frac{9}{21}$ and $\frac{3}{7}$ are <u>equivalent fractions</u>.

CHAPTER 4 Study Guide and Review

Lesson-by-Lesson Review

4-1 Prime Factorization (pp. 181–184)

Find the prime factorization of each number.

8. 54
9. 128
10. 68
11. 95
12. **ALGEBRA** Factor $36x^2yz^3$.
13. **PLANTS** The palm tree *raffia* has leaves up to 65 feet long. Write this length as a product of primes.

Example 1 Find the prime factorization of 18.

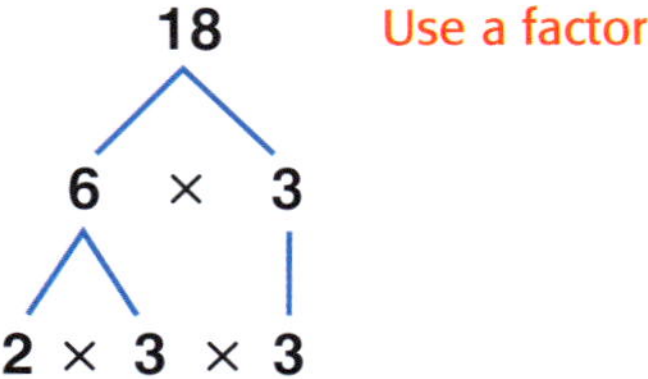

The prime factorization of 18 is 2×3^2.

4-2 Greatest Common Factor (p. 186–189)

Find the GCF of each set of numbers.

14. 18, 27
15. 30, 72
16. 28, 70, 98
17. 42, 63, 105
18. **ALGEBRA** Find the GCF of $18w$ and $54w^2y$.
19. **CLOTHING** Maria spent a total of $24 on earrings, $36 on shirts, and $48 on shorts. If each item cost the same amount, what is the greatest possible price per item?

Example 2 Find the GCF of 24 and 56.

First, make a list of all the factors of 24 and 56.

factors of 24: **1**, **2**, 3, **4**, 6, **8**, 12, 24
factors of 56: **1**, **2**, **4**, 7, **8**, 14, 28, 56
common factors: 1, 2, 4, 8
The GCF of 24 and 56 is 8.

4-3 PSI: Make an Organized List (pp. 190–191)

Solve by making an organized list.

20. **SEATING** In how many ways can four friends sit in a row at the movies?
21. **TELEPHONES** A phone company offers 5 different types of long-distance plans and 3 different caller features (call waiting, caller ID, and call forward). How many different kinds of plans can be set up that include a long-distance service and a caller feature?

Example 3 In how many ways can the letters A, B, and C be arranged?

The possible outcomes are written below.

ABC ACB
BAC BCA
CAB CBA

There are 6 different ways to arrange the letters.

Mixed Problem Solving
For mixed problem-solving practice, see page 707.

4-4 Simplifying Fractions (pp. 192–195)

Write each fraction in simplest form.

22. $\frac{12}{15}$ 23. $\frac{35}{60}$ 24. $\frac{11}{121}$
25. $\frac{14}{63}$ 26. $\frac{37}{45}$ 27. $\frac{55}{110}$

28. **CATS** The average household cat sleeps 18 hours a day. Write a fraction in simplest form comparing the number of hours a household cat sleeps to the number of hours in a day.

Example 4 Write $\frac{24}{32}$ in simplest form.

Find the GCF of the numerator and denominator.

24 = 1, 2, 3, 4, 6, 8, 12, 24
32 = 1, 2, 4, 8, 16, 32

$\frac{24}{32} = \frac{24 \div 8}{32 \div 8} = \frac{3}{4}$ Divide the numerator and denominator by the GCF.

4-5 Fractions and Decimals (pp. 196–200)

Write each fraction or mixed number as a decimal. Use bar notation if the decimal is a repeating decimal.

29. $\frac{3}{4}$ 30. $\frac{7}{8}$ 31. $\frac{5}{9}$
32. $4\frac{1}{3}$ 33. $6\frac{2}{5}$ 34. $1\frac{6}{7}$

Write each decimal as a fraction in simplest form.

35. 0.7 36. 0.44 37. 0.05
38. 0.18 39. 0.54 40. 0.08

41. **RUNNING** Jeremy ran a mile in 5 minutes and 8 seconds. Write this time in minutes as a decimal.

Example 5 Write $\frac{3}{8}$ as a decimal.

$$\begin{array}{r} 0.375 \\ 8\overline{)3.000} \\ -\underline{24} \\ 60 \\ -\underline{56} \\ 40 \\ -\underline{40} \\ 0 \end{array}$$

So, $\frac{3}{8} = 0.375$.

Example 6 Write 0.64 as a fraction.

$0.64 = \frac{64}{100}$ Write as a fraction with a denominator of 100.

$= \frac{16}{25}$ Simplify.

4-6 Fractions and Percents (pp. 202–205)

Write each fraction as a percent.

42. $\frac{32}{100}$ 43. $\frac{11}{25}$ 44. $\frac{47}{50}$ 45. $\frac{8}{20}$

Write each percent as a fraction in simplest form.

46. 68% 47. 95% 48. 42% 49. 16%

50. **LUNCH** In Mrs. Soulise's class, 56% of the students buy their lunch. Write this percent as a fraction in simplest form.

Example 7 Write $\frac{27}{50}$ as a percent.

$\frac{27}{50} = \frac{54}{100}$ Write an equivalent fraction with a denominator of 100.

$= 54\%$ Definition of percent

Example 8 Write 96% as a fraction.

$96\% = \frac{96}{100}$ Definition of percent

$= \frac{24}{25}$ Simplify.

CHAPTER 4

Study Guide and Review

4-7 Percents and Decimals (pp. 206–210)

Write each percent as a decimal.

51. 48%

52. 7%

53. 12.5%

54. $75\frac{1}{4}\%$

Write each decimal as a percent.

55. 0.61

56. 0.055

57. 0.19

58. 0.999

59. **FOOD** A serving of oatmeal contains 3 grams of fiber. This is 12% of the recommended daily allowance. Write this percent as a decimal.

Example 9 **Write 35% as a decimal.**

$35\% = \frac{35}{100}$ Write the percent as a fraction.

$= 0.35$ Write the fraction as a decimal.

Example 10 **Write 0.625 as a percent.**

$0.625 = 0.625$ Multiply by 100.

$= 62.5\%$ Add the % symbol.

4-8 Least Common Multiple (pp. 211–214)

Find the LCM of each set of numbers.

60. 9, 15

61. 4, 8

62. 16, 24

63. 3, 8, 12

64. 4, 9, 12

65. 15, 24, 30

66. **BREAKFAST** At a bakery, muffins come in dozens and individual serving containers of orange juice come in packs of 8. If Avery needs to have the same amount of muffins as orange juice containers, what is the least possible number of sets of each he needs to buy?

Example 11 **Find the LCM of 8 and 36.**

Write each prime factorization.

$8 = 2 \times 2 \times 2 = 2^3$

$36 = 2 \times 2 \times 3 \times 3 = 2^2 \times 3^2$

LCM: $2^3 \times 3^2 = 72$

The LCM of 8 and 36 is 72.

4-9 Comparing and Ordering Rational Numbers (pp. 215–220)

Replace each ● with <, >, or = to make a true sentence.

67. $\frac{3}{8}$ ● $\frac{2}{3}$

68. -0.45 ● $-\frac{9}{20}$

69. $\frac{8}{9}$ ● 85%

70. $-3\frac{3}{4}$ ● $-3\frac{5}{8}$

71. **SCHOOL** Michael received a $\frac{26}{30}$ on his English quiz and received 81% on his biology test. In which class did he receive the higher score?

Example 12 **Replace ● with <, >, or = to make $\frac{3}{5}$ ● $\frac{5}{8}$ a true sentence.**

Find equivalent fractions. The LCD is 40.

$\frac{3}{5} = \frac{3 \times 8}{5 \times 8} = \frac{24}{40}$ $\frac{5}{8} = \frac{5 \times 5}{8 \times 5} = \frac{25}{40}$

Since $\frac{24}{40} < \frac{25}{40}$, then $\frac{3}{5} < \frac{5}{8}$.

Chapter 4 Practice Test

Math Online glencoe.com
• Chapter Test

1. Find the prime factorization of 72.

2. Find the GCF of 24 and 40.

3. **SCHEDULES** Farijah registered for French, Pre-Algebra, Life Science, English, and Social Studies. French is only offered first period, Pre-Algebra is only offered fifth period, and she must have lunch fourth period. How many different schedules can she create out of a six period day? Use the *make an organized list* strategy.

Write each fraction in simplest form.

4. $\frac{24}{60}$

5. $\frac{64}{72}$

Write each fraction, mixed number, or percent as a decimal. Use bar notation if the decimal is a repeating decimal.

6. $\frac{7}{9}$

7. $4\frac{5}{8}$

8. 91%

9. **COINS** The United States Mint released a new quarter every ten weeks from 1999 to 2008 commemorating the 50 states. By the end of 2006, 40 state coins had been released. What percent of the coins is this?

Write each decimal or percent as a fraction in simplest form.

10. 0.84

11. 0.006

12. 42%

13. **MULTIPLE CHOICE** Which of the following is equivalent to the decimal 0.087?

A 0.87%
B 8.7%
C 87%
D 870%

Write each fraction or decimal as a percent.

14. $\frac{15}{25}$

15. 0.26

16. 0.135

17. **FLOORING** Mr. Daniels is putting new floor tiles in his bathroom. He has already tiled 34 square feet of the floor measuring 5 feet by 10 feet. What percent of the floor has he tiled?

18. **MULTIPLE CHOICE** What percent of the figure below is unshaded?

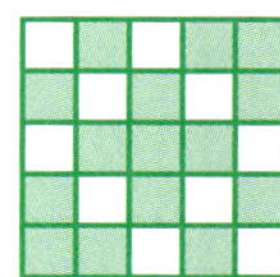

F 15%
G 30%
H 40%
J 60%

Find the LCM of each set of numbers.

19. 18, 42

20. 4, 5, 12

21. **PRACTICE** Rico has track practice every 3 days. He has saxophone practice every 4 days. If Rico has both track and saxophone practice today, after how many days will Rico have both track and saxophone practice again?

Replace each ● with <, >, or = to make a true sentence.

22. $-\frac{3}{5}$ ● $-\frac{5}{9}$

23. $4\frac{7}{12}$ ● $4\frac{6}{8}$

24. $\frac{13}{20}$ ● 65%

25. **BASKETBALL** To make it past the first round of tryouts for the basketball team, Paul must make at least 35% of his free-throw attempts. During the first round of tryouts he makes 17 out of 40 attempts. Did Paul make it to the next round of tryouts? Explain your reasoning.

CHAPTER 4

Test Practice
Cumulative, Chapters 1–4

Math Online glencoe.com
• Test Practice

PART 1 Multiple Choice

Read each question. Then fill in the correct answer on the answer sheet provided by your teacher or on a sheet of paper.

1. A large school system estimates that 0.706 of its students will take the bus to school throughout the school year. Which number is greater than 0.706?

   A $\frac{706}{1,000}$

   B $-1\frac{6}{7}$

   C $\frac{76}{100}$

   D -7.06

2. Debra is working on three different art projects. She has completed $\frac{1}{4}$, $\frac{3}{8}$, and $\frac{1}{2}$ of these projects, respectively. Which list shows the percent of work completed on these projects from least to greatest?

   F 37.5%, 50%, 25%

   G 50%, 37.5%, 25%

   H 25%, 37.5%, 50%

   J 25%, 50%, 87.5%

3. Which of the following is the prime factored form of the lowest common denominator of $\frac{1}{6}$ and $\frac{3}{8}$?

   A $2^2 \times 3 \times 5$ C 2×6

   B $2^3 \times 5$ D $2^3 \times 3$

TEST-TAKING TIP

Question 3 Eliminate any answer choices that you know are incorrect. Since the LCD, 24, does not have a factor of 5, you can eliminate answer choices A and B.

4. Solve the equation $x + 7 = -3$. What is the value of x?

   F 4   H -4

   G 3   J -10

5. At a wedding reception, the number of seats s is equal to 8 times the number of tables t. Which equation matches this situation?

   A $s = 8 + t$

   B $t = 8 \cdot s$

   C $s = 8 \cdot t$

   D $t = 8 - t$

6. Which problem situation matches the equation below?

$$x + 12 = 35$$

   F The difference between two numbers is 35. One of the numbers is 12. What is x, the other number?

   G Laura is 12 years younger than her brother. If Laura is 35 years old, find her brother's age x.

   H The sum of a number, x, and 12 is 35. What is the value of x?

   J Karen had $35. If she received $12, what is x, the total amount she now has?

7. Which of the following is true when evaluating the expression $3 \cdot 4^2 - 12 \div 6$?

   A Multiply 3 by 4 first since multiplication comes before subtraction.

   B Evaluate 4^2 first since it is a power.

   C Divide 12 by 6 first since division comes before multiplication.

   D Multiply 3 by 4 first since all operations occur in order from left to right.

Preparing for Standardized Tests

For test-taking strategies and practice, see pages 716–733.

8. Which sequence follows the rule $2n + 5$, where n represents the position of a term in the sequence?

F 3, 5, 7, 9, 11, ...
G 6, 8, 10, 12, 14, ...
H 7, 9, 11, 13, 15, ...
J 8, 12, 16, 20, 24, ...

9. Nicholas used the Distributive Property to evaluate the expression 5(12 + 7) mentally. Which of the following is a correct use of the Distributive Property to evaluate this expression?

A $5(12 + 7) = 5(12) + 5(7) = 60 + 35$ or 95
B $5(12 + 7) = 5(12) + 7 = 60 + 7$ or 67
C $5(12 + 7) = 12 + 5(7) = 12 + 35$ or 47
D $5(12 + 7) = 5 + 60 + 5 + 7 = 65 + 12$ or 77

10. Which of the following relationships is represented by the data in the table?

x	y
1	5,280
2	10,560
3	15,840
4	21,120
5	26,400

F conversion of miles to feet
G conversion of inches to yards
H conversion of feet to miles
J conversion of yards to inches

11. If $g = 4$, $m = 3$, and $n = 6$, then $\frac{mn + 2}{g} + 1$ is equivalent to which of the following?

A 6
B 5
C 3
D 2

PART 2 Short Response/Grid In

Record your answers on the answer sheet provided by your teacher or on a sheet of paper.

12. Write 7.2% as a decimal.

13. Jeremy expects 8 out of the 10 friends he invited to come to his party. What percent of his friends does he expect to come?

PART 3 Extended Response

Record your answers on the answer sheet provided by your teacher or on a sheet of paper. Show your work.

14. The prime factorization of 24 is $2 \times 2 \times 2 \times 3$. The table lists each unique prime factor and the products of all possible unique combinations of two, three, and four prime factors.

Unique Prime Factors	2, 3
Products of Two Factors	2×2, 2×3
Products of Three Factors	$2 \times 2 \times 2$, $2 \times 2 \times 3$
Product of Four Factors	$2 \times 2 \times 2 \times 3$

a. Find each product.

b. What do the products have in common?

c. What other numbers are factors of 24?

d. Explain how you can use the prime factors of a number to find all of its factors. Test your conjecture by finding the factors of 60.

NEED EXTRA HELP?														
If You Missed Question...	1	2	3	4	5	6	7	8	9	10	11	12	13	14
Go to Lesson...	4-9	4-9	4-2	3-2	3-1	3-1	1-4	1-9	1-8	2-6	1-4	4-7	4-6	4-9

Applying Fractions

- Add, subtract, multiply, and divide to solve fraction problems.

Key Vocabulary

compatible numbers (p. 232)
like fractions (p. 236)
reciprocal (p. 258)
unlike fractions (p. 237)

Real-World Link

Baking The measurements found on measuring cups and spoons are written as fractions. You will use fractions to find how much of each ingredient is needed when you make part of a whole recipe.

Applying Fractions Make this Foldable to help you organize your notes. Begin with a plain sheet of 11″ by 17″ paper, four index cards, and glue.

1. **Fold** the paper in half widthwise.

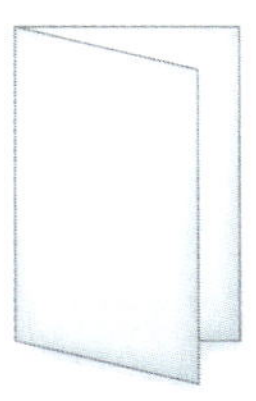

2. **Open** and fold along the length about $2\frac{1}{2}$″ from the bottom.

3. **Glue** the edge on each side to form two pockets.

4. **Label** the pockets *Fractions* and *Mixed Numbers*, respectively. Place two index cards in each pocket.

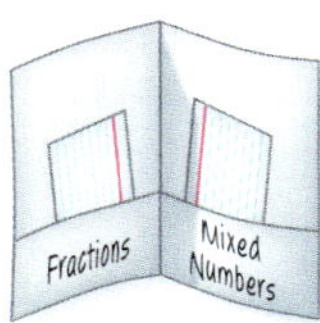

GET READY for Chapter 5

Diagnose Readiness You have two options for checking Prerequisite Skills.

Option 2

Math Online Take the Online Readiness Quiz at glencoe.com.

Option 1

Take the Quick Quiz below. Refer to the Quick Review for help.

QUICK Quiz

Find the LCD of each pair of fractions. (Lesson 4-8)

1. $\frac{5}{7}, \frac{3}{5}$
2. $\frac{1}{2}, \frac{4}{9}$
3. $\frac{8}{15}, \frac{1}{6}$
4. $\frac{3}{4}, \frac{7}{10}$

Multiply or divide. (Prior Grade)

5. 1.8×12
6. $99 \div 12$
7. $83 \div 100$
8. 4.6×0.3
9. **MEASUREMENT** How many 1.6-meter sections of rope can be cut from a length of rope 6.4 meters? (Prior Grade)
10. **COINS** Manuel owes each of 8 friends \$0.35. How much does he owe in all? (Prior Grade)

Complete to show equivalent mixed numbers. (Prior Grade)

11. $3\frac{1}{5} = 2\frac{■}{5}$
12. $9\frac{2}{3} = ■\frac{5}{3}$
13. $6\frac{1}{4} = 5\frac{■}{4}$
14. $8\frac{6}{7} = 7\frac{■}{7}$
15. **RECIPES** A recipe calls for $4\frac{2}{3}$ cups of flour. This is equivalent to 3 cups of flour plus an additional how many cups of flour? (Prior Grade)

QUICK Review

Example 1

Find the LCD of $\frac{5}{6}$ and $\frac{3}{10}$.

The LCD is the LCM of the denominators, 6 and 10, or 30.

Example 2

Find $7.8 \div 0.25$.

$$\begin{array}{r} 31.2 \\ 0.25\overline{)7.80\,0} \\ -7\,5 \\ \hline 30 \\ -25 \\ \hline 50 \\ -50 \\ \hline 0 \end{array}$$

Move the decimal point 2 places to the right and divide as with whole numbers.

Example 3

Complete $4\frac{2}{9} = ■\frac{11}{9}$ to show equivalent mixed numbers.

$$\begin{aligned} 4\frac{2}{9} &= 3 + 1\frac{2}{9} \\ &= 3 + \frac{9}{9} + \frac{2}{9} \\ &= 3 + \frac{11}{9} \\ &= 3\frac{11}{9} \end{aligned}$$

5-1 Estimating with Fractions

MAIN IDEA

Estimate sums, differences, products, and quotients of fractions and mixed numbers.

New Vocabulary

compatible numbers

Math Online

glencoe.com

- Extra Examples
- Personal Tutor
- Self-Check Quiz

GET READY for the Lesson

MAMMALS The table below lists the average length for a few mammals.

1. Graph $9\frac{1}{4}$ on a number line. To the nearest whole number, how long is an American Bison?
2. Graph $3\frac{3}{4}$ on a number line. To the nearest whole number, how long is a dingo?
3. About how much longer is the American bison than a dingo?

Mammal	Length (ft)
Brown Bear	$6\frac{1}{2}$
American Bison	$9\frac{1}{4}$
Opossum	$2\frac{1}{2}$
Dingo	$3\frac{3}{4}$

To estimate the sum, difference, product, or quotient of mixed numbers, round the mixed numbers to the nearest whole number.

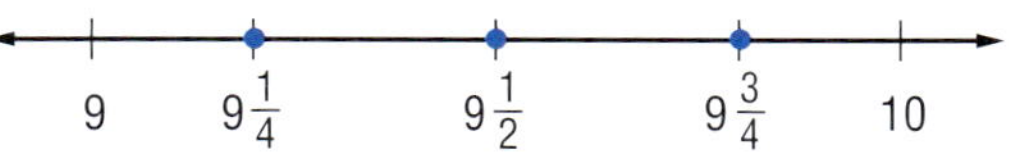

Round down.
$9\frac{1}{4} \approx 9$

Round up.
$9\frac{1}{2} \approx 10,\ 9\frac{3}{4} \approx 10$

EXAMPLES Estimate with Mixed Numbers

1 Estimate $3\frac{2}{3} + 5\frac{1}{6}$.

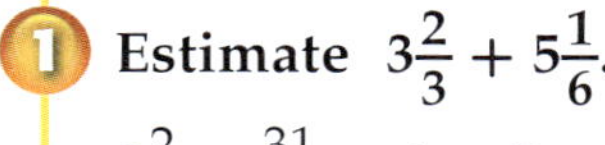

$3\frac{2}{3} + \frac{31}{6} \approx 4 + 5$ or 9

The sum is *about* 9.

2 Estimate $6\frac{2}{5} \times 1\frac{7}{8}$.

$6\frac{2}{5} \times 1\frac{7}{8} \approx 6 \times 2$ or 12

The product is *about* 12.

CHECK Your Progress

Estimate.

a. $2\frac{1}{5} + 3\frac{1}{2}$

b. $4\frac{3}{8} \times 5\frac{1}{4}$

c. $8\frac{7}{9} \div 2\frac{3}{4}$

To estimate the sum, difference, product, or quotient of fractions, round each fraction to 0, $\frac{1}{2}$, or 1, whichever is closest. Number lines and fraction models, like the ones shown below, can help you decide how to round.

Fractions Close to 0	Fractions Close to $\frac{1}{2}$	Fractions Close to 1
0 $\frac{1}{6}$ 1	0 $\frac{1}{2}$ $\frac{5}{8}$ 1	0 $\frac{9}{10}$ 1
$\frac{1}{7}$	$\frac{4}{9}$	$\frac{5}{6}$
The numerator is much smaller than the denominator.	The numerator is about half of the denominator.	The numerator is almost as large as the denominator.

EXAMPLES Estimate with Fractions

3 Estimate $\frac{1}{8} + \frac{2}{3}$.

1 is much smaller than 8, so $\frac{1}{8} \approx 0$.

2 is close to half of 3, so $\frac{2}{3} \approx \frac{1}{2}$.

$\frac{1}{8} + \frac{2}{3} \approx 0 + \frac{1}{2} = \frac{1}{2}$ The sum is *about* $\frac{1}{2}$.

Study Tip

Estimating with Fractions If one of the fractions is a mixed number, such as $3\frac{5}{8} + \frac{2}{3}$, round the mixed number to the nearest whole number and the fraction to the nearest half. $3\frac{5}{8} + \frac{2}{3} \approx 4 + \frac{1}{2}$ or about $4\frac{1}{2}$.

4 Estimate $\frac{6}{7} - \frac{7}{10}$.

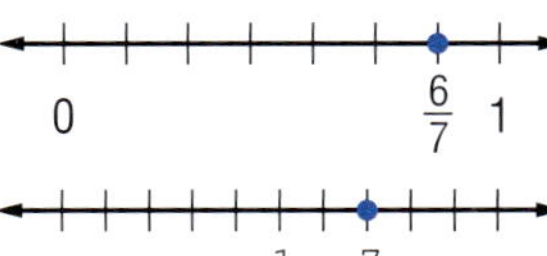

6 is almost as large as 7, so $\frac{6}{7} \approx 1$.

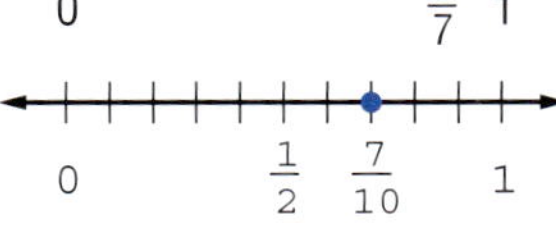

7 is about half of 10, so $\frac{7}{10} \approx \frac{1}{2}$.

$\frac{6}{7} - \frac{7}{10} \approx 1 - \frac{1}{2} = \frac{1}{2}$ The difference is *about* $\frac{1}{2}$.

5 Estimate $\frac{8}{9} \div \frac{5}{6}$.

$\frac{8}{9} \div \frac{5}{6} \approx 1 \div 1 = 1$ $\frac{8}{9} \approx 1$ and $\frac{5}{6} \approx 1$.

The quotient is *about* 1.

CHECK Your Progress

Estimate.

d. $\frac{1}{7} + \frac{3}{5}$ e. $\frac{7}{8} - \frac{5}{9}$ f. $\frac{3}{5} \times \frac{11}{12}$ g. $\frac{7}{8} \div \frac{2}{5}$

Compatible numbers, or numbers that are easy to compute mentally, can also be used to estimate.

EXAMPLES Use Compatible Numbers

Estimate using compatible numbers.

6 $\frac{1}{3} \cdot 14$ — **THINK** What is $\frac{1}{3}$ of 14?

$\frac{1}{3} \cdot 14 \approx \frac{1}{3} \cdot 15$ or 5 — Round 14 to 15, since 15 is divisible by 3. $\frac{1}{3}$ of 15 is $15 \div 3$ or 5.

7 $9\frac{7}{8} \div 4\frac{1}{5}$

$9\frac{7}{8} \div 4\frac{1}{5} \approx 10 \div 4\frac{1}{5}$ — Round $9\frac{7}{8}$ to 10.

$\approx 10 \div 5$ or 2 — Round $4\frac{1}{5}$ to 5, since 10 is divisible by 5.

Study Tip

Compatible Numbers When dividing mixed numbers, round so that the dividend is a multiple of the divisor.

CHECK Your Progress

Estimate using compatible numbers.

h. $\frac{1}{4} \cdot 21$

i. $\frac{1}{3} \cdot 17$

j. $12 \div 6\frac{2}{3}$

Real-World EXAMPLE

8 **MONSTER TRUCKS** The height of the wheels on the monster truck at the left is about $\frac{2}{3}$ of the total height of the truck. Estimate the height of the wheels.

Real-World Link... The monster truck shown is $15\frac{1}{2}$ feet tall and weighs 28,000 pounds.
Source: Monster Trucks UK

Words	Wheel height is $\frac{2}{3}$ of the truck height.
Variable	Let x represent the wheel height.
Equation	$x = \frac{2}{3} \cdot 15\frac{1}{2}$

$x \approx \frac{2}{3} \cdot 15$ — Round $15\frac{1}{2}$ to 15, since 15 is divisible by 3.

$x \approx 10$ — $\frac{1}{3}$ of 15 is 5, so $\frac{2}{3}$ of 15 is $2 \cdot 5$ or 10.

The wheels are about 10 feet high.

CHECK Your Progress

k. **MEASUREMENT** The area of a rectangle is $19\frac{3}{4}$ square feet. The width of the rectangle is $5\frac{1}{4}$ feet. What is the approximate length of the rectangle?

CHECK Your Understanding

Examples 1–5 (p. 230–231)

Estimate.

1. $8\frac{3}{8} + 1\frac{4}{5}$
2. $2\frac{5}{6} - 1\frac{1}{8}$
3. $5\frac{5}{7} \cdot 2\frac{7}{8}$
4. $9\frac{2}{7} \div 2\frac{2}{3}$
5. $\frac{1}{6} + \frac{2}{5}$
6. $\frac{6}{7} - \frac{1}{5}$
7. $\frac{5}{8} \cdot \frac{8}{9}$
8. $\frac{4}{5} \div \frac{6}{7}$

Examples 6, 7 (p. 232)

Estimate using compatible numbers.

9. $\frac{1}{4} \cdot 15$
10. $21\frac{5}{6} \div 9\frac{3}{4}$

Example 8 (p. 232)

11. **BIRDS** A seagull's wingspan is about $\frac{2}{3}$ of a bald eagle's wingspan. The eagle's wingspan is shown at the right. Estimate the wingspan of a seagull.

Practice and Problem Solving

HOMEWORK HELP

For Exercises	See Examples
12–19	1, 2
20–29	3–5
30–35	6–8

Estimate.

12. $3\frac{3}{4} + 4\frac{5}{6}$
13. $1\frac{1}{8} + 5\frac{11}{12}$
14. $5\frac{1}{3} - 3\frac{1}{6}$
15. $4\frac{2}{5} - 1\frac{1}{2}$
16. $2\frac{2}{3} \cdot 6\frac{1}{3}$
17. $1\frac{4}{5} \cdot 3\frac{1}{4}$
18. $6\frac{1}{8} \div 1\frac{2}{3}$
19. $8\frac{1}{2} \div 2\frac{5}{8}$
20. $\frac{3}{4} + \frac{3}{8}$
21. $\frac{5}{8} + \frac{3}{7}$
22. $\frac{5}{9} - \frac{1}{6}$
23. $\frac{3}{4} - \frac{3}{5}$
24. $\frac{1}{8} \cdot \frac{3}{4}$
25. $\frac{4}{9} \cdot \frac{11}{12}$
26. $\frac{4}{5} \div \frac{7}{8}$
27. $\frac{1}{10} \div \frac{5}{6}$

28. **COOKING** Joaquim wants to make the macaroni and cheese shown at the right, but he has only about $1\frac{3}{4}$ cups of macaroni. About how much more macaroni does he need?

Macaroni & Cheese
3 tbsp butter
$2\frac{1}{2}$ c uncooked macaroni
1 tbsp salt
$\frac{1}{4}$ tbsp pepper
1 qt milk
$\frac{1}{2}$ lb cheese

29. **MEASUREMENT** Isabella is sewing a trim that is $1\frac{1}{8}$ inches wide on the bottom of a skirt that is $15\frac{7}{8}$ inches long. Approximately how long will the skirt be?

Estimate using compatible numbers.

30. $\frac{1}{4} \cdot 39$
31. $\frac{1}{6} \cdot 37$
32. $23\frac{2}{9} \div 3$
33. $25\frac{3}{10} \div 5\frac{2}{3}$

34. **MONEY** Arleta has \$22. She uses $\frac{1}{3}$ of her money to buy a pair of earrings. About how much money did she spend on the earrings?

35. **SNACKS** A cereal company has 24 pounds of granola to package in bags that contain $1\frac{3}{4}$ pounds of granola. About how many bags will they have?

36. **FIND THE DATA** Refer to the Data File on pages 16–19. Choose some data and write a real-world problem in which you would estimate with fractions.

37. **SPORTS** Paquito and Jeff are on a basketball team. The table shows the approximate fraction of the team's points that each of them scored in a game. If the team scored a total of 72 points, about how many did Paquito and Jeff score together?

Player's Names	Fraction of Total Points Scored
Paquito	$\frac{3}{8}$
Jeff	$\frac{1}{6}$

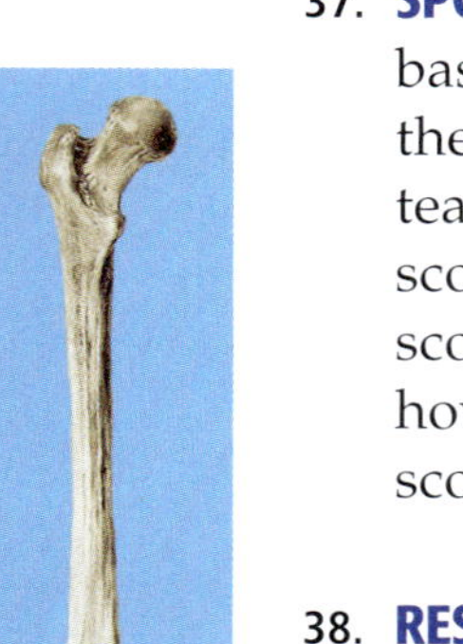

Real-World Link The femur or thigh bone is the longest in length, largest in volume, and strongest bone of the human body.

38. **RESEARCH** Research the statistics of any basketball team. How can you use fractions to analyze the statistics?

39. **COOKING** Kathryn baked the sheet of brownies shown. She wants to cut it into brownies that are about 2 inches square. How many brownies will there be?

ANALYZE TABLES For Exercises 40–43, use the following information and the table shown.

The adult human skeleton is made up of 206 bones. The table shows the approximate fraction of the bones that each body part(s) makes up.

Body Part(s)	Fraction of Total Bones
Feet	$\frac{1}{4}$
Hands & Feet	$\frac{1}{2}$

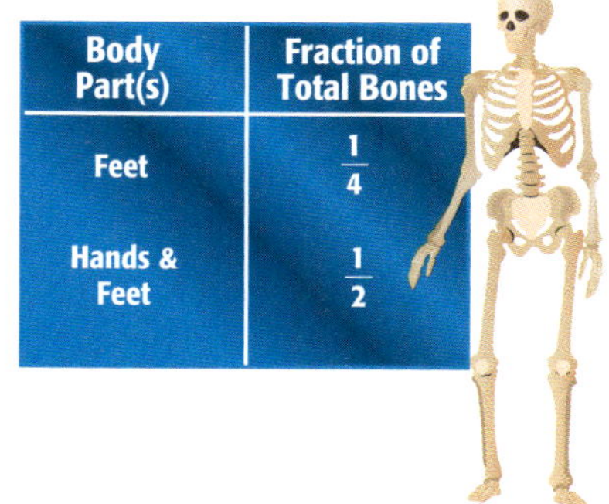

40. About how many bones are in the feet?

41. About how many bones are in both hands and feet?

42. About how many bones are in one hand?

43. The length of your thighbone is equal to $\frac{1}{4}$ of your height. About how many inches long is your thighbone?

See pages 679, 708.

H.O.T. Problems

44. **CHALLENGE** In a division expression, the divisor is rounded up and the dividend is rounded down. How does the new quotient compare to the original quotient? Explain.

45. **OPEN ENDED** Select two fractions whose estimated difference and product is $\frac{1}{2}$. Justify your selection.

46. **NUMBER SENSE** Decide which of the following have sums that are less than 1. Explain.

a. $\frac{1}{3} + \frac{2}{5}$

b. $\frac{7}{8} + \frac{1}{2}$

c. $\frac{5}{6} + \frac{2}{3}$

d. $\frac{1}{7} + \frac{3}{9}$

47. **SELECT A TECHNIQUE** To make the crust for a peach cobbler, Dion needs $3\frac{1}{4}$ cups of flour, $1\frac{2}{3}$ cups of sugar, and $1\frac{2}{3}$ cups of hot water. He needs to mix all of these in a large bowl. The largest bowl he can find holds 6 cups. Which of the following techniques might Dion use to determine whether he can use this bowl to mix the ingredients? Justify your selection(s). Then use the technique(s) to solve the problem.

48. **WRITING IN MATH** Explain when estimation would *not* be the best method for solving a problem. Then give an example.

TEST PRACTICE

49. **SHORT RESPONSE** A chef has $15\frac{2}{3}$ cups of penne pasta and $22\frac{1}{4}$ cups of rigatoni pasta. About how much pasta is there altogether?

50. On a full tank of gasoline, a certain car can travel 360 miles. The needle on its gasoline gauge is shown. Without refueling, which is the best estimate of how far the car can travel?

A 150 miles

B 180 miles

C 240 miles

D 329 miles

Spiral Review

Replace each ● with <, >, or = to make a true sentence. (Lesson 4-9)

51. $2\frac{7}{8}$ ● 2.75
52. $\frac{-1}{3}$ ● $\frac{-7}{3}$
53. $\frac{5}{7}$ ● $\frac{4}{5}$
54. $3\frac{6}{11}$ ● $3\frac{9}{14}$

55. **SHOPPING** A store sells a 3-pack of beaded necklaces and a 5-pack of beaded bracelets. How many packages of each must you buy so that you have the same number of necklaces and bracelets? (Lesson 4-8)

Write each decimal as a percent. (Lesson 4-7)

56. 0.56
57. 0.375
58. 0.07
59. 0.019

GET READY for the Next Lesson

PREREQUISITE SKILL Find the LCD of each pair of fractions. (Lesson 4-9)

60. $\frac{3}{4}, \frac{5}{12}$
61. $\frac{1}{2}, \frac{7}{10}$
62. $\frac{1}{6}, \frac{1}{8}$
63. $\frac{4}{5}, \frac{2}{3}$

5-2 Adding and Subtracting Fractions

MAIN IDEA

Add and subtract fractions.

New Vocabulary

like fractions
unlike fractions

Math Online

glencoe.com

- Extra Examples
- Personal Tutor
- Self-Check Quiz
- Reading in the Content Area

GET READY for the Lesson

INSTANT MESSENGER Sean surveyed ten classmates to find which abbreviation they use most when they instant message.

Abbreviation	Number
L8R	5
LOL	3
BRB	2

1. What fraction uses L8R? BRB?
2. What fraction uses either L8R or BRB?

Fractions that have the same denominators are called **like fractions**.

Add and Subtract Like Fractions — Key Concept

Words To add or subtract like fractions, add or subtract the numerators and write the result over the denominator.

Examples

Numbers	Algebra
$\frac{5}{10} + \frac{2}{10} = \frac{5+2}{10}$ or $\frac{7}{10}$	$\frac{a}{c} + \frac{b}{c} = \frac{a+b}{c}$, where $c \neq 0$
$\frac{11}{12} - \frac{4}{12} = \frac{11-4}{12}$ or $\frac{7}{12}$	$\frac{a}{c} - \frac{b}{c} = \frac{a-b}{c}$, where $c \neq 0$

EXAMPLES Add and Subtract Like Fractions

1 Add $\frac{5}{9} + \frac{2}{9}$. Write in simplest form.

$\frac{5}{9} + \frac{2}{9} = \frac{5+2}{9}$ Add the numerators.

$= \frac{7}{9}$ Write the sum over the denominator.

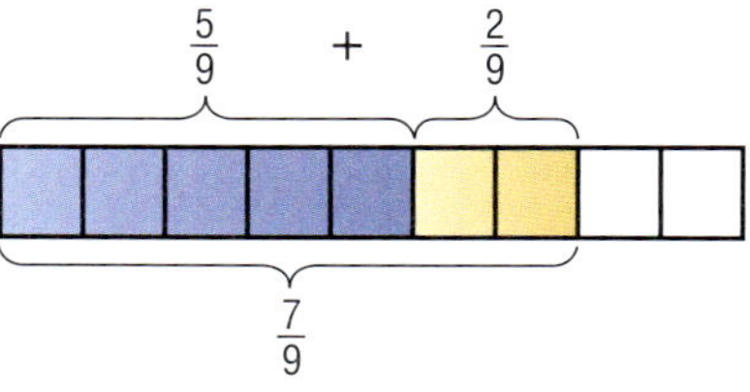

2 Subtract $\frac{9}{10} - \frac{1}{10}$. Write in simplest form.

$\frac{9}{10} - \frac{1}{10} = \frac{9-1}{10}$ Subtract the numerators.

$= \frac{8}{10}$ Write the difference over the denominator.

$= \frac{4}{5}$ Simplify.

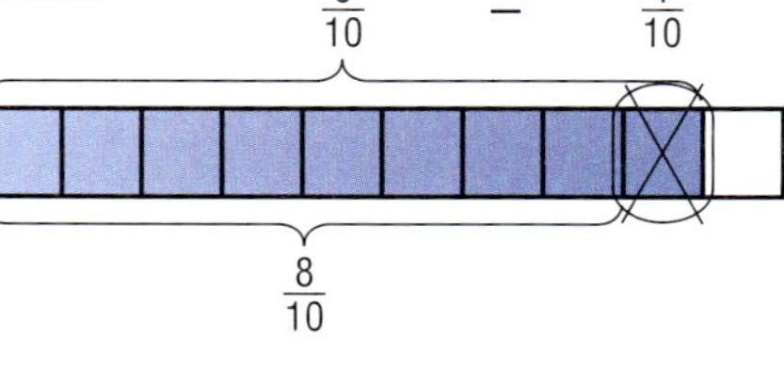

CHECK Your Progress

a. $\frac{1}{6} + \frac{3}{6}$

b. $\frac{3}{7} - \frac{1}{7}$

Review Vocabulary

LCD the least common multiple of the denominators of two or more fractions; *Example*: the LCD of $\frac{1}{4}$ and $\frac{2}{3}$ is 12. (Lesson 4-9)

To add or subtract **unlike fractions**, or fractions with different denominators, rename the fractions using the LCD. Then add or subtract as with like fractions.

EXAMPLES Add and Subtract Unlike Fractions

3 **Add $\frac{1}{2} + \frac{1}{6}$. Write in simplest form.** **Estimate** $\frac{1}{2} + 0 = \frac{1}{2}$

METHOD 1 **Use a model.**

$$\begin{array}{r} \frac{1}{2} \\ + \frac{1}{6} \\ \hline \frac{4}{6} \text{ or } \frac{2}{3} \end{array}$$

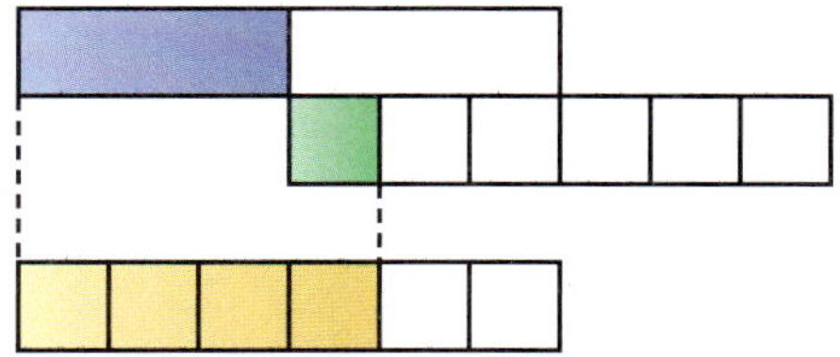

METHOD 2 **Use the LCD.**

The least common denominator (LCD) of $\frac{1}{2}$ and $\frac{1}{6}$ is 6.

Rename using the LCD, 6. Add.

$$\frac{1}{2} \rightarrow \frac{1 \times 3}{2 \times 3} = \frac{3}{6} \rightarrow \frac{3}{6}$$

$$+\frac{1}{6} \rightarrow \frac{1 \times 1}{6 \times 1} = +\frac{1}{6} \rightarrow +\frac{1}{6}$$

$$\frac{4}{6} \text{ or } \frac{2}{3}$$

So, $\frac{1}{2} + \frac{1}{6} = \frac{2}{3}$. **Check for Reasonableness** $\frac{2}{3} \approx \frac{1}{2}$ ✔

Study Tip

Renaming Fractions To rename a fraction, multiply both the numerator and the denominator of the original fraction by the same number. By doing so, the renamed fraction has the same value as the original fraction.

4 **Subtract $\frac{11}{12} - \frac{3}{8}$. Write in simplest form.** **Estimate** $1 - \frac{1}{2} = \frac{1}{2}$

Since $12 = 2^2 \cdot 3$ and $8 = 2^3$, the LCM of 12 and 8 is $2^3 \cdot 3$ or 24. Rename each fraction using a denominator of 24. Then subtract.

Think: $12 \times 2 = 24$, so $\frac{11 \times 2}{12 \times 2}$ or $\frac{22}{24}$.

Think: $8 \times 3 = 24$, so $\frac{3}{8} = \frac{3 \times 3}{8 \times 3}$ or $\frac{9}{24}$.

$\frac{11}{12} - \frac{3}{8} = \frac{11 \times 2}{12 \times 2} - \frac{3 \times 3}{8 \times 3}$ The LCD of $\frac{11}{12}$ and $\frac{3}{8}$ is 24.

$= \frac{22}{24} - \frac{9}{24}$ Rename the fractions using LCD, 24.

$= \frac{13}{24}$ Subtract the fractions.

Check for Reasonableness $\frac{13}{24} \approx \frac{1}{2}$ ✔

CHOOSE Your Method

c. $\frac{8}{9} - \frac{2}{3}$

d. $\frac{5}{6} - \frac{3}{8}$

e. $\frac{7}{8} + \frac{3}{4}$

Real-World EXAMPLES

SURVEYS In a recent survey, students were asked what they would choose for a healthy lunch. The results are shown in the graph.

Study Tip

Key Words The phrase *what fraction more* suggests subtraction.

5 What fraction more of the students chose salad bar rather than a deli sandwich?

$$\frac{9}{20} - \frac{3}{25} = \frac{9 \times 5}{20 \times 5} - \frac{3 \times 4}{25 \times 4}$$ The LCD of $\frac{9}{20}$ and $\frac{3}{25}$ is 100.

$$= \frac{45}{100} - \frac{12}{100}$$ Rename the fractions using the LCD.

$$= \frac{33}{100}$$ Subtract the numerators.

So, $\frac{33}{100}$ more students chose salad bar rather than a deli sandwich.

6 What fraction of students chose pizza or chicken nuggets?

$$\frac{3}{20} + \frac{1}{10} = \frac{3}{20} + \frac{2}{20}$$ Rename.

$$= \frac{5}{20}$$ Add.

$$= \frac{1}{4}$$ Simplify.

So, $\frac{1}{4}$ of the students chose pizza or chicken nuggets combined.

CHECK Your Progress

f. **SURVEYS** What fraction more of the students chose a deli sandwich rather than a burger and fries?

CHECK Your Understanding

Examples 1–4 (pp. 236–237)

Add or subtract. Write in simplest form.

1. $\frac{4}{9} + \frac{2}{9}$
2. $\frac{5}{6} + \frac{4}{9}$
3. $\frac{3}{8} - \frac{1}{8}$
4. $\frac{4}{5} - \frac{2}{5}$
5. $\frac{1}{6} + \frac{3}{8}$
6. $\frac{2}{3} + \frac{5}{6}$
7. $\frac{5}{6} - \frac{7}{12}$
8. $\frac{3}{4} - \frac{1}{3}$

Examples 5, 6 (p. 238)

For Exercises 9 and 10, choose an operation to solve each problem. Explain your reasoning. Then solve the problem.

9. **MEASUREMENT** Cassandra cuts $\frac{5}{16}$ inch off the top of a photo and $\frac{3}{8}$ inch off the bottom. How much smaller is the total height of the photo now?

10. **CHORES** A bucket was $\frac{7}{8}$ full with soapy water. After washing the car, the bucket was only $\frac{1}{4}$ full. What part of the water was used?

Practice and Problem Solving

HOMEWORK HELP	
For Exercises	See Examples
11–14	1, 2
15–22	3, 4
23–26	5, 6

Add or subtract. Write in simplest form.

11. $\frac{3}{7} + \frac{1}{7}$
12. $\frac{5}{8} + \frac{7}{8}$
13. $\frac{5}{6} - \frac{1}{6}$
14. $\frac{7}{10} - \frac{3}{10}$
15. $\frac{1}{15} + \frac{3}{5}$
16. $\frac{7}{12} + \frac{7}{10}$
17. $\frac{5}{8} + \frac{11}{12}$
18. $\frac{7}{9} + \frac{5}{6}$
19. $\frac{7}{9} - \frac{1}{3}$
20. $\frac{4}{5} - \frac{1}{6}$
21. $\frac{4}{9} - \frac{2}{15}$
22. $\frac{3}{10} - \frac{1}{4}$

For Exercises 23–26, choose an operation to solve each problem. Explain your reasoning. Then solve the problem.

23. **MEASUREMENT** Ebony is building a shelf to hold the two boxes shown. What is the smallest width she should make the shelf?

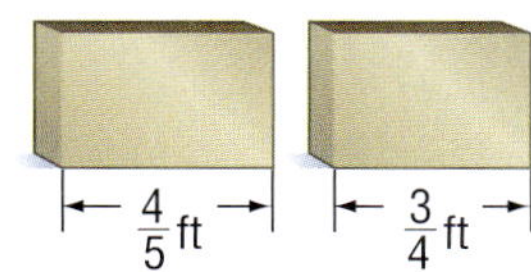

24. **WEATHER** Using the information under the photo, find the difference of the average precipitation for Boise in February and November.

25. **MEASUREMENT** Makayla bought $\frac{1}{4}$ pound of ham and $\frac{5}{8}$ pound of turkey. How much more turkey did she buy?

26. **ANIMALS** The three-toed sloth can travel $\frac{3}{20}$ miles per hour while a giant tortoise can travel $\frac{17}{100}$ miles per hour. How much faster, in miles per hour, is the giant tortoise?

Real-World Link . . . The average precipitation for February and November for Boise, Idaho, is $\frac{4}{10}$ and $\frac{7}{10}$ inches, respectively.

Source: The Weather Channel

Simplify.

27. $\frac{1}{7} + \frac{1}{2} + \frac{5}{28}$
28. $\frac{1}{4} + \frac{5}{6} + \frac{7}{12}$
29. $\frac{1}{6} + \left(\frac{2}{3} - \frac{1}{4}\right)$
30. $\frac{5}{6} - \left(\frac{1}{2} + \frac{1}{3}\right)$

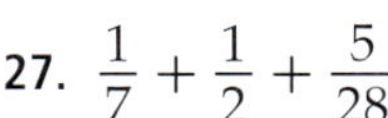

31. $1 + \frac{1}{4}$
32. $1 - \frac{5}{8}$
33. $2 + \frac{2}{3}$
34. $3 - \frac{1}{6}$

35. **MONEY** Chellise saves $\frac{1}{5}$ of her allowance and spends $\frac{2}{3}$ of her allowance at the mall. What fraction of her allowance remains?

36. **ANALYZE TABLES** Pepita and Francisco each spend an equal amount of time on homework. The table shows the fraction of their time they spend on each subject. Determine the missing fraction for each student.

Homework	Fraction of Time	
	Pepita	Francisco
Math	■	$\frac{1}{2}$
English	$\frac{2}{3}$	■
Science	$\frac{1}{6}$	$\frac{3}{8}$

ALGEBRA Evaluate each expression if $a = \frac{3}{4}$ and $b = \frac{5}{6}$.

37. $\frac{1}{2} + a$
38. $b - \frac{7}{10}$
39. $b - a$
40. $a + b$

41. **BOOK REPORTS** Four students were scheduled to give book reports in a 1-hour class period. After the first report, $\frac{2}{3}$ hour remained. If the next two students' reports took $\frac{1}{6}$ hour and $\frac{1}{4}$ hour, respectively, what fraction of the hour remained after the final students' report? Justify your answer.

42. **MEASUREMENT** Mrs. Escalante was riding a bicycle on a bike path. After riding $\frac{2}{3}$ of a mile, she discovered that she still needed to travel $\frac{3}{4}$ of a mile to reach the end of the path. How long is the bike path?

43. **CELL PHONES** One hundred sixty cell phone owners were surveyed. What fraction of owners prefers using their cell phone for text messaging or taking pictures?

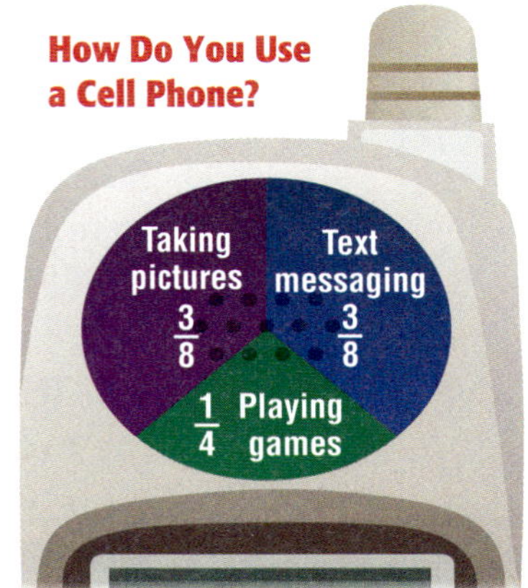

44. **MEASUREMENT** LaTasha and Eric are jogging on a track. LaTasha jogs $\frac{1}{4}$ of a mile and then stops. Eric jogs $\frac{5}{8}$ of a mile, stops and then turns around and jogs $\frac{1}{2}$ of a mile. Who is farther ahead on the track? How much farther?

See pages 679, 708.

H.O.T. Problems

45. **CHALLENGE** Fractions, such as $\frac{1}{2}$ or $\frac{1}{3}$, whose numerators are 1, are called *unit fractions*. Describe a method you can use to add two unit fractions mentally. Explain your reasoning and use your method to find $\frac{1}{99} + \frac{1}{100}$.

46. **OPEN ENDED** Provide a counterexample to the following statement.

The sum of three fractions with odd numerators is never $\frac{1}{2}$.

47. **FIND THE ERROR** Meagan and Lourdes are finding $\frac{1}{4} + \frac{3}{5}$. Who is correct? Explain.

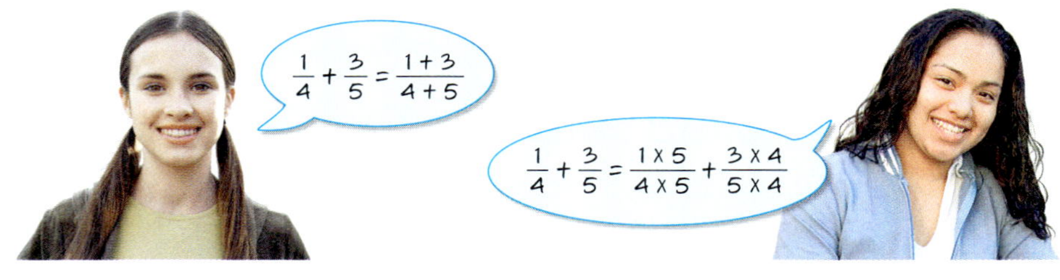

Meagan Lourdes

48. **WRITING IN MATH** To make a cake, Felicia needs 1 cup of flour but she only has a $\frac{2}{3}$-measuring cup and a $\frac{3}{4}$-measuring cup. Which method will bring her closest to having the amount of flour she needs? Explain.

a. Fill the $\frac{2}{3}$-measuring cup twice.
b. Fill the $\frac{2}{3}$-measuring cup once.
c. Fill the $\frac{3}{4}$-measuring cup twice.
d. Fill the $\frac{3}{4}$-measuring cup once.

TEST PRACTICE

49. The table gives the number of hours Orlando spent at football practice for one week.

Day	Time (hours)
Monday	$1\frac{1}{2}$
Tuesday	2
Wednesday	$2\frac{1}{3}$
Thursday	$1\frac{5}{6}$
Friday	$2\frac{1}{2}$
Saturday	$1\frac{3}{4}$

How many more hours did he practice over the last three days than he did over the first three days?

A $\frac{1}{4}$ h

B $\frac{1}{2}$ h

C $\frac{2}{3}$ h

D $\frac{3}{4}$ h

50. Which of the following is the prime factored form of the lowest common denominator of $\frac{7}{12} + \frac{11}{18}$?

F 2×3

G 2×3^2

H $2^2 \times 3^2$

J $2^3 \times 3$

51. Find $\frac{5}{6} - \frac{1}{8}$.

A $\frac{4}{7}$

B $\frac{3}{8}$

C $\frac{7}{12}$

D $\frac{17}{24}$

Spiral Review

Estimate. (Lesson 5-1)

52. $\frac{6}{7} - \frac{5}{12}$ **53.** $4\frac{1}{9} + 3\frac{3}{4}$ **54.** $16\frac{2}{3} \div 8\frac{1}{5}$ **55.** $5\frac{4}{5} \cdot 3\frac{1}{3}$

56. **WEATHER** The table shows about how much rain falls in Albuquerque and Denver. Which city has the greater fraction of inches of rain per day? Explain. (Lesson 4-9)

City	Amount of Rain (in.)	Number of Days
Albuquerque, NM	9	60
Denver, CO	15	90

Source: The Weather Channel

57. Write 0.248 as a percent. (Lesson 4-7)

ALGEBRA **Find each sum if $a = -3$ and $b = 2$.** (Lessons 2-4 and 2-5)

58. $a + b$ **59.** $a - b$ **60.** $b - a$

GET READY for the Next Lesson

PREREQUISITE SKILL **Complete.**

61. $5\frac{2}{3} = 5 + \blacksquare$ **62.** $1 = \frac{\blacksquare}{9}$ **63.** $1 = \frac{\blacksquare}{5}$ **64.** $\blacksquare = 4 + \frac{3}{8}$

5-3 Adding and Subtracting Mixed Numbers

MAIN IDEA

Add and subtract mixed numbers.

Math Online

glencoe.com

- Extra Examples
- Personal Tutor
- Self-Check Quiz

GET READY for the Lesson

BABIES The birth weights of several babies in the hospital nursery are shown.

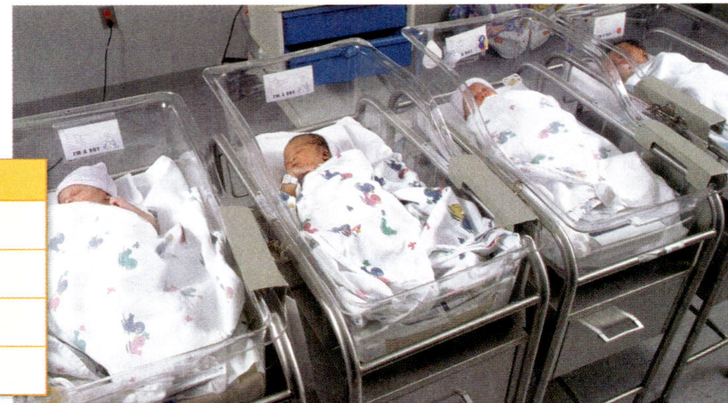

Birth Weight (pounds)	
Jackson	$8\frac{1}{8}$
Nicolás	$7\frac{15}{16}$
Rebekah	$6\frac{13}{16}$
Mia	$5\frac{7}{8}$

1. Write an expression to find how much more Nicolás weighs than Mia.
2. Rename the fractions using the LCD.
3. Find the difference of the fractional parts of the mixed numbers.
4. Find the difference of the whole numbers.
5. **MAKE A CONJECTURE** Explain how to find $7\frac{15}{16} - 5\frac{7}{8}$. Then use your conjecture to find the difference.

To add or subtract mixed numbers, first add or subtract the fractions. If necessary, rename them using the LCD. Then add or subtract the whole numbers and simplify if necessary.

EXAMPLES Add and Subtract Mixed Numbers

1 **Find $7\frac{4}{9} + 10\frac{2}{9}$. Write in simplest form.**

Estimate $7 + 10 = 17$

$$\begin{array}{r} 7\frac{4}{9} \\ +\ 10\frac{2}{9} \\ \hline 17\frac{6}{9} \end{array}$$

Add the whole numbers and fractions separately.

$17\frac{6}{9}$ or $17\frac{2}{3}$ Simplify.

Check for Reasonableness $17\frac{2}{3} \approx 17$ ✔

CHECK Your Progress

a. $6\frac{1}{8} + 2\frac{5}{8}$

b. $5\frac{1}{5} + 2\frac{3}{10}$

c. $1\frac{5}{9} + 4\frac{1}{6}$

2 Find $8\frac{5}{6} - 2\frac{1}{3}$. Write in simplest form.

Estimate $9 - 2 = 7$

$$\begin{array}{rcr} 8\frac{5}{6} & \rightarrow & 8\frac{5}{6} \\ -2\frac{1}{3} & \rightarrow & -2\frac{2}{6} \\ \hline & & 6\frac{3}{6} \text{ or } 6\frac{1}{2} \end{array}$$

Rename the fraction using the LCD. Then subtract.

Simplify.

Check for Reasonableness $6\frac{1}{2} \approx 7$ ✔

Subtract. Write in simplest form.

d. $5\frac{4}{5} - 1\frac{3}{10}$ e. $13\frac{7}{8} - 9\frac{3}{4}$ f. $8\frac{2}{3} - 2\frac{1}{2}$

g. $7\frac{3}{4} - 4\frac{1}{3}$ h. $11\frac{5}{6} - 3\frac{1}{8}$ i. $9\frac{4}{7} - 5\frac{1}{2}$

Study Tip

Improper Fractions An improper fraction has a numerator that is greater than or equal to the denominator. Examples of improper fractions are $\frac{5}{4}$ and $2\frac{6}{5}$.

Sometimes when you subtract mixed numbers, the fraction in the first mixed number is less than the fraction in the second mixed number. In this case, rename the first fraction as an improper fraction in order to subtract.

EXAMPLES Rename Mixed Numbers to Subtract

3 Find $2\frac{1}{3} - 1\frac{2}{3}$.

Estimate $2 - 1\frac{1}{2} = \frac{1}{2}$

Since $\frac{1}{3}$ is less than $\frac{2}{3}$, rename $2\frac{1}{3}$ before subtracting.

Change 1 to $\frac{3}{3}$.

$2\frac{1}{3} = 1\frac{3}{3} + \frac{1}{3}$ or $1\frac{4}{3}$

$$\begin{array}{rcr} 2\frac{1}{3} & \rightarrow & 1\frac{4}{3} \\ -1\frac{2}{3} & \rightarrow & -1\frac{2}{3} \\ \hline & & \frac{2}{3} \end{array}$$

Rename $2\frac{1}{3}$ as $1\frac{4}{3}$.

Subtract the whole numbers and then the fractions.

Check for Reasonableness $\frac{2}{3} \approx \frac{1}{2}$ ✔

4 Find $8 - 3\frac{3}{4}$. **Estimate** $8 - 4 = 4$

Using the denominator of the fraction in the subtrahend, $8 = 8\frac{0}{4}$.

Since $\frac{0}{4}$ is less than $\frac{3}{4}$, rename 8 before subtracting.

$$\begin{array}{rcr} 8 & \rightarrow & 7\frac{4}{4} \\ -3\frac{3}{4} & \rightarrow & -3\frac{3}{4} \\ \hline & & 4\frac{1}{4} \end{array}$$

Rename 8 as $7 + \frac{4}{4}$ or $7\frac{4}{4}$.

Subtract.

Check for Reasonableness $4\frac{1}{4} \approx 4$ ✔

CHECK Your Progress

j. $11\frac{2}{5} - 2\frac{3}{5}$

k. $5\frac{3}{8} - 4\frac{11}{12}$

l. $7 - 1\frac{1}{2}$

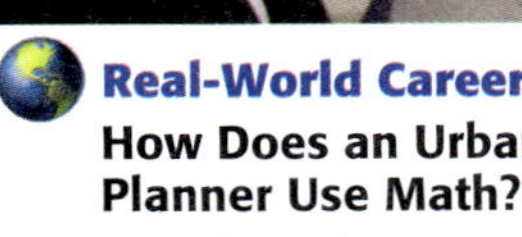

Real-World Career

How Does an Urban Planner Use Math?

An urban planner uses math to measure and draw site plans for future development.

Math Online

For more information, go to glencoe.com.

Real-World EXAMPLE

5 **MEASUREMENT** **An urban planner is designing a skateboard park. What will be the length of the park and the parking lot combined?**

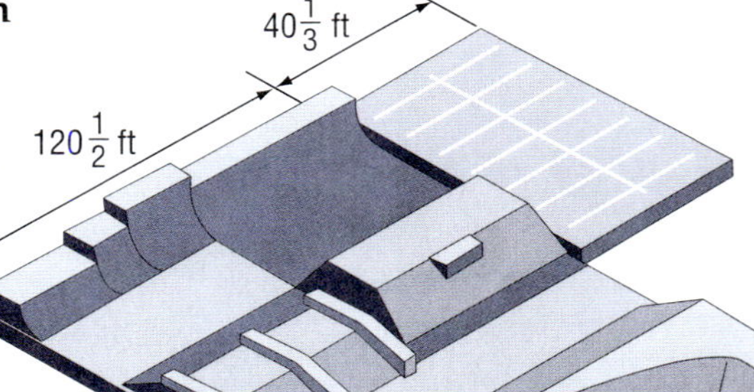

$$\begin{aligned} 120\frac{1}{2} + 40\frac{1}{3} &= 120\frac{3}{6} + 40\frac{2}{6} \\ &= 160 + \frac{5}{6} \\ &= 160\frac{5}{6} \end{aligned}$$

The total length is $160\frac{5}{6}$ feet.

CHECK Your Progress

m. **MEASUREMENT** Jermaine walked $1\frac{5}{8}$ miles on Saturday and $2\frac{1}{2}$ miles on Sunday. How many more miles did he walk on Sunday?

CHECK Your Understanding

Examples 1–4 (pp. 242–244)

Add or subtract. Write in simplest form.

1. $1\frac{5}{7} + 8\frac{1}{7}$
2. $8\frac{1}{2} + 3\frac{4}{5}$
3. $7\frac{5}{6} - 3\frac{1}{6}$
4. $9\frac{4}{5} - 2\frac{3}{4}$
5. $3\frac{1}{4} - 1\frac{3}{4}$
6. $5\frac{2}{3} - 2\frac{3}{5}$
7. $11 - 6\frac{3}{8}$
8. $16 - 5\frac{5}{6}$

Example 5 (p. 244)

9. **CARS** A hybrid car's gas tank can hold $11\frac{9}{10}$ gallons of gasoline. It contains $8\frac{3}{4}$ gallons of gasoline. How much more gasoline is needed to fill the tank?

Practice and Problem Solving

HOMEWORK HELP	
For Exercises	See Examples
10–17	1, 2
18–23	3
24–25	4
26–29	5

Add or subtract. Write in simplest form.

10. $2\frac{1}{9} + 7\frac{4}{9}$
11. $3\frac{2}{7} + 4\frac{3}{7}$
12. $10\frac{4}{5} - 2\frac{1}{5}$
13. $8\frac{6}{7} - 6\frac{5}{7}$
14. $9\frac{4}{5} - 2\frac{3}{10}$
15. $11\frac{3}{4} - 4\frac{1}{3}$
16. $8\frac{5}{12} + 11\frac{1}{4}$
17. $8\frac{3}{8} + 10\frac{1}{3}$
18. $9\frac{1}{5} - 2\frac{3}{5}$
19. $6\frac{1}{4} - 2\frac{3}{4}$
20. $6\frac{3}{5} - 1\frac{2}{3}$
21. $4\frac{3}{10} - 1\frac{3}{4}$
22. $14\frac{1}{6} - 7\frac{1}{3}$
23. $12\frac{1}{2} - 6\frac{5}{8}$
24. $8 - 3\frac{2}{3}$
25. $13 - 5\frac{5}{6}$

For Exercises 26–29, choose an operation to solve each problem. Explain your reasoning. Then solve the problem.

26. **HIKING** If Sara and Maggie hiked both of the trails listed in the table, how far did they hike altogether?

Trail	Length (mi)
Woodland Park	$3\frac{2}{3}$
Mill Creek Way	$2\frac{5}{6}$

27. **JEWELRY** Margarite made the jewelry shown at the right. If the necklace is $10\frac{5}{8}$ inches longer than the bracelet, how long is the necklace that Margarite made?

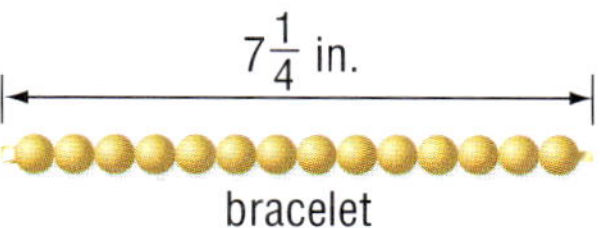

28. **GARDENS** The length of Kasey's garden is $4\frac{5}{8}$ feet. Find the width of Kasey's garden if it is $2\frac{7}{8}$ feet shorter than the length.

29. **HAIRSTYLES** Before Alameda got her haircut, the length of her hair was $9\frac{3}{4}$ inches. After her haircut, the length was $6\frac{1}{2}$ inches. How many inches did she have cut?

Add or subtract. Write in simplest form.

30. $10 - 3\frac{5}{11}$
31. $24 - 8\frac{3}{4}$
32. $6\frac{1}{6} + 1\frac{2}{3} + 5\frac{5}{9}$
33. $3\frac{1}{4} + 2\frac{5}{6} - 4\frac{1}{3}$

34. **TIME** Karen wakes up at 6:00 A.M. It takes her $1\frac{1}{4}$ hours to shower, get dressed, and comb her hair. It takes her $\frac{1}{2}$ hour to eat breakfast, brush her teeth, and make her bed. At what time will she be ready for school?

MEASUREMENT **Find the perimeter of each figure.**

35.

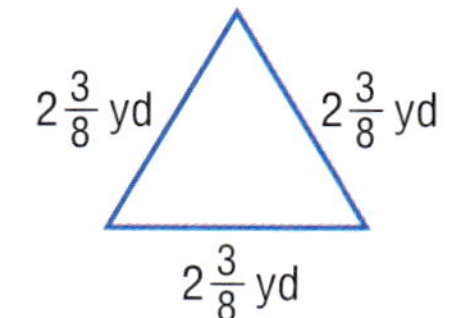

36.

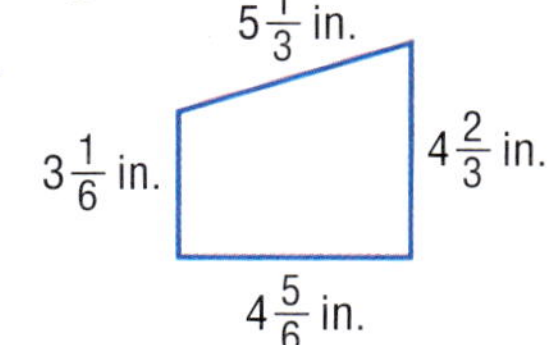

EXTRA PRACTICE
See pages 680, 708.

H.O.T. Problems

37. **NUMBER SENSE** Which of the following techniques could be used to determine whether $6\frac{3}{4} + \frac{4}{5}$ is *greater than, less than,* or *equal to* $2\frac{1}{9} + 6\frac{7}{8}$? Justify your selection(s). Then use the technique(s) to solve the problem.

number sense | mental math | estimation

38. **CHALLENGE** A string is cut in half. One of the halves is thrown away. One fifth of the remaining half is cut away and the piece left is 8 feet long. How long was the string initially? Justify your answer.

39. **WRITING IN MATH** The fence of a rectangular garden is constructed from 12 feet of fencing wire. Suppose that one side of the garden is $2\frac{5}{12}$ feet long. Explain how to find the length of the other side.

TEST PRACTICE

40. The distance from home plate to the pitcher's mound is 60 feet 6 inches and from home plate to second base is 127 feet $3\frac{3}{8}$ inches. Find the distance from the pitcher's mound to second base.

A 68 ft $3\frac{1}{4}$ in.

B 67 ft $8\frac{3}{4}$ in.

C 67 ft $2\frac{5}{8}$ in.

D 66 ft $9\frac{3}{8}$ in.

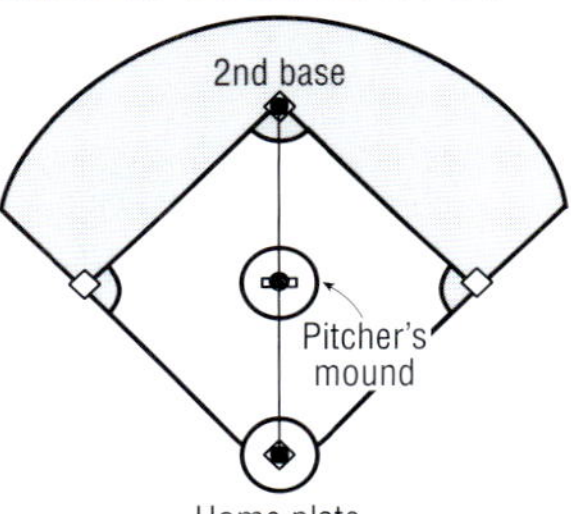

41. A recipe for party mix calls for $4\frac{3}{4}$ cups of cereal. The amount of peanuts needed is $1\frac{2}{3}$ cups less than the amount of cereal needed. How many cups of peanuts and cereal are needed?

F $3\frac{1}{12}$ cups

G $6\frac{1}{2}$ cups

H $7\frac{5}{6}$ cups

J $8\frac{1}{2}$ cups

Spiral Review

42. **SCHOOL** Kai did $\frac{1}{5}$ of her homework in class and $\frac{1}{3}$ more of it on the bus. What fraction of homework does she still need to do? (Lesson 5-2)

Estimate. (Lesson 5-1)

43. $\frac{8}{9} \div \frac{9}{10}$

44. $3\frac{1}{2} + 6\frac{2}{3}$

45. $8\frac{4}{5} \times 7\frac{1}{9}$

46. $4\frac{2}{9} - 1\frac{1}{4}$

47. **MEASUREMENT** To carpet a living room with a length of 17 feet, 255 square feet of carpet is needed. Find the width of the living room. (Lesson 3-6)

GET READY for the Next Lesson

48. **PREREQUISITE SKILL** Andre needs to be at the train station by 5:30 P.M. It takes him $\frac{1}{3}$ hour to pack and $1\frac{1}{4}$ hours to get to the station. Find the latest time he should begin packing. Use the *work backward* strategy. (Lesson 3-4)

CHAPTER 5

Mid-Chapter Quiz

Lessons 5-1 through 5-3

1. **MONEY** Latisha spends $\frac{3}{4}$ of her money on a birthday present for her brother. If she has $33, estimate the amount she spends on her brother's present. (Lesson 5-1)

Estimate. (Lesson 5-1)

2. $5\frac{1}{9} + 1\frac{7}{8}$
3. $13\frac{1}{2} \div 7\frac{2}{9}$
4. $\frac{11}{20} - \frac{5}{8}$
5. $4\frac{2}{3} \times 1\frac{3}{4}$
6. $7\frac{3}{4} \div 1\frac{4}{5}$
7. $\frac{8}{9} + 2\frac{13}{15}$

8. **MULTIPLE CHOICE** Mrs. Ortega is making 5 batches of muffins for the school bake sale. Each batch uses $2\frac{1}{4}$ cups sugar and $1\frac{1}{2}$ cups milk. Which is the best estimate of the total amount of sugar and milk Mrs. Ortega uses for the muffins? (Lesson 5-1)

   A less than 15 cups

   B between 15 and 20 cups

   C between 20 and 25 cups

   D more than 25 cups

Add or subtract. Write in simplest form. (Lesson 5-2)

9. $\frac{11}{15} - \frac{1}{15}$
10. $\frac{4}{7} - \frac{3}{14}$
11. $\frac{1}{2} + \frac{2}{9}$
12. $\frac{5}{8} + \frac{3}{4}$

13. **SCIENCE** $\frac{39}{50}$ of Earth's atmosphere is made up of nitrogen while only $\frac{21}{100}$ is made up of oxygen. What fraction of Earth's atmosphere is either nitrogen or oxygen? (Lesson 5-2)

Add or subtract. Write in simplest form. (Lesson 5-3)

14. $8\frac{3}{4} - 2\frac{5}{12}$
15. $5\frac{1}{6} - 1\frac{1}{3}$
16. $2\frac{5}{9} + 1\frac{2}{3}$
17. $2\frac{3}{5} + 6\frac{13}{15}$

18. **MULTIPLE CHOICE** The table shows the weight of a newborn infant for the first year. (Lesson 5-3)

Month	Weight (lb)
0	$7\frac{1}{4}$
3	$12\frac{1}{2}$
6	$16\frac{5}{8}$
9	$19\frac{4}{5}$
12	$23\frac{3}{20}$

During which three-month period was the infant's weight gain the greatest?

   F 0–3 months

   G 3–6 months

   H 6–9 months

   J 9–12 months

19. **MEASUREMENT** How much does a $50\frac{1}{4}$-pound suitcase weigh after $3\frac{7}{8}$ pounds is removed? (Lesson 5-3)

20. **MULTIPLE CHOICE** The table gives the average annual snowfall for several U.S. cities. (Lesson 5-3)

City	Average Snowfall (in.)
Anchorage, AK	$70\frac{4}{5}$
Mount Washington, NH	$259\frac{9}{10}$
Buffalo, NY	$93\frac{3}{5}$
Birmingham, AL	$1\frac{1}{2}$

Source: Fact Monster

On average, how many more inches of snow does Mount Washington, New Hampshire, receive than Anchorage, Alaska?

   A $330\frac{7}{10}$ in.

   B $189\frac{1}{10}$ in.

   C $166\frac{3}{10}$ in.

   D $92\frac{1}{10}$ in.

Problem-Solving Investigation

MAIN IDEA: Solve problems by eliminating possibilities.

P.S.I. TEAM +

e-Mail: ELIMINATE POSSIBILITIES

MADISON: I am making school pennants to decorate the cafeteria. I use $1\frac{1}{4}$ yards of fabric for each pennant.

YOUR MISSION: Eliminate possibilities to find the greatest number of pennants Madison can make with 12 yards of fabric. Is it 6, 9, or 12?

Understand	You know she has 12 yards of fabric. Each pennant uses $1\frac{1}{4}$ yards of fabric.
Plan	Eliminate the answers that are not reasonable.
Solve	Madison needs more than 1 yard of fabric for each pennant. So, she needs more than 12 yards for 12 pennants. Eliminate this choice. Now check the choice of 9 pennants. • $1\frac{1}{4} + 1\frac{1}{4} + 1\frac{1}{4} + 1\frac{1}{4} = 5$. So, Madison can make 4 pennants with 5 yards of fabric. Therefore, she can make 8 pennants out of 10 yards of fabric. • She can also make 1 more pennant with the remaining 2 yards. So, Madison can make 8 + 1 or 9 pennants.
Check	Making 6 pennants would take $1\frac{1}{4} + 1\frac{1}{4} + 1\frac{1}{4} + 1\frac{1}{4} + 1\frac{1}{4} + 1\frac{1}{4} = 7\frac{1}{2}$ yards. This is not the greatest number she can make. So, making 6 pennants is *not* reasonable.

Analyze The Strategy

1. Describe different ways that you can eliminate possibilities when solving problems.
2. Explain how the strategy of eliminating possibilities is useful for taking multiple-choice tests.
3. **WRITING IN MATH** Write a problem that could be solved by eliminating possibilities.

Mixed Problem Solving

EXTRA PRACTICE
See pages 679, 681.

Eliminate possibilities to solve Exercises 4–6.

4. **TRAINS** A train passes through an intersection at the rate of 3 cars per 30 seconds. Assume that it takes 5 minutes for the train to completely pass through the intersection. How many cars does the train have altogether?

   A 6 cars **C** 30 cars
   B 15 cars **D** 45 cars

5. **PIZZA** A pizza shop used 100 pounds of pizza dough to make 125 pizzas. If a large pizza requires 1 pound of dough and a medium pizza requires $\frac{1}{2}$ pound, how many large- and medium-sized pizzas were made?

   F 40 large, 85 medium
   G 65 large, 60 medium
   H 55 large, 70 medium
   J 75 large, 50 medium

6. **PILLOWS** Pat is making pillows out of fabric. He uses $\frac{3}{4}$ yard of fabric for each pillow. What is the greatest number of pillows Pat can make with 9 yards of fabric: 9, 12, or 15?

Use any strategy to solve Exercises 7–14. Some strategies are shown below.

7. **MEASUREMENT** The diagram shows a shelf that holds CDs. Each shelf is $\frac{1}{8}$ inch thick, and the distance between shelves is as shown. How much space is available on each layer of the shelf for a CD?

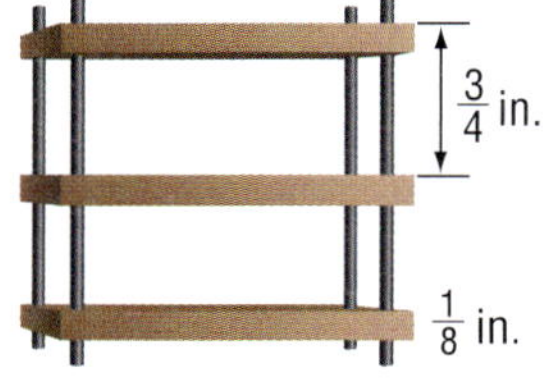

8. **BRIDGES** A covered bridge has a maximum capacity of 48,000 pounds. If an average school bus weighs 10,000 pounds, about how many school buses could a covered bridge hold?

9. **GEOMETRY** Draw the next two figures in the pattern.

10. **SLEEP** A 9-month-old infant needs about 14 hours of sleep each day while a teenager needs about 10 hours of sleep each day. How much more sleep does a 9-month-old need than a teenager? Write as a fraction of a day.

11. **PRECIPITATION** In Olympia, Washington, the average annual precipitation is $50\frac{3}{5}$ inches. Is $\frac{1}{49}$ inch, 1 inch, or 14 inches the best estimate for the average precipitation per day?

12. **MONEY** Kristen has $15 to go to the movies. Her ticket costs $7.25, drinks are $3.50, popcorn is $5.75, and pretzels are $4.25. Which two items can Kristen get from the concession stand?

13. **PIZZA** Sebastian ate $\frac{2}{5}$ of a pizza while his sister ate $\frac{1}{3}$ of the same pizza. The remainder was stored in the refrigerator. What fraction of the pizza was stored in the refrigerator?

14. **GRADES** Jerome had an average of 88 on his first three science tests. His score on the second and third tests were 92 and 87. What was his score on the first test?

Explore 5-5

Math Lab
Multiplying Fractions

MAIN IDEA

Use area models to multiply fractions and mixed numbers.

Math Online

glencoe.com

- Concepts In Motion

Just as the product of 3×4 is the number of square units in a rectangle, the product of two fractions can be shown using area models.

ACTIVITY

1 **Find $\frac{3}{4} \times \frac{2}{3}$ using a geoboard.**

The first factor is 3 *fourths* and the second factor is 2 *thirds*.

STEP 1 Use one geoband to show fourths and another to show thirds on the geoboard.

STEP 2 Use geobands to form a rectangle. Place one geoband on the peg to show 3 fourths and another on the peg to show 2 thirds.

STEP 3 Connect the geobands to show a small rectangle.

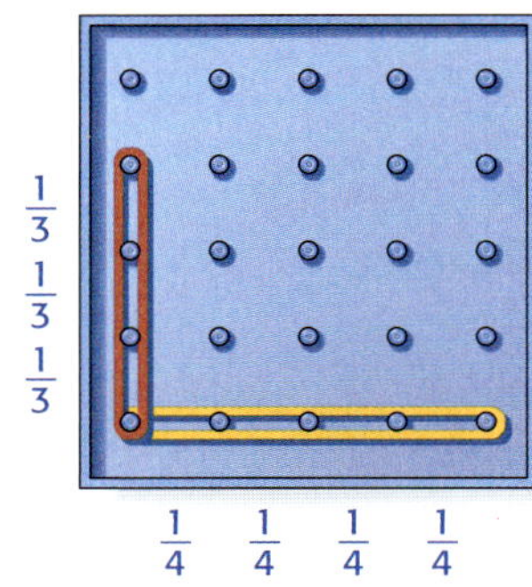

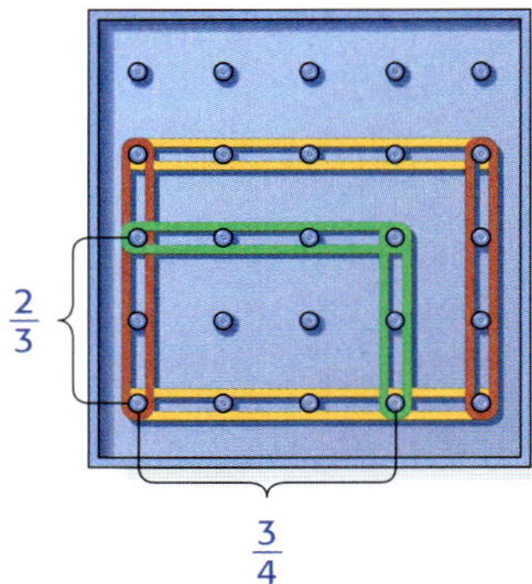

The area of the small square is 6 square units. The area of the large rectangle is 12 square units. So, $\frac{3}{4} \times \frac{2}{3} = \frac{6}{12}$ or $\frac{1}{2}$.

CHECK Your Progress

Find each product using a geoboard.

a. $\frac{1}{4} \times \frac{1}{3}$ b. $\frac{1}{2} \times \frac{1}{2}$ c. $\frac{3}{4} \times \frac{1}{2}$ d. $\frac{2}{3} \times \frac{1}{4}$

ACTIVITY

2 **Find $2 \times \frac{1}{4}$ using an area model.**

STEP 1 To represent 2 or $\frac{2}{1}$, draw 2 large rectangles, side by side. Divide each rectangle horizontally into fourths. Color both large rectangles blue.

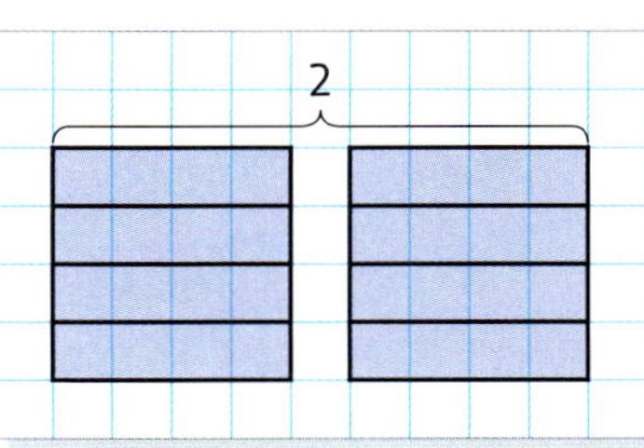

STEP 2 Color 1 fourth of each large rectangle yellow.

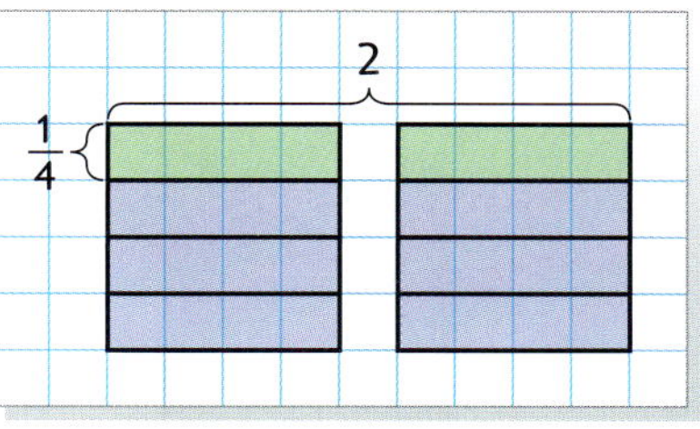

The fraction that compares the number of green sections, 2, to the number of sections in one rectangle, 4, is $\frac{2}{4}$ or $\frac{1}{2}$. So, $2 \times \frac{1}{4} = \frac{1}{2}$.

CHECK Your Progress

Find each product using a model.

e. $3 \times \frac{2}{3}$ f. $2 \times \frac{2}{5}$ g. $4 \times \frac{1}{2}$ h. $3 \times \frac{3}{4}$

ACTIVITY

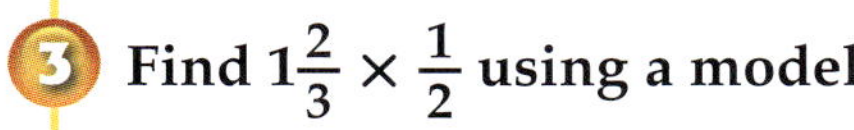

3 **Find $1\frac{2}{3} \times \frac{1}{2}$ using a model.**

STEP 1 Draw 2 rectangles divided vertically into thirds and horizontally into halves. Color $1\frac{2}{3}$ of the squares blue.

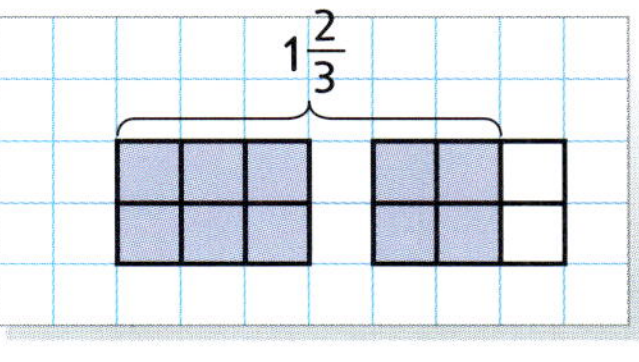

STEP 2 Color $\frac{1}{2}$ of the squares yellow. Then count the small squares that are green.

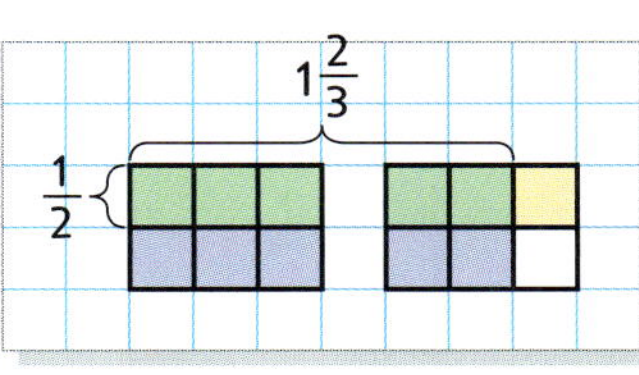

Since the green area is $\frac{3}{6}$ of the first rectangle and $\frac{2}{6}$ of the second rectangle, the total area shaded green is $\frac{3}{6} + \frac{2}{6}$ or $\frac{5}{6}$. So, $1\frac{2}{3} \times \frac{1}{2} = \frac{5}{6}$.

CHECK Your Progress

Find each product using a model.

i. $1\frac{1}{4} \times \frac{1}{5}$ j. $2\frac{1}{2} \times \frac{3}{4}$ k. $1\frac{2}{3} \times \frac{1}{3}$

ANALYZE THE RESULTS

1. Analyze Exercises a–k. What is the relationship between the numerators of the factors and of the product? between the denominators of the factors and of the product?

2. **MAKE A CONJECTURE** Write a rule you can use to multiply two fractions.

5-5 Multiplying Fractions and Mixed Numbers

MAIN IDEA

Multiply fractions and mixed numbers.

Math Online

glencoe.com

- Extra Examples
- Personal Tutor
- Self-Check Quiz

GET READY for the Lesson

LUNCH Two thirds of the students at the lunch table ordered a hamburger for lunch. One half of those students ordered cheese on their hamburgers.

1. What fraction of the students at the lunch table ordered a cheeseburger?
2. How are the numerators and denominators of $\frac{2}{3}$ and $\frac{1}{2}$ related to the fraction in Exercise 1?

Multiply Fractions — Key Concept

Words To multiply fractions, multiply the numerators and multiply the denominators.

Examples

Numbers

$\frac{1}{2} \times \frac{2}{3} = \frac{1 \times 2}{2 \times 3}$ or $\frac{2}{6}$

Algebra

$\frac{a}{b} \cdot \frac{c}{d} = \frac{a \cdot c}{b \cdot d}$ or $\frac{ac}{bd}$, where $b, d \neq 0$

EXAMPLES Multiply Fractions

Multiply. Write in simplest form.

1 $\frac{1}{2} \times \frac{1}{3}$

$\frac{1}{2} \times \frac{1}{3} = \frac{1 \times 1}{2 \times 3}$ ← Multiply the numerators. ← Multiply the denominators.

$= \frac{1}{6}$ Simplify.

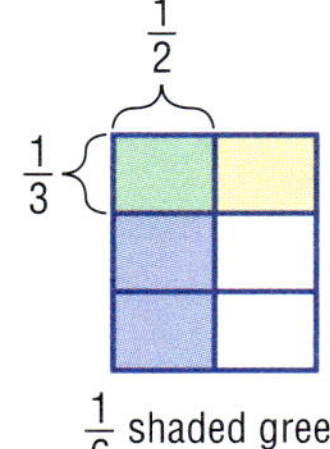

$\frac{1}{6}$ shaded green

2 $2 \times \frac{3}{4}$

$2 \times \frac{3}{4} = \frac{2}{1} \times \frac{3}{4}$ Write 2 as $\frac{2}{1}$.

$= \frac{2 \times 3}{1 \times 4}$ ← Multiply the numerators. ← Multiply the denominators.

$= \frac{6}{4}$ or $1\frac{1}{2}$ Simplify.

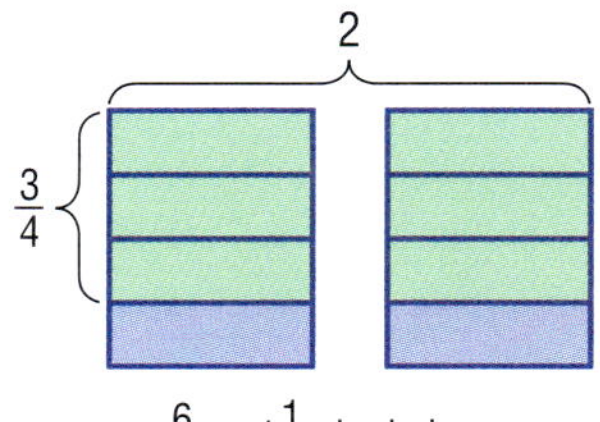

$\frac{6}{4}$ or $1\frac{1}{2}$ shaded green

Study Tip

Whole Numbers When multiplying a fraction by a whole number, write the whole number as a fraction with a denominator of 1.

CHECK Your Progress

a. $\frac{3}{5} \times \frac{1}{2}$

b. $\frac{1}{3} \times \frac{3}{4}$

c. $\frac{2}{3} \times 4$

If the numerator and denominator of either fraction have common factors, you can simplify before multiplying.

Review Vocabulary

GCF the greatest of the common factors of two or more numbers; *Example:* the GCF of 8 and 12 is 4. (Lesson 4-2)

EXAMPLE Simplify Before Multiplying

3 **Find $\frac{2}{7} \times \frac{3}{8}$. Write in simplest form.**

$\frac{2}{7} \times \frac{3}{8} = \frac{\overset{1}{\cancel{2}}}{7} \times \frac{3}{\underset{4}{\cancel{8}}}$ Divide 2 and 8 by their GCF, 2.

$= \frac{1 \times 3}{7 \times 4}$ or $\frac{3}{28}$ Multiply.

CHECK Your Progress

Multiply. Write in simplest form.

d. $\frac{1}{3} \times \frac{3}{7}$ e. $\frac{4}{9} \times \frac{1}{8}$ f. $\frac{5}{6} \times \frac{3}{5}$

EXAMPLE Multiply Mixed Numbers

4 **Find $\frac{1}{2} \times 4\frac{2}{5}$. Write in simplest form.** **Estimate** $\frac{1}{2} \times 4 = 2$

METHOD 1 **Rename the mixed number.**

$\frac{1}{2} \times 4\frac{2}{5} = \frac{1}{\underset{1}{\cancel{2}}} \times \frac{\overset{11}{\cancel{22}}}{5}$ Rename $4\frac{2}{5}$ as an improper fraction, $\frac{22}{5}$. Divide 2 and 22 by their GCF, 2.

$= \frac{1 \times 11}{1 \times 5}$ Multiply.

$= \frac{11}{5}$ or $2\frac{1}{5}$ Simplify.

METHOD 2 **Use mental math.**

The mixed number $4\frac{2}{5}$ is equal to $4 + \frac{2}{5}$.

So, $\frac{1}{2} \times 4\frac{2}{5} = \frac{1}{2}\left(4 + \frac{2}{5}\right)$. Use the Distributive Property to multiply, then add mentally.

$\frac{1}{2}\left(4 + \frac{2}{5}\right) = 2 + \frac{1}{5}$ **THINK** Half of 4 is 2 and half of 2 fifths is 1 fifth.

$= 2\frac{1}{5}$ Rewrite the sum as a mixed number.

So, $\frac{1}{2} \times 4\frac{2}{5} = 2\frac{1}{5}$. **Check for Reasonableness** $2\frac{1}{5} \approx 2$ ✔

Study Tip

Simplifying
If you forget to simplify before multiplying, you can always simplify the final answer. However, it is usually easier to simplify before multiplying.

CHOOSE Your Method

Multiply. Write in simplest form.

g. $\frac{1}{4} \times 8\frac{4}{9}$ h. $5\frac{1}{3} \times 3$ i. $1\frac{7}{8} \times 2\frac{2}{5}$

Real-World EXAMPLES

Study Tip

Meaning of Multiplication Recall that one meaning of 3×4 is three groups with 4 in each group. In Example 5, there are $365\frac{1}{4}$ groups with $\frac{1}{3}$ in each group.

5 **SLEEP** **Humans sleep about $\frac{1}{3}$ of each day. If each year is equal to $365\frac{1}{4}$ days, determine the number of days in a year the average human sleeps.**

Words	Humans sleep about $\frac{1}{3}$ of $365\frac{1}{4}$ days.
Variable	Let d represent the number of days a human sleeps.
Equation	$d = \frac{1}{3} \cdot 365\frac{1}{4}$

$d = \frac{1}{3} \cdot 365\frac{1}{4}$ — Write the equation.

$d = \frac{1}{3} \cdot \frac{1,461}{4}$ — Rename the mixed number as an improper fraction.

$d = \frac{1}{\cancel{3}_{1}} \cdot \frac{\cancel{1,461}^{487}}{4}$ — Divide 3 and 1,461 by their GCF, 3.

$d = \frac{487}{4}$ or $121\frac{3}{4}$ — Multiply. Then rename as a mixed number.

The average human sleeps $121\frac{3}{4}$ days each year.

Real-World Link The average group of lions, called a pride, consists of about 15 lions with about $\frac{2}{3}$ of the pride being female.
Source: *African Wildlife Foundation*

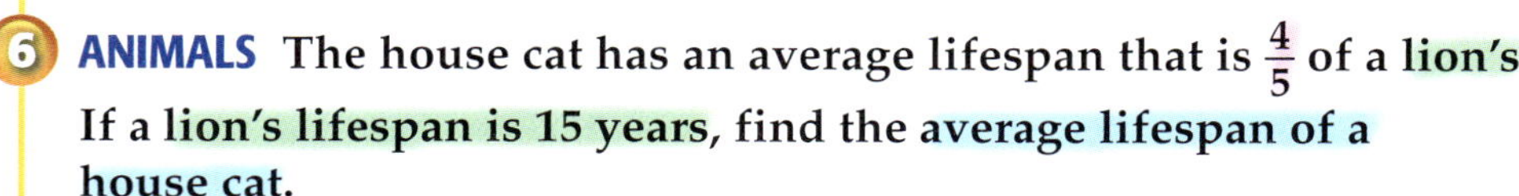

6 **ANIMALS** **The house cat has an average lifespan that is $\frac{4}{5}$ of a lion's. If a lion's lifespan is 15 years, find the average lifespan of a house cat.**

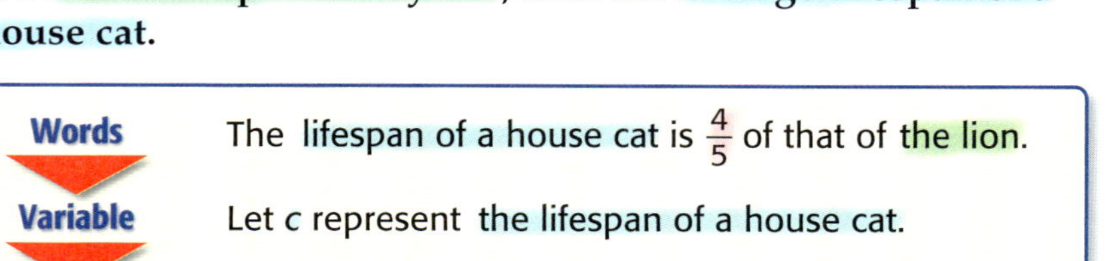

Words	The lifespan of a house cat is $\frac{4}{5}$ of that of the lion.
Variable	Let c represent the lifespan of a house cat.
Equation	$c = \frac{4}{5} \cdot 15$

$c = \frac{4}{5} \cdot 15$ — Write the equation.

$c = \frac{4}{5} \cdot \frac{15}{1}$ — Write the whole number 15 as an improper fraction.

$c = \frac{4}{\cancel{5}_{1}} \cdot \frac{\cancel{15}^{3}}{1}$ — Divide 5 and 15 by their GCF, 5.

$c = \frac{12}{1}$ or 12 — Multiply, then simplify.

The average lifespan of a house cat is 12 years.

CHECK Your Progress

j. **COOKING** Sofia wishes to make $\frac{1}{2}$ of a recipe. If the original recipe calls for $3\frac{3}{4}$ cups of flour, how many cups should she use?

Examples 1–4 (pp. 252–253)

Multiply. Write in simplest form.

1. $\frac{2}{3} \times \frac{1}{3}$
2. $2 \times \frac{2}{5}$
3. $\frac{1}{6} \times 4$
4. $\frac{1}{4} \times \frac{8}{9}$
5. $2\frac{1}{4} \times \frac{2}{3}$
6. $1\frac{5}{6} \times 3\frac{3}{5}$

Examples 5, 6 (p. 254)

7. **WEIGHT** The weight of an object on Mars is about $\frac{2}{5}$ its weight on Earth. How much would an 80-pound dog weigh on Mars?

Practice and Problem Solving

HOMEWORK HELP

For Exercises	See Examples
8–11	1, 2
12–19	3, 4
20–23	5, 6

Multiply. Write in simplest form.

8. $\frac{3}{4} \times \frac{1}{8}$
9. $\frac{2}{5} \times \frac{2}{3}$
10. $9 \times \frac{1}{2}$
11. $\frac{4}{5} \times 6$
12. $\frac{1}{5} \times \frac{5}{6}$
13. $\frac{4}{9} \times \frac{1}{4}$
14. $\frac{2}{3} \times \frac{1}{4}$
15. $\frac{1}{12} \times \frac{3}{5}$
16. $\frac{4}{7} \times \frac{7}{8}$
17. $\frac{2}{5} \times \frac{15}{16}$
18. $\frac{3}{8} \times \frac{10}{27}$
19. $\frac{9}{10} \times \frac{5}{6}$

20. **DVDs** Each DVD storage case is about $\frac{1}{5}$ inch thick. What will be the height of 12 cases sold together in plastic wrapping?

21. **PIZZA** Mark left $\frac{3}{8}$ of a pizza in the refrigerator. On Friday, he ate $\frac{1}{2}$ of what was left of the pizza. What fraction of the entire pizza did he eat on Friday?

22. **MEASUREMENT** The width of a vegetable garden is $\frac{1}{3}$ times its length. If the length of the garden is $7\frac{3}{4}$ feet, what is the width?

23. **RECIPES** A recipe to make one batch of blueberry muffins calls for $4\frac{2}{3}$ cups of flour. How many cups of flour are needed to make 3 batches of blueberry muffins?

Multiply. Write in simplest form.

24. $4\frac{2}{3} \times \frac{4}{7}$
25. $\frac{5}{8} \times 2\frac{1}{2}$
26. $14 \times 1\frac{1}{7}$
27. $3\frac{3}{4} \times 8$
28. $9 \times 4\frac{2}{3}$
29. $4 \times 7\frac{5}{6}$
30. $3\frac{1}{4} \times 2\frac{2}{3}$
31. $5\frac{1}{3} \times 3\frac{3}{4}$

32. **MEASUREMENT** The width of the fish tank is $\frac{2}{5}$ of its length. What is the width of the fish tank?

33. **BICYCLING** Philip rode his bicycle at $9\frac{2}{5}$ miles per hour. If he rode for $\frac{3}{4}$ of an hour, how many miles did he cover?

Evaluate each verbal expression.

34. one half of five eighths
35. four sevenths of two thirds
36. nine tenths of one fourth
37. one third of eleven sixteenths

MEASUREMENT Find the perimeter and area of each rectangle.

38.

$3\frac{1}{2}$ ft

$5\frac{1}{4}$ ft

39.

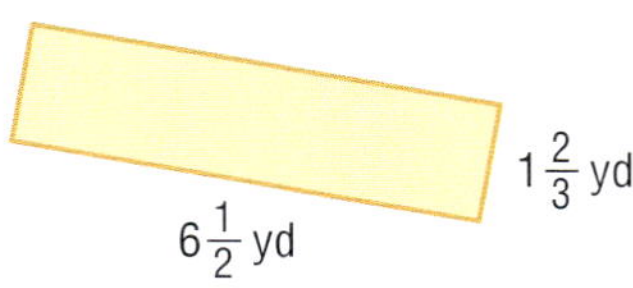

$1\frac{2}{3}$ yd

$6\frac{1}{2}$ yd

Real-World Link There are an estimated 5 million in-ground swimming pools in the U.S.

Source: *Pool & Spa Service Industry News*

40. **POOLS** A community swimming pool is $90\frac{2}{5}$ feet long and $55\frac{1}{2}$ feet wide. If Natalie swims the perimeter of the pool four times, what is the total number of feet she will swim? Explain how you solved the problem.

MEASUREMENT For Exercises 41–44, use measurement conversions.

41. Find $\frac{1}{2}$ of $\frac{1}{4}$ of a gallon.
42. What is $\frac{1}{60}$ of $\frac{1}{24}$ of a day?
43. Find $\frac{1}{100}$ of $\frac{1}{1,000}$ of a kilometer.
44. What is $\frac{1}{12}$ of $\frac{1}{3}$ of a yard?

ALGEBRA Evaluate each expression if $a = 4$, $b = 2\frac{1}{2}$, and $c = 5\frac{3}{4}$.

45. $a \times b + c$
46. $b \times c - a$
47. $2bc$

48. **TELEVISION** One evening, $\frac{2}{3}$ of the students in Rick's class watched television, and $\frac{3}{8}$ of those students watched a reality show, of which $\frac{1}{4}$ taped the show. What fraction of the students in Rick's class watched and taped a reality TV show?

49. **FOOD** Alano wants to make one and a half recipes of the pasta salad recipe shown at the right. How much of each ingredient will Alano need? Explain how you solved the problem.

Pasta Salad Recipe

Ingredient	Amount
broccoli	$1\frac{1}{4}$ c
cooked pasta	$3\frac{3}{4}$ c
salad dressing	$\frac{2}{3}$ c
cheese	$1\frac{1}{3}$ c

50. **FIND THE DATA** Refer to the Data File on pages 16–19. Choose some data and write a real-world problem in which you would multiply fractions.

Write and evaluate a multiplication expression to represent each model. Explain how the models show the multiplication process.

51.

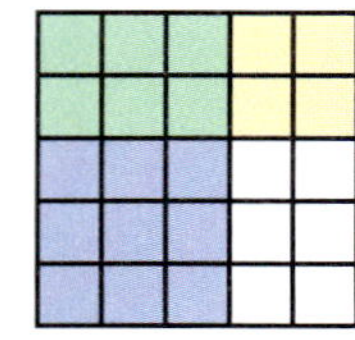

52.

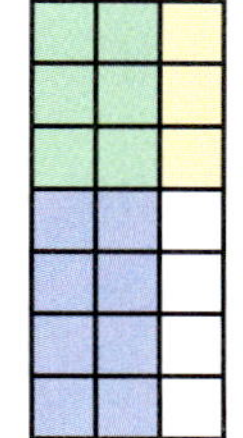

EXTRA PRACTICE
See pages 680, 708.

H.O.T. Problems

53. **CHALLENGE** Two improper fractions are multiplied. Is the product *sometimes*, *always*, or *never* less than 1? Explain your reasoning.

54. **OPEN ENDED** Write a word problem that involves finding the product of $\frac{3}{4}$ and $\frac{1}{8}$.

55. **WRITING IN MATH** Refer to Example 2. Explain how the model represents the meaning of the multiplication process.

TEST PRACTICE

56. Of the dolls in Marjorie's doll collection, $\frac{1}{5}$ have red hair. Of these, $\frac{3}{4}$ have green eyes. What fraction of Marjorie's doll collection has both red hair and green eyes?

A $\frac{2}{9}$

B $\frac{3}{20}$

C $\frac{4}{9}$

D $\frac{19}{20}$

57. Which description gives the relationship between a term and n, its position in the sequence?

Position	1	2	3	4	5	n
Value of Term	$\frac{1}{4}$	$\frac{1}{2}$	$\frac{3}{4}$	1	$1\frac{1}{4}$	

F Subtract 4 from n.

G Add $\frac{1}{4}$ to n.

H Multiply n by $\frac{1}{4}$.

J Divide n by $\frac{1}{4}$.

Spiral Review

58. **MEASUREMENT** Find which room dimensions would give an area of $125\frac{3}{8}$ square feet. Use the *eliminate possibilities* strategy. (Lesson 5-4)

A $11\frac{1}{2}$ feet by $10\frac{3}{8}$ feet

B $10\frac{7}{8}$ feet by $12\frac{1}{4}$ feet

C $13\frac{5}{8}$ feet by 9 feet

D $14\frac{3}{4}$ feet by $8\frac{1}{2}$ feet

59. **MEASUREMENT** How much longer is a $2\frac{1}{2}$-inch-long piece of string than a $\frac{2}{5}$-inch-long piece of string? (Lesson 5-3)

Replace each ● with <, >, or = to make a true sentence. (Lesson 4-9)

60. $\frac{5}{12}$ ● $\frac{2}{5}$

61. $\frac{3}{16}$ ● $\frac{1}{8}$

62. $3\frac{7}{6}$ ● $3\frac{6}{5}$

63. **PHONES** A long-distance telephone company charges a flat monthly fee of \$4.95 and \$0.06 per minute on all long-distance calls. Write and solve an equation to find the number of monthly minutes spent talking long-distance if the bill total was \$22.95. (Lesson 3-5)

GET READY for the Next Lesson

PREREQUISITE SKILL **Solve each equation mentally.** (Lesson 1-7)

64. $x + 2 = 8$

65. $9 + m = 12$

66. $7 - w = 2$

5-6 Algebra: Solving Equations

MAIN IDEA

Solve equations with rational number solutions.

New Vocabulary

multiplicative inverse
reciprocal

Math Online

glencoe.com

- Extra Examples
- Personal Tutor
- Self-Check Quiz

GET READY for the Lesson

HOMEWORK Shawnda spends $\frac{1}{2}$ hour doing homework after school. Then she spends another $\frac{1}{2}$ hour doing homework before bed.

1. Write a multiplication expression to find how much time Shawnda spends doing homework. Then find the product.
2. Copy and complete the table below.

$\frac{3}{2} \times \frac{2}{3} = \blacksquare$	$\frac{1}{5} \times \blacksquare = 1$	$\frac{5}{6} \times \frac{6}{5} = \blacksquare$	$\frac{7}{8} \times \frac{8}{7} = \blacksquare$
$\blacksquare \times \frac{5}{7} = 1$	$\frac{2}{6} \times \frac{6}{2} = \blacksquare$	$\frac{7}{1} \times \blacksquare = 1$	$\blacksquare \times 8 = 1$

3. What is true about the numerators and denominators in the fractions in Exercise 2?

Two numbers with a product of 1 are called **multiplicative inverses**, or **reciprocals**.

Inverse Property of Multiplication (Key Concept)

Words The product of a number and its multiplicative inverse is 1.

Examples

Numbers	Algebra
$\frac{3}{4} \times \frac{4}{3} = 1$	$\frac{a}{b} \cdot \frac{b}{a} = 1$, for $a, b \neq 0$

EXAMPLES Find Multiplicative Inverses

1 **Find the multiplicative inverse of $\frac{2}{5}$.**

$\frac{2}{5} \cdot \frac{5}{2} = 1$ Multiply $\frac{2}{5}$ by $\frac{5}{2}$ to get the product 1.

The multiplicative inverse of $\frac{2}{5}$ is $\frac{5}{2}$, or $2\frac{1}{2}$.

2 **Find the multiplicative inverse of $2\frac{1}{3}$.**

$2\frac{1}{3} = \frac{7}{3}$ Rename the mixed number as an improper fraction.

$\frac{7}{3} \cdot \frac{3}{7} = 1$ Multiply $\frac{7}{3}$ by $\frac{3}{7}$ to get the product 1.

The multiplicative inverse of $2\frac{1}{3}$ is $\frac{3}{7}$.

CHECK Your Progress

a. $\frac{5}{6}$ b. $1\frac{1}{2}$ c. 8 d. $\frac{4}{3}$

In Chapter 3, you learned to solve equations using the Addition, Subtraction, and Division Properties of Equality. You can also solve equations by multiplying each side by the same number. This is called the **Multiplication Property of Equality**.

Multiplication Property of Equality

Key Concept

Words If you multiply each side of an equation by the same nonzero number, the two sides remain equal.

Examples

Numbers	Algebra	
$5 = 5$	$\frac{x}{2} = -3$	$\frac{2}{3}x = 4$
$5 \cdot 2 = 5 \cdot 2$	$\frac{x}{2}(2) = -3(2)$	$\frac{3}{2} \cdot \frac{2}{3}x = \frac{3}{2} \cdot 4$
$10 = 10$	$x = -6$	$x = 6$

Study Tip

Fractions The fraction bar indicates division. So, $\frac{x}{2}$ means x divided by 2.

EXAMPLES Solve a Division Equation

3 **Solve $7 = \frac{n}{4}$. Check your solution.**

$7 = \frac{n}{4}$ Write the equation.

$7 \cdot 4 = \frac{n}{4} \cdot 4$ Multiply each side of the equation by 4.

$28 = n$ Simplify.

Check $7 = \frac{n}{4}$ Write the original equation.

$7 \stackrel{?}{=} \frac{28}{4}$ Replace n with 28.

$7 = 7$ ✔ Is this sentence true?

4 **Solve $\frac{d}{3.5} = 4.2$.**

$\frac{d}{3.5} = 4.2$ Write the equation.

$\frac{d}{3.5} \cdot 3.5 = 4.2 \cdot 3.5$ Multiply each side by 3.5.

$d = 14.7$ Simplify.

The solution is 14.7.

Check $\frac{d}{3.5} = 4.2$ Write the original equation.

$\frac{14.7}{3.5} \stackrel{?}{=} 4.2$ Replace d with 14.7.

$4.2 = 4.2$ ✔ Is this sentence true?

CHECK Your Progress

Solve each equation. Check your solution.

e. $6 = \frac{m}{8}$ f. $\frac{p}{2.8} = 1.5$ g. $\frac{k}{4.7} = 2.3$

EXAMPLE Solve a Multiplication Equation

Solve $\frac{3}{4}x = \frac{12}{20}$.

$\frac{3}{4}x = \frac{12}{20}$	Write the equation.
$\left(\frac{4}{3}\right) \cdot \frac{3}{4}x = \left(\frac{4}{3}\right) \cdot \frac{12}{20}$	Multiply each side by the reciprocal of $\frac{3}{4}$, $\frac{4}{3}$.
$\frac{\overset{1}{\cancel{4}}}{\underset{1}{\cancel{3}}} \cdot \frac{\overset{1}{\cancel{3}}}{\underset{1}{\cancel{4}}}x = \frac{\overset{1}{\cancel{4}}}{\underset{1}{\cancel{3}}} \cdot \frac{\overset{4}{\cancel{12}}}{\underset{5}{\cancel{20}}}$	Divide by common factors.
$x = \frac{4}{5}$	Simplify.

Study Tip

Fractions as Coefficients The expression $\frac{3}{4}x$ can be read as $\frac{3}{4}$ of x, $\frac{3}{4}$ multiplied by x, $3x$ divided by 4, or $\frac{x}{4}$ multiplied by 3.

CHECK Your Progress

Solve each equation. Check your solution.

h. $\frac{1}{2}x = 8$

i. $\frac{3}{4}x = 9$

j. $\frac{7}{8}x = \frac{21}{64}$

TEST EXAMPLE

Valerie needs $\frac{2}{3}$ yard of fabric to make each hat for the school play. How many hats can she make with 6 yards of fabric?

A 12

B 9

C 8

D 4

Read the Item

Each hat needs $\frac{2}{3}$ yard of fabric. Given the number of hats, you would multiply by $\frac{2}{3}$ to find the number of yards of fabric needed.

Solve the Item

Write and solve a multiplication equation.

$\frac{2}{3}n = 6$	Write the equation.
$\left(\frac{3}{2}\right) \cdot \frac{2}{3}n = \left(\frac{3}{2}\right) \cdot 6$	Multiply each side by $\frac{3}{2}$.
$n = 9$	Simplify.

So, the answer is B.

Test-Taking Tip

Verify Your Answer It is a good idea to verify your answer by checking the other answer choices. By doing so, you can greatly reduce your chances of making an error.

CHECK Your Progress

k. Wilson has 9 pounds of trail mix. How many $\frac{3}{4}$-pound bags of trail mix can he make?

F 3

G 6

H 9

J 12

CHECK Your Understanding

Examples 1, 2 (p. 258)

Find the multiplicative inverse of each number.

1. $\frac{8}{5}$
2. $\frac{2}{9}$
3. $5\frac{4}{5}$
4. 9

Examples 3–5 (p. 259–260)

Solve each equation. Check your solution.

5. $\frac{k}{16} = 2$
6. $4 = \frac{y}{3}$
7. $\frac{b}{8.2} = 2.5$
8. $0.5 = \frac{h}{3.6}$
9. $\frac{3}{8}a = \frac{12}{40}$
10. $6 = \frac{4}{7}x$

Example 5 (p. 260)

11. **FRUIT** Three fourths of the fruit in a refrigerator are apples. There are 24 apples in the refrigerator. The number of pieces of fruit is given by the equation $\frac{3}{4}f = 24$. How many pieces of fruit are in the refrigerator?

Example 6 (p. 260)

12. **MULTIPLE CHOICE** Dillon deposited $\frac{3}{4}$ of his paycheck into the bank. The deposit slip shows how much he deposited. What was the amount of his paycheck?

A $15
B $33.75
C $60
D $75

Practice and Problem Solving

HOMEWORK HELP	
For Exercises	See Examples
13–20	1, 2
21–26, 33–34	3, 4
27–32	5
51–52	6

Find the multiplicative inverse of each number.

13. $\frac{5}{6}$
14. $\frac{11}{2}$
15. $\frac{1}{6}$
16. $\frac{1}{10}$
17. 3
18. 14
19. $5\frac{1}{8}$
20. $6\frac{2}{3}$

Solve each equation. Check your solution.

21. $\frac{x}{12} = 3$
22. $28 = \frac{d}{4}$
23. $\frac{b}{2.4} = 6$
24. $5 = \frac{w}{4.9}$
25. $0.8 = \frac{h}{3.6}$
26. $\frac{m}{4.6} = 2.8$
27. $\frac{2}{5}t = \frac{12}{25}$
28. $\frac{24}{16} = \frac{3}{4}a$
29. $\frac{7}{8}k = \frac{5}{6}$
30. $\frac{2}{3} = \frac{8}{3}b$
31. $\frac{1}{2}g = 3\frac{1}{3}$
32. $\frac{3}{5}c = 6\frac{1}{4}$

33. **DISTANCE** The distance d Toya travels in her car while driving 60 miles per hour for 3.25 hours is given by the equation $\frac{d}{3.25} = 60$. How far did she travel?

34. **ANIMALS** An adult Fitch ferret weighs about 1.8 kilograms. To find its weight in pounds p, you can use the equation $\frac{p}{1.8} = 2.2$. How many pounds does an adult Fitch ferret weigh?

Solve each equation. Check your solution.

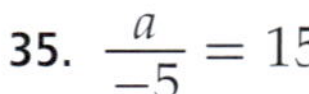

35. $\frac{a}{-5} = 15$

36. $-8 = \frac{r}{-2}$

37. $34.5 = \frac{5}{6}m$

38. $\frac{5}{7}x = -1.5$

39. $\frac{1}{4}t = \frac{3}{8}$

40. $\frac{3}{8}m = 1\frac{1}{2}$

For Exercises 41–46, define a variable and write an equation. Then solve.

41. **CAVES** The self-guided Mammoth Cave Discovery Tour includes an elevation change of 140 feet. This is $\frac{7}{15}$ of the elevation change on the Wild Cave Tour. What is the elevation change on the Wild Cave Tour?

Real-World Link
Kentucky's Mammoth Cave is the longest recorded cave system in the world, with more than 360 miles explored and mapped. The Wild Cave Tour requires visitors to crawl through an opening only 9 inches high.
Source: National Park Service

42. **MUSEUMS** Twenty-four students brought their permission slips to attend the class field trip to the local art museum. If this represented $\frac{4}{5}$ of the class, how many students are in the class?

43. **MEASUREMENT** If one serving of cooked rice is $\frac{3}{4}$ cup, how many servings will $16\frac{1}{2}$ cups of rice yield?

44. **HIKING** After Alana hiked $2\frac{5}{8}$ miles along a hiking trail, she realized that she was only $\frac{3}{4}$ of the way to the end of the trail. How long is the trail?

45. **SLEEP** The average person spends $\frac{1}{3}$ of his life asleep. According to this, if a person has spent 26 years asleep, how old is he?

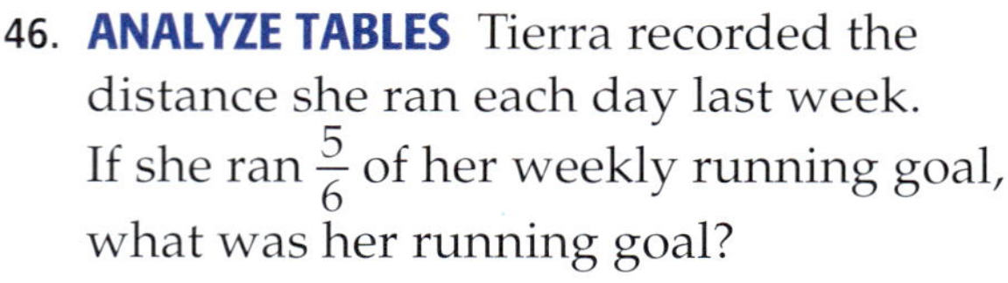

46. **ANALYZE TABLES** Tierra recorded the distance she ran each day last week. If she ran $\frac{5}{6}$ of her weekly running goal, what was her running goal?

Distance Ran in One Week

Day	Distance (mi)
Monday	$1\frac{3}{4}$
Wednesday	2
Friday	$1\frac{1}{2}$
Saturday	$2\frac{1}{4}$

EXTRA PRACTICE
See pages 681, 708.

H.O.T. Problems

47. **REASONING** Complete the statement: If $8 = \frac{m}{4}$, then $m - 12 = $ ■. Explain your reasoning.

48. **Which One Doesn't Belong?** Identify the pair of numbers that does not belong with the other three. Explain.

$\frac{9}{6}, \frac{6}{9}$	$4, \frac{1}{4}$	$\frac{3}{5}, 5$	$\frac{2}{7}, \frac{7}{2}$

49. **CHALLENGE** The formula for the area of a trapezoid is $A = \frac{1}{2}h(b_1 + b_2)$, where b_1 and b_2 are both bases and h is the height. Find the value of h in terms of A, b_1, and b_2. Justify your answer.

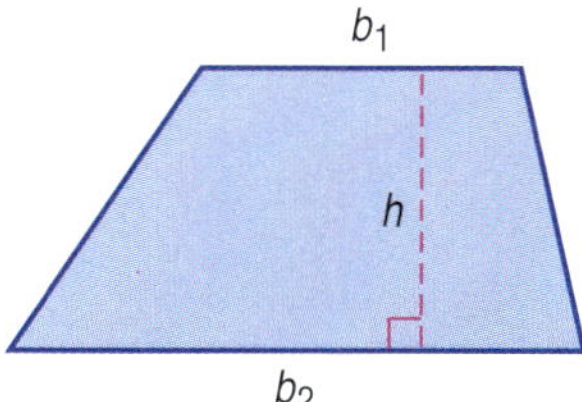

50. **WRITING IN MATH** Explain the Multiplication Property of Equality. Then give an example of an equation in which you would use this property to solve the equation.

51. Audrey drove 200 miles in 3.5 hours. Which equation can you use to find the rate r at which Audrey was traveling?

A $200 = 3.5r$

B $200 \cdot 3.5 = r$

C $\frac{r}{3.5} = 200$

D $200r = 3.5$

52. The table shows the results of a survey.

Music Preference	
Type	**Fraction of Students**
pop	$\frac{5}{8}$
jazz	$\frac{1}{8}$
rap	$\frac{1}{4}$

If there are 420 students surveyed, which equation can be used to find the number of students s who prefer rap?

F $\frac{1}{4}s = 420$

H $s + \frac{1}{4} = 420$

G $s = \frac{1}{4} \cdot 420$

J $420 + s = \frac{1}{4}$

Spiral Review

Multiply. Write in simplest form. (Lesson 5-5)

53. $\frac{3}{8} \times \frac{4}{9}$ **54.** $1\frac{1}{2} \times 6$ **55.** $2\frac{2}{5} \times \frac{1}{6}$ **56.** $1\frac{1}{2} \times 1\frac{7}{9}$

57. COOKING Lawana had $4\frac{2}{3}$ cups of chopped walnuts. She used $1\frac{1}{4}$ cups in a recipe. How many cups of chopped walnuts are left? (Lesson 5-3)

Write each percent as a decimal. (Lesson 4-7)

58. 25% **59.** 8% **60.** 25.6% **61.** 123%

62. MEASUREMENT A farmer has a rectangular pumpkin field with a perimeter of 3,800 feet. If the width of the pumpkin field is 800 feet, what is the length of the field? (Lesson 3-6)

ALGEBRA Solve each equation. Check your solution. (Lesson 3-2)

63. $7 = x + 8$ **64.** $k - 3 = -14$ **65.** $-2 = m + 6$

66. ALGEBRA The table shows the time needed to complete 4 art projects. If the pattern continues, how much time is needed to complete the fifth art project? (Lesson 2-7)

Project	1	2	3	4	5
Time (min)	8	25	42	59	■

GET READY for the Next Lesson

PREREQUISITE SKILL Estimate. (Lesson 5-1)

67. $18\frac{1}{6} \div 3$ **68.** $24\frac{3}{8} \div 11\frac{7}{9}$ **69.** $\frac{2}{11} \div \frac{11}{12}$ **70.** $\frac{9}{10} \div \frac{6}{7}$

READING to SOLVE PROBLEMS

Meaning of Division

You know that one meaning of division is to *put objects into equal groups*. But there are other meanings too. Look for these meanings when you're solving a word problem.

- **To share**

  Zach and his friend are going to share 3 apples equally. How many apples will each boy have?

- **To take away equal amounts**

  Isabel is making bookmarks from a piece of ribbon. Each bookmark is 6.5 centimeters long. How many bookmarks can she make from a piece of ribbon that is 27 centimeters long?

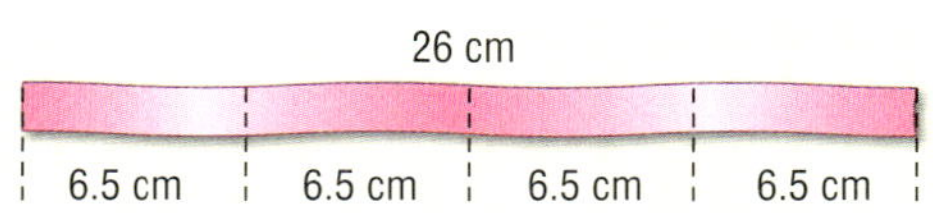

- **To find how many times greater**

  The Nile River, the longest river on Earth, is 4,160 miles long. The Rio Grande River is 1,900 miles long. About how many times longer is the Nile than the Rio Grande?

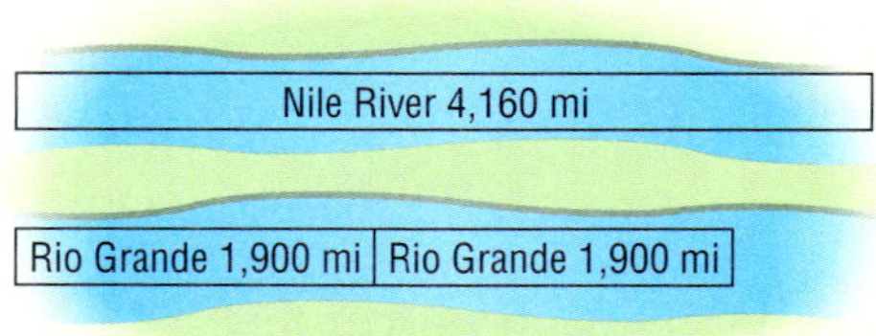

PRACTICE

1. Solve each problem above.

Identify the meaning of division shown in each problem. Then solve the problem.

2. A landscape architect wants to make a border along one side of a garden using bricks that are 0.25 meter long. If the garden is 11.25 meters long, how many bricks does she need?
3. The Jackson family wants to buy a flat-screen television that costs $1,200. They plan to pay in six equal payments. What will be the amount of each payment?
4. A full-grown blue whale can weigh 150 tons. An adult African elephant weighs about 5 tons. How many times greater does a blue whale weigh than an African elephant?
5. Each story in an office building is about 4 meters tall. The Eiffel Tower in Paris, France, is 300 meters tall. How many stories tall is the Eiffel Tower?

5-7 Dividing Fractions and Mixed Numbers

MAIN IDEA

Divide fractions and mixed numbers.

Math Online

glencoe.com

- Concepts In Motion
- Extra Examples
- Personal Tutor
- Self-Check Quiz

MINI Lab

Cut two paper plates into four equal pieces each to show $2 \div \frac{1}{4}$.

1. How many $\frac{1}{4}$'s are in 2 plates?
2. How would you model $3 \div \frac{1}{2}$?
3. What is true about $3 \div \frac{1}{2}$ and 3×2?

Dividing 8 by 2 gives the same result as multiplying 8 by $\frac{1}{2}$, which is the reciprocal of 2. In the same way, dividing 4 by $\frac{1}{3}$ is the same as multiplying 4 by the reciprocal of $\frac{1}{3}$, or 3.

reciprocals

$8 \div 2 = 4 \qquad 8 \cdot \frac{1}{2} = 4$

same result

reciprocals

$4 \div \frac{1}{3} = 12 \qquad 4 \cdot 3 = 12$

same result

Is this pattern true for any division expression?

Consider $\frac{7}{8} \div \frac{3}{4}$, which can be rewritten as $\frac{\frac{7}{8}}{\frac{3}{4}}$.

$$\frac{\frac{7}{8}}{\frac{3}{4}} = \frac{\frac{7}{8} \times \frac{4}{3}}{\frac{3}{4} \times \frac{4}{3}}$$

Multiply the numerator and denominator by the reciprocal of $\frac{3}{4}$, which is $\frac{4}{3}$.

$$= \frac{\frac{7}{8} \times \frac{4}{3}}{1}$$

$\frac{3}{4} \times \frac{4}{3} = 1$

$$= \frac{7}{8} \times \frac{4}{3}$$

So, $\frac{7}{8} \div \frac{3}{4} = \frac{7}{8} \times \frac{4}{3}$. These examples suggest the following rule.

Divide by Fractions

Key Concept

Words To divide by a fraction, multiply by its multiplicative inverse, or reciprocal.

Examples

Numbers	Algebra
$\frac{7}{8} \div \frac{3}{4} = \frac{7}{8} \cdot \frac{4}{3}$	$\frac{a}{b} \div \frac{c}{d} = \frac{a}{b} \cdot \frac{d}{c}$, where $b, c, d \neq 0$

EXAMPLE Divide by a Fraction

1 **Find $\frac{3}{4} \div \frac{1}{2}$. Write in simplest form.**

Estimate $1 \div \frac{1}{2} = \blacksquare$

Think: How many groups of $\frac{1}{2}$ are in 1? $1 \div \frac{1}{2} = 2$

$\frac{3}{4} \div \frac{1}{2} = \frac{3}{4} \cdot \frac{2}{1}$ Multiply by the reciprocal of $\frac{1}{2}$, which is $\frac{2}{1}$.

$= \frac{3}{\cancel{4}_2} \cdot \frac{\cancel{2}^1}{1}$ Divide 4 and 2 by their GCF, 2.

$= \frac{3}{2}$ or $1\frac{1}{2}$ Multiply.

Check for Reasonableness $1\frac{1}{2} \approx 2$ ✔

CHECK Your Progress

Divide. Write in simplest form.

a. $\frac{3}{4} \div \frac{1}{4}$ b. $\frac{4}{5} \div \frac{8}{9}$ c. $\frac{5}{6} \div \frac{2}{3}$

To divide by a mixed number, first rename the mixed number as an improper fraction. Then multiply the first fraction by the reciprocal, or multiplicative inverse, of the second fraction.

EXAMPLE Divide by Mixed Numbers

2 **Find $\frac{2}{3} \div 3\frac{1}{3}$. Write in simplest form.**

Estimate $\frac{1}{2} \div 3 = \frac{1}{2} \times \frac{1}{3}$ or $\frac{1}{6}$

$\frac{2}{3} \div 3\frac{1}{3} = \frac{2}{3} \div \frac{10}{3}$ Rename $3\frac{1}{3}$ as an improper fraction.

$= \frac{2}{3} \cdot \frac{3}{10}$ Multiply by the reciprocal of $\frac{10}{3}$, which is $\frac{3}{10}$.

$= \frac{\cancel{2}^1}{\cancel{3}_1} \cdot \frac{\cancel{3}^1}{\cancel{10}_5}$ Divide out common factors.

$= \frac{1}{5}$ Multiply.

Check for Reasonableness $\frac{1}{5}$ is close to $\frac{1}{6}$. ✔

CHECK Your Progress

Divide. Write in simplest form.

d. $5 \div 1\frac{1}{3}$ e. $-\frac{3}{4} \div 1\frac{1}{2}$ f. $2\frac{1}{3} \div 5$

g. **NUTS** In planning for a party, $5\frac{1}{4}$ pounds of cashews will be divided into $\frac{3}{4}$-pound bags. How many such bags can be made?

Study Tip

Dividing by a Whole Number
Remember that a whole number can be written as a fraction with a 1 in the denominator.

So, $2\frac{1}{3} \div 5$ can be rewritten as $2\frac{1}{3} \div \frac{5}{1}$.

3 WOODWORKING **Students in a woodworking class are making butterfly houses. The side pieces of the house need to be $8\frac{1}{4}$ inches long. How many side pieces can be cut from a board measuring $49\frac{1}{2}$ inches long?**

To find how many side pieces can be cut, divide $49\frac{1}{2}$ by $8\frac{1}{4}$.

Estimate Use compatible numbers. $48 \div 8 = 6$

$49\frac{1}{2} \div 8\frac{1}{4} = \frac{99}{2} \div \frac{33}{4}$ — Rename the mixed numbers as improper fractions.

$= \frac{99}{2} \cdot \frac{4}{33}$ — Multiply by the reciprocal of $\frac{33}{4}$, which is $\frac{4}{33}$.

$= \frac{\overset{3}{\cancel{99}}}{\underset{1}{\cancel{2}}} \cdot \frac{\overset{2}{\cancel{4}}}{\underset{1}{\cancel{33}}}$ — Divide out common factors.

$= \frac{6}{1}$ or 6 — Multiply.

So, 6 side pieces can be cut.

Check for Reasonableness The answer matches the estimate. ✔

CHECK Your Progress

h. **FOOD** Suppose a small box of cereal contains $12\frac{2}{3}$ cups of cereal. How many $1\frac{1}{3}$-cup servings are in the box?

i. **MEASUREMENT** The area of a rectangular bedroom is $146\frac{7}{8}$ square feet. If the width of the bedroom is $11\frac{3}{4}$ feet, find the length.

CHECK Your Understanding

Examples 1–3 (pp. 266–267)

Divide. Write in simplest form.

1. $\frac{1}{8} \div \frac{1}{3}$
2. $\frac{3}{5} \div \frac{1}{4}$
3. $3 \div \frac{6}{7}$
4. $\frac{3}{4} \div 6$
5. $\frac{1}{2} \div 7\frac{1}{2}$
6. $\frac{4}{7} \div 1\frac{2}{7}$
7. $5\frac{3}{5} \div 4\frac{2}{3}$
8. $6\frac{1}{2} \div 3\frac{5}{7}$

Example 2 (p. 266)

9. **FOOD** Deandre has 7 apples, and each apple is divided evenly into eighths. How many apple slices does Deandre have?

Example 3 (p. 267)

10. **WALKING** On Saturday, Lindsay walked $3\frac{1}{2}$ miles in $1\frac{2}{5}$ hours. What was her walking pace, in miles per hour?

Practice and Problem Solving

HOMEWORK HELP	
For Exercises	See Examples
11–14	1
15–32	2, 3

Divide. Write in simplest form.

11. $\frac{3}{8} \div \frac{6}{7}$
12. $\frac{5}{9} \div \frac{5}{6}$
13. $\frac{2}{3} \div \frac{1}{2}$
14. $\frac{7}{8} \div \frac{3}{4}$
15. $6 \div \frac{1}{2}$
16. $\frac{4}{9} \div 2$
17. $2\frac{2}{3} \div 4$
18. $5 \div 1\frac{1}{3}$

19. **FOOD** Mason has 8 cups of popcorn kernels to divide into $\frac{2}{3}$-cup portions. How many portions will there be?

20. **MOVIES** Cheryl is organizing her movie collection. If each movie case is $\frac{3}{4}$ inch wide, how many movies can fit on a shelf 5 feet wide?

Divide. Write in simplest form.

21. $\frac{2}{3} \div 2\frac{1}{2}$
22. $\frac{8}{9} \div 5\frac{1}{3}$
23. $4\frac{1}{2} \div 6\frac{3}{4}$
24. $5\frac{2}{7} \div 2\frac{1}{7}$
25. $3\frac{4}{5} \div 1\frac{1}{3}$
26. $9\frac{1}{2} \div 2\frac{5}{6}$
27. $5\frac{1}{5} \div \frac{2}{3}$
28. $6\frac{7}{8} \div \frac{3}{4}$

29. **ICE CREAM** Vinh bought $4\frac{1}{2}$ gallons of ice cream to serve at his birthday party. If a pint is $\frac{1}{8}$ of a gallon, how many pint-sized servings can be made?

30. **BEVERAGES** William has $8\frac{1}{4}$ cups of fruit juice. If he divides the juice into $\frac{3}{4}$-cup servings, how many servings will he have?

BIRDS **For Exercises 31 and 32, use the table that gives information about several types of birds of prey found at the Woodland Park Zoo in Seattle, Washington.**

Bird	Maximum Weight (lb)
Golden Eagle	$13\frac{9}{10}$
Northern Bald Eagle	$9\frac{9}{10}$
Red-Tailed Hawk	$3\frac{1}{2}$

Source: Woodland Park Zoo

31. How many times as heavy is the Golden Eagle as the Red-tailed Hawk?
32. How many times as heavy is the Golden Eagle as the Northern Bald Eagle?

Real-World Link
Red-tailed hawks are large, stocky birds with long, broad wings and short, broad tails. Females are larger than males and can weigh up to $3\frac{1}{2}$ pounds.
Source: Woodland Park Zoo

Draw a model of each verbal expression and then evaluate the expression. Explain how the model shows the division process.

33. one half divided by two fifths
34. five eighths divided by one fourth
35. one and three eighths divided by one half
36. two and one sixth divided by two thirds

37. **PIZZA** A concession stand sells three types of pizza. The diagram shows how much pizza of each type is left after the concession stand was open for one hour. If the pizza is sold in slices that are $\frac{1}{8}$ of a whole pizza, how many more slices can be sold?

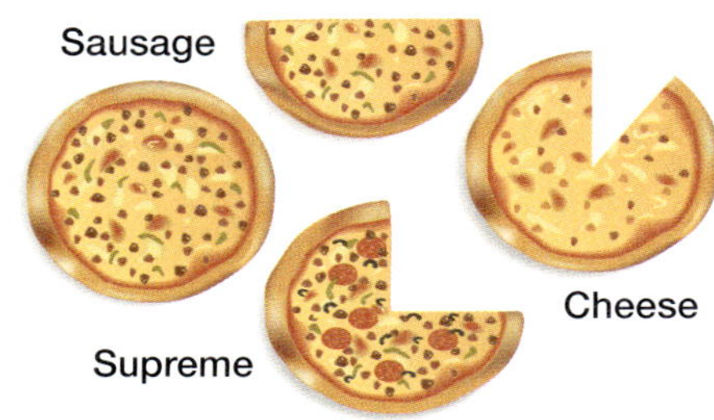

ALGEBRA Evaluate each expression if $g = \frac{1}{6}$, $h = \frac{1}{2}$, and $j = 3\frac{2}{3}$.

38. $j \div h$
39. $g \div j$
40. $3g \div h$
41. $h \div \left(\frac{1}{2}j\right)$

42. **SHOPPING** A supermarket sells pretzels in $\frac{3}{4}$-ounce snack-sized bags or $12\frac{1}{2}$-ounce regular-sized bags. How many times larger is the regular-sized bag than the snack-sized bag?

43. **MEASUREMENT** A recipe calls for $2\frac{2}{3}$ cups of brown sugar and $\frac{2}{3}$ cup of confectioner's sugar. How many times greater is the number of cups of brown sugar in the recipe than of confectioner's sugar?

SCHOOL For Exercises 44 and 45, use the table that shows the number of hours students spend studying each week during the school year.

Weekly Study Hours

Hours	Fraction of Students
none	$\frac{1}{50}$
1–2	$\frac{2}{25}$
3–5	$\frac{11}{50}$
6–7	$\frac{17}{100}$
8–10	$\frac{1}{5}$
Over 10	$\frac{1}{5}$
Not sure	$\frac{3}{25}$

Source: *Time Magazine*

44. How many times greater was the number of students who spent over 10 hours each week studying than those who spent only 1–2 hours each week studying?

45. How many times greater was the number of students who spent 3 or more hours each week studying than those who spent less than 3 hours each week studying?

46. **SCHOOL SUPPLIES** Tara bought a dozen folders. She took $\frac{1}{3}$ of the dozen and then divided the remaining folders equally among her four friends. What fraction of the dozen did each of her four friends receive and how many folders was this per person?

See pages 681, 708.

47. **WEATHER** A meteorologist has issued a thunderstorm warning. So far, the storm has traveled 35 miles in $\frac{1}{2}$ hour. If it is currently 5:00 P.M., and the storm is 105 miles away from you, at what time will the storm reach you? Explain how you solved the problem.

H.O.T. Problems

48. **CHALLENGE** If $\frac{5}{6}$ is divided by a certain fraction $\frac{a}{b}$, the result is $\frac{1}{4}$. What is the fraction $\frac{a}{b}$?

49. **SELECT A TOOL** Reynaldo cut a rope to make the running knot shown. The rope used to make the knot was $1\frac{1}{2}$ feet long and was $\frac{3}{4}$ of the original rope length. Which of the following tools could be used to determine the rope's original length? Justify your selection(s). Then use your tool(s) to find the length.

paper and pencil | model | calculator | real object

50. **FIND THE ERROR** Evan and José are finding $\frac{4}{5} \div \frac{6}{7}$. Who is correct? Explain your reasoning.

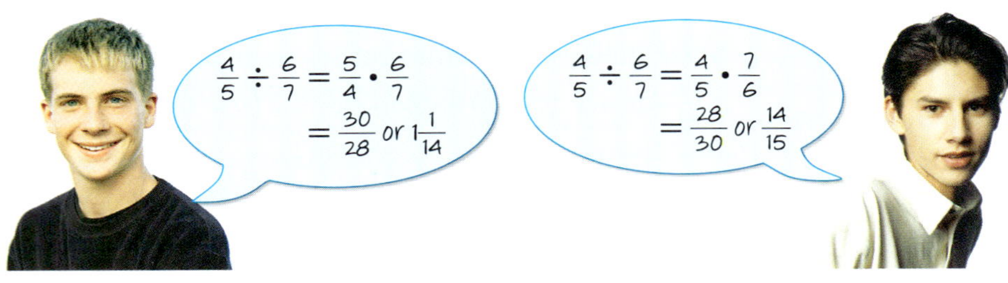

51. **WRITING IN MATH** If you divide a proper fraction by another proper fraction, is it possible to get a mixed number as an answer? Explain your reasoning.

TEST PRACTICE

52. The Corbett family owns 300 acres of land that they plan to rent to people for their horses. How many $7\frac{1}{2}$-acre lots can they make using the 300 acres?

A 21 **C** $40\frac{1}{2}$

B 40 **D** $292\frac{1}{2}$

53. How many $1\frac{1}{8}$-pound boxes of peanuts can be made using $6\frac{3}{4}$ pounds of peanuts?

F 4 **H** 6

G 5 **J** 7

Spiral Review

Find the multiplicative inverse of each number. (Lesson 5-6)

54. $\frac{6}{7}$ 55. $\frac{4}{13}$ 56. 8 57. $5\frac{1}{4}$

58. Find $\frac{1}{10} \times \frac{5}{8}$. Write in simplest form. (Lesson 5-5)

59. **MEASUREMENT** Find the length of a rectangular flower bed if the perimeter is 12 feet and the width is 1.5 feet. (Lesson 3-6)

60. **ANIMALS** An elephant herd can move 50 miles in a day. At this rate, about how many miles can an elephant herd move each hour? (Lesson 1-1)

Problem Solving in Geography

A Traveling We Will Go It's time to complete your project. Use the data you have gathered about schedules and costs to prepare a travel brochure for your vacation destination. Be sure to include a paragraph describing why you chose your vacation spot.

Math Online Unit Project at glencoe.com

CHAPTER 5 Study Guide and Review

Math Online glencoe.com
- STUDY TO GO
- Vocabulary Review

GET READY to Study

Be sure the following Big Ideas are noted in your Foldable.

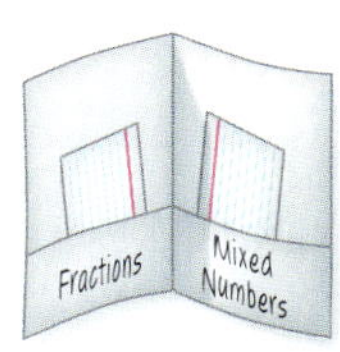

BIG Ideas

Estimating with Fractions (Lesson 5-1)

- When the numerator is much smaller than the denominator, round the fraction to 0.
- When the numerator is about half of the denominator, round the fraction to $\frac{1}{2}$.
- When the numerator is almost as large as the denominator, round the fraction to 1.

Adding and Subtracting Fractions (Lessons 5-2 and 5-3)

- To add or subtract like fractions, add or subtract the numerators and write the result over the denominator.
- To add or subtract unlike fractions, rename the fractions using the LCD. Then add or subtract as with like fractions.
- To add or subtract mixed numbers, first add or subtract the fractions. If necessary, rename them using the LCD. Then add or subtract the whole numbers and simplify if necessary.

Multiplying and Dividing Fractions (Lessons 5-5 and 5-7)

- To multiply fractions, multiply the numerators and multiply the denominators.
- The product of a number and its multiplicative inverse is 1.
- To divide by a fraction, multiply by its multiplicative inverse, or reciprocal.

Solving Equations (Lesson 5-6)

If you multiply each side of an equation by the same nonzero number, the two sides remain equal.

Key Vocabulary

compatible numbers (p. 232)
like fractions (p. 236)
multiplicative inverse (p. 258)
reciprocal (p. 258)
unlike fractions (p. 237)

Vocabulary Check

Choose the correct term or number to complete each sentence.

1. To add like fractions, add the (numerators, denominators).
2. The symbol ≈ means (*approximately, exactly*) *equal to*.
3. When dividing by a fraction, multiply by its (value, reciprocal).
4. When estimating, if the numerator of a fraction is much smaller than the denominator, round the fraction to $\left(0, \frac{1}{2}\right)$.
5. Fractions with different denominators are called (like, unlike) fractions.
6. The multiplicative inverse of $\frac{5}{6}$ is $\left(\frac{6}{5}, -\frac{5}{6}\right)$.
7. The mixed number $2\frac{4}{7}$ can be renamed as $\left(2\frac{7}{7}, 1\frac{11}{7}\right)$.
8. When multiplying fractions, multiply the numerators and (multiply, keep) the denominators.
9. The reciprocal of $\frac{1}{3}$ is $(-3, 3)$.
10. The fractions $\frac{4}{16}$ and $\frac{2}{4}$ are (like, unlike) fractions.
11. Another word for multiplicative inverse is (reciprocal, denominator).
12. The fraction $\frac{x}{2}$ can be read x *multiplied by* $\left(2, \frac{1}{2}\right)$.

CHAPTER 5 Study Guide and Review

Lesson-by-Lesson Review

5-1 Estimating with Fractions (pp. 230–235)

Estimate.

13. $2\frac{9}{10} \div 1\frac{1}{8}$
14. $6\frac{2}{9} - 5\frac{1}{7}$
15. $\frac{13}{15} \times \frac{1}{5}$
16. $\frac{1}{2} + \frac{3}{8}$
17. $\frac{1}{2} \cdot 25$
18. $15\frac{6}{7} \div 7\frac{1}{3}$
19. **MEASUREMENT** Gina wishes to carpet her living room. It has a length of $18\frac{5}{8}$ feet and the width of her living room is $9\frac{1}{2}$ feet. About how many square feet of carpet would be needed for her living room?
20. **FOOTBALL** Jamil practiced football for $1\frac{3}{4}$ hours on Saturday and $2\frac{2}{3}$ hours on Sunday. About how many more hours did he practice on Sunday than on Saturday?

Example 1 Estimate $5\frac{1}{12} + 2\frac{5}{6}$.

1 is much smaller than 12, so $5\frac{1}{12} \approx 5$.

5 is almost as large as 6, so $2\frac{5}{6} \approx 3$.

$5\frac{1}{12} + 2\frac{5}{6} \approx 5 + 3$ or 8

The sum is *about* 8.

Example 2 Estimate $\frac{7}{8} - \frac{4}{7}$.

7 is almost as large as 8, so $\frac{7}{8} \approx 1$.

4 is about half of 7, so $\frac{4}{7} \approx \frac{1}{2}$.

$\frac{7}{8} - \frac{4}{7} \approx 1 - \frac{1}{2}$ or $\frac{1}{2}$

The difference is *about* $\frac{1}{2}$.

5-2 Adding and Subtracting Fractions (pp. 236–241)

Add or subtract. Write in simplest form.

21. $\frac{2}{6} - \frac{1}{6}$
22. $\frac{3}{7} + \frac{9}{14}$
23. $\frac{1}{9} + \frac{5}{9}$
24. $\frac{9}{10} - \frac{3}{10}$
25. $\frac{5}{8} - \frac{5}{12}$
26. $\frac{3}{4} + \frac{7}{20}$
27. **RAIN** At 8 A.M., Della's rain gauge read $\frac{1}{8}$ inch. By 4 P.M., the gauge read $\frac{3}{4}$ inch. How much rain fell between 8 A.M. and 4 P.M.?
28. **PIZZA** Owen ate $\frac{1}{8}$ of a pizza Tuesday night. The next day, he ate an additional $\frac{1}{2}$ of the pizza. What fraction of the pizza has he eaten?

Example 3 Find $\frac{1}{6} + \frac{2}{3}$.

Use a model.

$\frac{1}{6}$

$+\frac{2}{3}$

$\frac{5}{6}$

Example 4 Find $\frac{3}{10} - \frac{1}{4}$.

$\frac{3}{10} - \frac{1}{4} = \frac{6}{20} - \frac{5}{20}$ Rename the fractions using the LCD, 20.

$= \frac{1}{20}$ Subtract the numerators.

Mixed Problem Solving
For mixed problem-solving practice, see page 708.

5-3 Adding and Subtracting Mixed Numbers (pp. 242–246)

Add or subtract. Write in simplest form.

29. $3\frac{2}{15} + 6\frac{9}{15}$
30. $4\frac{1}{3} - 2\frac{2}{3}$
31. $8\frac{2}{7} + 1\frac{6}{7}$
32. $7\frac{11}{12} - 4\frac{3}{12}$
33. $7\frac{3}{5} - 5\frac{1}{3}$
34. $5\frac{3}{4} + 1\frac{1}{6}$
35. $3\frac{5}{8} + 11\frac{1}{2}$
36. $4\frac{3}{10} - 2\frac{4}{5}$
37. **BABYSITTING** Lucas watched his little sister for $2\frac{1}{2}$ hours on Friday, $3\frac{2}{3}$ hours on Saturday, and $1\frac{3}{4}$ hours on Sunday. How many hours did Lucas watch his little sister?

Example 5 Find $5\frac{2}{3} + 3\frac{1}{2}$.

$5\frac{2}{3} + 3\frac{1}{2} = 5\frac{4}{6} + 3\frac{3}{6}$ Rename the fractions.

$= 8\frac{7}{6}$ Add the whole numbers and add the fractions.

$= 9\frac{1}{6}$ $8\frac{7}{6} = 8 + 1\frac{1}{6}$ or $9\frac{1}{6}$

Example 6 Find $4\frac{1}{5} - 2\frac{3}{5}$.

$4\frac{1}{5} - 2\frac{3}{5} = 3\frac{6}{5} - 2\frac{3}{5}$ Rename $4\frac{1}{5}$ as $3\frac{6}{5}$.

$= 1\frac{3}{5}$ Subtract the whole numbers and subtract the fractions.

5-4 PSI: Eliminate Possibilities (pp. 248–249)

Solve by eliminating possibilities.

38. **SCHOOL** It takes Beth 15 minutes to walk to school, $\frac{1}{2}$ mile away. What is her walking pace?
    - A 2 miles per hour
    - B 1 mile per hour
    - C 7.5 miles per hour
    - D 30 miles per hour
39. **COOKING** Which of the following would yield a larger batch of bagels?
    - F Multiply a recipe by $\frac{1}{2}$.
    - G Divide a recipe by $\frac{1}{2}$.
    - H Multiply a recipe by $\frac{3}{4}$.
    - J Divide a recipe by 3.

Example 7 **A group of friends went to a theme park. Six of the friends rode the Ferris wheel. If this was $\frac{2}{3}$ of the group, how many friends were in the group?**

A 3

B 6

C 9

D 12

Since 6 friends rode the Ferris wheel and this was $\frac{2}{3}$ of the total number of friends in the group, the number of friends in the group must be greater than 6. So, eliminate choices A and B.

If there were 12 friends in the group, the 6 that rode the Ferris wheel would represent $\frac{1}{2}$ of the group. So, eliminate choice D.

Choice C is the only remaining possibility. Since 6 out of 9 is $\frac{6}{9}$ or $\frac{2}{3}$, C is correct.

Chapter 5 Study Guide and Review

5-5 Multiplying Fractions and Mixed Numbers (pp. 252–257)

Multiply. Write in simplest form.

40. $\frac{3}{5} \times \frac{2}{7}$
41. $\frac{5}{12} \times \frac{4}{9}$
42. $\frac{3}{5} \times \frac{10}{21}$
43. $4 \times \frac{13}{20}$
44. $2\frac{1}{3} \times \frac{3}{4}$
45. $4\frac{1}{2} \times 2\frac{1}{12}$
46. **FOOD** An average slice of American cheese is about $\frac{1}{8}$ inch thick. What is the height of a package containing 20 slices?

Example 8 Find $\frac{5}{9} \times \frac{2}{3}$.

$\frac{5}{9} \times \frac{2}{3} = \frac{5 \times 2}{9 \times 3}$ Multiply the numerators and multiply the denominators.

$= \frac{10}{27}$ Simplify.

Example 9 Find $3\frac{1}{2} \times 2\frac{3}{4}$.

$3\frac{1}{2} \times 2\frac{3}{4} = \frac{7}{2} \times \frac{11}{4}$ Rename $3\frac{1}{2}$ and $2\frac{3}{4}$.

$= \frac{7 \times 11}{2 \times 4}$ Multiply the numerators and multiply the denominators.

$= \frac{77}{8}$ or $9\frac{5}{8}$ Simplify.

5-6 Algebra: Solving Equations (pp. 258–263)

Find the multiplicative inverse of each number.

47. $\frac{7}{12}$
48. 5
49. $3\frac{1}{3}$

Solve each equation. Check your solution.

50. $8 = \frac{w}{2}$
51. $\frac{4}{5}b = 12$
52. $-7.6 = \frac{n}{3}$
53. $\frac{x}{0.3} = 2.5$
54. **BOOKS** Of the books on a shelf, $\frac{2}{3}$ are mysteries. If there are 10 mystery books, how many books are on the shelf?

Example 10 Find the multiplicative inverse of $\frac{9}{5}$.

$\frac{9}{5} \cdot \frac{5}{9} = 1$ The product of $\frac{9}{5}$ and $\frac{5}{9}$ is 1.

The multiplicative inverse of $\frac{9}{5}$ is $\frac{5}{9}$.

Example 11 Solve $\frac{3}{4}g = 2$.

$\frac{3}{4}g = 2$ Write the equation.

$\frac{4}{3} \cdot \frac{3}{4}g = \frac{4}{3} \cdot 2$ Multiply each side by the reciprocal of $\frac{3}{4}$.

$g = \frac{8}{3}$ or $2\frac{2}{3}$ Simplify.

5-7 Dividing Fractions and Mixed Numbers (pp. 265–270)

Divide. Write in simplest form.

55. $\frac{3}{5} \div \frac{6}{7}$
56. $4 \div \frac{2}{3}$
57. $2\frac{3}{4} \div \frac{5}{6}$
58. $-\frac{2}{5} \div 3$
59. $4\frac{3}{10} \div 2\frac{1}{5}$
60. $-\frac{2}{7} \div \frac{8}{21}$
61. **MEASUREMENT** How many $\frac{1}{8}$-inch lengths are in $6\frac{3}{4}$ inches?

Example 12 Find $2\frac{4}{5} \div \frac{7}{10}$.

$2\frac{4}{5} \div \frac{7}{10} = \frac{14}{5} \div \frac{7}{10}$ Rename $2\frac{4}{5}$.

$= \frac{\overset{2}{\cancel{14}}}{\underset{1}{\cancel{5}}} \cdot \frac{\overset{2}{\cancel{10}}}{\underset{1}{\cancel{7}}}$ Multiply by the reciprocal of $\frac{7}{10}$.

$= \frac{4}{1}$ or 4 Simplify.

CHAPTER 5 Practice Test

Math Online glencoe.com
• Chapter Test

Estimate.

1. $5\frac{7}{9} - 1\frac{2}{13}$
2. $3\frac{1}{12} + 6\frac{5}{7}$
3. $\frac{3}{7} \times \frac{13}{15}$
4. $5\frac{2}{3} \div 1\frac{4}{5}$
5. **BAKING** A restaurant uses $2\frac{3}{4}$ pounds of flour to make a batch of dinner rolls. About how many pounds of flour are needed if 3 batches of dinner rolls are to be made?

Add, subtract, multiply, or divide. Write in simplest form.

6. $\frac{4}{15} + \frac{8}{15}$
7. $\frac{7}{10} - \frac{1}{6}$
8. $\frac{5}{8} \times \frac{2}{5}$
9. $6 \times \frac{8}{21}$
10. $4\frac{5}{12} - 2\frac{1}{12}$
11. $6\frac{7}{9} + 3\frac{5}{12}$
12. $8\frac{4}{7} - 1\frac{5}{14}$
13. $4\frac{5}{6} \times 1\frac{2}{3}$
14. $\frac{8}{9} \div 5\frac{1}{3}$
15. $\frac{1}{6} \div 5$
16. **MULTIPLE CHOICE** Seth drove $5\frac{3}{4}$ miles to the bank, $6\frac{1}{3}$ miles to the post office, and $4\frac{5}{6}$ miles to the park. What is the total distance Seth drove?

    A $15\frac{9}{13}$ miles

    B $\frac{7}{12}$ miles

    C $\frac{11}{12}$ miles

    D $16\frac{11}{12}$ miles

17. **SPORTS** Tyler's football practice lasted $2\frac{1}{2}$ hours. If $\frac{1}{4}$ of the time was spent catching passes, how many hours were spent catching passes?
18. **MEASUREMENT** The floor of a moving van is $11\frac{1}{3}$ feet long and $7\frac{5}{12}$ feet wide. Find the area of the moving van floor.
19. **MULTIPLE CHOICE** For his birthday, Keith received a check from his grandmother. Of this amount, the table shows how he spent or saved the money.

Fraction of Check	How Spent or Saved
$\frac{2}{5}$	spent on baseball cards
$\frac{1}{4}$	spent on a CD
$\frac{7}{20}$	deposited into savings account

Two weeks later, he withdrew $\frac{2}{3}$ of the amount he had deposited into his savings account. What fraction of the original check did he withdraw from his savings account?

F $\frac{2}{3}$

G $\frac{9}{23}$

H $\frac{7}{30}$

J $\frac{7}{40}$

20. **MEASUREMENT** An ounce is $\frac{1}{16}$ of a pound. How many ounces are in $8\frac{3}{4}$ pounds?

ALGEBRA Solve each equation. Check your solution.

21. $\frac{y}{3.7} = 8.1$
22. $6 = \frac{2}{5}m$
23. $\frac{3}{4} = \frac{5}{8}x$
24. $3\frac{1}{6} = \frac{2}{3}p$
25. **MULTIPLE CHOICE** Maria is making a mural that is $9\frac{2}{3}$ feet long. She wants to divide the mural into sections that are each $\frac{5}{8}$ foot. Which equation can be used to find n, the number of sections in Maria's mural?

    A $\frac{5}{8}n = 9\frac{2}{3}$

    B $9\frac{2}{3}n = \frac{5}{8}$

    C $\frac{5}{8} + n = 9\frac{2}{3}$

    D $n - \frac{5}{8} = 9\frac{2}{3}$

CHAPTER 5 Test Practice
Cumulative, Chapters 1–5

Math Online glencoe.com
• Test Practice

PART 1 Multiple Choice

Read each question. Then fill in the correct answer on the answer sheet provided by your teacher or on a sheet of paper.

1. Mrs. Brown needs to make two different desserts for a dinner party. The first recipe requires $2\frac{1}{4}$ cups of flour, and the second recipe requires $\frac{3}{4}$ cup less than the first. Which equation can be used to find n, the number of cups of flour needed for the second recipe?

   A $n = 2\frac{1}{4} - \frac{3}{4}$

   B $n = 2\frac{1}{4} \cdot \frac{3}{4}$

   C $n = 2\frac{1}{4} + \frac{3}{4}$

   D $n = 2\frac{1}{4} \div \frac{3}{4}$

2. Which of the following is true concerning the least common multiple of 6 and 9?

   F It is greater than the least common multiple of 8 and 12.

   G It is greater than the least common multiple of 5 and 15.

   H It is less than the least common multiple of 4 and 6.

   J It is less than the least common multiple of 3 and 4.

3. Kyle's hockey team has 6 sixth graders, 9 seventh graders, and 5 eighth graders. Which statement below is true?

   A One fourth of the team members are sixth graders.

   B More than half of the team members are seventh graders.

   C 25% of the team members are eighth graders.

   D 30% of the team members are seventh graders.

4. The fraction $\frac{5}{6}$ is found between which pair of fractions on a number line?

   F $\frac{1}{4}$ and $\frac{5}{8}$

   G $\frac{1}{3}$ and $\frac{4}{9}$

   H $\frac{11}{12}$ and $\frac{31}{36}$

   J $\frac{7}{12}$ and $\frac{17}{18}$

5. The table shows the distance Kelly swam over a four-day period. What was the total distance, in miles, Kelly swam?

Kelly's Swimming	
Day	**Distance (miles)**
Monday	1.5
Tuesday	$2\frac{3}{4}$
Wednesday	2.3
Thursday	$3\frac{1}{2}$

   A 10.5 miles

   B $10\frac{1}{4}$ miles

   C $10\frac{1}{20}$ miles

   D 9 miles

6. Which of the following gives the correct meaning of the expression $\frac{5}{8} \div \frac{1}{3}$?

   F $\frac{5}{8} \div \frac{1}{3} = \frac{8}{5} \times \frac{3}{1}$

   G $\frac{5}{8} \div \frac{1}{3} = \frac{5}{8} \times \frac{3}{1}$

   H $\frac{5}{8} \div \frac{1}{3} = \frac{5+1}{8+3}$

   J $\frac{5}{8} \div \frac{1}{3} = \frac{5}{8} \times \frac{1}{3}$

Preparing for Standardized Tests

For test-taking strategies and practice, see pages 716–733.

7. What is the value of the expression $(3 + 4)^2 \div 7 - 2 \times 6$?

   A -9
   B -5
   C 30
   D 1

8. Which line contains the ordered pair $(-1, 2)$?

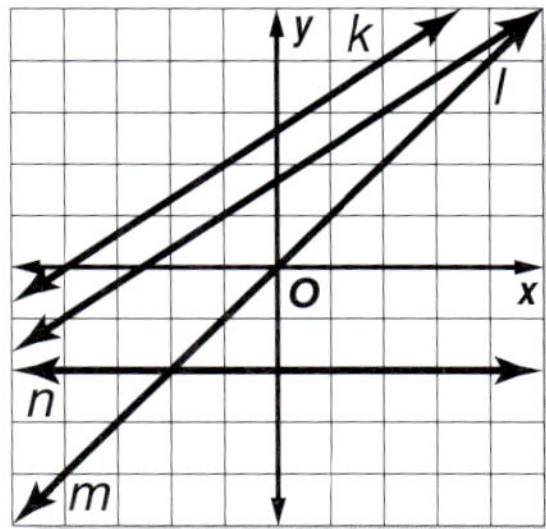

   F Line k
   G Line l
   H Line m
   J Line n

9. A pizza shop tried 45 new types of pizza during the past year and 20% of them became popular. Which best represents the fraction of pizzas that did *not* become popular?

   A $\frac{1}{5}$
   B $\frac{4}{9}$
   C $\frac{3}{5}$
   D $\frac{4}{5}$

TEST-TAKING TIP

Question 9 Be sure to pay attention to emphasized words, or words that are italicized. In Question 9, you are asked to find which answer is *not* correct.

PART 2 Short Response/Grid In

Record your answers on the answer sheet provided by your teacher or on a sheet of paper.

10. Write an equation using two variables to show the relationship between the position x and the value of a term y.

Position (x)	1	2	3	4	5	n
Value of Term (y)	5	9	13	17	21	

11. Evan runs $2\frac{3}{8}$ miles each week. He runs $\frac{3}{4}$ mile on Mondays and $\frac{3}{4}$ mile on Tuesdays. How far does he run, in miles, if the only other day he runs each week is Thursday?

12. Find $15 \div (-5)$.

PART 3 Extended Response

Record your answers on the answer sheet provided by your teacher or on a sheet of paper. Show your work.

13. A box of laundry detergent contains 35 cups. It takes $1\frac{1}{4}$ cups per load of laundry.

    a. Write an equation to represent how many loads ℓ you can wash with one box.

    b. How many loads can you wash with one box?

    c. How many loads can you wash with 3 boxes?

NEED EXTRA HELP?													
If You Missed Question...	1	2	3	4	5	6	7	8	9	10	11	12	13
Go to Lesson...	5-2	4-8	4-6	4-9	4-5	5-7	1-4	3-7	4-6	1-10	5-2	2-8	5-7

Unit 3

Algebra and Number Sense: Proportions and Percents

Focus

Develop an understanding of and apply proportionality.

CHAPTER 6
Ratios and Proportions

BIG Idea Use ratio and proportionality to solve problems, including those with tables and graphs.

CHAPTER 7
Applying Percents

BIG Idea Solve percent problems using ratios and proportions.

Problem Solving in Art

Real-World Unit Project

It's Golden! On this adventure, you'll learn about the Golden Ratio in art and nature. Along the way, you'll research how artists use the Golden Ratio to create masterpieces. Also, you'll learn how the Golden Ratio occurs in nature as well. Our adventure will begin soon, so pack your art supplies and math tool kit. This is one golden adventure!

Math Online Log on to glencoe.com to begin.

Ratios and Proportions

BIG Idea

- Use ratio and proportionality to solve problems, including those with tables and graphs.

Key Vocabulary

rate (p. 287)
ratio (p. 282)
proportional (p. 310)

Real-World Link

Statues A bronze replica of the Statue of Liberty can be found in Paris, France. The replica has the ratio 1 : 4 with the Statue of Liberty that stands in New York Harbor.

Ratios and Proportions Make this Foldable to help you organize your notes. Begin with a sheet of notebook paper.

1. **Fold** lengthwise to the holes.

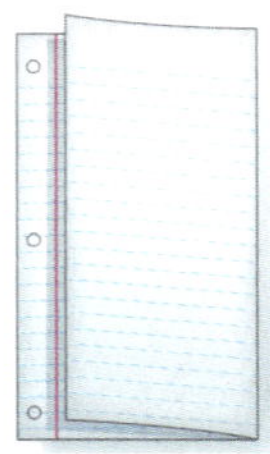

2. **Cut** along the top line and then make equal cuts to form 7 tabs.

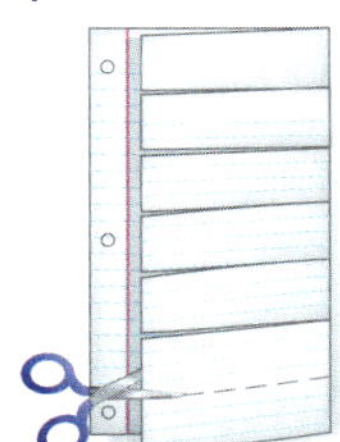

3. **Label** the major topics as shown.

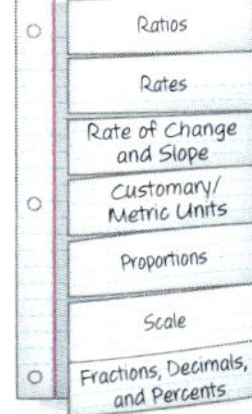

GET READY for Chapter 6

Diagnose Readiness You have two options for checking Prerequisite Skills.

Option 2

Math Online Take the Online Readiness Quiz at glencoe.com.

Option 1

Take the Quick Quiz below. Refer to the Quick Review for help.

QUICK Quiz

Evaluate each expression. Round to the nearest tenth if necessary. (Lesson 1-4)

1. $100 \times 25 \div 52$
2. $10 \div 4 \times 31$
3. $\frac{63 \times 4}{34}$
4. $\frac{2 \times 100}{68}$

Write each fraction in simplest form. (Lesson 4-4)

5. $\frac{9}{45}$
6. $\frac{16}{24}$
7. $\frac{38}{46}$
8. **AGES** Mikhail is 14 years old. His father is 49 years old. What fraction, in simplest form, of his father's age is Mikhail? (Lesson 4-4)

Write each decimal as a fraction in simplest form. (Lesson 4-5)

9. 0.78
10. 0.320
11. 0.06
12. **SAVINGS** Belinda has saved 0.92 of the cost of a new bicycle. What fraction, in simplest form, represents her savings? (Lesson 4-5)

Multiply. (Lesson 1-2)

13. 4.5×10^2
14. 1.78×10^3
15. 0.22×10^4
16. 0.03×10^5

QUICK Review

Example 1 **Evaluate $15 \times 32 \div 40$.**

$15 \times 32 \div 40 = 480 \div 40$ Multiply 15 by 32.

$= 12$ Divide.

Example 2 **Write $\frac{16}{44}$ in simplest form.**

$\frac{16}{44} = \frac{4}{11}$ (÷ 4 numerator and denominator) Divide the numerator and denominator by their GCF, 4.

Example 3 **Write 0.62 as a fraction in simplest form.**

$0.62 = \frac{62}{100}$ 0.62 is sixty-two hundredths.

$= \frac{31}{50}$ Divide the numerator and denominator by their GCF, 2.

Example 4 **Find 3.9×10^3.**

$3.9 \times 10^3 = 3.900$ Move the decimal point 3 places to the right. Annex two zeros.

$= 3{,}900$

6-1 Ratios

MAIN IDEA

Write ratios as fractions in simplest form and determine whether two ratios are equivalent.

New Vocabulary

ratio
equivalent ratios

Math Online

glencoe.com

- Extra Examples
- Personal Tutor
- Self-Check Quiz
- Reading in the Content Area

GET READY for the Lesson

SCHOOL The student-teacher ratio of a school compares the total number of students to the total number of teachers.

Middle School	Students	Teachers
Prairie Lake	396	22
Green Brier	510	30

1. Write the student-teacher ratio of Prairie Lake Middle School as a fraction. Then write this fraction with a denominator of 1.
2. Can you determine which school has the lower student-teacher ratio by examining just the number of teachers at each school? just the number of students at each school? Explain.

Ratios — Key Concept

Words A **ratio** is a comparison of two quantities by division.

Examples

Numbers 3 to 4 3:4 $\frac{3}{4}$

Algebra a to b $a:b$ $\frac{a}{b}$

Ratios can express part to part, part to whole, or whole to part relationships and are often written as fractions in simplest form.

EXAMPLE Write Ratios in Simplest Form

1 GRILLING **Seasonings are often added to meat prior to grilling. Using the recipe, write a ratio comparing the amount of garlic powder to the amount of dried oregano as a fraction in simplest form.**

$$\frac{\text{garlic powder}}{\text{dried oregano}} \quad \frac{4 \text{ tsp}}{6 \text{ tsp}} = \frac{\overset{2}{\cancel{4 \text{ tsp}}}}{\underset{3}{\cancel{6 \text{ tsp}}}} \text{ or } \frac{2}{3}$$

The ratio of garlic powder to dried oregano is $\frac{2}{3}$, 2:3, or 2 to 3. That is, for every 2 units of garlic powder there are 3 units of dried oregano.

CHECK Your Progress

Use the recipe to write each ratio as a fraction in simplest form.

a. pepper : garlic powder

b. oregano : pepper

Ratios that express the same relationship between two quantities are called **equivalent ratios**. Equivalent ratios have the same value.

EXAMPLE Identify Equivalent Ratios

Study Tip

Writing Ratios Ratios greater than 1 are expressed as improper fractions and not as mixed numbers.

2 **Determine whether the ratios 250 miles in 4 hours and 500 miles in 8 hours are equivalent.**

METHOD 1 **Compare the ratios written in simplest form.**

250 miles : 4 hours $= \frac{250 \div 2}{4 \div 2}$ or $\frac{125}{2}$ Divide the numerator and denominator by the GCF, 2

500 miles : 8 hours $= \frac{500 \div 4}{8 \div 4}$ or $\frac{125}{2}$ Divide the numerator and denominator by the GCF, 4

The ratios simplify to the same fraction.

METHOD 2 **Look for a common multiplier relating the two ratios.**

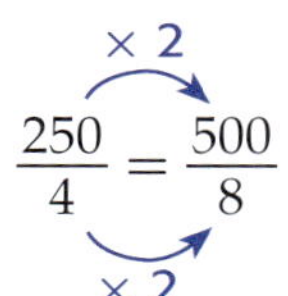

$\frac{250}{4} = \frac{500}{8}$ (× 2, × 2) The numerator and denominator of the ratios are related by the same multiplier, 2.

The ratios are equivalent.

CHOOSE Your Method

Determine whether the ratios are equivalent.

c. 20 nails for every 5 shingles, 12 nails for every 3 shingles

d. 2 cups flour to 8 cups sugar, 8 cups flour to 14 cups sugar

Real-World EXAMPLE

Real-World Link In 2006, the New York Yankees had a 0.285 batting average as a team.

Source: Major League Baseball

3 **BASEBALL** **Derek Jeter of the New York Yankees had 32 hits out of 93 times at bat. Jorge Posada had 11 hits out of 31 times at bat. Are these ratios equivalent? Justify your answer.**

Derek Jeter

$32:93 = \frac{32}{93}$

Jorge Posada

$11:31 = \frac{11 \times 3}{31 \times 3}$ or $\frac{33}{93}$

Since $\frac{32}{93} \neq \frac{33}{93}$, the ratios are not equivalent.

CHECK Your Progress

e. **SWIMMING** A community pool requires there to be at least 3 lifeguards for every 20 swimmers. There are 60 swimmers and 9 lifeguards at the pool. Is this the correct number of lifeguards based on the above requirement? Justify your answer.

CHECK Your Understanding

Example 1 (p. 282)

FIELD TRIPS **Use the information in the table to write each ratio as a fraction in simplest form.**

Field Trip Statistics	
Students	180
Adults	24
Buses	4

1. adults : students
2. students : buses
3. buses : people
4. adults : people

Example 2 (p. 283)

Determine whether the ratios are equivalent. Explain.

5. 12 out of 20 doctors agree
   6 out of 10 doctors agree
6. 2 DVDs to 7 CDs
   10 DVDs to 15 CDs

Example 3 (p. 283)

7. **SHOPPING** A grocery store has a brand-name cereal on sale at 2 boxes for \$5. You buy 6 boxes and are charged \$20. Based on the price ratio indicated, were you charged the correct amount? Justify your answer.

Practice and Problem Solving

HOMEWORK HELP	
For Exercises	See Examples
8–17	1
18–21	2
22–23	3

SOCCER **Use the Madison Mavericks team statistics to write each ratio as a fraction in simplest form.**

Madison Mavericks Team Statistics	
Wins	10
Losses	12
Ties	8

8. wins : losses
9. losses : ties
10. losses : games played
11. wins : games played

CARNIVALS **Use the following information to write each ratio as a fraction in simplest form.**

At its annual carnival, Brighton Middle School had 6 food booths and 15 games booths. A total of 66 adults and 165 children attended. The carnival raised a total of \$1,600. Of this money, \$550 came from ticket sales.

12. children : adults
13. food booths : games booths
14. children : games booths
15. booths : money raised
16. people : children
17. non-ticket sale money : total money

Determine whether the ratios are equivalent. Explain.

18. 20 female lions to 8 male lions,
    34 female lions to 10 male lions
19. \$4 for every 16 ounces,
    \$10 for every 40 ounces
20. 27 students to 6 microscopes,
    18 students to 4 microscopes
21. 8 roses to 6 babies breath,
    12 roses to 10 babies breath
22. **BAKING** It is recommended that a ham be baked 1 hour for every 2 pounds of meat. Latrell baked a 9-pound ham for 4.5 hours. Did he follow the above recommendation? Justify your answer.
23. **FISHING** Kamala catches two similar looking fish. The larger fish is 12 inches long and 3 inches wide. The smaller fish is 6 inches long and 1 inch wide. Do these fish have an equivalent length to width ratio? Justify your answer.

MEASUREMENT The *aspect ratio* of a television is a ratio comparing the width and height. A wide screen television has an aspect ratio of 16:9. Televisions without the same aspect ratio crop the image to fit the screen. Determine which television sizes have a full 16:9 image. Justify your answers.

24. 32″ × 18″
25. 71″ × 42″
26. 48″ × 36″

MAMMALS For Exercises 27 and 28, use the information below.

Mammal	Average Brain Weight (lb)	Average Body Weight (lb)
Adult Human	3	150
Adult Orca Whale	12	5,500

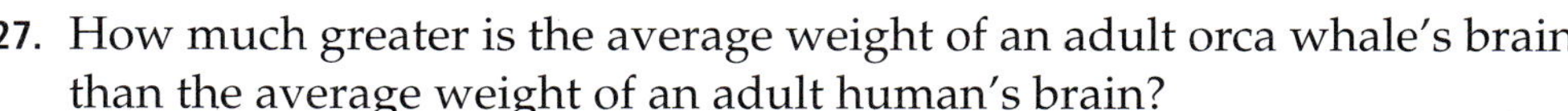

27. How much greater is the average weight of an adult orca whale's brain than the average weight of an adult human's brain?

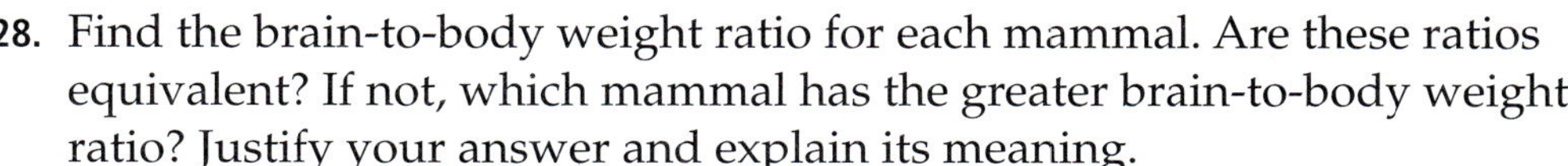

28. Find the brain-to-body weight ratio for each mammal. Are these ratios equivalent? If not, which mammal has the greater brain-to-body weight ratio? Justify your answer and explain its meaning.

Real-World Link An orca whale, also called a killer whale, is not really a whale, but a dolphin. Its average birth weight is 300 pounds.

29. **MUSIC** The pitch of a musical note is measured by the number of sound waves per second, or *hertz*. If the ratio of the frequencies of two notes can be simplified, the two notes are harmonious. Use the information at the right to find if notes E and G are harmonious. Explain.

E : 330 Hertz

G : 396 Hertz

30. **FOOD** The ratio of the number of cups of chopped onion to the number of cups of chopped cilantro in a salsa recipe is 4:3. If the recipe calls for $\frac{2}{3}$ cup chopped onion, how many cups of chopped cilantro are needed?

ANALYZE TABLES For Exercises 31–33, use the table below that shows the logging statistics for three areas of forest.

Area	Estimated Number of Trees Left to Grow	Estimated Number of Trees Removed for Timber
A	440	1,200
B	1,625	3,750
C	352	960

31. For which two areas was the growth-to-removal ratio the same? Explain.
32. Which area had the greatest growth-to-removal ratio? Justify your answer.
33. Find the additional number of trees that should be planted and left to grow in area A so that its growth-to-removal ratio is the same as area B's. Justify your answer.

EXTRA PRACTICE
See pages 681, 709.

H.O.T. Problems

34. **FIND THE ERROR** Cleveland and Luis are determining whether the ratios $\frac{6}{4}$ and $\frac{18}{16}$ are equivalent. Who is correct? Explain.

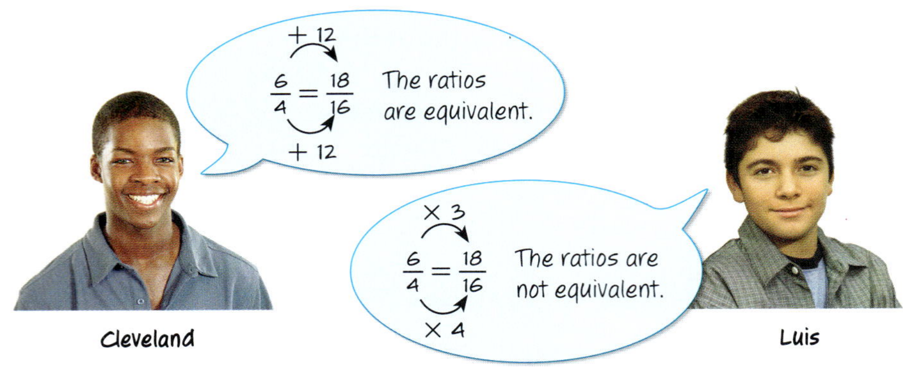

35. **CHALLENGE** Find the missing number in the following pattern. Explain your reasoning. (*Hint*: Look at the ratios of successive numbers.)

20, 40, 120, 480, ■

36. **WRITING IN MATH** Refer to the application in Exercises 31–33. What would a growth-to-removal ratio greater than 1 indicate?

TEST PRACTICE

37. Which of the following ratios does *not* describe a relationship between the marbles in the jar?

A 8 white : 5 black

B 2 white : 5 black

C 5 black : 13 total

D 8 white : 13 total

38. A class of 24 students has 15 boys. What ratio compares the number of girls to boys in the class?

F 3:5 **H** 3:8

G 5:3 **J** 8:3

Spiral Review

39. Find $1\frac{4}{7} \div 1\frac{5}{6}$. Write in simplest form. (Lesson 5-7)

ALGEBRA Solve each equation. Check your solution. (Lesson 5-6)

40. $\frac{y}{4} = 7$

41. $\frac{1}{3}x = \frac{5}{9}$

42. $4 = \frac{p}{2.7}$

43. $2\frac{5}{6} = \frac{1}{2}a$

44. **MONEY** Grant and his brother put together their money to buy a present for their mom. If they had a total of \$18 and Grant contributed \$10, how much did his brother contribute? (Lesson 3-2)

GET READY for the Next Lesson

PREREQUISITE SKILL Divide. (p. 676)

45. 9.8 ÷ 2

46. \$4.30 ÷ 5

47. \$12.40 ÷ 40

48. 27.36 ÷ 3.2

6-2 Rates

MAIN IDEA

Determine unit rates.

New Vocabulary

rate
unit rate

Math Online

glencoe.com

- Extra Examples
- Personal Tutor
- Self-Check Quiz

MINI Lab

Choose a partner and take turns taking each other's pulse for 2 minutes.

1. Count the number of beats for each of you.
2. Write the ratio *beats* to *minutes* as a fraction.

A ratio that compares two quantities with different kinds of units is called a **rate**.

$\frac{\text{160 beats}}{\text{2 minutes}}$ — The units *beats* and *minutes* are different.

When a rate is simplified so that it has a denominator of 1 unit, it is called a **unit rate**.

$\frac{\text{80 beats}}{\text{1 minute}}$ — The denominator is 1 unit.

The table below shows some common unit rates.

Rate	Unit Rate	Abbreviation	Name
$\frac{\text{number of miles}}{\text{1 hour}}$	miles per hour	mi/h or mph	average speed
$\frac{\text{number of miles}}{\text{1 gallon}}$	miles per gallon	mi/gal or mpg	gas mileage
$\frac{\text{number of dollars}}{\text{1 pound}}$	price per pound	dollars/lb	unit price
$\frac{\text{number of dollars}}{\text{1 hour}}$	dollars per hour	dollars/h	hourly wage

Real-World EXAMPLE Find a Unit Rate

1 WORKING Desiree earns \$280 in 40 hours. What is her hourly pay rate?

$\$280 \text{ in } 40 \text{ hours} = \frac{\$280}{40 \text{ h}}$ — Write the rate as a fraction.

$= \frac{\$280 \div 40}{40 \text{ h} \div 40}$ — Divide the numerator and the denominator by 40.

$= \frac{\$7}{1 \text{ h}}$ — Simplify.

Desiree's hourly pay rate is \$7.

CHECK Your Progress

Find each unit rate. Round to the nearest hundredth if necessary.

a. \$300 for 6 hours

b. 220 miles on 8 gallons

Real-World EXAMPLE Find a Unit Rate

JUICE **Find the unit price if it costs \$2 for eight juice boxes. Round to the nearest cent if necessary.**

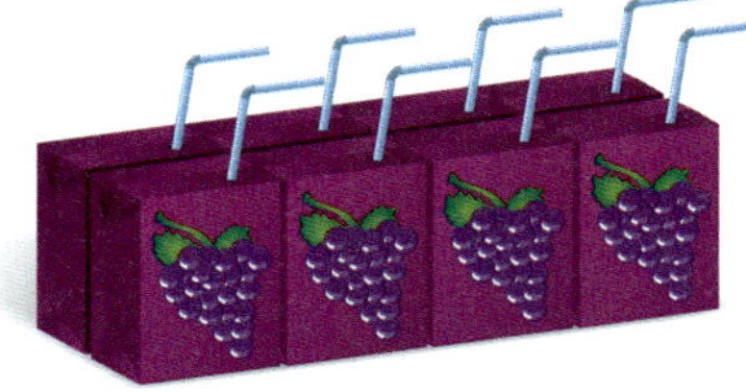

$\$2 \text{ for eight boxes} = \frac{\$2}{8 \text{ boxes}}$ Write the rate as a fraction.

$= \frac{\$2 \div 8}{8 \text{ boxes} \div 8}$ Divide the numerator and the denominator by 8.

$= \frac{\$0.25}{1 \text{ box}}$ Simplify.

The unit price is \$0.25 per juice box.

CHECK Your Progress

c. **ESTIMATION** Find the unit price if a 4-pack of mixed fruit sells for \$2.12.

Unit rates are useful when you want to make comparisons.

TEST EXAMPLE Compare Using Unit Rates

The prices of 3 different bags of dog food are given in the table. Which size bag has the lowest price per pound?

A the 40-lb bag

B the 20-lb bag

C the 8-lb bag

D All three bag sizes have the same price per pound.

Dog Food Prices	
Bag Size (pounds)	Price
40	\$49.00
20	\$23.44
8	\$9.88

Read the Item

To determine the lowest price per pound, find and compare the unit price for each size bag.

Solve the Item

40-pound bag $\$49.00 \div 40 \text{ pounds} = \$1.225 \text{ per pound}$

20-pound bag $\$23.44 \div 20 \text{ pounds} = \$1.172 \text{ per pound}$

8-pound bag $\$9.88 \div 8 \text{ pounds} = \$1.235 \text{ per pound}$

At \$1.172 per pound, the 20-pound bag sells for the lowest price per pound.

The answer is B.

Test-Taking Tip

Alternative Method
One 40-lb bag is equivalent to two 20-lb bags or five 8-lb bags. The cost for one 40-lb bag is \$49, the cost for two 20-lb bags is about 2 × \$23 or \$46, and the cost for five 8-lb bags is about 5 × \$10 or \$50. So the 20-lb bag has the lowest price per pound.

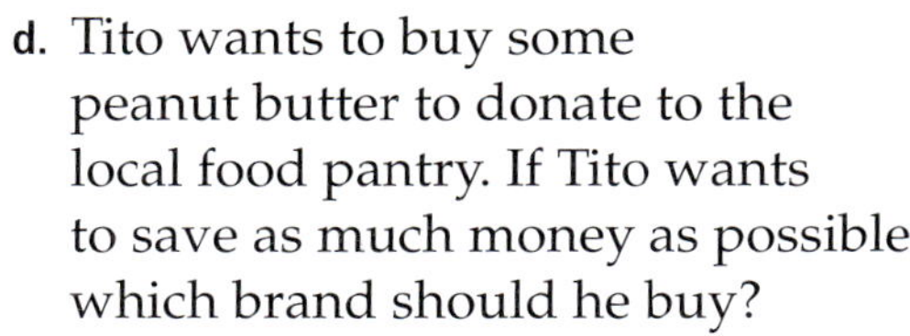

CHECK Your Progress

d. Tito wants to buy some peanut butter to donate to the local food pantry. If Tito wants to save as much money as possible, which brand should he buy?

Peanut Butter Sales	
Brand	**Sale Price**
Nutty	12 ounces for \$2.19
Grandma's	18 ounces for \$2.79
Bee's	28 ounces for \$4.69
Save-A-Lot	40 ounces for \$6.60

F Nutty, because the quality of the peanut butter is better

G Grandma's, because the price per ounce is about \$0.16

H Bee's, because the price per ounce is about \$0.14

J Save-A-Lot, because he wants to buy 40 ounces

Real-World Link Face paint can be made from 1 teaspoon cornstarch and $\frac{1}{2}$ teaspoon each of water and cold cream.

Real-World EXAMPLE Use a Unit Rate

4 FACE PAINTING Lexi painted 3 faces in 12 minutes at the Crafts Fair. At this rate, how many faces can she paint in 40 minutes?

Find the unit rate. Then multiply this unit rate by 40 to find the number of faces she can paint in 40 minutes.

3 faces in 12 minutes $= \frac{3 \text{ faces} \div 12}{12 \text{ min} \div 12} = \frac{0.25 \text{ faces}}{1 \text{ min}}$ Find the unit rate.

$\frac{0.25 \text{ faces}}{1 \text{ min}} \cdot 40 \text{ min} = 10 \text{ faces}$ Divide out the common units.

Lexi can paint 10 faces in 40 minutes.

CHECK Your Progress

e. **SCHOOL SUPPLIES** Kimbel bought 4 notebooks for \$6.32. At this same unit price, how much would he pay for 5 notebooks?

CHECK Your Understanding

Examples 1, 2 (pp. 287–288)

Find each unit rate. Round to the nearest hundredth if necessary.

1. 90 miles on 15 gallons
2. 1,680 kilobytes in 4 minutes
3. 5 pounds for \$2.49
4. 152 feet in 16 seconds

Example 3 (pp. 288–289)

5. **MULTIPLE CHOICE** Four stores offer customers bulk CD rates. Which store offers the best buy?

A CD Express C Music Place

B CD Rack D Music Shop

Bulk CD Offers	
Store	**Offer**
CD Express	4 CDs for \$60
Music Place	6 CDs for \$75
CD Rack	5 CDs for \$70
Music Shop	3 CDs for \$40

Example 4 (p. 289)

6. **TRAVEL** After 3.5 hours, Pasha had traveled 217 miles. At this same speed, how far will she have traveled after 4 hours?

Practice and Problem Solving

HOMEWORK HELP	
For Exercises	See Examples
7–16	1, 2
17–20	3
21–24	4

Find each unit rate. Round to the nearest hundredth if necessary.

7. 360 miles in 6 hours
8. 6,840 customers in 45 days
9. 152 people for 5 classes
10. 815 Calories in 4 servings
11. 45.5 meters in 13 seconds
12. $7.40 for 5 pounds
13. $1.12 for 8.2 ounces
14. 144 miles in 4.5 gallons

15. **ESTIMATION** Estimate the unit rate if 12 pairs of socks sell for $5.79.

16. **ESTIMATION** Estimate the unit rate if a 26-mile marathon was completed in 5 hours.

17. **SPORTS** The results of a swim meet are shown. Who swam the fastest? Explain your reasoning.

Name	Event	Time (s)
Tawni	50-m Freestyle	40.8
Pepita	100-m Butterfly	60.2
Susana	200-m Medley	112.4

18. **MONEY** A grocery store sells three different packages of bottled water. Which package costs the least per bottle? Explain your reasoning.

6-pack for $3.79

9-pack for $4.50

12-pack for $6.89

NUTRITION **For Exercises 19 and 20, use the table at the right.**

19. Which soft drink has about twice the amount of sodium per ounce than the other two? Explain.

20. Which soft drink has the least amount of sugar per ounce? Explain.

Soft Drink Nutritional Information			
Soft Drink	Serving Size (oz)	Sodium (mg)	Sugar (g)
A	12	40	22
B	8	24	15
C	7	42	30

Real-World Link North Carolina has approximately 8.9 million people living in 48,718 square miles.
Source: U.S. Census Bureau

21. **WORD PROCESSING** Ben can type 153 words in 3 minutes. At this rate, how many words can he type in 10 minutes?

22. **FABRIC** Marcus buys 3 yards of fabric for $7.47. Later he realizes that he needs 2 more yards. How much will he pay for the extra fabric?

23. **ESTIMATION** A player scores 87 points in 6 games. At this rate, about how many points would she score in the next 4 games?

24. **JOBS** Dalila earns $94.20, for working 15 hours as a holiday helper wrapping gifts. If she works 18 hours the next week, how much money will she earn?

25. **POPULATION** Use the information at the left. What is the *population density* or number of people per square mile in North Carolina?

ESTIMATION Estimate the unit price for each item. Justify your answers.

26. 

27. 

28. 

29. **RECIPES** A recipe that makes 10 mini-loaves of banana bread calls for $1\frac{1}{4}$ cups flour. How much flour is needed to make 2 dozen mini-loaves using this recipe?

Real-World Link
The record for the Boston Marathon's wheelchair division is 1 hour, 18 minutes, and 27 seconds.
Source: Boston Athletic Association

SPORTS For Exercises 30 and 31, use the information at the left.

30. The wheelchair division for the Boston Marathon is 26.2 miles long. What was the average speed of the record winner of the wheelchair division? Round to the nearest hundredth.

31. At this rate, about how long would it take this competitor to complete a 30 mile race?

32. **MONEY** Suppose that 1 European euro is worth $1.25. In Europe, a book costs 19 euro. In Los Angeles, the same book costs $22.50. In which location is the book less expensive?

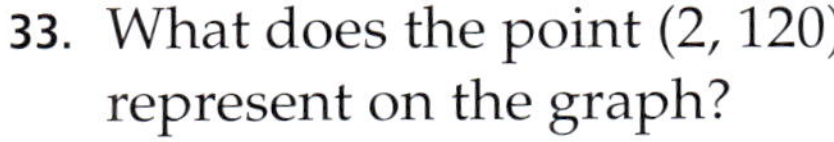

ANIMALS For Exercises 33–37, use the graph that shows the average number of heartbeats for an active adult brown bear and a hibernating brown bear.

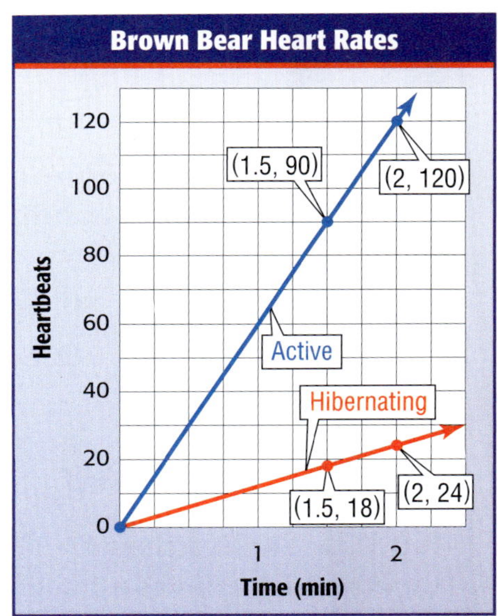

33. What does the point (2, 120) represent on the graph?

34. What does the point (1.5, 18) represent on the graph?

35. What does the ratio of the y-coordinate to the x-coordinate for each pair of points on the graph represent?

36. Use the graph to find the bear's average heart rate when it is active and when it is hibernating.

37. When is the bear's heart rate greater, when it is active or when it is hibernating? How can you tell this from the graph?

38. **TIRES** At Tire Depot, a pair of new tires sells for $216. The manager's special advertises the same tires selling at a rate of $380 for 4 tires. How much do you save per tire if you purchase the manager's special?

39. **FIND THE DATA** Refer to the Data File on pages 16–19. Choose some data and write a real-world problem in which you would compare unit rates or ratios.

See pages 682, 709.

H.O.T. Problems

CHALLENGE **Determine whether each statement is *sometimes*, *always*, or *never* true. Give an example or a counterexample.**

40. A ratio is a rate.

41. A rate is a ratio.

42. **OPEN ENDED** Create a rate and then convert it to a unit rate.

43. **NUMBER SENSE** In which situation will the rate $\frac{x \text{ feet}}{y \text{ minutes}}$ increase? Give an example to explain your reasoning.
    a. x increases, y is unchanged
    b. x is unchanged, y increases

44. **WRITING IN MATH** Describe, using an example, how a *rate* is a measure of one quantity per unit of another quantity.

TEST PRACTICE

45. Mrs. Ross needs to buy dish soap. There are four different size containers at a store.

Dish Soap Prices	
Brand	**Price**
Lots of Suds	$0.98 for 8 ounces
Bright Wash	$1.29 for 12 ounces
Spotless Soap	$3.14 for 30 ounces
Lemon Bright	$3.45 for 32 ounces

Mrs. Ross wants to buy the one that costs the least per ounce. Which brand should she buy?

A Lots of Suds
B Bright Wash
C Spotless Soap
D Lemon Bright

46. The table shows the total distance traveled by a car driving at a constant rate of speed.

Time (h)	Distance (mi)
2	130
3.5	227.5
4	260
7	455

Based on this information, how far will the car have traveled after 10 hours?

F 520 miles
G 585 miles
H 650 miles
J 715 miles

Spiral Review

FLOWERS **For Exercises 47–50, use the information in the table to write each ratio as a fraction in simplest form.** (Lesson 6-1)

Flower Arrangement	
Lilies	4
Roses	18
Snapdragons	6

47. lilies : roses

48. snapdragons : lilies

49. roses : flowers

50. flowers : snapdragons

51. **SANDWICHES** Lawanda is making subs. She puts $1\frac{1}{2}$ slices of cheese on each sub. If she has 12 slices of cheese, how many subs can she make? (Lesson 5-6)

GET READY for the Next Lesson

PREREQUISITE SKILL **Write each fraction in simplest form.** (Lesson 4-3)

52. $\frac{8}{12}$

53. $\frac{9}{18}$

54. $\frac{25}{35}$

55. $\frac{10}{40}$

6-3 Rate of Change and Slope

MAIN IDEA

Identify rate of change and slope using tables and graphs.

New Vocabulary

rate of change
slope

Math Online

glencoe.com

- Extra Examples
- Personal Tutor
- Self-Check Quiz

GET READY for the Lesson

HEIGHTS The table shows Stephanie's height at ages 9 and 12.

Age (yr)	9	12
Height (in.)	53	59

1. What is the change in Stephanie's height from ages 9 to 12?
2. Over what number of years did this change take place?
3. Write a rate that compares the change in Stephanie's height to the change in age. Express your answer as a unit rate and explain its meaning.

A **rate of change** is a rate that describes how one quantity changes in relation to another. A rate of change is usually expressed as a unit rate.

EXAMPLE Find Rate of Change from a Table

1 **FUNDRAISING** **The table shows the amount of money a Booster Club made washing cars for a fundraiser. Use the information to find the rate of change in dollars per car.**

Cars Washed	
Number	Money ($)
5	40
10	80
15	120
20	160

(Number: +5, +5, +5; Money: +40, +40, +40)

Find the unit rate to determine the rate of change.

$\frac{\text{change in money}}{\text{change in cars}} = \frac{40 \text{ dollars}}{5 \text{ cars}}$ The money earned increases by \$40 for every 5 cars.

$= \frac{8 \text{ dollar}}{1 \text{ car}}$ Write as a unit rate.

So, the number of dollars earned increases by \$8 for every car washed.

CHECK Your Progress

a. **PLANES** The table shows the number of miles a plane traveled while in flight. Use the information to find the approximate rate of change in miles per minute.

Time (min)	30	60	90	120
Distance (mi)	290	580	870	1,160

Reading Math

Ordered Pairs The ordered pair (2, 120) represents traveling 120 miles in 2 hours.

EXAMPLE Find Rate of Change from a Graph

2 DRIVING The graph represents the distance traveled while driving on a highway. Use the graph to find the rate of change in miles per hour.

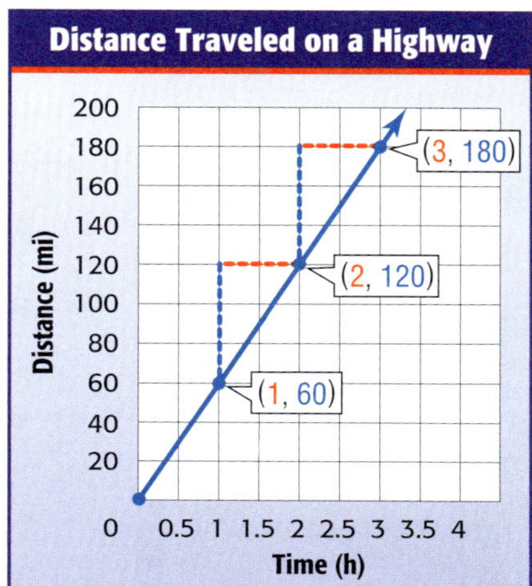

To find the rate of change, pick any two points on the line, such as (1, 60) and (2, 120).

$$\frac{\text{change in miles}}{\text{change in hours}} = \frac{(120 - 60) \text{ miles}}{(2 - 1) \text{ hours}}$$

$$= \frac{60 \text{ miles}}{1 \text{ hour}}$$

The distance increases by 60 miles in 1 hour. So, the rate of traveling on a highway is 60 miles per hour.

CHECK Your Progress

b. **DRIVING** Use the graph to find the rate of change in miles per hour while driving in the city.

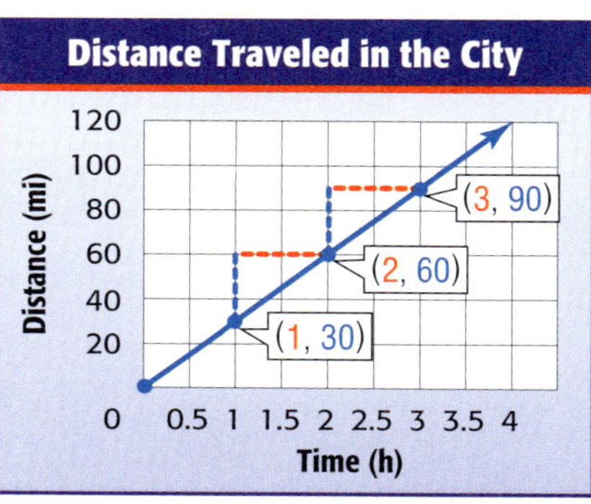

Notice that the graph in Example 2 about driving on a highway represents a rate of change of 60 mph. The graph in Check Your Progress about driving in the city is not as steep. It represents a rate of change of 30 mph.

The constant rate of change in y with respect to the constant change x is also called the slope of a line. Slope is a number that tells how steep the line is. The slope is the same for any two points on a straight line.

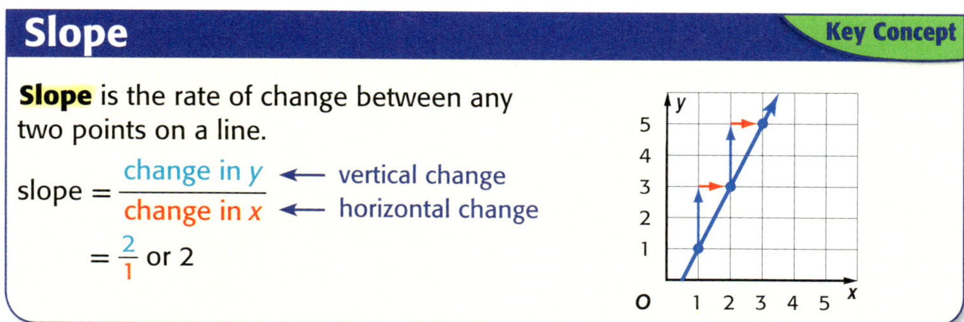

Slope

Key Concept

Slope is the rate of change between any two points on a line.

$$\text{slope} = \frac{\text{change in } y}{\text{change in } x} \leftarrow \text{vertical change} \atop \leftarrow \text{horizontal change}$$

$$= \frac{2}{1} \text{ or } 2$$

Real-World EXAMPLE Find Slope

3 **PHYSICAL SCIENCE** **The table below shows the relationship between the number of seconds y it takes to hear the thunder after a lightning strike and the distance x you are from the lightning.**

Distance (x)	0	1	2	3	4	5
Seconds (y)	0	5	10	15	20	25

Graph the data. Then find the slope of the line. Explain what the slope represents.

$\text{slope} = \frac{\text{change in } y}{\text{change in } x}$ Definition of slope

$= \frac{25 - 10}{5 - 2}$ Use (2, 10) and (5, 25).

$= \frac{15}{3}$ ← seconds, ← miles

$= \frac{5}{1}$ Simplify.

So, for every 5 seconds between a lightning flash and the sound of the thunder, there is 1 mile between you and the lightning strike.

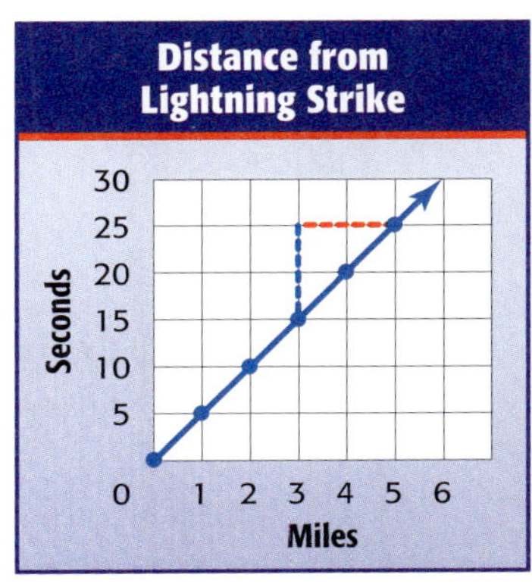

Real-World Link

Lightning strikes somewhere on the surface of Earth about 100 times every second.

Source: National Geographic

CHECK Your Progress

c. **WATER** Graph the data. Then find the slope of the line. Explain what the slope represents.

Water Level Loss	
Week	**Water Loss (cm)**
1	1.5
2	3
3	4.5
4	6

CHECK Your Understanding

Example 1 (p. 293)

1. Use the information in the table to find the rate of change in degrees per hour.

Temperature (°F)	54	57	60	63
Time	6 A.M.	8 A.M.	10 A.M.	12 P.M.

Example 2 (p. 294)

2. **DISTANCE** The graph shows Benito's distance from the starting line. Use the graph to find the rate of change.

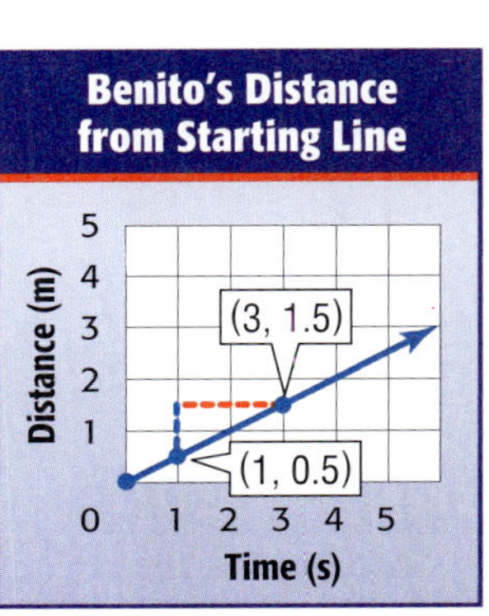

Example 3 (p. 295)

3. **SNACKS** The table below shows the number of small packs of fruit snacks y per box x. Graph the data. Then find the slope of the line. Explain what the slope represents.

Boxes (x)	3	5	7	9
Packs (y)	24	40	56	72

Practice and Problem Solving

HOMEWORK HELP

For Exercises	See Examples
4–6	1
7, 8	2
9, 10	3

For Exercises 4 and 5, find the rate of change for each table.

4.

Time (s)	Distance (m)
0	6
1	12
2	18
3	24

5.

Time (h)	Wage ($)
0	0
1	9
2	18
3	27

6. The number of minutes included in different cell phone plans and the costs are shown in the table. What is the approximate rate of change in cost per minute?

Cost ($)	38	50	62	74	86
Minutes	1,000	1,500	2,000	2,500	3,000

For Exercises 7 and 8, find the rate of change for each graph.

7.

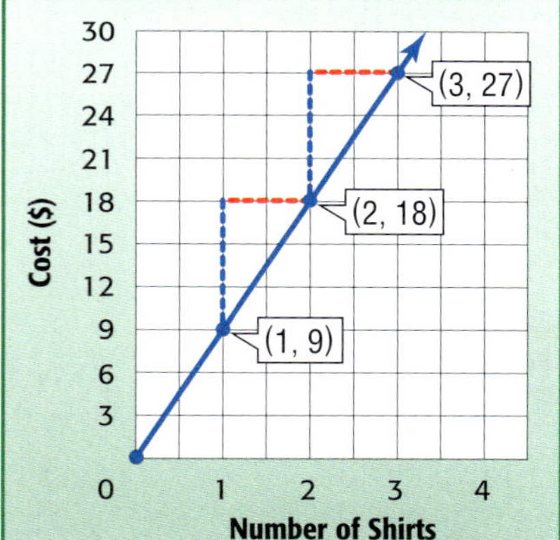

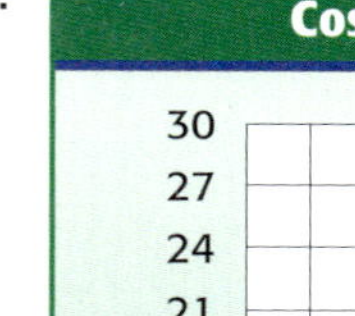

8.

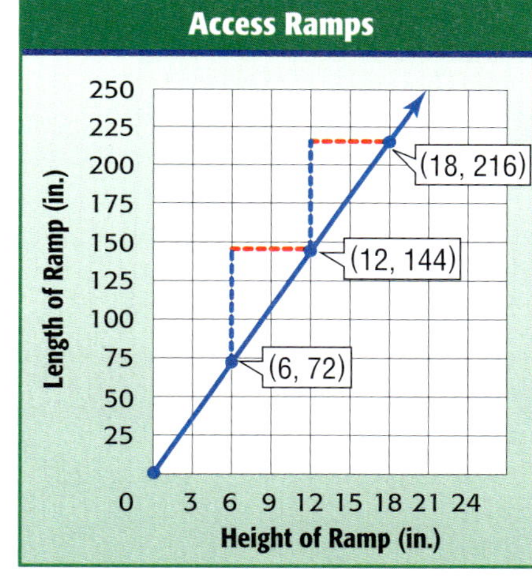

9. **CYCLING** The table shows the distance y Cheryl traveled in x minutes while competing in the cycling portion of a triathlon. Graph the data. Then find the slope of the line. Explain what the slope represents.

Time (min)	45	90	135	180
Distance (km)	5	10	15	20

10. **MAPS** The table shows the key for a map. Graph the data. Then find the slope of the line.

Distance on Map (in.)	2	4	6	8
Actual Distance (mi)	40	80	120	160

11. **WATER** At 1:00, the water level in a pool is 13 inches. At 2:30, the water level is 28 inches. What is the rate of change?

12. **MONEY** Dwayne opens a savings account with $75. He makes the same deposit every month and makes no withdrawals. After 3 months, he has $150. After 6 months, he has $300. After 9 months, he has $450 dollars. What is the rate of change?

H.O.T. Problems

13. **OPEN ENDED** Make a table where the rate of change is 6 inches for every foot.

14. **WRITING IN MATH** Write a problem to represent a rate of change of $15 per item.

TEST PRACTICE

15. Use the information in the table to find the rate of change.

Number of Apples	Number of Seeds
3	30
7	70
11	110

A $\frac{10}{1}$

B $\frac{1}{10}$

C $\frac{40}{4}$

D $\frac{4}{40}$

16. **SHORT RESPONSE** Find the slope of the line below that shows the distance Jairo traveled while jogging.

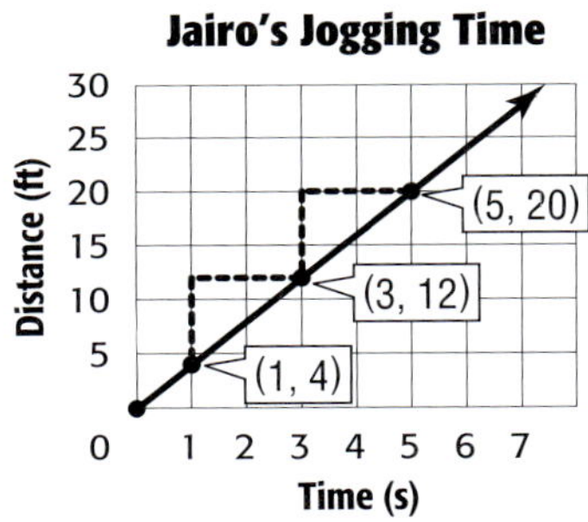

Spiral Review

17. **GROCERIES** Three pounds of pears cost $3.57. At this rate, how much would 10 pounds cost? (Lesson 6-2)

Write each ratio as a fraction in simplest form. (Lesson 6-1)

18. 9 feet in 21 minutes

19. 36 calls in 2 hours

20. 14 SUVs out of 56 vehicles

GET READY for the Next Lesson

PREREQUISITE SKILL **Solve.** (Page 674)

21. 2.5×20

22. 3.5×4

23. $104 \div 16$

24. $4{,}200 \div 2{,}000$

6-4 Measurement: Changing Customary Units

MAIN IDEA

Change units in the customary system.

New Vocabulary

unit ratio

Math Online

glencoe.com

- Extra Examples
- Personal Tutor
- Self-Check Quiz

GET READY for the Lesson

ANIMALS The table shows the approximate weights in tons of several large land animals. One ton is equivalent to 2,000 pounds.

Animal	Weight (T)
Grizzly Bear	1
White Rhinoceros	4
Hippopotamus	5
African Elephant	8

You can use a *ratio table*, which have columns filled with ratios that have the same value, to convert each weight from tons to pounds.

1. Copy and complete the ratio table. The first two ratios are done for you.

×4

Tons	1	4	5	8
Pounds	2,000	8,000	■	■

×4

To produce equivalent ratios, multiply the quantities in each row by the same number.

2. Then graph the ordered pairs (tons, pounds) from the table. Label the horizontal axis *Weight in Tons* and the vertical axis *Weight in Pounds*. Connect the points. What do you notice about the graph of these data?

The relationships among the most commonly used customary units of length, weight, and capacity are shown in the table below.

Customary Units — Key Concept

Type of Measure	Larger Unit	→	Smaller Unit
Length	1 foot (ft)	=	12 inches (in.)
	1 yard (yd)	=	3 feet
	1 mile (mi)	=	5,280 feet
Weight	1 pound (lb)	=	16 ounces (oz)
	1 ton (T)	=	2,000 pounds
Capacity	1 cup (c)	=	8 fluid ounces (fl oz)
	1 pint (pt)	=	2 cups
	1 quart (qt)	=	2 pints
	1 gallon (gal)	=	4 quarts

Each of the relationships above can be written as a unit ratio. Like a unit rate, a **unit ratio** is one in which the denominator is 1 unit.

$$\frac{3 \text{ ft}}{1 \text{ yd}} \qquad \frac{2{,}000 \text{ lb}}{1 \text{ T}} \qquad \frac{4 \text{ qt}}{1 \text{ gal}}$$

Notice that the numerator and denominator of each fraction above are equivalent, so the value of each ratio is 1. You can multiply by a unit ratio of this type to *convert* or change from larger units to smaller units.

Study Tip

Multiplying by 1
Although the number and units changed in Example 1, because the measure is multiplied by 1, the value of the converted measure is the same as the original.

EXAMPLES Convert Larger Units to Smaller Units

1 Convert 20 feet into inches.

Since 1 foot = 12 inches, the unit ratio is $\frac{12 \text{ in.}}{1 \text{ ft}}$.

$20 \text{ ft} = 20 \text{ ft} \cdot \frac{12 \text{ in.}}{1 \text{ ft}}$ — Multiply by $\frac{12 \text{ in.}}{1 \text{ ft}}$.

$= 20 \cancel{\text{ft}} \cdot \frac{12 \text{ in.}}{1 \cancel{\text{ft}}}$ — Divide out common units, leaving the desired unit, inches.

$= 20 \cdot 12 \text{ in. or } 240 \text{ in.}$ — Multiply.

So, 20 feet = 240 inches.

2 GARDENING Clarence mixes $\frac{1}{4}$ cup of fertilizer with soil before planting each bulb. How many ounces of fertilizer does he use per bulb?

$\frac{1}{4} \text{ c} = \frac{1}{4} \cancel{\text{c}} \cdot \frac{8 \text{ fl oz}}{1 \cancel{\text{c}}}$ — Since 1 cup = 8 fluid ounces, multiply by $\frac{8 \text{ fl oz}}{1 \text{ c}}$. Then, divide out common units.

$= \frac{1}{4} \cdot 8 \text{ fl oz or } 2 \text{ fl oz}$ — Multiply.

So, 2 fluid ounces of fertilizer are used per bulb.

CHECK Your Progress

Complete.

a. 36 yd = ▢ ft

b. $\frac{3}{4}$ T = ▢ lb

c. $1\frac{1}{2}$ qt = ▢ pt

Review Vocabulary

reciprocal The product of a number and its reciprocal is 1; *Example*: The reciprocal of $\frac{3}{5}$ is $\frac{5}{3}$. (Lesson 5-7)

To convert from smaller units to larger units, multiply by the reciprocal of the appropriate unit ratio.

EXAMPLES Convert Smaller Units to Larger Units

3 Convert 15 quarts into gallons.

Since 1 gallon = 4 quarts, the unit ratio is $\frac{4 \text{ qt}}{1 \text{ gal}}$, and its reciprocal is $\frac{1 \text{ gal}}{4 \text{ qt}}$.

$15 \text{ qt} = 15 \text{ qt} \cdot \frac{1 \text{ gal}}{4 \text{ qt}}$ — Multiply by $\frac{1 \text{ gal}}{4 \text{ qt}}$.

$= 15 \cancel{\text{qt}} \cdot \frac{1 \text{ gal}}{4 \cancel{\text{qt}}}$ — Divide out common units, leaving the desired unit, gallons.

$= 15 \cdot \frac{1}{4} \text{ gal or } 3.75 \text{ gal}$ — Multiplying 15 by $\frac{1}{4}$ is the same as dividing 15 by 4.

4 **COSTUMES** **Umeka needs $4\frac{1}{2}$ feet of fabric to make a costume for a play. How many yards of fabric does she need?**

$4\frac{1}{2}\text{ ft} = 4\frac{1}{2}\text{ ft} \cdot \frac{1\text{ yd}}{3\text{ ft}}$ Since 1 yard = 3 feet, multiply by $\frac{1\text{ yd}}{3\text{ ft}}$. Then, divide out common units.

$= \frac{\overset{3}{\cancel{9}}}{2} \cdot \frac{1}{\underset{1}{\cancel{3}}}\text{ yd}$ Write $4\frac{1}{2}$ as an improper fraction. Then divide out common factors.

$= \frac{3}{2}\text{ yd or } 1\frac{1}{2}\text{ yd}$ Multiply.

So Umeka needs $1\frac{1}{2}$ yards of fabric.

CHECK Your Progress

Complete.

d. 2,640 ft = ■ mi

e. 5 pt = ■ qt

f. 100 oz = ■ lb

g. 76c = ■ gal

h. 3 c = ■ pt

i. 18 in. = ■ ft

j. **FOOD** A 3-pound pork loin can be cut into 10 smaller pork chops of equal weight. How many ounces does each pork chop weigh?

You can also convert from one rate to another by multiplying by a unit rate or its reciprocal.

Real-World EXAMPLE Convert Rates

5 **HELICOPTERS** **A helicopter flies at a rate of 158 miles per hour. How many miles per second is this?**

Since 1 hour = 3,600 seconds, multiply by $\frac{1\text{ h}}{3{,}600\text{ s}}$.

$\frac{158\text{ mi}}{\text{h}} = \frac{158\text{ mi}}{1\text{ h}} \times \frac{1\text{ h}}{3{,}600\text{ s}}$ Multiply by $\frac{1\text{ h}}{3{,}600\text{ s}}$.

$= \frac{158\text{ mi}}{1\cancel{\text{h}}} \times \frac{1\cancel{\text{h}}}{3{,}600\text{ s}}$ Divide out common units.

$\approx \frac{0.04\text{ mi}}{1\text{ s}}$ Simplify.

So, a helicopter flies approximately 0.04 mile per second.

Real-World Link
A swordfish reaches a maximum size of 14 feet and almost 1,200 pounds.
Source: Sport Fishing Central

CHECK Your Progress

k. **FISH** A swordfish can swim at a rate of 60 miles per hour. How many feet per hour is this?

l. **WALKING** Ava walks at a speed of 7 feet per second. How many feet per hour is this?

CHECK Your Understanding

Examples 1, 2 (p. 299)

Complete.

1. 3 lb = ▒ oz
2. $5\frac{1}{3}$ yd = ▒ ft
3. 6.5 c = ▒ fl oz
4. **FISH** Grouper are members of the sea bass family. A large grouper can weigh $\frac{1}{3}$ ton. About how much does a large grouper weigh to the nearest pound?

Examples 3, 4 (pp. 299–300)

Complete.

5. 12 qt = ▒ gal
6. 28 in. = ▒ ft
7. 15 pt = ▒ qt
8. **VEHICLES** The world's narrowest electric vehicle is about 35 inches wide and is designed to move down narrow aisles in warehouses. About how wide is this vehicle to the nearest foot?

Example 5 (p. 300)

9. **RUNNING** The fastest a human has ever run is about 27 miles per hour. How many miles per minute is this?

Practice and Problem Solving

HOMEWORK HELP

For Exercises	See Examples
10–21	1–4
22–23	2
24–25	4
26–27	5

Complete.

10. 18 ft = ▒ yd
11. 72 oz = ▒ lb
12. 2 lb = ▒ oz
13. 4 gal = ▒ qt
14. $4\frac{1}{2}$ pt = ▒ c
15. 3 c = ▒ fl oz
16. 2 mi = ▒ ft
17. $1\frac{1}{4}$ mi = ▒ ft
18. 5,000 lb = ▒ T
19. 13 c = ▒ pt
20. $2\frac{3}{4}$ qt = ▒ pt
21. $3\frac{3}{8}$ T = ▒ lb
22. **PUMPKINS** One of the largest pumpkins ever grown weighed about $\frac{1}{2}$ ton. How many pounds did the pumpkin weigh?
23. **SKIING** Speed skiing takes place on a course that is $\frac{2}{3}$ mile long. How many feet long is the course?
24. **BOATING** A 40-foot power boat is for sale by owner. About how long is this boat to the nearest yard?
25. **BLOOD** A total of 35 pints of blood were collected at a local blood drive. How many quarts of blood is this?
26. **GO-KARTS** A go-kart's top speed is 607,200 feet per hour. How many miles per hour is this?
27. **BIRDS** A peregrine falcon can fly at over 200 miles per hour. How many feet per hour is this?

28. **PUNCH** Will a 2-quart pitcher hold the entire recipe of citrus punch given at the right? Explain your reasoning.

29. **WEATHER** On Monday, it snowed a total of 15 inches. On Tuesday and Wednesday, it snowed an additional $4\frac{1}{2}$ inches and $6\frac{3}{4}$ inches, respectively. A weather forecaster says that over the last three days, it snowed about $2\frac{1}{2}$ feet. Is this a valid claim? Justify your answer.

MEASUREMENT **Complete the following statements.**

30. If 16 c = 1 gal, then $1\frac{1}{4}$ gal = ■ c

31. If 1,760 yd = 1 mi, then 880 yd = ■ mi

32. If 36 in. = 1 yd, then 2.3 yd = ■ in.

33. **ESTIMATION** Cristos is a member of the swim team and trains by swimming an average of 3,000 yards a day. About how many miles would he swim by training at this rate for 5 days, to the nearest half-mile?

MEASUREMENT **For Exercises 34–37, use the graph at the right.**

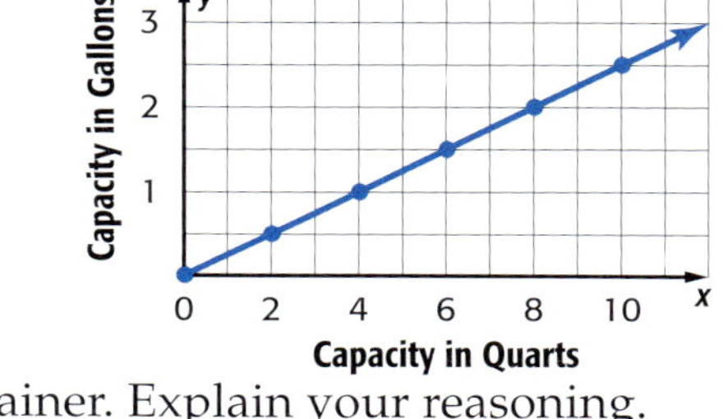

34. What does an ordered pair from this graph represent?

35. Find the slope of the line.

36. Use the graph to find the capacity in quarts of a 2.5-gallon container. Explain your reasoning.

37. Use the graph to predict the capacity in gallons of a 12-quart container. Explain your reasoning.

H.O.T. Problems

38. **OPEN ENDED** Write a problem about a real-world situation in which you would need to convert pints to cups.

REASONING **Replace each ● with <, >, or = to make a true sentence. Justify your answers.**

39. 16 in. ● $1\frac{1}{2}$ ft

40. $8\frac{3}{4}$ gal ● 32 qt

41. 2.7 T ● 86,400 oz

42. **CHALLENGE** To whiten fabrics, a certain Web site recommends that you soak them in a mixture of $\frac{3}{4}$ cup vinegar, 2 quarts water, and some salt. Does a mixture that contains 1.5 ounces vinegar and 16 ounces water have the same vinegar-to-water ratio as the recommended mixture? Explain.

43. **WRITING IN MATH** Use multiplication by unit ratios of equivalent measures to convert 5 square feet to square inches. Justify your answer.

44. Which situation is represented by the graph?

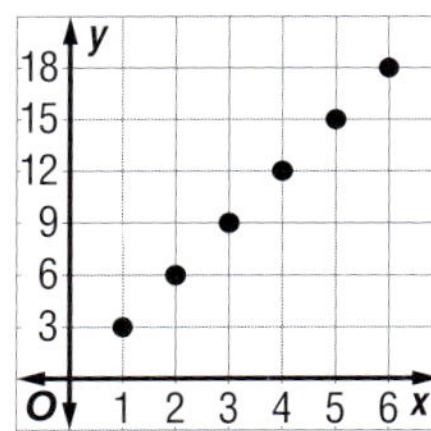

A conversion of inches to yards
B conversion of feet to inches
C conversion of miles to feet
D conversion of yards to feet

45. How many cups of milk are shown below?

F $\frac{3}{4}$ c
G $1\frac{1}{4}$ c
H $2\frac{1}{2}$ c
J 10 c

46. How many ounces are in $7\frac{3}{4}$ pounds?

A 124 oz
B 122 oz
C 120 oz
D 112 oz

Spiral Review

47. Use the information in the table to find the rate of change in dollars per hour. (Lesson 6-3)

Wage ($)	0	9	18	27
Time (h)	0	1	2	3

48. **GROCERIES** Find the unit price if Anju spent $2 for six oranges. Round to the nearest cent if necessary. (Lesson 6-2)

49. **MEASUREMENT** By doubling just the length of the rectangular ice skating rink in Will's backyard from 16 to 32 feet, he increased its area from 128 square feet to 256 square feet. Find the width of both rinks. (Lesson 3-6)

ALGEBRA For Exercises 50–52, use the pay stub at the right. (Lesson 3-3)

Martin, Grace — Employee #: 4211

Description:	Hours:	Earnings ($):
Regular hours:	40	300.00
Overtime hours:	2	22.50

50. Write and solve an equation to find the regular hourly wage.

51. Write and solve an equation to find the overtime hourly wage.

52. Write and solve an equation to find how many times greater Grace's overtime hourly wage is than her regular hourly wage.

GET READY for the Next Lesson

PREREQUISITE SKILL Multiply. (p. 674)

53. 14.5×8.2
54. 7.03×4.6
55. 9.29×15.3
56. 1.84×16.7

Measurement: Changing Metric Units

MAIN IDEA

Change metric units of length, capacity, and mass.

New Vocabulary

metric system
meter
liter
gram
kilogram

Math Online

glencoe.com

- Extra Examples
- Personal Tutor
- Self-Check Quiz

MINI Lab

The lengths of two objects are shown below.

Object	Length (millimeters)	Length (centimeters)
paper clip	45	4.5
CD case	144	14.4

1. Select three other objects. Find and record the width of all five objects to the nearest millimeter and tenth of a centimeter.
2. Compare the measurements of the objects, and write a rule that describes how to convert from millimeters to centimeters.
3. Measure the length of your classroom in meters. Make a conjecture about how to convert this measure to centimeters. Explain.

The **metric system** is a decimal system of measures. The prefixes commonly used in this system are kilo-, centi-, and milli-.

Prefix	Meaning In Words	Meaning In Numbers
kilo-	thousands	1,000
centi-	hundredths	0.01
milli-	thousandths	0.001

In the metric system, the base unit of *length* is the **meter** (m). Using the prefixes, the names of other units of length are formed. Notice that the prefixes tell you how the units relate to the meter.

Unit	Symbol	Relationship to Meter	
kilometer	km	1 km = 1,000 m	1 m = 0.001 km
meter	m	1 m = 1 m	
centimeter	cm	1 cm = 0.01 m	1 m = 100 cm
millimeter	mm	1 mm = 0.001 m	1 m = 1,000 mm

The **liter** (L) is the base unit of *capacity*, the amount of dry or liquid material an object can hold. The **gram** (g) measures *mass*, the amount of matter in an object. The prefixes can also be applied to these units. Whereas the meter and liter are the base units of length and capacity, the base unit of mass is the **kilogram** (kg).

To change a metric measure of length, mass, or capacity from one unit to another, you can use the relationship between the two units and multiplication by a power of 10.

EXAMPLES Convert Units in the Metric System

Study Tip

Metric Conversions When converting from a larger unit to a smaller unit, the power of ten being multiplied will be greater than 1.

When converting from a smaller unit to a larger unit, the power of ten will be less than 1.

1 Convert 4.5 liters to milliliters.

You need to convert liters to milliliters. Use the relationship 1 L = 1,000 mL.

$1 \text{ L} = 1{,}000 \text{ mL}$	Write the relationship.
$4.5 \times 1 \text{ L} = 4.5 \times 1{,}000 \text{ mL}$	Multiply each side by 4.5 since you have 4.5 L.
$4.5 \text{ L} = 4{,}500 \text{ mL}$	To multiply 4.5 by 1,000, move the decimal point 3 places to the right.

2 Convert 500 millimeters to meters.

You need to convert millimeters to meters. Use the relationship 1 mm = 0.001 m.

$1 \text{ mm} = 0.001 \text{ m}$	Write the relationship.
$500 \times 1 \text{ mm} = 500 \times 0.001 \text{ m}$	Multiply each side by 500 since you have 500 mm.
$500 \text{ mm} = 0.5 \text{ m}$	To multiply 500 by 0.001, move the decimal point 3 places to the left.

CHECK Your Progress

Complete.

a. 25.4 g = ■ kg

b. 158 mm = ■ m

Real-World EXAMPLE

Real-World Link The maximum weight of a grizzly bear is 521.64 kilograms.

Source: North American Bear Center

3 BEARS The California Grizzly Bear was designated the official state animal in 1953. Use the information at the left to find the maximum weight of a grizzly bear in grams.

You are converting kilograms to grams. Since the maximum weight of a grizzly bear is 521.64 kilograms, use the relationship 1 kg = 1,000 g.

$1 \text{ kg} = 1{,}000 \text{ g}$	Write the relationship.
$521.64 \times 1 \text{ kg} = 521.64 \times 1{,}000 \text{ g}$	Multiply each side by 521.64 since you have 521.64 kg.
$521.64 \text{ kg} = 521{,}640 \text{ g}$	To multiply 521.64 by 1,000, move the decimal point 3 places to the right.

So, the maximum weight of a grizzly bear is 521,640 grams.

CHECK Your Progress

c. **FOOD** A bottle contains 1.75 liters of juice. How many milliliters is this?

To convert measures between customary units and metric units, use the relationships below.

Customary and Metric Relationships

Key Concept

Type of Measure	Customary	→	Metric
Length	1 inch (in.)	≈	2.54 centimeters (cm)
	1 foot (ft)	≈	0.30 meter (m)
	1 yard (yd)	≈	0.91 meter (m)
	1 mile (mi)	≈	1.61 kilometers (km)
Weight/Mass	1 pound (lb)	≈	453.6 grams (g)
	1 pound (lb)	≈	0.4536 kilogram (kg)
	1 ton (T)	≈	907.2 kilograms (kg)
Capacity	1 cup (c)	≈	236.59 milliliters (mL)
	1 pint (pt)	≈	473.18 milliliters (mL)
	1 quart (qt)	≈	946.35 milliliters (mL)
	1 gallon (gal)	≈	3.79 liters (L)

EXAMPLES Convert Between Measurement Systems

4 Convert 17.22 inches to centimeters. Round to the nearest hundredth if necessary.

Use the relationship 1 inch ≈ 2.54 centimeters.

$1 \text{ inch} \approx 2.54 \text{ cm}$ — Write the relationship.

$17.22 \times 1 \text{ in.} \approx 17.22 \times 2.54 \text{ cm}$ — Multiply each side by 17.22 since you have 17.22 in.

$17.22 \text{ in.} \approx 43.7388 \text{ cm}$ — Simplify.

So, 17.22 inches is approximately 43.74 centimeters.

Study Tip

Alternative Method When converting 17.22 inches to centimeters, you can use the relationship 1 in. ≈ 2.54 cm or the unit ratio $\frac{2.54 \text{ cm}}{1 \text{ in.}}$.

5 Convert 828.5 milliliters to cups. Round to the nearest hundredth if necessary.

Since 1 cup ≈ 236.59 milliliters, multiply by $\frac{1 \text{ c}}{236.59 \text{ mL}}$.

$828.5 \text{ mL} \approx 828.5 \cancel{\text{mL}} \cdot \frac{1 \text{ c}}{236.59 \cancel{\text{mL}}}$ — Multiply by $\frac{1 \text{ c}}{236.59 \text{ mL}}$.

$\approx \frac{828.5 \text{ c}}{236.59}$ or 3.5 c — Simplify.

So, 828.5 milliliters is approximately 3.5 cups.

CHECK Your Progress

Complete. Round to the nearest hundredth if necessary.

d. 7.44 c ≈ ▢ mL e. 22.09 lb ≈ ▢ kg f. 35.85 L ≈ ▢ gal

Real-World Link Before the seventeenth century, people thought light was transmitted instantly. Now, we know that light is too fast for the delay to be noticeable.

Source: University of California, Riverside

Real-World EXAMPLE Convert with Rates

6 **LIGHT** **The speed of light is about 186,000 miles per second. Find the approximate speed of light in kilometers per second.**

Since 1 mile ≈ 1.61 kilometers, multiply by $\frac{1.61 \text{ km}}{1 \text{ mi}}$.

$$\frac{186{,}000 \text{ mi}}{\text{s}} \approx \frac{186{,}000 \text{ mi}}{1 \text{ s}} \times \frac{1.61 \text{ km}}{1 \text{ mi}} \quad \text{Multiply by } \frac{1.61 \text{ km}}{1 \text{ mi}}.$$

$$\approx \frac{299{,}460 \text{ km}}{1 \text{ s}} \quad \text{Simplify.}$$

So, the speed of light is approximately 299,460 kilometers per second.

CHECK Your Progress

g. **RUNNING** Chuck runs at a speed of 3 meters per second. About how many feet per second does Chuck run?

CHECK Your Understanding

Examples 1, 2, 4, 5 (pp. 305–306)

Complete. Round to the nearest hundredth if necessary.

1. 3.7 m = ▒ cm
2. 550 m = ▒ km
3. 1,460 mg = ▒ g
4. 2.34 kL = ▒ L
5. 9.36 yd ≈ ▒ m
6. 11.07 pt ≈ ▒ mL
7. 58.14 kg ≈ ▒ lb
8. 38.44 cm ≈ ▒ in.

Examples 3, 6 (pp. 305, 307)

9. **SPORTS** About how many feet does a team of athletes run in a 1,600-meter relay race?

Practice and Problem Solving

HOMEWORK HELP

For Exercises	See Examples
10–23	1, 2, 4, 5
24–27	3, 6

Complete. Round to the nearest hundredth if necessary.

10. 720 cm = ▒ m
11. 983 mm = ▒ m
12. 3.2 m = ▒ cm
13. 0.03 g = ▒ mg
14. 997 g = ▒ kg
15. 82.1 g = ▒ kg
16. 9.1 L = ▒ mL
17. 130.5 kL = ▒ L
18. 3.75 c ≈ ▒ mL
19. 41.8 in. ≈ ▒ cm
20. 156.25 lb ≈ ▒ kg
21. 9.5 gal ≈ ▒ L
22. 680.4 g ≈ ▒ lb
23. 4.725 m ≈ ▒ ft

24. **WATERFALLS** At 979 meters tall, Angel Falls in Venezuela is the highest waterfall in the world. How many kilometers tall is the waterfall?

25. **FOOD** An 18-ounce jar contains 510 grams of grape jelly. How many kilograms of grape jelly does the jar contain?

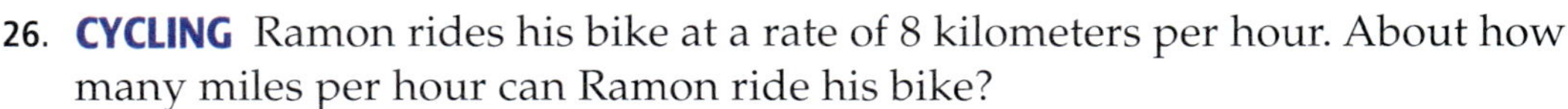
26. **CYCLING** Ramon rides his bike at a rate of 8 kilometers per hour. About how many miles per hour can Ramon ride his bike?

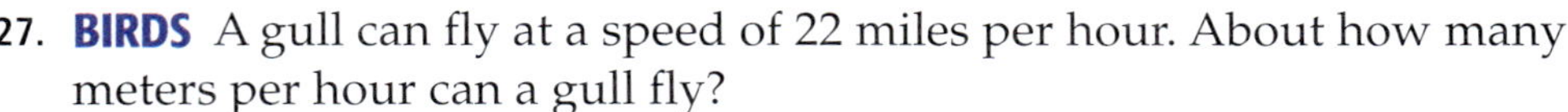
27. **BIRDS** A gull can fly at a speed of 22 miles per hour. About how many meters per hour can a gull fly?

Complete. Round to the nearest hundredth if necessary.

28. 8.18 qt ≈ ■ L
29. 15.09 km ≈ ■ yd
30. 72.26 cm ≈ ■ ft
31. 0.445 T ≈ ■ g

Order each set of measures from least to greatest.

32. 0.02 km, 50 m, 3,000 cm
33. 660 mL, 0.06 L, 6.6 kL
34. 0.32 kg, 345 g, 35,100 mg
35. 2,650 mm, 130 cm, 5 m

Real-World Link The Mackinac Bridge opened on November 1, 1957. It is the longest two-tower suspension bridge between bases in the Western Hemisphere.
Source: *Encyclopaedia Britannica*

36. **ANALYZE TABLES** The table shows the lengths of bridges in the United States. Which bridges are about 1 kilometer in length? Justify your answer.

Bridge	Length (m)
Mackinac, MI	1,158
George Washington, NY	1,067
Tacoma Narrows II, WA	853
Oakland Bay, CA	704
Pennybacker, TX	345
Sunshine Skyway, FL	8,712
Golden Gate, CA	2,780

37. **CARPENTRY** Jacinta needs a 2.5-meter pole for a birdfeeder that she is building. How many centimeters will she need to cut off a 3-meter pole in order to use it for the birdfeeder?

See pages 683, 709.

38. **BAKING** A bakery uses 900 grams of peaches per cobbler. How many cobblers can be made using 10.5 pounds of peaches?

H.O.T. Problems

39. **FIND THE ERROR** Jake and Gerardo are converting 3.25 kilograms to grams. Who is correct? Explain your reasoning.

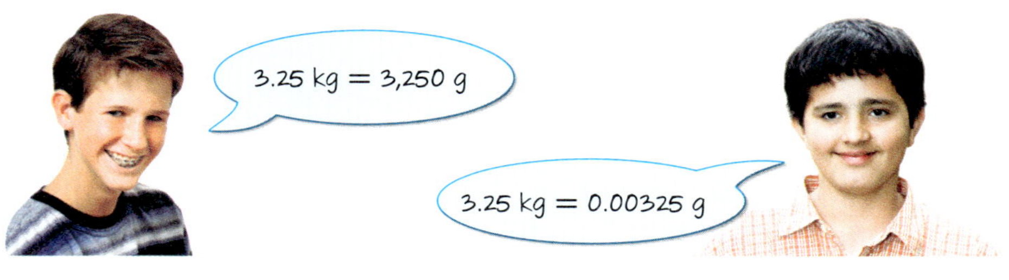

CHALLENGE For Exercises 40–42, use the following information.
The metric prefix *giga* refers to something one billion times larger than the base unit.

40. How many meters are in one gigameter?
41. About how many miles are in one gigameter? Round to the nearest hundredth.
42. The distance from Earth to the Sun is approximately 93 million miles. About how many gigameters is this? Round to the nearest hundredth.

43. **WRITING IN MATH** Explain why it makes sense to multiply by a power of 10 that is greater than 1 when changing from a larger unit to a smaller unit.

44. The table shows the mass of four wireless telephones. Find the approximate total mass of the telephones in kilograms.

Telephone Owner	Mass (g)
Elena	100.4
Kevin	70.8
Marissa	95.6
Corey	120.4

A 0.39 kilogram

B 3.9 kilograms

C 39.0 kilograms

D 390.0 kilograms

45. Which relationship between the given units of measure is correct?

F One gram is $\frac{1}{100}$ of a centigram.

G One meter is $\frac{1}{100}$ of a centimeter.

H One gram is $\frac{1}{1,000}$ of a kilogram.

J One milliliter is $\frac{1}{100}$ of a liter.

Spiral Review

46. **MEASUREMENT** A certain car weighs 3,200 pounds. What is the weight of the car in tons? (Lesson 6-4)

47. **MEASUREMENT** The table shows the number of inches per foot. Graph the data. Then find the slope of the line. Explain what slope represents. (Lesson 6-3)

Feet (x)	1	2	3	4
Inches (y)	12	24	36	48

Add or subtract. Write in simplest form. (Lesson 5-3)

48. $3\frac{4}{7} + 1\frac{1}{7}$

49. $8\frac{3}{5} - 2\frac{2}{5}$

50. $9\frac{1}{6} + 4\frac{3}{8}$

51. $11\frac{7}{10} - 5\frac{3}{4}$

52. **BASKETBALL** Jared made thirty-seven percent of his free-throw attempts during basketball practice. Write this percent as a decimal. (Lesson 4-7)

GET READY for the Next Lesson

PREREQUISITE SKILL **Solve each equation.** (Lesson 3-3)

53. $5 \cdot 4 = x \cdot 2$

54. $9 \cdot 24 = 27 \cdot x$

55. $x \cdot 15 = 12 \cdot 4$

56. $8\frac{1}{2} \cdot x = 11 \cdot 17$

6-6 Algebra: Solving Proportions

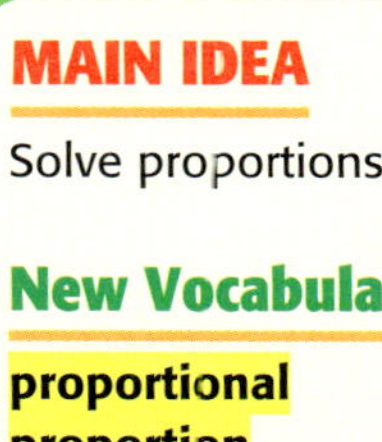

MAIN IDEA

Solve proportions.

New Vocabulary

proportional
proportion
cross product

Math Online

glencoe.com

- Extra Examples
- Personal Tutor
- Self-Check Quiz

GET READY for the Lesson

NUTRITION The amount of calcium in different servings of milk is shown.

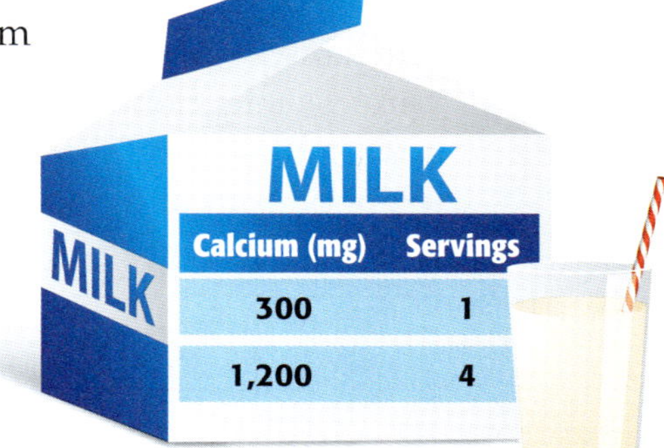

Calcium (mg)	Servings
300	1
1,200	4

1. Write the rate $\frac{\text{calcium}}{\text{number of servings}}$ for each amount of milk.
2. Find the number of milligrams per cup for each serving size. What do you notice?

Two quantities are **proportional** if they have a constant rate or ratio. In the example above, notice that the number of servings and amount of calcium change or *vary* in the same way.

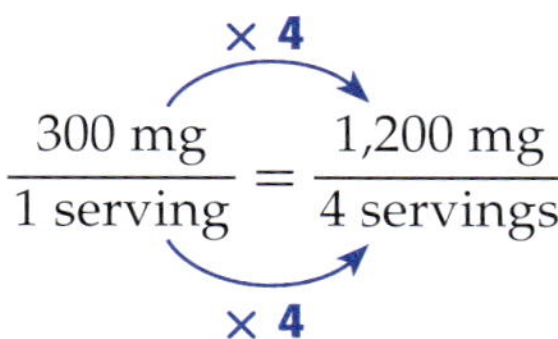

$$\frac{300 \text{ mg}}{1 \text{ serving}} = \frac{1{,}200 \text{ mg}}{4 \text{ servings}} \quad (\times 4)$$

The unit rates for these different-sized servings are the same, a constant 300 milligrams per serving. So, the amount of calcium is proportional to the serving size.

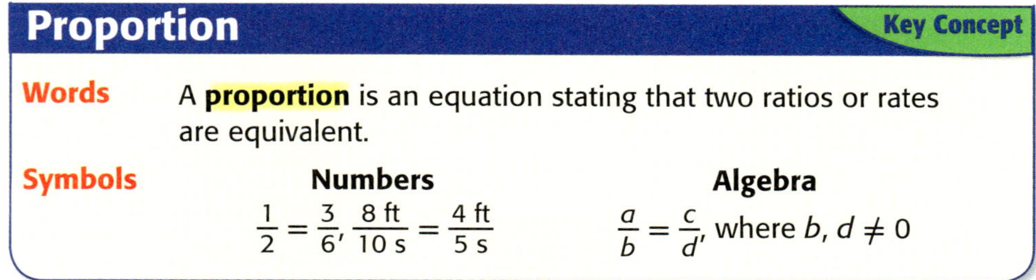

Proportion — Key Concept

Words A **proportion** is an equation stating that two ratios or rates are equivalent.

Symbols

Numbers $\frac{1}{2} = \frac{3}{6}$, $\frac{8 \text{ ft}}{10 \text{ s}} = \frac{4 \text{ ft}}{5 \text{ s}}$

Algebra $\frac{a}{b} = \frac{c}{d}$, where $b, d \neq 0$

Consider the following proportion.

$$\frac{a}{b} = \frac{c}{d}$$

$$\frac{a}{b} \cdot bd = \frac{c}{d} \cdot bd \quad \text{Multiply each side by } bd.$$

$$ad = bc \quad \text{Simplify.}$$

The products ad and bc are called the **cross products** of this proportion. The cross products of any proportion are equal. You can compare unit rates or cross products to identify proportional relationships.

EXAMPLE Identify Proportional Relationships

Reading Math

Nonproportional When ratios do not form a proportion, they are called nonproportional.

1 **RECREATION** **A carousel makes 4 complete turns after 64 seconds and 5 complete turns after 76 seconds. Based on this information, is the number of turns made by this carousel proportional to the time in seconds? Explain.**

METHOD 1 **Compare unit rates.**

$\frac{\text{seconds}}{\text{complete turns}} \rightarrow \frac{64 \text{ s}}{4 \text{ turns}} = \frac{16 \text{ s}}{1 \text{ turn}} \qquad \frac{76 \text{ s}}{5 \text{ turns}} = \frac{15.2 \text{ s}}{1 \text{ turn}}$

Since the unit rates are not equal, the number of turns is not proportional to the time in seconds.

METHOD 2 **Compare ratios by comparing cross products.**

seconds → $\frac{64}{4} \stackrel{?}{=} \frac{76}{5}$ ← seconds
complete turns → ← complete turns

$64 \cdot 5 \stackrel{?}{=} 4 \cdot 76$ Find the cross products.

$320 \neq 304$ Multiply.

Since the cross products are not equal, the number of turns is not proportional to the time in seconds.

CHOOSE Your Method

Determine if the quantities in each pair of ratios are proportional. Explain.

a. 60 voted out of 100 registered and 84 voted out of 140 registered

b. $12 for 16 yards of fabric and $9 for 24 yards fabric

You can also use cross products to find a missing value in a proportion. This is known as *solving the proportion.*

Study Tip

Mental Math Some proportions can be solved using mental math.

$\frac{2.5}{10} = \frac{x}{30}$

×3

$\frac{2.5}{10} = \frac{7.5}{30}$

×3

EXAMPLES Solve a Proportion

2 **Solve** $\frac{21}{5} = \frac{c}{7}$.

$\frac{21}{5} = \frac{c}{7}$ Write the proportion.

$21 \cdot 7 = 5 \cdot c$ Find the cross products.

$147 = 5c$ Multiply.

$\frac{147}{5} = \frac{5c}{5}$ Divide each side by 5.

$29.4 = c$ Simplify.

Check for Reasonableness Since $\frac{21}{5} \approx \frac{20}{5}$ or $\frac{4}{1}$ and $\frac{29.4}{7} \approx \frac{28}{7}$ or $\frac{4}{1}$, the answer is reasonable. ✔

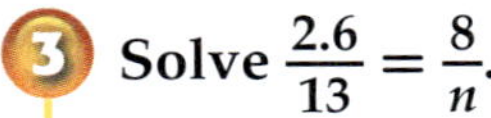

3 Solve $\frac{2.6}{13} = \frac{8}{n}$.

$\frac{2.6}{13} = \frac{8}{n}$	Write the proportion.
$2.6 \cdot n = 13 \cdot 8$	Find the cross products.
$2.6n = 104$	Multiply.
$\frac{2.6n}{2.6} = \frac{104}{2.6}$	Divide each side by 2.6.
$n = 40$	Simplify.

CHECK Your Progress

c. $\frac{16}{k} = \frac{2}{3}$ d. $\frac{2}{6} = \frac{5}{h}$ e. $\frac{10}{k} = \frac{2.5}{4}$

Real-World Career
How Does a Physician's Assistant Use Math?
A physician's assistant uses math when calculating safe dosages of medications.

Math Online
For more information visit, glencoe.com.

Real-World EXAMPLE

4 **MEDICINE** For every 18 people who have a sore throat, there are 2 people who actually have strep throat. If 72 patients have sore throats, how many of these would you expect to have strep throat?

METHOD 1 **Write and solve a proportion.**

Let s represent strep throat.

$\frac{2 \text{ strep throats}}{18 \text{ sore throats}} = \frac{s}{72 \text{ sore throats}}$	Write a proportion.
$2 \cdot 72 = 18 \cdot s$	Find the cross products.
$144 = 18s$	Multiply.
$8 = s$	Divide each side by 18.

METHOD 2 **Find and use a unit rate or ratio.**

$\frac{2 \text{ strep throats} \div 2}{18 \text{ sore throats} \div 2} = \frac{1}{9}$ The ratio of strep throats to sore throats is 1 : 9.

Words	For every 9 sore throats, there is 1 strep throat.
Variable	Let s represent the number of strep throats.
Equation	$s = \frac{1}{9} \cdot 72$

$s = \frac{1}{9} \cdot 72$ or 8 Multiply.

So, you would expect 8 people to have strep throat.

CHOOSE Your Method

f. **RUNNING** Salvador can run 120 meters in 24 seconds. At this rate, how many seconds will it take him to run a 300-meter race?

CHECK Your Understanding

Example 1 (p. 311)

Determine if the quantities in each pair of ratios are proportional. Explain.

1. 2 adults for 10 children and 3 adults for 12 children
2. 12 inches by 8 inches and 18 inches by 12 inches
3. 8 feet in 21 seconds and 12 feet in 31.5 seconds
4. $5.60 for 5 pairs of socks and $7.12 for 8 pairs of socks

Examples 2, 3 (pp. 311–312)

Solve each proportion.

5. $\frac{5}{6} = \frac{t}{18}$
6. $\frac{6}{k} = \frac{24}{28}$
7. $\frac{21}{5} = \frac{c}{7}$
8. $\frac{15}{w} = \frac{2}{5}$
9. $\frac{3}{n} = \frac{2.7}{18}$
10. $\frac{0.2}{3} = \frac{3}{d}$

Example 4 (p. 312)

11. **GROCERIES** Orange juice is on sale at 3 half-gallons for $5. At this rate, find the cost of 5 half-gallons of orange juice to the nearest cent.
12. **TRAVEL** Franco drove 203 miles in 3.5 hours. At this rate, how long will it take him to drive another 29 miles to the next town?

Practice and Problem Solving

HOMEWORK HELP

For Exercises	See Examples
13–20	1
21–32	2, 3
33–36	4

Determine if the quantities in each pair of ratios are proportional. Explain.

13. 20 children from 6 families to 16 children from 5 families
14. 5 pounds of dry ice melts in 30 hours and 4 pounds melts in 24 hours
15. 16 winners out of 200 entries and 28 winners out of 350 entries
16. 5 meters in 7 minutes and 25 meters in 49 minutes
17. 1.4 tons produced every 18 days and 10.5 tons every 60 days
18. 3 inches for every 4 miles and 7.5 inches for every 10 miles
19. **READING** Leslie reads 25 pages in 45 minutes. After 60 minutes, she has read a total of 30 pages. Is her time proportional to the number of pages she reads? Explain.
20. **PETS** A store sells 2 hamsters for $11 and 6 hamsters for $33. Is the cost proportional to the number of hamsters sold? Explain.

Solve each proportion.

21. $\frac{3}{8} = \frac{b}{40}$
22. $\frac{x}{12} = \frac{12}{4}$
23. $\frac{c}{7} = \frac{18}{42}$
24. $\frac{5}{k} = \frac{10}{22}$
25. $\frac{3}{8} = \frac{n}{4}$
26. $\frac{15}{4} = \frac{3}{g}$
27. $\frac{45}{5} = \frac{d}{7}$
28. $\frac{30}{a} = \frac{8}{20}$
29. $\frac{1.6}{m} = \frac{2}{3}$
30. $\frac{4.5}{5} = \frac{t}{7}$
31. $\frac{2.5}{4.5} = \frac{7.5}{x}$
32. $\frac{3.8}{5.2} = \frac{7.6}{z}$
33. **SCHOOL** If 4 notebooks weigh 2.8 pounds, how much do 6 of the same notebooks weigh?
34. **COOKING** There are 6 teaspoons in 2 tablespoons. How many teaspoons are in 1.5 tablespoons?

35. **SCIENCE** The ratio of salt to water in a certain solution is 4 to 15. If the solution contains 6 ounces of water, how many ounces of salt does it contain?

36. **CONCERTS** Alethia purchased 7 advanced tickets for herself and her friends to a concert and paid $164.50. If the total cost of tickets to the concert is proportional to the number purchased, how many tickets to the same concert did Serefina purchase if she paid a total of $94?

ANALYZE GRAPHS For Exercises 37–40, use the graph. It shows the cost of several pizzas, with and without a delivery fee.

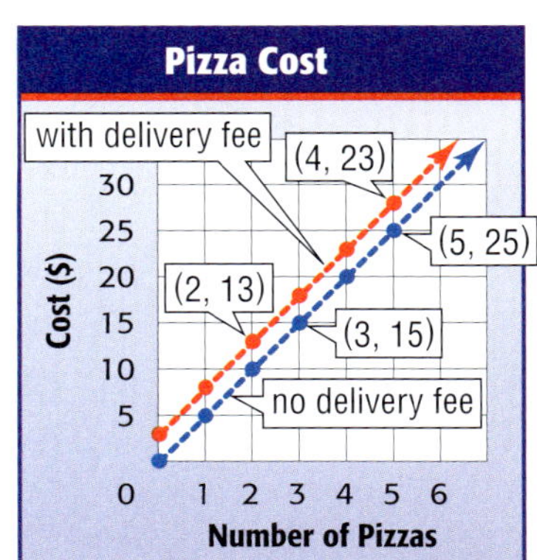

37. What do the points (3, 15) and (5, 25) represent on the graph? Is this situation proportional? Explain.

38. What do the points (2, 13) and (4, 23) represent on the graph? Is this situation proportional? Explain.

39. What is the slope of each line? What does the slope represent?

40. What is the delivery fee? Explain.

Real-World Link Film for an IMAX projection system passes through the projector at the rate of 330 feet per minute or 5.5 feet per second.
Source: IMAX Corporation

41. **SAVINGS** Pao spent $140 of his paycheck and put the remaining $20 in his savings account. If the number of dollars he spends is proportional to the number he saves, how much of a $156-paycheck will he put into savings?

42. **MOVIES** After 30 seconds, 720 frames of film have passed through a movie projector. At this rate, what is the approximate running time in minutes of a movie made up of 57,000 frames of film?

43. **SCHOOL** There are 325 students and 13 teachers at a school. Next school year, the enrollment is expected to increase by 100 students. Write and solve a proportion to find the number of teachers that must be hired so the student-teacher ratio remains the same.

See pages 683, 709.

44. **FIND THE DATA** Refer to the Data File on pages 16–19. Choose some data and write a real-world problem in which you would solve a proportion.

H.O.T. Problems

45. **Which One Doesn't Belong?** Identify the rate that is not proportional to the other three. Explain your reasoning.

$4.50 for 5 lb	$2.88 for 3.2 lb	$5.70 for 6 lb	$4.86 for 5.4 lb

46. **CHALLENGE** In a cleaning solution, the ratio of bleach to water is 1:5. If there are 36 cups of cleaning solution, how many cups of water are needed? Explain your reasoning.

47. **SELECT A TECHNIQUE** Sweet corn is on sale at $2.50 for a dozen at a farmer's market. Select one or more of the following technique(s) to determine how many ears you can buy for $10. Then use this technique to solve the problem.

mental math | estimation | number sense

48. **WRITING IN MATH** Explain why the cross products of a proportion are equal. Use the term *multiplicative inverse* in your explanation.

TEST PRACTICE

49. Mirma gives away 84 flyers over a 3-hour period. If the number of flyers she is able to give away per hour remains the same, which proportion can be used to find x, the number of flyers that she would give away over a 5-hour period?

A $\frac{3}{84} = \frac{x}{5}$ **C** $\frac{5}{3} = \frac{84}{x}$

B $\frac{84}{3} = \frac{x}{5}$ **D** $\frac{3}{84} = \frac{x}{8}$

50. A recipe that makes 16 muffins calls for $\frac{1}{2}$ cup of flour. How much flour is needed to make 3 dozen muffins using this recipe?

F $1\frac{1}{8}$ c

G 1 c

H $1\frac{1}{4}$ c

J $1\frac{1}{2}$ c

Spiral Review

51. **MEASUREMENT** Felicia bought 5 pounds of onions. About how many kilograms of onions did she buy? (Lesson 6-5)

MEASUREMENT **Complete.** (Lesson 6-4)

52. 5 qt = ▒ pt 53. $3\frac{1}{2}$ lb = ▒ oz 54. 28 c = ▒ qt

Multiply. Write in simplest form. (Lesson 5-5)

55. $3\frac{1}{2} \times 5\frac{7}{8}$ 56. $1\frac{2}{3} \times 5\frac{4}{5}$ 57. $2\frac{1}{4} \times 7\frac{5}{8}$

GET READY for the Next Lesson

58. **PREREQUISITE SKILL** Mr. Andres is filling up his car with gas that costs $2.50 per gallon. His car's gas gauge before filling up is shown at the right. If his car's gas tank holds 16 gallons, about how much will Mr. Andres pay to fill up his tank? Use the *eliminate possibilities* strategy. (Lesson 5-4)

A $15.00 **C** $27.00

B $25.00 **D** $35.00

Extend 6-6

Math Lab
Inverse Proportionality

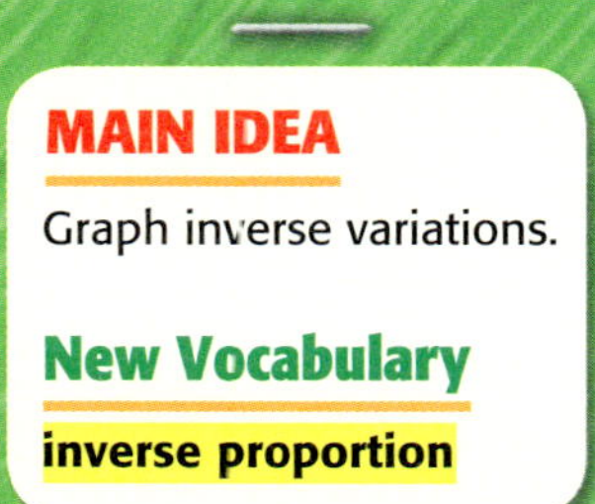

Jackie walks at an average rate of 4 miles per hour. This situation can be represented by the equation $d = 4t$, where d is the distance in miles, and t is the time in hours. The number of miles is proportional to the number of hours because the ratios are equal.

Let's vary the situation a little. Suppose Jackie wants to walk 12 miles each day, at varying speeds. How long will it take her to walk 12 miles? The answer depends on how fast she walks.

ACTIVITY

STEP 1 Copy and complete the table for the equation $12 = rt$.

t (hours)	12	8	6				
r (miles per hour)	1	1.5	2	2.5	3	3.5	4

STEP 2 Copy and complete the graph of the ordered pairs from Step 1. Connect the line with a smooth curve. The first three points are done for you.

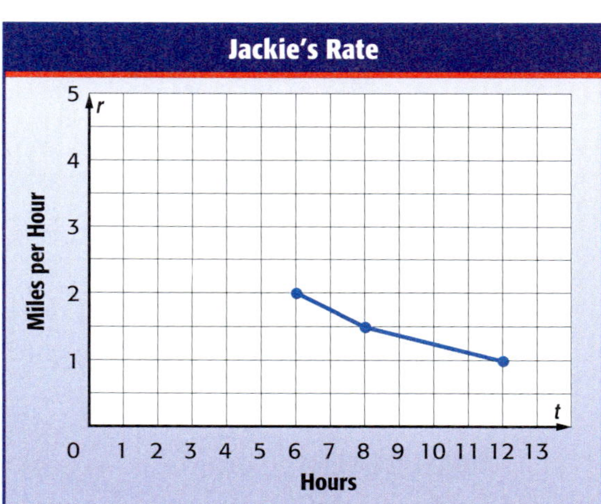

Analyze the Results

1. Is the time proportional to the rate? Explain why or why not.
2. When the product of two variables is a constant, the relationship forms an **inverse proportion.** Which situation is an inverse proportion: Jackie walking at 4 miles per hour or walking 12 miles at varying rates? Identify the constants in each situation.
3. Mr. Anwar agrees to pay Rob a flat fee of $240 to do some yard work. Mr. Sloan agrees to pay Rob's brother $10 per hour to do some yard work. Make a table of ordered pairs and a graph for each situation. Then decide whether each relationship is a proportion or an inverse proportion.

Chapter 6 Mid-Chapter Quiz

Lessons 6-1 through 6-6

RECIPE For Exercises 1–3, use the information in the table to write each ratio as a fraction in simplest form. (Lesson 6-1)

Cherry Punch Recipe	
Cherry Juice	4 cups
Apple Juice	2 cups
Ginger Ale	16 cups

1. cherry juice : apple juice
2. apple juice : ginger ale
3. cherry juice : ginger ale

Determine whether the ratios are equivalent. Explain. (Lesson 6-1)

4. 6 out of 9 words spelled correctly
   2 out of 3 words spelled correctly
5. 150 athletes to 15 coaches
   3 athletes to 1 coach
6. 24 points in 4 games
   72 points in 8 games
7. **MULTIPLE CHOICE** Which amount of chocolate shown in the table has the best unit price? (Lesson 6-2)

Weight (oz)	Cost ($)
12	2.50
18	3.69
24	4.95
30	6.25

A 12 oz
B 18 oz
C 24 oz
D 36 oz

8. Use the graph to find the rate of change in cost per magazine. (Lesson 6-3)

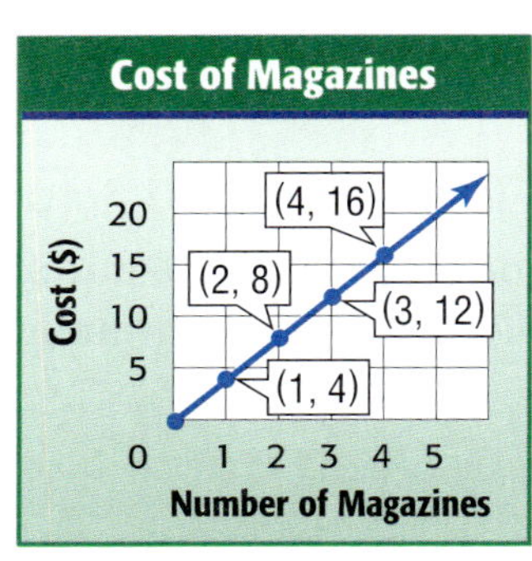

Complete. (Lesson 6-4)

9. 42 ft = ▒ yd
10. 9 pt = ▒ qt
11. 7,600 lb = ▒ T
12. $7\frac{1}{2}$ gal = ▒ qt

13. **MULTIPLE CHOICE** Which situation is best represented by the graph? (Lesson 6-4)

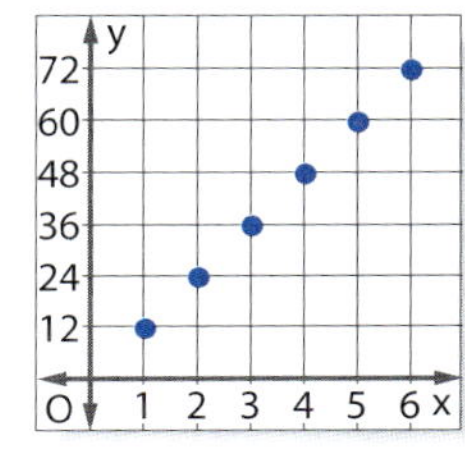

F conversion of inches to yards
G conversion of feet to inches
H conversion of inches to miles
J conversion of yards to feet

Complete. Round to the nearest hundredth if necessary. (Lesson 6-5)

14. 12.5 mi ≈ ▒ km
15. 4.75 gal ≈ ▒ L
16. 76 cm ≈ ▒ in.
17. 31.8 kg ≈ ▒ lb

Determine if the quantities in each pair of ratios are proportional. Explain. (Lesson 6-6)

18. 8 pages in 5 minutes and 40 pages in 25 minutes
19. 40 blank CDs for $9.60 and 24 blank CDs for $4.80

Solve each proportion. (Lesson 6-6)

20. $\frac{3}{d} = \frac{12}{20}$
21. $\frac{7}{8} = \frac{m}{48}$
22. $\frac{w}{8} = \frac{1}{3}$

23. **MEASUREMENT** It took 45 minutes to fill a circular pool of uniform depth to a level of 18 inches. At this rate, how long will it take to fill the pool to a level of 35 inches? (Lesson 6-6)

6-7 Problem-Solving Investigation

MAIN IDEA: Solve problems by drawing a diagram.

P.S.I. TEAM +

e-Mail: DRAW A DIAGRAM

CACEY: I dropped a ball from a height of 12 feet. It hits the ground and bounces up half as high as it fell. This is true for each successive bounce.

YOUR MISSION: Draw a diagram to find the height the ball reaches after the fourth bounce.

Understand	You know the ball is dropped from a height of 12 feet. It bounces up half as high as it falls.
Plan	Draw a diagram to show the height of the ball after each bounce.
Solve	12 ft; 6 ft; 3 ft; $1\frac{1}{2}$ ft; $\frac{3}{4}$ ft; 1, 2, 3, 4 The ball reaches a height of $\frac{3}{4}$ foot after the fourth bounce.
Check	Start at 12 feet. Multiply by $\frac{1}{2}$ for each bounce: $12 \cdot \frac{1}{2} \cdot \frac{1}{2} \cdot \frac{1}{2} \cdot \frac{1}{2} = \frac{12}{16}$ or $\frac{3}{4}$. So, the solution is correct.

Analyze The Strategy

1. Determine what height a ball would reach after the fourth bounce if it is dropped from 12 feet and bounces up $\frac{2}{3}$ as high. Draw a new diagram for this situation.
2. **WRITING IN MATH** Write a problem that could be solved by drawing a diagram. Exchange your problem with a classmate and solve.

Mixed Problem Solving

Solve Exercises 3–5. Use the *draw a diagram* strategy.

3. **TRAVEL** Mr. Garcia has driven 60 miles, which is $\frac{2}{3}$ of the way to his sister's house. How much farther does he have to drive to get to his sister's house?

4. **DISTANCE** Alejandro and Pedro are riding their bikes to school. After 1 mile, they are $\frac{4}{5}$ of the way there. How much farther do they have to go?

5. **VOLUME** A swimming pool is being filled with water. After 25 minutes, $\frac{1}{6}$ of the swimming pool is filled. How much longer will it take to completely fill the pool, assuming the water rate is constant?

Use any strategy to solve Exercises 6–10. Some strategies are shown below.

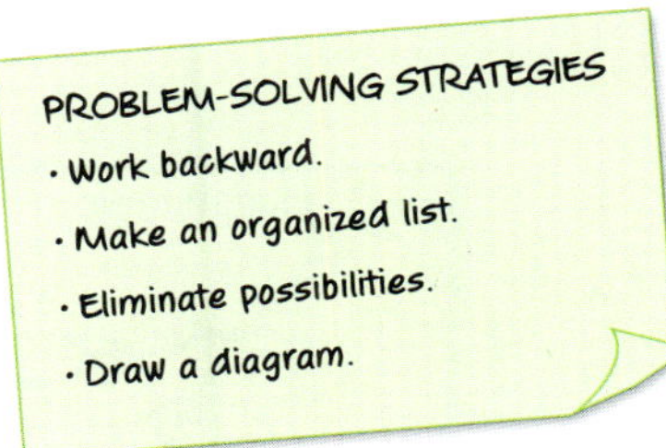

6. **BASEBALL** Of Lee's baseball cards, $\frac{1}{5}$ show California players. Of these, $\frac{3}{8}$ show San Diego Padres players. Is the fraction of Lee's collection that show Padres players $\frac{23}{40}$, $\frac{4}{13}$, or $\frac{3}{40}$?

7. **GAMES** Eight members of a chess club are having a tournament. In the first round, every player will play a chess game against every other player. How many games will be in the first round of the tournament?

8. **MEASUREMENT** Kiaya is adding a 2-inch border to the length and width of a photograph as shown.

Which expression represents the area of the border to be added to the original photograph?

A $(8 + 4)(10 + 4)$

B $(8 + 4)(10 + 4) - (8)(10)$

C $(8 - 4)(10 - 4)$

D $(8 - 4)(10 - 4) - (8)(10)$

9. **RACES** Anna, Isabela, Mary, and Pilar ran a race. Anna is just ahead of Pilar. Pilar is two places behind Isabela. Isabela is a few seconds behind the leader, Mary. Use the table to place the girls in order from first to last.

10. **FRACTIONS** Marta ate a quarter of a whole pie. Edwin ate $\frac{1}{4}$ of what was left. Cristina then ate $\frac{1}{3}$ of what was left. What fraction of the pie remains?

6-8 Scale Drawings

MAIN IDEA

Solve problems involving scale drawings.

New Vocabulary

scale drawing
scale model
scale
scale factor

Math Online

glencoe.com

- Concepts In Motion
- Extra Examples
- Personal Tutor
- Self-Check Quiz

MINI Lab

- Measure the length of each item in a room, such as a gymnasium.
- Record each length to the nearest $\frac{1}{2}$ foot.

1. Let 1 unit on the grid paper represent 2 feet. So, 4 units = 8 feet. Convert all your measurements to units.
2. On grid paper, make a drawing of your gymnasium like the one shown at the right.

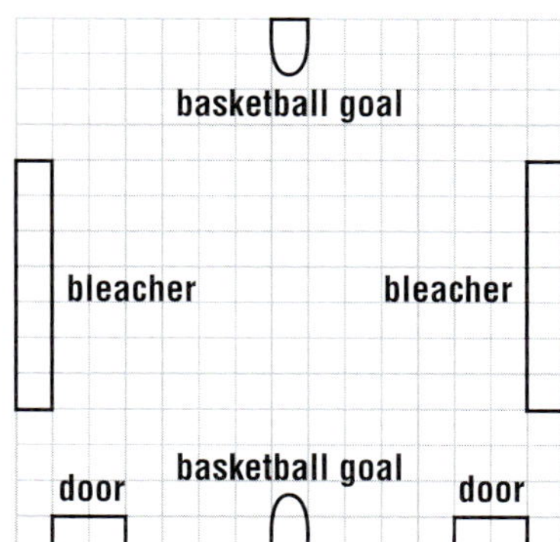

A map is an example of a scale drawing. **Scale drawings** and **scale models** are used to represent objects that are too large or too small to be drawn or built at actual size. The **scale** gives the ratio that compares the measurements of the drawing or model to the measurements of the real object. The measurements on a drawing or model are proportional to measurements of the actual object.

EXAMPLE Use a Map Scale

1 **MAPS** **What is the actual distance between Hagerstown and Annapolis?**

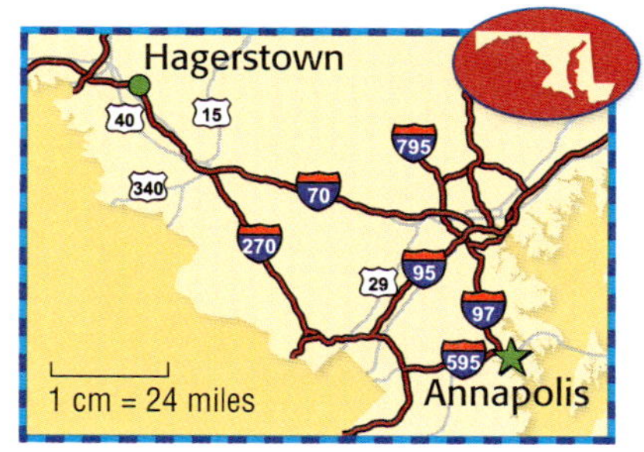

Step 1 Use a centimeter ruler to find the map distance between the two cities. The map distance is about 4 centimeters.

Step 2 Write and solve a proportion using the scale. Let d represent the actual distance between the cities.

	Scale		Length	
map → / actual →	$\frac{1 \text{ centimeter}}{24 \text{ miles}}$	=	$\frac{4 \text{ centimeters}}{d \text{ miles}}$	← map / ← actual

$$1 \times d = 24 \times 4 \quad \text{Cross products}$$

$$d = 96 \quad \text{Simplify.}$$

The distance between the cities is about 96 miles.

CHECK Your Progress

a. **MAPS** On the map of Arkansas shown, find the actual distance between Clarksville and Little Rock. Use a ruler to measure.

> **Study Tip**
>
> **Scale** A map scale can be written in different ways, including the following:
>
> 1 cm = 20 mi
>
> 1 cm : 20 mi
>
> $\frac{1 \text{ cm}}{20 \text{ mi}}$

A blueprint is another example of a scale drawing.

EXAMPLE Use a Blueprint Scale

2 **DECKS On the blueprint of the deck, each square has a side length of $\frac{1}{2}$ inch. What is the actual width of the deck?**

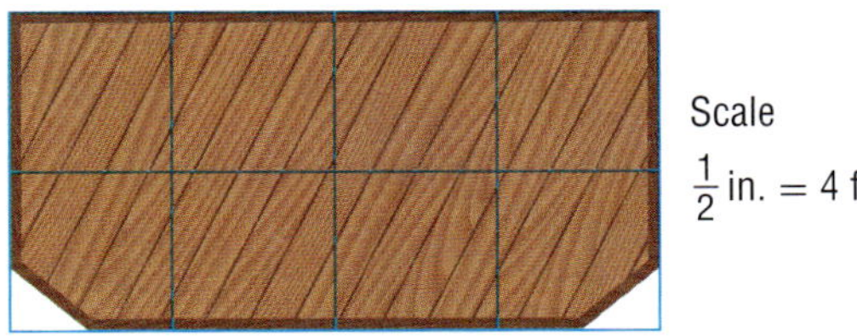

The deck on the blueprint is 2 inches wide. Write and solve a proportion using the scale. Let w represent the actual width of the deck.

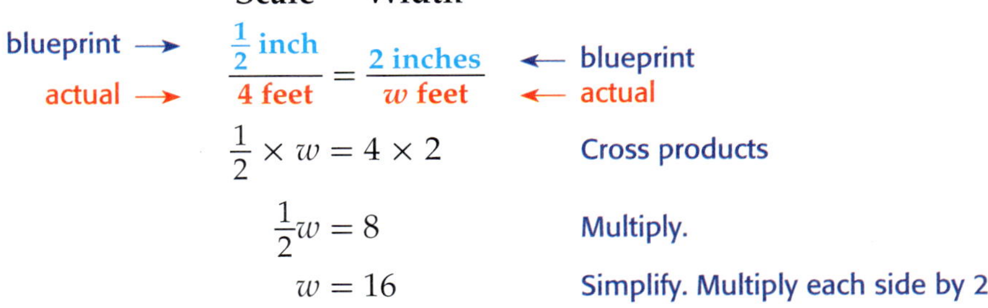

	Scale		Width	
blueprint →	$\frac{1}{2}$ inch	=	2 inches	← blueprint
actual →	4 feet		w feet	← actual

$\frac{1}{2} \times w = 4 \times 2$ Cross products

$\frac{1}{2}w = 8$ Multiply.

$w = 16$ Simplify. Multiply each side by 2.

The actual width of the deck is 16 feet.

> **Study Tip**
>
> **Scales** Scales and scale factors are always written so that the drawing length comes first in the ratio.

CHECK Your Progress

b. **INTERIOR DESIGN** On the blueprint of the living room, each square has a side length of $\frac{1}{4}$ inch. What are the actual dimensions of the living room?

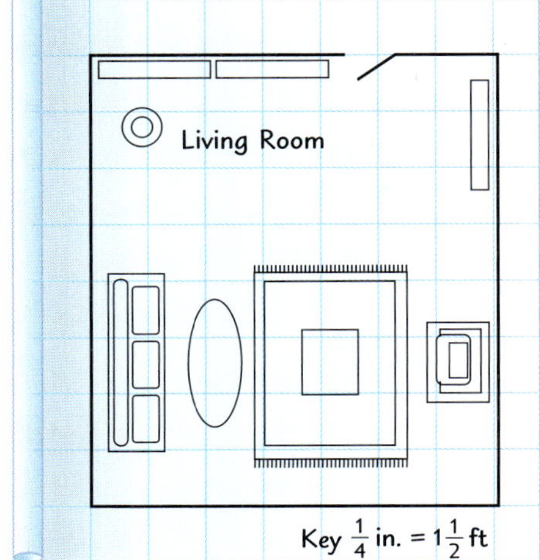

EXAMPLE Use a Scale Model

Study Tip

Scale The scale is the ratio of the drawing/model measure to the actual measure. It is not always the ratio of a smaller measure to a larger measure.

3 **PHONES** **A graphic artist is creating an advertisement for a new cell phone. If she uses a scale of 5 inches = 1 inch, what is the length of the cell phone on the advertisement?**

Write a proportion using the scale. Let a represent the length of the advertisement cell phone.

	Scale		Length	
advertisement →	5 inches	=	a inches	← advertisement
actual →	1 inch		4 inches	← actual

$$\frac{5 \text{ inches}}{1 \text{ inch}} = \frac{a \text{ inches}}{4 \text{ inches}}$$

$5 \cdot 4 = 1 \cdot a$ Cross products

$20 = a$ Multiply.

The length of the cell phone on the advertisement is 20 inches long.

CHECK Your Progress

c. **SCOOTERS** A scooter is $3\frac{1}{2}$ feet long. Find the length of a scale model of the scooter if the scale is 1 inch = $\frac{3}{4}$ feet.

In Lesson 6-4, you used ratios to convert units. You can use a similar method to simplify a scale. A scale written as a ratio without units in simplest form is called the **scale factor**.

scale: $\dfrac{\frac{1}{4}\text{ inch}}{2 \text{ feet}} = \dfrac{\frac{1}{4}\text{ inch}}{24 \text{ inches}}$ Convert 2 feet to inches.

$= \dfrac{4}{4} \cdot \dfrac{\frac{1}{4}\text{ inch}}{24 \text{ inches}}$ Multiply by $\frac{4}{4}$ to eliminate the fraction in the numerator. Divide out the common units.

$= \dfrac{1}{96}$ scale factor

EXAMPLE Find a Scale Factor

Study Tip

Equivalent Scales The scales below are equivalent because their scale factors are equal, $\frac{1}{72}$.

- 1 inch = 6 feet
- $\frac{1}{2}$ inch = 3 feet

4 **SAILBOATS** **Find the scale factor of a model sailboat if the scale is 1 inch = 6 feet.**

$\dfrac{1 \text{ inch}}{6 \text{ feet}} = \dfrac{1 \text{ inch}}{72 \text{ inches}}$ Convert 6 feet to inches.

$= \dfrac{1}{72}$ Divide out the common units.

The scale factor is $\frac{1}{72}$.

CHECK Your Progress

d. **CARS** What is the scale factor of a model car if the scale is 1 inch = 2 feet?

CHECK Your Understanding

Example 1 (pp. 320–321)

GEOGRAPHY **Find the actual distance between each pair of cities in New Mexico. Use a ruler to measure.**

1. Carlsbad and Artesia
2. Hobbs and Eunice
3. Artesia and Eunice
4. Lovington and Carlsbad

Example 2 (p. 321)

BLUEPRINTS **For Exercises 5 and 6, use the blueprint. Each square has a side length of $\frac{1}{4}$ inch.**

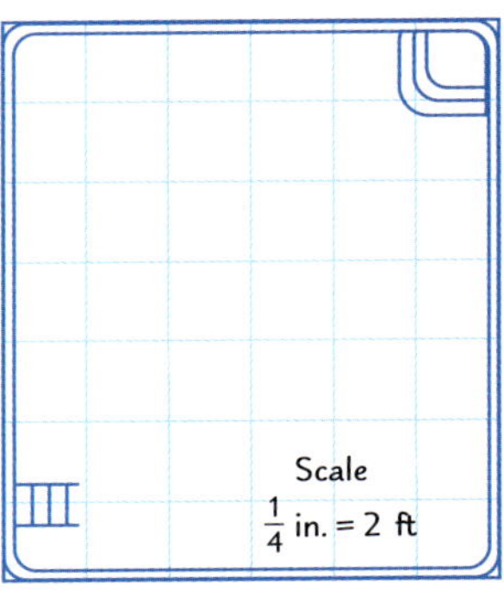

5. What is the actual length of the pool?
6. What is the actual width of the pool?

Example 3 (p. 322)

BRIDGES **For Exercises 7 and 8, use the following information.**

An engineer makes a model of the bridge using a scale of 1 inch = 3 yards.

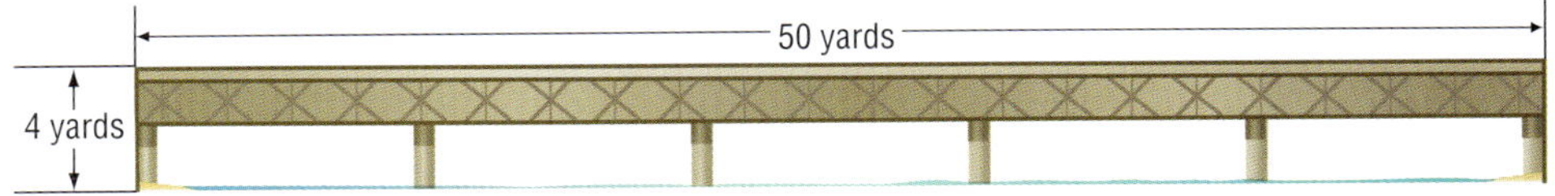

7. What is the length of the model?
8. What is the height of the model?

Example 4 (p. 322)

Find the scale factor of each scale drawing or model.

9. 

1 inch = 4 feet

10. 

1 centimeter = 15 millimeters

11. **CITY PLANNING** In the aerial view of a city block at the right, the length of Main Street is 2 inches. If Main Street's actual length is 2 miles, find the scale factor of the drawing.

Practice and Problem Solving

HOMEWORK HELP

For Exercises	See Examples
12–15	1
16–17	2
18–24	3, 4

GEOGRAPHY **Find the actual distance between each pair of locations in South Carolina. Use a ruler to measure.**

12. Columbia and Charleston
13. Hollywood and Sumter
14. Congaree Swamp and Charleston
15. Sumter and Columbia

For Exercises 16–18, use the blueprint of an apartment at the right. Each square has a side length of $\frac{1}{4}$ inch.

16. What is the actual length of the living room?
17. Find the actual dimensions of the master bedroom.
18. Find the scale factor for this blueprint.

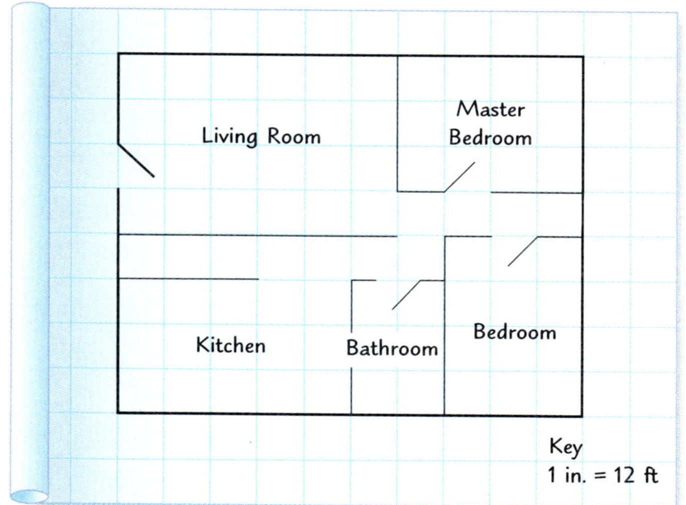

Find the length of each model. Then find the scale factor.

19.

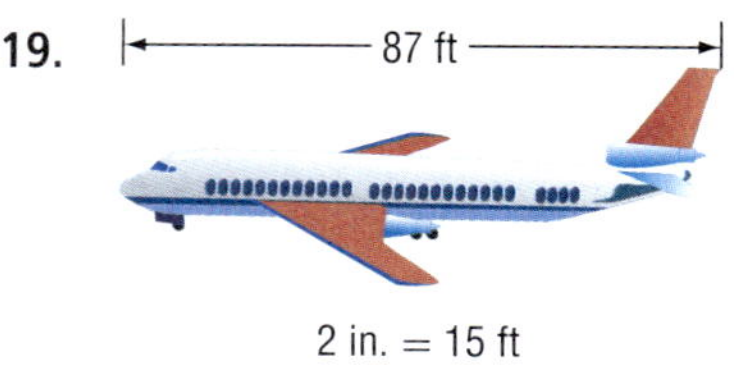

2 in. = 15 ft

20.

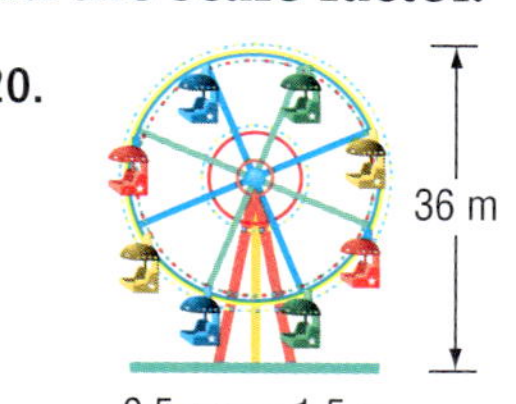

0.5 cm = 1.5 m

21.

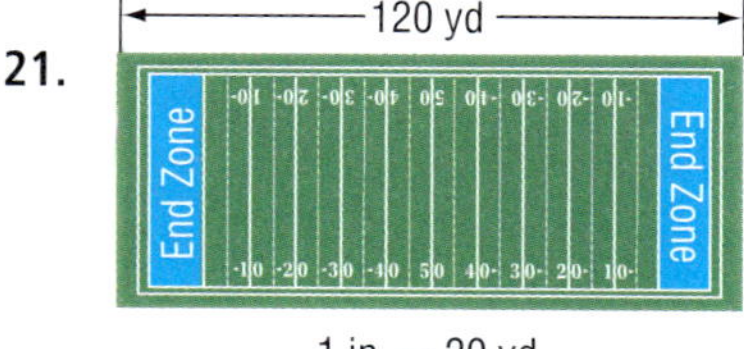

1 in. = 20 yd

22.

$5\frac{7}{8}$ in.

1 in. = 0.5 in.

Real-World Link The statue of Thomas Jefferson inside the Jefferson Memorial in Washington, D.C., was made using a scale of 3 feet : 1 foot.

Source: National Register of Historic Places

23. **GEOGRAPHY** A map of Bakersfield, California, has a scale of 1 inch to 5 miles. If the city is $5\frac{1}{5}$ inches across on the map, what is the actual distance across the actual city? Use estimation to check your answer.

24. **TREES** A model of a tree is made using a scale of 1 inch : 25 feet. What is the height of the actual tree if the height of the model is $4\frac{3}{8}$ inches?

25. **STATUES** Refer to the information at the left. Find the scale factor and the actual height of Thomas Jefferson if the height of the statue is 19 feet.

26. **GEOGRAPHY** Lexington and Elizabethtown, Kentucky, are 79 miles apart. If the distance on the map is $2\frac{1}{2}$ inches, find the scale of the map.

27. **RESEARCH** Find the dimensions of any U.S. presidential monument. Give an appropriate scale that can be used to make a scale model of the monument. State the dimensions of the model using your scale.

28. **BUILDINGS** If you are making a model of your bedroom, which would be an appropriate scale: 1 inch = 2 feet, or 1 inch = 12 feet?

29. **LIFE SCIENCE** A scale drawing of a red blood cell is shown below. If the blood cell's actual diameter is 0.008 millimeter, use a ruler to find the scale factor of the drawing.

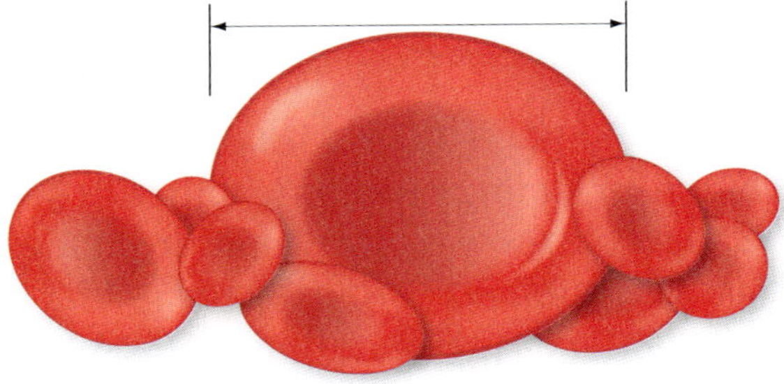

EXTRA PRACTICE See pages 684, 709.

H.O.T. Problems

30. **OPEN ENDED** On grid paper, create a scale drawing of a room in your home. Include the scale that you used.

31. **CHALLENGE** Montoya constructed three models, A, B, and C, of the same figure, with scales of 0.5 cm = 1 mm, 1.5 mm = 4 cm, and 0.25 cm = 2.5 mm, respectively.
    a. Which model is larger than the actual figure? Justify your answer.
    b. Which model is smaller than the actual figure? Justify your answer.
    c. Which model is the same size as the actual figure? Justify your answer.

32. **REASONING** Compare and contrast the terms *scale* and *scale factor*. Include an example in your comparison.

33. **WRITING IN MATH** Explain how you could use estimation to find the actual distance between San Diego, California, and Seattle, Washington, on a map.

34. A scale drawing of a doctor's office is shown.

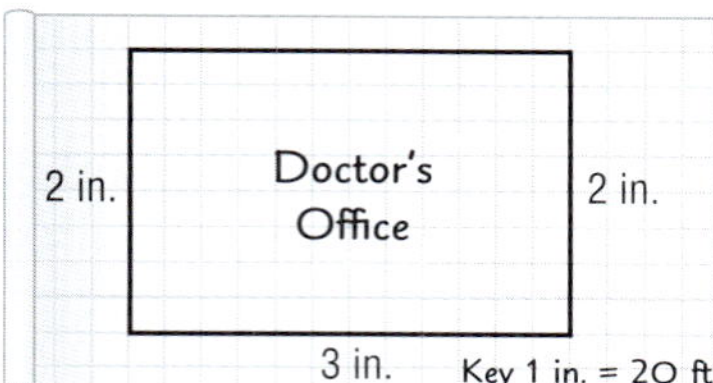

What are the actual dimensions of the doctor's office?

A 24 feet by 48 feet

B 30 feet by 52 feet

C 40 feet by 60 feet

D 37.5 feet by 65 feet

35. A certain map has a scale of $\frac{1}{4}$ inch = 30 miles. How many miles are represented by 4 inches on this map?

F 480 miles

G 120 miles

H 30 miles

J 16 miles

36. Ernesto drew a map of his school. He used a scale of 1 inch : 50 feet. What distance on Ernesto's map should represent the 625 feet between the cafeteria and the science lab?

A 8 in.

B 10.5 in.

C 12.5 in.

D 15 in.

Spiral Review

37. **FAMILY** At Nelia's family reunion, $\frac{4}{5}$ of the people are 18 years of age or older. Half of the remaining people are under 12 years old. If 20 children are under 12 years old, how many people are at the reunion? Use the *draw a diagram* strategy. (Lesson 6-7)

Solve each proportion. (Lesson 6-6)

38. $\frac{5}{7} = \frac{a}{35}$

39. $\frac{12}{p} = \frac{36}{45}$

40. $\frac{3}{9} = \frac{21}{k}$

41. **JOGGING** The table shows the number of miles Tonya jogged each week for the past several weeks. Estimate the total number of miles she jogged. (Lesson 5-1)

Week	Miles
1	$7\frac{1}{6}$
2	$8\frac{3}{4}$
3	10
4	$12\frac{1}{4}$
5	$6\frac{2}{3}$

Find the LCM of each set of numbers. (Lesson 4-8)

42. 2, 4

43. 4, 8, 12

44. 3, 7, 5

45. 5, 10, 15

46. 2, 6, 9

47. 3, 15, 20

GET READY for the Next Lesson

PREREQUISITE SKILL **Divide. Write in simplest form.** (Lesson 5-7)

48. $2\frac{3}{4} \div 10$

49. $4\frac{1}{3} \div 10$

50. $30\frac{2}{3} \div 100$

51. $87\frac{1}{2} \div 100$

Spreadsheet Lab
Scale Drawings

MAIN IDEA

Use a spreadsheet to calculate measurements for scale drawings.

A computer spreadsheet is a useful tool for calculating measures for scale drawings. You can change the scale factors and the dimensions, and the spreadsheet will automatically calculate the new values.

ACTIVITY

Suppose you want to make a scale drawing of your school. Set up a spreadsheet like the one shown below. In this spreadsheet, the actual measures are in feet, and the scale drawing measures are in inches.

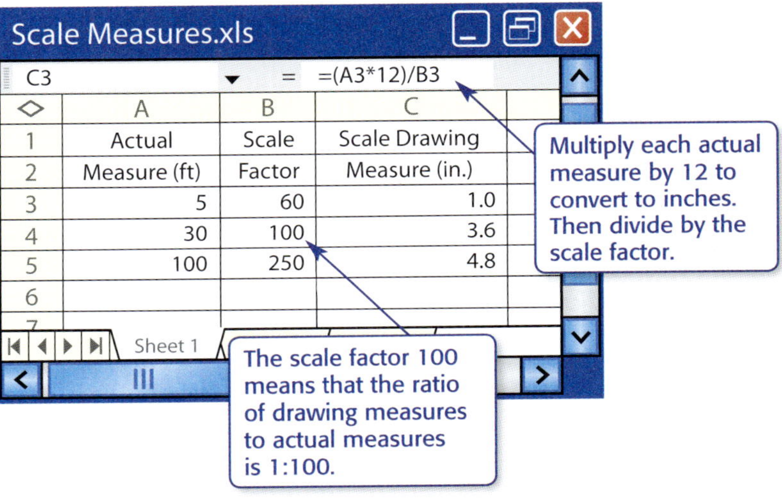

	A	B	C
1	Actual	Scale	Scale Drawing
2	Measure (ft)	Factor	Measure (in.)
3	5	60	1.0
4	30	100	3.6
5	100	250	4.8
6			

Analyze the Results

1. The length of one side of the school building is 100 feet. If you use a scale factor of 1:250, what is the length on your scale drawing?
2. The length of a classroom is 30 feet. What is the scale factor if the length of the classroom on a scale drawing is 3.6 inches?
3. Calculate the length of a 30-foot classroom on a scale drawing if the scale factor is 1:10.
4. The width of a hallway is 20 feet. What is the scale factor if the width of the hallway on a scale drawing is 2.5 inches?
5. Suppose the actual measures of your school are given in meters. Describe how you could use a spreadsheet to calculate the scale drawing measures in centimeters using a scale factor of 1:50.
6. Choose three rooms in your home and use a spreadsheet to make scale drawings. First, choose an appropriate scale and calculate the scale factor. Include a sketch of the furniture drawn to scale in each room.

6-9 Fractions, Decimals, and Percents

MAIN IDEA

Write percents as fractions, and decimals and vice versa.

Math Online

glencoe.com

- Extra Examples
- Personal Tutor
- Self-Check Quiz

GET READY for the Lesson

SURVEYS The graph shows the results of a survey about favorite type of TV show.

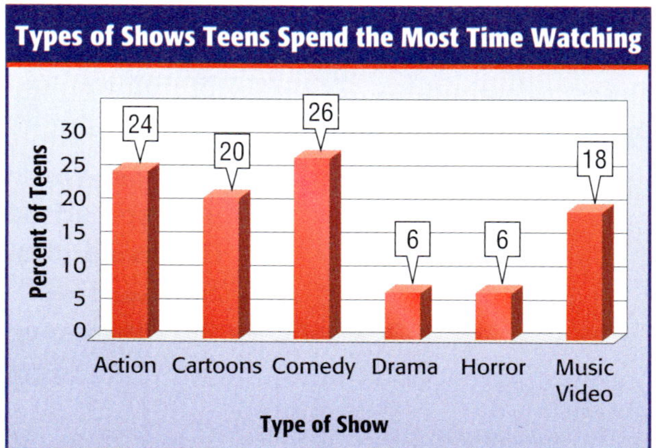

Source: Kids USA Survey

1. What percent of the teens chose comedy?
2. Write this percent as a ratio in simplest form.

In Lesson 4-6, you wrote percents like 26% as fractions by writing fractions with denominators of 100 and then simplifying. You can use the same method to write percents like $8\frac{1}{3}\%$ and 190% as fractions.

EXAMPLES Percents as Fractions

1 **Write $8\frac{1}{3}\%$ as a fraction in simplest form.**

$$8\frac{1}{3}\% = \frac{8\frac{1}{3}}{100} \quad \text{Write a fraction.}$$

$$= 8\frac{1}{3} \div 100 \quad \text{Divide.}$$

$$= \frac{25}{3} \div 100 \quad \text{Write } 8\frac{1}{3} \text{ as an improper fraction.}$$

$$= \frac{25}{3} \cdot \frac{1}{100} \quad \text{Multiply by the reciprocal of 100, which is } \frac{1}{100}.$$

$$= \frac{25}{300} \text{ or } \frac{1}{12} \quad \text{Simplify.}$$

2 **TOYS** **A collectible action figure sold for 190% of its original price. Write this percent as a fraction in simplest form.**

$$190\% = \frac{190}{100} \quad \text{Definition of percent}$$

$$= \frac{19}{10} \text{ or } 1\frac{9}{10} \quad \text{Simplify.}$$

A percent greater than 100 is equal to a number greater than 1.

So, the toy sold for $1\frac{9}{10}$ of its original price.

CHECK Your Progress

Write each percent as a fraction in simplest form.

a. 150% b. $17\frac{1}{2}\%$ c. $33\frac{1}{3}\%$

To write a fraction like $\frac{8}{25}$ as a percent, multiply the numerator and the denominator by a number so that the denominator is 100. If the denominator is not a factor of 100, you can write fractions as percents by using a proportion.

EXAMPLES Fractions as Percents

3 **Write $\frac{4}{15}$ as a percent. Round to the nearest hundredth.**

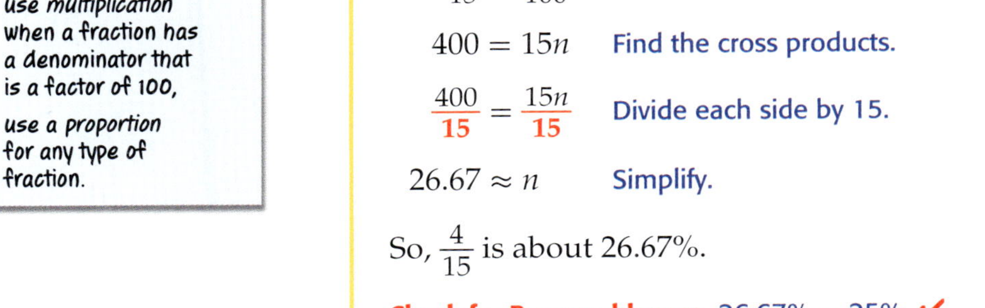

Study Tip

Choose the Method To write a fraction as a percent,
- use multiplication when a fraction has a denominator that is a factor of 100,
- use a proportion for any type of fraction.

Estimate $\frac{4}{15}$ is about $\frac{4}{16}$, which equals $\frac{1}{4}$ or 25%.

$\frac{4}{15} = \frac{n}{100}$ Write a proportion.

$400 = 15n$ Find the cross products.

$\frac{400}{15} = \frac{15n}{15}$ Divide each side by 15.

$26.67 \approx n$ Simplify.

So, $\frac{4}{15}$ is about 26.67%.

Check for Reasonableness 26.67% ≈ 25% ✔

4 **BLOGGING** **In Boston, $\frac{89}{100{,}000}$ residents blog. Write this fraction as a percent.**

$\frac{89}{100{,}000} = \frac{n}{100}$ Write a proportion.

$8{,}900 = 100{,}000n$ Find the cross products.

$\frac{8{,}900}{100{,}000} = \frac{100{,}000n}{100{,}000}$ Divide each side by 100,000.

$0.089 = n$ Simplify.

So, 0.089% of Boston's residents blog.

A percent less than 1% is equal to a number less than 0.01 or $\frac{1}{100}$.

CHECK Your Progress

Write each fraction as a percent. Round to the nearest hundredth if necessary.

d. $\frac{2}{15}$ e. $\frac{7}{1{,}600}$ f. $\frac{17}{25}$

Study Tip

Look Back You can review writing fractions as decimals in lesson 4-3.

In this lesson, you have written percents as fractions and fractions as percents. In Chapter 4, you wrote percents and fractions as decimals. You can also write a fraction as a percent by first writing the fraction as a decimal and then writing the decimal as a percent.

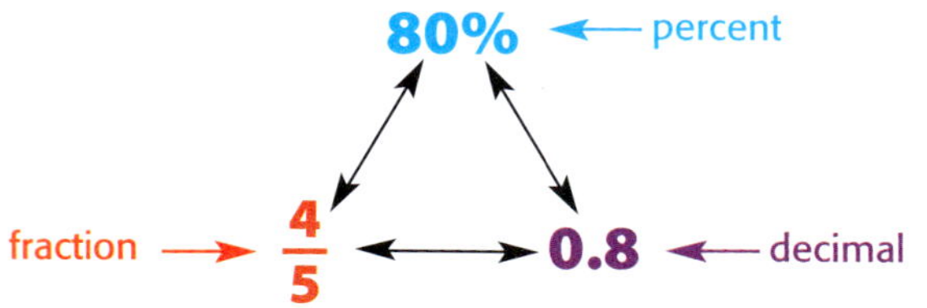

Percents, fractions, and decimals are different names that represent the same number.

EXAMPLES Fractions as Percents

5 **Write $\frac{5}{6}$ as a percent. Round to the nearest hundredth.**

$\frac{5}{6} = 0.833333333...$ Write $\frac{5}{6}$ as a decimal.

$\approx 83.33\%$ Multiply by 100 and add the %.

6 **BOOKS** **Bryce has read $\frac{3}{5}$ of a book. What percent of the book has he read?**

$\frac{3}{5} = 0.6$ Write the fraction as a decimal.

$= 60\%$ Multiply by 100 and add the %.

So, Bryce has read 60% of the book.

CHECK Your Progress

Write each fraction as a percent. Round to the nearest hundredth if necessary.

g. $\frac{5}{16}$ h. $\frac{7}{12}$ i. $\frac{2}{9}$

j. **LAWNS** Mika is mowing lawns to earn extra money. She has mowed 6 out of 13 lawns. What percent of the lawns has she mowed?

Some fractions with denominators that are not factors of 100 are used often in everyday situations. It is helpful to memorize these fractions and their equivalent decimals and percents. These common equivalents are shown below.

Common Equivalents (Key Concept)

Fraction	Decimal	Percent	Fraction	Decimal	Percent
$\frac{1}{3}$	$0.\overline{3}$	$33\frac{1}{3}\%$	$\frac{3}{8}$	0.375	$37\frac{1}{2}\%$
$\frac{2}{3}$	$0.\overline{6}$	$66\frac{2}{3}\%$	$\frac{5}{8}$	0.625	$62\frac{1}{2}\%$
$\frac{1}{8}$	0.125	$12\frac{1}{2}\%$	$\frac{7}{8}$	0.875	$87\frac{1}{2}\%$

CHECK Your Understanding

Examples 1, 2 (pp. 328–329)

Write each percent as a fraction in simplest form.

1. 135%
2. 18.75%
3. $7\frac{1}{2}\%$
4. $66\frac{2}{3}\%$
5. **FOOD** Steven and Rebecca ate 62.5% of a pizza. What fraction of the pizza did they eat?

Examples 3–5 (pp. 329–330)

Write each fraction as a percent. Round to the nearest hundredth if necessary.

6. $\frac{3}{4}$
7. $\frac{4}{2{,}500}$
8. $\frac{4}{11}$
9. $\frac{1}{9}$

Example 6 (p. 330)

10. **SCHOOL** Moses has finished 11 out of 15 homework questions. To the nearest hundredth, what percent of the homework is complete?

Practice and Problem Solving

HOMEWORK HELP

For Exercises	See Examples
11–14, 19	1
15–18, 20	2
21–32	3–6
33–34	3

Write each percent as a fraction in simplest form.

11. 62.5%
12. 6.2%
13. 28.75%
14. 56.25%
15. $33\frac{1}{3}\%$
16. $16\frac{2}{3}\%$
17. $93\frac{3}{4}\%$
18. $78\frac{3}{4}\%$
19. **ENVIRONMENT** Freshwater from lakes only accounts for 0.1% of the world's water supply. Write this percent as a fraction in simplest form.
20. **ATTENDANCE** At last year's spring dance, $78\frac{1}{3}\%$ of the student body attended. What fraction of the student body is this?

Write each fraction as a percent. Round to the nearest hundredth if necessary.

21. $\frac{111}{20}$
22. $\frac{180}{25}$
23. $\frac{30}{8}$
24. $\frac{210}{40}$
25. $\frac{29}{30}$
26. $\frac{8}{9}$
27. $\frac{5}{7}$
28. $\frac{1}{16}$
29. $\frac{1}{800}$
30. $\frac{57}{20{,}000}$
31. $\frac{5}{1{,}200}$
32. $\frac{7}{1{,}500}$
33. **FOOD** The size of a large milkshake is $\frac{7}{5}$ times the size of a medium milkshake. Write $\frac{7}{5}$ as a percent.
34. **PETS** In a class, 28 out of 32 students had a pet. What percent is this?

Replace each ● with >, <, or = to make a true statement.

35. 0.86 ● $\frac{7}{8}$
36. $\frac{9}{20}$ ● 45%
37. 5% ● 0.004

Order each set of numbers from least to greatest.

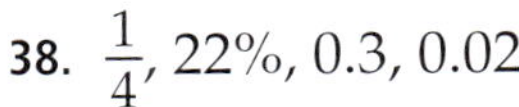

38. $\frac{1}{4}$, 22%, 0.3, 0.02
39. 0.48, $\frac{1}{2}\%$, 0.5, $\frac{2}{5}$
40. **GEOGRAPHY** Use the information at the left. What percent of the states in the United States do *not* border an ocean or the Gulf of Mexico?

Real-World Link Out of the 50 states, 23 states border an ocean or the Gulf of Mexico.
Source: The US50

41. **FIND THE DATA** Refer to the Data File on pages 16–19. Choose some data and write a real-world problem in which you would write a fraction as a percent.

CARS For Exercises 42 and 43, use the table, which shows the percent of people in a recent survey who kept the listed items in their car.

Items in Car	Percent of People
Pen/Pencil	73.0%
Cassette Tapes/CDs	66.1%
First-Aid Kit	38.2%
Sports Equipment	28.9%

42. What fraction of people kept a first-aid kit in their car?

43. Approximately 26 out of 125 people surveyed kept a hairbrush in their car. Is this greater or less than the percent who kept sports equipment? Explain.

See pages 684, 709.

H.O.T. Problems

44. **CHALLENGE** For what value of x does $\frac{1}{x} = x\%$?

45. **WRITING IN MATH** Explain why 80%, 0.8, and $\frac{4}{5}$ all represent the same value.

TEST PRACTICE

46. Ms. Gallagher made 64 ounces of punch. The punch contained 17 ounces of apple juice. Which equation can be used to find x, the percent of apple juice in the punch?

A $\frac{x}{100} = \frac{64}{17}$

B $\frac{x}{17} = \frac{64}{100}$

C $\frac{x}{64} = \frac{17}{100}$

D $\frac{x}{100} = \frac{17}{64}$

47. A group of 150 students were asked if they own a pet. The results are shown.

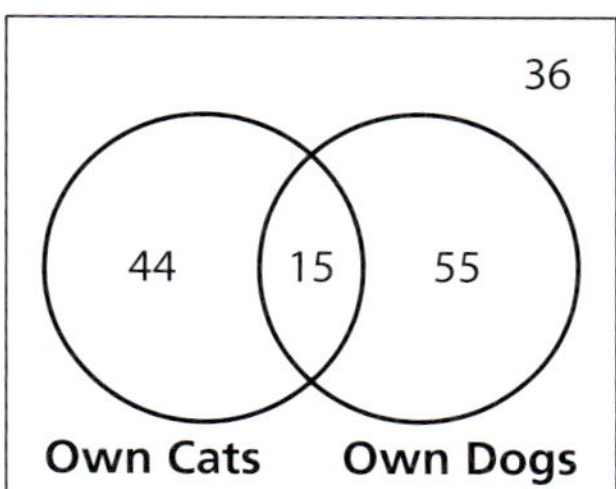

What percent of those surveyed own dogs?

F 50% H 36.7%

G 46.7% J 30%

Spiral Review

48. **COMPUTERS** Designers are creating a larger model of the computer memory board. They use a scale of 20 inches = 1 inch. If the actual board is $5\frac{1}{4}$ inches long, what is the length of the model? (Lesson 6-8)

49. **RECIPES** Camila is making soup. She has added $\frac{2}{3}$ of the ingredients. If she has added 4 ingredients, how many more does she have to add to be finished? (Lesson 6-7)

GET READY for the Next Lesson

PREREQUISITE SKILL **Write each fraction in simplest form.** (Lesson 4-4)

50. $\frac{8}{10}$ 51. $\frac{45}{100}$ 52. $\frac{450}{100}$ 53. $\frac{175}{100}$

Chapter 6 Study Guide and Review

Math Online glencoe.com
- STUDY TO GO
- Vocabulary Review

Be sure the following Big Ideas are noted in your Foldable.

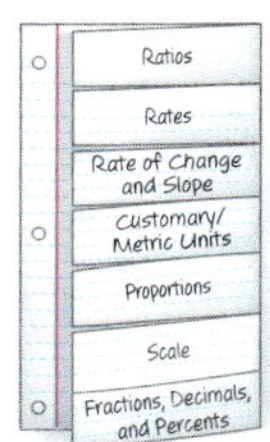

BIG Ideas

Ratios and Rates (Lessons 6-1 and 6-2)
- A ratio is a comparison of two quantities by division.
- A rate is a ratio comparing two quantities with different kinds of units.

Slope and Rate of Change (Lesson 6-3)
- Slope is the rate of change between any two points on a line.

Changing Customary Units (Lesson 6-4)
- To convert from larger units to smaller units, multiply by the appropriate unit ratio.
- To convert from smaller units to larger units, multiply by the reciprocal of the appropriate unit ratio.

Changing Metric Units (Lesson 6-5)
- When converting metric units, multiply by the appropriate power of 10.
- When converting between customary and metric units, use the appropriate unit ratio or relationship.

Proportions (Lesson 6-6)
- Proportions are equations that state two ratios or rates are equivalent.

Scale Drawings (Lesson 6-8)
- Scale drawings represent something that is too large or too small to be drawn at actual size.

Key Vocabulary

- cross products (p. 310)
- equivalent ratios (p. 283)
- inverse proportion (p. 316)
- proportion (p. 310)
- proportional (p. 310)
- rate (p. 287)
- rate of change (p. 293)
- ratio (p. 282)
- scale (p. 320)
- scale drawing (p. 320)
- scale factor (p. 322)
- scale model (p. 320)
- slope (p. 294)
- unit rate (p. 287)
- unit ratio (p. 299)

Vocabulary Check

Choose the term from the list above that best matches each phrase.

1. a comparison of two quantities by division
2. two ratios that have the same value
3. a ratio of two measurements with different units
4. an equation that shows that two ratios or rates are equivalent
5. used to represent something that is too large or too small for an actual-size drawing
6. the ratio of the distance on a map to the actual distance
7. a scale written as a ratio in simplest form without units of measurement
8. the constant rate of change in y with respect to the constant change in x
9. a rate that is simplified so that it has a denominator of 1
10. two quantities that have a constant rate or ratio

CHAPTER 6 Study Guide and Review

Lesson-by-Lesson Review

6-1 Ratios (pp. 282–286)

Write each ratio as a fraction in simplest form.

11. 16 dogs : 12 cats
12. 5 ft : 25 ft
13. 50 boys : 75 girls
14. 36 ft : 6 ft.
15. Determine whether the ratios 18 out of 24 and 5 out of 20 are equivalent.

Example 1 Write the ratio 32 to 18 as a fraction in simplest form.

$32 \text{ to } 18 = \frac{32}{18}$ Write the ratio as a fraction.

$= \frac{16}{9}$ Simplify.

Example 2 Determine whether 5 : 6 and 15 : 18 are equivalent.

$5:6 = \frac{5}{6}$ $\quad 15:18 = \frac{15}{18}$ or $\frac{5}{6}$

The ratios in simplest form both equal $\frac{5}{6}$. So, 5 : 6 and 15 : 18 are equivalent.

6-2 Rates (pp. 287–292)

Find each unit rate.

16. \$23.75 for 5 pounds
17. 810 miles in 9 days
18. **SHAMPOO** Which bottle of shampoo shown at the right costs the least per ounce?

Bottle	Price
8 oz	\$1.99
12 oz	\$2.59
16 oz	\$3.19

Example 3 Find the unit price of a 16-ounce box of pasta that is on sale for 96 cents.

$\text{16-ounce box for 96 cents} = \frac{96 \text{ cents} \div 16}{16 \text{ ounces} \div 16}$

$= \frac{6 \text{ cents}}{1 \text{ ounce}}$

The unit price is 6 cents per ounce.

6-3 Rate of Change and Slope (pp. 293–297)

Complete.

19. **MONEY** The table shows the amount of money José saved over a period of time. Graph the data. Then find the slope of the line. Explain what the slope represents.

Amount (\$)	30	60	90
Weeks	1	2	3

Example 4 Find the rate of change in degrees per hour.

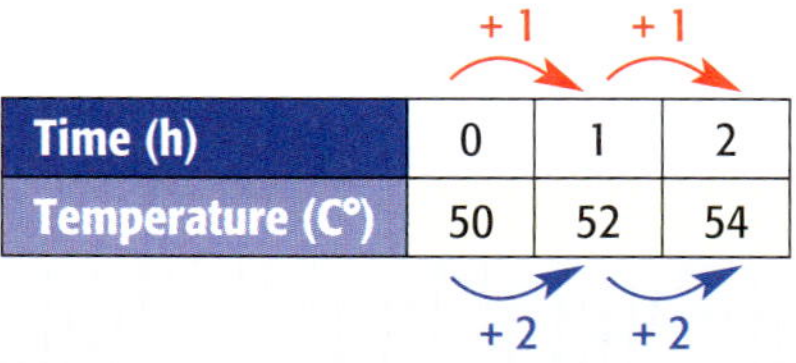

Time (h)	0	1	2
Temperature (C°)	50	52	54

$\frac{\text{change in temperature}}{\text{change in time}} = \frac{2° \text{ Celsius}}{1 \text{ hour}}$

So, the temperature increases by 2° Celsius each hour.

Mixed Problem Solving
For mixed problem-solving practice, see page 709.

6-4 Measurement: Changing Customary Units (pp. 298–303)

Complete.

20. 4 qt = ▢ pt
21. 6 gal = ▢ qt
22. 48 oz = ▢ lb
23. 9 c = ▢ pt

24. **RUNNING** Kimi runs at a speed of 30 feet per second. About how many yards per second does Kimi run?

25. **ESTIMATION** One bushel of apples weighs about 40 pounds. About how many bushels of apples would weigh 1 ton?

Example 5 **Complete: 32 qt = ▢ gal**

Since 1 gallon = 4 quarts, multiply by $\frac{1 \text{ gal}}{4 \text{ qt}}$.

$32 \text{ qt} = 32 \text{ qt} \cdot \frac{1 \text{ gal}}{4 \text{ qt}}$ Multiply by $\frac{1 \text{ gal}}{4 \text{ qt}}$.

$= \overset{8}{\cancel{32}}\ \cancel{\text{qt}} \cdot \frac{1 \text{ gal}}{\underset{1}{\cancel{4}}\ \cancel{\text{qt}}}$ Divide out common factors and units.

$= 8 \text{ gal}$ Multiply.

6-5 Measurement: Changing Metric Units (pp. 304–309)

Complete. Round to the nearest hundredth if necessary.

26. 18.25 ft ≈ ▢ m
27. 113.6 lb ≈ ▢ g
28. 24 L ≈ ▢ gal
29. 46.8 cm ≈ ▢ in.

30. **RUNNING** Justine ran a 5-kilometer race. About how many miles did she run?

31 **BIRDS** The world's largest bird is the ostrich, whose mass can be as much as 156.5 kilograms. What is the approximate weight in pounds?

Example 6 **Complete: 48.8 c ≈ ▢ mL**

Use the relationship 1 c ≈ 236.59 mL.

$1 \text{ c} \approx 236.59 \text{ mL}$

$48.8 \times 1 \text{ c} \approx 48.8 \times 236.59 \text{ mL}$

$48.8 \text{ c} \approx 11{,}545.592 \text{ mL}$

So, 48.8 cups is approximately 11,545.59 milliliters.

6-6 Algebra: Solving Proportions (pp. 310–315)

Solve each proportion.

32. $\frac{x}{10} = \frac{3}{5}$
33. $\frac{4}{9} = \frac{24}{m}$
34. $\frac{2}{t} = \frac{8}{50}$
35. $\frac{15}{w} = \frac{35}{21}$
36. $\frac{12}{8} = \frac{a}{6}$
37. $\frac{7}{18} = \frac{d}{6}$

38. **WEIGHT** If 3 televisions weigh 240.6 pounds, how much do 9 of the same televisions weigh?

Example 7 **Solve $\frac{6}{9} = \frac{n}{12}$.**

$\frac{6}{9} = \frac{n}{12}$ Write the proportion.

$6 \cdot 12 = 9 \cdot n$ Find the cross products.

$72 = 9n$ Multiply.

$\frac{72}{9} = \frac{9n}{9}$ Divide each side by 9.

$8 = n$ Simplify.

Study Guide and Review

6-7 PSI: Draw a Diagram (pp. 318–319)

Solve each problem by drawing a diagram.

39. **PAINTING** Marian is painting a fence that is 72 feet long. She has already painted $\frac{5}{8}$ of the fence. How many feet of fence does she have left to paint?

40. **COOKIES** A cookie jar contains three types of cookies: oatmeal, chocolate chip, and sugar. 60 percent are chocolate chip. Half of the remaining cookies are oatmeal. If there are 9 oatmeal cookies, how many cookies are in the jar?

Example 8 **Ramiro has filled $\frac{1}{3}$ or 50 gallons of his fish tank. Find the total capacity of the fish tank.**

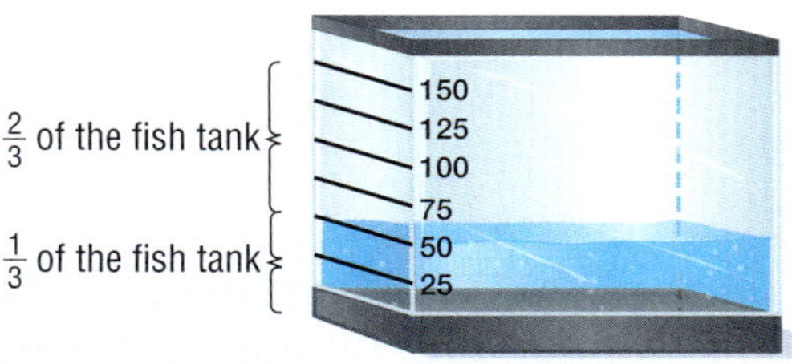

If $\frac{1}{3}$ of the fish tank is 50 gallons, then $\frac{2}{3}$ of the fish tank is 100 gallons. So, the missing two thirds must be 100 gallons. The total capacity of the fish tank is 50 + 100, or 150 gallons.

6-8 Scale Drawings (pp. 320–326)

41. **MAPS** Washington, D.C, and Baltimore, Maryland, are 2 inches apart on a map. If the scale is $\frac{1}{2}$ inch : 6 miles, what is the actual distance between the cities?

42. **MODELS** A Boeing 747 jet is 70.5 meters long and has a wingspan of 60 meters. A model of the 747 has a wingspan of 80 centimeters. What is the length of the model?

Example 9 **On a map, the distance between two cities is 10.9 centimeters. If the scale is 1 centimeter = 250 kilometers, what is the actual distance?**

Scale / Distance

map → $\frac{1 \text{ cm}}{250 \text{ km}} = \frac{10.9 \text{ cm}}{n \text{ km}}$ ← map
actual → ← actual

$$1 \cdot n = 250 \cdot 10.9$$

$$n = 2{,}725$$

The actual distance is 2,725 kilometers.

6-9 Fractions, Decimals, and Percents (pp. 328–332)

Write each percent as a fraction in simplest form.

43. 27.5% 44. 5.40% 45. $45\frac{1}{4}\%$

46. **COINS** A quarter is made of $\frac{1}{12}$ nickel, and the rest is copper. Write the portion of a quarter that is copper as a percent. Round to the nearest hundredth if necessary.

Example 10 **Write 82.5% as a fraction in simplest form.**

$82.5\% = \frac{82.5}{100}$ Write a fraction with a denominator of 100.

$= \frac{825}{1{,}000}$ Multiply 82.5 and 100 by 10 to eliminate the decimal.

$= \frac{33}{40}$ Simplify.

CHAPTER 6 Practice Test

Math Online glencoe.com
• Chapter Test

LAWN CARE **For Exercises 1 and 2, use the following information to write each ratio as a fraction in simplest form.**

A bag of fertilizer nutrients contains 18 pounds of nitrogen, 6 pounds of phosphorus, and 12 pounds of potassium.

1. nitrogen : potassium
2. phosphorus : nitrogen

Find each unit rate. Round to the nearest hundredth if necessary.

3. 24 greeting cards for $4.80
4. 330 miles on 15 gallons of gasoline
5. **MULTIPLE CHOICE** The population of bacteria in 4 different-sized lab dishes are given. Which dish has the lowest density of bacteria or bacteria per square inch?

Dish	Bacteria	Dish Area
1	100	205 sq in.
2	50	125 sq in.
3	35	75 sq in.
4	180	300 sq in.

A Dish 1 C Dish 3
B Dish 2 D Dish 4

6. The graph shows the relationship between time and water level of a pool. Find the rate of change.

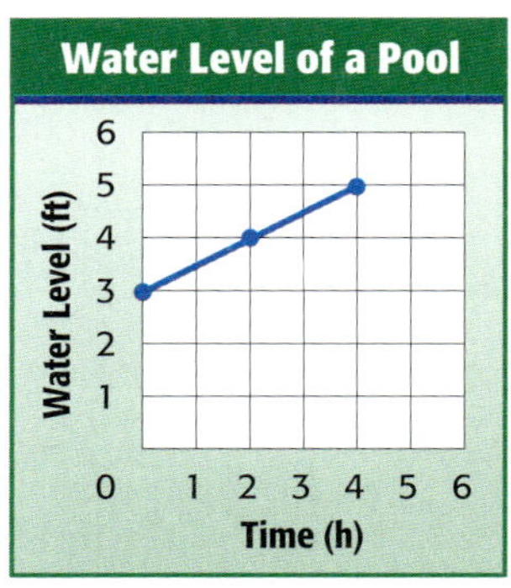

MEASUREMENT **Complete. Round to the nearest tenth if necessary.**

7. 7.62 yd ≈ ■ m
8. 50.8 lb ≈ ■ kg
9. 3,600 mL ≈ ■ qt
10. 19.25 m ≈ ■ ft

ALGEBRA **Solve each proportion.**

11. $\frac{2}{3} = \frac{x}{42}$
12. $\frac{t}{21} = \frac{15}{14}$

13. **NUTRITION** If an 8-ounce glass of orange juice has 72 milligrams of vitamin C, how much vitamin C is in a 7-ounce glass?

14. **MAPS** The table shows the key for a map. Graph the data. Then find the slope of the line.

Distance on Map (cm)	1	2	3	4
Actual Distance (km)	20	40	60	80

BLUEPRINTS **For Exercises 15 and 16, use the following blueprint of a room.**

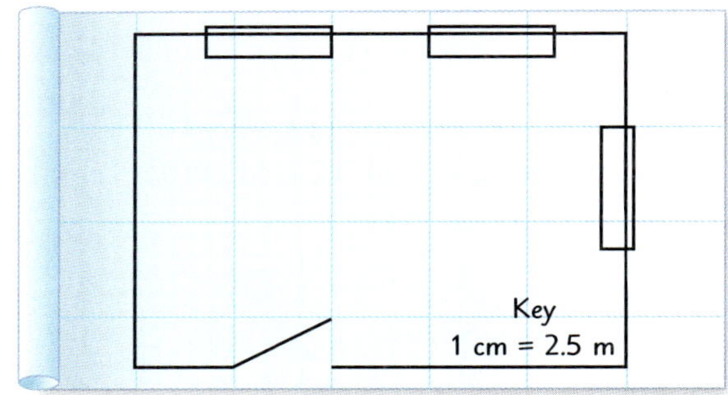

15. Use a centimeter ruler to find the length of the wall with 2 windows.
16. How wide would a 1.4-meter-wide dresser appear on this drawing?

Write each fraction as a percent. Round to the nearest hundredth if necessary.

17. $\frac{5}{8}$
18. $\frac{7}{15}$

19. **GUM** A company test-marketed 7 new flavors of gum last year. Only 2 of these received favorable ratings. Which represents the percent of flavors that did *not* receive favorable ratings?

20. **STOCKS** A company's stock increased 0.83% last month. Write 0.83% as a decimal.

CHAPTER 6

Test Practice
Cumulative, Chapters 1–6

Math Online glencoe.com
• Test Practice

PART 1 Multiple Choice

Read each question. Then fill in the correct answer on the answer sheet provided by your teacher or on a sheet of paper.

1. Francesca typed 496 words in 8 minutes. Which of the following is a correct understanding of this rate?

   A On average, it takes 62 minutes for Francesca to type one word.

   B On average, Francesca can type 62 words in 8 minutes.

   C On average, Francesca can type 62 words in one minute.

   D On average, Francesca can type 8 words in one minute.

2. The table shows the prices of 3 different boxes of cereal. Which box of cereal has the highest price per ounce?

Cereal Box Size (ounces)	Price ($)
48	5.45
32	3.95
20	3.10

   F The 20-ounce box

   G The 32-ounce box

   H The 48-ounce box

   J All three boxes have the same price per ounce.

3. A bakery sells 6 bagels for a total of $2.99 and 4 muffins for a total of $3.29. If you bought 4 dozen bagels and 16 muffins, what is the total cost of the bagels and muffins, not including tax?

   A $64.60 C $31.10

   B $37.08 D $26.50

4. Mrs. Black is making 2 pasta salads for a picnic. The first pasta salad requires $4\frac{2}{3}$ cups of pasta, and the second pasta salad requires $\frac{1}{3}$ cup more than the first. Which of the following equations can be used to find n, the number of cups of pasta needed for the second recipe?

   F $n = 4\frac{2}{3} \div \frac{1}{3}$

   G $n = 4\frac{2}{3} + \frac{1}{3}$

   H $n = 4\frac{2}{3} - \frac{1}{3}$

   J $n = 4\frac{2}{3} \times \frac{1}{3}$

5. Simplify the expression below.

$$8 + 3(15 - 5) - 3^2$$

   A 101 C 39

   B 44 D 29

6. A shoe store had to increase prices. The table shows the regular price r and the new price n of several shoes. Which of the following formulas can be used to calculate the new price?

Shoe	Regular Price (r)	New Price (n)
A	$25.00	$27.80
B	$30.00	$32.80
C	$35.00	$37.80
D	$40.00	$42.80

   F $n = r - 2.80$ H $n = r \times 0.1$

   G $n = r + 2.80$ J $n = r \div 0.1$

7. Annika can run 2 miles in 15 minutes. At this rate, about how long will it take her to run $3\frac{1}{2}$ miles?

   A 26 minutes C 36 minutes

   B 32 minutes D 45 minutes

Preparing for Standardized Tests

For test-taking strategies and practice, see pages 716–733.

8. A building is 55 meters tall. About how tall is the building in feet (ft) and inches (in.)? (1 meter ≈ 39 inches)

   F 179 ft 0 in.

   G 178 ft 9 in.

   H 178 ft 8 in.

   J 178 ft 6 in.

9. You can drive your car 21.75 miles with one gallon of gasoline. How many miles can you drive with 13.2 gallons of gasoline?

   A 13.2

   B 21.75

   C 150.2

   D 287.1

10. The table shows the number of yards of material Leah used each day last week. What was the total number of yards Leah used last week?

Day	Material (yd)
Monday	2.3
Tuesday	$1\frac{3}{4}$
Wednesday	2.8
Thursday	3.1
Friday	$3\frac{1}{4}$
Saturday	1.7
Sunday	$4\frac{1}{2}$

   F 19.4 yd

   G 17 yd

   H 16.5 yd

   J 16 yd

PART 2 Short Response/Grid In

Record your answers on the answer sheet provided by your teacher or on a sheet of paper.

11. Some employees work 40 hours a week. If there are 168 hours in one week, about what part of the week do they work?

12. During a visit to his favorite bookstore, Kevin bought 3 hardback books priced at \$14.99 each and 4 paperbacks priced at \$7.99 each. Find the total of Kevin's purchase, in dollars, before tax is included.

PART 3 Extended Response

Record your answers on the answer sheet provided by your teacher or on a sheet of paper. Show your work.

13 Pistachios cost \$3.99 a pound at the local health food store.

   a. Set up a proportion to find the cost of 3 pounds.

   b. Solve the proportion. How much do 3 pounds of pistachios cost?

   c. If the pistachios are on sale for \$3.09 a pound, how much money will you save if you buy 3 pounds of pistachios?

TEST-TAKING TIP

Question 13 When a question involves information from a previous part of a question, make sure to check that information before you move on.

NEED EXTRA HELP?													
If You Missed Question...	1	2	3	4	5	6	7	8	9	10	11	12	13
Go to Lesson...	6-2	6-2	1-1	5-2	1-4	1-10	6-2	6-8	6-6	5-2	6-9	6-7	6-2

Applying Percents

BIG Idea

- Solve percent problems using ratios and proportionalities.

Key Vocabulary

percent equation (p. 361)
percent of change (p. 369)
percent proportion (p. 350)

Real-World Link

Boogie Boards You can buy a boogie board in Myrtle Beach, South Carolina, for $25. You will also pay a sales tax of 5%.

Applying Percents Make this Foldable to help you organize your notes. Begin with a piece of 11" by 17" paper.

1. **Fold** the paper in half lengthwise.

2. **Open** and refold the paper into fourths along the opposite axis.

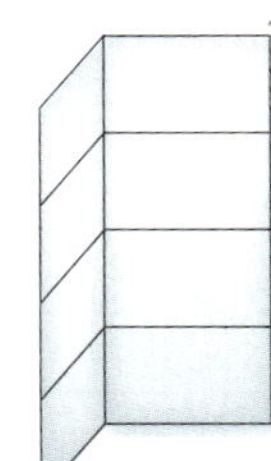

3. **Trace** along the fold lines and label each section with a lesson title or number.

7-1	7-2
7-3	7-4
7-5	7-6
7-7	7-8

GET READY for Chapter 7

Diagnose Readiness You have two options for checking Prerequisite Skills.

Option 2

Math Online Take the Online Readiness Quiz at glencoe.com.

Option 1

Take the Quick Quiz below. Refer to the Quick Review for help.

QUICK Quiz

Multiply. (Prior Grade)

1. $300 \times 0.02 \times 8$
2. $85 \times 0.25 \times 3$
3. $560 \times 0.6 \times 4.5$
4. $154 \times 0.12 \times 5$
5. **MONEY** If Nicole saves \$0.05 every day, how much money will she have in 3 years? (Prior Grade)

Simplify. Write as a decimal. (Prior Grade)

6. $\frac{22-8}{8}$
7. $\frac{50-33}{50}$
8. $\frac{35-7}{35}$
9. **BASEBALL CARDS** Tim has 56 baseball cards. He gives 14 of them away. What decimal represents the portion he has left? (Prior Grade)

ALGEBRA Solve. Round to the nearest tenth if necessary. (Lesson 3-3)

10. $0.4m = 52$
11. $21 = 0.28a$
12. $13 = 0.06s$
13. $0.95z = 37$

Write each percent as a decimal. (Lesson 4-7)

14. 40%
15. 17%
16. 110%
17. 157%
18. 3.25%
19. 7.5%
20. **FOOD** Approximately 92% of a watermelon is water. What decimal represents this amount? (Lesson 4-7)

QUICK Review

Example 1

Evaluate $240 \times 0.03 \times 5$.

$240 \times 0.03 \times 5$
$= 7.2 \times 5$ Multiply 240 by 0.03.
$= 36$ Simplify.

Example 2

Simplify $\frac{17-8}{8}$. Write as a decimal.

$\frac{17-8}{8} = \frac{9}{8}$ Subtract 8 from 17.
$= 1.125$ Divide 9 by 8.

Example 3

Solve $0.6k = 7.8$

$0.6k = 7.8$ Write the equation.
$k = 13$ Divide each side by 0.6.

Example 4

Write 9.8% as a decimal.

$9.8\% = 0.098$ Move the decimal point two places to the left and remove the percent symbol.

Explore 7-1

Math Lab
Percent of a Number

MAIN IDEA

Use a model to find the percent of a number.

Do you enjoy shopping? If so, you may have seen sales or other discounts represented as percents. For example, consider the following situation. A backpack is on sale for 30% off the original price. If the original price of the backpack is $50, how much will you save?

In this situation, you know the percent. You need to find what part of the original price you will save. In this lab, you will use a model to find the percent of a number or *part* of a whole.

ACTIVITY

1 Find 30% of $50 using a model.

STEP 1 Draw a 1-by-10 rectangle as shown on grid paper. Label the units on the right from 0% to 100% as shown.

Part	Percent
	0%
	10%
	20%
	30%
	40%
	50%
	60%
	70%
	80%
	90%
	100%

STEP 2 Since $50 represents the original price, mark equal units from $0 to $50 on the left side of the model as shown.

STEP 3 Draw a line from 30% on the right side to the left side of the model as shown and shade the portion of the rectangle above this line.

Part	Percent
$0	0%
$5	10%
$10	20%
$15	30%
$20	40%
$25	50%
$30	60%
$35	70%
$40	80%
$45	90%
$50	100%

The model shows that 30% of $50 is $15. So, you will save $15.

CHECK Your Progress

Draw a model to find the percent of each number.

a. 20% of 120 b. 60% of 70 c. 90% of 400

Suppose a bicycle is on sale for 35% off the original price. How much will you save if the original price of the bicycle is $180?

ACTIVITY

2 **Find 35% of $180 using a model.**

STEP 1 Draw a 1-by-10 rectangle as shown on grid paper. Label the units on the right from 0% to 100% as shown.

Part	Percent
	0%
	10%
	20%
	30%
	40%
	50%
	60%
	70%
	80%
	90%
	100%

Study Tip

Equal Units
For the model at the right, use an interval of $18 since $180 ÷ 10 = $18.

STEP 2 The original price is $180. So, mark equal units from $0 to $180 on the left side of the model as shown.

STEP 3 Draw a line from 35% on the right side to the left side of the model.

Part	Percent
$0	0%
$18	10%
$36	20%
$54	30%
$72	40%
$90	50%
$108	60%
$126	70%
$144	80%
$162	90%
$180	100%

The model shows that 35% of $180 is halfway between $54 and $72, or $63.

So, you will save $63.

CHECK Your Progress

Draw a model to find the percent of each number. If it is not possible to find an exact answer from the model, estimate.

d. 25% of 140 e. 7% of 50 f. 0.5% of 20

Analyze the Results

1. Tell how to determine the units that get labeled on the left side of a percent model.
2. Explain how to find 40% of 30 using a model.
3. **REASONING** How does knowing 10% of a number help you find the percent of the number when the percent is a multiple of 10%?

7-1 Percent of a Number

MAIN IDEA

Find the percent of a number.

Math Online

glencoe.com

- Extra Examples
- Personal Tutor
- Self-Check Quiz

GET READY for the Lesson

PETS Some students are collecting money for a local pet shelter. The model shows that they have raised 60% of their \$2,000 goal or \$1,200.

Pet Shelter Fundraiser

0%	20%	40%	60%	80%	100%
0	400	800	1,200	1,600	2,000

1. Sketch the model and label using decimals instead of percents.
2. Sketch the model using fractions instead of percents.
3. Use these models to write two multiplication sentences that are equivalent to 60% of 2,000 = 1,200.

To find the percent of a number such as 60% of 2,000, you can use one of the following methods.

- Write the percent as a fraction and then multiply, or
- Write the percent as a decimal and then multiply.

EXAMPLE Find the Percent of a Number

1 Find 5% of 300.

To find 5% of 300, you can use either method.

METHOD 1 Write the percent as a fraction.

$5\% = \frac{5}{100}$ or $\frac{1}{20}$

$\frac{1}{20}$ of $300 = \frac{1}{20} \times 300$ or 15

METHOD 2 Write the percent as a decimal.

$5\% = \frac{5}{100}$ or 0.05

0.05 of $300 = 0.05 \times 300$ or 15

So, 5% of 300 is 15.

CHOOSE Your Method

Find the percent of each number.

a. 40% of 70

b. 15% of 100

c. 55% of 160

EXAMPLE Use Percents Greater Than 100%

2 **Find 120% of 75.**

Study Tip

Check for Reasonableness 120% is a little more than 100%. So, the answer should be a little more than 100% of 75 or a little more than 75.

METHOD 1 **Write the percent as a fraction.**

$$120\% = \frac{120}{100} \text{ or } \frac{6}{5}$$

$$\frac{6}{5} \text{ of } 75 = \frac{6}{5} \times 75$$

$$= \frac{6}{5} \times \frac{75}{1} \text{ or } 90$$

METHOD 2 **Write the percent as a decimal.**

$$120\% = \frac{120}{100} \text{ or } 1.2$$

$$1.2 \text{ of } 75 = 1.2 \times 75 \text{ or } 90$$

So, 120% of 75 is 90. Use a model to check the answer.

CHOOSE Your Method

Find each number.

d. 150% of 20

e. 160% of 35

Real-World EXAMPLE

3 **ANALYZE GRAPHS** **Refer to the graph. If 275 students took the survey, how many can be expected to have 3 televisions each in their houses?**

Survey Results of Number of Televisions in House

Number	Percent
0	2%
1	9%
2	17%
3	23%
4	20%
More than 4	25%

(one television symbol = 5%)

To find 23% of 275, write the percent as a decimal. Then multiply.

$$23\% \text{ of } 275 = 23\% \times 275$$

$$= 0.23 \times 275$$

$$= 63.25$$

So, about 63 students can be expected to have 3 televisions each in their houses.

CHECK Your Progress

f. **ANALYZE GRAPHS** Refer to the graph above. Suppose 455 students took the survey. How many can be expected to have more than 4 televisions each in their houses?

CHECK Your Understanding

Find each number. Round to the nearest tenth if necessary.

Examples 1–2 (pp. 344–345)

1. 8% of 50
2. 95% of 40
3. 42% of 263
4. 110% of 70
5. 115% of 20
6. 130% of 78

Example 3 (p. 345)

7. **TAXES** Mackenzie wants to buy a new backpack that costs \$50. If the tax rate is 6.5%, how much tax will she pay when she buys the backpack?

Practice and Problem Solving

HOMEWORK HELP

For Exercises	See Examples
8–13, 20–25	1
14–19	2
26–27	3

Find each number. Round to the nearest tenth if necessary.

8. 65% of 186
9. 45% of \$432
10. 23% of \$640
11. 54% of 85
12. 12% of \$230
13. 98% of 15
14. 130% of 20
15. 175% of 10
16. 150% of 128
17. 250% of 25
18. 108% of \$50
19. 116% of \$250
20. 3.2% of 40
21. 5.4% of 65
22. 23.5% of 128
23. 75.2% of 130
24. 67.5% of 76
25. 18.5% of 500

26. **BASEBALL** Tomás got on base 60% of the times he was up to bat. If he was up to bat 5 times, how many times did he get on base?

27. **TELEVISION** In a recent year, 17.7% of households watched the finals of a popular reality series. There are 110.2 million television households in the United States. How many households watched the finals?

Find each number. Round to the nearest hundredth if necessary.

28. $\frac{4}{5}$% of 500
29. $5\frac{1}{2}$% of 60
30. $20\frac{1}{4}$% of 3
31. 1,000% of 99
32. 100% of 79
33. 520% of 100
34. 0.15% of 250
35. 0.3% of 80
36. 0.28% of 50

37. **TIPPING** A customer wants to tip 15% of the restaurant bill. How much change should there be after the tip if the customer pays with a \$50 bill?

Sal's Bistro

Herbed Salmon	\$16.25
Chicken Pasta	15.25
Iced Tea	1.75
Iced Tea	1.75
Total	\$35.00

38. **INTERNET** A family pays \$19 each month for Internet access. Next month, the cost will increase 5%. After this increase, what will be the cost for the Internet access?

39. **BUSINESS** A store sells a certain brand of a lawn mower for \$275. Next year, the cost of the lawn mower will increase by 8%. What will be the cost of the lawn mower next year?

ANALYZE GRAPHS **For Exercises 40–42, use the graph below that shows the results of a poll of 2,632 listeners. Round to the nearest whole number.**

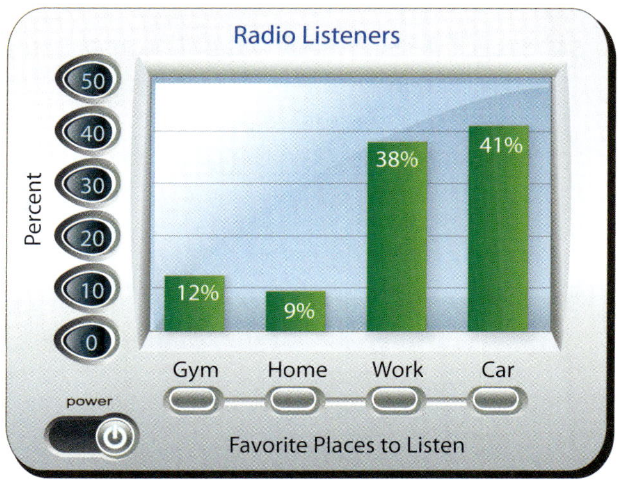

40. How many people listen to the radio during work?
41. How many people like to listen to the radio while they are at the gym?
42. Determine how many more people listen to the radio in the car than at home.

Use mental math to find each percent. Justify your answer.

43. 53% of 60
44. 24% of 48
45. 75% of 19

Real-World Link
California, the largest producer of peaches, produces about 60% of all the peaches, grown in the U.S.
Source: California Tree Fruit Agreement

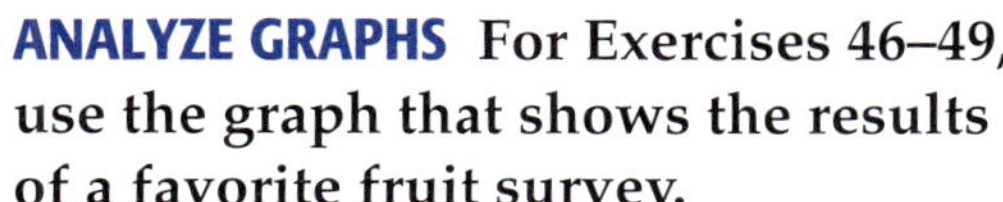

ANALYZE GRAPHS **For Exercises 46–49, use the graph that shows the results of a favorite fruit survey.**

46. How many people were surveyed?
47. Of those surveyed, how many people prefer peaches?
48. Which type of fruit did more than 100 people prefer?
49. Of those surveyed, how many people did *not* prefer cherries? Explain how you arrived at the answer.
50. **SHOPPING** The Leather Depot sells a certain leather coat for $179.99. If sales tax is 6.25%, what will be the approximate total cost of the coat?
51. **SCHOOL** Suppose there are 20 questions on a multiple-choice test. If 25% of the answers are choice B, how many of the answers are *not* choice B?
52. **COMMISSION** In addition to her salary, Ms. Lopez earns a 3% *commission*, or fee paid based on a percent of her sales, on every vacation package that she sells. One day, she sold the three vacation packages shown. What was her total commission?

Package #1	Package #2	Package #3
$2,375	$3,950	$1,725

H.O.T. Problems

53. **OPEN ENDED** Give two examples of real-world situations in your life in which you would find the percent of a number.

54. **SELECT A TECHNIQUE** Maggie uses a $50 gift card to buy a pair of shoes that costs $24.99 and a purse that costs $19.99. If the tax rate is 7%, will the gift card cover the entire purchase? Select and use one or more of the following techniques to solve the problem. Justify your selection(s).

mental math	number sense	estimation

55. **CHALLENGE** Suppose you add 10% of a number to the number, and then you subtract 10% of the total. Is the result *greater than*, *less than*, or *equal to* the original number? Explain your reasoning.

56. **WRITING IN MATH** Explain which method you prefer to use to find the percent of a number: write the percent as a fraction or write the percent as a decimal. Explain your reasoning.

TEST PRACTICE

57. Reggie has memorized 60% of the 50 state capitals for a social studies test. How many more capitals does Reggie need to memorize before the test?

A 35 C 20

B 30 D 18

58. **SHORT RESPONSE** Tanner has 200 baseball cards. Of those, 42% are in mint condition. How many of the cards are *not* in mint condition?

Spiral Review

59. **PETS** In Rebecca's class, 17 out of 24 students have pets. What percent of the students have pets? Round to the nearest percent. (Lesson 6-9)

60. **MODELS** On a scale model of a building, 3 in. = 12 ft. If the model is 8 inches tall, how tall is the actual building? (Lesson 6-8)

Add or subtract. Write in simplest form. (Lesson 6-2)

61. $\frac{7}{10} - \frac{1}{10}$

62. $\frac{20}{21} - \frac{3}{7}$

63. $\frac{5}{6} - \frac{1}{8}$

64. **ALGEBRA** What are the next three numbers in the pattern 3, 10, 17, 24, …? (Lesson 1-9)

GET READY for the Next Lesson

PREREQUISITE SKILL **Solve each equation.** (Lesson 3-3)

65. $12b = 144$

66. $9x = 630$

67. $8{,}100 = 100k$

READING to SOLVE PROBLEMS

Meaning of Percent

When you solve percent problems, look for three parts: the *part*, the *whole*, and the *percent*. Consider this example.

The table at the right shows the results of a survey about favorite flavor of sugarless gum.

Favorite Flavor of Sugarless Gum	
Flavor	**Number**
Cinnamon	10
Peppermint	18
Watermelon	12
Total	40

- **Part**

  Ten students chose cinnamon as their favorite.

- **Whole**

  Forty students were surveyed.

- **Percent**

  25% of the students who were surveyed (10 out of 40) chose cinnamon as their favorite.

Using all three parts, 25% of 40 is 10.

PRACTICE

Identify each statement as the *part*, the *whole*, or the *percent*. Then write a sentence using all three parts.

1. The table at the right shows the results of a survey about which "bugs" people dislike most.
   a. Fifty people were surveyed.
   b. 60% disliked spiders the most.
   c. Thirty people disliked spiders.

Least Favorite "Bug"	
Kind	**Number**
Centipede	2
Cockroach	18
Spider	30
Total	50

2. Suppose you find a sale at the mall.
   a. Everything was 20% off.
   b. The original price of a jacket was $30.
   c. You saved $6.

3. You and your family are eating at a restaurant.
   a. The meal cost $34.
   b. You want to leave a tip of 15%.
   c. The tip is $5.10.

4. Your sister plays basketball.
   a. She usually makes 75% of her free throws.
   b. In the last game, she made 6 free throws.
   c. She had 8 free throws.

7-2 The Percent Proportion

MAIN IDEA

Solve problems using the percent proportion.

New Vocabulary

percent proportion

Math Online

glencoe.com

- Extra Examples
- Personal Tutor
- Self-Check Quiz
- Reading in the Content Area

GET READY for the Lesson

MONSTER TRUCKS The tires on a monster truck weigh approximately 3,600 pounds. The entire truck weighs about 11,000 pounds.

1. Write the ratio of tire weight to total weight as a fraction.
2. Use a calculator to write the fraction as a decimal to the nearest hundredth.
3. What percent of the monster truck's weight is the tires?

In a **percent proportion**, one ratio or fraction compares part of a quantity to the whole quantity, also called the *base*. The other ratio is the equivalent percent written as a fraction with a denominator of 100.

4 out of **5** is **80%.**

part → 4, whole → 5: $\frac{4}{5} = \frac{80}{100}$ } percent

When given two of these pieces of information—part, whole, or percent—you can use the proportion to find the missing information.

EXAMPLE Find the Percent

1 What percent of \$15 is \$9?

The number 15 comes after the word *of*, so the whole is 15. You are asked to find the percent, so the part is the remaining number, 9.

Words	What percent of \$15 is \$9?
Variable	Let n% represent the percent.
Proportion	part → 9, whole → 15: $\frac{9}{15} = \frac{n}{100}$ } percent

$\frac{9}{15} = \frac{n}{100}$	Write the proportion.
$9 \cdot 100 = 15 \cdot n$	Find the cross products.
$900 = 15n$	Simplify.
$\frac{900}{15} = \frac{15n}{15}$	Divide each side by 15.
$60 = n$	

So, \$9 is 60% of \$15.

CHECK Your Progress

Find each number. Round to the nearest tenth if necessary.

a. What percent of 25 is 20?

b. \$12.75 is what percent of \$50?

EXAMPLE Find the Part

2 **What number is 40% of 120?**

The percent is 40%. Since the number 120 comes after the word *of*, the whole is 120. You are asked to find the part.

Words	What number is 40% of 120?
Variable	Let p represent the part.
Proportion	$\frac{\text{part}}{\text{whole}} \rightarrow \frac{p}{120} = \frac{40}{100} \}$ percent

$$\frac{p}{120} = \frac{40}{100}$$ Write the proportion.

$$p \cdot 100 = 120 \cdot 40$$ Find the cross products.

$$100p = 4{,}800$$ Simplify.

$$\frac{100p}{100} = \frac{4{,}800}{100}$$ Divide each side by 100.

$$p = 48$$

So, 48 is 40% of 120.

CHECK Your Progress

Find each number. Round to the nearest tenth if necessary.

c. What number is 5% of 60?

d. 12% of 85 is what number?

Study Tip

The Percent Proportion The part usually comes before or after the word *is* and the whole usually comes before or after the word *of*.

EXAMPLE Find the Whole

3 **18 is 25% of what number?**

The percent is 25%. The words *what number* come after the word *of*. So, you are asked to find the whole. Thus, 18 is the part.

Words	18 is 25% of what number?
Variable	Let w represent the whole.
Proportion	$\frac{\text{part}}{\text{whole}} \rightarrow \frac{18}{w} = \frac{25}{100} \}$ percent

(continued on the next page)

$$\frac{18}{w} = \frac{25}{100}$$ Write the proportion.

$$18 \cdot 100 = w \cdot 25$$ Find the cross products.

$$1{,}800 = 25w$$ Simplify.

$$\frac{1{,}800}{25} = \frac{25w}{25}$$ Divide each side by 25.

$$72 = w$$

So, 18 is 25% of 72.

CHECK Your Progress

Find each number. Round to the nearest tenth if necessary.

e. 40% of what number is 26?

f. 80 is 75% of what number?

Real-World EXAMPLE

Real-World Link Male Western Lowland gorillas weigh about 350–400 pounds. Females weigh about 160–200 pounds.

Source: Columbus Zoo and Aquarium

4 **ANIMALS** **The average adult male Western Lowland gorilla eats about 33.5 pounds of fruit each day. How much food does the average adult male gorilla eat each day?**

Western Lowland Gorilla's Diet	
Food	**Percent**
Fruit	67%
Seeds, Leaves, Stems, and Pith	17%
Insects/ Insect Larvae	16%

You know that 33.5 pounds of fruit is 67% of the total amount eaten daily. So, the problem asks 33.5 is 67% of what number. Thus, you need to find the whole.

$$\frac{33.5}{w} = \frac{67}{100}$$ Write the proportion.

$$33.5 \cdot 100 = w \cdot 67$$ Find the cross products.

$$3{,}350 = 67w$$ Simplify.

$$\frac{3{,}350}{67} = \frac{67w}{67}$$ Divide each side by 67.

$$50 = w$$

So, the average adult male gorilla eats 50 pounds of food each day.

CHECK Your Progress

g. **ZOO** If 200 of the 550 reptiles in a zoo are on display, what percent of the reptiles are on display? Round to the nearest whole number.

Types of Percent Problems

Key Concept

Type	Example	Proportion
Find the Percent	What percent of 6 is 3?	$\frac{3}{6} = \frac{n}{100}$
Find the Part	What number is 50% of 6?	$\frac{p}{6} = \frac{50}{100}$
Find the Whole	3 is 50% of what number?	$\frac{3}{w} = \frac{50}{100}$

Examples 1–3 (pp. 350–352)

Find each number. Round to the nearest tenth if necessary.

1. What percent of 50 is 18?
2. What percent of \$90 is \$9?
3. What number is 2% of 35?
4. What number is 25% of 180?
5. 9 is 12% of which number?
6. 62 is 90.5% of what number?

Example 4 (p. 352)

7. **MEASUREMENT** If a box of Brand A cereal contains 10 cups of cereal, how many more cups of cereal are in a box of Brand B cereal?

Practice and Problem Solving

HOMEWORK HELP	
For Exercises	See Examples
8–11	1, 2
12–17	3
18–21	4
22, 23	5

Find each number. Round to the nearest tenth if necessary.

8. What percent of 60 is 15?
9. \$3 is what percent of \$40?
10. What number is 15% of 60?
11. 12% of 72 is what number?
12. 9 is 45% of what number?
13. 75 is 20% of what number?
14. **SCHOOL** Roman has 2 red pencils in his backpack. If this is 25% of the total number of pencils, how many pencils are in his backpack?
15. **BASKETBALL** Lisa and Michelle scored 48% of their team's points. If their team had a total of 50 points, how many points did they score?
16. **SHOES** A pair of sneakers are on sale as shown. This is 75% of the original price. What was the original price of the shoes?

17. **BOOKS** Of the 60 books on a bookshelf, 24 are nonfiction. What percent of the books are nonfiction?

Find each number. Round to the nearest hundredth if necessary.

18. What percent of 25 is 30?
19. What number is 8.2% of 50?
20. 40 is 50% of what number?
21. 12.5% of what number is 24?
22. What number is 0.5% of 8?
23. What percent of 300 is 0.6?
24. **BUSINESS** The first week of June, there were 404 customers at an ice cream parlor. Eight weeks later, the number of customers was 175% of this amount. How many customers were there eight weeks later?
25. **MONEY** Ajamu saves 40% of his allowance each week. If he saves \$16 in 5 weeks, how much allowance does Ajamu receive each week?
26. **SCHOOL** A class picture includes 95% of the students. Seven students were absent. How many students are in the class?

ASTRONOMY For Exercises 27–29, use the table shown.

Planet	Radius (km)
Mercury	2,440
Mars	3,397
Jupiter	71,492

27. Mercury's radius is what percent of Jupiter's radius?

28. If the radius of Mars is about 13.7% of Neptune's radius, what is the radius of Neptune?

29. Earth's radius is about 261.4% of Mercury's radius. What is the radius of Earth?

H.O.T. Problems

30. **OPEN ENDED** Write a proportion that can be used to find the percent scored on a science quiz that has 10 questions.

31. **CHALLENGE** Without calculating, arrange the following from greatest to least value. Justify your reasoning.

20% of 100, 20% of 500, 5% of 100

32. **WRITING IN MATH** Create a problem involving a percent that can be solved by using the proportion $\frac{3}{b} = \frac{15}{100}$.

33. Of the 273 students in a school, 95 volunteered to work the book sale. About what percent of the students did *not* volunteer?

A 55%

B 65%

C 70%

D 75%

34. A customer at a restaurant leaves a tip of $2.70. This amount is 15% of the total bill. Which equation can be used to find x, the total amount of the food bill?

F $\frac{2.70}{15} = \frac{15}{100}$

G $\frac{2.70}{x} = \frac{15}{100}$

H $\frac{15}{2.70} = \frac{x}{100}$

J $\frac{x}{2.70} = \frac{15}{100}$

Spiral Review

Find each number. Round to the nearest tenth if necessary. (Lesson 7-1)

35. What is 25% of 120?

36. Find 45% of 70.

37. **PLANTS** A plant was 275% taller than the month before. What decimal represents this percent? (Lesson 6-9)

MEASUREMENT **Complete.** (Lesson 6-4)

38. 3,000 lb = ▒ T

39. 36 in. = ▒ ft

40. $4\frac{1}{2}$ lb = ▒ oz

GET READY for the Next Lesson

PREREQUISITE SKILL **Multiply.** (Lesson 5-5)

41. $\frac{1}{2} \cdot 60$

42. $\frac{3}{4} \cdot 28$

43. $\frac{2}{5} \cdot 45$

7-3 Percent and Estimation

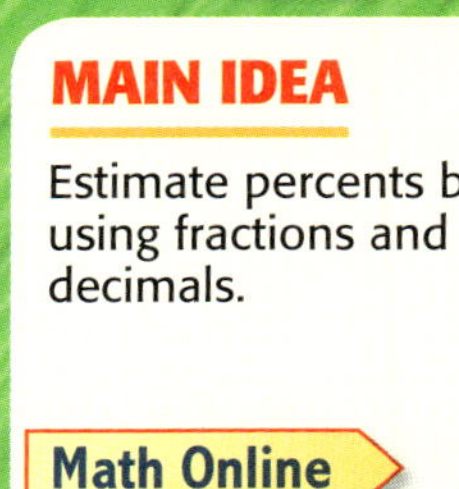

MAIN IDEA

Estimate percents by using fractions and decimals.

Math Online

glencoe.com

- Extra Examples
- Personal Tutor
- Self-Check Quiz

GET READY for the Lesson

MUSIC Refer to the graph below.

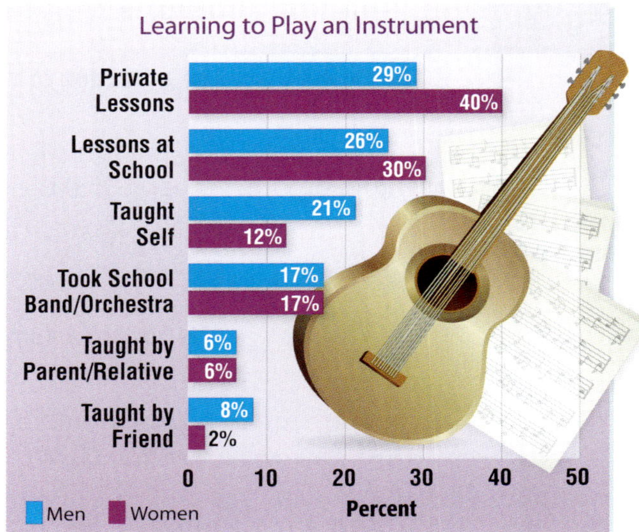

1. What fraction of women took lessons at school? If 200 women were surveyed, how many of them took lessons at school?
2. Use a fraction to estimate the number of men who took lessons at school. Assume 200 men were surveyed.

Sometimes an exact answer is not needed when using percents. One way to estimate the percent of a number is to use a fraction.

Real-World EXAMPLE

1 **SPORTS** **In a recent year, quarterback Carson Palmer completed 62% of his passes. He threw 520 passes. About how many did he complete?**

62% of $520 \approx 60\%$ of 520	$62\% \approx 60\%$
$\approx \frac{3}{5} \cdot 520$	$60\% = \frac{6}{10}$ or $\frac{3}{5}$
≈ 312	Multiply.

So, Carson Palmer completed about 312 out of 520 passes.

CHECK Your Progress

a. **REPTILES** Box turtles have been known to live for 120 years. American alligators have been known to live 42% as long as box turtles. About how long can an American alligator live?

Another method for estimating the percent of a number is to first find 10% of the number and then multiply. For example, 70% = 7 • 10%. So, 70% of a number equals 7 times 10% of the number.

Real-World Link In a recent year, the Internal Revenue Service estimated that Americans paid $15.37 billion in tips.

Real-World EXAMPLE

2 **MONEY** **Marita decides to leave a 20% tip on a restaurant bill of $14.72. About how much money should she tip the restaurant server?**

You need to estimate 20% of $14.72.

METHOD 1 **Use a fraction to estimate.**

20% is $\frac{2}{10}$ or $\frac{1}{5}$.

20% of $14.72 $\approx \frac{1}{5} \cdot$ $15.00 — 20% = $\frac{1}{5}$ and round $14.72 to $15.00.

$\approx$ $3.00 — Multiply.

METHOD 2 **Use 10% of a number to estimate.**

Step 1 Find 10% of the number.
$14.72 is about $15.00.
10% of $15.00 = 0.1 • $15.00
= $1.50
To multiply by 10%, move the decimal point one place to the left.

Step 2 Multiply.
20% of $15.00 is 2 times 10% of $15.00.
2 • $1.50 = $3.00

So, Marita should tip the restaurant server about $3.00.

b. **MONEY** Dante plans to put 80% of his paycheck into a savings account. His paycheck this week was $295. About how much money will he put into his savings account?

You can also estimate percents of numbers when the percent is greater than 100 or the percent is less than 1.

Study Tip

Check for Reasonableness When estimating the percent of a number and the percent is greater than 100, the estimate will always be greater than the number.

EXAMPLES Percents Greater Than 100 or Less Than 1

3 **Estimate 122% of 50.**

122% is about 120%.

120% of 50 = (100% of 50) + (20% of 50) — 120% = 100% + 20%

$= (1 \cdot 50) + \left(\frac{1}{5} \cdot 50\right)$ — 100% = 1 and 20% = $\frac{1}{5}$

= 50 + 10 or 60 — Simplify.

So, 122% of 50 is about 60.

4 **Estimate $\frac{1}{4}\%$ of 589.**

$\frac{1}{4}\%$ is one fourth of 1%. 589 is about 600.

$1\% \text{ of } 600 = 0.01 \cdot 600$ Write 1% as 0.01.

$= 6$ To multiply by 1%, move the decimal point two places to the left.

One fourth of 6 is $\frac{1}{4} \cdot 6$ or 1.5. So, $\frac{1}{4}\%$ of 589 is about 1.5.

Estimate.

c. 174% of 200 d. 298% of 45 e. 0.25% of 789

Real-World EXAMPLE

5 **CELL PHONES** **In a recent year, there were about 200 million people in the U.S. with cell phones. Of those, about 0.5% used their phone as an MP3 player. Estimate the number of people who used their phone as an MP3 player.**

0.5% is half of 1%.

$1\% \text{ of } 200 \text{ million} = 0.01 \cdot 200{,}000{,}000$

$= 2{,}000{,}000$

So, 0.5% of 200,000,000 is about $\frac{1}{2}$ of 2,000,000 or 1,000,000.

So, about 1,000,000 people used their phone as an MP3 player.

f. **ATTENDANCE** Last year, 639 students attended a summer camp. Of those who attended this year, 0.9% also attended last year. About how many people attended the camp two years in a row?

CHECK Your Understanding

Examples 1–4 (pp. 355–357)

Estimate.

1. 52% of 10
2. 7% of 20
3. 38% of 62
4. 79% of 489
5. 151% of 70
6. $\frac{1}{2}\%$ of 82

Example 1 (p. 355)

7. **BUSINESS** A bicycle store increases its prices by 23%. About how much more will a customer pay for a bicycle that originally costs $200?

Example 2 (p. 356)

8. **BIRTHDAYS** Of the 78 teenagers at a youth camp, 63% have birthdays in the spring. About how many have birthdays in the spring?

Example 5 (p. 357)

9. **GEOGRAPHY** About 0.8% of the land in Maine is federally owned. If Maine is 19,847,680 acres, about how many acres are federally owned?

Practice and Problem Solving

HOMEWORK HELP	
For Exercises	See Examples
10–21	1, 3
22–23	2
24–25	3
26–27, 30	4
28–29, 31	5

Estimate.

10. 47% of 70
11. 21% of 90
12. 39% of 120
13. 76% of 180
14. 57% of 29
15. 92% of 104
16. 24% of 48
17. 28% of 121
18. 88% of 207
19. 62% of 152
20. 65% of 152
21. 72% of 238

22. **MONEY** Jessica spent $42 at the hair salon. About how much money should she tip the hair stylist if she wants to leave a 15% tip?

23. **HEALTH** You use 43 muscles to frown. When you smile, you use 32% of these same muscles. About how many muscles do you use when you smile?

Estimate.

24. 132% of 54
25. 224% of 320
26. $\frac{1}{2}$% of 412
27. $\frac{3}{4}$% of 168
28. 0.4% of 510
29. 0.9% of 74

30. **GEOGRAPHY** The United States has 12,383 miles of coastline. If $\frac{4}{5}$% of the U.S. coastline is located in Georgia, about how many miles of coastline are in Georgia?

31. **BIRDS** During migration, 450,000 sandhill cranes stop to rest in Nebraska. About 0.6% of these cranes stop to rest in Oregon. About how many sandhill cranes stop in Oregon during migration?

Estimate.

32. 67% of 8.7
33. 54% of 76.8
34. 32% of 89.9
35. 10.5% of 238
36. 22.2% of 114
37. 98.5% of 45

ANALYZE GRAPHS **For Exercises 38–40, use the graph shown.**

Amanda's Day

Real-World Link About 75% of the entire world sandhill crane population stops to rest in Nebraska during migration.
Source: *World Book of Records*

38. About how many hours does Amanda spend doing her homework each day?
39. About how many more hours does Amanda spend sleeping than doing the activities in the "other" category? Justify your answer.
40. What is the approximate number of minutes Amanda spends each day on extracurricular activities?

41. **ANALYZE GRAPHS** 2,075 tennis fans were asked to name the greatest all time female tennis player. The top five responses are shown. About how many more people chose Martina Navratilova than Steffi Graf?

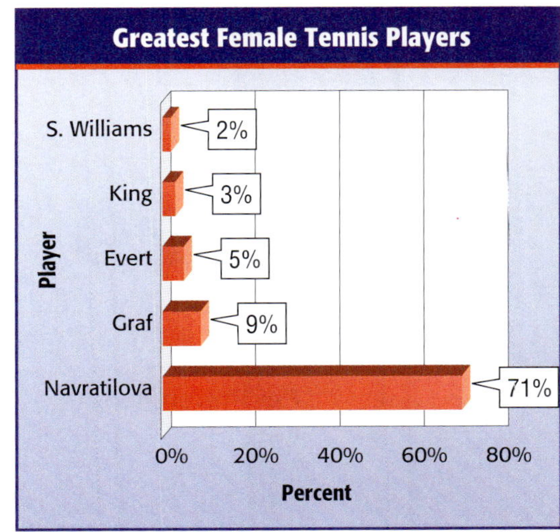

42. **ANIMALS** The average white rhinoceros gives birth to a single calf that weighs about 3.8% as much as its mother. If the mother rhinoceros weighs 3.75 tons, about how many pounds does its calf weigh?

43. **POPULATION** According to the 2000 U.S. Census, about 7.8% of the people in Minnesota live in Minneapolis. If the population of Minnesota is about 4,920,000, estimate the population of Minnesota.

CLEANING For Exercises 44 and 45, use the following information.

A cleaning solution is made up of 0.9% chlorine bleach.

44. About how many ounces of bleach are in 189 ounces of cleaning solution?

45. About how many ounces of bleach would be found in 412 ounces of cleaning solution?

EXTRA PRACTICE
See pages 685, 710.

H.O.T. Problems

46. **OPEN ENDED** Write a real-world problem in which the answer can be found by estimating 12% of 50.

47. **CHALLENGE** Explain how you could find $\frac{3}{8}\%$ of $800.

48. **FIND THE ERROR** Tom and Elsa are estimating 1.5% of 210. Who is correct? Explain.

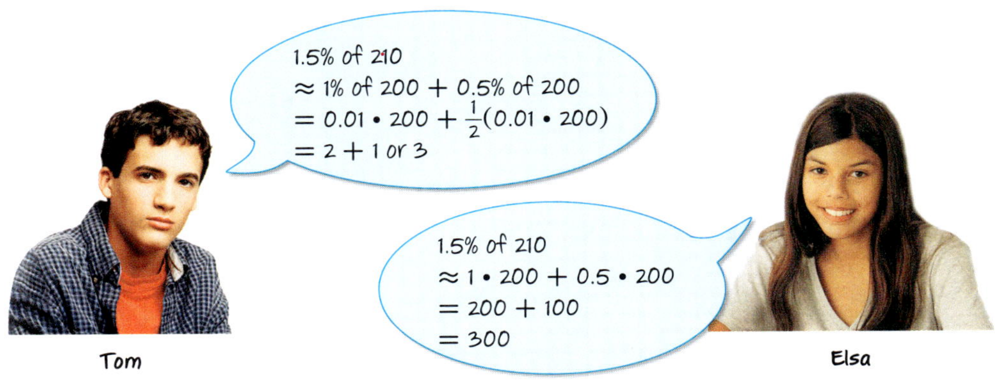

49. **NUMBER SENSE** Is an estimate for the percent of a number *always*, *sometimes*, or *never* greater than the actual percent of the number? Give an example or a counterexample to support your answer.

50. **WRITING IN MATH** Estimate 22% of 136 using two different methods. Justify the steps used in each method.

51. The graph shows the results of a survey of 510 students.

Pet Preferences

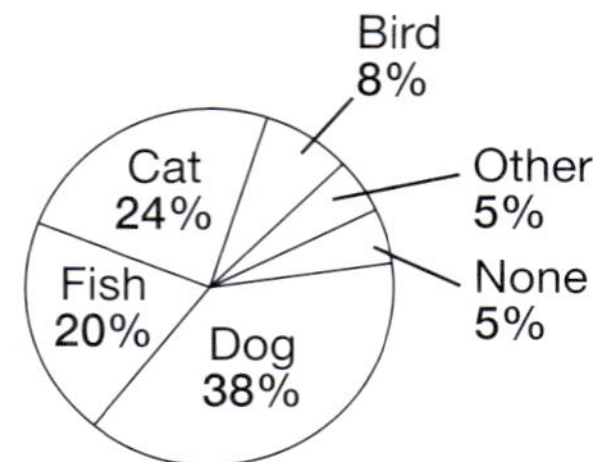

Which is the best estimate for the number of students who prefer cats?

A 75 **C** 225

B 125 **D** 450

52. Megan is buying an entertainment system for $1,789.43. The speakers are 39.7% of the total cost. Which is the best estimate for the cost of the speakers?

F $540 **H** $720

G $630 **J** $810

53. Daniel decides to leave a 20% tip for a restaurant bill of $28.92. About how much money should he tip the restaurant server?

A $2.00 **C** $4.00

B $3.00 **D** $6.00

Spiral Review

Find each number. Round to the nearest tenth if necessary. (Lesson 7-2)

54. 6 is what percent of 15?

55. Find 72% of 90.

56. What number is 120% of 60?

57. 35% of what number is 55?

58. **HEALTH** Adults have 32 teeth. Children have 62.5% as many teeth as adults. How many teeth do children have? (Lesson 7-1)

Estimate. (Lesson 5-1)

59. $\frac{8}{9} + \frac{1}{12}$

60. $\frac{4}{7} + \frac{7}{16}$

61. $\frac{7}{8} - \frac{7}{16}$

62. $\frac{4}{5} - \frac{9}{10}$

Solve. Round to the nearest tenth if necessary. (Lesson 3-3)

63. $40 = 0.8x$

64. $10r = 61$

65. $0.07t = 25$

66. $56 = 0.32n$

GET READY for the Next Lesson

Solve each equation. Check your solution. (Lesson 3-3)

67. $14 = n \cdot 20$

68. $25 = n \cdot 40$

69. $28.5 = n \cdot 38$

70. $36 = n \cdot 80$

7-4

Algebra: The Percent Equation

MAIN IDEA

Solve problems by using the percent equation.

New Vocabulary

percent equation

Math Online

glencoe.com

- Extra Examples
- Personal Tutor
- Self-Check Quiz

GET READY for the Lesson

ARTHROPODS There are about 854,000 different species of spiders, insects, crustaceans, millipedes, and centipedes on Earth. The graph shows that 88% of the total numbers of species of arthropods are insects.

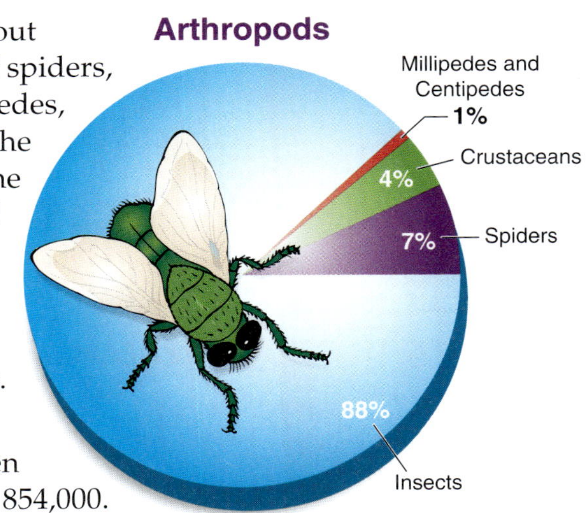

1. Use the percent proportion to find how many species are insects.
2. Express the percent of insects as a decimal. Then multiply the decimal by 854,000.

In Lesson 7-2, you used a percent proportion to find the missing part, percent, or whole. You can also use an equation. The percent equation is another form of the percent proportion.

$\frac{\text{part}}{\text{whole}} = \text{percent}$ The percent must be written as a decimal or fraction.

$\frac{\text{part}}{\text{whole}} \cdot \textbf{whole} = \text{percent} \cdot \textbf{whole}$ Multiply each side by the whole.

$\text{part} = \text{percent} \cdot \text{whole}$ ← This form is called the **percent equation**.

EXAMPLE Find the Part

1 **What number is 12% of 150?** **Estimate** 12% of 150 ≈ 0.1 · 150 or 15

Write 12% as a decimal, 0.12. The whole is 150. You need to find the part. Let p represent the part.

part = percent · whole

$p = 0.12 \cdot 150$ Write the percent equation.

$p = 18$ Multiply. The part is 18.

So, 18 is 12% of 150. **Check for Reasonableness** 18 is close to 15. ✔

Study Tip

Percent Equation

A percent must always be converted to a decimal or a fraction when it is used in an equation.

CHECK Your Progress

Write an equation for each problem. Then solve. Round to the nearest tenth if necessary.

a. What is 6% of 19?

b. Find 72% of 90.

EXAMPLE Find the Percent

2 **21 is what percent of 40?** **Estimate** $\frac{21}{40} \approx \frac{1}{2}$ or 50%

The part is 21. The whole is 40. You need to find the percent. Let n represent the percent.

$$\underbrace{\text{part}} = \underbrace{\text{percent}} \cdot \underbrace{\text{whole}}$$

$21 = n \cdot 40$	Write the percent equation.
$\frac{21}{40} = \frac{40n}{40}$	Divide each side by 40.
$0.525 = n$	Since n represents the decimal form, the percent is 52.5%.

So, 21 is 52.5% of 40.

Check for Reasonableness 52.5% ≈ 50% ✔

Percent
Remember to write the decimal as a percent in your final answer.

CHECK Your Progress

Write an equation for each problem. Then solve. Round to the nearest tenth if necessary.

c. 35 is what percent of 70?

d. What percent of 125 is 75?

e. What percent of 40 is 9?

f. 27 is what percent of 150?

EXAMPLE Find the Whole

3 **13 is 26% of what number?** **Estimate** $\frac{1}{4}$ of 48 = 12

The part is 13. The percent is 26, which when written as a decimal, is 0.26. You need to find the whole. Let w represent the whole.

$$\underbrace{\text{part}} = \underbrace{\text{percent}} \cdot \underbrace{\text{whole}}$$

$13 = 0.26 \cdot w$	Write the percent equation. 26% = 0.26
$\frac{13}{0.26} = \frac{0.26w}{0.26}$	Divide each side by 0.26.
$50 = w$	The number is 50.

So, 13 is 26% of 50.

Check for Reasonableness 50 is close to 48. ✔

CHECK Your Progress

Write an equation for each problem. Then solve. Round to the nearest tenth if necessary.

g. 39 is 84% of what number?

h. 26% of what number is 45?

i. 14% of what number is 7?

j. 24 is 32% of what number?

Real-World Link
In the U.S., Anchorage, Alaska, has the highest percent of cell phone users.
Source: Polk's Research

Real-World EXAMPLE

4 **CELL PHONES** **A survey found that 25% of people age 18–24 gave up their home phone and only use a cell phone. If 3,264 people only use a cell phone, how many people were surveyed?**

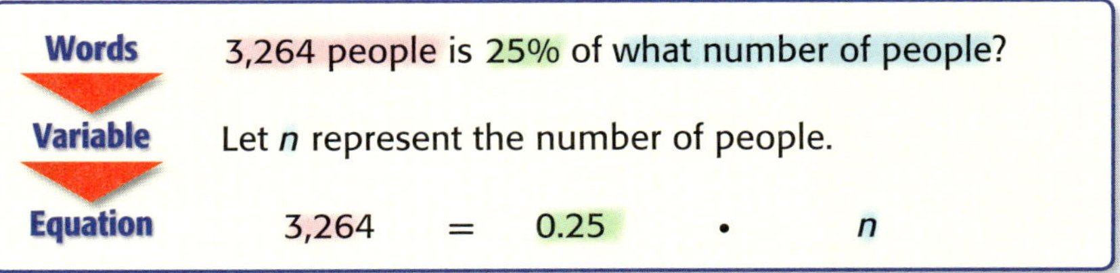

$3{,}264 = 0.25 \cdot n$	Write the percent equation. 25% = 0.25
$\dfrac{3{,}264}{0.25} = \dfrac{0.25n}{0.25}$	Divide each side by 0.25. Use a calculator.
$13{,}056 \approx n$	Simplify.

The number of people surveyed is about 13,056.

CHECK Your Progress

k. **POPULATION** The Louisville-Jefferson County metropolitan area contains 17.2% of the population of Kentucky. If the population of Kentucky is about 4,040,000 people, what is the population of the Louisville-Jefferson County metropolitan area?

Types of Percent Problems — Concept Summary

Type	Example	Equation
Find the Part	What number is 50% of 6?	$p = 0.5 \cdot 6$
Find the Percent	3 is what percent of 6?	$3 = n \cdot 6$
Find the Whole	3 is 50% of what number?	$3 = 0.5 \cdot w$

Examples 1–3 (pp. 361–362)

Write an equation for each problem. Then solve. Round to the nearest tenth if necessary.

1. What number is 88% of 300?
2. What number is 12% of 250?
3. 75 is what percent of 150?
4. 24 is what percent of 120?
5. 3 is 12% of what number?
6. 84 is 60% of what number?

Example 4 (p. 363)

7. **BUSINESS** A local bakery sold 60 loaves of bread in one day. If 65% of these were sold in the afternoon, how many loaves were sold in the afternoon?

Practice and Problem Solving

HOMEWORK HELP	
For Exercises	See Examples
8–11	1
12–15	2
16–19	3
20–23	4

Write an equation for each problem. Then solve. Round to the nearest tenth if necessary.

8. What number is 65% of 98?
9. Find 39% of 65.
10. Find 24% of 25.
11. What number is 53% of 470?
12. 9 is what percent of 45?
13. What percent of 96 is 26?
14. What percent of 392 is 98?
15. 30 is what percent of 64?
16. 33% of what number is 1.45?
17. 84 is 75% of what number?
18. 17 is 40% of what number?
19. 80% of what number is 64?

20. **BOOKS** Emma bought 6 new books for her collection. This increased her collection by 12%. How many books did she have before her purchases?

21. **VIDEO GAMES** A store sold 550 video games during the month of December. If this made up 12.5% of their yearly video game sales, about how many video games did the store sell all year?

22. **MEASUREMENT** The length of Giselle's arm is 27 inches. The length of her lower arm is 17 inches. About what percent of Giselle's arm is her lower arm?

23. **LOBSTERS** Approximately 0.02% of North Atlantic lobsters are born bright blue in color. Out of 5,000 North Atlantic lobsters, how many would you expect to be blue in color?

Write an equation for each problem. Then solve. Round to the nearest tenth if necessary.

24. Find 135% of 64.
25. What number is 0.4% of 82.1?
26. 450 is 75.2% of what number?
27. What percent of 200 is 230?

28. **SALARY** Suppose you earn $6 per hour at your part-time job. What will your new hourly rate be after a 2.5% raise?

ANALYZE GRAPHS About 672 million metric tons of corn was produced worldwide in 2006. For Exercises 29–31, use the graph at the right.

29. About what percent of corn was produced in the United States?
30. About what percent of corn was produced in Mexico?
31. What percent of the world's corn production do Brazil and China make together?

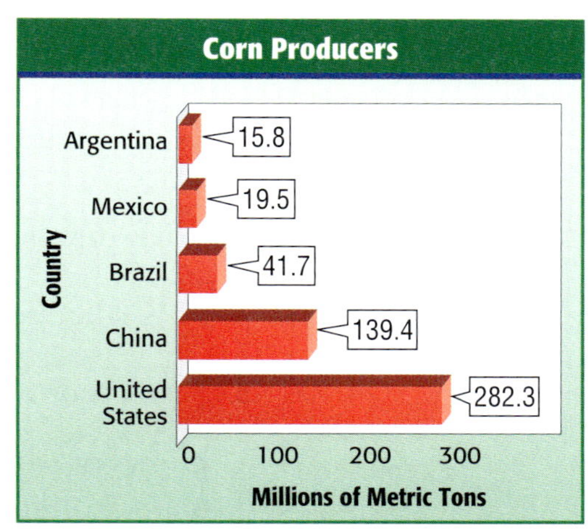

32. **MEASUREMENT** A pool that holds 320 cubic feet of water is 84% filled to capacity. Another pool that holds 400 cubic feet of water is 82.5% filled to capacity. Which pool contains more water? How much more?

H.O.T. Problems

33. **OPEN ENDED** Write a percent problem for which the percent is greater than 100% and the part is known. Use the percent equation to solve your problem to find the base.

34. **CHALLENGE** If you need to find the percent of a number, explain how you can predict whether the part will be less than, greater than, or equal to the number.

35. **WRITING IN MATH** Compare the percent equation and the percent proportion. Then explain when it might be easier to use the percent equation rather than the percent proportion.

TEST PRACTICE

36. In a survey, 100 students were asked to choose their favorite take-out food. The table shows the results.

Favorite Take-Out Food	
Type of Food	**Percent**
Pizza	40
Sandwiches	32
Fried chicken	28

Based on this data, predict how many out of 1,800 students would choose sandwiches.

A 504 **C** 680

B 576 **D** 720

37. If 60% of a number is 18, what is 90% of the number?

F 3 **H** 27

G 16 **J** 30

38. Taryn's grandmother took her out to dinner. If the dinner was $34 and she left a 20% tip, how much money did Taryn's grandmother spend?

A $6.80 **C** $39.50

B $27.20 **D** $40.80

Spiral Review

39. **RESTAURANT** Mitchell spent $13 on dinner. About how much money should he tip the server if he wants to leave a 15% tip? (Lesson 7-3)

Find each number. Round to the nearest hundredth if necessary. (Lesson 7-2)

40. What percent of 15 is 20?

41. 20.5% of what number is 35?

42. What number is 0.5% of 10?

GET READY for the Next Lesson

43. **PREREQUISITE SKILL** To estimate the age of a dog in human years, count the first year as 15 human years, the second year as 10 human years, and all of the following years as 3 human years. How old in human years is a 6-year-old dog? (Lesson 1-1)

Problem-Solving Investigation

MAIN IDEA: Solve problems by determining reasonable answers.

P.S.I. TEAM +

e-Mail: DETERMINE REASONABLE ANSWERS

Doug: My dad painted 25% of my bedroom in 28 minutes. I think the whole project will take about 3 hours.

YOUR MISSION: Determine whether it is reasonable for Doug's dad to paint the bedroom in 3 hours.

Understand	Twenty-five percent of the room has been painted in 28 minutes. Doug thinks it will take a total of 3 hours to paint the whole room.
Plan	Since 25% or $\frac{1}{4}$ of the room was painted in about 30 minutes, use a model of 25%.
Solve	Round 28 minutes to 30 minutes 25% (30 min) → 25% 25% 25% 25% (30 min 30 min 30 min 30 min) $30 \text{ minutes} \times 4 = 120 \text{ minutes}$ $120 \text{ min} = 2 \text{ h}$ So, 2 hours would be a better estimate than 3 hours.
Check	Thirty minutes is $\frac{1}{2}$ hour. Since $\frac{1}{2} \times 4 = 2$, 2 hours is reasonable answer. ✔

Analyze The Strategy

1. Describe other problem-solving strategies that you could use to determine whether answers are reasonable.
2. WRITING IN MATH Write two word problems. One should have a reasonable answer and the other should not.

Mixed Problem Solving

See pages 686, 710.

Determine reasonable answers for Exercises 3–6.

3. **SAVING** Aliayah saves \$11 each month for her class trip. What is a reasonable estimate for the amount of money she will have saved after a year: about \$100, \$120, or \$160? Explain.

4. **SCHOOL** Of 423 students, 57.6% live within 5 miles of the school. What is a reasonable estimate for the number of students living within 5 miles of the school? Explain.

5. **EXERCISE** A survey showed that 61% of middle school students do some kind of physical activity every day. If there are 828 middle school students in your school, would the number of students who exercise be about 300, 400, or 500? Explain.

6. **ANALYZE GRAPHS** A travel agency surveyed 140 families about their favorite vacation spots. Is 60, 70, or 80 families a reasonable estimate for the number of families that did *not* choose Hawaii?

Favorite Vacation Spots

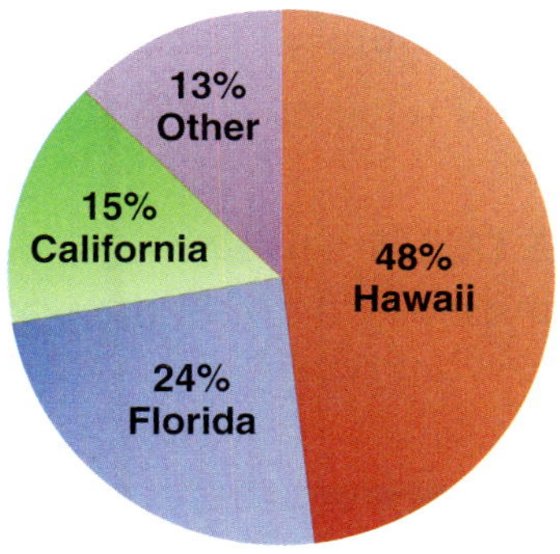

Use any strategy to solve Exercises 7–13. Some strategies are shown below.

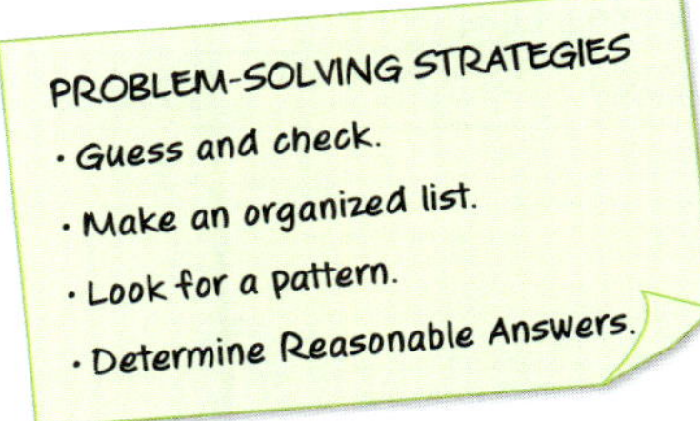

7. **COINS** John has 10 coins that total \$0.83. What are the coins?

8. **ANALYZE GRAPHS** Refer to the graph. A pie is set out to cool. Is it reasonable to estimate that the pie will be 90°F after ten minutes of cooling?

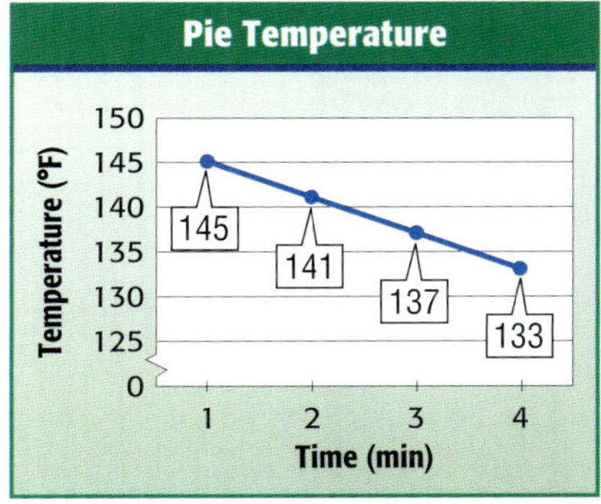

9. **SHOPPING** Deshawn wants to buy a shirt that has a regular price of \$41, but is now on sale for 25% off. Is \$25, \$30, or \$35 the best estimate for the cost of the shirt?

10. **BOWLING** In bowling, you get a spare when you knock down the ten pins in two throws. How many possible ways are there to get a spare?

11. **TIPS** Shawnda decides to leave a 20% tip on a restaurant bill of \$17.50. How much should she tip the restaurant server?

12. **FUNDRAISER** During a popcorn sale for a fundraiser, the soccer team gets to keep 25% of the sales. One box of popcorn sells for \$1.50, and the team has sold 510 boxes so far. Has the team raised a total of \$175?

13. **MEASUREMENT** How many square yards of carpet are needed to carpet the two rooms described below? Explain.

Room	Dimensions
living room	15 ft by 18 ft
TV room	18 ft by 20 ft

CHAPTER 7

Mid-Chapter Quiz

Lessons 7-1 through 7-5

Find each number. Round to the nearest tenth if necessary. (Lesson 7-1)

1. Find 17% of 655.
2. What is 235% of 82?
3. Find 75% of 160.
4. What number is 162.2% of 55?

5. **MULTIPLE CHOICE** Ayana has 220 coins in her piggy bank. Of those, 45% are pennies. How many coins are not pennies? (Lesson 7-1)

   A 121   **C** 109

   B 116   **D** 85

Find each number. Round to the nearest tenth if necessary. (Lesson 7-2)

6. What percent of 84 is 12?
7. 15 is 25% of what number?
8. 85% of 252 is what number?

ANALYZE GRAPHS **For Exercises 9 and 10, refer to the graph that shows the results of a survey of 200 students' favorite DVDs.**

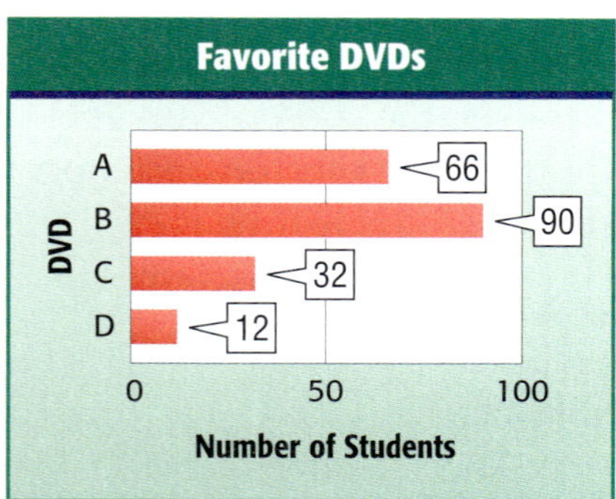

9. What percent of students preferred DVD A?
10. Which DVD did about 15% of students prefer?

Estimate. (Lesson 7-3)

11. 20% of 392
12. 78% of 112
13. 52% of 295
14. 30% of 42
15. 79% of 88
16. 41.5% of 212

17. **MULTIPLE CHOICE** A football player has made about 75% of the field goals he has attempted in his career. If he attempts 41 field goals in one season, about how many would he be expected to make?

   A 35   **C** 25

   B 30   **D** 20

Write an equation for each problem. Then solve. Round to the nearest tenth if necessary. (Lesson 7-4)

18. What number is 35% of 72?
19. 16.1 is what percent of 70?
20. 27.2 is 68% of what number?
21. 16% of 32 is what number?
22. 55% of what number is 1.265?
23. 17 is 40% of what number?

24. **ANALYZE TABLES** The table shows the costs of owning a dog over an average 11-year lifespan. What percent of the total cost is veterinary bills? (Lesson 7-4)

Dog Ownership Costs

Item	Cost ($)
Food	4,020
Veterinary Bills	3,930
Grooming, Equipment	2,960
Training	1,220
Other	2,470

Source: American Kennel Club

25. **SHOPPING** A desktop computer costs $849.75 and the hard drive is 61.3% of the total cost. What is a reasonable estimate for the cost of the hard drive? (Lesson 7-5)

7-6 Percent of Change

MAIN IDEA

Find the percent of increase or decrease.

New Vocabulary

percent of change
percent of increase
percent of decrease

Math Online

glencoe.com

- Concepts In Motion
- Extra Examples
- Personal Tutor
- Self-Check Quiz

MINI Lab

You can model a 50% increase using straws.

100%

50%

150%

- Begin with two straws. The first straw will represent 100%.
- Cut the second straw in half. One part represents 50%.
- Tape the two straws together. This new straw represents a 50% increase or 150% of the original straw.

Model each percent of change.

1. 25% increase
2. 75% increase
3. 30% increase
4. Describe a model that represents a 100% increase, a 200% increase, and a 300% increase.
5. Describe how this process would change to show percent of decrease.

One way to describe a change in quantities is to use percent of change.

Percent of Change — Key Concept

Words A **percent of change** is a ratio that compares the change in quantity to the original amount.

Equation $\text{percent of change} = \frac{\text{amount of change}}{\text{original amount}}$

The percent of change is based on the original amount. If the original quantity is increased, then it is called a **percent of increase**. If the original quantity is decreased, then it is called a **percent of decrease**.

$$\text{percent of increase} = \frac{\text{amount of increase}}{\text{original amount}}$$ ← new − original

$$\text{percent of decrease} = \frac{\text{amount of decrease}}{\text{original amount}}$$ ← original − new

EXAMPLE Find Percent of Increase

1 **GASOLINE** **Find the percent of change in the cost of gasoline from 1981 to 2007. Round to the nearest whole percent if necessary.**

Since the 2007 price is greater than the 1981 price, this is a percent of increase. The amount of increase is \$2.85 - \$1.30 or \$1.55.

$$\text{percent of increase} = \frac{\text{amount of increase}}{\text{original amount}}$$

$= \frac{\$1.55}{\$1.30}$ Substitution

≈ 1.19 Simplify.

$\approx 119\%$ Write 1.19 as a percent.

The cost of gasoline increased 119% from 1981 to 2007.

Percents
In the percent of change formula, the decimal representing the percent of change must be written as a percent.

 CHECK Your Progress

a. **MEASUREMENT** Find the percent of change from 10 yards to 13 yards.

EXAMPLE Find Percent of Decrease

2 **DVD RECORDER** **Yusuf bought a DVD recorder for \$280. Now, it is on sale for \$220. Find the percent of change in the price. Round to the nearest whole percent if necessary.**

Since the new price is less than the original price, this is a percent of decrease. The amount of decrease is \$280 - \$220 or \$60.

$$\text{percent of decrease} = \frac{\text{amount of decrease}}{\text{original amount}}$$

$= \frac{\$60}{\$280}$ Substitution

≈ 0.21 Simplify.

$\approx 21\%$ Write 0.21 as a percent.

The price of the DVD recorder decreased by about 21 percent.

b. **MONEY** Find the percent of change from \$20 to \$15.

TEST EXAMPLE

3 **The table shows about how many people attended the home games of a high school football team for five consecutive years. Which statement is supported by the information in the table?**

Attendance of Home Games	
Year	**Total Attendance (thousands)**
2003	16.6
2004	16.4
2005	15.9
2006	17.4
2007	17.6

A The attendance in 2006 was 15% greater than the attendance in 2005.

B The greatest decrease in attendance occurred from 2003 to 2004.

C The attendance in 2005 was 3% less than the attendance in 2004.

D The greatest increase in attendance occurred from 2006 to 2007.

Read the Item

You need to determine which statement is best supported by the information given in the table.

Solve the Item

- Check **A**. The percent of change from 2005 to 2006 was $\frac{17.4 - 15.9}{15.9}$ or about 10%, not 15%.
- Check **B**.
  From 2003 to 2004, the decrease was 16.6 − 16.4 or 0.2.
  From 2004 to 2005, the decrease was 16.4 − 15.9 or 0.5.
  This statement is not supported by the information.
- Check **C**. The percent of change from 2004 to 2005 was $\frac{16.4 - 15.9}{16.4}$ or about 3%. This statement is supported by the information.
- Check **D**.
  From 2005 to 2006, the increase was 17.4 − 15.9 or 1.5.
  From 2006 to 2007, the increase was 17.6 − 17.4 or 0.2.
  This statement is not supported by the information.

The solution is **C**.

Test-Taking Tip

Check the Results If you have time, check all of the choices given. By doing so, you will verify that your choice is correct.

CHECK Your Progress

c. Which of the following represents the greatest percent of change?

F A savings account that had \$500 now has \$470.

G An MP3 player that stored 15 GB now stores 30 GB.

H A plant grew from 3 inches to 8 inches in one month.

J An airplane ticket that was originally priced at \$345 is now \$247.

CHECK Your Understanding

Find each percent of change. Round to the nearest whole percent if necessary. State whether the percent of change is an *increase* or a *decrease*.

Examples 1, 2 (p. 370)

1. 30 inches to 24 inches
2. 20.5 meters to 35.5 meters
3. \$126 to \$150
4. \$75.80 to \$94.75

Example 3 (p. 371)

5. **MULTIPLE CHOICE** The table shows the number of youth 7 years and older who played soccer from 1998 to 2006. Which statement is supported by the information in the table?

Playing Soccer	
Year	**Number (millions)**
1998	13.2
2000	12.9
2002	13.7
2004	13.3
2006	14.0

Source: National Sporting Goods Association

A The greatest decrease in the number of players occurred from 1998 to 2000.

B There were 7% fewer youth playing soccer in 2004 than in 2002.

C The number of players in 2002 was 6% greater than the number of players in 2000.

D There were 10% more youth playing soccer in 2000 than in 1998.

Practice and Problem Solving

HOMEWORK HELP	
For Exercises	**See Examples**
6–7, 14–15 18–19	1
8–13 16–17	2
39, 40	3

For Exercises 6–19, find each percent of change. Round to the nearest whole percent if necessary. State whether the percent of change is an *increase* or a *decrease*.

6. 15 yards to 18 yards
7. 100 acres to 140 acres
8. \$12 to \$6
9. 48 notebooks to 14 notebooks
10. 125 centimeters to 87.5 centimeters
11. \$15.60 to \$11.70
12. 1.6 hours to 0.95 hour
13. 132 days to 125.4 days
14. \$240 to \$320
15. 624 feet to 702 feet
16. **BOOKS** On Monday, Kenya spent 60 minutes reading her favorite book. Today, she spent 45 minutes reading this book.
17. **EXERCISE** Three months ago, Ernesto could walk 2 miles in 40 minutes. Today he can walk 2 miles in 25 minutes.
18. **SCHOOL** Last school year the enrollment of Gilboa Middle School was 465 students. This year the enrollment is 525.
19. **MONEY** Jake had \$782 in his checking account. He now has \$798.

Find each percent of change. Round to the nearest whole percent if necessary. State whether the percent of change is an *increase* or a *decrease*.

20. $\frac{1}{2}$ to $\frac{1}{4}$
21. $\frac{4}{6}$ to $\frac{1}{6}$
22. $\frac{1}{5}$ to $\frac{4}{5}$
23. $\frac{2}{3}$ to $\frac{5}{3}$

MEASUREMENT For Exercises 24 and 25, refer to the rectangle at the right. Suppose the side lengths are doubled.

8 cm

3 cm

24. Find the percent of change in the perimeter.

25. Find the percent of change in the area.

26. **MUSIC PHONES** Between 2006 and 2007, music phone owners increased from 6.8 million to 33 million. Find the percent of increase. Round to the nearest whole percent.

27. **FIND THE DATA** Refer to the Data File on pages 16–19. Choose some data and write a real-world problem in which you would find the percent of change.

28. **ANALYZE GRAPHS** Use the graphic shown to find the percent of change in CD sales from 2005 to 2006.

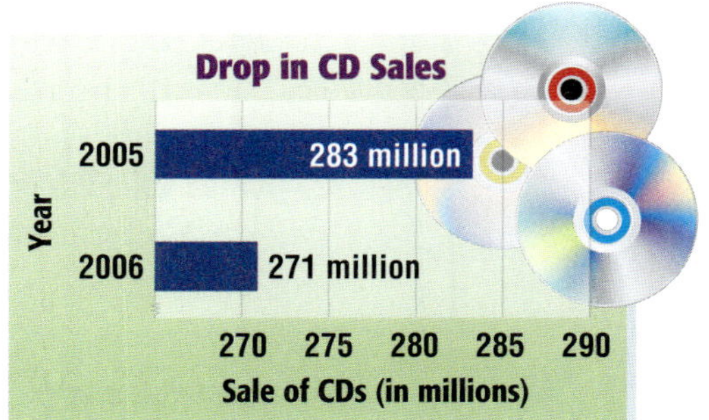

Source: Fox News

29. **SHOES** In 2009, shoe sales for a certain company were $25.9 billion. Sales are expected to increase by about 20% from 2009 to 2010. Find the projected amount of shoe sales in 2010.

30. **BABYSITTING** The table shows how many hours Catalina spent babysitting during the months of April and May. If Catalina charges $6.50 per hour, what is the percent of change in the amount of money earned from April to May?

Month	Hours Worked
April	40
May	32

ANALYZE GRAPHS For Exercises 31–33, refer to the graph.

31. Find the percent of decrease of truck sales from 2004 to 2005. Round to the nearest whole percent.

32. Find the percent of increase of truck sales from 2003 to 2004. Round to the nearest whole percent.

33. Between which two consecutive years is the percent of increase the greatest? What is the percent of increase? Round to the nearest whole percent.

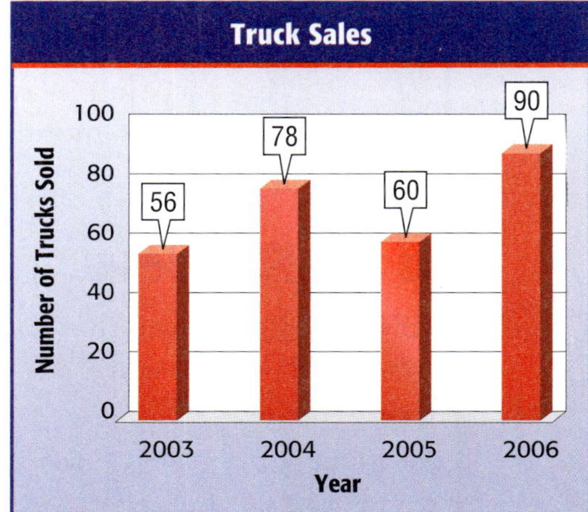

EXTRA PRACTICE
See pages 686, 710.

H.O.T. Problems

34. **OPEN ENDED** Write a percent of change problem using the quantities 14 and 25, and state whether there is a percent of increase or decrease. Find the percent of change.

35. **NUMBER SENSE** The costs of two different sound systems were decreased by $10. The original costs of the systems were $90 and $60, respectively. Without calculating, which had greater percent of decrease? Explain.

36. **FIND THE ERROR** Sade and Trish are finding the percent of change from \$52 to \$125. Who is correct? Explain.

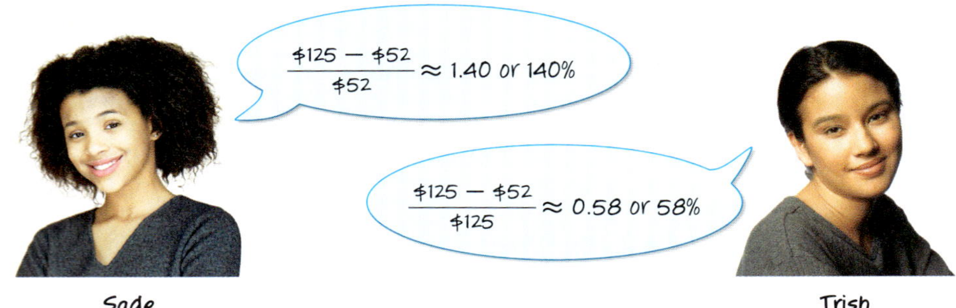

37. **CHALLENGE** If a quantity increases by 10% and then decreases by 10%, will the result be the original quantity? Explain.

38. **WRITING IN MATH** Explain how you know whether a percent of change is a percent of increase or a percent of decrease.

39. Which of the following represents the least percent of change?

A A coat that was originally priced at \$90 is now \$72.

B A puppy who weighed 6 ounces at birth now weighs 96 ounces.

C A child grew from 54 inches to 60 inches in 1 year.

D A savings account increased from \$500 to \$550 in 6 months.

40. If each dimension of the rectangle is doubled, what is the percent of increase in the area?

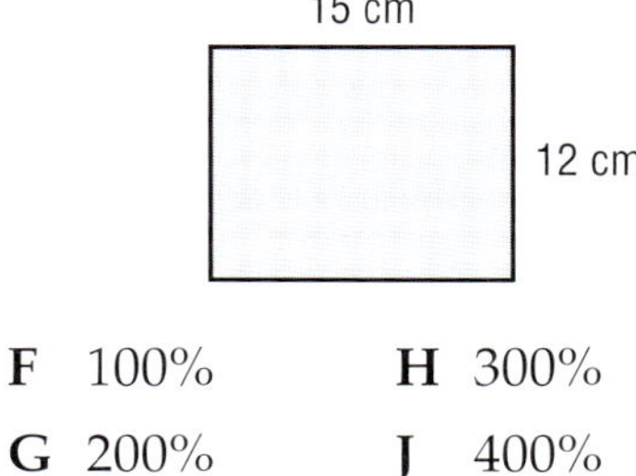

F 100% H 300%

G 200% J 400%

Spiral Review

ALGEBRA Write an equation for each problem. Then solve. Round to the nearest tenth if necessary. (Lesson 7-4)

41. **FOOD** Of 823 students 47.2% of the students chose pizza as their favorite food. What is a reasonable estimate for the number of students who chose pizza as their favorite food? Explain. (Lesson 7-5)

42. 30% of what number is 17?

43. What is 21% of 62?

44. **SHOPPING** Four pounds of pecans cost \$12.75. How much is this per pound? (Lesson 6-2)

GET READY for the Next Lesson

PREREQUISITE SKILL Write each percent as a decimal. (Lesson 6-8)

45. 6.5%

46. $5\frac{1}{2}\%$

47. $8\frac{1}{4}\%$

48. $6\frac{3}{4}\%$

7-7 Sales Tax and Discount

MAIN IDEA

Solve problems involving sales tax and discount.

New Vocabulary

sales tax
discount

Math Online

glencoe.com

- Extra Examples
- Personal Tutor
- Self-Check Quiz

GET READY for the Lesson

KAYAKS Horatio plans to buy a new kayak that costs $1,849. He lives in North Carolina where there is a 4.25% sales tax.

1. Calculate the sales tax by finding 4.25% of $1,849. Round to the nearest cent.
2. What will be the total cost including the sales tax?
3. Multiply 1.0425 and 1,849. How does the result compare to your answer in Exercise 2?

Sales tax is an additional amount of money charged on items that people buy. The total cost of an item is the regular price plus the sales tax.

EXAMPLE Find the Total Cost

ELECTRONICS A DVD player costs $140, and the sales tax is 5.75%. What is the total cost of the DVD player?

METHOD 1 **Add sales tax to the regular price.**

First, find the sales tax.

5.75% of $140 = 0.0575 × 140 — Write 5.75% as a decimal.
= 8.05 — The sales tax is $8.05.

Next, add the sales tax to the regular price.
$8.05 + $140 = $148.05

METHOD 2 **Add the percent of tax to 100%.**

100% + 5.75% = 105.75% — Add the percent of tax to 100%.

The total cost is 105.75% of the regular price.

105.75% of $140 = 1.0575 × $140 — Write 105.75% as a decimal.
= $148.05 — Multiply.

So, the total cost of the DVD player is $148.05.

CHOOSE Your Method

a. **CLOTHES** What is the total cost of a sweatshirt if the regular price is $42 and the sales tax is $5\frac{1}{2}$%?

Study Tip

Sales Tax and Discount If both are represented as percents, sales tax is a percent of increase, and discount is a percent of decrease.

Discount is the amount by which the regular price of an item is reduced. The sale price is the regular price minus the discount.

EXAMPLE Find the Sale Price

BOOGIE BOARDS **A boogie board that has a regular price of $69 is on sale at a 35% discount. What is the sale price of the boogie board?**

METHOD 1 **Subtract the discount from the regular price.**

First, find the amount of the discount.

35% of $69 = 0.35 • $69	Write 35% as a decimal.
= $24.15	The discount is $24.15.

Next, subtract the discount from the regular price.
$69 – $24.15 = $44.85

METHOD 2 **Subtract the percent of discount from 100%.**

100% – 35% = 65%	Subtract the discount from 100%.

The sale price is 65% of the regular price.

65% of $69 = 0.65 • $69	Write 65% as a decimal.
= 44.85	Multiply.

So, the sale price of the boogie board is $44.85.

CHOOSE Your Method

b. **MUSIC** A CD that has a regular price of $15.50 is on sale at a 25% discount. What is the sale price of the CD?

Study Tip

Percent Equation Remember that, in the percent equation, the percent must be written as a decimal. Since the sale price is 70% of the original price, use 0.7 to represent 70% in the percent equation.

EXAMPLE Find the Original Price

CELL PHONES **A cell phone is on sale for 30% off. If the sale price is $239.89, what is the original price?**

The sale price is 100% – 30% or 70% of the original price.

Words $239.89 is 70% of what price?

Variable Let p represent the original price.

Equation $239.89 = 0.7 × p

$239.89 = 0.7p$	Write the equation.
$\frac{239.89}{0.7} = \frac{0.7p}{0.7}$	Divide each side by 0.7.
$342.70 = p$	Simplify.

The original price is $342.70.

CHECK Your Progress

c. Find the original price if the sale price of the cell phone is $205.50.

CHECK Your Understanding

Find the total cost or sale price to the nearest cent.

Example 1 (p. 375)

1. $2.95 notebook; 5% tax
2. $46 shoes; 2.9% tax

Example 2 (p. 376)

3. $1,575 computer; 15% discount
4. $119.50 skateboard; 20% off

Example 3 (p. 376)

5. **IN-LINE SKATES** A pair of in-line skates is on sale for $90. If this price represents a 9% discount from the original price, what is the original price to the nearest cent?

Practice and Problem Solving

HOMEWORK HELP

For Exercises	See Examples
6–13	1–2
14–17	3

Find the total cost or sale price to the nearest cent.

6. $58 ski lift ticket; 20% discount
7. $1,500 computer; 7% tax
8. $99 CD player; 5% tax
9. $12.25 pen set; 60% discount
10. $4.30 makeup; 40% discount
11. $7.50 meal; 6.5% tax
12. $39.60 sweater; 33% discount
13. $89.75 scooter; $7\frac{1}{4}$% tax
14. **COSMETICS** A bottle of hand lotion is on sale for $2.25. If this price represents a 50% discount from the original price, what is the original price to the nearest cent?
15. **TICKETS** At a movie theater, the cost of admission to a matinee is $5.25. If this price represents a 30% discount from the evening price, find the evening price to the nearest cent.

Find the original price to the nearest cent.

16. calendar: discount, 75%
    sale price, $2.25
17. telescope: discount, 30%
    sale price, $126
18. **VIDEO GAMES** What is the sales tax of a $178.90 video game system if the tax rate is 5.75%?
19. **RESTAURANTS** A restaurant bill comes to $28.35. Find the total cost if the tax is 6.25% and a 20% tip is left on the amount before tax.

SKATEBOARDS For Exercises 20–22, use the information in the table at the right.

A skateboard costs $320, not including the sales tax.

State	2007 Sales Tax Rate
Washington	6.5%
Kansas	5.3%
North Carolina	4.25%

Source: Federation of Tax Administrators

20. What is the total cost of the skateboard, including tax in Washington?
21. What is the total cost of the skateboard, including tax, in North Carolina?
22. A store in Kansas has the skateboard on sale for 20% off. If the sales tax is calculated after the discount, what is the cost of the skateboard?

EXTRA PRACTICE See pages 686, 710.

H.O.T. Problems

23. **CHALLENGE** A gift store is having a sale in which all items are discounted 20%. Including tax, Colin paid $21 for a picture frame. If the sales tax rate is 5%, what was the original price of the picture frame?

24. **OPEN ENDED** Give an example of the regular price of an item and the total cost including sales tax if the tax rate is 5.75%.

25. **Which One Doesn't Belong?** In each pair, the first value is the regular price of an item and the second value is the sale price. Identify the pair that does not have the same percent of discount as the other three. Explain.

$24, $18	$50, $25	$12, $9	$80, $60

26. **WRITING IN MATH** Describe two methods for finding the sale price of an item that is discounted 30%. Which method do you prefer? Explain.

TEST PRACTICE

27. A computer software store is having a sale. The table shows the regular price, r, and the sales price, s, of various items.

Item	Regular Price (r)	Sale Price (s)
A	$5.00	$4.00
B	$8.00	$6.40
C	$10.00	$8.00
D	$15.00	$12.00

Which formula can be used to calculate the sale price?

A $s = r \times 0.2$ **C** $s = r \times 0.8$

B $s = r - 0.2$ **D** $s = r - 0.8$

28. A chair that costs $210 was reduced by 40% for a one day sale. After the sale, the sale price was increased by 40%. What is the price of the chair?

F $176.40 **H** $205.50

G $185.30 **J** $210.00

29. Juanita paid $10.50 for a T-shirt at the mall. It was on sale for 30% off. What was the original price before the discount?

A $3.15 **C** $15.00

B $7.35 **D** $35.00

Spiral Review

Find each percent of change. Round to the nearest whole percent if necessary. State whether the percent of change is an *increase* or *decrease*. (Lesson 7-6)

30. 4 hours to 6 hours

31. $500 to $456

32. 20.5 meters to 35.5 meters

33. **TRAVEL** Out of a 511-mile trip, Mya drove about 68% on Monday. Determine a reasonable estimate for the number of miles she drove on Monday. (Lesson 7-5)

GET READY for the Next Lesson

PREREQUISITE SKILL Multiply. Write in simplest form. (Lesson 5-5)

34. $\frac{2}{7} \cdot \frac{4}{5}$

35. $\frac{1}{8} \cdot \frac{4}{9}$

36. $\frac{6}{11} \cdot \frac{9}{24}$

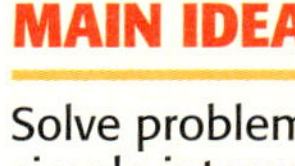

7-8 Simple Interest

MAIN IDEA

Solve problems involving simple interest.

New Vocabulary

principal
simple interest

Math Online

glencoe.com

- Extra Examples
- Personal Tutor
- Self-Check Quiz

GET READY for the Lesson

INVESTING Suni plans to save the $200 she received for her birthday. The graphs shows the average yearly rates at three different banks.

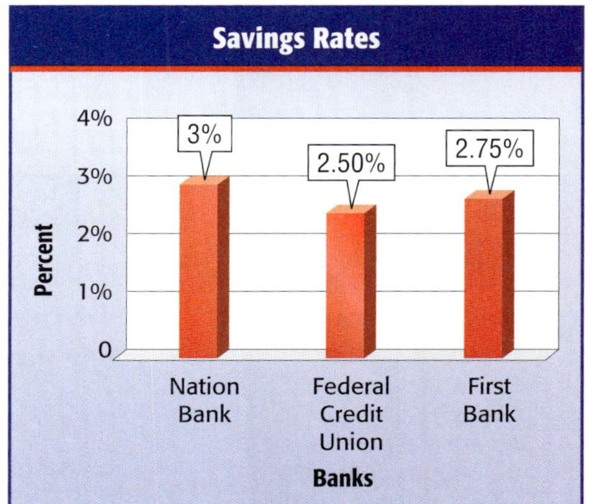

1. Calculate 2.50% of $200 to find the amount of money Suni can earn in one year at Federal Credit Bank.
2. Calculate 2.75% of $200 to find the amount of money Suni can earn in one year at First Bank.

Principal is the amount of money deposited or borrowed. **Simple interest** is the amount paid or earned for the use of money. To find simple interest I, use the following formula.

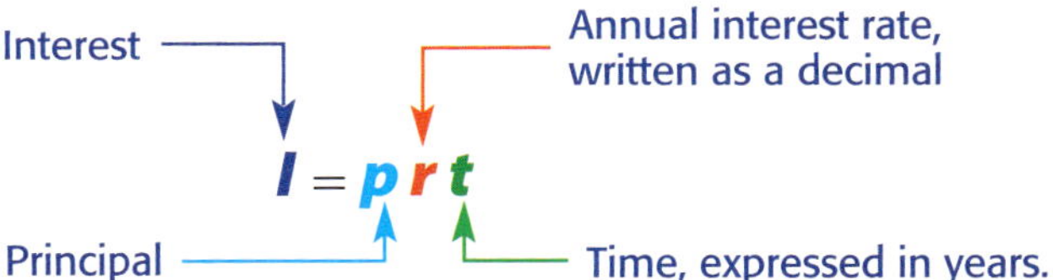

EXAMPLES Find Interest Earned

CHECKING **Arnold has $580 in a savings account that pays 3% simple interest. How much interest will he earn in each amount of time?**

1 **5 years**

$I = prt$	Formula for simple interest
$I = 580 \cdot 0.03 \cdot 5$	Replace p with $580, r with 0.03, and t with 5.
$I = 87$	Simplify.

Arnold will earn $87 in interest in 5 years.

2 **6 months**

6 months $= \frac{6}{12}$ or 0.5 year	Write the time as years.
$I = prt$	Formula for simple interest
$I = 580 \cdot 0.03 \cdot 0.5$	$p = \$580$, $r = 0.03$, $t = 0.5$
$I \approx 8.7$	Simplify.

Arnold will earn $8.70 in interest in 6 months.

SAVINGS **Jenny has \$1,560 in a savings account that pays 2.5% simple interest. How much interest will she earn in each amount of time?**

a. 3 years

b. 6 months

Real-World Career . . .
How does a Car Salesperson Use Math?
A car salesperson must be able to determine values of cars, calculate interest rates, and determine monthly payments.

For more information go to glencoe.com.

The formula $I = prt$ can also be used to find the interest owed when you borrow money. In this case, p is the amount of money borrowed, and t is the amount of time the money is borrowed.

EXAMPLE Find Interest Paid on a Loan

3 **LOANS** **Rondell's parents borrow \$6,300 from the bank for a new car. The interest rate is 6% per year. How much simple interest will they pay if they take 2 years to repay the loan?**

$I = prt$ — Formula for simple interest

$I = 6{,}300 \cdot 0.06 \cdot 2$ — Replace p with \$6,300, r with 0.06, and t with 2.

$I = 756$ — Simplify.

Rondell's parents will pay \$756 in interest in 2 years.

c. **LOANS** Mrs. Hanover borrows \$1,400 at a rate of 5.5% per year. How much simple interest will she pay if it takes 8 months to repay the loan?

EXAMPLE Find Total Paid on a Credit Card

4 **CREDIT CARDS** **Derrick's dad bought new tires for \$900 using a credit card. His card has an interest rate of 19%. If he has no other charges on his card and does not pay off his balance at the end of the month, how much money will he owe after one month?**

Study Tip
Fractions of Years
Remember to express 1 month as $\frac{1}{12}$ year in the formula.

$I = prt$ — Formula for simple interest

$I = 900 \cdot 0.19 \cdot \frac{1}{12}$ — Replace p with \$900, r with 0.19, and t with $\frac{1}{12}$.

$I = 14.25$ — Simplify.

The interest owed after one month is \$14.25. So, the total amount owed would be \$900 + \$14.25 or \$914.25.

CHECK Your Progress

d. **CREDIT CARDS** An office manager charged \$425 worth of office supplies on a charge card with an interest rate of 9.9%. How much money will he owe if he makes no other charges on the card and does not pay off the balance at the end of the month?

CHECK Your Understanding

Examples 1, 2 (pp. 379–380)

Find the simple interest earned to the nearest cent for each principal, interest rate, and time.

1. \$640, 3%, 2 years
2. \$1,500, 4.25%, 4 years
3. \$580, 2%, 6 months
4. \$1,200, 3.9%, 8 months

Example 3 (p. 380)

Find the simple interest paid to the nearest cent for each loan, interest rate, and time.

5. \$4,500, 9%, 3.5 years
6. \$290, 12.5%, 6 months

Example 4 (p. 380)

7. **FINANCES** The Masters family financed a computer that costs \$1,200. If the interest rate is 19%, how much will the family owe after one month if no payments are made?

Practice and Problem Solving

HOMEWORK HELP	
For Exercises	See Examples
8–9	1
10–11	2
12–15	3
16–17	4

Find the simple interest earned to the nearest cent for each principal, interest rate, and time.

8. \$1,050, 4.6%, 2 years
9. \$250, 2.85%, 3 years
10. \$500, 3.75%, 4 months
11. \$3,000, 5.5%, 9 months

Find the simple interest paid to the nearest cent for each loan, interest rate, and time.

12. \$1,000, 7%, 2 years
13. \$725, 6.25%, 1 year
14. \$2,700, 8.2%, 3 months
15. \$175.80, 12%, 8 months

16. **CREDIT CARDS** Leon charged \$75 at an interest rate of 12.5%. How much will Leon have to pay after one month if he makes no payments?

17. **TRAVEL** A family charged \$1,345 in travel expenses. If no payments are made, how much will they owe after one month if the interest rate is 7.25%?

BANKING For Exercises 18 and 19, use the table.

Home Savings and Loan	
Time	Rate
6 months	2.4%
9 months	2.9%
12 months	3.0%
18 months	3.1%

18. What is the simple interest earned on \$900 for 9 months?
19. Find the simple interest earned on \$2,500 for 18 months.

INVESTING For Exercises 20 and 21, use the following information.

Ramon has \$4,200 to invest for college.

20. If Ramon invests \$4,200 for 3 years and earns \$630, what was the simple interest rate?
21. Ramon's goal is to have \$5,000 after 4 years. Is this possible if he invests with a rate of return of 6%? Explain.

EXTRA PRACTICE
See pages 687, 711.

H.O.T. Problems

22. **OPEN ENDED** Suppose you earn 3% on a $1,200 deposit for 5 years. Explain how the simple interest is affected if the rate is increased by 1%. What happens if the time is increased by 1 year?

23. **CHALLENGE** Mrs. Antil deposits $800 in a savings account that earns 3.2% interest annually. At the end of the year, the interest is added to the principal or original amount. She keeps her money in this account for three years without withdrawing any money. Find the total in her account after each year for three years.

24. **WRITING IN MATH** List the steps you would use to find the simple interest on a $500 loan at 6% interest rate for 18 months. Then find the simple interest.

25. Jada invests $590 in a money market account. Her account pays 7.2% simple interest. If she does not add or withdraw any money again, how much interest will Jada's account earn after 4 years of simple interest?
    A $75.80
    B $158.67
    C $169.92
    D $220.67

26. Mr. Sprockett borrows $3,500 from his bank to buy a used car. The loan has a 7.4% annual simple interest rate. If it takes Mr. Sprockett two years to pay back the loan, what is the total amount he will be paying?
    F $3,012
    G $4,018
    H $4,550
    J $3,598

27. Find the total cost of a $19.99 DVD if the tax rate is 7%. (Lesson 7-7)

Find each percent of change. Round to the nearest whole percent if necessary. State whether the percent of change is an increase or decrease. (Lesson 7-6)

28. 35 birds to 45 birds
29. 60 inches to 38 inches
30. $2.75 to $1.80

Divide. Write in simplest form. (Lesson 5-7)

31. $\frac{3}{5} \div \frac{1}{2}$
32. $\frac{4}{7} \div \frac{5}{8}$
33. $2\frac{2}{3} \div 1\frac{1}{4}$

Problem Solving in Art

It's Golden! It's time to complete your project. Use the information and data you have gathered about the Golden Ratio to prepare a Power Point presentation. Be sure to include your reports and calculations in your presentation.

Math Online **Unit Project at** glencoe.com

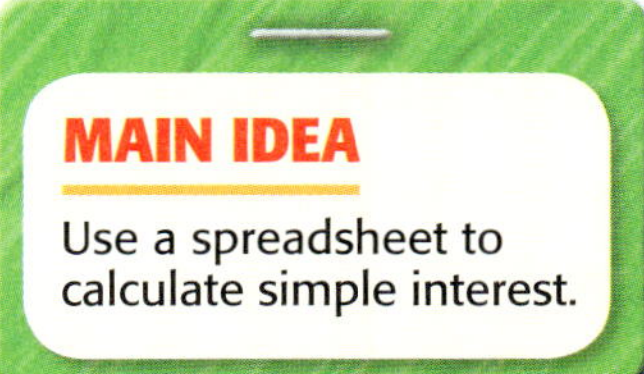

Spreadsheet Lab
Simple Interest

MAIN IDEA

Use a spreadsheet to calculate simple interest.

A computer spreadsheet is a useful tool for quickly calculating simple interest for different values of principal, rate, and time.

ACTIVITY

Max plans on opening a "Young Savers" account at his bank. The current rate on the account is 4%. He wants to see how different starting balances, rates, and times will affect his account balance. To find the balance at the end of 2 years for different principal amounts, he enters the values B2 = 4 and C2 = 2 into the spreadsheet below.

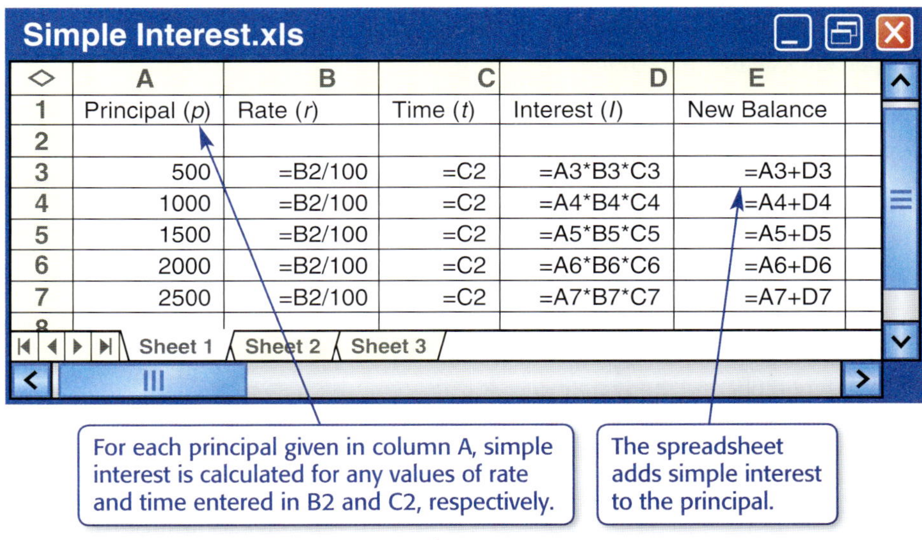

	A	B	C	D	E
1	Principal (*p*)	Rate (*r*)	Time (*t*)	Interest (*I*)	New Balance
2					
3	500	=B2/100	=C2	=A3*B3*C3	=A3+D3
4	1000	=B2/100	=C2	=A4*B4*C4	=A4+D4
5	1500	=B2/100	=C2	=A5*B5*C5	=A5+D5
6	2000	=B2/100	=C2	=A6*B6*C6	=A6+D6
7	2500	=B2/100	=C2	=A7*B7*C7	=A7+D7

Analyze the Results

1. Why is the rate in column B divided by 100?
2. What is the balance in Max's account after 2 years if the principal is \$1,500 and the simple interest rate is 4%?
3. How much interest does Max earn in 2 years if his account has a principal of \$2,000 and a simple interest rate of 4%?
4. Is the amount of principal proportional to the interest Max earns if his account earns 4% simple interest over 2 years? Explain.
5. Is the amount of principal proportional to the balance in Max's account if it earns 4% simple interest over 2 years? Explain.
6. What entries for cells B2 and C2 would you use to calculate the simple interest on a principal of \$1,500 at a rate of 7% for a 9-month period?
7. What is the balance of this account at the end of the 9 months?

Chapter 7 Study Guide and Review

Math Online glencoe.com
• STUDY TO GO
• Vocabulary Review

GET READY to Study

Be sure the following Big Ideas are noted in your Foldable.

7-1	7-2
7-3	7-4
7-5	7-6
7-7	7-8

BIG Ideas

Percent of a Number (Lesson 7-1)
- To find the percent of a number, first write the percent as either a fraction or decimal and then multiply.

Percent Proportion (Lesson 7-2)

$$\frac{\text{part}}{\text{whole}} = \left.\frac{n}{100}\right\} \text{percent}$$

Percent and Estimation (Lesson 7-3)
- One way to estimate the percent of a number is to use a fraction. The other way is to first find 10% of the number and then multiply.

Percent Equation (Lesson 7-4)

$$\text{part} = \text{percent} \cdot \text{whole}$$

Percent of Change (Lesson 7-6)
- A percent of change is a ratio that compares the change in quantity to the original amount.

$$\text{percent of change} = \frac{\text{amount of change}}{\text{original amount}}$$

Sales Tax and Discount (Lesson 7-7)
- Sales tax is an additional amount of money charged on items. The total cost of an item is the regular price plus the sales tax.
- Discount is the amount by which the regular price of an item is reduced. The sale price is the regular price minus the discount.

Simple Interest (Lesson 7-8)
- Simple interest is the amount paid or earned for the use of money.

$$I = prt$$

Key Vocabulary

discount (p. 375)
percent equation (p. 361)
percent of change (p. 369)
percent of decrease (p. 369)
percent of increase (p. 369)
percent proportion (p. 350)
principal (p. 379)
sales tax (p. 375)
simple interest (p. 379)

Vocabulary Check

State whether each sentence is *true* or *false*. If *false*, replace the underlined word or number to make a true sentence.

1. The sale price of a discounted item is the regular price <u>minus</u> the discount.
2. A ratio that compares the change in quantity to the original amount is called the <u>percent of change</u>.
3. A <u>percent proportion</u> compares part of a quantity to the whole quantity using a percent.
4. The formula for simple interest is <u>$I = prt$</u>.
5. A method for estimating the percent of a number is to find <u>21%</u> of the number and then multiply.
6. The equation part = percent • whole is known as the <u>principal</u> equation.
7. The <u>principal</u> is the amount of money deposited or borrowed.
8. A <u>tax</u> is the amount by which the regular price of an item is reduced.
9. To find a percent of increase, compare the amount of the increase to the <u>new</u> amount.
10. If the new amount is greater than the original amount, then the percent of change is percent of <u>decrease</u>.

Lesson-by-Lesson Review

7-1 Percent of a Number (pp. 344–348)

Find each number. Round to the nearest tenth if necessary.

11. Find 78% of 50.
12. 45.5% of 75 is what number?
13. What is 225% of 60?
14. 0.75% of 80 is what number?

Example 1 **Find 24% of 200.**

24% of 200

$= 24\% \times 200$ Write the expression.

$= 0.24 \times 200$ Write 24% as a decimal.

$= 48$ Multiply.

So, 24% of 200 is 48.

7-2 The Percent Proportion (pp. 350–354)

Find each number. Round to the nearest tenth if necessary.

15. **SOCCER** A soccer team lost 30% of their games. If they played 20 games, how many did they win?
16. 6 is what percent of 120?
17. Find 0.8% of 35.
18. What percent of 375 is 40?
19. **PHONE SERVICE** A family pays \$21.99 each month for their long distance phone service. This is 80% of the original price of the phone service. What is the original price of the phone service? Round to the nearest cent if necessary.

Example 2 **What percent of 90 is 18?**

$\frac{18}{90} = \frac{n}{100}$ Write the proportion.

$18 \cdot 100 = 90 \cdot n$ Find the cross products.

$1{,}800 = 90n$ Simplify.

$\frac{1{,}800}{90} = \frac{90n}{90}$ Divide each side by 90.

$20 = n$ So, 18 is 20% of 90.

Example 3 **52 is 65% of what number?**

$\frac{52}{w} = \frac{65}{100}$ Write the proportion.

$52 \cdot 100 = w \cdot 65$ Find the cross products.

$5{,}200 = 65w$ Simplify.

$\frac{5{,}200}{65} = \frac{65w}{65}$ Divide each side by 65.

$80 = w$ So, 52 is 65% of 80.

7-3 Percent and Estimation (pp. 355–360)

Estimate.

20. 25% of 81
21. 33% of 122
22. 77% of 38
23. 19.5% of 96

Estimate by using 10%.

24. 12% of 77
25. 88% of 400
26. **BOOKS** About 26% of the 208 books in Deja's collection are nonfiction. Estimate how many of Deja's books are nonfiction.

Example 4 **Estimate 52% of 495.**

$52\% \approx 50\%$ or $\frac{1}{2}$, and $495 \approx 500$.

52% of $495 \approx \frac{1}{2} \cdot 500$ or 250

So, 52% of 495 is about 250.

Example 5 **Estimate 68% of 80.**

10% of $80 = 0.1 \cdot 80$ or 8 Find 10% of 80.

68% is about 70%.

$7 \cdot 8 = 56$ 70% of 80 $\approx 7 \cdot$ (10% of 80)

So, 68% of 80 is about 56.

CHAPTER 7 Study Guide and Review

7-4 Algebra: The Percent Equation (pp. 361–365)

Write an equation for each problem. Then solve. Round to the nearest tenth if necessary.

27. 32 is what percent of 50?
28. 65% of what number is 39?
29. Find 42% of 300.
30. 7% of 92 is what number?
31. 12% of what number is 108?
32. **SALONS** A local hair salon increased their sales of hair products by about 12.5% this week. If they sold 48 hair products, how many hair products did they sell last week?

Example 6 **27 is what percent of 90?**

27 is the part and 90 is the base.

Let n represent the percent.

$$\underbrace{\text{part}} = \underbrace{\text{percent}} \cdot \underbrace{\text{base}}$$

$27 = n \cdot 90$ — Write an equation.

$\frac{27}{90} = \frac{90n}{90}$ — Divide each side by 90.

$0.3 = n$ — The percent is 30%.

So, 27 is 30% of 90.

7-5 PSI: Determine Reasonable Answers (pp. 366–367)

Determine a reasonable answer for each problem.

33. **CABLE TV** In a survey of 1,813 consumers, 18% said that they would be willing to pay more for cable if they got more channels. Is 3.3, 33, or 333 a reasonable estimate for the number of consumers willing to pay more for cable?
34. **SCHOOL** There are 880 students at Medina Middle School. If 68% of the students are involved in sports, would the number of students involved in sports be about 510, 630, or 720?
35. **VACATION** Suppose you are going on vacation for $689 and the airfare accounts for 43.5% of the total cost. What is a reasonable cost of the airfare?

Example 7 **Mr. Swanson harvested 1,860 pounds of apples from one orchard, 1,149 pounds from another, and 905 pounds from a third. The apples will be placed in crates that hold 42 pounds of apples. Will Mr. Swanson need 100, 200, or 400 crates?**

Since an exact answer is not needed, we can estimate the total of pounds.

1,860	→	1,900
1,149	→	1,100
+ 905	→	+ 900
		3,900

Since 3,900 ÷ 40 is about 100, it is reasonable that 100 crates need to be ordered.

Mixed Problem Solving
For mixed problem-solving practice, see page 710.

7-6 Percent of Change (pp. 369–374)

Find each percent of change. Round to the nearest whole percent if necessary. State whether the percent of change is an *increase* or *decrease*.

36. original: 172
new: 254

37. original: $200
new: $386

38. original: 75
new: 60

39. original: $49.95
new: $54.95

40. Tyree bought a collectible comic book for $49.62 last year. This year, he sold it for $52.10. Find the percent of change of the price of the comic book. Round to the nearest percent.

Example 8 **A magazine that originally cost $2.75 is now $3.55. Find the percent of change. Round to the nearest whole percent.**

The new price is greater than the original price, so this is a percent of increase.

amount of increase = 3.55 − 2.75 or 0.80

$$\text{percent of increase} = \frac{\text{amount of increase}}{\text{original amount}}$$

$$= \frac{0.80}{2.75} \quad \text{Substitution}$$

$$\approx 0.29 \quad \text{Simplify.}$$

The percent of increase is about 29%.

7-7 Sales Tax and Discount (pp. 375–378)

Find the total cost or sale price to the nearest cent.

41. $25 backpack; 7% tax
42. $210 bicycle; 15% discount
43. $8,000 car; $5\frac{1}{2}$% tax
44. $40 sweater; 33% discount

Find the percent of discount to the nearest percent.

45. shirt: regular price: $42
sale price: $36

46. boots: regular price: $78
sale price: $70

47. **MONEY** At the media store a certain DVD normally costs $21.99. This week the DVD is on sale for 25% off. Tara buys the DVD and pays using a $20 bill. Not including tax, how much change will she receive to the nearest cent?

Example 9 **A new computer system is priced at $2,499. Find the total cost if the sales tax is 6.5%.**

First, find the sales tax.

$$6.5\% \text{ of } \$2{,}499 = 0.065 \cdot 2{,}499$$

$$\approx 162.44$$

Next, add the sales tax. The total cost is 162.44 + 2,499 or $2,661.44.

Example 10 **A pass at a water park is $58. At the end of the season, the same pass costs $46.40. What is the percent of discount?**

$58 - 46.40 = 11.60$ Find the amount of discount.

Next, find what percent of 58 is 11.60.

$11.60 = n \cdot 58$ Write an equation.

$0.2 = n$ Divide each side by 58.

The percent of discount is 20%.

7-8 Simple Interest (pp. 379–382)

Find the interest earned to the nearest cent for each principal, interest rate, and time.

48. \$475, 5%, 2 years
49. \$5,000, 10%, 3 years
50. \$2,500, 11%, $1\frac{1}{2}$ years
51. **SAVINGS** Tonya deposited \$450 into a savings account earning 3.75% annual simple interest. How much interest will she earn in 6 years?

Find the interest paid to the nearest cent for each loan balance, interest rate, and time.

52. \$3,200, 8%, 4 years
53. \$1,980, 21%, 9 months
54. **CREDIT CARDS** David bought a computer for \$600 using his credit card. The interest rate on his credit card is 19%. How much will he pay in all for the computer, if he pays off the balance at the end of 2 years?

Example 11 **Find the interest earned on \$400 at 9% for 3 years.**

$I = prt$ Simple interest formula

$I = 400 \cdot 0.09 \cdot 3$ $p = \$400, r = 0.09, t = 3$

$I = 108$ Simplify.

The interest earned is \$108.

Example 12 **Elisa has a loan for \$1,300. The interest rate is 7%. If she pays it off in 6 months, how much interest will she pay?**

$I = prt$ Simple interest formula

$I = 1{,}300 \cdot 0.07 \cdot 0.5$ $p = \$1{,}300, r = 0.07, t = 0.5$

$I = 45.5$ Simplify.

The interest she will pay after 6 months is \$45.50.

CHAPTER 7 Practice Test

Math Online glencoe.com
• Chapter Test

Find each number. Round to the nearest tenth if necessary.

1. Find 55% of 164.
2. What is 355% of 15?
3. Find 25% of 80.

4. **MULTIPLE CHOICE** Of 365 students, 210 bought a hot lunch. About what percent of the students did *not* buy a hot lunch?

   A 35%
   B 42%
   C 56%
   D 78%

Estimate.

5. 18% of 246
6. 145% of 81
7. 71% of 324
8. 56% of 65.4

9. **COMMUNICATION** Theresa makes a long distance phone call and talks for 50 minutes. Of these minutes, 25% were spent talking to her brother. Would the time spent talking with her brother be about 8, 12, or 15 minutes? Explain your reasoning.

Write an equation for each problem. Then solve. Round to the nearest tenth if necessary.

10. Find 14% of 65.
11. What number is 36% of 294?
12. 82% of what number is 73.8?
13. 75 is what percent of 50?

Find each percent of change. Round to the nearest whole percent if necessary. State whether the percent of change is an *increase* or a *decrease*.

14. $60 to $75
15. 145 meters to 216 meters
16. 48 minutes to 40 minutes

FOOD For Exercises 17 and 18, use the table below. It shows the results of a survey in which 175 students were asked what type of food they wanted for their class party.

Type of Food	Percent
Subs	32%
Tex-Mex	56%
Italian	12%

17. How many of the 175 students chose Italian food for their class party?
18. How many students chose Tex-Mex food for the party?

Find the total cost or sale price to the nearest cent.

19. $2,200 computer, $6\frac{1}{2}$% sales tax
20. $16 hat, 55% discount
21. $35.49 jeans, 33% discount

Find the simple interest earned to the nearest cent for each principal, interest rate, and time.

22. $750, 3%, 4 years
23. $1,050, 4.6%, 2 years
24. $2,600, 4%, 3 months

25. **MULTIPLE CHOICE** Mr. Jackson borrows $3,500 to renovate his home. His loan has an annual simple interest rate of 15%. If he pays off the loan after 6 months, about how much will he pay in all?

   F $3,763
   G $3,500
   H $3,720
   J $4,025

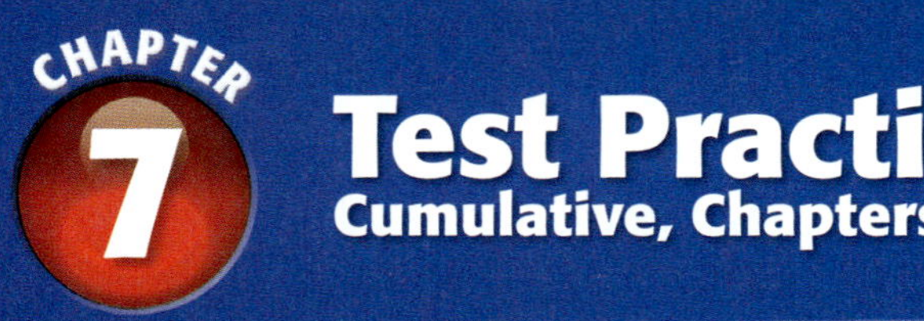

Chapter 7 Test Practice
Cumulative, Chapters 1–7

Math Online glencoe.com
• Test Practice

PART 1 Multiple Choice

Read each question. Then fill in the correct answer on the answer document provided by your teacher or on a sheet of paper.

1. Sarah wants to buy pillows for her living room. Which store offers the best buy on pillows?

Store	Sale Price
A	3 pillows for $40
B	4 pillows for $50
C	2 pillows for $19
D	1 pillow for $11

A Store A
B Store B
C Store C
D Store D

2. The graph below shows the attendance at a summer art festival from 2002 to 2007. If the trend in attendance continues, which is the best prediction of the attendance at the art festival in 2010?

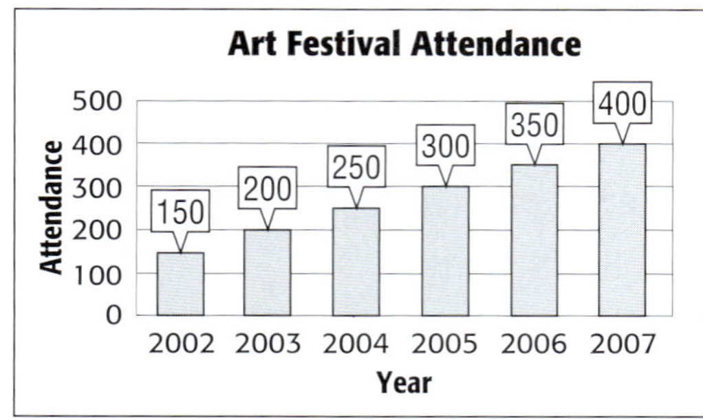

F Fewer than 200
G Between 500 and 600
H Between 700 and 800
J More than 800

3. At their annual car wash, the science club washes 30 cars in 45 minutes. At this rate, how many cars will they wash in 1 hour?

A 40
B 45
C 50
D 60

4. The cost of Ken's haircut was $23.95. If he wants to give his hair stylist a 15% tip, about how much of a tip should he leave?

F $2.40
G $3.60
H $4.60
J $4.80

5. At a pet store, 38% of the animals are dogs. If there are a total of 88 animals at the pet store, which equation can be used to find x, the number of dogs at the pet store?

A $\frac{x}{88} = \frac{100}{38}$
B $\frac{38}{88} = \frac{100}{x}$
C $\frac{x}{88} = \frac{38}{100}$
D $\frac{100}{88} = \frac{x}{38}$

6. An architect made a model of an office building using a scale of 1 inch equals 3 meters. If the height of the model is 12.5 inches, which of the following represents the actual height of the building?

F 40.0 m
G 37.5 m
H 36.0 m
J 28.4 m

7. Mrs. Stewart painted the door to her deck. The door is a rectangle with length x feet and width y feet. In the middle of the door, there is a rectangular panel of glass that measures 5 feet by 2 feet. Which expression gives the painted area of the door in square feet?

A $x + y - 10$
B $xy + 10$
C $xy - 10$
D $x + y + 10$

Preparing for Standardized Tests

For test-taking strategies and practice, see pages 716–733.

8. At a grocery store, half-gallons of milk are on sale 5 for \$4. Find the cost of 7 half-gallons of milk to the nearest cent.

   F \$2.86 **H** \$5.40
   G \$4.75 **J** \$5.60

9. If point B is translated 3 units to the left and 2 units up, what will be point B's new coordinates?

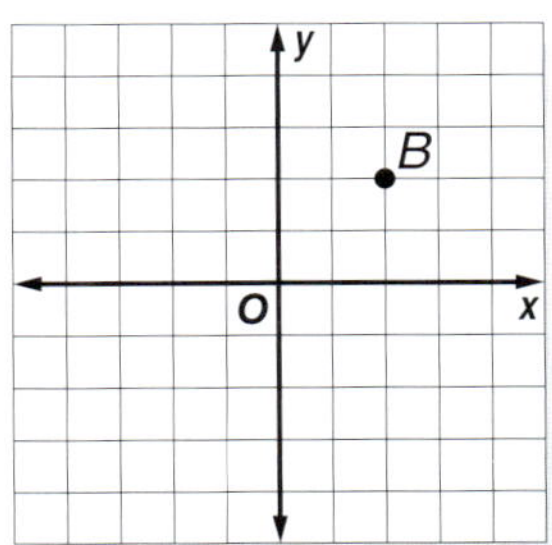

   A $(-3, 2)$ **C** $(4, -1)$
   B $(5, 0)$ **D** $(-1, 4)$

10. In Nadia's DVD collection, she has 8 action DVDs, 12 comedy DVDs, 7 romance DVDs, and 3 science fiction DVDs. What percent of Nadia's DVD collection are comedies?

   F 25% **H** 35%
   G 30% **J** 40%

11. Cassandra bought 2 dozen juice boxes priced at 6 juice boxes for \$2.29 and 24 snack packages priced at 8 snack packages for \$6.32. What is the total amount, not including tax, she spent on juice boxes and snack packages?

   A \$34.44 **C** \$28.12
   B \$32.15 **D** \$25.83

PART 2 Short Response/Grid In

Record your answers on the answer sheet provided by your teacher or on a sheet of paper.

12. The average cost of a 2-bedroom apartment in Grayson was \$625 last year. This year, the average cost is \$650. What is the percent of increase from last year to this year?

13. A necklace regularly sells for \$18.00. The store advertises a 15% discount. What is the sale price of the necklace in dollars?

PART 3 Extended Response

Record your answers on the answer sheet provided by your teacher or on a sheet of paper. Show your work.

TEST-TAKING TIP

Question 14 Remember to show all of your work. You may be able to get partial credit for your answers, even if they are not entirely correct.

14. Cable Company A increases their rates from \$98 a month to \$101.92 a month.

    a. What is the percent of increase?

    b. Cable Company B offers their cable for \$110 dollars a month, but gives a 10% discount for new customers. Describe two ways to find the cost for new customers.

    c. If you currently use Cable Company A, would it make sense to change to Cable Company B?

NEED EXTRA HELP?														
If You Missed Question...	1	2	3	4	5	6	7	8	9	10	11	12	13	14
Go to Lesson...	6-2	2-6	6-2	7-1	7-2	6-8	3-6	6-6	2-3	7-5	6-1	7-6	7-7	7-6

Unit 4

Statistics, Data Analysis, and Probability

Focus

Use statistical measures and probability to describe data.

CHAPTER 8
Statistics: Analyzing Data

BIG Idea Use measures of central tendency and range to describe a set of data.

BIG Idea Create and read graphs that depict data.

CHAPTER 9
Probability

BIG Idea Students use probability and proportions to make predictions.

Problem Solving in Science

Real-World Unit Project

Math Genes What's math have to do with genetics? Well, you're about to find out. You'll research basic genetics and learn how to use a Punnett square. Then you'll create sample genes for pet traits. You'll make predictions based on the pets' traits to determine the traits of their offspring. So, put on your lab coat and grab your math tool kit to begin this adventure.

Math Online Log on to glencoe.com to begin.

Statistics: Analyzing Data

- Use measures of central tendency and range to describe data.
- Create and read graphs that depict data.

Key Vocabulary

histogram (p. 416)

measures of central tendency (p. 402)

range (p. 397)

scatter plot (p. 427)

Real-World Link

Amusement Parks Hershey Park in Pennsylvania has over 60 rides and attractions. You can use a bar graph to display and then compare the speeds of these rides.

FOLDABLES® Study Organizer

Statistics: Analyzing Data Make this Foldable to help you organize your notes. Begin with nine sheets of notebook paper.

1. **Fold** 9 sheets of paper in half along the width.

2. **Cut** a 1″ tab along the left edge through one thickness.

3. **Glue** the 1″ tab down. Write the lesson number and title on the front tab.

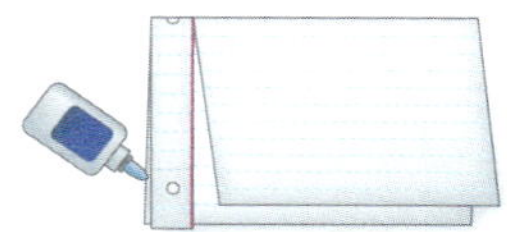

4. **Repeat** Steps 2 and 3 for the remaining sheets. Staple them together on the glued tabs to form a booklet.

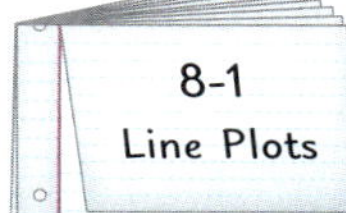

GET READY for Chapter 8

Diagnose Readiness You have two options for checking Prerequisite Skills.

Option 2

Math Online Take the Online Readiness Quiz at glencoe.com.

Option 1

Take the Quick Quiz below. Refer to the Quick Review for help.

QUICK Quiz

Order from least to greatest. (Lesson 4-9)

1. 96.2, 96.02, 95.89
2. 5.61, 5.062, 5.16
3. 22.02, 22, 22.012
4. **JEANS** A store sells boot-cut jeans for $49.97, classic for $49.79, and flared for $47.99. Write these prices in order from least to greatest. (Lesson 4-9)

Order from greatest to least. (Lesson 4-9)

5. 74.65, 74.67, 74.7
6. 1.26, 1.026, 10.26
7. 3.304, 3.04, 3.340

Evaluate each expression. (Lesson 1-4)

8. $\frac{23 + 44 + 37 + 45}{4}$
9. $\frac{1.7 + 2.6 + 2.4 + 3.1 + 1.8}{5}$
10. **PIZZA** Four friends ordered a large pizza for $14.95, a salad for $3.75, and two bottles of soda for $2.25 each. If they split the cost evenly, how much does each person owe? (Lesson 1-4)

QUICK Review

Example 1

Order 47.7, 47.07, and 40.07 from least to greatest.

47.7
47.07
40.07

Line up the decimal points and compare place value.

The numbers in order from least to greatest are 40.07, 47.07, and 47.7.

Example 2

Order 2.08, 20.8, 0.28 from greatest to least.

2.08
20.8
0.28

Line up the decimal points and compare place value.

The numbers in order from greatest to least are 20.8, 2.08, and 0.28.

Example 3

Evaluate $\frac{3.4 + 4.5 + 3.8}{3}$.

$\frac{3.4 + 4.5 + 3.8}{3} = \frac{11.7}{3}$ Add 3.4, 4.5, and 3.8.

$= 3.9$ Divide 11.7 by 3.

8-1 Line Plots

MAIN IDEA

Display and analyze data using a line plot.

New Vocabulary

- statistics
- data
- line plot
- outlier
- cluster
- range
- analyze

Math Online

glencoe.com

- Concepts In Motion
- Extra Examples
- Personal Tutor
- Self-Check Quiz
- Reading in the Content Area

GET READY for the Lesson

BUILDINGS The table shows the number of stories in 20 of the tallest buildings in Boston, Massachusetts.

Boston's Tallest Buildings (Number of Stories)				
60	38	40	35	38
46	26	41	36	52
33	33	32	37	37
46	40	36	40	32

Source: Emporis Buildings

1. Do any of the values seem much greater or much less than the other data values?
2. Do some of the buildings have the same height? Is this easy to see? Explain.

Statistics deals with collecting, organizing, and interpreting data. **Data** are pieces of information, which are often numerical. One way to show how data are spread out is to use a line plot. A **line plot** is a diagram that shows the data on a number line.

EXAMPLE Display Data Using a Line Plot

1 **BUILDINGS** **Make a line plot of the data shown above.**

Step 1 Draw a number line. The shortest building in the table has 26 stories, and the tallest has 60. You can use a scale of 25 to 65 and an interval of 5. Other scales and intervals could also be used.

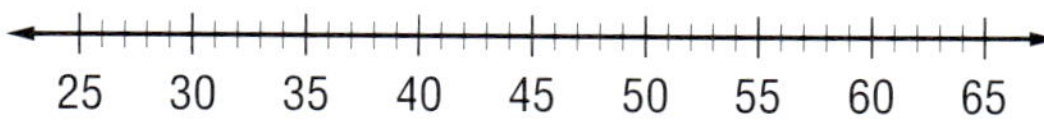

Step 2 Put an × above the number that represents the number of stories in each building. Include a title.

Boston's Tallest Buildings
Number of Stories

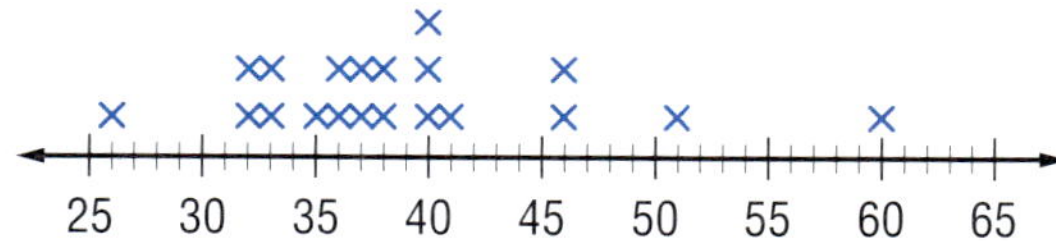

CHECK Your Progress

a. **BUILDINGS** The number of stories in the 15 tallest buildings in the world are listed at the right. Display the data in a line plot.

World's Tallest Buildings (Number of Stories)				
101	88	88	110	88
88	80	69	102	78
72	54	73	85	80

Source: *The World Almanac*

You can make some observations about the *distribution* of data, or how data are grouped together or spread out. Consider the line plot below.

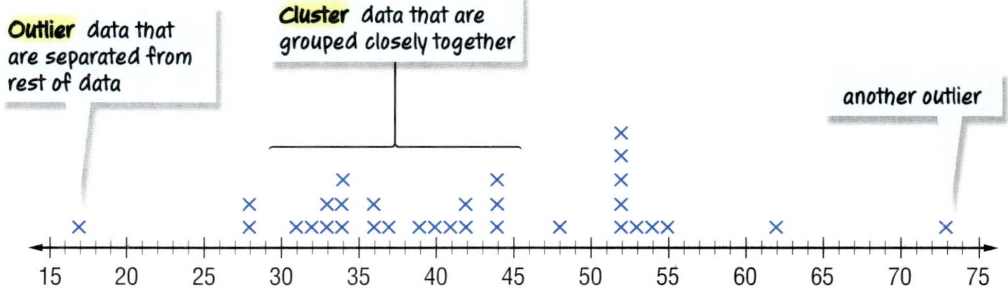

In a line plot, you can easily find the **range**, or spread, of the data, which is the difference between the greatest and least numbers. When you **analyze** data, you use these observations to describe and compare data.

Vocabulary Link
Range
Everyday Meaning in music, all the notes between the high and low notes, as in a singer with a wide range.
Math Use the difference between the greatest number and least number in a set of data.

EXAMPLES Use a Plot to Analyze Data

2 **ANIMALS The line plot below shows the life spans for different animals. Identify any clusters, gaps, and outliers and find the range.**

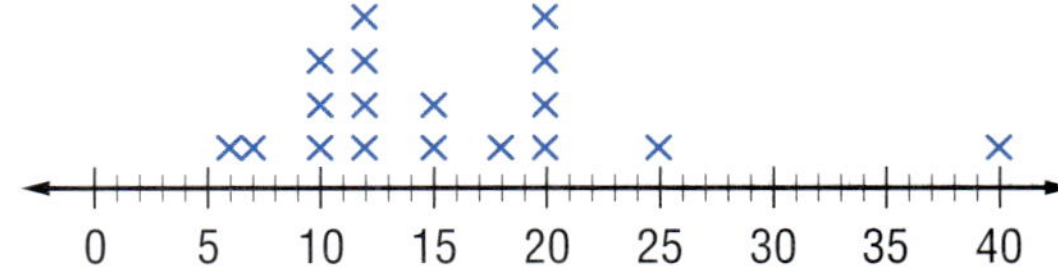

Many of the data cluster between 10 and 12 years.

There is a gap between 25 and 40 years.

Since 40 is apart from the rest of the data, it is an outlier.

The greatest age is 40 years, and the least age is 6 years. So, the range of the ages is 40 − 6 or 34.

Study Tip
Clusters You can describe a cluster by stating a range of values or by giving a single value around which the data appear to be grouped.

3 **Describe how the range would change if the data value 54 was added to the data set in Example 2.**

The greatest age would change to 54, and the least age would remain the same at 6. So, the range of the ages would change from 34 to 54 − 6 or 48.

CHECK Your Progress

Refer to Example 1.

b. Identify any clusters, gaps, and outliers and find the range.

c. Describe how the range would change if the data value 50 was added to the data set.

CHECK Your Understanding

Example 1 (p. 396) Display each set of data in a line plot.

1.

Costs of Video Games ($)			
20	29	40	50
45	20	50	50
20	25	50	40

2.

Sizes of Tennis Shoes					
8	10	9	8	7	6
9	10	9	6	5	7
7	8	11	6	8	7

MUSIC For Exercises 3 and 4, analyze the line plot below.

Number of Music CDs Owned

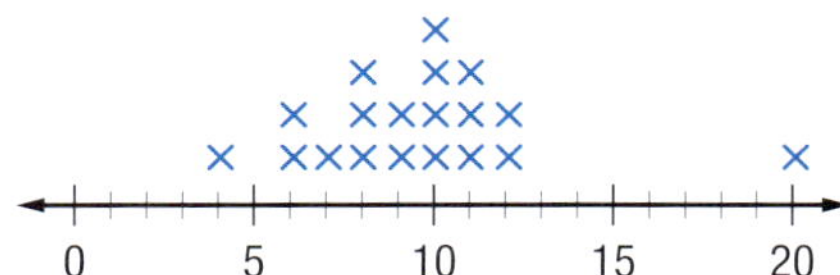

Example 2 (p. 397)

3. Identify any clusters, gaps, and outliers and find the range of the data.

Example 3 (p. 397)

4. Describe how the range would change if the data value 3 was added to the data set.

SURVEYS For Exercises 5–8, analyze the line plot at the right and use the information below.

Jamie asked her classmates how many glasses of water they drink on a typical day. The results are shown.

Glasses of Water Consumed

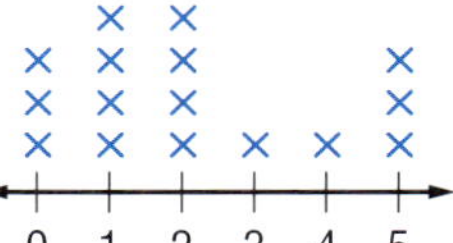

Example 2 (p. 397)

5. What was the most frequent response?
6. What was the least frequent response?
7. What is the range?

Example 3 (p. 397)

8. Describe how the range would change if an additional data value of 4 was added to the data set.

Practice and Problem Solving

HOMEWORK HELP

For Exercises	See Examples
9–12	1
13–20	2–3

Display each set of data in a line plot.

9.

Snowfall (in.)				
2	10	1	5	2
4	1	2	3	4
6	3	12	2	1

10.

Drink Size (oz)				
12	16	8	24	32
20	12	12	16	24
8	20	48	16	12

11.

Basketball Scores (points)				
101	105	99	130	120
100	108	126	135	98
120	122	115	129	97

12.

Ages of Students (y)					
12	13	13	13	12	14
13	12	13	13	12	12
13	14	12	13	12	12

Real-World Link Death Valley National Park is the site of the highest temperature ever recorded in the United States, 134°F.

Source: Death Valley Chamber of Commerce

WEATHER **For Exercises 13–16, analyze the line plot that shows the record high temperatures recorded by weather stations in each of the fifty states.**

Record High Temperatures (°F)

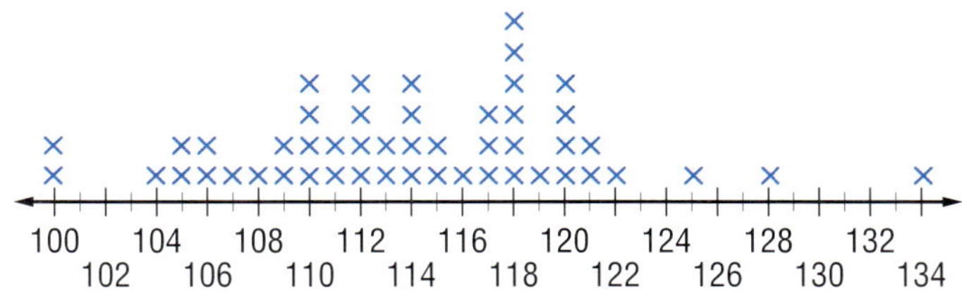

Source: *The World Almanac*

13. What is the range of the data?
14. What temperature occurred most often?
15. Identify any clusters, gaps, or outliers.
16. Describe how the range of the data would change if 134°F were not part of the data set.

MOVIES **For Exercises 17–20, analyze the line plot below that shows the number of digital video discs various students have in their DVD collection.**

Digital Video Disc (DVD) Collection

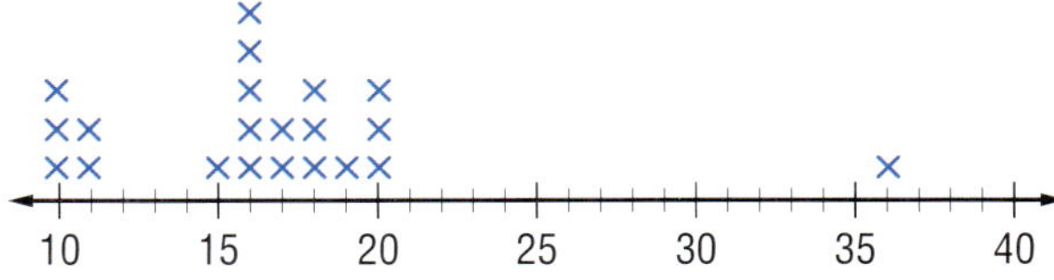

17. Find the range of the data.
18. What number of DVDs occurred most often?
19. How many students have more than 15 DVDs in their collection?
20. Describe how the range would change if the data value 38 was added to the data set.

Determine whether each statement is *sometimes*, *always*, or *never* true. Explain your reasoning.

21. If a new piece of data is added to a data set, the range will change.
22. If there is a cluster, it will appear in the center of the line plot.

BOOKS **For Exercises 23–25, analyze the line plot at the right.**

Number of Books Read

0 1 2 3 4 5 6 7 8

23. How many students read 4 or more books?
24. How many more students read 1–2 books than 5–6 books?
25. About what percent of the students read less than 5 books?

GOVERNMENT For Exercises 26–28, refer to the table showing the number of representatives for each of the Northeast states.

The House of Representatives Northeast States

State	Number	State	Number	State	Number
CT	5	MA	10	PA	19
DE	1	NH	2	RI	2
ME	2	NJ	13	VT	1
MD	8	NY	29		

26. Display the data in a line plot.
27. Find the range and determine any clusters, gaps, or outliers.
28. Use the line plot to summarize the data.
29. The number of House of Representatives for the ten Southwestern states is quite different. The Southwestern states have 4, 8, 53, 7, 7, 3, 3, 5, 32, and 3 representatives. Display this data in a line plot. Compare this line plot to the line plot you made in Exercise 26. Include a discussion about clusters, outliers, range, and gaps in data.

30. **COLLECT THE DATA** Conduct a survey of your classmates to determine how many hours of television they watch on a typical school night. Then display and analyze the data in a line plot. Use your analysis of the data to write a convincing argument about television viewing on a school night.

H.O.T. Problems

31. **REASONING** Explain how the inclusion or exclusion of outliers affects the computation of the range of a data set.

32. **FIND THE ERROR** Elena and Rashaun are analyzing the data shown in the line plot at the right. Who is correct? Explain.

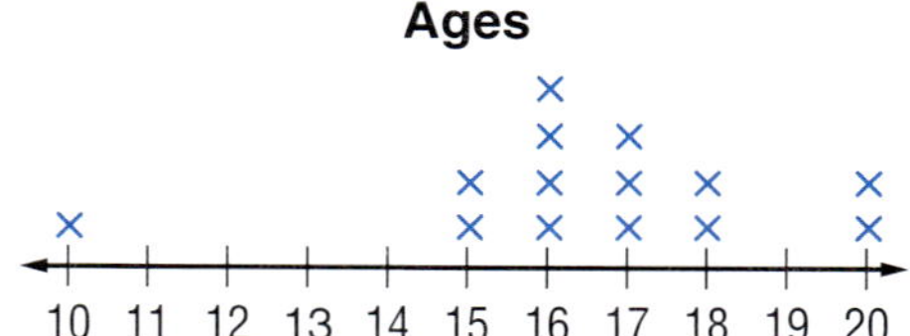

33. **CHALLENGE** Compare and contrast line plots and frequency tables. Include a discussion about what they show and when it is better to use each one.

34. **WRITING IN MATH** The number of fundraising items sold by two grades is shown. Describe which grade is more consistent and explain how you know.

Fundraising Items

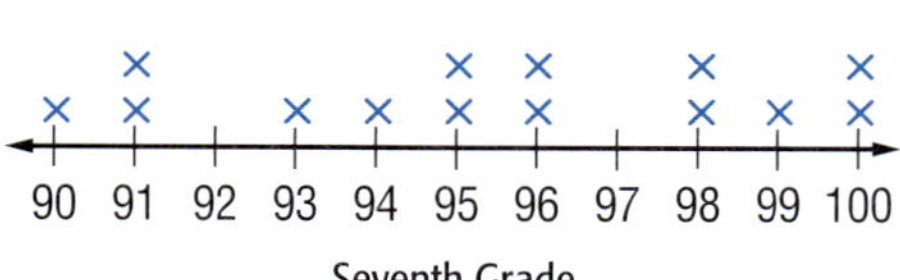

Fundraising Items

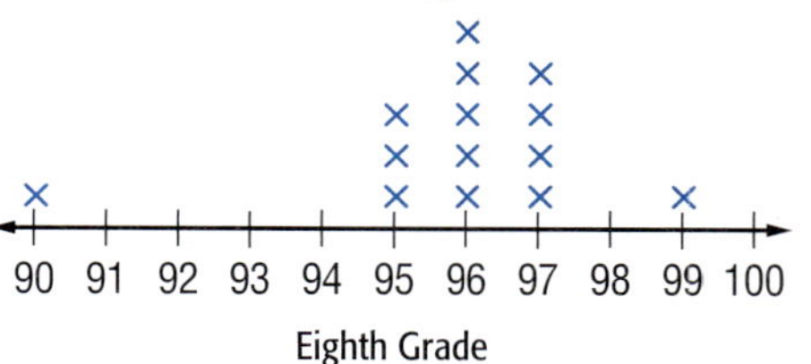

TEST PRACTICE

35. The graph shows the weight of the emperor penguins at a zoo.

Emperor Penguins Weight (kg)

23 25 27 29 31 33 35 37 39 41 43 45 47 49

Which statement is *not* valid?

A More than half of these penguins weigh at least 41 kilograms.

B There are 16 emperor penguins at the zoo.

C Of these penguins, 30% weigh between 30 and 38 kilograms.

D The range of the emperor penguins' weight is 49 − 23 or 26 kilograms.

36. The table shows the math scores for 24 students in Mr. Baker's class.

Math Test Scores							
90	86	96	89	85	91	82	89
100	65	73	85	85	93	77	93
71	70	75	80	82	99	84	75

How would the range of the test scores change if a score of 83 was added?

F The range would remain unchanged at 45.

G The range would remain unchanged at 35.

H The range would change from 45 to 83.

J The range would change from 35 to 17.

Spiral Review

Find the interest earned to the nearest cent for each principal, interest rate, and time. (Lesson 7-8)

37. \$300, 10%, 2 years

38. \$900, 5.5%, 4.5 years

39. **BASEBALL CARDS** What is the total cost of a package of baseball cards if the regular price is \$4.19 and the sales tax is 6.5%? (Lesson 7-7)

40. Solve $m + 18 = 33$ mentally. (Lesson 1-7)

GET READY for the Next Lesson

PREREQUISITE SKILL **Add or divide. Round to the nearest tenth if necessary.**

41. $16 + 14 + 17$

42. $4.6 + 2.5 + 9$

43. $\frac{202}{16}$

44. $\frac{255}{7}$

8-2 Measures of Central Tendency and Range

MAIN IDEA

Describe a set of data using mean, median, mode, and range.

New Vocabulary

measures of central tendency
mean
median
mode

Math Online

glencoe.com

- Extra Examples
- Personal Tutor
- Self-Check Quiz

MINI Lab

The number of pennies in each cup represents Jack's scores for five math quizzes.

Move the pennies among the cups so that each cup has the same number of pennies.

1. What was Jack's average score for the five quizzes?
2. If Jack scores 14 points on the next quiz, how many pennies would be in each cup?

A number used to describe the *center* of a set of data is a **measure of central tendency**. The most common of these measures is the mean.

Mean — Key Concept

Words The **mean** of a set of data is the sum of the data divided by the number of items in the data set. The mean is also referred to as *average*.

Examples data set: 1 cm, 1 cm, 5 cm, 2 cm, 2 cm, 4 cm, 2 cm, 5 cm

mean: $\frac{1 + 1 + 5 + 2 + 2 + 4 + 2 + 5}{8}$ or 2.75 cm

EXAMPLE Find the Mean

QUIZ SCORES The table shows the quiz scores for 16 students. Find the mean.

Quiz Scores			
47	40	43	45
49	41	49	44
43	41	44	49
44	50	41	44

$$\text{mean} = \frac{47 + 40 + ... + 44}{16}$$ ← sum of data ← number of data items

$$= \frac{714}{16} \text{ or } 44.625$$

CHECK Your Progress

a. **MONEY** Adam earned $14, $10, $12, $15, and $13 by doing chores around the house. What is the mean amount Adam earned doing these chores?

Two other common measures of central tendency are median and mode.

Median

Everyday Use the middle paved or planted section of a highway, as in median strip.

Math Use the middle number of the ordered data.

Median

Key Concept

Words In a data set that has been ordered from least to greatest, the **median** is the middle number if there is an odd number of data items. If there is an even number of data items, the median is the mean of the two numbers closest to the middle.

Example data set: 7 yd, 11 yd, 15 yd, 17 yd, 20 yd, 20 yd

median: $\frac{15 + 17}{2}$ or 16 yd — The median divides the data in half.

Mode

Words The **mode** of a set of data is the number that occurs most often. If there are two or more numbers that occur most often, all of them are modes.

Example data set: 50 mi, 45 mi, 45 mi, 52 mi, 49 mi, 56 mi, 56 mi

modes: 45 mi and 56 mi

EXAMPLE Find the Mean, Median, and Mode

2 **MOVIE RENTALS** The number of DVDs rented during one week at Star Struck Movie Rental is shown in the table. What are the mean, median, and mode of the data?

Star Struck Movie Rental Daily DVD Rentals

S	M	T	W	TH	F	S
55	34	35	34	57	78	106

mean: $\frac{55 + 34 + 35 + 34 + 57 + 78 + 106}{7} = \frac{399}{7}$ or 57

median: 34, 34, 35, 55, 57, 78, 106 — First, write the data in order. (55 is the median)

mode: 34 — It is the only value that occurs more than once.

The mean is 57 DVDs, the median is 55 DVDs, and the mode is 34 DVDs.

CHECK Your Progress

b. **BICYCLES** The sizes of the bicycles owned by the students in Ms. Garcia's class are listed in the table. What are the mean, median, and mode of the data?

Students' Bicycle Sizes (in.)			
20	24	20	26
24	24	24	26
24	29	26	24

c. **FOOTBALL** The points scored in each game by Darby Middle School's football team for 9 games are 21, 35, 14, 17, 28, 14, 7, 21, and 14. Find the mean, median, and mode.

TEST EXAMPLE

3 The maximum length in feet of several whales is listed below.

46, 53, 33, 53, 79

If the maximum length of the Blue Whale, 98 feet, is added to this list, which of the following statements would be true?

A The mode would decrease.
B The median would decrease.
C The mean would increase.
D The mean would decrease.

Test-Taking Tip

Comparing Measures Another way to solve Example 3 is to find the measures *before* 98 is added to the data set. Then find the measures *after* 98 is added to the data set. Then compare.

Read the Item

You are asked to identify which statement would be true if the data value 98 was added to the data set.

Solve the Item

Use number sense to eliminate possibilities.
The mode, 53, will remain unchanged since the new data value occurs only once. So, eliminate answer choice A.

Since the new data value is greater than each value in the data set, the median will not decrease. So, eliminate answer choice B.

The remaining two answer choices refer to the mean. Since 98 is greater than each value in the data set, the mean will increase, not decrease. So, the answer is C.

CHECK Your Progress

d. If the maximum length of the Orca Whale, 30 feet, is added to the list in Example 3, which of the following statements would be true?

F The mode would decrease.
G The median would increase.
H The mean would increase.
J The mean would decrease.

In addition to the mean, median, and mode, you can also use the range to describe a set of data. Below are some guidelines for using these measures.

Mean, Median, Mode, and Range — Concept Summary

Measure	Most Useful When...
Mean	• data set has no outliers
Median	• data set has outliers • there are no big gaps in the middle of the data
Mode	• data set has many identical numbers
Range	• describing the spread of the data

Study Tip

Median When there is an odd number of data, the median is the middle number of the ordered set. When there is an even number of data, the median is the mean of the two middle numbers.

EXAMPLE Choose Mean, Median, Mode, or Range

4 PLANTS The line plot shows the height of desert cacti. Would the mean, median, mode, or range best represent the heights?

Heights of Desert Cacti (ft)

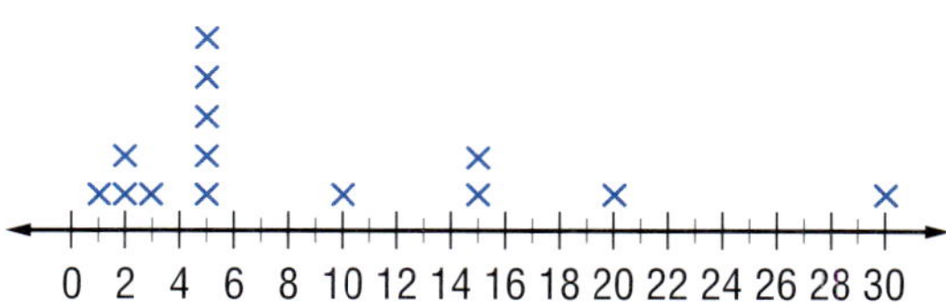

mean: $\frac{1 + 2 + 2 + ... + 30}{14}$ or 8.8

median: $\frac{\text{7th term} + \text{8th term}}{2} = \frac{5 + 5}{2}$ or 5

mode: 5

range: $30 - 1$ or 29

The mean of 8.8 misrepresents the score. The median or mode represents the height of the cacti well.

 **CHECK Your Progress**

e. **GAMES** The table shows the cost of various board games. Would the mean, median, mode, or range best represent the costs? Explain.

Board Game Costs ($)			
12	15	40	22
14	40	15	17
20	18	40	19
16	21	19	16

CHECK Your Understanding

Examples 1, 2 (pp. 402–403)

Find the mean, median, and mode for each set of data. Round to the nearest tenth if necessary.

1. Miles traveled on the weekend: 29, 14, 80, 59, 78, 30, 59, 69, 55, 50

2.

Team	Number of Wins
Eagles	10
Hawks	8
Zipps	9
Falcons	11

3. **Minutes Spent Walking**

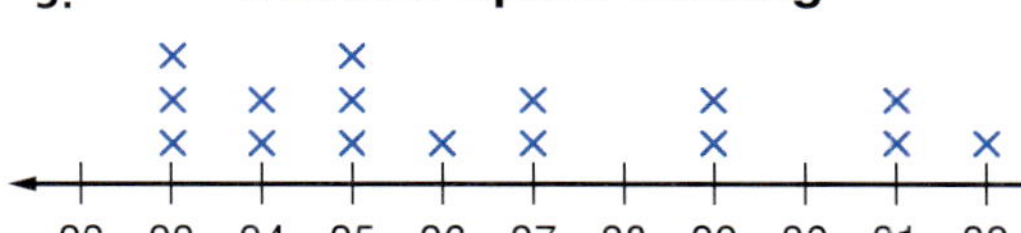

Example 3 (p. 404)

4. **MULTIPLE CHOICE** During the week, the daily low temperatures were 52°F, 45°F, 51°F, 45°F, and 48°F. If Saturday's low temperature of 51°F is added, which statement about the data set would be true?

A The mean would decrease.
B The median would decrease.
C The mode would increase.
D The mode would decrease.

Example 4 (p. 405)

5. **SHOES** The line plot shows the price of athletic shoes. Which measure best describes the data: mean, median, mode, or range? Explain.

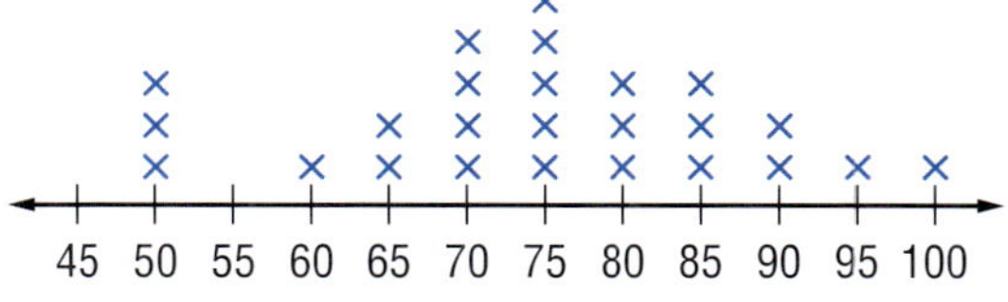

Practice and Problem Solving

HOMEWORK HELP	
For Exercises	See Examples
6–11	1, 2
30–32	3
12–13	4

Find the mean, median, and mode for each set of data. Round to the nearest tenth if necessary.

6. Number of dogs groomed each week: 65, 56, 57, 75, 76, 66, 64
7. Daily number of boats in a harbor: 93, 84, 80, 91, 94, 90, 78, 93, 80
8. Scores earned on a math test: 95, 90, 92, 94, 91, 90, 98, 88, 89, 100
9. Prices of books: \$10, \$18, \$11, \$6, \$6, \$5, \$10, \$11, \$46, \$7, \$6, \$8

10.

Cost	Number of Coats
\$75	8
\$80	3
\$85	6

11. **Springdale Middle School Basketball Scores**

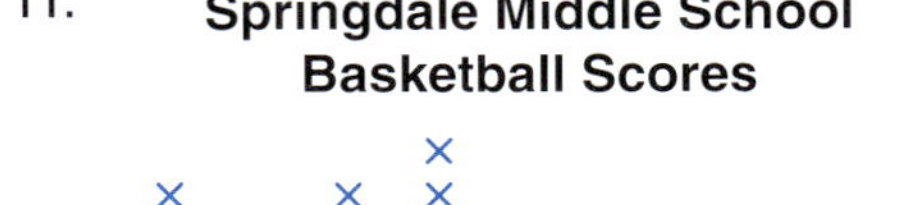

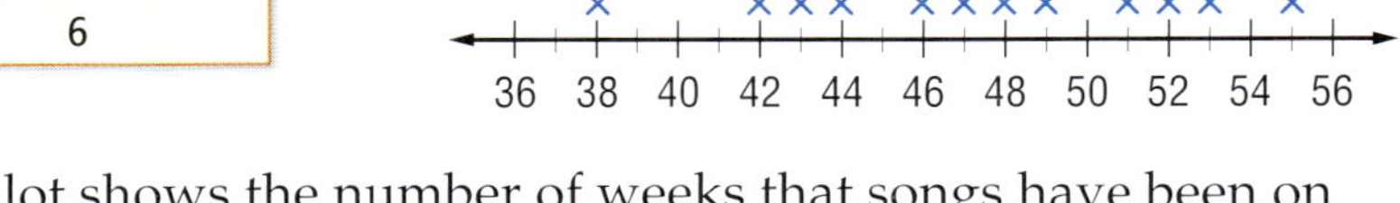

12. **MUSIC** The line plot shows the number of weeks that songs have been on the Top 20 Country Songs list. Would the mean, median, mode, or range best represent the data? Explain.

Country Songs
Number of Weeks in Top 20

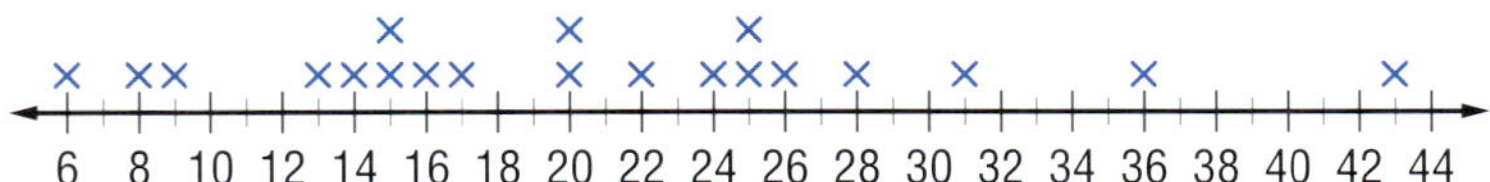

Real-World Link The International Space Station measures 356 feet by 290 feet, and contains almost an acre of solar panels.
Source: *The World Almanac*

13. **SPACE** Twenty-seven countries have sent people into space. The table shows the number of individuals from each country. Which measure best describes the data: mean, median, mode, or range? Explain.

People in Space								
267	1	9	8	1	1	1	1	1
97	1	1	1	3	1	1	2	1
11	2	1	1	5	1	1	1	1

Source: *The World Almanac*

Find the mean, median, and mode for each set of data. Round to the nearest tenth if necessary.

14. Weight in ounces of various insects: 6.1, 5.2, 7.2, 7.2, 3.6, 9.0, 6.5, 7.4, 5.4
15. Prices of magazines: \$3.50, \$3.75, \$3.50, \$4.00, \$3.00, \$3.50, \$3.25
16. Daily low temperatures: −2°F, −8°F, −2°F, 0°F, −1°F, 1°F, −2°F, −1°F

REASONING Determine whether each statement is *always*, *sometimes*, or *never* true about the data set {8, 12, 15, 23}. Explain your reasoning.

17. If a value greater than 23 is added, the mean will increase.
18. If a value less than or equal to 8 is added, the mean will decrease.
19. If a value between 8 and 23 is added, the mean will remain unchanged.

DINOSAURS For Exercises 20–22, use the lengths of the dinosaurs shown below.

20. What is the mean length of the dinosaurs?

21. One of the largest dinosaurs ever is the Brachiosaurus. Its length was 960 inches. If this data value is added to the lengths of the dinosaurs above, how will it affect the mean? Explain your reasoning.

22. Which measure best describes the data if the length of the Brachiosaurus is included: mean, median, mode, or range? If the length of the Brachiosaurus is *not* included? Explain any similarities or differences.

23. **SPORTS** The table shows the points scored by a lacrosse team so far this season. The team will play 14 games this season. How many points need to be scored during the last game so that the average number of points scored this season is 12? Explain.

Hawks Lacrosse Team Points Scored						
11	15	12	10	10	10	13
14	13	13	10	15	12	■

24. **FIND THE DATA** Refer to the Data File on pages 16–19. Choose some data and then describe it using the mean, median, mode, and range.

H.O.T. Problems

25. **OPEN ENDED** Give an example of a set of data in which the mean is not the best representation of the data set. Explain why not.

26. **Which One Doesn't Belong?** Identify the term that does not have the same characteristic as the other three. Explain your reasoning.

27. **REASONING** Determine whether the median is *sometimes*, *always*, or *never* part of the data set. Explain your reasoning.

28. **CHALLENGE** Without calculating, would the mean, median, or mode be most affected by eliminating 1,000 from the data shown? Which would be the least affected? Explain your reasoning.

50, 100, 75, 60, 75, 1,000, 90, 100

29. **WRITING IN MATH** According to the U.S. Census Bureau, the typical number of family members per household is 2.59. State whether this measure is a mean or mode. Explain how you know.

TEST PRACTICE

30. The table below shows the number of soup labels collected in one week by each homeroom in grade 7.

Classroom	Number of Soup Labels
Mr. Martin	138
Ms. Davis	125
Mr. Cardona	89
Mrs. Turner	110
Mr. Wilhelm	130
Mrs. LaBash	?

Which number could be added to the set of data in order for the mode and median of the set to be equal?

A 89 **C** 125

B 110 **D** 130

31. An antique dealer purchased 5 antiques for a total of $850.00. He later bought another antique for $758.00. What is the mean cost of all the antiques?

F $151.60 **H** $268.00

G $170.00 **J** $321.60

32. Gina found the mean and median of the following list of numbers.

5, 7, 7

If the number 11 was added to this list, which of the following statements would be true?

A The mean would increase.

B The mean would decrease.

C The median would increase.

D The median would decrease.

Spiral Review

33. TEMPERATURE The table shows record high temperatures for Kentucky in July. Make a line plot of the data. (Lesson 8-1)

July Temperatures				
99	98	96	98	98
97	100	103	103	103
100	95	100	103	105

Find the simple interest earned to the nearest cent for each principal, interest rate, and time. (Lesson 7-8)

34. $1,250, 3.5%, 2 years

35. $569, 5.5%, 4 months

36. FOOD The United States produced almost 11 billion pounds of apples in a recent year. Use the information in the graph to find how many pounds of apples were used to make juice and cider. (Lesson 7-1)

Uses of Apples in the United States

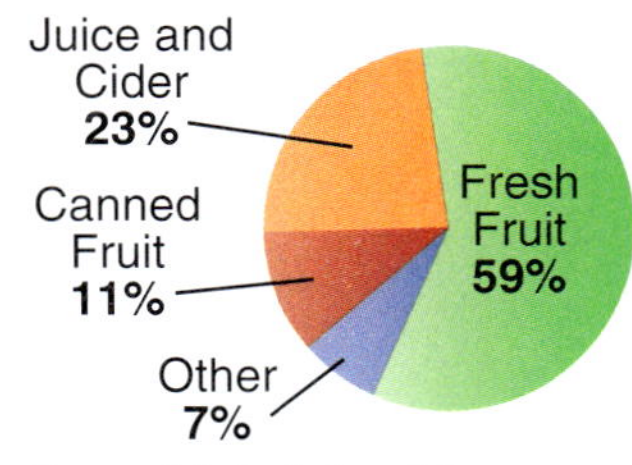

Source: U.S. Apple Association

37. Name the property shown by the statement $4 \times 6 = 6 \times 4$. (Lesson 1-8)

GET READY for the Next Lesson

PREREQUISITE SKILL **Name the place value of the underlined digit.** (p. 669)

38. $\underline{5}81$ **39.** $6{,}29\underline{5}$ **40.** $\underline{4}{,}369$ **41.** $2.\underline{8}4$

Extend 8-2

Graphing Calculator Lab
Mean and Median

MAIN IDEA

Use technology to calculate the mean and median of a set of data.

You can more efficiently calculate the mean and median of a large set of data using a graphing calculator.

ACTIVITY

COMPUTERS **Kendrick surveys thirty seventh graders and asks them how many times they had to wait longer than 5 minutes during the previous week to use a computer in the school library. The results are shown below.**

Number of Times a Student Had to Wait to Use the Library Computer									
5	2	9	1	1	2	1	2	5	2
3	4	2	1	4	0	4	2	2	5
4	2	2	3	2	1	3	9	5	2

Find the mean and median of the data.

STEP 1 Clear list L1 by pressing STAT ENTER ▲ CLEAR ENTER

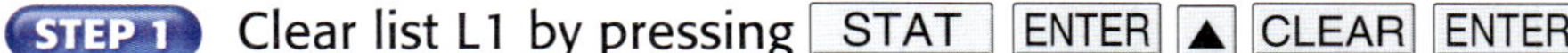

STEP 2 Enter the number of times students had to wait in L1. Press 5 ENTER 2 ENTER . . . 2 ENTER.

STEP 3 Display a list of statistics for the data by pressing STAT ▶ ENTER 1 ENTER.

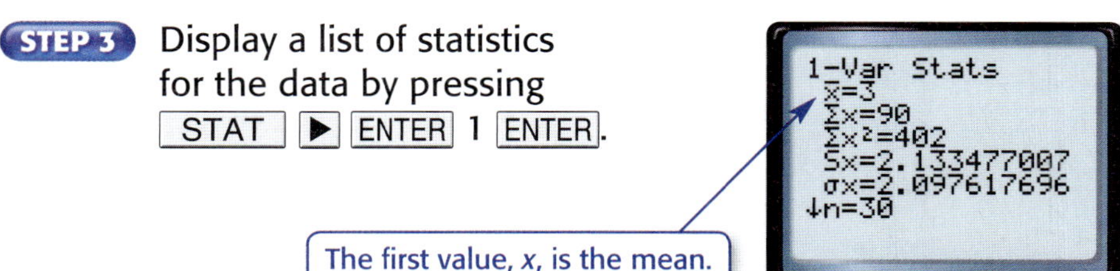

Use the down arrow key to locate **Med**. The mean number of times a student waited was 3 and the median number of times was 2.

Analyze the Results

1. **WRITING IN MATH** Kendrick claims that, on average, students had to wait more than 5 minutes about 3 times last week. Based on your own analysis of the data, write a convincing argument to dispute his claim. (*Hint*: Create and use a line plot of the data to support your argument.)

2. **COLLECT THE DATA** Collect some numerical data from your classmates. Then use a graphing calculator to calculate the mean and median of the data. After analyzing the data, write a convincing argument to support a claim you can make about your data.

8-3 Stem-and-Leaf Plots

MAIN IDEA

Display and analyze data in a stem-and-leaf plot.

New Vocabulary

stem-and-leaf plot
leaf
stem

Math Online

glencoe.com

- Extra Examples
- Personal Tutor
- Self-Check Quiz

GET READY for the Lesson

BIRDS The table shows the average chick weight in grams of sixteen different species of birds.

1. Which chick weight is the lightest?
2. How many of the weights are less than 10 grams?

Chick Weight (g)			
19	6	7	10
11	13	18	25
21	12	5	12
20	21	11	12

In a **stem-and-leaf plot**, the data are organized from least to greatest. The digits of the least place value usually form the **leaves**, and the next place-value digits form the **stems**.

EXAMPLE Display Data in a Stem-and-Leaf Plot

1 **BIRDS** **Display the data in the table above in a stem-and-leaf plot.**

Step 1 Choose the stems using digits in the tens place, 0, 1, and 2. The least value, 5, has 0 in the tens place. The greatest value, 25, has 2 in the tens place.

Step 2 List the stems from least to greatest in the *Stem* column. Write the leaves, the ones digits to the right of the corresponding stems.

Stem	Leaf
0	6 7 5
1	9 0 1 3 8 2 2 1 2
2	5 1 0 1

Step 3 Order the leaves and write a *key* that explains how to read the stems and leaves. Include a title.

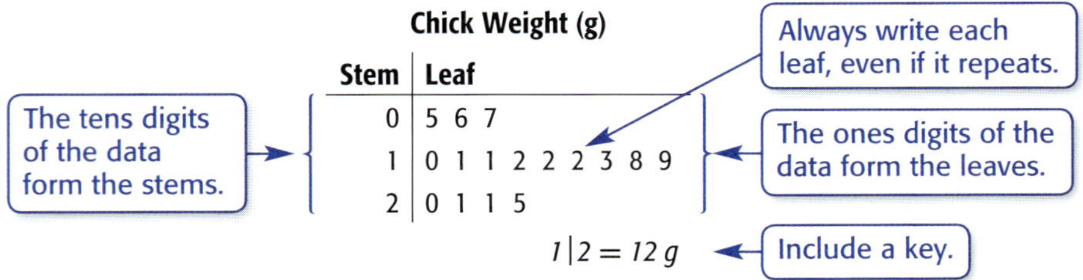

CHECK Your Progress

a. **HOMEWORK** The number of minutes the students in Mr. Blackwell's class spent doing their homework one night is shown. Display the data in a stem-and-leaf plot.

Homework Time (min)				
42	5	75	30	45
47	0	24	45	51
56	23	39	30	49
58	55	75	45	35

Stem-and-leaf plots are useful in analyzing data because you can see all the data values, including the greatest, least, mode, and median value.

EXAMPLE Describe Data

2 **CHESS** **The stem-and-leaf plot shows the number of chess matches won by members of the Avery Middle School Chess Team. Find the range, median, and mode of the data.**

Chess Matches Won

Stem	Leaf
0	8 8 9
1	9
2	0 0 2 4 4 8 9
3	1 1 2 4 5 5 6 6 7 7 8
4	0 0 0 3 8 9
5	2 4
6	1

3|2 = 32 wins

range: greatest wins − least wins
= 61 − 8 or 53

median: middle value, or 35 wins

mode: most frequent value, 40

CHECK Your Progress

b. **BIRDS** Find the range, median, and mode of the data in Example 1.

Real-World Career
How Does a Sports Scout Use Math?
Sports scouts review game records and statistics and evaluate athletes' skills.

Math Online For more information, go to glencoe.com.

EXAMPLE Effect of Outliers

3 **SPORTS** **The stem-and-leaf plot shows the number of points scored by a college basketball player. Which measure of central tendency is most affected by the outlier?**

Basketball Points

Stem	Leaf
0	2
1	2 2 3 5 8
2	0 0 1 1 3 4 6 6 6 8 9
3	0 0 1

1|2 = 12 points

The mode, 26, is not affected by the inclusion of the outlier, 2.

Calculate the mean and median each without the outlier, 2. Then calculate them including the outlier and compare.

	without the outlier	including the outlier
mean:	$\frac{12 + 12 + ... + 31}{19} \approx 22.37$	$\frac{2 + 12 + 12 + ... + 31}{20} = 21.35$
median:	23	22

The mean decreased by 22.37 − 21.35, or 1.02, while the median decreased by 23 − 22, or 1. Since 1.02 > 1, the mean is most affected.

CHECK Your Progress

c. **CHESS** Refer to Example 2. If an additional student had 84 wins, which measure of central tendency would be most affected?

CHECK Your Understanding

Example 1 (p. 410)

Display each set of data in a stem-and-leaf plot.

1.

Height of Trees (ft)				
15	25	8	12	20
10	16	15	8	18

2.

Cost of Shoes ($)				
42	47	19	16	21
23	25	25	29	31
33	34	35	39	48

Examples 2, 3 (p. 411)

CAMP The stem-and-leaf plot at the right shows the ages of students in a pottery class.

Ages of Students

Stem	Leaf
0	9 9 9
1	0 1 1 1 1 2 2 3 3 4

1|0 = 10 years

3. What is the range of the ages of the students?
4. Find the median and mode of the data.
5. If an additional student was 6 years old, which measure of central tendency would be most affected?

Practice and Problem Solving

HOMEWORK HELP

For Exercises	See Examples
6–9	1
10, 11, 13, 14, 16–18	2
12, 15, 19	3

Display each set of data in a stem-and-leaf plot.

6.

Quiz Scores (%)			
70	96	72	91
80	80	79	93
76	95	73	93
90	93	77	91

7.

Low Temperatures (°F)				
15	13	28	32	38
30	31	13	36	35
38	32	38	24	20

8.

Floats at Annual Parade			
151	158	139	103
111	134	133	154
157	142	149	159

9.

School Play Attendance			
225	227	230	229
246	243	269	269
267	278	278	278

CYCLING The number of Tour de France titles won by eleven countries is shown.

Tour de France Titles Won by Eleven Countries

Stem	Leaf
0	1 1 1 2 2 4 8 9
1	0 8
2	
3	6

0|4 = 4 titles

10. Find the range of titles won.
11. Find the median and mode of the data.
12. Which measure of central tendency is most affected by the outlier?

ELECTRONICS For Exercises 13–15, use the stem-and-leaf plot that shows the costs of various DVD players at an electronics store.

Costs of DVD Players

Stem	Leaf
8	2 5 5
9	9 9
10	0 0 2 5 6 8
11	0 0 5 5 5 9 9
12	5 7 7

11|5 = $115

13. What is the range of the prices?
14. Find the median and mode of the data.
15. If an additional DVD player cost $153, which measure of central tendency would be most affected?

HISTORY For Exercises 16–19, refer to the stem-and-leaf plot below.

Real-World Link The saltwater crocodile is the largest living reptile. Some measuring 27–30 feet in length have been recorded in the wild.
Source: PBS

Ages of Signers of Declaration of Independence

Stem	Leaf
2	6 6 9
3	0 1 3 3 3 4 4 5 5 5 5 7 7 8 8 9 9
4	0 1 1 1 2 2 2 4 5 5 5 5 6 6 6 6 7 8 9
5	0 0 0 0 2 2 3 3 5 7
6	0 0 2 3 5 6
7	0

$3|1 = 31$ *years*

16. How many people signed the Declaration of Independence?
17. What was the age of the youngest signer?
18. What is the range of the ages of the signers?
19. Based on the data, can you conclude that the majority of the signers were 30–49 years old? Explain your reasoning.
20. **GYMNASTICS** The scores for 10 girls in a gymnastics event are 9.3, 10.0, 9.9, 8.9, 8.7, 9.0, 8.7, 8.5, 8.8, 9.3. Analyze a stem-and-leaf plot of the data to draw two conclusions about the scores.
21. **REPTILES** The average lengths of certain species of crocodiles are given in the table. Analyze a stem-and-leaf plot of this data to write a convincing argument about a reasonable length for a crocodile.

Crocodile Average Lengths (ft)			
8.1	16.3	16.3	9.8
16.3	16.3	11.4	6.3
13.6	9.8	19.5	16.0

Source: Crocodilian Species List

22. **FIND THE DATA** Refer to the Data File on pages 16–19. Choose some data that can be presented in a stem-and-leaf plot. Then analyze the stem-and-leaf plot to draw two conclusions about the data.

H.O.T. Problems

23. **FIND THE ERROR** Rosita and Diana are analyzing the data in the stem-and-leaf plot at the right. Diana says half of the pieces of ribbon are between 20 and 30 inches in length. Rosita says there are no pieces of ribbon more than 50 inches in length. Who is correct? Explain.

Cut Ribbon Length

Stem	Leaf
2	6 6 9
3	
4	6
5	3 6

$2|6 = 26$ *in.*

24. **CHALLENGE** Create a stem-and-leaf plot in which the median of the data is 25.
25. **WRITING IN MATH** Present the data shown at the right in a line plot and a stem-and-leaf plot. Describe the similarities and differences among the representations. Which representation do you prefer to use? Explain your reasoning.

Fiber in Cereal (g)				
5	5	4	3	3
3	1	1	1	2
1	1	1	1	0

26. **COLLECT THE DATA** Collect a set of data that represents the heights in inches of the people in your math class. Then write a question that can be solved by analyzing a stem-and-leaf plot of the data. Be sure to explain how the stem-and-leaf plot would be used to solve your problem.

TEST PRACTICE

27. Denzell's science quiz scores are 11, 12, 13, 21, and 35. Which stem-and-leaf plot best represents this data?

A

Stem	Leaf
1	1
2	1
3	5

$3|5 = 35$

B

Stem	Leaf
1	3
2	1
3	5

$3|5 = 35$

C

Stem	Leaf
1	1 2 3
2	1
3	5

$3|5 = 35$

D

Stem	Leaf
1	1
2	1 1
3	5

$3|5 = 35$

28. The stem-and-leaf plot shows the points scored by the Harding Middle School basketball team.

Points Scored

Stem	Leaf
4	7 8 8 8
5	0 0 2 3 7 9
6	1 6
7	
8	4

$7|0 = 70$

Which one of the following statements is true concerning how the measures of central tendency are affected by the inclusion of the outlier?

F The mode is most affected.

G The median is not affected.

H The mean is most affected.

J None of the measures of central tendency are affected.

Spiral Review

Find the mean, median, and mode for each set of data. Round to the nearest tenth if necessary. (Lesson 8-2)

29. 80, 23, 55, 58, 45, 32, 40, 55, 50

30. 3.6, 2.4, 3.0, 7.9, 7.8, 2.4, 3.6, 3.9

31. Make a line plot of the test scores shown. (Lesson 8-1)

Test Scores				
83	94	78	78	85
86	88	83	82	92
90	77	83	81	89
90	88	87	88	85
84	81	83	85	91

32. **SCHOOL** The ratio of boys to girls in the sixth grade is 7 to 8. How many girls are in the sixth grade if there are 56 boys? (Lesson 6-1)

33. Write $\frac{9}{24}$ in simplest form. (Lesson 4-4)

GET READY for the Next Lesson

PREREQUISITE SKILL **Choose an appropriate interval and scale for each set of data.** (Lesson 8-1)

34. 9, 0, 18, 19, 2, 9, 8, 13, 4

35. 30, 20, 60, 80, 90, 120, 40

8-4 Bar Graphs and Histograms

MAIN IDEA

Display and analyze data using bar graphs and histograms.

New Vocabulary

bar graph
histogram

Math Online

glencoe.com

- Extra Examples
- Personal Tutor
- Self-Check Quiz

GET READY for the Lesson

FOOTBALL The table shows 5 teams that scored the greatest number of points in the Super Bowl.

Team	Score
San Francisco	55
Dallas	52
Tampa Bay	48
Chicago	46
Washington	42

Source: National Football League

1. What is the greatest and least scores in the table?
2. How can you summarize the data with a visual representation?
3. Do any of these representations show both the team and its score?

A **bar graph** is a method of comparing data by using solid bars to represent quantities.

EXAMPLE Display Data Using a Bar Graph

1 **Display the data in the table above in a bar graph.**

Step 1 Draw a horizontal axis and a vertical axis. Label the axes as shown. In this case, the scale on the vertical axis is chosen so that it includes all the scores. Add a title.

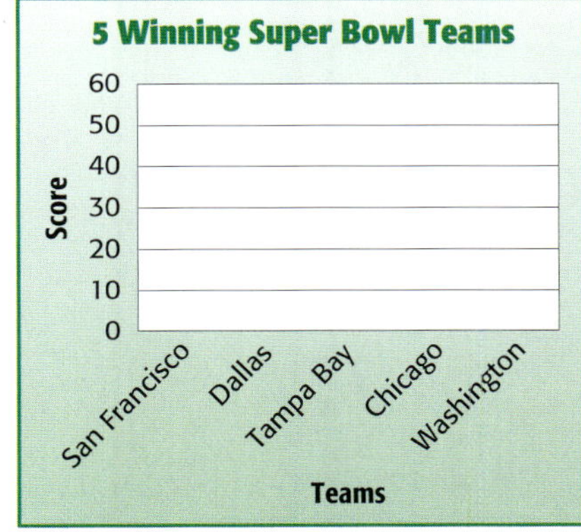

Step 2 Draw a bar to represent each category. In this case, a bar is used to represent the score of each team.

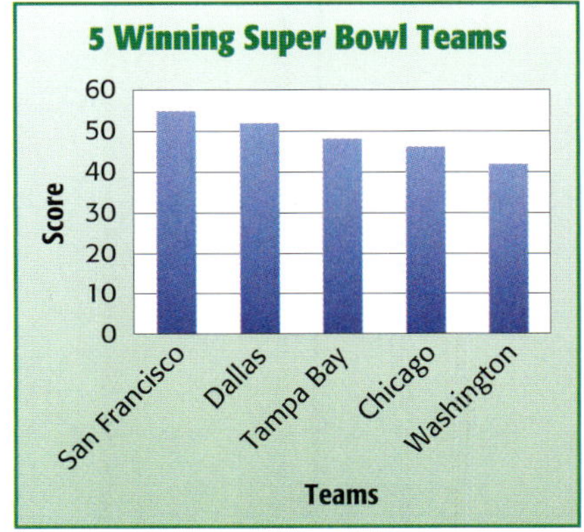

a. **FLOWERS** The table shows the diameters of the world's largest flowers. Display the data in a bar graph.

Flower	Maximum Size (in.)
Rafflesia	36
Sunflower	19
Giant Water Lily	18
Brazilian Dutchman	14
Magnolia	10

Source: *Book of World Records*

Reading Math

Frequency
Frequency refers to the number of data items in a particular interval. In Example 2, the frequency of 7 in the third row means that there are 7 games with a score of 31–40.

A special kind of bar graph, called a **histogram**, uses bars to represent the frequency of numerical data that have been organized in intervals.

EXAMPLE Display Data Using a Histogram

2 **FOOTBALL** **The winning scores of twenty recent Super Bowl games have been organized into a frequency table. Display the data in a histogram.**

Score	Frequency
11–20	3
21–30	4
31–40	7
41–50	4
51–60	2

Source: National Football League

Study Tip

Histograms
Because the intervals are equal, all of the bars have the same width, with no space between them.

Step 1 Draw and label horizontal and vertical axes. Add a title.

Step 2 Draw a bar to represent the frequency of each interval.

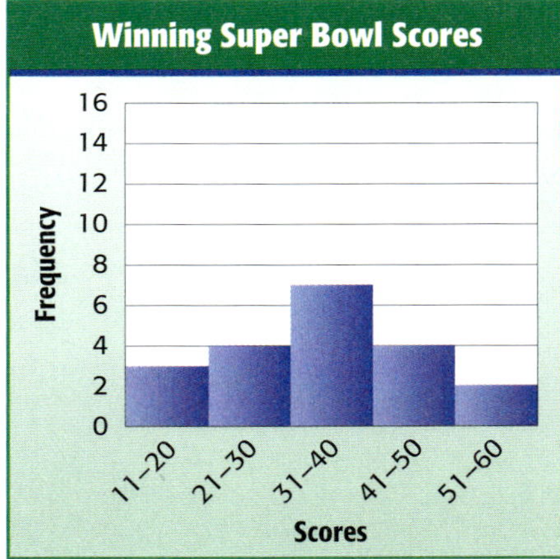

The three highest bars represent a majority of the data. From the graph, you can easily see that most of the scores were between 21 and 50 points.

b. **EARTHQUAKES** The magnitudes of the largest U.S. earthquakes are organized into the frequency table shown. Display the data in a histogram.

Magnitude	Frequency
7.0–7.4	4
7.5–7.9	14
8.0–8.4	5
8.5–8.9	2
9.0–9.4	1

Source: National Earthquake Information Center

Study Tip

Alternate Method
You can also use a proportion to find the percent in Example 4.

$\frac{6}{30} = \frac{x}{100}$

$6 \cdot 100 = 30 \cdot x$

$600 = 30x$

$20 = x$

EXAMPLES Interpret Histograms and Bar Graphs

MALLS The histogram shows the number of stores in the largest malls in the U.S.

Source: Directory of Major Malls

3 How many malls are represented in the histogram? Justify your answer.

Find the sum of the heights of the bars in the histogram.
So, $10 + 14 + 4 + 1 + 1 = 30$.

4 What percent of the malls had more than 274 stores?

$\frac{6}{30}$ → number of malls with more than 274 stores
→ total number of malls

$\frac{6}{30} = 0.2$ Write the fraction as a decimal.

$0.2 = 20\%$ Write the decimal as a percent.

So, 20% of the malls had more than 274 stores.

CHECK Your Progress

NASCAR The histogram shows the average winning times for the Daytona 500.

c. How many winning times are represented in the histogram? Explain your reasoning.

d. What percent of the winning speeds were faster than 150 miles per hour?

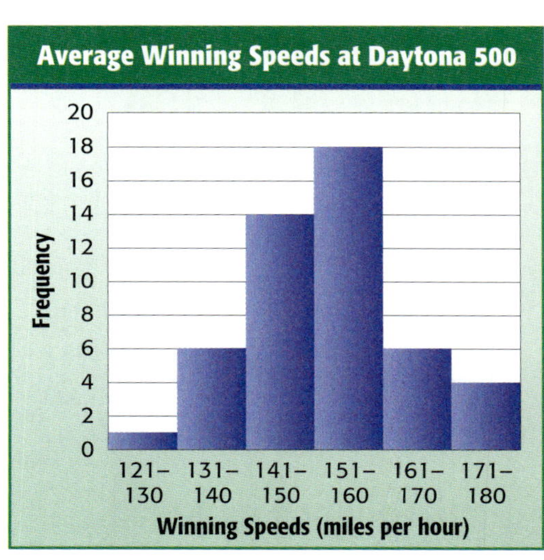

CHECK Your Understanding

Examples 1, 2 (pp. 415–417)

Select the appropriate graph to display each set of data: bar graph or histogram. Then display the data in the appropriate graph.

1.

State Sales Tax Rates	
Percent	**States**
2.0–2.9	1
3.0–3.9	0
4.0–4.9	12
5.0–5.9	12
6.0–6.9	16
7.0–7.9	4

Source: Federation of Tax Administrators

2.

Men's Grand Slam Titles	
Player	**Titles**
Pete Sampras	14
Roy Emerson	12
Bjorn Borg	11
Rod Laver	11
Andre Agassi	8

Source: *Book of World Records*

Examples 3, 4 (p. 417)

TEXTBOOKS **For Exercises 3 and 4, use the bar graph that shows the average number of pages in various textbooks.**

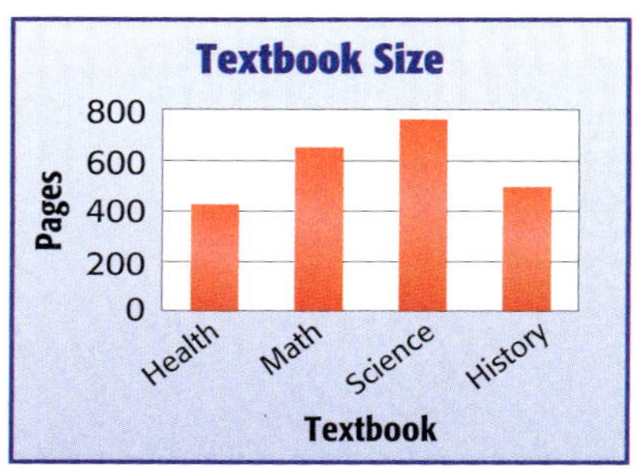

3. On average, which textbook has the least number of pages?

4. Is it reasonable to say that on average, a health textbook has half as many pages as a science textbook? Explain.

Practice and Problem Solving

HOMEWORK HELP	
For Exercises	**See Examples**
5–8	1, 2
9–15	3, 4

Select the appropriate graph to display each set of data: bar graph or histogram. Then display the data in the appropriate graph.

5.

Most Threatened Reptiles	
Country	**Number of Species**
Australia	38
China	31
Indonesia	28
U.S.	27
India	25

Source: *Top 10 of Everything*

6.

Home Run Leaders	
Home Runs	**Frequency**
31–36	1
37–42	4
43–48	7
49–54	5
55–60	3

7.

Major U.S. Rivers	
Length (mi)	**Frequency**
600–999	15
1,000–1,399	5
1,400–1,799	3
1,800–2,199	3
2,200–2,599	2

Source: *The World Almanac*

8.

City Skyscrapers	
City	**Skyscrapers**
New York	176
Hong Kong	163
Chicago	81
Shanghai	49
Tokyo	44

Source: *Book of World Records*

Real-World Link
Giraffes live for 10–15 years in the wild, but average 25 years at zoos.

Source: Woodland Park Zoo

HEIGHT **For Exercises 9-12, use the histogram that shows the heights of students in a classroom.**

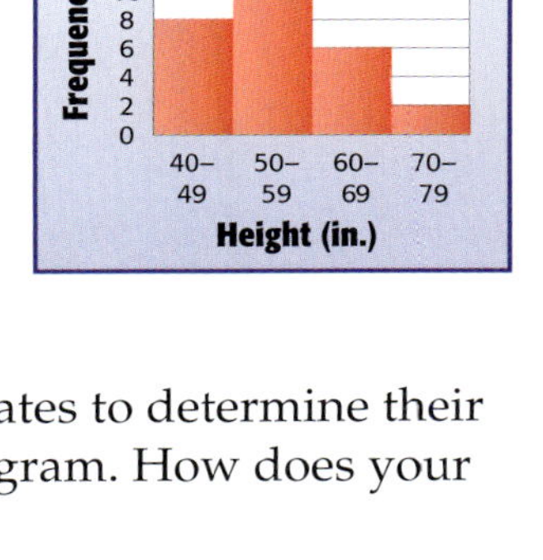

9. How many students are from 50 to 59 inches tall?

10. What percent of students are at least 60 inches tall?

11. Write a statement comparing the 70–79 interval to the 60–69 interval.

12. **COLLECT THE DATA** Conduct a survey of your classmates to determine their height. Then display and analyze the data in a histogram. How does your data compare to the histogram above?

ZOOS **For Exercises 13–15, use the histogram that shows the attendance at the major U.S. zoos in a recent year.**

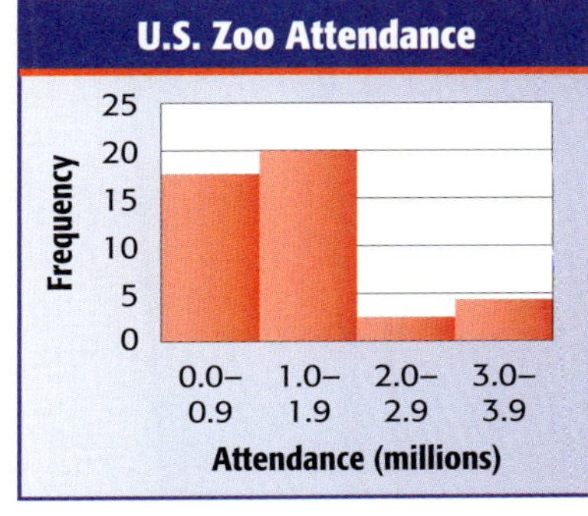

Source: *The World Almanac*

13. About how many zoos does the graph represent?

14. What is the range of attendance for most of the zoos?

15. Compare the number of zoos with 0.0–0.9 million visitors to the number of zoos with 3.0–3.9 million visitors.

Match each characteristic to the appropriate graph(s).

16. data display based upon place value
17. shows the frequency of data on a number line
18. compares data using solid bars
19. data are organized using intervals

a. line plot
b. histogram
c. stem-and-leaf plot
d. bar graph

DISTANCE **For Exercises 20 and 21, use the histogram shown below.**

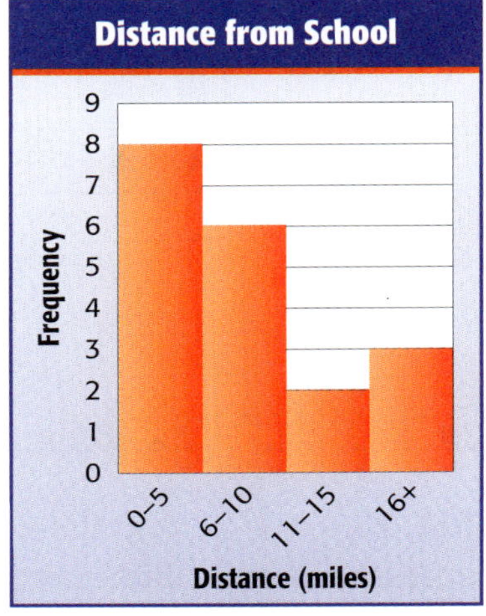

20. How many students live 6–10 miles from school?

21. What percent of students live 16 or more miles from school?

FOOD **For Exercises 22 and 23, use the multiple-bar graph that compares boys' and girls' favorite pizza toppings**

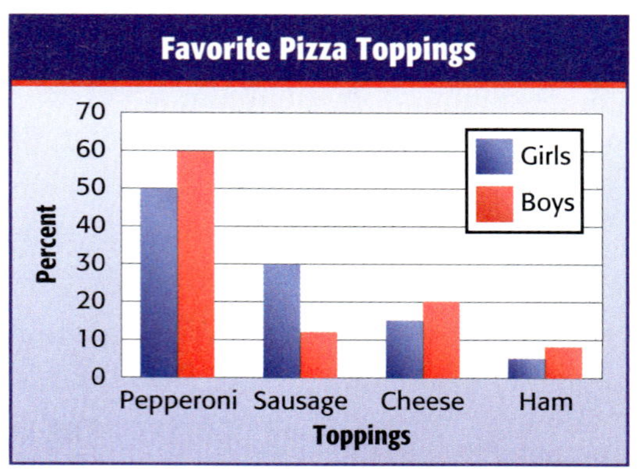

22. For which topping is the difference in girls' and boys' favorites the greatest? Explain.

23. Describe an advantage of using a multiple-bar graph rather than two separate graphs to compare data.

EXERCISE **For Exercises 24–27, refer to the graph below.**

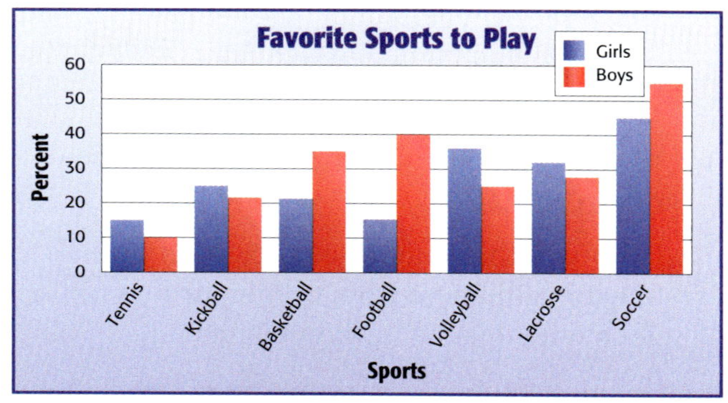

24. Which sport did the girls surveyed prefer the most?

25. Which sport is the least favorite for the boys?

26. Based on this survey, boys prefer football 4 times more than what sport?

27. Is it reasonable to say that almost twice as many boys prefer basketball than girls? Explain.

H.O.T. Problems

28. **CHALLENGE** The histograms show players' salaries for two major league baseball teams. Compare the salary distributions of the two teams.

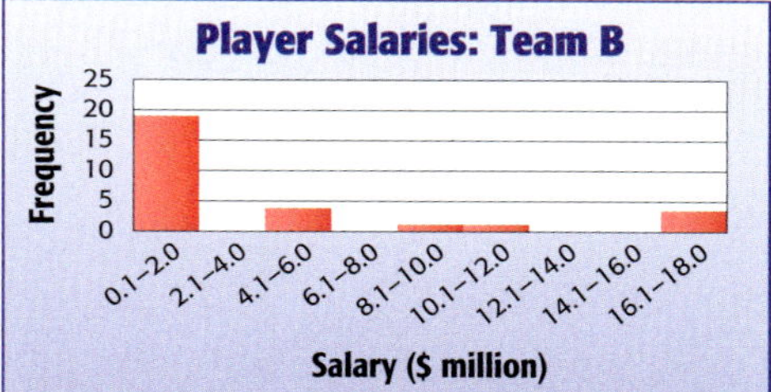

29. **DATA SENSE** Describe how to determine the number of values in a data set that is represented by a histogram.

30. **WRITING IN MATH** Can any data set be displayed using a histogram? If yes, explain why. If no, give a counterexample and explain why not.

TEST PRACTICE

31. The results of a survey are displayed in the graph.

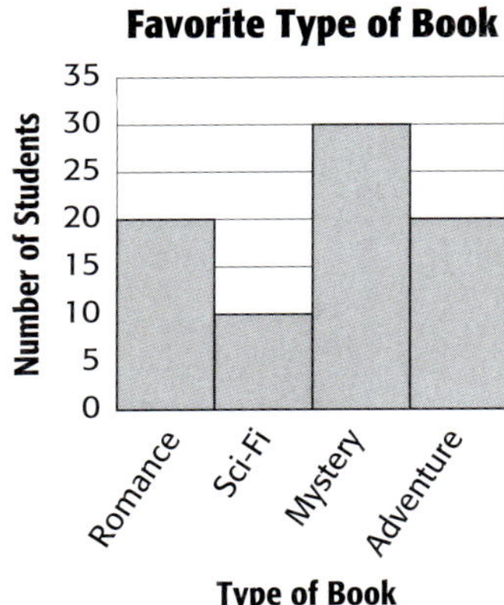

Which statement is valid about the survey?

A Twice as many students enjoy reading mysteries than romance.

B Most students enjoy reading adventure books.

C Twice as many students enjoy reading romance books than science fiction.

D Half as many students enjoy reading mysteries than romance.

32. **SHORT RESPONSE** The graph shows the average car sales per month at a car dealership.

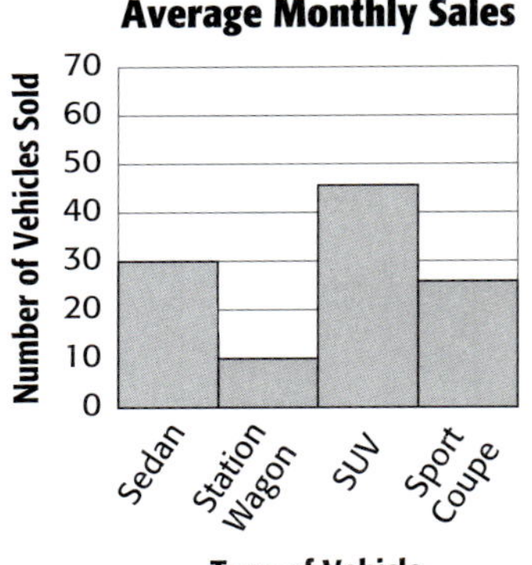

What is the best prediction for the number of station wagons the dealer sells in a year?

Spiral Review

SPORTS For Exercises 33 and 34, refer to the table that lists the number of games won by each team in a baseball league.

Number of Wins					
25	36	46	15	30	53
40	32	17	45	41	31
56	50	52	47	26	40
43	56	51	50	55	50
44	47	53	23	19	

33. Make a stem-and-leaf plot of the data. (Lesson 8-3)

34. What is the mean, median, and mode of the data? (Lesson 8-2)

35. **SELECT A TECHNIQUE** The video game that Neil wants to buy costs \$50. He has saved $\frac{1}{5}$ of the amount he needs. Which of the following techniques might Neil use to find how much more money he will need to buy the game? Justify your selection(s). Then use the technique(s) to solve the problem. (Lesson 5-5)

mental math | number sense | estimation

GET READY for the Next Lesson

36. **WEATHER** At 5:00 P.M., the outside temperature was 81°F. At 6:00 P.M., it was 80°F. At 7:00 P.M., it was 79°F. Use the *look for a pattern* strategy to predict the outside temperature at 8:00 P.M. (Lesson 2-7)

Extend 8-4

Spreadsheet Lab
Circle Graphs

MAIN IDEA

Use technology to create circle graphs.

Another type of display used to compare categories of data is a *circle graph*. Circle graphs are useful when comparing parts of a whole.

ACTIVITY

MAGAZINES **The table shows the results of a survey in which students were asked to indicate their favorite type of magazine. Use a spreadsheet to make a circle graph of these data.**

Magazine Preferences	
Type	**Frequency**
Comics	2
Fashion	7
Entertainment	5
News	3
Sports	6
Other	1

STEP 1 Enter the data in a spreadsheet as shown.

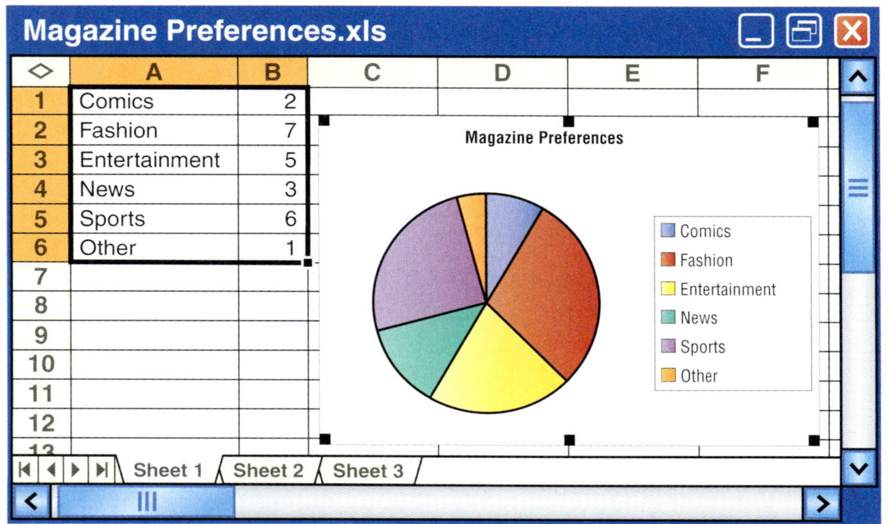

STEP 2 Select the information in cells A1 to B6. Click on the Chart Wizard icon. Choose the Pie chart type. Click Next twice. Enter the title Magazine Preferences. Then click Next and Finish.

Analyze the Results

1. **MAKE A CONJECTURE** Use the graph to determine which types of magazines were preferred by about $\frac{1}{3}$ and 25% of the students surveyed. Explain your reasoning. Then check your answers.

2. **COLLECT THE DATA** Collect some data that can be displayed in either a circle or bar graph. Record the data in a spreadsheet. Then use the spreadsheet to make both types of displays. Which display is more appropriate? Justify your selection.

CHAPTER 8

Mid-Chapter Quiz

Lessons 8-1 through 8-4

1. **MULTIPLE CHOICE** The table shows quiz scores of a math class. What is the range of test scores? (Lesson 8-1)

Math Scores						
89	92	67	75	95	89	82
92	88	89	80	91	79	90

A 89
B 82
C 67
D 28

For Exercises 2–4, use the data below. (Lesson 8-1)

Age Upon Receiving Driver's License									
16	17	16	16	18	21	16	16	18	18
17	25	16	17	17	17	17	16	20	16

2. Make a line plot of the data.
3. Identify any clusters, gaps, or outliers.
4. Describe how the range of data would change if 25 was not part of the data set.

5. **MULTIPLE CHOICE** The table shows the average April rainfall for 12 cities. If the value 4.2 is added to this list, which of the following would be true? (Lesson 8-2)

Average Rain (in.)					
0.5	0.6	1.0	1.0	2.5	3.7
2.6	3.3	2.0	1.4	0.7	0.4

F The mode would increase.
G The mean would increase.
H The mean would decrease.
J The median would decrease.

6. **TREES** The heights, in meters, of several trees are 7.6, 6.8, 6.5, 7.0, 7.9, and 6.8. Find the mean, median, and mode. Round to the nearest tenth if necessary. (Lesson 8-2)

7. **SPEED** Display the data shown in a stem-and-leaf plot and write one conclusion based on the data. (Lesson 8-3)

Car Highway Speeds				
65	72	76	68	65
59	70	69	71	74
68	65	71	74	69

MAMMALS For Exercises 8–10, refer to the stem-and-leaf plot that shows the maximum weight in kilograms of several rabbits.

Maximum Weight of Rabbits (kg)

Stem	Leaf
0	8 9
1	0 2 4 6 8
2	7
3	
4	
5	4

$0|8 = 0.8$ kg

8. Find the range of weights.
9. Find the median and mode of the data.
10. Which measure of central tendency is most affected by the inclusion of the outlier? Explain.

ATTENDANCE For Exercises 11 and 12, refer to the graph. (Lesson 8-4)

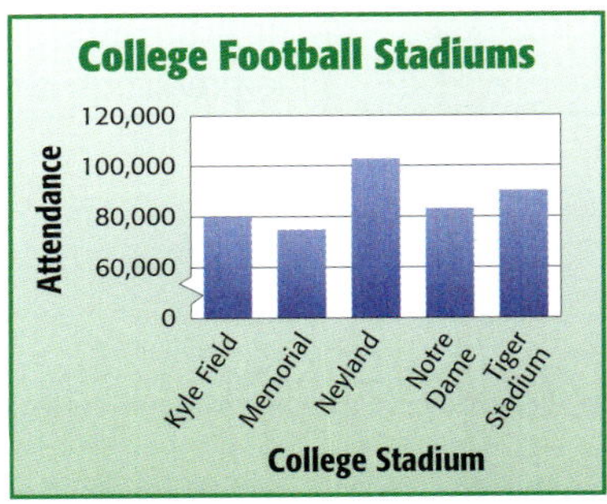

Source: MSNBC

11. About how many people does the graph represent?
12. Which two stadiums house about the same number of people?

Problem-Solving Investigation

MAIN IDEA: Solve problems by using a graph.

P.S.I. TEAM +

e-Mail: USE A GRAPH

RICK: The table shows the study times and test scores of 13 students in Mrs. Collins's English class.

YOUR MISSION: Use a graph to predict the test score of a student who studied for 80 minutes.

Study Time and Test Scores											
Study Time (min)	120	30	60	95	70	55	90	45	75	60	10
Test Score (%)	98	77	91	93	77	78	95	74	87	83	65

Understand	You know the number of minutes studied. You need to predict the test score.
Plan	Organize the data in a graph so you can easily see any trends.
Solve	The graph shows that as the study times progress, the test scores increase. You can predict that the test score of a student who studied for 80 minutes is about 88%.
Check	Draw a line that is close to as many of the points as possible, as shown. The estimate is close to the line so the prediction is reasonable.

Study Time and Test Scores

y: Test Score (%) — 65, 75, 85, 95

x: Study Time (min) — 0, 20, 40, 60, 80, 100

Analyze The Strategy

1. Explain why analyzing a graph is a useful way to quickly make conclusions about a set of data.
2. **WRITING IN MATH** Write a problem in which using a graph would be a useful way to check a solution.

Mixed Problem Solving

See pages 688, 711.

For Exercises 3 and 4, use the table. It shows the relationship between Celsius and Fahrenheit temperatures.

Temperature	
Celsius	Fahrenheit
0	32
10	50
20	68
30	86
40	104

3. Make a graph of the data.

4. Suppose the temperature is 25° Celsius. Estimate the temperature in Fahrenheit.

5. **FUNDRAISING** The graph shows how many boxes of popcorn were sold by four students for a fundraiser. Which student sold about half as many boxes as Alyssa?

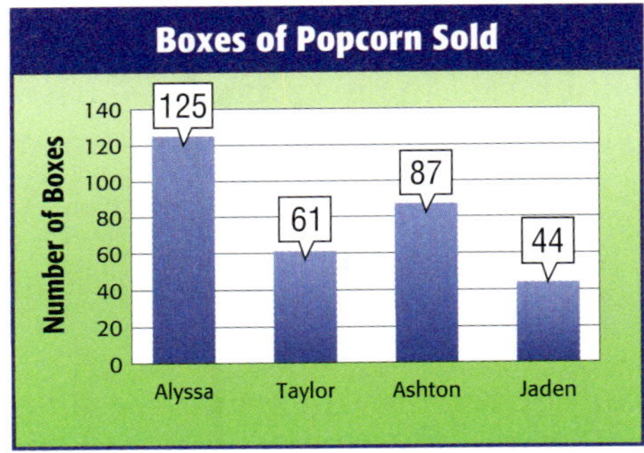

Use any strategy to solve Exercises 6–12. Some strategies are shown below.

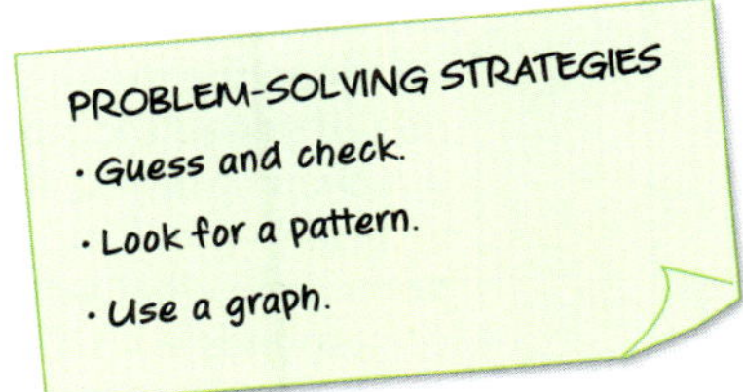

6. **ALGEBRA** What are the next two numbers in the pattern 8, 18, 38, 78, ...?

7. **EXERCISE** Emma walked 8 minutes on Sunday and plans to walk twice as long each day than she did the previous day. On what day will she walk over 1 hour?

8. **EXERCISE** The graph shows the number of minutes Jacob exercised during one week. According to the graph, which two days did he exercise about the same amount of time?

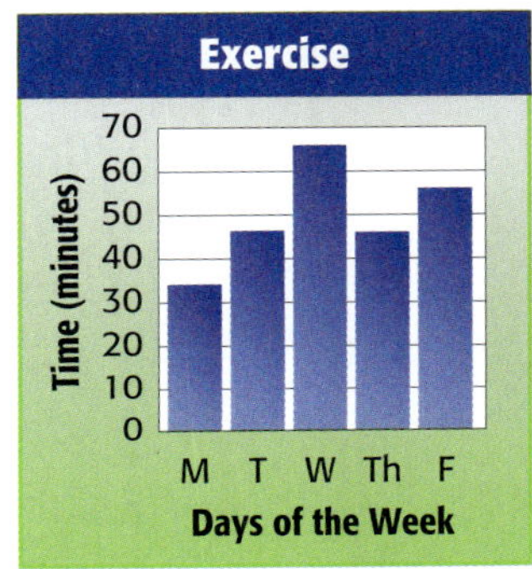

9. **ALGEBRA** Find two numbers with a sum of 56 and with a product of 783.

10. **HELICOPTERS** A helicopter has a maximum freight capacity of 2,400 pounds. How many crates, each weighing about 75 pounds, can the helicopter hold?

11. **SKATING** Moses and some of his friends are going to the movies. Suppose they each buy nachos and a beverage. They spend $36. How many friends are going to the movies with Moses?

Movie Costs	
Item	Price
ticket	$6.00
beverage	$2.25
nachos	$3.75

12. **NUMBER THEORY** A number is squared and the result is 324. Find the number.

8-6 Using Graphs to Predict

MAIN IDEA

Analyze line graphs and scatter plots to make predictions and conclusions.

New Vocabulary

line graph
scatter plot

Math Online

glencoe.com

- Extra Examples
- Personal Tutor
- Self-Check Quiz

MINI Lab

- Pour 1 cup of water into the drinking glass.
- Measure the height of the water, and record it in a table like the one shown.
- Place 5 marbles in the glass. Measure the height of the water. Record.
- Continue adding marbles, 5 at a time, until there are 20 marbles in the glass. After each time, measure and record the height of the water.

Number of Marbles	Height of Water (cm)
0	
5	
10	
15	
20	

1. By how much did the water's height change after each addition of marbles?
2. Predict the height of the water when 30 marbles are in the drinking glass. Explain how you made your prediction.
3. Test your prediction by placing 10 more marbles in the glass.
4. Draw a graph of the data that you recorded in the table.

You created a line graph in the Mini Lab. **Line graphs** can be useful in predicting future events because they show relationships or trends over time.

EXAMPLES Use a Line Graph to Predict

1 **TEMPERATURE** **The relationship between temperature readings in °C and °F is shown below. Use the line graph to predict the temperature reading 35°C in °F.**

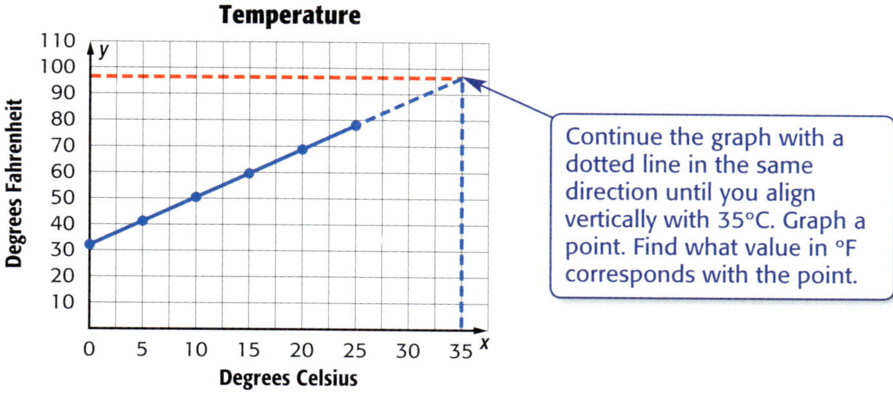

The temperature reading 35°C is equivalent to 95°F.

2 **SCHOOL** **The graph shows the student enrollment at McDaniel Middle School for the past several years. If the trend continues, what will be the enrollment in 2010?**

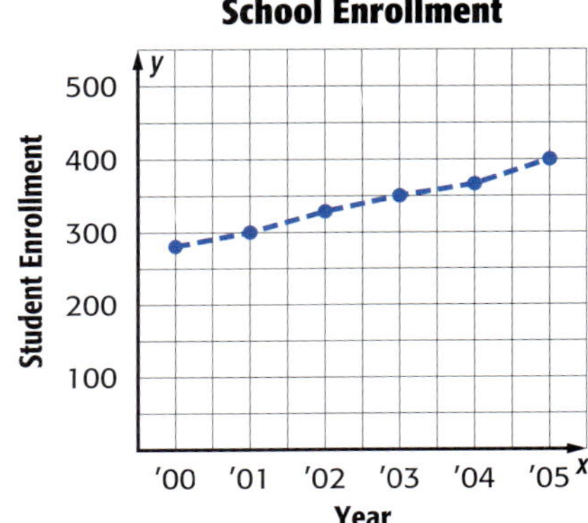

If the trend continues, the enrollment in 2010 will be about 525 students.

Study Tip

Broken Lines
In Example 2, there are no data points between the points that represent enrollment. So, a broken line was used to help you easily see trends in the data.

CHECK Your Progress

a. **READING** Kerry is reading *The Game of Sunken Places* over summer break. The graph shows the time it has taken her to read the book so far. Predict the time it will take her to read 150 pages.

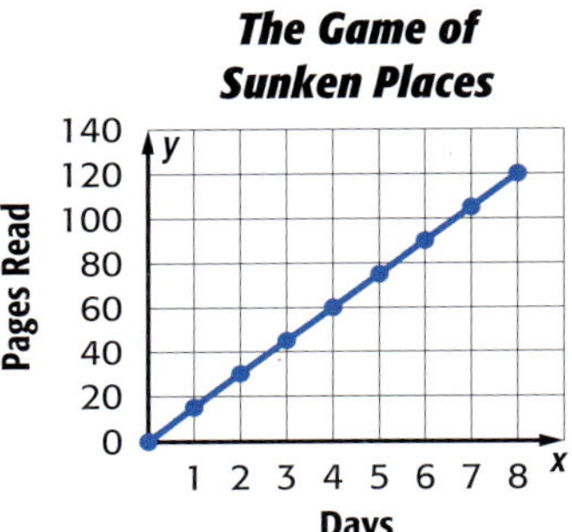

b. **JUICE BOXES** The table shows the number of juice boxes a cafeteria sold in a five-week period. Display the data in a line graph. If the trend continues, how many juice boxes will be sold in week 8?

Juice Box Sales

Week	Number Sold
1	50
2	52
3	56
4	60
5	62

A **scatter plot** displays two sets of data on the same graph. Like line graphs, scatter plots are useful for making predictions because they show trends in data. If the points on a scatter plot come close to lying on a straight line, the two sets of data are related.

Study Tip

Scatter Plots
In a positive relationship, as the value of *x* increases, so does the value of *y*. In a negative relationship, as the value of *x* increases, the value of *y* decreases.

Types of Relationships

Concept Summary

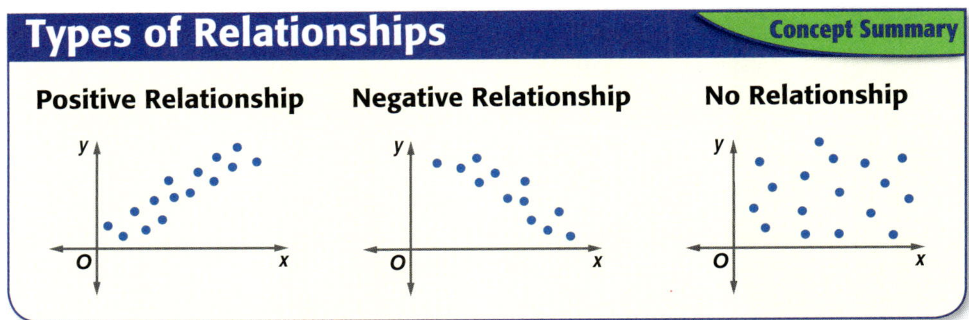

Reading Math

Scatter Plots Another name for scatter plot is *scattergram*.

EXAMPLE 3 Use a Scatter Plot to Predict

NASCAR **The scatter plot shows the earnings for the winning driver for the Nextel Cup Series from 1986 to 2006. Predict the winning earnings for the next Nextel Cup Series.**

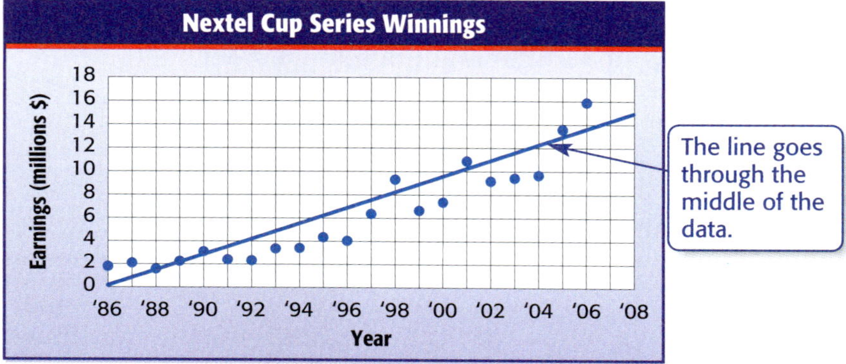

By looking at the pattern, we can predict the winning earnings for 2008 will be about $16,500,000.

CHECK Your Progress

c. **NASCAR** Use the scatter plot above to predict winning earnings for 2010.

CHECK Your Understanding

Examples 1, 2 (pp. 426–427)

POPULATION **Delaware is a fast growing city in Ohio. The graph shows its increase in population.**

1. Describe the relationship between the two sets of data.
2. If the trend continues, what will be the population in 2010?

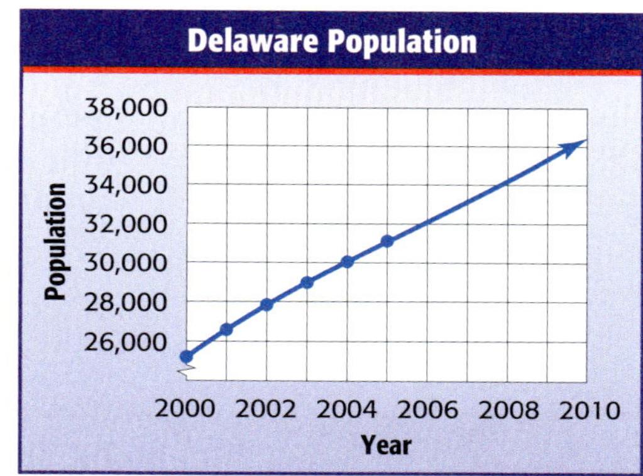

Example 3 (p. 428)

3. **PICNICS** The scatter plot shows the number of people who attended a neighborhood picnic each year. How many people should be expected to attend the picnic in 2007?

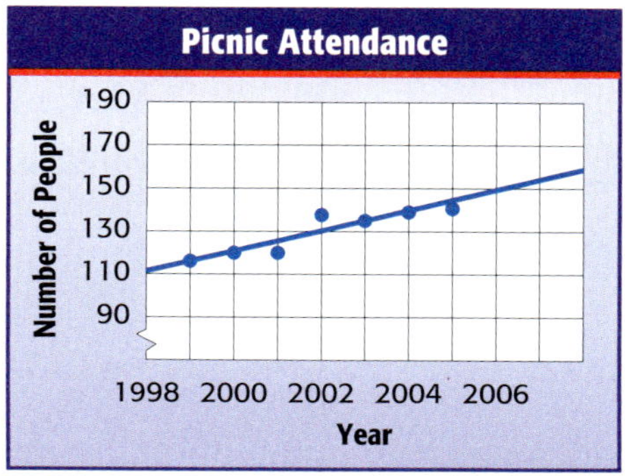

Practice and Problem Solving

HOMEWORK HELP	
For Exercises	See Examples
4–5	1, 2
6–7	3

MONUMENTS For Exercises 4 and 5, use the graph that shows the time it takes Ciro to climb the Statue of Liberty.

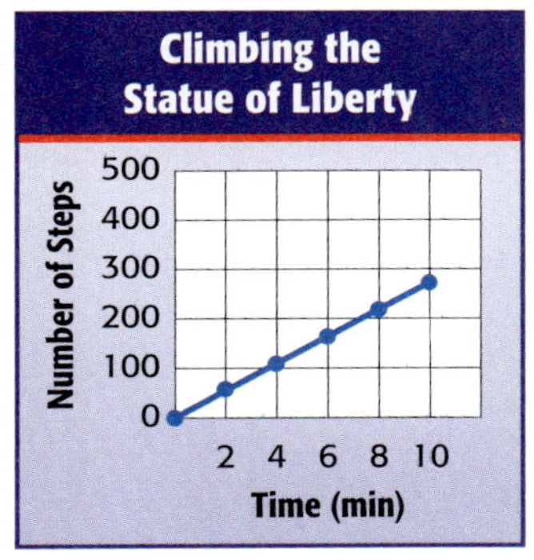

4. Predict the time it will take Ciro to climb 354 steps to reach the top.
5. How many steps will he have climbed after 14 minutes?

SCHOOL For Exercises 6 and 7, use the graph that shows the time students spent studying for a test and their test score.

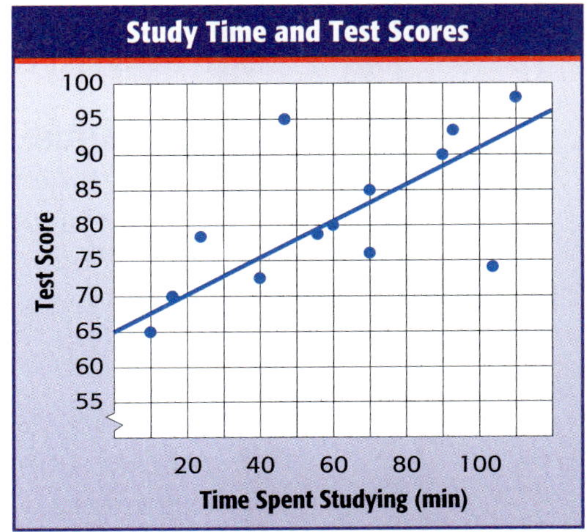

6. What score should a student who studies for 1 hour be expected to earn?
7. If a student scored 90 on the test, about how much time can you assume the student spent studying?

SLEEP For Exercises 8–10, use the table that shows the relationship between hours of sleep before and scores on a math test.

Hours of Sleep	Math Test Score
9	96
8	88
7	76
6	71

8. Display the data in a scatter plot.
9. Describe the relationship, if any, between the two sets of data.
10. Predict the test score for someone that sleeps 5 hours.

BASKETBALL For Exercises 11–13, use the table at the right.

11. Make a scatter plot of the data to show the relationship between free throws made and free throw attempts.
12. Predict the number of free throws made if 500 free throws were attempted.
13. Describe the trend in the data.

Player	Free Throws Made	Free Throw Attempts
T. Duncan	362	568
S. Nash	222	247
Y. Ming	356	413
B. Davis	275	369
A. Jamison	226	307
D. Williams	227	296
D. Howard	390	666
J. Howard	243	294

Source: National Basketball Association

SCHOOLS For Exercises 14 and 15, use the graphic that shows public school teachers' average salaries for the past few years.

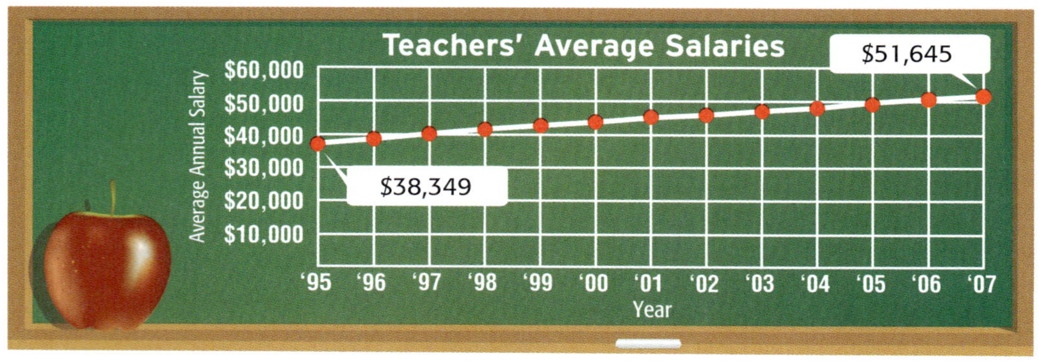

14. Describe the relationship, if any, between the two sets of data.
15. If the trend continues, what will be the average annual salary in 2011?
16. **POPULATION** The multiple line graph at the right shows the population of San Diego, California, and Phoenix, Arizona, from 1980 to 2005. What can you conclude from the graph?

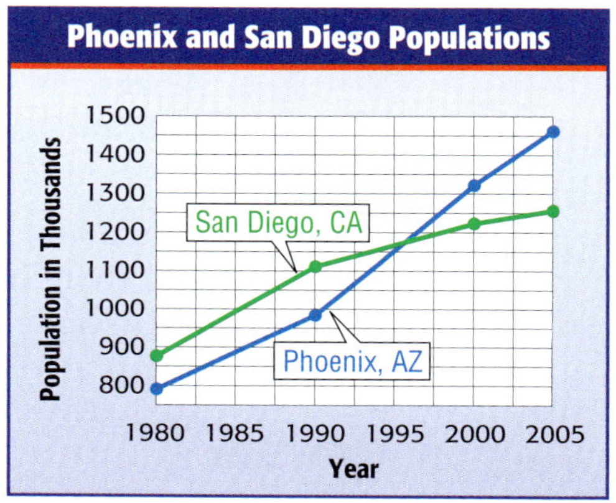

17. **RESEARCH** Use the Internet or another source to find a real-world example of a scatter plot. Write a description of what the graph displays and extend the graph to show where the data will be in the future.

EXTRA PRACTICE
See pages 689, 711.

H.O.T. Problems

18. **OPEN ENDED** Name two sets of data that can be graphed on a scatter plot.
19. **Which One Doesn't Belong?** Identify the term that does not have the same characteristic as the other three. Explain your reasoning.

line plot	mode	bar graph	scatter plot

20. **CHALLENGE** What can you conclude about the relationship between pet owner age and number of pets shown in the scatter plot at the right?

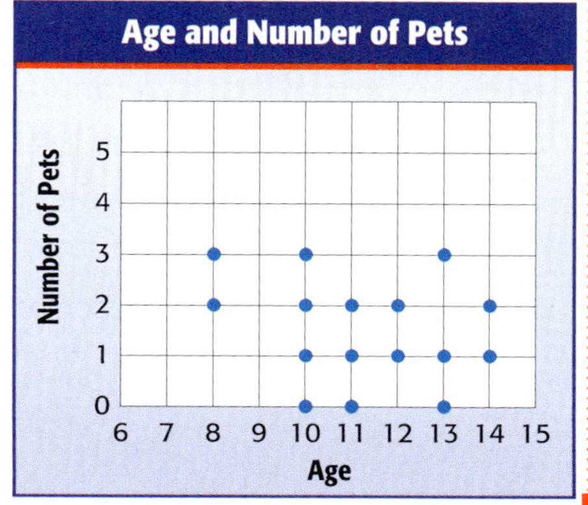

21. **WRITING IN MATH** Explain how a graph can be used to make predictions.

TEST PRACTICE

22. The number of laps Gaspar has been swimming each day is shown.

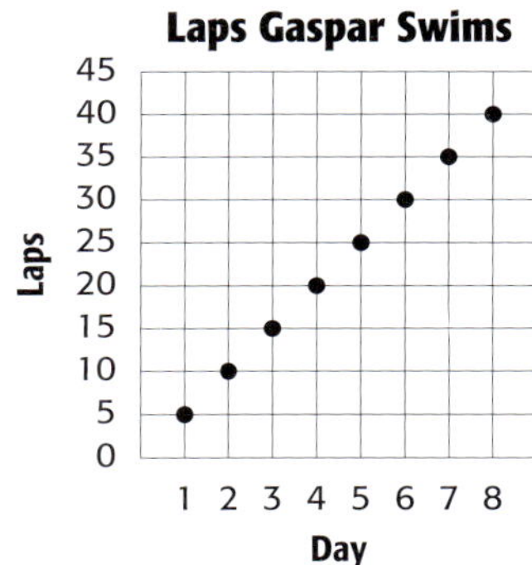

If the trend shown in the graph continues, what is the best prediction for the number of laps he will swim on day 10?

A 50

B 65

C 75

D 100

23. The number of people at the pool at different times during the day is shown.

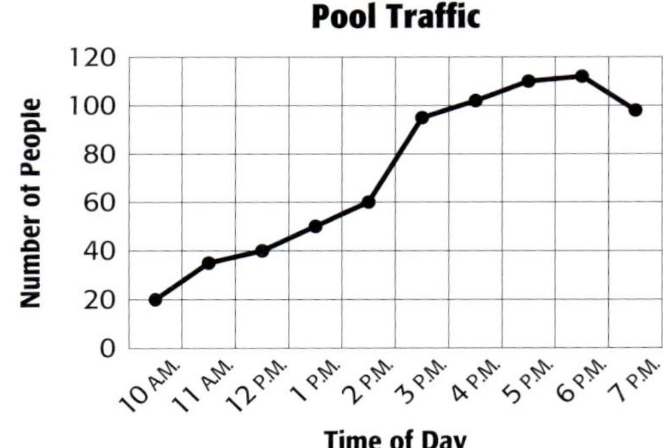

If an extra lifeguard is needed when the number of people at the pool exceeds 100, between which hours is an extra lifeguard needed?

F 10:00 A.M.–12:00 P.M.

G 12:00 P.M.–3:00 P.M.

H 2:00 P.M.–5:00 P.M.

J 4:00 P.M.–6:00 P.M.

Spiral Review

24. **SKATING** Use the *use a graph* strategy to compare the number of people who skate in California to the number of people who skate in Texas. (Lesson 8-5)

25. **COLORS** Of 57 students, 13 prefer the color red, 16 prefer blue, 20 prefer green, and 8 prefer yellow. Display this data in a bar graph. (Lesson 8-4)

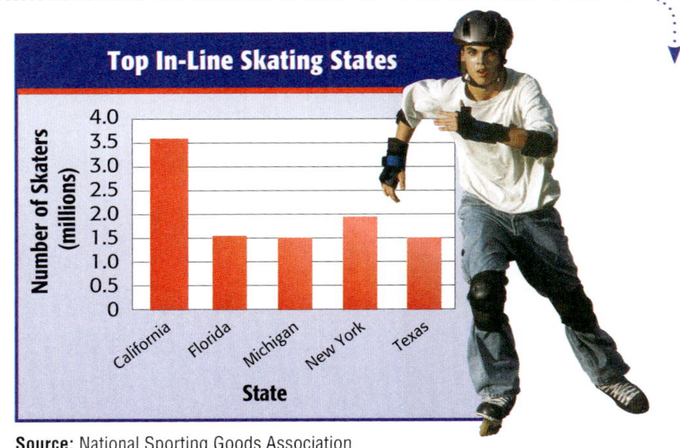

Source: National Sporting Goods Association

GET READY for the Next Lesson

PREREQUISITE SKILL **Find the mean and median for each set of data.** (Lesson 8-2)

26. 89 ft, 90 ft, 74 ft, 81 ft, 68 ft

27. 76°, 90°, 88°, 84°, 82°, 78°

Extend 8-6

Spreadsheet Lab
Multiple-Line and -Bar Graphs

MAIN IDEA

Use a spreadsheet to make a multiple-line graph and a multiple-bar graph.

In Lessons 8-4 and 8-6, you interpreted data in a multiple-bar graph and in a multiple-line graph, respectively. You can use a spreadsheet to make these two types of graphs.

ACTIVITY

1 The stopping distances for a car on dry pavement and on wet pavement are shown in the table at the right.

Speed (mph)	Stopping Distance (ft)	
	Dry Pavement	Wet Pavement
50	200	250
60	271	333
70	342	430
80	422	532

Source: Continental Teves

Set up a spreadsheet like the one shown below.

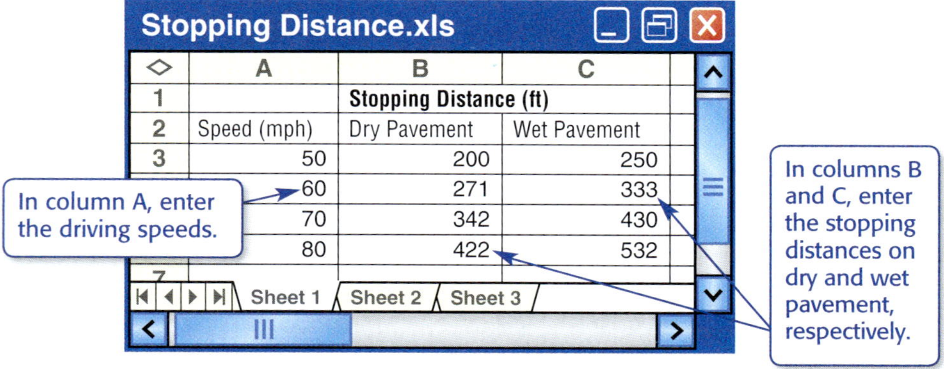

The next step is to "tell" the spreadsheet to make a double-line graph for the data.

1. Highlight the data in columns B and C, from B2 through C6.
2. Click on the Chart Wizard icon.
3. Choose the line graph and click Next.
4. To set the x-axis, choose the Series tab and press the icon next to the Category (X) axis labels.
5. On the spreadsheet, highlight the data in column A, from A3 through A6.
6. Press the icon on the bottom of the Chart Wizard box to automatically paste the information.
7. Click Next and enter the chart title and labels for the x- and y-axes.
8. Click Next and then Finish.

This tells the spreadsheet to read the data in columns B and C.

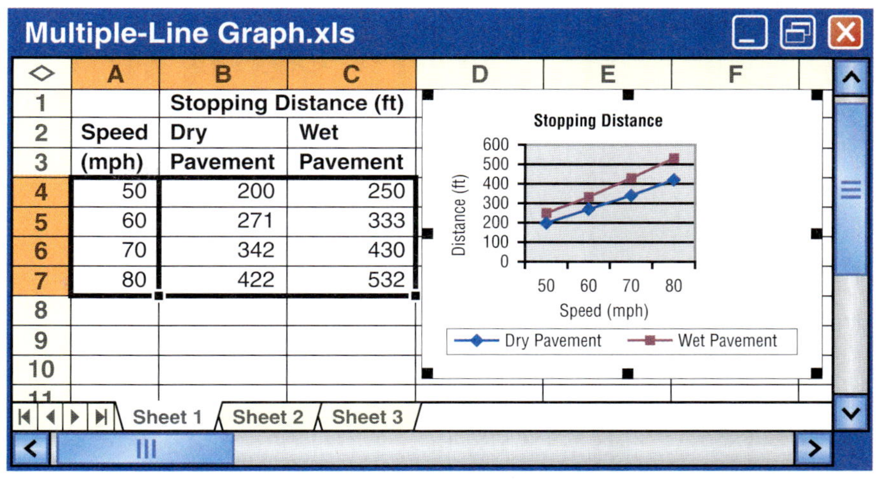

Multiple-Line Graph.xls

	A	B	C
1		Stopping Distance (ft)	
2	Speed	Dry	Wet
3	(mph)	Pavement	Pavement
4	50	200	250
5	60	271	333
6	70	342	430
7	80	422	532

ACTIVITY

2 Use the same data to make a multiple-bar graph.

- Highlight the data in columns B and C, from B2 through C6.
- Click on the Chart Wizard icon.
- Click on Column and Next to choose the vertical bar graph.
- Complete steps 4–8 from Activity 1.

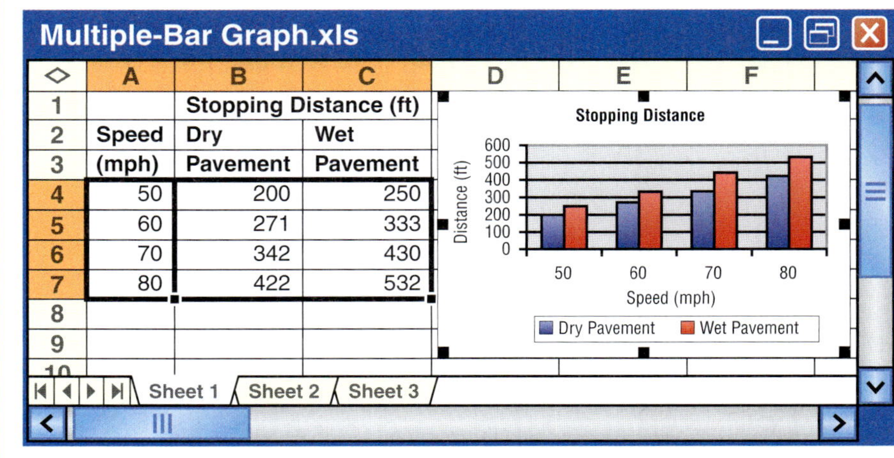

Multiple-Bar Graph.xls

	A	B	C
1		Stopping Distance (ft)	
2	Speed	Dry	Wet
3	(mph)	Pavement	Pavement
4	50	200	250
5	60	271	333
6	70	342	430
7	80	422	532

Analyze the Results

1. Explain the steps you would take to make a multiple-line graph of the stopping distances that include the speeds 55, 65, and 75.

2. **COLLECT THE DATA** Collect two sets of data that represent the number of boys and the number of girls in your class born in the spring, summer, fall, and winter. Use a spreadsheet to make a multiple-line or -bar graph of the data. Justify your selection.

8-7 Using Data to Predict

MAIN IDEA

Predict actions of a larger group by using a sample.

New Vocabulary

survey
population

Math Online

glencoe.com

- Extra Examples
- Personal Tutor
- Self-Check Quiz

GET READY for the Lesson

TELEVISION The circle graph shows the results of a survey in which children ages 8 to 12 were asked whether they have a television in their bedroom.

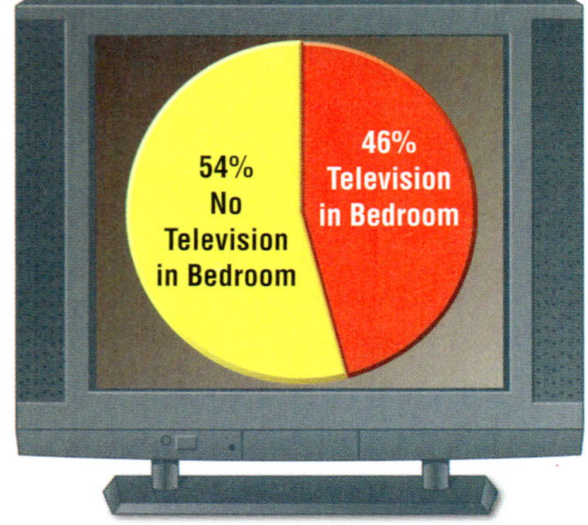

Source: National Institute on Media and the Family

1. Can you tell how many were surveyed? Explain.
2. Describe how you could use the graph to predict how many students in your school have a television in their bedroom.

A **survey** is designed to collect data about a specific group of people, called the **population**. If a survey is conducted at random, or without preference, you can assume that the survey represents the population. In this lesson, you will use the results of randomly conducted surveys to make predictions about the population.

Real-World EXAMPLE

1 **TELEVISION** **Refer to the graphic above. Predict how many out of 1,725 students would not have a television in their bedrooms.**

You can use the percent proportion and the survey results to predict what part p of the 1,725 students have no TV in their bedrooms.

part of the population → p; whole population → 1,725

$\frac{p}{1,725} = \frac{54}{100}$ Survey results: 54%

$p \cdot 100 = 1,725 \cdot 54$ Find the cross products.

$100p = 93,150$ Simplify.

$\frac{100p}{100} = \frac{93,150}{100}$ Divide each side by 100.

$p = 931.5$ Simplify.

About 932 students do not have a television in their bedrooms.

CHECK Your Progress

a. **TELEVISION** Refer to the same graphic. Predict how many out of 1,370 students have a television in their bedrooms.

Real-World EXAMPLE

2 INSTANT MESSAGING Use the information at the left to predict how many of the 2,450 students at Washington Middle School use emoticons on their instant messengers.

You need to predict how many of the 2,450 students use emoticons.

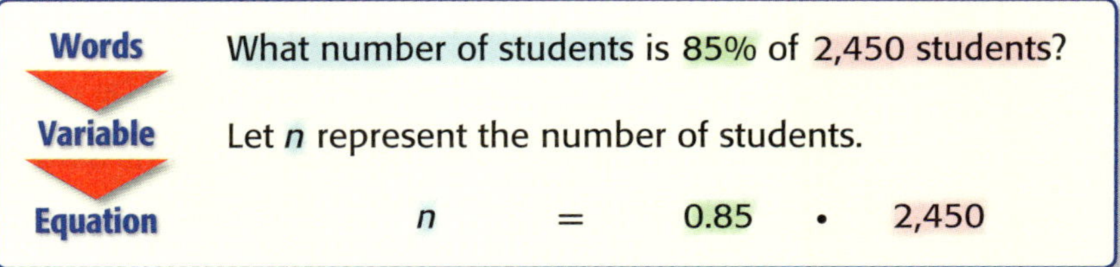

$n = 0.85 \cdot 2{,}450$ Write the percent equation.

$n = 2{,}082.5$ Multiply.

About 2,083 of the students use emoticons.

Real-World Link A survey found that 85% of people use emoticons on their instant messengers.

CHECK Your Progress

b. **INSTANT MESSAGING** This same survey found that 59% of people use sound on their instant messengers. Predict how many of the 2,450 students use sound on their instant messengers.

CHECK Your Understanding

Example 1 (p. 434)

SPENDING For Exercises 1 and 2, use the circle graph that shows the results of a poll to which 60,000 teens responded.

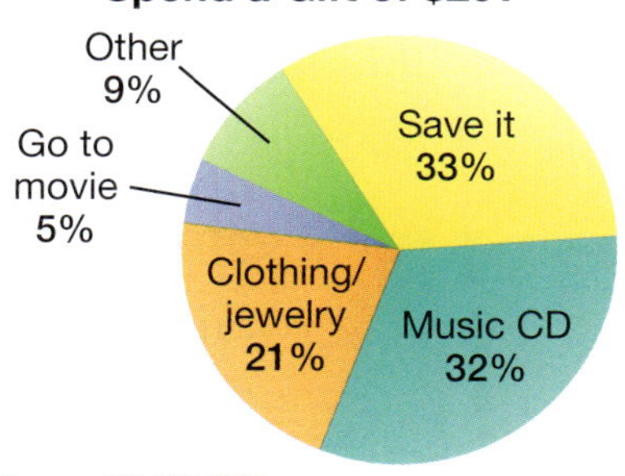

1. How many of the teens surveyed said that they would save their money?
2. Predict how many of the approximately 28 million teens in the United States would buy a music CD if they were given $20.

Example 2 (p. 435)

FOOD For Exercises 3 and 4, use the bar graph that shows the results of a survey in which students at Vail Middle School were asked their favorite ice cream flavor.

3. Out of 538 students at Vail Middle School, predict how many prefer strawberry ice cream.
4. Predict how many students prefer chocolate ice cream.

Practice and Problem Solving

HOMEWORK HELP	
For Exercises	See Examples
5–8	1, 2

RECREATION **In a survey, 250 people from a town were asked if they thought the town needed a recreation center. The results are shown in the table.**

Recreation Center Needed	
Response	**Percent**
yes	44%
no	38%
undecided	18%

5. Predict how many of the 3,225 people in the town think a recreation center is needed.
6. About how many of the people would be undecided?
7. **MP3 PLAYERS** In a survey, 82% of teens said they own an MP3 player. Predict how many of 346,000 teens do *not* own an MP3 player.
8. **VOLUNTEERING** A survey showed that 90% of teens donate money to a charity during the holidays. Based on that survey, how many teens in a class of 400 will donate money the next holiday season?

Match each situation with the appropriate equation or proportion.

9. 27% of MP3 owners download music weekly. Predict how many MP3 owners out of 238 owners download music weekly.
10. 27 MP3s is what percent of 238 MP3s?
11. 238% of 27 is what number?

a. $n = 27 \cdot 2.38$

b. $\frac{27}{100} = \frac{p}{238}$

c. $\frac{27}{238} = \frac{n}{100}$

CATS **For Exercises 12 and 13, use the graph that shows the percent of cat owners who train their cats in each category.**

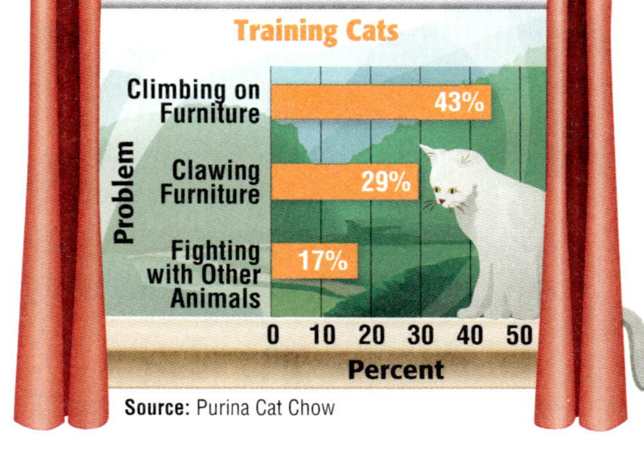

12. Out of 255 cat owners, predict how many owners trained their cat not to climb on furniture.
13. Out of 316 cat owners, predict how many more cat owners have trained their cat not to claw on furniture than have trained their cat not to fight with other animals.

14. **FIND THE DATA** Refer to the Data File on pages 16–19. Choose some data and write a real-world problem in which you could use the percent proportion or percent equation to make a prediction.

H.O.T. Problems

15. **CHALLENGE** A survey found that 80% of teens enjoy going to the movies in their free time. Out of 5,200 teens, predict how many said that they do not enjoy going to the movies in their free time.
16. **OPEN ENDED** Select a newspaper or magazine article that contains a table or graph. Identify the population and explain how you think the results were found.

17. **SELECT A TOOL** A survey showed that 15% of the people in Tennessee over the age of 16 belong to a fitness center. Predict how many of the 5,900,962 people in Tennessee over the age of 16 belong to a fitness center. Select one or more of the following tools to solve the problem. Justify your selection(s).

make a model | calculator | paper/pencil | real objects

18. **WRITING IN MATH** Explain how to use a sample to predict what a group of people prefer. Then give an example of a situation in which it makes sense to use a sample.

TEST PRACTICE

19. The table shows how students spend time with their family.

How Students Spend Time with Family	
Dinner	34%
TV	20%
Talking	14%
Sports	14%
Taking Walks	4%
Other	14%

Source: Kids USA Survey

Of the 515 students surveyed, predict about how many spend time with their family at dinner.

A 17 **C** 119

B 34 **D** 175

20. Yesterday, a bakery baked 54 loaves of bread in 20 minutes. Today, the bakery needs to bake 375 loaves of bread. At this rate, predict how long it will take to bake the bread.

F 1.5 hours **H** 3.0 hours

G 2.3 hours **J** 3.75 hours

21. Of the 357 students in a freshman class, about 82% plan to go to college. How many students plan on going to college?

A 224 **C** 314

B 293 **D** 325

Spiral Review

RUNNING For Exercises 22–24, refer to the table that shows the time it took Dale to run each mile of a 5-mile run.

Mile	Time
1	4 min 19 s
2	4 min 28 s
3	4 min 39 s
4	4 min 54 s
5	5 min 1 s

22. Make a scatter plot of the data. (Lesson 8-6)

23. Describe the relationship, if any, between the two sets of data. (Lesson 8-6)

24. Suppose the trend continues. Predict the time it would take Dale to run a sixth mile. (Lesson 8-5)

Multiply. (Lesson 2-6)

25. -4×6

26. $5 \times (-8)$

27. $-6 \times (-9)$

28. 8×3

GET READY for the Next Lesson

PREREQUISITE SKILL **Simplify.** (Lesson 1-4)

29. $\frac{10 - 7}{10}$

30. $\frac{50 - 18}{50}$

31. $\frac{22 - 4}{4}$

32. $\frac{39 - 15}{15}$

8-8 Using Sampling to Predict

MAIN IDEA

Predict the actions of a larger group by using a sample.

New Vocabulary

sample
unbiased sample
simple random sample
biased sample
convenience sample
voluntary response sample

Math Online

glencoe.com

- Extra Examples
- Personal Tutor
- Self-Check Quiz

GET READY for the Lesson

CELL PHONES The manager of a local cell phone company wants to conduct a survey to determine what kind of musical ring tones people typically use.

What Kind of Musical Ring Tone Do You Use?
Classical
Rock
Rap/Hip-Hop
Dance
Other

1. Suppose she decides to survey the listeners of a rock radio station. Do you think the results would represent the entire population? Explain.
2. Suppose she decides to survey a group of people standing in line for a symphony. Do you think the results would represent the entire population? Explain.
3. Suppose she decides to mail a survey to every 100th household in the area. Do you think the results would represent the entire population? Explain.

The manager of the cell phone company cannot survey everyone. A smaller group called a **sample** is chosen. A sample should be representative of the population.

Population	Sample
United States citizens	registered voters
California residents	homeowners
Six Flags Marine World visitors	teenagers

For valid results, a sample must be chosen very carefully. An **unbiased sample** is selected so that it is representative of the entire population. A simple random sample is the most common type of unbiased sample.

Unbiased Samples

Concept Summary

Type	Description	Example
Simple Random Sample	Each item or person in the population is as likely to be chosen as any other.	Each student's name is written on a piece of paper. The names are placed in a bowl, and names are picked without looking.

Bias

Everyday Use a tendency or prejudice.

Math Use error introduced by selecting or encouraging a specific outcome.

In a **biased sample**, one or more parts of the population are favored over others. Two ways to pick a biased sample are listed below.

Biased Samples

Concept Summary

Type	Description	Example
Convenience Sample	A convenience sample includes members of a population who are easily accessed.	To represent all the students attending a school, the principal surveys the students in one math class.
Voluntary Response Sample	A voluntary response sample involves only those who want to participate in the sampling.	Students at a school who wish to express their opinion are asked to complete an online survey.

EXAMPLES Determine Validity of Conclusions

Determine whether each conclusion is valid. Justify your answer.

1 **To determine what kind of movies people like to watch, every tenth person who walks into a video rental store is surveyed. The store carries all kinds of movies. Out of 180 customers surveyed, 62 stated that they prefer action movies. The store manager concludes that about a third of all customers prefer action movies.**

The conclusion is valid. Since the population is every tenth customer of a video rental store, the sample is an unbiased random sample.

2 **A television program asks its viewers to visit a Web site to indicate their preference for two presidential candidates. 76% of the viewers who responded preferred candidate A, so the television program announced that most people prefer candidate A.**

The conclusion is not valid. The population is restricted to viewers who have Internet access, it is a voluntary response sample, and is biased. The results of a voluntary response sample do not necessarily represent the entire population.

CHECK Your Progress

Determine whether each conclusion is valid. Justify your answer.

a. To determine what people like to do in their leisure time, people at a local mall are surveyed. Of these, 82% said they like to shop. The mall manager concludes that most people like to shop during their leisure time.

b. To determine what kind of sport junior high school students like to watch, 100 students are randomly selected from each of four junior high schools in a city. Of these, 47% like to watch football. The superintendent concludes that about half of all junior high students like to watch football.

In Lesson 8-7, you used the results of a random sampling method to make predictions. In this lesson, you will first determine if a sampling method is valid and if so, use the results to make predictions.

Study Tip

Misleading Predictions Predictions based on biased samples can be misleading. If the students surveyed were all boys, the predictions generated by the survey would not be valid, since both girls and boys attend the junior high school.

Real-World EXAMPLE

3 **MASCOTS** **The Student Council at a new junior high school surveyed 5 students from each of the 10 homerooms to determine what mascot students would prefer. The results of the survey are shown at the right. If there are 375 students at the school, predict how many students prefer a tiger as the school mascot.**

Mascot	Number
Tornadoes	15
Tigers	28
Twins	7

The sample is an unbiased random sample since students were randomly selected. Thus, the sample is valid.

$\frac{28}{50}$ or 56% of the students prefer a tiger. So, find 56% of 375.

$0.56 \times 375 = 210$ 56% of 375 = 0.56×375

So, about 210 students would prefer a tiger as the school mascot.

CHECK Your Progress

c. **AIRLINES** During flight, a pilot determined that 20% of the passengers were traveling for business and 80% were traveling for pleasure. If there are 120 passengers on the next flight, how many can be expected to be traveling for pleasure?

CHECK Your Understanding

Examples 1, 2 (p. 439)

Determine whether each conclusion is valid. Justify your answer.

1. To determine the number of umbrellas the average household in the United States owns, a survey of 100 randomly selected households in Arizona is conducted. Of the households, 24 said that they own 3 or more umbrellas. The researcher concluded that 24% of the households in the United States own 3 or more umbrellas.

2. A researcher randomly surveys ten employees from each floor of a large company to determine the number of employees who carpool to work. Of these, 31% said that they carpool. The researcher concludes that most employees do not carpool.

Example 3 (p. 440)

3. **LUNCH** Jared randomly surveyed some students to determine their lunch habits. The results are shown in the table. If there are 268 students in the school, predict how many bring their lunch from home.

Lunch Habit	Number
Bring Lunch from Home	19
Buy Lunch in the Cafeteria	27
Other	4

Practice and Problem Solving

HOMEWORK HELP	
For Exercises	See Examples
4–9	1, 2
10, 11	3

Determine whether each conclusion is valid. Justify your answer.

4. The principal of a high school randomly selects 50 students to participate in a school improvement survey. Of these, 38 said that more world language courses should be offered. As a result, the principal decides to offer both Japanese and Italian language classes.

5. To evaluate their product, the manufacturer of light bulbs inspects the first 50 light bulbs produced on one day. Of these, 2 are defective. The manufacturer concludes that about 4% of light bulbs produced are defective.

6. To evaluate its service, a restaurant asks its customers to call a number and complete a telephone survey. The majority of those who replied said that they prefer broccoli instead of carrots as the vegetable side dish. As a result, the restaurant decides to offer broccoli instead of carrots.

7. To determine which type of pet is preferred by most customers, the manager of a pet store surveys every 15th customer that enters the store.

8. To determine which school dance theme most students favor, 20 students from each grade level at Lakewood Middle School are surveyed. The results are shown in the table. Based on these results, the student council decides that the dance theme should be *Unforgettable*.

Theme	Number
Starry Night	23
Unforgettable	26
At the Hop	11

9. To determine whether 15 boxes of porcelain tea sets have not been cracked during shipping, the owner of an antique store examines the first two boxes. None of the tea sets have been cracked, so the owner concludes that none of the tea sets in the remaining boxes are cracked.

10. **LAWNS** A researcher randomly surveyed 100 households in a small community to determine the number of households that use a professional lawn service. Of these, 27% of households use a professional lawn service. If there are 786 households in the community, how many can be expected to use a professional lawn service?

Real-World Link There are more than 600 shapes of pasta produced worldwide.

11. **PASTA** A grocery store asked every 20th person entering the store what kind of pasta they preferred. The results are shown in the table. If the store decides to restock their shelves with 450 boxes of pasta, how many boxes of lasagna should they order?

Pasta	Number
Macaroni	38
Spaghetti	56
Rigatoni	12
Lasagna	44

12. **FURNITURE** The manager of a furniture store asks the first 25 customers who enter the store if they prefer dining room tables made of oak, cherry, or mahogany wood. Of these, 17 said they prefer cherry. If the store manager orders 80 dining room tables in the next shipment, how many should be made of cherry wood?

13. **RADIO** A radio station asks its listeners to dial one of two numbers to indicate their preference for one of two candidates in an upcoming election. Of the responses received, 76% favored candidate A. If there are 1,500 registered voters, how many will vote for candidate A?

14. **HOBBIES** Pedro wants to conduct a survey about the kinds of hobbies that sixth graders enjoy. Describe a valid sampling method he could use.

AMUSEMENT PARKS For Exercises 15 and 16,use the following information.

The manager of an amusement park mailed 2,000 survey forms to households near the park. The results of the survey are shown in the graph at the right.

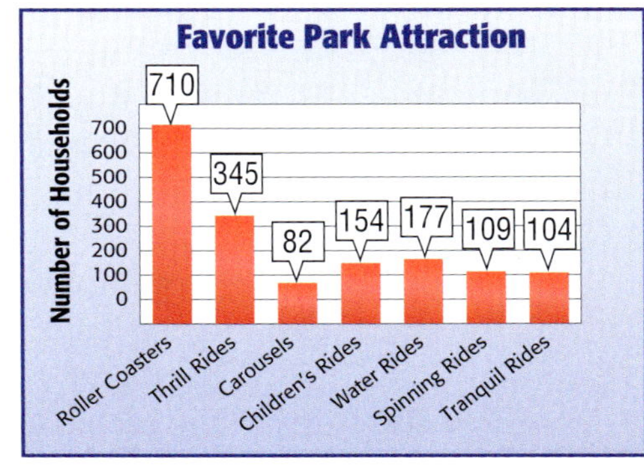

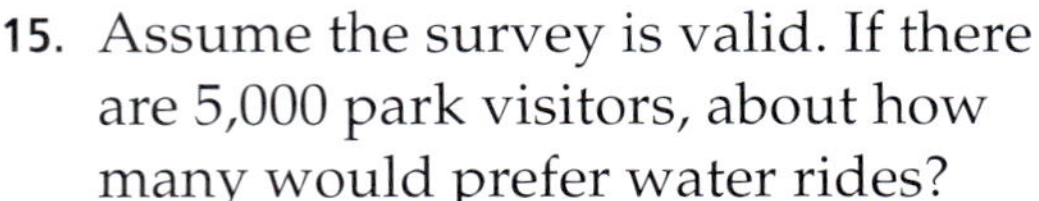

15. Assume the survey is valid. If there are 5,000 park visitors, about how many would prefer water rides?

16. Based on the survey results, the manager concludes that about 36% of park visitors prefer roller coasters. Is this a valid conclusion? Explain.

INTERNET For Exercises 17–19, use the following information.

A survey is to be conducted to find out how many hours students at a school spend on the Internet each weeknight. Describe the sample and explain why each sampling method might not be valid.

17. Ten randomly selected students from each grade level are asked to keep a log during their winter vacation.

18. Randomly selected parents are mailed a questionnaire and asked to return it.

19. A questionnaire is handed out to all students on the softball team.

COMPARE SAMPLES For Exercises 20–23, use the following information.

Suppose you were asked to determine the approximate percent of students in your school who are left-handed without surveying every student in the school.

20. Describe three different samples of the population that you could use to approximate the percent of students who are left-handed.

21. Would you expect the percent of left-handed students to be the same in each of these three samples? Explain your reasoning.

22. Describe any additional similarities and differences in your three samples.

23. You could have surveyed every student in your school to determine the percent of students who are left-handed. Describe a situation in which it makes sense to use a sample to describe aspects of a population instead of using the entire population.

See pages 701, 722.

24. **FIND THE DATA** Refer to the Data File on pages 16–19. Choose some data and write a real-world problem in which you would make a prediction based on samples.

H.O.T. Problems

25. **CHALLENGE** Is it possible to create an unbiased random sample that is also a convenience sample? Explain and cite an example, if possible.

26. **WRITING IN MATH** Explain why the way in which a survey question is asked might influence the results that are obtained. Cite at least two examples in your explanation.

TEST PRACTICE

27. Yolanda wants to conduct a survey to determine what type of salad dressing is preferred by most students at her school. Which of the following methods is the best way for her to choose a random sample of the students at her school?

 A Select students in her math class.

 B Select members of the Spanish Club.

 C Select ten students from each homeroom.

 D Select members of the girls basketball team.

28. The manager of a zoo wanted to know which animals are most popular among visitors. She surveyed every 10th visitor to the reptile exhibit. Of these, she found that 75% like snakes. If there are 860 visitors to the zoo, which of the following claims is valid?

 F About 645 zoo visitors like snakes.

 G The reptile exhibit is the most popular exhibit.

 H 25% of zoo visitors prefer mammals.

 J No valid prediction can be made since the sample is a convenience sample.

Spiral Review

29. **SCHOOL** In a survey of 120 randomly selected students at Jefferson Middle School, 34% stated that science was their favorite class. Predict how many of the 858 students in the school would choose science as their favorite class. (Lesson 8-7)

30. **HEALTH** Use the scatter plot at the right to predict the height of a 16-year-old. (Lesson 8-6)

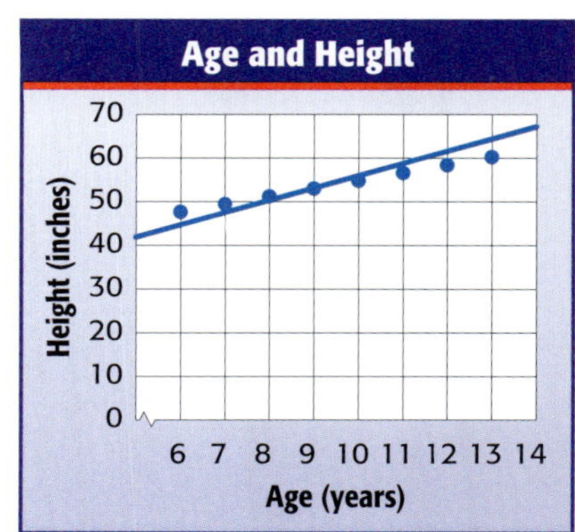

31. **SHOPPING** Nora bought a pair of running shoes that was discounted 35%. If the original price of the shoes was $89.90, find the discounted price to the nearest cent. (Lesson 7-7)

Write each percent as a fraction in simplest form. (Lesson 6-9)

32. 17%

33. 62.5%

34. 12.8%

GET READY for the Next Lesson

PREREQUISITE SKILL **Determine whether each statement is *true* or *false*.** (Lesson 8-6)

35. The vertical scale on a line graph must have equal intervals.

36. You do not need to label the axes of a line graph.

8-9 Misleading Statistics

MAIN IDEA

Recognize when statistics and graphs are misleading.

Math Online

glencoe.com

- Extra Examples
- Personal Tutor
- Self-Check Quiz

GET READY for the Lesson

HOCKEY The graph shows the all-time Stanley Cup playoff leaders.

1. According to the size of the hockey players, how many times more points does Mark Messier appear to have than Jari Kurri? Explain.
2. Do you think this graph is representative of the players' number of points?

Source: *ESPN Sports Almanac*

Graphs let readers analyze and interpret data easily, but are sometimes drawn to influence conclusions by misrepresenting the data. The use of different scales can influence conclusions drawn from graphs.

EXAMPLE Changing the Interval of Graphs

1 **SCHOOL DANCES** **The graphs show how the price of spring dance tickets increased.**

Graph A

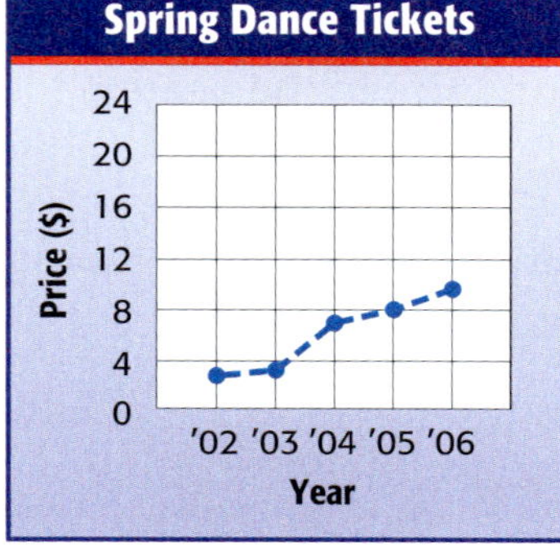

Graph B

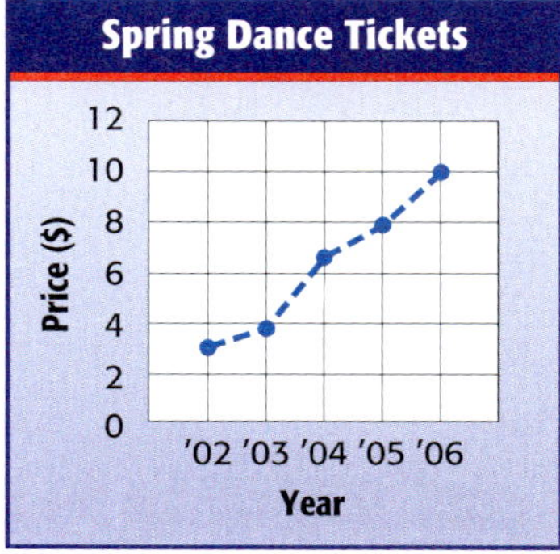

Do the graphs show the same data? If so, explain how they differ.
The graphs show the same data. However, the graphs differ in that Graph A uses an interval of 4, and Graph B uses an interval of 2.

Which graph makes it appear that the prices increased more rapidly? Graph B makes it appear that the prices increased more rapidly even though the price increase is the same.

Which graph might Student Council use to show that while ticket prices have risen, the increase is not significant? Explain. They might use Graph A. The scale used on the vertical axis of this graph makes the increase appear less significant.

CHECK Your Progress

a. **BUSINESS** The line graphs show monthly profits of a company from October to March. Which graph suggests that the business is extremely profitable? Is this a valid conclusion? Explain.

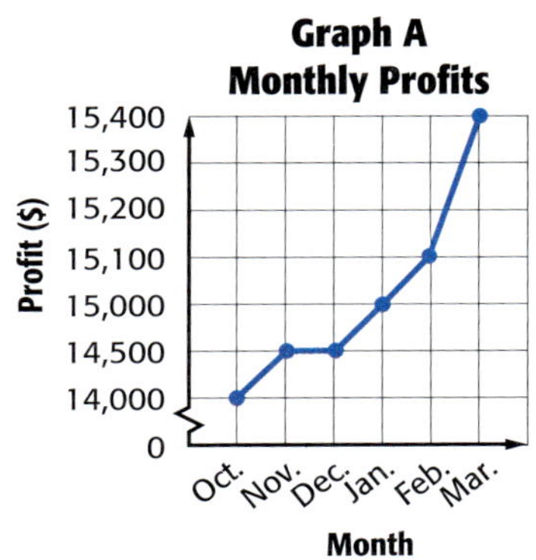

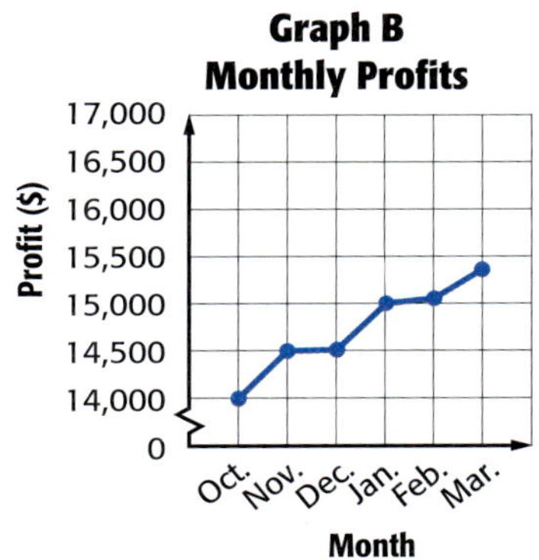

Study Tip

Changing Scales To emphasize a change over time, reduce the scale interval on the vertical axis.

Sometimes the data used to create the display comes from a biased sample. In these cases, the data and the display are both biased and should be considered invalid.

EXAMPLE Identify Biased Displays

2 **FITNESS** **The president of a large company mailed a survey to 500 of his employees in order to determine if they use the fitness room at work. The results are shown in the graph. Identify any sampling errors and explain why the sample and the display might be biased.**

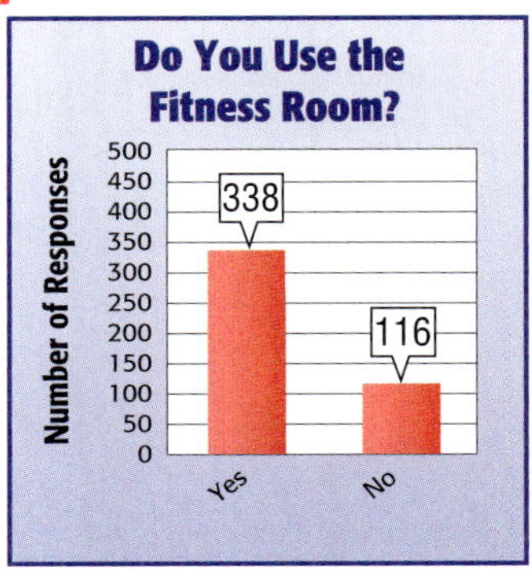

Not all of the surveys were returned since $338 + 116 < 500$. This is a biased, voluntary response sample. The sample is not representative of the entire population since only those who wanted to participate in the survey are involved in the sampling.

The display is biased because the data used to create the display came from a biased sample.

b. MOVIES The manager of a movie theater asked 100 of his customers what they like to do on a Saturday night. The results are shown in the graph. Identify any sampling errors and explain why the sample and the display might be biased.

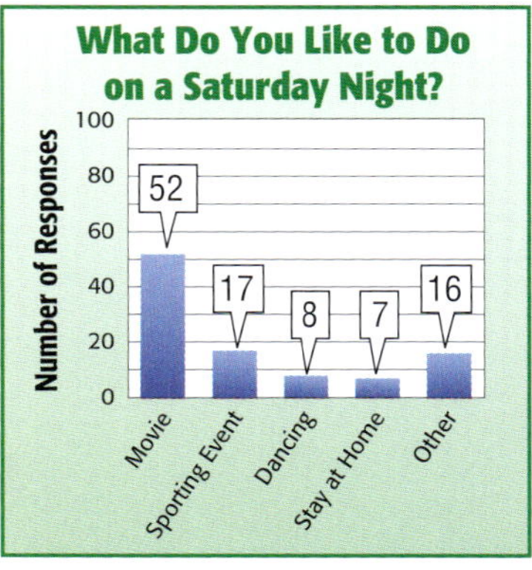

Statistics can also be used to influence conclusions.

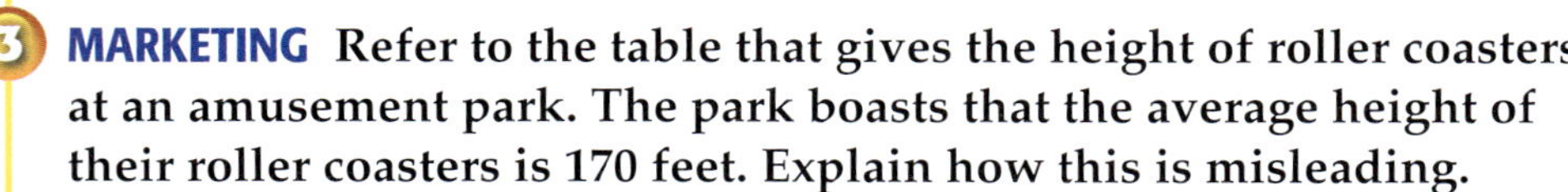

3 MARKETING Refer to the table that gives the height of roller coasters at an amusement park. The park boasts that the average height of their roller coasters is 170 feet. Explain how this is misleading.

Real-World Link The tallest roller coaster in the world is the Kingda Ka in Jackson, New Jersey, with a height of 456 feet.
Source: Ultimate Roller Coaster

Park Roller Coaster Heights	
Coaster	**Height (ft)**
Viper	109
Monster	135
Red Zip	115
Tornado	365
Riptide	126

mean: $\frac{109 + 135 + 115 + 365 + 126}{5} = \frac{850}{5}$
$= 170$

median: 109, 115, 126, 135, 365

mode: none

The average used by the park was the mean. This measure is much greater than most of the heights listed because of the outlier, 365 feet. So, it is misleading to use this measure to attract visitors.

A more appropriate measure to describe the data would be the median, 126 feet, which is closer to the height of most of the coasters.

CHECK Your Progress

c. FOOD A restaurant claims its average menu price is $3.50. Use the table to explain how this is misleading.

Menu	
Burger	$4.00
Fish Sandwich	$4.45
Chicken Sandwich	$4.35
Garden Salad	$3.90
Coffee	$0.80

Example 1 (pp. 444–445)

1. **BASEBALL** Refer to the graphs below. Which graph suggests that Cy Young had three times as many wins as Jim Galvin? Is this a valid conclusion? Explain.

Graph A

Most Career Wins by a Pitcher
Pitchers: Cy Young, Walter Johnson, Grover Alexander, Christy Mathewson, Jim Gavin
Wins: 0, 200, 400, 600

Graph B

Most Career Wins by a Pitcher
Pitchers: Cy Young, Walter Johnson, Grover Alexander, Christy Mathewson, Jim Gavin
Wins: 350, 400, 450, 500, 550

Example 2 (pp. 445–446)

2. **PHONES** The manager of a telephone company mailed a survey to 400 households asking each household how they prefer to pay their monthly bill. The results are shown in the graph at the right. Identify any sampling errors and explain why the sample and the display might be biased.

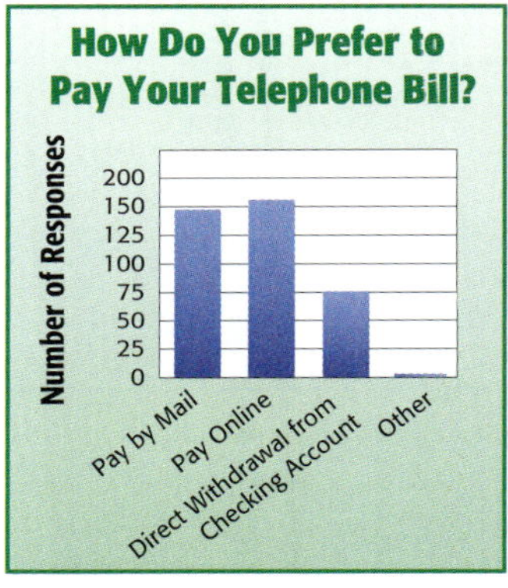

Example 3 (p. 446)

3. **TUNNELS** The table lists the five largest land vehicle tunnels in the U.S. Write a convincing argument for which measure of central tendency you would use to emphasize the average length of the tunnels.

U.S. Vehicle Tunnels on Land

Name	Length (ft)
Anton Anderson Memorial	13,300
E. Johnson Memorial	8,959
Eisenhower Memorial	8,941
Allegheny	6,072
Liberty Tubes	5,920

Practice and Problem Solving

HOMEWORK HELP

For Exercises	See Examples
4, 8	1
5, 9	2
6, 7	3

4. **GAS** The bar graph shows monthly gas prices for 2006–2007. Why is the graph misleading?

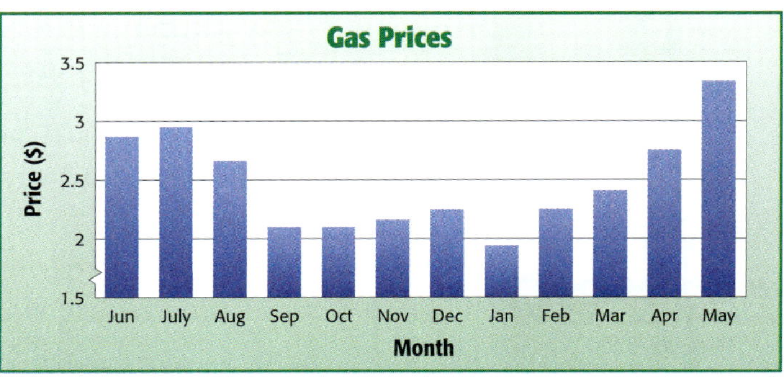

5. **SCHOOL** To determine how often his students are tardy, Mr. Kessler considered his first period class. The results are shown in the graph at the right. Identify any sampling errors and explain why the sample and the display might be biased.

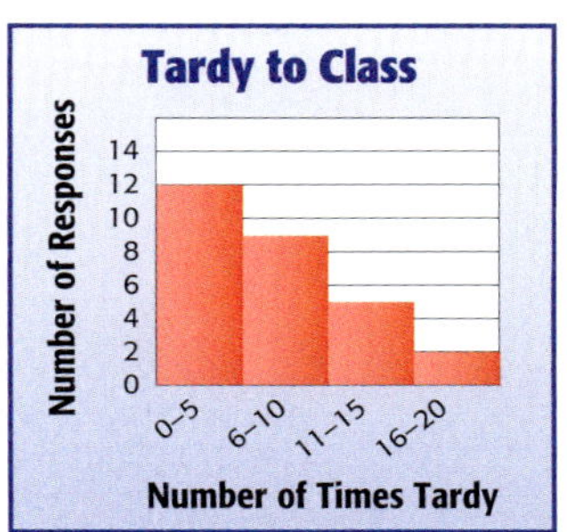

TRAVEL **For Exercises 6 and 7, use the table.**

6. Find the mean, median, and mode of the data. Which measure might be misleading in describing the average annual number of visitors who visit these sights? Explain.

7. Which measure would be best if you wanted a value close to the most number of visitors? Explain.

Annual Sight-Seeing Visitors	
Sight	**Visitors***
Cape Cod	4,600,000
Grand Canyon	4,500,000
Lincoln Memorial	4,000,000
Castle Clinton	4,600,000
Smoky Mountains	10,200,000

Source: *The World Almamac*
*Approximation

8. **STOCK** The graphs below show the increases and decreases in the monthly closing prices of Skateboard Depot's stock.

Graph A

Monthly Stock Prices
Price per Share ($): 50, 40, 30, 20, 10, 0
Month: Jan., Feb., Mar., Apr., May

Graph B

Monthly Stock Prices
Price per Share ($): 29, 28, 27, 26, 25, 0
Month: Jan., Feb., Mar., Apr., May

Suppose you are a stockbroker and want to show a customer that the price of the stock has been fairly stable since January. Write a convincing argument as to which graph you should show the customer.

9. **MANUFACTURING** To evaluate their product, the manager of an assembly line inspects the first 100 batteries that are produced out of 30,000 total batteries produced that day. He displays the results in the graph at the right and then releases it to the local newspaper. Identify any sampling errors and explain why the sample and the display might be biased.

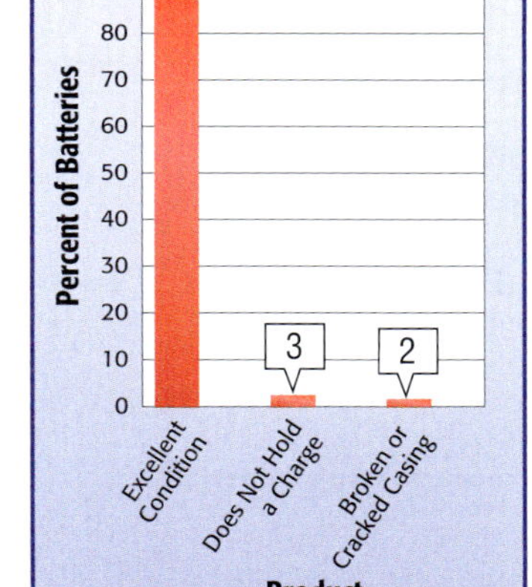

APARTMENTS **For Exercises 10 and 11, create a display that would support each argument given the monthly costs to rent an apartment for the last five years are \$500, \$525, \$560, \$585, and \$605.**

10. Rent has remained fairly stable.

11. Rent has increased dramatically.

H.O.T. Problems

12. **CHALLENGE** Does adding values that are much greater or much less than the other values in a set of data affect the median of the set? Give an example to support your answer.

13. **WRITING IN MATH** Describe at least two ways in which the display of data can influence the conclusions reached.

14. The bar graph shows the average number of hours each week that a group of students attend an extracurricular activity after school.

Time Spent on Extracurricular Activities

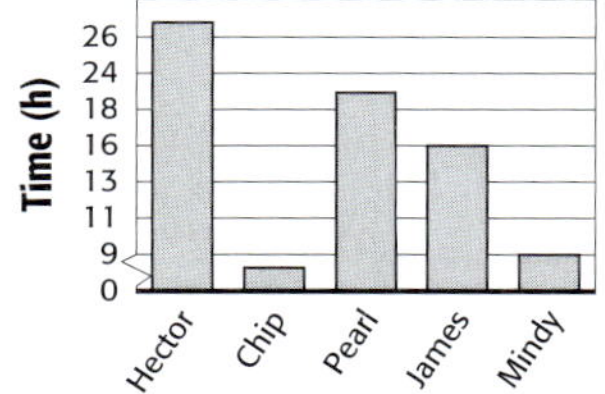

Which statement best tells why the graph may be misleading if you want to use the graph to compare the number of hours the students attend an extracurricular activity?

A The vertical scale should show days instead of hours.

B The graph does not show which activity each person attended.

C The intervals on the vertical scale are inconsistent.

D The graph's title is misleading.

15. A department store mailed 100 surveys to teenagers about their preferred style of jeans. The graph shows the results.

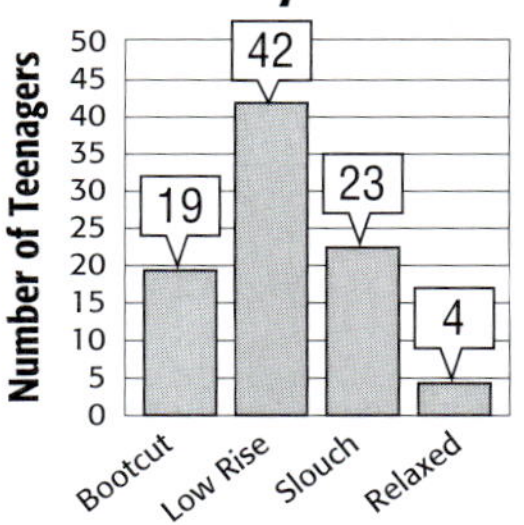

Which of the following is true concerning the sample and the display?

F Both the display and the sample are unbiased.

G The display is biased because the sample is a biased, voluntary response sample.

H The display is biased because the sample is a biased, convenience sample.

J The sample is biased but the display is unbiased.

Spiral Review

16. **CARS** To determine what kind of automobile is preferred by most customers, the owner of an auto dealership surveys every 10th person who enters the dealership. Of these, 54% state that they prefer 4-door sedans. Based on these results, if the dealership stocks 150 cars, about how many of them should be 4-door sedans? (Lesson 8-8)

17. **MP3 PLAYERS** In a survey, 46% of randomly selected teens said they own an MP3 player. Predict how many of the 850 teens at Harvey Middle School own an MP3 player. (Lesson 8-7)

Chapter 8 Study Guide and Review

Math Online glencoe.com
- STUDY TO GO
- Vocabulary Review

GET READY to Study

Be sure the following Big Ideas are noted in your Foldable.

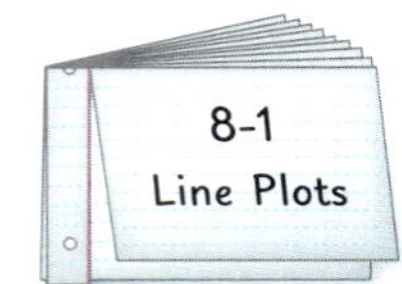

BIG Ideas

Mean, Median, and Mode (Lesson 8-2)
- The mean of a set of data is the sum of the data divided by the number of items in the set.
- The median of a set of data is the middle number of the ordered data if there is an odd number of values, or the mean of the middle two numbers if there is an even number of values.
- The mode of a set of data is the number or numbers that occur most often. If there are two or more numbers that occur most often, all of them are modes.

Statistical Displays (Lessons 8-1, 8-3 through 8-9)
- Line plots show how many times each number occurs in a data set.
- Stem-and-leaf plots list all individual numerical data in a condensed form.
- Bar graphs show the data in specific categories.
- Histograms show the frequency of data divided into smaller intervals.
- Circle graphs compare data parts to the whole.
- Line graphs show change over a period of time.
- Scatter plots determine if there is a relationship between two sets of data.

Sampling Methods (Lesson 8-8)
- In a random sample, each item or person in the population is as likely to be chosen as any other.
- A convenience sample includes members of a population who are easily accessed.
- A voluntary response sample involves only those who want to participate in the sampling.

Key Vocabulary

analyze (p. 397)
bar graph (p. 415)
cluster (p. 397)
convenience sample (p. 439)
data (p. 396)
histogram (p. 416)
leaf (p. 410)
line graph (p. 426)
line plot (p. 396)
mean (p. 402)
measures of central tendency (p. 402)
median (p. 403)
mode (p. 403)
outlier (p. 397)
random sample (p. 438)
range (p. 397)
scatter plot (p. 427)
statistics (p. 396)
stem (p. 410)
stem-and-leaf plot (p. 410)
voluntary response sample (p. 439)

Vocabulary Check

State whether each sentence is *true* or *false*. If *false*, replace the underlined word or number to make a true sentence.

1. The range is the difference between the greatest and the least values in a set of data.
2. The mode divides a set of data in half.
3. A graph that uses bars to make comparisons is a bar graph.
4. A scatter plot shows two sets of related data.
5. The median is a data value that is quite separated from the rest of the data.
6. The mean is the arithmetic average of a set of data.
7. The number or item that appears most often in a set of data is the mode.
8. The range is the middle number of the ordered data, or the mean of the middle two numbers.

Lesson-by-Lesson Review

8-1 Line Plots (pp. 396–401)

Display each set of data in a line plot. Identify any clusters, gaps, or outliers.

9. 10°, 12°, 10°, 8°, 13°, 10°, 8°, 12°.
10. 7 ft, 8 ft, 8 ft , 9 ft, 14 ft, 9 ft, 8 ft, 7 ft
11. Number of Calories: 43, 41, 42, 45, 43, 42, 43, 46, 44, 44

Example 1 **Display the test scores 72, 75, 72, 74, 73, 68, 73, 74, 74, 75, and 73 in a line plot. Identify any clusters, gaps, or outliers.**

Test Scores

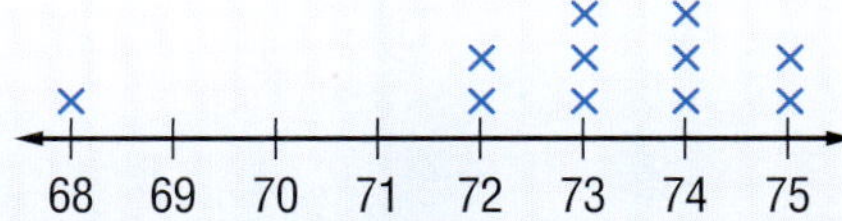

There is a cluster from 72 to 75, a gap between 68 and 72, and an outlier at 68.

8-2 Measures of Central Tendency and Range (pp. 402–408)

Find the mean, median, and mode. Round to the nearest tenth if necessary.

12. Number of siblings: 2, 3, 4, 3, 4, 3, 8, 7, 2
13. 89°, 76°, 93°, 100°, 72°, 86°, 74°
14. **MONEY** Which measure, mean, median, mode, or range best represents the amount of money students spent on clothing?

Money Spent ($)			
125	108	172	136
121	112	218	172

Example 2 **Find the mean, median, and mode for the following college students' ages: 23, 22, 19, 19, and 20.**

mean: $\frac{23 + 22 + 19 + 19 + 20}{5}$ or 20.6 years

median: 20, the middle value of the ordered set

mode: 19, the data value that occurs most often

8-3 Stem-and-Leaf Plots (pp. 410–414)

Display each set of data using a stem-and-leaf plot.

15. Hours worked: 29, 54, 31, 26, 38, 46, 23, 21, 32, 37
16. Number of points: 75, 83, 78, 85, 87, 92, 78, 53, 87, 89, 91
17. Birth dates: 9, 5, 12, 21, 18, 7, 16, 24, 11, 10, 3, 14

Example 3 **Display the number of pages read 12, 15, 17, 20, 22, 22, 23, 25, 27, and 35 in a stem-and-leaf plot.**

The tens digits form the stems, and the ones digits form the leaves.

Pages Read

Stem	Leaf
1	2 5 7
2	0 2 2 3 5 7
3	5

2|3 = 23 pages

Study Guide and Review

8-4 Bar Graphs and Histograms (pp. 415–421)

ATTENDANCE For Exercises 18–20, refer to the graph.

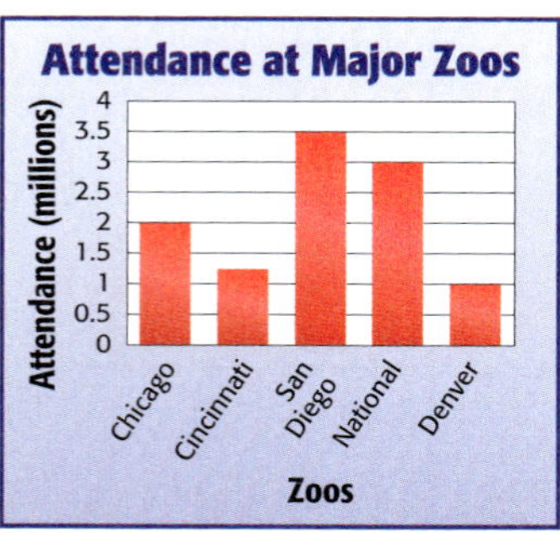

18. Which zoo did the most people attend?
19. About what was the total attendance for all five zoos?
20. Write a statement comparing the attendance at the National Zoo to the attendance at the Denver Zoo.

Example 4 The graph shows the number of bordering states for each of the fifty states.

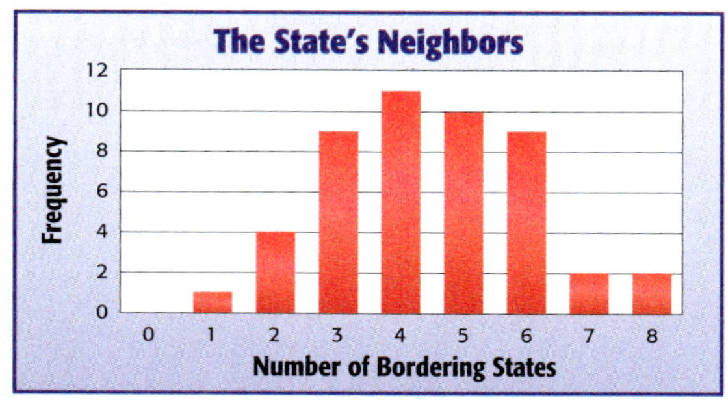

What is the greatest number of states that border any state?

8 states

How many states are bordered by 6 states?

9 states

8-5 PSI: Use a Graph (pp. 424–425)

STATUES For Exercises 21 and 22, use the graph that shows the heights of free-standing statues in the world.

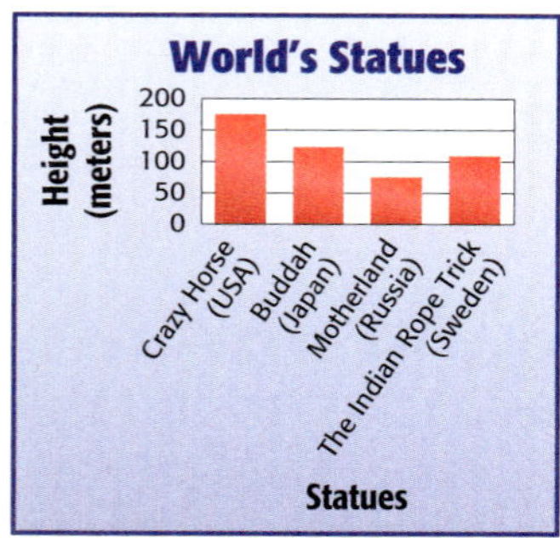

21. Which statue is the tallest?
22. Compare the height of the Motherland statue to the height of the Crazy Horse statue.

Example 5 The graph shows the results of a survey about favorite vacation places.

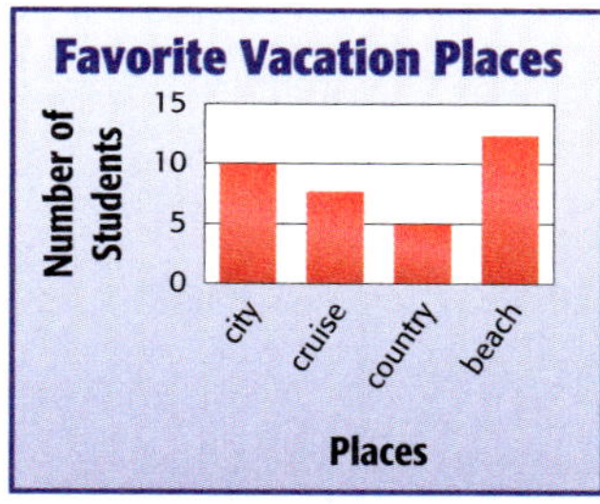

Which place was favored by most students?

The beach was favored by 12 students, which was the greatest number.

Mixed Problem Solving
For mixed problem-solving practice, see page 711.

8-6 Using Graphs to Predict (pp. 426–431)

PHONE CALLS For Exercises 23 and 24, use the graph showing the number of people in a family and the number of weekly calls.

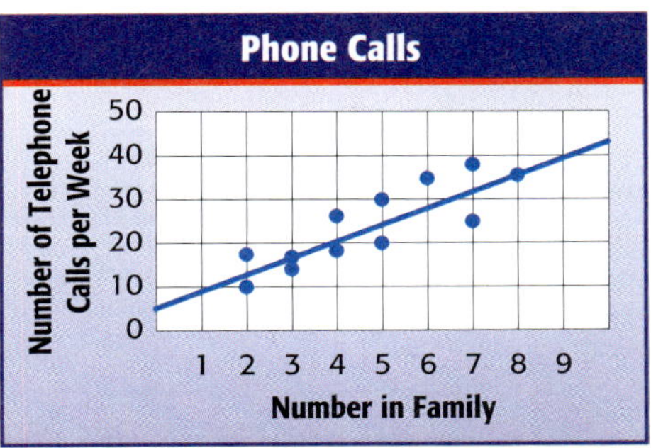

23. Describe the relationship between the two sets of data.
24. Predict the number of weekly phone calls for a family of 10.

Example 6 The scatter plot below shows the keyboarding speeds in words per minute of 12 students.

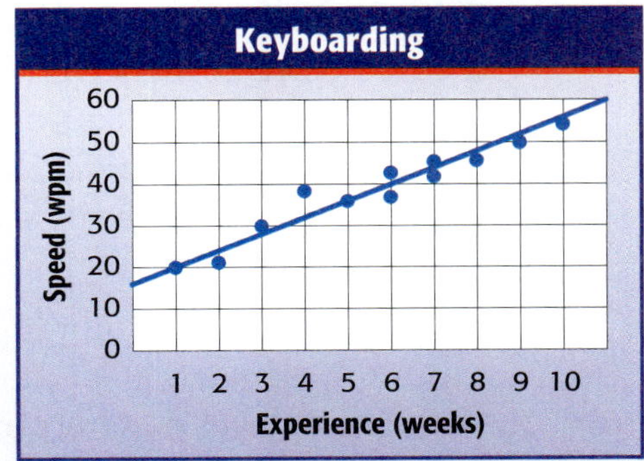

Describe the relationship between the two sets of data.

The graph shows a positive relationship. That is, as the weeks pass, speed increases.

8-7 Using Data to Predict (pp. 434–437)

CAREERS For Exercises 25 and 26, use the table that shows the results of a university survey of incoming freshmen.

Career Goal	Percent
Elementary teacher	5.5%
Engineer	6.4%

25. Predict how many of the 3,775 freshmen would choose a career as an elementary teacher.
26. How many of the 3,775 freshmen would you expect to choose a career as an engineer?
27. **SHOES** A survey showed that 72% of teens bought new athletic shoes for the new school year. Based on that survey, how many teens in group of 225 bought new athletic shoes for the new school year?

Example 7 The circle graph shows the results of a survey to which 150 students at McAuliffe Middle School responded. Predict how many of the 644 students at the school have after-school jobs.

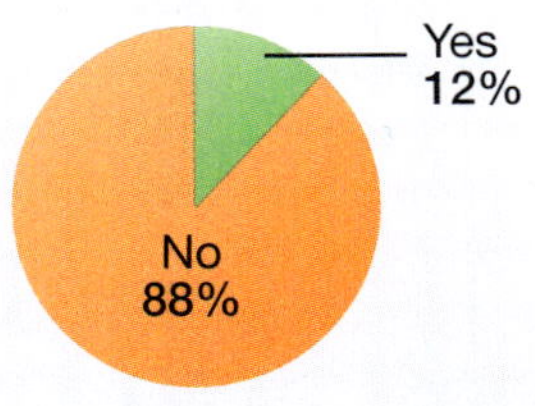

Find 12% of 644.

$n = 0.12 \cdot 644$ Write an equation.

$= 77.28$ Multiply.

So, you could predict that about 77 students at McAuliffe Middle School have after-school jobs.

Study Guide and Review

8-8 Using Sampling to Predict (pp. 438–443)

Determine whether each conclusion is valid. Justify your answer.

28. To determine the number of vegetarians in a city, a restaurant owner surveys the first 50 customers who enter the restaurant. Of these, 6 said they are vegetarians, so the owner concludes that about 12% of the city's population are vegetarians.
29. The principal of a junior high school randomly surveys 40 students from each grade level to determine how many students are interested in after-school tutoring. Of these, 88% are interested, so the principal decides to offer after-school tutoring.
30. **BOOKS** The owner of a bookstore surveyed every 10th person that entered the store to determine her customers' preferred type of book. Of these, 32% preferred mysteries. If the owner will order 500 new books, about how many should be mysteries?

Example 8 **To determine the preference of her customers, a florist mails surveys to 100 of her customers. The results are shown in the table. Based on these results, the florist decides to stock more roses.**

Type of Flower	Number
Roses	45
Tulips	26
Lilacs	17

This conclusion is invalid. This is a biased voluntary response sample. Not all surveys were returned.

8-9 Misleading Statistics (pp. 444–449)

31. **UTILITIES** The line graph shows the monthly electric bill for the condominium that Toshiko is interested in renting. Why is the graph misleading?

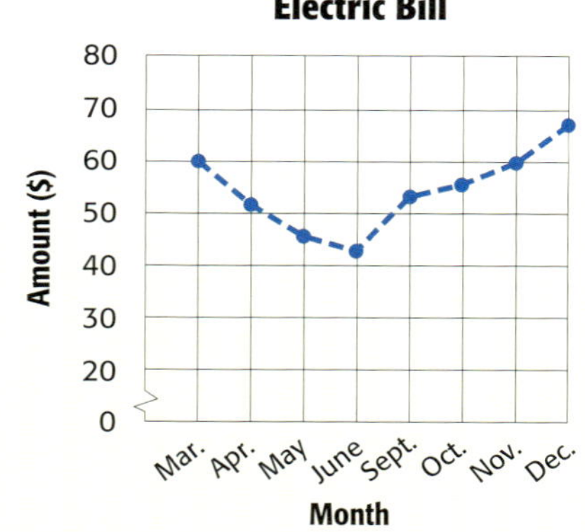

Example 9 **The graph shows the number of motorcycles produced in each decade. Why might this graph be misleading?**

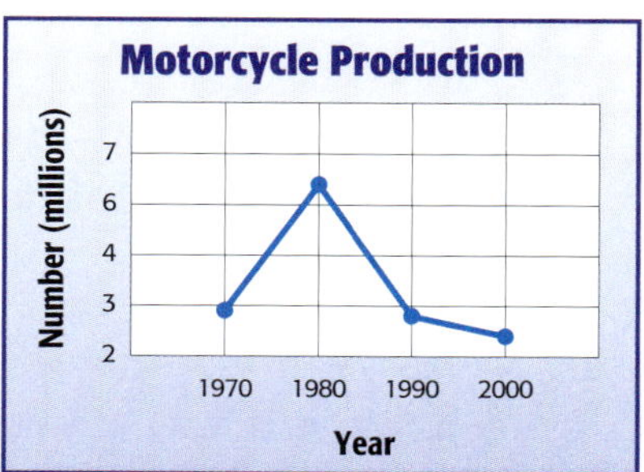

The scale does not start at zero and does not increase by the same amount each time.

CHAPTER 8 Practice Test

Math Online glencoe.com
• Chapter Test

For Exercises 1 and 2, use the line plot that shows the number of hours students spend listening to the radio per week.

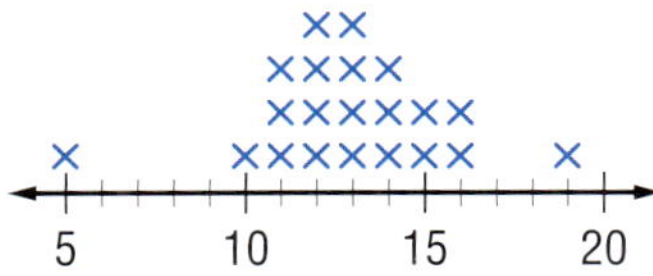

1. Identify any clusters, gaps, or outliers.
2. Describe how the range of data would change if 5 was not part of the data set.
3. **INSECTS** The lengths in inches of several insects are given below. Find the mean, median, and mode of the data set. Round to the nearest tenth if necessary.

   0.75, 1.24, 0.95, 2.6, 1.18, 1.3

Display each data set in a stem-and-leaf plot.

4. 37°, 59°, 26°, 42°, 57°, 53°, 31°, 58°
5. \$461, \$422, \$430, \$425, \$425, \$467, \$429
6. **MULTIPLE CHOICE** Refer to the data below. Which of the following statements is true concerning the measures of central tendency?

   41, 45, 42, 38, 77, 44, 36, 43

   A The mode is most affected by the inclusion of the outlier.
   B The median is not affected by the inclusion of the outlier.
   C The mean is most affected by the inclusion of the outlier.
   D None of the measures of central tendency are affected by the inclusion of the outlier.

7. **GRADES** Make a histogram for the following French test grades: 95, 76, 82, 90, 83, 76, 79, 82, 95, 85, 93, 81, and 63.
8. **EMPLOYMENT** The line graph shows the percent of women who had jobs outside the home from 1975 to 2000. Use the graph to predict the number of women who will have jobs outside the home in 2010.

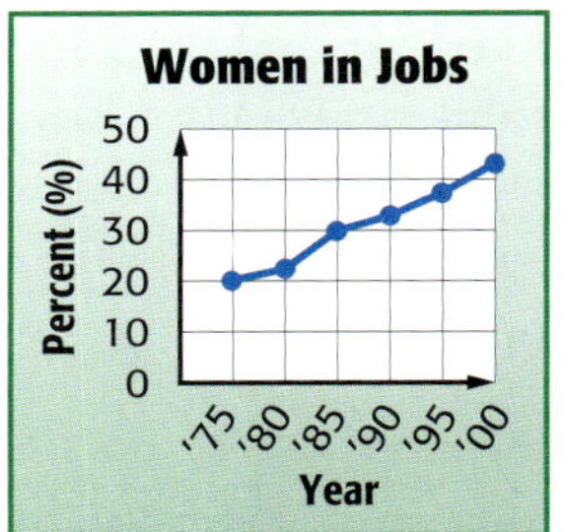

9. **AMUSEMENT PARKS** A researcher asked 250 students at Lake Valley Middle School to dial one of four telephone numbers to indicate their preference for the type of amusement park rides that they enjoy. Of these, 19% said they prefer the Ferris wheel. The researcher concludes that about $\frac{1}{5}$ of the students prefer the Ferris wheel. Is the conclusion valid?
10. **MULTIPLE CHOICE** The line graph shows ship sales at Marvin's Marina in thousands of dollars. Which of the following statements best tells why the graph is misleading?

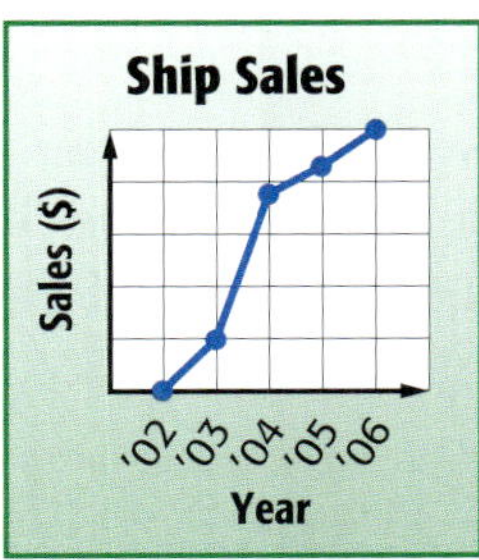

   F The graph's title is misleading.
   G The intervals on the horizontal scale are inconsistent.
   H The graph does not show any data.
   J The vertical axis is not labeled.

Chapter 8 Test Practice
Cumulative, Chapters 1–8

Math Online glencoe.com
• Test Practice

PART 1 Multiple Choice

Read each question. Then fill in the correct answer on the answer sheet provided by your teacher or on a sheet of paper.

1. Ed's Used Car Lot bought 5 used cars for \$32,000. The business later bought another used car for \$4,600. What was the mean cost of all of the used cars?

   A \$3,200.00 C \$6,100.00
   B \$4,600.00 D \$8,500.00

2. A fitness club charges a membership fee of \$50 plus \$25 each month you belong to the club. Which expression could be used to find the total cost of belonging to the club for 10 months?

   F $50(10) + 25$
   G $50 - 25(10)$
   H $50 + 25(10)$
   J $50(10) + 25(10)$

3. Sierra has 11.5 yards of fabric. She will use 20% of the fabric to make a flag. How many yards of fabric will she use?

   A 9.2 yd C 4.5 yd
   B 8.6 yd D 2.3 yd

4. Ms. Thompson made 17 liters of punch for a party. The punch contained 5 liters of orange juice. Which equation could be used to find y, the percent of orange juice in the punch?

   F $\frac{17}{5} = \frac{y}{100}$
   G $\frac{5}{17} = \frac{y}{100}$
   H $\frac{5}{17} = \frac{100}{y}$
   J $\frac{17}{y} = \frac{100}{5}$

5. The number of students in each grade level at Hampton Middle School is shown in the graph below.

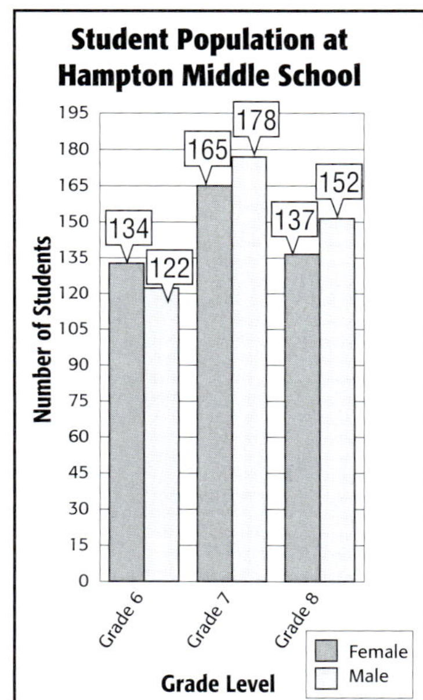

Which statement is true based on this information?

   A There are more total students in the 6th grade than there are in the 8th grade.
   B The female 7th graders outnumber the male 8th graders.
   C The student population decreases by the same amount as each grade level increases.
   D There are more female students in each grade level than male students.

6. A football team scored 20, 32, 28, 21, and 24 points in their first five games. How many points should they score in the next game so that the median and mode scores are equal?

   F 32 H 21
   G 24 J 20

Preparing for Standardized Tests

For test-taking strategies and practice, see pages 716–733.

7. Regina priced six MP3 players. The prices are shown below.

$120.00, $90.00, $75.00, $105.00, $85.00, $150.00

What is the median price?

A $90.00

B $97.50

C $104.17

D $105.00

8. Which of the following is the prime factorization of the lowest common denominator of $\frac{3}{8} + \frac{5}{6}$?

F 2×3

G $2 \times 2 \times 2$

H $2 \times 2 \times 2 \times 3$

J $2 \times 2 \times 2 \times 2 \times 3$

9. If a is a negative number and b is a negative number, which of the following expressions is always negative?

A $a + b$

B $a - b$

C $a \times b$

D $a \div b$

10. The numbers of monthly minutes Gary used on his cell phone for the last eight months are shown below.

400, 550, 450, 620, 550, 600, 475, 425

What is the mode of this data?

F 550

G 475

H 450

J 400

PART 2 Short Response/Grid In

Record your answers on the answer sheet provided by your teacher or on a sheet of paper.

11. Taylor spends between $125 and $200 per month on food. Which is the best estimate of how much she spends on food in 6 months?

12. A store has 2,545 CDs. On Saturday, the store sold $12\frac{1}{2}\%$ of the CDs. What fraction of the CDs were sold on Saturday?

PART 3 Extended Response

Record your answers on the answer sheet provided by your teacher or a sheet of paper. Show your work.

13. The table shows how values of a painting increased over ten years.

Year	Value	Year	Value
1997	$350	2002	$1,851
1998	$650	2003	$2,151
1999	$950	2004	$2,451
2000	$1,200	2005	$2,752
2001	$1,551	2006	$3,052

a. Make a line graph of the data.

b. Use the graph to predict what the value of the painting will be in 2010.

TEST-TAKING TIP

Question 13 If you find that you cannot answer every part of an open-ended question, do as much as you can. You may earn partial credit.

NEED EXTRA HELP?													
If You Missed Question...	1	2	3	4	5	6	7	8	9	10	11	12	13
Go to Lesson...	8-2	1-6	7-1	7-2	8-6	8-2	8-2	4-1	2-4	8-2	1-1	6-8	8-6

Probability

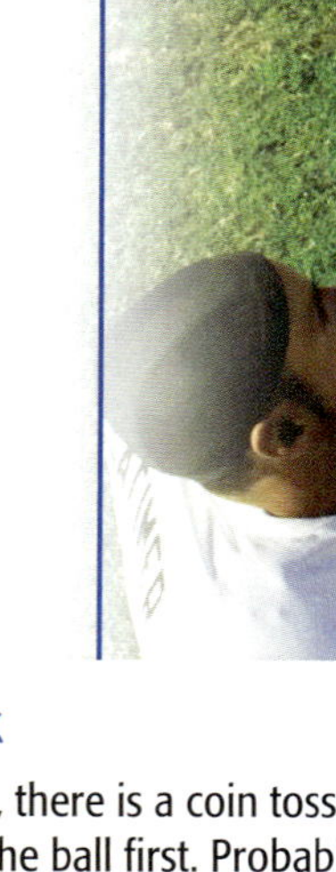

- Students use theoretical and experimental probabilities to make predictions about events.

Key Vocabulary

compound event (p. 492)
independent event (p. 492)
probability (p. 460)
sample space (p. 465)

Real-World Link

Sports Before a football game, there is a coin toss to determine which team gets the ball first. Probability tells you that each team has a 50% chance of winning the coin toss.

Probability Make this Foldable to help you organize your notes. Begin with five sheets of $8\frac{1}{2}''$ by $11''$ paper.

1. **Stack** five sheets of paper $\frac{3}{4}$ inch apart.

2. **Roll** up bottom edges so that all tabs are the same size.

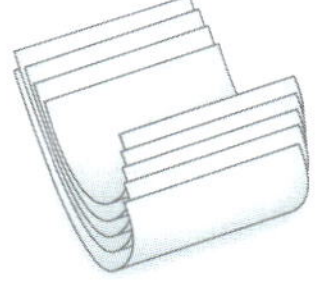

3. **Crease** and staple along the fold.

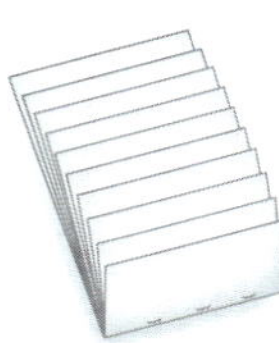

4. **Write** the chapter title on the front. Label each tab with a lesson number and title. Label the last tab *Vocabulary.*

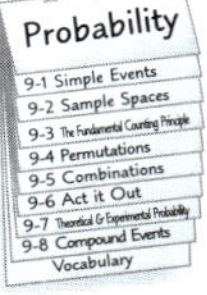

GET READY for Chapter 9

Diagnose Readiness You have two options for checking Prerequisite Skills.

Option 2

Math Online Take the Online Readiness Quiz at glencoe.com.

Option 1

Take the Quick Quiz below. Refer to the Quick Review for help.

QUICK Quiz

Multiply. (Prior Grade)

1. 7×15
2. 24×6
3. 13×4
4. 8×21
5. 5×32
6. 30×8
7. $7 \times 6 \times 5$
8. $8 \times 7 \times 6$
9. $6 \times 5 \times 4 \times 3$
10. $4 \times 3 \times 2 \times 1$
11. $10 \times 9 \times 8 \times 7$
12. $11 \times 10 \times 9$
13. **JOBS** If you earn $9 an hour and work 5 hours each day for 7 days, how much have you earned? (Prior Grade)

Write each fraction in simplest form. Write *simplified* if the fraction is already in simplest form. (Lesson 4-4)

14. $\frac{8}{12}$
15. $\frac{3}{18}$
16. $\frac{4}{9}$
17. $\frac{5}{15}$
18. **SLEEP** If the average adult gets 8 hours of sleep, what fraction of the day, in simplest form, is spent asleep? (Lesson 4-4)

Find each value. (Prior Grade)

19. $\frac{6 \times 5}{3 \times 2}$
20. $\frac{9 \times 8 \times 7}{5 \times 4 \times 3}$
21. $\frac{4 \times 3 \times 2}{3 \times 2 \times 1}$
22. $\frac{7 \times 6 \times 5 \times 4}{4 \times 3 \times 2 \times 1}$

QUICK Review

Example 1 **Multiply $7 \times 6 \times 5 \times 4$.**

$$\begin{aligned} 7 \times 6 \times 5 \times 4 &= 42 \times 5 \times 4 \\ &= 210 \times 4 \\ &= 840 \end{aligned}$$

Multiply from left to right.

Example 2 **Write $\frac{21}{28}$ in simplest form.**

$$\frac{21}{28} = \frac{3}{4} \quad (\div 7)$$

Divide the numerator and denominator by the GCF, 7.

Example 3 **Find the value of $\frac{6 \times 5 \times 4}{3 \times 2 \times 1}$.**

$$\frac{6 \times 5 \times 4}{3 \times 2 \times 1} = \frac{120}{6}$$

← Multiply the numerator.
← Multiply the denominator.

$$= 20$$

Simplify.

9-1 Simple Events

MAIN IDEA

Find the probability of a simple event.

New Vocabulary

outcome
simple event
probability
random
complementary event

Math Online

glencoe.com

- Concepts In Motion
- Extra Examples
- Personal Tutor
- Self-Check Quiz

GET READY for the Lesson

FOOD A cheesecake has four slices of each type as shown.

Cheesecake	
original	raspberry
chocolate	turtle

1. What fraction of the cheesecake is chocolate? Write in simplest form.
2. Suppose your friend gives you the first piece of cheesecake without asking which type you prefer. Are your chances of getting original the same as getting raspberry?

An **outcome** is any one of the possible results of an action. A **simple event** is one outcome or a collection of outcomes. For example, getting a piece of chocolate cheesecake is a simple event. The chance of that event happening is called its **probability**.

Probability — Key Concept

Words If all outcomes are equally likely, the probability of a simple event is a ratio that compares the number of favorable outcomes to the number of possible outcomes.

Symbols $P(\text{event}) = \dfrac{\text{number of favorable outcomes}}{\text{number of possible outcomes}}$

EXAMPLE Find Probability

1 What is the probability of rolling an even number on a number cube marked with 1, 2, 3, 4, 5, and 6 on its faces?

$$P(\text{even number}) = \frac{\text{even numbers possible}}{\text{total numbers possible}}$$
$$= \frac{3}{6} \text{ or } \frac{1}{2}$$

The probability of rolling an even number is $\frac{1}{2}$, 0.5, or 50%.

CHECK Your Progress

Use the number cube above to find each probability. Write as a fraction in simplest form.

a. P(odd number) b. P(5 or 6) c. P(prime number)

Outcomes occur at **random** if each outcome occurs by chance. For example, rolling a number on a number cube occurs at random.

Real-World EXAMPLE

2 **TALENT COMPETITION** **Simone and her three friends were deciding how to pick the song they will sing for their school's talent show. They decide to roll a number cube. The person with the lowest number chooses the song. If her friends rolled a 6, 5, and 2, what is the probability that Simone will get to choose the song?**

The possible outcomes of rolling a number cube are 1, 2, 3, 4, 5, and 6.

In order for Simone to be able to choose the song, she will need to roll a 1.

Let $P(A)$ be the probability that Simone chooses the song.

$$P(A) = \frac{\text{number of favorable outcomes}}{\text{number of possible outcomes}}$$

$$= \frac{1}{6} \quad \text{There are 6 possible outcomes, and 1 of them is favorable.}$$

The probability that Simone will choose the song is $\frac{1}{6}$, or about 17%.

Real World Link Founded in 1842, the New York Philharmonic is the oldest symphony orchestra in the United States. They have performed over 14,000 concerts.

Source: New York Philharmonic

CHECK Your Progress

MUSIC **The table shows the numbers of brass instrument players in the New York Philharmonic. Suppose one brass instrument player is randomly selected to be a featured performer. Find the probability of each event. Write as a fraction in simplest form.**

New York Philharmonic Brass Instrument Players	
Horn	6
Trombone	4
Trumpet	3
Tuba	1

Source: New York Philharmonic

d. $P(\text{trumpet})$

e. $P(\text{brass})$

f. $P(\text{flute})$

g. $P(\text{horn or tuba})$

The probability that an event will happen can be any number from 0 to 1, including 0 and 1, as shown on the number line below. Notice that probabilities can be written as fractions, decimals, or percents.

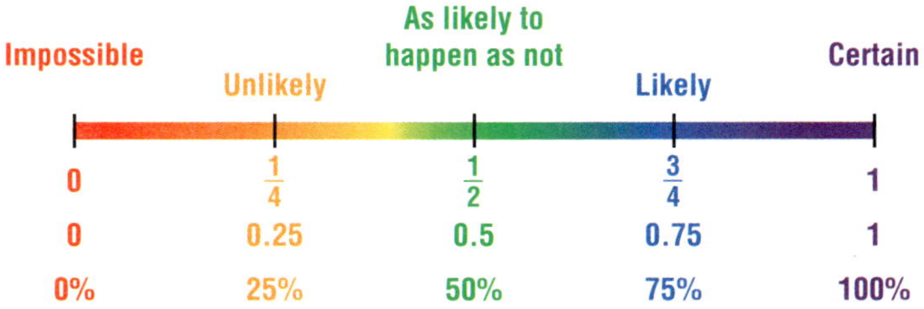

Either Simone will go first or she will *not* go first. These two events are **complementary events**. The sum of the probabilities of an event and its complement is 1 or 100%. In symbols, $P(A) + P(not\ A) = 1$.

Study Tip

Complement of an Event The probability that event A will not occur is noted as $P(not\ A)$. Since $P(A) + P(not\ A) = 1$, $P(not\ A) = 1 - P(A)$. $P(not\ A)$ is read as the probability of the complement of A.

EXAMPLE Complementary Events

3 TALENT COMPETITION Refer to Example 2. Find the probability that Simone will *not* choose the song.

The probability that Simone will *not* choose the song is the complement of the probability that Simone will choose the song.

$P(A) + P(not\ A) = 1$ — Definition of complementary events

$\frac{1}{6} + P(not\ A) = 1$ — Replace $P(A)$ with $\frac{1}{6}$.

$-\frac{1}{6} \qquad -\frac{1}{6}$ — Subtract $\frac{1}{6}$ from each side.

$P(not\ A) = \frac{5}{6}$ — $1 - \frac{1}{6}$ is $\frac{6}{6} - \frac{1}{6}$ or $\frac{5}{6}$

The probability that Simone will *not* choose the song is $\frac{5}{6}$, or about 83%.

CHECK Your Progress

SCHOOL Ramón's teacher uses a spinner similar to the one shown at the right to determine the order in which each group will make their presentation. Use the spinner to find each probability. Write as a fraction in simplest form.

h. $P(not$ group 4)

i. $P(not$ group 1 or group 3)

CHECK Your Understanding

Example 1 (p. 460)

Use the spinner to find each probability. Write as a fraction in simplest form.

1. $P(M)$
2. $P(Q$ or $R)$
3. P(vowel)

Examples 2, 3 (pp. 461–462)

MARBLES Robert has a bag that contains 7 blue, 5 purple, 12 red, and 6 orange marbles. Find each probability if he draws one marble at random from the bag. Write as a fraction in simplest form.

4. P(purple)
5. P(red or orange)
6. P(green)
7. P(*not* blue)
8. P(*not* red or orange)
9. P(*not* yellow)

Example 3 (p. 462)

10. **SURVEYS** Shanté asked her classmates how many pets they own. The responses are in the table. If a student in her class is selected at random, what is the probability that the student does *not* own 3 or more pets?

Number of Pets	Response
None	6
1–2	15
3 or more	4

Practice and Problem Solving

HOMEWORK HELP	
For Exercises	See Examples
11–14	1
17–22	2
15–16, 23–26	3

A set of 20 cards is numbered 1, 2, 3, . . ., 20. Suppose you pick a card at random without looking. Find the probability of each event. Write as a fraction in simplest form.

11. $P(1)$
12. $P(3 \text{ or } 13)$
13. $P(\text{multiple of } 3)$
14. $P(\text{even number})$
15. $P(\textit{not } 20)$
16. $P(\textit{not} \text{ a factor of } 10)$

RAFFLE **The table shows those students in seventh grade who entered in the school drawing to win lunch with the principal. Suppose that only one student is randomly selected to win. Find the probability of each event. Write as a fraction in simplest form.**

Lunch Raffle	
girls	25
boys	15
Room 10	10
Room 11	16
Room 12	14

17. $P(\text{girl})$
18. $P(\text{boy})$
19. $P(\text{Room } 12)$
20. $P(\text{Room } 10)$
21. $P(\text{girl or boy})$
22. $P(\text{Room } 11)$
23. $P(\textit{not} \text{ Room } 10)$
24. $P(\text{Room } 10 \text{ or } 11)$

25. **SOUP** A cupboard contains 20 soup cans. Seven are tomato, 4 are cream of mushroom, 5 are chicken, and 4 are vegetable. If one can is chosen at random from the cupboard, what is the probability that it is *neither* cream of mushroom *nor* vegetable soup? Write as a percent.

26. **VIDEOS** In a drawing, one name is randomly chosen from a jar of 75 names to receive free video rentals for a month. If Enola entered her name 8 times, what is the probability that she is *not* chosen to receive the free rentals? Write as a fraction in simplest form.

27. **PETS** The graph shows the last 33 types of pets that were purchased at a local pet store. Based on this, what is the probability that the next pet purchased will be a dog? Write as a fraction in simplest form.

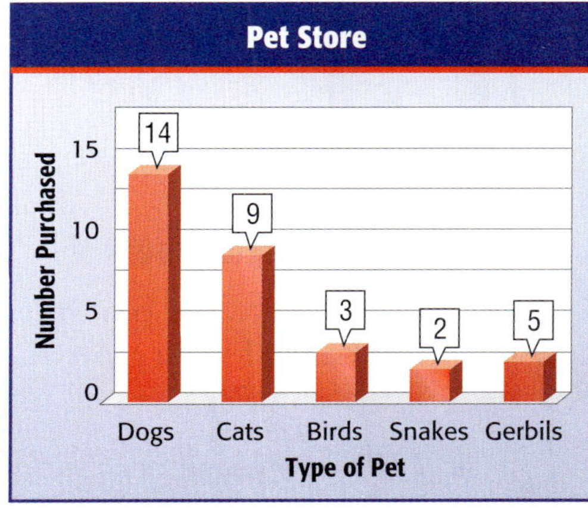

28. **GAMES** For a certain game, the probability of choosing a card with the number 13 is 0.008. What is the probability of *not* choosing card 13?

29. **WEATHER** The forecast for tomorrow says that there is a 37% chance of rain. Describe the complementary event and predict its probability.

30. **ANNOUNCEMENTS** There are 90 students in the seventh grade. Fifty-two of those students are girls. If one student will be chosen at random to read the morning announcements for the week, what is the probability that the student is a boy?

See pages 690, 712.

H.O.T. Problems

31. **REASONING** A *leap year* has 366 days and occurs in non-century years that are evenly divisible by 4. The extra day is added as February 29th. Determine whether each probability is 0 or 1. Explain your reasoning.

    a. P(there will be 29 days in February in 2032)

    b. P(there will be 29 days in February in 2058)

32. **CHALLENGE** A bag contains 6 red marbles, 4 blue marbles, and 8 green marbles. How many marbles of each color should be added so that the total number of marbles is 27, but the probability of randomly selecting one marble of each color remains unchanged? Explain your reasoning.

33. **Which One Doesn't Belong?** Identify the pair of probabilities that does not represent probabilities of complementary events. Explain your reasoning.

$\frac{3}{5}, \frac{2}{5}$	$0.625, \frac{3}{8}$	$\frac{6}{8}, \frac{1}{4}$	0.33, 0.44

34. **WRITING IN MATH** Marissa has 5 black T-shirts, 2 purple T-shirts, and 1 orange T-shirt. Without calculating, determine whether each of the following probabilities is reasonable if she randomly selects one T-shirt. Explain your reasoning.

    a. $P(\text{black T-shirt}) = \frac{1}{3}$ b. $P(\text{orange T-shirt}) = \frac{4}{5}$ c. $P(\text{purple T-shirt}) = \frac{1}{4}$

TEST PRACTICE

35. A bag contains 8 blue marbles, 15 red marbles, 10 yellow marbles, and 3 brown marbles. If a marble is randomly selected, what is the probability that it will be brown?

    A 0.27 C $0.08\overline{3}$

    B 11% D $\frac{3}{8}$

36. What is the probability of the spinner landing on a number less than 3?

    F 25% H 50%

    G 37.5% J 75%

Spiral Review

37. **RAIN** The scatter plot shows the relationship between rainfall and lawn growth. Why might the graph be misleading? (Lesson 8-9)

Rainfall and Lawn Growth

Height of Grass (in.)

y

0 1 2 3 4 x

Amount of Rain (in.)

38. **PARKS** A researcher randomly selected 100 households near a city park. Of these, 26% said they visit the park daily. If there are 500 households near the park, about how many visit it daily? (Lesson 8-8)

GET READY for the Next Lesson

PREREQUISITE SKILL **Write each fraction in simplest form.** (Lesson 4-4)

39. $\frac{2}{6}$ 40. $\frac{6}{8}$ 41. $\frac{15}{30}$ 42. $\frac{6}{16}$ 43. $\frac{18}{32}$

9-2 Sample Spaces

MAIN IDEA

Find sample spaces and probabilities.

New Vocabulary

sample space
tree diagram

Math Online

glencoe.com

- Extra Examples
- Personal Tutor
- Self-Check Quiz

MINI Lab

Here is a probability game for two players.

- Place two green marbles into Bag A. Place one green and one red marble into Bag B.
- Without looking, player 1 chooses a marble from each bag. If both marbles are the same color, player 1 wins a point. If the marbles are different colors, player 2 wins a point. Record your results and place the marbles back in the bag.
- Player 2 then pulls a marble from each bag and records the results. Continue alternating turns until each player has pulled from the bag 10 times. The player with the most points wins.

1. Make a conjecture. Do you think this is a fair game? Explain.
2. Now, play the game. Who won? What was the final score?

The set of all of the possible outcomes in a probability experiment is called the **sample space**. A table or grid can be used to list the outcomes in the sample space.

EXAMPLE Find the Sample Space

1 **ICE CREAM** **A vendor sells vanilla and chocolate ice cream. Customers can choose from a waffle or sugar cone and either hot fudge or caramel topping. Find the sample space for all possible orders of one scoop of ice cream in a cone with one topping.**

Make a table that shows all of the possible outcomes.

Outcomes		
Vanilla	Waffle	Hot Fudge
Vanilla	Waffle	Caramel
Vanilla	Sugar	Hot Fudge
Vanilla	Sugar	Caramel
Chocolate	Waffle	Hot Fudge
Chocolate	Waffle	Caramel
Chocolate	Sugar	Hot Fudge
Chocolate	Sugar	Caramel

CHECK Your Progress

a. **PETS** The animal shelter has both male and female Labradors in yellow, brown, or black. Find the sample space for all possible Labradors available at the shelter.

A **tree diagram** can also be used to display the sample space.

TEST EXAMPLE

2 A car comes in silver, red, or purple as a convertible or hardtop. Which list shows all possible color-top outcomes?

A

Outcomes	
silver	convertible
silver	hardtop
red	convertible
red	hardtop
purple	convertible
purple	hardtop

C

Outcomes	
silver	convertible
red	hardtop
purple	convertible
silver	hardtop
purple	convertible

B

Outcomes	
silver	convertible
red	hardtop
purple	convertible

D

Outcomes	
silver	convertible
red	hardtop
purple	convertible
silver	hardtop

Test-Taking Tip

Educated Guess Find out if there is a penalty for incorrect answers. If there is no penalty, making an educated guess can only increase your score, or at worst, leave your score the same.

Read the Item

The car comes in 3 colors: silver, red, or purple, and 2 tops: convertible or hardtop. Find all of the color-top combinations.

Solve the Item

Make a tree diagram to show the sample space.

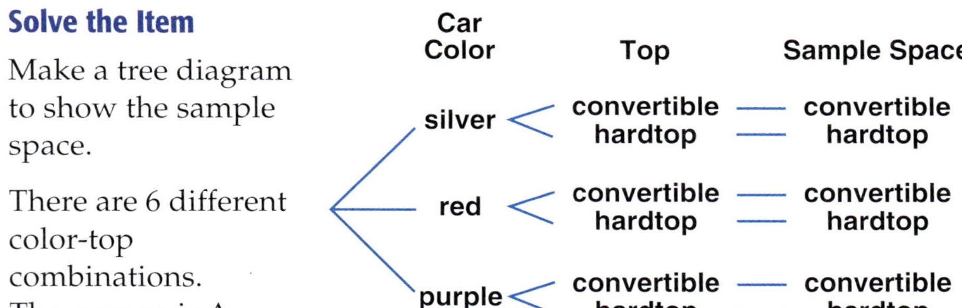

There are 6 different color-top combinations. The answer is A.

CHECK Your Progress

b. For dessert, you can have apple or cherry pie with or without ice cream. Which list shows all the possible outcomes of choosing pie and ice cream?

F

Outcomes	
apple	with ice cream
cherry	without ice cream

H

Outcomes	
apple	without ice cream
cherry	with ice cream

G

Outcomes	
apple	with ice cream
apple	without ice cream
cherry	with ice cream
cherry	without ice cream

J

Outcomes	
apple	with ice cream
cherry	with ice cream
apple	without ice cream

You can use a table or a tree diagram to find the probability of an event.

EXAMPLE Find Probability

3 GAMES Refer to the Mini Lab at the start of this lesson. Find the sample space. Then find the probability that player 2 wins.

There are 4 equally likely outcomes with 2 favoring each player. So, the probability that player 2 wins is $\frac{2}{4}$, or $\frac{1}{2}$.

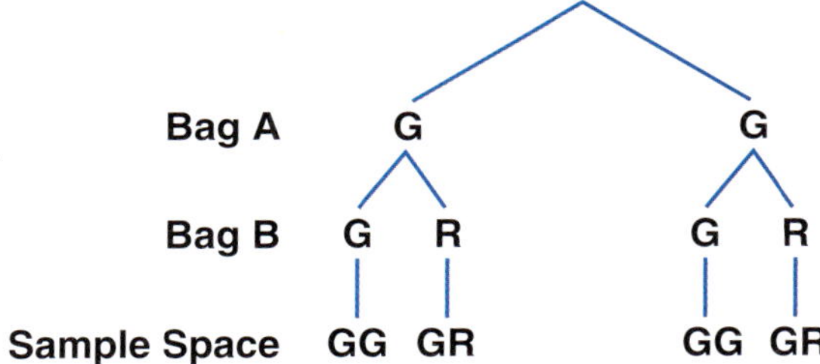

Study Tip

Fair Game A fair game is one in which each player has an equal chance of winning. This game is a fair game.

CHECK Your Progress

c. **GAMES** Marcos tosses three coins. If all three coins show up heads, Marcos wins. Otherwise, Kara wins. Find the sample space. Then find the probability that Marcos wins.

CHECK Your Understanding

Examples 1, 2 (pp. 465–466)

For each situation, find the sample space using a table or tree diagram.

1. A number cube is rolled twice.
2. A pair of brown or black sandals are available in sizes 7, 8, or 9.

Example 2 (p. 466)

3. **MULTIPLE CHOICE** Sandwiches can be made with ham or turkey on rye, white, or sourdough breads. Which list shows all the possible outcomes?

A

Outcomes	
ham	rye
turkey	white
ham	sourdough
ham	rye
turkey	white
turkey	sourdough

B

Outcomes	
ham	rye
turkey	white
turkey	sourdough

C

Outcomes	
ham	rye
turkey	rye
ham	white
turkey	white
ham	sourdough
turkey	sourdough

D

Outcomes	
ham	rye
turkey	white
ham	sourdough

Example 3 (p. 467)

4. **GAMES** Brianna spins a spinner with four sections of equal size twice, labeled A, B, C, and D. If letter A is spun at least once, Brianna wins. Otherwise, Odell wins. Find the probability that Odell wins.

Practice and Problem Solving

HOMEWORK HELP	
For Exercises	See Examples
5–12	1, 2
28	2
13–14	3

For each situation, find the sample space using a table or tree diagram.

5. tossing a coin, and spinning the spinner from the choices at the right
6. choosing left or right and either boots, gym shoes, or dress shoes
7. tossing a coin and rolling a number cube
8. picking a number from 1 to 5 and choosing the color red, white, or blue

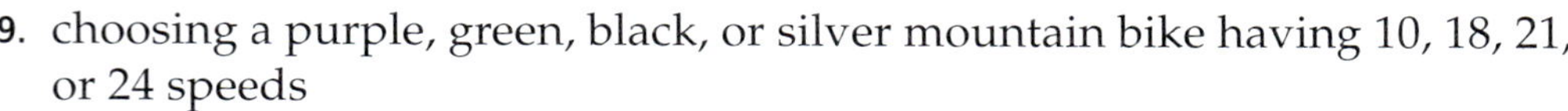

9. choosing a purple, green, black, or silver mountain bike having 10, 18, 21, or 24 speeds
10. choosing a letter from the word SPACE and choosing a consonant from the word MATH

11. **CLOTHES** Jerry can buy a school T-shirt with either short sleeves or long sleeves in either gray or white and in small, medium, or large. Find the sample space for all possible T-shirts he can buy.

12. **FOOD** Three-course dinners can be made from the menu shown. Find the sample space for a dinner consisting of an appetizer, entrée, and dessert.

Appetizers	Entrees	Desserts
Soup	Steak	Carrot Cake
Salad	Chicken	Cheesecake
	Fish	

Real-World Link The average family size in the United States is 2.59 people.
Source: U.S. Census Bureau

For each game, find the sample space. Then find the indicated probability.

13. Elba tosses a quarter, a dime, and a nickel. If tails comes up at least twice, Steve wins. Otherwise Elba wins. Find P(Elba wins).
14. Ming rolls a number cube, tosses a coin, and chooses a card from two cards marked A and B. If an even number and heads appears, Ming wins, no matter which card is chosen. Otherwise Lashonda wins. Find P(Ming wins).

FAMILIES Mr. and Mrs. Romero are expecting triplets. Suppose the chance of each child being a boy is 50% and of being a girl is 50%. Find each probability.

15. P(all three children will be boys)
16. P(at least one boy and one girl)
17. P(two boys and one girl)
18. P(at least two girls)
19. P(the first two born are boys and the last born is a girl)

20. **GAMES** The following is a game for two players. Find the probability that each player wins.
    - Three counters are labeled according to the table at the right.
    - Toss the three counters.
    - If exactly 2 counters match, Player 1 scores a point. Otherwise, Player 2 scores a point.

	Side 1	Side 2
Counter 1	red	blue
Counter 2	red	yellow
Counter 3	blue	yellow

UNIFORMS **For Exercises 21 and 22, use the information below.**

The University of Oregon's football team has many different uniforms. The coach can choose from four colors of jerseys and pants: green, yellow, white, and black. There are three helmet options: green, white, and yellow. Also, there are four colors of socks and two colors of shoes.

21. How many jersey/pant combinations are there?

22. If the coach picks a jersey/pant combination at random, what is the probability he will pick a yellow jersey with green pants?

23. **RESEARCH** Use the Internet or another resource to find the number of jerseys and pants your favorite college or professional sports team has as part of its uniform. How many jersey/pants combinations are there for the team you chose?

H.O.T. Problems

24. **CHALLENGE** Refer to Exercise 20. A *fair game* is one in which each player has an equal chance of winning. Adjust the scoring of the game so that it is fair.

25. **SELECT A TOOL** Mei wants to determine the probability of guessing correctly on two true-false questions on her history test. Which of the following tools might Mei use to determine the probability of answering both questions correctly by guessing? Justify your selection(s). Then use the tool(s) to solve the problem.

draw a model | calculator | real objects

26. **FIND THE ERROR** Rhonda and Elise are finding all the possible unique outcomes of rolling an even number on a number cube and landing on A or B on the spinner shown. Who is correct? Explain your reasoning.

Rhonda

Outcomes	
Number Cube	Spinner
2	A
2	B
4	C
4	A
6	B
6	C

Elise

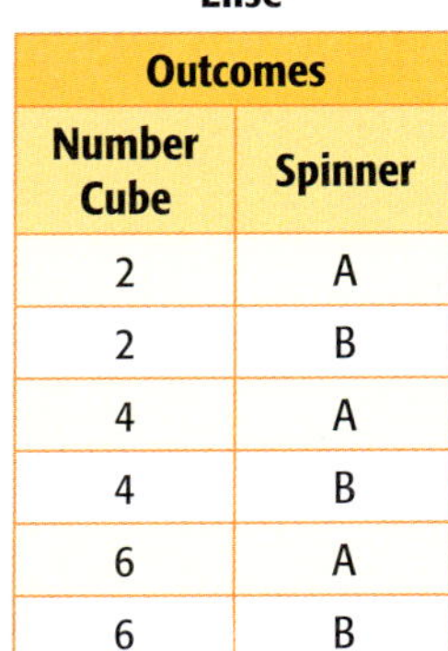

Outcomes	
Number Cube	Spinner
2	A
2	B
4	A
4	B
6	A
6	B

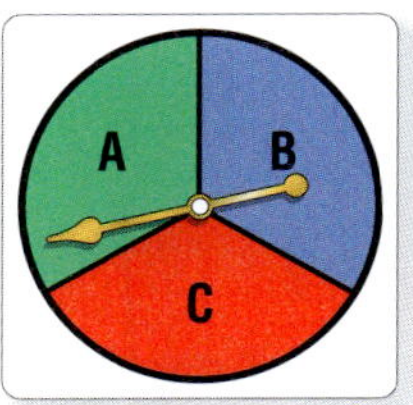

27. **WRITING IN MATH** Describe a game between two players using one coin in which each player has an equal chance of winning.

28. Mr. Zajac will choose one student from each of the two groups below to present their history reports to the class.

Group 1
Julia
Antoine
Greg

Group 2
Keith
Isabel

Which set shows all the possible choices?

A {(Julia, Keith), (Antoine, Keith), (Greg, Keith)}

B {(Julia, Antoine), (Antoine, Greg), (Isabel, Keith)}

C {(Julia, Keith), (Antoine, Keith), (Greg, Keith), (Julia, Isabel), (Antoine, Isabel), (Greg, Isabel)}

D {(Isabel, Antoine), (Keith, Greg), (Julia, Isabel), (Keith, Antoine)}

PROBABILITY A spinner is equally likely to stop on each of its regions numbered 1 to 20. Find each probability as a fraction in simplest form. (Lesson 9-1)

29. a prime number
30. GCF(12, 18)
31. multiple of 2 or 3
32. *not* a multiple of 4
33. factor of 10 or 6
34. *not* an even number

UTILITIES For Exercises 35 and 36, use the graph that shows the prices for natural gas charged by an Illinois natural gas supplier. (Lesson 8-6)

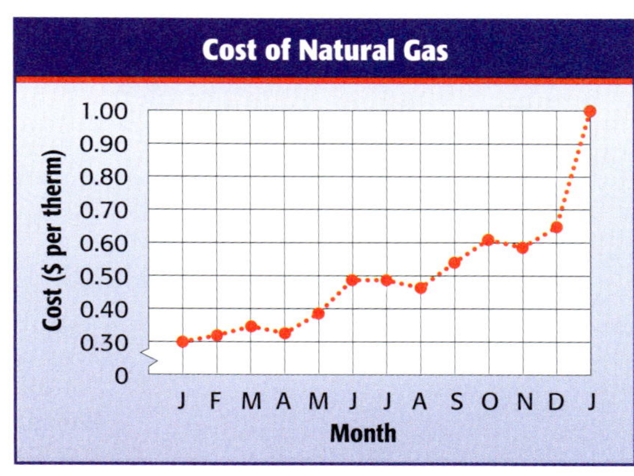

35. What trend seems to be revealed in the line graph?

36. What problems might there be in using this information to predict future prices of natural gas?

37. **SAVINGS** Amare invests $3,400 in a savings account that pays 3.5 % simple interest. After four years, how much money will be in his account?

Find each number. Round to the nearest tenth if necessary. (Lesson 7-1)

38. 43% of 266
39. 17% of 92
40. 2.5% of 44

GET READY for the Next Lesson

PREREQUISITE SKILL Multiply.

41. 7 • 22
42. 11 • 16
43. 23 • 20
44. 131 • 4

The Fundamental Counting Principle

MAIN IDEA

Use multiplication to count outcomes and find probabilities.

New Vocabulary

Fundamental Counting Principle

Math Online

glencoe.com

- Extra Examples
- Personal Tutor
- Self-Check Quiz
- Reading in the Content Area

GET READY for the Lesson

SALES The Shoe Warehouse sells sandals in different colors and styles.

Color	Style
black	platform
brown	slides
tan	wedges
white	
red	

1. According to the table, how many colors of sandals are available?
2. How many styles are available?
3. Find the product of the two numbers you found in Exercises 1 and 2.
4. Draw a tree diagram to find the number of different color and style combinations. How does the number of outcomes compare to the product you found above?

In the activity above, you discovered that multiplication, instead of a tree diagram, can be used to find the number of possible outcomes in a sample space. This is called the **Fundamental Counting Principle**.

Fundamental Counting Principle — Key Concept

Words If event M has m possible outcomes and event N has n possible outcomes, then event M followed by event N has $m \times n$ possible outcomes.

EXAMPLE Find the Number of Outcomes

1 **Find the total number of outcomes when a coin is tossed and a number cube is rolled.**

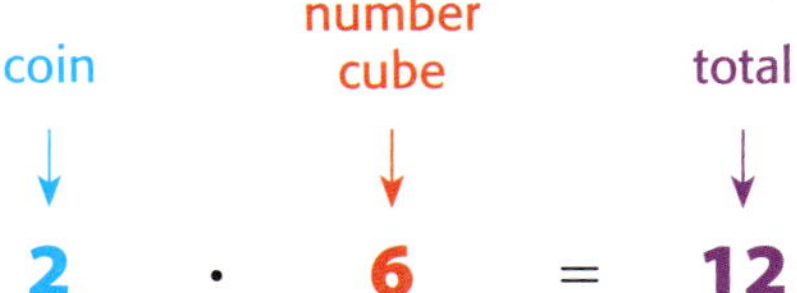

Fundamental Counting Principle

There are 12 different outcomes.

Check Draw a tree diagram to show the sample space.

CHECK Your Progress

a. Find the total number of outcomes when choosing from bike helmets that come in three colors and two styles.

The Fundamental Counting Principle can be used to find the number of possible outcomes and solve probability problems in more complex problems, when there are more than two events.

Real-World EXAMPLE

2 **JEANS** **The Jean Shop sells young men's jeans in different sizes, styles, and lengths, as shown in the table. Find the number of jeans available. Then find the probability of selecting a size 32 × 34 slim fit.**

The Jeans Shop

Waist Size	Length (in.)	Style
30	30	slim fit
32	32	bootcut
34	34	loose fit
36		
38		

$$5 \cdot 3 \cdot 3 = 45 \quad \text{Fundamental Counting Principle}$$

There are 45 different types of jeans to choose from. Out of the 45 possible outcomes, only one is favorable. So, the probability of randomly selecting a 32 × 34 slim fit is $\frac{1}{45}$.

Study Tip

Jean size
In mens' jeans, the size is labeled waist × length. So, a 32 × 34 is a 32-inch waist with a 34-inch length.

CHECK Your Progress

b. **JEANS** If the Jean Shop adds relaxed fit jeans to its selection, find the number of available jeans. Then find the probability of randomly selecting a 36 × 30 relaxed fit pair of jeans.

CHECK Your Understanding

Example 1 (p. 471)

Use the Fundamental Counting Principle to find the total number of outcomes in each situation.

1. tossing a quarter, a dime, and a nickel
2. choosing scrambled, sunny-side up, or poached eggs with bacon or sausage and milk or orange juice
3. choosing a number on a number cube and picking a marble from the bag at the right

Example 2 (p. 472)

4. **CLOTHES** Beth has 3 sweaters, 4 blouses, and 6 skirts that coordinate. Find the number of different outfits consisting of a sweater, blouse, and skirt that are possible. Then find the probability of randomly selecting a particular sweater-blouse-skirt outfit.

Practice and Problem Solving

HOMEWORK HELP

For Exercises	See Examples
5–10	1
11–12	2

Use the Fundamental Counting Principle to find the total number of outcomes in each situation.

Bagels	Cream Cheese
plain	plain
blueberry	chive
cinnamon raisin	sun-dried tomato
garlic	

5. choosing a bagel with one type of cream cheese from the list shown in the table
6. choosing a number from 1 to 20 and a color from 7 colors
7. picking a month of the year and a day of the week
8. choosing from a comedy, horror, or action movie each shown in four theaters
9. rolling a number cube and tossing two coins
10. choosing iced tea in regular, raspberry, lemon, or peach flavors; sweetened or unsweetened; and in a glass or a plastic container

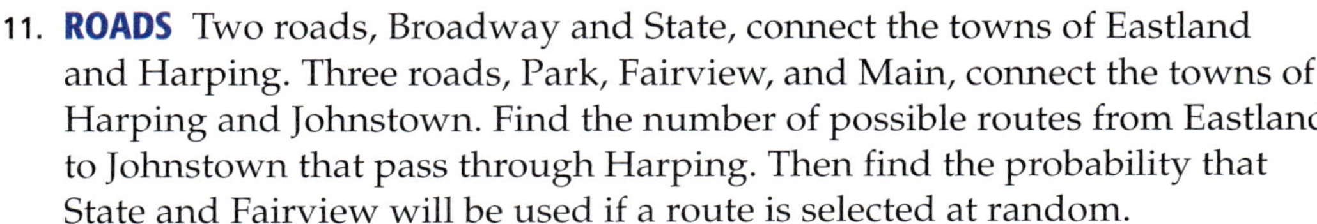

11. **ROADS** Two roads, Broadway and State, connect the towns of Eastland and Harping. Three roads, Park, Fairview, and Main, connect the towns of Harping and Johnstown. Find the number of possible routes from Eastland to Johnstown that pass through Harping. Then find the probability that State and Fairview will be used if a route is selected at random.

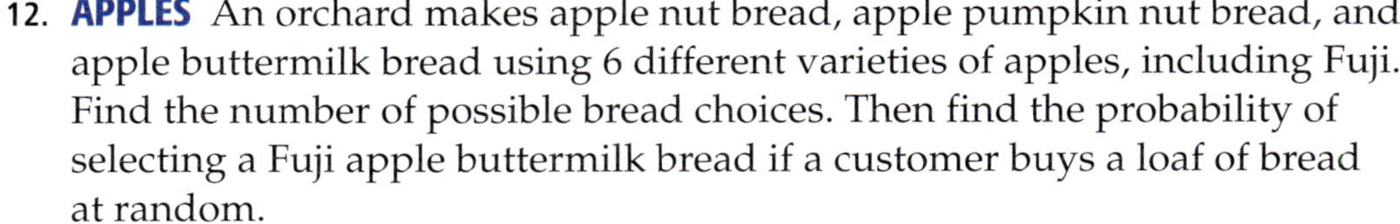

12. **APPLES** An orchard makes apple nut bread, apple pumpkin nut bread, and apple buttermilk bread using 6 different varieties of apples, including Fuji. Find the number of possible bread choices. Then find the probability of selecting a Fuji apple buttermilk bread if a customer buys a loaf of bread at random.

Real-World Link

A popular orchard in Wapato, Washington, grows 7 varieties of apples including Granny Smith and Fuji.

Source: All About Apples

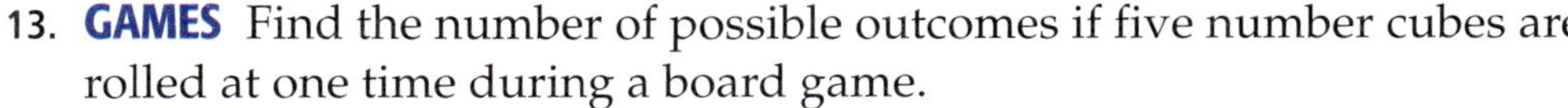

13. **GAMES** Find the number of possible outcomes if five number cubes are rolled at one time during a board game.
14. **PASSWORDS** Find the number of possible choices for a 2-digit password that is greater than 19. Then find the number of possible choices for a 4-digit Personal Identification Number (PIN) if the digits *cannot* be repeated.
15. **T-SHIRTS** A store advertises that they have a different T-shirt for each day of the year. The store offers 32 different T-shirt designs and 11 choices of color. Is the advertisement true? Explain.
16. **ANALYZE TABLES** The table shows cell phone options offered by a wireless phone company. If a phone with one payment plan and one accessory is given away at random, predict the probability that it will be Brand B and have a headset. Explain your reasoning.

Phone Brands	Payment Plans	Accessories
Brand A	Individual	Leather Case
Brand B	Family	Car Mount
Brand C	Business	Headset
	Government	Travel Charger

EXTRA PRACTICE

See pages 691, 712.

H.O.T. Problems

17. **CHALLENGE** Determine the number of possible outcomes for tossing one coin, two coins, and three coins. Then determine the number of possible outcomes for tossing n coins. Describe the strategy you used.

18. **Which One Doesn't Belong?** Identify the choices for event M and N that do *not* result in the same number of outcomes as the other two. Explain your reasoning.

9 drinks, 8 desserts	18 shirts, 4 pants	10 groups, 8 activities

19. **WRITING IN MATH** Explain when you might choose to use the Fundamental Counting Principle to find the number of possible outcomes and when you might choose to use a tree diagram.

TEST PRACTICE

20. A bakery offers white, chocolate, or yellow cakes with white or chocolate icing. There are also 24 designs that can be applied to a cake. If all orders are equally likely, what is the probability that a customer will order a white cake with white icing in a specific design?

    A $\frac{1}{30}$ C $\frac{1}{120}$

    B $\frac{1}{64}$ D $\frac{1}{144}$

21. **SHORT RESPONSE** Hat World sells 9 different styles of hats in several different colors for 2 different sports teams. If the company makes 108 kinds of hats, how many different colors do they make?

Spiral Review

22. **SCHOOL** Horacio can choose from 2 geography, 3 history, and 2 statistics classes. Find the sample space for all possible schedules. (Lesson 9-2)

PROBABILITY Find the probability that the spinner shown at the right will stop on each of the following. Write as a fraction in simplest form. (Lesson 9-1)

23. a vowel

24. red

Order each set of numbers from least to greatest. (Lesson 6-8)

25. 27%, $\frac{1}{5}$, 0.22, 20.1

26. $\frac{19}{20}$, 88%, 0.85, $\frac{3}{4}$

GET READY for the Next Lesson

PREREQUISITE SKILL Multiply.

27. $3 \cdot 2 \cdot 1$

28. $9 \cdot 8 \cdot 7$

29. $5 \cdot 4 \cdot 3 \cdot 2$

30. $7 \cdot 6 \cdot 5 \cdot 4$

9-4 Permutations

MAIN IDEA

Find the number of permutations of a set of objects and find probabilities.

New Vocabulary

permutation

Math Online

glencoe.com

- Extra Examples
- Personal Tutor
- Self-Check Quiz

MINI Lab

How many different ways are there to arrange your first 3 classes if they are math, science, and language arts?

STEP 1 Write math, science, and language arts on the index cards.

MATH	SCIENCE	LANGUAGE ARTS

STEP 2 Find and record all arrangements of classes by changing the order of the index cards.

1. When you first started to make your list, how many choices did you have for your first class?
2. Once your first class was selected, how many choices did you have for the second class? then, the third class?

A **permutation** is an arrangement, or listing, of objects in which order is important. In the example above, the arrangement science, math, language arts is a permutation of math, science, language arts because the order of the classes is different. You can use the Fundamental Counting Principle to find the number of possible permutations.

EXAMPLE Find a Permutation

1 **SCHEDULES** **Find the number of possible arrangements of classes in the Mini Lab above using the Fundamental Counting Principle.**

There are **3** choices for the first class.

There are **2** choices that remain for the second class.

There is **1** choice that remains for the third class.

$3 \cdot 2 \cdot 1 = 6$ ← The number of permutations of 3 classes

There are 6 possible arrangements, or permutations, of the 3 classes.

CHECK Your Progress

a. **VOLLEYBALL** In how many ways can the starting six players of a volleyball team stand in a row for a picture?

You can use a permutation to find the probability of an event.

Real-World EXAMPLE Find Probability

2 **SWIMMING** **The finals of the Northwest Swimming League features 8 swimmers. If each swimmer has an equally likely chance of finishing in the top two, what is the probability that Yumii will be in first place and Paquita in second place?**

Northwest League Finalists	
Octavia	Eden
Natasha	Paquita
Calista	Samantha
Yumii	Lorena

There are **8** choices for first place.

There are **7** choices that remain for second place.

$8 \cdot 7 = 56$ ← The number of permutations of the 2 places

There are 56 possible arrangements, or permutations, of the 2 places.

Since there is only one way of having Yumii come in first and Paquita second, the probability of this event is $\frac{1}{56}$.

CHECK Your Progress

b. **LETTERS** Two different letters are randomly selected from the letters in the word *math*. What is the probability that the first letter selected is *m* and the second letter is *h*?

CHECK Your Understanding

Example 1 (p. 475)

1. **AMUSEMENT PARKS** Seven friends are waiting to ride the new roller coaster. In how many ways can they board the ride, once it is their turn?

2. **COMMITTEES** In how many ways can a president, vice president, and secretary be randomly selected from a class of 25 students?

Example 2 (p. 476)

3. **DVDs** You have five seasons of your favorite TV show on DVD. If you randomly select two of them from a shelf, what is the probability that you will select season one first and season two second?

4. **PASSWORDS** A password consists of four letters, of which none are repeated. What is the probability that a person could guess the entire password by randomly selecting the four letters?

Practice and Problem Solving

HOMEWORK HELP

For Exercises	See Examples
5–8	1
9–12	2

5. **CONTESTS** In the Battle of the Bands contest, in how many ways can the four participating bands be ordered?

6. **CODES** A garage door code has 5 digits. If no digit is repeated, how many codes are possible?

7. **LETTERS** How many permutations are possible of the letters in the word *friend*?

8. **NUMBERS** How many different 3-digit numbers can be formed using the digits 9, 3, 4, 7, and 6? Assume no number can be used more than once.

9. **CAPTAINS** The members of the Evergreen Junior High Quiz Bowl team are listed at the right. If a captain and an assistant captain are chosen at random, what is the probability that Walter is selected as captain and Mi-Ling as co-captain?

Evergreen Junior High Quiz Bowl Team	
Jamil	Luanda
Savannah	Mi-Ling
Tucker	Booker
Ferdinand	Nina
Walter	Meghan

10. **BASEBALL** Adriano, Julián, and three of their friends will sit in a row of five seats at a baseball game. If each friend is equally likely to sit in any seat, what is the probability that Adriano will sit in the first seat and Julián will sit in the second seat?

11. **GAMES** Alex, Aiden, Dexter, and Dion are playing a video game. If they each have an equally likely chance of getting the highest score, what is the probability that Dion will get the highest score and Alex the second highest?

Real-World Link
In 2006, Stephen Clarke set the record for the fastest time to carve a face into a pumpkin. It took him 24.03 seconds.

Source: Guinness World Records

12. **BLOCKS** A child has wooden blocks with the letters *G*, *R*, *T*, *I*, and *E*. Find the probability that the child randomly arranges the letters in the order *TIGER*.

13. **SELECT A TOOL** Refer to the information in the table. There are four ribbons passed out to participants in the Perfect Pumpkin competition. Which of the following tools might you use to find the number of ways a ribbon can be awarded to a pumpkin in the Perfect Pumpkin competition? Justify your selection(s) to solve the problem.

Pumpkin Festival	
Competition	Number of Participants
Perfect Pumpkin	24
Biggest Pumpkin	17
Heaviest Pumpkin	15
Pumpkin Carving	5

calculator | mental math | estimation

EXTRA PRACTICE
See pages 691, 712.

14. **PHOTOGRAPHY** A family discovered they can stand in a row for their portrait in 720 different ways. How many members are in the family?

15. **STUDENT ID** Hamilton Middle School assigns a four-digit identification number to each student. The number is made from the digits 1, 2, 3, and 4, and no digit is repeated. If assigned randomly, what is the probability that an ID number will end with a 3?

H.O.T. Problems

16. **CHALLENGE** There are 1,320 ways for three students to win first, second, and third place during a debate match. How many students are there on the debate team? Explain your reasoning.

17. **WRITING IN MATH** Describe a real-world situation that has 6 permutations. Justify your answer.

TEST PRACTICE

18. The five finalists in a random drawing are shown. Find the probability that Sean is awarded first prize and Teresa is awarded second prize.

Finalists
Cesar
Teresa
Sean
Nikita
Alfonso

A $\frac{1}{5}$

B $\frac{1}{10}$

C $\frac{2}{5}$

D $\frac{1}{20}$

19. A baseball coach is deciding on the batting order for his nine starting players with the pitcher batting last. How many batting orders are possible?

F 8

G 72

H 40,320

J 362,880

Spiral Review

20. **BREAKFAST** Find the total number of outcomes if you can choose from 8 kinds of bagels, 3 toppings, and 4 beverages. (Lesson 9-3)

21. **LUNCH** Make a tree diagram showing different ways to make a sandwich with turkey, ham, or salami and either cheddar or Swiss cheese. (Lesson 9-2)

22. **PROBABILITY** What is the probability of rolling a number greater than four on a number cube? (Lesson 9-1)

Find each product. Write in simplest form. (Lesson 5-5)

23. $\frac{4}{5} \times 2\frac{1}{3}$

24. $11\frac{1}{8} \times \frac{1}{2}$

25. $4\frac{5}{6} \times \frac{7}{8}$

GET READY for the Next Lesson

PREREQUISITE SKILL Find each value. (Lesson 1-4)

26. $\frac{5 \cdot 4}{2 \cdot 1}$

27. $\frac{8 \cdot 7 \cdot 6}{3 \cdot 2 \cdot 1}$

28. $\frac{5 \cdot 4 \cdot 3}{4 \cdot 3 \cdot 2}$

29. $\frac{10 \cdot 9 \cdot 8 \cdot 7}{8 \cdot 7 \cdot 6 \cdot 5}$

CHAPTER 9

Mid-Chapter Quiz

Lessons 9-1 through 9-4

A number cube is rolled. Find each probability. Write as a fraction in simplest form. (Lesson 9-1)

1. *P*(an odd number)
2. *P*(a number not greater than 4)
3. *P*(a number less than 6)
4. *P*(a multiple of 2)

5. **BOOKS** Brett owns 5 science-fiction books, 3 biographies, and 12 mysteries. If he randomly picks a book to read, what is the probability that he will *not* pick a science-fiction book? Write as a percent.

For each situation, find the sample space using a table or tree diagram. (Lesson 9-2)

6. Two coins are tossed.
7. The spinner shown is spun, and a digit is randomly selected from the number 803.

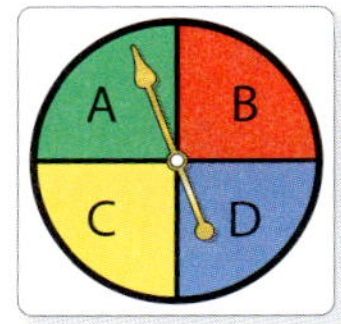

8. **MULTIPLE CHOICE** At a diner, a customer can choose from eggs or pancakes as an entrée and from ham or sausage as a side. Which set shows all the possible choices of one entrée and one side? (Lesson 9-2)

   A {(eggs, pancakes), (ham, sausage)}

   B {(eggs, ham), (eggs, sausage), (pancakes, ham), (pancakes, sausage)}

   C {(eggs, ham), (eggs, pancakes), (sausage, pancakes)}

   D {(eggs, ham), (pancakes, sausage)}

9. **GAMES** Abbey rolls a number cube and chooses a card from among cards marked *A*, *B*, and *C*. If an odd number and a vowel turn up, Abbey wins. Otherwise, Benny wins. Find the sample space. Then find the probability that Benny wins. (Lesson 9-2)

For Exercises 10 and 11, use the Fundamental Counting Principle to find the total number of possible outcomes in each situation. (Lesson 9-3)

10. A customer chooses a paper color, size, and binding style for some copies.

Color	Size	Binding
white	8.5″ x 11″	paper clip
yellow	8.5″ x 14″	binder clip
green	8.5″ x 17″	staple

11. A number cube is rolled and three coins are tossed.

12. **CARS** A certain car model comes in the colors in the table and either automatic or manual transmission. Find the probability that a randomly selected car will have a black exterior, tan interior, and manual transmission if all combinations are equally likely. (Lesson 9-3)

Exterior	Interior
Black	Gray
White	Tan
Red	
Silver	

13. **COMPETITION** How many ways can 6 swimmers come in first, second, or third place?

14. **MULTIPLE CHOICE** Noriko packed five different sweaters for her weekend vacation. If she randomly selects one sweater to wear each day, what is the probability that she will select the brown sweater on Friday, the orange sweater on Saturday, and the pink sweater on Sunday? She will not wear each sweater more than once. (Lesson 9-4)

    F $\frac{1}{60}$

    G $\frac{1}{120}$

    H $\frac{3}{5}$

    J $\frac{1}{5}$

9-5 Combinations

MAIN IDEA

Find the number of combinations of a set of objects and find probabilities.

New Vocabulary

combination

Math Online

glencoe.com

- Extra Examples
- Personal Tutor
- Self-Check Quiz

GET READY for the Lesson

FOOD Mr. Rius is making a salad for a party. He has tomatoes, green peppers, cucumbers, and radishes. He starts with lettuce and then decides to add three of the above ingredients to his salad.

1. Use the first letter of each vegetable to list all of the permutations of the ingredients added to the lettuce. How many are there?
2. Cross out any arrangement that contains the same letters as another one in the list. How many are there now?
3. Explain the difference between the two lists.

An arrangement, or listing, of objects in which order is not important is called a **combination**. In the activity above, choosing cucumbers and radishes is the same as choosing radishes and cucumbers.

Permutations and combinations are related. You can find the number of combinations of objects by dividing the number of permutations of the entire set by the number of ways the smaller set can be arranged.

EXAMPLE Find the Number of Combinations

FOOD Terrence's Pizza Parlor is offering the special shown in the table. How many different two-topping pizzas are possible?

This is a combination problem because the order of the toppings on the pizza is not important.

METHOD 1 **Make a list.**

Use the first letter of each topping to list all of the permutations of the toppings taken two at a time. Then cross out the pizzas that are the same as another one.

p, s	~~s, p~~	~~g, p~~	~~o, p~~	~~m, p~~
p, o	s, o	~~g, s~~	~~o, s~~	~~m, s~~
p, m	s, m	~~g, o~~	o, m	~~m, o~~
p, g	s, g	~~g, m~~	o, g	m, g

So, there are 10 different two-topping pizzas.

METHOD 2 **Use a permutation.**

Step 1 Find the number of permutations of the entire set.

$5 \cdot 4 = 20$ A permutation of 5 toppings, taken 2 at time

Step 2 Find the number of permutations of the smaller set.

$2 \cdot 1 = 2$ Number of ways to arrange 2 toppings

Step 3 Find the number of combinations.

$\frac{20}{2}$ or 10 Divide the number of permutations of the entire set by the number of permutations of each smaller set.

So, there are 10 different two-topping pizzas.

CHOOSE Your Method

a. **FOOD** How many different three-topping pizzas are possible if Terrence adds ham and anchovies to the topping choices?

Real-World Link The Last Man Standing One-on-One Basketball Tournament is held in New York. The top 16 players from preliminary competition play in a championship tournament in Madison Square Garden.

Real-World EXAMPLES

2 **BASKETBALL A one-on-one basketball tournament has six players from the regional finals. Each player will play every opponent once. The 2 players with the best records will then play in the championship. How many one-on-one games will be played?**

Find the number of ways 2 players can be chosen from a group of 6.

There are 6 · 5 ways to choose 2 people. →
There are 2 · 1 ways to arrange 2 people. →

$$\frac{6 \cdot 5}{2 \cdot 1} = \frac{30}{2} = 15$$

There are 15 games plus 1 final game to determine the overall winner. So, there will be 16 games played.

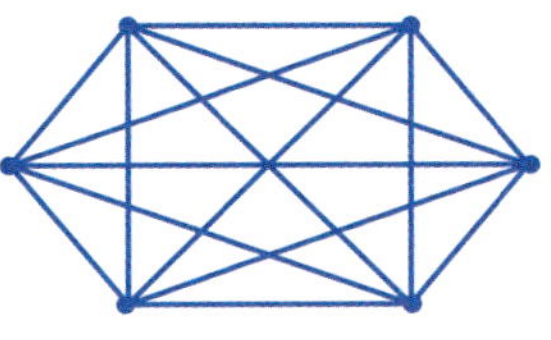

Check Make a diagram in which each person is represented by a point. Draw a line segment between each pair of points to represent all the games. This produces 15 line segments, or 15 games. Then add the final game to make a total of 16 games.

3 **If the players in Example 2 are selected at random, what is the probability that player 3 will play player 6 in the first game?**

There are 15 possible first games and only one favorable outcome. So, the probability is $\frac{1}{15}$.

CHECK Your Progress

b. **BASKETBALL** What is the probability that player 3 will play against player 12 in the first game if 12 people play in the tournament?

Check Your Understanding

Example 1 (pp. 480–481)

1. **STICKERS** In how many ways can you pick 2 stickers from a package of 7?
2. **CRAFT FAIR** In how many ways can 3 out of 10 students be chosen to present their projects at a craft fair?

Examples 2, 3 (p. 481)

PAINTING For Exercises 3 and 4, use the information below.

Jade is going to paint her room two different colors from among white, gray, sage, or yellow.

3. How many combinations of two paint colors are there?
4. Find the probability that two colors chosen randomly will be white and sage.

Practice and Problem Solving

HOMEWORK HELP

For Exercises	See Examples
5–8	1, 2
9–10	3

5. **VOLUNTEERS** In how many ways can you select 4 volunteers out of 10?
6. **ART** In how many ways can four drawings out of 15 be chosen for display?
7. **INTERNET** Of 12 Web sites, in how many ways can you choose to visit 6?
8. **SPORTS** On an 8-member volleyball team, how many different 6-player starting teams are possible?
9. **STUDENT COUNCIL** The students listed are members of Student Council. Three will be chosen at random to form a committee. Find the probability that the three students chosen will be Placido, Maddie, and Akira.

Roster
Leon
Placido
Maddie
Adrahan
Matt
Akira

10. **FOOD** At a hot dog stand, customers can select three toppings from among chili, onions, cheese, mustard, or relish. What is the probability that three toppings selected at random will include onions, mustard, and relish?
11. **MUSIC** Marissa practiced the five pieces listed at the right for a recital. Find the number of different ways that three pieces will be randomly chosen for her to play. Then find the probability that all three were composed by Beethoven.

Recital Piece	Composer
Fur Elise	Ludwig van Beethoven
First Piano Sonata	Sergei Rachmaninoff
The Four Seasons	Antonio Vivaldi
Cappricio	Ludwig van Beethoven
Moonlight Sonata	Ludwig van Beethoven

Tell whether each problem represents a *permutation* or a *combination*. Then solve the problem.

12. Six children remain in a game of musical chairs. If two chairs are removed, how many different groups of four children can remain?
13. How many ways can first and second chair positions be awarded in a band that has 10 flute players?
14. How many ways can 12 books be stacked in a single pile?

See pages 692, 712.

H.O.T. Problems

15. **CHALLENGE** How many people were at a party if each person shook hands exactly once with every other person and there were 105 handshakes?

16. **FIND THE ERROR** Ling and Daniela are calculating the number of ways that a 4-member committee can be chosen from an 8-member club. Who is correct? Explain your reasoning.

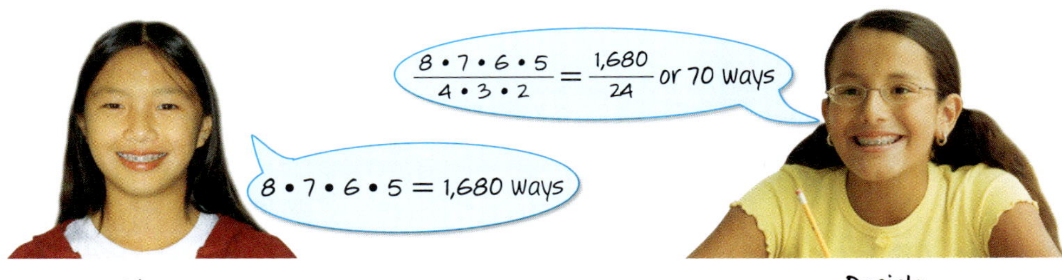

17. **WRITING IN MATH** Write about a real-world situation that can be solved using a combination. Then solve the problem.

TEST PRACTICE

18. Three cheerleaders will be randomly selected to represent the squad at a game. If there are 12 cheerleaders, find the probability that the three members chosen are Kameko, Lynn, and Tory.

    A $\frac{1}{220}$ **C** $\frac{1}{4}$

    B $\frac{3}{110}$ **D** $\frac{1}{3}$

19. Four students are to be chosen from a roster of 9 students to attend a science camp. In how many ways can these 4 students be chosen?

    F 5   **H** 126

    G 36   **J** 3,024

Spiral Review

20. **TRACK** Six sprinters are entered in a 100-meter dash. In how many different ways can the race be completed? Assume there are no ties. (Lesson 9-4)

21. **T-SHIRTS** A clothing company makes T-shirts with the choices as shown in the table. How many different T-shirts are possible? (Lesson 9-3)

Size	Color	Style	Material
S	Orange	Crew	Cotton
M	Pink	V-Neck	Polyester
L	Lime Green	Tank-Top	
XL			

Estimate. (Lesson 5-1)

22. $\frac{1}{10} + \frac{7}{8}$

23. $\frac{5}{12} - \frac{1}{9}$

GET READY for the Next Lesson

PREREQUISITE SKILL For Exercises 24 and 25, use the graph. (Lesson 8-5)

24. How many students were surveyed?

25. Find the probability that a student's favorite picnic game is sack racing.

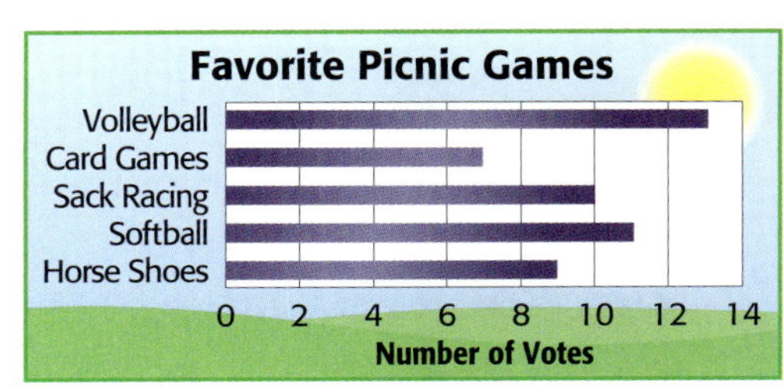

9-6 Problem-Solving Investigation

MAIN IDEA: Solve problems by acting it out.

P.S.I. TEAM +

e-Mail: ACT IT OUT

EDDIE: I've been practicing free throws every day after school. Now I can make an average of 3 out of every 4 free throws I try. I wonder how many times I usually make two free throws in a row.

YOUR MISSION: Act it out to determine the probability that Eddie makes two free throws in a row.

Understand	You know that Eddie makes an average of 3 out of every 4 free throws. You could have Eddie actually make free throws, but that requires a basketball hoop. You could also act it out with a spinner.
Plan	Spin a spinner, numbered 1 to 4, two times. If the spinner lands on 1, 2, or 3, he makes the free throw. If the spinner lands on 4, he doesn't make it. Repeat the experiment 10 times.
Solve	Spin the spinner and make a table of the results.
Check	Repeat the experiment several times to see whether the results agree.

Trials	1	2	3	4	5	6	7	8	9	10
First Spin	4	1	4	3	1	2	2	1	3	2
Second Spin	2	3	3	2	1	4	1	4	3	3

The highlighted columns show that six out of the 10 trials resulted in two free throws in a row. So, the probability is 60%.

Analyze The Strategy

1. Explain whether the results of the experiment would be the same if it were repeated.
2. WRITING IN MATH Write a problem that can be solved by acting it out. Then solve the problem by acting it out.

Mixed Problem Solving

For Exercises 3–6, use the *act it out* strategy.

3. **TESTS** Determine whether using a spinner with four equal sections is a good way to answer a 5-question multiple-choice quiz if each question has choices A, B, C, and D. Justify your answer.

4. **BOOKS** There are 6 students in a book club. Two of them order books, and the delivery comes to the classroom teacher. However, the teacher cannot remember which 2 students ordered the books. Is it a good idea for the teacher to randomly pass out the books to any two students? Explain. What is the probability that the teacher will give the correct books to the students?

5. **RUNNING** Six runners are entered in a race. Assuming no ties, in how many different ways can first and second places be awarded?

6. **MOVIES** In how many different ways can four friends sit in a row of four seats at the movies if two of the friends insist on sitting next to each other?

Use any strategy to solve Exercises 7–14. Some strategies are shown below.

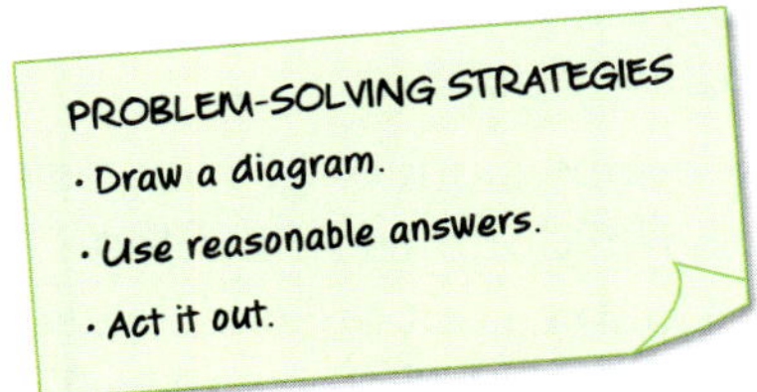

7. **FESTIVALS** The Student Council will have a booth set up at the town festival. They surveyed 160 students to find out their preference for the booth. The results are shown below. Is 35, 65, or 95 a reasonable answer for the number of students who would prefer a dunking booth? Explain.

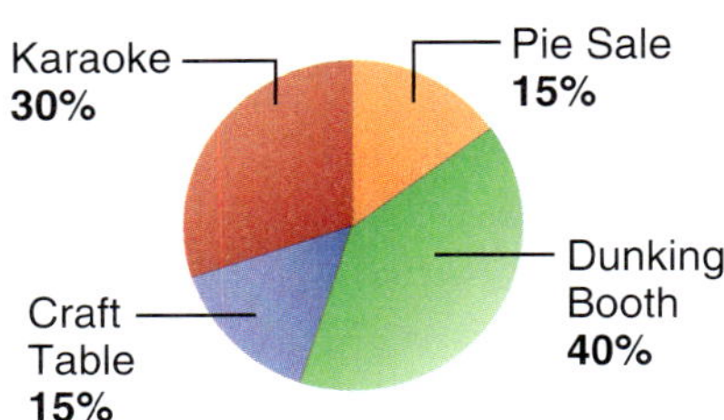

8. **TRANSPORTATION** There are 4 students waiting at a subway stop. How many different ways can they board the subway?

9. **ALGEBRA** The pattern below is known as Pascal's Triangle. Would 1, 6, 10, 10, 6, 1 be a reasonable conjecture for the numbers in the 6th row? Justify your answer.

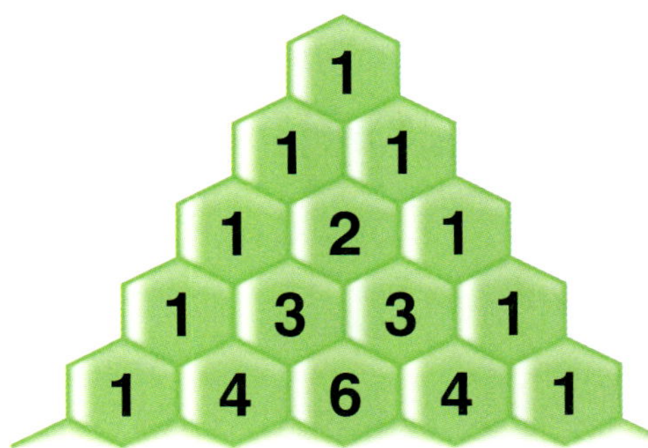

10. **CHESS** A chess tournament is held, and 32 students participate. The tournament will be single-elimination, which means if a player loses one match, he or she will be eliminated. How many total games will be played in the tournament?

11. **SCHOOL** Suppose rolling an even number on a number cube corresponds to an answer of *true* and rolling an odd number corresponds to an answer of *false*. Determine whether rolling this number cube is a good way to answer a 5-question true-false quiz. Justify your answer.

12. **CABLE** A cable company is running a special for new customers. For the first 3 months they will get a discount of 20% off their regular bill. Would \$50, \$60, or \$70 be a reasonable estimate for the first bill if their regular bill is \$95? Explain.

13. **MONEY** If you save \$1.25 every week in a piggy bank, how much money will you have after 3 years?

14. **MUSIC** Liseta has an equal number of jazz, country, rap, pop, and R&B songs on her MP3 player. She listens to her MP3 player on random mode on both Wednesday and Thursday nights. What is the probability Liseta will hear a rap song first on Wednesday night?

Theoretical and Experimental Probability

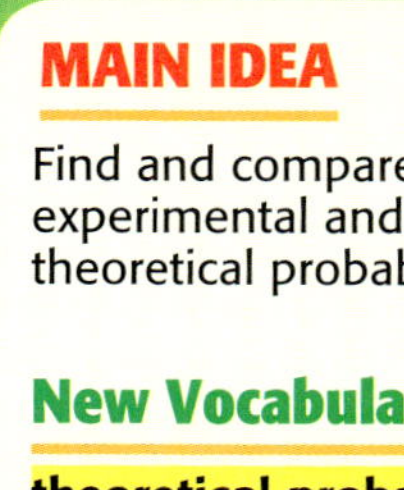

MAIN IDEA

Find and compare experimental and theoretical probabilities.

New Vocabulary

theoretical probability
experimental probability

Math Online

glencoe.com

- Extra Examples
- Personal Tutor
- Self-Check Quiz

MINI Lab

Follow the steps to determine how many times doubles are expected to turn up when two number cubes are rolled.

Step 1 Use the table to help you find the expected number of times doubles should turn up when rolling two number cubes 36 times. The top row represents one number cube, and the left column represents the other number cube.

	1	2	3	4	5	6
1	1, 1	1, 2	1, 3	1, 4	1, 5	1, 6
2	2, 1	2, 2	2, 3	2, 4	2, 5	2, 6
3	3, 1	3, 2	3, 3	3, 4	3, 5	3, 6
4	4, 1	4, 2	4, 3	4, 4	4, 5	4, 6
5	5, 1	5, 2	5, 3	5, 4	5, 5	5, 6
6	6, 1	6, 2	6, 3	6, 4	6, 5	6, 6

Step 2 Roll two number cubes 36 times. Record the number of times doubles turn up.

1. Compare the number of times you *expected* to roll doubles with the number of times you *actually* rolled doubles.
2. Write the probability of rolling doubles out of 36 rolls using the number of times you *expected* to roll doubles from Step 1. Then write the probability of rolling doubles out of 36 rolls using the number of times you *actually* rolled doubles from Step 2.

In the Mini Lab above, you found both the theoretical probability and the experimental probability of rolling doubles using two number cubes. **Theoretical probability** is based on what *should* happen when conducting a probability experiment. This is the probability you have been using since Lesson 9-1. **Experimental probability** is based on what *actually* occurred during such an experiment.

Theoretical Probability

$\frac{6}{36}$ ← 6 rolls *should* occur

Experimental Probability

$\frac{n}{36}$ ← n rolls *actually* occurred

The theoretical probability and the experimental probability of an event may or may not be the same. As the number of times an experiment is conducted increases, the theoretical probability and the experimental probability should become closer in value.

EXAMPLE Experimental Probability

1 **Two number cubes are rolled 75 times, and a sum of 9 is rolled 10 times. What is the experimental probability of rolling a sum of 9?**

$$P(9) = \frac{\text{number of times a sum of 9 occurs}}{\text{total number of rolls}}$$

$$= \frac{10}{75} \text{ or } \frac{2}{15}$$

The experimental probability of rolling a sum of 9 is $\frac{2}{15}$.

CHECK Your Progress

a. In the above experiment, what is the experimental probability of rolling a sum that is *not* 9?

b. In the above experiment, what is the experimental probability of rolling a sum that is *not* six if a sum of six was rolled 18 times?

EXAMPLES Experimental and Theoretical Probability

Study Tip

Trials
A *trial* is one experiment in a series of successive experiments.

2 **The graph shows the results of an experiment in which a spinner with 3 equal sections is spun sixty times. Find the experimental probability of spinning red for this experiment.**

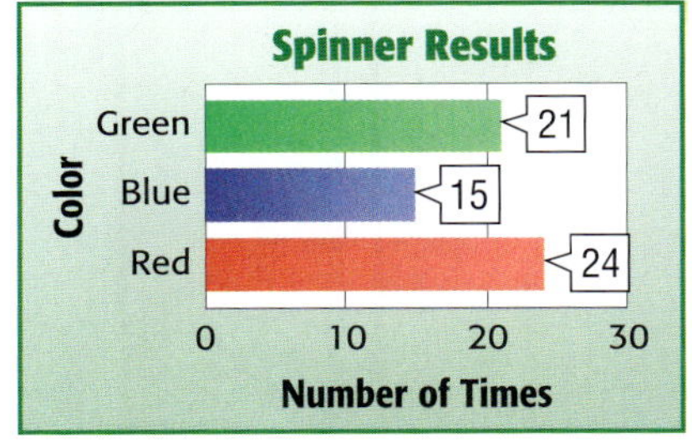

The graph indicates that the spinner landed on red 24 times, blue 15 times, and green 21 times.

$$P(\text{red}) = \frac{\text{number of times red occurs}}{\text{total number of spins}}$$

$$= \frac{24}{60} \text{ or } \frac{2}{5}$$

The experimental probability of spinning red was $\frac{2}{5}$.

3 **Compare the experimental probability you found in Example 2 to its theoretical probability.**

The spinner has three possible outcomes, red, blue, or green. So, the theoretical probability of spinning red is $\frac{1}{3}$. Since $\frac{2}{5} \approx \frac{1}{3}$, the experimental probability is close to the theoretical probability.

CHECK Your Progress

c. Refer to Example 2. If the spinner was spun 3 more times and landed on green each time, find the experimental probability of spinning green for this experiment.

d. Compare the experimental probability you found in Exercise c to its theoretical probability.

Theoretical and experimental probability can be used to make predictions about future events.

Real-World Career. . .
How Does a Media Buyer Use Math? A media buyer looks at previous sales to make predictions on how many items to buy in the future.

Math Online
For more information, go to glencoe.com.

Real-World EXAMPLES Predict Future Events

4 MEDIA A media buyer examines last year's DVD sales to decide how many DVDs of each type to buy this year. Last year's sales are shown in the table. What is the probability that a person buys a comedy DVD?

DVDs Sold	
Type	**Number**
action	670
comedy	580
drama	450
horror	300

There were 2,000 DVDs sold and 580 chose comedy. So, the probability is $\frac{580}{2,000}$ or $\frac{29}{100}$.

5 Suppose the media buyer expects to sell 5,000 DVDs this year. How many drama DVDs should she buy?

$\frac{450}{2,000} = \frac{x}{5,000}$ Write a proportion.

$450 \cdot 5,000 = 2,000 \cdot x$ Find the cross products.

$2,250,000 = 2,000x$ Multiply.

$1,125 = x$ Divide each side by 2,000.

She should buy about 1,125 drama DVDs.

CHECK Your Progress

e. What is the probability that a person buys a horror DVD?

f. If the media buyer expects to sell 3,000 DVDs this year, about how many action movies should she buy?

CHECK Your Understanding

Examples 1–3 (p. 487)

For Exercises 1–3, a coin is tossed 50 times, and it lands on heads 28 times.

1. Find the experimental probability of the coin landing heads.
2. Find the theoretical probability of the coin landing heads.
3. Compare the probabilities in Exercises 1 and 2.

FOOD For Exercises 4 and 5, use the table showing the types of muffins that customers bought one morning from their local bakery.

Muffin	Number of People
blueberry	22
poppyseed	17
banana	11

Example 4 (p. 488)

4. What is the probability that a customer buys a blueberry muffin?
5. If 100 customers buy muffins tomorrow, about how many would you expect to buy a banana muffin?

Practice and Problem Solving

HOMEWORK HELP	
For Exercises	See Examples
6–7	1–3
8–9	4
10–11	5

For Exercises 6 and 7, a number cube is rolled 20 times and lands on 1 two times and on 5 four times.

6. Find the experimental probability of landing on 5. Compare the experimental probability to the theoretical probability.
7. Find the experimental probability of *not* landing on 1. Compare the experimental probability to the theoretical probability.

ZOO For Exercises 8–11, use the graph of a survey of 70 zoo visitors who were asked to name their favorite animal exhibit.

What is your Favorite Animal Exhibit?

Exhibit	Tally	Frequency
bears	卌 I	6
elephants	卌 卌 卌 II	17
monkeys	卌 卌 卌 卌 I	21
penguins	卌 卌 III	13
snakes	卌 卌 III	13

8. What is the probability that the elephant exhibit is someone's favorite?
9. What is the probability that the bear exhibit is someone's favorite?
10. Suppose 540 people visit the zoo. Predict how many people will choose the monkey exhibit as their favorite.
11. Suppose 720 people visit the zoo. Predict how many people will choose the penguin exhibit as their favorite.

For Exercises 12–14, a spinner with three equal-sized sections marked A, B, and C is spun 100 times.

Section	Frequency
A	24
B	50
C	26

12. What is the theoretical probability of landing on A?
13. The results of the experiment are shown in the table. What is the experimental probability of landing on A? of landing on C?
14. Make a drawing of what the spinner might look like based on its experimental probabilities. Explain your reasoning.

GIFTS For Exercises 15–17, use the graph at the right.

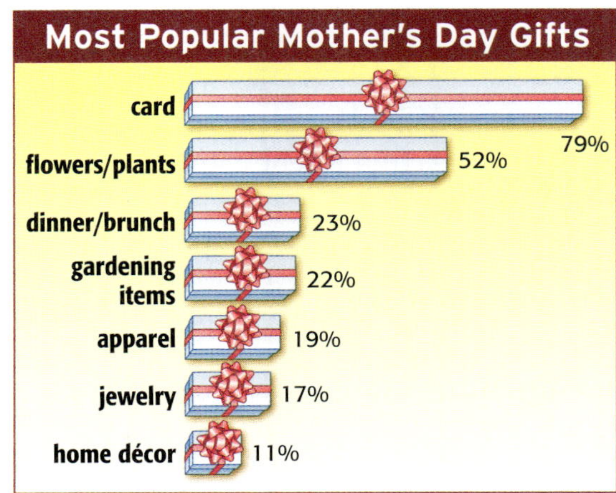

Source: Carlton Cards

15. What is the probability that a mother will receive a gift of flowers or plants? Write the probability as a fraction.
16. Out of 400 mothers that receive gifts, predict how many will receive flowers or plants.
17. Out of 750 mothers that receive gifts, is it reasonable to expect 250 mothers to receive jewelry? Why or why not?

H.O.T. Problems

18. **CHALLENGE** The experimental probability of a coin landing on heads is $\frac{7}{12}$. If the coin landed on tails 30 times, find the number of tosses.

19. **REASONING** Twenty sharpened pencils are placed in a box containing an unknown number of unsharpened pencils. Suppose 15 pencils are taken out at random, of which five are sharpened. Based on this, is it reasonable to assume that the number of unsharpened pencils was 40? Explain your reasoning.

20. **WRITING IN MATH** Compare and contrast experimental probability and theoretical probability.

TEST PRACTICE

21. The frequency table shows Mitch's record for the last thirty par-3 holes he has played.

Mitch's Golf Results	
Score	**Number of Holes**
2	4
3	14
4	9
5	3

Based on this record, what is the probability that Mitch will score a 2 or 3 on the next par-3 hole?

A $\frac{7}{9}$ C $\frac{3}{10}$

B $\frac{3}{5}$ D $\frac{9}{50}$

22. J.R. tossed a coin 100 times and graphed the results.

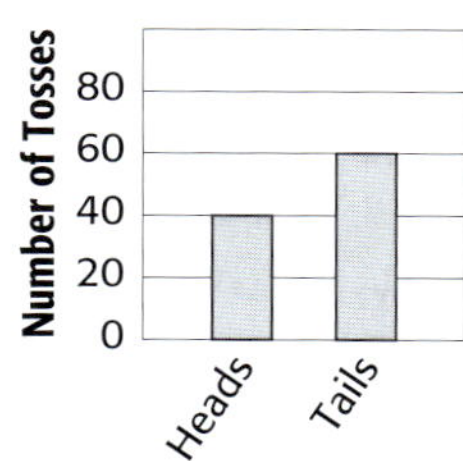

Based on this information, what is the experimental probability of tossing tails on the next toss?

F $\frac{1}{5}$ H $\frac{3}{5}$

G $\frac{2}{3}$ J $\frac{4}{5}$

Spiral Review

23. **SPINNERS** In how many ways could the colors in the spinner shown be arranged so that red and blue remain in the same places? (Lesson 9-6)

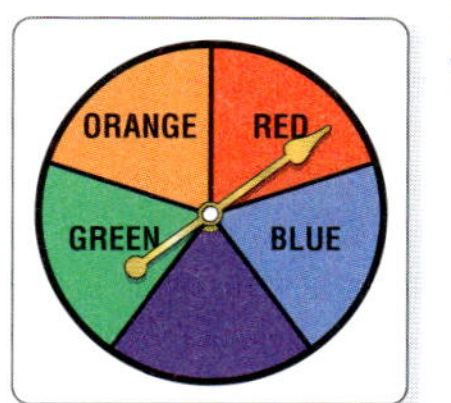

24. **BASEBALL** How many ways can a baseball coach select four starting pitchers from a pitching staff of eight? (Lesson 9-5)

25. **CLOTHES** A pair of jeans comes in 4 different styles, 3 different colors, and 5 different sizes. How many unique outcomes are possible? (Lesson 9-3)

GET READY for the Next Lesson

PREREQUISITE SKILL **Write each fraction as a percent.** (Lesson 6-9)

26. $\frac{4}{5}$ 27. $\frac{11}{20}$ 28. $\frac{7}{8}$ 29. $\frac{39}{50}$

Extend 9-7

Probability Lab
Simulations

MAIN IDEA

Investigate experimental probability by conducting a simulation.

A *simulation* is a way of acting out a problem situation. Simulations often use models to act out events that would be difficult or impractical to perform. In this lab, you will simulate purchasing a box of cereal and getting one of four possible prizes inside.

ACTIVITY

STEP 1 Place four different colored cubes into a paper bag.

STEP 2 Without looking, draw a cube from the bag, record its color, and then place the cube back in the bag.

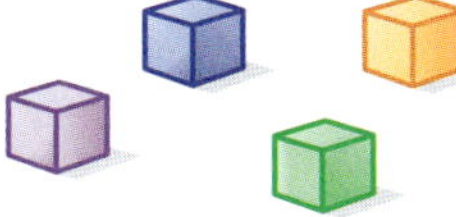

STEP 3 Repeat steps 1 and 2 until you have drawn a cube from the bag a total of four times.

Analyze the Results

1. Based on your results, predict the probability of getting each prize.
2. What is the theoretical probability of getting each prize?
3. How do your probabilities in Exercises 1 and 2 compare?
4. **MAKE A PREDICTION** Predict the probability of selecting all four prizes in four boxes of cereal.
5. Repeat the simulation above 20 times. Use this data to predict the probability of selecting all four prizes in four boxes of cereal.
6. Calculate the experimental probability described in Exercise 5 using the combined data of five different groups. How does this probability compare with your prediction?
7. Describe a simulation that could be used to predict the probability of taking a five question true/false test and getting all five questions correct by guessing. Choose from among two-sided counters, number cubes, coins, or spinners as your model.
8. **COLLECT THE DATA** Conduct 50 trials of the experiment you described in Exercise 7. Then calculate the experimental probability of getting all five questions correct by guessing.

9-8 Compound Events

MAIN IDEA

Find the probability of independent and dependent events.

New Vocabulary

compound event
independent events
dependent events
disjoint events

Math Online

glencoe.com

- Extra Examples
- Personal Tutor
- Self-Check Quiz

GET READY for the Lesson

MONEY Reginald has 3 state quarters, one from Colorado, one from Montana, and one from Washington.

1. If Reginald picks one quarter without looking, what is the probability it is from Colorado?
2. Suppose he tosses the coin. What is the probability it lands heads up?
3. Make a tree diagram to find the probability of choosing a Colorado quarter that lands heads up.
4. How are the answers to Exercises 1, 2, and 3 related?

In the example above, choosing a quarter and tossing heads is a compound event. A **compound event** consists of two or more simple events. Since choosing a quarter does not affect tossing heads, the two events are called **independent events**. The outcome of one event does not affect the outcome of the other event.

EXAMPLE Independent Events

1 **A coin is tossed, and the spinner shown is spun. Find the probability of tossing heads and spinning a consonant.**

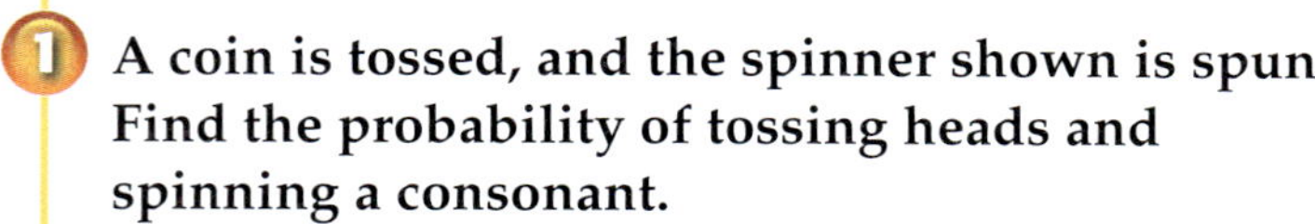

List the sample space. Use H for heads and T for tails.

H, A	H, B	H, C
T, A	T, B	T, C

$$P(\text{H and a consonant}) = \frac{\text{number of times heads and a consonant occurs}}{\text{number of possible outcomes}}$$

$$P(\text{H and a consonant}) = \frac{2}{6} \text{ or } \frac{1}{3}$$

So, the probability is $\frac{1}{3}$ or about 33%.

CHECK Your Progress

A number cube is rolled, and the spinner in Example 1 is spun. Find each probability.

a. $P(4 \text{ and a consonant})$

b. $P(\text{odd and a B})$

The probability in Example 1 can also be found by multiplying the probabilities of each event. $P(\text{H}) = \frac{1}{2}$ and $P(\text{consonant}) = \frac{1}{3}$ and so $P(\text{H and C}) = \frac{1}{2} \cdot \frac{1}{3}$ or $\frac{1}{6}$. This leads to the following.

Probability of Independent Events

Key Concept

Words The probability of two independent events can be found by multiplying the probability of the first event by the probability of the second event.

Symbols $P(A \text{ and } B) = P(A) \cdot P(B)$

Real-World EXAMPLE

2 **SHOPPING** **Brianna is buying a new outfit. She is choosing among 2 red, 1 purple, 3 pink, or 4 yellow tops. For pants, she is choosing between jeans or capris. If Brianna chooses a top and capris at random, find the probability that she chooses a yellow top and jeans.**

$P(\text{yellow top and jeans})$

$= P(\text{yellow top}) \cdot P(\text{jeans})$

$= \frac{4}{10} \cdot \frac{1}{2}$ — 4 out of 10 tops are yellow. 1 out of 2 pants are jeans.

$= \frac{\overset{2}{\cancel{4}}}{10} \cdot \frac{1}{\underset{1}{\cancel{2}}} = \frac{2}{10}$ or $\frac{1}{5}$ — Simplify.

So, the probability is $\frac{1}{5}$ or about 20%.

Reasonable Answer
You can check your answer in Example 2 by listing the sample space or by making a tree diagram.

CHECK Your Progress

c. **SHOPPING** If khakis and shorts are added to Brianna's pant choices, find the probability that she chooses a red top and capris.

If the outcome of one event affects the outcome of a second event, the events are called **dependent events**. Just as in independent events, the probabilities of dependent events can be found by multiplying the probabilities of each event. However, now the probability of the second event depends on the fact that the first event has already occurred.

Probability of Dependent Events

Key Concept

Words If two events, A and B, are dependent, then the probability of both events occurring is the product of the probability of A and the probability of B after A occurs.

Symbols $P(A \text{ and } B) = P(A) \cdot P(B \text{ following } A)$

EXAMPLE Dependent Events

3 There are 2 red, 5 green, and 8 yellow marbles in a jar. Martina randomly selects two marbles without replacing the first marble. What is the probability that she selects two green marbles?

Since the first marble is not replaced, the first event affects the second event. These are dependent events.

$P(\text{first marble is green}) = \frac{5}{15}$ ← number of green marbles / ← total number of marbles

$P(\text{second marble is green}) = \frac{4}{14}$ ← number of green marbles after one green marble is removed / ← total number of marbles after one green marble is removed

$P(\text{two green marbles}) = \frac{\overset{1}{\cancel{5}}}{\underset{3}{\cancel{15}}} \cdot \frac{\overset{2}{\cancel{4}}}{\underset{7}{\cancel{14}}} \text{ or } \frac{2}{21}$

So, the probability of selecting two green marbles is $\frac{2}{21}$, or about 9.5%.

CHECK Your Progress

d. There are 4 blueberry, 6 raisin, and 2 plain bagels in a bag. Javier randomly selects two bagels without replacing the first bagel. Find the probability that he selects a raisin bagel and then a plain bagel.

Sometimes two events cannot happen at the same time. For example, when a coin is tossed, the outcome of heads cannot happen at the same time as tails. Either heads *or* tails will turn up. Tossing heads and tossing tails are examples of **disjoint events**, or events that cannot happen at the same time. Disjoint events are also called *mutually exclusive events*.

Study Tip

Disjoint Events When finding the probabilities of disjoint events, the word *or* is usually used.

EXAMPLE Disjoint Events

4 A number cube is rolled. What is the probability of rolling an odd number or a 6?

These are disjoint events since it is impossible to roll an odd number and a 6 at the same time.

$P(\text{odd number or } 6) = \frac{4}{6}$ ← There are four favorable outcomes: 1, 3, 5, or 6. / ← There are 6 total possible outcomes.

So, the probability of rolling an odd number or a 6 is $\frac{4}{6}$, or $\frac{2}{3}$.

CHECK Your Progress

e. Twenty-six cards are labeled, each with a letter of the alphabet, and placed in a box. A single card is randomly selected. What is the probability that the card selected will be labeled with the letter M or the letter T?

Study Tip

Probability
The probability of two disjoint events is the sum of the two individual probabilities. The probability of two independent events is the product of the two individual probabilities.

Notice that the probability in Example 4 can also be found by adding the probabilities of each event.

Probability of Disjoint Events — Key Concept

Words If two events, *A* and *B*, are disjoint, then the probability that either *A* or *B* occurs is the sum of their probabilities.

Symbols $P(A \text{ or } B) = P(A) + P(B)$

CHECK Your Understanding

Example 1 (p. 492)

A number cube is rolled, and the spinner is spun. Find each probability.

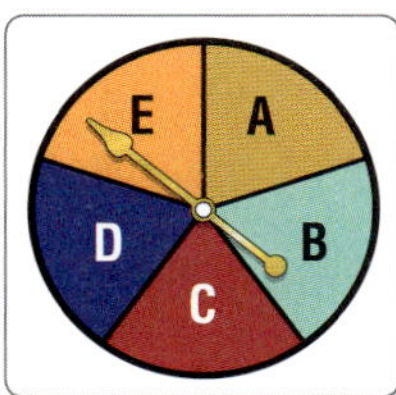

1. P(5 and E)
2. P(2 and vowel)
3. P(3 and a consonant)
4. P(factor of 6 and D)

Example 2 (p. 493)

5. **CLOTHES** Loretta has 2 pairs of black pants, 3 pairs of blue pants, and 1 pair of tan pants. She also has 4 white and 2 red shirts. If Loretta chooses a pair of pants and a shirt at random, what is the probability that she will choose a pair of black pants and a white shirt?

6. **MARBLES** A jar contains 12 marbles. Four are red, 3 are white, and 5 are blue. A marble is randomly selected, its color recorded, and then the marble is returned to the jar. A second marble is randomly selected. Find the probability that both marbles selected are blue.

Example 3 (p. 494)

7. The digits 0–9 are each written on a slip of paper and placed in a hat. Two slips of paper are randomly selected, without replacing the first. What is the probability that the number 0 is drawn first and then a 7 is drawn?

Example 4 (p. 494)

A number cube is rolled. Find each probability.

8. P(4 or 5)
9. P(3 or even number)
10. P(1 or multiple of 2)
11. P(6 or number less than 3)

Practice and Problem Solving

HOMEWORK HELP

For Exercises	See Examples
12–17	1
18–19	2
20–21	3
22–25	4

A coin is tossed, and a number cube is rolled. Find each probability.

12. P(heads and 1)
13. P(tails and multiple of 3)

A set of five cards is labeled 1–5. A second set of ten cards contains the following colors: 2 red, 3 purple, and 5 green. One card from each set is selected. Find each probability.

14. P(5 and green)
15. P(odd and red)
16. P(prime and purple)
17. P(even and yellow)

18. **MUSIC** Denzel is listening to a CD that contains 12 songs. If he presses the random button on his CD player, what is the probability that the first two songs played will be the first two songs listed on the album?

19. **JUICE POPS** Lakita has two boxes of juice pops with an equal number of pops in each flavor. Find the probability of randomly selecting a grape juice pop from the first box and randomly selecting a juice pop from the second box that is *not* grape.

20. **FRUIT** Francesca randomly selects two pieces of fruit from a basket containing 8 oranges and 4 apples without replacing the first fruit. Find the probability that she selects two oranges.

21. **SCHOOL** The names of 24 students, of which 14 are girls and 10 are boys, in Mr. Santiago's science class are written on cards and placed in a jar. Mr. Santiago randomly selects two cards without replacing the first to determine which students will present their lab reports today. Find the probability that two boys are selected.

A day of the week is randomly selected. Find each probability.

22. P(Monday or Tuesday)
23. P(a day beginning with T or Friday)
24. P(a weekday or Saturday)
25. P(Wednesday or a day with 6 letters)

A coin is tossed twice, and a letter is randomly picked from the word *event*. Find each probability.

26. P(two heads and T)
27. P(tails, *not* tails, consonant)
28. P(heads, tails, *not* V)
29. P(two tails and vowel)

FAMILY For Exercises 30–32, use the fact that the probability for a boy or a girl is each $\frac{1}{2}$.

30. Copy and complete the table that gives the probability that all the children in a family are boys given the number of children in the family.

Number of Children	P(all boys)
1	$\frac{1}{2}$
2	$\frac{1}{2} \cdot \frac{1}{2}$ or $\frac{1}{4}$
3	■
4	■
5	■

31. Predict the probability that, in a family of ten children, all ten are boys.

32. Predict the probability that, in a family of n children, all n are boys.

33. **LIGHTING** Gene has set two of his lights on timers. He always has at least one light on between the hours of 8:00 P.M. and 7:00 A.M. Light A is on 30% of the time, and Light B is on 70% of the time. What is the probability both lights are on at the same time?

34. **RESEARCH** The *contiguous* United States consists of all states excluding Alaska and Hawaii. If one of these contiguous states is chosen at random, what is the probability that it will end with the letter A or O? Write as a percent.

EXTRA PRACTICE
See pages 693, 712.

H.O.T. Problems

CHALLENGE For Exercises 35 and 36, use the spinner.

35. Use a tree diagram to construct the sample space of all the possible outcomes of three successive spins.

36. Suppose the spinner is designed so that for each spin there is a 40% probability of spinning red and a 20% chance of spinning blue. What is the probability of spinning two reds and then one blue?

37. **WRITING IN MATH** A shelf has books A, B, and C on it. You pick a book at random, place it on a table, and then pick a second book. Explain why the probability that you picked books A and B is *not* $\frac{1}{9}$.

38. A jar contains 8 white marbles, 4 green marbles, and 2 purple marbles. If Darla picks one marble from the jar without looking, what is the probability that it will be either white or purple?

A $\frac{5}{7}$ C $\frac{2}{7}$

B $\frac{4}{7}$ D $\frac{1}{7}$

39. What is the probability of spinning a red, the number 1, and the letter A on the three spinners below?

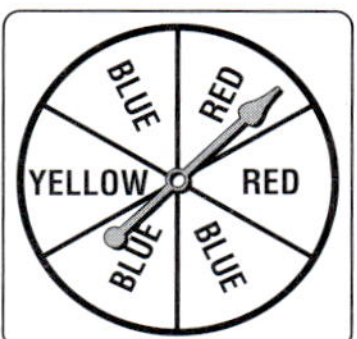

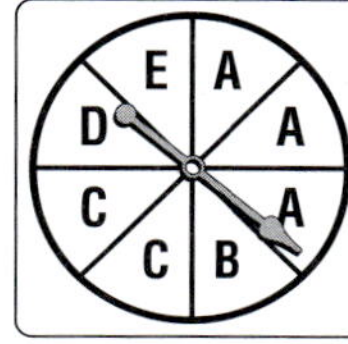

F $\frac{1}{3}$ G $\frac{1}{32}$ H $\frac{1}{12}$ J $\frac{1}{64}$

Spiral Review

40. **PROBABILITY** Ella is going to roll a number cube 30 times. How many times should she expect to roll a number greater than 2? (Lesson 9-7)

41. **CHORES** This weekend, Brennen needs to do laundry, mow the lawn, and clean his room. How many different ways can he do these three chores? (Lesson 9-6)

ALGEBRA Evaluate each expression if $a = 6$, $b = -4$, and $c = -3$. (Lesson 1-6)

42. $9c$ 43. $-8a$ 44. $2bc$ 45. $5b^2$

Problem Solving in Science

Math Genes It's time to complete your project. Use the information and data you have gathered about genetics and pet traits to prepare a poster. Be sure to include a chart displaying your data with your project.

Math Online Unit Project at glencoe.com

CHAPTER 9

Study Guide and Review

Math Online glencoe.com

• STUDY TO GO
• Vocabulary Review

GET READY to Study

Be sure the following Big Ideas are noted in your Foldable.

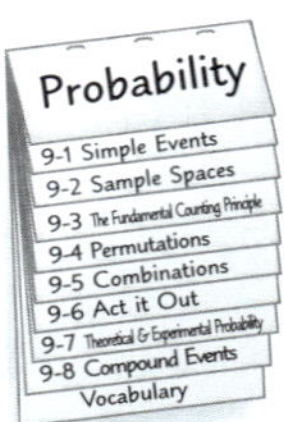

BIG Ideas

Probability (Lesson 9-1)

- The probability of a simple event is a ratio that compares the number of favorable outcomes to the number of possible outcomes.

Fundamental Counting Principle (Lesson 9-3)

- If event M has m possible outcomes and is followed by event N that has n possible outcomes, then the event M followed by N has $m \times n$ possible outcomes.

Theoretical and Experimental Probability (Lesson 9-7)

- Theoretical probability is based on what *should* happen when conducting a probability experiment.
- Experimental probability is based on what *actually occurred* during a probability experiment.

Independent Events (Lesson 9-8)

- The probability of two independent events can be found by multiplying the probability of the first event by the probability of the second event.

Dependent Events (Lesson 9-8)

- If two events, A and B, are dependent, then the probability of both events occurring is the product of the probability of A and the probability of B after A occurs.

Disjoint Events (Lesson 9-8)

- If two events are disjoint, then the probability that either event will occur is the sum of their individual probabilities.

Key Vocabulary

combination (p. 480)
complementary events (p. 462)
compound event (p. 492)
dependent events (p. 493)
disjoint events (p. 494)
experimental probability (p. 486)
Fundamental Counting Principle (p. 471)
independent events (p. 492)
outcome (p. 460)
permutation (p. 475)
probability (p. 460)
random (p. 461)
sample space (p. 465)
simple event (p. 460)
theoretical probability (p. 486)
tree diagram (p. 466)

Vocabulary Check

State whether each sentence is *true* or *false*. If *false*, replace the underlined word or number to make a true sentence.

1. Compound events consist of two or more simple events.
2. A random outcome is an outcome that occurs by chance.
3. P(not A) is read the permutation of the complement of A.
4. The Fundamental Counting Principle counts the number of possible outcomes using the operation of addition.
5. Events in which the outcome of the first event does not affect the outcome of the other event(s) are simple events.
6. The sample space of an event is the set of outcomes not included in the event.
7. Events that cannot occur at the same time are called dependent events.

Lesson-by-Lesson Review

9-1 Simple Events (pp. 460–464)

A bag of animal crackers contains 5 monkeys, 4 giraffes, 6 elephants, and 3 tigers. Suppose you draw a cracker at random. Find the probability of each event. Write as a fraction in simplest form.

8. P(monkey)
9. P(tiger)
10. P(giraffe or elephant)
11. P(*not* monkey)
12. P(monkey, giraffe, or elephant)
13. **ARRIVALS** The probability that a plane will arrive at the airport on time is $\frac{23}{25}$. Find the probability that the plane will *not* arrive on time. Write as a percent.

Example 1 **What is the probability of rolling a number less than 3 on a number cube?**

$$P(1 \text{ or } 2) = \frac{\text{numbers less than 3}}{\text{total number of possible outcomes}}$$

$= \frac{2}{6}$ Two numbers are less than 3.

$= \frac{1}{3}$ Simplify.

Therefore, $P(1 \text{ or } 2) = \frac{1}{3}$.

9-2 Sample Spaces (pp. 465–470)

For each situation, find the sample space using a table or tree diagram.

14. rolling a number cube and tossing a coin
15. choosing from pepperoni, mushroom, or cheese pizza and water, juice, or milk
16. **GAMES** Eliza and Zeke are playing a game in which Zeke spins the spinner shown and rolls a number cube. If the sum of the numbers is less than six, Eliza wins. Otherwise Zeke wins. Find the sample space. Then find the probability that Zeke wins.

Example 2 **Ginger and Micah are playing a game in which a coin is tossed twice. If heads comes up exactly once, Ginger wins. Otherwise, Micah wins. Find the sample space. Then find the probability that Ginger wins.**

Make a tree diagram.

First Toss	Second Toss	Sample Space	
H	H	HH	Micah wins.
	T	HT	Ginger wins.
T	H	TH	Ginger wins.
	T	TT	Micah wins.

There are four equally likely outcomes with 2 favoring each player. The probability that Ginger wins is $\frac{2}{4}$ or $\frac{1}{2}$.

CHAPTER 9 Study Guide and Review

9-3 The Fundamental Counting Principle (pp. 471–474)

Use the Fundamental Counting Principle to find the total number of outcomes in each situation.

17. rolling two number cubes
18. creating an outfit from 6 different shirts and 4 different pants
19. **TUXEDOS** A tuxedo shop offers a tuxedo in three colors, black, gray, and white. The tie can be a bow tie or a regular tie. The tuxedo can come with tails or no tails. If a tuxedo is selected at random, what is the probability that it will be black, with a bow tie, and no tails?

Example 3 **Use the Fundamental Counting Principle to find the total number of outcomes for a coin that is tossed four times.**

There are 2 possible outcomes, heads or tails, each time a coin is tossed. For a coin that is tossed four times, there are $2 \cdot 2 \cdot 2 \cdot 2$, or 16 outcomes.

Example 4 **Find the probability that, in a family of four children, all four children are girls.**

There are 16 outcomes. There is one possible outcome resulting in four girls. So, the probability that all four children are girls is $\frac{1}{16}$.

9-4 Permutations (pp. 475–478)

20. **PORTRAITS** In how many ways can a family of five arrange themselves in a line for a family portrait?
21. **LETTERS** How many permutations are there of the letters in the word *computer*?
22. **RUNNING** Jacinda and Raul are entered in a race with 5 other runners. If each runner is equally likely to win, what is the probability that Jacinda will finish first and Raul will finish second?

Example 5 **Nathaniel needs to choose two of the chores shown to do after school. If he is equally likely to choose the chores, what is the probability that he will walk the dog first and rake the leaves second?**

Chores
Walk the Dog
Do Homework
Clean the Kitchen
Rake the Leaves

There are $4 \cdot 3$, or 12, arrangements in which Nathaniel can complete the chores. There is one way in which he will walk the dog first and rake the leaves second. So, the probability that he will walk the dog first and rake the leaves second is $\frac{1}{12}$.

Mixed Problem Solving
For mixed problem-solving practice, see page 712.

9-5 Combinations (pp. 480–483)

23. **DVD** In how many ways can Toni select 2 DVDs from the 15 in her collection?

24. **SPORTS** How many ways can a coach select 3 players from a roster of 9?

25. **GAMES** Marcus has enough money on his gift card to purchase 3 new games from the 14 displayed in the New Release section. In how many ways can Marcus select 3 different games?

26. **QUIZ** Frances must answer 3 of the 5 questions on a quiz, numbered 1–5. What is the probability that Frances will answer questions 2, 3, and 4?

Example 6 Caitlin and Román are playing a game in which Román chooses four different numbers from 1–15. What is the probability that Caitlin will guess all four numbers correctly?

There are $15 \cdot 14 \cdot 13 \cdot 12$ permutations of four numbers chosen from 15 numbers.

There are $4 \cdot 3 \cdot 2 \cdot 1$ ways to arrange the 4 numbers.

$$\frac{15 \cdot 14 \cdot 13 \cdot 12}{4 \cdot 3 \cdot 2 \cdot 1} = \frac{32{,}760}{24} \text{ or } 1{,}365$$

There are 1,365 ways to choose four numbers from 15 numbers. There is one way to guess all four numbers correctly, so the probability that Caitlin will guess all four numbers correctly is $\frac{1}{1{,}365}$.

9-6 PSI: Act It Out (pp. 484–485)

Solve each problem. Use the *act it out* strategy.

27. **QUIZ** Determine whether tossing a coin is a good way to answer a 6-question true-false quiz. Justify your answer.

28. **FAMILY PORTRAIT** In how many ways can the Maxwell family pose for a portrait if Mr. and Mrs. Maxwell are sitting in the middle and their three children are standing behind them?

29. **AMUSEMENT PARK** In how many ways can 4 friends be seated in 2 rows of 2 seats each on a roller coaster if Judy and Harold must ride together?

Example 7 In how many ways can three females and two males sit in a row of five seats at a concert if the females must sit in the first three seats?

Place five desks or chairs in a row. Have three females and two males sit in any of the seats as long as the females sit in the first three seats. Continue rearranging until you find all the possibilities. Record the results.

$F_1\ F_2\ F_3\ M_1\ M_2$ $F_2\ F_3\ F_1\ M_1\ M_2$
$F_1\ F_2\ F_3\ M_2\ M_1$ $F_2\ F_3\ F_1\ M_2\ M_1$
$F_1\ F_3\ F_2\ M_1\ M_2$ $F_3\ F_2\ F_1\ M_1\ M_2$
$F_1\ F_3\ F_2\ M_2\ M_1$ $F_3\ F_2\ F_1\ M_2\ M_1$
$F_2\ F_1\ F_3\ M_1\ M_2$ $F_3\ F_1\ F_2\ M_1\ M_2$
$F_2\ F_1\ F_3\ M_2\ M_1$ $F_3\ F_1\ F_2\ M_2\ M_1$

There are 12 possible arrangements.

CHAPTER 9

Study Guide and Review

9-7 Theoretical and Experimental Probability (pp. 486–490)

The student council surveyed their classmates to find what they want to eat for their end-of-year celebration. The results are shown in the table. Find the experimental probability of each event.

Meal	Number of Students
pizza	26
chicken	20
hamburger	13
hot dog	5

30. P(hot dog)
31. P(chicken)
32. P(hamburger)
33. P(hot dog or hamburger)
34. P(*not* pizza)
35. P(pizza or chicken)

36. **PROBABILITY** If a spinner has four equal sections labeled 1–4, what is the theoretical probability of landing on 2?

Example 8 **A coin is tossed 65 times, and it lands on tails 40 times. What is the experimental probability of the coin landing on heads?**

The coin landed on heads 25 times.

$$P(\text{heads}) = \frac{\text{number of times heads occurs}}{\text{total number of possible outcomes}}$$

$$= \frac{25}{65} \text{ or } \frac{5}{13}$$

So, the experimental probability of the coin landing on heads is $\frac{5}{13}$ or about 38%.

9-8 Compound Events (pp. 492–497)

A bag contains 6 green, 8 white, and 2 blue counters. Two are randomly drawn. Find each probability if the first counter is replaced before the second counter is drawn. Then find each probability if the first counter is not replaced.

37. P(green, blue)
38. P(2 white)
39. P(blue, *not* white)
40. P(white, *not* green)

41. **PROBABILITY** A coin is tossed and a number cube is rolled. Find the probability that tails and a number less than 5 comes up.

42. **COMPUTERS** A computer randomly generates a digit from 0–9. Find the probability that an odd number or the number 8 is generated.

Example 9 **A number cube is rolled and a spinner with 8 equal sections labeled A through H is spun. Find the probability of rolling an even number and spinning a vowel.**

$P(\text{even}) = \frac{3}{6}$

$P(\text{vowel}) = \frac{2}{8}$

$\frac{3}{6} \cdot \frac{2}{8} = \frac{6}{48} \text{ or } \frac{1}{8}$

So, the probability of rolling an even number and spinning a vowel is $\frac{1}{8}$, or about 12.5%.

Practice Test

Math Online glencoe.com
• Chapter Test

The spinner shown has an equal chance of landing on each number. Find each probability.

1. P(odd number)
2. P(1 or 7)
3. P(*not* a prime number)
4. P(number greater than 1)

For each situation, use a table or a tree diagram to find the sample space.

5. A coin is tossed two times.
6. A letter is chosen from the word *GAME* and then a digit from the number 123.

7. **GAMES** Randall and Lucy are playing a game in which Lucy rolls a number cube and selects a card from the cards *A* and *B*. If a number less than 4 and a consonant comes up, Lucy wins. Otherwise Randall wins. Find the sample space. Then find the probability that Lucy wins.

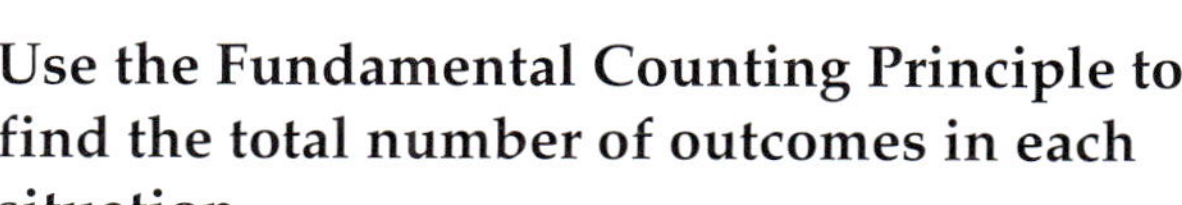

Use the Fundamental Counting Principle to find the total number of outcomes in each situation.

8. A 4-digit security code is chosen.
9. A number cube is rolled five times.

10. **MULTIPLE CHOICE** A cooler contains 8 grape juice boxes, 12 orange juice boxes, and 4 apple juice boxes. If a juice box is selected at random, what is the probability that it will be grape?

    A 50% **C** $0.1\overline{6}$
    B $\frac{1}{3}$ **D** $\frac{5}{6}$

11. **DOGS** There are 40 dogs entered in a dog show. How many ways can a first place and a second place ribbon be awarded?

12. **MULTIPLE CHOICE** There is a choice of 8 toppings for a pizza. Which of the following gives the number of ways you can order a pizza with 3 different toppings?

    F 336 **H** 56
    G 58 **J** 24

13. **CAMPING** Four campers are chosen from nine to pitch the tents. If Sandy, Jarrod, Dyami, and Clara are among the nine campers, find the probability that they are chosen.

14. **SCHOOL** Determine whether spinning a spinner with five equal sections would be a good way to answer a 5-question multiple-choice quiz. Justify your answer.

15. **PROBABILITY** A spinner is spun 60 times. The results are shown in the table. What is the experimental probability that the spinner lands on section C? Write as a percent.

Section	Number of Times
A	12
B	17
C	12
D	4
E	15

16. **PRIZES** Josh is choosing from two prize bags that each contain 5 packs of baseball cards, 11 packages of putty, and 9 hats. What is the probability that Josh randomly picks a hat from the first bag and a pack of baseball cards from the second bag?

CHAPTER 9

Test Practice

Cumulative, Chapters 1–9

Math Online glencoe.com

• Test Practice

PART 1 Multiple Choice

Read each question. Then fill in the correct answer on the answer sheet provided by your teacher or on a sheet of paper.

1. Jessica played a game where she spun each of the spinners shown below once. If she spins an even number on Spinner 1, red or yellow on Spinner 2, and a B on Spinner 3, how many possible unique combinations are there?

Spinner 1

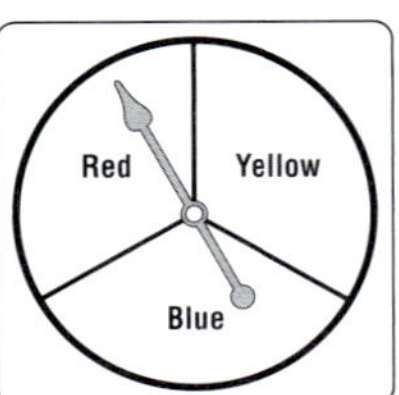

Spinner 2

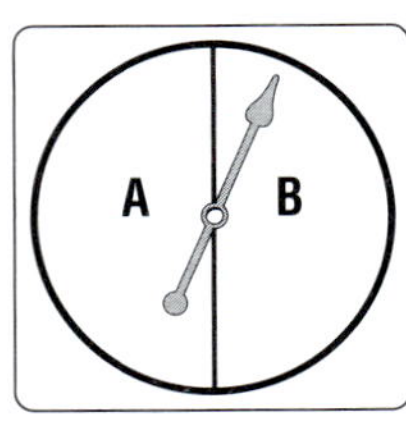

Spinner 3

A 4
B 8
C 10
D 16

2. Mr. Campos bought 40 pencils priced at 8 for \$0.99 and 3 dozen notebooks priced at 4 for \$2.49. Find the total amount, not including tax, Mr. Campos spent on pencils and notebooks.

F \$28.86
G \$27.36
H \$17.88
J \$15.96

3. In a movie theater there are 168 seats. If 75% of the theater is filled, how many people are sitting in the movie theater?

A 156
B 148
C 134
D 126

4. Mr. Blackwell gave his math students a pop quiz. The students' scores are listed below. What is the median quiz score?

23	19	18	12	21	24	25

F 12
G 21
H 24
J 25

5. The results of an election for student body president showed that Trey received 250 votes, Marta 100 votes, and Ed 50 votes. Which of the following correctly displays the election results?

A
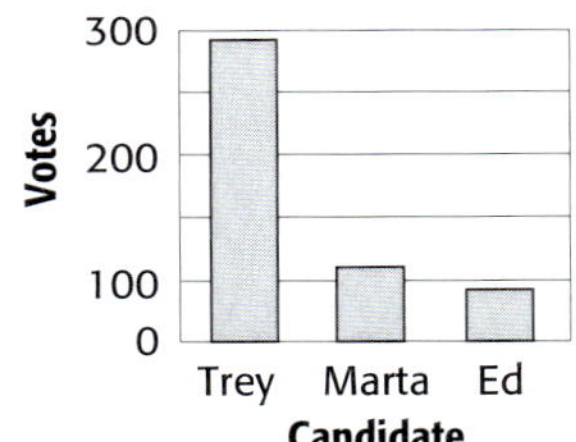

B
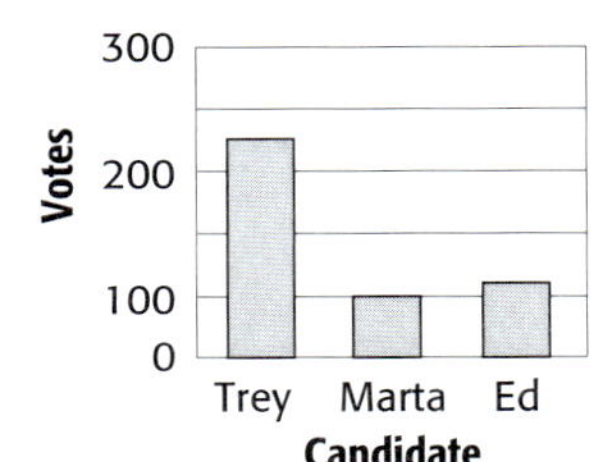

C
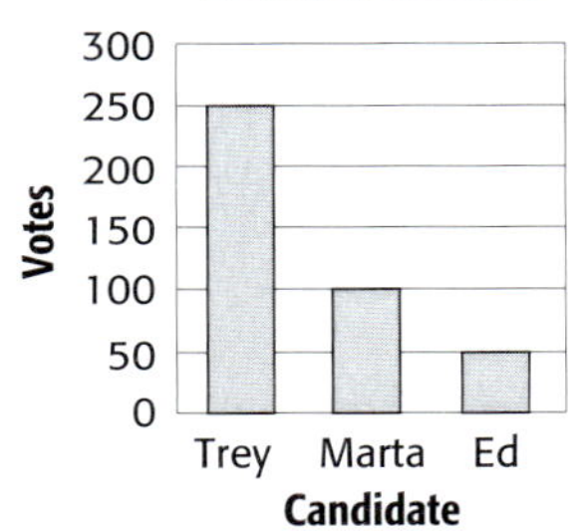

D
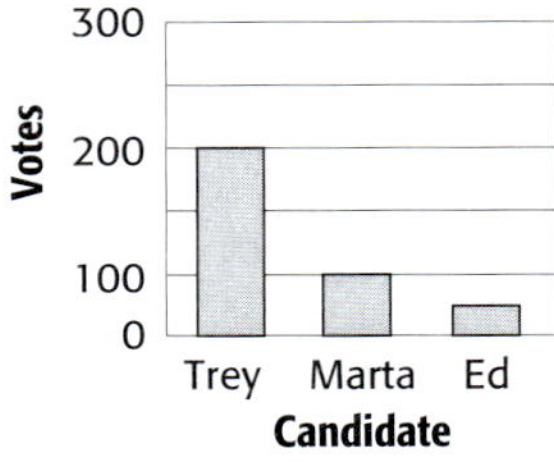

6. What is $4 \div \frac{1}{3}$?

F $\frac{1}{12}$
G $\frac{4}{3}$
H 7
J 12

Preparing for Standardized Tests

For test-taking strategies and practice, see pages 716–733.

7. Hanako spins each spinner shown below once. Find the total possible letter/number combinations that could have resulted from Hanako's spins.

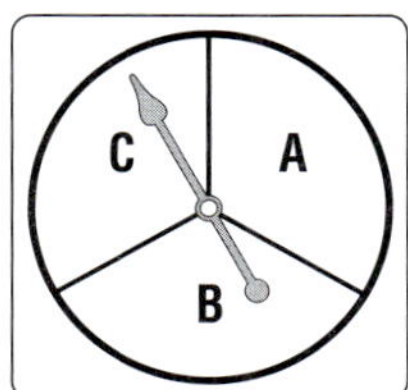

First Spinner

1 2 3

Second Spinner

A 3
B 6
C 9
D 12

8. Juan rolled a number cube four times. Each time, the number 3 appeared. If Juan rolls the number cube one more time, what is the probability that the number 3 will appear?

F $\frac{2}{3}$
G $\frac{1}{2}$
H $\frac{1}{6}$
J $\frac{5}{6}$

TEST-TAKING TIP

Question 8 You may want to find your own answer before looking at the answer choices. This keeps you from choosing an answer that looks correct, but is still wrong.

9. The owner of a fruit stand has x pounds of apples on display. She sells 30 pounds and then adds $4y$ pounds of apples to the display. Which of the following expressions represents the weight in pounds of the apples that are now on the display?

A $x + 30 + 4y$
B $x - 30 + 4y$
C $x + 30 - 4y$
D $x - 30 - 4y$

PART 2 Short Response/Grid In

Record your answers on the answer sheet provided by your teacher or on a sheet of paper.

10. A building is 182 meters tall. About how tall is the building in feet and inches? (1 meter $\approx$ 39 inches)

11. Wilson has 7 different pieces of fruit in his refrigerator. If he randomly selects 3 pieces of fruit, how many possible unique combinations are there?

12. In how many ways can you select 3 flowers out of 9?

PART 3 Extended Response

Record your answers on the answer sheet provided by your teacher or on a sheet of paper. Show your work.

13. Audrey is going on vacation. She packs 4 shirts and 3 pairs of pants. The shirts are red, green, yellow, and pink. The pants are black, white, and brown.

   a. Make a tree diagram that shows all of the outfits that Audrey can make.

   b. If Audrey chooses a shirt and pair of pants at random, what is the probability that she will wear a red shirt with white pants on the first day of her vacation?

   c. Audrey does not repeat outfits. What is the probability that she will wear a yellow shirt with black pants on the first day and a green shirt with brown pants on the second day?

NEED EXTRA HELP?													
If You Missed Question...	1	2	3	4	5	6	7	8	9	10	11	12	13
Go to Lesson...	9-2	1-1	7-1	8-2	8-4	5-7	9-2	9-8	3-1	6-8	9-2	9-5	9-8

Unit 5

Geometry and Measurement

Focus

Use formulas to determine surface areas and volumes of three-dimensional shapes.

CHAPTER 10
Geometry: Polygons

BIG Idea Identify and describe properties of two-dimensional figures.

CHAPTER 11
Measurement: Two- and Three-Dimensional Figures

BIG Idea Use formulas to determine area and volume of two- and three-dimensional figures.

BIG Idea Derive and determine the area of a circle.

CHAPTER 12
Looking Ahead to Next Year: Geometry and Measurement

BIG Idea Find length using the Pythagorean Theorem.

BIG Idea Find surface areas of rectangular prisms and cylinders.

Problem Solving in Life Skills

Real-World Unit Project

Design That House Are you ready to become an architect? You've been selected to design and decorate a dream house. Along the way, you'll determine actual angle measures and wall lengths of the blueprint you'll be creating of your dream house. Your journey will begin soon, so pack your geometry tool kit.

Math Online **Log on to glencoe.com to begin.**

Geometry: Polygons

- Identify and describe properties of two-dimensional figures.

Key Vocabulary

complementary angles (p. 514)
line of symmetry (p. 558)
similar figures (p. 540)
supplementary angles (p. 514)

Real-World Link

Tulips Holland, Michigan, hosts a Tulip Time Festival each May. Geometry is used to explain how a tulip shows rotational symmetry.

FOLDABLES® Study Organizer

Geometry: Polygons Make this Foldable to help you organize your notes. Begin with a piece of 11″ by 17″ paper.

1. **Fold** a 2″ tab along the long side of the paper.

2. **Unfold** the paper and fold in thirds widthwise.

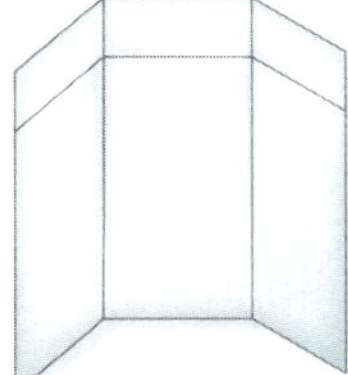

3. **Open** and draw lines along the folds. Label the head of each column as shown. Label the front of the folded table with the chapter title.

What I Know About Polygons	What I Need to Know	What I've Learned

GET READY for Chapter 10

Diagnose Readiness You have two options for checking Prerequisite Skills.

Option 2

Math Online Take the Online Readiness Quiz at glencoe.com.

Option 1

Take the Quick Quiz below. Refer to the Quick Review for help.

QUICK Quiz

Multiply or divide. Round to the nearest hundredth if necessary. (Prior Grade)

1. 360×0.85
2. $48 \div 191$
3. $24 \div 156$
4. 0.37×360
5. $33 \div 307$
6. 0.69×360

Solve each equation. (Lesson 3-2)

7. $122 + x + 14 = 180$
8. $45 + 139 + k + 17 = 360$
9. **SCHOOL** There are 180 school days at Lee Middle School. If school has been in session for 62 days and there are 13 days until winter break, how many school days are after the break? (Lesson 3-2)

Solve each proportion. (Lesson 6-5)

10. $\frac{4}{a} = \frac{3}{9}$
11. $\frac{7}{16} = \frac{h}{32}$
12. $\frac{5}{8} = \frac{15}{y}$
13. $\frac{t}{42} = \frac{6}{7}$
14. **READING** Sandra can read 28 pages of a novel in 45 minutes. At this rate, how many pages can she read in 135 minutes? (Lesson 6-6)

QUICK Review

Example 1

Find 0.92 × 360.

$$\begin{array}{r} 360 \\ \times\ 0.92 \\ \hline 720 \\ +\ 32400 \\ \hline 331.20 \end{array}$$

0.92 ← two decimal places

331.20 ← two decimal places

So, $0.92 \times 360 = 331.2$.

Example 2

Solve the equation.
46 + 90 + p = 180.

$46 + 90 + p = 180$	Write the equation.
$136 + p = 180$	Add 46 and 90.
$-136 \quad -136$	Subtract 136 from each side.
$p = 44$	

The solution to the equation $46 + 90 + p = 180$ is $p = 44$.

Example 3

Solve the proportion $\frac{3}{8} = \frac{g}{48}$.

$\frac{3}{8} = \frac{g}{48}$ Write a proportion.

×6

$\frac{3}{8} = \frac{18}{48}$ Since $8 \times 6 = 48$, multiply 3 by 6 to find g.

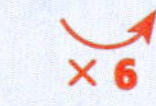

×6

So, $g = 18$.

10-1 Angle Relationships

MAIN IDEA

Classify angles and identify vertical and adjacent angles.

New Vocabulary

angle
degrees
vertex
congruent angles
right angle
acute angle
obtuse angle
straight angle
vertical angles
adjacent angles

Math Online

glencoe.com

- Extra Examples
- Personal Tutor
- Self-Check Quiz
- Reading in the Content Area

GET READY for the Lesson

ROLLER COASTERS The angles of descent of a roller coaster are shown.

1. The roller coaster at the right shows two angles of descent. Draw an angle between 44° and 70°.
2. Some roller coasters have an angle of descent that is 90°, known as a vertical angle of descent. Draw a vertical angle of descent.

An **angle** has two sides that share a common endpoint and is measured in units called **degrees**. If a circle were divided into 360 equal-sized parts, each part would have an angle measure of 1 degree (1°).

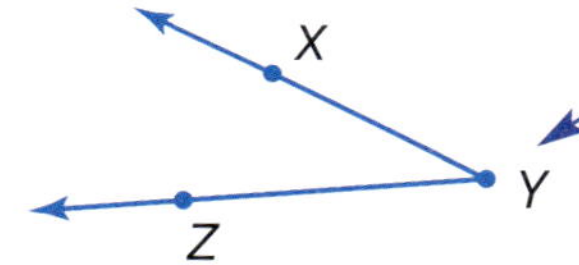

A **vertex** is the point where the sides meet.

An angle can be named in several ways. The symbol for angle is ∠.

EXAMPLE Naming Angles

1 **Name the angle at the right.**

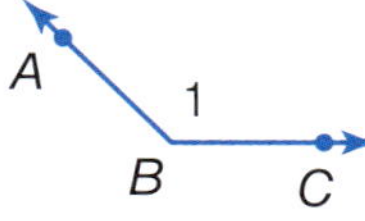

- Use the vertex as the middle letter and a point from each side.
  $\angle ABC$ or $\angle CBA$
- Use the vertex only.
  $\angle B$
- Use a number.
  $\angle 1$

The angle can be named in four ways: $\angle ABC$, $\angle CBA$, $\angle B$, or $\angle 1$.

CHECK Your Progress

a. Name the angle shown in four ways.

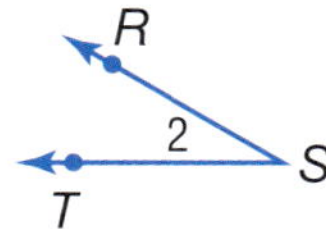

Angles are classified according to their measure. Two angles that have the same measure are said to be **congruent**.

Types of Angles

Key Concept

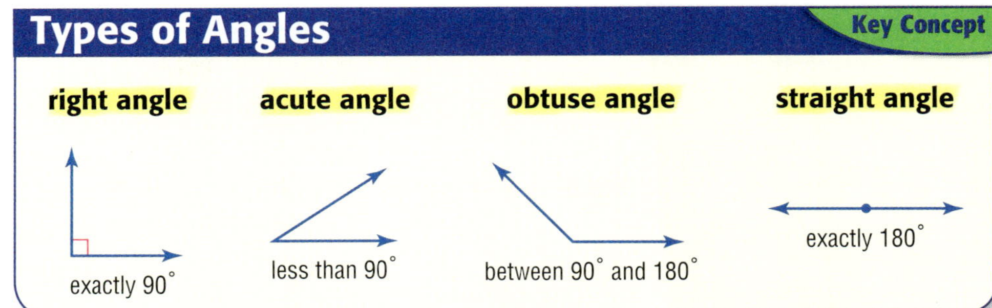

Study Tip

Right Angles The square corner indicates a right angle.

EXAMPLES Classify Angles

Classify each angle as *acute, obtuse, right,* or *straight*.

2 The angle is less than 90°, so it is an acute angle.

3 The angle is between 90° and 180°, so it is an obtuse angle.

CHECK Your Progress

Classify each angle as *acute, obtuse, right,* or *straight*.

b. c. d.

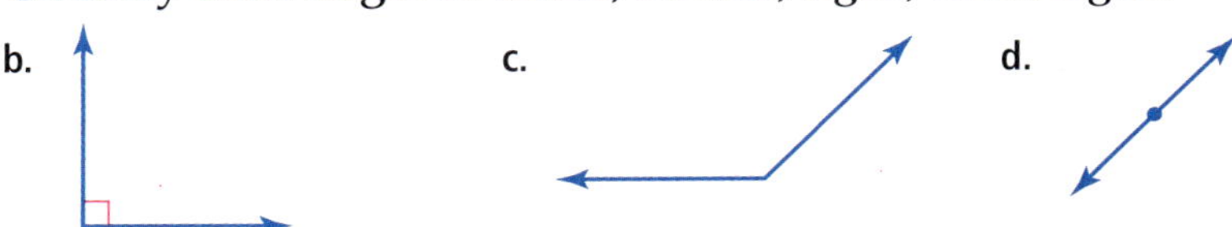

Study Tip

Classifying Angles You do not need to use a protractor to measure an angle in order to classify it as acute, obtuse, right, or straight.

Vertical Angles

Key Concept

Words Two angles are **vertical** if they are opposite angles formed by the intersection of two lines.

Examples

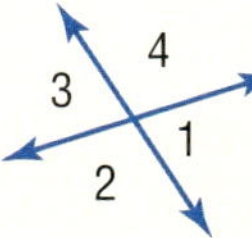

∠1 and ∠3 are vertical angles.
∠2 and ∠4 are vertical angles.

Adjacent Angles

Words Two angles are **adjacent** if they share a common vertex, a common side, and do not overlap.

Examples

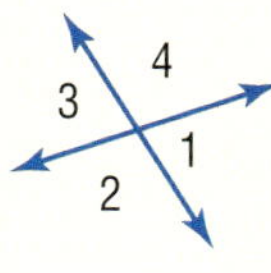

Adjacent angle pairs are ∠1 and ∠2, ∠2 and ∠3, ∠3 and ∠4, and ∠4 and ∠1.

∠5 and ∠6 are adjacent angles.

4 INTERSECTIONS Identify a pair of vertical angles in the diagram at the right. Justify your response.

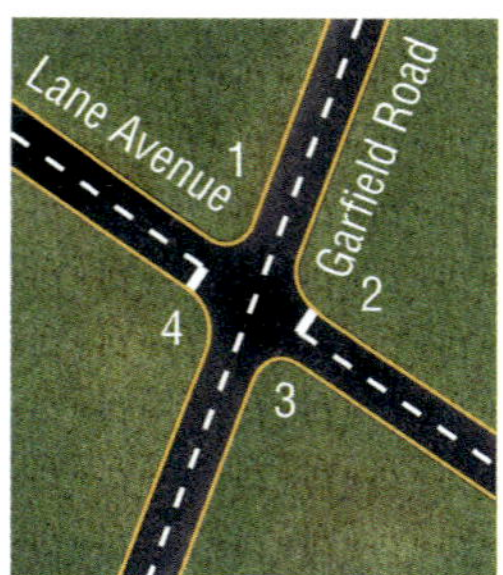

Since ∠2 and ∠4 are opposite angles formed by the intersection of two lines, they are vertical angles. Similarly, ∠1 and ∠3 are also vertical angles.

Refer to the diagram at the right. Identify each of the following. Justify your response.

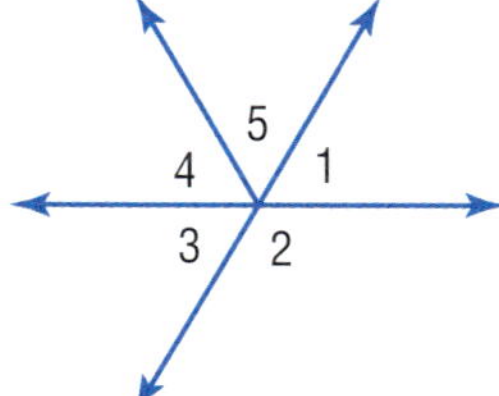

e. a pair of vertical angles

f. a pair of adjacent angles

CHECK Your Understanding

Examples 1–3 (pp. 510–511)

Name each angle in four ways. Then classify the angle as *acute*, *right*, *obtuse*, or *straight*.

1. 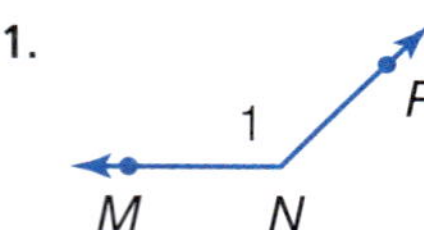

2. S R T 3

Example 4 (p. 512)

3. **RAILROADS** Identify a pair of vertical angles on the railroad crossing sign. Justify your response.

Practice and Problem Solving

HOMEWORK HELP	
For Exercises	See Examples
4–9	1–3
10–17	4

Name each angle in four ways. Then classify the angle as *acute*, *right*, *obtuse*, or *straight*.

4. 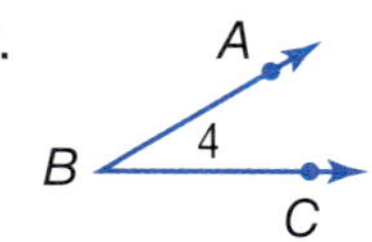

5. 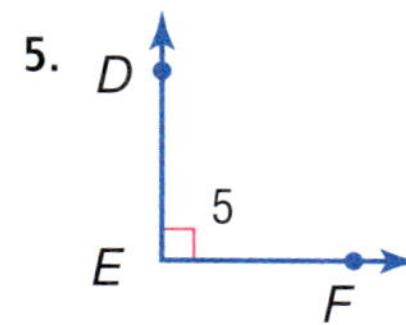

6. 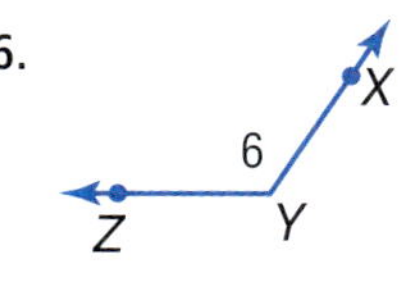

7. M 7 P N

8. 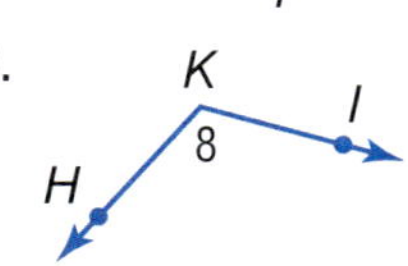

9. 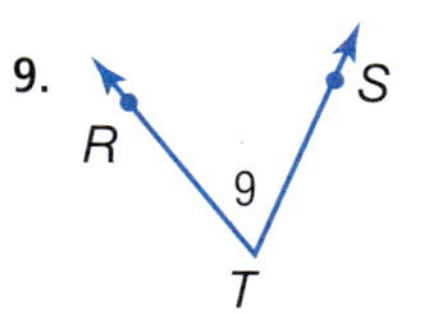

For Exercises 10–15, refer to the diagram at the right. Identify each angle pair as *adjacent*, *vertical*, or *neither*.

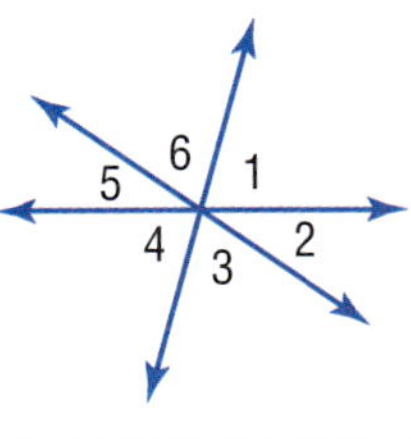

10. ∠2 and ∠5
11. ∠4 and ∠6
12. ∠3 and ∠4
13. ∠5 and ∠6
14. ∠1 and ∠3
15. ∠1 and ∠4

GEOGRAPHY For Exercises 16 and 17, use the diagram at the right and the following information.

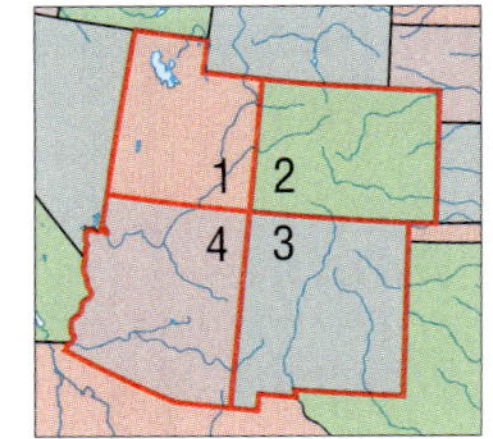

The corner where the states of Utah, Arizona, New Mexico, and Colorado meet is called the Four Corners.

EXTRA PRACTICE
See pages 693, 713.

16. Identify a pair of vertical angles. Justify your response.
17. Identify a pair of adjacent angles. Justify your response.

H.O.T. Problems

CHALLENGE For Exercises 18 and 19, determine whether each statement is *true* or *false*. If the statement is true, provide a diagram to support it. If the statement is false, explain why.

18. A pair of obtuse angles can also be vertical angles.
19. A pair of straight angles can also be adjacent angles.
20. **WRITING IN MATH** Describe the differences between vertical and adjacent angles.

TEST PRACTICE

21. Which word best describes the angle marked in the figure?

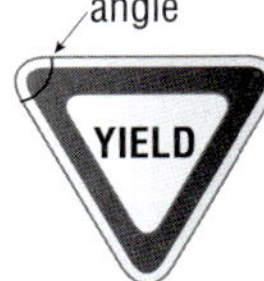

A acute

B obtuse

C right

D straight

22. Which statement is true?

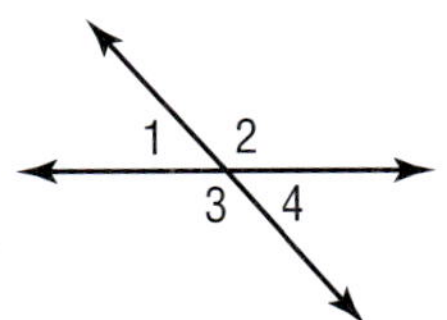

F ∠1 and ∠4 are adjacent angles.

G ∠2 and ∠3 are vertical angles.

H ∠3 and ∠4 are vertical angles.

J ∠2 and ∠3 are adjacent angles.

Spiral Review

A coin is tossed twice and a number cube is rolled. Find each probability. (Lesson 9-8)

23. P(2 heads and 6)
24. P(1 head, 1 tail, and a 3)
25. P(2 tails and *not* 4)

26. **PROBABILITY** A spinner is spun 20 times, and it lands on the color red 5 times. What is the experimental probability of *not* landing on red? (Lesson 9-7)

GET READY for the Next Lesson

ALGEBRA Solve each equation. Check your solution. (Lesson 3-2)

27. $44 + x = 90$
28. $117 + x = 180$
29. $90 = 36 + x$
30. $180 = 75 + x$

10-2 Complementary and Supplementary Angles

MAIN IDEA

Identify complementary and supplementary angles and find missing angle measures.

New Vocabulary

complementary angles
supplementary angles

Math Online

glencoe.com

- Extra Examples
- Personal Tutor
- Self-Check Quiz

MINI Lab

GEOMETRY Refer to ∠A shown at the right.

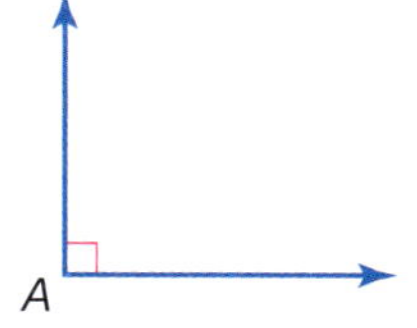

1. Classify it as *acute, right, obtuse,* or *straight.*
2. Copy the angle onto a piece of paper. Then draw a ray that separates the angle into two congruent angles. Label these angles ∠1 and ∠2.
3. What is $m\angle 1$ and $m\angle 2$?
4. What is the sum of $m\angle 1$ and $m\angle 2$?
5. Copy the original angle onto a piece of paper. Then draw a ray that separates the angle into two non-congruent angles. Label these angles ∠3 and ∠4.
6. What is true about the sum of $m\angle 3$ and $m\angle 4$?
7. Complete Exercises 1–6 for ∠B shown at the right.

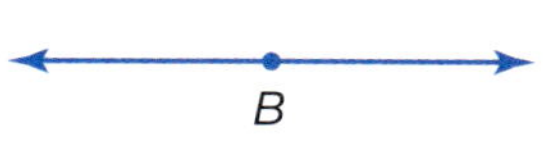

A special relationship exists between two angles whose sum is 90°. A special relationship also exists between two angles whose sum is 180°.

Complementary Angles

Key Concept

Words Two angles are **complementary** if the sum of their measures is 90°.

Examples

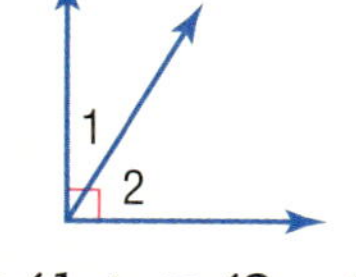

$m\angle 1 + m\angle 2 = 90°$

55° 35°

$55° + 35° = 90°$

Supplementary Angles

Words Two angles are **supplementary** if the sum of their measures is 180°.

Examples

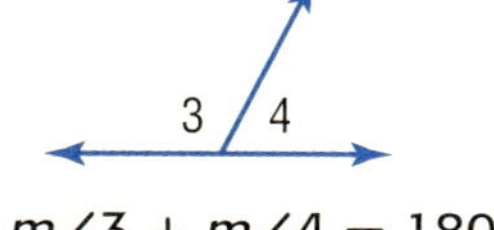

$m\angle 3 + m\angle 4 = 180°$

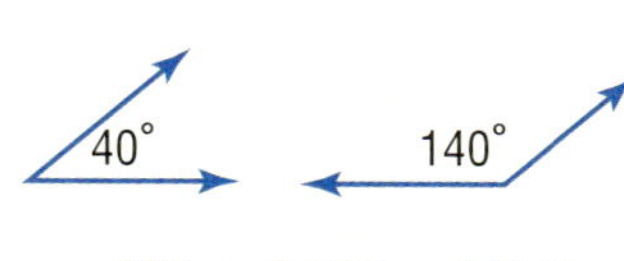

$40° + 140° = 180°$

Reading Math

Angle Measure The notation $m\angle 1$ is read *the measure of angle 1.*

You can use these relationships to identify complementary and supplementary angles.

EXAMPLES Identify Angles

Identify each pair of angles as *complementary*, *supplementary*, or *neither*.

1

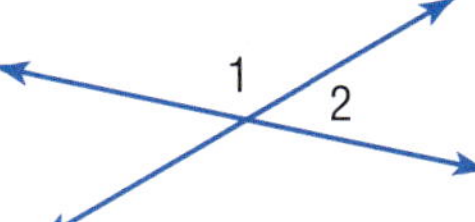

∠1 and ∠2 form a straight angle. So, the angles are supplementary.

2

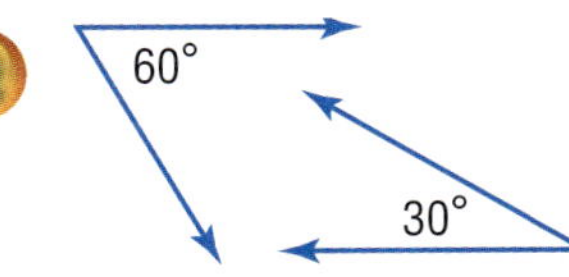

$60° + 30° = 90°$
The angles are complementary.

CHECK Your Progress

Identify each pair of angles as *complementary*, *supplementary*, or *neither*.

a.

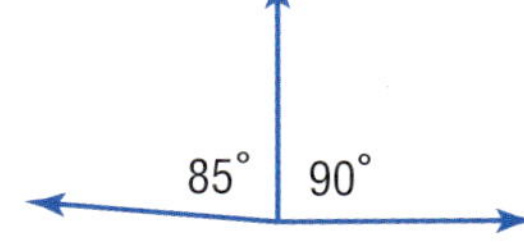

b.

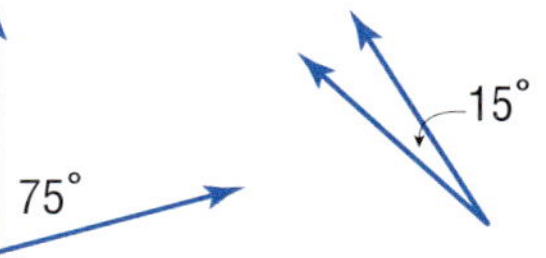

You can use angle relationships to find missing measures.

EXAMPLE Find a Missing Angle Measure

3 **ALGEBRA** **Find the value of x.**

Since the two angles form a right angle, they are complementary.

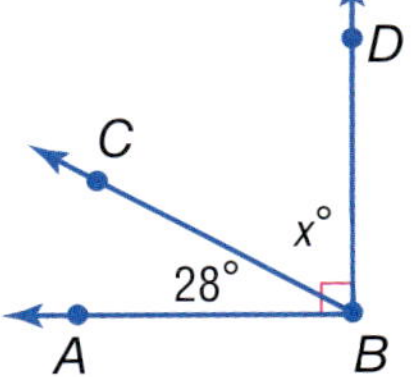

Words	The sum of the measures of ∠ABC and ∠CBD	is	90°.
Variable	Let x represent the measure of ∠CBD.		
Equation	$28 + x$	=	90

$$\begin{aligned} 28 + x &= 90 \\ -28 \quad &\;\; -28 \\ x &= 62 \end{aligned}$$

Write the equation.
Subtract 28 from each side.

So, the value of x is 62.

Reading Math

Perpendicular Lines or sides that meet to form right angles are perpendicular.

CHECK Your Progress

c. **ALGEBRA** Find the value of x.

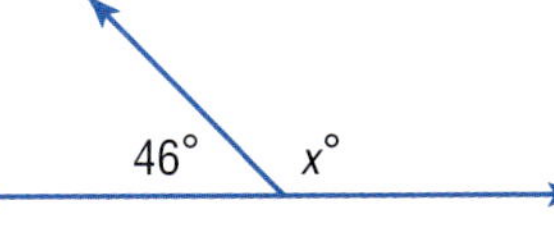

d. **ALGEBRA** If ∠J and ∠K are complementary and the measure of ∠K is 65°, what is the measure of ∠J?

CHECK Your Understanding

Examples 1, 2 (p. 515)

Identify each pair of angles as *complementary*, *supplementary*, or *neither*.

1. 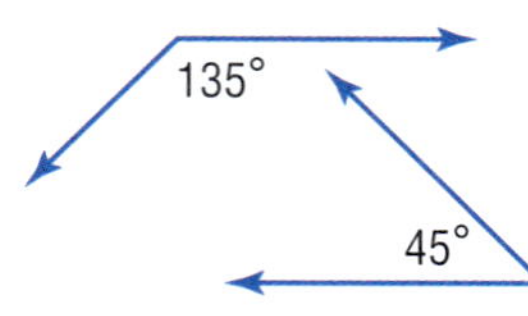

2. 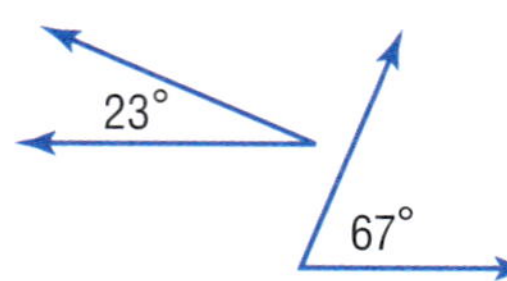

Example 3 (p. 515)

3. **ALGEBRA** Find the value of x.

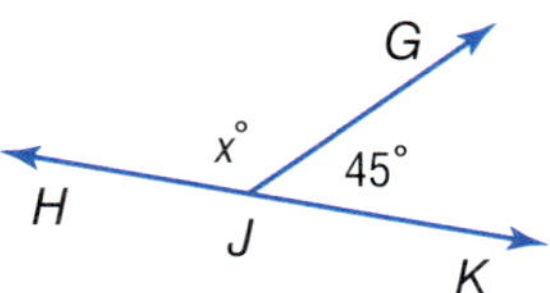

Practice and Problem Solving

HOMEWORK HELP	
For Exercises	See Examples
4–9	1, 2
10–11	3

Identify each pair of angles as *complementary*, *supplementary*, or *neither*.

4. 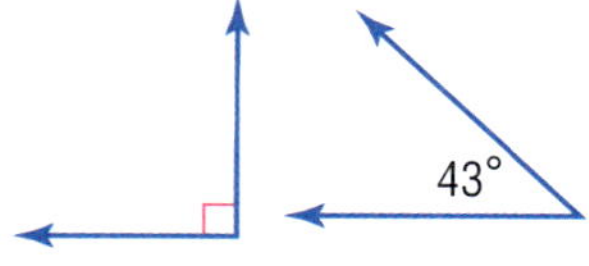

5. 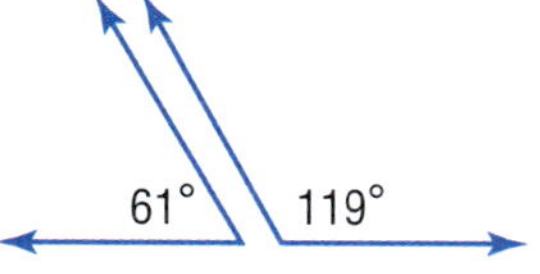

6. 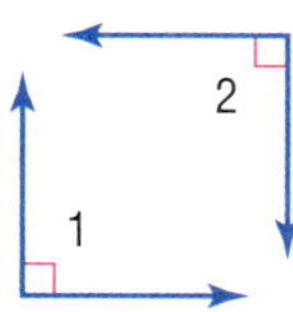

7. 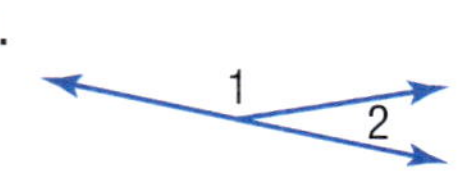

8. 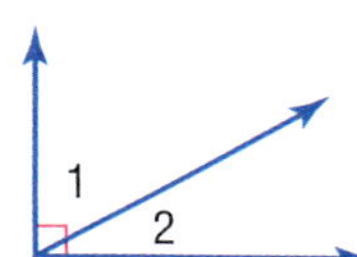

9. 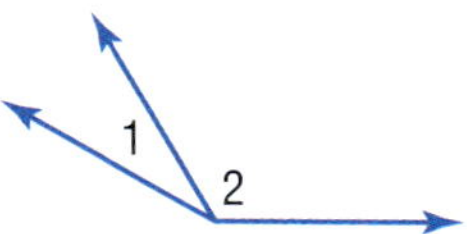

10. **ALGEBRA** If $\angle A$ and $\angle B$ are complementary and the measure of $\angle B$ is 67°, what is the measure of $\angle A$?

11. **ALGEBRA** What is the measure of $\angle J$ if $\angle J$ and $\angle K$ are supplementary and the measure of $\angle K$ is 115°?

12. **SCHOOL SUPPLIES** What is the measure of the angle given by the opening of the scissors, x?

13. **SKATEBOARDING** A skateboard ramp forms a 43° angle as shown. Find the unknown angle.

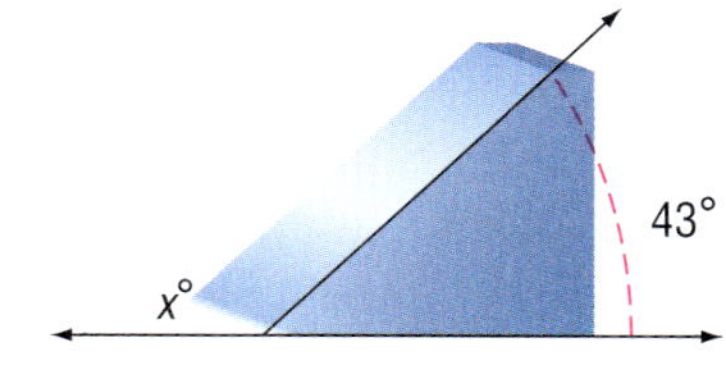

Use the figure at the right to name the following.

14. a pair of supplementary angles
15. a pair of complementary angles
16. a pair of vertical angles

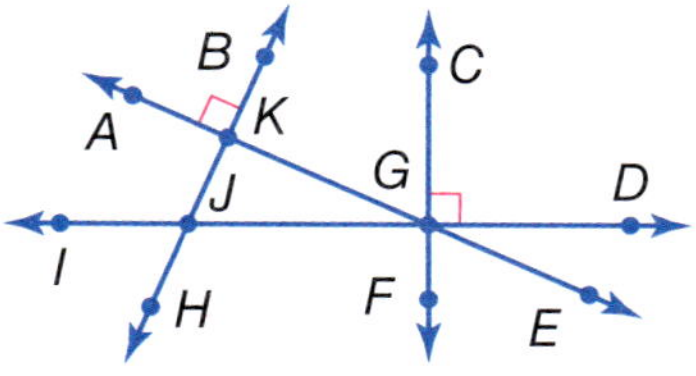

GEOMETRY **For Exercises 17–20, use the figure at the right.**

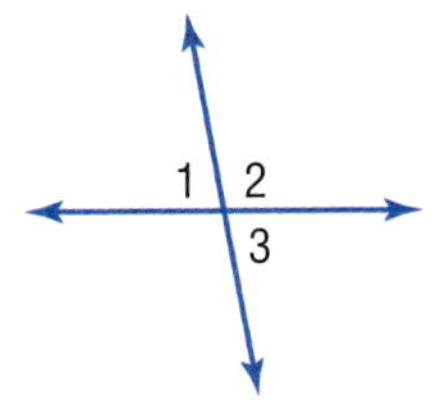

17. Are $\angle 1$ and $\angle 2$ vertical angles, adjacent angles, or neither? $\angle 2$ and $\angle 3$? $\angle 1$ and $\angle 3$?

18. Write an equation representing the sum of $m\angle 1$ and $m\angle 2$. Then write an equation representing the sum of $m\angle 2$ and $m\angle 3$.

19. Solve the equations you wrote in Exercise 18 for $m\angle 1$ and $m\angle 3$, respectively. What do you notice?

20. **MAKE A CONJECTURE** Use your answer to Exercise 19 to make a conjecture as to the relationship between vertical angles.

H.O.T. Problems

21. **CHALLENGE** Angles E and F are complementary. If $m\angle E = x - 10$ and $m\angle F = x + 2$, find the measure of each angle.

22. **WRITING IN MATH** Describe a strategy for determining whether two angles are *complementary*, *supplementary*, or *neither* without knowing or measuring each angle using a protractor.

23. In the figure below, $m\angle YXZ = 35°$ and $m\angle WXV = 40°$. What is $m\angle ZXW$?

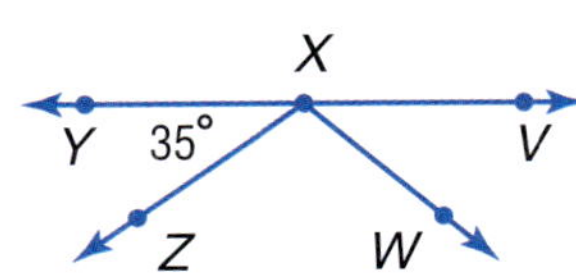

A 180° **C** 75°

B 105° **D** 15°

24. Which is a true statement about angles 1 and 2 shown below?

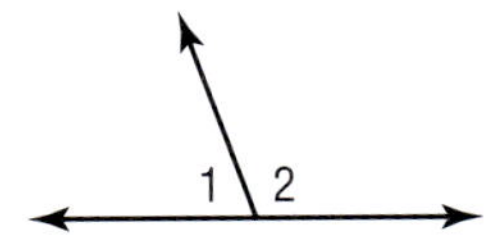

F $\angle 1$ is complementary to $\angle 2$.

G $\angle 1$ and $\angle 2$ are vertical angles.

H $\angle 1$ is supplementary to $\angle 2$.

J Both angles are obtuse.

Spiral Review

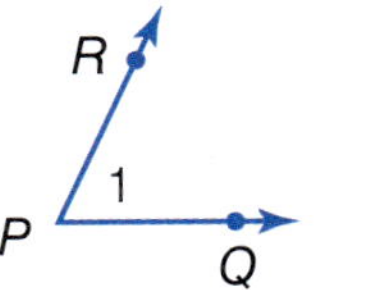

25. Name the angle at the right in four ways. Then classify it as *acute*, *right*, *obtuse*, or *straight*. (Lesson 10-1)

26. **MEASUREMENT** A house for sale has a rectangular lot with a length of 250 feet and a width of 120 feet. What is the area of the lot? (Lesson 3-6)

GET READY for the Next Lesson

PREREQUISITE SKILL **Multiply or divide. Round to the nearest hundredth if necessary.** (pp. 674 and 676)

27. $0.62 \cdot 360$

28. $360 \cdot 0.25$

29. $17 \div 146$

30. $63 \div 199$

10-3 Statistics: Display Data in a Circle Graph

MAIN IDEA

Construct and interpret circle graphs.

New Vocabulary

circle graph

Math Online

glencoe.com

- Extra Examples
- Personal Tutor
- Self-Check Quiz

GET READY for the Lesson

VEGETABLES The students at Pine Ridge Middle School were asked to identify their favorite vegetable. The table shows the results of the survey.

1. Explain how you know that each student only selected one favorite vegetable.
2. If 400 students participated in the survey, how many students preferred carrots?

Favorite Vegetable	
Vegetable	**Percent**
Carrots	45%
Green Beans	23%
Peas	17%
Other	15%

A graph that shows data as parts of a whole is called a **circle graph**. In a circle graph, the percents add up to 100.

EXAMPLE Display Data in a Circle Graph

1 **VEGETABLES** **Display the data above in a circle graph.**

- There are 360° in a circle. Find the degrees for each part.

  45% of 360° = 0.45 • 360° or 162°

  23% of 360° = 0.23 • 360° or 83° Round to the nearest whole degree.

  17% of 360° = 0.17 • 360° or about 61°

  15% of 360° = 0.15 • 360° or about 54°

- Draw a circle with a radius as shown. Then use a protractor to draw the first angle, in this case 162°. Repeat this step for each section or *sector*.

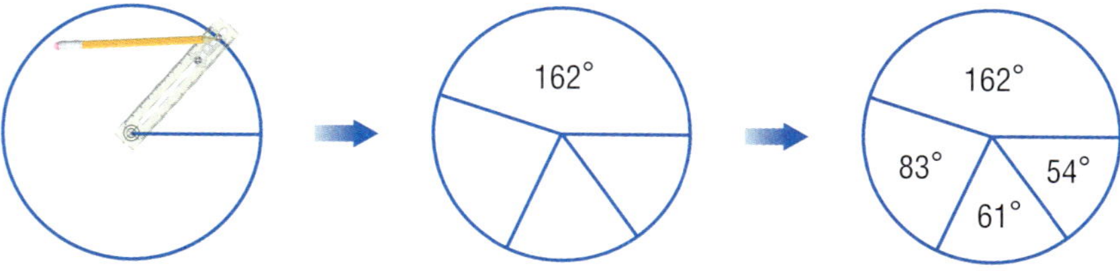

- Label each section of the graph with the category and percent it represents. Give the graph a title.

Check The sum of the angle measures should equal to 360°.
162° + 83° + 61° + 54° = 360°

Favorite Vegetable

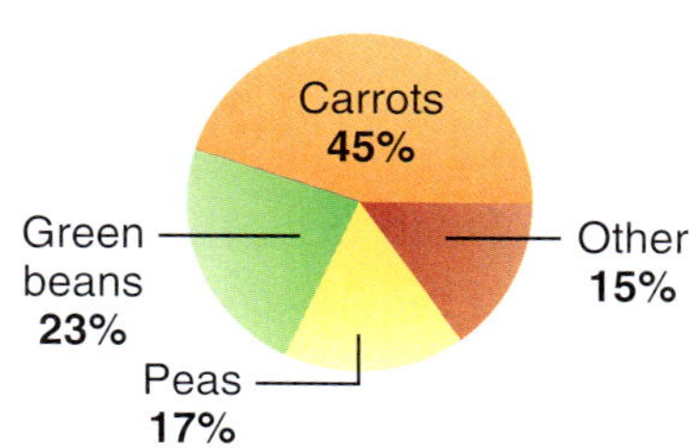

CHECK Your Progress

a. **SCIENCE** The table shows the present composition of Earth's atmosphere. Display the data in a circle graph.

Composition of Earth's Atmosphere	
Element	**Percent**
Nitrogen	78%
Oxygen	21%
Other gases	1%

When constructing a circle graph, you may need to first convert the data to ratios and decimals and then to degrees and percents.

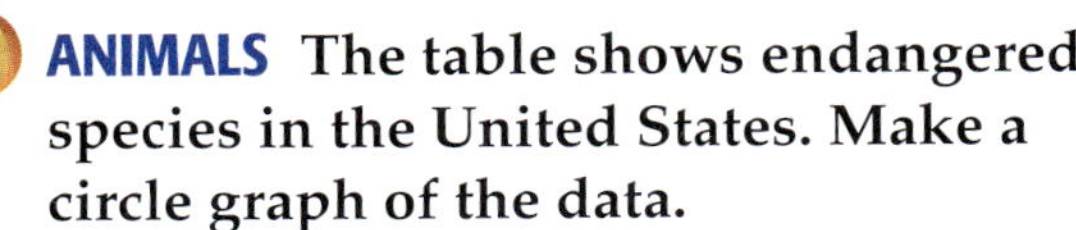

EXAMPLE Construct a Circle Graph

2 **ANIMALS The table shows endangered species in the United States. Make a circle graph of the data.**

Species	Number of Species
Mammals	68
Birds	77
Reptiles	14
Amphibians	11

Source: U.S. Fish & Wildlife Service

- Find the total number of species:
  $68 + 77 + 14 + 11 = 170$.
- Find the ratio that compares each number with the total. Write the ratio as a decimal rounded to the nearest hundredth.
  mammals: $\frac{68}{170} = 0.40$ birds: $\frac{77}{170} \approx 0.45$
  reptiles: $\frac{14}{170} \approx 0.08$ amphibians: $\frac{11}{170} \approx 0.06$
- Find the number of degrees for each section of the graph.
  mammals: $0.40 \cdot 360° = 144°$
  birds: $0.45 \cdot 360° \approx 162°$
  reptiles: $0.08 \cdot 360° \approx 29°$
  amphibians: $0.06 \cdot 360° \approx 22°$
  Because of rounding, the sum of the degrees is 357°.
- Draw the circle graph.
  $0.40 = 40\%$, $0.45 = 45\%$,
  $0.08 = 8\%$, $0.06 = 6\%$

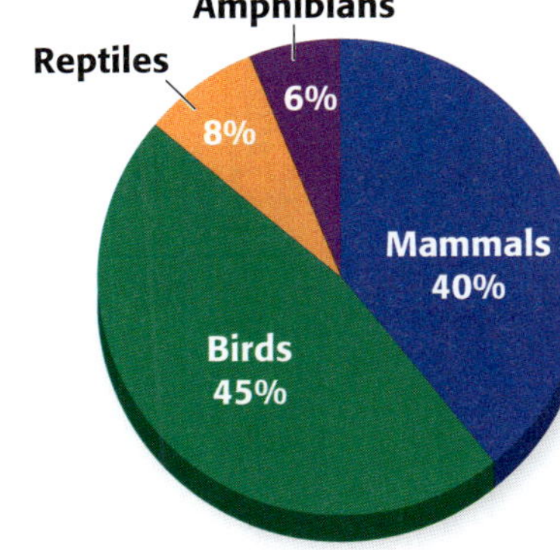

Check After drawing the first two sections, you can measure the last section of a circle graph to verify that the angles have the correct measures.

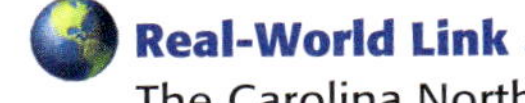

Real-World Link

The Carolina Northern and Virginian Northern Flying Squirrel are both endangered. The northern flying squirrel is a small nocturnal gliding mammal that is about 10 to 12 inches in total length and weighs about 3–5 ounces.

Source: U.S. Fish and Wildlife Service

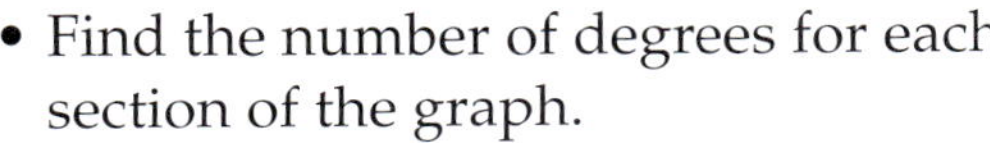

CHECK Your Progress

b. **OLYMPICS** The number of Winter Olympic medals won by the U.S. from 1924 to 2006 is shown in the table. Display the data in a circle graph.

U.S. Winter Olympic Medals	
Type	**Number**
Gold	78
Silver	81
Bronze	59

EXAMPLES Analyze a Circle Graph

AUTOMOBILES The graph shows the percent of automobiles registered in the western United States in a recent year.

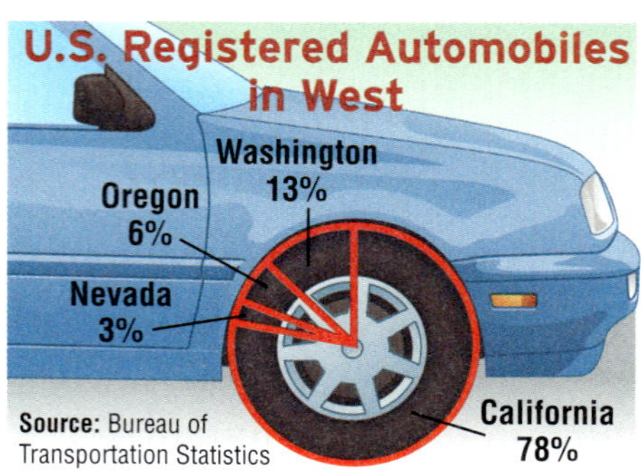

3 **Which state had the most registered automobiles?**

The largest section of the circle is the one representing California. So, California has the most registered automobiles.

4 **If 24.0 million automobiles were registered in these states, how many more automobiles were registered in California than Oregon?**

California: 78% of 24.0 million → 0.78×24.0, or 18.72 million

Oregon: 6% of 24.0 million → 0.06×24.0, or 1.44 million

There were 18.72 million − 1.44 million, or 17.28 million more registered automobiles in California than in Oregon.

Study Tip

Check for Reasonableness To check Example 4, you can estimate and solve the problem another way.

$78\% - 6\% \approx 70\%$
70% of 24 is about 17.

Since 17.28 is about 17, the answer is reasonable.

CHECK Your Progress

c. Which state had the least number of registered automobiles? Explain.

d. What was the total number of registered automobiles in Washington and Oregon?

CHECK Your Understanding

Examples 1, 2 (pp. 518–519) Display each set of data in a circle graph.

1.

Blood Types in the U.S.	
Blood Type	**Percent**
O	44%
A	42%
B	10%
AB	4%

Source: Stanford School of Medicine

2.

Favorite Musical Instrument	
Type	**Number of Students**
Piano	54
Guitar	27
Drum	15
Flute	24

Examples 3, 4 (p. 520) **COLORS** For Exercises 3 and 4, use the graph that shows the results of a survey.

3. What color is most favored?

4. If 400 people were surveyed, how many more people favored purple than red?

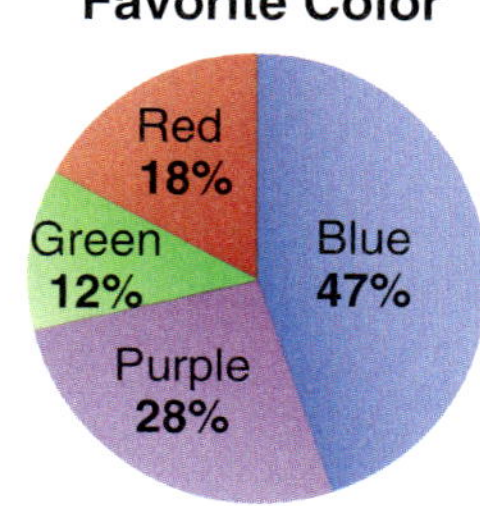

Practice and Problem Solving

HOMEWORK HELP	
For Exercises	See Examples
5–6	1
7–8	2
9–14	3,4

Display each set of data in a circle graph.

5.

U.S. Steel Roller Coasters	
Type	**Percent**
Sit down	86%
Inverted	8%
Other	6%

6.

U.S. Orange Production	
State	**Orange Production**
California	18%
Florida	81%
Texas	1%

Source: National Agriculture Statistics Service

7.

Animals in Pet Store	
Animal	**Number of Pets**
Birds	13
Cats	11
Dogs	9
Fish	56
Other	22

8.

Favorite Games	
Type of Game	**Number of Students**
Card	7
Board	9
Video	39
Sports	17
Drama	8

LANDFILLS **For Exercises 9-11, use the circle graph that shows what is in United States landfills.**

9. What takes up the most space in landfills?
10. About how many times more paper is there than food and yard waste?
11. If a landfill contains 200 million tons of trash, how much of it is plastic?

What is in U.S. Landfills?

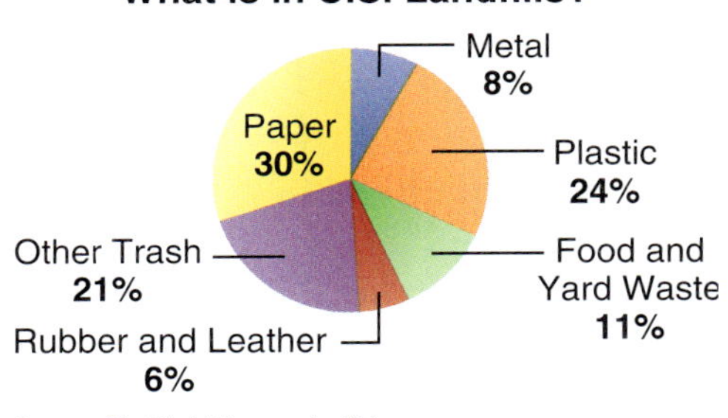

Source: *The World Almanac for Kids*

MONEY **For Exercises 12–14, use the graph that shows the results of a survey about a common currency for North America.**

Do Americans Favor Common North American Currency?

Source: Coinstar

12. What percent of Americans favor a common North American currency?
13. Based on these results, about how many of the approximately 298 million Americans would say "Don't Know" in response to this survey?
14. About how many more Americans oppose a common currency than favor it?

DATA SENSE For each graph, find the missing values.

15.

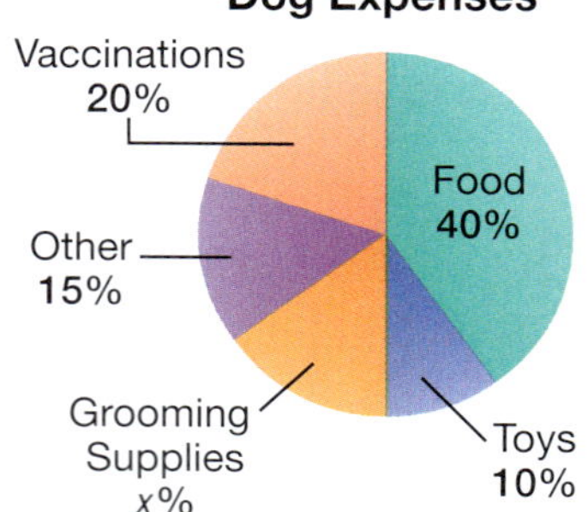

16.

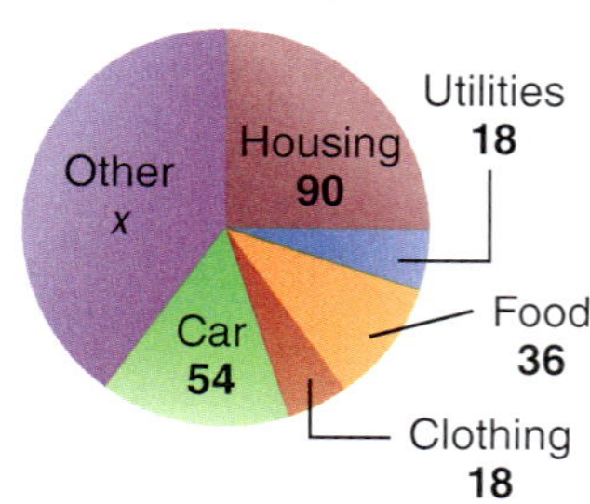

Select an appropriate type of graph to display each set of data: line graph, bar graph, or circle graph. Then display the data using the graph.

17.

Top 5 Presidential Birth States	
Place	**Presidents**
Virginia	8
Ohio	7
Massachusetts	4
New York	4
Texas	3

Source: *The World Book of Facts*

18.

Tanya's Day	
Activity	**Percent**
School	25%
Sleep	33%
Homework	12%
Sports	8%
Other	22%

GEOGRAPHY For Exercises 19–21, use the table.

19. Display the data in a circle graph.

20. Use your graph to find which two lakes equal the size of Lake Superior.

21. Compare the size of Lake Ontario to the size of Lake Michigan.

Sizes of U.S. Great Lakes	
Lake	**Size (sq mi)**
Erie	9,930
Huron	23,010
Michigan	22,400
Ontario	7,520
Superior	31,820

POLITICS For Exercises 22 and 23, use the graph and information below.

A group of students were asked whether people their age could make a difference in the political decisions of elected officials.

22. How many students participated in the survey?

23. Write a convincing argument explaining whether or not it is reasonable to say that 50% more students said they could make a difference than those who said they could not make a difference.

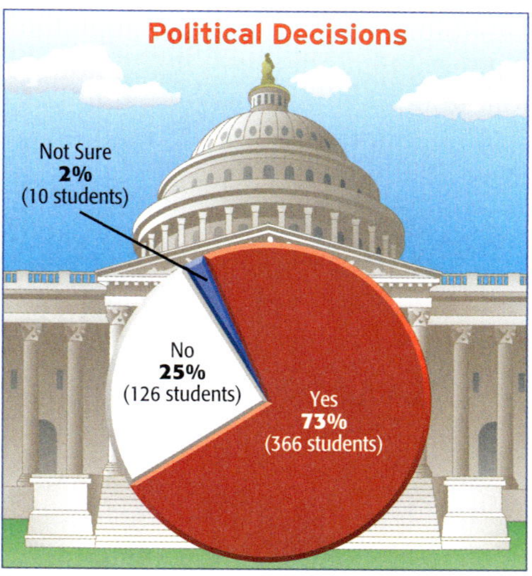

Source: *Mom's Life* and *Mothering Magazine*

24. **FIND THE DATA** Refer to the Data File on pages 16–19. Choose some data that can be displayed in a circle graph. Then display the data in a circle graph and write one statement analyzing the data.

H.O.T. Problems

25. **CHALLENGE** The graph shows the results of a survey about students' favorite school subject. About what percent of those surveyed said that math was their favorite subject? Explain your reasoning.

Favorite Subject

Other
Math
English
Science

26. **COLLECT THE DATA** Collect some data from your classmates that can be represented in a circle graph. Then create the circle graph and write one statement analyzing the data.

27. **WRITING IN MATH** The table shows the percent of people that like each type of fruit juice. Can the data be represented in a circle graph? Justify your answer.

Fruit Juice	Percent
Apple	54%
Grape	48%
Orange	37%
Cranberry	15%

TEST PRACTICE

28. The graph shows the type of vehicles that used Highway 82 during one month.

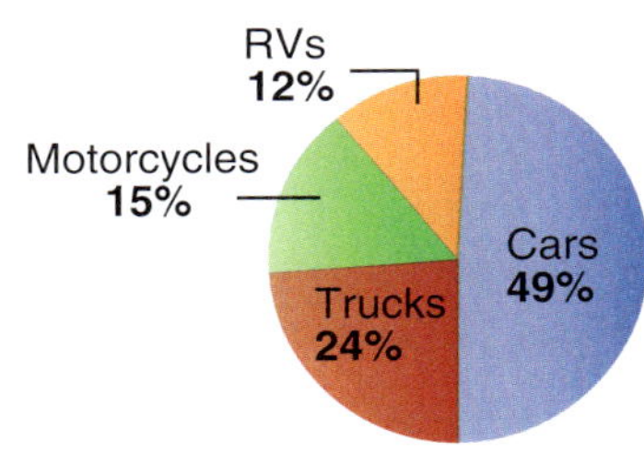

Which statement is true according to the circle graph shown?

A More cars used the highway than RVs and trucks combined.

B More than half the vehicles that used the highway were cars.

C More RVs used the highway than trucks.

D More trucks used the highway than cars.

Spiral Review

29. **GEOMETRY** Refer to the diagram at the right. Identify a pair of vertical angles. (Lesson 10-1)

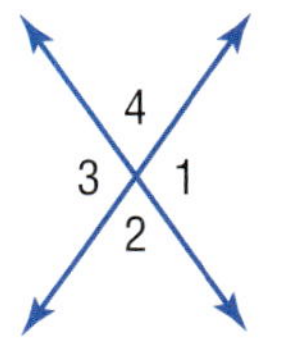

30. **ALGEBRA** $\angle A$ and $\angle B$ are complementary. If $m\angle A = 15°$, find $m\angle B$. (Lesson 10-2)

GET READY for the Next Lesson

PREREQUISITE SKILL **Solve each equation.** (Lesson 3-2)

31. $x + 112 = 180$

32. $50 + t = 180$

33. $180 = 79 + y$

34. $180 = h + 125$

10-4 Triangles

MAIN IDEA

Identify and classify triangles.

New Vocabulary

- triangle
- congruent segments
- acute triangle
- right triangle
- obtuse triangle
- scalene triangle
- isosceles triangle
- equilateral triangle

Math Online

glencoe.com

- Extra Examples
- Personal Tutor
- Self-Check Quiz

MINI Lab

STEP 1 Use a straightedge to draw a triangle with three acute angles. Label the angles A, B, and C. Cut out the triangle.

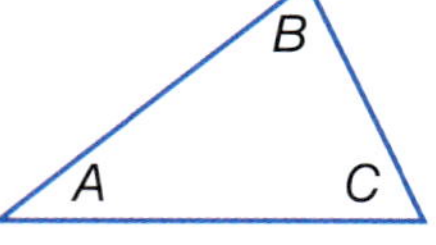

STEP 2 Fold $\angle A$, $\angle B$, and $\angle C$ so the vertices meet on the line between angles A and C.

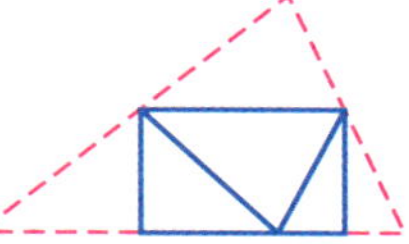

1. What kind of angle is formed where the three vertices meet?
2. Repeat the activity with another triangle. Make a conjecture about the sum of the measures of the angles of any triangle.

A **triangle** is a figure with three sides and three angles. The symbol for triangle is △. There is a relationship among the three angles in a triangle.

Angles of a Triangle — Key Concept

Words The sum of the measures of the angles of a triangle is 180°.

Algebra $x + y + z = 180$

Model

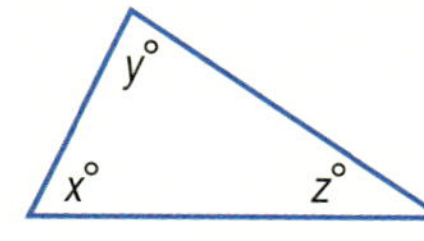

EXAMPLE Find a Missing Measure

1 ALGEBRA Find $m\angle Z$ in the triangle.

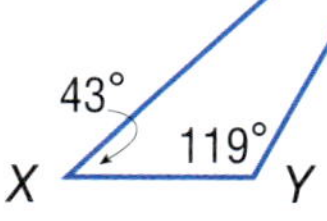

Since the sum of the angle measures in a triangle is 180°, $m\angle Z + 43° + 119° = 180°$.

$m\angle Z + 43° + 119° = 180°$		Write the equation.
$m\angle Z + 162° = 180°$		Simplify.
$-162° = -162°$		Subtract 162° from each side.
$m\angle Z = 18°$		

So, $m\angle Z$ is 18°.

CHECK Your Progress

a. **ALGEBRA** In $\triangle ABC$, if $m\angle A = 25°$ and $m\angle B = 108°$, what is $m\angle C$?

TEST EXAMPLE

2 The Alabama state flag is constructed with the triangles shown. What is the missing measure in the design?

A 145° C 35°

B 75° D 25°

Read the Item

To find the missing measure, write and solve an equation.

Solve the Item

$x + 110 + 35 = 180$ The sum of the measures is 180.

$x + 145 = 180$ Simplify.

$-145 = -145$ Subtract 145 from each side.

$x = 35$

The answer is C.

Test-Taking Tip

Check the Results To check the results, add the three angle measures to see if their sum is 180.

35 + 110 + 35 = 180 ✔

The answer is correct.

CHECK Your Progress

b. The frame of a bicycle shows a triangle. What is the missing measure?

F 31° H 45°

G 40° J 50°

Every triangle has at least two acute angles. One way you can classify a triangle is by using the third angle. Another way to classify triangles is by their sides. Sides with the same length are **congruent segments**.

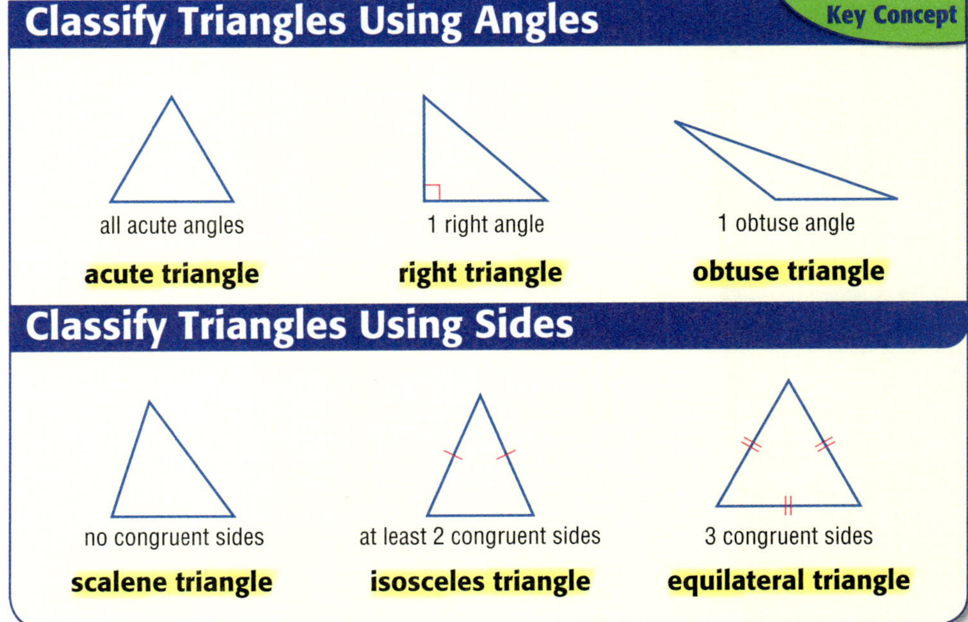

Study Tip

Congruent Segments The marks on the sides of the triangle indicate that those sides are congruent.

Real-World Link
There are two main types of roofs—flat and pitched. Most houses have pitched, or sloped, roofs. A pitched roof generally lasts 15 to 20 years.

Source: National Association of Certified Home Inspectors

Real-World EXAMPLE

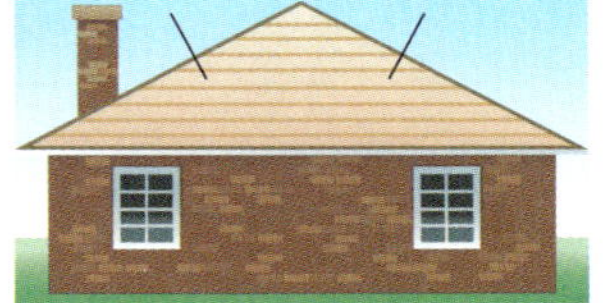

3 **Classify the marked triangle at the right by its angles and by its sides.**

The triangle on the side of a house has one obtuse angle and two congruent sides. So, it is an obtuse, isosceles triangle.

CHECK Your Progress

c. 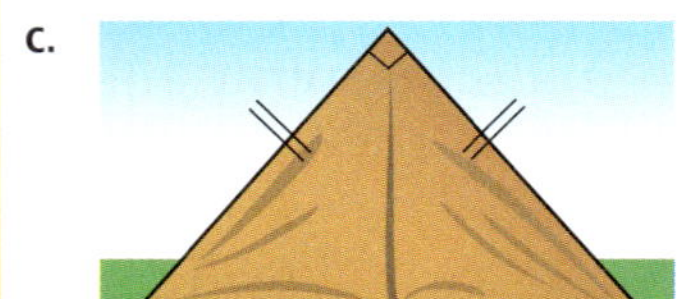

d. 

EXAMPLES Draw Triangles

4 **Draw a triangle with one right angle and two congruent sides. Then classify the triangle.**

Draw a right angle. The two segments should be congruent.

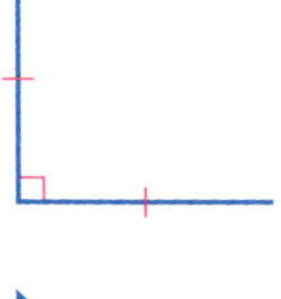

Connect the two segments to form a triangle.

The triangle is a right isosceles triangle.

5 **Draw a triangle with one obtuse angle and no congruent sides. Then classify the triangle.**

Draw an obtuse angle. The two segments of the angle should have different lengths.

Connect the two segments to form a triangle.

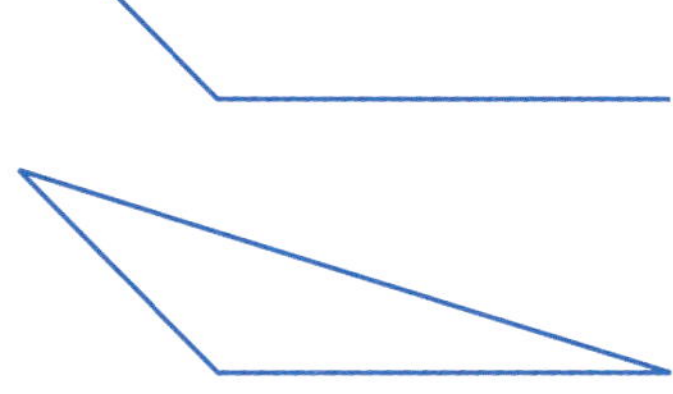

The triangle is an obtuse scalene triangle.

CHECK Your Progress

Draw a triangle that satisfies each set of conditions below. Then classify each triangle.

e. a triangle with three acute angles and three congruent sides

f. a triangle with one right angle and no congruent sides

CHECK Your Understanding

Example 1 (p. 524)

Find the value of *x*.

1.

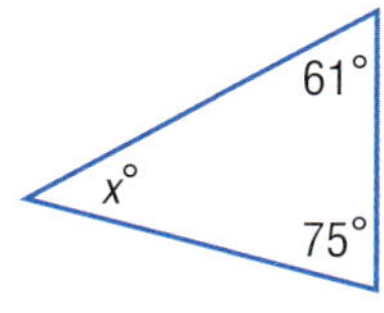

2.

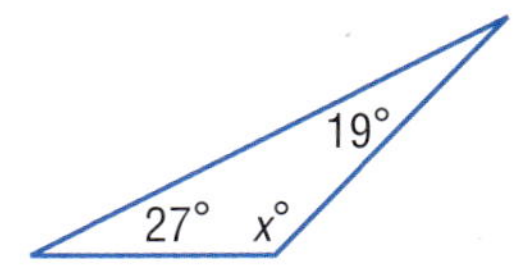

3.

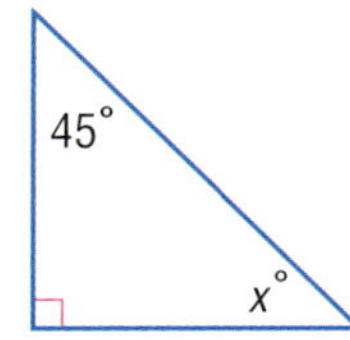

4. **ALGEBRA** Find $m\angle T$ in $\triangle RST$ if $m\angle R = 37°$ and $m\angle S = 55°$.

Example 2 (p. 525)

5. **MULTIPLE CHOICE** A triangle is used in the game of pool to rack the pool balls. Find the missing measure of the triangle.

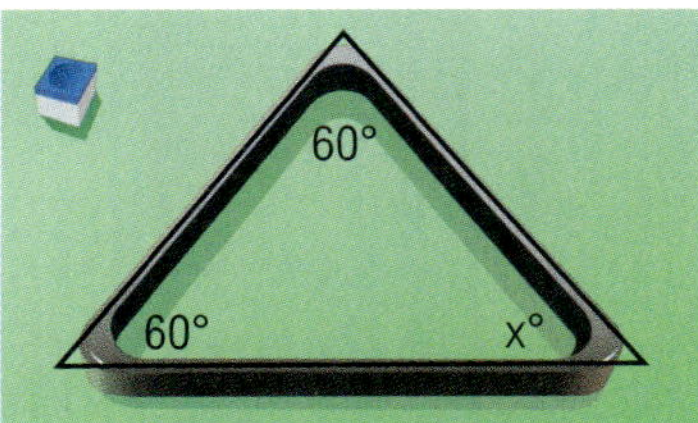

A 30° **C** 60°

B 40° **D** 75°

Example 3 (p. 526)

NATURE **Classify the marked triangle in each object by its angles and by its sides.**

6.

7.

8.

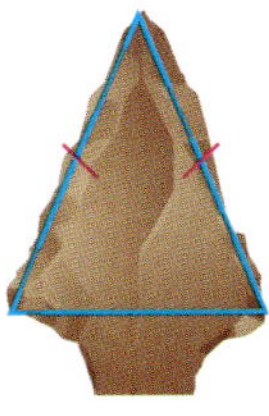

Examples 4, 5 (p. 526)

DRAWING TRIANGLES **For Exercises 9 and 10, draw a triangle that satisfies each set of conditions. Then classify each triangle.**

9. a triangle with three acute angles and two congruent sides

10. a triangle with one obtuse angle and two congruent sides

Practice and Problem Solving

HOMEWORK HELP

For Exercises	See Examples
11–18, 47, 48	1–2
19–26	3
27–30	4, 5

Find the value of *x*.

11.

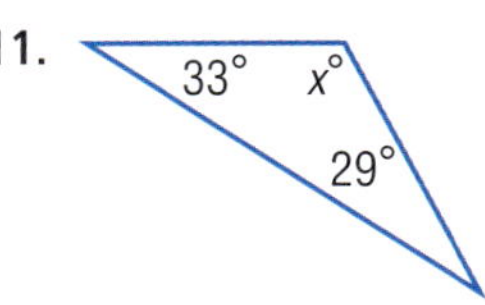

12.

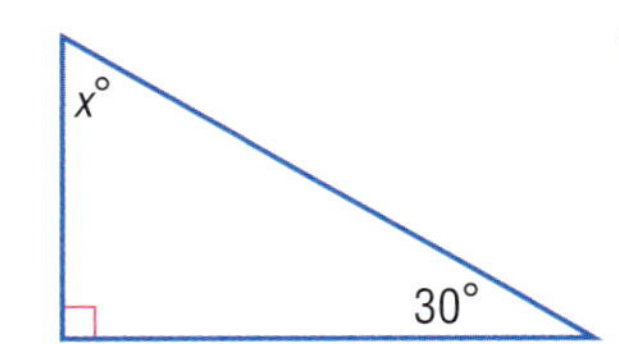

13.

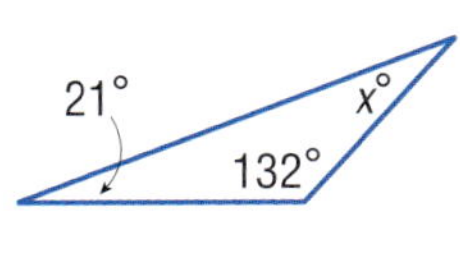

14.

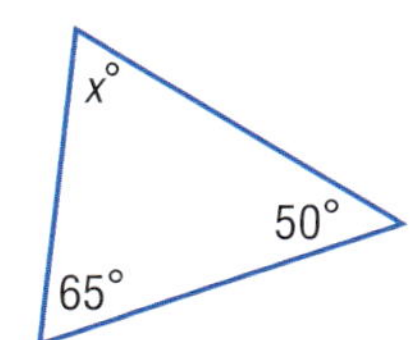

15.

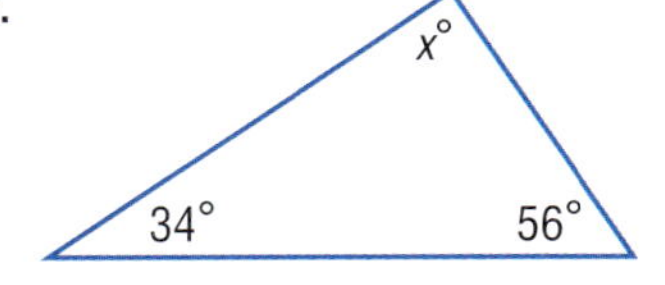

16.

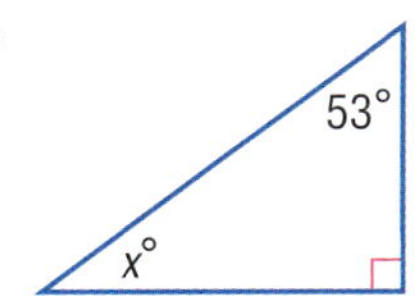

17. **ALGEBRA** Find $m\angle Q$ in $\triangle QRS$ if $m\angle R = 25°$ and $m\angle S = 102°$.

18. **ALGEBRA** In $\triangle EFG$, $m\angle F = 46°$ and $m\angle G = 34°$. What is $m\angle E$?

Classify the marked triangle in each object by its angles and by its sides.

19. 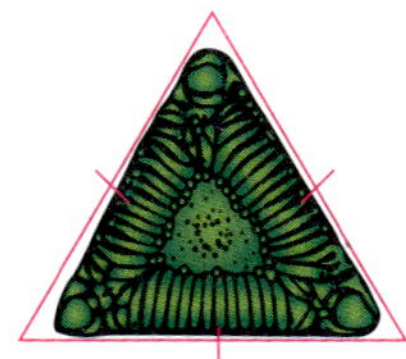

20. 

21. 

22. 

23. 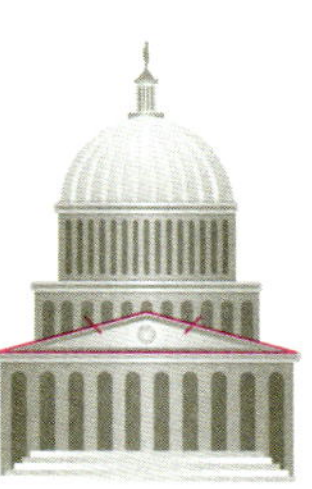

24. 

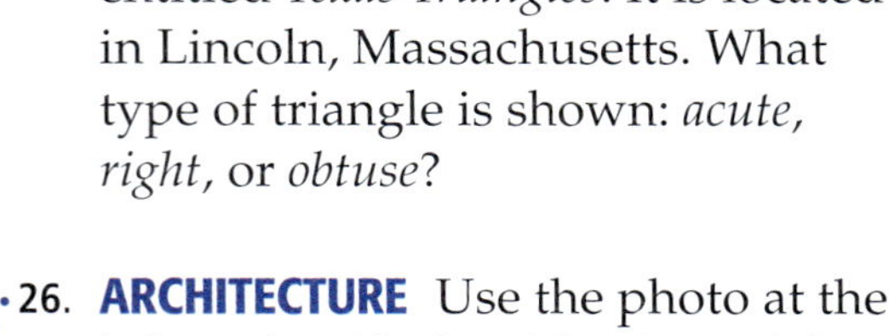

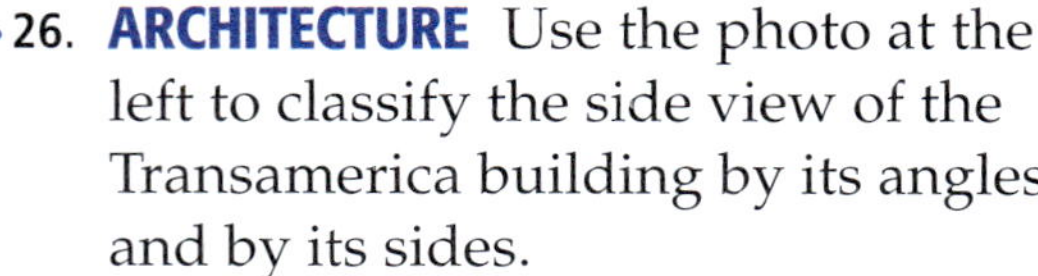

Real-World Link The Transamerica building in San Francisco is 853 feet tall.

Source: Transamerica Corporation

25. **ART** The sculpture at the right is entitled *Texas Triangles*. It is located in Lincoln, Massachusetts. What type of triangle is shown: *acute*, *right*, or *obtuse*?

Source: DeCordova Museum and Sculpture Park

26. **ARCHITECTURE** Use the photo at the left to classify the side view of the Transamerica building by its angles and by its sides.

DRAWING TRIANGLES For Exercises 27–30, draw a triangle that satisfies each set of conditions. Then classify each triangle.

27. a triangle with three acute angles and no congruent sides
28. a triangle with one obtuse angle and two congruent sides
29. a triangle with three acute angles and three congruent sides
30. a triangle with one right angle and no congruent sides

Find the missing measure in each triangle with the given angle measures.

31. $80°, 20.5°, x°$
32. $75°, x°, 50.2°$
33. $x°, 10.8°, 90°$
34. $45.5°, x°, 105.6°$
35. $x°, 140.1°, 18.6°$
36. $110.2°, x°, 35.6°$

37. **ALGEBRA** Find the third angle measure of a right triangle if one of the angles measures is 10°.

38. **ALGEBRA** What is the third angle measure of a right triangle if one of the angle measures is 45.8°?

ALGEBRA Find the value of x in each triangle.

39. 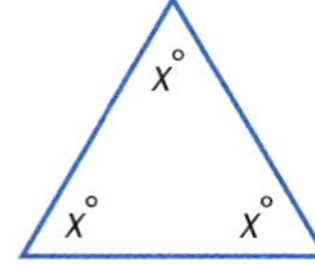

40. 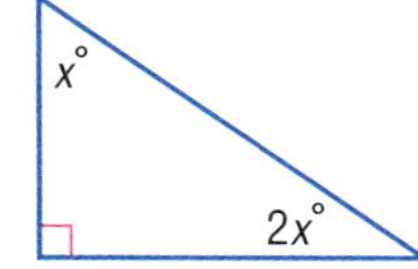

41. 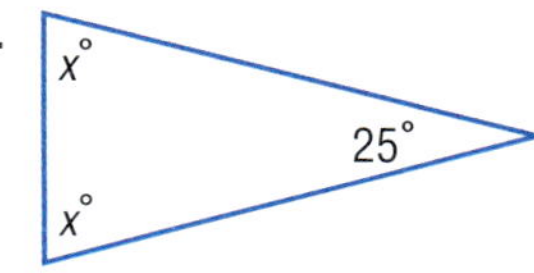

EXTRA PRACTICE
See pages 694, 713.

H.O.T. Problems

42. **CHALLENGE** Apply what you know about triangles to find the missing angle measures in the figure.

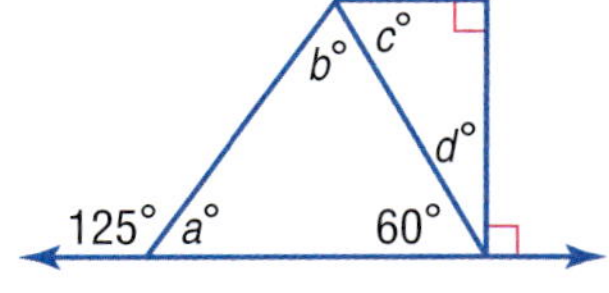

43. **OPEN ENDED** Draw an acute scalene triangle. Describe the angles and sides of the triangle.

REASONING Determine whether each statement is *sometimes*, *always*, or *never* true. Justify your answer.

44. It is possible for a triangle to have two right angles.

45. It is possible for a triangle to have two obtuse angles.

46. **WRITING IN MATH** An equilateral triangle not only has three congruent sides, but also has three congruent angles. Based on this, explain why it is impossible to draw an equilateral triangle that is either right or obtuse.

TEST PRACTICE

47. How would you find $m\angle R$?

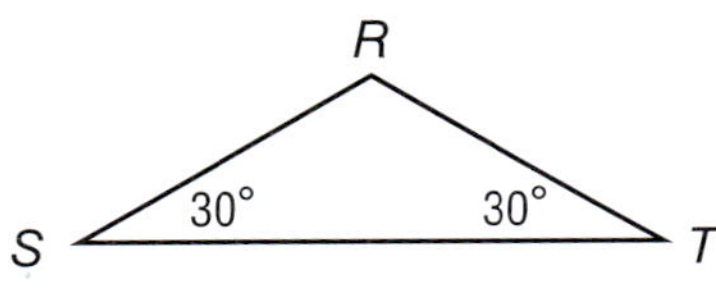

A Add 30° to 180°.

B Subtract 60° from 180°.

C Subtract 30° from 90°.

D Subtract 180° from 60°.

48. Which of the following is an acute triangle?

F 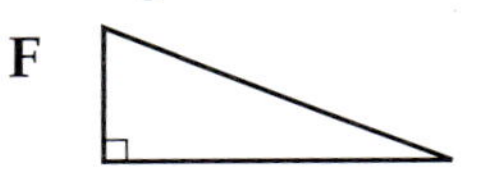

H 

G 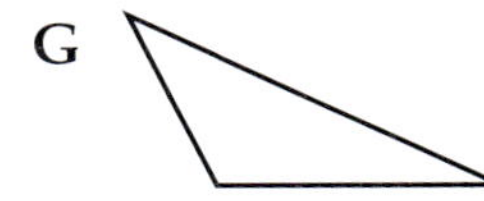

J 

Spiral Review

49. **SURVEYS** A circle graph shows that 28% of people chose tea as their favorite drink. What is the measure of the angle of the tea section of the graph? (Lesson 10-3)

Classify each pair of angles as *complementary*, *supplementary*, or *neither*. (Lesson 10-2)

50. 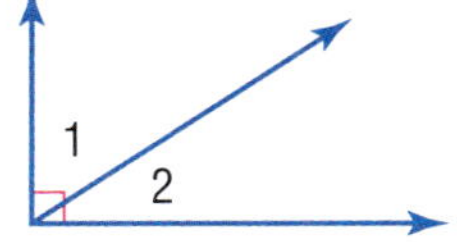

51. 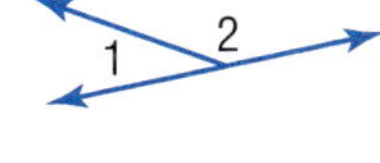

52. 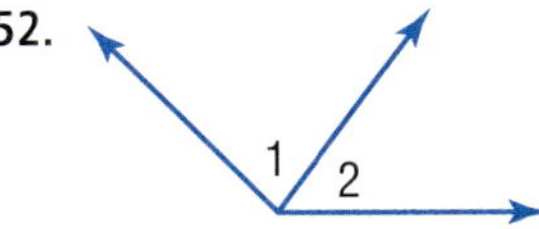

GET READY for the Next Lesson

53. **PREREQUISITE SKILL** If Jade buys 5 notebooks at $1.75 each, what will be the total cost of the notebooks; about $6, $7, or $9? (Lesson 7-5)

10-5 Problem-Solving Investigation

MAIN IDEA: Solve problems by using logical reasoning.

P.S.I. TEAM +

e-Mail: USE LOGICAL REASONING

SANTOS: I know that at least two sides of an isosceles triangle are congruent. It also looks like two of the angles in an isosceles triangle are congruent.

YOUR MISSION: Use logical reasoning to find if the angles in an isosceles triangles are congruent.

Understand	Isosceles triangles have at least two congruent sides. We need to find if there is a relationship between the angles.
Plan	Draw several isosceles triangles and measure their angles.
Solve	In each triangle, two angles are congruent. So, it seems like an isosceles triangle has two congruent angles.
Check	Try drawing several more isosceles triangles and measuring their angles. Although this is not a proof, it is likely your conclusion is valid.

Analyze The Strategy

1. When you use *inductive reasoning*, you make a rule after seeing several examples. When you use *deductive reasoning*, you use a rule to make a decision. What type of reasoning did Santos use to solve the problem? Explain your reasoning.
2. Explain how the *look for a pattern* strategy is similar to inductive reasoning.

Mixed Problem Solving

See pages 694, 713.

For Exercises 3–5, use logical reasoning to solve the problem. Justify your response.

3. **GEOMETRY** Draw several scalene triangles and measure their angles. What do you notice about the measures of the angles of a scalene triangle?

4. **HOUSE NUMBERS** Rico's house number contains four digits. The digits are 5, 8, 3, and 2. If his house number is odd, divisible by 3, and the middle two numbers are a perfect square, what is his house number?

5. **FRUIT** Julio, Rashanda, and Perry each brought a fruit with their lunch. The fruits brought were a mango, a banana, and an orange. If Perry did not bring a banana and Julio brought a mango, what type of fruit did each student bring?

Use any strategy to solve Exercises 6–14. Some strategies are shown below.

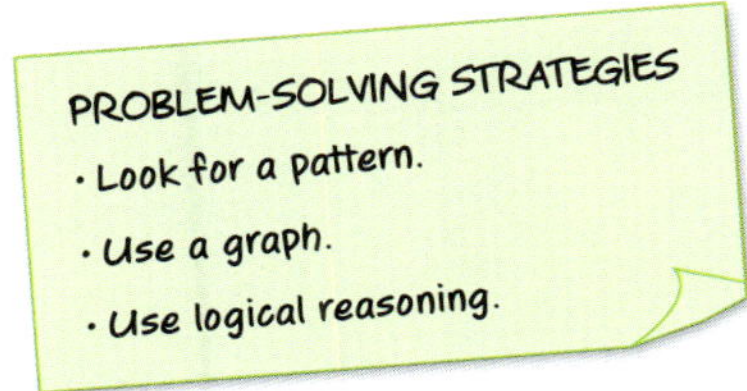

6. **GEOMETRY** Draw several rectangles and measure their diagonals. Find a relationship between the diagonals of a rectangle.

7. **MONEY** Corelia has twice as many quarters in her purse as dimes and half as many nickels as dimes. If she has 12 quarters in her purse, what is the total amount of money she has?

8. **ALGEBRA** Find the next three numbers in the pattern below.

   71, 64, 57, 50, ■, ■, ■

9. **MEASUREMENT** The large square has been divided into 9 squares. The lengths of the squares are given. Find the area of the entire square.

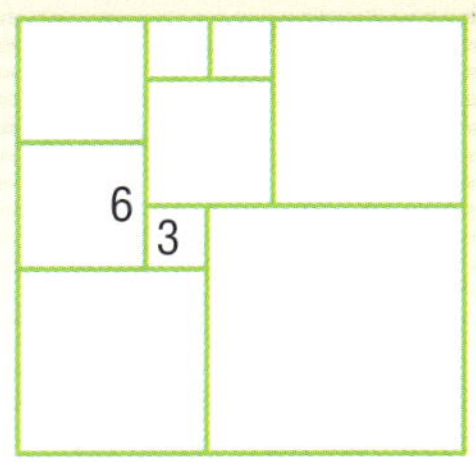

10. **READING** Sonia read 10 pages of a 150-page book on Monday. She plans to read twice as many pages each day than she did the previous day. On what day will she finish the book?

11. **SUPPLIES** Bianca has $55 to buy school supplies. She bought a backpack for $23.50, a combination lock for $6.25, and 4 binders that are $3.99 each. If the costs include tax and mechanical pencils are $2.50 per pack, how many packs can she buy?

12. **BOWLING** Colin and three of his friends are going bowling, and they have a total of $70 to spend. Suppose they buy a large pizza, four beverages, and each rent bowling shoes. How many games can they bowl if they all bowl the same number of games?

Bowling Costs

Item	Price
large pizza	$15.75
beverage	$1.50
shoe rental	$3.50
game	$4.00

13. **STATISTICS** David has earned scores of 73, 85, 91, and 82 on the first four out of five math tests for the grading period. He would like to finish the grading period with a test average of at least 82. What is the minimum score David needs to earn on the fifth test in order to achieve his goal?

14. **ALLOWANCE** Samantha earns $520 in allowance yearly. Her parents promise to give her a $60 raise each year. At this rate, what will her yearly allowance be in 4 years?

Explore 10-6

Geometry Lab
Investigating Quadrilaterals

MAIN IDEA

Investigate the properties of special quadrilaterals.

Four-sided figures are called *quadrilaterals*. In this lab, you will explore the properties of different types of quadrilaterals.

ACTIVITY

STEP 1 Draw the quadrilaterals shown on grid paper.

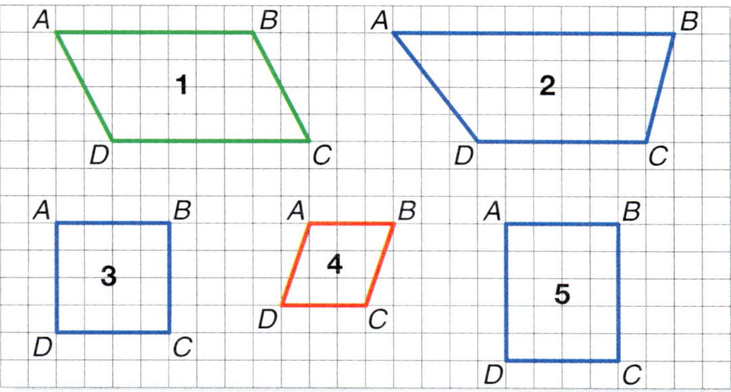

STEP 2 Use a ruler and a protractor to measure the sides and angles of each quadrilateral. Record your results in a table.

Quadrilateral	m∠A	m∠B	m∠C	m∠D	AB	BC	CD	DA
1								
2								

Analyze the Results

1. Describe any similarities or patterns in the angle measurements.
2. Describe any similarities or patterns in the side measurements.
3. **MAKE A VENN DIAGRAM** Cut out the quadrilaterals you drew in the activity. Then sort them into categories according to their similarities and differences. Arrange and record your categories in a two-circled Venn diagram. Be sure to label each circle with its category.
4. Create two other Venn diagrams illustrating two different ways of categorizing these quadrilaterals.
5. **WRITING IN MATH** Did you find shapes that did not fit a category? Where did you place these shapes? Did any shapes have properties allowing them to belong to more than one category? Could you arrange these quadrilaterals into a three-circled Venn diagram? If so, how?

10-6 Quadrilaterals

MAIN IDEA

Identify and classify quadrilaterals.

New Vocabulary

quadrilateral
parallelogram
trapezoid
rhombus

Math Online

glencoe.com

- Extra Examples
- Personal Tutor
- Self-Check Quiz

GET READY for the Lesson

VIDEO GAMES The general shape of a video game controller is shown.

1. Describe the angles inside the four-sided figure.
2. Which sides of the figure appear to be parallel?
3. Which sides appear to be congruent?

A **quadrilateral** is a closed figure with four sides and four angles. Quadrilaterals are named based on their sides and angles. The diagram shows how quadrilaterals are related. Notice how it goes from the most general to the most specific.

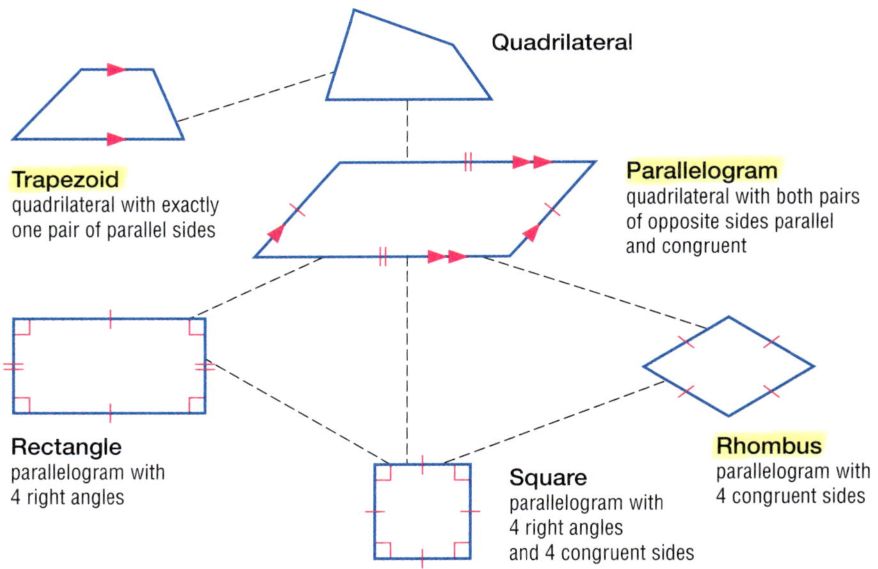

The name that *best* describes a quadrilateral is the one that is most specific.

- If a quadrilateral has all the properties of a parallelogram and a rhombus, then the *best* description of the quadrilateral is a rhombus.
- If a quadrilateral has all the properties of a parallelogram, rhombus, rectangle, and square, then the *best* description of the quadrilateral is a square.

Study Tip

Parallel Lines The sides with matching arrows are parallel.

 EXAMPLES Draw and Classify Quadrilaterals

Draw a quadrilateral that satisfies each set of conditions. Then classify each quadrilateral with the name that best describes it.

1 a parallelogram with four right angles and four congruent sides

Draw one right angle. The two segments should be congruent.

Draw a second right angle that shares one of the congruent segments. The third segment drawn should be congruent to the first two segments drawn.

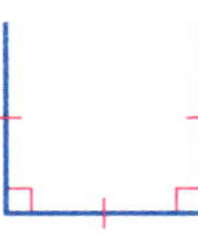

Connect the fourth side of the quadrilateral. All four angles should be right angles, and all four sides should be congruent.

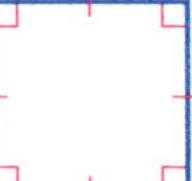

The figure is a square.

Study Tip

Check for Reasonableness *Use a ruler and a protractor to measure the sides and angles to verify that your drawing satisfies the given conditions.*

2 a quadrilateral with opposite sides parallel

Draw two parallel sides of equal length.

Connect the endpoints of these two sides so that two new parallel sides are drawn.

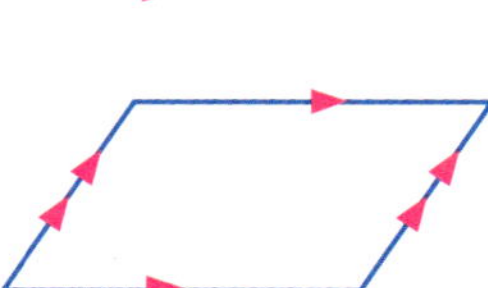

The figure is a parallelogram.

 **CHECK Your Progress**

Draw a quadrilateral that satisfies each set of conditions. Then classify each quadrilateral with the name that best describes it.

a. a quadrilateral with exactly one pair of parallel sides

b. a parallelogram with four congruent sides

A quadrilateral can be separated into two triangles, A and B. Since the sum of the angle measures of each triangle is 180°, the sum of the angle measures of the quadrilateral is $2 \cdot 180$, or 360°.

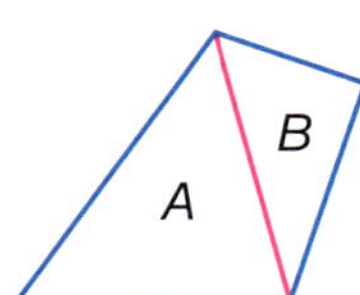

Angles of a Quadrilateral — Key Concept

Words The sum of the measures of the angles of a quadrilateral is 360°.

Algebra $w + x + y + z = 360$

Model $w°$, $x°$, $y°$, $z°$

EXAMPLE Find a Missing Measure

3 ALGEBRA Find the value of x in the quadrilateral shown.

Write and solve an equation.

Words	The sum of the measures is 360°.
Variable	Let x represent the missing measure.
Equation	$85 + 73 + 59 + x = 360$

$85 + 73 + 59 + x = 360$	Write the equation.
$217 + x = 360$	Simplify.
$-217 = -217$	Subtract 217 from each side.
$x = 143$	

So, the missing angle measure is 143°.

Study Tip

Check for Reasonableness Since $\angle x$ is an obtuse angle, $m\angle x$ should be between 90° and 180°. Since $90° < 143° < 180°$, the answer is reasonable.

CHECK Your Progress

c. **ALGEBRA** Find the value of x in the quadrilateral shown.

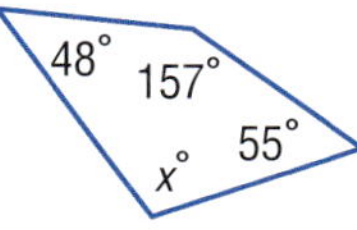

CHECK Your Understanding

Examples 1, 2 (p. 534) **Classify each quadrilateral with the name that best describes it.**

1. 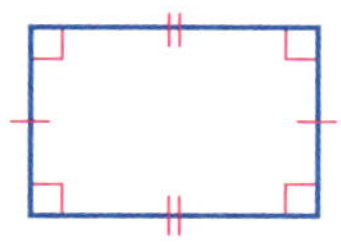

2. 

3. 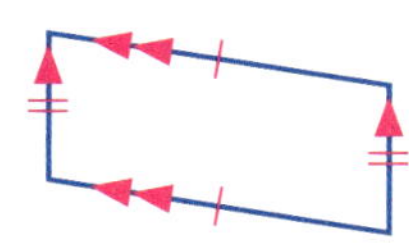

4. **BOATS** The photo shows a sailboat called a schooner. What type of quadrilateral does the indicated sail best represent?

Example 3 (p. 535)

5. **ALGEBRA** In quadrilateral $DEFG$, $m\angle D = 57°$, $m\angle E = 78°$, $m\angle G = 105°$. What is $m\angle F$?

ALGEBRA Find the missing angle measure in each quadrilateral.

6. 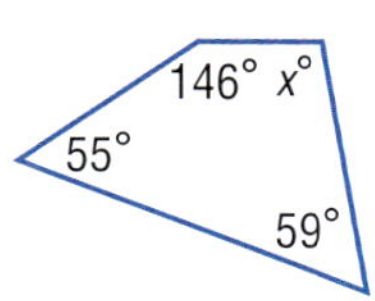

7. 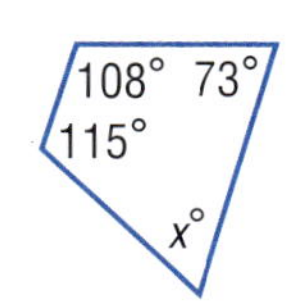

8. 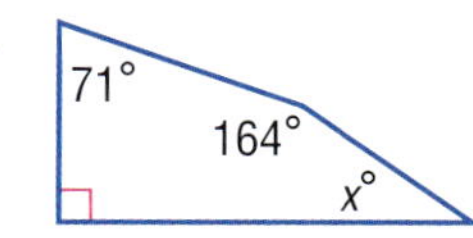

Practice and Problem Solving

HOMEWORK HELP	
For Exercises	See Examples
9–14, 23–24	1, 2
15–22	3

Classify each quadrilateral with the name that best describes it.

9\.

10\. 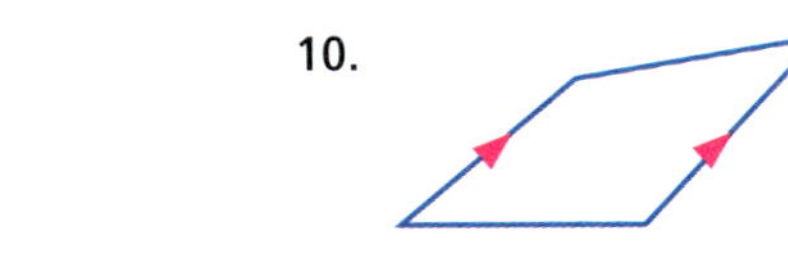

11\. 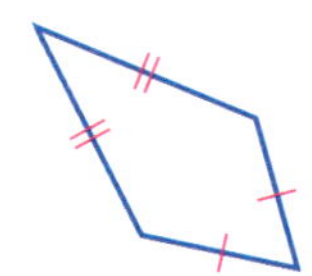

12\.

13\. 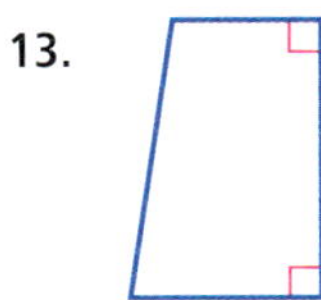

14\. 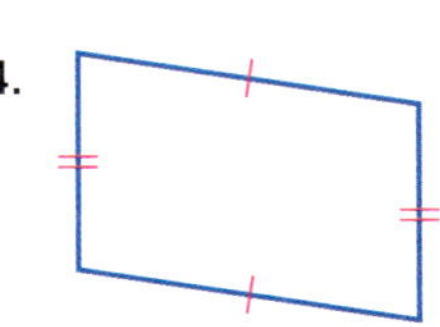

ALGEBRA **Find the missing angle measure in each quadrilateral.**

15\. 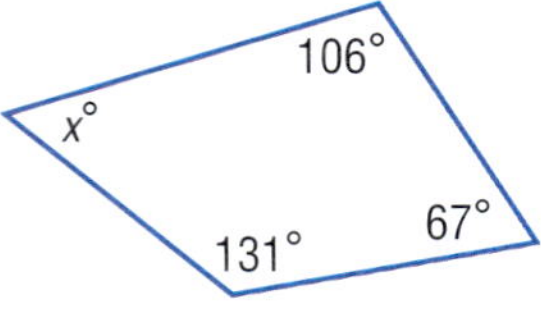

16\. 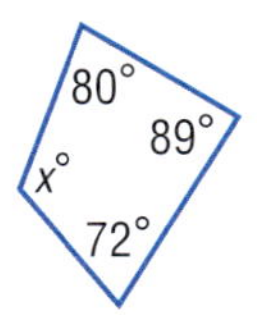

17\. 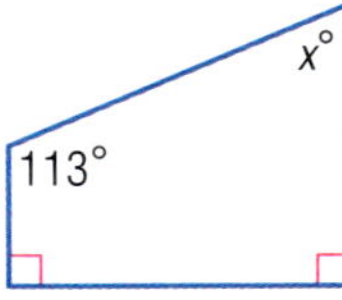

18\.

19\. 

20\. 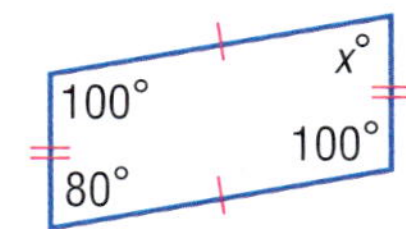

21\. **ALGEBRA** Find $m\angle B$ in quadrilateral $ABCD$ if $m\angle A = 87°$, $m\angle C = 135°$, and $m\angle D = 22°$.

22\. **ALGEBRA** What is $m\angle X$ in quadrilateral $WXYZ$ if $m\angle W = 45°$, $m\angle Y = 128°$, and $\angle Z$ is a right angle?

23\. **LANDSCAPE** Identify the shapes of the bricks used in the design at the right. Use the name that *best* describes each brick.

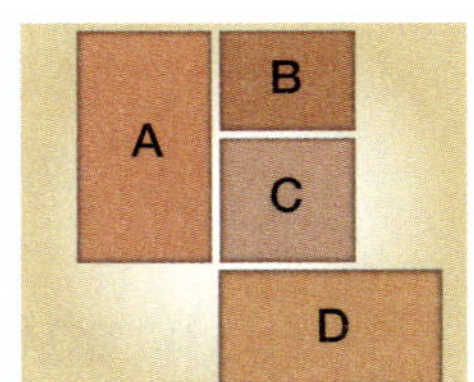

24\. **MEASUREMENT** Find each of the missing angle measures a, b, c, and d in the figure at the right. Justify your answers.

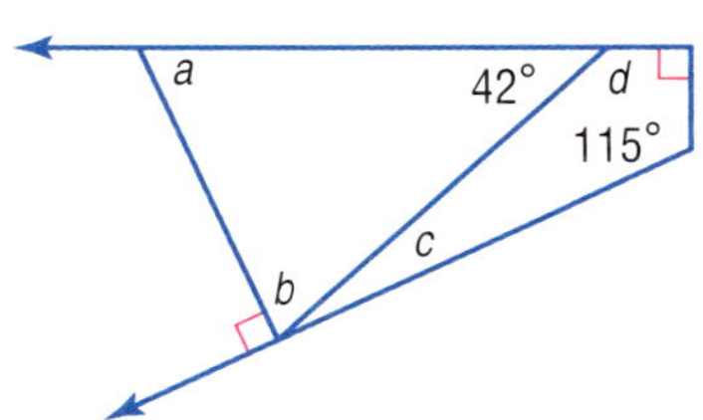

Find the missing measure in each quadrilateral with the given angle measures.

25\. 37.5°, 78°, 115.4°, $x°$

26\. $x°$, 108.3°, 49.8°, 100°

27\. 25.5°, $x°$, 165.9°, 36.8°

28\. 79.1°, 120.8°, $x°$, 65.7°

ART **For Exercises 29–31, identify the types of triangles and quadrilaterals used in each quilt block pattern. Use the names that *best* describe the figures.**

29. 

30. 

31. 

DRAWING QUADRILATERALS **Determine whether each figure described below can be drawn. If the figure can be drawn, draw it. If not, explain why not.**

32. a quadrilateral that is both a rhombus and a rectangle

33. a trapezoid with three right angles

34. a trapezoid with two congruent sides

ALGEBRA **Find the value of x in each quadrilateral.**

35. $2x°$ $2x°$ $2x°$ $2x°$

36. 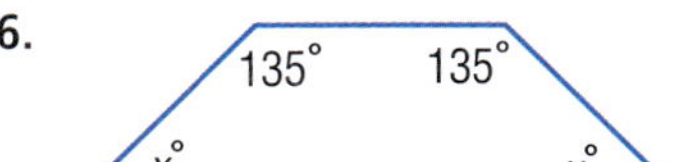

37. $100°$ $x°$ $x°$ $100°$

H.O.T. Problems

CHALLENGE **For Exercises 38 and 39, refer to the table that gives the properties of several parallelograms. Property A states that both pairs of opposite sides are parallel and congruent.**

Parallelogram	Properties
1	A, C
2	A, B, C
3	A, B

38. If property C states that all four sides are congruent, classify parallelograms 1–3. Justify your response.

39. If parallelogram 3 is a rectangle, describe Property B. Justify your response.

REASONING **Determine whether each statement is *sometimes*, *always*, or *never* true. Explain your reasoning.**

40. A quadrilateral is a trapezoid.

41. A trapezoid is a parallelogram.

42. A square is a rectangle.

43. A rhombus is a square.

44. **FIND THE ERROR** Isabelle and John are describing a rectangle. Who is more accurate? Explain.

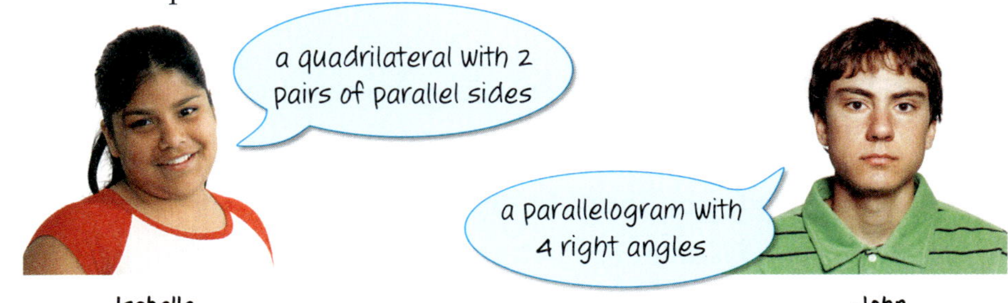

45. **WRITING IN MATH** The diagonals of a rectangle are congruent, and the diagonals of a rhombus are perpendicular. Based on this information, what can you conclude about the diagonals of a square? of a parallelogram? Explain your reasoning.

46. Identify the name that does *not* describe the quadrilateral shown.

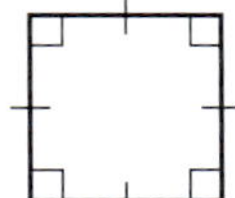

A square

B rectangle

C rhombus

D trapezoid

47. Which statement is always true about a rhombus?

F It has 4 right angles.

G The sum of the measures of the angles is 180°.

H It has exactly one pair of parallel sides.

J It has 4 congruent sides.

48. Which of the following is a correct drawing of a quadrilateral with all sides congruent and with four right angles?

A 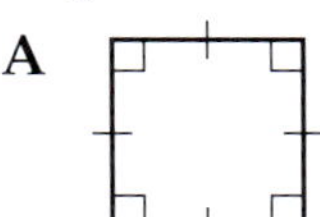

B 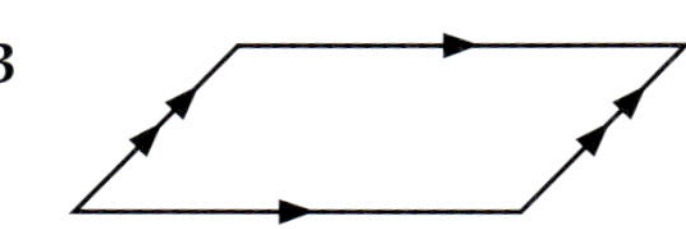

C 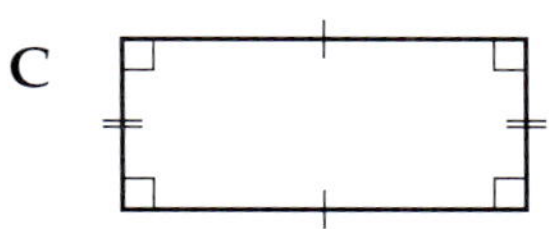

D 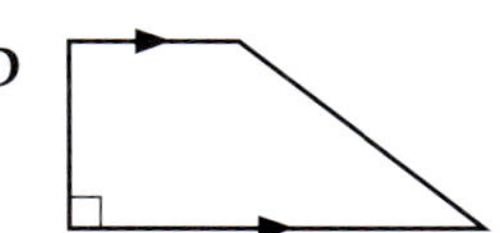

Spiral Review

49. **REASONING** Neva, Sophie, and Seth have a turtle, a dog, and a hamster for a pet, but not in that order. Sophie's pet lives in a glass aquarium and does not have fur. Neva never has to give her pet a bath. Who has what pet? Use the *logical reasoning* strategy. (Lesson 10-5)

Classify each triangle by its angles and by its sides. (Lesson 10-4)

50. 

51. 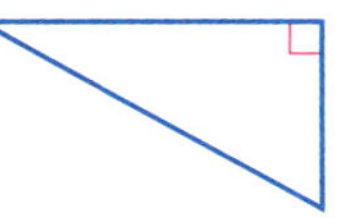

52. 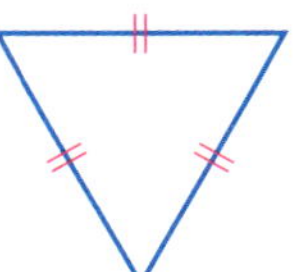

53. **LETTERS** How many permutations are possible of the letters in the word *Fresno?* (Lesson 9-4)

Find the sales tax or discount to the nearest cent. (Lesson 7-7)

54. \$54 jacket; 7% sales tax

55. \$23 hat; 15% discount

GET READY for the Next Lesson

PREREQUISITE SKILL **Solve each proportion.** (Lesson 6-6)

56. $\frac{3}{5} = \frac{x}{75}$

57. $\frac{a}{7} = \frac{18}{42}$

58. $\frac{7}{9} = \frac{28}{m}$

59. $\frac{3.5}{t} = \frac{16}{32}$

60. $\frac{3}{6} = \frac{c}{5}$

Chapter 10 Mid-Chapter Quiz

Lessons 10-1 through 10-6

Name each angle in four ways. Then classify each angle as *acute*, *obtuse*, *right*, or *straight*. (Lesson 10-1)

1. 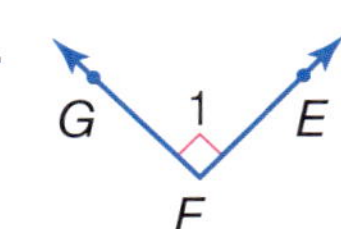

2. 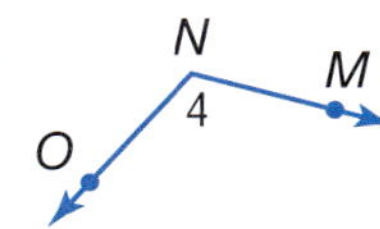

3. **MULTIPLE CHOICE** Which angle is complementary to $\angle CBD$? (Lesson 10-2)

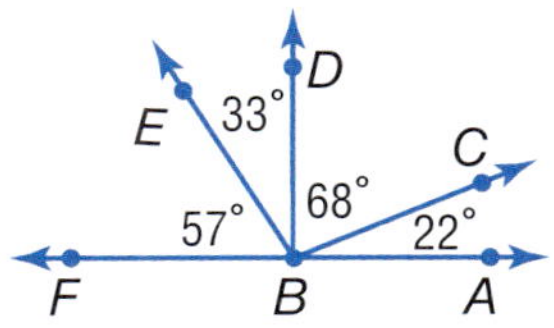

A $\angle ABC$ **C** $\angle DBE$

B $\angle FBC$ **D** $\angle EBF$

4. **SOCCER** Display the data in a circle graph. (Lesson 10-3)

Injuries of High School Girls' Soccer Players	
Position	**Percent**
Halfbacks	37%
Fullbacks	23%
Forward Line	28%
Goalkeepers	12%

EDUCATION For Exercises 5 and 6, use the circle graph that shows the percent of students by grade level in U.S. schools. (Lesson 10-3)

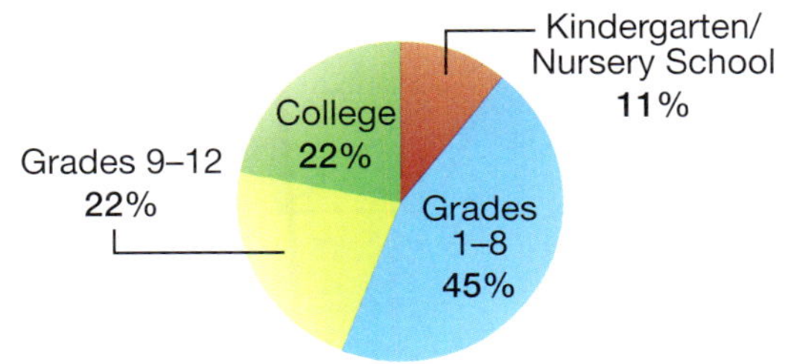

5. In which grades are most students?
6. How many times as many students are there in grades 1–8 than in grades 9–12?

ALGEBRA Find the value of x. (Lesson 10-4)

7. 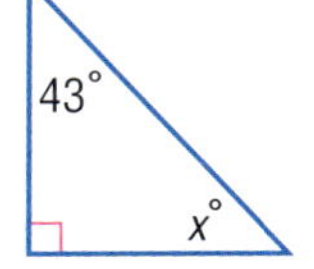

8. 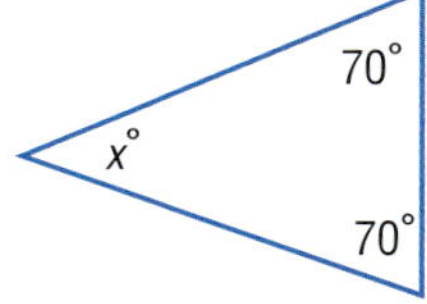

9. **MULTIPLE CHOICE** In triangle ABC, $m\angle A = 62°$ and $m\angle C = 44°$. What is $m\angle B$? (Lesson 10-4)

F 90° **H** 64°

G 74° **J** 42°

10. **RACES** Norberto, Isabel, Fiona, Brock, and Elizabeth were the first five finishers of a race. From the given clues, find the order in which they finished. Use the *logical reasoning* strategy. (Lesson 10-5)
    - Norberto passed Fiona just before the finish line.
    - Elizabeth finished 5 seconds ahead of Norberto.
    - Isabel crossed the finish line after Fiona.
    - Brock was fifth at the finish line.

Classify the quadrilateral with the name that best describes it. (Lesson 10-6)

11. 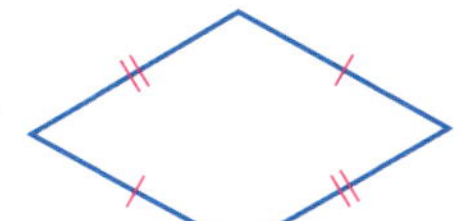

12. 

ALGEBRA Find the value of x in each quadrilateral. (Lesson 10-6)

13. 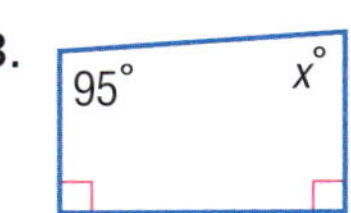

14. 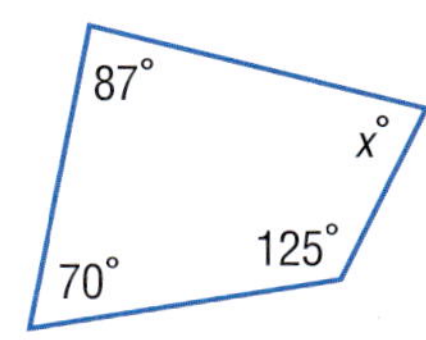

15. **ALGEBRA** What is $m\angle A$ in quadrilateral $ABCD$ if $m\angle B = 36°$, $m\angle C = 74°$, and $\angle D$ is a right angle? (Lesson 10-6)

10-7 Similar Figures

MAIN IDEA

Determine whether figures are similar and find a missing length in a pair of similar figures.

New Vocabulary

similar figures
corresponding sides
corresponding angles
indirect measurement

Math Online

glencoe.com

- Extra Examples
- Personal Tutor
- Self-Check Quiz

MINI Lab

The figures in each pair below have the same shape but different sizes. Copy each pair onto dot paper. Then find the measure of each angle using a protractor and the measure of each side using a centimeter ruler.

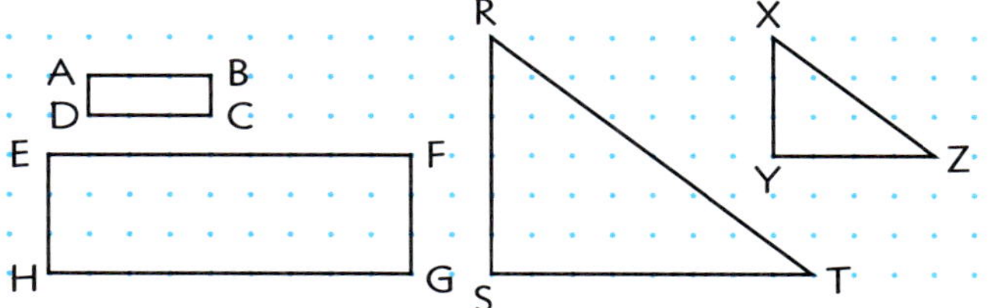

1. $\overline{AB}$ on the smaller rectangle matches $\overline{EF}$ on the larger rectangle. Name all pairs of matching sides in each pair of figures.
   The notation $\overline{AB}$ means the segment with endpoints at *A* and *B*.
2. Write each ratio in simplest form.
   The notation *AB* means the *measure* of segment *AB*.
   a. $\frac{AB}{EF}, \frac{BC}{FG}, \frac{DC}{HG}, \frac{AD}{EH}$ b. $\frac{RS}{XY}, \frac{ST}{YZ}, \frac{RT}{XZ}$
3. What do you notice about the ratios of matching sides?
4. Name all pairs of matching angles in the figures above. What do you notice about the measure of these angles?
5. **MAKE A CONJECTURE** about figures that have the same shape but not necessarily the same size.

Figures that have the same shape but not necessarily the same size are **similar figures**. In the figures below, triangle *RST* is similar to triangle *XYZ*. We write this as $\triangle RST \sim \triangle XYZ$.

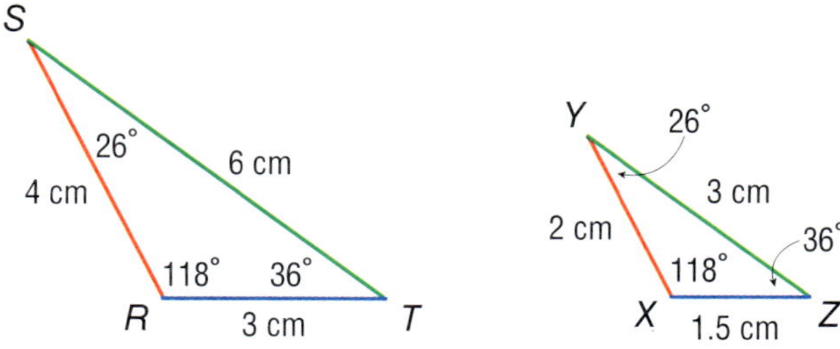

The matching sides are $\overline{ST}$ and $\overline{YZ}$, $\overline{SR}$ and $\overline{YX}$, and $\overline{RT}$ and $\overline{XZ}$. The sides of similar figures that "match" are called **corresponding sides**.

The matching angles are $\angle S$ and $\angle Y$, $\angle R$ and $\angle X$, and $\angle T$ and $\angle Z$. The angles of similar figures that "match" are called **corresponding angles**.

The Mini Lab illustrates the following statements.

Similar Figures

Key Concept

Words If two figures are similar, then

- the corresponding sides are proportional, and
- the corresponding angles are congruent.

Models

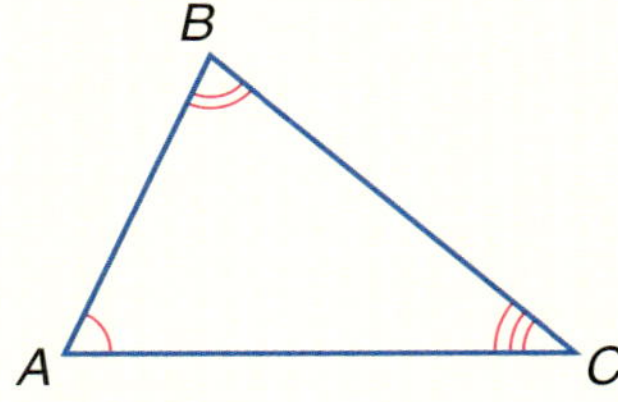

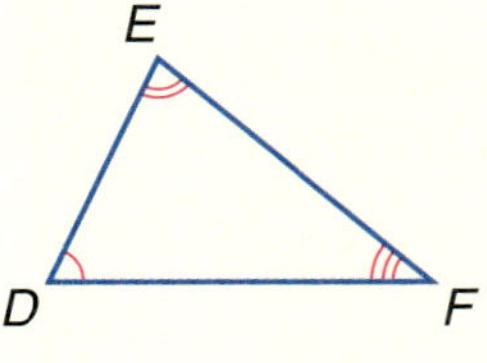

Symbols $\triangle ABC \sim \triangle DEF$ The symbol $\sim$ means *is similar to*.

corresponding sides: $\frac{AB}{DE} = \frac{BC}{EF} = \frac{AC}{DF}$

corresponding angles: $\angle A \cong \angle D$; $\angle B \cong \angle E$; $\angle C \cong \angle F$

Reading Math

Geometry Symbols

$\sim$ is similar to

$\cong$ is congruent to

EXAMPLE Identify Similar Figures

1 **Which trapezoid below is similar to trapezoid *DEFG*?**

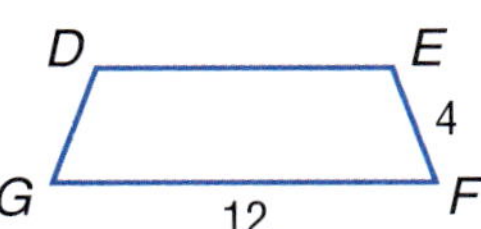

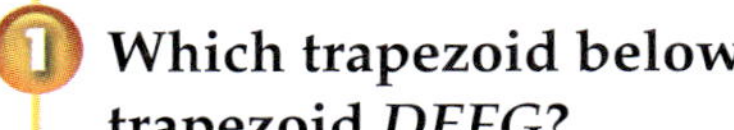

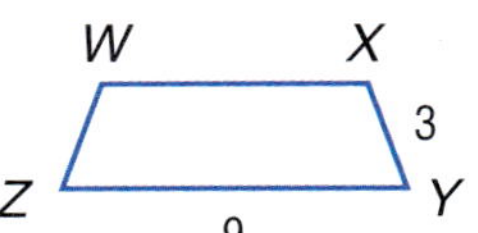

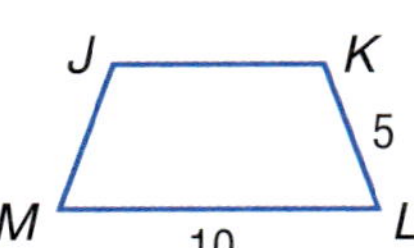

Find the ratios of the corresponding sides to see if they form a constant ratio.

Trapezoid *PQRS*

$\frac{EF}{QR} = \frac{4}{6}$ or $\frac{2}{3}$

$\frac{FG}{RS} = \frac{12}{14}$ or $\frac{6}{7}$

Not similar

Trapezoid *WXYZ*

$\frac{EF}{XY} = \frac{4}{3}$

$\frac{FG}{YZ} = \frac{12}{9}$ or $\frac{4}{3}$

Similar

Trapezoid *JKLM*

$\frac{EF}{KL} = \frac{4}{5}$

$\frac{FG}{LM} = \frac{12}{10}$ or $\frac{6}{5}$

Not similar

So, trapezoid *WXYZ* is similar to trapezoid *DEFG*.

CHECK Your Progress

a. Which triangle below is similar to triangle *DEF*?

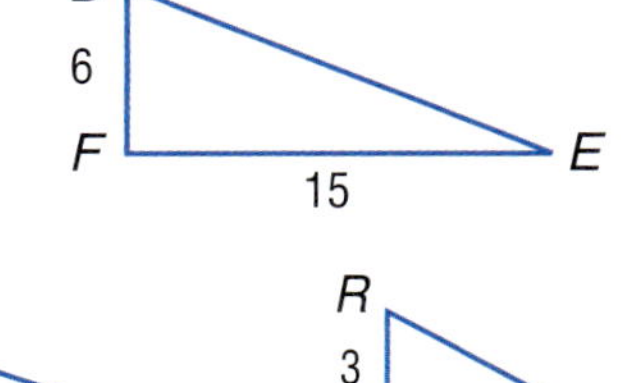

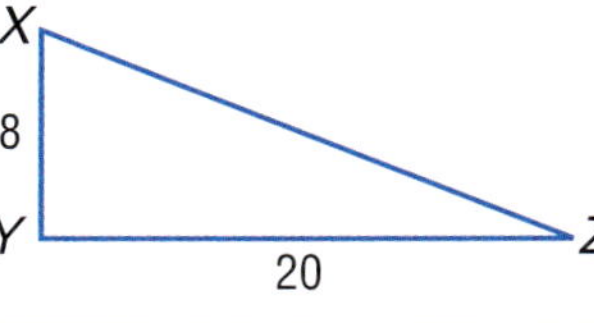

A
4
C
12
B

R
3
T
6
S

EXAMPLE Find Side Measures of Similar Triangles

2 If $\triangle RST \sim \triangle XYZ$, find the length of $\overline{XY}$.

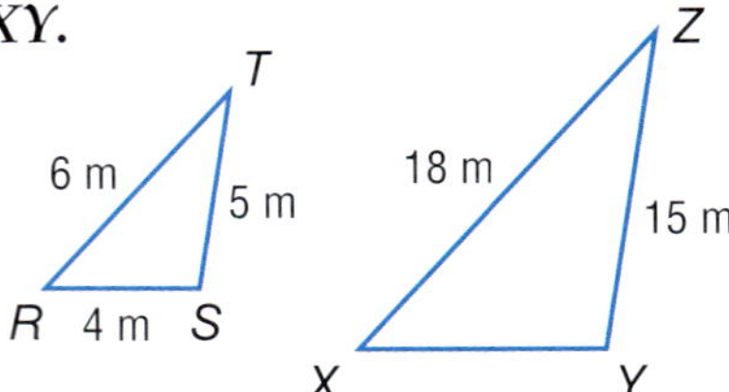

Since the two triangles are similar, the ratios of their corresponding sides are equal. Write and solve a proportion to find XY.

$\frac{RT}{XZ} = \frac{RS}{XY}$ Write a proportion.

$\frac{6}{18} = \frac{4}{n}$ Let n represent the length of $\overline{XY}$. Then substitute.

$6n = 18(4)$ Find the cross products.

$6n = 72$ Simplify.

$n = 12$ Divide each side by 6. The length of $\overline{XY}$ is 12 meters.

> **Reading Math**
>
> **Geometry Symbols**
>
> Just as the measure of angle A can be written as $m\angle A$, there is a special way to indicate the measure of a segment. The measure of $\overline{AB}$ is written as AB, without the bar over it.

CHECK Your Progress

b. If $\triangle ABC \sim \triangle EFD$, find the length of $\overline{AC}$.

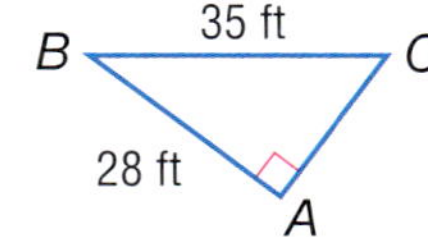

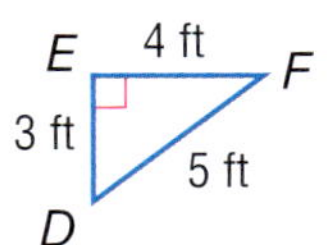

Indirect measurement uses similar figures to find the length, width, or height of objects that are too difficult to measure directly.

Real-World EXAMPLE

3 GEYSERS Old Faithful in Yellowstone National Park shoots water 60 feet into the air that casts a shadow of 42 feet. What is the height of a nearby tree that casts a shadow 63 feet long? Assume the triangles are similar.

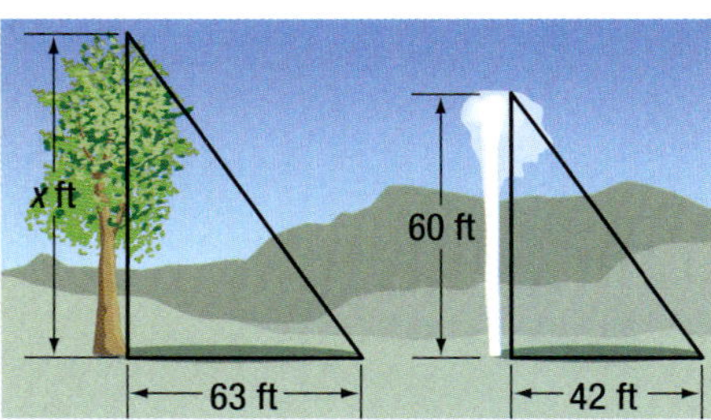

Tree Old Faithful

$\frac{x}{63} = \frac{60}{42}$ ← height ← shadow

$42x = 60(63)$ Find the cross products.

$42x = 3{,}780$ Simplify.

$x = 90$ Divide each side by 42.

The tree is 90 feet tall.

CHECK Your Progress

c. **PHOTOGRAPHY** Destiny wants to resize a 4-inch wide by 5-inch long photograph for the school newspaper. It is to fit in a space that is 2 inches wide. What is the length of the resized photograph?

CHECK Your Understanding

Example 1 (p. 541)

1. Which rectangle below is similar to rectangle $ABCD$?

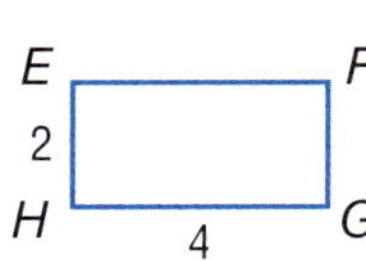

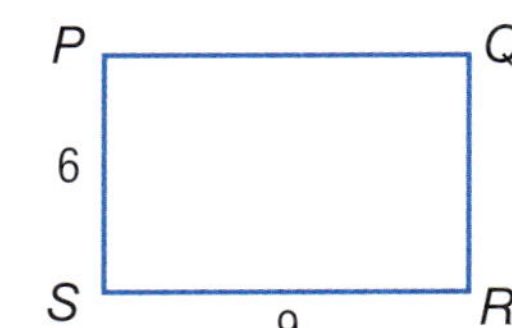

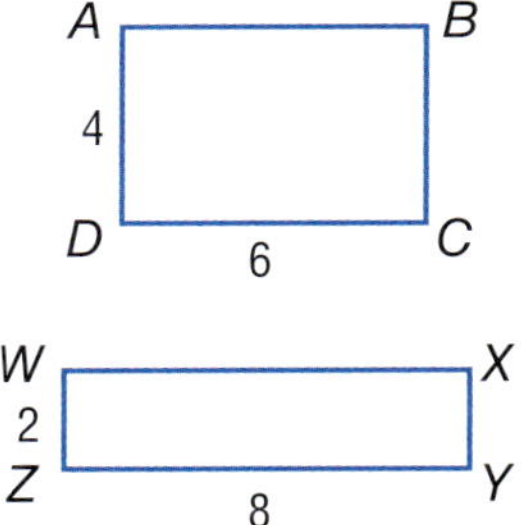

Example 2 (p. 542)

ALGEBRA Find the value of x in each pair of similar figures.

2. 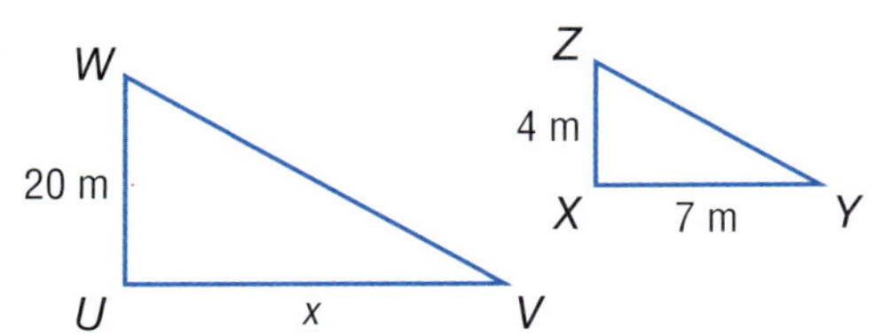

3. 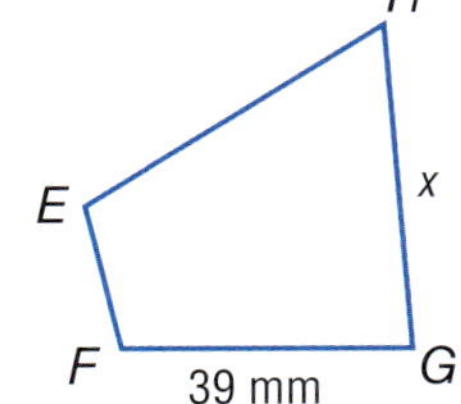

Example 3 (p. 542)

4. **SHADOWS** A flagpole casts a 20-foot shadow. At the same time, Humberto, who is 6 feet tall, casts a 5-foot shadow. What is the height of the flagpole? Assume the triangles are similar.

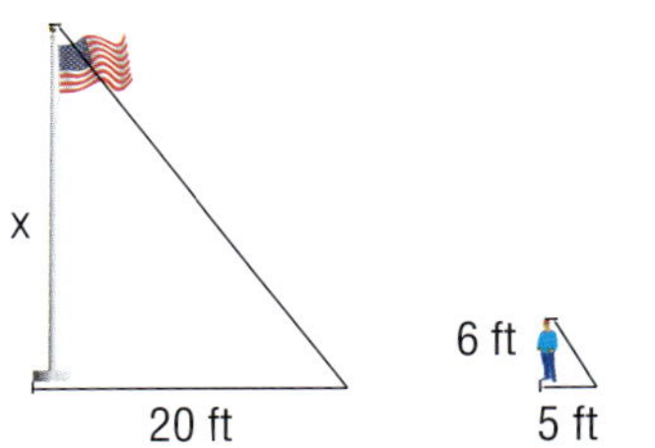

Practice and Problem Solving

HOMEWORK HELP	
For Exercises	See Examples
5–6	1
7–10	2
11–12	3

5. Which triangle below is similar to triangle FGH?

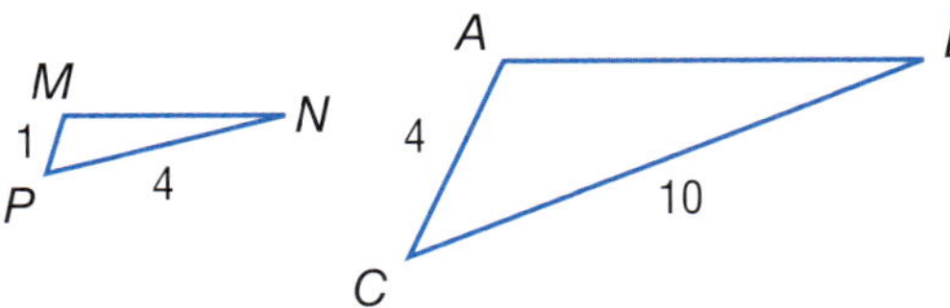

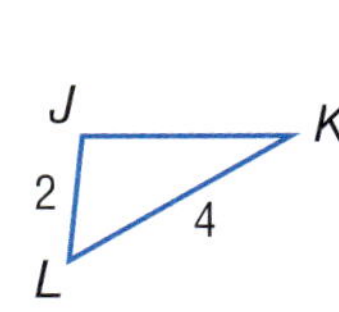

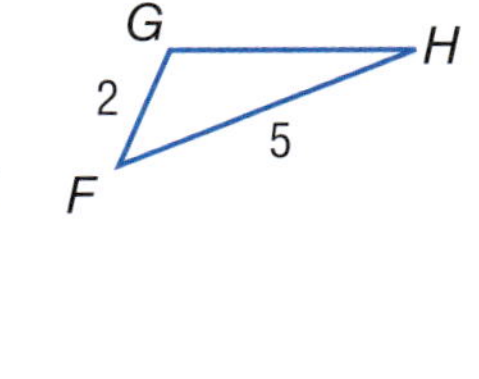

6. Which parallelogram below is similar to parallelogram $HJKM$?

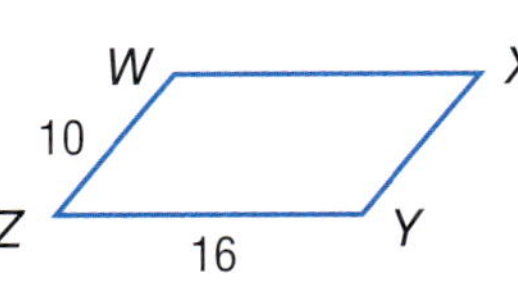

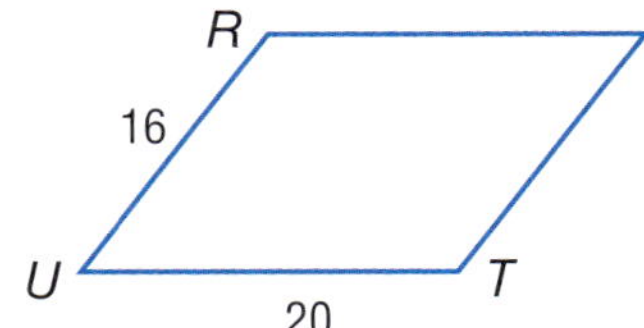

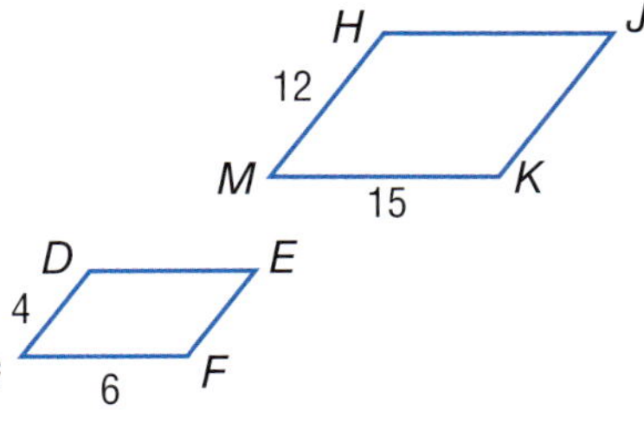

ALGEBRA Find the value of x in each pair of similar figures.

7. Q, 5 mi, 6 mi, O, P; T, x, 30 mi, R, S

8. 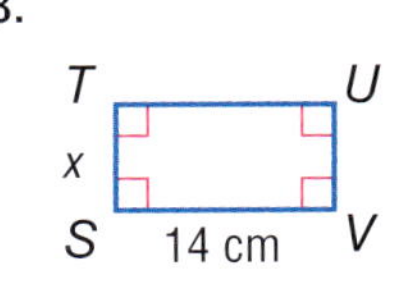

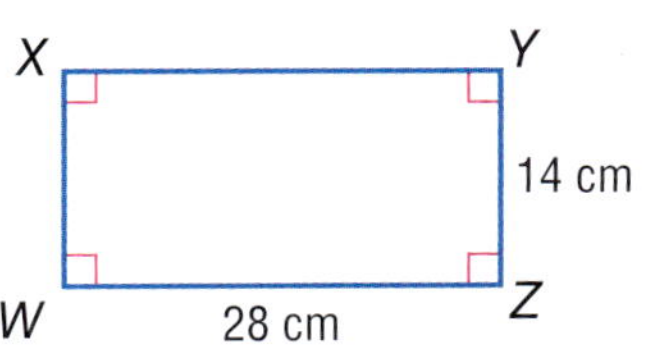

ALGEBRA **Find the value of x in each pair of similar figures.**

9.

10.

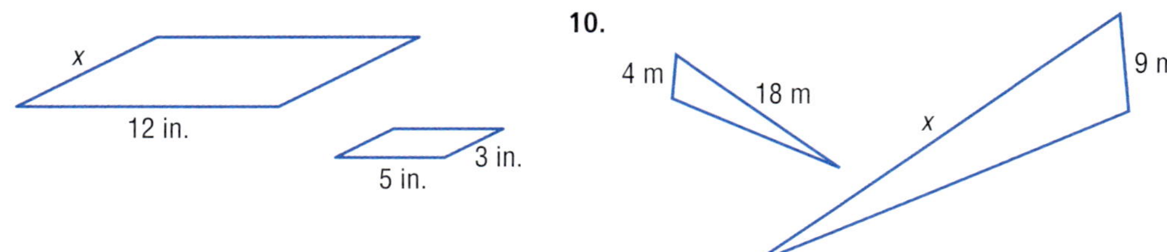

11. **PARKS** Ruth is at the park standing next to a slide. Ruth is 5 feet tall, and her shadow is 4 feet long. If the shadow of the slide is 4.8 feet long, what is the height of the slide? Assume the triangles are similar.

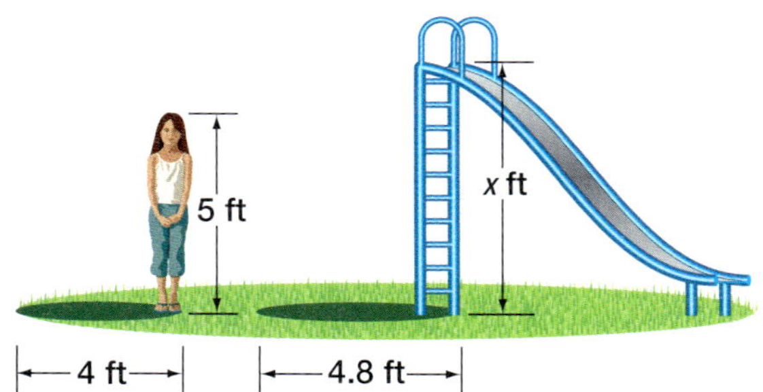

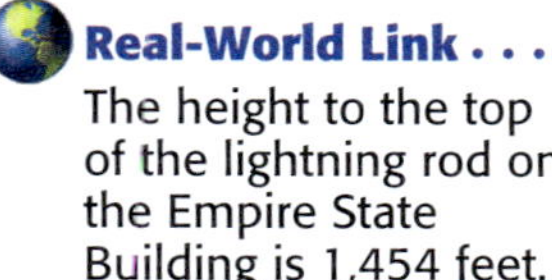

Real-World Link
The height to the top of the lightning rod on the Empire State Building is 1,454 feet.

Source: Wired New York

12. **FURNITURE** A child's desk is made so that it is a replica of a full-size adult desk. Suppose the top of the full-size desk measures 54 inches long by 36 inches wide. If the top of a child's desk is 24 inches wide and is similar to the full-size desk, what is the length?

ALGEBRA **Find the value of x in each pair of similar figures.**

13.

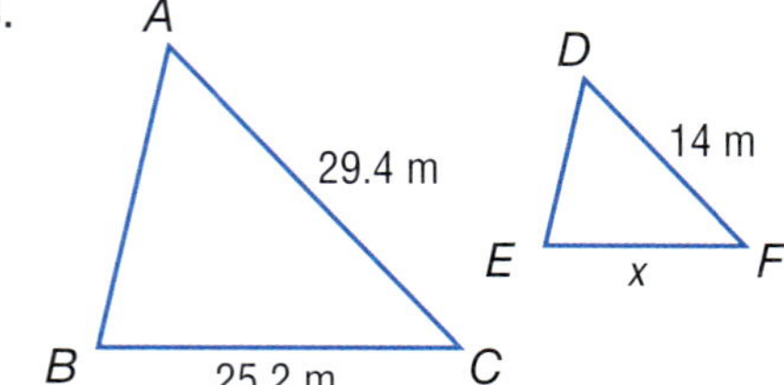

14.

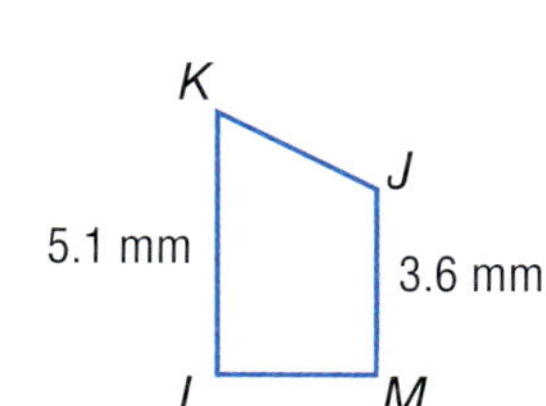

SKYSCRAPERS **For Exercises 15 and 16, use the information below and at the left.**

Tricia has a miniature replica of the Empire State Building. The replica is 10 inches tall, and the height of the observation deck is 8.3 inches.

15. About how tall is the actual observation deck?

16. Tricia's sister has a larger replica in which the height of the observation deck is 12 inches. How tall is the larger replica?

EXTRA PRACTICE
See pages 695, 713.

17. **MEASUREMENT** The ratio of the length of square A to the length of square B is 3:5. If the length of square A is 18 meters, what is the perimeter of square B?

H.O.T. Problems

CHALLENGE For Exercises 18 and 19, use the following information.

Two rectangles are similar. The ratio of their corresponding sides is 1:4.

18. Find the ratio of their perimeters.

19. What is the ratio of their areas?

20. **WRITING IN MATH** Write a problem about a real-world situation that could be solved using proportions and the concept of similarity. Then use what you have learned in this lesson to solve the problem.

TEST PRACTICE

21. Which rectangle is similar to the rectangle shown?

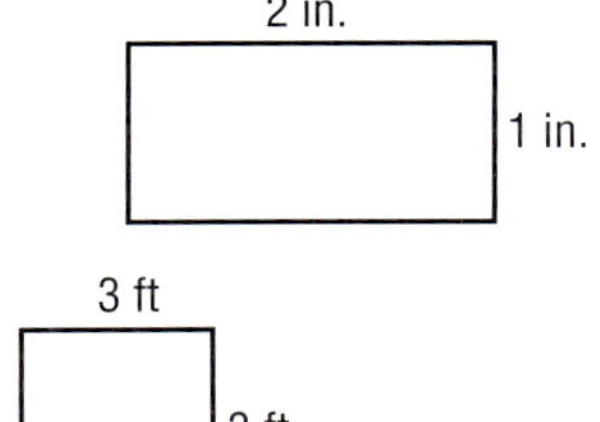

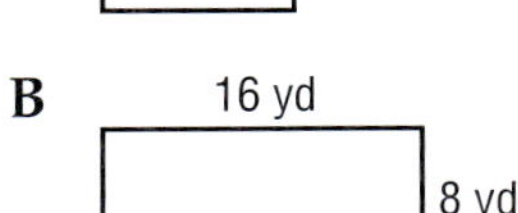

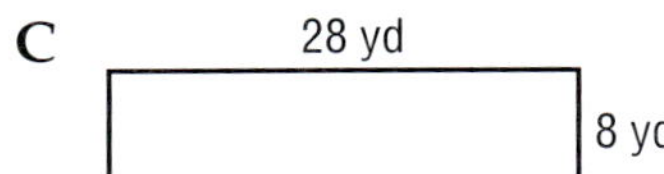

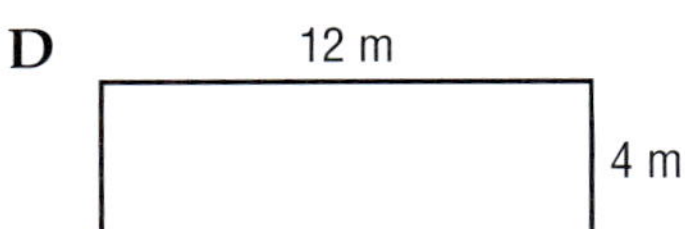

22. Which of the following equations is a correct use of cross-multiplication in solving the proportion $\frac{12}{15} = \frac{m}{6}$?

F $12 \cdot m = 15 \cdot 6$

G $12 \cdot 6 = m \cdot 15$

H $12 \cdot 15 = m \cdot 6$

J $12 \div 6 = m \div 15$

23. Horatio is 6 feet tall and casts a shadow 3 feet long. What is the height of a nearby tower if it casts a shadow 25 feet long at the same time?

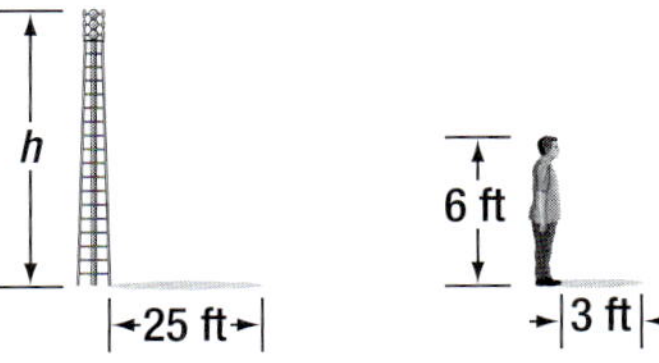

A 25 feet

B 45 feet

C 50 feet

D 75 feet

Spiral Review

GEOMETRY Classify the quadrilateral using the name that *best* describes it. (Lesson 10-6)

24. 

25. 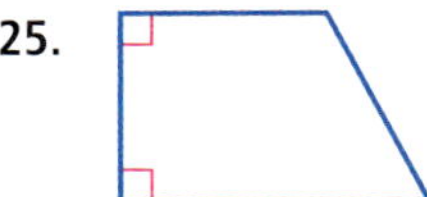

26. 

27. **MEASUREMENT** A triangular-shaped sail has angle measures of 44° and 67°. Find the measure of the third angle. (Lesson 10-4)

GET READY for the Next Lesson

PREREQUISITE SKILL Solve each equation. (Lesson 3-3)

28. $5a = 120$

29. $360 = 4x$

30. $940 = 8n$

31. $6t = 720$

10-8 Polygons and Tessellations

MAIN IDEA

Classify polygons and determine which polygons can form a tessellation.

New Vocabulary

polygon
pentagon
hexagon
heptagon
octagon
nonagon
decagon
regular polygon
tessellation

Math Online

glencoe.com

- Extra Examples
- Personal Tutor
- Self-Check Quiz

GET READY for the Lesson

POOLS Prairie Pools designs and builds swimming pools in various shapes and sizes. The shapes of five swimming pool styles are shown in their catalog.

Aquarius

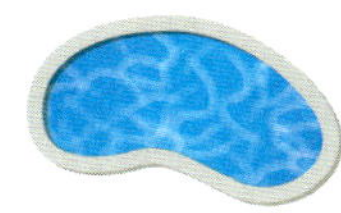
Kidney

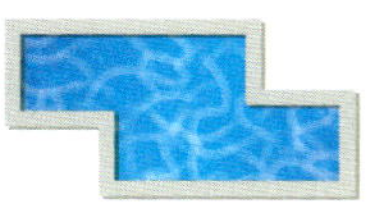
Roman

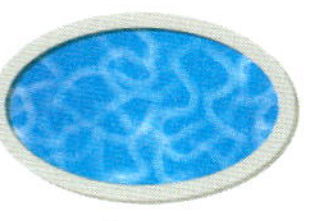
Oval

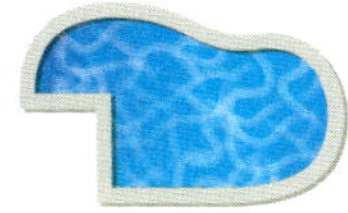
Rustic

1. In the pool catalog, the Aquarius and the Roman styles are listed under Group A. The remaining three pools are listed under Group B. Describe one difference between the shapes of the pools in the two groups.
2. Create your own drawing of the shape of a pool that would fit into Group A. Group B.

A **polygon** is a simple, closed figure formed by three or more straight line segments. A *simple figure* does not have lines that cross each other. You have drawn a *closed figure* when your pencil ends up where it started.

Polygons	Not Polygons
• Line segments are called sides. • Sides meet only at their endpoints. • Points of intersection are called vertices.	• Figures with sides that cross each other. • Figures that are open. • Figures that have curved sides.

A polygon can be classified by the number of sides it has.

Words	pentagon	hexagon	heptagon	octagon	nonagon	decagon
Number of Sides	5	6	7	8	9	10
Models						

A **regular polygon** has all sides congruent and all angles congruent. Equilateral triangles and squares are examples of regular polygons.

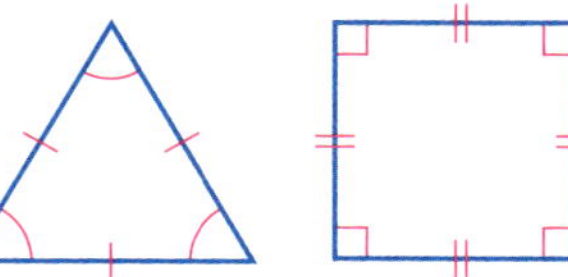

EXAMPLES Classify Polygons

Determine whether each figure is a polygon. If it is, classify the polygon and state whether it is regular. If it is not a polygon, explain why.

Reading Math

Regular Polygons Since regular polygons have *equal–sized angles*, they are also called *equiangular*.

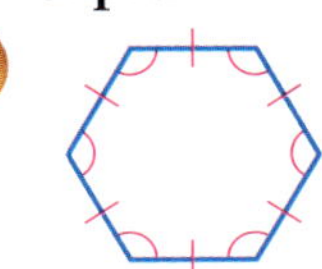

The figure has 6 congruent sides and 6 congruent angles. It is a regular hexagon.

The figure is not a polygon since it has a curved side.

CHECK Your Progress

Determine whether each figure is a polygon. If it is, classify the polygon and state whether it is regular. If it is *not* a polygon, explain why.

a. 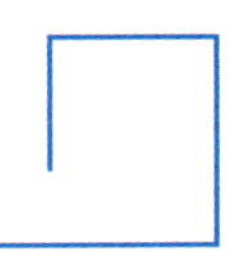

b. 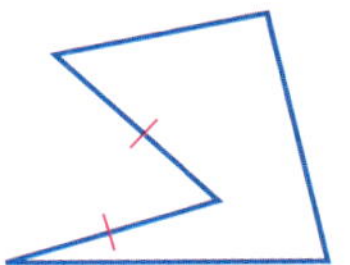

The sum of the measures of the angles of a triangle is 180°. You can use this relationship to find the measures of the angles of regular polygons.

EXAMPLE Angle Measures of a Polygon

Study Tip

Angle Measures
The number of triangles formed is 2 less than the number of sides in the polygon. The equation $(n - 2) + 180 = s$ gives the sum s of angle measures in a polygon with n sides.

3 **ALGEBRA Find the measure of each angle of a regular pentagon.**

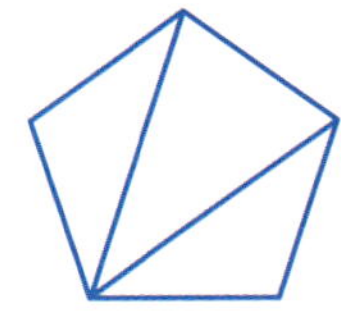

- Draw all of the diagonals from one vertex as shown and count the number of triangles formed.
- Find the sum of the angle measures in the polygon.

number of triangles formed × 180° = sum of angle measures in polygon

$$3 \times 180° = 540°$$

- Find the measure of each angle of the polygon. Let n represent the measure of one angle in the pentagon.

$5n = 540$ There are five congruent angles.

$n = 108$ Divide each side by 5.

The measure of each angle in a regular pentagon is 108°.

CHECK Your Progress

Find the measure of an angle in each polygon.

c. regular octagon

d. equilateral triangle

A repetitive pattern of polygons that fit together with no overlaps or holes is called a **tessellation**. The surface of these bricks is an example of a tessellation of squares.

The sum of the measures of the angles where the vertices meet in a tessellation is 360°.

90° 90°
90° 90°

$4 \times 90° = 360°$

Real-World Career **How Does a Textile Designer Use Math?** A textile designer uses math when creating tile patterns for flooring and walls.

Math Online For more information, go to glencoe.com.

Real-World EXAMPLE

4 **DESIGN** **Ms. Evans wants to design a floor tile using pentagons. Can Ms. Evans make a tessellation using pentagons?**

The measure of each angle in a regular pentagon is 108°.

The sum of the measures of the angles where the vertices meet must be 360°. So, solve $108°n = 360$.

$108n = 360$ Write the equation.

$\frac{108n}{108} = \frac{360}{108}$ Divide each side by 108.

$n \approx 3.3$ Use a calculator.

Since 108° does not divide evenly into 360°, the sum of the measures of the angles where the vertices meets is not 360°. So, Ms. Evans cannot make a tessellation using the pentagons.

Check

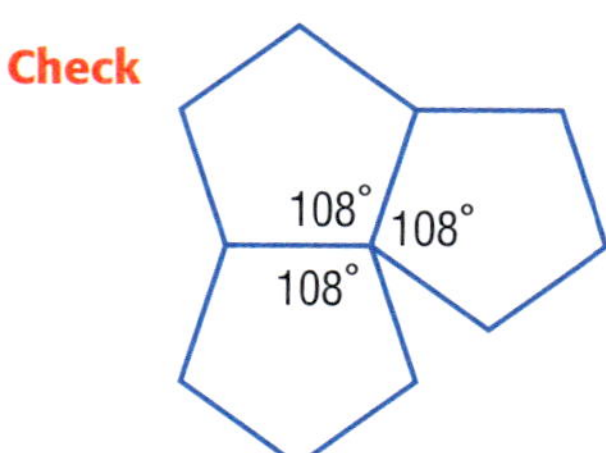

CHECK Your Progress

e. **DESIGN** Can Ms. Evans use tiles that are equilateral triangles to cover the floor? Explain.

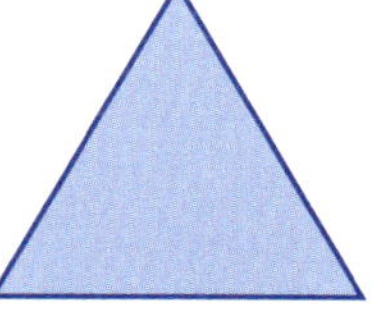

Check Your Understanding

Examples 1, 2 (p. 547)

Determine whether each figure is a polygon. If it is, classify the polygon and state whether it is regular. If it is *not* a polygon, explain why.

1. 
2. 
3. 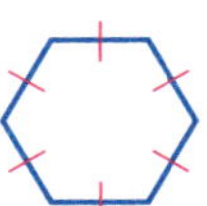

Example 3 (p. 547)

Find the measure of an angle in each polygon if the polygon is regular. Round to the nearest tenth of a degree if necessary.

4. hexagon
5. heptagon

Example 4 (p. 548)

6. **ART** In art class, Trisha traced and then cut several regular octagons out of tissue paper. Can she use the figures to create a tessellation? Explain.

Practice and Problem Solving

HOMEWORK HELP	
For Exercises	See Examples
7–12	1, 2
13–16	3
17–18	4

Determine whether each figure is a polygon. If it is, classify the polygon and state whether it is regular. If it is *not* a polygon, explain why.

7. 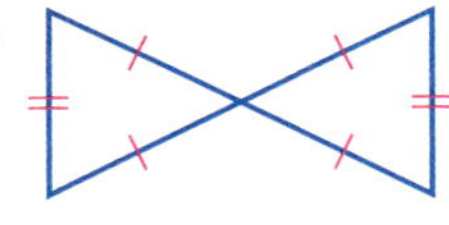
8. 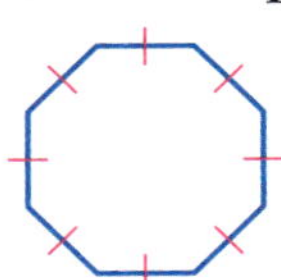
9. 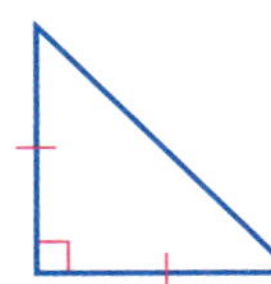
10. 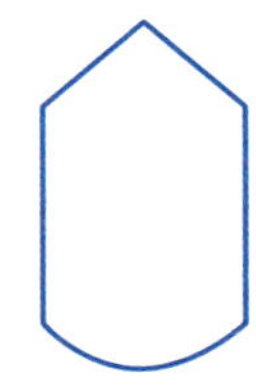
11. 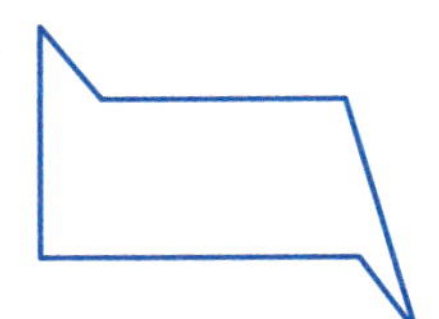
12. 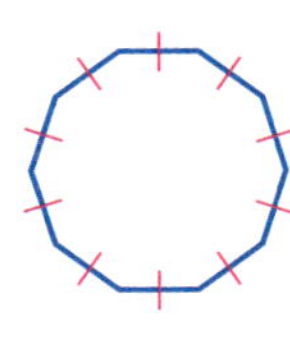

Find the measure of an angle in each polygon if the polygon is regular. Round to the nearest tenth of a degree if necessary.

13. decagon
14. nonagon
15. quadrilateral
16. 11-gon

17. **TOYS** Marty used his magnetic building set to build the regular decagon at the right. Assume he has enough building parts to create several of these shapes. Can the figures be arranged in a tessellation? Explain.

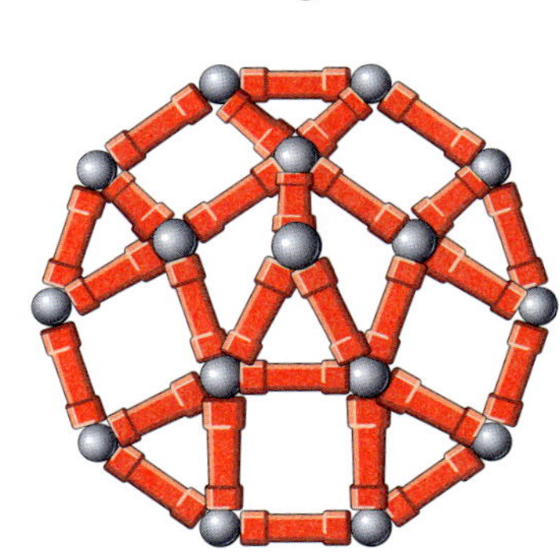

18. **COASTERS** Paper coasters are placed under a beverage glass to protect the table surface. The coasters are shaped like regular heptagons. Can the coasters be arranged in a tessellation? Explain your reasoning.

Classify the polygons that are used to create each tessellation.

19. 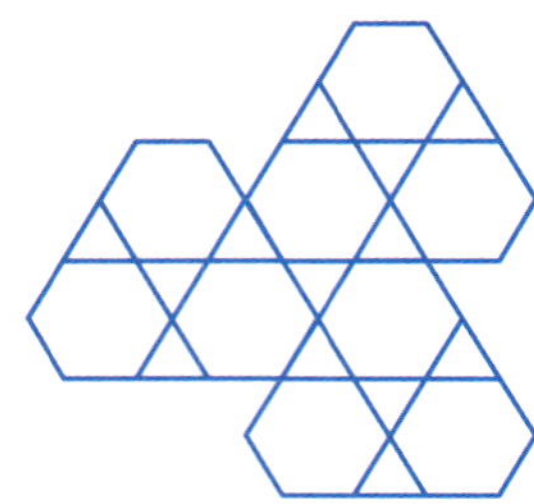

20. 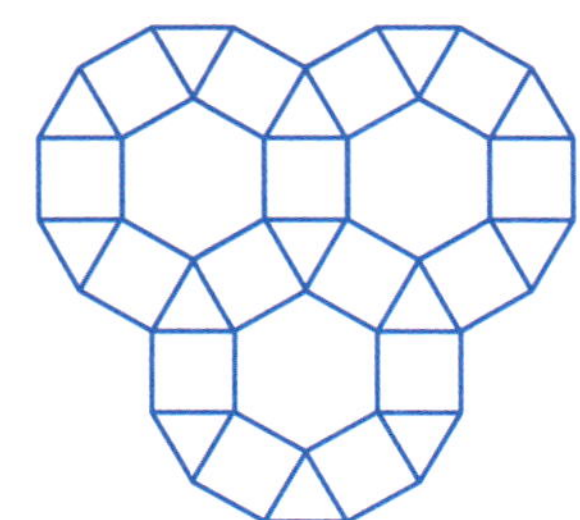

21. 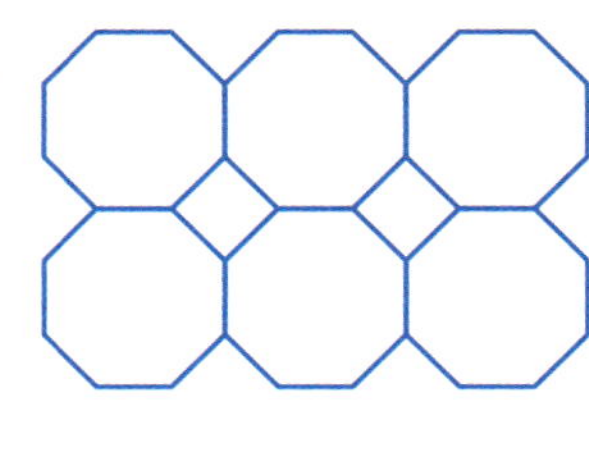

22. What is the perimeter of a regular nonagon with sides 4.8 centimeters?

23. Find the perimeter of a regular pentagon having sides $7\frac{1}{4}$ yards long.

24. **ART** The mosaic shown at the right is from a marble floor in Venice, Italy. Name the polygons used in the floor.

25. **SIGNS** Refer to the photo at the left. Stop signs are made from large sheets of steel. Suppose one sheet of steel is large enough to cut nine signs. Can all nine signs be arranged on the sheet so that none of the steel goes to waste? Explain.

26. **RESEARCH** Use the Internet or another source to find the shape of other road signs. Name the type of sign, its shape, and state whether or not it is regular.

Real-World Link

All stop signs have the same shape and meaning. In Spanish-speaking countries, the signs read "ALTO" (halt) or "PARE" (stop).

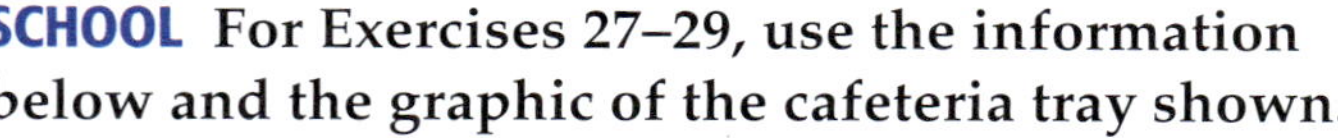

SCHOOL For Exercises 27–29, use the information below and the graphic of the cafeteria tray shown.

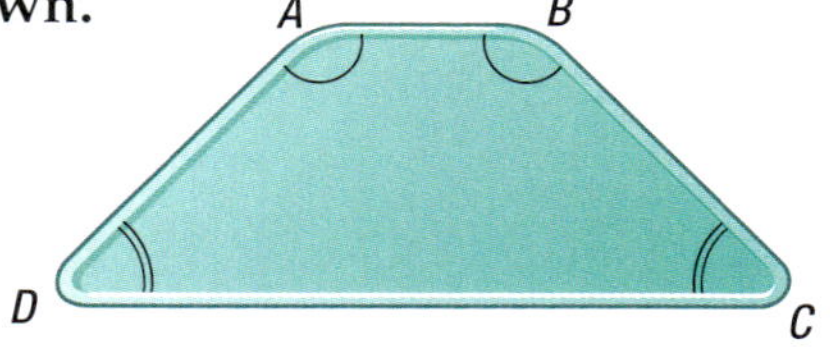

A company designs cafeteria trays so that four students can place their trays around a square table without bumping corners. The top and bottom sides of the tray are parallel.

27. Classify the shape of the tray.

28. If $\angle A \cong \angle B$, $\angle C \cong \angle D$, and $m\angle A = 135°$, find $m\angle B$, $m\angle C$, and $m\angle D$.

29. Name the polygon formed by the outside of four trays when they are placed around the table with their sides touching. Justify your answer.

EXTRA PRACTICE

See pages 695, 713.

H.O.T. Problems

30. **REASONING** *True* or *False*? Only a regular polygon can tessellate a plane.

31. **OPEN ENDED** Draw examples of a pentagon and a hexagon that represent real-world objects.

32. **CHALLENGE** You can make a tessellation with equilateral triangles. Can you make a tessellation with any isosceles or scalene triangles? If so, explain your reasoning and make a drawing.

33. **WRITING IN MATH** Analyze the parallelogram at the right and then explain how you know the parallelogram can be used by itself to make a tessellation.

TEST PRACTICE

34. **SHORT RESPONSE** What is the measure of $\angle 1$?

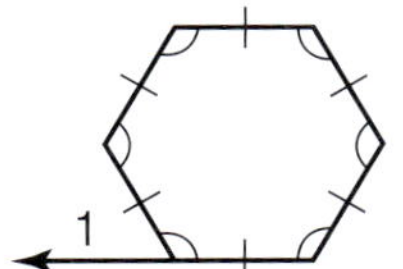

35. Which statement is *not* true about polygons?

A A polygon is classified by the number of sides it has.

B The sides of a polygon overlap.

C A polygon is formed by 3 or more line segments.

D The sides of a polygon meet only at its endpoints.

Spiral Review

For Exercises 36 and 37, use the figures at the right.

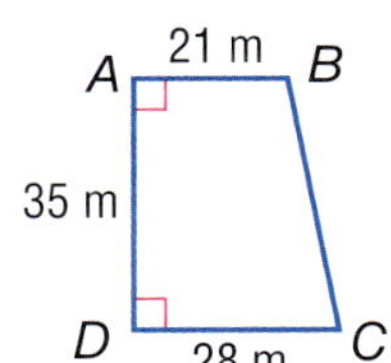

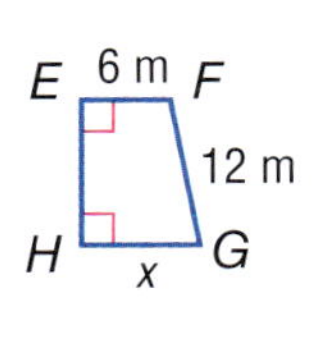

36. **ALGEBRA** The quadrilaterals are similar. Find the value of x. (Lesson 10-7)

37. **GEOMETRY** Classify figure $ABCD$. (Lesson 10-6)

38. **PROBABILITY** Two students will be randomly selected from a group of seven to present their reports. If Carla and Pedro are in the group of 7, what is the probability that Carla will be selected first and Pedro selected second? (Lesson 9-4)

39. **RUNNING** Use the information in the table to find the rate of change. (Lesson 6-3)

Distance (m)	15	30	45	60
Time (s)	10	20	30	40

Add or subtract. Write each sum or difference in simplest form. (Lesson 5-3)

40. $3\frac{2}{9} + 5\frac{4}{9}$

41. $5\frac{1}{3} - 2\frac{1}{6}$

42. $1\frac{3}{7} + 6\frac{1}{4}$

43. $9\frac{4}{5} - 4\frac{7}{8}$

GET READY for the Next Lesson

PREREQUISITE SKILL **Graph and label each point on the same coordinate plane.** (Lesson 2-3)

44. $A(-2, 3)$

45. $B(4, 3)$

46. $C(2, -1)$

47. $D(-4, -1)$

Geometry Lab
Tessellations

MAIN IDEA

Create tessellations.

In this lab, you will create tessellations.

ACTIVITY

STEP 1 Draw a square on the back of an index card. Then draw a triangle on the inside of the square and a trapezoid on the bottom of the square as shown.

STEP 2 Cut out the square. Then cut out the triangle and slide it from the right side of the square to the left side of the square. Cut out the trapezoid and slide it from the bottom to the top of the square.

STEP 3 Tape the figures together to form a pattern.

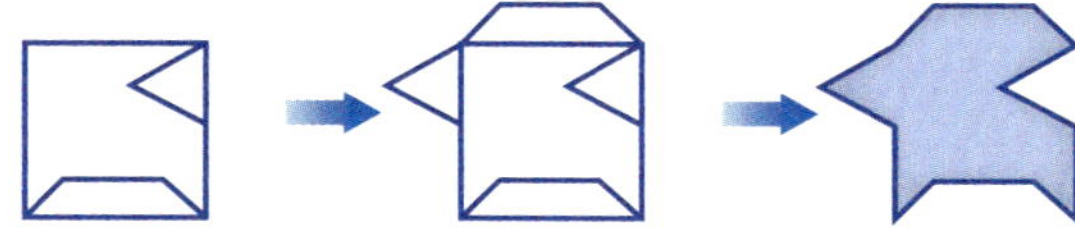

STEP 4 Trace this pattern onto a sheet of paper as shown to create a tessellation.

CHECK Your Progress

Create a tessellation using each pattern.

a. 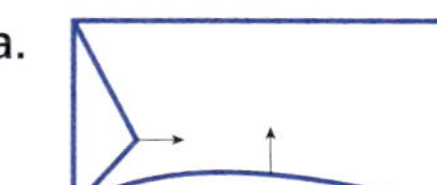

b. 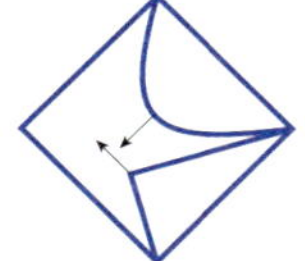

c. 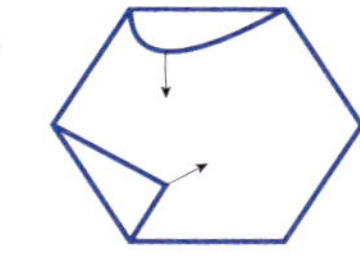

Analyze the Results

1. Design and describe your own tessellation pattern.
2. **MAKE A CONJECTURE** *Congruent figures* have corresponding sides of equal length and corresponding angles of equal measure. Explain how congruent figures are used in your tessellation.

10-9 Translations

MAIN IDEA

Graph translations of polygons on a coordinate plane.

New Vocabulary

transformation
translation
congruent figures

Math Online

glencoe.com

- Concepts In Motion
- Extra Examples
- Personal Tutor
- Self-Check Quiz

MINI Lab

STEP 1 Trace a parallelogram-shaped pattern block onto a coordinate grid. Label the vertices *ABCD*.

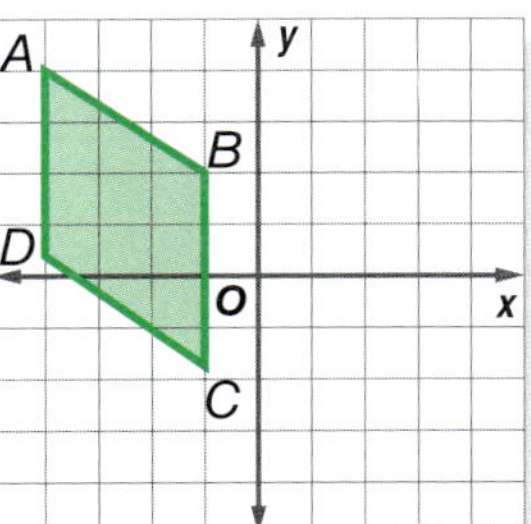

STEP 2 Slide the pattern block over 5 units to the right and 2 units down.

STEP 3 Trace the figure in its new position. Label the vertices *A′*, *B′*, *C′*, and *D′*.

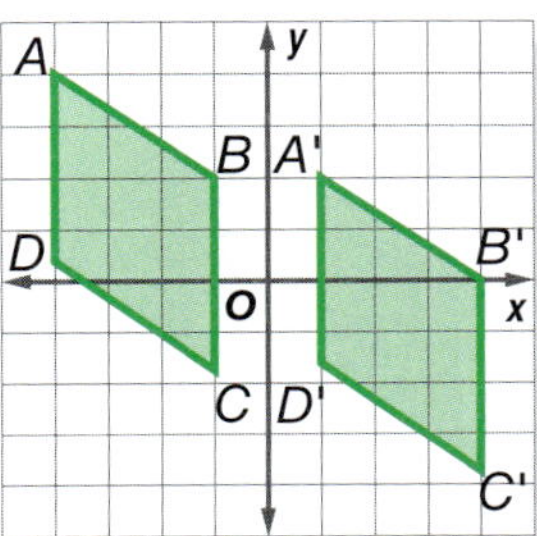

1. Trace the horizontal and vertical path between corresponding vertices. What do you notice?
2. Add 5 to each x-coordinate of the vertices of the original figure. Then subtract 2 from each y-coordinate of the vertices of the original figure. What do you notice?

A **transformation** maps one figure onto another. When you move the figure without turning it, the motion is called a **translation**.

When translating a figure, every point of the original figure is moved the same distance and in the same direction.

EXAMPLE Graph a Translation

1 **Translate quadrilateral *HIJK* 2 units left and 5 units up. Graph quadrilateral *H′ I′ J′ K′*.**

- Move each vertex of the figure 2 units left and 5 units up. Label the new vertices H', I', J', and K'.
- Connect the vertices to draw the trapezoid. The coordinates of the vertices of the new figure are $H'(-4, 1)$, $I'(-3, 4)$, $J'(1, 3)$, and $K'(-1, 1)$.

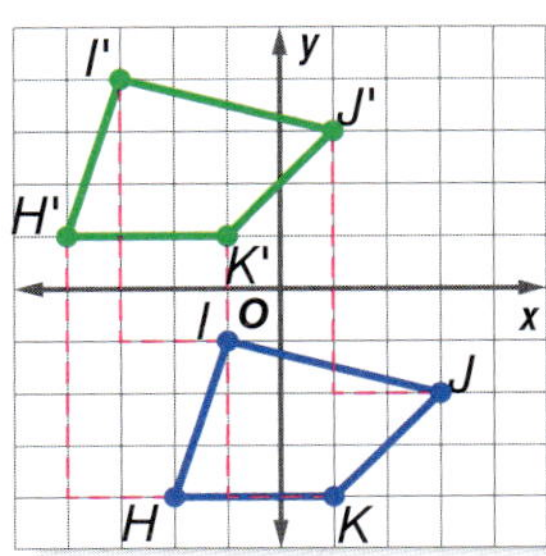

CHECK Your Progress

a. Translate quadrilateral *HIJK* 4 units up and 2 units right. Graph quadrilateral $H' I' J' K'$.

Reading Math

Prime Symbols Use prime symbols for vertices in a transformed image.

$A \rightarrow A'$
$B \rightarrow B'$
$C \rightarrow C'$

A' is read *A prime*.

When a figure has been translated, the original figure and the translated figure, or *image*, are congruent. **Congruent figures** have the same size and same shape, and the corresponding sides and angles have equal measures.

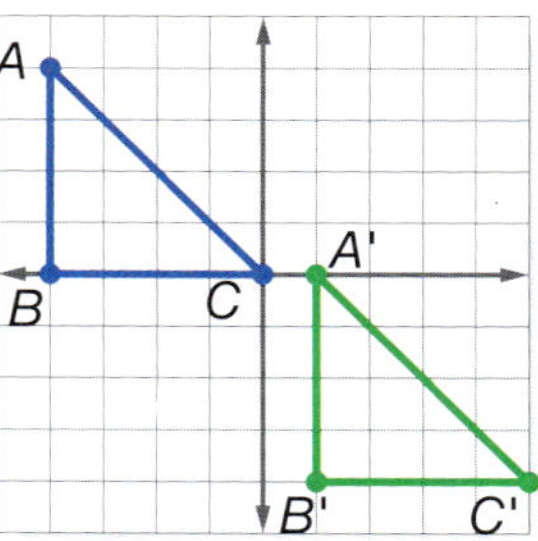

$\triangle ABC \cong \triangle A'B'C'$

You can increase or decrease the coordinates of the vertices of a figure by a fixed amount to find the coordinates of the translated vertices.

A *positive* integer describes a translation right or up on a coordinate plane. A *negative* integer describes a translation left or down.

EXAMPLE Find Coordinates of a Translation

2 Triangle LMN has vertices $L(-1, -2)$, $M(6, -3)$, and $N(2, -5)$. Find the vertices of $\triangle L'M'N'$ after a translation of 6 units left and 4 units up. Then graph the figure and its translated image.

The vertices can be found by adding -6 to the x-coordinates and 4 to the y-coordinates.

Add -6 to each x-coordinate.

Add 4 to each y-coordinate.

Vertices of $\triangle LMN$	$(x + (-6), y + 4)$	Vertices of $\triangle L'M'N'$
$L(-1, -2)$	$(-1 + (-6), -2 + 4)$	$L'(-7, 2)$
$M(6, -3)$	$(6 + (-6), -3 + 4)$	$M'(0, 1)$
$N(2, -5)$	$(2 + (-6), -5 + 4)$	$N'(-4, -1)$

Study Tip

Transformations
A transformation of the form $(x', y') = (x + a, y + b)$ is a translation which moves the point (x, y) a units horizontally and b units vertically.

Use the vertices of $\triangle LMN$ and of $\triangle L'M'N'$ to graph each triangle.

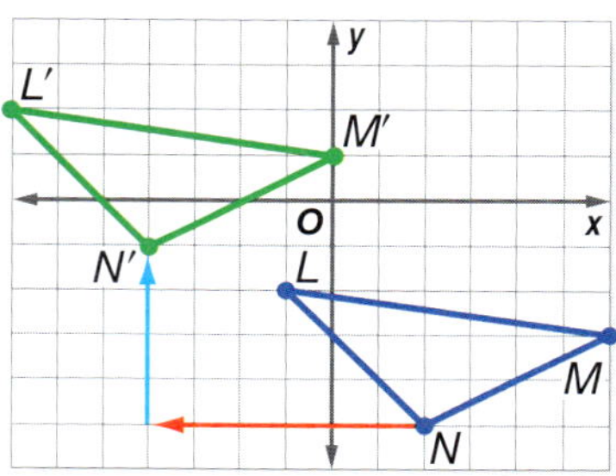

CHECK Your Progress

b. Triangle TUV has vertices $T(6, -3)$, $U(-2, 0)$, and $V(-1, 2)$. Find the vertices of $\triangle T'U'V'$ after a translation of 3 units right and 4 units down. Then graph the figure and its translated image.

In Example 2, $\triangle LMN$ was translated 6 units left and 4 units up. This translation can be described using the ordered pair $(-6, 4)$. In Check Your Progress b., $\triangle TUV$ was translated 3 units right and 4 units down. This translation can be described using the ordered pair $(3, -4)$.

CHECK Your Understanding

Example 1 (p. 553)

1. Translate $\triangle ABC$ 3 units left and 3 units down. Graph $\triangle A'B'C'$.

Example 2 (p. 554)

Quadrilateral *DEFG* has vertices $D(1, 0)$, $E(-2, -2)$, $F(2, 4)$, and $G(6, -3)$. Find the vertices of $D'E'F'G'$ after each translation. Then graph the figure and its translated image.

2. 4 units right, 5 units down
3. 6 units right

4. **MAPS** Nakos explores part of the Denver Zoo in Colorado as shown. He starts at the felines and then visits the hoofed animals. Describe this translation in words and as an ordered pair.

Practice and Problem Solving

HOMEWORK HELP

For Exercises	See Examples
5–6	1
7–12	2

5. Translate $\triangle HIJ$ 2 units right and 6 units down. Graph $\triangle H'I'J'$.

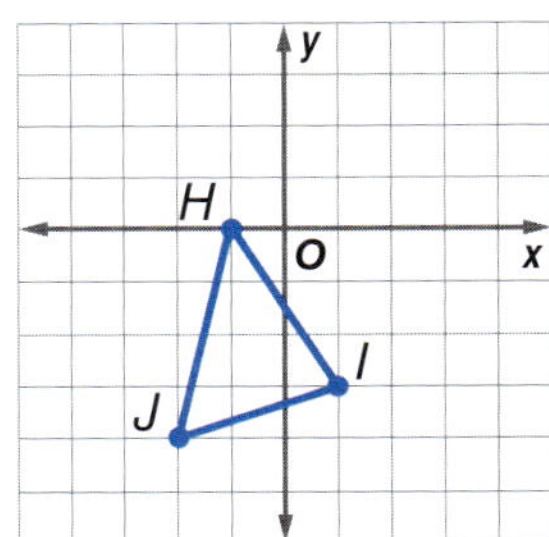

6. Translate rectangle *KLMN* 1 unit left and 3 units up. Graph rectangle $K'L'M'N'$.

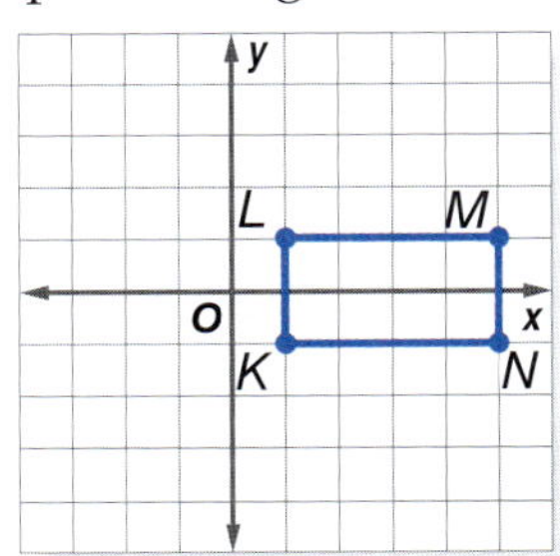

Triangle *PQR* has vertices $P(0, 0)$, $Q(5, -2)$, and $R(-3, 6)$. Find the vertices of $P'Q'R'$ after each translation. Then graph the figure and its translated image.

7. 6 units right, 5 units up
8. 8 units left, 1 unit down
9. 3 units left
10. 9 units down

GAMES When playing the game shown at the right, the player can move horizontally or vertically across the board. Describe each of the following as a translation in words and as an ordered pair.

11. Green player
12. Orange player

13. Triangle ABC is translated 2 units left and 3 units down. Then the translated figure is translated 3 units right. Graph the resulting triangle.

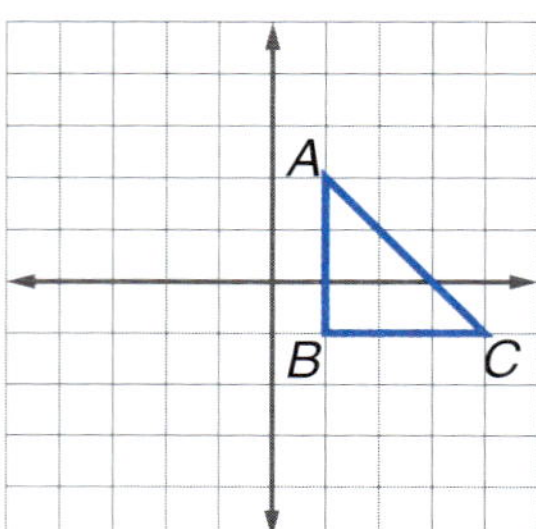

14. Parallelogram $RSTU$ is translated 3 units right and 5 units up. Then the translated figure is translated 2 units left. Graph the resulting parallelogram.

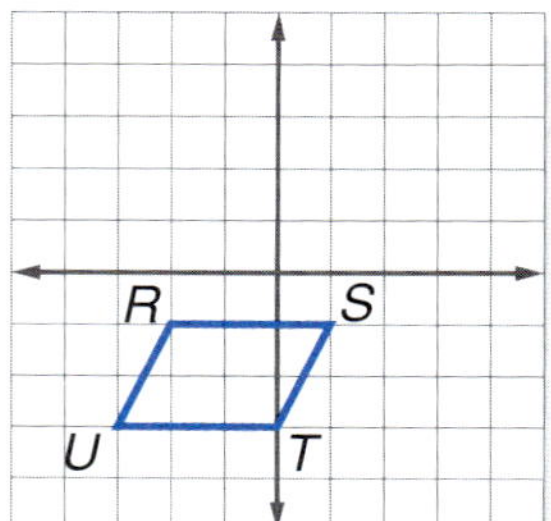

15. **ART** Marjorie Rice creates art using tessellations. At the right is her artwork of fish. Explain how translations and tessellations were used in the figure.

16. **RESEARCH** Use the Internet or another source to find other pieces of art that contain tessellations of translations. Describe how the artists incorporated both ideas into their work.

17. Triangle FGH has vertices $F(7, 6)$, $G(3, 4)$, $H(1, 5)$. Find the coordinates of $\triangle F'G'H'$ after a translation $1\frac{1}{2}$ units right and $3\frac{1}{2}$ units down. Then graph the figure and its translated image.

REASONING The coordinates of a point and its image after a translation are given. Describe the translation in words and as an ordered pair.

See pages 696, 713.

18. $N(0, -3) \rightarrow N'(2, 2)$
19. $M(2, 4) \rightarrow M'(-3, 1)$
20. $P(-2, -1) \rightarrow P'(3, -2)$
21. $Q(-4, 0) \rightarrow Q'(1, 4)$

H.O.T. Problems

22. **CHALLENGE** Is it possible to make a tessellation with translations of an equilateral triangle? Explain your reasoning.

23. **Which One Doesn't Belong?** Identify the transformation that is not the same as the other three. Explain your reasoning.

A

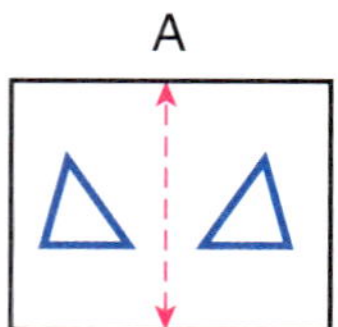

B

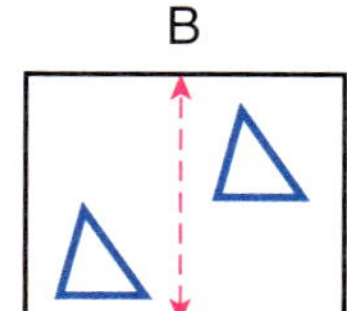

C

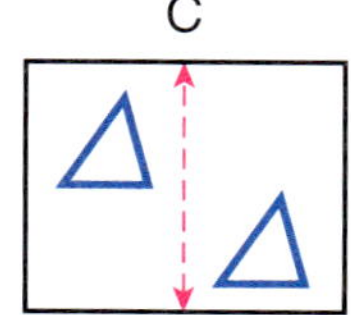

D

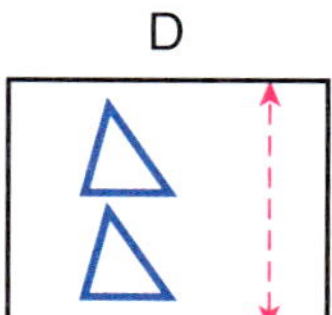

24. **WRITING IN MATH** Triangle ABC is translated 4 units right and 2 units down. Then the translated image is translated again 7 units left and 5 units up. Describe the final translated image in words.

TEST PRACTICE

25. Which graph shows a translation of the letter Z?

A

C

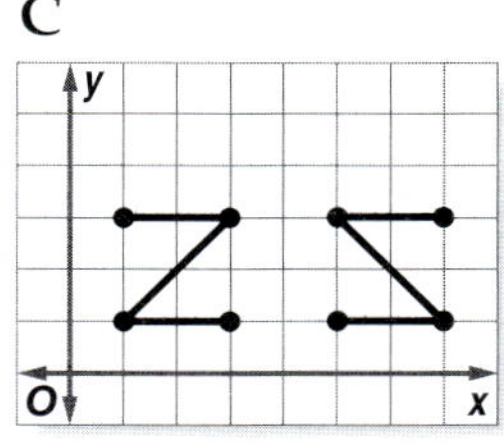

B

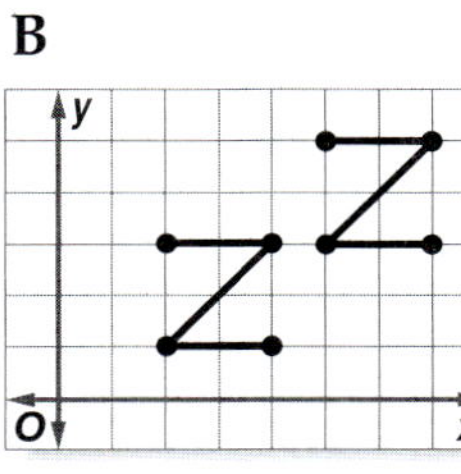

D

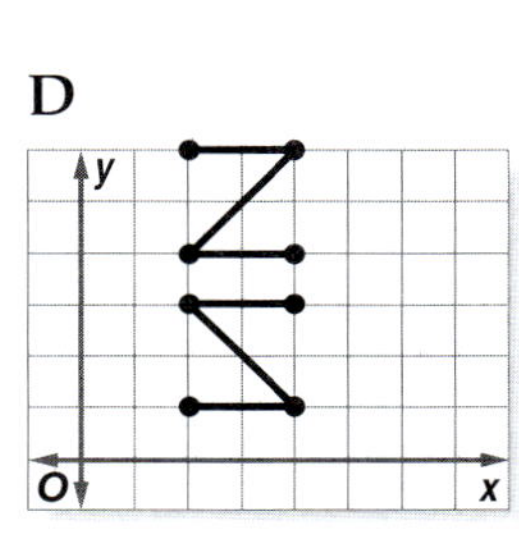

26. If point A is translated 4 units left and 3 units up, what will be the coordinates of point A in its new position?

F $(4, 4)$

G $(-5, 5)$

H $(-5, -1)$

J $(-4, 3)$

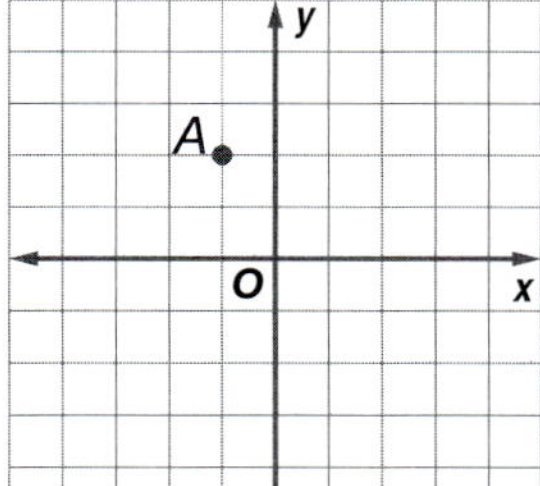

Spiral Review

27. **GEOMETRY** What is the name of a polygon with eight sides? (Lesson 10-8)

28. **GEOMETRY** The triangles at the right are similar. What is the measure of $\angle F$? (Lesson 10-7)

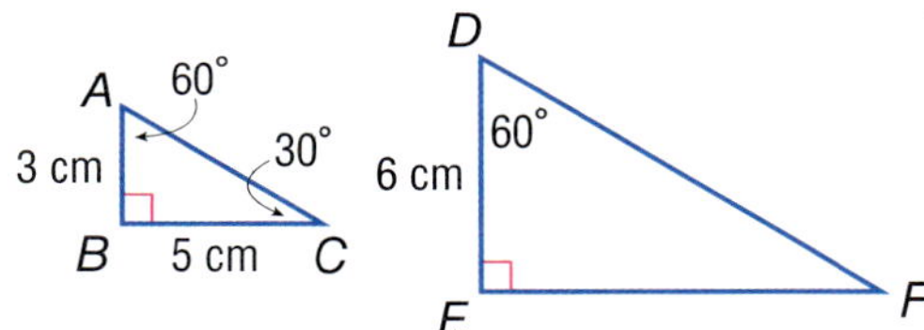

29. **FOOD** For dinner, you can choose one of two appetizers, one of four entrées, and one of three desserts. How many possible unique dinners can you choose? (Lesson 9-3)

For each set of data, describe how the range would change if the value 15 was added to the data set. (Lesson 8-2)

30. $\{8, 17, 32\}$

31. $\{22, 38, 41, 77\}$

32. $\{10, 10, 19\}$

33. $\{7, 11, 13\}$

Write each percent as a decimal. (Lesson 4-7)

34. 83.8%

35. 56.7%

36. 3.8%

37. 102.6%

GET READY for the Next Lesson

PREREQUISITE SKILL **Determine whether each figure can be folded in half so that one side matches the other. Write *yes* or *no*.**

38. 

39. 

40. 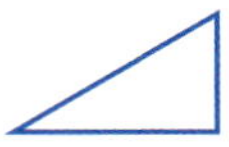

41. 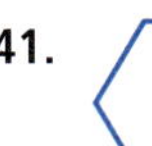

10-10 Reflections

MAIN IDEA

Identify figures with line symmetry and graph reflections on a coordinate plane.

New Vocabulary

line symmetry
line of symmetry
reflection
line of reflection

Math Online

glencoe.com

- Extra Examples
- Personal Tutor
- Self-Check Quiz

MINI Lab

VISION Scientists have determined that the human eye uses symmetry to see. It is possible to understand what you are looking at, even if you do not see all of it.

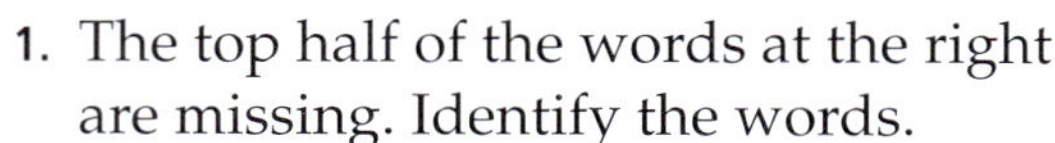

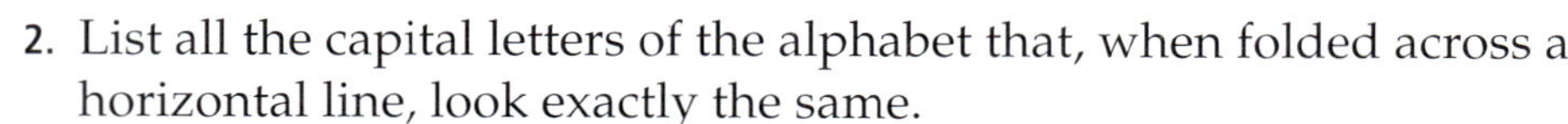

1. The top half of the words at the right are missing. Identify the words.
2. List all the capital letters of the alphabet that, when folded across a horizontal line, look exactly the same.
3. On a piece of paper, write the bottom half of other words that, when reflected across a horizontal line, look exactly the same.

Figures that match exactly when folded in half have **line symmetry**. The figures at the right have line symmetry.

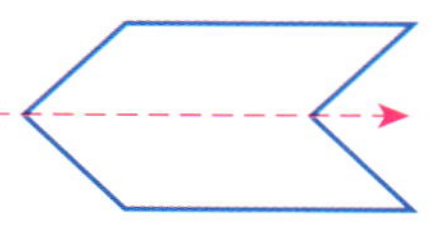

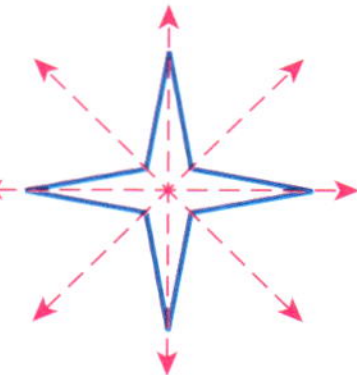

Each fold line is called a **line of symmetry**.

Real-World EXAMPLES

GRAPHIC DESIGN **Determine whether each figure has line symmetry. If so, copy the figure and draw all lines of symmetry.**

no symmetry

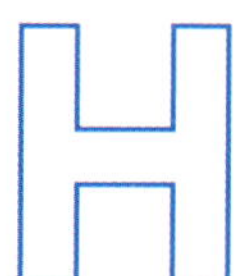

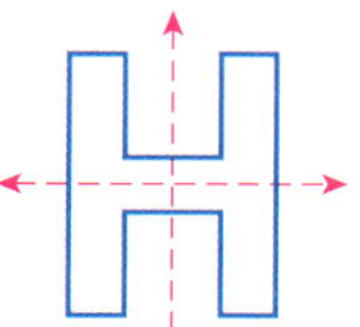

CHECK Your Progress

a.

b.

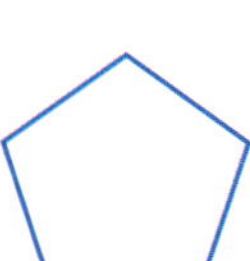

c.

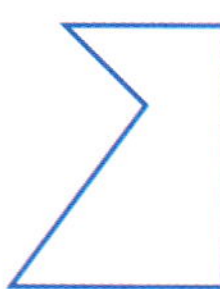

Study Tip

Congruent Figures As with translations, the original figure and the reflected image are congruent.

A **reflection** is a mirror image of the original figure. It is the result of a transformation of a figure over a line called a **line of reflection**.

EXAMPLE Reflect a Figure Over the x-axis

4 **Triangle ABC has vertices $A(5, 2)$, $B(1, 3)$, and $C(-1, 1)$. Graph the figure and its reflected image over the x-axis. Then find the coordinates of the vertices of the reflected image.**

The x-axis is the line of reflection. So, plot each vertex of $A'B'C'$ the same distance from the x-axis as its corresponding vertex on ABC.

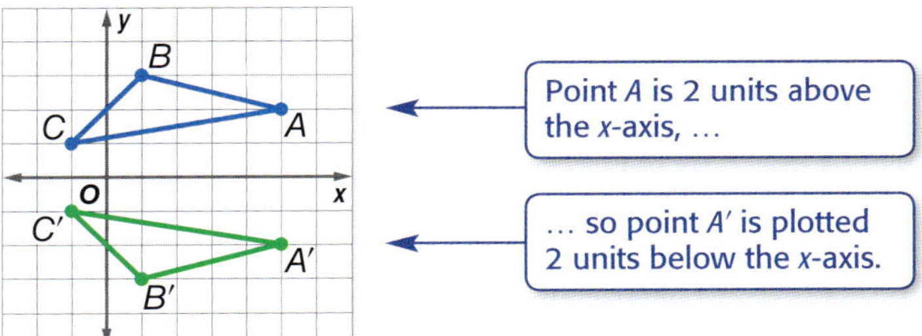

The coordinates are $A'(5, -2)$, $B'(1, -3)$, and $C'(-1, -1)$.

CHECK Your Progress

d. Rectangle $GHIJ$ has vertices $G(3, -4)$, $H(3, -1)$, $I(-2, -1)$, and $J(-2, -4)$. Graph the figure and its image after a reflection over the x-axis. Then find the coordinates of the reflected image.

EXAMPLE Reflect a Figure Over the y-axis

5 **Quadrilateral $KLMN$ has vertices $K(2, 3)$, $L(5, 1)$, $M(4, -2)$, and $N(1, -1)$. Graph the figure and its reflected image over the y-axis. Then find the coordinates of the vertices of the reflected image.**

The y-axis is the line of reflection. So, plot each vertex of $K'L'M'N'$ the same distance from the y-axis as its corresponding vertex on $KLMN$.

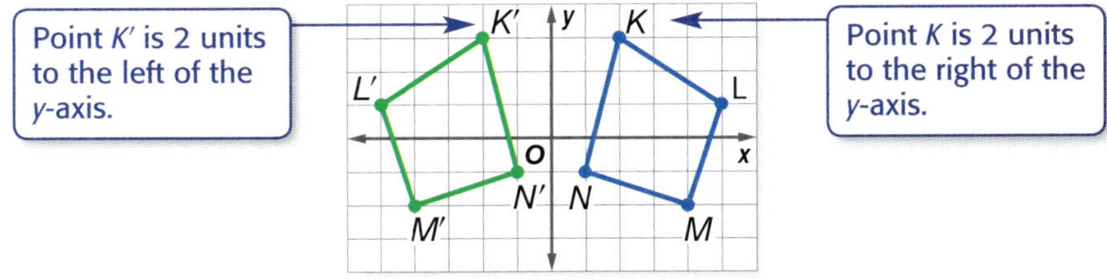

The coordinates are $K'(-2, 3)$, $L'(-5, 1)$, $M'(-4, -2)$, and $N'(-1, -1)$.

CHECK Your Progress

e. Triangle PQR has vertices $P(1, 5)$, $Q(3, 7)$, and $R(5, -1)$. Graph the figure and its reflection over the y-axis. Then find the coordinates of the reflected image.

CHECK Your Understanding

Examples 1–3 (p. 558) **Determine whether each figure has line symmetry. If so, copy the figure and draw all lines of symmetry.**

1. 

2. 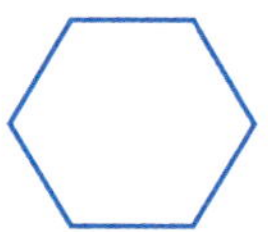

3. 

4. **INSECTS** Identify the number of lines of symmetry in the photo of the butterfly at the right.

Example 4 (p. 559) **Graph each figure and its reflection over the x-axis. Then find the coordinates of the reflected image.**

5. $\triangle ABC$ with vertices $A(5, 8)$, $B(1, 2)$, and $C(6, 4)$

6. quadrilateral $DEFG$ with vertices $D(-4, 6)$, $E(-2, -3)$, $F(2, 2)$, and $G(4, 9)$

Example 5 (p. 559) **Graph each figure and its reflection over the y-axis. Then find the coordinates of the reflected image.**

7. $\triangle QRS$ with vertices $Q(2, -5)$, $R(5, -5)$, and $S(2, 3)$

8. parallelogram $WXYZ$ with vertices $W(-4, -2)$, $X(-4, 3)$, $Y(-2, 4)$, and $Z(-2, -1)$

Practice and Problem Solving

HOMEWORK HELP

For Exercises	See Examples
9–14, 23–24	1, 3
15–18	4
19–22	5

Determine whether each figure has line symmetry. If so, copy the figure and draw all lines of symmetry.

9. 

10. 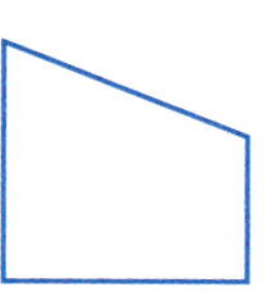

11. 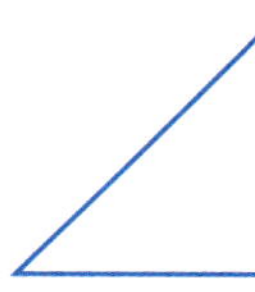

12. 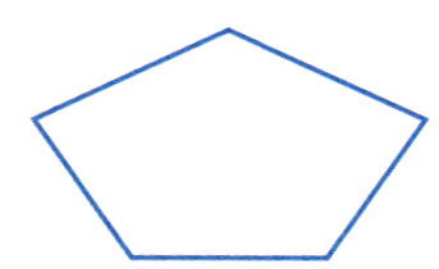

13. 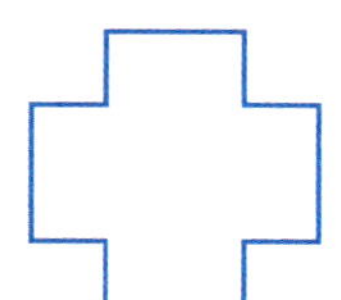

14. 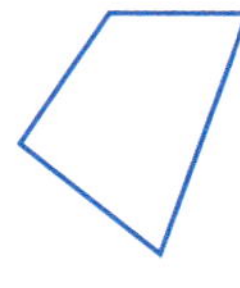

Graph each figure and its reflection over the x-axis. Then find the coordinates of the reflected image.

15. TUV with vertices $T(-6, -1)$, $U(-2, -3)$, and $V(5, -4)$

16. MNP with vertices $M(2, 1)$, $N(-3, 1)$, and $P(-1, 4)$

17. square $ABCD$ with vertices $A(2, 4)$, $B(-2, 4)$, $C(-2, 8)$, and $D(2, 8)$

18. $WXYZ$ with vertices $W(-1, -1)$, $X(4, 1)$, $Y(4, 5)$, and $Z(1, 7)$

Graph each figure and its reflection over the y-axis. Then find the coordinates of the reflected image.

19. $\triangle RST$ with vertices $R(-5, 3)$, $S(-4, -2)$, and $T(-2, 3)$
20. $\triangle GHJ$ with vertices $G(4, 2)$, $H(3, -4)$, and $J(1, 1)$
21. parallelogram $HIJK$ with vertices $H(-1, 3)$, $I(-1, -1)$, $J(2, -2)$, and $K(2, 2)$
22. quadrilateral $DEFG$ with vertices $D(1, 0)$, $E(1, -5)$, $F(4, -1)$, and $G(3, 2)$

23. **GATES** Describe the location of the line(s) of symmetry in the photograph of Brandenburg Gate in Berlin, Germany.
24. **FLAGS** Flags of some countries have line symmetry. Of the flags shown below, which flags have line symmetry? Copy and draw all lines of symmetry.

Nigeria

Ghana

Japan

Mexico

Real-World Link A violin is usually around 14 inches long.

25. **MUSIC** Use the photo at the left to determine how many lines of symmetry the body of a violin has.

For Exercises 26–29, use the graph shown at the right.

26. Identify the pair(s) of figures for which the x-axis is the line of reflection.
27. For which pair(s) of figures is the line of reflection the y-axis?
28. What type of transformation do figures B and C represent?
29. Describe the possible transformation(s) required to move figure A onto figure D.
30. $\triangle RST$ is reflected over the x-axis and then translated 3 units to the left and 2 units down. Graph the resulting triangle.

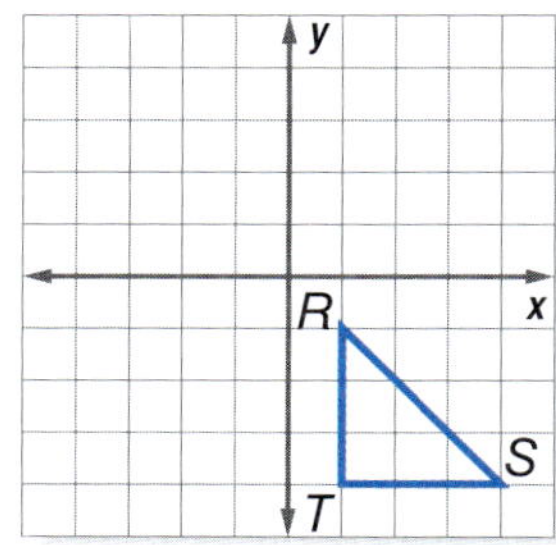

31. $\triangle MNP$ is translated 2 units right and 3 units up. Then the translated figure is reflected over the y-axis. Graph the resulting triangle.

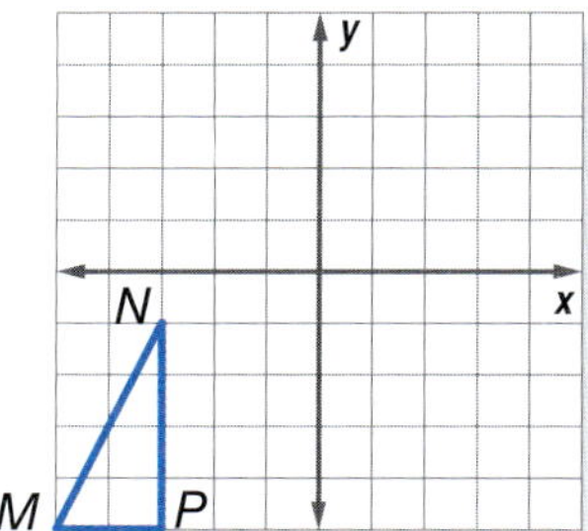

The coordinates of a point and its image after a reflection are given. Describe the reflection as over the x-axis or y-axis.

32. $A(-3, 5) \rightarrow A'(3, 5)$

33. $M(3, 3) \rightarrow M'(3, -3)$

34. $X(-1, -4) \rightarrow X'(-1, 4)$

35. $W(-4, 0) \rightarrow W'(4, 0)$

H.O.T. Problems

36. **OPEN ENDED** Make a tessellation using a combination of translations and reflections of polygons. Explain your method.

37. **CHALLENGE** Triangle JKL has vertices $J(-7, 4)$, $K(7, 1)$, and $L(2, -2)$. Without graphing, find the new coordinates of the vertices of the triangle after a reflection first over the x-axis and then over the y-axis.

38. **WRITING IN MATH** Draw a figure on a coordinate plane and its reflection over the y-axis. Explain how the x- and y-coordinates of the reflected figure relate to the x- and y-coordinates of the original figure. Then repeat, this time reflecting the figure over the x-axis.

39. The figure shown was transformed from quadrant II to quadrant III.

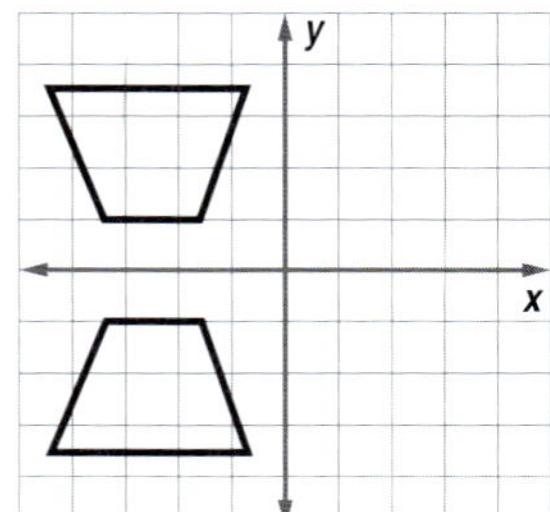

This transformation best represents which of the following?

A translation

B tessellation

C reflection

D rotation

40. If $ABCD$ is reflected over the x-axis and translated 5 units to the right, which is the resulting image of point B?

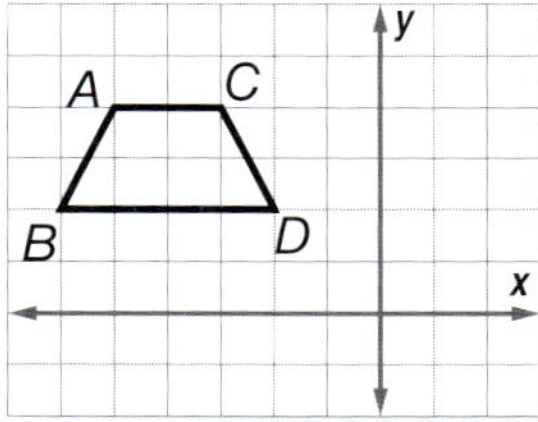

F $(-1, -2)$

G $(-11, 2)$

H $(-1, 2)$

J $(11, 2)$

Spiral Review

41. **GEOMETRY** Triangle FGH has vertices $F(-3, 7)$, $G(-1, 5)$, and $H(-2, 2)$. Graph the figure and its image after a translation 4 units right and 1 unit down. Write the ordered pairs for the vertices of the image. (Lesson 10-9)

42. **GEOMETRY** Melissa wishes to construct a tessellation for a wall hanging made only from regular decagons. Is this possible? Explain. (Lesson 10-8)

Estimate. (Lesson 5-1)

43. $\frac{4}{9} + 8\frac{1}{9}$

44. $\frac{1}{9} \times \frac{2}{5}$

45. $12\frac{1}{4} \div 5\frac{6}{7}$

CHAPTER 10 Study Guide and Review

Math Online glencoe.com
- STUDY TO GO
- Vocabulary Review

GET READY to Study

Be sure the following Big Ideas are noted in your Foldable.

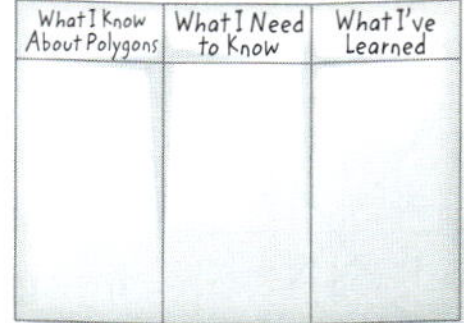

BIG Ideas

Angles (Lessons 10-1 and 10-2)
- Two angles are adjacent if they have the same vertex, share a common side, and do not overlap.
- Two angles are vertical if they are opposite angles formed by the intersection of two lines.
- Two angles are complementary if the sum of their measures is 90°.
- Two angles are supplementary if the sum of their measures is 180°.

Triangles (Lesson 10-4)
- The sum of the measures of the angles of a triangle is 180°.

Quadrilaterals (Lesson 10-6)
- The sum of the measures of the angles of a quadrilateral is 360°.

Similar Figures (Lesson 10-7)
- If two figures are similar then the corresponding sides are proportional and the corresponding angles are congruent.

Transformations (Lessons 10-9 and 10-10)
- When translating a figure, every point in the original figure is moved the same distance in the same direction.
- When reflecting a figure, every point in the original figure is the same distance from the line of reflection as its corresponding point on the original figure.

Key Vocabulary

acute angle (p. 511)
angle (p. 510)
circle graph (p. 518)
complementary angles (p. 514)
congruent angles (p. 511)
congruent figures (p. 554)
degrees (p. 510)
hexagon (p. 546)
indirect measurement (p. 542)
line of symmetry (p. 558)
line symmetry (p. 558)
obtuse angle (p. 511)
octagon (p. 546)
parallelogram (p. 533)
pentagon (p. 546)
polygon (p. 546)
quadrilateral (p. 533)
reflection (p. 559)
regular polygon (p. 546)
rhombus (p. 533)
right angle (p. 511)
similar figures (p. 540)
straight angle (p. 511)
supplementary angles (p. 514)
tessellation (p. 548)
transformation (p. 553)
translation (p. 553)
trapezoid (p. 533)
triangle (p. 524)
vertex (p. 510)

Vocabulary Check

State whether each sentence is *true* or *false*. If *false*, replace the underlined word or number to make a true sentence.

1. Two angles with measures adding to 180° are called <u>complementary angles</u>.
2. A <u>hexagon</u> is a polygon with 6 sides.
3. An angle with a measure of less than 90° is called a <u>right angle</u>.
4. The <u>vertex</u> is where the sides of an angle meet.
5. The point (3, −2) when translated up 3 units and to the left 5 units becomes <u>(6, −7)</u>.
6. A <u>trapezoid</u> has both pairs of opposite sides parallel.

Lesson-by-Lesson Review

10-1 Angle Relationships (pp. 510–513)

For Exercises 7 and 8, refer to the figure at the right to identify each pair of angles. Justify your response.

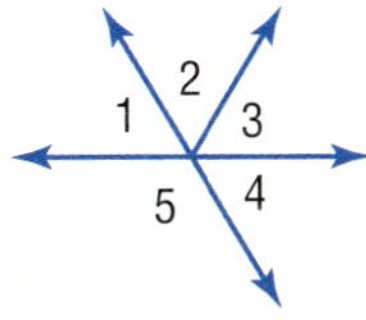

7. a pair of vertical angles
8. a pair of adjacent angles

Example 1 Refer to the figure below. Identify a pair of vertical angles.

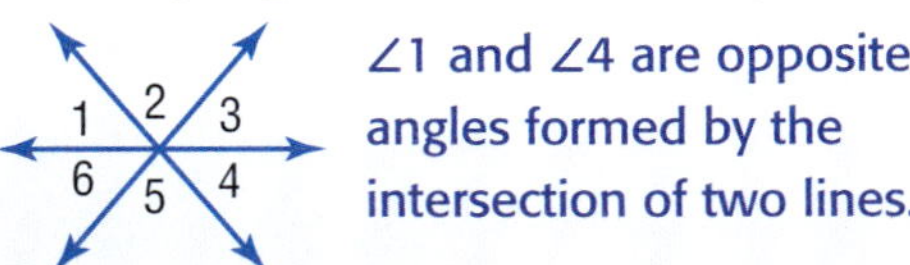

$\angle 1$ and $\angle 4$ are vertical angles.

10-2 Complementary and Supplementary Angles (pp. 514–517)

Classify each pair of angles as *complementary*, *supplementary*, or *neither*.

9. 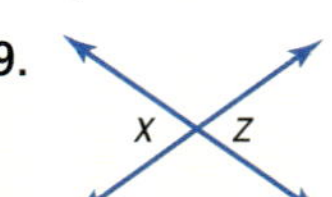

10. 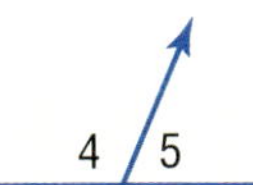

Example 2 Find the value of x.

$$\begin{aligned} x + 27 &= 90 \\ -27 &= -27 \\ \hline x &= 63 \end{aligned}$$

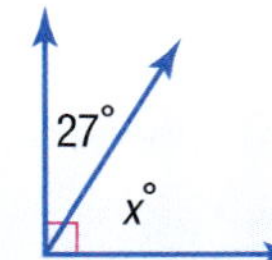

10-3 Statistics: Display Data in a Circle Graph (pp. 518–523)

11. **COLORS** The table shows favorite shades of blue. Display the set of data in a circle graph.

Shade	Percent
Navy	35%
Sky/Light Blue	30%
Aquamarine	17%
Other	18%

Example 3 Which pizza was chosen by about twice as many people as supreme?

Pepperoni was chosen by about twice as many people as supreme.

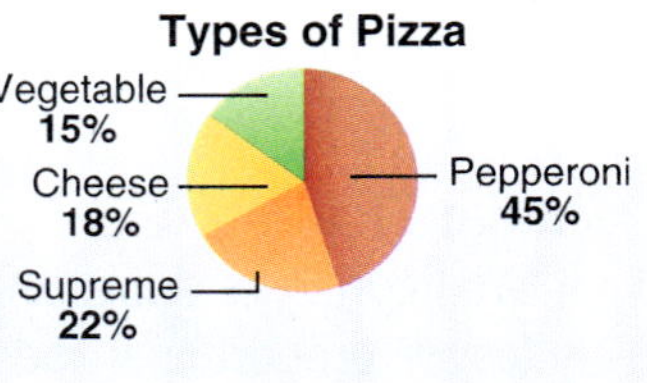

10-4 Triangles (pp. 524–529)

ALGEBRA Find the value of x.

12. 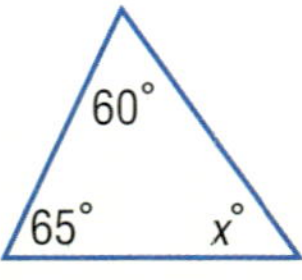

13. 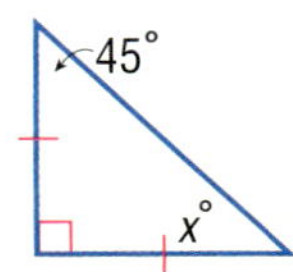

Example 4 Find the value of x.

$$\begin{aligned} x + 64 + 67 &= 180 \\ x + 131 &= 180 \\ -131 &= -131 \\ \hline x &= 49 \end{aligned}$$

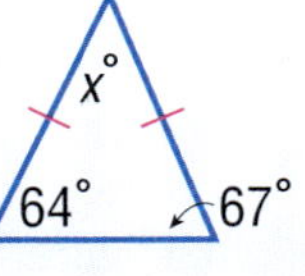

Mixed Problem Solving
For mixed problem-solving practice, see page 713.

10-5 PSI: Logical Reasoning (pp. 530–531)

14. **SPORTS** Donnie, Jenna, Milo, and Barbara play volleyball, field hockey, golf, and soccer but not in that order. Use the clues given below to find the sport each person plays.
    - Donnie does not like golf, volleyball, or soccer.
    - Neither Milo nor Jenna likes golf.
    - Milo does not like soccer.

15. **FOOD** Angelo's Pizza Parlor makes square pizzas. After baking, the pizzas are cut along one diagonal into two triangles. Classify the triangles made.

Example 5 **Todd, Virginia, Elaine, and Peter are siblings. Todd was born after Peter, but before Virginia. Elaine is the oldest. Who is the youngest in the family?**

Use logical reasoning to determine the youngest of the family.

You know that Elaine is the oldest, so she is first on the list. Todd was born after Peter, but before Virginia. So, Peter was second and then Todd was born. Virginia is the youngest of the family.

10-6 Quadrilaterals (pp. 533–538)

Classify the quadrilateral with the name that best describes it.

16. 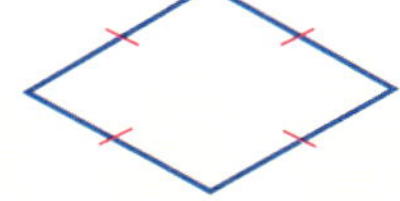

17. 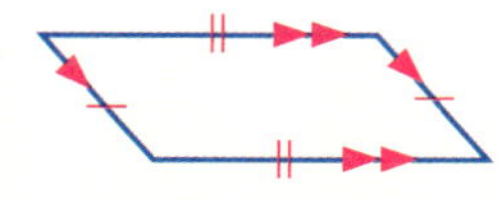

18. **GEOMETRY** What quadrilateral does not have opposite sides congruent?

Example 6 **Classify the quadrilateral using the name that *best* describes it.**

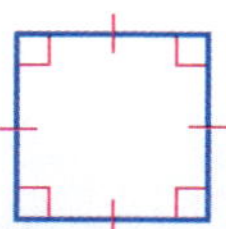

The quadrilateral is a parallelogram with 4 right angles and 4 congruent sides. It is a square.

10-7 Similar Figures (pp. 540–545)

Find the value of x in each pair of similar figures.

19.–20.

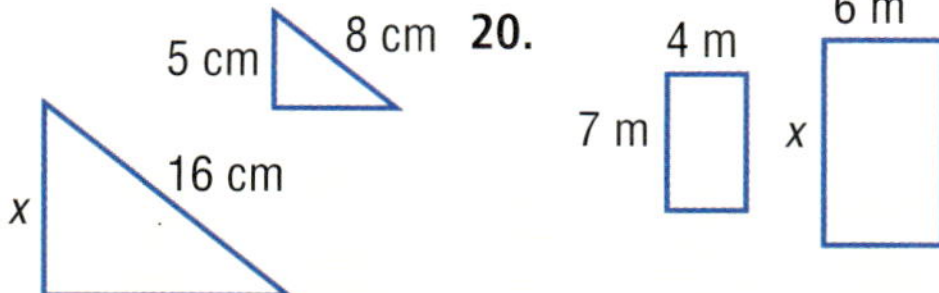

21. **FLAGPOLES** Hiroshi is 1.6 meters tall and casts a shadow 0.53 meter in length. How tall is a flagpole if it casts a shadow 2.65 meters in length?

Example 7

Find the value of x in the pair of similar figures.

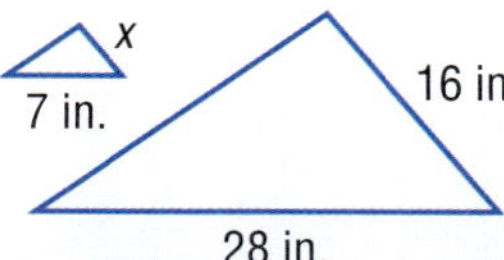

$\frac{7}{28} = \frac{x}{16}$ Write a proportion.

$28 \cdot x = 7 \cdot 16$ Find the cross products.

$28x = 112$ Simplify.

$\frac{28x}{28} = \frac{112}{28}$ Divide each side by 28.

$x = 4$ Simplify.

So, the value of x is 4.

CHAPTER 10 Study Guide and Review

10-8 Polygons and Tessellations (pp. 546–551)

Determine whether each figure is a polygon. If it is, classify the polygon and state whether it is regular. If it is *not* a polygon, explain why.

22. 

23. 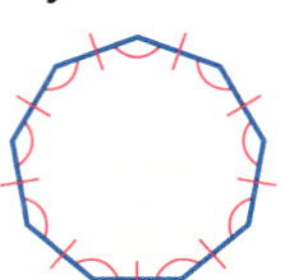

24. **ALGEBRA** Find the measure of each angle of a regular 12-gon.

Example 8 **Determine whether the figure is a polygon. If it is, classify the polygon and state whether it is regular. If it is *not* a polygon, explain why.**

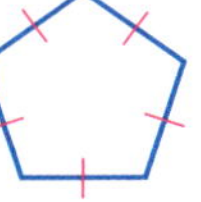

Since the polygon has 5 congruent sides and 5 congruent angles, it is a regular pentagon.

10-9 Translations (pp. 553–557)

Triangle PQR has coordinates $P(4, -2)$, $Q(-2, -3)$, and $R(-1, 6)$. Find the coordinates of $P'Q'R'$ after each translation. Then graph each translation.

25. 6 units left, 3 units up
26. 4 units right, 1 unit down
27. 3 units left
28. 7 units down

Example 9 **Find the coordinates of $\triangle G'H'I'$ after a translation of 2 units left and 4 units up.**

The vertices of $\triangle G'H'I'$ are $G'(-2, 7)$, $H'(2, 3)$, and $I'(-4, 1)$.

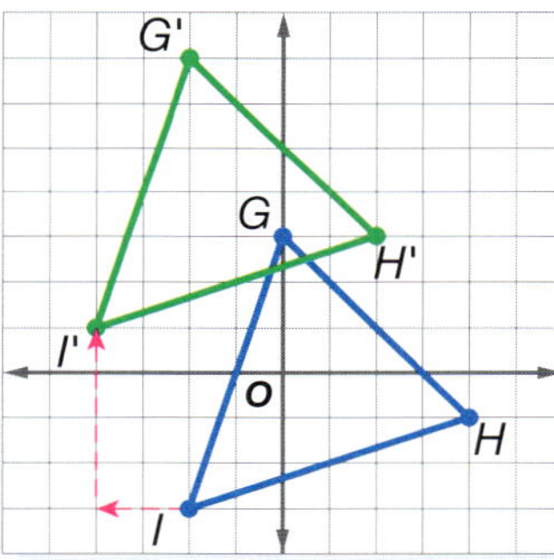

10-10 Reflections (pp. 558–562)

Find the coordinates of each figure after a reflection over the given axis. Then graph the figure and its reflected image.

29. $\triangle RST$ with coordinates $R(-1, 3)$, $S(2, 6)$, and $T(6, 1)$; x-axis
30. parallelogram $ABCD$ with coordinates $A(1, 3)$, $B(2, -1)$, $C(5, -1)$, and $D(4, 3)$; y-axis
31. rectangle $EFGH$ with coordinates $E(4, 2)$, $F(-2, 2)$, $G(-2, 5)$, and $H(4, 5)$; x-axis

Example 10 **Find the coordinates of $\triangle C'D'E'$ after a reflection over the y-axis. Then graph its reflected image.**

The vertices of $\triangle C'D'E'$ are $C'(-3, 4)$, $D'(-2, 1)$, and $E'(-5, 3)$.

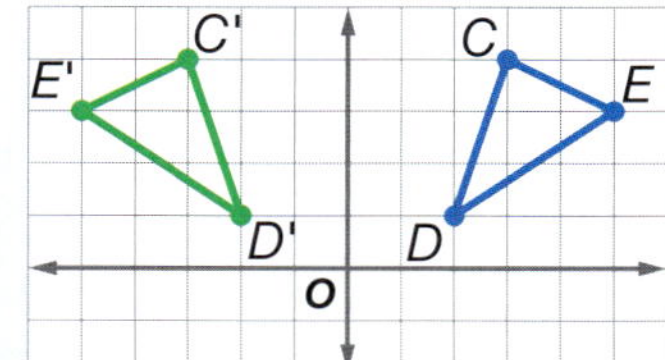

CHAPTER 10

Practice Test

Math Online glencoe.com
• Chapter Test

Name each angle in four ways. Then classify each angle as *acute*, *obtuse*, *right*, or *straight*.

1. 

2. 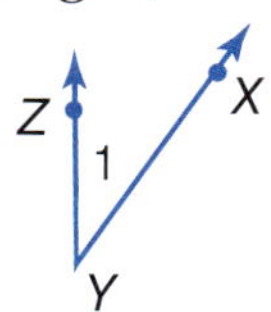

Classify each pair of angles as *complementary*, *supplementary*, or *neither*.

3. 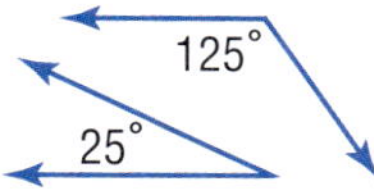

4. 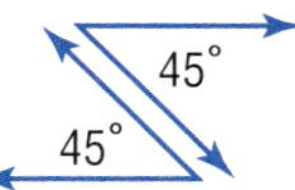

5. **GEOMETRY** Classify the angle pair at the right as *vertical*, *adjacent*, or *neither*.

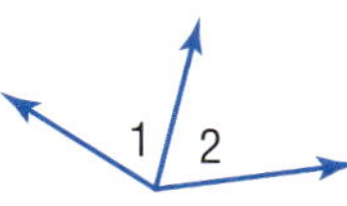

6. **MULTIPLE CHOICE** The table shows the results of a survey. The results are to be displayed in a circle graph. Which statement about the graph is *not* true?

Favorite Type of Bagels	
Type	**Students**
blueberry	8
cinnamon raisin	9
everything	18
plain	32

A About 12% of students chose blueberry as their favorite bagel.
B The blueberry section on the graph will have an angle measure of about 43°.
C The everything and plain sections on the circle graph form supplementary angles.
D Plain bagels were preferred more than any other type of bagel.

ALGEBRA Find the missing measure in each triangle with the given angle measures.

7. 75°, 25.5°, $x°$
8. 23.5°, $x°$, 109.5°

9. **ALGEBRA** Numbers ending in zero or five are divisible by five. Are the numbers 25, 893, and 690 divisible by 5? Use the *logical reasoning* strategy.

ALGEBRA Find the value of x in each quadrilateral.

10. 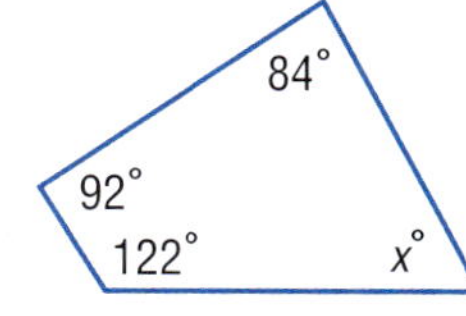

11. 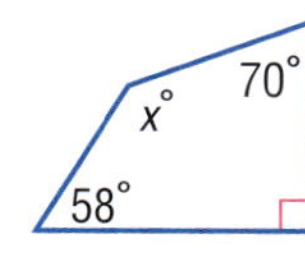

12. **ART** A drawing is enlarged so that it is 14 inches long and 11 inches wide. If the original length of the drawing is 8 inches, what is its width?

13. **GEOMETRY** Can a regular heptagon, with angle measures that total 900°, be used by itself to make a tessellation? Explain.

14. **MULTIPLE CHOICE** Which quadrilateral does *not* have opposite sides congruent?

F parallelogram
G square
H trapezoid
J rectangle

15. **ALGEBRA** Square *ABCD* is shown. What are the vertices of *A′B′C′D′* after a translation 2 units right and 2 units down? Graph the translated image.

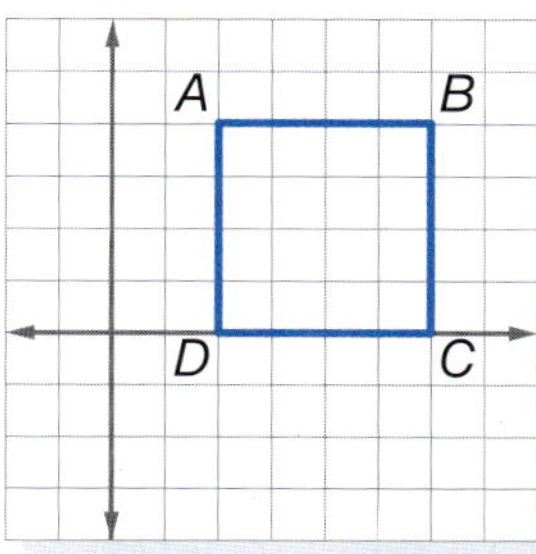

16. **GEOMETRY** Draw a figure with one line of symmetry. Then draw a figure with no lines of symmetry.

CHAPTER 10

Test Practice
Cumulative, Chapters 1–10

Math Online glencoe.com
• Test Practice

PART 1 Multiple Choice

Read each question. Then fill in the correct answer on the answer document provided by your teacher or on a sheet of paper.

1. Which of the following two angles are complementary?

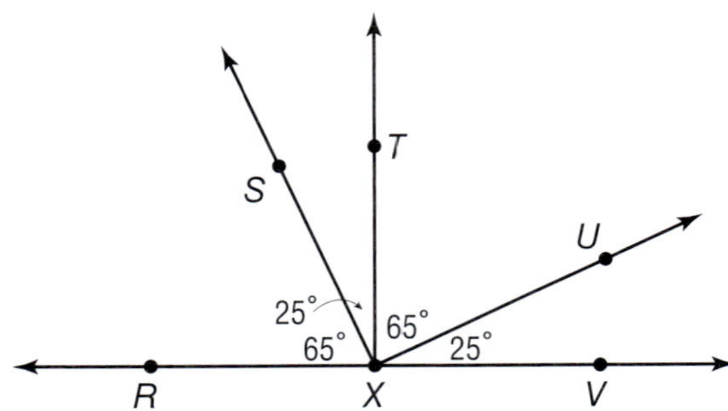

A $\angle RXS$ and $\angle TXU$

B $\angle SXT$ and $\angle TXU$

C $\angle RXS$ and $\angle SXV$

D $\angle SXR$ and $\angle SXV$

2. A square is divided into 9 congruent squares. Which of the following methods can be used to find the area of the larger square, given the area of one of the smaller squares?

F Multiply the area of the larger square by 9.

G Add 9 to the area of one of the smaller squares.

H Multiply the area of one of the smaller squares by 9.

J Add the area of the larger square to the sum of the areas of each of the 9 smaller squares.

3. Which of the following groups does *not* contain equivalent fractions, decimals, and percents?

A $\frac{9}{20}$, 0.45, 45%

B $\frac{3}{10}$, 0.3, 30%

C $\frac{7}{8}$, 0.875, 87.5%

D $\frac{1}{100}$, 0.1, 1%

4. The table below shows all the possible outcomes when tossing two fair coins at the same time.

1st Coin	2nd Coin
H	H
H	T
T	H
T	T

Which of the following must be true?

F The probability that both coins have the same outcome is $\frac{1}{4}$.

G The probability of getting at least one tail is higher than the probability of getting two heads.

H The probability that exactly one coin will turn up heads is $\frac{3}{4}$.

J The probability of getting at least one tail is lower than the probability of getting two tails.

5. Seth has $858.60 in his savings account. He plans to spend 15% of his savings on a bicycle. Which of the following represents the amount Seth plans to spend on the bicycle?

A $182.79

B $171.72

C $128.79

D $122.79

Preparing for Standardized Tests

For test-taking strategies and practice, see pages 716–733.

6. A manager took an employee to lunch. If the lunch was $48 and she left a 20% tip, how much money did she spend on lunch?

   F $68.00
   G $57.60
   H $55.80
   J $38.40

7. What is the measure of $\angle 1$ in the figure below?

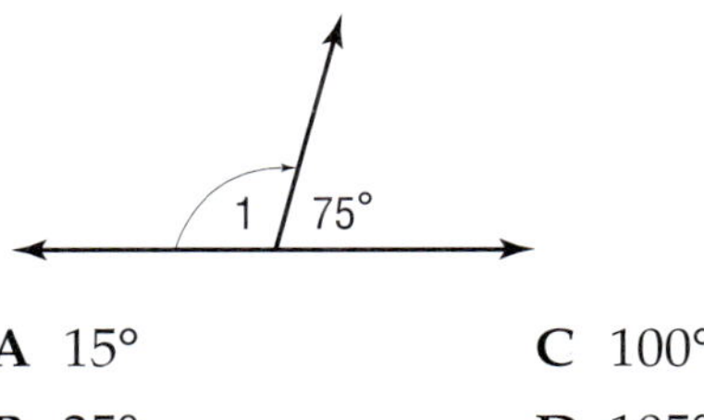

   A 15°
   B 25°
   C 100°
   D 105°

8. Josiah found the mean and median of the following list of numbers.

   11, 17, 17

   If the number 25 is added to this list, then which of the following statements would be true?

   F The mean would increase.
   G The mean would decrease.
   H The median would increase.
   J The median would decrease.

TEST-TAKING TIP

Question 8 Sometimes, it is not necessary to perform any calculations in order to answer the question correctly. In Question 8, you can use number sense to eliminate certain answer choices. Not having to perform calculations can help save time during a test.

PART 2 Short Response/Grid In

Record your answers on the answer sheet provided by your teacher or on a sheet of paper.

9. Three students are to be chosen from 8 auditions to star in the school play. In how many ways can these 3 students be chosen?

PART 3 Extended Response

Record your answers on the answer sheet provided by your teacher or on a sheet of paper. Show your work.

10. Use triangle XYZ to answer the following questions.

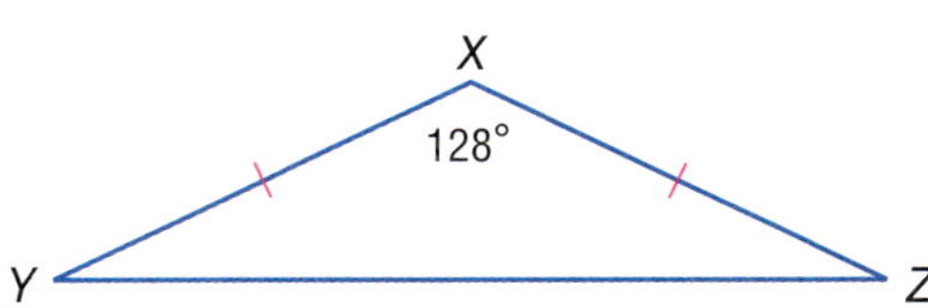

   a. Classify angle X.
   b. Classify angle Y.
   c. Classify the triangle by its sides and angles.
   d. If $\angle Y$ is congruent to $\angle Z$, find the measure of $\angle Z$. Explain.
   e. Can triangle XYZ be used by itself to make a tesselation? If so, include a drawing of the tesselation. If not, explain why not.

NEED EXTRA HELP?										
If You Missed Question...	1	2	3	4	5	6	7	8	9	10
Go to Lesson...	10-1	10-5	6-8	9-1	7-1	7-4	10-2	8-2	9-5	10-5

Measurement: Two- and Three-Dimensional Figures

- Use formulas to determine area and volume of two- and three-dimensional figures.
- Derive and use the area of a circle.

Key Vocabulary

circumference (p. 584)
cylinder (p. 604)
pyramid (p. 603)
volume (p. 613)

Real-World Link

Architecture If you visit the Jay Pritzker Pavilion in Chicago, Illinois, you will see examples of three-dimensional figures used in architecture.

Measurement: Two- and Three-Dimensional Figures Make this Foldable to help you organize your notes. Begin with a sheet of $8\frac{1}{2}$" by 11" construction paper and two sheets of notebook paper.

1. **Fold** the construction paper in half lengthwise. Label the chapter title on the outside.

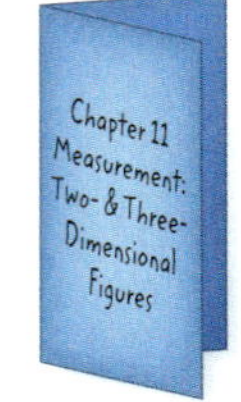

2. **Fold** the sheets of notebook paper in half lengthwise. Then fold top to bottom twice.

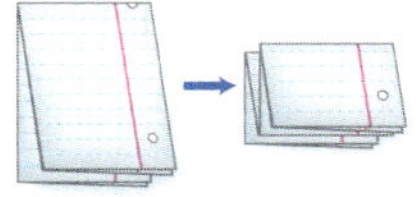

3. **Open** the notebook paper. Cut along the second folds to make four tabs.

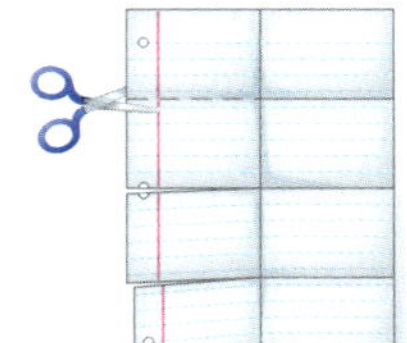

4. **Glue** the uncut notebook paper side by side onto the construction paper. Label each tab as shown.

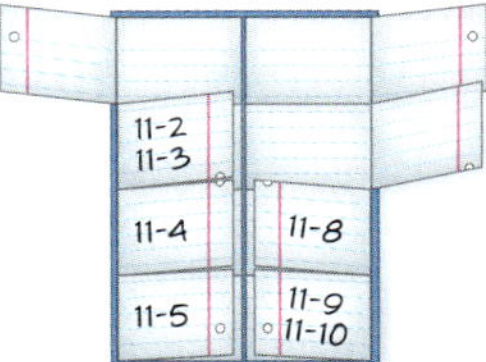

GET READY for Chapter 11

Diagnose Readiness You have two options for checking Prerequisite Skills.

Option 2

Math Online Take the Online Readiness Quiz at glencoe.com.

Option 1

Take the Quick Quiz below. Refer to the Quick Review for help.

QUICK Quiz

Evaluate each expression. (Prior Grade)

1. 8×17
2. 5.6×9.8
3. $12 \times 4 \times 26$
4. $4.5 \times 3.2 \times 1.7$
5. $\left(\frac{1}{2}\right)(11)(14)$
6. $\left(\frac{1}{2}\right)(8.8)(2.3)$
7. **SHOPPING** Margo bought 3 sweaters that originally cost $27.78 each. If they were on sale for half the price, what was the total cost of the sweaters, not including tax? (Prior Grade)

Evaluate each expression. (Lesson 1-2)

8. 3^2
9. 11 squared
10. 5 to the third power
11. 6 to the second power
12. **CHESS** If a chessboard has 8^2 squares, how many squares is this? (Lesson 1-2)

Use the π button on your calculator to evaluate each expression. Round to the nearest tenth. (Prior Grade)

13. $\pi \times 4$
14. $\pi \times 13.8$
15. $(2)(\pi)(5)$
16. $(2)(\pi)(1.7)$
17. $\pi \times 9^2$
18. $\pi \times 6^2$

QUICK Review

Example 1 **Find 1.2 • 3.4.**

$$\begin{array}{r} 1.2 \\ \times\ 3.4 \\ \hline 48 \\ 36 \\ \hline 4.08 \end{array}$$

1.2 ← 1 decimal place
× 3.4 ← +1 decimal place
4.08 ← 2 decimal places

Example 2 **Find $\left(\frac{1}{2}\right)(26)(19)$.**

$\left(\frac{1}{2}\right)(26)(19) = (13)(19)$ Multiply $\frac{1}{2}$ by 26.

$= 247$ Multiply 13 by 19.

Example 3 **Evaluate 7^3.**

$7^3 = 7 \cdot 7 \cdot 7$ or 343

Example 4 **Evaluate 2 to the fourth power.**

2 to the fourth power is written 2^4.

$2^4 = 2 \cdot 2 \cdot 2 \cdot 2$ or 16

Example 5 **Use the π button on your calculator to evaluate $\pi \times 5^2$. Round to the nearest tenth.**

$\pi \cdot 5^2 = \pi \cdot 25$ $5^2 = 25$

$= 78.5$ Multiply π by 25.

Area of Parallelograms

MAIN IDEA

Find the areas of parallelograms.

New Vocabulary

base
height

Math Online

glencoe.com

- Extra Examples
- Personal Tutor
- Self-Check Quiz

MINI Lab

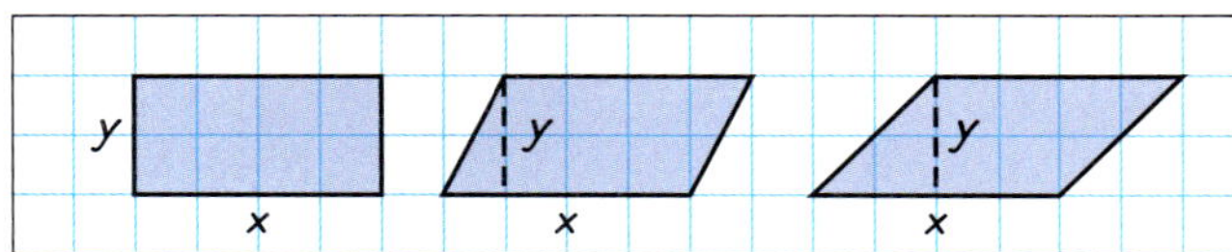

1. What is the value of x and y for each parallelogram?
2. Count the grid squares to find the area of each parallelogram.
3. On grid paper, draw three different parallelograms in which $x = 5$ units and $y = 4$ units. Find the area of each.
4. **MAKE A CONJECTURE** Explain how to find the area of a parallelogram if you know the values of x and y.

You can find the area of a parallelogram by using the values for the base and height, as described below.

The **base** is any side of a parallelogram.

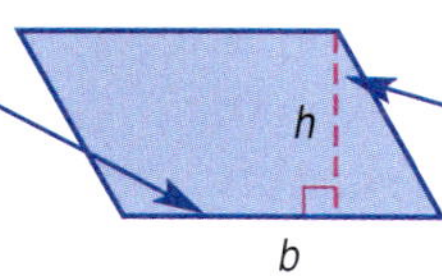

The **height** is the length of the segment perpendicular to the base with endpoints on opposite sides.

Area of a Parallelogram — Key Concept

Words The area A of a parallelogram equals the product of its base b and height h.

Symbols $A = bh$

Model

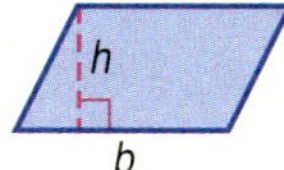

EXAMPLES Find the Area of a Parallelogram

 **Find the area of the parallelogram.**

5.8 cm

13 cm

Estimate $A = 13 \cdot 6$ or 78 cm^2

$A = bh$ Area of a parallelogram

$A = 13 \cdot 5.8$ Replace b with 13 and h with 5.8.

$A = 75.4$ Multiply.

The area is 75.4 square centimeters.

Check for Reasonableness $75.4 \approx 78$ ✔

Study Tip

Common Error When finding the area of a parallelogram, be sure to use the base and the height, not the base and a side.

2 **Find the area of the parallelogram.**

The base is 11 inches, and the height is 9 inches.

Estimate $A = 10 \cdot 10$ or 100 in^2

$A = bh$ Area of a parallelogram

$A = 11 \cdot 9$ Replace b with 11 and h with 9.

$A = 99$ Multiply.

The area of the parallelogram is 99 square inches.

Check for Reasonableness $99 \approx 100$ ✓

CHECK Your Progress

Find the area of each parallelogram.

a. 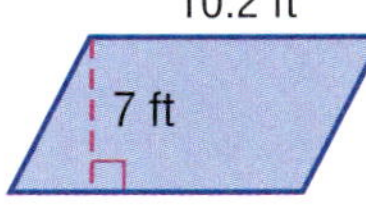

b. 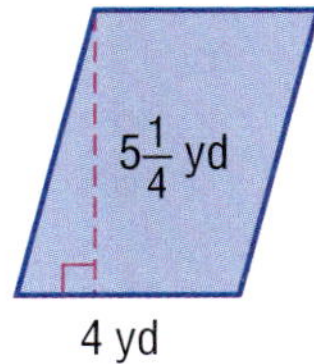

Real-World Link In 2006, there were 1,105 tornadoes in the U.S. with 245 of these occurring in April.
Source: NOAA

Real-World EXAMPLE

3 **WEATHER** **The map shows the region of a state that is under a tornado warning. What is the area of this region?**

Estimate $A = 30 \cdot 30$ or 900 mi^2

$A = bh$ Area of a parallelogram

$A = 27.5 \cdot 30.6$ Replace b with 27.5 and h with 30.6.

$A = 841.5$ Multiply.

The area of the region is 841.5 square miles.

Check for Reasonableness $841.5 \approx 900$ ✓

CHECK Your Progress

c. **SAFETY** A street department painted the pavement markings shown at the right on the surface of a highway to reduce traffic speeds and crashes. What is the area inside one of the markings?

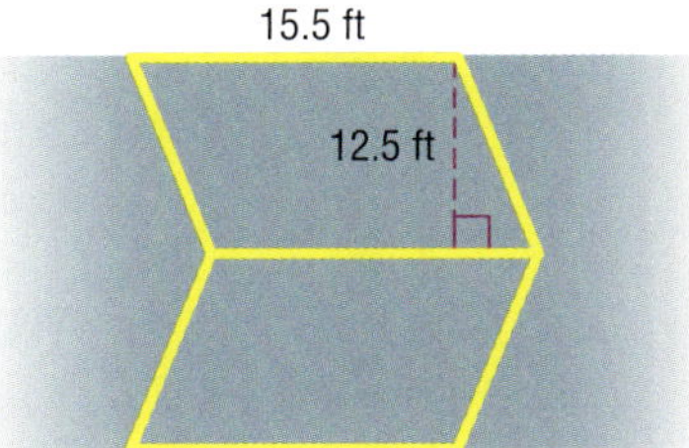

CHECK Your Understanding

Example 1 (p. 572) **Find the area of each parallelogram. Round to the nearest tenth if necessary.**

1. 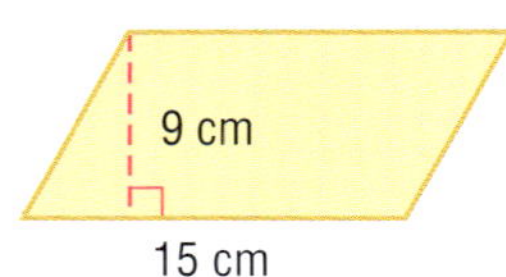

2. 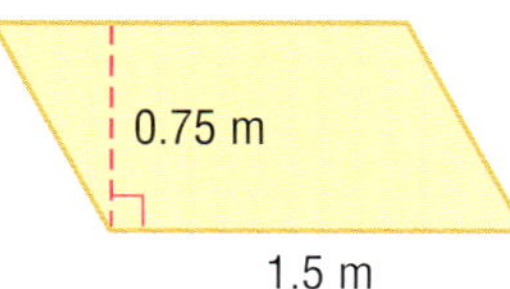

Example 2 (p. 573)

3. 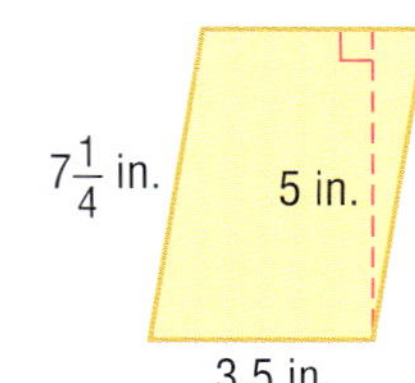

4. 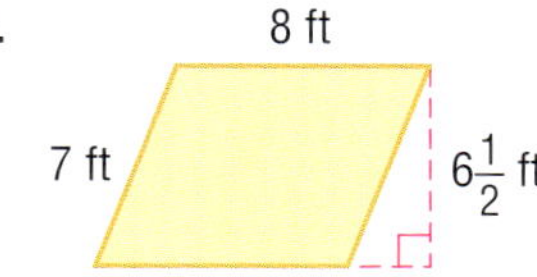

Example 3 (p. 573)

5. **ART** Martina designs uniquely-shaped ceramic wall tiles. What is the area of the tile shown?

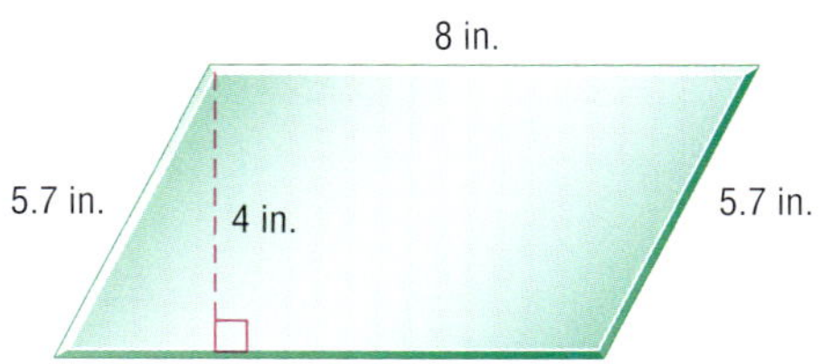

Practice and Problem Solving

HOMEWORK HELP	
For Exercises	See Examples
6–9, 12–13	1
10–11	2
14–15	3

Find the area of each parallelogram. Round to the nearest tenth if necessary.

6. 7. 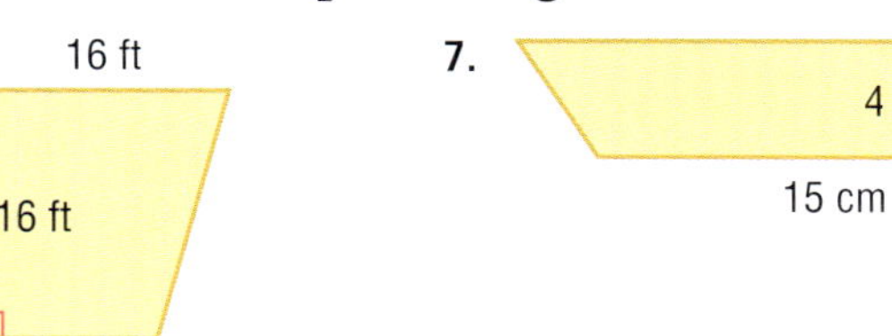

8. 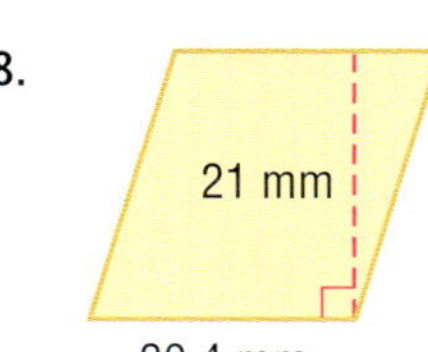

9.

10. 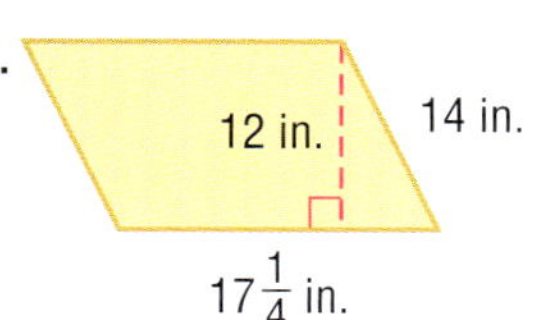

11. 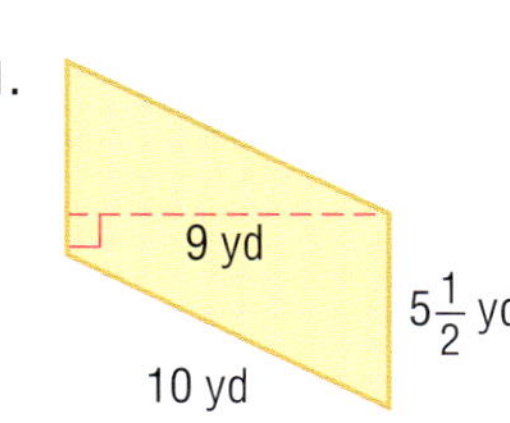

12. What is the area of a parallelogram with base $10\frac{3}{4}$ yards and height 7 yards?

13. Find the area of a parallelogram with base 12.5 meters and height 15.25 meters.

14. **WALLPAPER** The design of the wallpaper border at the right contains parallelograms. How much space on the border is covered by the parallelograms?

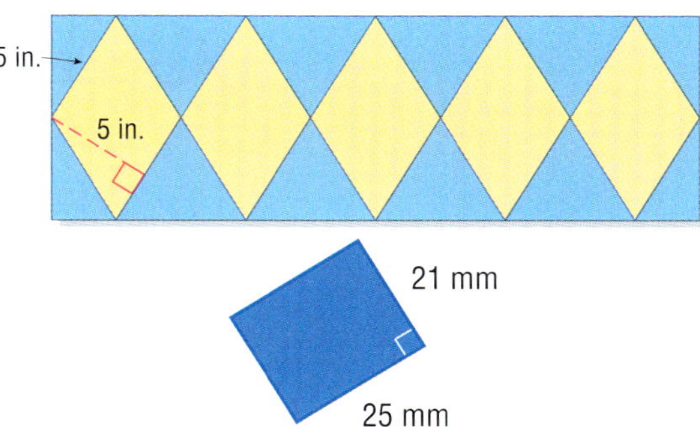

15. **PATTERN BLOCKS** What is the area of the parallelogram-shaped pattern block shown at the right?

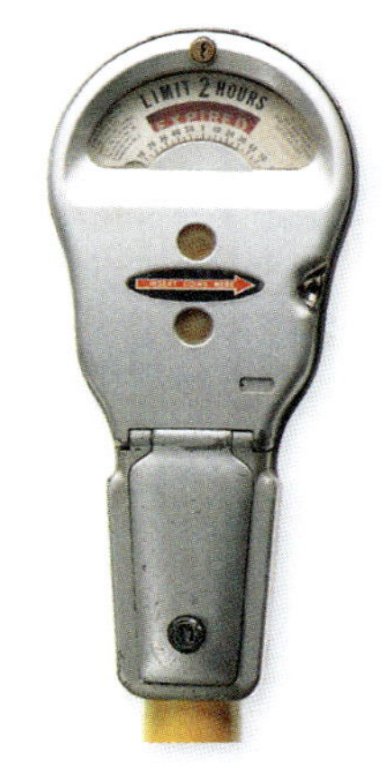

Real-World Link The first parking meter was installed in Oklahoma City, Oklahoma in 1935.

16. **PARKING SPACES** A city ordinance requires that each parking space has a minimum area of 162 square feet. Do the measurements of the parking spaces shown below meet the requirements? Explain.

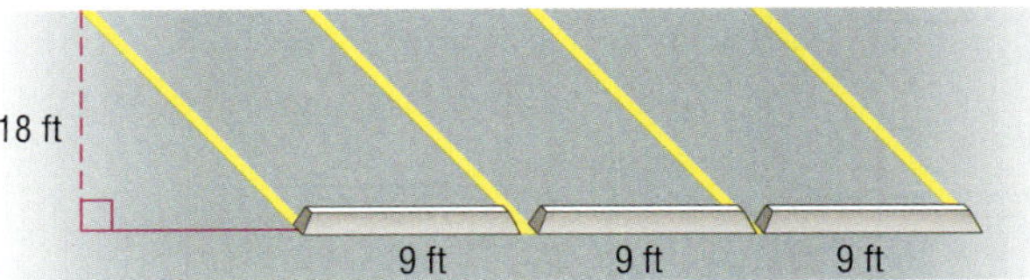

Find the area of each parallelogram. Round to the nearest tenth if necessary.

17.

18.
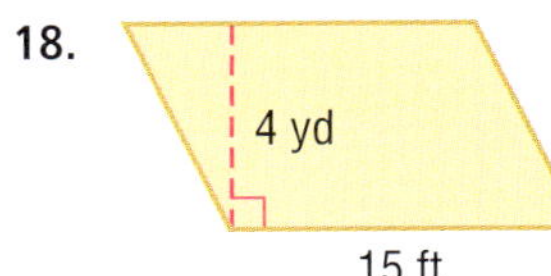

19.
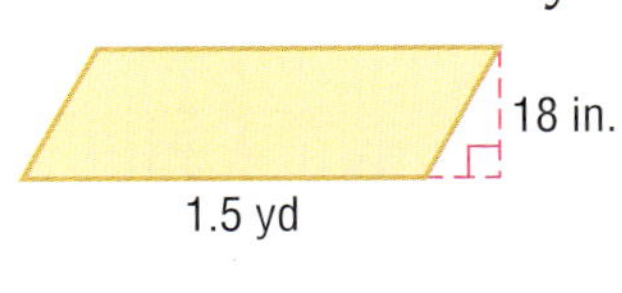

GEOGRAPHY **Estimate the area of each state.**

20.
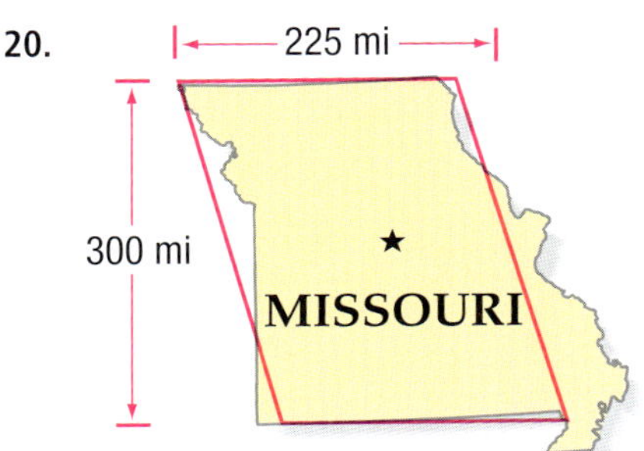

21.

22. **ALGEBRA** A parallelogram has an area of 75 square feet. Find the base of the parallelogram if the height is 3 feet.

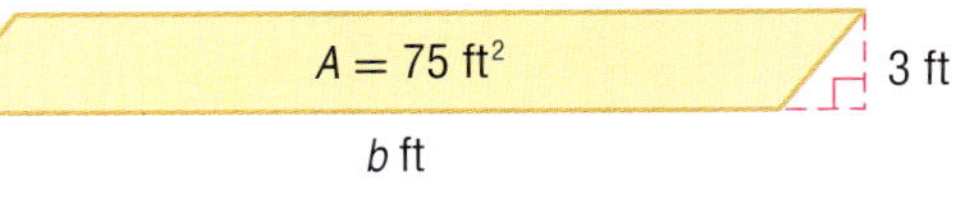

23. **ALGEBRA** What is the height of a parallelogram if the base is 24 inches and the area is 360 square inches?

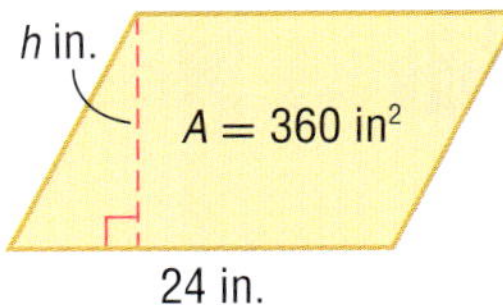

QUILTING **For Exercises 24 and 25, use the four quilt blocks shown and the following information.**

Each quilt block uses eight parallelogram-shaped pieces of fabric that have a height of $1\frac{1}{2}$ inches and a base of $4\frac{2}{3}$ inches.

24. Find the amount of fabric in square inches needed to make the parallelogram-shaped pieces for one quilt block.

25. How much fabric is needed to make the parallelogram pieces for a quilt that is made using 30 blocks? Write in square feet. (*Hint*: $144 \text{ in}^2 = 1 \text{ ft}^2$)

EXTRA PRACTICE
See pages 697, 714.

H.O.T. Problems

26. **OPEN ENDED** Draw three different parallelograms, each with an area of 24 square units.

27. **CHALLENGE** *True* or *False*? The area of a parallelogram doubles if you double the base and the height. Explain or give a counterexample to support your answer.

28. **WRITING IN MATH** Compare and contrast the formula for the area of a rectangle and a parallelogram.

29. A scale drawing of a piece of land is shown below.

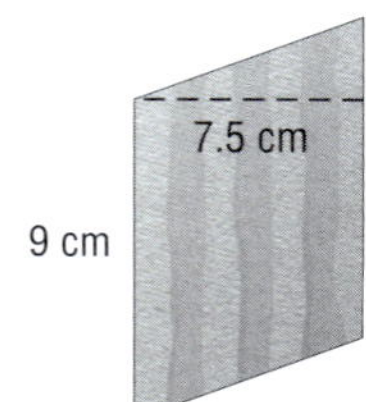

What is the actual area of the land if the scale on the drawing is 10 km = 1 cm?

A 67.5 cm^2 **C** 675 km^2

B 67.5 km^2 **D** 6,750 km^2

30. Ms. Cruz painted one wall in her living room. She did not paint the window.

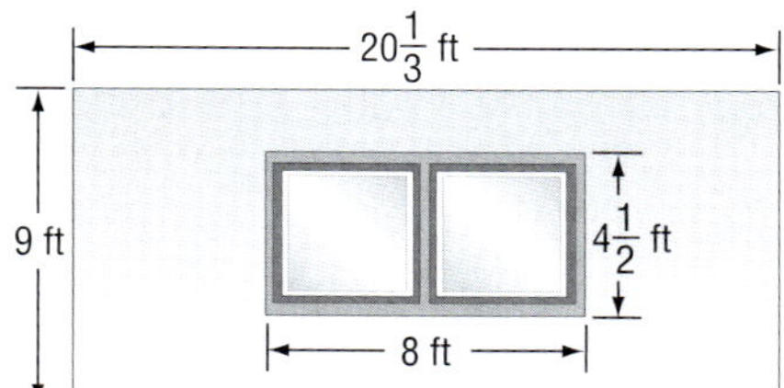

Which of the following is closest to the painted area of the wall in square feet?

F 180 ft^2 **H** 120 ft^2

G 150 ft^2 **J** 34 ft^2

Spiral Review

For Exercises 31 and 32, refer to $\triangle ABC$ at the right. Find the vertices of $\triangle A'B'C'$ after each transformation. Then graph the triangle and its reflected or translated image.

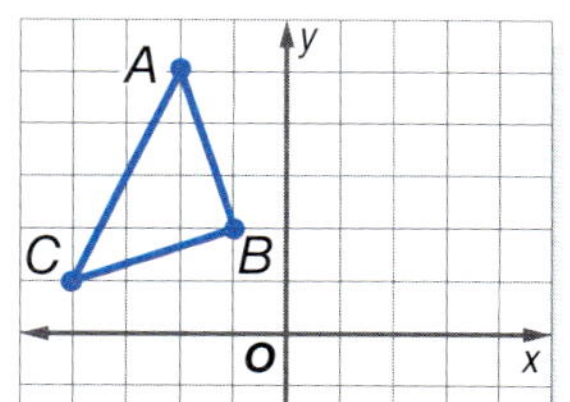

31. $\triangle ABC$ reflected over the y-axis (Lesson 10-10)

32. $\triangle ABC$ translated 5 units right and 1 unit up (Lesson 10-9)

33. **GEOMETRY** Explain how to determine whether a regular octagon tessellates the plane. (Lesson 10-8)

34. **FRUIT** If 2 out of every 3 pieces of fruit in a fruit basket are oranges, how many oranges are there if the fruit basket has 18 pieces of fruit? (Lesson 6-5)

GET READY for the Next Lesson

PREREQUISITE SKILL **Find each value.** (Lesson 1-4)

35. $6(4 + 10)$

36. $\frac{1}{2}(8)(8)$

37. $\frac{1}{2}(24 + 15)$

38. $\frac{1}{2}(5)(13 + 22)$

Explore 11-2

Measurement Lab
Triangles and Trapezoids

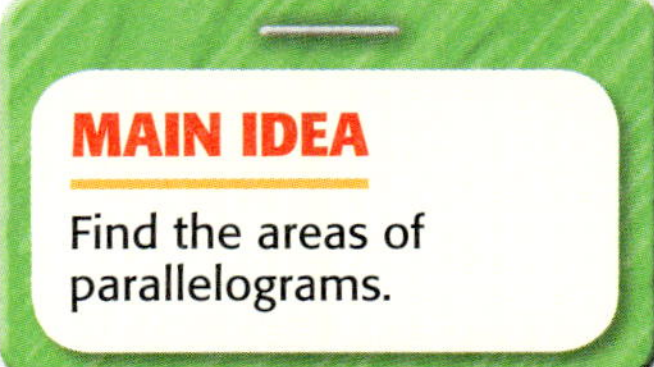

ACTIVITY

STEP 1 On grid paper, draw a triangle with a base of 6 units and a height of 3 units. Label the base *b* and the height *h* as shown.

STEP 2 Fold the grid paper in half and cut out the triangle through both sheets so that you have two congruent triangles.

STEP 3 Turn the second triangle upside down and tape it to the first triangle.

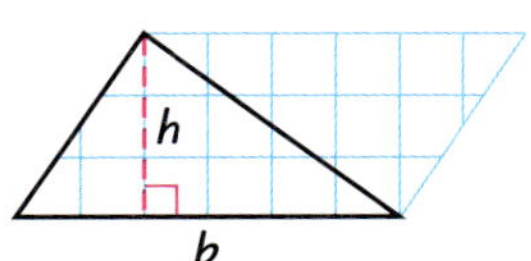

Analyze the Results

1. What figure is formed by the two triangles?
2. Write the formula for the area of the figure. Then find the area.
3. What is the area of each of the triangles? How do you know?
4. Repeat the activity above, drawing a different triangle in Step 1. Then find the area of each triangle.
5. Compare the area of a triangle to the area of a parallelogram with the same base and height.
6. **MAKE A CONJECTURE** Write a formula for the area of a triangle with base b and height h.

For Exercises 7–10, refer to the information below.

On grid paper, cut out two identical trapezoids. Label the bases b_1 and b_2, respectively, and label the heights h. Then turn one trapezoid upside down and tape it to the other trapezoid as shown.

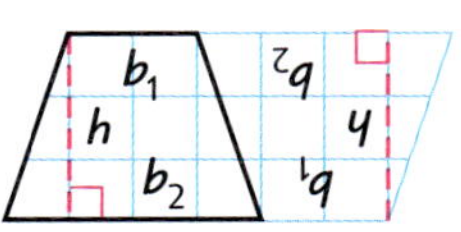

7. Write an expression to represent the base of the parallelogram.
8. Write a formula for the area A of the parallelogram using b_1, b_2, and h.
9. How does the area of each trapezoid compare to the area of the parallelogram?
10. **MAKE A CONJECTURE** Write a formula for the area A of a trapezoid with bases b_1 and b_2, and height h.

11-2 Area of Triangles and Trapezoids

MAIN IDEA

Find the areas of triangles and trapezoids.

Math Online

glencoe.com

- Concepts In Motion
- Extra Examples
- Personal Tutor
- Self-Check Quiz

MINI Lab

- Draw a parallelogram with a base of 6 units and a height of 4 units.
- Draw a diagonal as shown.
- Cut out the parallelogram.

1. What is the area of the parallelogram?
2. Cut along the diagonal. What is true about the triangles formed?
3. What is the area of each triangle?
4. If the area of a parallelogram is bh, then write an expression for the area A of each of the two congruent triangles that form the parallelogram.

You can find the area of a triangle by using the base and height.

The base of a triangle can be any of its sides.

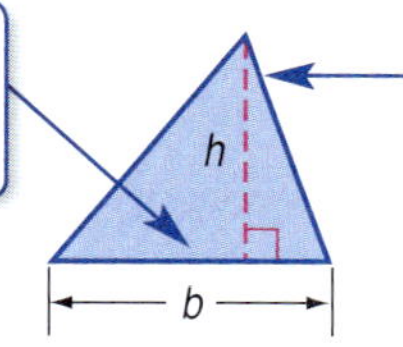

The height is the perpendicular distance from the vertex opposite the base to the line containing the base.

Area of a Triangle — Key Concept

Words The area A of a triangle equals half the product of its base b and height h.

Symbols $A = \frac{1}{2}bh$

Model

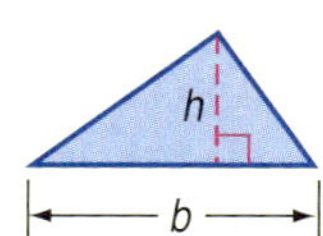

EXAMPLE Find the Area of a Triangle

1 **Find the area of the triangle shown.**

Estimate $A = \frac{1}{2}(10)(7)$ or 35

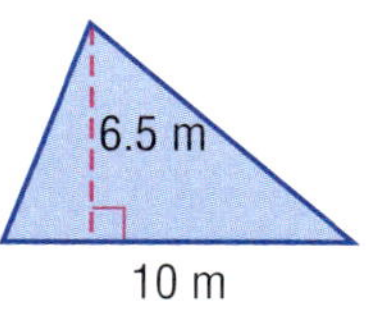

$A = \frac{1}{2}bh$ Area of a triangle

$A = \frac{1}{2}(10)(6.5)$ Replace b with 10 and h with 6.5.

$A = 32.5$ Multiply.

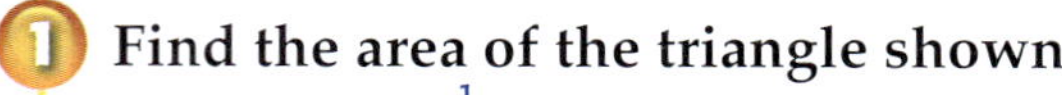

The area of the triangle is 32.5 square meters.

Check for Reasonableness $32.5 \approx 35$ ✔

Find the area of each triangle. Round to the nearest tenth if necessary.

a.
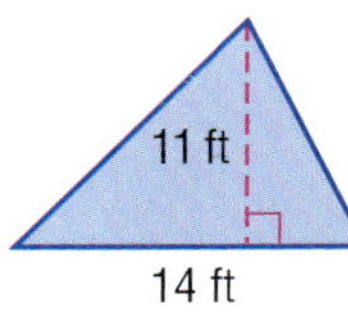

b.
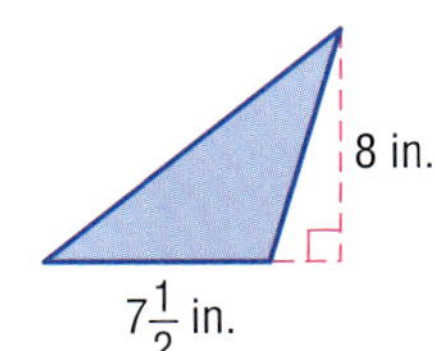

A trapezoid has two bases, b_1 and b_2. The bases are always the two sides that are parallel. The height of a trapezoid is the perpendicular distance between the bases.

Area of a Trapezoid

Key Concept

Words The area A of a trapezoid equals half the product of the height h and the sum of the bases $b_1 + b_2$.

Symbols $A = \frac{1}{2}h(b_1 + b_2)$

Model

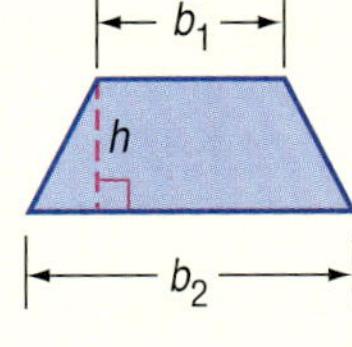

Reading Math

Subscripts Read b_1 as *b sub 1*. Read b_2 as *b sub 2*. The subscripts mean that b_1 and b_2 represent different variables.

EXAMPLE Find the Area of a Trapezoid

2 **Find the area of the trapezoid.**

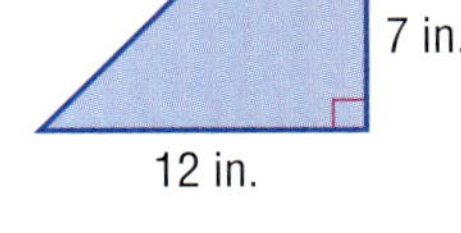

The bases are 5 inches and 12 inches. The height is 7 inches.

$A = \frac{1}{2}h(b_1 + b_2)$	Area of a trapezoid
$A = \frac{1}{2}(7)(5 + 12)$	Replace h with 7, b_1 with 5, and b_2 with 12.
$A = \frac{1}{2}(7)(17)$	Add 5 and 12.
$A = 59.5$	Multiply.

The area of the trapezoid is 59.5 square inches.

CHECK Your Progress

Find the area of each trapezoid. Round to the nearest tenth if necessary.

c.
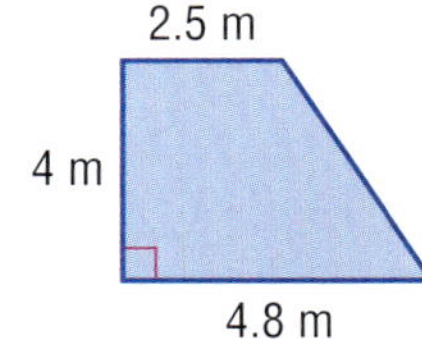

d.
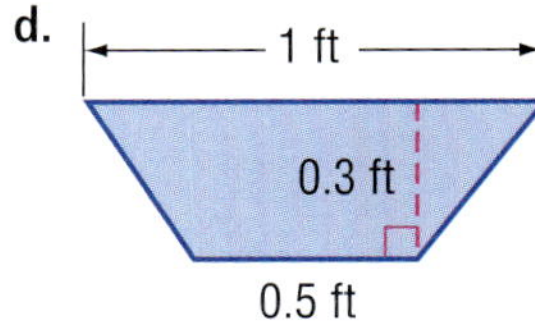

3 **GEOGRAPHY** The shape of Iron County, Michigan, resembles a trapezoid. Find the approximate area of this county.

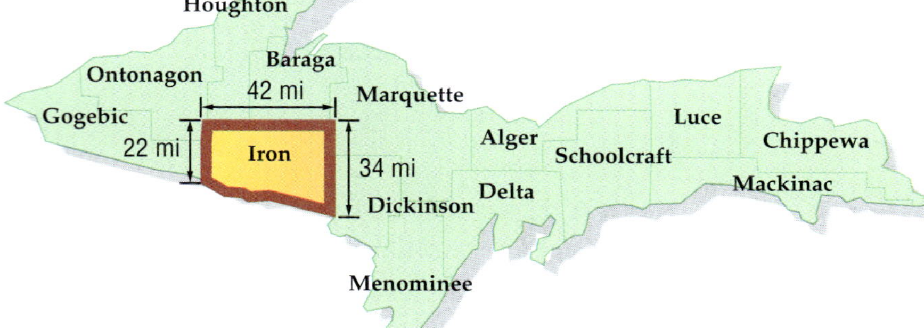

Real-World Link On average, there are approximately 11 persons per square mile in Iron County. The average number of persons per square mile in the state of Michigan is 175.
Source: U.S. Census Bureau

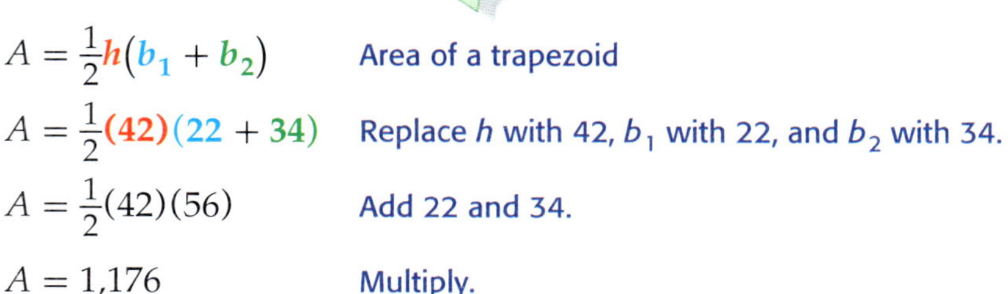

$A = \frac{1}{2}h(b_1 + b_2)$ Area of a trapezoid

$A = \frac{1}{2}(42)(22 + 34)$ Replace h with 42, b_1 with 22, and b_2 with 34.

$A = \frac{1}{2}(42)(56)$ Add 22 and 34.

$A = 1{,}176$ Multiply.

The area of Iron County is approximately 1,176 square miles.

CHECK Your Progress

e. **GEOGRAPHY** The shape of the state of Arkansas resembles a trapezoid. Find the approximate area of Arkansas.

CHECK Your Understanding

Examples 1, 2 (pp. 578–579)

Find the area of each figure. Round to the nearest tenth if necessary.

1. 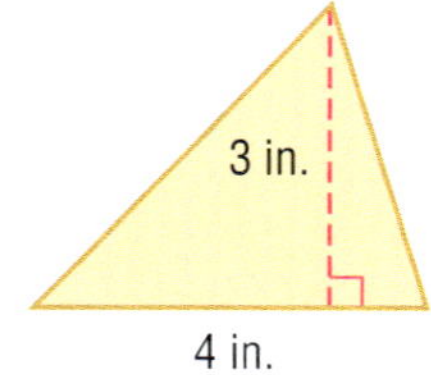

2. 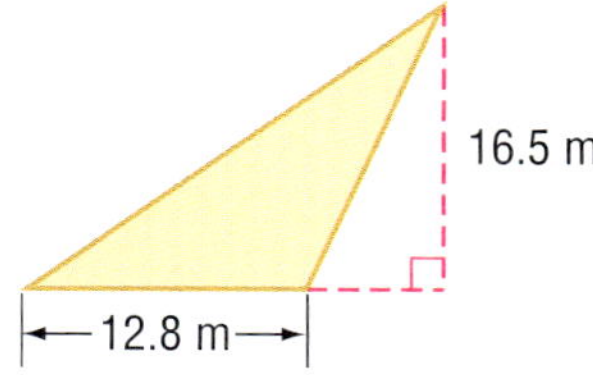

3. 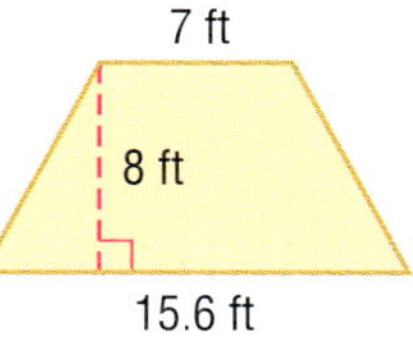

Example 3 (p. 580)

4. **HOCKEY** In the National Hockey League, goaltenders can play the puck behind the goal line only in a trapezoid-shaped area, as shown at the right. Find the area of the trapezoid.

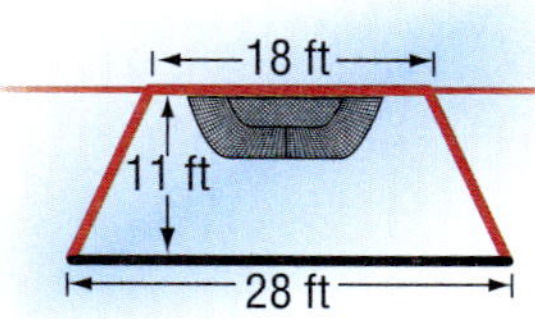

Practice and Problem Solving

HOMEWORK HELP

For Exercises	See Examples
5, 6, 9	1
7, 8, 10	2
11, 12	3

Find the area of each figure. Round to the nearest tenth if necessary.

5. 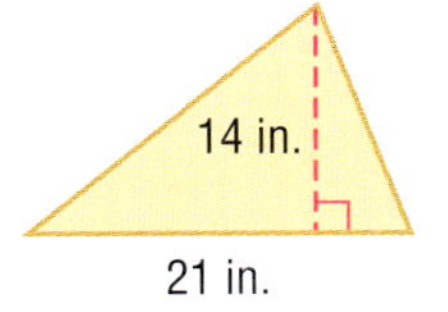

6. 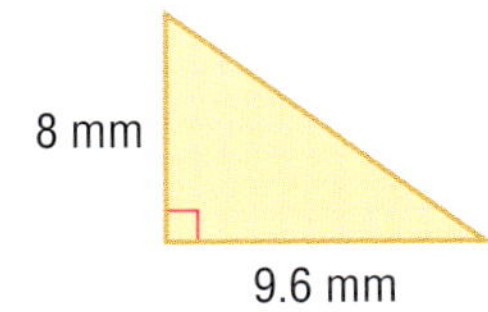

7. 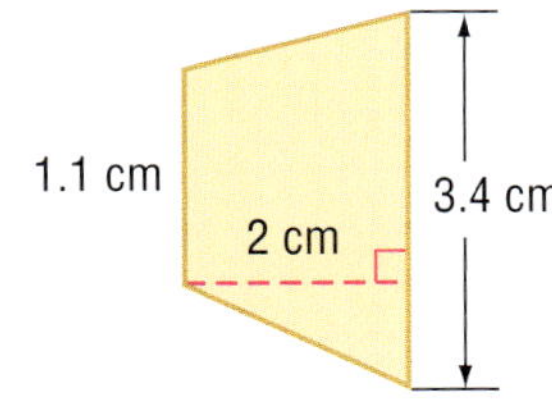

8. 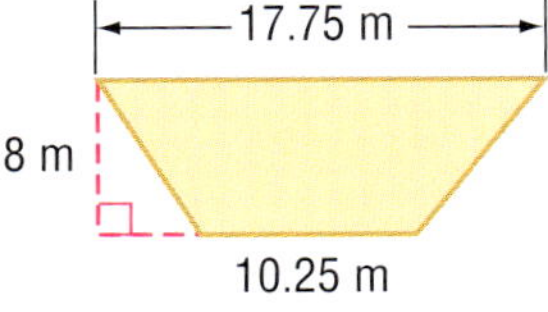

9. 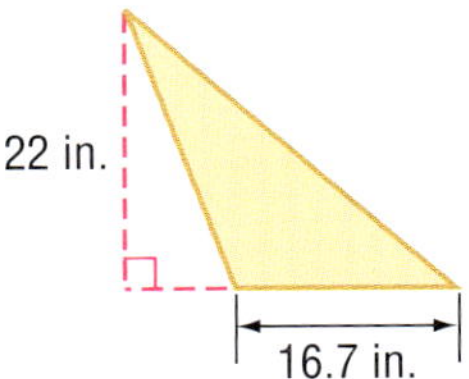

10. 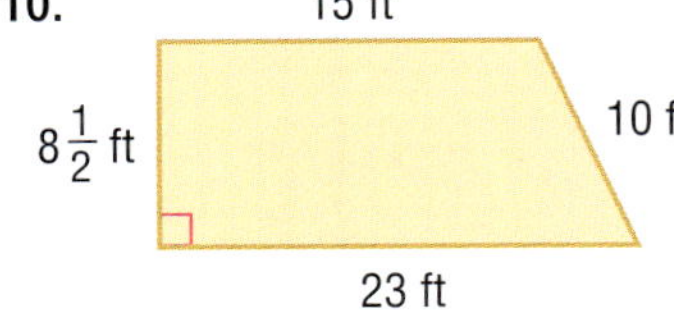

11. **GEOGRAPHY** The shape of Idaho is roughly triangular with a base of 380 miles and a height of 500 miles. Find the approximate area of Idaho.

12. **ALGEBRA** Find the area of a trapezoid with bases 13 inches and 15 inches and a height of 7 inches.

ALGEBRA Find the height of each figure.

13. 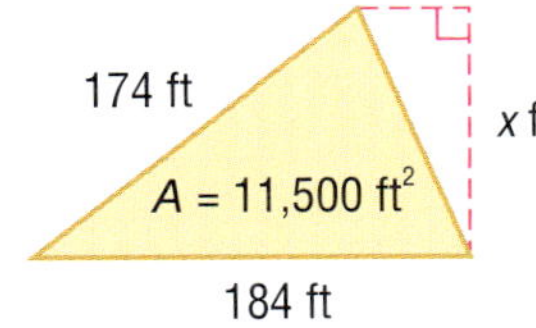

14. 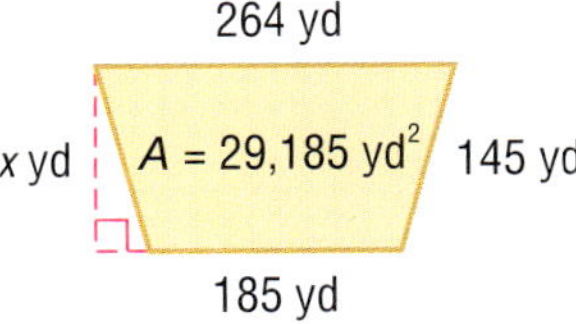

Draw and label each figure. Then find the area.

15. a triangle with no right angles and an area less than 12 square centimeters
16. a trapezoid with a right angle and an area greater than 40 square meters
17. a trapezoid with no right angles and an area less than 25 square feet

18. **TENTS** A play tent is shown at the right. How much fabric was used to make the front and back of the play tent?

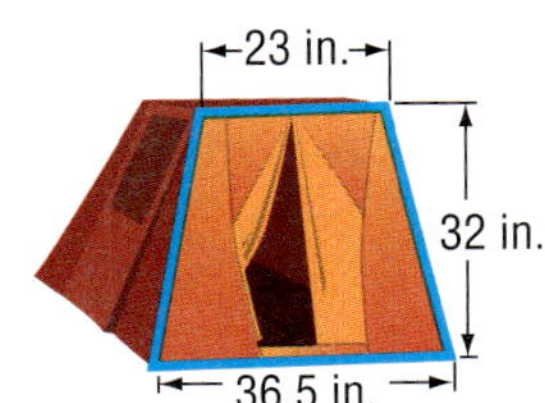

LANDSCAPING For Exercises 19 and 20, use the diagram that shows the lawn that surrounds an office building.

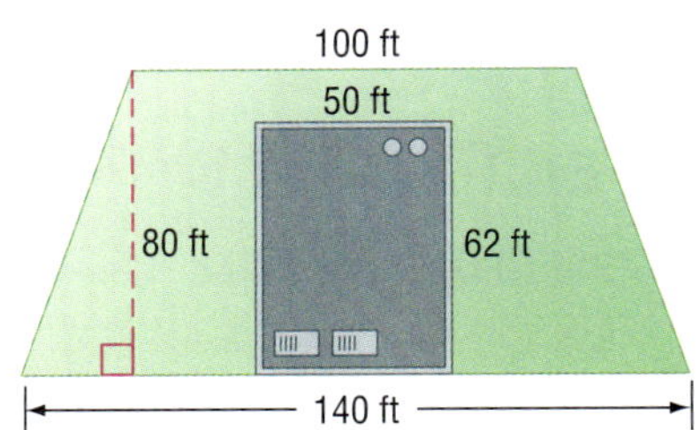

19. What is the area of the lawn?
20. If one bag of grass seed covers 2,000 square feet, how many bags are needed to seed the lawn?

EXTRA PRACTICE
See pages 697, 714.

H.O.T. Problems

21. **CHALLENGE** Triangle ABC has a base of 4 units and a height of 8 units. Triangle DEF has twice the base and height. Describe how the ratio of the bases is related to the ratio of the areas.

22. **REASONING** Apply what you know about rounding to explain how to estimate the height h of the trapezoid shown if the area is 235.5 in^2.

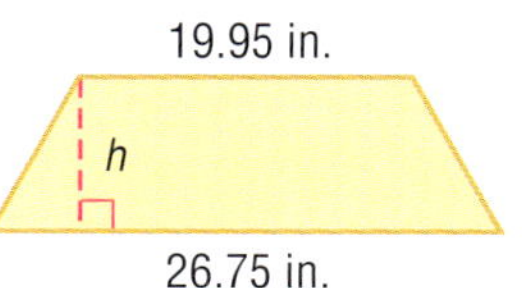

23. **WRITING IN MATH** Describe the relationship between the area of a parallelogram and the area of a triangle with the same height and base.

TEST PRACTICE

24. $\triangle FGH$ and $\triangle JKM$ are similar.

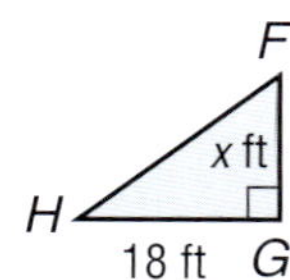

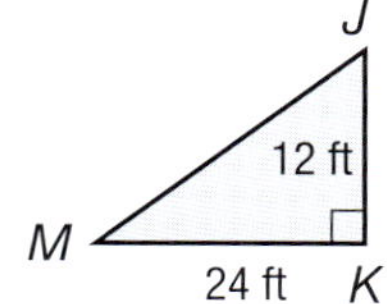

Which choice shows the equations that can be used to find the area of $\triangle FGH$?

A $\frac{18}{24} = \frac{12}{x}$ and then $\frac{1}{2}(18x)$

B $\frac{18}{24} = \frac{x}{12}$ and then $18x$

C $\frac{18}{24} = \frac{x}{12}$ and then $\frac{1}{2}(18x)$

D $\frac{18}{24} = \frac{12}{x}$ and then $18x$

25. **SHORT RESPONSE** Randy was hired to put in sod on a piece of land shaped like a trapezoid as shown. How many square feet of sod are needed?

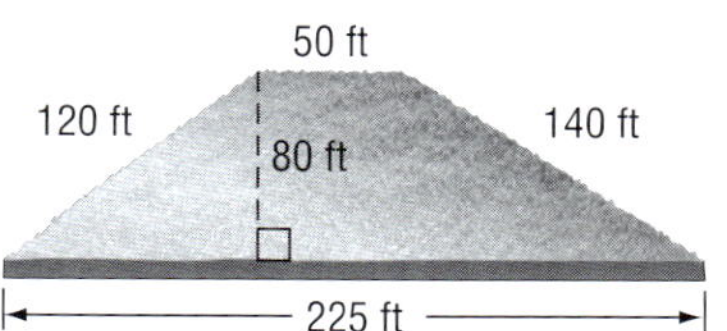

Spiral Review

26. **MEASUREMENT** Find the area of a parallelogram having a base of 2.3 inches and a height of 1.6 inches. Round to the nearest tenth. (Lesson 11-1)

27. **GEOMETRY** Graph $\triangle JLK$ with vertices $J(-1, -4)$, $L(3, -2)$ and $K(1, 1)$, and its reflection over the x-axis. Write the ordered pairs for the vertices of the new figure. (Lesson 10-10)

Find each number. Round to the nearest tenth if necessary. (Lesson 7-2)

28. What number is 56% of 600?
29. 24.5 is what percent of 98?
30. 72 is 45% of what number?
31. 62.5% of 250 is what number?

GET READY for the Next Lesson

PREREQUISITE SKILL **Use a calculator to find each product to the nearest tenth.** (Lesson 1-4)

32. $\pi \cdot 13$
33. $\pi \cdot 29$
34. $\pi \cdot 16^2$
35. $\pi \cdot 4.8^2$

Explore 11-3

Measurement Lab
Circumference of Circles

MAIN IDEA

Find a relationship between circumference and diameter.

In this lab, you will investigate how the *circumference*, or the distance around a circle, is related to its *diameter*, or the distance across a circle through its center.

ACTIVITY

STEP 1 Use a ruler to measure the diameter of a circular object. Record the length in a table like the one shown below.

Object	Diameter (cm)	Circumference (cm)

STEP 2 Make a small mark at the edge of the circular object. Place a measuring tape on a flat surface. Place the mark you made on the circular object at the beginning of the measuring tape. Roll the object along the tape for one revolution, until you reach the mark again.

STEP 3 Record the length in the table. This is the circumference.

STEP 4 Repeat this activity with circular objects of various sizes.

ANALYZE THE RESULTS

1. For each object, divide the circumference by the diameter. Add another column to your table and record the results. Round to the nearest tenth if necessary.
2. What do you notice about the ratio of each circumference to each diameter?
3. Graph the ordered pair (diameter, circumference) on a coordinate plane for each object. What do you notice?
4. Use the graph to predict the circumference of a circular object that has a diameter of 18 centimeters.
5. **MAKE A CONJECTURE** Write a rule describing how you would find the circumference C of a circle if you know the diameter d.
6. Use your rule to approximate the circumference of a circular object that has a diameter of 45 centimeters.

11-3 Circles and Circumference

MAIN IDEA

Find the circumference of circles.

New Vocabulary

circle
center
diameter
circumference
radius
π (pi)

Math Online

glencoe.com

- Extra Examples
- Personal Tutor
- Self-Check Quiz

GET READY for the Lesson

CLOCKS Big Ben is a famous clock tower in London, England. The diameter of the clock face is 23 feet.

1. Which point appears at the middle of Big Ben?
2. How does the distance from A to C compare to the distance from B to D?
3. Find the distance from D to C.

A **circle** is the set of all points in a plane that are the same distance from a given point, called the **center**.

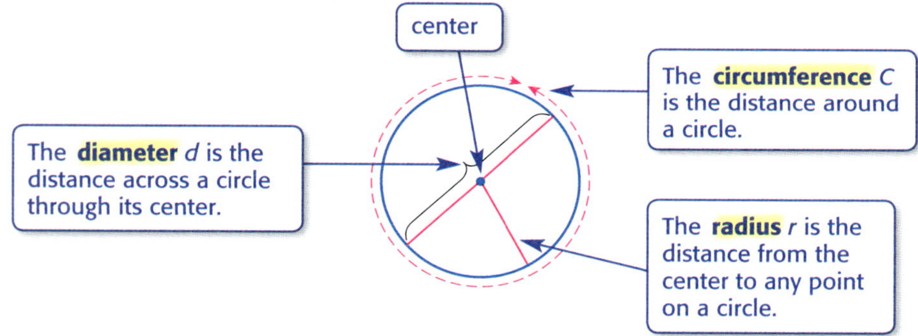

The diameter of a circle is 2 times the radius, or $d = 2r$. Another relationship that is true of all circles is $\frac{C}{d} = 3.1415926\ldots$. This nonterminating and nonrepeating number is represented by the Greek letter **π (pi)**. An approximation often used for π is 3.14.

Circumference of a Circle — Key Concept

Words	The circumference C of a circle is equal to its diameter d times π, or 2 times its radius r times π.
Symbols	$C = \pi d$ or $C = 2\pi r$

When finding the circumference of a circle, it is necessary to use an approximation of π since its exact value cannot be determined.

Study Tip

Estimation To estimate the circumference of a circle, you can use 3 for π since $\pi \approx 3$.

Real-World EXAMPLE Find Circumference

1 **CLOCKS** **Refer to the lesson opener. Find the circumference of Big Ben's clock face.**

Estimate $C = 3 \cdot 23$ or 69 ft

$C = \pi d$	Circumference of a circle
$C \approx 3.14(23)$	Replace π with 3.14 and d with 23.
$C \approx 72.22$	Multiply.

So, the distance around the clock is about 72.22 feet.

Check for Reasonableness $72.22 \approx 69$ ✔

CHECK Your Progress

Find the circumference of each circle. Use 3.14 for π. Round to the nearest tenth if necessary.

a.

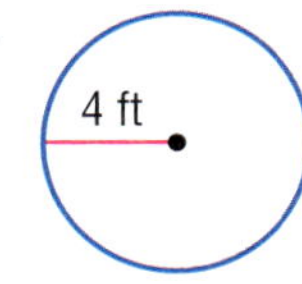

b.

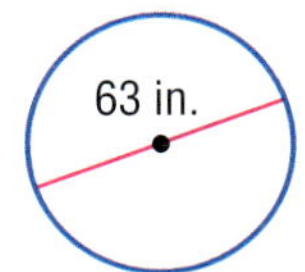

Another approximation for π is $\frac{22}{7}$. Use this value when the radius or diameter is a multiple of 7 or has a multiple of 7 in its numerator if the radius is a fraction.

Study Tip

Technology You can use a calculator to find the circumference. To find 2π (21), press 2 [2nd] [π] [×] 21 [ENTER]. The circumference is about 131.9468915.

EXAMPLE Find Circumference

2 **Find the circumference of a circle with a radius of 21 inches.**

Since 21 is a multiple of 7, use $\frac{22}{7}$ for π.

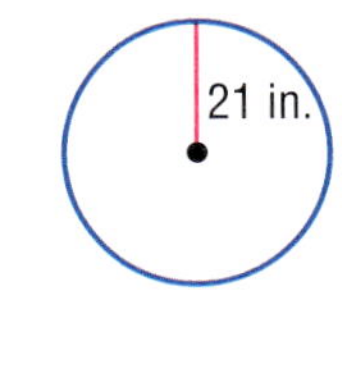

$C = 2\pi r$	Circumference of a circle
$C \approx 2 \cdot \frac{22}{7} \cdot 21$	Replace π with $\frac{22}{7}$ and r with 21.
$C \approx 2 \cdot \frac{22}{\cancel{7}_1} \cdot \frac{\cancel{21}^3}{1}$	Divide by the GCF, 7.
$C \approx 132$	Simplify.

The circumference of the circle is about 132 inches.

CHECK Your Progress

Find the circumference of each circle. Use $\frac{22}{7}$ for π.

c.

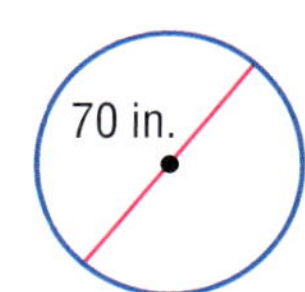

d. ($\frac{7}{8}$ ft radius circle)

CHECK Your Understanding

Examples 1, 2 (p. 585)

Find the circumference of each circle. Use 3.14 or $\frac{22}{7}$ for π. Round to the nearest tenth if necessary.

1. 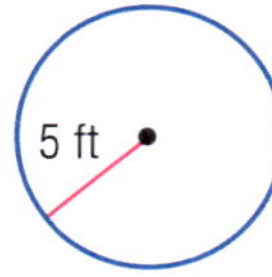

2. 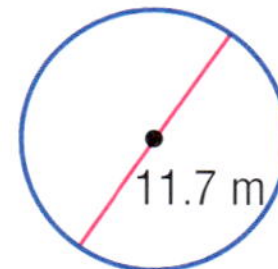

3. 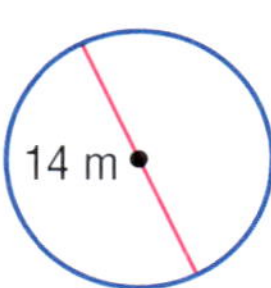

4. 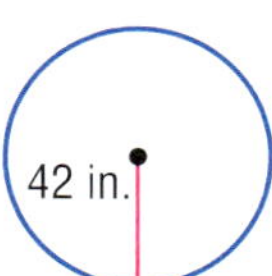

5. **CLOCKS** To the nearest tenth, how many centimeters does the tip of the minute hand of the clock shown travel each hour?

Practice and Problem Solving

HOMEWORK HELP	
For Exercises	See Examples
6–9, 14–15 20–21	1
10–13, 16–19	2

Find the circumference of each circle. Use 3.14 or $\frac{22}{7}$ for π. Round to the nearest tenth if necessary.

6. 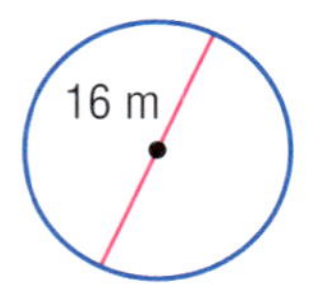

7. 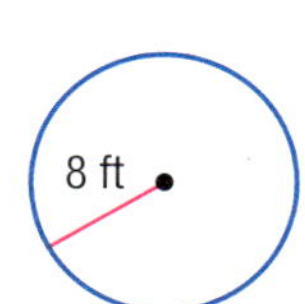

8. 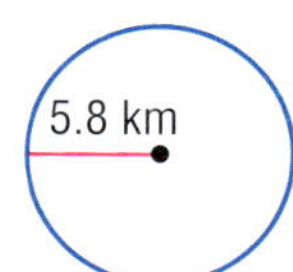

9. 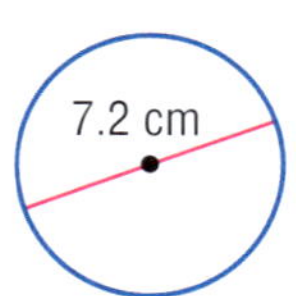

10. 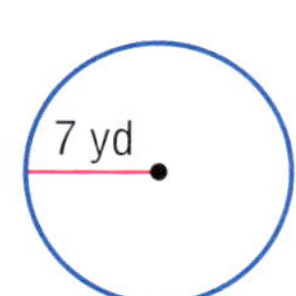

11. 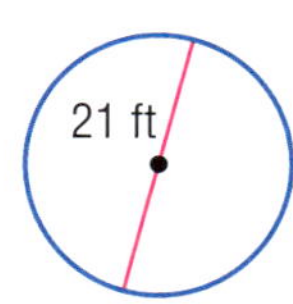

12. radius = $1\frac{3}{4}$ in.
13. diameter = $10\frac{1}{2}$ in.
14. diameter = 15.1 m
15. diameter = 10.8 km
16. radius = $2\frac{5}{8}$ in.
17. diameter = $12\frac{1}{4}$ mi
18. **SPORTS** A flying disc has a diameter of $9\frac{5}{8}$ inches. Find its circumference.
19. **WHEELS** A hamster wheel has a radius of $4\frac{1}{2}$ inches. How far will the wheel turn in one revolution?
20. **PATCHES** A National Guard military patch has a diameter of 2.5 inches. What is its circumference to the nearest tenth?
21. **POOLS** The Cole family owns an above-ground circular swimming pool that has walls made of aluminum. Find the length ℓ of aluminum surrounding the pool as shown if the radius is 15 feet. Round to the nearest tenth.

LABELS Determine the length of each can's label.

22. 

23. 

24. 

Real-World Link The record for the longest unicycle ride is 9,126 miles.
Source: Guinness World Records

MEASUREMENT For Exercises 25–28, perform each of the following steps.

a. Use a centimeter ruler to measure the diameter of each circular object listed.

b. Estimate to find the approximate circumference of each circle.

c. Calculate the circumference of each circle. Use 3.14 for π.

d. Cut a piece of string the length of the circumference of each circle. Use a centimeter ruler to measure the length of the string to the nearest tenth of a centimeter. Compare this actual length to the calculated length.

25. soup can lid
26. quarter
27. CD or DVD
28. button

ALGEBRA Find the diameter or radius of each circle. Use 3.14 for π. Round to the nearest tenth if necessary.

29. $C = 25$ ft, diameter = ▒ ft
30. $C = 54$ cm, diameter = ▒ cm
31. $C = 30$ yd, radius = ▒ yd
32. $C = 48$ km, radius = ▒ km

33. **UNICYCLES** A unicycle wheel has a radius of 10 inches. How many feet will the unicycle travel in 5 revolutions? Explain how you solved this problem.

34. **ROUNDABOUTS** A roundabout is a one-way circular intersection. About how many feet would a car travel if it drove once around the roundabout?

35. **FIND THE DATA** Refer to the Data File on pages 16–19. Choose some data and write a real-world problem in which you would find the circumference of a circle.

EXTRA PRACTICE See pages 697, 714.

H.O.T. Problems

36. **OPEN ENDED** Select a real-world situation in which finding the circumference of a circle would be useful.

37. **FIND THE ERROR** Logan and Elsa are finding the circumference of a circle with a radius of 7 inches. Who is correct? Explain.

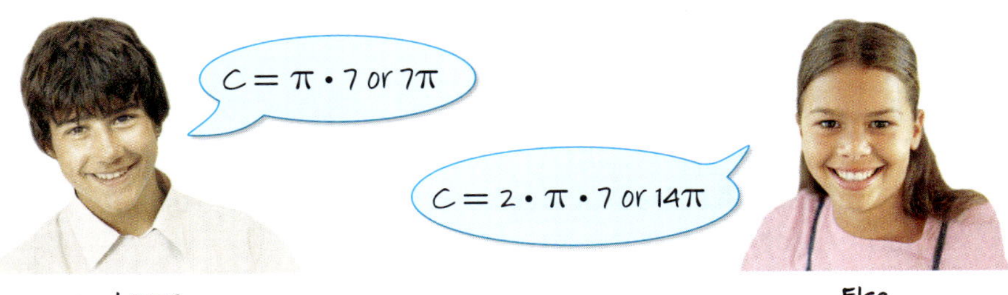

CHALLENGE **For Exercises 38 and 39, use the circle at the right.**

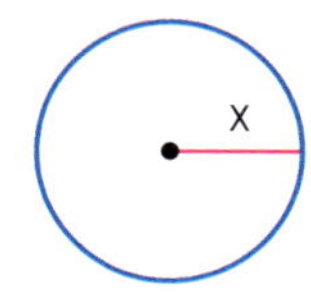

38. How many lengths x will fit on the circle's circumference?

39. If the value of x is doubled, what effect will this have on the diameter? on the circumference? Explain your reasoning.

40. **WRITING IN MATH** A *constant* is a quantity whose value never changes. In the formula for the circumference of a circle, identify any constants. Justify your response.

TEST PRACTICE

41. Malik's bike tire has a radius of 8 inches. Which equation could be used to find the circumference of the tire in inches?

A $C = \pi \cdot 4$ **C** $C = \pi \cdot 16$

B $C = \pi \cdot 16 \times 2$ **D** $C = \pi \cdot 8$

42. Each wheel on Nina's car has a diameter of 18 inches. Which expression could be used to find the circumference of the wheel?

F $2 \times 9 \times \pi$ **H** $9 \times 9 \times \pi$

G $2 \times 18 \times \pi$ **J** $18 \times 18 \times \pi$

43. Which measure is *closest* to the circumference of the dreamcatcher shown below?

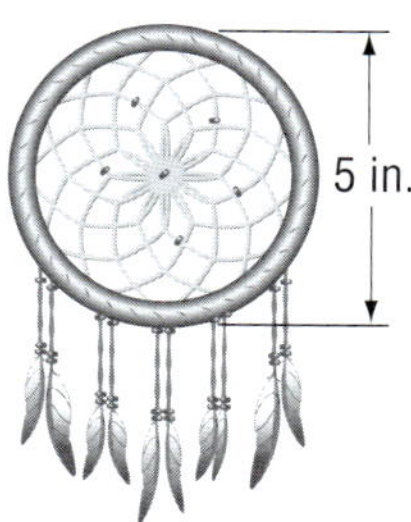

A 7.9 in. **C** 34.1 in.

B 15.7 in. **D** 62.8 in.

Spiral Review

MEASUREMENT **Find the area of each figure. Round to the nearest tenth if necessary.** (Lesson 11-2)

44.

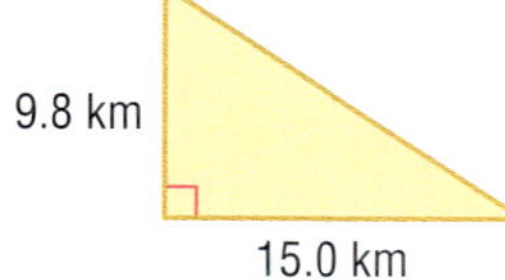

45.

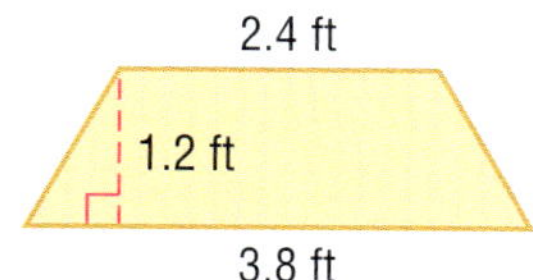

46. **MEASUREMENT** Find the area of a parallelogram with base 6.5 meters and height 7.0 meters. (Lesson 11-1)

47. **PROBABILITY** Jorge rolled a number cube several times and recorded the results in the table shown. Find the experimental probability that an odd number turned up. (Lesson 9-7)

Outcome	Frequency
1	𝍸 |
2	|||
3	𝍸 ||
4	𝍸
5	||
6	||||

GET READY for the Next Lesson

PREREQUISITE SKILL **Use a calculator to find each product to the nearest tenth.** (Lesson 1-4)

48. $\pi \cdot 5^2$

49. $\pi \cdot 7^2$

50. $\pi \cdot (2.4)^2$

51. $\pi \cdot (4.5)^2$

11-4 Area of Circles

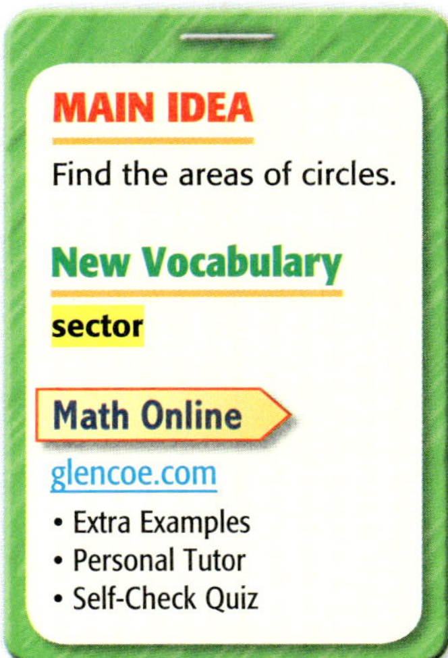

MINI Lab

- Fold a paper plate in half four times to divide it into 16 equal-sized sections.
- Label the radius r as shown. Let C represent the circumference of the circle.
- Cut out each section; reassemble to form a parallelogram-shaped figure.

1. What is the measurement of the base and the height?

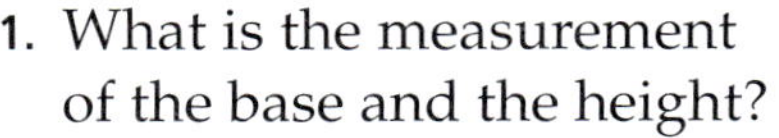

2. Substitute these values into the formula for the area of a parallelogram.

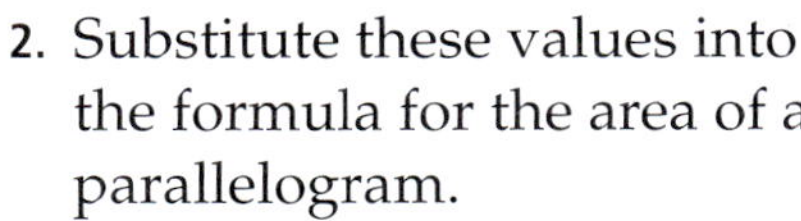

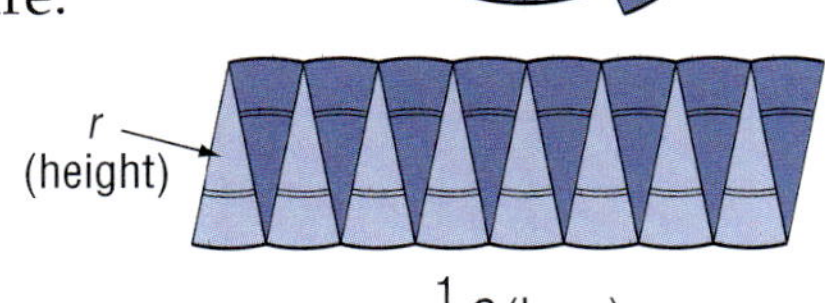

3. Replace C with the expression for the circumference of a circle, $2\pi r$. Simplify the equation and describe what it represents.

In the Mini Lab, the formula for the area of a parallelogram was used to develop a formula for the area of a circle.

Area of a Circle — Key Concept

Words The area A of a circle equals the product of π and the square of its radius r.

Symbols $A = \pi r^2$

Model (circle with radius r)

EXAMPLE Find the Area of a Circle

1 Find the area of the circle.

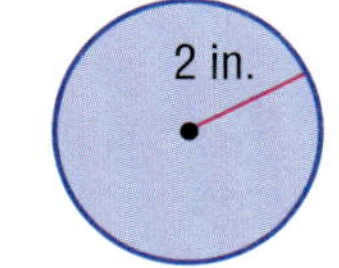

$A = \pi r^2$ Area of a circle

$A = \pi \cdot 2^2$ Replace r with 2.

[2nd] [π] [×] 2 [x^2] [ENTER] 12.56637061

The area of the circle is approximately 12.6 square inches.

CHECK Your Progress

a. Find the area of a circle with a radius of 3.2 centimeters. Round to the nearest tenth.

Real-World EXAMPLE

2 **COINS** **Find the area of the face of the Wisconsin quarter shown.**

The diameter of the quarter is 24 millimeters, so the radius is $\frac{1}{2}(24)$ or 12 millimeters.

$A = \pi r^2$ Area of a circle

$A = \pi \cdot 12^2$ Replace r with 12.

$A \approx 452.4$ Use a calculator.

The area is approximately 452.4 square millimeters.

CHECK Your Progress

b. **POOLS** The bottom of a circular swimming pool with diameter 30 feet is painted blue. How many square feet are blue?

> **Study Tip**
>
> **Radii** The plural form of radius is radii.

A **sector** of a circle is a region of a circle bounded by two radii.

TEST EXAMPLE

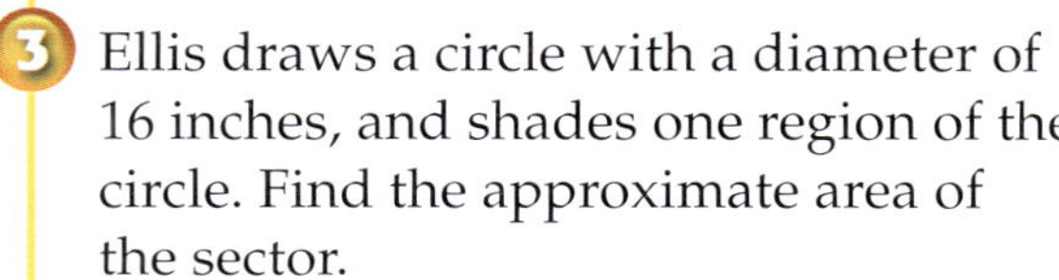

3 Ellis draws a circle with a diameter of 16 inches, and shades one region of the circle. Find the approximate area of the sector.

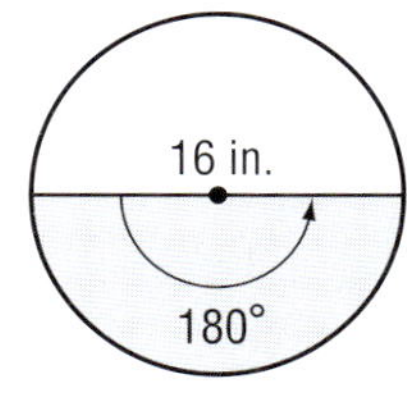

A 100 in^2 **C** 402 in^2

B 201 in^2 **D** 804 in^2

> **Test-Taking Tip**
>
> **Identifying What is Given** Before finding area, be sure to read the question carefully and identify if the radius or diameter is given.

Read the Item

The diameter of the circle is 16 inches. Since there are 360° in a circle, the sector is $\frac{180°}{360°}$ or $\frac{1}{2}$ the area of the entire circle.

Solve the Item

$A = \pi r^2$ Area of a circle

$A = \pi \cdot 8^2$ Replace r with 16 ÷ 2 or 8.

$A \approx 200$ Multiply. Use 3.14 for π.

The area of the sector is approximately $\frac{1}{2}(200)$ or 100 square inches. The answer is A.

CHECK Your Progress

c. Ray drew one circle with a radius of 7 centimeters and another circle with a radius of 10 centimeters. Find the approximate difference between the areas of the circles.

F 28 cm^2 **G** 40 cm^2 **H** 160 cm^2 **J** 254 cm^2

Examples 1, 2 (pp. 589–590)

Find the area of each circle. Round to the nearest tenth.

1. 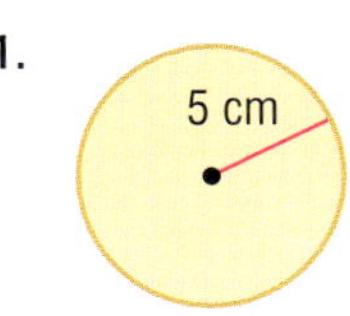

2. 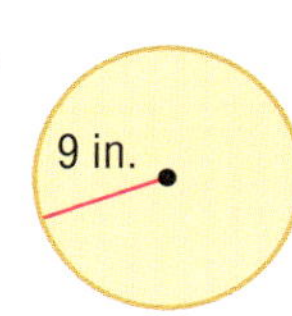

3. diameter = 16 m

4. diameter = 13 ft

Example 3 (p. 590)

5. **MULTIPLE CHOICE** Kenneth draws the circle shown at the right. He shades one region of the circle. What is the approximate area of the sector?

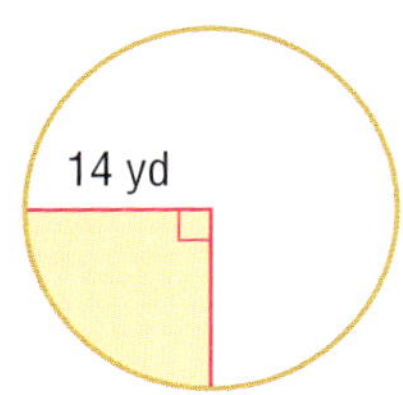

A 88 yd^2 **C** 310 yd^2

B 154 yd^2 **D** 615 yd^2

Practice and Problem Solving

HOMEWORK HELP	
For Exercises	**See Examples**
6–7, 10–11, 14–15, 19	1
8–9, 12–13, 16–18	2
36–38	3

Find the area of each circle. Round to the nearest tenth.

6. 8 cm

7. 3 in.

8. 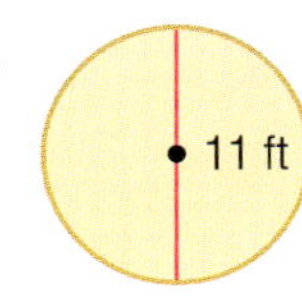

9. 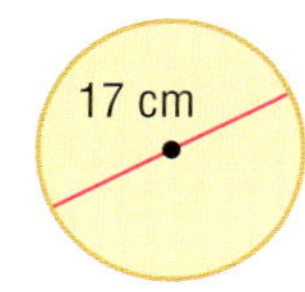

10. 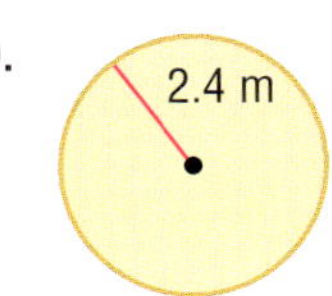

11. 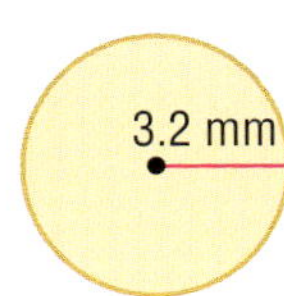

12. diameter = 8.4 m

13. diameter = 12.6 cm

14. radius = $4\frac{1}{2}$ in.

15. radius = $3\frac{3}{4}$ ft

16. diameter = $9\frac{1}{4}$ mi

17. diameter = $20\frac{3}{4}$ yd

18. **PATCHES** Find the area of the Girl Scout patch shown if the diameter is 1.25 inches. Round to the nearest tenth.

19. **TOOLS** A sprinkler that sprays water in a circular area can be adjusted to spray up to 30 feet. To the nearest tenth, what is the maximum area of lawn that can be watered by the sprinkler?

ESTIMATION **Estimate to find the approximate area of each circle.**

20. 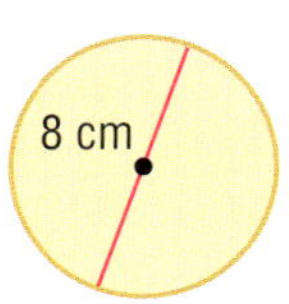

21. 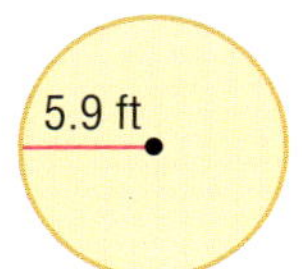

22. 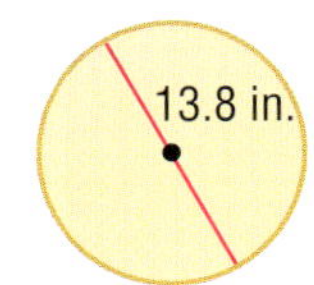

For Exercises 23–26, use a compass to draw the circle shown on centimeter grid paper.

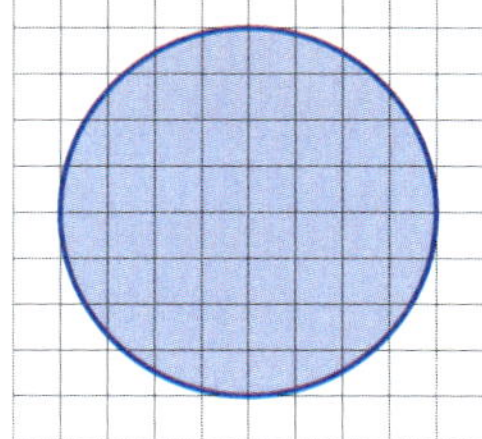

23. Count the number of squares that lie completely within the circle. Then count the number of squares that lie completely within or contain the circle.
24. Estimate the area of the circle by finding the mean of the two values you found in Exercise 23.
25. Find the area of the circle by using the area formula.
26. How do the areas you found in Exercises 24 and 25 compare to one another?
27. A *semicircle* is half a circle. Find the area of the semicircle to the nearest tenth.

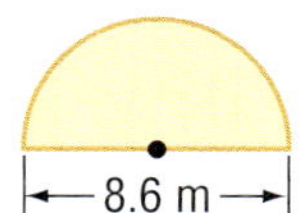

28. Which has a greater area, a triangle with a base of 100 feet and a height of 100 feet or a circle with diameter of 100 feet? Justify your selection.

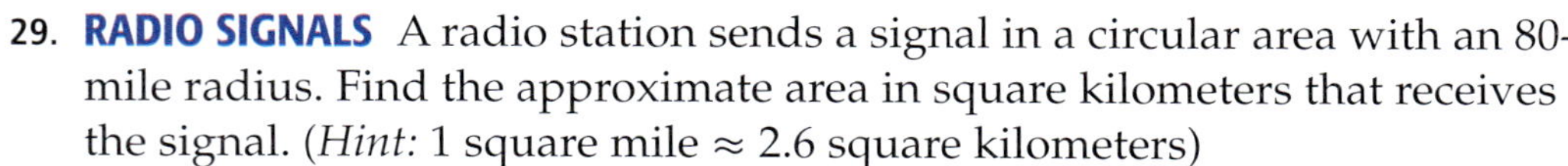

29. **RADIO SIGNALS** A radio station sends a signal in a circular area with an 80-mile radius. Find the approximate area in square kilometers that receives the signal. (*Hint:* 1 square mile ≈ 2.6 square kilometers)

H.O.T. Problems

30. **REASONING** If the length of the radius of a circle is tripled, does the area also triple? Explain your reasoning.

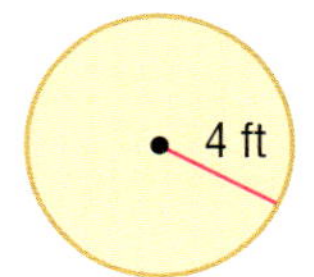

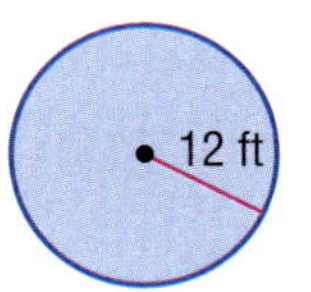

CHALLENGE **Find the area of the shaded region in each figure. Round to the nearest tenth.**

31.

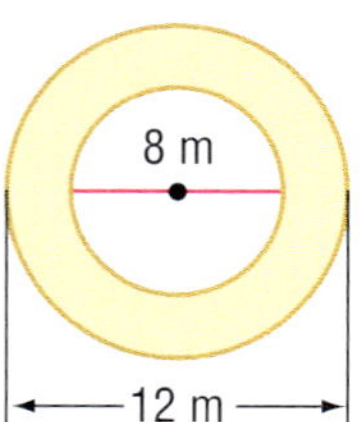

32.

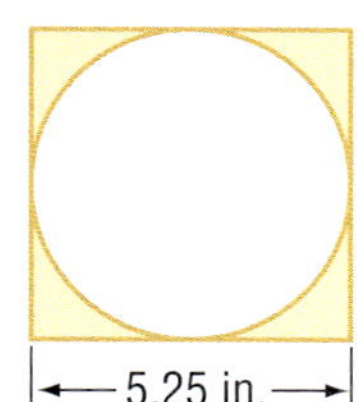

33.

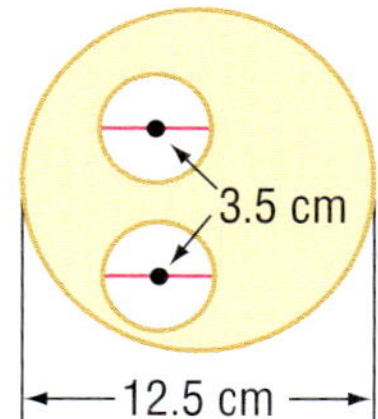

34. **FIND THE ERROR** Dasan and Carmen are finding the area of a circle that has a diameter of 16 centimeters. Who is correct? Explain.

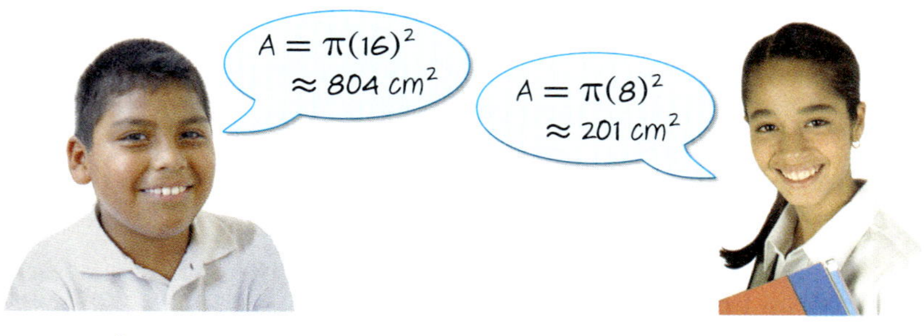

35. **WRITING IN MATH** Write and solve a real-world problem in which you would solve the problem by finding the area of a circle.

TEST PRACTICE

36. The radius of the half dollar in centimeters is given below. Find the approximate area of the shaded sector.

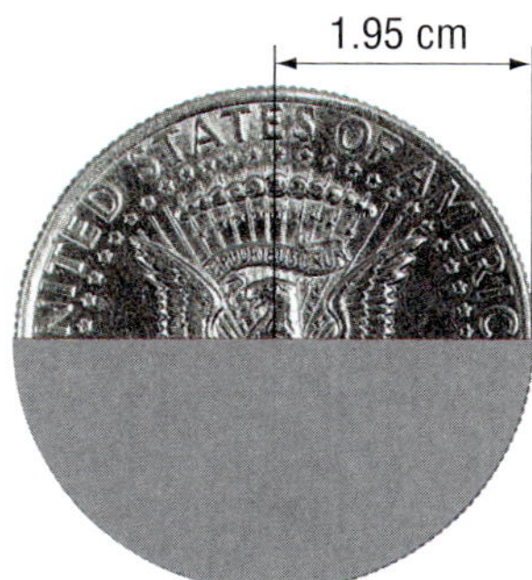

A 6 cm^2 **C** 14 cm^2
B 12 cm^2 **D** 28 cm^2

37. Which equation could be used to find the area in square inches of a circle with a radius of 12 inches?

F $A = 6 \times \pi$ **H** $A = 12 \times \pi$
G $A = \pi \times 6^2$ **J** $A = \pi \times 12^2$

38. Which two figures have the same area shaded?

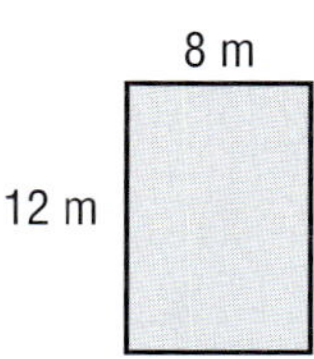

Figure I

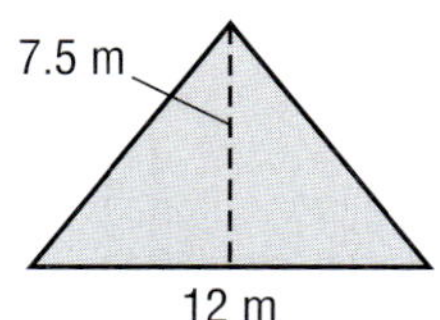

Figure II

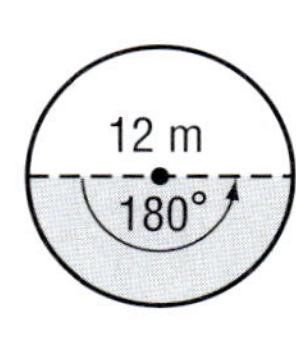

Figure III

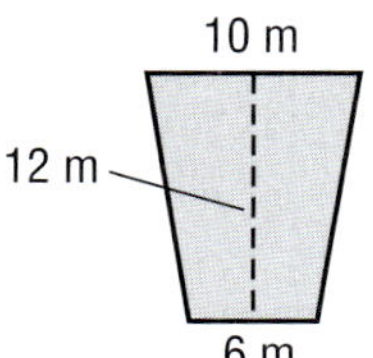

Figure IV

A Figure I and Figure IV
B Figure I and Figure II
C Figure II and Figure IV
D Figure II and Figure III

Spiral Review

39. **MEASUREMENT** What is the circumference of a circle that has a radius of 8 yards? Use 3.14 for π and round to the nearest tenth if necessary. (Lesson 11-3)

40. **MEASUREMENT** Find the area of a triangle with a base of 21 meters and a height of 27 meters. (Lesson 11-2)

Find the area of each parallelogram. Round to the nearest tenth if necessary. (Lesson 11-1)

41. 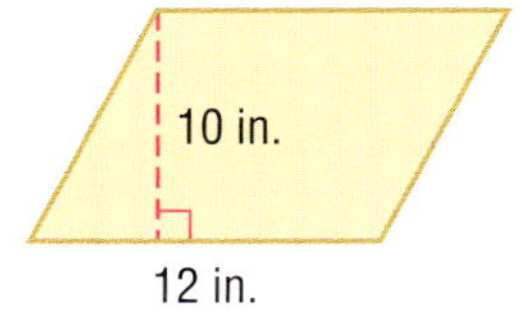

42. 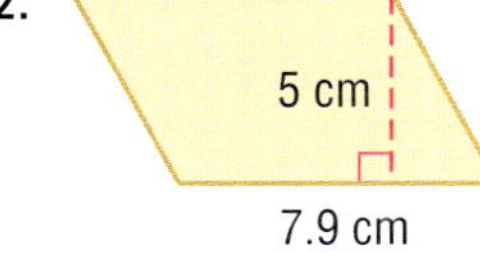

43. 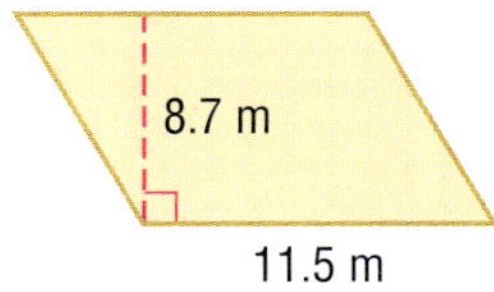

GET READY for the Next Lesson

PREREQUISITE SKILL **Simplify each expression.** (Lessons 1-2, 1-3, and 1-4)

44. 8.5^2

45. $3.14 \cdot 6^2$

46. $\frac{1}{2} \cdot 5.4^2 + 11$

47. $\frac{1}{2} \cdot 7^2 + (9)(14)$

Problem-Solving Investigation

MAIN IDEA: Solve problems by solving a simpler problem.

P.S.I. TEAM +

e-Mail: SOLVE A SIMPLER PROBLEM

LIAM: For a service project, I am helping mulch the play area at the community center. We need to know how large the play area is in order to buy the right amount of mulch. The diagram shows the dimensions of the play area.

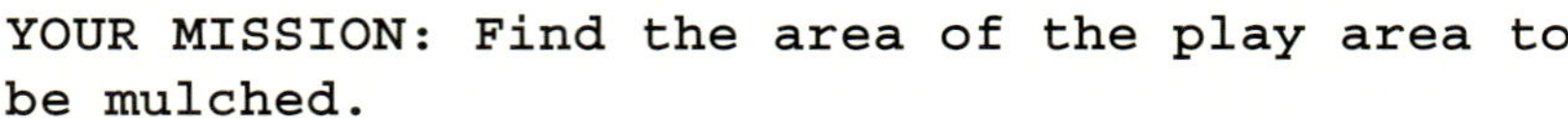

YOUR MISSION: Find the area of the play area to be mulched.

Understand	You know that the play area is made of two rectangles.	13 ft 7 ft 10 ft 8 ft 5 ft
Plan	Find the area of the two rectangles, and then add.	
Solve	Area of Rectangle 1 $A = \ell w$ $A = 5 \cdot 10$ $A = 50$ The total area is $50 + 56$ or 106 square feet. So, we need to buy enough mulch for at least 106 square feet.	Area of Rectangle 2 $A = \ell w$ $A = 8 \cdot 7$ $A = 56$
Check	The play area is less than $13 \cdot 10$ or 130 square feet. So, an answer of 106 square feet is reasonable.	

Analyze The Strategy

1. Why is breaking this problem into simpler parts a good strategy to solve it?
2. Describe another way that the problem could have been solved by breaking it into simpler parts.
3. **WRITING IN MATH** Write a problem that can be solved by breaking it into simpler parts. Solve the problem and explain your answer.

Mixed Problem Solving

See pages 698, 714.

Solve Exercises 4 and 5. Use the *solve a simpler problem* strategy.

4. **WALLPAPER** Brianna is wallpapering a wall in her house. What is the area that will be wallpapered?

5. **CONTINENTS** The table lists each continent and its percent of the world's land area. The land area of Earth is 57,505,708 square miles. Find the approximate land area of each continent.

Continent	Percent of Earth's Land
Asia	30
Africa	20.2
North America	16.5
South America	12
Antarctica	8.9
Europe	6.7
Australia/Oceana	5.3

Use any strategy to solve Exercises 6–10. Some strategies are shown below.

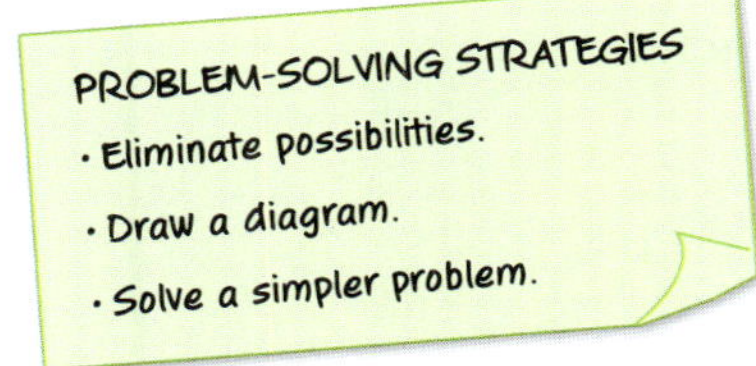

6. **DRIVING** Tara is driving from New Orleans to Atlanta. The driving distance is 480 miles. After driving 6 hours, she is $\frac{3}{4}$ of the way there. How much longer does she have to drive to reach Atlanta?

7. **ZOO** The table shows the cost of admission.

Ticket	Cost
adult	\$10.50
child	\$7.00
senior	\$8.50

A family spent \$33.00 on admission. What combination is possible for the number of tickets that they purchased?

A 2 adult, 1 child, 1 senior

B 1 adult, 2 child, 1 senior

C 1 adult, 1 child, 2 senior

D 2 adult, 2 child

8. **MUSIC** On Mondays, you practice piano for 45 minutes. For each successive day of the week, you practice $\frac{1}{3}$ hour more than the day before. How many hours and minutes do you practice the piano on Saturdays?

9. **FOUNTAINS** Mr. Flores has a circular fountain with a radius of 5 feet. He plans on installing a brick path around the fountain. What will be the area of the path? Use 3.14 for π.

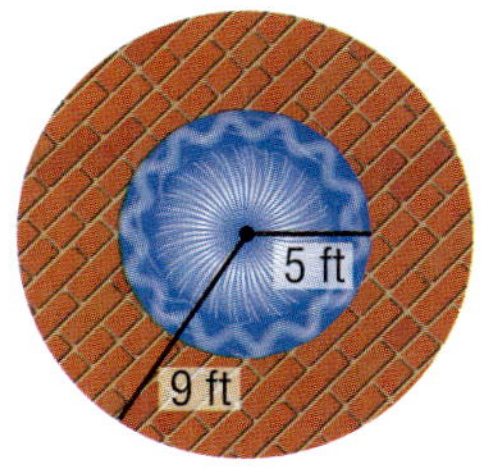

10. **VIDEO GAMES** The graph shows the results of a survey in which 347 students were asked to name their favorite type of video game. About how many students chose adventure as their favorite type of game?

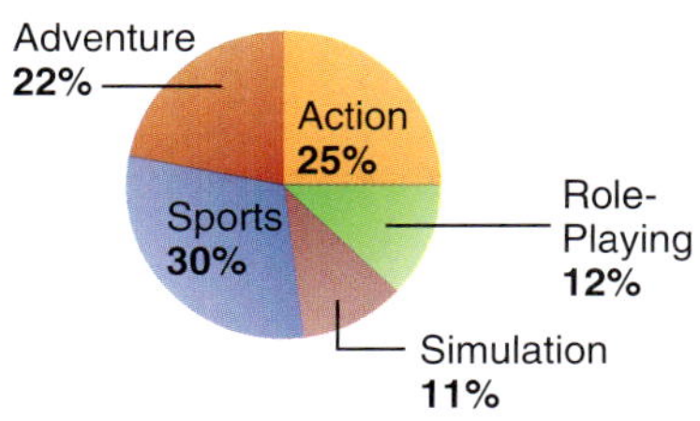

11-6 Area of Composite Figures

MAIN IDEA

Find the areas of composite figures.

New Vocabulary

composite figure
semicircle

Math Online

glencoe.com

- Extra Examples
- Personal Tutor
- Self-Check Quiz

GET READY for the Lesson

POOLS The dimensions of a pool at the recreation center are shown.

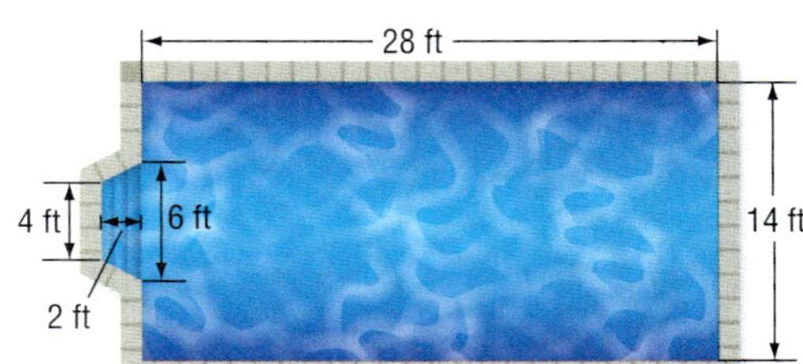

1. Describe the shape of the pool.
2. How could you determine the area of the pool's floor?

A **composite figure** is made of triangles, quadrilaterals, semicircles, and other two-dimensional figures. A **semicircle** is half of a circle.

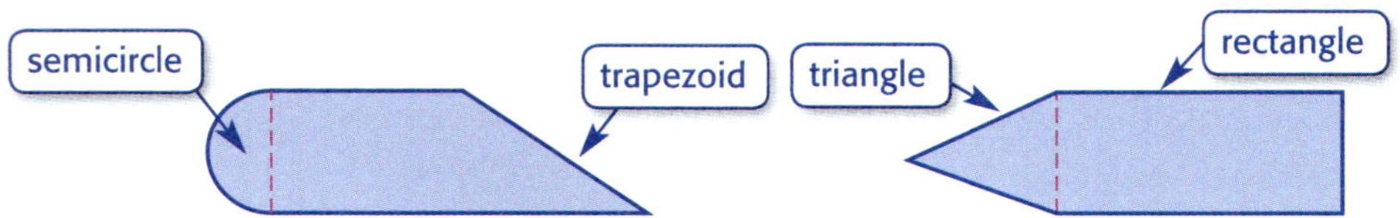

To find the area of a composite figure, separate it into figures with areas you know how to find, and then add those areas.

EXAMPLE Find the Area of a Composite Figure

1 **Find the area of the figure at the right.**

The figure can be separated into a rectangle and a triangle. Find the area of each.

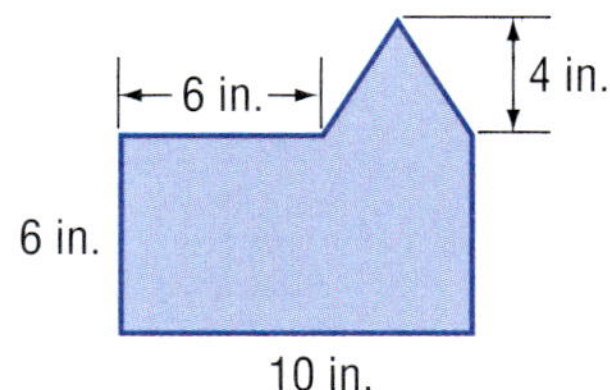

Area of Rectangle

$A = \ell w$

$A = 10 \cdot 6$ or 60

Area of Triangle

$A = \frac{1}{2}bh$

$A = \frac{1}{2}(4)(4)$ or 8

The base of the triangle is 10 − 6 or 4 inches.

The area is 60 + 8 or 68 square inches.

CHECK Your Progress

Find the area of each figure.

a.

10 ft
8 ft
4 ft
12 ft

b.

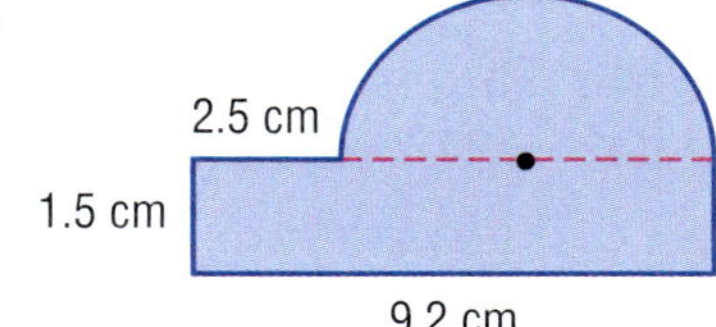

Real-World EXAMPLE

2 **POOLS** **The diagram of the pool from the beginning of the lesson is shown at the right. Find the area of the pool's floor.**

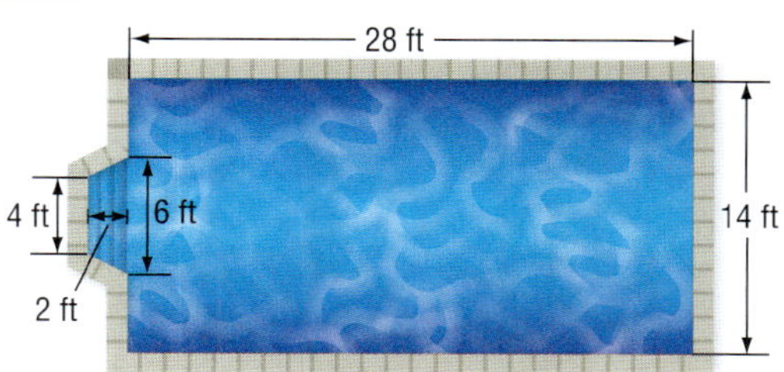

The figure can be separated into a rectangle and a trapezoid.

Area of Rectangle	**Area of Trapezoid**
$A = \ell w$	$A = \frac{1}{2}h(b_1 + b_2)$
$A = 28 \cdot 14$	$A = \frac{1}{2}(2)(4 + 6)$
$A = 392$	$A = \frac{1}{2}(2)(10)$
	$A = 10$

The area is 392 + 10 or 402 square feet.

c. **DECKS** Find the area of the deck shown.

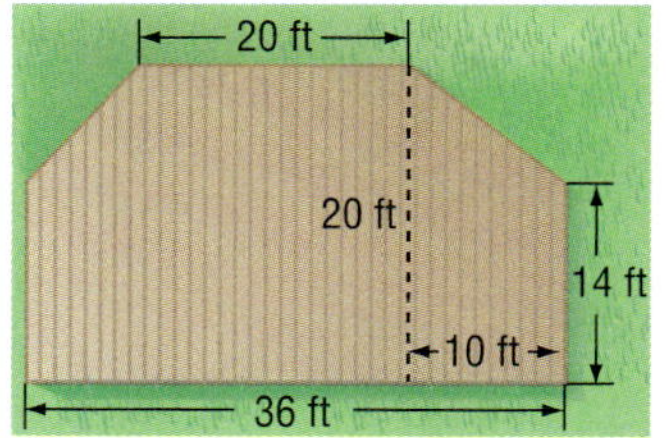

CHECK Your Understanding

Example 1 (p. 596)

Find the area of each figure. Round to the nearest tenth if necessary.

1.

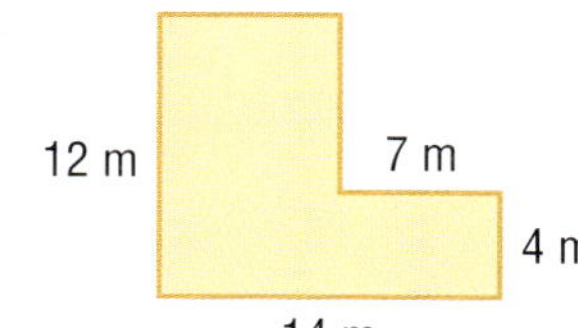

2.

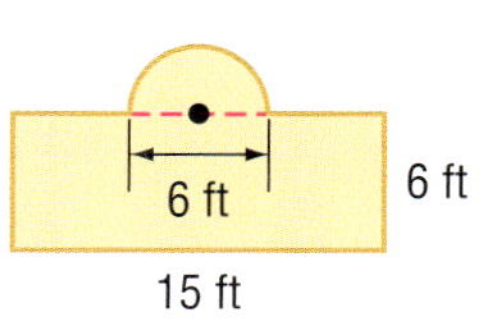

3.

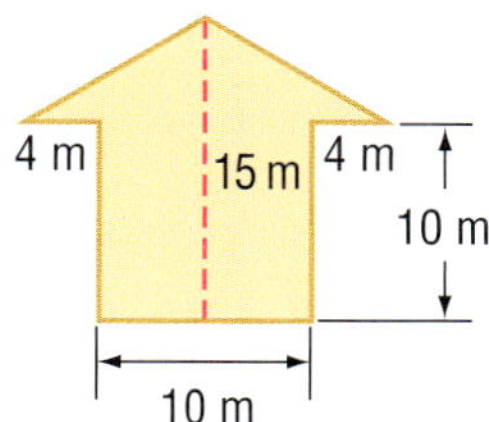

Example 2 (p. 597)

4. **APARTMENTS** The manager of an apartment complex will install new carpeting in a studio apartment. The floor plan is shown at the right. What is the total area that needs to be carpeted?

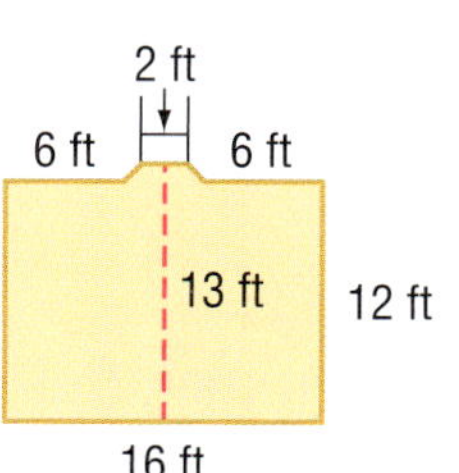

5. **TILING** A kitchen, shown at the right, has a bay window. If the entire kitchen floor is to be tiled, including the section by the bay window, how many square feet of tile are needed?

Practice and Problem Solving

HOMEWORK HELP	
For Exercises	See Examples
6–11	1
12–13	2

Find the area of each figure. Round to the nearest tenth if necessary.

6.
7. 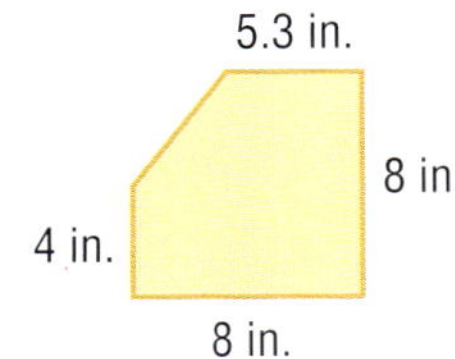

8. 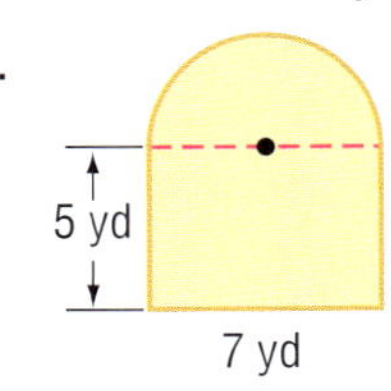

9.
10. 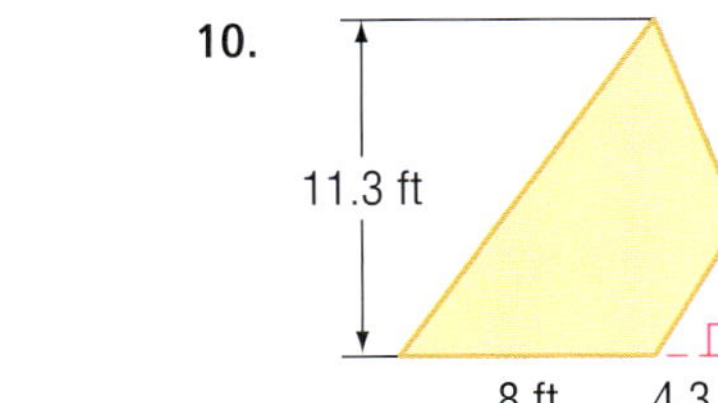

11. 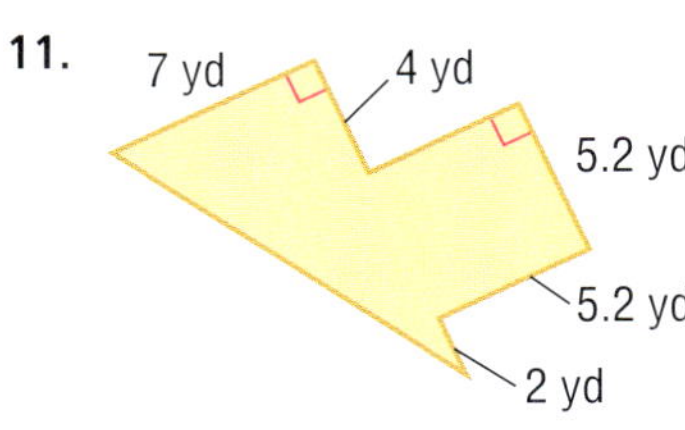

12. **BLUEPRINTS** On a blueprint, a rectangular room 14 feet by 12 feet has a semicircular sitting area attached with a diameter of 12 feet. What is the total area of the room and the sitting area?

13. **POOLS** The diagram at the right gives the dimensions of a swimming pool. If a cover is needed for the pool, what will be the approximate area of the cover?

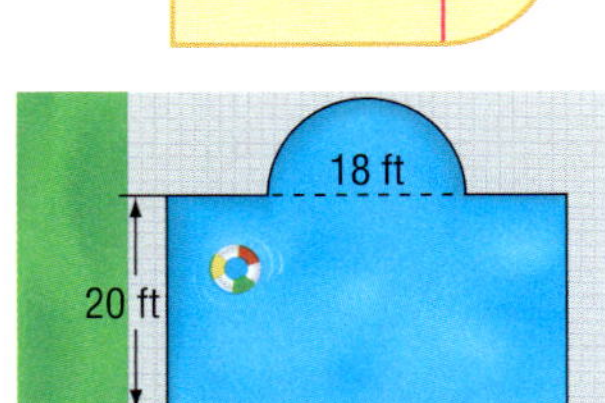

Find the area of the shaded region. Round to the nearest tenth if necessary.

14. 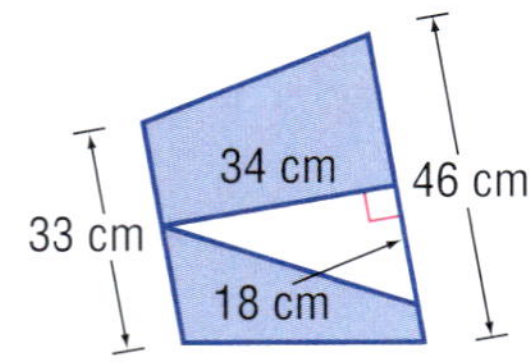

15. 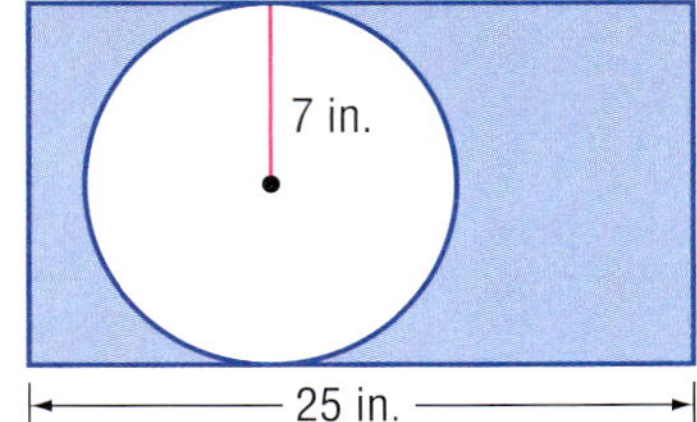

For each figure, write an algebraic expression that represents the area in square centimeters of the shaded region.

16. 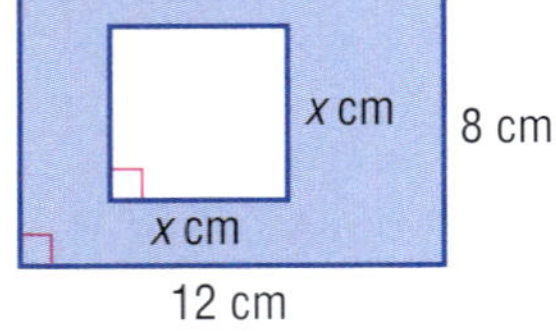

17. 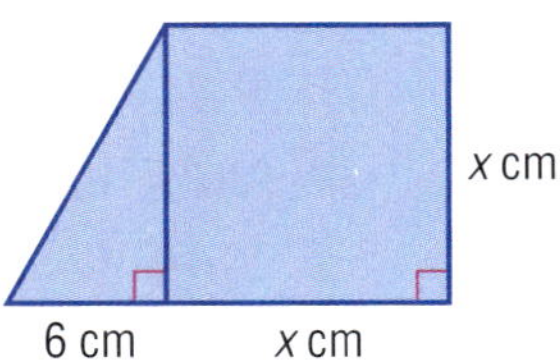

PAINTING For Exercises 18 and 19, use the diagram that shows one side of a storage barn.

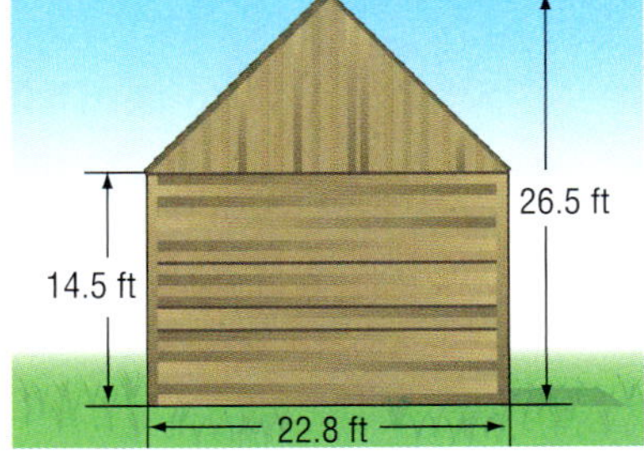

18. This side of the storage barn needs to be painted. Find the total area to be painted.

19. Each gallon of paint costs $20 and covers 350 square feet. Find the total cost to paint this side once. Justify your answer.

EXTRA PRACTICE
See pages 699, 714.

H.O.T. Problems

CHALLENGE **Describe the figures each state can be separated into. Then use these figures to estimate the area of each state if one square unit equals 2,400 square miles. Justify your answer.**

20. 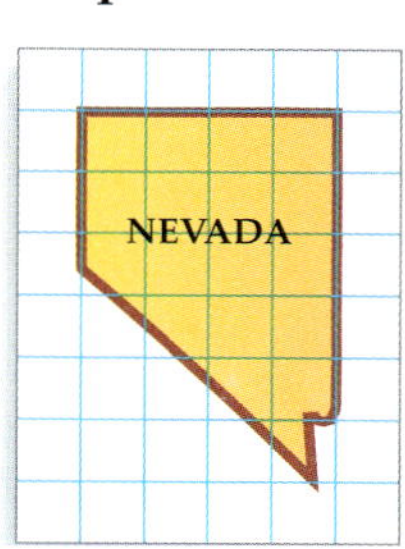

21. 

22. **WRITING IN MATH** Describe how you would find the area of the figure shown at the right.

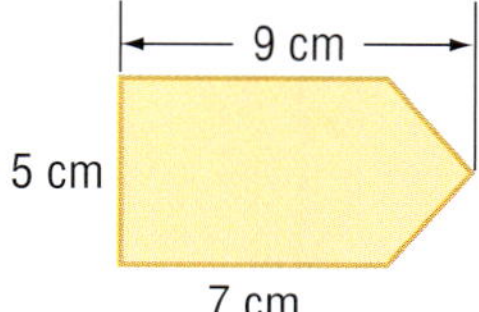

TEST PRACTICE

23. Which expression represents the area, in square feet, of the recreation room in terms of x?

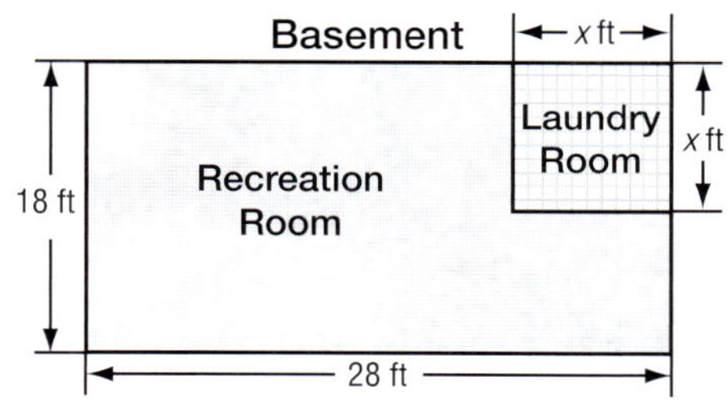

A $504 - 2x$ **C** $504 + x^2$

B $504 - x^2$ **D** $504 + 4x$

24. The shaded part of the grid represents the plans for a fish pond.

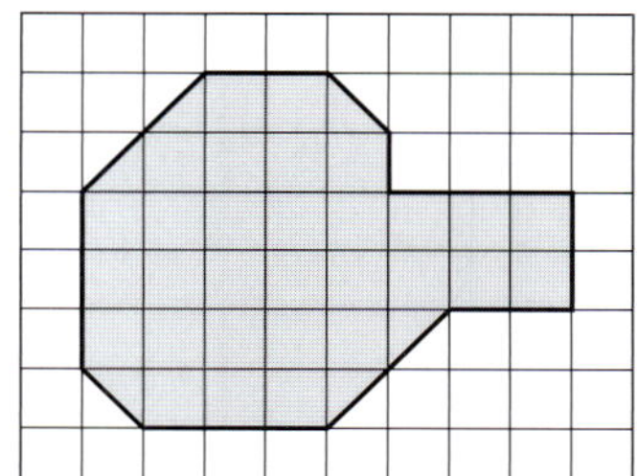

If each square on the grid represents 5 square feet, what is the approximate area of the fish pond?

F 175 ft^2 **H** 150 ft^2

G 165 ft^2 **J** 33 ft^2

Spiral Review

25. **MONEY** Over the weekend, Mrs. Lobo spent $534. Of that, about 68% was spent on groceries. About how much money was *not* spent on groceries? Use the *solve a simpler problem* strategy. (Lesson 11-5)

Find the area of each circle. Round to the nearest tenth. (Lesson 11-4)

26. radius = 4.7 cm
27. radius = 12 in.
28. diameter = 15 in.

GET READY for the Next Lesson

PREREQUISITE SKILL **Sketch each object.**

29. ice cream cone
30. shoe box
31. drinking straw

Extend 11-6

Measurement Lab
Nets and Surface Area

MAIN IDEA

Use nets to find the surface area of rectangular prisms.

Suppose you cut a cardboard box along its edges, open it up, and lay it flat.

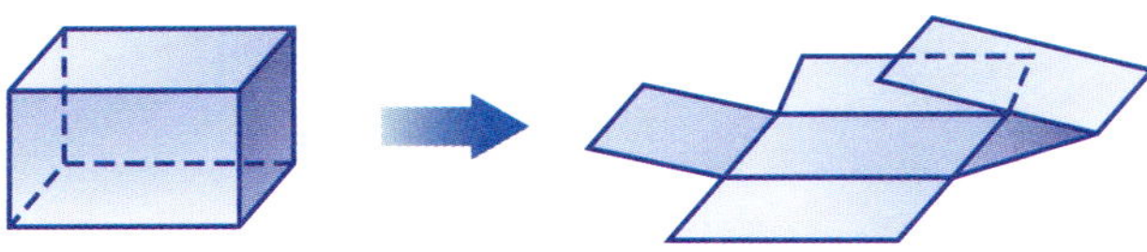

The result is a complex figure called a *net*. A net can help you see the regions or faces that make up the surface of a figure.

ACTIVITY

STEP 1 Place the box in the middle of a large sheet of paper as shown. Trace the outline of the bottom of the box.

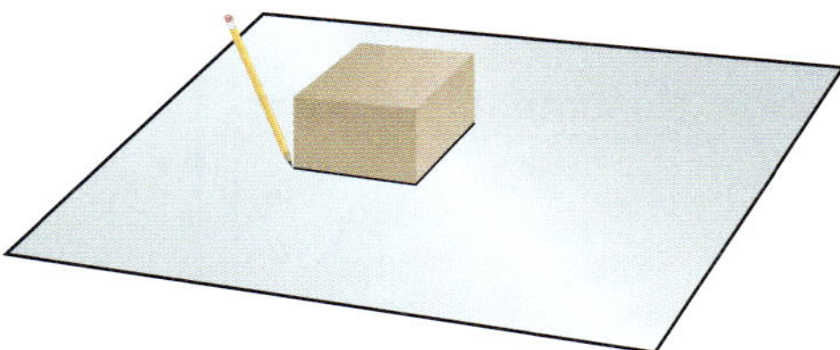

STEP 2 Roll the box onto its right side and label the outline you traced "Bottom". Trace and label each of the sides and top in this same way as shown below.

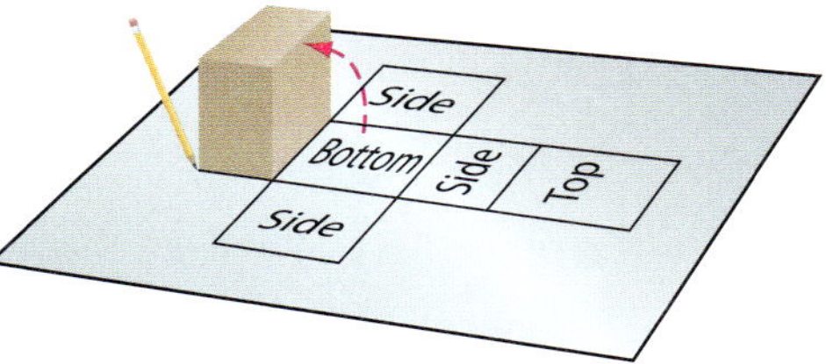

STEP 3 Cut out the resulting complex figure.

a–b. Make nets for two other rectangular boxes.

Check Your Net
To check that you have created a correct net for a figure, cut out the net, fold it, and tape it together to form the figure.

Analyze the Results

1. The net shown in the Activity is made of rectangles. How many rectangles are in the net?

2. Explain how you can find the total area of the rectangles.

Draw a net for each figure. Find the area of the net.

3. 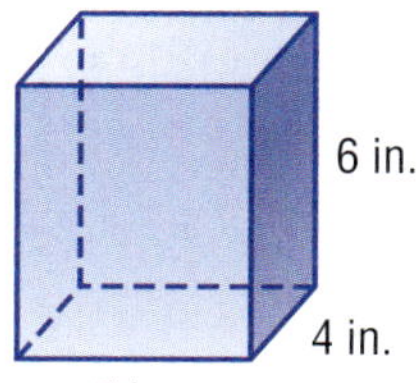

4. 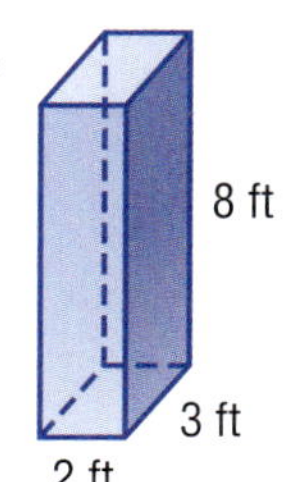

5. 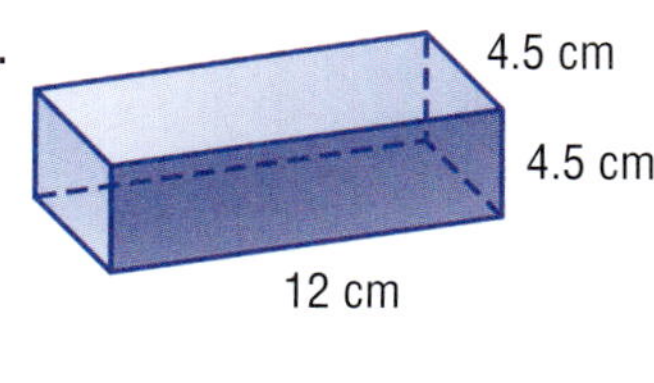

6. The *surface area* of a prism is the total area of its net. Write an equation that shows how to find the surface area of the prism below using the length ℓ, width w, and height h.

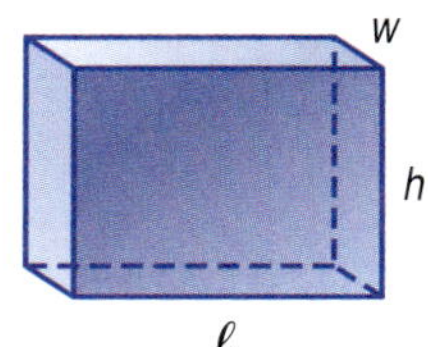

7. Find the surface areas of cubes whose edges are 1 unit, 2 units, and 3 units, and graph the ordered pairs (side length, surface area) on a coordinate plane. Describe the graph.

8. **MAKE A CONJECTURE** Describe what happens to the surface area of a cube as its dimensions are doubled? tripled?

Draw a net for each figure.

9. 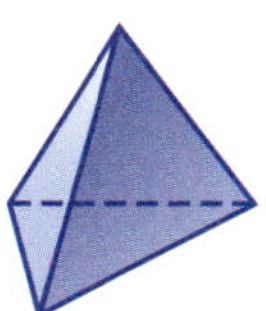

tetrahedron

10. 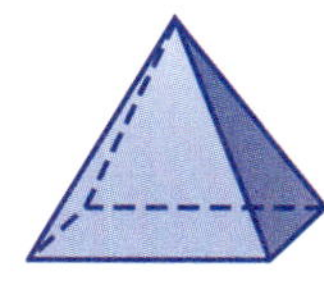

square-based pyramid

11. Explain how the net of a tetrahedron differs from the net of a square-based pyramid.

12. Describe how you could find the surface area of a tetrahedron.

13. Describe how you could find the surface area of a square-based pyramid.

14. Find the surface area of a square-based pyramid if the square base has a side length of 8 centimeters and the height of each triangular side of the pyramid has a height of 5 centimeters.

CHAPTER 11

Mid-Chapter Quiz

Lessons 11-1 through 11-6

Find the area of each parallelogram. Round to the nearest tenth if necessary. (Lesson 11-1)

1. base = 7 cm height = 4 cm
2. base = 4.3 in. height = 9 in.
3. base = $11\frac{3}{4}$ ft height = $8\frac{1}{3}$ ft

4. **MULTIPLE CHOICE** A scale drawing of a deck is shown. What is the actual area of the deck if the scale drawing is 10 m = 1 mm? (Lesson 11-1)

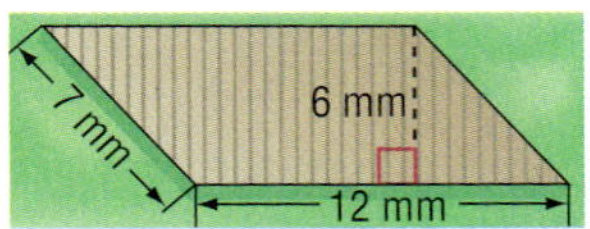

A $7{,}200\ m^2$

B $720\ m^2$

C $720\ mm^2$

D $24\ m^2$

Find the area of each figure. Round to the nearest tenth if necessary. (Lesson 11-2)

5.

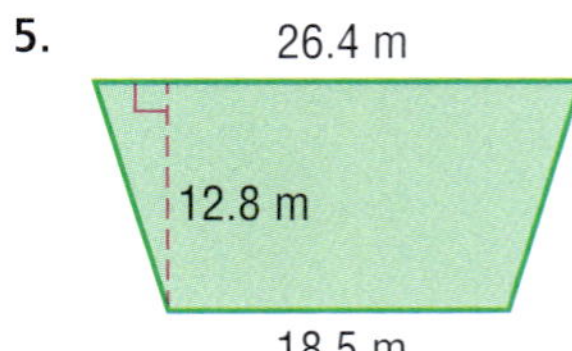

6.

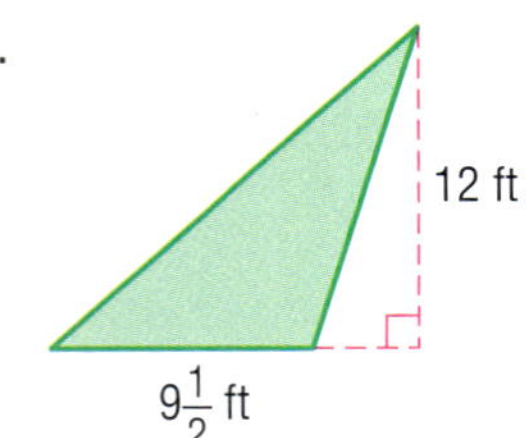

7. **ALGEBRA** Find the area of a triangle with a base of 23 centimeters and a height of 18 centimeters. (Lesson 11-2)

Find the circumference of each circle. Use 3.14 or $\frac{22}{7}$ for π. Round to the nearest tenth if necessary. (Lesson 11-3)

8. radius = $10\frac{7}{8}$ in.
9. diameter = 21 ft

10.

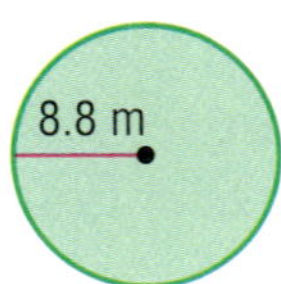

11.

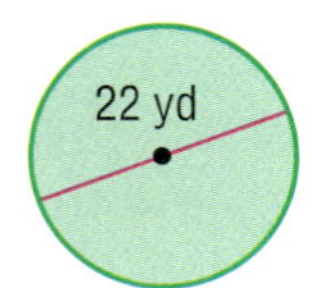

12. **MULTIPLE CHOICE** Which expression could be used to find the circumference of a circular patio table with a diameter of 8.9 feet? (Lesson 11-3)

F $2 \times \pi \times 8.9$

G $\pi \times 8.9$

H $\pi \times 8.9 \times 8.9$

J $\pi \times 4.45 \times 4.45$

Find the area of each circle. Round to the nearest tenth. (Lesson 11-4)

13. radius = $4\frac{1}{4}$ cm
14. diameter = $6\frac{4}{5}$ ft
15. diameter = 14.6 m
16. radius = $7\frac{3}{4}$ yd

17. **SALES** A manager at the local cell phone store reported to his employees that sales had increased 19.5% over last month's total of $25,688. About how much did the store sell this month? Use the *solve a simpler problem* strategy. (Lesson 11-5)

For Exercises 18 and 19, find the area of the shaded region for each figure. (Lesson 11-6)

18.

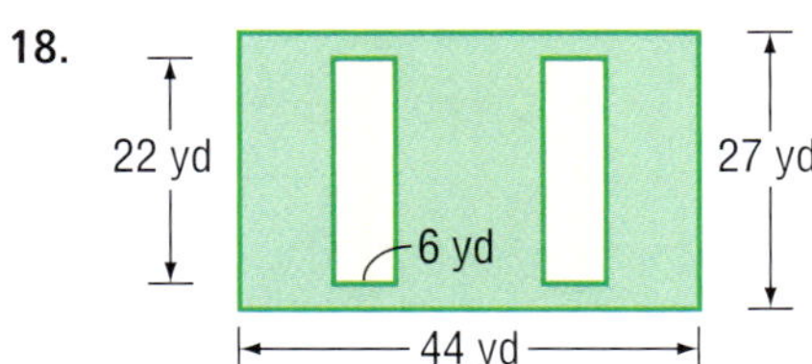

19.

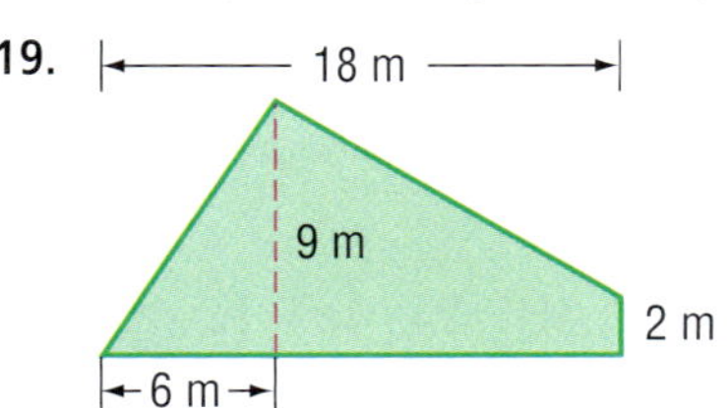

20. **MEASUREMENT** How many square feet of glass is needed to make the window shown? Round to the nearest tenth. (Lesson 11-6)

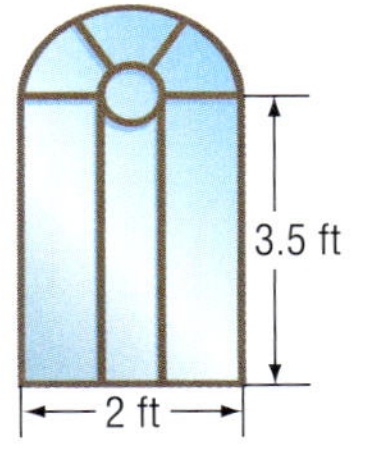

11-7 Three-Dimensional Figures

MAIN IDEA

Build three-dimensional figures given the top, side, and front views.

New Vocabulary

three-dimensional figure
face
edge
lateral face
vertex (vertices)
prism
base
pyramid
cone
cylinder
sphere
center

Math Online

glencoe.com

- Extra Examples
- Personal Tutor
- Self-Check Quiz

GET READY for the Lesson

Study the shape of each common object below.
Then compare and contrast the properties of each object.

Many common shapes are **three-dimensional figures**. That is, they have length, width, and depth (or height). Some terms associated with three-dimensional figures are shown below.

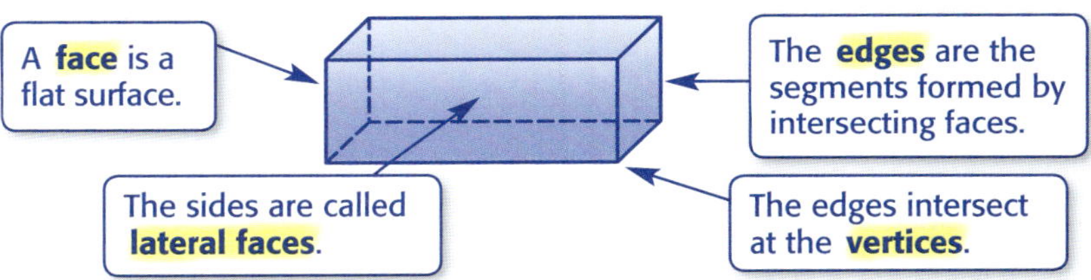

Two types of three-dimensional figures are prisms and pyramids.

Prisms and Pyramids — Key Concept

Figure	Properties
Prism	• Has at least three lateral faces that are parallelograms. • The top and bottom faces, called the **bases**, are congruent parallel polygons. • The shape of the base tells the name of the prism. Rectangular prism · Triangular prism · Square prism or cube
Pyramid	• Has at least three lateral faces that are triangles. • Has only one base, which is a polygon. • The shape of the base tells the name of the pyramid. Triangular pyramid · Square pyramid

Some three-dimensional figures have curved surfaces.

Cones, Cylinders, and Spheres

Key Concept

Figure	Properties
Cone	• Has only one base. • The base is a circle. • Has one vertex.
Cylinder	• Has only two bases. • The bases are congruent circles. • Has no vertices and no edges.
Sphere	• All of the points on a sphere are the same distance from the **center**. • No faces, bases, edges, or vertices.

Study Tip

Three-Dimensional Figures In three-dimensional figures, dashed lines are used to indicate edges that are hidden from view.

Study Tip

Prisms and Pyramids Prisms and pyramids are examples of *polyhedra*, or solids with flat surfaces that are polygonal regions. Cones, cylinders, and spheres are not examples of polyhedra.

EXAMPLES Classify Three-Dimensional Figures

For each figure, identify the shape of the base(s). Then classify the figure.

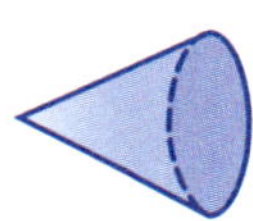

The figure has one circular base, no edge, and one vertex.

The figure is a cone.

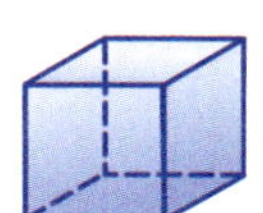

The base and all other faces are squares.

The figure is a square prism or cube.

CHECK Your Progress

a.  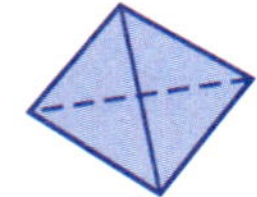

b. 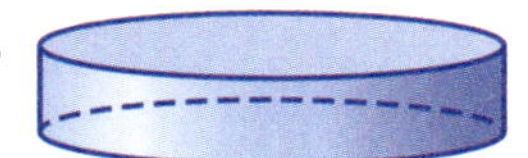

Real-World EXAMPLE

3 CAMERAS Classify the shape of the body of the digital camera, not including the lens, as a three-dimensional figure.

The body of the camera is a rectangular prism.

CHECK Your Progress

c. Classify the shape of the zoom lens as a three-dimensional figure.

Examples 1, 2 (p. 604)

For each figure, identify the shape of the base(s). Then classify the figure.

1. 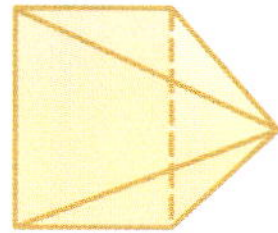

2. 

3. 

Example 3 (p. 604)

4. **SPORTS** An official major league baseball has 108 stitches. Classify the shape of a baseball as a three-dimensional figure.

Practice and Problem Solving

HOMEWORK HELP

For Exercises	See Examples
5–8	1–2
9–10	3

For each figure, identify the shape of the base(s). Then classify the figure.

5. 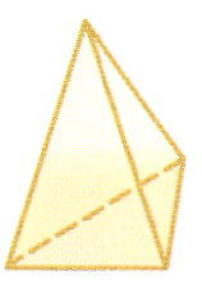

6. 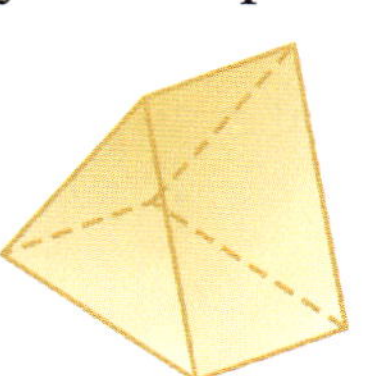

7. 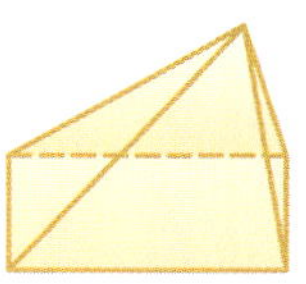

8. 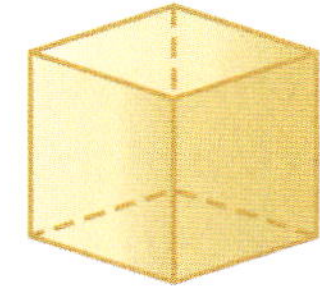

9. **FOOD** What three-dimensional figure describes the item at the right?

10. **SCHOOL SUPPLIES** Classify the shape of your math textbook as a three-dimensional figure.

For each figure, identify the shape of the base(s). Then classify the figure.

11. 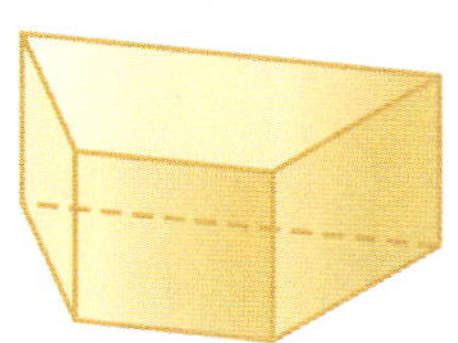

12. 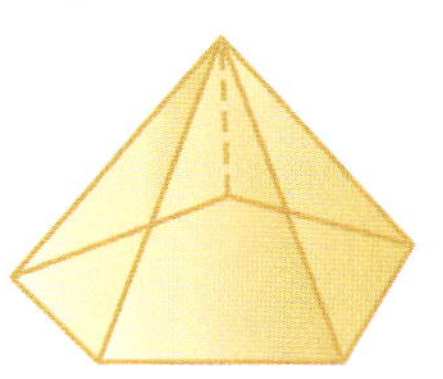

13. 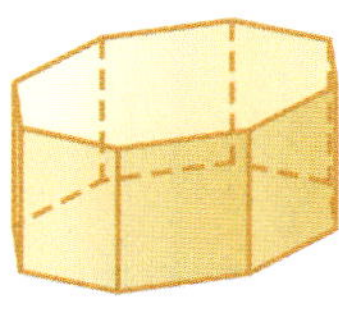

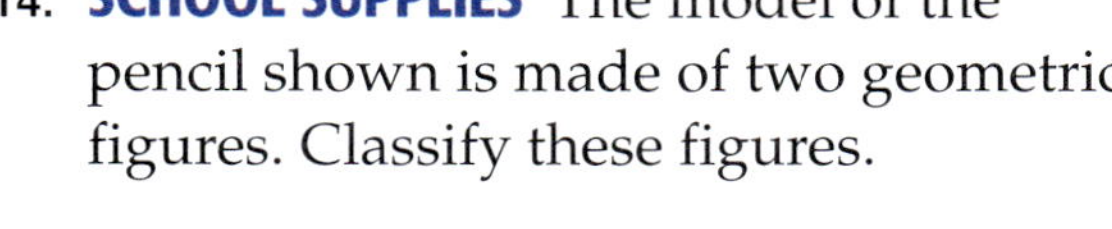

14. **SCHOOL SUPPLIES** The model of the pencil shown is made of two geometric figures. Classify these figures.

15. **HOUSES** The model of the house shown is made of two geometric figures. Classify these figures.

H.O.T. Problems

16. **REASONING** Two sets of figures were sorted according to a certain rule. The figures in Set A follow the rule and the figures in Set B do not follow the rule. Describe the rule.

Set A	Prism	Pyramid	Cube
Set B	Cylinder	Cone	Sphere

17. **CHALLENGE** What figure is formed if only the height of a cube is increased? Draw a figure to justify your answer.

18. **OPEN ENDED** Select one three-dimensional figure in which you could use the term *congruent* to describe the bases of the figure. Then write a sentence using *congruent* to describe the figure.

19. **WRITING IN MATH** Apply what you know about the properties of geometric figures to compare and contrast cones and pyramids.

20. Which statement is true about all triangular prisms?
    - **A** All of the edges are congruent line segments.
    - **B** There are exactly 6 faces.
    - **C** The bases are congruent triangles.
    - **D** All of the faces are triangles.

21. Which figure is shown?
    - **F** triangular pyramid
    - **G** square pyramid
    - **H** rectangular pyramid
    - **J** triangular prism

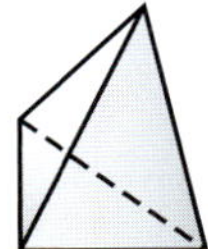

Spiral Review

22. **MEASUREMENT** Find the area of the figure shown at the right if each triangle has a height of 3.5 inches and the square has side lengths of 4 inches. (Lesson 11-6)

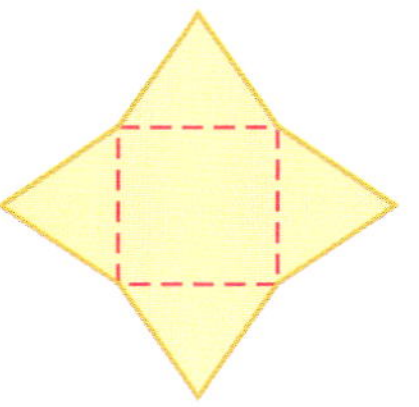

23. **MEASUREMENT** Find the area of a circle with a radius of 5.7 meters. Round to the nearest tenth. (Lesson 11-4)

ALGEBRA Find the missing angle measure in each quadrilateral. (Lesson 10-6)

24. 

25. 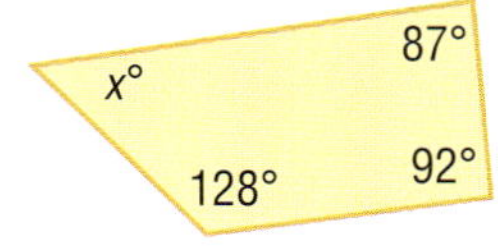

26. 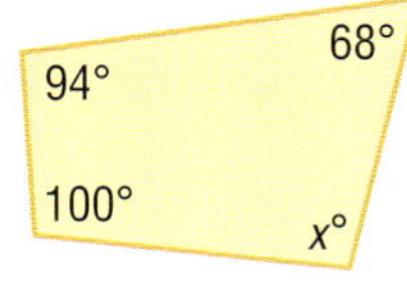

GET READY for the Next Lesson

PREREQUISITE SKILL **Describe the shape seen when each object is viewed from the top.**

27. number cube
28. cereal box
29. soup can

Explore 11-8

Geometry Lab
Three-Dimensional Figures

MAIN IDEA

Build three-dimensional figures given the top, side, and front views.

Cubes are examples of three-dimensional figures because they have length, width, and depth. In this lab, you will use centimeter cubes to build other three-dimensional figures.

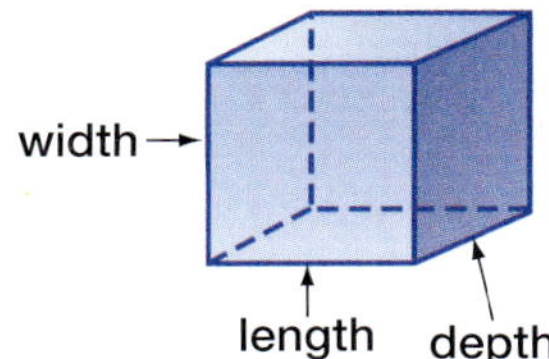

ACTIVITY

The top view, side view, and front view of a three-dimensional figure are shown below. Use centimeter cubes to build the figure. Then make a sketch of the figure.

top

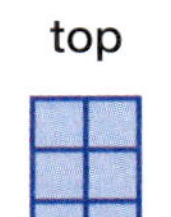

side

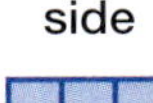

front

STEP 1 Use the top view to build the figure's base.

STEP 2 Use the side view to complete the figure.

STEP 3 Use the front view to check the figure.

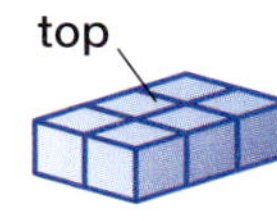

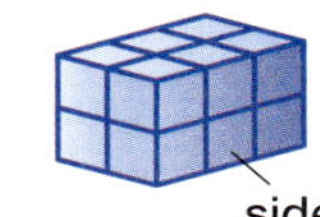

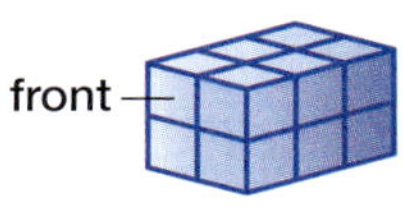

CHECK Your Progress

a. top

side

front

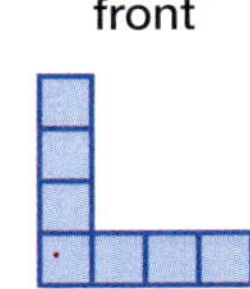

b. top

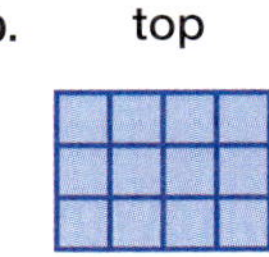

side

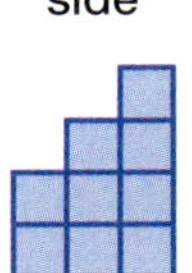

front

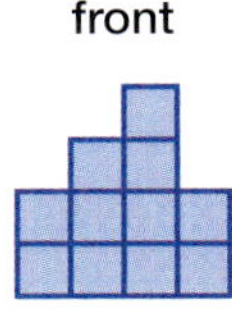

ANALYZE THE RESULTS

1. Explain how you began building the figures in Exercises a and b.
2. Determine whether there is more than one way to build each model. Explain your reasoning.
3. Build two different models that would look the same from two views, but not the third view. Draw a top view, side view, and front view of each model.
4. Describe a real-world situation where it might be necessary to draw a top, side, and front view of a three-dimensional figure.

Drawing Three-Dimensional Figures

MAIN IDEA

Draw a three-dimensional figure given the top, side, and front views.

Math Online

glencoe.com

- Concepts In Motion
- Extra Examples
- Personal Tutor
- Self-Check Quiz

GET READY for the Lesson

MONUMENTS The front view of the Wright Brothers Memorial in Kittyhawk, North Carolina, is shown.

1. Describe the two-dimensional figure(s) that make up the front view.
2. The monument is a three-sided building. Sketch what you think the top view might look like.

You can draw different views of three-dimensional figures. The most common views drawn are the top, side, and front views.

EXAMPLE Draw a Three-Dimensional Figure

1 **Draw a top, a side, and a front view of the figure at the right.**

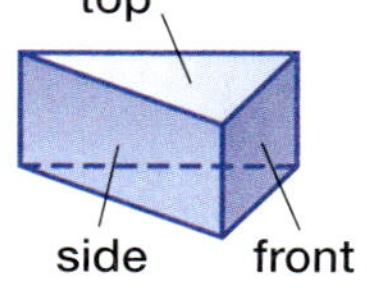

The top view is a triangle.

The side and front view are rectangles.

top

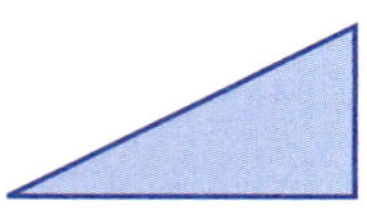

side

front

CHECK Your Progress

Draw a top, a side, and a front view of each solid.

a.

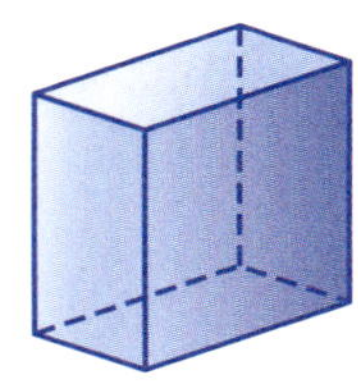

b.

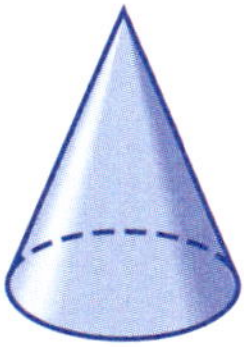

Study Tip

Plane Figures In geometry, three-dimensional figures are solids and two-dimensional figures such as triangles, circles, and squares are plane figures.

Real-World EXAMPLE

2 **VIDEO GAMES** **Draw a top, a side, and a front view of the video console shown.**

The top view is a rectangle.

The side and front views are two rectangles.

CHECK Your Progress

c. **TENTS** Draw a top, a side, and a front view of the tent shown.

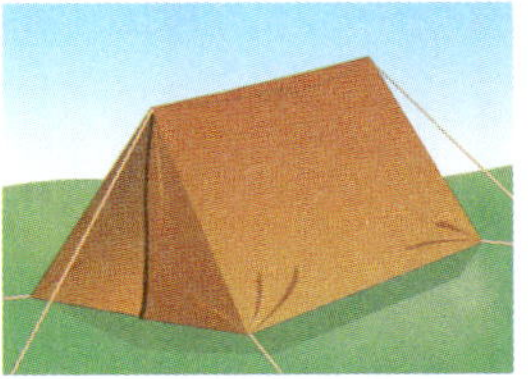

The top, side, and front views of a three-dimensional figure can be used to draw a corner view of the figure.

EXAMPLE Draw a Three-Dimensional Figure

3 **Draw a corner view of the three-dimensional figure whose top, side, and front views are shown.**

top side front

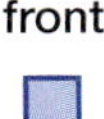

Study Tip

Paper Use isometric dot paper for the drawings in this lesson, as shown at the right.

Step 1 Use the top view to draw the base of the figure, a 1-by-3 rectangle.

Step 2 Add edges to make the base a solid figure.

Step 3 Use the side and front views to complete the figure.

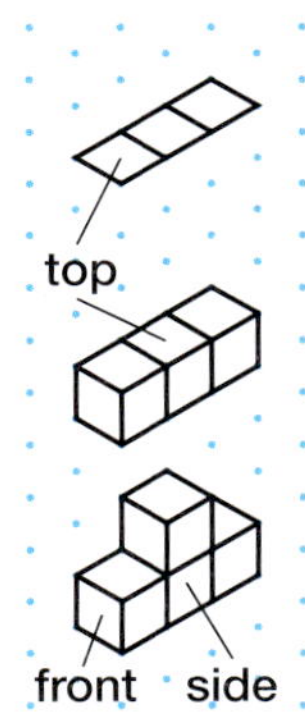

CHECK Your Progress

d. Draw a corner view of the three-dimensional figure whose top, side, and front views are shown.

top side front

CHECK Your Understanding

Example 1 (p. 608)

Draw a top, a side, and a front view of each solid.

1. 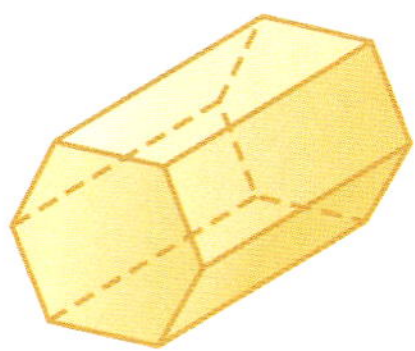

2. 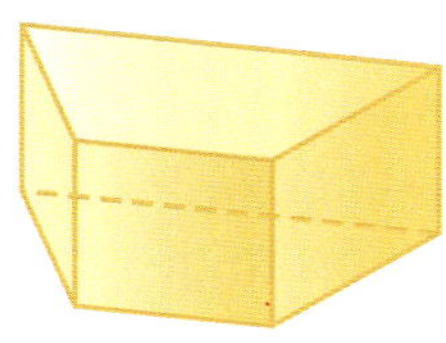

Example 2 (p. 609)

3. **SCIENCE** A transparent prism can be used to refract or disperse a beam of light. Draw a top, a side, and a front view of the prism shown at the right.

Example 3 (p. 609)

4. Draw a corner view of the three-dimensional figure whose top, side, and front views are shown.

top side front

Practice and Problem Solving

HOMEWORK HELP

For Exercises	See Examples
5–10	1
15–16	2
11–14	3

Draw a top, a side, and a front view of each solid.

5. 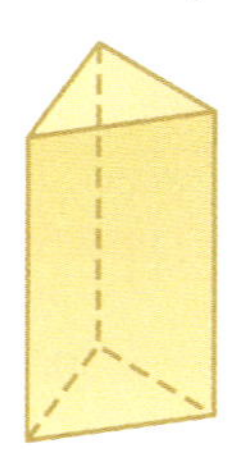

6. 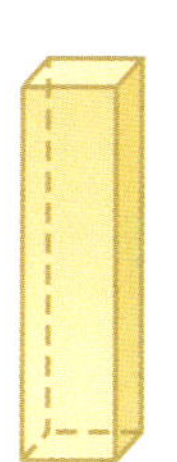

7. 

8. 

9. 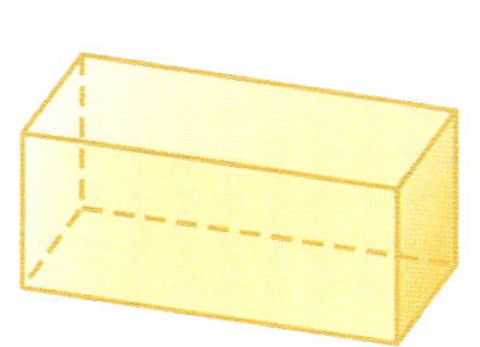

10. 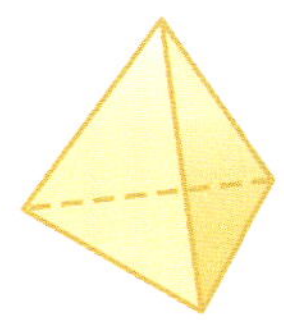

Draw a corner view of each three-dimensional figure whose top, side, and front views are shown. Use isometric dot paper.

11. top side front

12. top side front

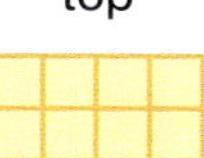

13. top side front

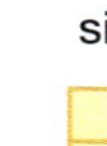

14. top side front

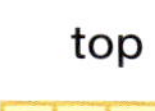

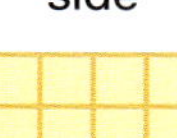

15. **SCHOOL** Draw a top, a side, and a front view of the eraser shown.

16. **TABLES** Draw a top, a side, and a front view of a square table.

Draw a corner view of each three-dimensional figure whose top, side, and front views are shown. Use isometric dot paper.

17. top side front

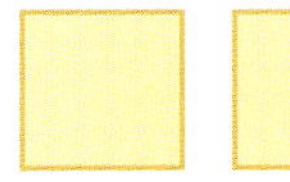

18. top side front

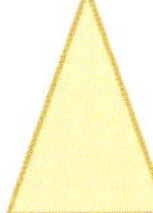
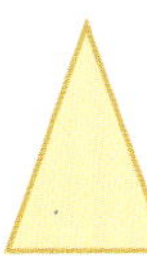

19. **ARCHITECTURE** The Quetzalcoatl pyramid in Mexico is the largest pyramid in the world. Use the photo at the left to sketch views from the top, side, and front of the pyramid.

Real-World Link The Quetzalcoatl pyramid is about 30 meters tall. It was constructed by the Mayans 1000–1200 A.D.
Source: Guinness World Records

20. **RESEARCH** Use the Internet or another source to find a photograph of a United States monument. Draw a top view, a side view, and a front view of the monument.

Draw a top, a side, and a front view of each solid.

21.

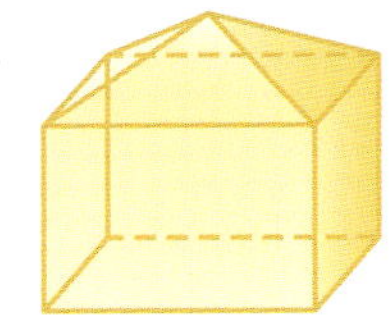

22.

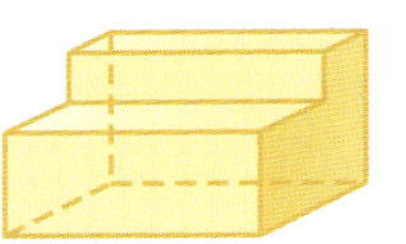

23.

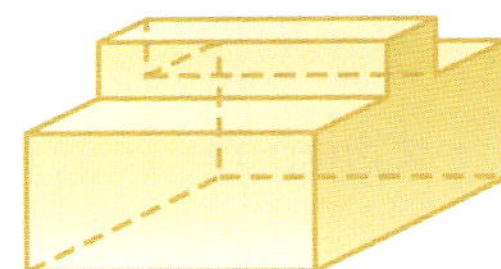

24. **TRANSPORTATION** Sketch views of the top, side, and front of the school bus shown at the right.

H.O.T. Problems

25. **CHALLENGE** Draw a three-dimensional figure in which the front and top views each have a line of symmetry but the side view does not. (*Hint*: Refer to Lesson 10-10 to review line symmetry).

26. **Which One Doesn't Belong?** Identify the figure that does not have the same characteristic as the other three. Explain your reasoning.

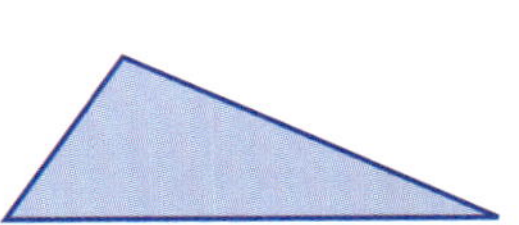
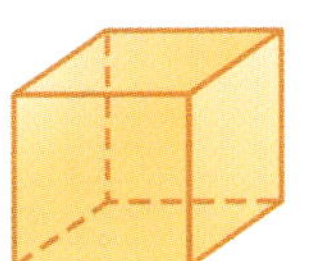

27. **OPEN ENDED** Choose an object in your classroom or in your home. Sketch any view of the object. Choose among a top, a side, or a front view.

28. **WRITING IN MATH** Apply what you have learned about views of three-dimensional figures to write a problem about the bridge shown.

29. The top, side, and front view of a solid figure made of cubes are shown.

top 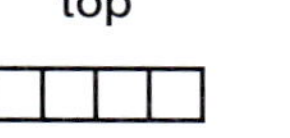

side 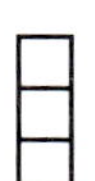

front 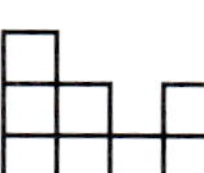

Which solid figure is best represented by these views?

A 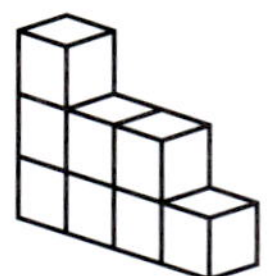

C 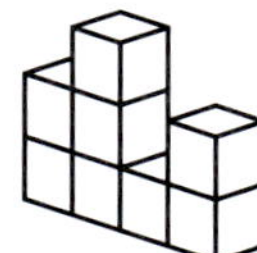

B 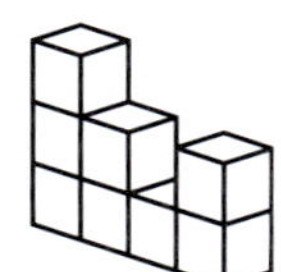

D 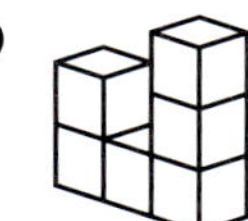

Spiral Review

Classify each figure. (Lesson 11-7)

30. 

31. 

32. 

MEASUREMENT **Find the area of each composite figure. Round to the nearest tenth if necessary.** (Lesson 11-6)

33. 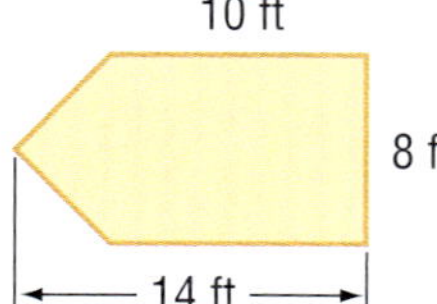

34. 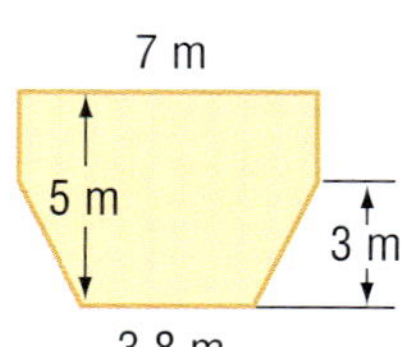

35. 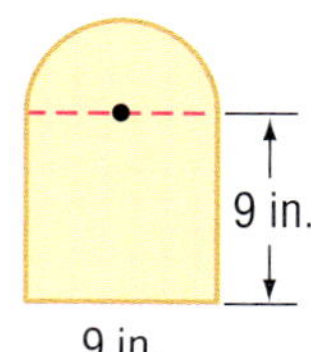

36. **STATISTICS** Jordan buys a soccer ball for \$15, a baseball for \$8, a basketball for \$18, and a football for \$19. Find the mean amount spent. (Lesson 8-2)

37. **SAVINGS** Ernesto deposited \$75 into a savings account earning 4.25% annual interest. What is his balance 9 months later if he makes no withdrawals and no more deposits? Round to the nearest cent. (Lesson 7-8)

GET READY for the Next Lesson

PREREQUISITE SKILL **Multiply.** (Lesson 5-5)

38. $7\frac{1}{2} \cdot 6$

39. $8 \cdot 2\frac{3}{4}$

40. $\frac{5}{6} \cdot 1\frac{4}{5}$

41. $10\frac{1}{5} \cdot 6\frac{2}{3}$

11-9 Volume of Prisms

MAIN IDEA

Find the volumes of rectangular and triangular prisms.

New Vocabulary

volume
rectangular prism
triangular prism

Math Online

glencoe.com

- Extra Examples
- Personal Tutor
- Self-Check Quiz
- Reading in the Content Area

MINI Lab

- On a piece of grid paper, cut out a square that is 10 centimeters on each side.
- Cut a 1-centimeter square from each corner. Fold the paper and tape the corners together to make a box.

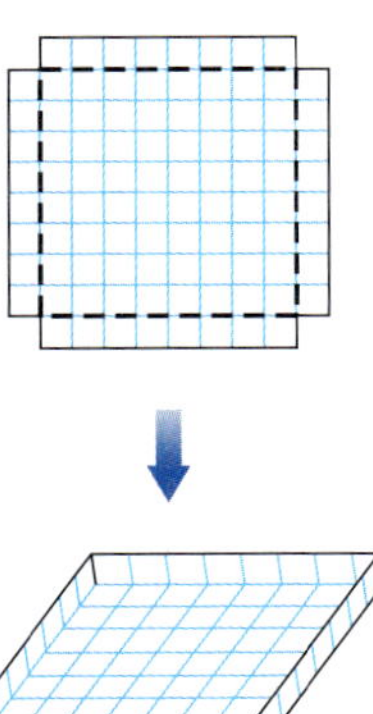

1. What is the area of the base, or bottom, of the box? What is the height of the box?
2. How many centimeter cubes fit in the box?
3. What do you notice about the product of the base area and the height of the box?

The **volume** of a three-dimensional figure is the measure of space occupied by it. It is measured in cubic units such as cubic centimeters (cm^3) or cubic inches (in^3). The volume of the figure at the right can be shown using cubes.

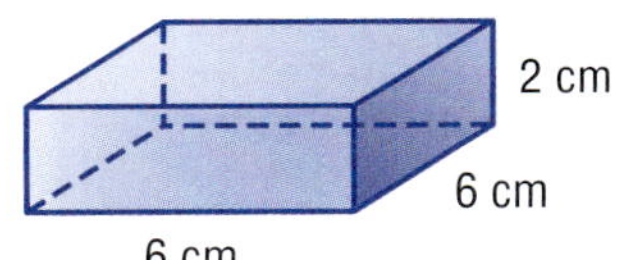

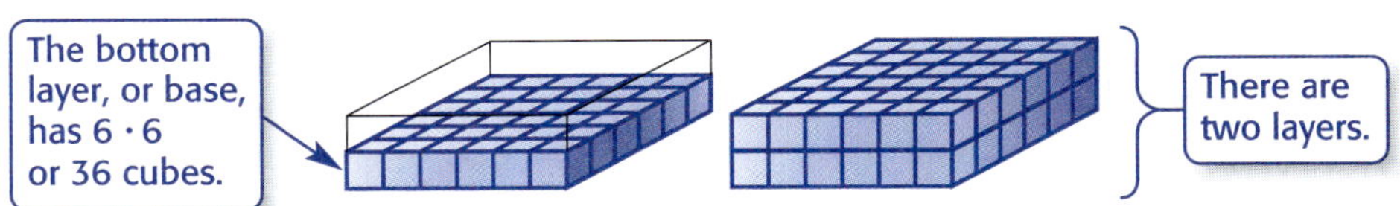

It takes 36 · 2 or 72 cubes to fill the box. So, the volume of the box is 72 cubic centimeters.

The figure above is a rectangular prism. A **rectangular prism** is a prism that has rectangular bases.

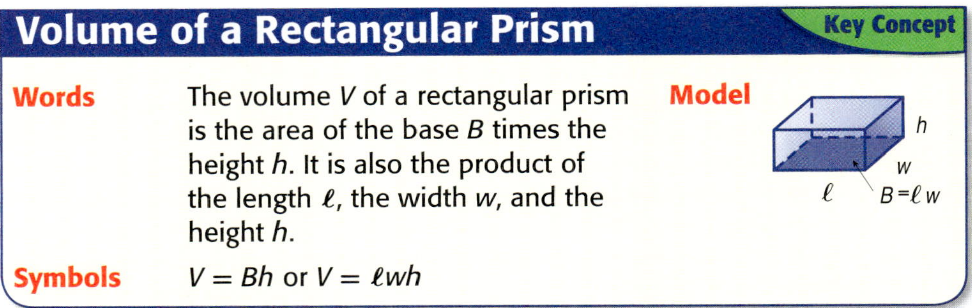

Volume of a Rectangular Prism — Key Concept

Words The volume V of a rectangular prism is the area of the base B times the height h. It is also the product of the length ℓ, the width w, and the height h.

Model

Symbols $V = Bh$ or $V = \ell wh$

You can use the formula $V = Bh$ or $V = \ell wh$ to find the volume of a rectangular prism.

EXAMPLE Volume of a Rectangular Prism

1 **Find the volume of the rectangular prism.**

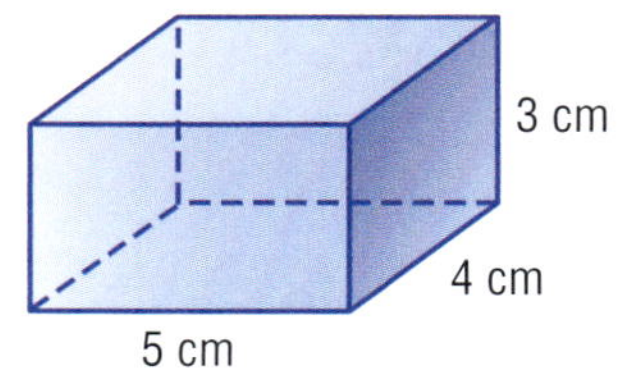

$V = \ell wh$	Volume of a prism
$V = 5 \cdot 4 \cdot 3$	$\ell = 5$, $w = 4$, and $h = 3$
$V = 60$	Multiply.

The volume is 60 cubic centimeters or 60 cm^3.

CHECK Your Progress

a. Find the volume of the rectangular prism at the right.

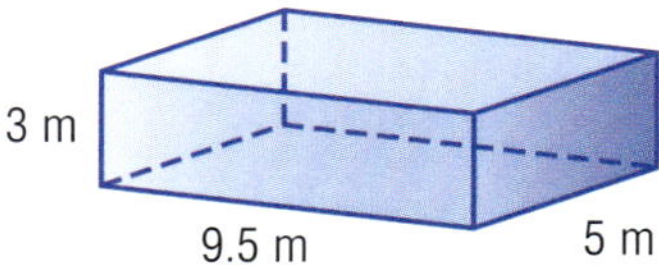

Real-World Career . . . .
How Does a Market Researcher Use Math?
Market researchers use tools such as statistics, surveys, focus groups, and product tests to determine what influences people to buy a product.

Math Online
For more information, go to glencoe.com.

Real-World EXAMPLE

2 **MARKETING** **A company needs to decide which size lunch box to manufacture. Which lunch box shown will hold more food?**

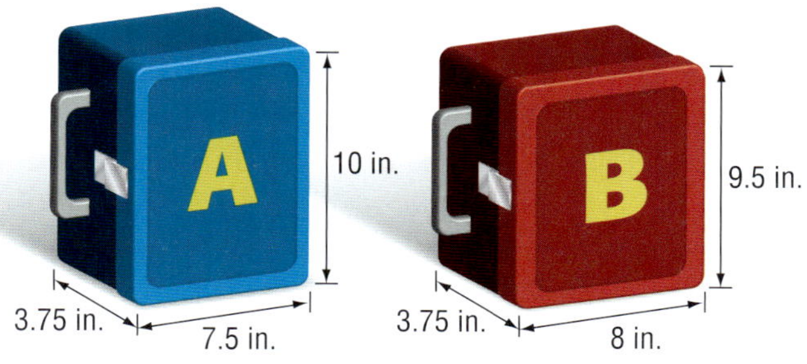

Find the volume of each lunch box. Then compare.

Lunch Box A

$V = \ell wh$	Volume of a rectangular prism
$V = 7.5 \cdot 3.75 \cdot 10$	$\ell = 7.5$, $w = 3.75$, and $h = 10$
$V = 281.25 \text{ in}^3$	Multiply.

Lunch Box B

$V = \ell wh$	Volume of a rectangular prism
$V = 8 \cdot 3.75 \cdot 9.5$	$\ell = 8$, $w = 3.75$, and $h = 9.5$
$V = 285 \text{ in}^3$	Multiply.

Since $285 \text{ in}^3 > 281.25 \text{ in}^3$, Lunch Box B will hold more food.

CHECK Your Progress

b. **PACKAGING** A movie theater serves popcorn in two different container sizes. Which container holds more popcorn? Justify your answer.

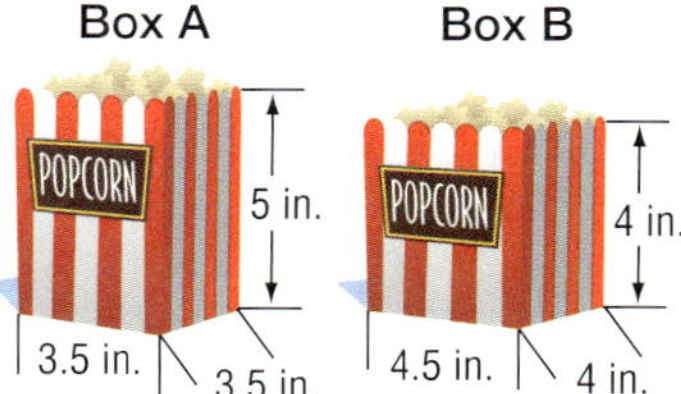

Study Tip

Height Do not confuse the height of the triangular base with the height of the prism.

A **triangular prism** is a prism that has triangular bases. The diagram below shows that the volume of a triangular prism is also the product of the area of the base B and the height h of the prism.

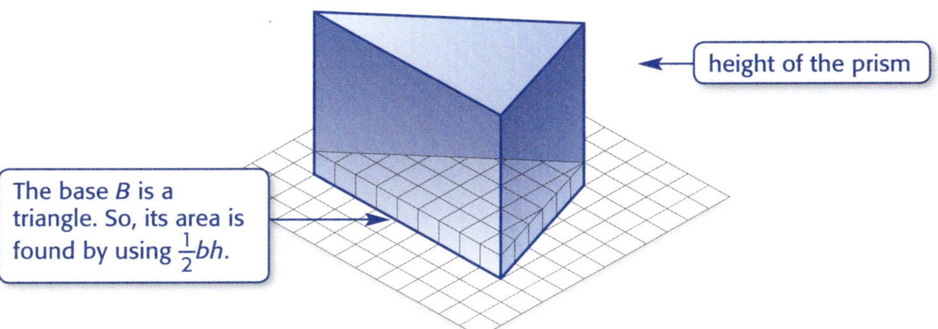

Volume of a Triangular Prism

Key Concept

Words The volume V of a triangular prism is the area of the base B times the height h.

Symbols $V = Bh$

Model

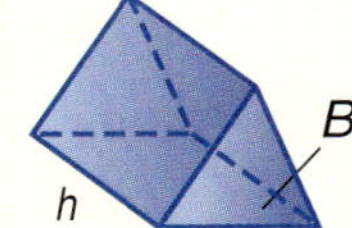

EXAMPLE Volume of a Triangular Prism

Study Tip

Base Before finding the volume of a prism, identify the base. In Example 3, the base is a triangle so you replace B with $\frac{1}{2}bh$.

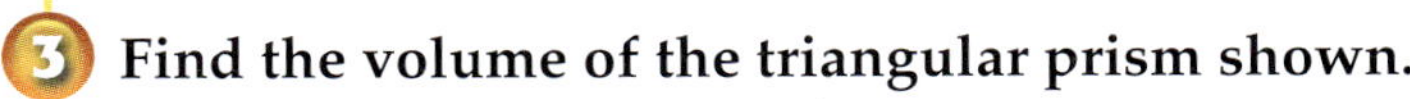

3 **Find the volume of the triangular prism shown.**

The area of the triangle is $\frac{1}{2} \cdot 6 \cdot 8$ so replace B with $\frac{1}{2} \cdot 6 \cdot 8$.

6 ft, 8 ft, 9 ft

$V = Bh$	Volume of a prism
$V = \left(\frac{1}{2} \cdot 6 \cdot 8\right)h$	Replace B with $\frac{1}{2} \cdot 6 \cdot 8$.
$V = \left(\frac{1}{2} \cdot 6 \cdot 8\right)9$	The height of the prism is 9.
$V = 216$	Multiply.

The volume is 216 cubic feet or 216 ft^3.

CHECK Your Progress

Find the volume of each triangular prism.

c.

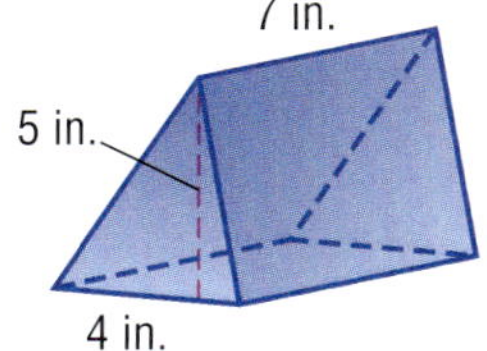

d. 6 mm, 5.2 mm, 3 mm

CHECK Your Understanding

Example 1 (p. 614)

Find the volume of each prism. Round to the nearest tenth if necessary.

1. 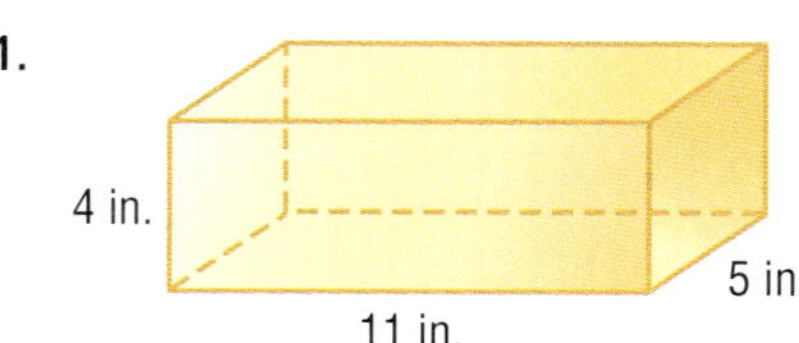

2. 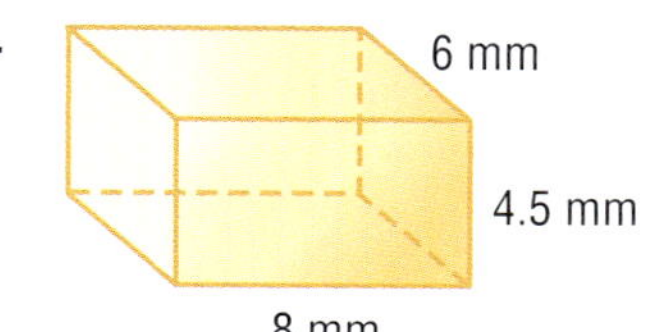

Example 3 (p. 615)

3. 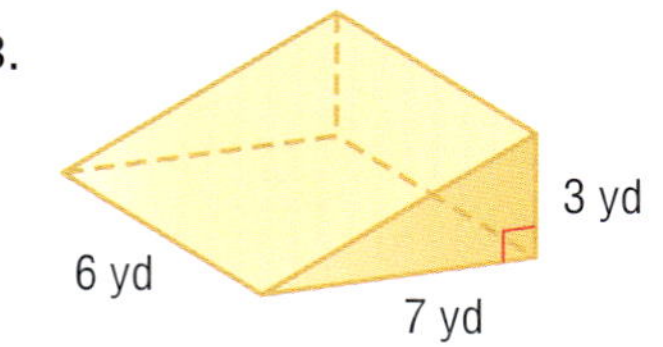

4. 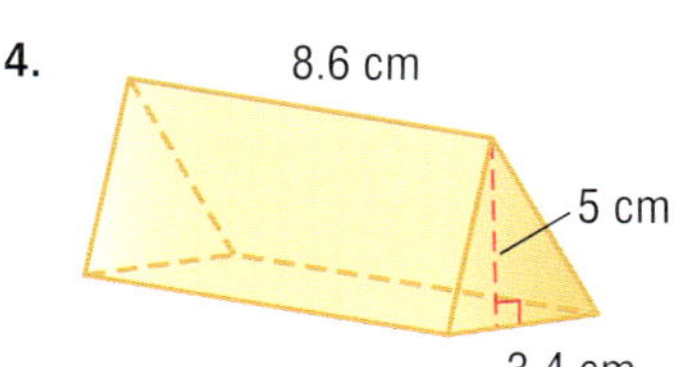

Example 2 (p. 614)

5. **STORAGE** One cabinet measures 3 feet by 2.5 feet by 5 feet. A second measures 4 feet by 3.5 feet by 4.5 feet. Which cabinet has the greater volume?

Practice and Problem Solving

HOMEWORK HELP

For Exercises	See Examples
6–9	1
14–15	2
10–13	3

Find the volume of each prism. Round to the nearest tenth if necessary.

6. 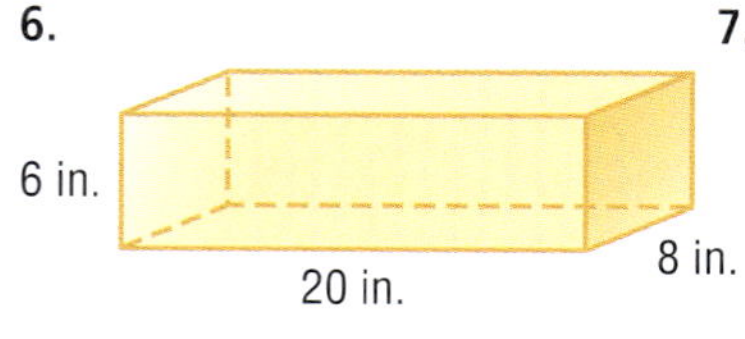

7. 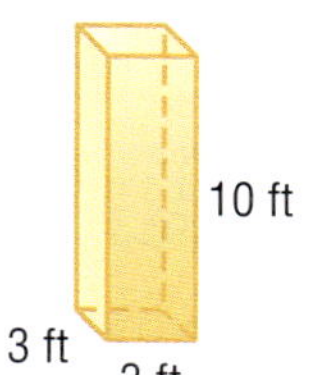

8. 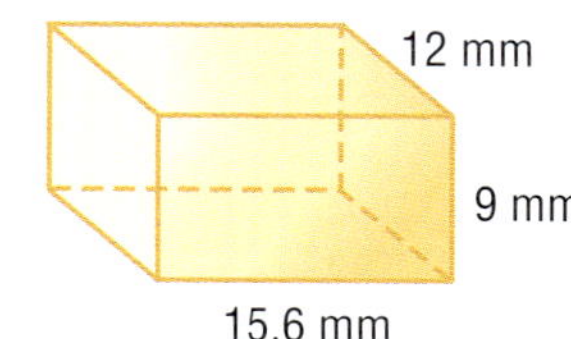

9. 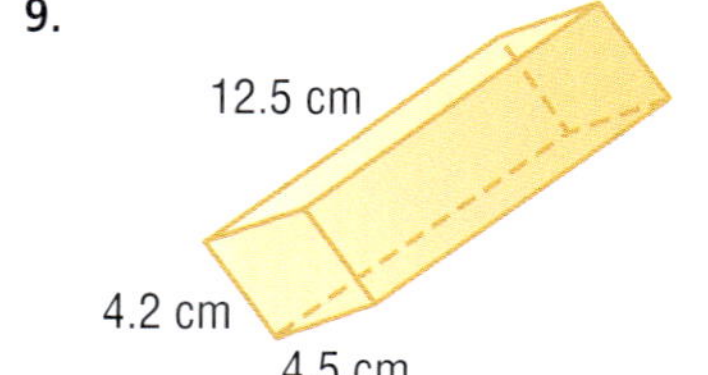

10. 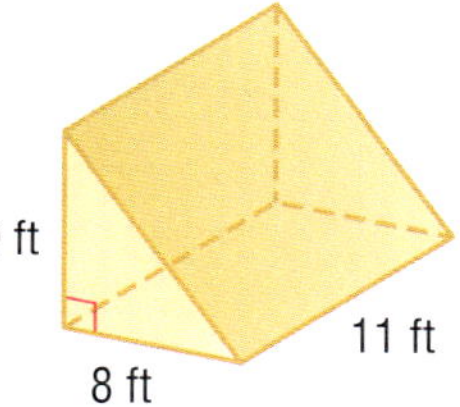

11. 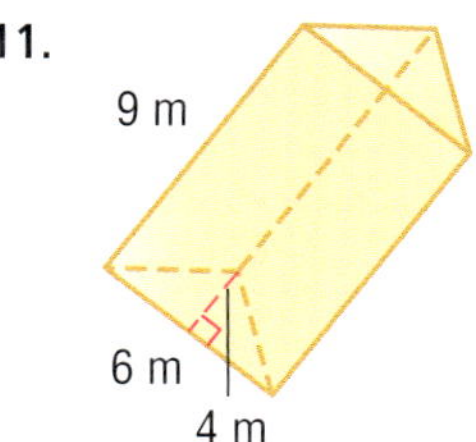

12. 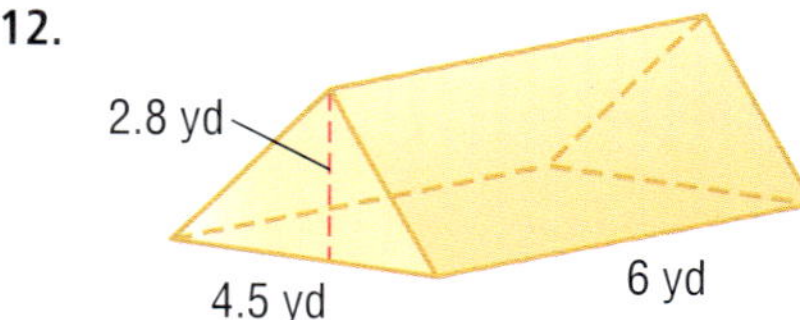

13. 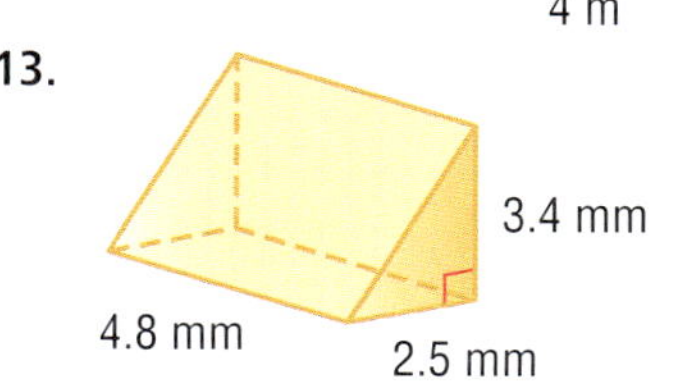

14. **PACKAGING** A soap company sells laundry detergent in two different containers. Which container holds more detergent? Justify your answer.

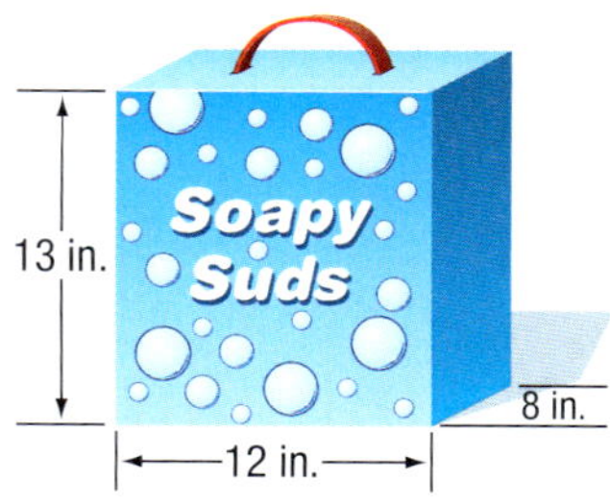

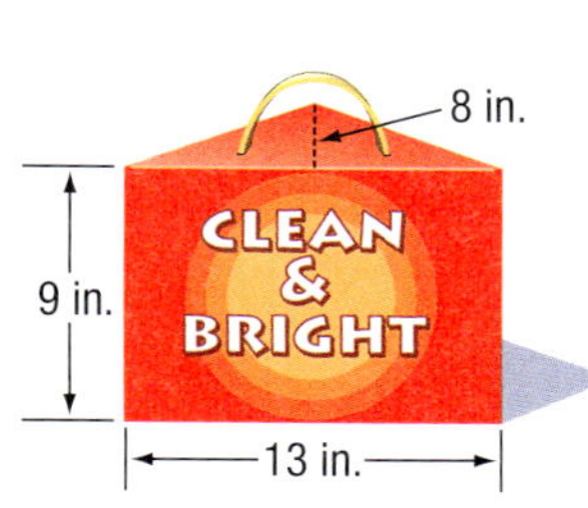

Real-World Math The Flatiron Building in New York City resembles a triangular prism.

15. **TOYS** A toy company makes rectangular sandboxes that measure 6 feet by 5 feet by 1.2 feet. A customer buys a sandbox and 40 cubic feet of sand. Did the customer buy too much or too little sand? Justify your answer.

Find the volume of each prism.

16. 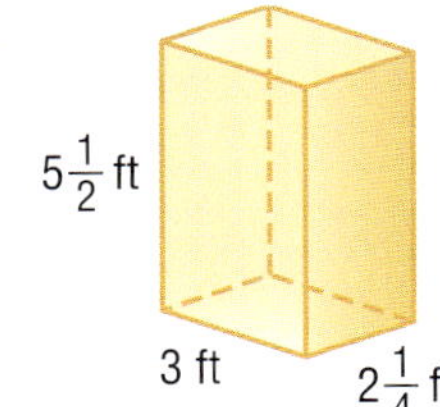

17. 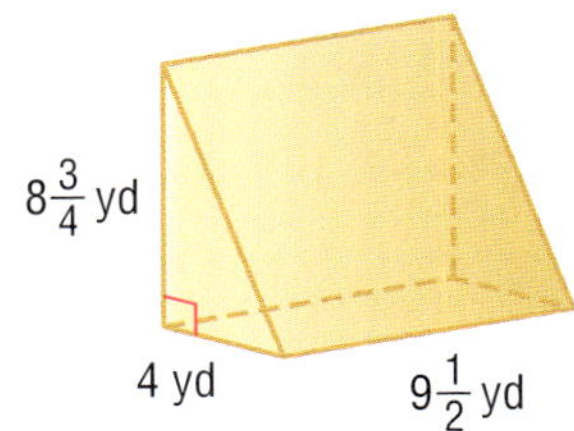

18. 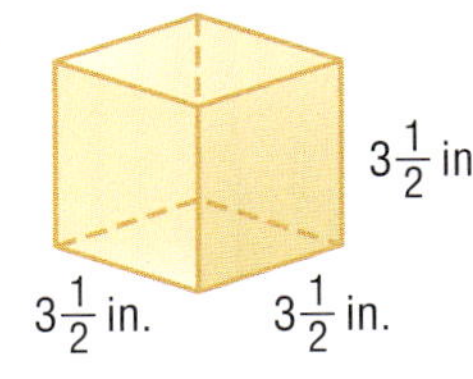

ARCHITECTURE For Exercises 19 and 20, use the diagram at the right that shows the approximate dimensions of the Flatiron Building in New York City.

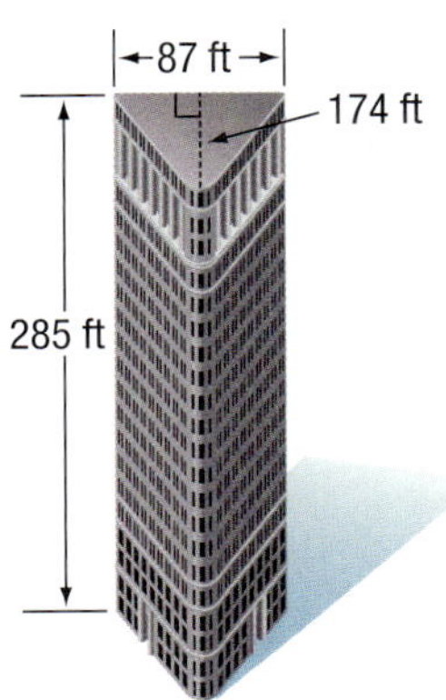

19. What is the approximate volume of the Flatiron Building?

20. The building is a 22-story building. Estimate the volume of each story.

21. **ALGEBRA** The base of a rectangular prism has an area of 19.4 square meters and a volume of 306.52 cubic meters. Write an equation that can be used to find the height h of the prism. Then find the height of the prism.

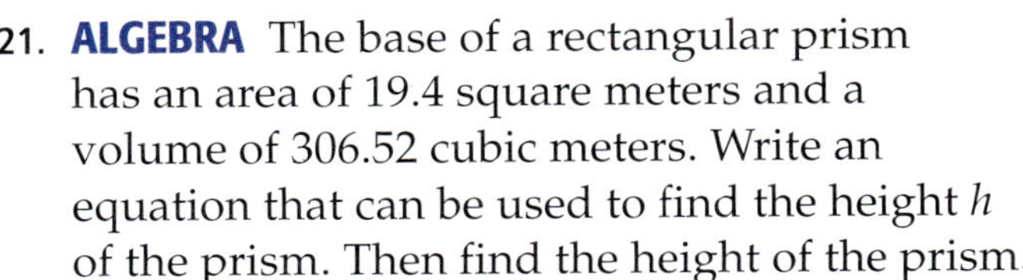

ESTIMATION Estimate to find the approximate volume of each prism.

22. 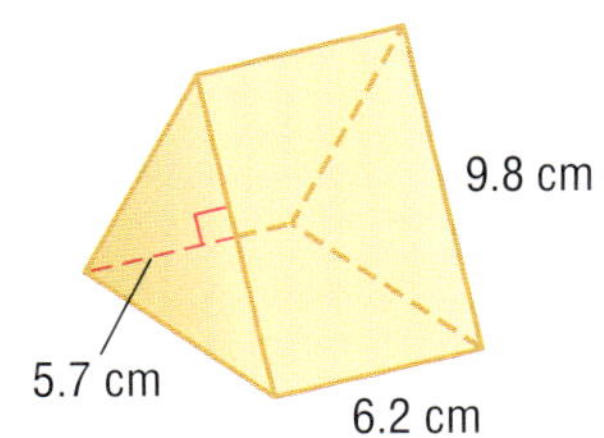

23. 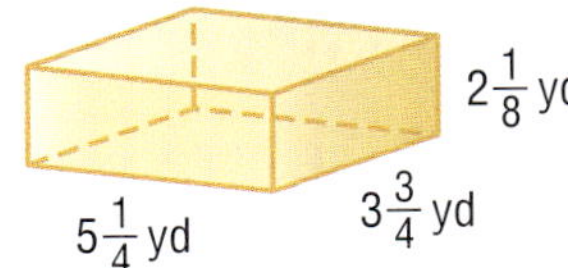

24. **MONEY** The diagram shows the dimensions of an office. It costs about 11¢ per year to air condition one cubic foot of space. On average, how much does it cost to air condition the office for one month?

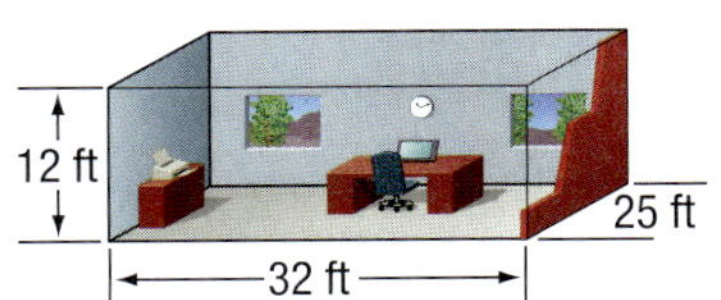

25. **MEASUREMENT** The Garrett family is building a pool in the shape of a rectangular prism in their backyard. The pool will cover an area 18 feet by 25 feet and will hold 2,700 cubic feet of water. If the pool is equal depth throughout, find that depth.

See pages 700, 714.

H.O.T. Problems

26. **CHALLENGE** How many cubic inches are in a cubic foot?

27. **REASONING** Two rectangular prisms are shown at the right. When the dimensions of Prism A are doubled, does the volume also double? Explain your reasoning.

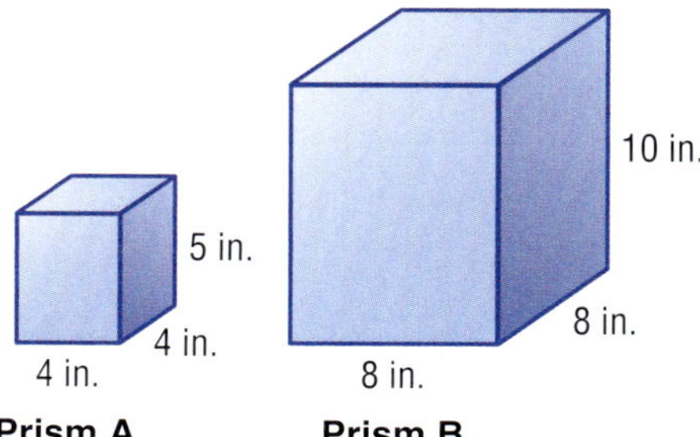

28. **WRITING IN MATH** Explain the similarities and differences in finding the volume of a rectangular prism and a triangular prism.

TEST PRACTICE

29. A fish aquarium is shown below.

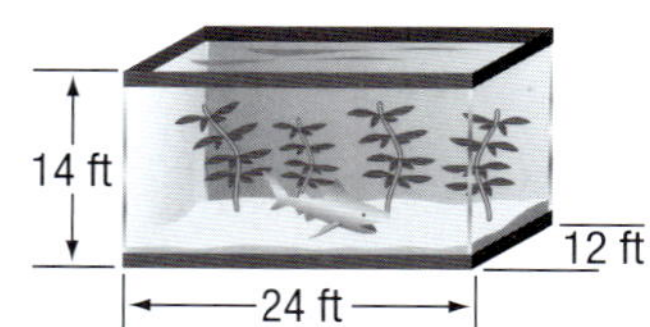

What is the volume of the aquarium?

A 168 ft^3 **C** 2,016 ft^3

B 342 ft^3 **D** 4,032 ft^3

30. Use a ruler to measure the dimensions of the paper clip box in centimeters.

Which is closest to the volume of the box?

F 1.5 cm^3 **H** 4.5 cm^3

G 2.5 cm^3 **J** 5.5 cm^3

Spiral Review

31. **GEOMETRY** The top, side, and front view of a three-dimensional figure are shown at the right. Draw a corner view of the figure. (Lesson 11-8)

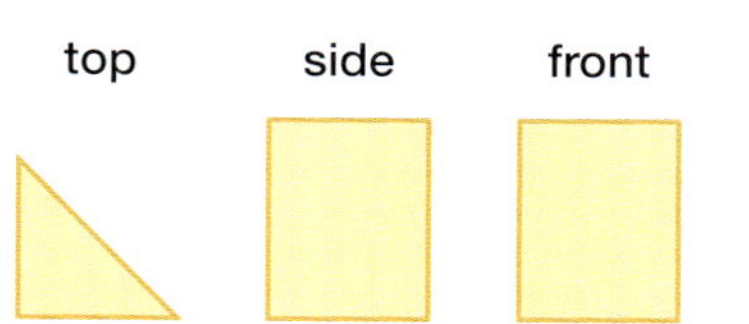

For each figure, identify the shape of the base(s). Then classify the figure. (Lesson 11-7)

32. 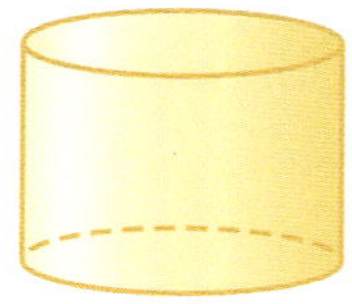

33. 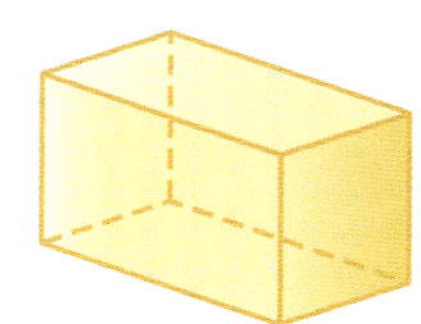

34. 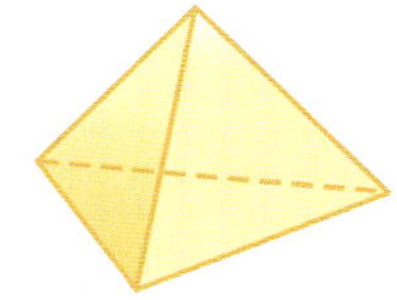

35. **RATES** A car travels 180 miles in 3.6 hours. What is the average rate of speed in miles per hour? (Lesson 6-2)

GET READY for the Next Lesson

PREREQUISITE SKILL **Estimate.** (page 674)

36. $3.14 \cdot 6$

37. $5 \cdot 2.7^2$

38. $9.1 \cdot 8.3$

39. $3.1 \cdot 1.75^2 \cdot 2$

11-10 Volume of Cylinders

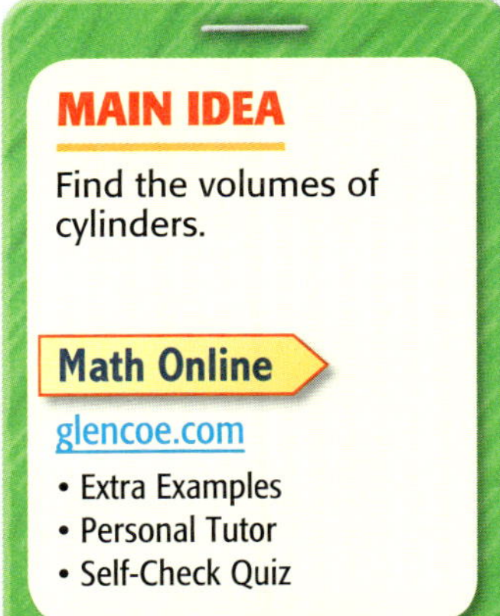

MAIN IDEA

Find the volumes of cylinders.

Math Online

glencoe.com

- Extra Examples
- Personal Tutor
- Self-Check Quiz

MINI Lab

Set a vegetable can on a piece of grid paper and trace around the base, as shown at the right.

1. Estimate the number of centimeter cubes that would fit at the bottom of the can. Include parts of cubes.
2. If each layer is 1 centimeter high, how many layers would it take to fill the cylinder?

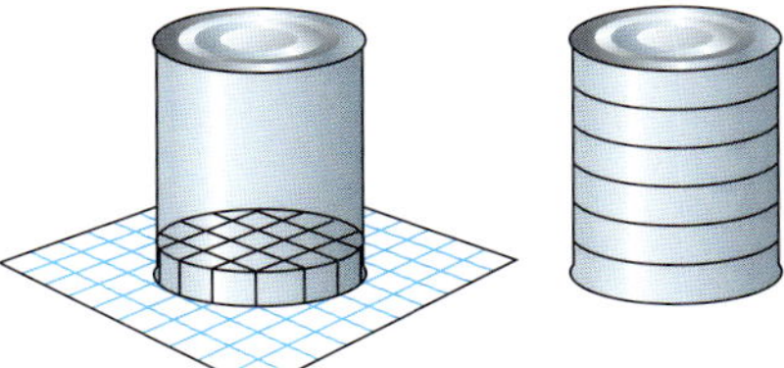

3. **MAKE A CONJECTURE** How can you find the volume of the can?

As with prisms, the area of the base of a cylinder tells the number of cubic units in one layer. The height tells how many layers there are in the cylinder.

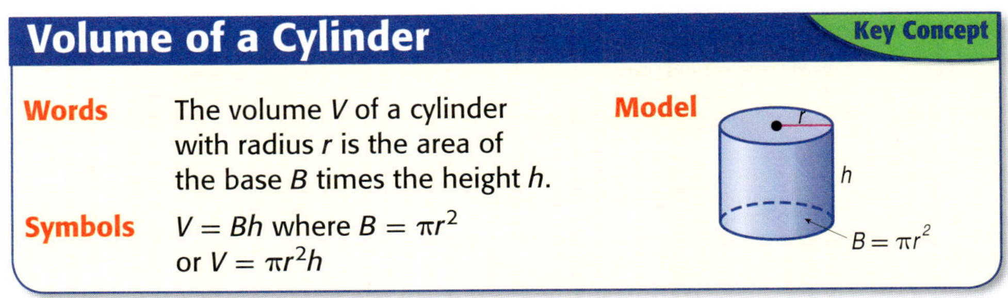

Volume of a Cylinder

Key Concept

Words The volume V of a cylinder with radius r is the area of the base B times the height h.

Symbols $V = Bh$ where $B = \pi r^2$ or $V = \pi r^2 h$

Model

EXAMPLE Find the Volume of a Cylinder

1 **Find the volume of the cylinder. Round to the nearest tenth.**

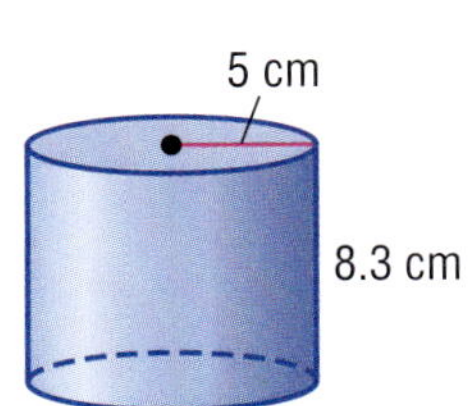

$V = \pi r^2 h$ Volume of a cylinder

$V = \pi(5)^2(8.3)$ Replace r with 5 and h with 8.3.

Use a calculator.

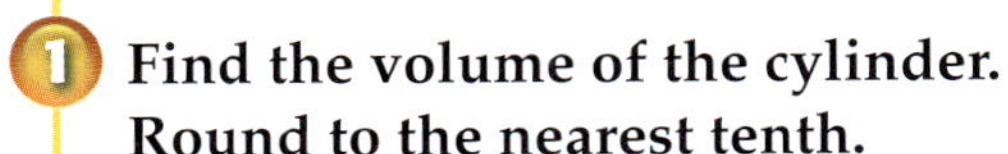

[2nd] [π] [X] 5 [x^2] [ENTER] 651.8804756

The volume is about 651.9 cubic centimeters.

CHECK Your Progress

Find the volume of each cylinder. Round to the nearest tenth.

a. 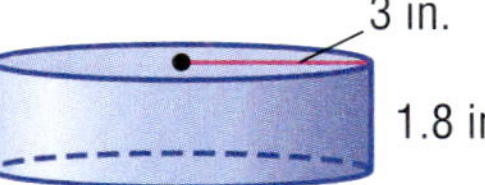

b. 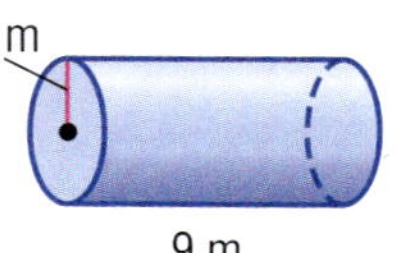

Real-World EXAMPLE

Study Tip

Circles Recall that the radius is half the diameter.

2 WEATHER The decorative rain gauge shown has a height of 13 centimeters and a diameter of 3 centimeters. How much water can the rain gauge hold?

$V = \pi r^2 h$ Volume of a cylinder

$V = \pi(1.5)^2 13$ Replace r with 1.5 and h with 13.

$V \approx 91.9$ Simplify.

The rain gauge can hold about 91.9 cubic centimeters.

CHECK Your Progress

c. **PAINT** Find the volume of a cylinder-shaped paint can that has a diameter of 4 inches and a height of 5 inches.

CHECK Your Understanding

Find the volume of each cylinder. Round to the nearest tenth.

Example 1 (pp. 619–620)

1. 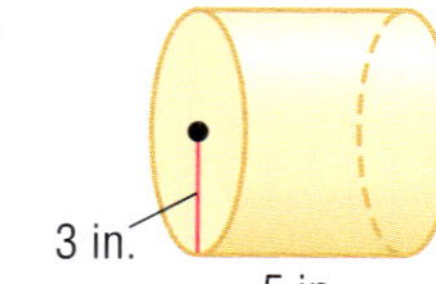

2. 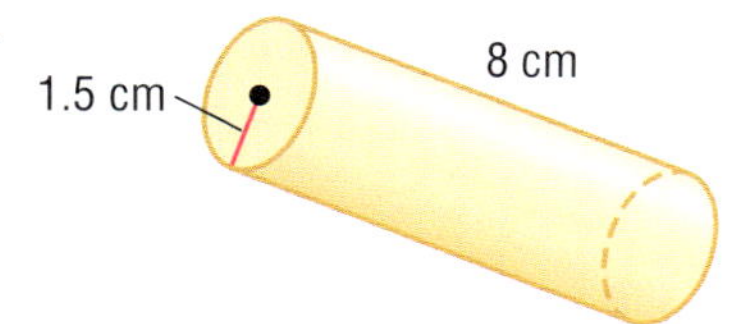

3. 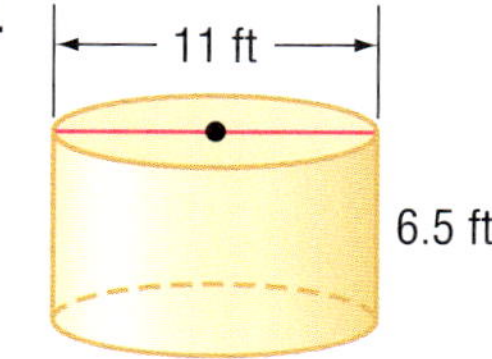

Example 2 (p. 620)

4. **CONTAINERS** A can of concentrated orange juice has the dimensions shown at the right. Find the volume of the can of orange juice to the nearest tenth.

5. **CANDLES** A scented candle is in the shape of a cylinder. The radius is 4 centimeters and the height is 12 centimeters. Find the volume of the candle.

Practice and Problem Solving

HOMEWORK HELP	
For Exercises	See Examples
6–10	1
16–17	2

Find the volume of each cylinder. Round to the nearest tenth.

6.
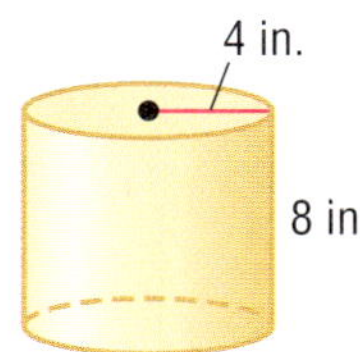

7.
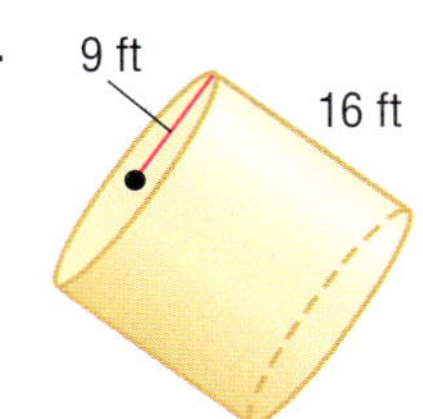

8.
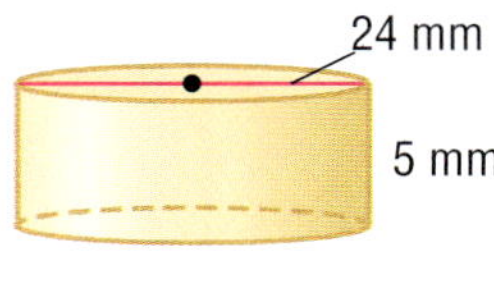

9.
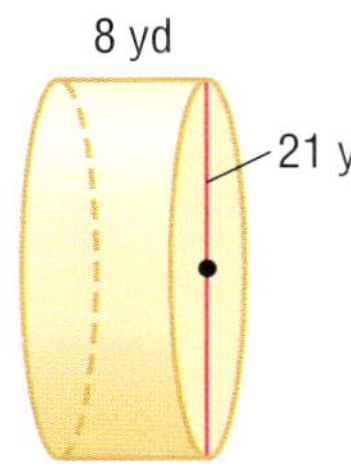

10.
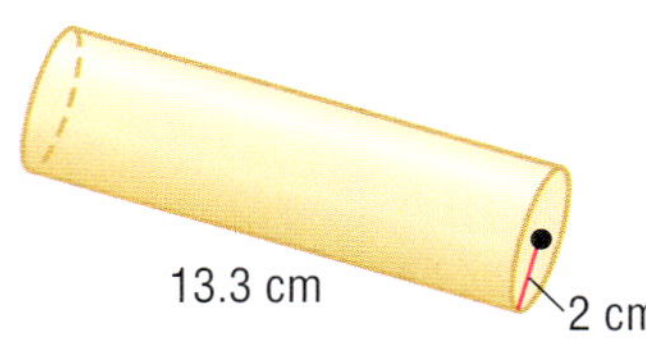

11.
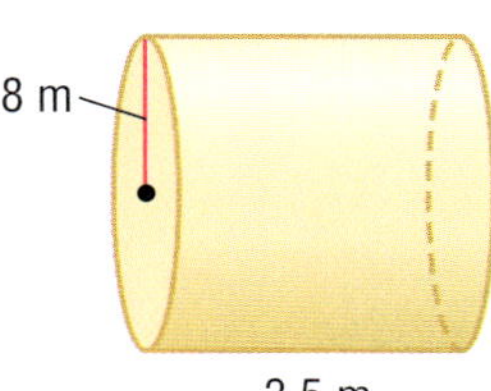

12. diameter = 15 mm
height = 4.8 mm

13. diameter = 4.5 m
height = 6.5 m

14. radius = 6 ft
height = $5\frac{1}{3}$ ft

15. radius = $3\frac{1}{2}$ in.
height = $7\frac{1}{2}$ in.

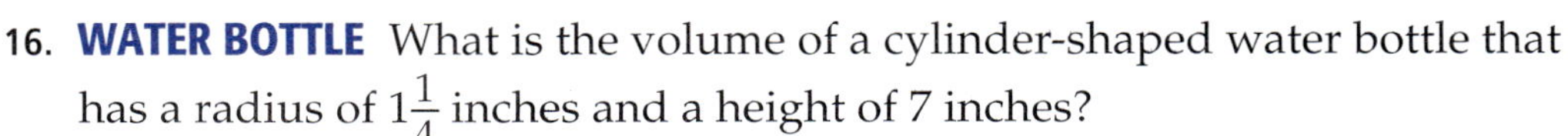

16. **WATER BOTTLE** What is the volume of a cylinder-shaped water bottle that has a radius of $1\frac{1}{4}$ inches and a height of 7 inches?

17. **BIRDS** A cylinder-shaped bird feeder has a diameter of 4 inches and a height of 18 inches. How much bird seed can the feeder hold?

Real-World Link Bird feeders can attract many species of birds. There are over 800 species of birds in North America.

Find the volume of each cylinder. Round to the nearest tenth.

18.
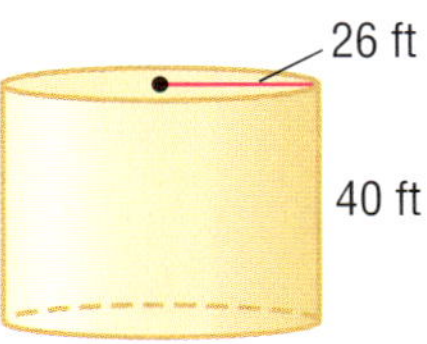

19.
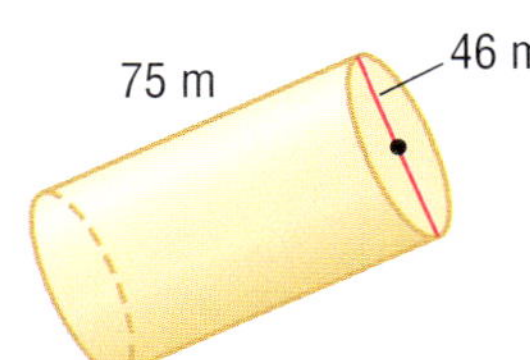

20.
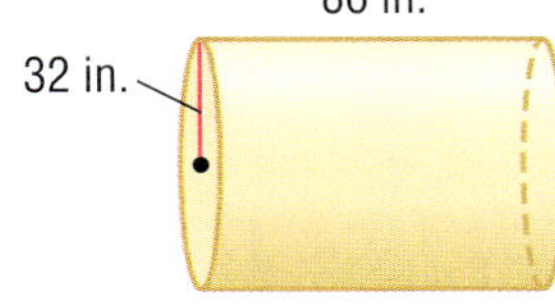

ESTIMATION Match each cylinder with its approximate volume.

21. radius = 4.1 ft, height = 5 ft
22. diameter = 8 ft, height = 2.2 ft
23. diameter = 6.2 ft, height = 3 ft
24. radius = 2 ft, height = 3.8 ft

a. 91 ft^3
b. 48 ft^3
c. 111 ft^3
d. 264 ft^3

25. **POTTERY** A vase in the shape of a cylinder has a diameter of 11 centimeters and a height of 250 millimeters. Find the volume of the vase to the nearest cubic centimeter. Use 3.14 for π.

26. **BAKING** Which will hold more cake batter, the rectangular pan or the two round pans? Explain.

27. **ALGEBRA** Cylinder A has a radius of 4 inches and a height of 2 inches. Cylinder B has a radius of 2 inches. What is the height of Cylinder B if both cylinders have the same volume?

ANALYZE TABLES For Exercises 28 and 29, use the table at the right and the following information.

The volume, using 3.14 for π, of four cylinders is shown at the right.

Radius (cm)	Height (cm)	Volume $(cm)^3$
2	4	50.24
4	8	401.92
8	16	3,215.36
16	32	25,722.88

28. Describe how the radius and the height increase for each successive cylinder.

EXTRA PRACTICE
See pages 701, 714.

29. As the radius and the height increase, how does the volume of each cylinder increase?

H.O.T. Problems

30. **CHALLENGE** Two equal-size sheets of construction paper are rolled along the length and along the width, as shown. Which cylinder do you think has the greater volume? Explain.

31. **OPEN ENDED** Draw and label a cylinder that has a larger radius, but less volume than the cylinder shown at the right.

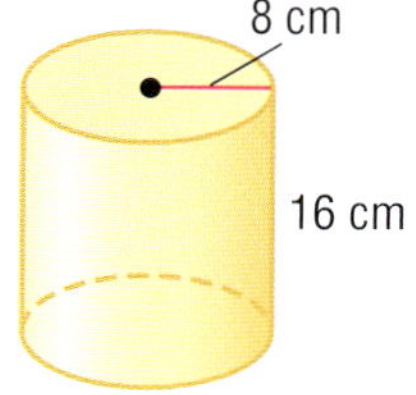

32. **NUMBER SENSE** What is the ratio of the volume of a cylinder to the volume of a cylinder having twice the height but the same radius?

33. **NUMBER SENSE** Suppose cylinder A has the same height but twice the radius of cylinder B. What is the ratio of the volume of cylinder B to cylinder A?

34. **WRITING IN MATH** Explain how the formula for the volume of a cylinder is similar to the formula for the volume of a rectangular prism.

TEST PRACTICE

35. The oatmeal container shown has a diameter of $3\frac{1}{2}$ inches and a height of 9 inches.

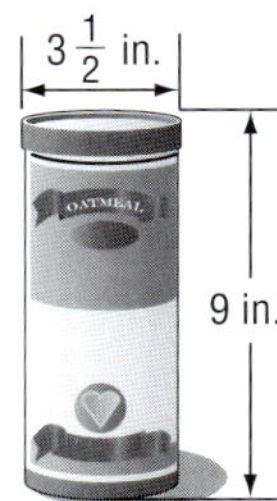

Which is closest to the number of cubic inches it will hold when filled?

A 32 **C** 75.92

B 42.78 **D** 86.55

36. Which statement is true about the volumes of the cylinders shown?

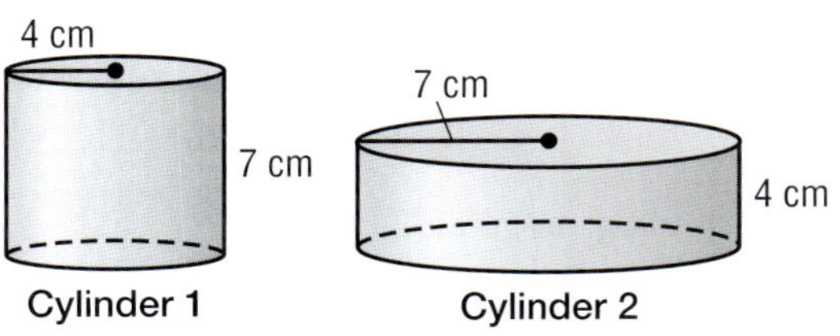

F The volume of cylinder 1 is greater than the volume of cylinder 2.

G The volume of cylinder 2 is greater than the volume of cylinder 1.

H The volumes are equal.

J The volume of cylinder 1 is twice the volume of cylinder 2.

Spiral Review

37. MEASUREMENT Find the volume of a rectangular prism with a length of 6 meters, a width of 4.9 meters, and a height of 5.2 meters. (Lesson 11-9)

Draw a corner view of each three-dimensional figure using the top, side, and front views shown. (Lesson 11-8)

38. top 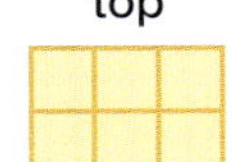 side 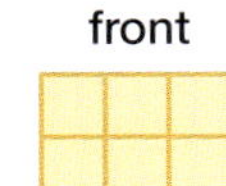 front

39. top 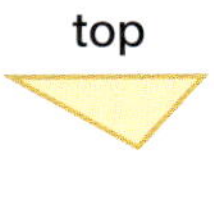 side  front

PROBABILITY A coin is tossed and a number cube is rolled. Find the probability of each of the following. (Lesson 9-8)

40. P(heads and 4)

41. P(tails and an odd number)

42. P(heads and *not* 5)

43. P(*not* tails and not 2)

44. TEST SCORES The list gives the scores on a recent history test. Find each measure of central tendency and range. Round to the nearest tenth if necessary. Then state which measure best represents the data. Explain your reasoning. (Lesson 8-2)

History Test Scores									
78	92	83	88	89	91	96	72	74	99
81	88	86	95	73	97	78	78	60	
84	85	90	92	98	74	76	80	83	

Graphing Calculator Lab
Graphing Geometric Relationships

MAIN IDEA

Use technology to graph data in order to demonstrate geometric relationships.

In this lab, you will use a TI-83/84 Plus graphing calculator to analyze geometric relationships among the base, height, and area of several parallelograms.

ACTIVITY

STEP 1 Draw five parallelograms that each have a height of 4 centimeters on centimeter grid paper.

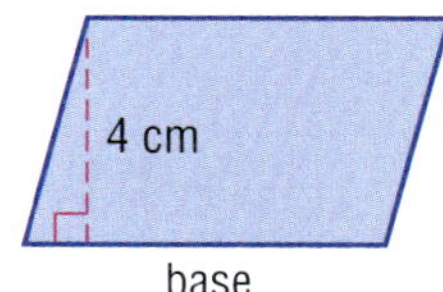

STEP 2 Copy and complete the table shown for each parallelogram.

Base (cm)	Height (cm)	Area (cm^2)
	4	
	4	
	4	
	4	
	4	

STEP 3 Next enter the data into your graphing calculator. Press STAT 1 and enter the length of each base in L1. Then enter the area of each parallelogram in L2.

STEP 4 Turn on the statistical plot by pressing 2nd [STAT PLOT] ENTER ENTER. Select the scatter plot and enter or confirm L1 as the Xlist and L2 as the Ylist.

STEP 5 Graph the data by pressing ZOOM 9. Use the Trace feature and the left and right arrow keys to move from one point to another.

Analyze the Results

1. What does an ordered pair on your graph represent?
2. Sketch and describe the shape of the graph.
3. **MAKE A CONJECTURE** Write an equation for your graph. Check your equation by pressing Y=, entering your equation into Y1, and then pressing Graph. What does this equation mean?
4. As the length of the base of the parallelogram increases, what happens to its area? Does this happen at a constant rate? How can you tell this from the table? from the graph?

Study Tip

Proportions Activity 2 is an example of an *inverse proportion* since the product of the length and width remains constant. You studied inverse proportions in Extend 6-6.

ACTIVITY

2 **STEP 1** Draw five rectangles that each have an area of 36 square centimeters on centimeter grid paper. The length should be greater than or equal to its width.

$A = 36 \text{ cm}^2$
width
length

STEP 2 Copy and complete the table shown for each rectangle.

Base (cm)	Height (cm)	Area (cm^2)
		36
		36
		36
		36
		36

STEP 3 Clear list L1 and L2 by pressing STAT 4 2nd [L1], 2nd [L2] ENTER. Then press STAT 1 and enter the length of each rectangle in L1 and the width of each rectangle in L2.

STEP 4 Follow Steps 4 and 5 of Activity 1 to graph the data.

Analyze the Results

5. What does an ordered pair on your graph represent?

6. Sketch and describe the shape of the graph.

7. **MAKE A CONJECTURE** Write an equation for your graph. Use the calculator to graph and check your equation. What does this equation mean?

8. As the length of the rectangle increases, what happens to its width? Does this happen at a constant rate? How can you tell this from the table? from the graph?

9. **MAKE A PREDICTION** Draw five cubes with different edge lengths. Predict the shape of the graph of the relationship between the edge length and volume of the cube.

10. Create a table to record the edge length and volume of each cube. Then graph the data to show the relationship between the edge length and volume of the cube. Sketch and describe the shape of the graph.

11. **MAKE A CONJECTURE** Write an equation for your graph. Use the calculator to graph and check your equation. What does this equation mean?

12. If the length of the cube's edge doubles, what happens to the volume? Explain.

CHAPTER 11 Study Guide and Review

Math Online glencoe.com
- STUDY TO GO
- Vocabulary Review

GET READY to Study

Be sure the following Big Ideas are noted in your Foldable.

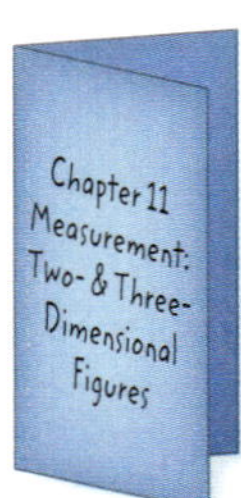

BIG Ideas

Area (Lessons 11-1, 11-2, and 11-6)

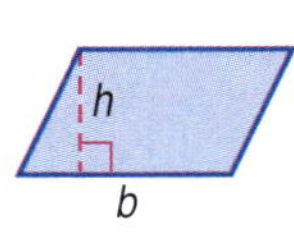

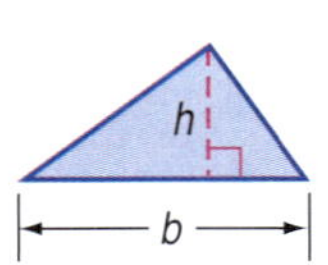

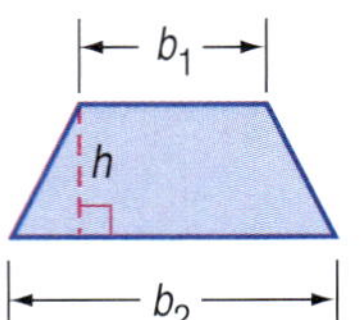

parallelogram	triangle	trapezoid
$A = bh$	$A = \frac{1}{2}bh$	$A = \frac{1}{2}h(b_1 + b_2)$

Circles (Lessons 11-3 and 11-4)

- circumference
  $C = \pi d$ or $C = 2\pi r$
- area
  $A = \pi r^2$

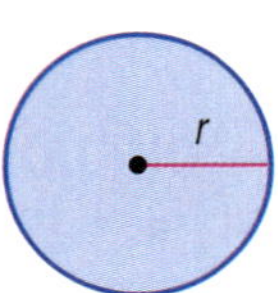

Volume (Lessons 11-9 and 11-10)

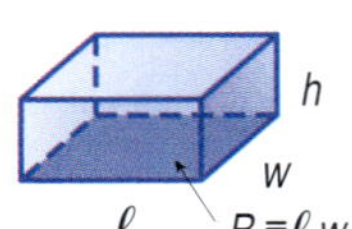

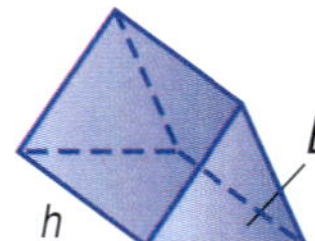

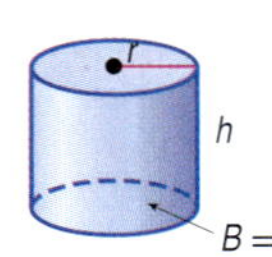

rectangular prism, triangular prism: $V = Bh$

cylinder: $V = Bh$ or $\pi r^2 h$

Key Vocabulary

base (p. 572)
center (p. 584)
circle (p. 584)
circumference (p. 584)
composite figure (p. 596)
cone (p. 604)
cylinder (p. 604)
diameter (p. 584)
edge (p. 603)
face (p. 603)
height (p. 572)
lateral face (p. 603)
π (pi) (p. 584)
prism (p. 603)
pyramid (p. 603)
radius (p. 584)
rectangular prism (p. 613)
sector (p. 590)
semicircle (p. 596)
sphere (p. 604)
three-dimensional figure (p. 603)
triangular prism (p. 615)
vertex (p. 603)
volume (p. 613)

Vocabulary Check

Choose the correct term or number to complete each sentence.

1. A (rectangular prism, rectangle) is a three-dimensional figure that has three sets of parallel congruent sides.
2. The (volume, surface area) of a three-dimensional figure is the measure of the space occupied by it.
3. $A = \frac{1}{2}h(b_1 + b_2)$ is the formula for the area of a (triangle, trapezoid).
4. Volume is measured in (square, cubic) units.
5. A (cylinder, prism) is a three-dimensional figure that has two congruent, parallel circles as its bases.
6. The volume of a rectangular prism is found by (adding, multiplying) the length, the width, and the height.
7. The formula for the area of a (square, circle) is $A = \pi r^2$.

Lesson-by-Lesson Review

11-1 Area of Parallelograms (pp. 572–576)

Find the area of each parallelogram. Round to the nearest tenth if necessary.

8. 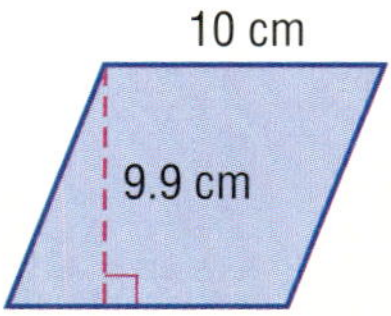

9. 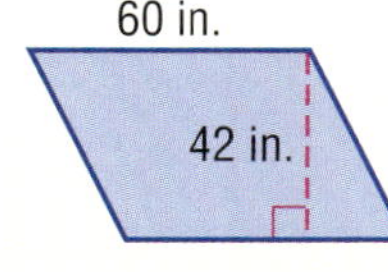

10. **ALGEBRA** A parallelogram has an area of 57 square inches. Find the base of the parallelogram if the height is 6 inches.

Example 1 **Find the area of a parallelogram if the base is 15 inches and the height is 8 inches.**

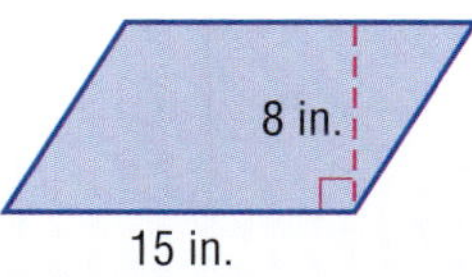

$A = bh$ Area of a parallelogram

$A = 15 \cdot 8$ Replace b with 15 and h with 8.

$A = 120 \text{ in}^2$. Multiply.

11-2 Area of Triangles and Trapezoids (pp. 578–582)

Find the area of each figure. Round to the nearest tenth if necessary.

11. 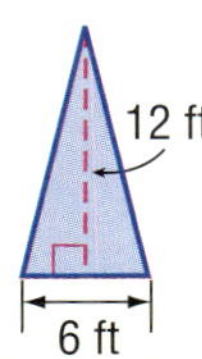

12. 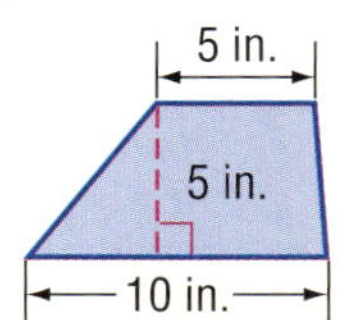

13. trapezoid: bases 22 yd and 35 yd height 18.5 yd

14. **ALGEBRA** The area of a triangle is 26.9 square inches. If the base is 9.6 inches, what is the height of the triangle?

Example 2 **Find the area of a triangle with a base of 8 meters and a height of 11.2 meters.**

$A = \frac{1}{2}bh$ Area of a triangle

$A = \frac{1}{2}(8)(11.2)$ or 44.8 m^2 $b = 8, h = 11.2$

Example 3 **Find the area of the trapezoid.**

$A = \frac{1}{2}h(b_1 + b_2)$

$A = \frac{1}{2}(3)(2 + 10)$ $h = 3, b_1 = 2, b_2 = 10$

$A = \frac{1}{2}(3)(12)$ or 18 in^2 Simplify.

11-3 Circles and Circumference (pp. 584–588)

Find the circumference of each circle. Use 3.14 or $\frac{22}{7}$ for π. Round to the nearest tenth if necessary.

15. radius = 12 in.
16. diameter = 28 m
17. diameter = $8\frac{2}{5}$ ft
18. radius = 4.4 cm
19. **LIFE SCIENCE** A circular nest built by bald eagles has a diameter of $9\frac{1}{2}$ feet. Find the nest's circumference.

Example 4 **Find the circumference of a circle with a diameter of 12.2 meters.**

12.2 m

$C = \pi d$ Circumference of a circle

$C \approx 3.14(12.2)$ $\pi \approx 3.14$ and $d = 12.2$

$C \approx 38.3$ Multiply.

The circumference is about 38.3 meters.

Chapter 11 Study Guide and Review

11-4 Area of Circles (pp. 589–593)

Find the area of each circle. Round to the nearest tenth.

20. radius = 11.4 in.
21. diameter = 44 cm
22. **CONCERTS** During an outdoor concert, a band can be heard within a 2-mile radius. What is the area of the region that can hear the concert? Round to the nearest tenth.

Example 5 **Find the area of a circle with a radius of 5 inches.**

5 in.

$A = \pi r^2$ Area of a circle

$A = \pi(5)^2$ Replace r with 5.

$A \approx 78.5$ Multiply.

The area of the circle is about 78.5 square inches.

11-5 PSI: Solve a Simpler Problem (pp. 594–595)

23. **BAKING** The local baker can make 10 cakes in 2 days. How many cakes can 8 bakers make working at the same rate in 20 days?
24. **TRAVEL** Mrs. Whitmore left Chicago at 6:45 A.M. and arrived in St. Louis at 11:15 A.M., driving a distance of approximately 292 miles. Find her approximate average speed.
25. **SHOPPING** Mercedes spent \$175.89 over the weekend. Of the money she spent, 40% was spent on shoes. About how much money was *not* spent on shoes?

Example 6 **A total of 950 residents voted on whether to build a neighborhood playground. Of those that voted, 70% voted for the playground. How many residents voted for the playground?**

Find 10% of 950 and then use the result to find 70% of 950.

10% of 950 = 95

Since there are seven 10s in 70%, multiply 95 by 7.

So, 95×7 or 665 residents voted for the playground.

11-6 Area of Composite Figures (pp. 596–599)

Find the area of each figure. Round to the nearest tenth if necessary.

26. 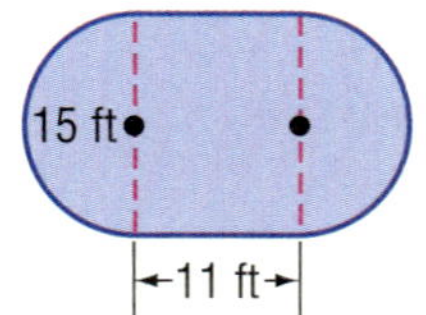

27. 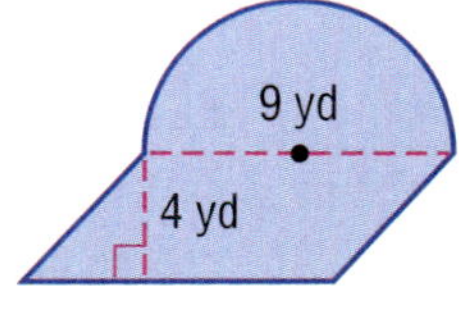

28. **PATIOS** The McAllister family is installing a brick patio like the one shown. What is the total area of the patio?

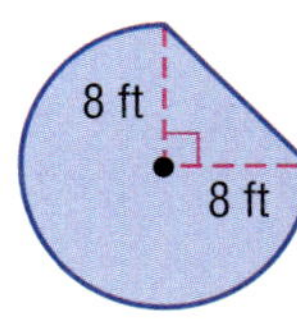

Example 7 **Find the area of the figure. Round to the nearest tenth.**

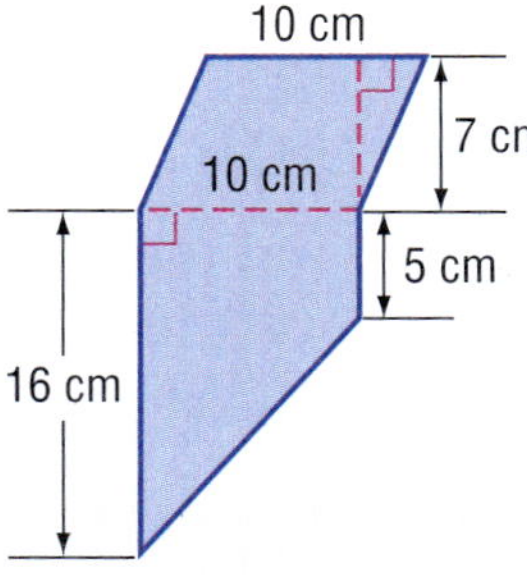

The figure can be separated into a parallelogram and a trapezoid.

parallelogram: $A = 10 \cdot 7$ or 70

trapezoid: $A = \frac{1}{2}(10)(16 + 5)$ or 105

The area is 70 + 105 or 175 cm^2.

Mixed Problem Solving
For mixed problem-solving practice, see page 627.

11-7 Three-Dimensional Figures (pp. 603–606)

For each figure, identify the shape of the base(s). Then classify the figure.

29.

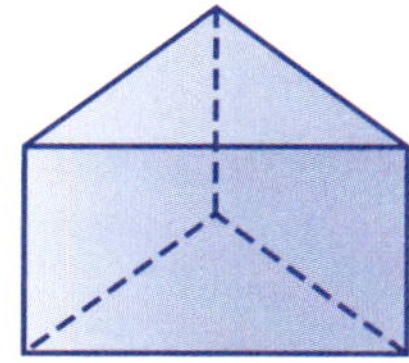

30.

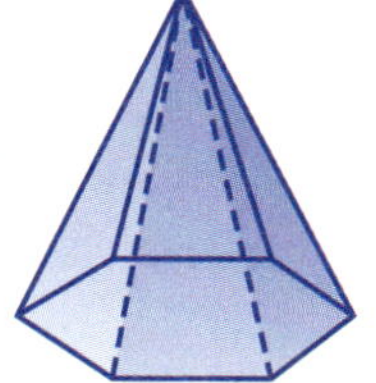

31. **VEGETABLES** Classify the shape of a can of green beans.

DOGHOUSES For Exercises 32 and 33, use the figure of the doghouse shown.

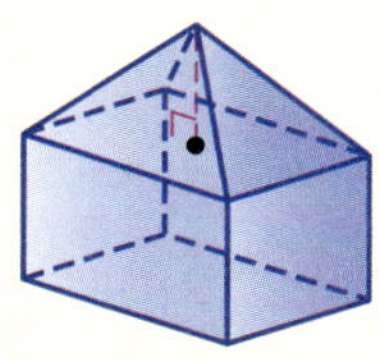

32. What geometric figure is represented by the main part of the doghouse?
33. Identify the top figure of the doghouse.

Example 8 **For the figure, identify the shape of the base(s). Then classify the figure.**

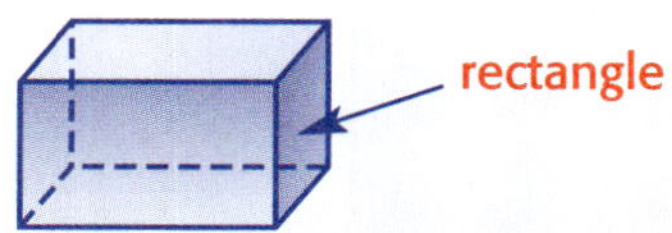

Since the figure has 6 rectangular faces, parallel bases, and a rectangular base, the figure is a rectangular prism.

Example 9 **Classify the shape of a basketball.**

The figure has no faces, bases, edges, or vertices. The figure is a sphere.

11-8 Drawing Three-Dimensional Figures (pp. 608–612)

Draw a top, a side, and a front view of each solid.

34.

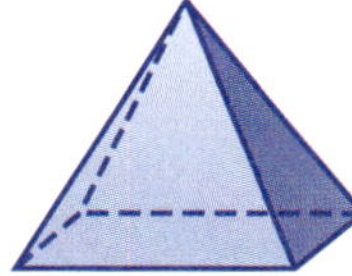

35.

36. Draw a corner view of the three-dimensional figure whose top, side, and front views shown. Use isometric dot paper.

top

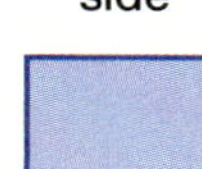

side

front

37. **CRAFTS** Alejandra put all of her craft supplies in the box shown. Draw a top, a side, and a front view of the box.

Example 10 **Draw a corner view of the three-dimensional figure using the top, side, and front views shown.**

top

side

front

The side view is a square. The top and front views are rectangles.

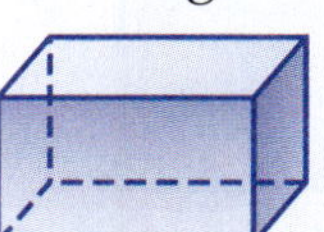

The figure drawn is a rectangular prism.

11-9 Volume of Prisms (pp. 613–618)

Find the volume of each prism. Round to the nearest tenth if necessary.

38. 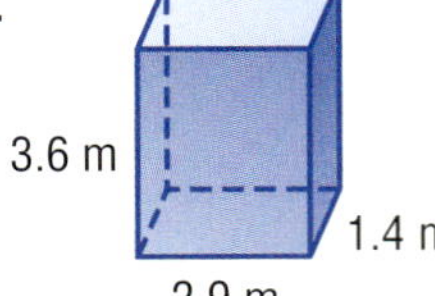

39. 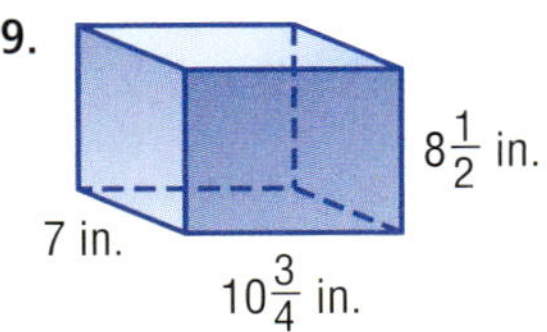

40. **CEREAL** A box of cereal is 8.5 inches long, 12.5 inches tall, and 3.5 inches wide. What is the maximum amount of cereal the box can contain?

41. **TRUCKS** The dimensions of the bed of a dump truck are length 20 feet, width 7 feet, and height $9\frac{1}{2}$ feet. What is the volume of the bed of the dump truck?

Example 11 A local city provides residents with a rectangular container for recycling products. Find the volume of the rectangular container.

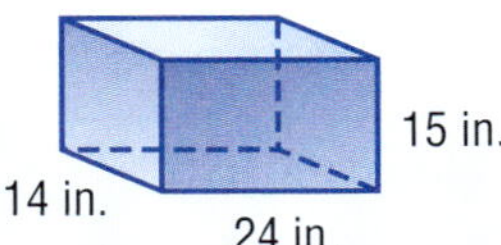

$V = \ell wh$	Volume of a rectangular prism
$V = (24)(14)(15)$	Replace ℓ with 24, w with 14 and h with 15.
$V = 5{,}040$	Multiply.

The volume of the rectangular container is 5,040 cubic inches.

11-10 Volume of Cylinders (pp. 619–623)

Find the volume of each cylinder. Round to the nearest tenth.

42. 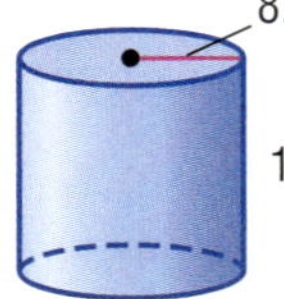

43. 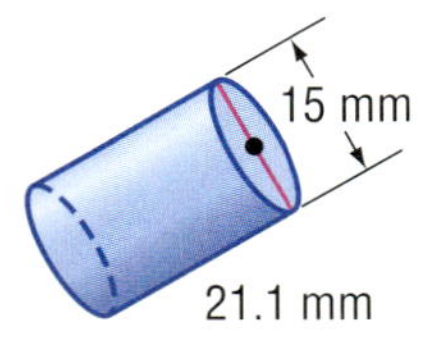

44. **CONTAINERS** A can of soup has a diameter of 3.5 inches, and a height of 5 inches. Find the volume of the soup can. Use 3.14 for π.

45. **COOKIES** Mrs. Delagado stores cookies in a cylinder-shaped jar that has a height of 12 inches and a diameter of 10 inches. Find the volume to the nearest cubic inch. Use 3.14 for π.

Example 12 Marquez stores his toys in a cylinder-shaped can like the one shown below. Find the volume of the cylinder-shaped can. Round to the nearest tenth.

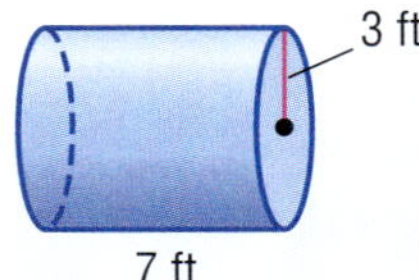

$V = \pi r^2 h$	Volume of a cylinder
$V = \pi 3^2(7)$	Replace r with 3 and h with 7.
$V \approx 197.9$	Multiply.

The volume of the cylinder-shaped can is 197.9 cubic feet.

CHAPTER 11 Practice Test

Math Online glencoe.com
• Chapter Test

Find the area of each figure. Round to the nearest tenth if necessary.

1. 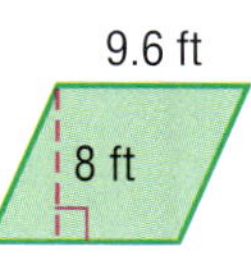

2. 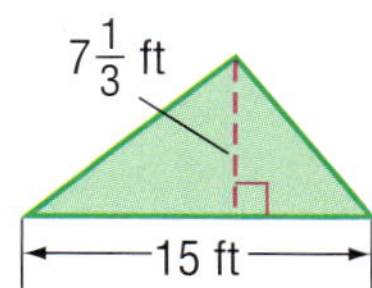

3. 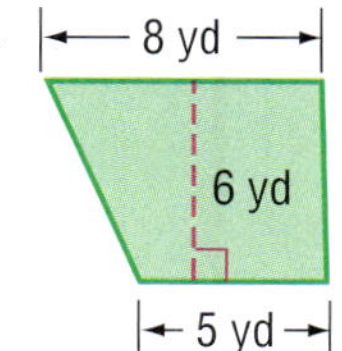

4. 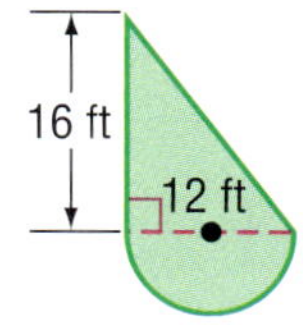

5. **MEASUREMENT** Mrs. Torres has a circular rug underneath her dining room table. What is the approximate circumference of the rug if it has a radius of $3\frac{1}{2}$ yards?

Find the area of each circle. Round to the nearest tenth.

6. radius = 9 ft
7. diameter = 5.2 m

8. **MULTIPLE CHOICE** A fountain is in the shape of a circle. If the fountain has a diameter of 8.8 meters, which equation could be used to find the area of the base of the fountain?

   A $A = \pi \times 8.8^2$
   B $A = \pi \times 4.4^2$
   C $A = 2 \times \pi \times 4.4$
   D $A = \pi \times 8.8$

9. **MEASUREMENT** The Gruseser family wants to build a swimming pool like the one shown below. If they have 85 square feet of land available for the pool, do they have enough space for the swimming pool? Justify your response.

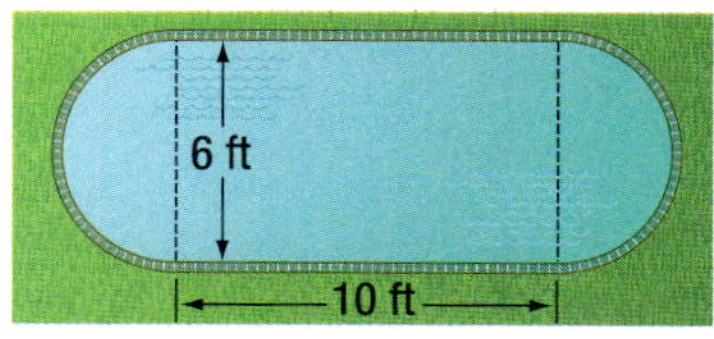

For each figure, identify the shape of the base(s). Then classify the figure.

10. 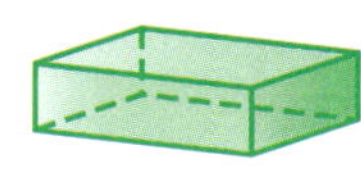

11. 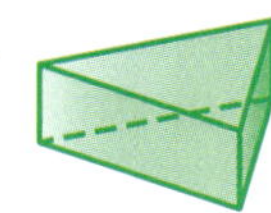

12. **GEOMETRY** Classify the shape of a roll of paper towels.

13. **GEOMETRY** Which geometric shape has at least three lateral faces that are triangles and only one base?

Draw a top, a side, and a front view of each solid.

14. 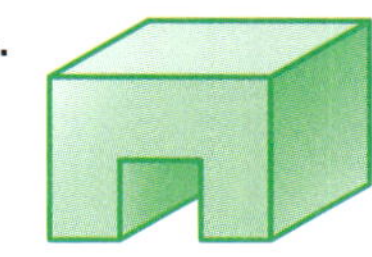

15. 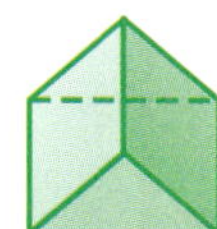

Find the volume of each prism and cylinder. Round to the nearest tenth.

16. 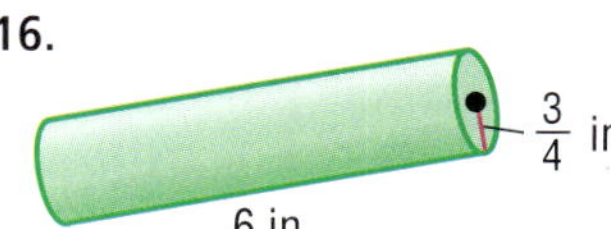

17. 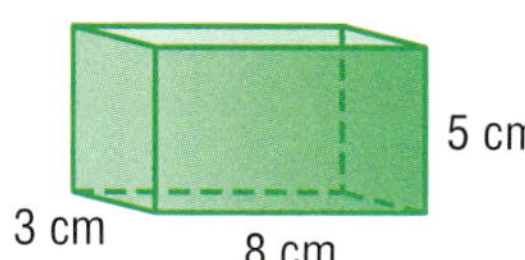

18. 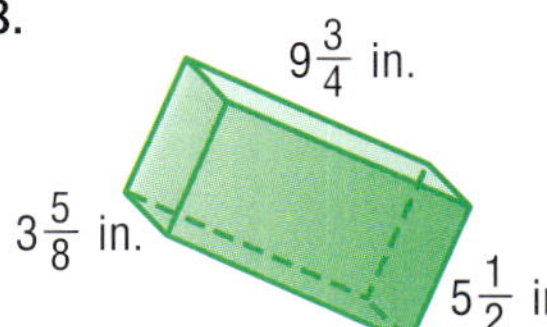

19. 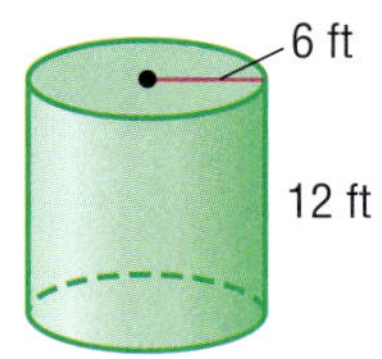

20. **MULTIPLE CHOICE** A cylinder-shaped coffee mug has a radius of 4 centimeters and a height of 10 centimeters. How much coffee is contained in the mug if it is only half full?

   F 0.2 in^3
   G 1.5 in^3
   H 3.4 in^3
   J 3.8 in^3

Chapter 11 Test Practice
Cumulative, Chapters 1–11

Math Online glencoe.com

• Test Practice

PART 1 Multiple Choice

Read each question. Then fill in the correct answer on the answer document provided by your teacher or on a sheet of paper.

1. Stephanie shaded part of a circle like the one shown below. What is the approximate area of the sector?

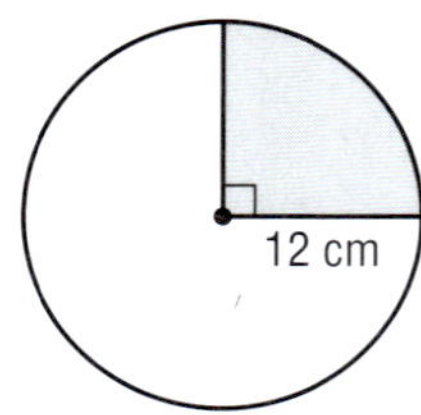

A 113 cm^2

B 364 cm^2

C 452 cm^2

D 728 cm^2

TEST-TAKING TIP

Question 1 Many tests include a Mathematics Chart in the test booklet. Refer to the chart for area and volume formulas.

2. The circular floor rug shown has a diameter of 6 feet. Which expression can be used to find its circumference, *C*, in feet?

F $C = 3 \times \pi$

G $C = 3^2 \times \pi$

H $C = 6 \times \pi$

J $C = 2 \times 6 \times \pi$

3. Angle *D* and angle *E* are complementary angles. If $\angle D$ is 35°, what is the measure of $\angle E$?

A 35° C 90°

B 55° D 145°

4. If the corresponding angles of 2 trapezoids are congruent and the lengths of the corresponding sides of the trapezoids are proportional, the trapezoids are —

F regular H symmetric

G congruent J similar

5. Which description shows the relationship between a term and *n*, its position in the sequence?

Position	1	2	3	4	5	*n*
Value of Term	2	5	8	11	14	

A Add 1 to *n*.

B Multiply *n* by 2 and add 3.

C Multiply *n* by 3 and subtract 1.

D Add 9 to *n*.

6. A metal toolbox has a length of 11 inches, a width of 5 inches, and a height of 6 inches. What is the volume of the toolbox?

F 22 in^3 H 210 in^3

G 121 in^3 J 330 in^3

7. A bag contains 5 red, 2 yellow, and 8 blue marbles. Xavier removed one blue marble from the bag and did not put it back. He then randomly removed another marble. What is the probability that the second marble removed was blue?

A $\frac{8}{14}$ C $\frac{1}{2}$

B $\frac{8}{15}$ D $\frac{7}{15}$

Preparing for Standardized Tests

For test-taking strategies and practice, see pages 716–733.

8. In the figure shown, all the corners form right angles. What is the area of the figure in square feet?

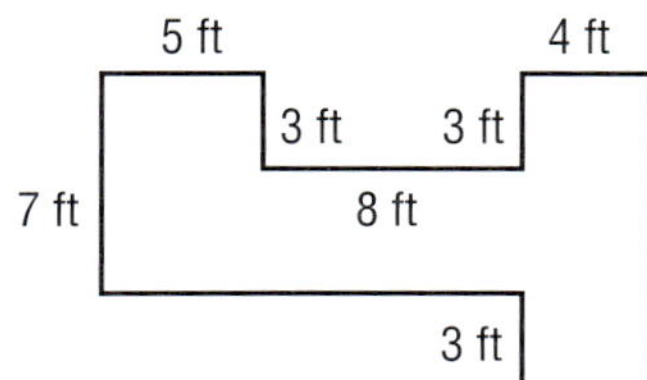

F 91 ft^2

G 107 ft^2

H 115 ft^2

J 122 ft^2

9. The circles shown have radii of 4 feet and 8 feet.

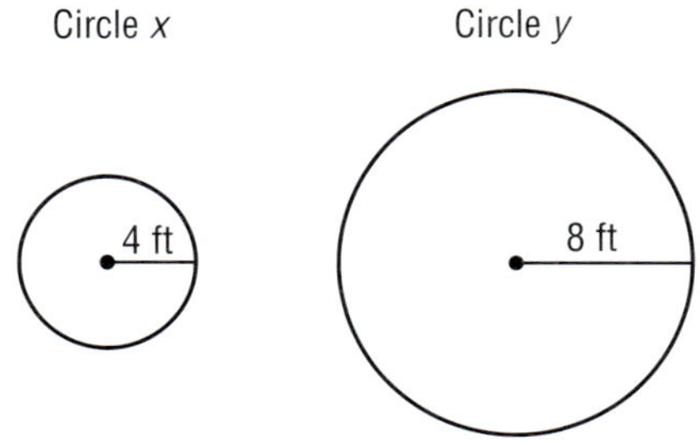

What is $\frac{\text{circumference of Circle } x}{\text{circumference of Circle } y}$?

A $\frac{\pi}{4}$

B $\frac{\pi}{2}$

C $\frac{1}{4}$

D $\frac{1}{2}$

10. Katie has 3 apples to serve to her friends. If Katie serves each friend $\frac{1}{3}$ of a whole apple, how many friends can she serve?

F 1

G 3

H 9

J 12

PART 2 Short Response/Grid In

Record your answers on the answer sheet provided by your teacher or on a sheet of paper.

11. Ms. Williams recorded the time it took four of her top students to complete a math quiz. What is the median time in minutes for these four students?

Math Quiz Times	
Student	**Time (minutes)**
1	12.8
2	23.1
3	19.6
4	15.7

PART 3 Extended Response

Record your answers on the answer sheet provided by your teacher or on a sheet of paper. Show your work.

12. A plastic cylinder-shaped pipe has the dimensions shown below.

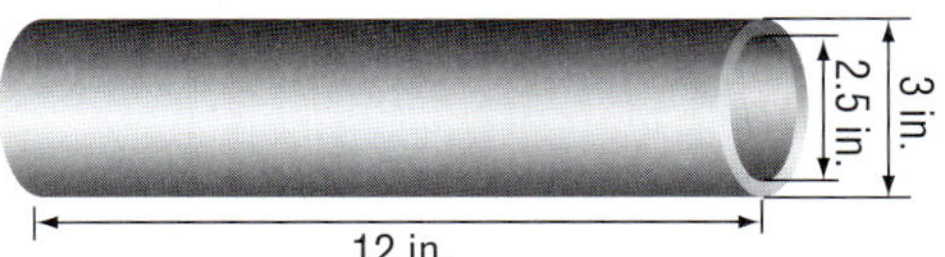

a. How much liquid can the pipe contain?

b. Describe how you could find the amount of plastic needed to make the pipe.

c. Use the method you described in part b to find the amount of plastic in the pipe.

NEED EXTRA HELP?												
If You Missed Question...	1	2	3	4	5	6	7	8	9	10	11	12
Go to Lesson...	11-4	11-6	10-1	10-6	1-9	11-9	9-1	11-6	11-3	5-7	8-2	11-2

Geometry and Measurement

BIG Idea

- Find length using the Pythagorean Theorem.

BIG Idea

- Find surface areas of rectangular prisms and cylinders.

Key Vocabulary

hypotenuse (p. 640)
irrational number (p. 637)
Pythagorean Theorem (p. 640)
surface area (p. 649)

Real-World Link

Spaghetti The shape of many spaghetti boxes are rectangular prisms, and the shape of many cans are cylinders. You can use the formula $S = 2lw + 2lh + 2wh$ to find the surface area of a box of spaghetti given the length l, the width w, and the height h of the box.

Geometry and Measurement Make this Foldable to help you organize your notes. Begin with a piece of 11″ by 17″ paper.

1. **Fold** the paper in fourths lengthwise.
2. **Open** and fold a 2″ tab along the short side. Then fold the rest in half.
3. **Draw** lines along the folds and label as shown.

GET READY for Chapter 12

Diagnose Readiness You have two options for checking Prerequisite Skills.

Option 2

Math Online Take the Online Readiness Quiz at glencoe.com.

Option 1

Take the Quick Quiz below. Refer to the Quick Review for help.

QUICK Quiz

Evaluate each expression. (Lesson 1-2)

1. 4^2
2. 7^2
3. 13^2
4. 24^2
5. $5^2 + 8^2$
6. $10^2 + 6^2$
7. $9^2 + 12^2$
8. $15^2 + 17^2$
9. **AGES** Samuel's mother is 7^2 years old, and his grandmother is 9^2 years old. Find the sum of their ages. (Lesson 1-2)

QUICK Review

Example 1

Evaluate $3^2 + 5^2$.

$3^2 + 5^2 = 9 + 25$ Evaluate 3^2 and 5^2.

$= 34$ Add 9 and 25.

Evaluate the expression $2ab + 2bc + 2ac$ for each value of the variables indicated. (Lesson 1-6)

10. $a = 4, b = 5, c = 8$
11. $a = 2, b = 7, c = 11$
12. $a = 3.1, b = 2.4, c = 9.9$
13. $a = 2.1, b = 1.7, c = 4.6$

Example 2

Evaluate the expression $2ab + 2bc + 2ac$ for $a = 3$, $b = 5$, and $c = 6$.

$2ab + 2bc + 2ac$

$= 2(3)(5) + 2(5)(6) + 2(3)(6)$ Replace a with 3, b with 5, and c with 6.

$= 30 + 60 + 36$ Multiply.

$= 126$ Add.

Use the π button on your calculator to evaluate each expression below. Round to the nearest tenth. (Lesson 11-3)

14. $(2)(\pi)(3^2) + (2)(\pi)(3)(8)$
15. $(2)(\pi)(7^2) + (2)(\pi)(7)(5)$

Example 3

Use the π button on your calculator to evaluate $(2)(\pi)(4^2) + (2)(\pi)(4)(6)$. Round to the nearest tenth.

$(2)(\pi)(4^2) + (2)(\pi)(4)(6)$

$= (2)(\pi)(16) + (2)(\pi)(4)(6)$ Evaluate 4^2.

$= (32)(\pi) + (48)(\pi)$ Multiply.

≈ 251.3 Multiply and add.

12-1 Estimating Square Roots

MAIN IDEA

Estimate square roots.

New Vocabulary

irrational number

glencoe.com

- Extra Examples
- Personal Tutor
- Self-Check Quiz
- Reading in the Content Area

MINI Lab

Estimate the square root of 27.

- Arrange 27 tiles into the largest square possible. You will use 25 tiles and 2 will remain.
- Add tiles to make the next larger square. So, add 9 tiles to make a square with 36 tiles.
- The square root of 27 is between 5 and 6. Since 27 is much closer to 25 than 36, we can expect that the square root of 27 is closer to 5 than 6.

The square root of 25 is 5.

The square root of 36 is 6.

Use algebra tiles to estimate the square root of each number to the nearest whole number.

1. 40
2. 28
3. 85
4. 62
5. Describe another method that you could use to estimate the square root of a number.

The square root of a perfect square is an integer. You can estimate the square root of a number that is *not* a perfect square.

EXAMPLE Estimate a Square Root

Estimate $\sqrt{78}$ to the nearest whole number.

List some perfect squares.

1, 4, 9, 16, 25, 36, 49, 64, 81, ...

$64 < 78 < 81$	78 is between the perfect squares 64 and 81.
$\sqrt{64} < \sqrt{78} < \sqrt{81}$	Find the square root of each number.
$8 < \sqrt{78} < 9$	$\sqrt{64} = 8$ and $\sqrt{81} = 9$

So, $\sqrt{78}$ is between 8 and 9. Since 78 is much closer to 81 than to 64, the best whole number estimate is 9. Verify with a calculator.

CHECK Your Progress

a. Estimate $\sqrt{50}$ to the nearest whole number.

A number that cannot be expressed as the quotient of two integers is an **irrational number**.

Vocabulary Link
Irrational
Everyday Use lacking usual or normal clarity, as in irrational thinking
Math Use a number that cannot be expressed as the quotient of two integers

Irrational Numbers $\sqrt{2}$, π, 0.636336333...

The square root of any number that is not a perfect square is an irrational number. You can use a calculator to estimate square roots that are irrational numbers.

EXAMPLE Graph Square Roots on a Number Line

2 **Graph $\sqrt{42}$ on a number line.**

2nd [$\sqrt{\ }$] 42 ENTER 6.480740698

$\sqrt{42} \approx 6.5$

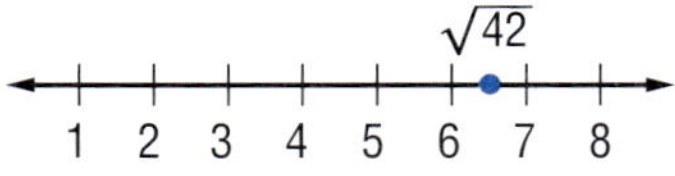

Check for Reasonableness
$6^2 = 36$ and $7^2 = 49$. Since 42 is between 36 and 49, the answer, 6.5, is reasonable.

Graph each square root on a number line.

b. $\sqrt{6}$ c. $\sqrt{23}$ d. $\sqrt{309}$

The Venn diagram shows the relationship among sets of numbers.

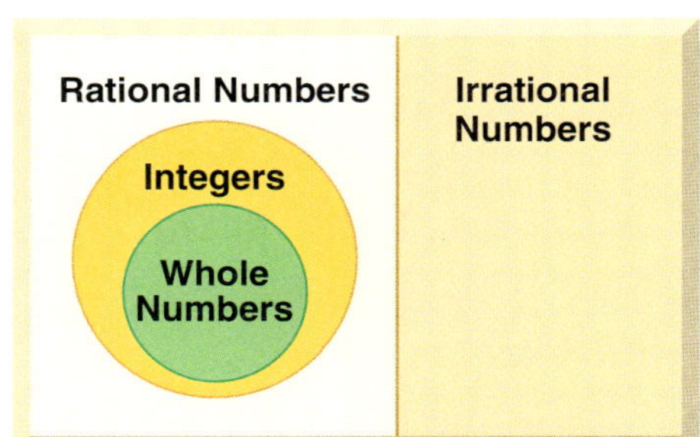

Whole Numbers: 0, 1, 2, 3, ...
Integers: ..., −2, −1, 0, 1, 2, ...
Rational Numbers: $\frac{1}{2}$, 0.25, −0.2, 0.333...
Irrational Numbers: π, $\sqrt{2}$, 0.124543...

CHECK Your Understanding

Example 1 (p. 636) **Estimate each square root to the nearest whole number.**

1. $\sqrt{39}$ 2. $\sqrt{106}$ 3. $\sqrt{90}$ 4. $\sqrt{140}$

Example 2 (p. 637) **Graph each square root on a number line.**

5. $\sqrt{7}$ 6. $\sqrt{51}$ 7. $\sqrt{135}$ 8. $\sqrt{462}$

9. **MEASUREMENT** The diagram at the right shows the floor plan of a square kitchen. What is the approximate length of one side of the kitchen floor to the nearest tenth?

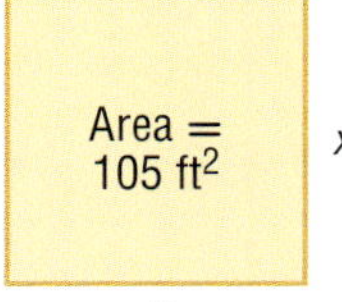

Practice and Problem Solving

HOMEWORK HELP	
For Exercises	See Examples
10–17, 26, 27	1
18–25	2

Estimate each square root to the nearest whole number.

10. $\sqrt{11}$
11. $\sqrt{20}$
12. $\sqrt{35}$
13. $\sqrt{65}$
14. $\sqrt{89}$
15. $\sqrt{116}$
16. $\sqrt{137}$
17. $\sqrt{409}$

Graph each square root on a number line.

18. $\sqrt{15}$
19. $\sqrt{8}$
20. $\sqrt{44}$
21. $\sqrt{89}$
22. $\sqrt{160}$
23. $\sqrt{573}$
24. $\sqrt{645}$
25. $\sqrt{2{,}798}$

26. **MEASUREMENT** The bottom of the square baking pan has an area of 67 square inches. What is the approximate length of one side of the pan?

27. **ALGEBRA** What whole number is closest to $\sqrt{m - n}$ if $m = 45$ and $n = 8$?

Estimate each square root to the nearest whole number.

28. $\sqrt{925}$
29. $\sqrt{2{,}480}$
30. $\sqrt{1{,}610}$
31. $\sqrt{6{,}500}$

Find each square root to the nearest tenth.

32. $\sqrt{0.25}$
33. $\sqrt{0.49}$
34. $\sqrt{1.96}$
35. $\sqrt{2.89}$

ALGEBRA For Exercises 36 and 37, estimate each expression to the nearest tenth if $a = 8$ and $b = 3.7$.

36. $\sqrt{a + b}$
37. $\sqrt{6b - a}$

STAMPS For Exercises 38 and 39, use the information below.

The Special Olympics' commemorative stamp is square in shape with an area of 1,008 square millimeters.

38. Find the length of one side of the postage stamp to the nearest tenth.
39. What is the length of one side in centimeters?

40. **ALGEBRA** The formula $D = 1.22 \times \sqrt{h}$ can be used to estimate the distance D in miles you can see from a point h feet above Earth's surface. Use the formula to find the distance D in miles you can see from the top of a 120-foot hill. Round to the nearest tenth.

EXTRA PRACTICE
See pages 701, 715.

41. **FIND THE DATA** Refer to the Data File on pages 16–19. Choose some data and write a real-world problem in which you would estimate a square root.

H.O.T. Problems

42. **Which One Doesn't Belong?** Identify the number that does not have the same characteristic as the other three. Explain your reasoning.

$\sqrt{5}$	π	$\sqrt{81}$	0.535335333...

43. **OPEN ENDED** Select three numbers with square roots between 4 and 5.

44. **NUMBER SENSE** Explain why 8 is the best whole number estimate for $\sqrt{71}$.

CHALLENGE A cube root of a number is one of three equal factors of that number. Estimate the cube root of each number to the nearest whole number.

45. $\sqrt[3]{9}$
46. $\sqrt[3]{26}$
47. $\sqrt[3]{120}$
48. $\sqrt[3]{500}$

49. **WRITING IN MATH** Apply what you know about numbers to explain why $\sqrt{30}$ is an irrational number.

TEST PRACTICE

50. Reina wrote four numbers on a piece of paper. She then asked her friend Tyron to select the number closest to 5. Which number should he select?

$\sqrt{56}$ $\sqrt{48}$ $\sqrt{37}$ $\sqrt{28}$

A $\sqrt{56}$
B $\sqrt{48}$
C $\sqrt{37}$
D $\sqrt{28}$

51. Which of the following is an irrational number?

F $\sqrt{25}$
G $\sqrt{7}$
H -13
J $\frac{4}{5}$

52. **SHORT RESPONSE** If the area of a square is 169 square inches, what is the length of the side of the square?

Spiral Review

53. **MEASUREMENT** Find the volume of a can of vegetables with a diameter of 3 inches and a height of 4 inches. Round to the nearest tenth. (Lesson 11-10)

54. **MEASUREMENT** A rectangular prism is 14 inches long, 4.5 inches wide, and 1 inch high. What is the volume of the prism? (Lesson 11-9)

GEOMETRY For Exercises 55–58, use the graph at the right. Classify the angle that represents each category as *acute*, *obtuse*, *right*, or *straight*. (Lesson 10-1)

55. 30–39 hours
56. 1–29 hours
57. 40 hours
58. 41–50 hours

Hours Worked in a Typical Week

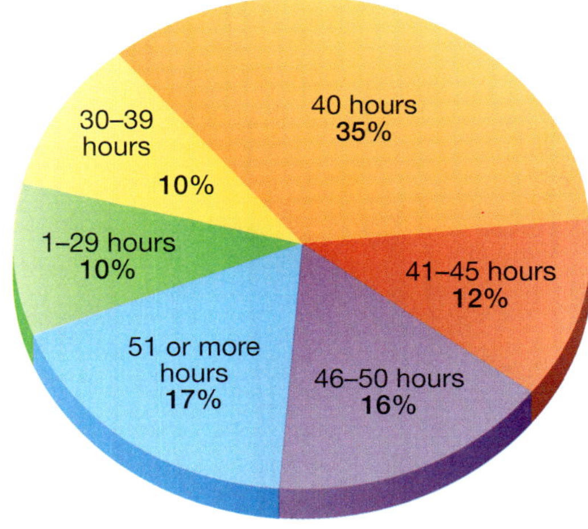

Source: Heldrich Work Trends Survey

GET READY for the Next Lesson

PREREQUISITE SKILL Solve each equation. (Lesson 1-7)

59. $7^2 + 5^2 = c$
60. $4^2 + b = 36$
61. $3^2 + a = 25$
62. $9^2 + 2^2 = c$

12-2 The Pythagorean Theorem

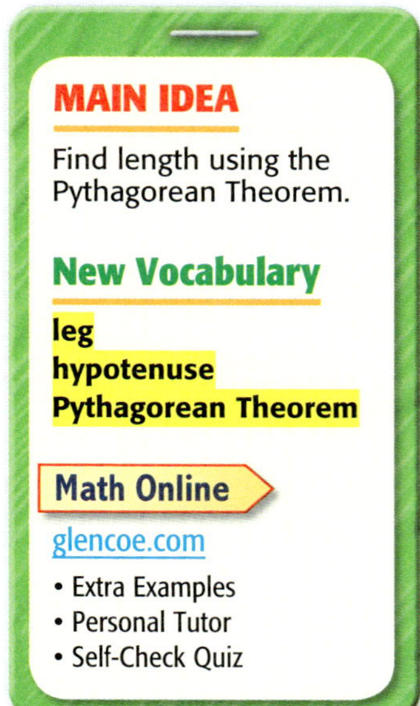

MINI Lab

Three squares with sides 3, 4, and 5 units are used to form the right triangle shown.

1. Find the area of each square.
2. How are the squares of the sides related to the areas of the squares?
3. Find the sum of the areas of the two smaller squares. How does the sum compare to the area of the larger square?
4. Use grid paper to cut out three squares with sides 5, 12, and 13 units. Form a right triangle with these squares. Compare the sum of the areas of the two smaller squares with the area of the larger square.

In a right triangle, the sides have special names.

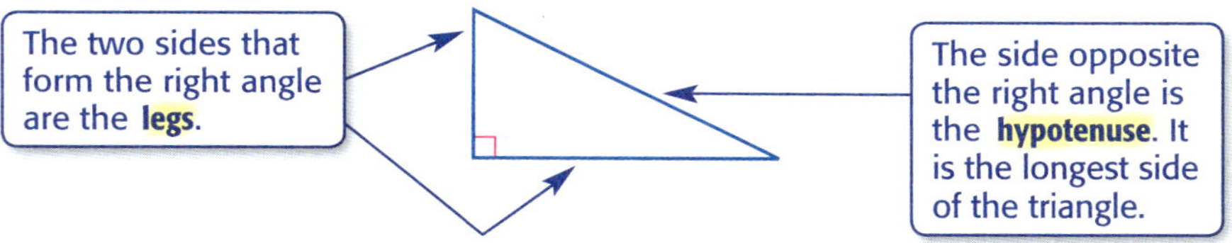

The **Pythagorean Theorem** describes the relationship between the length of the hypotenuse and the lengths of the legs.

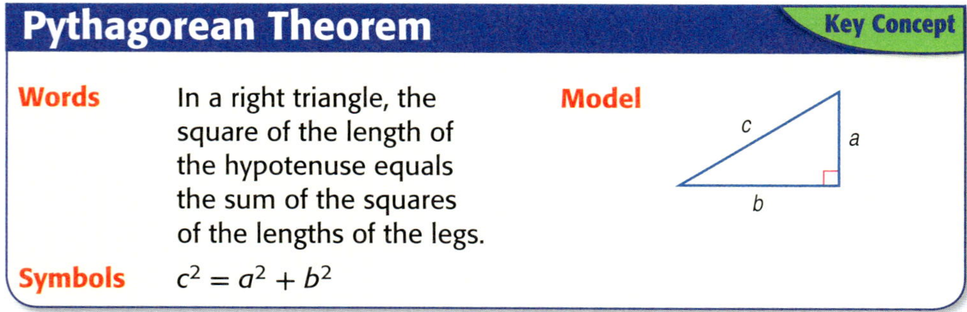

When using the Pythagorean Theorem, you will encounter equations that involve square roots. Every positive number has both a positive and a negative square root. By the definition of square roots, if $n^2 = a$, then $n = \pm\sqrt{a}$. The notation $\pm\sqrt{\ }$ indicates both the positive and negative square root of a number. You can use this relationship to solve equations that involve squares.

EXAMPLE Find the Length of the Hypotenuse

Study Tip

Check for Reasonableness You can eliminate −8.9 as a solution because the length of a side of a triangle cannot be a negative number.

1 **Find the length of the hypotenuse of the triangle.**

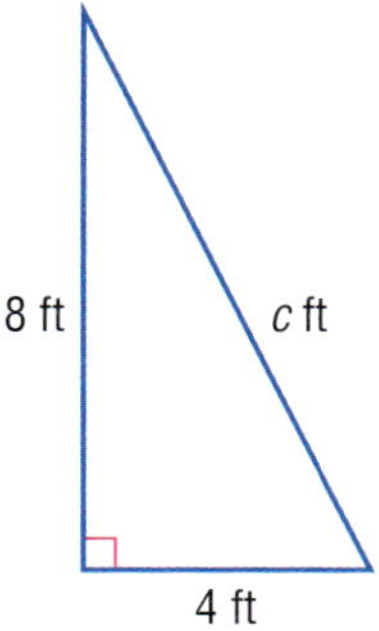

$c^2 = a^2 + b^2$	Pythagorean Theorem
$c^2 = 8^2 + 4^2$	Replace *a* with 8 and *b* with 4.
$c^2 = 64 + 16$	Evaluate 8^2 and 4^2.
$c^2 = 80$	Add.
$c = \pm\sqrt{80}$	Definition of square root
$c \approx \pm 8.9$	Simplify.

The length of the hypotenuse is about 8.9 feet.

CHECK Your Progress

a. Find the length of the hypotenuse of a right triangle with legs 5 yards and 7 yards. Round to the nearest tenth.

Real-World Career

How Does a Professional Diver Use Math? Professional divers must use formulas to compute pressure and air supply in order to determine safe diving depths and dive times.

Math Online For more information, go to glencoe.com.

Real-World EXAMPLE

2 **SCUBA DIVING A scuba diver dove 14 feet below the surface. Then, he swam 16 feet toward a coral formation. How far is the diver from his boat?**

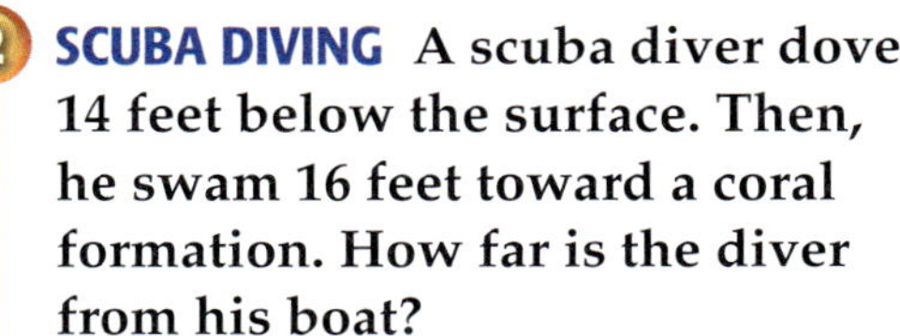

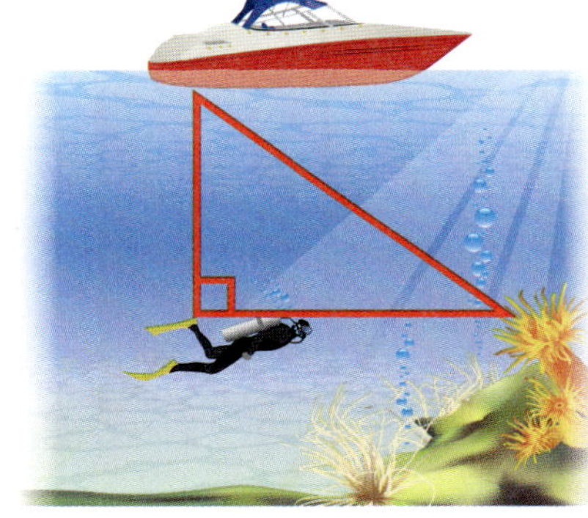

The diver's distance from the boat is the hypotenuse of a right triangle. Write and solve an equation for *x*.

$c^2 = a^2 + b^2$	Pythagorean Theorem
$x^2 = 14^2 + 16^2$	Replace *c* with *x*, *a* with 14, and *b* with 16.
$x^2 = 196 + 256$	Evaluate 14^2 and 16^2.
$x^2 = 452$	Add.
$x = \pm\sqrt{452}$	Definition of square root
$x \approx \pm 21.3$	Simplify.

The diver's distance from the boat is about 21.3 feet.

CHECK Your Progress

b. **SOFTBALL** A softball diamond is a square measuring 60 feet on each side. How far does a player on second base throw when she throws from second base to home? Round to the nearest tenth.

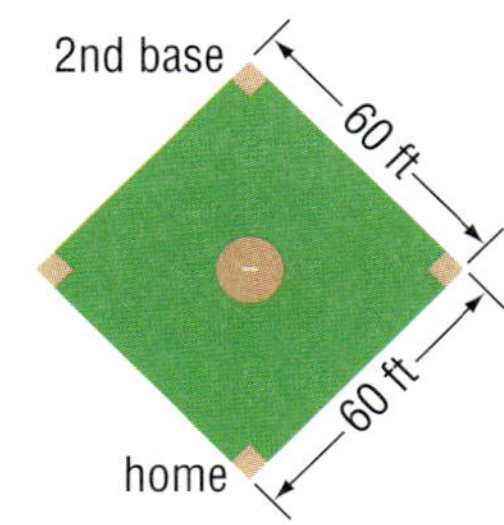

You can also use the Pythagorean Theorem to find the measure of a leg if the measure of the other leg and the hypotenuse are known.

EXAMPLE Find the Length of a Leg

3 **Find the missing measure of the triangle. Round to the nearest tenth if necessary.**

13 cm
5 cm
b cm

The missing measure is the length of a leg.

$c^2 = a^2 + b^2$	Pythagorean Theorem
$13^2 = 5^2 + b^2$	Replace a with 5 and c with 13.
$169 = 25 + b^2$	Evaluate 13^2 and 5^2.
$-25 = -25$	Subtract 25 from each side.
$144 = b^2$	Simplify.
$\pm\sqrt{144} = b$	Definition of square root
$12 = b$	Simplify.

The length of the leg is 12 centimeters.

CHECK Your Progress

c.

a ft
17 ft
15 ft

d.

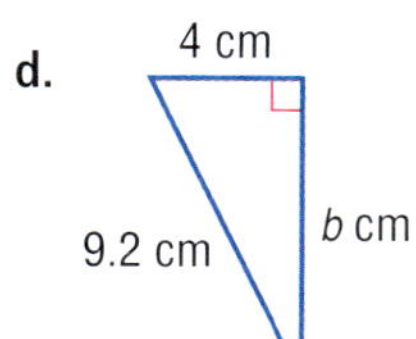

e. $b = 7$ in., $c = 25$ in.

TEST EXAMPLE

Test-Taking Tip

Formulas Some formulas will be given to you during the test. It is a good idea to familiarize yourself with the formulas before the test.

4 **Mr. Thomson created a mosaic tile in the shape of a square to place in his kitchen.**

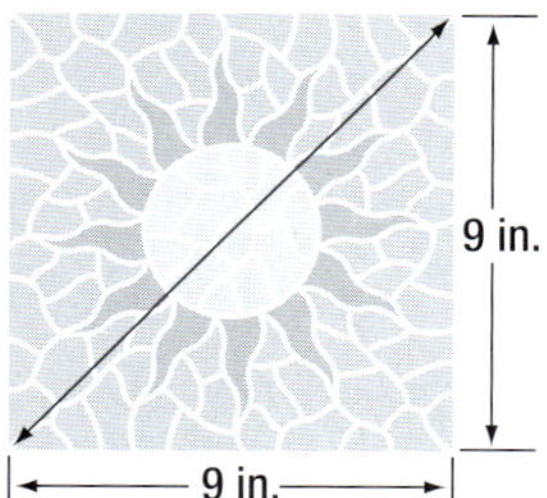

Which is closest to the length of the diagonal of the tile?

A 10 in.
B 13 in.
C 15 in.
D 17 in.

Read the Item

You need to use the Pythagorean Theorem to find the length of the diagonal.

Solve the Item

$c^2 = a^2 + b^2$	Pythagorean Theorem
$c^2 = 9^2 + 9^2$	Replace a with 9 and b with 9.
$c^2 = 81 + 81$	Evaluate 9^2 and 9^2.
$c^2 = 162$	Add.
$c = \pm\sqrt{162}$	Definition of square root
$c \approx \pm 12.7$	Simplify.

The length is about 12.7 inches.

The answer choice closest to 12.7 inches is 13 inches. So, the answer is B.

CHECK Your Progress

f. A painter leans a ladder against the side of a building. How far from the bottom of the building is the top of the ladder?

F 38.2 ft H 21.8 ft

G 28.0 ft J 20.0 ft

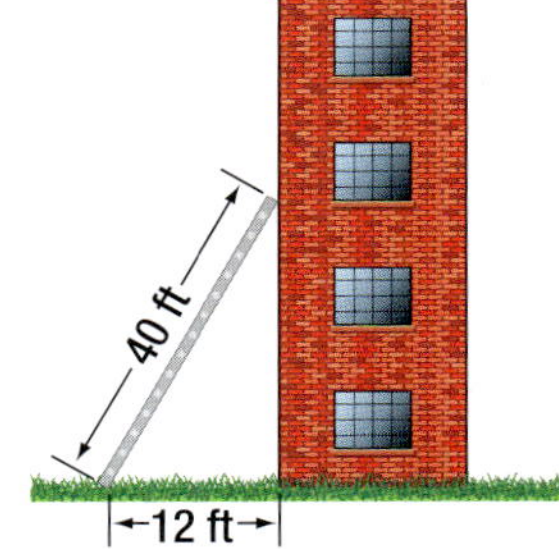

CHECK Your Understanding

Examples 1, 3 (pp. 641–642)

Find the missing measure of each triangle. Round to the nearest tenth if necessary.

1. 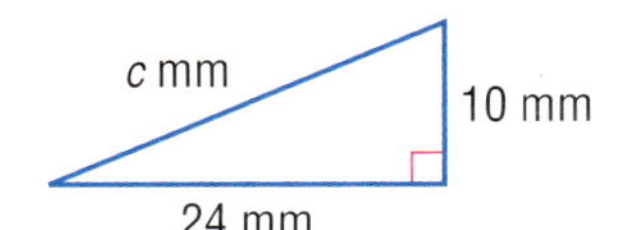

2. 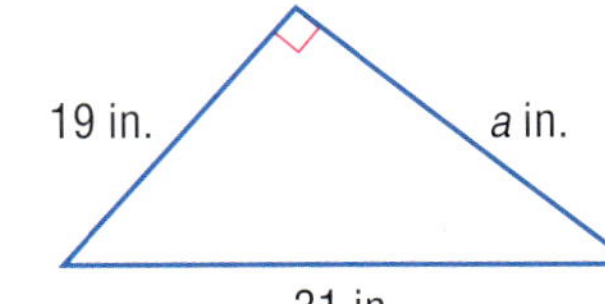

3. $b = 21$ cm, $c = 28$ cm

4. $a = 11$ yd, $b = 12$ yd

Example 2 (p. 641)

5. **ARCHITECTURE** What is the width of the the fence gate shown at the right? Round to the nearest tenth.

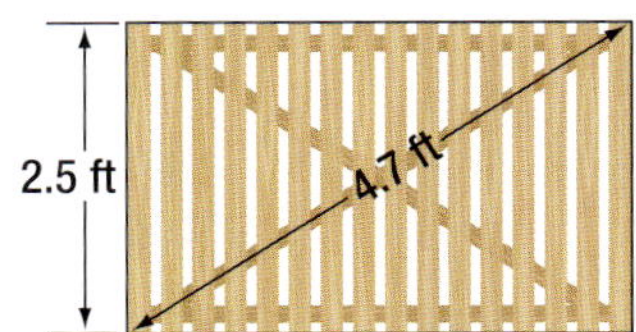

Example 4 (pp. 642–643)

6. **MULTIPLE CHOICE** A company designed a public play area in the shape of a square. The play area will include a pathway, as shown. Which is closest to the length of the pathway?

A 100 yd C 140 yd

B 125 yd D 175 yd

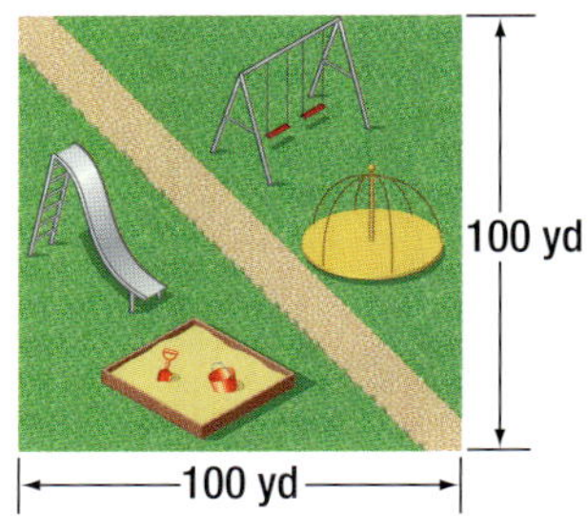

Practice and Problem Solving

HOMEWORK HELP	
For Exercises	**See Examples**
7–8, 11–12, 15–16	1
17–20	2
9–10, 13–14	3
26–27	4

Find the missing measure of each triangle. Round to the nearest tenth if necessary.

7. 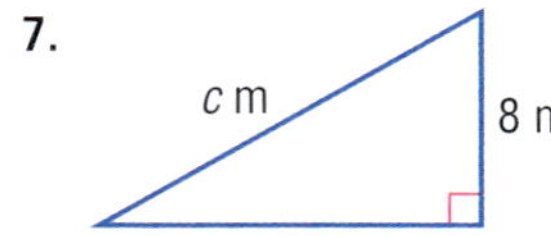

8. 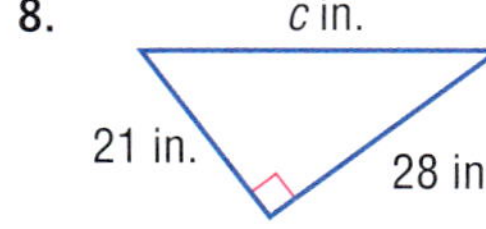

9. 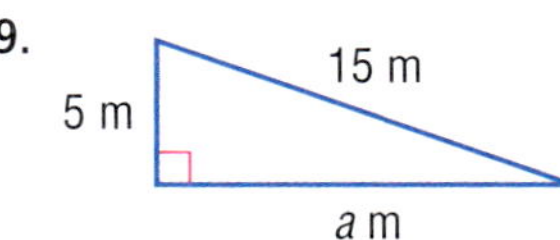

10. 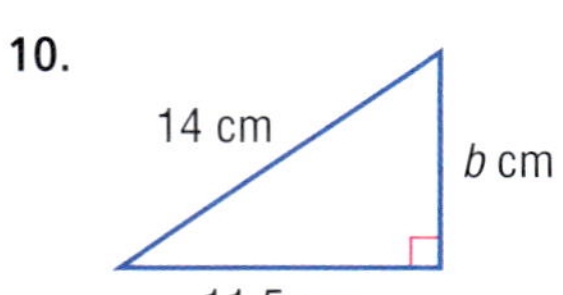

11. 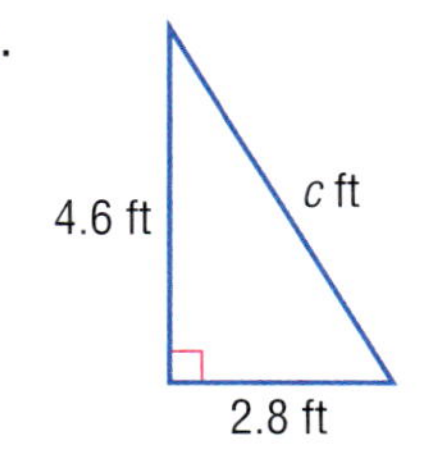

12. 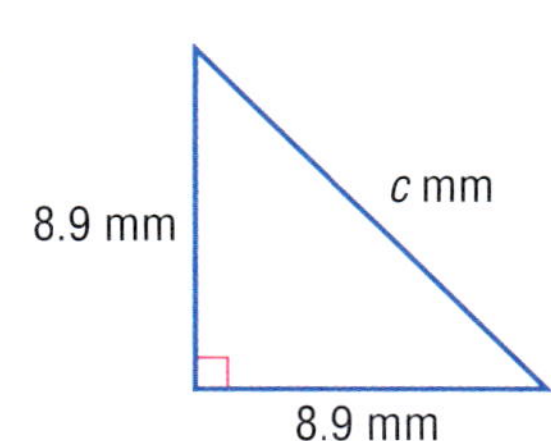

13. $a = 2.4$ yd, $c = 3.7$ yd
14. $b = 8.5$ m, $c = 10.4$ m
15. $a = 7$ in., $b = 24$ in.
16. $a = 13.5$ mm, $b = 18$ mm

MEASUREMENT **For Exercises 17 and 18, find each distance to the nearest tenth.**

17. 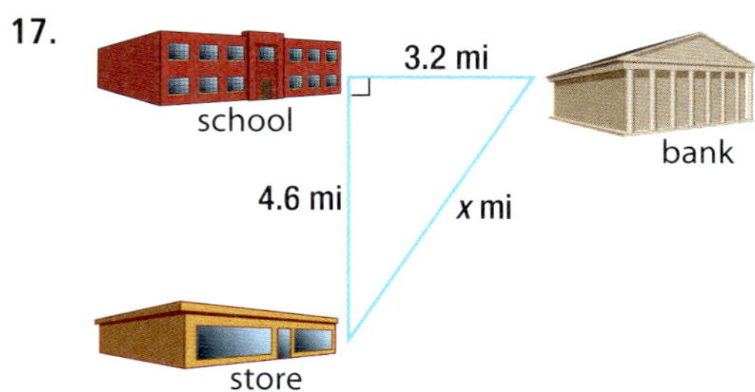

18. 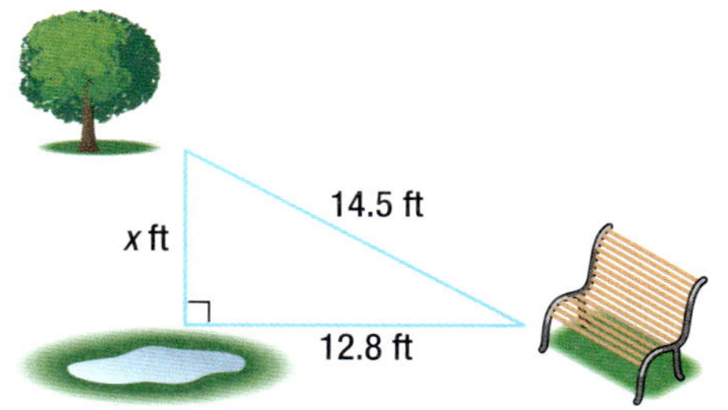

SPORTS **For Exercises 19 and 20, find the length or width of each piece of sports equipment. Round to the nearest tenth.**

19. 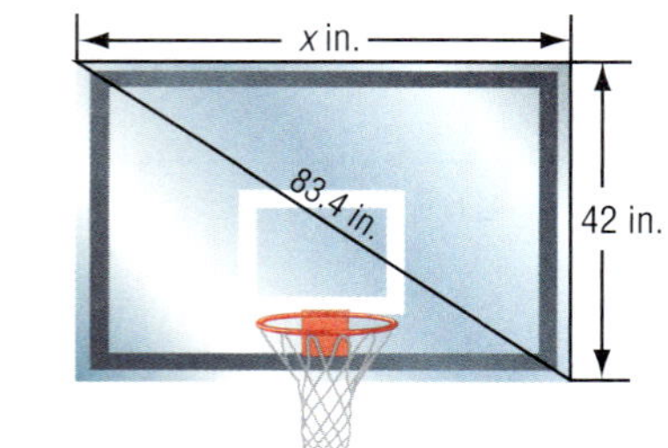

20. 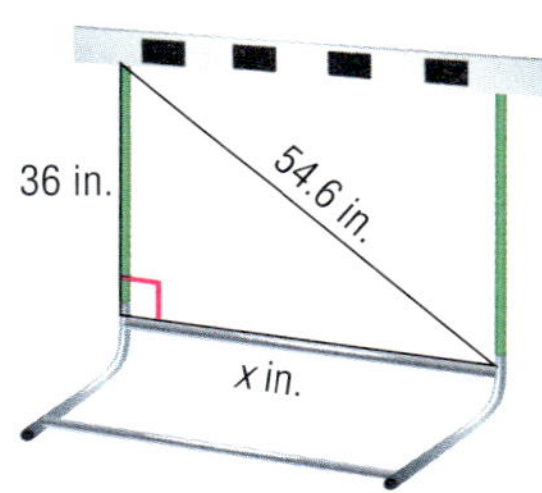

21. **MEASUREMENT** A barn door is 10 feet wide and 15 feet tall. A square plank 16 feet on each side must be taken through the doorway. Can the plank fit through the doorway? Justify your answer.

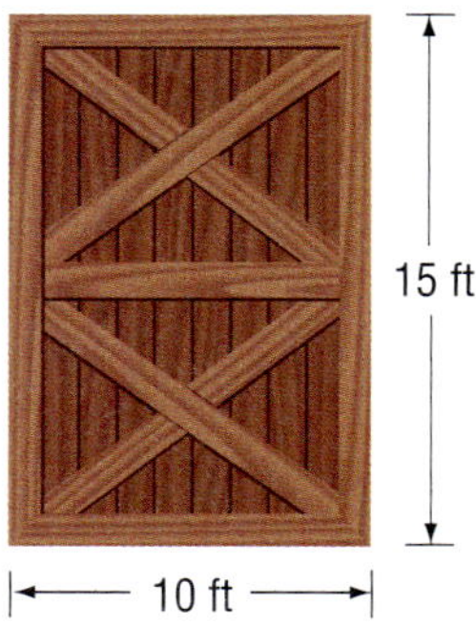

22. **MEASUREMENT** On a weekend trip around California, Sydney left her home in Modesto and drove 75 miles east to Yosemite National Park, then 70 miles south to Fresno, and finally 110 miles west to Monterey Bay. About how far is she from her starting point? Justify your answer with a drawing.

EXTRA PRACTICE
See pages 702, 715.

H.O.T. Problems

23. **CHALLENGE** What is the length of the diagonal shown in the cube at the right?

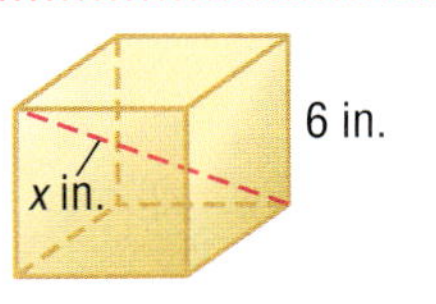

24. **FIND THE ERROR** Marcus and Aisha are writing an equation to find the missing measure of the triangle at the right. Who is correct? Explain.

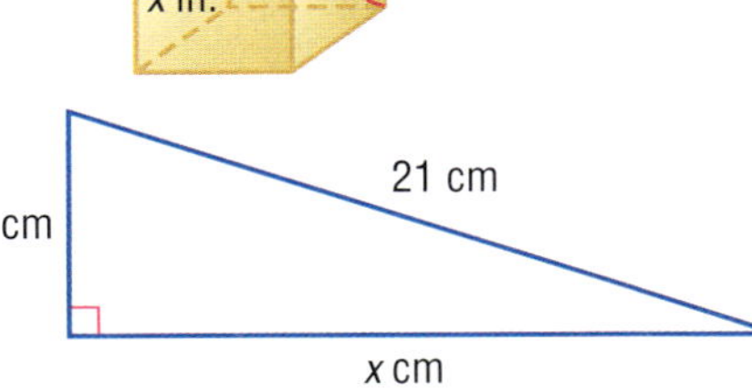

Marcus

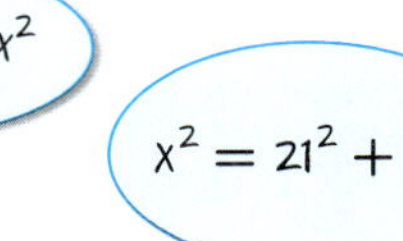

Aisha

25. **WRITING IN MATH** Write a problem about a real-world situation in which you would use the Pythagorean Theorem.

TEST PRACTICE

26. Which triangle has sides a, b, and c so that the relationship $a^2 + b^2 = c^2$ is true?

A 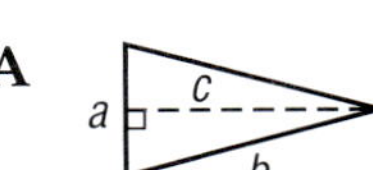

C 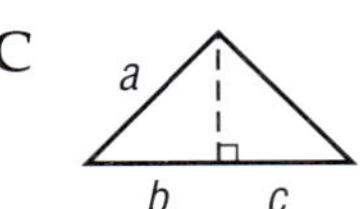

B 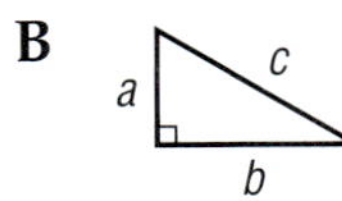

D 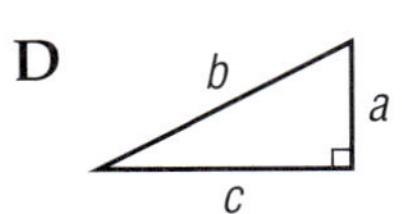

27. An isosceles right triangle has legs that are each 8 inches long. About how long is the hypotenuse?

F 12.8 inches

G 11.3 inches

H 8 inches

J 4 inches

Spiral Review

28. **ESTIMATION** Which is closer to $\sqrt{55}$: 7 or 8? (Lesson 12-1)

29. **MEASUREMENT** A cylinder-shaped popcorn tin has a height of 1.5 feet and a diameter of 10 inches. Find the volume to the nearest cubic inch. (Lesson 11-10)

Write each percent as a decimal. (Lesson 4-7)

30. 45%
31. 8%
32. 124%
33. 265%

GET READY for the Next Lesson

34. **PREREQUISITE SKILL** The average person takes about 15 breaths per minute. At this rate, how many breaths does the average person take in one week? Use the *solve a simpler problem* strategy. (Lesson 11-5)

12-3 Problem-Solving Investigation

MAIN IDEA: Solve problems by making a model.

P.S.I. TEAM +

e-Mail: MAKE A MODEL

AYITA: I am decorating the school's gymnasium for the spring dance with cubes that will hang from the ceiling.

YOUR MISSION: Make a model to find how much cardboard will be needed for each cube if the edge of one cube measures 12 inches.

Understand	You know that each cube is 12 inches long.
Plan	Make a cardboard model of a cube with sides 12 inches long. You will also need to determine where to put tabs so that all of the edges are glued together.
Solve	Start with a cube, then unfold it, to show the pattern. You know that 5 of the edges don't need tabs because they are the fold lines. The remaining 7 edges need a tab. Use $\frac{1}{2}$-inch tabs. $7 \times 12 \text{ in.} \times \frac{1}{2} \text{ in.} = 42 \text{ in}^2$ area of 7 tabs $6 \times 12 \text{ in.} \times 12 \text{ in.} = 864 \text{ in}^2$ area of 6 faces 906 in^2 total area (Figure labels: 12 in.; $\frac{1}{2}$ in.) So, 906 square inches of cardboard is needed to make one cube.
Check	Make another cube to determine whether all the edges can be glued together using your model.

Analyze The Strategy

1. How can making a model be useful when solving a word problem?
2. WRITING IN MATH Write a problem that can be solved by making a model. Then solve the problem.

Mixed Problem Solving

For Exercises 3–5, make a model to solve the problem.

3. **CARS** Fiona counted the number of vehicles in the parking lot at a store. She counted a total of 12 cars and motorcycles. If there was a total of 40 wheels, how many cars and motorcycles were there?

4. **ART** Miguel is making a drawing of his family room for a school project. The room measures 18 feet by 21 feet. If he uses a scale of 1 foot = $\frac{1}{2}$ inch, what are the dimensions of the family room on the drawing?

5. **MEASUREMENT** Francis has a photo that measures 10 inches by $8\frac{1}{2}$ inches. If the frame he uses is $1\frac{1}{4}$ inches wide, what is the perimeter of the framed picture?

Use any strategy to solve Exercises 6–13. Some strategies are shown below.

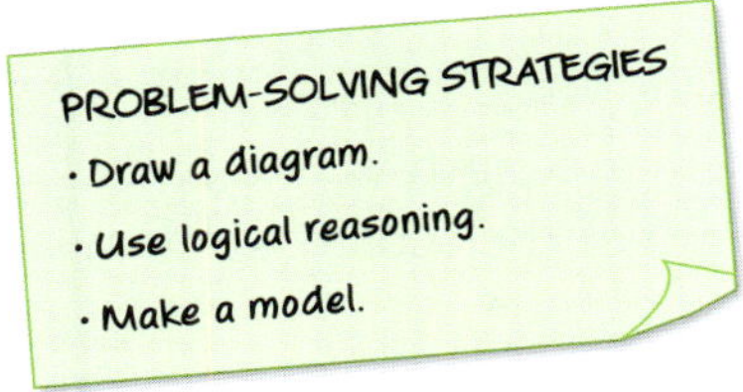

6. **DONATIONS** Hickory Point Middle School collected money for a local shelter. The table shows the total amount collected by each grade level. Suppose the school newspaper reported that $5,000 was collected. Is this estimate reasonable? Explain.

Grade	Dollars Collected
sixth	1,872
seventh	2,146
eighth	1,629

7. **TRACK** Wei can jog one 400-meter lap in $1\frac{1}{3}$ minutes. How long will it take her to run 1,600 meters at the same rate?

8. **BIRD HOUSES** About how many square inches of the bird house will be painted if only the outside of the wood is painted?

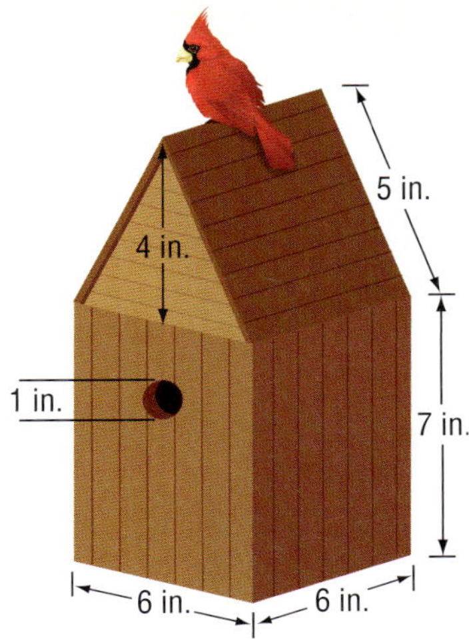

9. **BOXES** Juliet is placing 20 cereal boxes that measure 8 inches by 2 inches by 12 inches on a shelf that is 3 feet long and 11 inches deep. What is a possible arrangement for the boxes on the shelf?

10. **MONEY** At the beginning of the week, Marissa had $45.50. She spent $2.75 each of five days on lunch, bought a sweater for $14.95, and Jacob repaid her $10 that he owed her. How much money does she have at the end of the week?

11. **MEASUREMENT** How many square feet of wallpaper are needed to cover a wall that measures $15\frac{1}{4}$ feet by $8\frac{3}{4}$ feet and has a window that measures 2 feet by 4 feet?

12. **BASEBALL** A regulation baseball diamond is a square with an area of 8,100 square feet. If it is laid out on a field that is 172 feet wide and 301 feet long, how much greater is the distance around the whole field than the distance around the diamond?

13. **DVDs** Marc currently has 68 DVDs in his collection. By the end of the next four months, he wants to have 92 DVDs in his collection. How many DVDs must he buy each month to obtain his goal?

Chapter 12 Mid-Chapter Quiz

Lessons 12-1 through 12-3

Estimate each square root to the nearest whole number. (Lesson 12-1)

1. $\sqrt{32}$
2. $\sqrt{80}$
3. $\sqrt{105}$
4. $\sqrt{230}$

MEASUREMENT **Estimate the side length of each square to the nearest whole number.** (Lesson 12-1)

5. 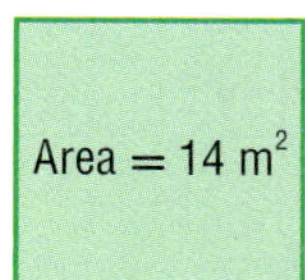

6. 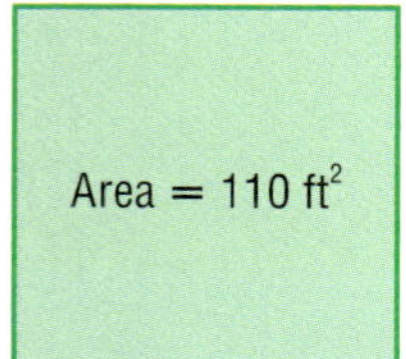

Graph each square root on a number line. (Lesson 12-1)

7. $\sqrt{18}$
8. $\sqrt{230}$

9. **MULTIPLE CHOICE** Imani is playing a review game in math class. She needs to pick the card that is labeled with a number closest to 8. Which should she pick? (Lesson 12-1)

$\sqrt{37}$ $\sqrt{52}$ 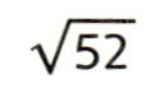 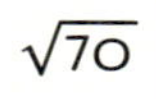

A $\sqrt{37}$
B $\sqrt{52}$
C $\sqrt{70}$
D $\sqrt{83}$

Find the length of the hypotenuse of each triangle. Round to the nearest tenth if necessary. (Lesson 12-2)

10. 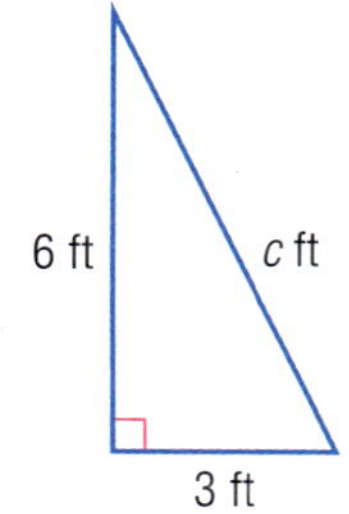

11. 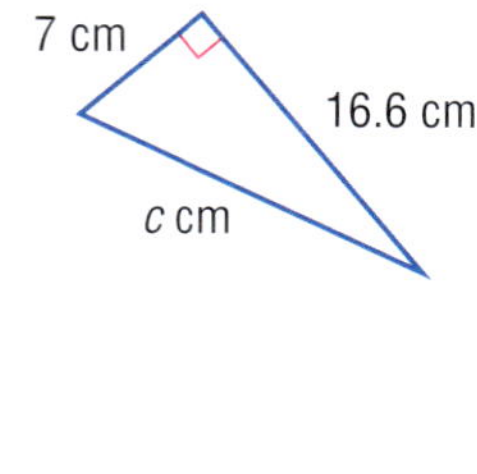

Find the missing measure of each triangle. Round to the nearest tenth if necessary. (Lesson 12-2)

12. 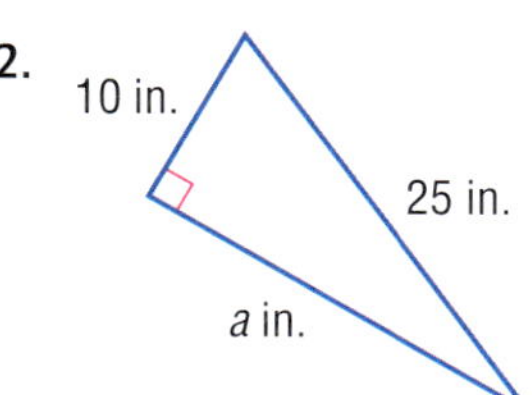

13. 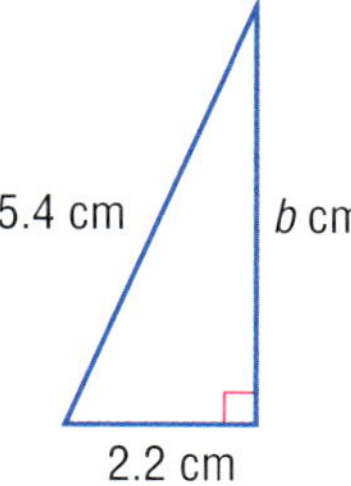

14. **MEASUREMENT** On a computer monitor, the diagonal measure of the screen is 17 inches.

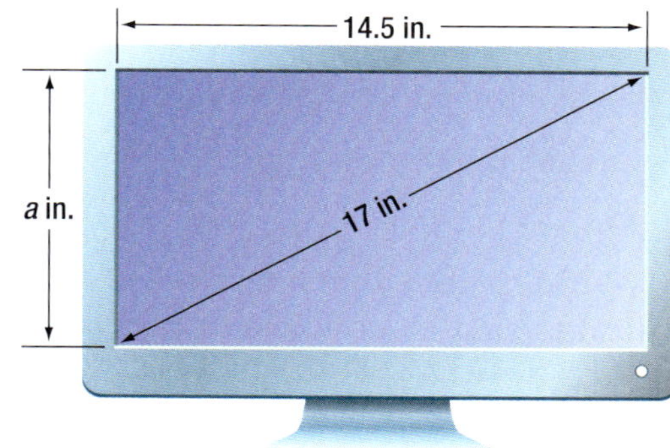

If the screen length is 14.5 inches, what is the height of the screen to the nearest tenth? (Lesson 12-2)

15. **MULTIPLE CHOICE** Eduardo jogs 5 kilometers north and 5 kilometers west. To the nearest kilometer, how far is he from his starting point? (Lesson 12-2)

F 25 km
G 10 km
H 7 km
J 5 km

16. **SCIENCE** A certain type of bacteria doubles every hour. If there are two bacteria initially in a sample, how many will be present after five hours? Use the *make a model* strategy. (Lesson 12-3)

17. **SCALE MODELS** A scale model is made of a building measuring 120 feet long, 75 feet wide, and 45 feet high. If the scale is 1 inch = 15 feet, what are the dimensions of the model? Use the *make a model* strategy. (Lesson 12-3)

Surface Area of Rectangular Prisms

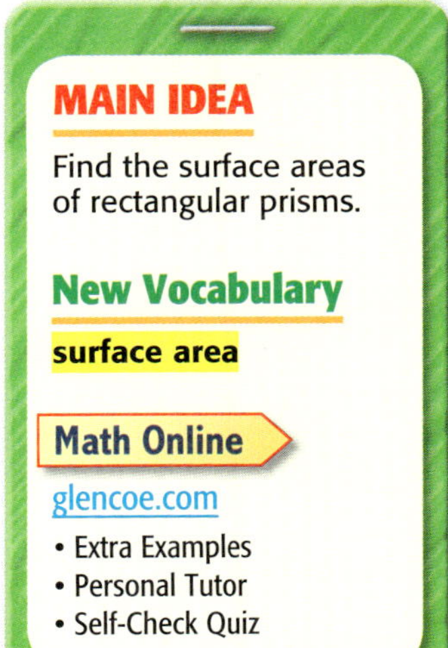

MINI Lab

- Use the cubes to build a rectangular prism with a length of 8 centimeters.
- Count the number of squares on the outside of the prism. The sum is the *surface area*.

1. Record the dimensions, volume, and surface area in a table.
2. Build two more prisms using all of the cubes. For each, record the dimensions, volume, and surface area.
3. Describe the prisms with the greatest and least surface areas.

The sum of the areas of all of the surfaces, or faces, of a three-dimensional figure is the **surface area**.

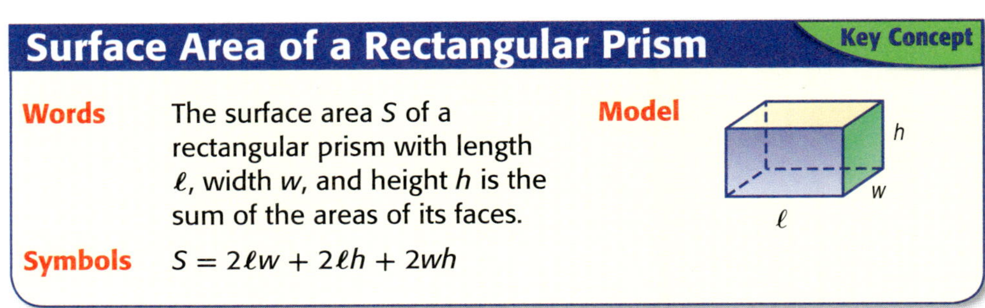

EXAMPLES Find Surface Area

1 **Find the surface area of the rectangular prism.**

There are three pairs of congruent faces.

- top and bottom
- front and back
- two sides

Faces	**Area**
top and bottom	$2(5 \cdot 4) = 40$
front and back	$2(5 \cdot 3) = 30$
two sides	$2(3 \cdot 4) = 24$
sum of the areas	$40 + 30 + 24 = 94$

The surface area is 94 square centimeters.

3 cm
4 cm
5 cm
5 cm
back
3 cm
3 cm
4 cm
side
bottom
side
4 cm
3 cm
front
4 cm
top
5 cm

2 **Find the surface area of the rectangular prism.**

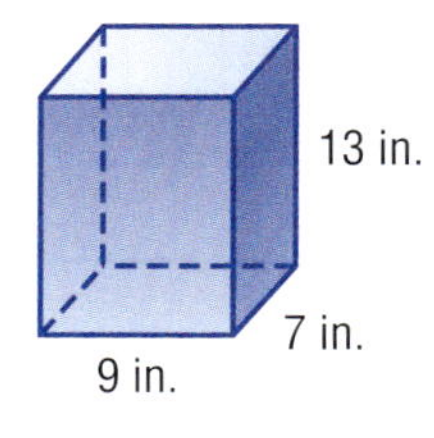

Replace ℓ, with 9, w with 7, and h with 13.

$$\begin{aligned}\text{surface area} &= 2\ell w + 2\ell h + 2wh \\ &= 2 \cdot 9 \cdot 7 + 2 \cdot 9 \cdot 13 + 2 \cdot 7 \cdot 13 \\ &= 126 + 234 + 182 \quad \text{Multiply first. Then add.} \\ &= 542\end{aligned}$$

The surface area of the prism is 542 square inches.

Study Tip

Surface Area When you find the surface area of a three-dimensional figure, the units are square units, not cubic units.

CHECK Your Progress

Find the surface area of each rectangular prism.

a. 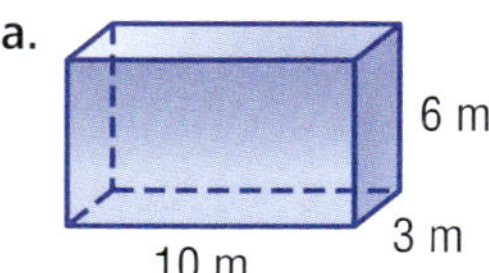

b. 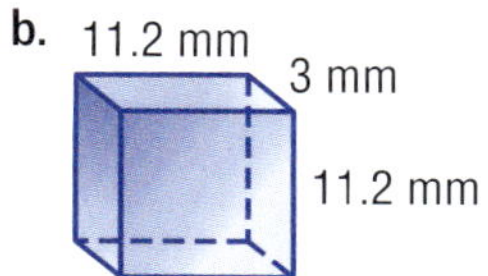

Real-World EXAMPLE

3 **PAINTING** **Domingo built a toy box 60 inches long, 24 inches wide, and 36 inches high. He has 1 quart of paint that covers about 87 square feet of surface. Does he have enough to paint the toy box? Justify your answer.**

STEP 1 Find the surface area of the toy box.

Replace ℓ with 60, w with 24, and h with 36.

$$\begin{aligned}\text{surface area} &= 2\ell w + 2\ell h + 2wh \\ &= 2 \cdot 60 \cdot 24 + 2 \cdot 60 \cdot 36 + 2 \cdot 24 \cdot 36 \\ &= 8{,}928 \text{ in}^2\end{aligned}$$

STEP 2 Find the number of square inches the paint will cover.

$$\begin{aligned}1 \text{ ft}^2 &= 1 \text{ ft} \times 1 \text{ ft} \quad \text{Replace 1 ft with 12 in.} \\ &= 12 \text{ in.} \times 12 \text{ in.} \quad \text{Multiply.} \\ &= 144 \text{ in}^2\end{aligned}$$

So, 87 square feet is equal to 87×144 or 12,528 square inches.

Since $12{,}528 > 8{,}928$, Domingo has enough paint.

Study Tip

Consistent Units Since the surface area of the toy box is expressed in inches, convert 87 ft^2 to square inches so that all measurements are expressed using the same units.

CHECK Your Progress

c. **BOXES** The largest corrugated cardboard box ever constructed measured about 23 feet long, 9 feet high, and 8 feet wide. Would 950 square feet of paper be enough to cover the box? Justify your answer.

d. **BOXES** If 1 foot was added to each dimension of the largest corrugated cardboard box ever constructed, would 950 square feet of paper still be enough to cover the box? Justify your answer.

EXAMPLE Use the Pythagorean Theorem

4 **Find the surface area of the rectangular prism.**

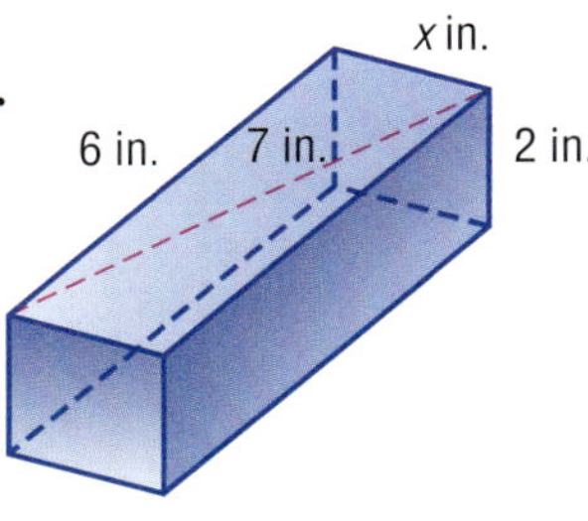

The width and height of the prism are given. To find the surface area, you need to find the length of the prism. Notice that the diagonal, length, and width of the top face of the prism form a right triangle.

$c^2 = a^2 + b^2$	Pythagorean Theorem
$7^2 = 6^2 + x^2$	Replace c with 7, a with 6, and b with x.
$49 = 36 + x^2$	Evaluate 7^2 and 6^2.
$49 - 36 = 36 + x^2 - 36$	Subtract 36 from each side.
$13 = x^2$	Simplify.
$\pm\sqrt{13} = x$	Definition of square root
$\pm 3.6 \approx x$	Simplify.

Study Tip

Square Roots The equation $13 = x^2$ has two solutions, 3.6 and −3.6. However, the length of the prism must be positive, so choose the positive solution.

The length of the prism is about 3.6 inches. Find the surface area.

$$\text{surface area} = 2\ell w + 2\ell h + 2wh$$
$$= 2(3.6)(6) + 2(3.6)(2) + 2(6)(2) \text{ or } 81.6$$

The surface area of the prism is about 81.6 square inches.

CHECK Your Progress

e. Find the surface area of the rectangular prism to the nearest tenth.

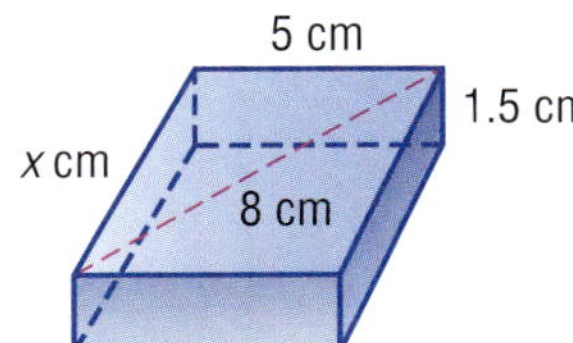

CHECK Your Understanding

Examples 1, 2 (pp. 649–650)

Find the surface area of each rectangular prism. Round to the nearest tenth if necessary.

1. 4 ft, 3 ft, 6 ft

2.

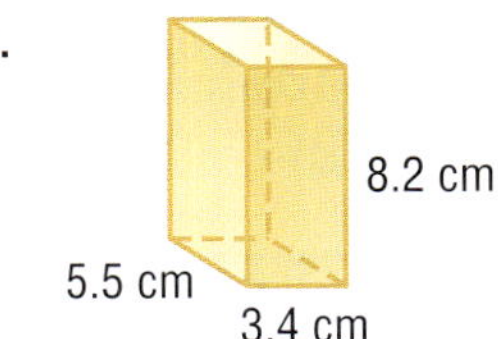

Example 3 (p. 650)

3. **GIFTS** Megan is wrapping a gift. She places it in a box 8 inches long, 2 inches wide, and 11 inches high. If Megan bought a roll of wrapping paper that is 1 foot wide and 2 feet long, did she buy enough paper to wrap the gift? Justify your answer.

Example 4 (p. 651)

4. **MEASUREMENT** Find the surface area of the rectangular prism at the right. Round to the nearest tenth if necessary.

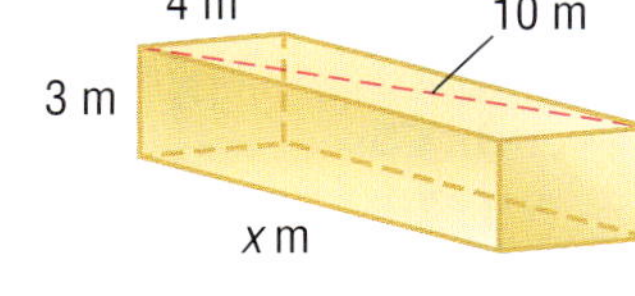

Practice and Problem Solving

HOMEWORK HELP	
For Exercises	See Examples
5–10	1, 2
11–12	3
13–14	4

Find the surface area of each rectangular prism. Round to the nearest tenth if necessary.

5. 8 cm, 9 cm, 5 cm

6. 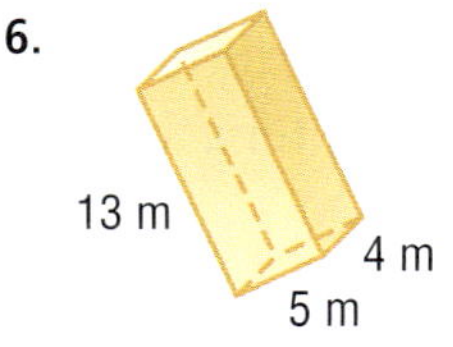

7. 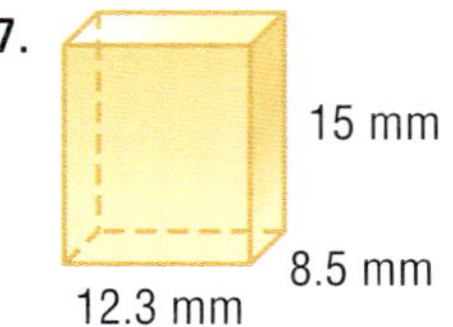

8. 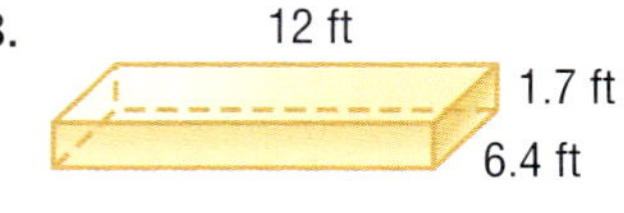

9. 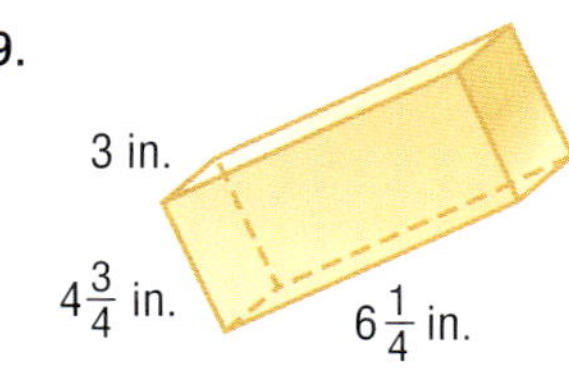

10. 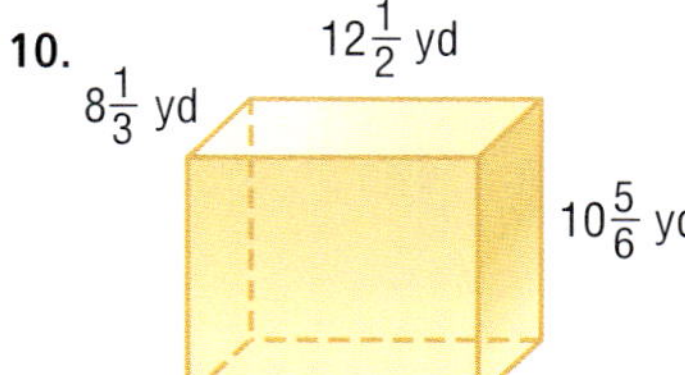

11. **BOOKS** When making a book cover, Anwar adds an additional 20 square inches to the surface area to allow for overlap. How many square inches of paper will Anwar use to make a book cover for a book 11 inches long, 8 inches wide, and 1 inch high?

12. **FENCES** If one gallon of paint covers 350 square feet, will 8 gallons of paint be enough to paint the inside and outside of the fence shown once? Explain.

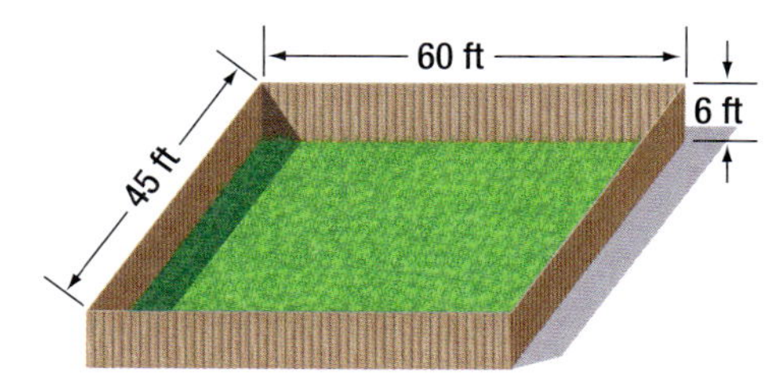

Find the surface area of each rectangular prism. Round to the nearest tenth if necessary.

13. 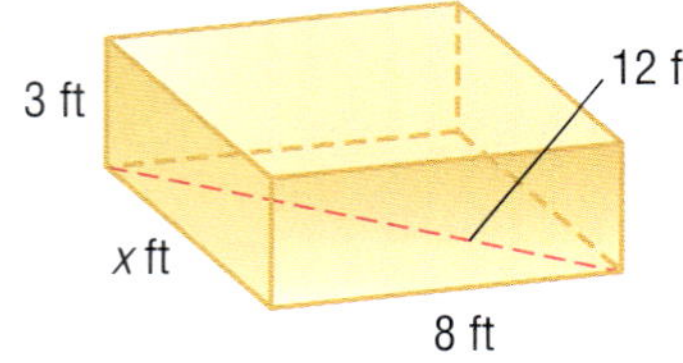

14. 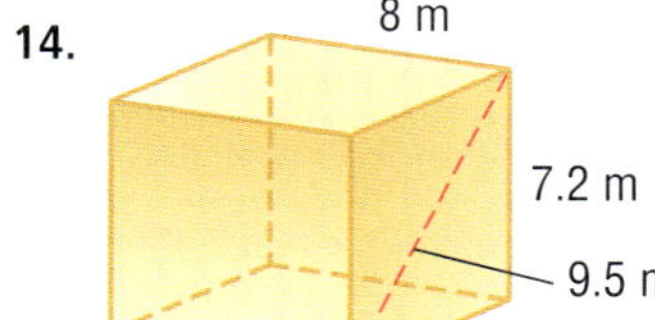

15. **MUSIC** To the nearest tenth, find the approximate amount of plastic covering the outside of the CD case.

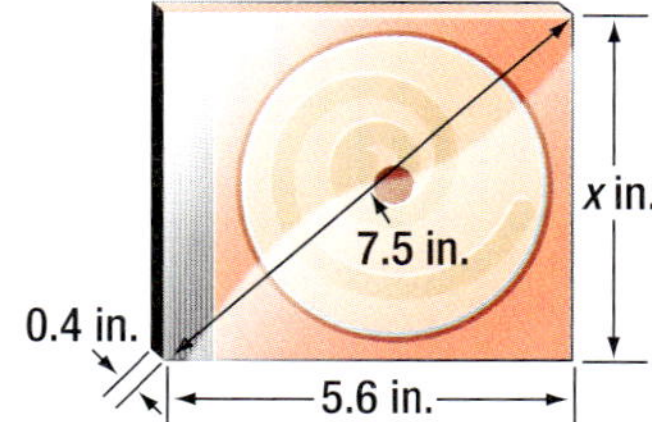

16. **MEASUREMENT** What is the surface area of a rectangular prism that has a length of 6.5 centimeters, a width of 2.8 centimeters, and a height of 9.7 centimeters?

Real-World Link In a recent year, 34% of all music sold was rock, 13% was country, and 11% was R&B. Also, 85.6% of all music formats sold were full-length CDs.
Source: Recording Industry Association of America

17. **ALGEBRA** Write a formula for the surface area s of a cube in which each side measures x units.

18. **PACKAGING** A company will make a cereal box with whole number dimensions and a volume of 100 cubic centimeters. If cardboard costs \$0.05 per 100 square centimeters, what is the least cost to make 100 boxes?

H.O.T. Problems

19. **REASONING** The bottom and sides of a pool in the shape of a rectangular prism will be painted blue. The length, width, and height of the pool are 18 feet, 12 feet, and 6 feet, respectively. Explain why the number of square feet to be painted is *not* equivalent to the expression 2(18)(12) + 2(18)(6) + 2(12)(6).

20. **CHALLENGE** The figure at the right is made by placing a cube with 12-centimeter sides on top of another cube with 15-centimeter sides. Find the surface area.

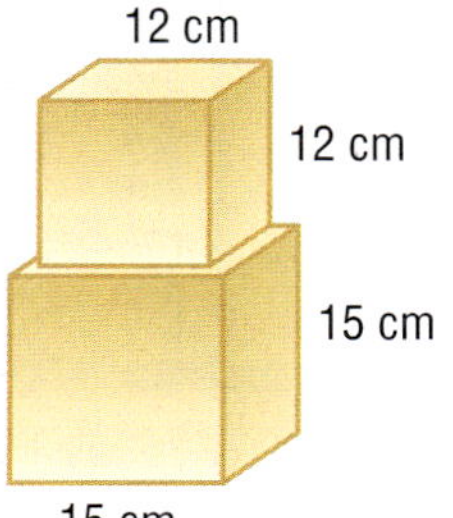

21. 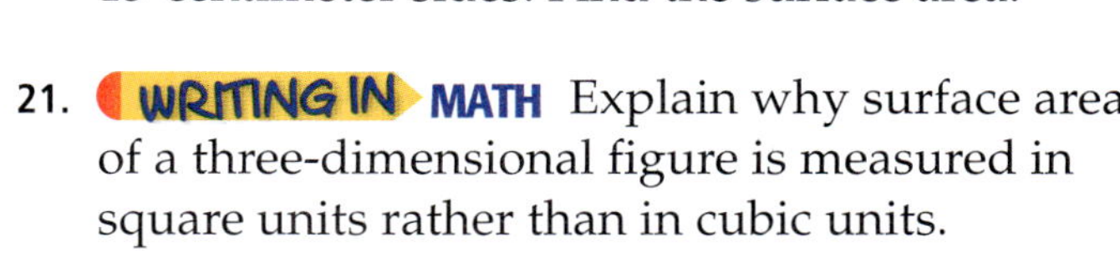 **WRITING IN MATH** Explain why surface area of a three-dimensional figure is measured in square units rather than in cubic units.

TEST PRACTICE

22. Which of the following expressions represents the surface area of a cube with side length w?

    A w^3

    B $6w^2$

    C $6w^3$

    D $2w + 4w^2$

23. How much cardboard is needed to make a box with a length of 2.5 feet, a width of 1.6 feet, and a height of 2 feet?

    F 37.5 square feet

    G 24.4 square feet

    H 8 square feet

    J 6.1 square feet

Spiral Review

24. **MEASUREMENT** A rectangular-shaped yard that measures 50 feet by 70 feet is bordered by a flowerbed that is 2 feet wide. What is the perimeter of the entire yard? Use the *make a model* strategy. (Lesson 12-3)

25. **MEASUREMENT** What is the missing measure of a right triangle in which $a = 13$ feet and $c = 18$ feet? Round to the nearest tenth. (Lesson 12-2)

26. **MEASUREMENT** What is the volume of the cylinder shown at the right? Round to the nearest tenth. (Lesson 11-10)

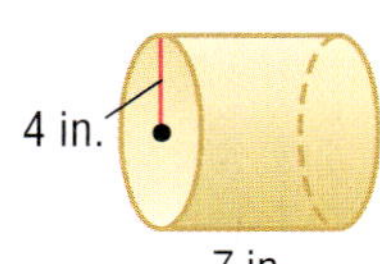

GET READY for the Next Lesson

PREREQUISITE SKILL **Find the area of each circle. Round to the nearest tenth.** (Lesson 11-4)

27. 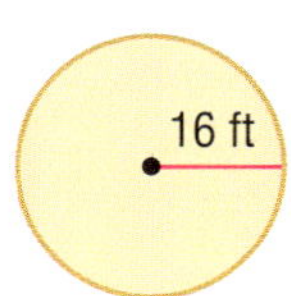

28. 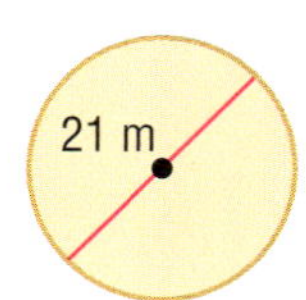

29. diameter = 13.6 yd

30. radius = 23 km

Extend 12-4

Measurement Lab
Changes in Scale

MAIN IDEA

Investigate how changes in scale affect volume and surface area.

Suppose you have a model of a rectangular prism and you are asked to create a similar model with dimensions that are twice as large. In this lab, you will investigate how the scale factor that relates the lengths in two similar objects affects how the surface areas and volumes are related.

ACTIVITY

STEP 1 Draw a cube on dot paper that measures 1 unit on each side. Calculate the volume and the surface area of the cube. Then record the data in a table like the one shown below.

STEP 2 Double the side lengths of the cube. Calculate the volume and the surface area of this cube. Record the data in your table.

STEP 3 Triple the side lengths of the original cube. Now each side measures 3 units long. Calculate the volume and the surface area of the cube and record the data.

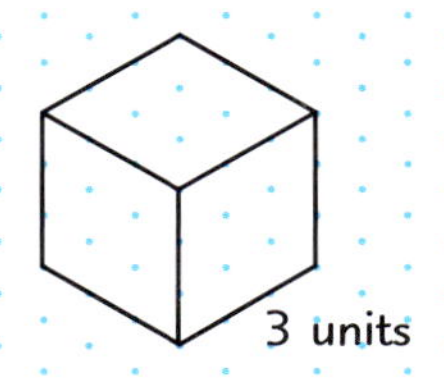

STEP 4 For each cube, write a ratio comparing the side length and the volume. Then write a ratio comparing the side length and the surface area. The first one is done for you.

Side Length (units)	Volume (units^3)	Surface Area (units^2)	Ratio of Side Length to Volume	Ratio of Side Length to Surface Area
1	$1^3 = 1$	$6(1^2) = 6$	1 : 1	1 : 6
2				
3				
4				
5				
s				

CHECK Your Progress

a. Complete the table above.

ACTIVITY

2 **STEP 1** Draw a cube on dot paper that measures 8 units on each side. Calculate the volume and the surface area of the cube. Record the data in a table like the one shown below.

STEP 2 Halve the side lengths of the cube in Step 1. Calculate the volume and the surface area of this cube and record the data.

STEP 3 Halve the side lengths of the cube in Step 2. Calculate the volume and the surface area of the cube and record the data.

STEP 4 For each cube, write a ratio comparing the side length and the volume and a ratio comparing the side length and the surface area. The first one is done for you.

Study Tip

Ratios If you're looking for a pattern among ratios, it is sometimes helpful to reduce each ratio first.

Side Length (units)	Volume (units^3)	Surface Area (units^2)	Ratio of Side Length to Volume	Ratio of Side Length to Surface Area
8	$8^3 = 512$	$6(8^2) = 384$	8 : 512 or 1 : 64	8 : 384 or 1 : 48
4				
2				
s				

CHECK Your Progress

b. Complete the table above.

ANALYZE THE RESULTS

1. Write a formula for the volume V of a cube with side length s.
2. Write a formula for the surface area A of a cube with side length s.

MAKE A CONJECTURE **Complete each sentence.**

3. If the side length of a cube is doubled, the volume is ▒ times greater.
4. If the side length of a cube is doubled, the surface area is ▒ times greater.
5. If the side length of a cube is tripled, the volume increases by ▒ times and the surface area increases by ▒ times.
6. If the side length of a cube decreases by $\frac{1}{2}$, the surface area decreases by ▒.

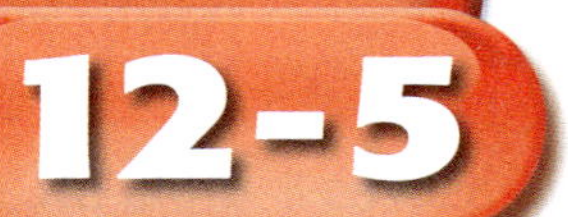

12-5 Surface Area of Cylinders

MAIN IDEA

Find the surface area of a cylinder.

Math Online

glencoe.com

- Extra Examples
- Personal Tutor
- Self-Check Quiz

MINI Lab

STEP 1 Trace the top and bottom of the can on grid paper. Then cut out the shapes.

STEP 2 Cut a long rectangle from the grid paper. The width of the rectangle should be the same as the height of the can. Wrap the rectangle around the side of the can. Cut off the excess paper so that the edges just meet.

1. Make a net of the cylinder.
2. Name the shapes in the net.
3. How is the length of the rectangle related to the circles?

You can put two circles and a rectangle together to make a cylinder.

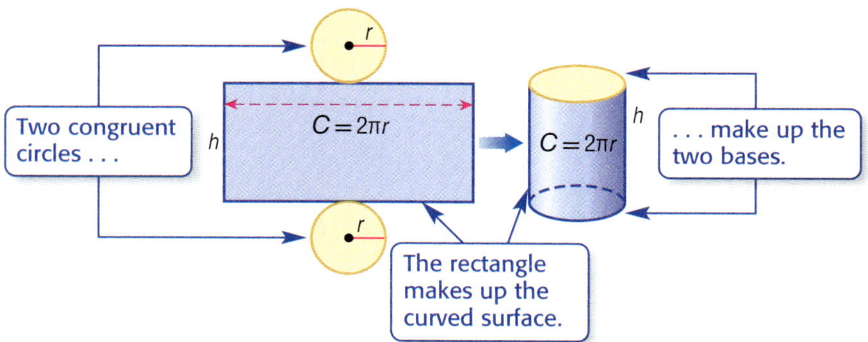

In the diagram above, the length of the rectangle is the same as the circumference of the circle. Also, the width of the rectangle is the same as the height of the cylinder.

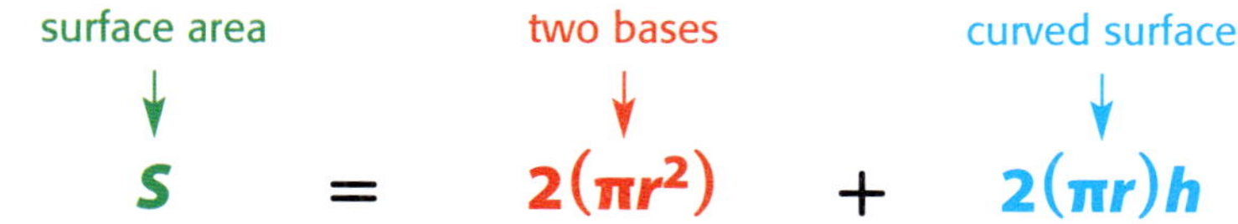

$$S = 2(\pi r^2) + 2(\pi r)h$$

Surface Area of a Cylinder — Key Concept

Words The surface area S of a cylinder with height h and radius r is the sum of the areas of the circular bases and the area of the curved surface.

Model (cylinder with radius r and height h)

Symbols $S = 2\pi r^2 + 2\pi rh$

EXAMPLE Find the Surface Area of a Cylinder

1 **Find the surface area of the cylinder. Round to the nearest tenth.**

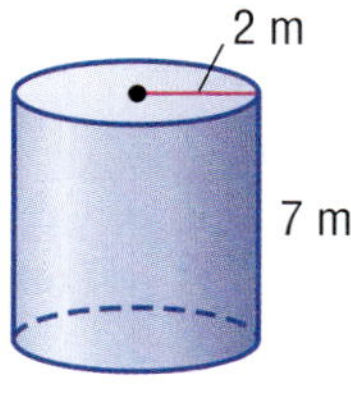

$S = 2\pi r^2 + 2\pi rh$	Surface area of a cylinder
$= 2\pi(2)^2 + 2\pi(2)(7)$	Replace r with 2 and h with 7.
≈ 113.1	Simplify.

The surface area is about 113.1 square meters.

CHECK Your Progress

a. Find the surface area of the cylinder. Round to the nearest tenth.

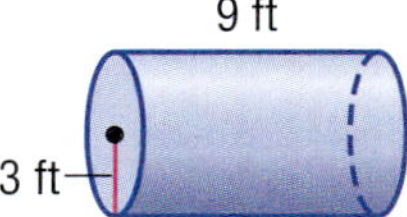

Real-World Link Of the 3,000 to 4,000 wooden carousels carved in America between 1885 and 1930, fewer than 150 operate today.
Source: National Carousel Association

Real-World EXAMPLE

2 **CAROUSELS A circular fence that is 2 feet high is to be built around the outside of a carousel. The distance from the center of the carousel to the edge of the fence will be 35 feet. How much fencing material is needed to make the fence around the carousel?**

The radius of the circular fence is 35 feet. The height is 2 feet.

$S = 2\pi rh$	Curved surface of a cylinder
$= 2\pi(35)(2)$	Replace r with 35 and h with 2.
≈ 439.8	Simplify.

So, about 439.8 square feet of material is needed to make the fence.

CHECK Your Progress

b. **DESIGN** Find the area of the label of a can of tuna with a radius of 5.1 centimeters and a height of 2.9 centimeters.

CHECK Your Understanding

Example 1 (p. 657)

Find the surface area of each cylinder. Round to the nearest tenth.

1.

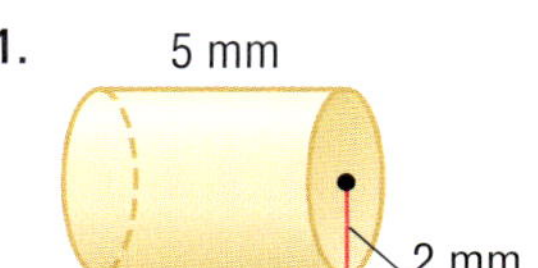

2.

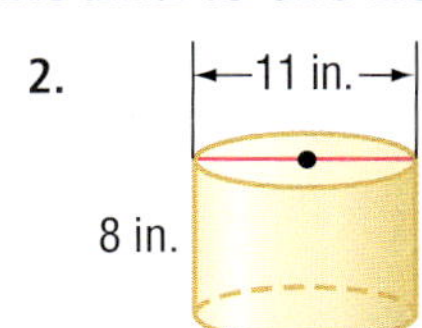

Example 2 (p. 657)

3. **STORAGE** The height of a water tank is 10 meters, and it has a diameter of 10 meters. What is the surface area of the tank?

Practice and Problem Solving

HOMEWORK HELP	
For Exercises	See Examples
4–9	1
10–11	2

Find the surface area of each cylinder. Round to the nearest tenth.

4. 6 yd
10 yd

5. 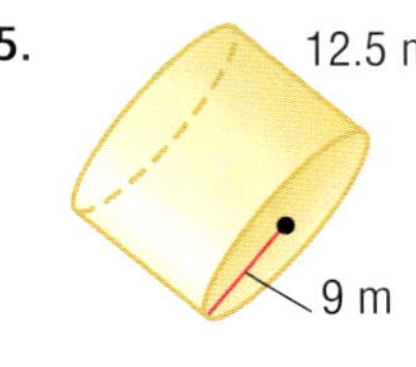

6. 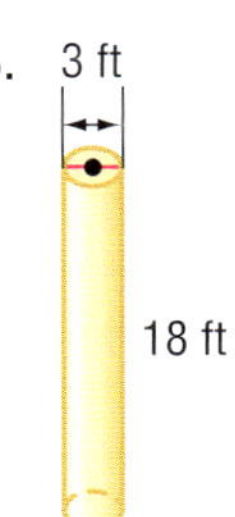

7. 8.7 mm
5.6 mm

8. 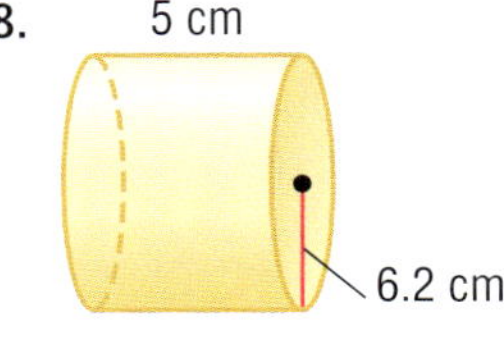

9. 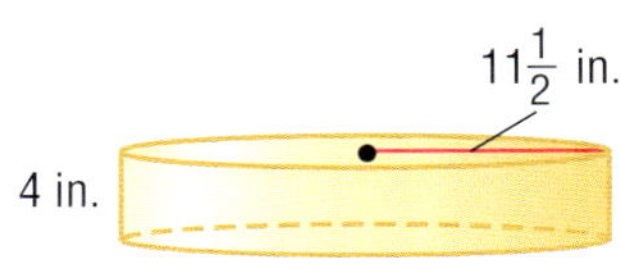

10. **CANDLES** A cylindrical candle has a diameter of 4 inches and a height of 7 inches. What is the surface area of the candle?

11. **PENCILS** Find the surface area of an unsharpened cylindrical pencil that has a radius of 0.5 centimeter and a height of 19 centimeters.

ESTIMATION Estimate the surface area of each cylinder.

12. 4.8 cm
2.2 cm

13. 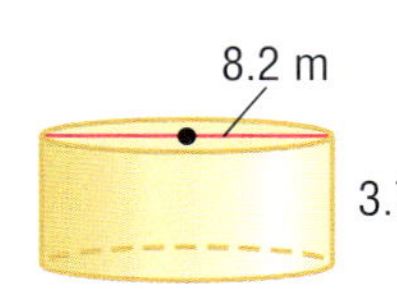

14. 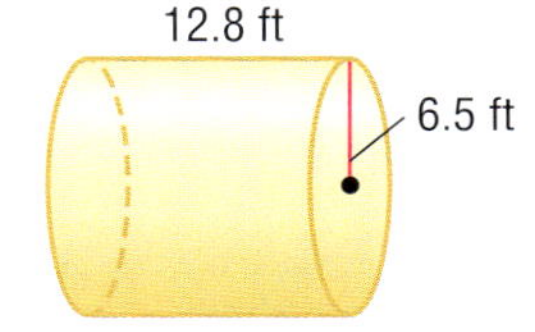

15. **BAKING** Mrs. Jones baked a cake 5 inches high and 9 inches in diameter. If Mrs. Jones covers the top and sides of the cake with frosting, find the area that the frosting covers to the nearest tenth.

16. **PACKAGING** The mail tube shown is made of cardboard and has plastic end caps. Approximately what percent of the surface area of the mail tube is cardboard?

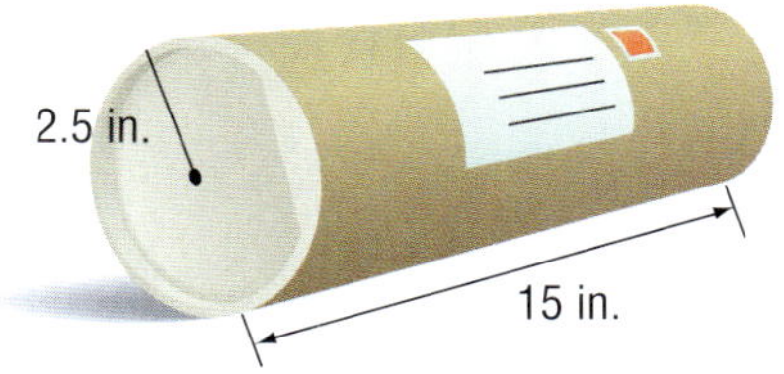

EXTRA PRACTICE
See pages 703, 715.

H.O.T. Problems

17. **CHALLENGE** If the height of a cylinder is doubled, will its surface area also double? Explain your reasoning.

18. **WRITING IN MATH** Write a problem about a real-world situation in which you would find the surface area of a cylinder. Be sure to include the answer to your problem.

19. **REASONING** Which has more surface area, a cylinder with radius 6 centimeters and height 3 centimeters or a cylinder with radius 3 centimeters and height 6 centimeters? Explain your reasoning.

TEST PRACTICE

20. Stacey has a cylindrical paper clip holder with the net shown. Use a centimeter ruler to measure the dimensions of the net in centimeters.

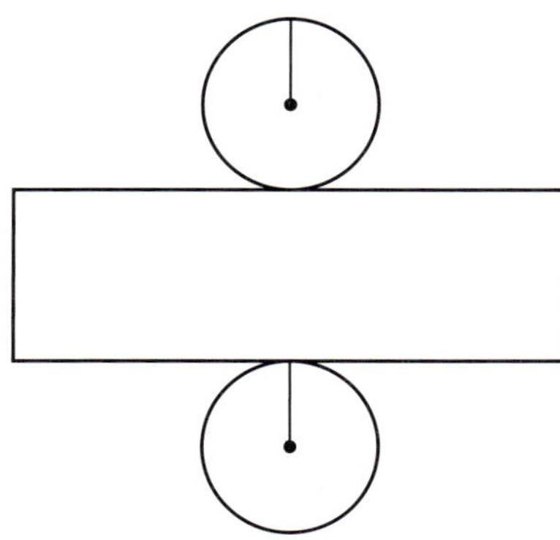

Which is closest to the surface area of the cylindrical paper clip holder?

A $6.0\ \text{cm}^2$

B $6.5\ \text{cm}^2$

C $7.5\ \text{cm}^2$

D $15.5\ \text{cm}^2$

21. The three containers below each hold about 1 liter of liquid. Which container has the greatest surface area?

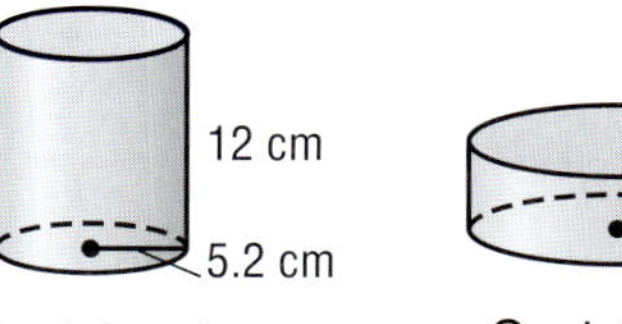

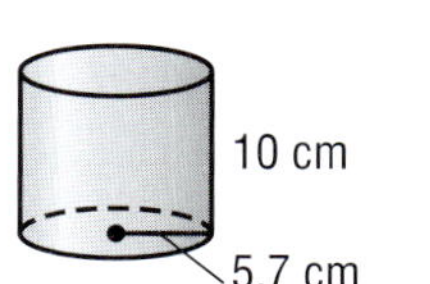

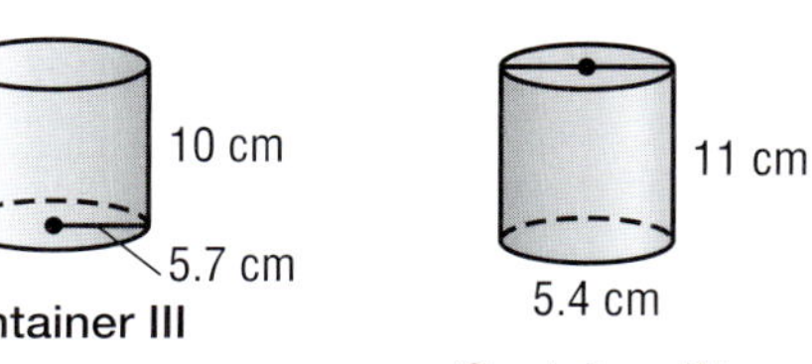

F Container I

G Container II

H Container III

J Container IV

Spiral Review

MEASUREMENT **Find the surface area of each rectangular prism.** (Lesson 12-4)

22.

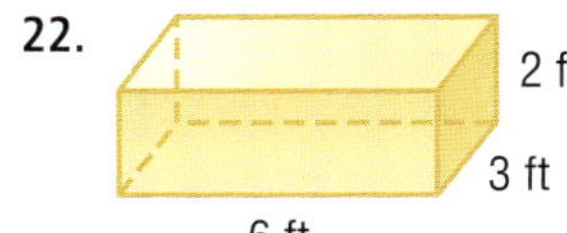

23.

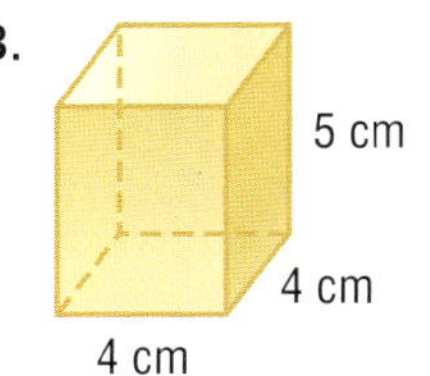

24.

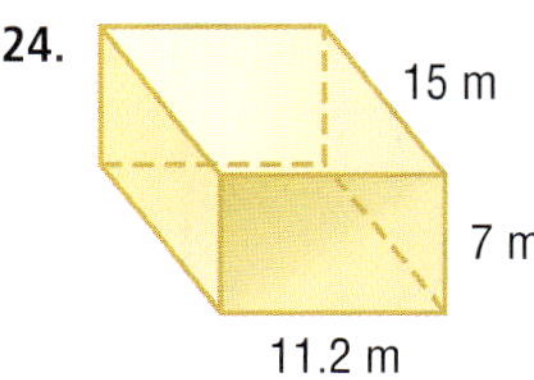

MEASUREMENT **Find the missing measure of each right triangle. Round to the nearest tenth if necessary.** (Lesson 12-2)

25. $a = 8$ in., $b = 10$ in.

26. $a = 12$ ft, $c = 20$ ft

27. $b = 12$ cm, $c = 14$ cm

Problem Solving in Life Skills

Design That House It's time to complete your project. Use the measurements you have gathered to create a blueprint of your dream house. Be sure to include the scale and actual measurements of your dream house.

Math Online **Unit Project at** glencoe.com

CHAPTER 12

Study Guide and Review

Math Online glencoe.com
- STUDY TO GO
- Vocabulary Review

GET READY to Study

Study Organizer

Be sure the following Big Ideas are noted in your Foldable.

Ch. 12	Rectangular Prisms	Cylinders
Draw Examples		
Find Volume		
Find Surface Area		

BIG Ideas

Irrational Numbers (Lesson 12-1)
- An irrational number is a number that cannot be written as a fraction.

Pythagorean Theorem (Lesson 12-2)
- In a right triangle, the square of the length of the hypotenuse equals the sum of the squares of the lengths of the legs.

Surface Area (Lessons 12-4, 12-5)
- The surface area S of a rectangular prism with length ℓ, width w, and height h is the sum of the areas of the faces. $S = 2\ell w + 2\ell h + 2wh$

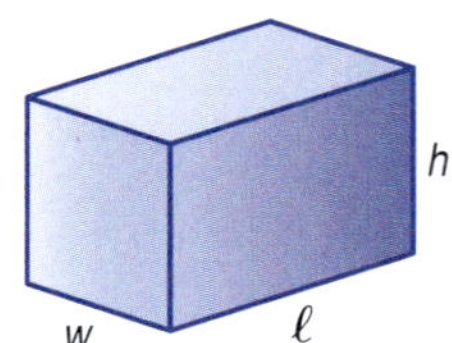

- The surface area S of a cylinder with height h and a radius r is the sum of the area of the circular bases and the area of the curved surface. $S = 2\pi r^2 + 2\pi rh$

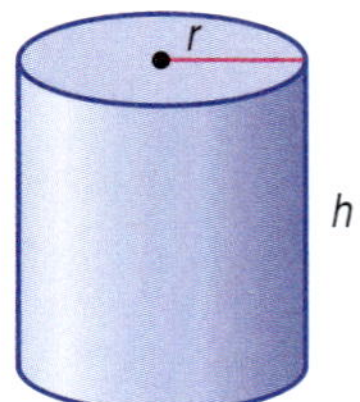

Key Vocabulary

hypotenuse (p. 640)
irrational number (p. 637)
leg (p. 640)
Pythagorean Theorem (p. 640)
surface area (p. 649)

Vocabulary Check

State whether each sentence is *true* or *false*. If *false*, replace the underlined word or number to make a true sentence.

1. The side opposite the right angle in a <u>scalene triangle</u> is called a hypotenuse.
2. Either of the two sides that form the right angle of a right triangle is called a <u>hypotenuse</u>.
3. An <u>irrational number</u> is a number that cannot be expressed as the quotient of two integers.
4. In a right triangle, the square of the length of the hypotenuse equals the <u>difference</u> of the squares of the lengths of the legs.
5. The sum of the areas of all the surfaces of a three-dimensional figure is called the <u>surface area</u>.
6. The formula for finding the surface area of a <u>cylinder</u> is $S = 2\ell w + 2\ell h + 2wh$.
7. Rational numbers include <u>only positive</u> numbers.
8. The <u>Pythagorean Theorem</u> can be used to find the length of the hypotenuse of a right triangle if the measures of both legs are known.
9. To find the surface area of a <u>rectangular prism</u>, you must know the measurements of the height and the radius.
10. The square root of a perfect square is a <u>rational number</u>.

Mixed Problem Solving
For mixed problem-solving practice, see page 715.

Lesson-by-Lesson Review

12-1 Estimating Square Roots (pp. 636–639)

Estimate each square root to the nearest whole number.

11. $\sqrt{6}$
12. $\sqrt{99}$
13. $\sqrt{48}$
14. $\sqrt{76}$
15. $\sqrt{19}$
16. $\sqrt{52}$

Graph each square root on a number line.

17. $\sqrt{61}$
18. $\sqrt{132}$
19. $\sqrt{444}$
20. $\sqrt{12}$
21. **SWIMMING POOL** The bottom of Marcia's square swimming pool has an area of 118 square feet. What is the approximate length of one of the sides?

Example 1 Estimate $\sqrt{29}$ to the nearest whole number.

$25 < 29 < 36$ — 29 is between the perfect squares 25 and 36.

$\sqrt{25} < \sqrt{29} < \sqrt{36}$ — Find the square root of each number.

$5 < \sqrt{29} < 6$ — $\sqrt{25} = 5$ and $\sqrt{36} = 6$

So, $\sqrt{29}$ is between 5 and 6. Since 29 is closer to 25 than to 36, the best whole number estimate is 5.

12-2 The Pythagorean Theorem (pp. 640–645)

Find the missing measure of each triangle. Round to the nearest tenth if necessary.

22.

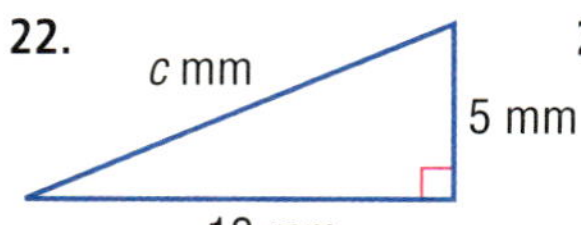

23.

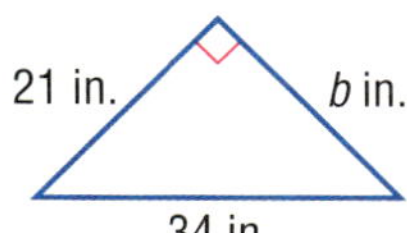

24. $b = 10$ yd, $c = 12$ yd
25. **COMMUNICATION** Find the length of the wire x that is attached to the telephone pole. Round to the nearest tenth.

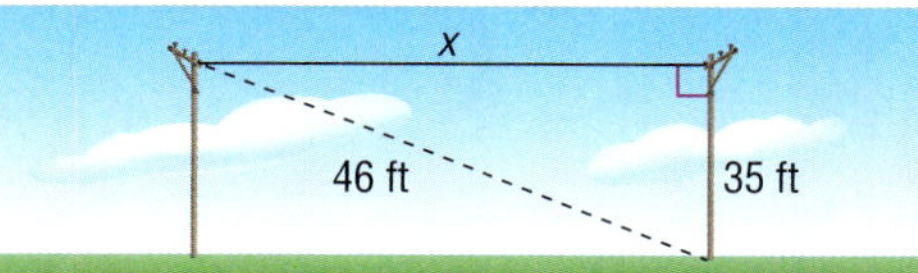

26. **LADDERS** Bartolo has a 26-foot ladder. He places it 10 feet away from the base of a building. What is the height of the building where the top of ladder rests?

Example 2 Find the missing measure of the triangle shown at the right. Round to the nearest tenth if necessary.

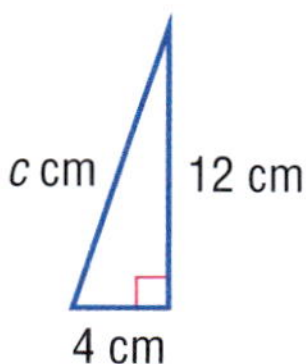

Use the Pythagorean Theorem to solve for c.

$c^2 = a^2 + b^2$ — Pythagorean Theorem

$c^2 = 4^2 + 12^2$ — $a = 4$ and $b = 12$

$c^2 = 16 + 144$ — Evaluate.

$c^2 = 160$ — Add.

$c = \pm\sqrt{160}$ — Definition of square root

$c \approx \pm 12.6$ — Simplify.

Since length cannot be negative, the length of the hypotenuse is about 12.6 centimeters.

Chapter 12 Study Guide and Review

12-3 PSI: Make a Model (pp. 646–647)

Solve the problem by using the *make a model* strategy.

27. **FRAMING** A painting 15 inches by 25 inches is bordered by a mat that is 3 inches wide. The frame around the mat is 2 inches wide. Find the area of the picture with the frame and mat.

28. **DVDs** A video store arranges its best-selling DVDs in their front window. In how many different ways can five best-seller DVDs be arranged in a row?

Example 3 The bottom layer of a display of soup cans has 6 cans in it. If there is one less can in each layer above it and there are 4 layers in the display, how many cans are there in the display?

So, based on the model, there are 18 cans.

12-4 Surface Area of Rectangular Prisms (pp. 649–653)

Find the surface area of each rectangular prism. Round to the nearest tenth if necessary.

29. 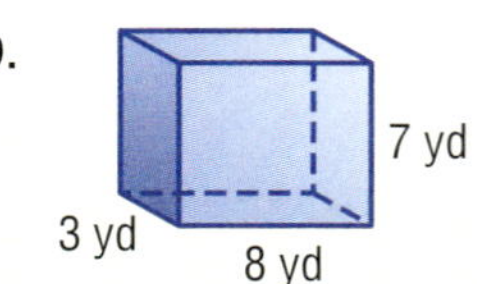

30. 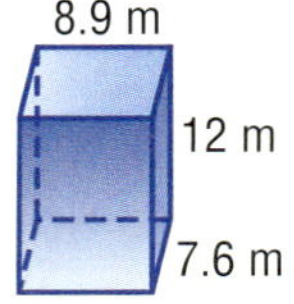

31. **MOVING** A large wardrobe box is 2.25 feet long, 2 feet wide, and 4 feet tall. How much cardboard is needed to make the box?

Example 4 Find the surface area of a rectangular prism.

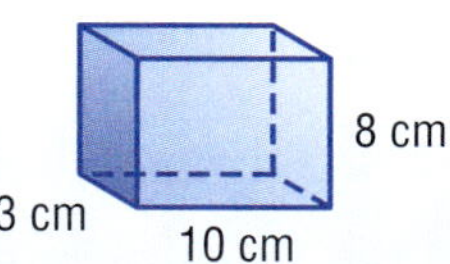

surface area

$= 2\ell w + 2\ell h + 2wh$

$= 2(10)(3) + 2(10)(8) + 2(3)(8)$

$= 268$

The surface area is 268 square centimeters.

12-5 Surface Area of Cylinders (pp. 656–659)

Find the surface area of each cylinder. Round to the nearest tenth.

32. 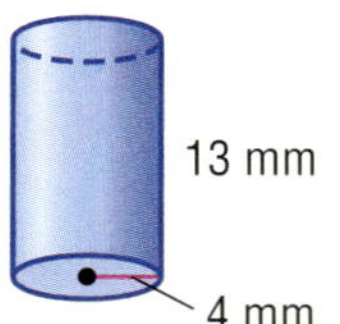

33. 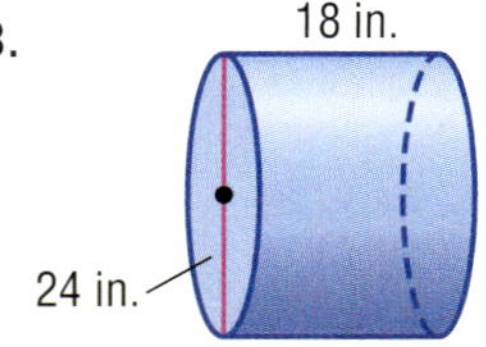

34. **DESIGN** A can of black beans is $5\frac{1}{2}$ inches high, and its base has a radius of 2 inches. How much paper is needed to make the label on the can?

Example 5 Find the surface area of the cylinder. Round to the nearest tenth.

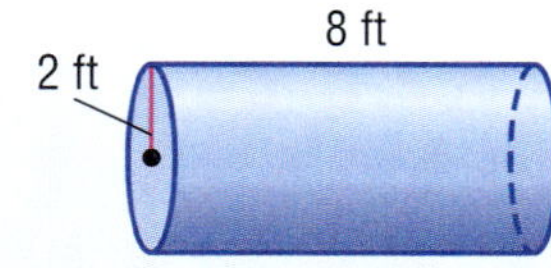

surface area $= 2\pi r^2 + 2\pi rh$

$= 2(\pi)(2^2) + 2(\pi)(2)8$

$\approx 125.7 \text{ ft}^2$

The surface area is about 125.7 square feet.

CHAPTER 12 Practice Test

Math Online glencoe.com
• Chapter Test

Estimate each square root to the nearest whole number.

1. $\sqrt{500}$
2. $\sqrt{95}$
3. $\sqrt{265}$

Graph each square root on the number line.

4. $\sqrt{570}$
5. $\sqrt{7}$
6. $\sqrt{84}$

7. **MULTIPLE CHOICE** The length of one side of a square sandbox is 7 feet. Which number is closest to the length of the diagonal of the sandbox?

   A $\sqrt{100}$
   B $\sqrt{50}$
   C $\sqrt{14}$
   D $\sqrt{7}$

Find the missing measure of each right triangle. Round to the nearest tenth if necessary.

8. $a = 5$ m, $b = 4$ m
9. $b = 12$ in., $c = 14$ in.
10. $a = 7$ in., $c = 13$ in.

11. **MEASUREMENT** Use the diagram below to find the distance from the library to the post office. Round to the nearest tenth.

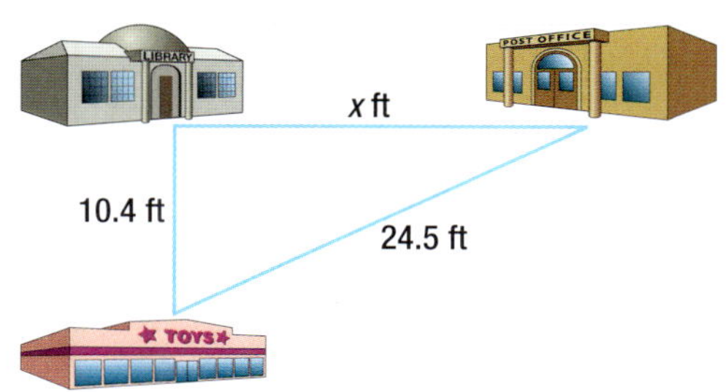

12. **CHAIRS** Chris is responsible for arranging the chairs at the meeting. There are 72 chairs, and he wants to have twice as many chairs in each row as he has in each column. How many chairs should he put in each row? How many rows does he need?

Find the surface area of each rectangular prism and cylinder. Round to the nearest tenth if necessary.

13.

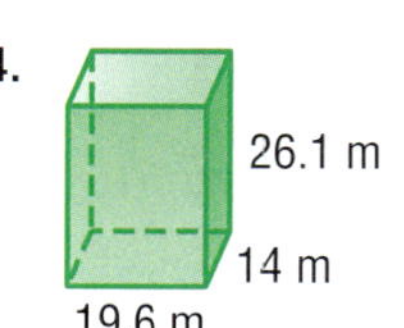

14.

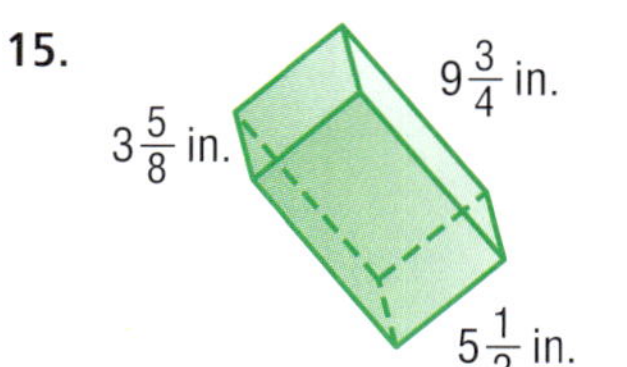

15.

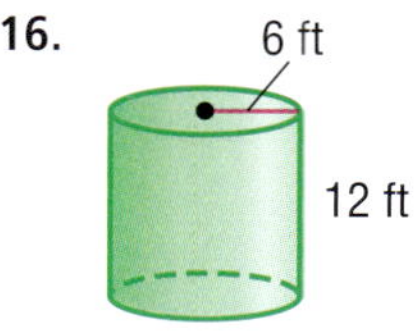

16.

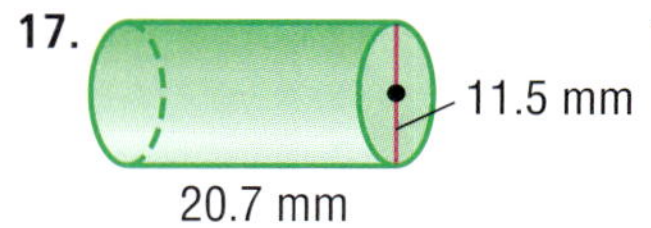

17.

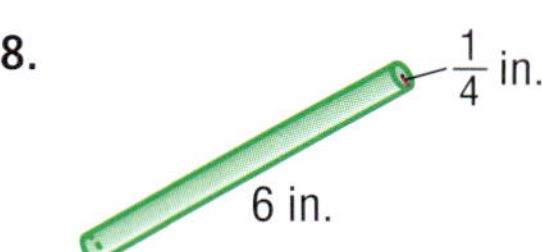

18.

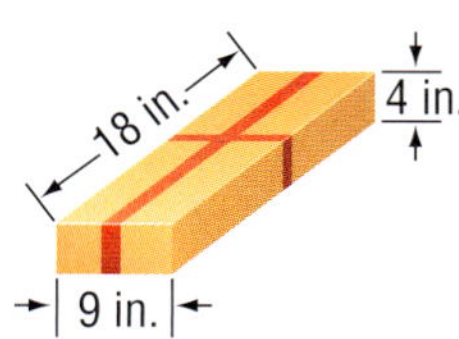

19. **PACKAGING** Mrs. Rodriguez is wrapping a gift. What is the least amount of wrapping paper she will need to wrap the box below?

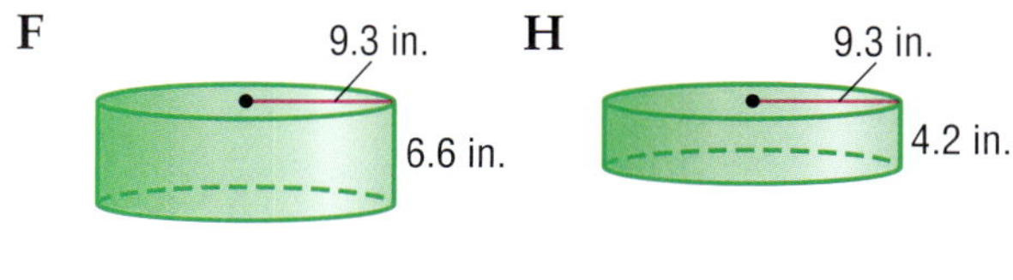

20. **MULTIPLE CHOICE** The dimensions of four containers are given below. Which container has the greatest surface area?

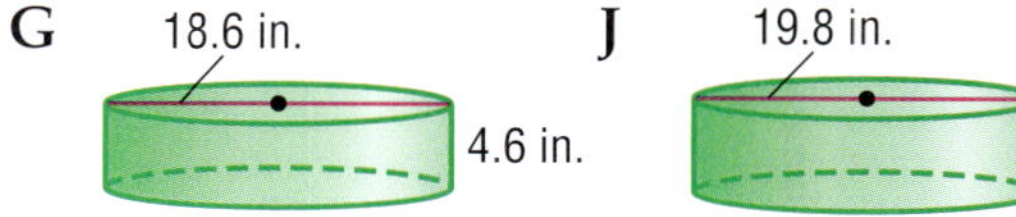

Test Practice

Cumulative, Chapters 1–12

Math Online glencoe.com
• Test Practice

PART 1 Multiple Choice

Read each question. Then fill in the correct answer on the answer document provided by your teacher or on a sheet of paper.

1. Which of the following three-dimensional figures could be formed from this net?

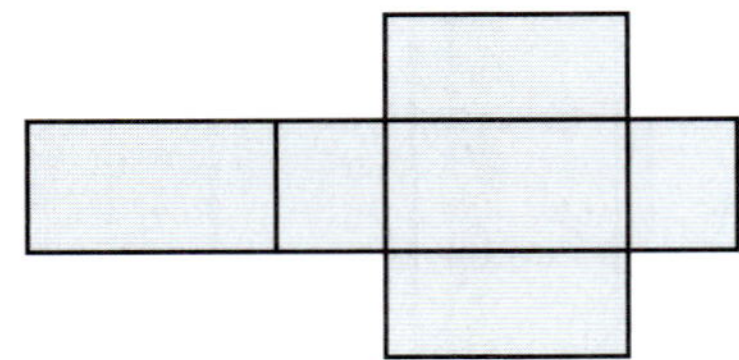

A cube
B rectangular pyramid
C triangular prism
D rectangular prism

2. Which of the following nets could be used to make a cylinder?

F

G

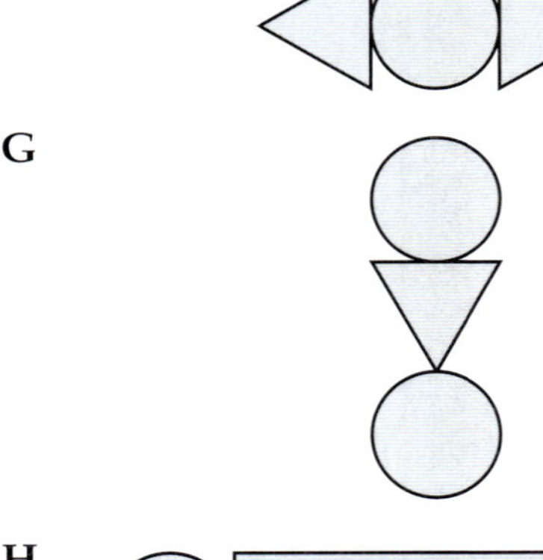

H

J

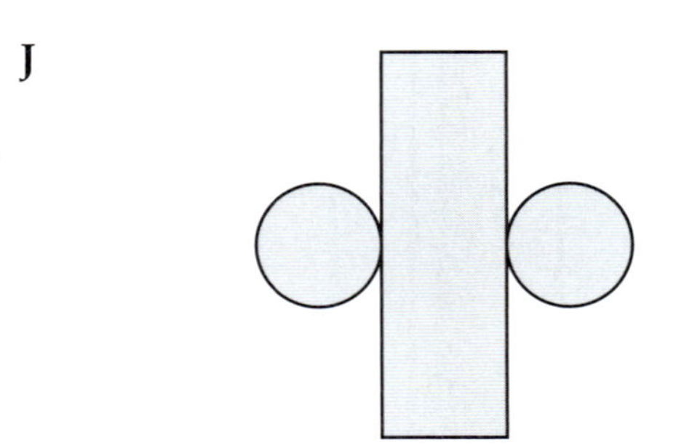

3. Carla has an above-ground swimming pool with a circumference of 20 feet. Which of the following equations could be used to find r, the radius of the pool?

A $r = \frac{10}{\pi}$
C $r = \frac{10}{2\pi}$
B $r = \frac{40}{\pi}$
D $r = \frac{\pi}{20}$

4. Of the following figures that Ryan drew, which 2 figures have the same area?

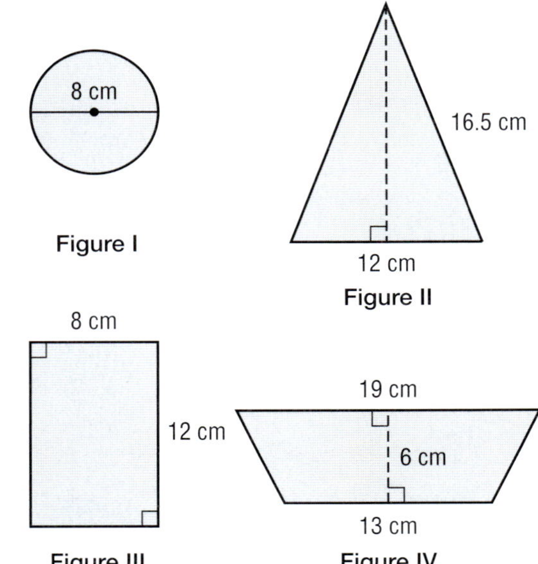

F Figure I and II
G Figure II and III
H Figure II and IV
J Figure III and IV

5. Cassandra drew a circle with a radius of 12 inches and another circle with a radius of 8 inches. What is the approximate difference between the areas of the 2 circles? Use $\pi = 3.14$.

A 452.16 in^2
C 50.24 in^2
B 251.2 in^2
D 25.12 in^2

Preparing for Standardized Tests

For test-taking strategies and practice, see pages 716–733.

6. Which equation could be used to find the area of a circle with a radius of 10 centimeters?

   F $A = 5 \times \pi$

   G $A = \pi \times 5^2$

   H $A = 10 \times \pi$

   J $A = \pi \times 10^2$

7. Dave can run 30 yards in 8.2 seconds. During a race, he ran 120 yards. If Dave's rate of speed remained the same, how long did it take him to run the race?

   A 43 seconds

   B 32.8 seconds

   C 24.6 seconds

   D 18.4 seconds

8. Which of the following equations gives the surface area S of a cube with side length m?

   F $S = m^3$

   G $S = 6m^2$

   H $S = 6m$

   J $S = 2m + 4m^2$

TEST-TAKING TIP

Question 9 Be sure to read each question carefully. In question 9, you are asked to find which statement is *not* true.

9. Which statement is *not* true about an equilateral triangle?

   A The sum of the angles is 180°.

   B It has three congruent angles.

   C It has one right angle.

   D It has exactly three congruent sides.

PART 2 Short Response/Grid In

Record your answers on the answer sheet provided by your teacher or on a sheet of paper.

10. Bill's Electronics bought 5 computers for a total of $3,000. The business later bought another computer for $600. What was the mean price of all the computers?

11. A jar contains 9 yellow marbles and 1 red marble. Ten students will each randomly select one marble to determine who goes first in a game. Whoever picks the red marble goes first. Lily will pick first and keep the marble that she picks. Heath will pick second. What is the probability that Lily will pick a yellow marble and Heath will pick the red marble?

PART 3 Extended Response

Record your answers on the answer sheet provided by your teacher or on a sheet of paper. Show your work.

12. A square with a side of y inches is inside a square with a side of 6 inches, as shown below.

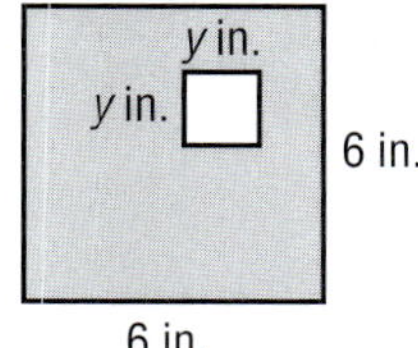

   a. Write an expression that can be used to find the area of the shaded region in terms of y.

   b. If the dimensions of both squares are doubled, write an expression that could be used to find the area of the new shaded region.

NEED EXTRA HELP?												
If You Missed Question...	1	2	3	4	5	6	7	8	9	10	11	12
Go to Lesson...	11-8	11-8	11-3	11-2	11-4	11-4	6-6	12-4	10-3	8-2	9-8	11-1

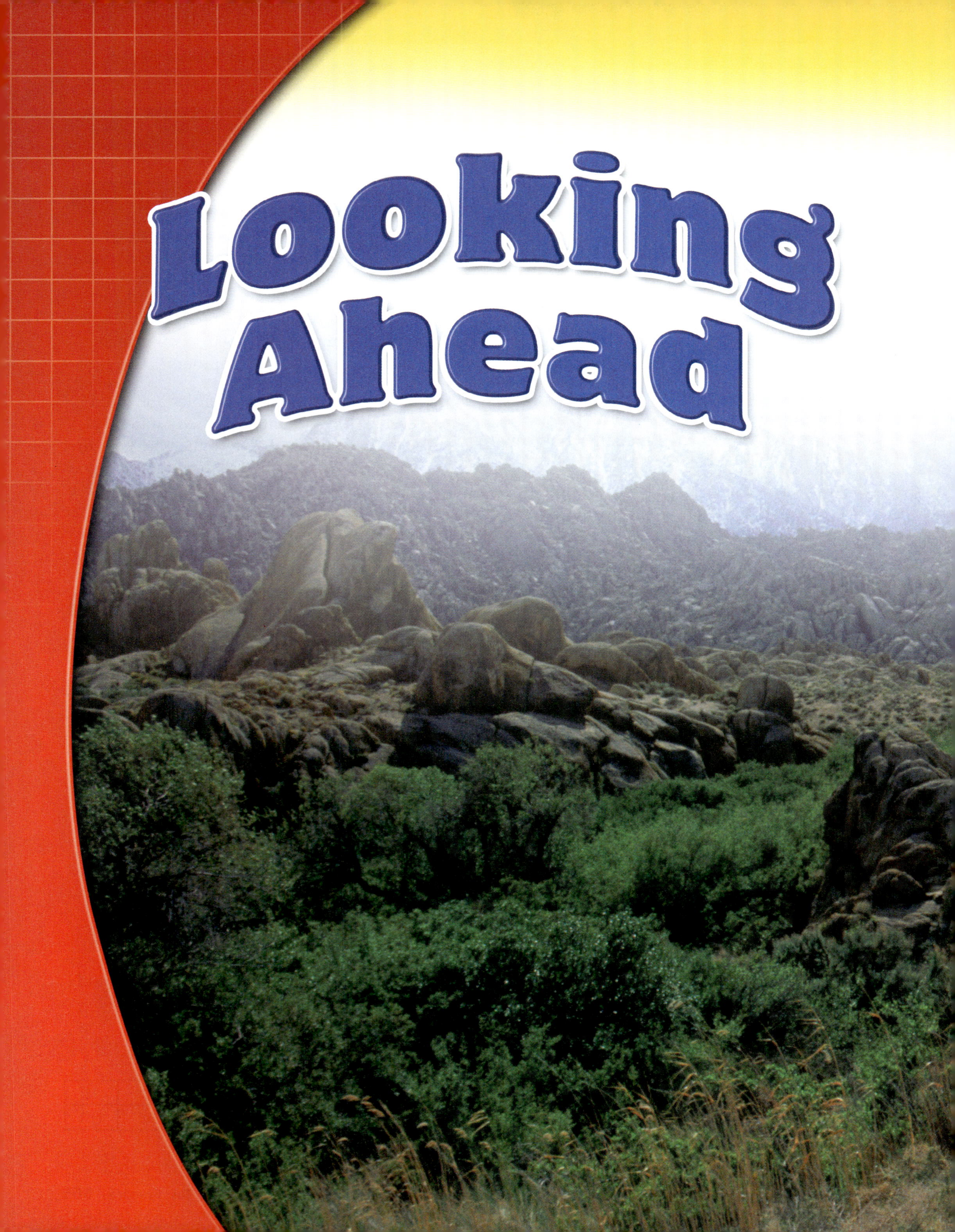
Looking
Ahead

Let's Look Ahead

Scientific Notation

MAIN IDEA

Express numbers in scientific notation and in standard form.

New Vocabulary

scientific notation

Math Online

glencoe.com

- Personal Tutor
- Self-Check Quiz
- Extra Examples

GET READY for the Lesson

More than 425 million pounds of gold has been discovered in the world. If all this gold were in one place, it would form a cube seven stories on each side.

1. Write 425 million in standard form.
2. Complete: $4.25 \times$ __?__ $= 425$ million.

When you deal with very large numbers like 425,000,000, it can be difficult to keep track of the zeros. You can express numbers such as this in **scientific notation** by writing the number as the product of a factor and a power of 10.

Scientific Notation — Key Concept

Words A number is expressed in scientific notation when it is written as the product of a factor and a power of 10. The factor must be greater than or equal to 1 and less than 10.

Symbols $a \times 10^n$, where $1 \le a < 10$ and n is an integer

Examples $425{,}000{,}000 = 4.25 \times 10^8$

EXAMPLE Express Large Numbers in Standard Form

1 **Express 2.16×10^5 in standard form.**

$2.16 \times 10^5 = 2.16 \times 100{,}000$ — $10^5 = 100{,}000$

$= 216{,}000$ — Move the decimal point 5 places to the right.

CHECK Your Progress

Express each number in standard form.

a. 7.6×10^6

b. 3.201×10^4

Scientific notation is also used to express very small numbers. Study the pattern of products at the right. Notice that multiplying by a negative power of 10 moves the decimal point to the left the same number of places as the absolute value of the exponent.

$1.25 \times 10^2 = 125$

$1.25 \times 10^1 = 12.5$

$1.25 \times 10^0 = 1.25$

$1.25 \times 10^{-1} = 0.125$

$1.25 \times 10^{-2} = 0.0125$

$1.25 \times 10^{-3} = 0.00125$

Study Tip

Move the Decimal Point The exponent tells you how many places to move the decimal point.

- If the exponent is positive, move the decimal point to the right.
- If the exponent is negative, move the decimal point to the left.

EXAMPLE Express Small Numbers in Standard Form

2 **Express 5.8×10^{-3} in standard form.**

$5.8 \times 10^{-3} = 5.8 \times 0.001$ — $10^{-3} = 0.001$

$= 0.0058$ — Move the decimal point 3 places to the left.

CHECK Your Progress

c. 4.7×10^{-5}

d. 9.0×10^{-4}

To write a number in scientific notation, place the decimal point after the first nonzero digit. Then find the power of 10.

EXAMPLES Express Numbers in Scientific Notation

Express each number in scientific notation.

3 **1,457,000**

$1{,}457{,}000 = 1.457 \times 1{,}000{,}000$ — The decimal point moves 6 places to the left.

$= 1.457 \times 10^6$ — The exponent is positive.

4 **0.00063**

$0.00063 = 6.3 \times 0.0001$ — The decimal point moves 4 places to the right.

$= 6.3 \times 10^{-4}$ — The exponent is negative.

CHECK Your Progress

e. 35,000

f. 0.00722

To compare numbers in scientific notation, first compare the exponents. With positive numbers, any number with a greater exponent is greater. If the exponents are the same, compare the factors.

Real-World EXAMPLE Compare Numbers in Scientific Notation

5 **OCEANS** **The Atlantic Ocean has an area of 3.18×10^7 square miles. The Pacific Ocean has an area of 6.4×10^7 square miles. Which ocean has the greater area?**

Since both exponents are the same, compare the factors.

$3.18 < 6.4 \rightarrow 3.18 \times 10^7 < 6.4 \times 10^7$

So, the Pacific Ocean has the greater area.

Real-World Link At the deepest point in the ocean, the pressure is greater than 8 tons per square inch and the temperature is only a few degrees above freezing.

Source: Ocean Planet Smithsonian

CHECK Your Progress

g. Replace ● with <, >, or = to make 4.13×10^{-2} ● 5.0×10^{-3} a true sentence.

CHECK Your Understanding

Examples 1, 2 (pp. LA2–LA3)

Express each number in standard form.

1. 3.754×10^5
2. 8.34×10^6
3. 1.5×10^{-4}
4. 2.68×10^{-3}

Examples 3, 4 (p. LA3)

Express each number in scientific notation.

5. 4,510,000
6. 0.00673
7. 0.000092
8. 11,620,000

9. **PHYSICAL SCIENCE** Light travels 300,000 kilometers per second. Write this number in scientific notation.

Example 5 (p. LA3)

10. **TECHNOLOGY** The distance between tracks on a CD and DVD are shown in the table. Which disc has the greater distance between tracks?

Disc	Distance (mm)
CD	1.6×10^{-3}
DVD	7.4×10^{-4}

Replace each ● with <, >, or = to make a true sentence.

11. 2.3×10^5 ● 1.7×10^5
12. 0.012 ● 1.4×10^{-1}

Practice and Problem Solving

HOMEWORK HELP	
For Exercises	See Examples
13–22	1, 2
23–32	3, 4
33–38	5

Express each number in standard form.

13. 6.1×10^4
14. 5.72×10^6
15. 3.3×10^{-1}
16. 5.68×10^{-3}
17. 9.014×10^{-2}
18. 1.399×10^5
19. 2.505×10^3
20. 7.4×10^{-5}

21. **SPIDERS** The diameter of a spider's thread is 1.0×10^{-3} inch. Write this number in standard form.

22. **DINOSAURS** The *Gigantosaurus* dinosaur weighed about 1.4×10^4 pounds. Write this number in standard form.

Express each number in scientific notation.

23. 499,000
24. 2,000,000
25. 0.006
26. 0.0125
27. 50,000,000
28. 39,560
29. 0.000078
30. 0.000425

31. **CHESS** The number of possible ways that a player can play the first four moves in a chess game is 3 billion. Write this number in scientific notation.

32. **SCIENCE** A particular parasite is approximately 0.025 inch long. Write this number in scientific notation.

SPORTS **For Exercises 33 and 34, use the table. Determine which category in each pair had a greater amount of sales.**

Category	Sales ($)
Camping	1.547×10^9
Golf	3.243×10^9
Tennis	3.73×10^8

Source: National Sporting Goods Assoc.

33. golf or tennis
34. camping or golf

Replace each ● with <, >, or = to make a true sentence.

35. 1.8×10^3 ● 1.9×10^{-1}

36. 5.2×10^2 ● 5000

37. 0.00701 ● 7.1×10^{-3}

38. 6.49×10^4 ● 649×10^2

39. **MEASUREMENT** The table at the right shows the values of different prefixes that are used in the metric system. Write the units attometer, gigameter, kilometer, nanometer, petameter, and picometer in order from greatest to least measure.

Metric Measures	
Prefix	**Meaning**
atto	10^{-18}
giga	10^9
kilo	10^3
nano	10^{-9}
peta	10^{15}
pico	10^{-12}

40. **NUMBER SENSE** Write the product of 0.00004 and 0.0008 in scientific notation.

41. **NUMBER SENSE** Order 6.1×10^4, 6100, 6.1×10^{-5}, 0.0061, and 6.1×10^{-2} from least to greatest.

PHYSICAL SCIENCE For Exercises 42 and 43, use the table.

The table shows the maximum amounts of lava in cubic meters per second that erupted from four volcanoes.

Volcanic Eruptions	
Volcano, Year	**Eruption Rate (m^3/s)**
Mount St. Helens, 1980	2.0×10^4
Ngauruhoe, 1975	2.0×10^3
Hekla, 1970	4.0×10^3
Agung, 1963	3.0×10^4

Source: University of Alaska

42. How many times greater was the Mount St. Helens eruption than the Ngauruhoe eruption?

43. How many times greater was the Hekla eruption than the Ngauruhoe eruption?

Write each number in standard form.

44. $(8 \times 10^0) + (4 \times 10^{-3}) + (3 \times 10^{-5})$

45. $(4 \times 10^4) + (8 \times 10^3) + (3 \times 10^2) + (9 \times 10^1) + (6 \times 10^0)$

H.O.T. Problems

46. **CHALLENGE** Convert the numbers in each expression to scientific notation. Then evaluate the expression. Express in scientific notation and in decimal notation.

a. $\dfrac{(420{,}000)(0.015)}{0.025}$

b. $\dfrac{(0.078)(8.5)}{0.16(250{,}000)}$

47. **REASONING** Which is a better estimate for the number of times per year that a person blinks: 6.25×10^{-2} times or 6.25×10^6 times? Explain your reasoning.

48. **OPEN ENDED** Describe a real-life value or measure using numbers in scientific notation and in standard form.

49. **WRITING IN MATH** Explain the relationship between a number in standard form and the sign of the exponent when the number is written in scientific notation.

Solving Multi-Step Equations

MAIN IDEA

Solve equations with the variable on each side.

Math Online

glencoe.com

- Personal Tutor
- Self-Check Quiz
- Extra Examples

GET READY for the Lesson

Jeremy bought two used video games for d dollars each. Alyssa bought one used video game for d dollars and a used CD for \$5. They both spent the same amount.

amount Jeremy spent		amount Alyssa spent
$2d$	$=$	$d + 5$

1. Use the expressions above to write an equation that represents this situation.
2. Use the *guess-and-check* strategy to solve the equation. What does the solution mean?

To solve equations with variables on each side, use the Addition or Subtraction Property of equality to write an equivalent equation with the variables on one side. Then solve.

EXAMPLES Equations with Variables on Each Side

Solve each equation. Check the solution.

1 $3x + 8 = 4x$

$3x + 8 = 4x$	Write the equation.
$3x - 3x + 8 = 4x - 3x$	Subtract $3x$ from each side.
$8 = x$	Simplify.

The solution is 8. **Check** $3(8) + 8 = 32$ and $4(8) = 32$ ✓

2 $4 + t = 3.5t - 2$

$4 + t = 3.5t - 2$	Write the equation.
$4 + t - t = 3.5t - t - 2$	Subtract t from each side.
$4 = 2.5t - 2$	Simplify.
$4 + 2 = 2.5t - 2 + 2$	Add 2 to each side.
$6 = 2.5t$	Simplify.
$\frac{6}{2.5} = \frac{2.5t}{2.5}$	Divide each side by 2.5.
$2.4 = t$	Simplify.

The solution is 2.4. **Check** $4 + 2.4 = 6.4$ and $3.5(2.4) - 2 = 6.4$ ✓

CHECK Your Progress

a. $7d - 13 = 3d + 7$

b. $12.6 - x = 2x$

You can use the Distributive Property to remove grouping symbols in equations.

EXAMPLE Use the Distributive Property

3 **Solve $2n = 10(n - 1)$.**

$2n = 10(n - 1)$	Write the equation.
$2n = 10(n) - 10(1)$	Use the Distributive Property.
$2n = 10n - 10$	Simplify.
$2n - 10n = 10n - 10n - 10$	Subtract $10n$ from each side.
$-8n = -10$	Simplify.
$\frac{-8n}{-8} = \frac{-10}{-8}$	Divide each side by –8.
$n = 1.25$	Simplify.

The solution is 1.25.

Study Tip

Check
Check your solution by replacing n with 1.25 in the original equation. Since $2(1.25) = 2.5$ and $10(1.25 - 1) = 2.5$, the solution is correct.

CHECK Your Progress

c. $3(k + 2) = 6k$

d. $3(a - 1) = 4(a - 1.5)$

Real-World EXAMPLE Use an Equation to Solve a Problem

4 **CAR RENTAL** **Suppose you can rent a car for either \$35 a day plus \$0.45 per mile or for \$50 a day plus \$0.25 per mile. What number of miles m results in the same cost for one day?**

\$35 a day plus \$0.45 per mile		\$50 a day plus \$0.25 per mile
$35 + 0.45m$	$=$	$50 + 0.25m$

$35 + 0.45m = 50 + 0.25m$	Write the equation.
$35 + 0.45m - 0.25m = 50 + 0.25m - 0.25m$	Subtract $0.25m$ from each side.
$35 + 0.2m = 50$	Simplify.
$35 - 35 + 0.2m = 50 - 35$	Subtract 35 from each side.
$0.2m = 15$	Simplify.
$\frac{0.2m}{0.2} = \frac{15}{0.2}$	Divide each side by 0.2.
$m = 75$	Simplify.

The cost is the same for 75 miles.

Study Tip

Alternative Method
In Example 4, you can also solve the equation by subtracting 35 from each side first, then subtracting $0.25m$ from each side.

CHECK Your Progress

e. **GEOMETRY** A rectangle's length is 30 centimeters longer than its width. The perimeter is 4.6 times the width. Find the dimensions.

Some equations have *no* solution. That is, no value of the variable results in a true sentence. This is shown by the symbol ∅ or { }. Other equations may have *every* number as the solution.

EXAMPLES No Solution or a Solution Set of All Numbers

Solve each equation.

5 $4x + \frac{1}{2} = 4x - 9$

$4x + \frac{1}{2} = 4x - 9$ Write the equation.

$4x - 4x + \frac{1}{2} = 4x - 4x - 9$ Subtract $4x$ from each side.

$\frac{1}{2} = -9$ Simplify.

The sentence $\frac{1}{2} = -9$ is *never* true. So, the solution set is ∅.

6 $8(r + 3) = 2(12 + 4r)$

$8(r + 3) = 2(12 + 4r)$ Write the equation.

$8r + 24 = 24 + 8r$ Use the Distributive Property.

$8r + 24 - 24 = 24 - 24 + 8r$ Subtract 24 from each side.

$8r = 8r$ Simplify.

$\frac{8r}{8} = \frac{8r}{8}$ Divide each side by 8.

$r = r$ Simplify.

The sentence $r = r$ is *always* true. So, the solution set is all numbers.

CHECK Your Progress

f. $3(x + 1) - 5 = 3x - 2$

g. $8y - 3 = 5(y - 1) + 3y$

CHECK Your Understanding

Examples 1, 2, 5, 6 (pp. LA6, LA8)

Solve each equation. Check the solution.

1. $4x - 7 = 5x$
2. $4x - 1 = 3x + 2$
3. $3.1w + 5 = 0.8 + w$
4. $12 - h = -h + 3$

Example 4 (p. LA7)

5. **BASKETBALL** Abigail has 6 more points than Victoria. Together, they have twice as many points as Hannah. If Hannah has 18 points, how many points does each of the other girls have?
6. **NUMBER THEORY** Twice a number is 220 less than six times the number. What is the number?

Examples 3, 5, 6 (pp. LA7, LA8)

Solve each equation. Check the solution.

7. $2(d + 6) = 3d - 1$
8. $g + 1 = 3(g - 3)$
9. $3(2a + 4) = 6(a + 2)$
10. $2(t - 3) + 5 = 3(t - 1)$

Practice and Problem Solving

HOMEWORK HELP	
For Exercises	See Examples
11–18	1, 2, 5, 6
19–20	4
21–28	3, 5, 6

Solve each equation. Check the solution.

11. $12x = 2x + 40$
12. $4x + 9 = 7x$
13. $4k + 24 = 6k - 10$
14. $2f - 6 = 7f + 24$
15. $12n - 24 = -14n + 28$
16. $n + 0.4 = -n + 1$
17. $-8b + 5 = 7 - 8b - 2$
18. $3y + \frac{1}{3} = 3y - \frac{1}{2}$

19. **GEOMETRY** The perimeter of a rectangle is 74 inches. Find the dimensions if the length is 7 inches longer than twice the width.

20. **NUMBER THEORY** Three times the sum of three consecutive integers is 72. What are the integers?

Solve each equation. Check the solution.

21. $3(x + 1) = 21$
22. $5(2c + 7) = 55$
23. $6(3d + 5) = 75$
24. $4(x - 2) = 3(1.5 + x)$
25. $3(s + 22) = 4(s + 12)$
26. $4.2x - 9 = 3(1.2x + 4)$
27. $4(f + 3) + 5 = 17 + 4f$
28. $3n + 4 = 5(n + 2) - 2n$

29. **GEOMETRY** The triangle and the rectangle have the same perimeter. Find the dimensions of the rectangle.

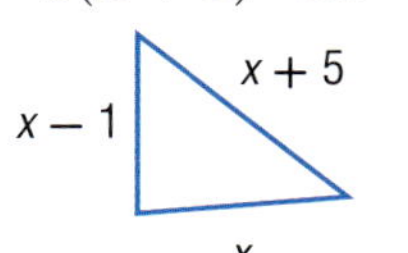

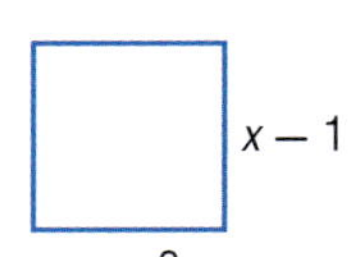

30. **RECREATION** Jennette begins in-line skating around a park path at a rate of 3 miles per hour. One hour later, one of her friends starts on the same path on her bike, riding at 12 miles per hour. Solve $3t = 12(t - 1)$ to find the time t Jennette's friend catches up to her.

Real-World Link In 1984, there were only about 20,000 in-line skaters in the United States. Today, there are more than 26 million in-line skaters.

Source: American Council of Exercise.

Solve each equation. Check the solution.

31. $-3(4b - 10) = \frac{1}{2}(-24b + 60)$
32. $\frac{3}{4}a + 4 = \frac{1}{4}(3a + 16)$
33. $\frac{d}{0.4} = 2d + 1.24$
34. $\frac{a - 6}{12} = \frac{a - 2}{4}$

H.O.T. Problems

35. **CHALLENGE** An apple costs the same as 2 oranges. Together, an orange and a banana cost 10¢ more than an apple. If $1.70 was spent on one apple, two oranges, and two bananas, what is the cost of one of each fruit?

36. **REASONING** Describe the steps used to solve $15x = -3x - 9$.

37. **OPEN ENDED** Write an equation that has parentheses and contains the variable b on both sides. Solve the equation.

38. **WRITING IN MATH** Describe how the Distributive Property is used to solve equations.

Parallel Lines and Transversals

MAIN IDEA

Analyze the relationships of angles formed by two parallel lines and a transversal.

New Vocabulary

- parallel lines
- transversal
- alternate interior angles
- alternate exterior angles
- corresponding angles
- vertical angles
- adjacent angles

Math Online

glencoe.com

- Personal Tutor
- Self-Check Quiz
- Extra Examples

GET READY for the Lesson

In the United States, the standard distance between rails on a railroad track is 4 feet 8.5 inches. The diagram at the right shows a road crossing over railroad tracks.

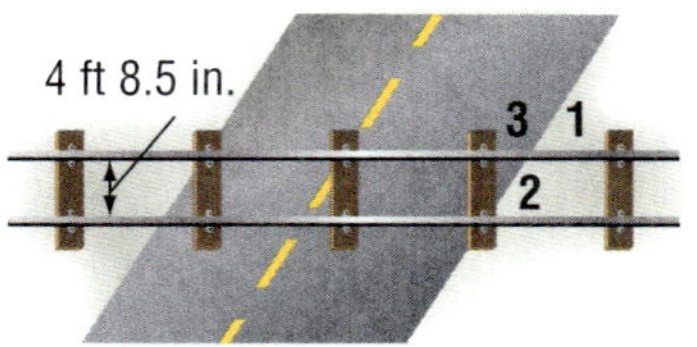

1. Measure angles 1 and 2. Record the measures. Then make a conjecture about the measure of angle 3. Then measure the angle to verify your conjecture.

Lines in a plane that never intersect are **parallel lines**. When two parallel lines are intersected by a third line, this line is called a **transversal**.

Names of Special Angles — Key Concept

If a pair of parallel lines is intersected by a transversal, this pair of angles are congruent.

Alternate interior angles are on opposite sides of the transversal and inside the parallel lines.

$\angle 3 \cong \angle 5$, $\angle 4 \cong \angle 6$

Alternate exterior angles are on opposite sides of the transversal and outside the parallel lines.

$\angle 1 \cong \angle 7$, $\angle 2 \cong \angle 8$

Corresponding angles are in the same position on the parallel lines in relation to the transversal.

$\angle 1 \cong \angle 5$, $\angle 2 \cong \angle 6$, $\angle 3 \cong \angle 7$, $\angle 4 \cong \angle 8$

EXAMPLE Find Measures of Angles

In the figure at the right, $p \parallel q$ and $m\angle 3 = 95°$. Find $m\angle 7$.

$m\angle 7$

$\angle 3$ and $\angle 7$ are alternate interior angles.

$m\angle 7 = m\angle 3 = 95°$

CHECK Your Progress

In the figure, $m\angle 4 = 85°$. Find each measure.

a. $m\angle 8$

b. $m\angle 2$

Vertical Angles and Adjacent Angles

Key Concept

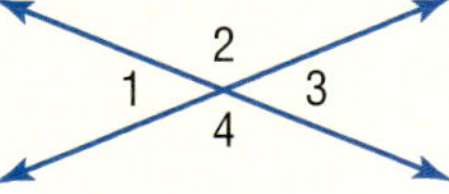

Vertical angles are opposite angles formed by the intersection of two lines. Vertical angles are congruent.

$\angle 1 \cong \angle 3$, $\angle 2 \cong \angle 4$

Two angles that have the same vertex, share a common side, and do not overlap are **adjacent angles**. Adjacent angles are supplementary.

$\angle 1$ and $\angle 2$, $\angle 2$ and $\angle 3$, $\angle 3$ and $\angle 4$, $\angle 4$ and $\angle 1$

EXAMPLES Use Vertical Angles and Adjacent Angles

Reading Math

Congruent Angles
- Angle 1 *is congruent to* angle 2: $\angle 1 \cong \angle 2$.
- The measure of $\angle 1$ *is equal to* the measure of $\angle 2$: $m\angle 1 = m\angle 2$.

In the figure at the right, $m\angle 1 = 70°$. Find each measure.

2 $m\angle 2$

$\angle 1$ and $\angle 2$ are vertical angles, so they are congruent. $m\angle 2 = m\angle 1 = 70°$

3 $m\angle 3$

$\angle 1$ and $\angle 3$ are adjacent angles, so they are supplementary.

$m\angle 1 + m\angle 3 = 180°$	Definition of supplementary angles
$70 + m\angle 3 = 180$	Replace $m\angle 1$ with 70.
$m\angle 3 = 110$	Subtract 70 from each side.

CHECK Your Progress

In the figure at the right, $m\angle 1 = 52°$. Find each measure.

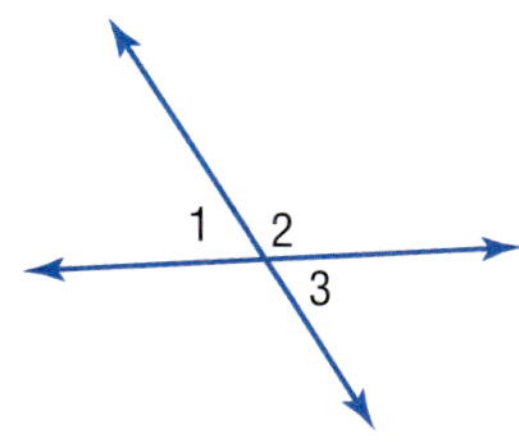

c. $m\angle 2$

d. $m\angle 3$

EXAMPLE Use Angle Relationships

4 **ALGEBRA In the figure at the right, $r \parallel s$. Find the value of x.**

The angles with measures $2x°$ and $110°$ are vertical angles, so they are congruent.

$2x = 110$	Congruent angles have equal measures.
$\frac{2x}{2} = \frac{110}{2}$	Divide each side by 2.
$x = 55$	Simplify.

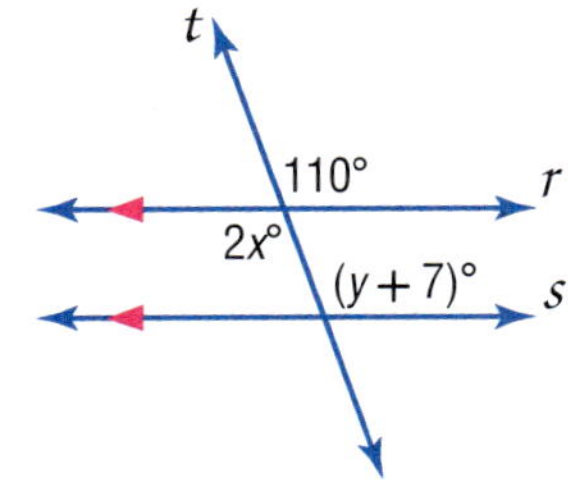

CHECK Your Progress

e. Find the value of y.

CHECK Your Understanding

Examples 1–3
(pp. LA10–LA11)

In the figure at the right, $\ell \parallel m$ and k is a transversal. If $m\angle 1 = 56°$, find each measure.

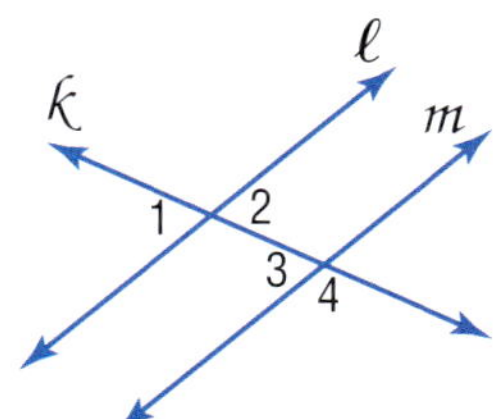

1. $m\angle 2$
2. $m\angle 3$
3. $m\angle 4$

In the figure at the right, $p \parallel q$ and ℓ is a transversal. If $m\angle 8 = 120°$, find each measure.

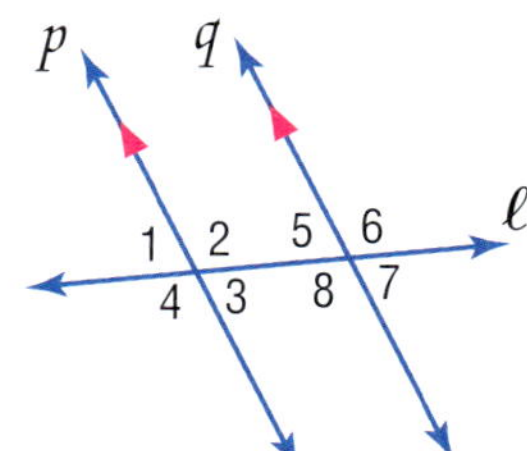

4. $m\angle 1$
5. $m\angle 3$
6. $m\angle 5$

Example 4
(p. LA11)

7. **SWIMMING** A swimmer crosses the lanes in a pool and swims from point A to point B, as shown in the figure. What is the value of x?

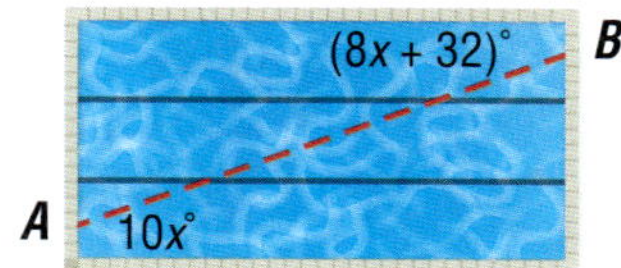

8. **ALGEBRA** Find the value of x in the figure at the right.

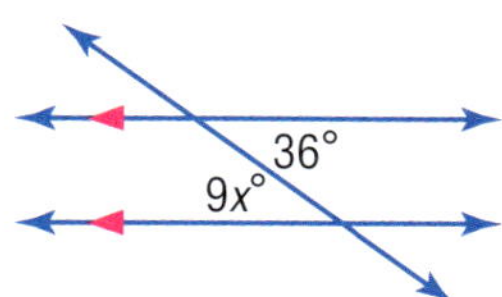

Practice and Problem Solving

HOMEWORK HELP

For Exercises	See Examples
9–18	1–3
19–26	4

In the figure at the right, if $m\angle 5 = 108°$, find each measure.

9. $m\angle 1$
10. $m\angle 3$
11. $m\angle 6$
12. $m\angle 7$

In the figure at the right, if $m\angle 2 = 74°$, find each measure.

13. $m\angle 8$
14. $m\angle 6$
15. $m\angle 4$
16. $m\angle 1$

17. **FURNITURE** In the chair at the right, $m\angle 4 = 106°$. Find $m\angle 6$ and $m\angle 3$.

18. **DRIVING** Ambulances can't safely make turns of less than 70°. The angle at the southeast corner of Delavan and Elmwood is 108°. Can an ambulance safely turn the northeast corner of Bidwell and Elmwood? Explain your reasoning.

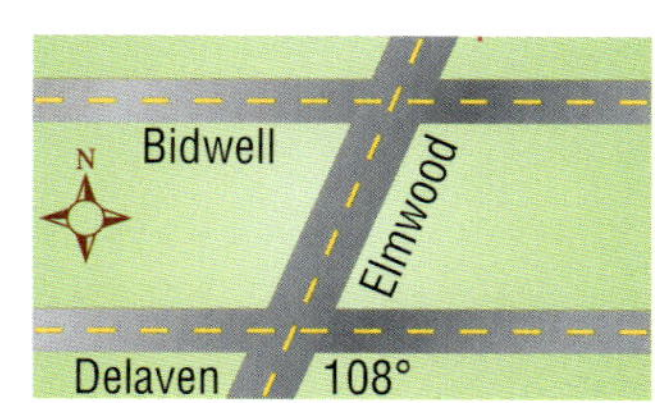

In the figure at the right, $m\angle 7 = 96°$. Find each measure.

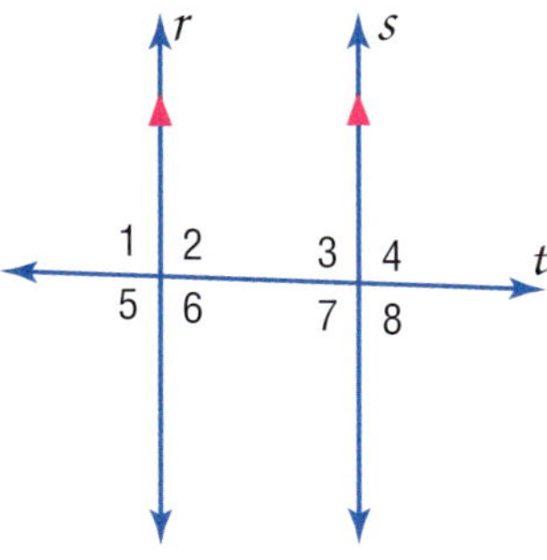

19. $m\angle 2$
20. $m\angle 5$
21. $m\angle 4$
22. $m\angle 8$

ALGEBRA **Find the value of x in each figure.**

23.

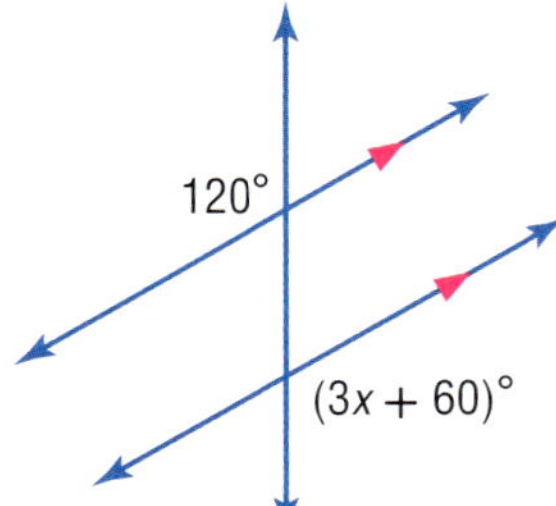

24.

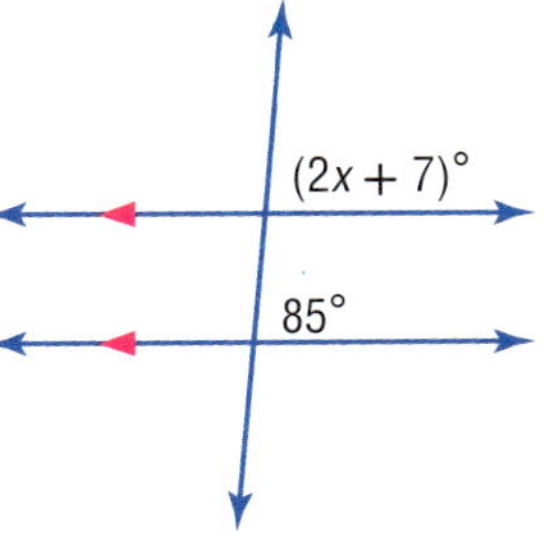

ALGEBRA **In the figure at the right, $m \parallel \ell$ and t is a transversal. Find the value of x for each of the following.**

Real-World Link
The area of Bosnia is 19,741 square miles. Until 1992, this country was a part of Yugoslavia.
Source: *Time for Kids Almanac*

25. $m\angle 2 = 2x + 3$ and $m\angle 4 = 4x - 7$
26. $m\angle 8 = 4x - 32$ and $m\angle 5 = 5x + 50$
27. **FLAGS** The flag at the right is the national flag of Bosnia. If $m\angle 1 = 135°$, what is $m\angle 2$? Explain how you found your answer.

28. **ALGEBRA** Find the value of x in the figure at the right.
29. **ALGEBRA** A transversal intersects two parallel lines and forms adjacent angles 5 and 6. If $m\angle 5 = (7x - 11)°$ and $m\angle 6 = (3x + 1)°$, find the measures of the angles.

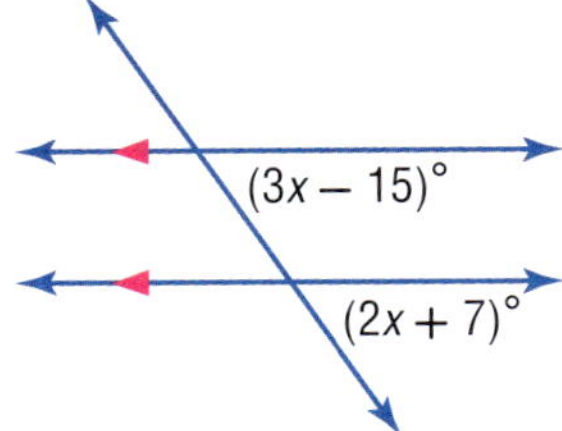

H.O.T. Problems

30. **CHALLENGE** Suppose two parallel lines are cut by a transversal. How are the interior angles on the same side of the transversal related?
31. **REASONING** Determine whether the following statement is *sometimes*, *always*, or *never* true. Explain your reasoning.

Vertical angles are supplementary.

32. **OPEN ENDED** Draw a pair of adjacent, supplementary angles. Label the angle measures.
33. **WRITING IN MATH** Summarize the angle relationships that are formed by parallel lines and a transversal. Describe which angles are congruent.

Congruent Polygons

MAIN IDEA

Identify similar and congruent polygons and use congruent polygons to solve problems.

New Vocabulary

congruent polygons
similar polygons
corresponding sides
corresponding angles

Math Online

glencoe.com

- Personal Tutor
- Self-Check Quiz
- Extra Examples

GET READY for the Lesson

Photo 1

Photo 2

Photo 3

1. Name two photos that are the same shape, but not the same size.
2. Name two photos that are not the same shape.

Polygons that are the same size and shape are **congruent polygons**. When polygons have the same shape but may be different in size, they are called **similar polygons**.

EXAMPLES Identify Congruent and Similar Polygons

Determine whether each pair of figures appears to be *congruent*, *similar*, or *neither*.

1

The figures are the same size and the same shape. So, they are congruent.

2

The figures are not the same shape. So, they are neither similar nor congruent.

CHECK Your Progress

a.

b.

The sides of similar or congruent figures that match are called **corresponding sides**. The angles of similar or congruent figures that match are called **corresponding angles**. Refer to the similar triangles.

- Side AB corresponds to side DE.
- Side BC corresponds to side EF.
- Side CA corresponds to side FD.
- Angles A, B, and C correspond to angles D, E, and F, respectively.

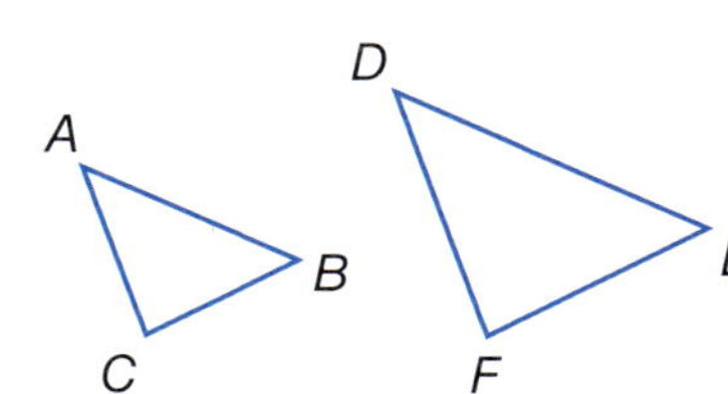

Study Tip

Similar and Congruent If two polygons are congruent, they are also similar.

Similar and Congruent Polygons

Key Concept

- Two polygons are *similar* if the corresponding angles are congruent and the ratios of corresponding sides are proportional.
- Two polygons are *congruent* if the corresponding angles are congruent and the corresponding sides are congruent.

EXAMPLES Apply Similarity and Congruence

Determine whether each pair of figures is *congruent*, *similar*, or *neither*.

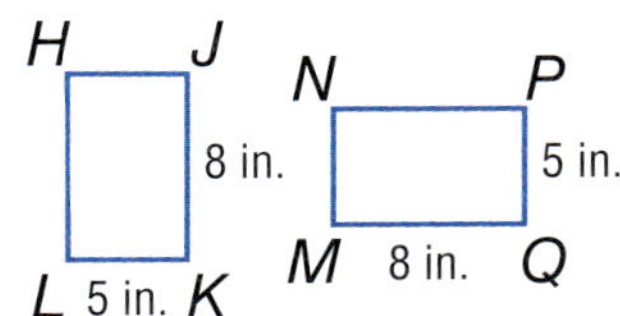

The corresponding sides are congruent. So, the figures are congruent.

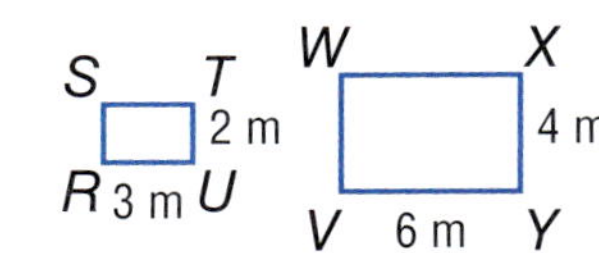

$\frac{TU}{XY} = \frac{2}{4}$ or $\frac{1}{2}$

$\frac{RU}{VY} = \frac{3}{6}$ or $\frac{1}{2}$

Since the ratios of the corresponding sides are equal, the figures are similar.

Study Tip

Rectangles All angles are congruent. So, to determine if two rectangles are similar, you need only to determine if corresponding sides are proportional.

CHECK Your Progress

c. Determine whether the pair of figures at the right is *congruent*, *similar*, or *neither*.

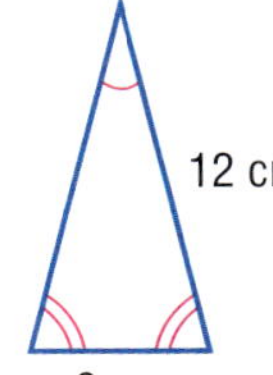

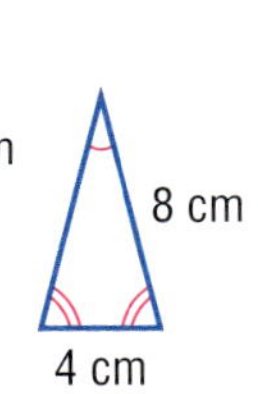

Real-World EXAMPLE Use Congruent Polygons to Solve Problems

GAMES **The table tennis tables at the right are congruent rectangles. What is the area of table A?**

Since the rectangles are congruent, the corresponding sides are congruent. So, $x = 9$. The area of table A is $5 \cdot 9$ or 45 square feet.

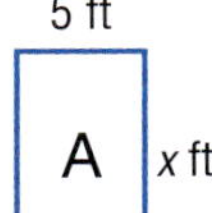

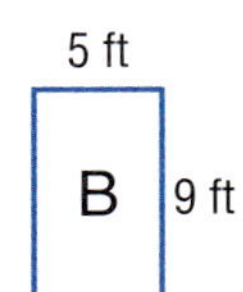

CHECK Your Progress

d. Triangle *A* has sides 2 centimeters, 3 centimeters, and 6 centimeters. Triangle *B* has sides 3 centimeters, *x* centimeters, and *y* centimeters. If the triangles are congruent, what is the perimeter of Triangle *B*?

CHECK Your Understanding

Examples 1, 2 (p. LA14)

Determine whether each pair of figures appears to be *congruent, similar,* or *neither*.

1. 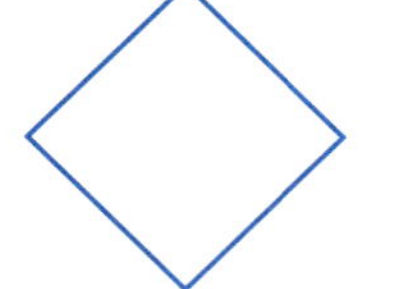

2. 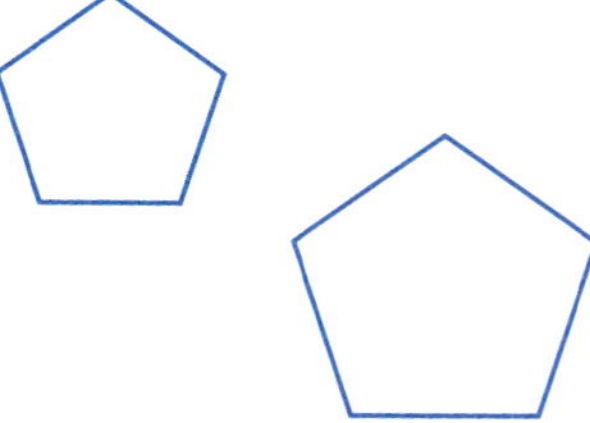

Examples 3, 4 (p. LA15)

3. **SCREENS** Determine whether the television screens shown below are *congruent, similar,* or *neither*.

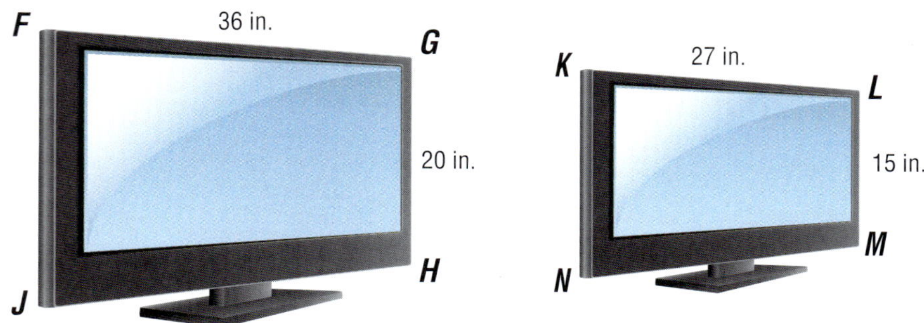

Determine whether each pair of figures is *congruent, similar,* or *neither*.

4. 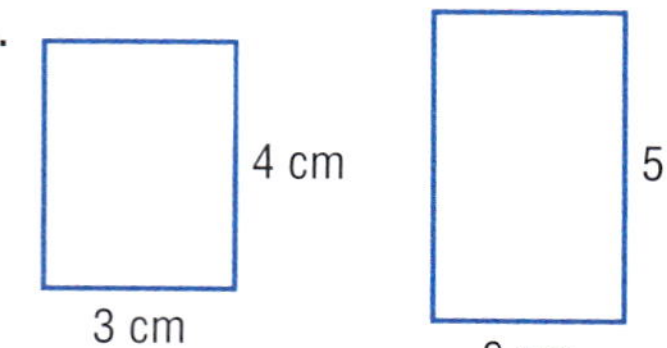

5. 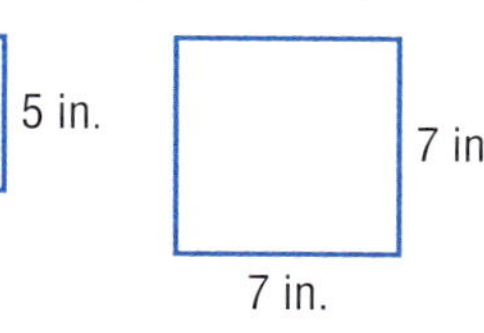

Example 5 (p. LA15)

6. Triangle *ABC* is congruent to triangle *RST*. What is the perimeter of triangle *ABC*?

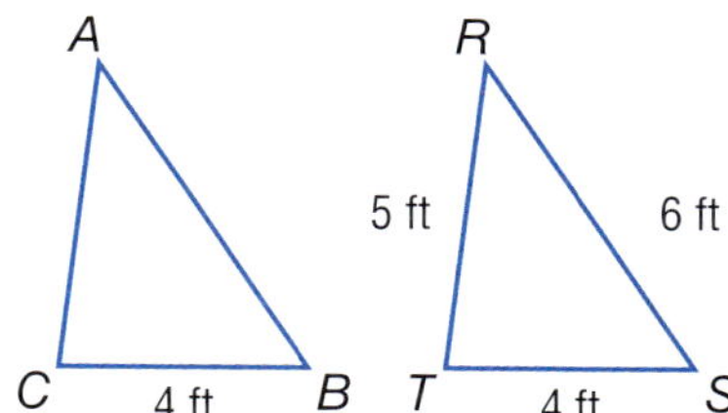

Practice and Problem Solving

HOMEWORK HELP	
For Exercises	See Examples
7–10	1, 2
11–14	3, 4
15, 16	5

Determine whether each pair of figures is *congruent, similar,* or *neither*.

7. 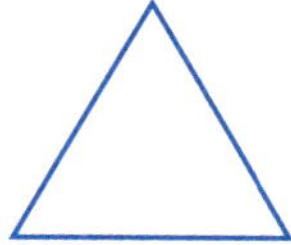 

8. 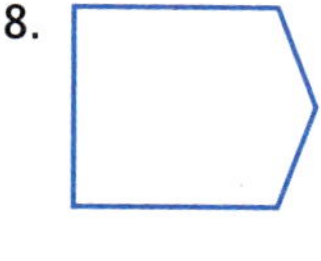 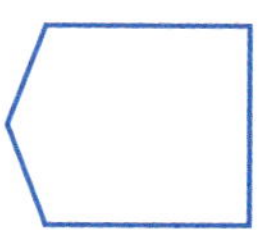

9.  

10. 

Determine whether each pair of figures is *congruent*, *similar*, or *neither*.

11. 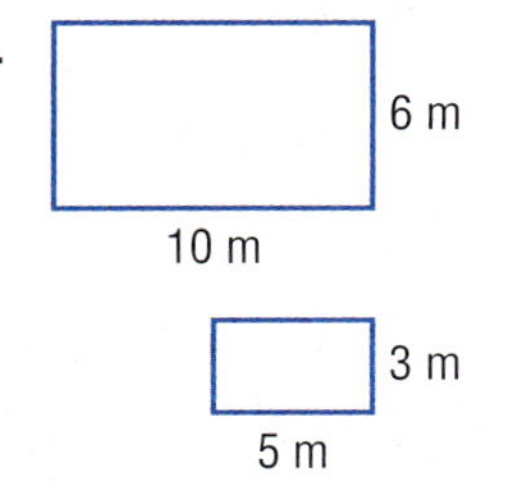

12. 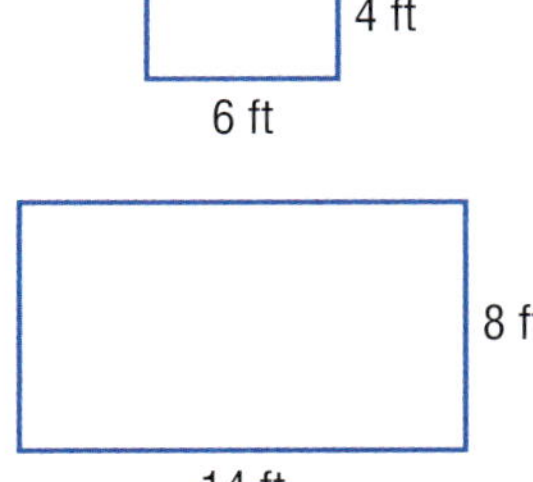

13. 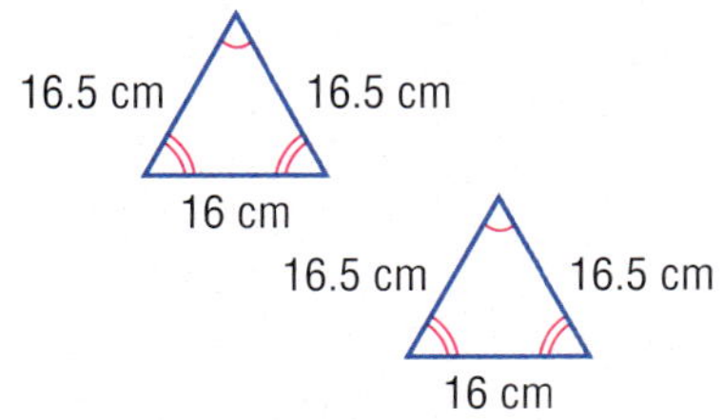

14. 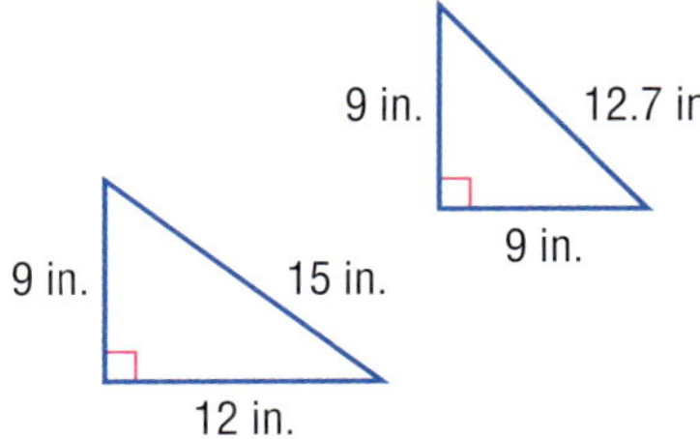

15. **MEASUREMENT** Two squares are congruent. If one square has an area of 100 square inches, what is the perimeter of the other square?

16. **MEASUREMENT** Two equilateral triangles are congruent. If one triangle has a perimeter of 24 centimeters, what are the side lengths of the other triangle?

17. **SIGNS** One stop sign has a perimeter of 48 inches. Another stop sign has a perimeter of 72 inches. Determine whether the stop signs are *congruent*, *similar*, or *neither*. Explain.

Each pair of figures is similar. Find the value of x.

18. 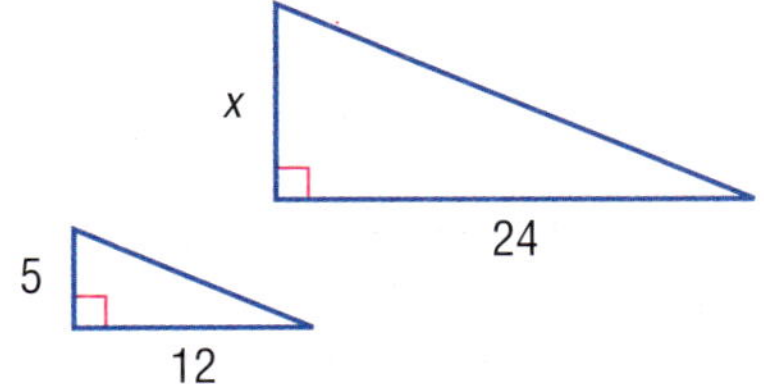

19. 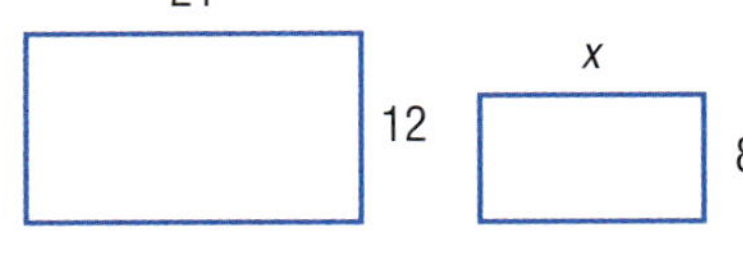

H.O.T. Problems

20. **CHALLENGE** Analyze the figure to determine the number of congruent triangles and the number of similar triangles there are in the figure. (It may be helpful to copy the figure and outline the triangles.)

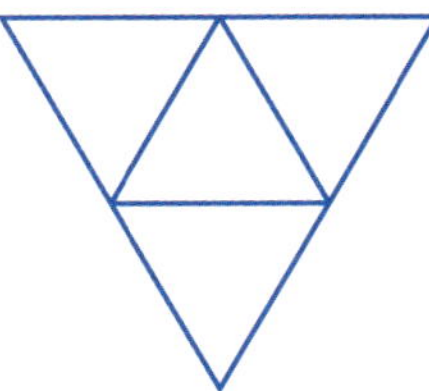

REASONING **Tell whether each statement is *sometimes*, *always*, or *never* true. Explain your reasoning.**

21. Two rectangles are similar.

22. Two squares are similar.

23. **OPEN ENDED** Draw two similar triangles and label the vertices. Then write a proportion that compares the corresponding sides.

24. **WRITING IN MATH** Compare and contrast similarity and congruence.

Converse of the Pythagorean Theorem

MAIN IDEA

Use the converse of the Pythagorean Theorem to determine whether a triangle is a right triangle.

New Vocabulary

converse

Math Online

glencoe.com

- Personal Tutor
- Self-Check Quiz
- Extra Examples

GET READY for the Lesson

A triangular flower bed is 4 feet by 6 feet by 10 feet.

1. If a right triangle has legs 4 feet and 6 feet, what is the measure of the hypotenuse?
2. Is the flower bed described above a right triangle? Explain.

According to the Pythagorean Theorem, if a triangle is a right triangle, the square of the length of the hypotenuse is equal to the sum of the squares of the lengths of the legs. If you reverse the statements after *if* and *then*, you have formed the **converse** of the Pythagorean Theorem.

Converse of Pythagorean Theorem — Key Concept

Words If the square of the length of the hypotenuse is equal to the sum of the squares of the lengths of the legs, then a triangle is a right triangle.

Symbols $c^2 = a^2 + b^2$

Example $5^2 = 3^2 + 4^2$

$25 = 9 + 16$

Model

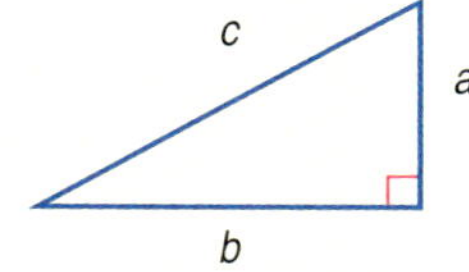

EXAMPLES Identify a Right Triangle

The measures of three sides of a triangle are given. Determine whether each triangle is a right triangle.

1 **9 cm, 12 cm, 15 cm**

$c^2 = a^2 + b^2$ Pythagorean Theorem

$15^2 \stackrel{?}{=} 9^2 + 12^2$ $c = 15, a = 9, b = 12$

$225 \stackrel{?}{=} 81 + 144$ Evaluate.

$225 = 225 \checkmark$ Simplify.

The triangle is a right triangle.

2 **3 in., 4 in., 6 in.**

$c^2 = a^2 + b^2$ Pythagorean Theorem

$6^2 \stackrel{?}{=} 3^2 + 4^2$ $c = 6, a = 3, b = 4$

$36 \stackrel{?}{=} 9 + 16$ Evaluate.

$36 \neq 25$ Simplify.

The triangle is *not* right.

CHECK Your Progress

a. 4 cm, 9 cm, 10 cm

b. 15 mm, 20 mm, 25 mm

Study Tip

Figures
Do not assume that if a triangle looks like a right triangle that it actually is a right triangle.

EXAMPLE Identify a Right Triangle

3 **Determine whether the triangle at the right is a right triangle.**

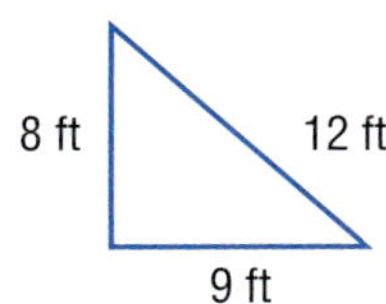

$c^2 = a^2 + b^2$	Pythagorean Theorem
$12^2 \stackrel{?}{=} 8^2 + 9^2$	$c = 12$, $a = 8$, $b = 9$
$144 \stackrel{?}{=} 64 + 81$	Evaluate.
$144 \neq 145$	The triangle is *not* a right triangle.

CHECK Your Progress

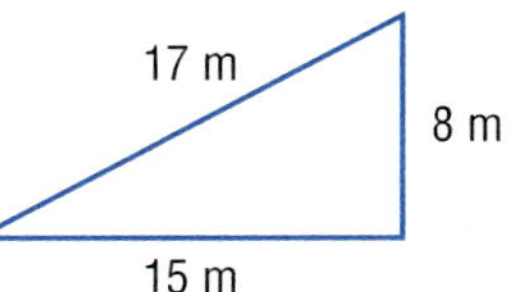

c. Determine whether the triangle at the right is a right triangle.

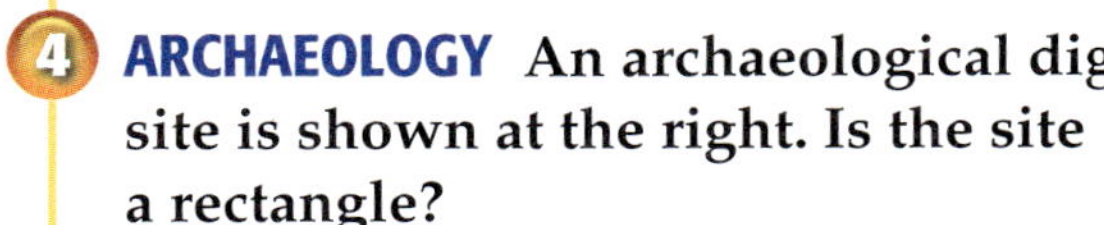

Real-World EXAMPLE Use the Converse

4 **ARCHAEOLOGY** **An archaeological dig site is shown at the right. Is the site a rectangle?**

35 ft
21 ft
28 ft

A rectangle has four right angles. Determine whether the triangle formed is a right triangle.

$c^2 = a^2 + b^2$	Pythagorean Theorem
$35^2 \stackrel{?}{=} 21^2 + 28^2$	$c = 35$, $a = 21$, $b = 28$
$1225 \stackrel{?}{=} 441 + 784$	Evaluate. Use a calculator.

$1225 = 1225$ The triangle *is* a right triangle. So, the area is a rectangle.

CHECK Your Progress

d. Another dig site is a quadrilateral that measures 12 yards on each side. If the diagonal is 15 yards, is this a square?

CHECK Your Understanding

Examples 1, 2 (p. LA18)

The lengths of three sides of a triangle are given. Determine whether each triangle is a right triangle.

1. $a = 12$ cm, $b = 16$ cm, $c = 20$ cm
2. $a = 2$ in., $b = 3$ in., $c = 4$ in.

Example 3 (p. LA19)

Determine whether each triangle is a right triangle.

3. 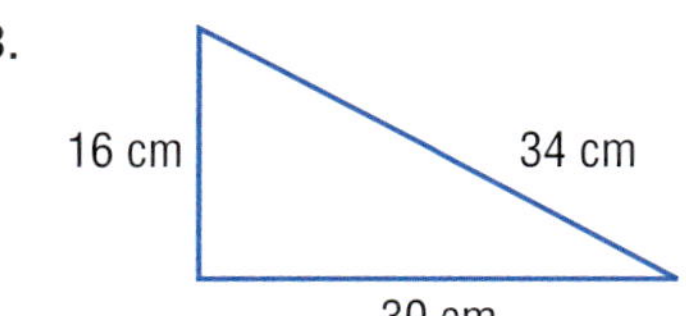

4. 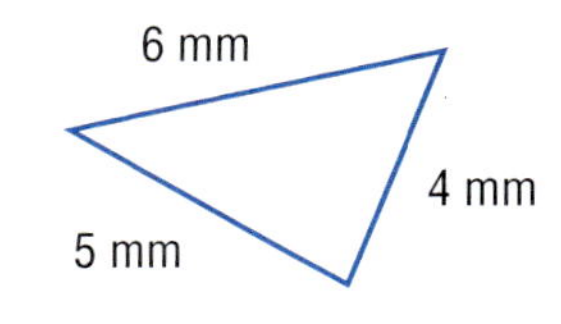

Example 4 (p. LA19)

5. **ART** A mosaic is made from triangles that have side lengths of 14 millimeters, 18 millimeters, and 20 millimeters. Are the triangles right?

Practice and Problem Solving

HOMEWORK HELP	
For Exercises	See Examples
6–13	1, 2
14–17	3
18–19	4

The lengths of three sides of a triangle are given. Determine whether each triangle is a right triangle.

6. $a = 9$ m, $b = 40$ m, $c = 41$ m
7. $a = 12$ km, $b = 35$ km, $c = 37$ km
8. $a = 6$ yd, $b = 11$ yd, $c = 13$ yd
9. $a = 18$ mm, $b = 24$ mm, $c = 30$ mm
10. $a = 5$ cm, $b = 9$ cm, $c = 12$ cm
11. $a = 14$ in., $b = 18$ in., $c = 22$ in.
12. $a = 16$ ft, $b = 30$ ft, $c = 34$ ft
13. $a = 10$ m, $b = 16$ m, $c = 24$ m

Determine whether each triangle is a right triangle.

14. 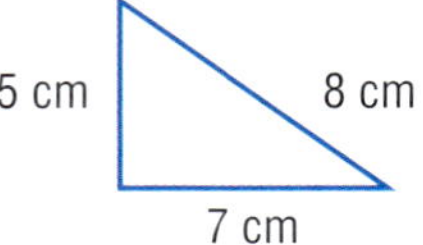

15. 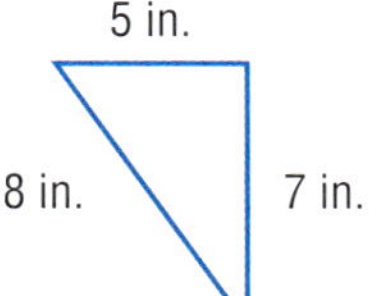

16. 

17. 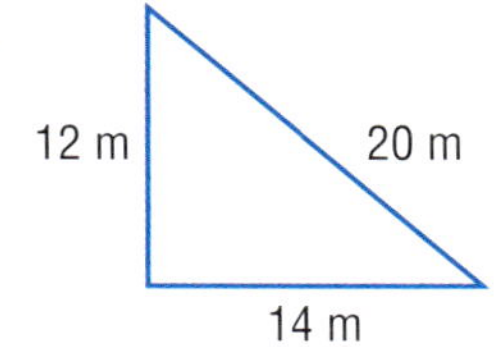

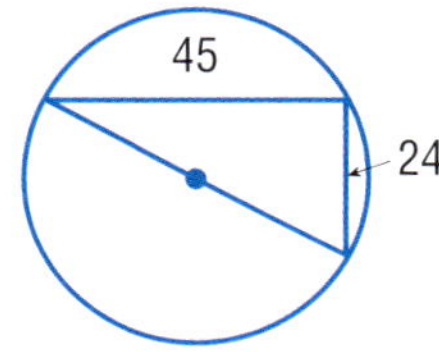

18. **GEOMETRY** The circle at the right has a diameter of 51 units. Is the triangle with vertices on the circle a right triangle?

19. **TRAVEL** Smithville is 28 miles from Littlefield and 26 miles from Alpine. The distance between Littlefield and Alpine is 32 miles. Do the segments connecting the three cities on the map form a right triangle?

20. **SEWING** A quilt is made from triangular pieces of cloth that have side lengths of 4 inches, 4 inches, and 4 inches. Are the pieces of cloth right triangles?

The lengths of three sides of a triangle are given. Determine whether each triangle is a right triangle.

21. $a = 5$ m, $b = 8$ m, $c = \sqrt{89}$ m
22. $a = 6$ in., $b = \sqrt{76}$ in., $c = \sqrt{112}$ in.

H.O.T. Problems

23. **CHALLENGE** A triangle has side lengths of x units. Is it possible for the triangle to be a right triangle? Explain.

24. **REASONING** Can you determine whether a triangle is a right triangle if you are given two side lengths? Explain.

25. **OPEN ENDED** Choose three numbers. Use the converse of the Pythagorean Theorem to determine whether the numbers could be measures of the sides of a right triangle.

26. **WRITING IN MATH** Explain how to use the converse of the Pythagorean Theorem to determine whether a triangle with three given measures is a right triangle.

Box-and-Whisker Plots

MAIN IDEA

Display and interpret data in box-and-whisker plots.

New Vocabulary

quartiles
lower quartile
upper quartile
interquartile range
box-and-whisker plot

Math Online

glencoe.com

- Personal Tutor
- Self-Check Quiz
- Extra Examples

GET READY for the Lesson

The lengths in millimeters of 10 ghost-faced bats are shown below.

62, 58, 65, 61, 61, 62, 62, 59, 63, 65

1. Order the numbers from least to greatest.
2. Divide the ordered list of numbers in half. What is the median of the lower half of the data?

In a set of data, the **quartiles** are the values that divide the data into four equal parts. The median of the lower half of a set of data is called the **lower quartile** or LQ. The median of the upper half of the data is called the **upper quartile** or UQ.

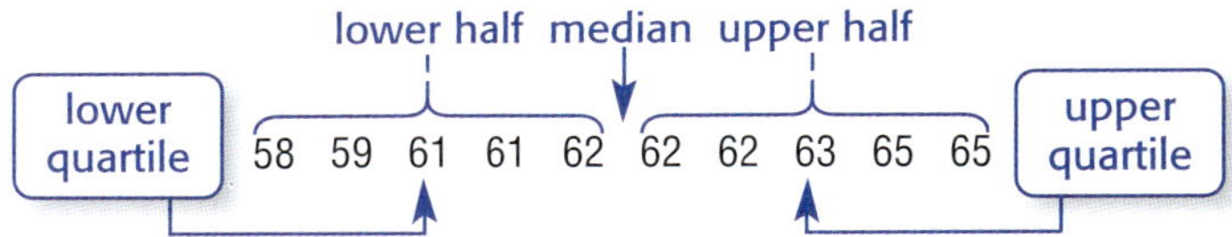

The **interquartile range** is the difference between the upper and lower quartiles. It is the range of the middle half of the data.

EXAMPLE Interquartile Range

1 **Find the median, upper and lower quartiles, and the interquartile range for the set of data {8, 11, 6, 23, 7, 2, 20, 4, 16}.**

STEP 1 List the data from least to greatest. Then find the median.

2 4 6 7 8 11 16 20 23

median = 8

STEP 2 Find the upper and lower quartiles.

lower half: 2 4 6 7   8   upper half: 11 16 20 23

$LQ = \frac{4 + 6}{2}$ or 5   median = 8 $UQ = \frac{16 + 20}{2}$ or 18

STEP 3 Find the interquartile range. UQ - LQ = 18 - 5 or 13

Study Tip

Common Misconception You may think that the median always divides the box in half. However, the median may not divide the box in half because the data may be clustered toward one quartile.

CHECK Your Progress

a. Find the median, upper and lower quartiles, and the interquartile range for the set of data {35, 27, 21, 37, 54, 47}.

A **box-and-whisker plot** divides a set of data into four parts using the median and quartiles. A *box* is drawn around the quartile values, and *whiskers* extend from each quartile to the extreme data points.

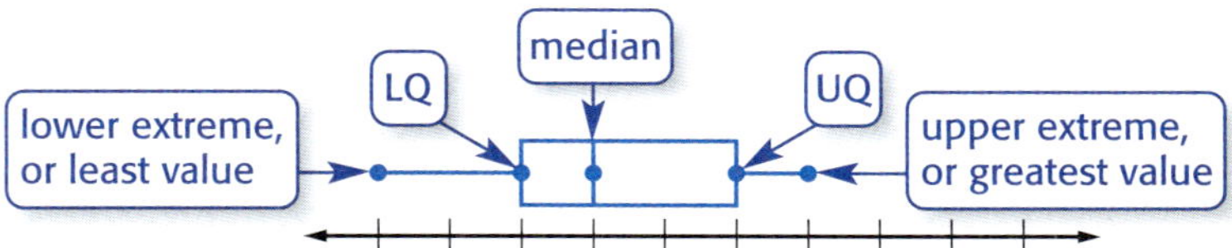

Real-World EXAMPLE **Draw a Box-and-Whisker Plot**

2 **DRIVING** **The list below shows the speeds of eleven cars. Draw a box-and-whisker plot of the data.**

25 35 27 22 34 40 20 19 23 25 30

STEP 1 Order the numbers from least to greatest. Then draw a number line that covers the range of the data.

10 15 20 25 30 35 40 45 50

STEP 2 Find the median, the extremes, and the upper and lower quartiles. Mark these points above the number line.

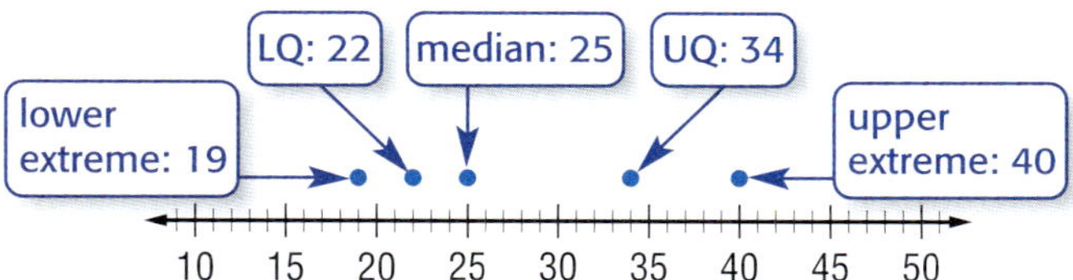

STEP 3 Draw the box so that it includes the quartile values. Draw a vertical line through the median value. Extend the whiskers from each quartile to the extreme data points.

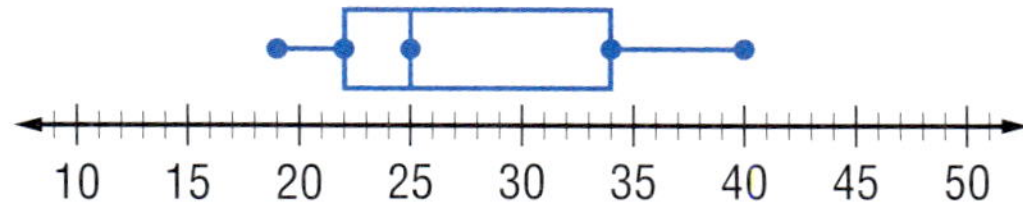

CHECK Your Progress

b. Draw a box-and-whisker plot of the data set below.
{\$25, \$30, \$27, \$35, \$19, \$23, \$25, \$22, \$40, \$34, \$20}

Study Tip

Box-and-Whisker Plots

- If the length of a whisker or the box is short, the values of the data in that part are concentrated.
- If the length of a whisker or the box is long, the values of the data in that part are spread out.

Box-and-whisker plots separate data into four parts. Even though the parts may differ in length, each part contains 25% of the data.

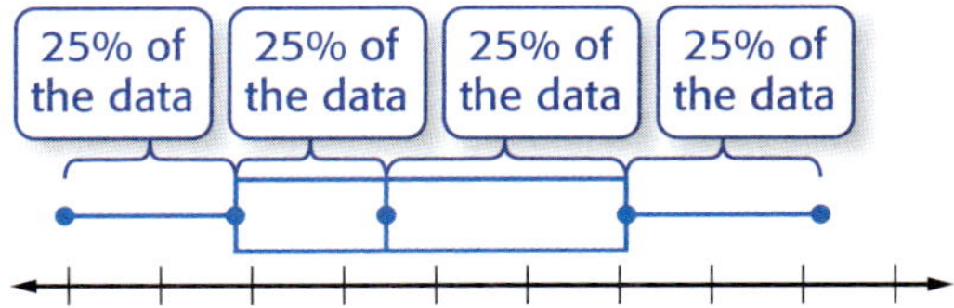

Real-World EXAMPLES Interpret Data

DRIVING **Refer to the box-and-whisker plot below from Example 2. It displays the speeds of eleven drivers.**

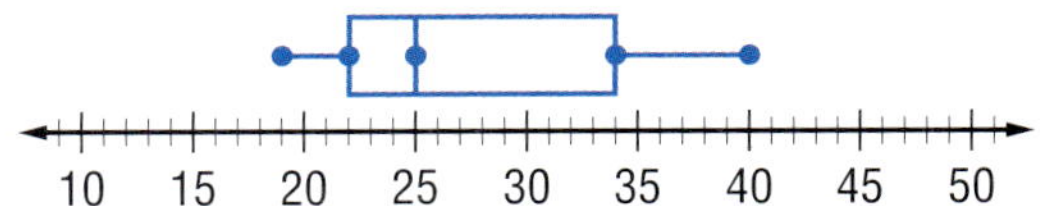

3 **Half of the drivers were driving faster than what speed?**

Half of the drivers were driving faster than 25 miles per hour.

4 **What does the length of the box-and-whisker plot tell about the data?**

The length of the left half of the box-and-whisker plot is short. This means that the speeds of the slowest half of the cars are concentrated. The speeds of the fastest half of the cars are spread out.

CHECK Your Progress

c. What percent of drivers were driving faster than 34 miles per hour?

CHECK Your Understanding

Example 1 (p. LA21) **Find the median, upper and lower quartiles, and the interquartile range for each set of data.**

1. {65, 64, 73, 34, 15, 43, 92}
2. {26, 48, 12, 32, 41, 35}

Example 2 (p. LA22) **Draw a box-and-whisker plot for each set of data.**

3. {29, 15, 22, 30, 32, 50, 26, 22, 36, 31}
4. {60, 60, 120, 80, 68, 90, 100, 69, 104, 99, 130}

Examples 3, 4 (p. LA23) **EARTH SCIENCE** **For Exercises 5–7, use the table.**

5. Make a box-and-whisker plot of the data.
6. What percent of the earthquakes were between 4 and 9 kilometers deep?
7. Write a sentence describing what the length of the box-and-whisker plot tells about the depths of the earthquakes.

Depth of Recent Earthquakes (km)		
5	15	11
10	7	9
1	9	5
7	5	4
2	3	

Source: Cooperative Central and Southeast U.S. Seismic Network

Practice and Problem Solving

HOMEWORK HELP	
For Exercises	See Examples
8–11	1
12–15	2
16–23	3, 4

Find the median, upper and lower quartiles, and the interquartile range for each set of data.

8. {10, 22, 9, 24, 36, 18, 15, 20}
9. {7, 12, 3, 2, 11, 9, 6, 4, 8}
10. {70, 65, 72, 70, 74, 75, 61, 60, 100, 88}
11. {46, 31, 59, 55, 40, 33, 36, 35, 48, 51, 52}

Draw a box-and-whisker plot for each set of data.

12. {26, 22, 31, 36, 22, 27, 15, 36, 32, 29, 30}
13. {65, 92, 74, 61, 55, 35, 88, 99, 97, 100, 96}

14.

Cost of MP3 Players ($)	
95	55
105	100
85	158
122	174
165	162

15.

Height of Waves (in.)		
80	51	77
72	55	65
42	78	67
40	81	68
63	73	59

TESTS **For Exercises 16–19, use the box-and-whisker plot. It summarizes the scores of a recent math test.**

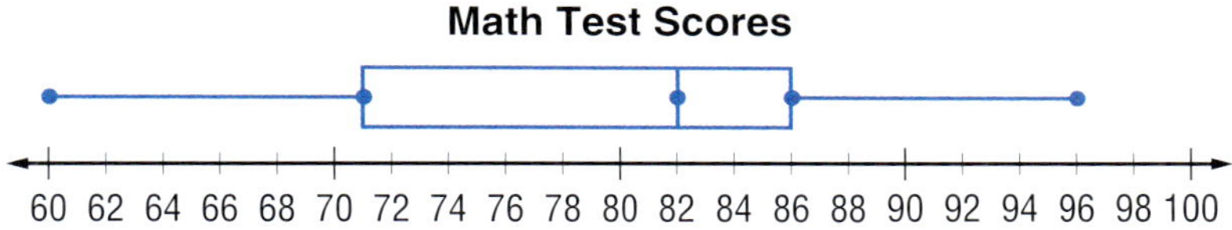

16. What was the greatest test score?
17. Explain why the median is not in the middle of the box.
18. What percent of the scores were between 71 and 96?
19. Half of the scores were higher than what percent?

Real-World Link
The total lengths of U.S. coastlines are shown below.
Atlantic Coast: 2069 mi
Gulf Coast: 1631 mi
Pacific Coast: 7623 mi
Arctic Coast: 1060 mi
Source: Fact Monster

GEOGRAPHY **For Exercises 20–23, use the table. It shows the length of coastline for the 13 states along the Atlantic Coast.**

Length of Coastline (mi)	
28	130
580	127
100	301
228	40
31	187
192	112
13	

Source: Cooperative Central and Southeast U.S. Seismic Network

20. Make a box-and-whisker plot of the data.
21. What percent of the coastline states have coastlines greater than 210 miles?
22. Half of the states have a coastline less than how many miles?
23. Write a sentence describing what the length of the box-and-whisker plot tells about the number of miles of coastline for states along the Atlantic coast.

24. **WORD PROCESSING** Find the median, upper and lower quartiles, and the interquartile range for the set of data in the stem-and-leaf plot shown at the right.

Words Typed per Minute

Stem	Leaf
4	0 2
5	1 5 9
6	3 5 7 8
7	2 3 7 8
8	0 1

4|0 = 40

TEMPERATURE For Exercises 25–27, use the table. It shows the average monthly temperatures for two cities.

Average Monthly Temperatures (°F)

	J	F	M	A	M	J	J	A	S	O	N	D
Tampa, FL	60	62	67	71	77	81	82	82	81	75	68	62
Caribou, ME	9	12	25	38	51	61	66	63	54	43	31	15

25. Find the low, high, and the median temperatures, and the upper and lower quartiles for each city.

26. On the same number line, draw a box-and-whisker plot for each set of data. Place the Caribou data above the Tampa data.

27. Write a few sentences comparing the average monthly temperatures displayed in the box-and-whisker plots.

ANIMALS For Exercises 28 and 29, use the box-and-whisker plots shown below. They summarizes the weights of Asiatic black bears and pandas.

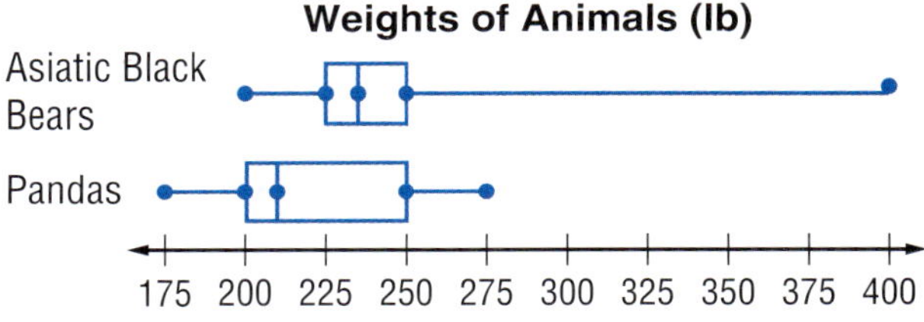

28. How do the weights of the two types of animals compare? Discuss how much most of the animals of each type weigh and the greatest weight of each.

29. Write a sentence or two describing what the length of the box-and-whisker plot tells about the weights of the animals.

H.O.T. Problems

30. **CHALLENGE** Write a set of data that contains 12 values for which the box-and-whisker plot has no whiskers. State the median, lower and upper quartiles, and lower and upper extremes.

31. **REASONING** Determine whether the following statement is *true* or *false*. Explain.

The median divides the box of a box-and-whisker plot in half.

32. **OPEN ENDED** Write a set of data that, when displayed in a box-and-whisker plot, will result in a long box and short whiskers. Draw the box-and-whisker plot.

33. **WRITING IN MATH** Explain how the information you can learn from a set of data shown in a box-and-whisker plot is different from what you can learn from the same set of data shown in a stem-and-leaf plot.

Student Handbook

Built-In Workbooks

Reference

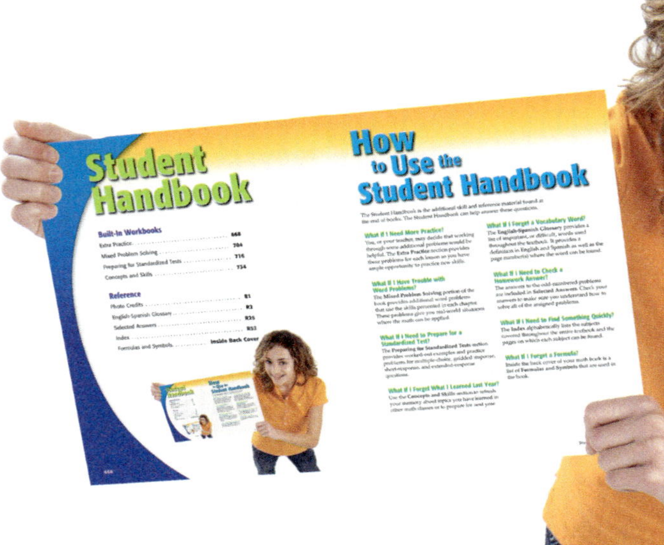

How to Use the Student Handbook

The Student Handbook is the additional skill and reference material found at the end of books. The Student Handbook can help answer these questions.

What If I Need More Practice?

You, or your teacher, may decide that working through some additional problems would be helpful. The **Extra Practice** section provides these problems for each lesson so you have ample opportunity to practice new skills.

What If I Have Trouble with Word Problems?

The **Mixed Problem Solving** portion of the book provides additional word problems that use the skills presented in each chapter. These problems give you real-world situations where the math can be applied.

What If I Need to Prepare for a Standardized Test?

The **Preparing for Standardized Tests** section provides worked-out examples and practice problems for multiple-choice, gridded response, short-response, and extended-response questions.

What If I Forget What I Learned Last Year?

Use the **Concepts and Skills** section to refresh your memory about topics you have learned in other math classes or to prepare for next year.

What If I Forget a Vocabulary Word?

The **English-Spanish Glossary** provides a list of important, or difficult, words used throughout the textbook. It provides a definition in English and Spanish as well as the page number(s) where the word can be found.

What If I Need to Check a Homework Answer?

The answers to the odd-numbered problems are included in **Selected Answers**. Check your answers to make sure you understand how to solve all of the assigned problems.

What If I Need to Find Something Quickly?

The **Index** alphabetically lists the subjects covered throughout the entire textbook and the pages on which each subject can be found.

What If I Forget a Formula?

Inside the back cover of your math book is a list of **Formulas and Symbols** that are used in the book.

Extra Practice

Extra Practice

Lesson 1-1

Pages 25–29

Use the four-step plan to solve each problem.

1. The Reyes family rode their bicycles for 9 miles to the park. The ride back was along a different route for 14 miles. How many miles did they ride in all?
2. Four hundred sixty people are scheduled to attend a banquet. If each table seats 8 people, how many tables are needed?
3. A group of 251 people is eating dinner at a school fund-raiser. If each person pays \$8.00 for their meal, how much money is raised?
4. Sherita's service charges a monthly fee of \$20.00 plus \$0.15 per minute. One monthly bill is \$31.25. How many minutes did Sherita use during the month?
5. ABC Car Rental charges \$25 per day to rent a mid-sized car plus \$0.20 per mile driven. Mr. Ruiz rents a mid-sized car for 3 days and drives a total of 72 miles. Find the amount of Mr. Ruiz's bill.

Lesson 1-2

Pages 30–33

Write each power as a product of the same factor.

1. 13^4
2. 9^6
3. 1^7
4. 12^2
5. 5^8
6. 15^4

Evaluate each expression.

7. 5^6
8. 17^3
9. 2^{12}
10. 3^5
11. 1^4
12. 5^3
13. 10^2
14. 2^8
15. 8^2
16. 7^4
17. 20^3
18. 42^3

Write each product in exponential form.

19. $2 \cdot 2 \cdot 2 \cdot 2 \cdot 2$
20. $3 \cdot 3$
21. $1 \cdot 1 \cdot 1 \cdot 1 \cdot 1 \cdot 1$
22. $18 \cdot 18 \cdot 18 \cdot 18$
23. $9 \cdot 9 \cdot 9 \cdot 9 \cdot 9 \cdot 9 \cdot 9 \cdot 9$
24. $10 \cdot 10 \cdot 10 \cdot 10 \cdot 10 \cdot 10$

Lesson 1-3

Pages 34–37

Find the square of each number.

1. 4
2. 19
3. 13
4. 25
5. 9
6. 2
7. 14
8. 24
9. 40
10. 50
11. 100
12. 250

Find each square root.

13. $\sqrt{324}$
14. $\sqrt{900}$
15. $\sqrt{2,500}$
16. $\sqrt{576}$
17. $\sqrt{8,100}$
18. $\sqrt{676}$
19. $\sqrt{100}$
20. $\sqrt{784}$
21. $\sqrt{1,024}$
22. $\sqrt{841}$
23. $\sqrt{2,304}$
24. $\sqrt{3,025}$

Lesson 1-4

Pages 38–41

Evaluate each expression.

1. $14 - (5 + 7)$
2. $(32 + 10) - 5 \times 6$
3. $(50 - 6) + (12 + 4)$
4. $12 - 2 \cdot 3$
5. $16 + 4 \times 5$
6. $(5 + 3) \times 4 - 7$
7. $2 \times 3 + 9 \times 2$
8. $6 \cdot (8 + 4) \div 2$
9. $7 \times 6 - 14$
10. $8 + (12 \times 4) \div 8$
11. $13 - 6 \cdot 2 + 1$
12. $(80 \div 10) \times 8$
13. $14 - 2 \cdot 7 + 0$
14. $156 - 6 \times 0$
15. $30 - 14 \cdot 2 + 8$
16. $3 \times 4 - 3^2$
17. $10^2 - 5$
18. $3 + (10 - 5 + 1)^2$
19. $(4 + 3)^2 \div 7$
20. 8×10^3
21. $10^4 \times 6$
22. 4.5×10^3
23. 1.8×10^2
24. $3 + 5(1.7 + 2.3)$
25. $4(3.6 + 5.4) - 9$
26. $10 + 3(6.1 + 3.7)$
27. $6(7.5 + 2.1) - 2.3$

Lesson 1-5

Pages 42–43

Use the *guess and check* strategy to solve each problem.

1. **NUMBERS** A number is divided by 3. Then 8 is added to the quotient. The result is 15. What is the number?
2. **NUMBERS** Benny is thinking of two numbers. Their product is 32 and their difference is 4. Find the numbers.
3. **MONEY** A theater is charging \$5 for children under 12 and \$8 for everyone else. If the total for a group of people was \$36, how many people under the age of 12 were in the group?
4. **PLACE VALUE** Mindy wrote down a decimal number. The digit in the tenth's place is half the digit in the hundredth's place. If the product of the two digits is 18, what is the number?
5. **MONEY** Penny has 14 coins totaling \$1.55. She has one more nickel than she has dimes, and three less quarters than nickels. How many quarters, dimes, and nickels does she have if these are the only coin types she has?
6. **SOUVENIRS** A souvenir shop sells standard-sized postcards in packages of 5 and large-sized postcards in packages of 3. If Juan bought 16 postcards, how many packages of each did he buy?

Lesson 1-6

Pages 44–47

Evaluate each expression if $a = 3$, $b = 4$, $c = 12$, and $d = 1$.

1. $a + b$
2. $c - d$
3. $a + b + c$
4. $b - a$
5. $c - ab$
6. $a + 2d$
7. $b + 2c$
8. ab
9. $a + 3b$
10. $6a + c$
11. $\frac{c}{d}$
12. abc
13. $2(a + b)$
14. $\frac{2c}{b}$
15. $144 - abc$
16. $2ab$
17. $\frac{b}{2}$
18. a^2
19. $c^2 - 100$
20. $a^3 + 3$
21. $2b^2$
22. $b^3 + c$
23. $\frac{a^2}{d}$
24. $5a^2 + 2d^2$
25. $\frac{4d^2}{b}$
26. $\frac{15}{a}$
27. $3a^2$
28. $10d^3$
29. $\frac{ab}{c}$
30. $\frac{(a + b)}{d}$
31. $2.5b + c$
32. $\frac{10}{d}$
33. $\frac{(2c + b)}{b}$
34. $\frac{(b^2 + 2d)}{a}$
35. $\frac{(2c + ab)}{c}$
36. $\frac{(3.5c + 2)}{11}$

Extra Practice

Lesson 1-7

Pages 49–52

Solve each equation mentally.

1. $b + 7 = 12$
2. $a + 3 = 15$
3. $s + 10 = 23$
4. $9 + n = 13$
5. $20 = 24 - n$
6. $4x = 36$
7. $2y = 10$
8. $15 = 5h$
9. $j \div 3 = 2$
10. $14 = w - 4$
11. $24 \div k = 6$
12. $b - 3 = 12$
13. $c \div 10 = 8$
14. $6 = t \div 5$
15. $14 + m = 24$
16. $3y = 39$
17. $\frac{f}{2} = 12$
18. $16 = 4v$
19. $81 = 80 + a$
20. $9 = \frac{72}{x}$
21. $66 = 22m$
22. $77 - 12 = a$
23. $9k = 81$
24. $95 + d = 100$
25. $b = \frac{72}{6}$
26. $z = 15 + 22$
27. $15b = 225$
28. $43 + s = 57$
29. $4w = 52$
30. $e - 10 = 0$
31. $62 - d = 12$
32. $14f = 14$
33. $48 \div n = 8$
34. $a - 82 = 95$
35. $\frac{x}{2} = 36$
36. $99 = c \div 2$

Lesson 1-8

Pages 53–56

Use the Distributive Property to evaluate each expression.

1. $3(4 + 5)$
2. $(2 + 8)6$
3. $4(9 - 6)$
4. $8(6 - 3)$
5. $5(200 - 50)$
6. $20(3 + 6)$
7. $(20 - 5)8$
8. $50(8 + 2)$
9. $15(1{,}000 - 200)$
10. $3(2{,}000 + 400)$
11. $12(1{,}000 + 10)$
12. $7(1{,}000 - 50)$

Find each expression mentally. Justify each step.

13. $(5 + 17) + 25$
14. $13 + (22 + 17)$
15. $(8 + 18) + 92$
16. $(11 + 32) + 9$
17. $4 + (15 + 76)$
18. $(25 + 56) + 75$
19. $(4 \cdot 21) \cdot 25$
20. $5 \cdot (40 \cdot 8)$
21. $(2 \cdot 38) \cdot 50$
22. $(12 \cdot 7) \cdot 5$
23. $25 \cdot (12 \cdot 4)$
24. $(15 \cdot 9) \cdot 2$

Lesson 1-9

Pages 57–61

Describe the relationship between the terms in each arithmetic sequence. Then write the next three terms in each sequence.

1. 5, 9, 13, 17, …
2. 3, 5, 7, 9, …
3. 10, 15, 20, 25, …
4. 90, 93, 96, 99, …
5. 8, 14, 20, 26, …
6. 4.5, 5.4, 6.3, 7.2, …
7. 0.3, 0.4, 0.5, …
8. 2.3, 3.4, 4.5, 5.6, …
9. 8.9, 9.1, 9.3, 9.5, …
10. 3, 11, 19, 27, …
11. 350, 375, 400, 425, …
12. 620, 635, 650, 665, …
13. 2, 7, 12, 17, …
14. 10, 17, 24, 31, …
15. 0, 7, 14, 21, …
16. 1, 7, 13, 19, …
17. 95, 101, 107, 113, …
18. 9, 90, 171, 252, …
19. 2.6, 2.8, 3.0, 3.2, …
20. 4.1, 4.6, 5.1, 5.6, …
21. 6.6, 7.7, 8.8, 9.9, …
22. 19.5, 21, 22.5, 24, …
23. 14.5, 14.8, 15.1, 15.4, …
24. 0.1, 0.4, 0.7, 1.0, …

Lesson 1-10

Pages 63–67

Copy and complete each function table. Then identify the domain and range.

1.

x	$2x$	y
0		
1		
2		
3		

2.

x	$3x + 1$	y
1		
2		
3		
4		

3.

x	$x - 2$	y
3		
4		
5		
6		

4.

x	$x + 0.1$	y
2		
3		
4		
5		

Lesson 2-1

Pages 80–83

Write an integer for each situation.

1. seven degrees below zero
2. a loss of 3 pounds
3. a loss of 20 yards
4. a profit of $25
5. 112°F above 0
6. 2,830 feet above sea level

Graph each set of integers on a number line.

7. $\{-2, 0, 2\}$
8. $\{1, 3, 5\}$
9. $\{-2, -5, 3\}$
10. $\{7, -1, 4\}$

Evaluate each expression.

11. $|1|$
12. $|-8|$
13. $|0|$
14. $|-82|$
15. $|64|$
16. $|-128|$
17. $|-22| + 5$
18. $|-40| - 8$
19. $|-18| + |10|$
20. $|-7| + |-1|$
21. $|98| - |-5|$
22. $|-49| - |-10|$

Lesson 2-2

Pages 84–87

Replace each ● with < or > to make a true sentence.

1. 7 ● −7
2. −8 ● 4
3. −4 ● −9
4. −3 ● 0
5. 8 ● 10
6. −5 ● −4
7. 6 ● −7
8. −12 ● −13
9. 3 ● 1
10. −2 ● 2
11. 7 ● −1
12. −15 ● −20
13. −40 ● 30
14. 0 ● −3
15. −5 ● 0
16. 85 ● −17

Order the integers from least to greatest.

17. −2, −8, 4, 10, −6, −12
18. 19, −19, −21, 32, −14, 18
19. 18, 23, 95, −95, −18, −23, 2
20. 46, −48, −47, −52, −18, 12
21. 0, −10, −6, −8, 12
22. −15, 18, −1, 0, 14, −20

Lesson 2-3

Pages 88–92

Write the ordered pair for each point graphed at the right. Then name the quadrant or axis on which each point is located.

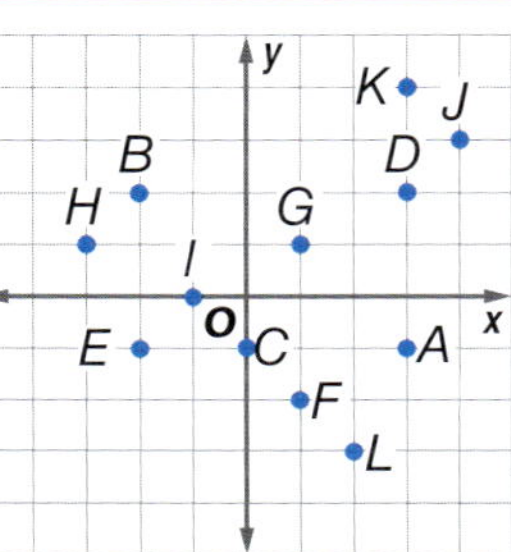

1. A 2. B 3. C
4. D 5. E 6. F
7. G 8. H 9. I
10. J 11. K 12. L

On graph paper, draw a coordinate plane. Then graph and label each point.

13. $N(-4, 3)$ 14. $K(2, 5)$ 15. $W(-6, -2)$ 16. $X(5, 0)$
17. $Y(4, -4)$ 18. $M(0, -3)$ 19. $Z(-2, 0.5)$ 20. $S(-1, -3)$
21. $A(0, 2)$ 22. $C(-2, -2)$ 23. $E(0, 1)$ 24. $G(1, -1)$

Lesson 2-4

Pages 95–99

Add.

1. $-4 + 8$ 2. $14 + 16$ 3. $-7 + (-7)$
4. $-9 + (-6)$ 5. $-18 + 11$ 6. $-36 + 40$
7. $42 + (-18)$ 8. $-42 + 29$ 9. $18 + (-32)$
10. $12 + (-9)$ 11. $-24 + 9$ 12. $-7 + (-1)$

Evaluate each expression if $a = 6$, $b = -2$, $c = -6$, and $d = 3$.

13. $-96 + a$ 14. $b + (-5)$ 15. $c + (-32)$
16. $d + 98$ 17. $-120 + b$ 18. $-120 + c$
19. $5 + b$ 20. $a + d$ 21. $c + a$
22. $d + (-9)$ 23. $b + c$ 24. $d + c$

Lesson 2-5

Pages 103–106

Subtract.

1. $3 - 7$ 2. $-5 - 4$ 3. $-6 - 2$
4. $8 - 13$ 5. $6 - (-4)$ 6. $12 - 9$
7. $-2 - 23$ 8. $63 - 78$ 9. $0 - (-14)$
10. $15 - 6$ 11. $18 - 20$ 12. $-5 - 8$
13. $21 - (-37)$ 14. $-60 - 32$ 15. $57 - 63$

Evaluate each expression if $k = -3$, $p = 6$, $n = 1$, and $d = -8$.

16. $55 - k$ 17. $p - 7$ 18. $d - 15$
19. $n - 12$ 20. $-51 - d$ 21. $k - 21$
22. $n - k$ 23. $-99 - k$ 24. $p - k$
25. $d - (-1)$ 26. $k - d$ 27. $n - d$

Lesson 2-6

Pages 107–111

Multiply.

1. $5(-2)$
2. $6(-4)$
3. $4(21)$
4. $-11(-5)$
5. $-6(5)$
6. $-50(0)$
7. $-5(-5)$
8. $-4(8)$
9. $3(-13)$
10. $12(-5)$
11. $-9(-12)$
12. $15(-8)$
13. $(-6)^2$
14. $(-2)^2$
15. $(-4)^3$
16. $(-5)^3$

Evaluate each expression if $a = -5$, $b = 2$, $c = -3$, and $d = 4$.

17. $-2d$
18. $6a$
19. $3ab$
20. $-12d$
21. $-4b^2$
22. $-5cd$
23. a^2
24. $13ab$

Lesson 2-7

Pages 112–113

Solve using the *look for a pattern* strategy.

1. **NUMBERS** Determine the next three numbers in the pattern below.

   15, 21, 27, 33, 39, …

2. **TIME** Determine the next two times in the pattern below.

   2:30 A.M., 2:50 A.M., 3:10 A.M., 3:30 A.M., …

3. **MONEY** The table shows Abigail's savings. If the pattern continues, what will be the total amount in week 6?

Week	Total ($)
1	$400
2	$800
3	$1,200
4	$1,600
5	$2,000
6	■

4. **SCIENCE** A single rotation of Earth takes about 24 hours. Copy and complete the table to determine the number of hours in a week.

Number of Days	Number of Hours
1	24
2	48
3	72
4	■
5	■
6	■
7	■

Lesson 2-8

Pages 114–118

Divide.

1. $4 \div (-2)$
2. $16 \div (-8)$
3. $-14 \div (-2)$
4. $\frac{32}{8}$
5. $18 \div (-3)$
6. $-18 \div 3$
7. $8 \div (-8)$
8. $0 \div (-1)$
9. $-25 \div 5$
10. $\frac{-14}{-7}$
11. $-32 \div 8$
12. $-56 \div (-8)$
13. $-81 \div 9$
14. $-42 \div (-7)$
15. $121 \div (-11)$
16. $-81 \div (-9)$
17. $18 \div (-2)$
18. $\frac{-55}{11}$
19. $\frac{25}{-5}$
20. $-21 \div 3$

Evaluate each expression if $a = -2$, $b = -7$, $x = 8$, and $y = -4$.

21. $-64 \div x$
22. $\frac{16}{y}$
23. $x \div 2$
24. $\frac{a}{2}$
25. $ax \div y$
26. $\frac{bx}{y}$
27. $2y \div 1$
28. $\frac{x}{ay}$
29. $-y \div a$
30. $x^2 \div y$
31. $\frac{ab}{1}$
32. $\frac{xy}{a}$

Lesson 3-1

Pages 128–133

Write each phrase as an algebraic expression.

1. six less than p
2. twenty more than c
3. the quotient of a and b
4. Juana's age plus 6
5. x increased by twelve
6. $1,000 divided by z
7. 3 divided into y
8. the product of 7 and m
9. the difference of f and 9
10. twenty-six less q
11. 19 decreased by z
12. two less than x

Write each sentence as an algebraic equation.

13. Three times a number less four is 17.
14. The sum of a number and 6 is 5.
15. Twenty more than twice a number is -30.
16. The quotient of a number and -2 is -42.
17. Four plus three times a number is 18.
18. Five times a number minus 15 is 92.
19. Eight times a number plus twelve is 36.
20. The difference of a number and 24 is -30.

Lesson 3-2

Pages 136–141

Solve each equation. Check your solution.

1. $r - 3 = 14$
2. $t + 3 = 21$
3. $s + 10 = 23$
4. $7 + a = -10$
5. $14 + m = 24$
6. $-9 + n = 13$
7. $s - 2 = -6$
8. $6 + f = 71$
9. $x + 27 = 30$
10. $a - 7 = 23$
11. $-4 + b = -5$
12. $w + 18 = -4$
13. $k - 9 = -3$
14. $j + 12 = 11$
15. $-42 + v = -42$
16. $s + 1.3 = 18$
17. $x + 7.4 = 23.5$
18. $p + 3.1 = 18$
19. $w - 3.7 = 4.63$
20. $m - 4.8 = 7.4$
21. $x - 1.3 = 12$
22. $y + 3.4 = 18$
23. $7.2 + g = 9.1$
24. $z - 12.1 = 14$
25. $v - 18 = 13.7$
26. $w - 0.1 = 0.32$
27. $r + 6.7 = 1.2$

Lesson 3-3

Pages 142–146

Solve each equation. Check your solution.

1. $2m = 18$
2. $-42 = 6n$
3. $72 = 8k$
4. $-20r = 20$
5. $420 = 5s$
6. $325 = 25t$
7. $-14 = -2p$
8. $18q = 36$
9. $40 = 10a$
10. $100 = 20b$
11. $416 = 4c$
12. $45 = 9d$
13. $0.5m = 3.5$
14. $1.8 = 0.6x$
15. $0.4y = 2$
16. $1.86 = 6.2z$
17. $-8x = 24$
18. $8.34 = 2r$
19. $1.67t = 10.02$
20. $243 = 27a$
21. $0.9x = 4.5$
22. $4.08 = 1.2y$
23. $8d = 112$
24. $5f = 180.5$
25. $59.66 = 3.14m$
26. $98.4 = 8p$
27. $208 = 26k$

Lesson 3-4

Pages 148–149

Use the *work backward* strategy to solve each problem.

1. **NUMBERS** A number is divided by 2. Then 4 is added to the quotient. Next, the sum of these numbers is multiplied by 3. The result is 21. Find the number.

2. **MONEY** Holly spent \$13.76 on a birthday present for her mom. She also spent \$3.25 on a snack for herself. If she now has \$7.74, how much money did she have initially?

3. **DVDs** Jack rented 2 times as many DVDs as Paloma last month. Paloma rented 4 fewer than Greg, but 4 more than Grace. Greg rented 9 DVDs. How many DVDs did each person rent?

4. **TIME** A portion of a shuttle bus schedule is shown. What is the earliest time after 9 A.M. when the bus departs?

Departs	Arrives
8:55 A.M.	9:20 A.M.
?	10:08 A.M.
10:31 A.M.	10:56 A.M.
11:19 A.M.	11:44 A.M.

5. **FOOD** After four days, 0.5 pound of lunch meat was left in the refrigerator. If half this amount was eaten on each of the previous four days, how much lunch meat was initially in the refrigerator?

Lesson 3-5

Pages 151–155

Solve each equation. Check your solution.

1. $3x + 6 = 6$
2. $2r - 7 = -1$
3. $-10 + 2d = 8$
4. $2b + 4 = -8$
5. $5w - 12 = 3$
6. $5t - 4 = 6$
7. $2q - 6 = 4$
8. $2g - 3 = -9$
9. $15 = 6y + 3$
10. $3s - 4 = 8$
11. $18 - 7f = 4$
12. $13 + 3p = 7$
13. $7.5r + 2 = -28$
14. $4.2 + 7z = 2.8$
15. $-9m - 9 = 9$
16. $32 + 0.2c = 1$
17. $5t - 14 = -14$
18. $-0.25x + 0.5 = 4$
19. $5w - 4 = 8$
20. $4d - 3 = 9$
21. $2g - 16 = -9$
22. $4k + 13 = 20$
23. $7 = 5 - 2x$
24. $8z + 15 = -1$
25. $92 - 16b = 12$
26. $14e + 14 = 28$
27. $1.1j + 2 = 7.5$

Lesson 3-6

Pages 156–161

Find the perimeter and area of each rectangle.

1. 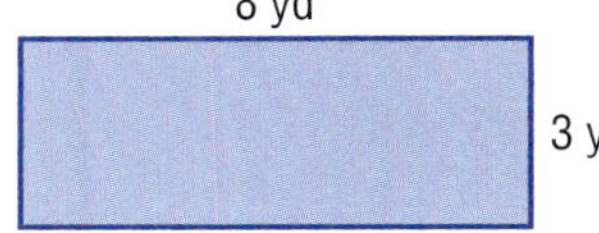

2. 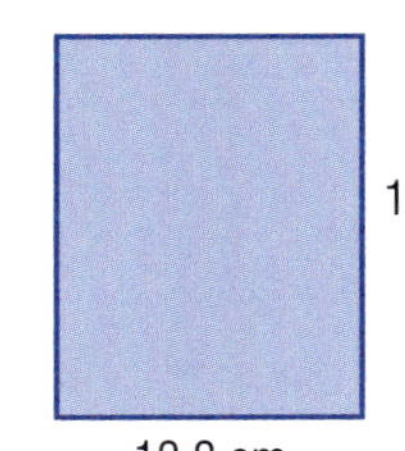

3. 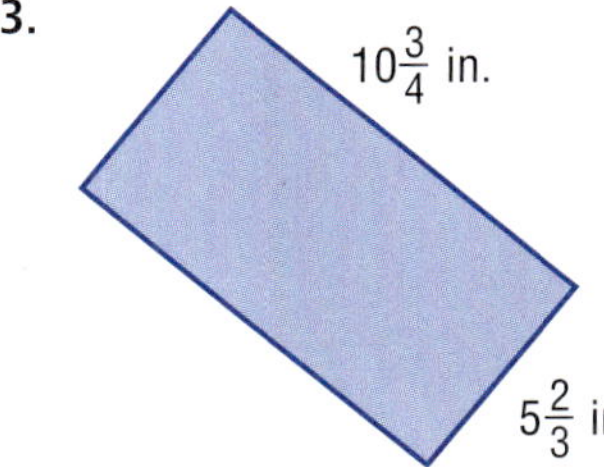

4. $\ell = 80$ yd, $w = 20$ yd
5. $\ell = 75$ cm, $w = 25$ cm
6. $\ell = 5.25$ km, $w = 1.5$ km
7. $\ell = 8.6$ cm, $w = 2.5$ cm
8. $\ell = 20.25$ m, $w = 4.75$ m
9. $\ell = 12$ ft, $w = 3$ ft
10. $\ell = 5\frac{1}{4}$ mi, $w = 2\frac{1}{2}$ mi
11. $\ell = 10\frac{2}{3}$ ft, $w = 5\frac{5}{6}$ ft

Extra Practice

Lesson 3-7

Pages 163–167

Graph the function represented by the table.

1.

Total Cost of Tennis Balls	
Number of Tennis Balls	Total Cost ($)
3	6
4	8
5	10
6	12

2.

Convert Gallons to Quarts	
Gallon	Quarts
1	4
2	8
3	12
4	16

Graph each equation.

3. $y = 3x$
4. $y = 2x + 3$
5. $y = -x$
6. $y = 0.5x + 2$
7. $y = -x + 3$
8. $y = 0.25x + 6$
9. $y = -3x + 6$
10. $y = -x + 1$
11. $y = 5 - 0.5x$

Lesson 4-1

Pages 181–184

Determine whether each number is *prime* or *composite*.

1. 32
2. 41
3. 52
4. 21
5. 71
6. 102
7. 239
8. 93
9. 123

Find the prime factorization of each number.

10. 81
11. 72
12. 144
13. 245
14. 423
15. 525
16. 750
17. 914
18. 975

Factor each expression.

19. $35xy$
20. $14a^2$
21. $30n$
22. $27cd^2$
23. $4s^2t^2$
24. $60p^2qr$

Lesson 4-2

Pages 186–189

Find the GCF of each set of numbers.

1. 12, 16
2. 63, 81
3. 225, 500
4. 37, 100
5. 32, 240
6. 412, 640
7. 36, 81
8. 140, 350
9. 72, 170
10. 12, 18, 42
11. 24, 56, 120
12. 48, 60, 84
13. 32, 80, 96
14. 14, 49, 70
15. 8, 10, 20

Find the GCF of each set of expressions.

16. $18b, 24b$
17. $2a, 3a$
18. $5n, 5mn$
19. $12cd, 24c$
20. $30x, 50x^2$
21. $15az, 25az$
22. $2c, 4ac, 8a$
23. $d, 6c^2d, 12d$
24. $10ab, 15bc, 20b^2$

Lesson 4-3

Pages 190–191

Use the *make a list* strategy to solve each problem.

1. **MEASUREMENT** Gabriel has to make deliveries to three neighbors. He lives at house b on the map. Find the shortest route to make the deliveries and return home?

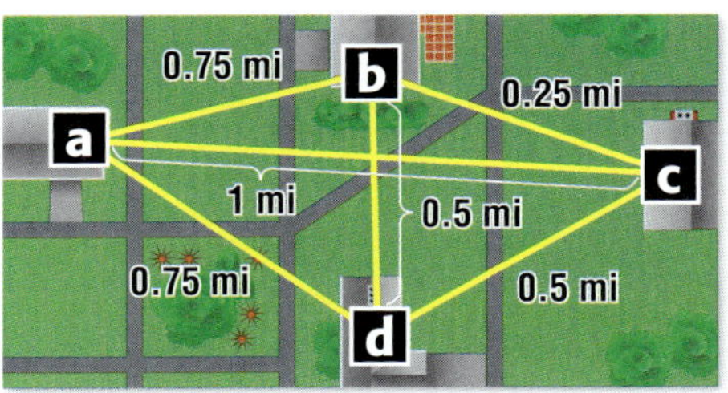

2. **FOOD** Daniel is making a peanut butter and jelly sandwich. His choices are creamy or crunchy peanut butter, white or wheat bread, and grape, apple, or strawberry jelly. How many different types of sandwiches can Daniel make?

3. **GAMES** On the game board, you plan to move two spaces away from square A. You can move horizontally, vertically, or diagonally. How many different moves can you make from square A? List them.

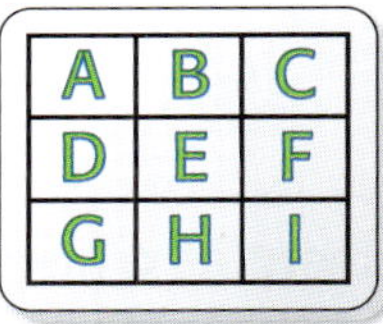

Lesson 4-4

Pages 192–195

Write each fraction in simplest form.

1. $\frac{14}{28}$
2. $\frac{15}{25}$
3. $\frac{100}{130}$
4. $\frac{14}{35}$
5. $\frac{9}{51}$
6. $\frac{54}{56}$
7. $\frac{75}{90}$
8. $\frac{24}{40}$
9. $\frac{180}{270}$
10. $\frac{312}{390}$
11. $\frac{240}{448}$
12. $\frac{71}{82}$
13. $\frac{333}{900}$
14. $\frac{85}{255}$
15. $\frac{84}{128}$
16. $\frac{64}{96}$
17. $\frac{99}{99}$
18. $\frac{3}{99}$
19. $\frac{44}{55}$
20. $\frac{57}{69}$
21. $\frac{15}{37}$
22. $\frac{204}{408}$
23. $\frac{5}{125}$
24. $\frac{144}{216}$
25. $\frac{15}{75}$

Lesson 4-5

Pages 196–200

Write each fraction or mixed number as a decimal. Use bar notation if the decimal is a repeating decimal.

1. $\frac{16}{20}$
2. $\frac{30}{120}$
3. $1\frac{7}{8}$
4. $\frac{1}{6}$
5. $\frac{11}{40}$
6. $5\frac{13}{50}$
7. $\frac{55}{300}$
8. $1\frac{1}{2}$
9. $\frac{5}{9}$
10. $2\frac{3}{4}$
11. $\frac{9}{11}$
12. $4\frac{1}{9}$

Write each decimal as a fraction or mixed number in simplest form.

13. 0.26
14. 0.75
15. 0.4
16. 0.1
17. 4.48
18. 9.8
19. 0.91
20. 11.15

Lesson 4-6

Pages 202–205

Write each ratio as a percent.

1. 39 out of 100
2. $\frac{23}{100}$
3. 17:100
4. 72 per 100
5. 4 to 100
6. 98 in 100

Write each fraction as a percent.

7. $\frac{1}{2}$
8. $\frac{2}{5}$
9. $\frac{60}{100}$
10. $\frac{17}{20}$
11. $\frac{7}{25}$
12. $\frac{1}{20}$
13. $\frac{8}{100}$
14. $\frac{7}{7}$
15. $\frac{9}{10}$
16. $\frac{1}{100}$
17. $\frac{50}{50}$
18. $\frac{49}{50}$

Write each percent as a fraction in simplest form.

19. 12%
20. 23%
21. 1%
22. 94%
23. 36%
24. 4%
25. 72%
26. 100%
27. 65%
28. 47%
29. 15%
30. 48%

Lesson 4-7

Pages 206–210

Write each percent as a decimal.

1. 42%
2. 100%
3. 8%
4. 20%
5. 35%
6. 3%
7. 62%
8. 50%
9. 28%
10. 87%
11. 7.5%
12. 87.5%
13. 1.8%
14. 99.9%
15. $85\frac{1}{4}\%$
16. $24\frac{1}{2}\%$
17. $64\frac{4}{5}\%$
18. $36\frac{3}{4}\%$
19. $1\frac{1}{5}\%$
20. $2\frac{1}{2}\%$

Write each decimal as a percent.

21. 0.16
22. 0.1
23. 0.5
24. 0.98
25. 0.31
26. 0.76
27. 0.07
28. 0.8
29. 0.07
30. 0.10
31. 0.90
32. 1.00
33. 0.666
34. 0.725
35. 0.138
36. 0.899
37. 0.256
38. 0.038
39. 0.0525
40. 0.017

Lesson 4-8

Pages 211–214

Find the LCM of each set of numbers.

1. 4, 9
2. 6, 16
3. 24, 36
4. 48, 84
5. 8, 9
6. 49, 56
7. 42, 66
8. 15, 39
9. 56, 64
10. 24, 42
11. 80, 250
12. 16, 24
13. 13, 14
14. 36, 48
15. 10, 100
16. 25, 200
17. 1, 2, 5
18. 2, 3, 7
19. 1, 9, 27
20. 2, 24, 36
21. 7, 21, 35
22. 12, 18, 28
23. 32, 80, 96
24. 5, 18, 45
25. 11, 22, 33
26. 35, 70, 140
27. 25, 200, 400
28. 100, 200, 300

Lesson 4-9

Pages 215–220

Replace each ● with <, >, or = to make a true sentence.

1. $-\frac{1}{5} \bullet -\frac{3}{5}$
2. $-\frac{7}{8} \bullet -\frac{5}{8}$
3. $-\frac{1}{6} \bullet -\frac{5}{6}$
4. $-\frac{3}{4} \bullet -\frac{1}{4}$
5. $-2\frac{1}{4} \bullet -2\frac{2}{8}$
6. $-4\frac{3}{7} \bullet -4\frac{2}{7}$
7. $-1\frac{4}{9} \bullet -1\frac{8}{9}$
8. $-3\frac{4}{5} \bullet -3\frac{2}{5}$
9. $\frac{7}{9} \bullet \frac{3}{5}$
10. $\frac{14}{25} \bullet \frac{3}{4}$
11. $\frac{8}{24} \bullet \frac{20}{60}$
12. $\frac{5}{12} \bullet \frac{4}{9}$
13. $\frac{18}{24} \bullet \frac{10}{18}$
14. $\frac{4}{6} \bullet \frac{5}{9}$
15. $\frac{11}{49} \bullet \frac{12}{42}$
16. $\frac{5}{14} \bullet \frac{2}{6}$

Order each set of numbers from least to greatest.

17. 70%, 0.6, $\frac{2}{3}$
18. 0.8, $\frac{17}{20}$, 17%
19. $\frac{61}{100}$, 0.65, 61.5%
20. $0.\overline{42}$, $\frac{3}{7}$, 42%
21. 2.15, 2.105, $2\frac{7}{50}$
22. $7\frac{1}{8}$, 7.81, 7.18

Lesson 5-1

Pages 230–235

Estimate.

1. $\frac{3}{7} + \frac{6}{8}$
2. $\frac{3}{9} + \frac{7}{8}$
3. $\frac{1}{8} + \frac{8}{9}$
4. $3\frac{1}{8} + 7\frac{6}{7}$
5. $4\frac{2}{3} + 6\frac{7}{8}$
6. $3\frac{2}{3} \times 2\frac{1}{3}$
7. $\frac{4}{5} \cdot 3$
8. $9\frac{7}{8} - 6\frac{2}{3}$
9. $\frac{3}{7} - \frac{1}{15}$
10. $\frac{3}{4} \cdot \frac{7}{8}$
11. $7\frac{1}{4} \div \frac{2}{3}$
12. $\frac{5}{6} \div \frac{2}{3}$
13. $9\frac{3}{5} + 3\frac{1}{8}$
14. $5\frac{1}{3} - 2\frac{3}{4}$
15. $13\frac{7}{8} - 2\frac{1}{3}$
16. $\frac{13}{15} \cdot \frac{3}{8}$
17. $\frac{1}{9} \div 2$
18. $\frac{5}{8} - \frac{1}{16}$
19. $9\frac{2}{3} + 4\frac{7}{8}$
20. $\frac{1}{2} \cdot 25$
21. $35\frac{1}{3} \div 6\frac{3}{4}$

Lesson 5-2

Pages 236–241

Add or subtract. Write in simplest form.

1. $\frac{5}{11} + \frac{9}{11}$
2. $\frac{5}{8} - \frac{1}{8}$
3. $\frac{7}{10} + \frac{7}{10}$
4. $\frac{9}{12} - \frac{5}{12}$
5. $\frac{2}{9} + \frac{1}{3}$
6. $\frac{1}{2} + \frac{3}{4}$
7. $\frac{1}{4} - \frac{3}{12}$
8. $\frac{3}{7} + \frac{6}{14}$
9. $\frac{1}{4} + \frac{3}{5}$
10. $\frac{4}{9} + \frac{1}{2}$
11. $\frac{5}{7} - \frac{4}{6}$
12. $\frac{3}{4} - \frac{1}{6}$
13. $\frac{3}{5} + \frac{3}{4}$
14. $\frac{2}{3} - \frac{1}{8}$
15. $\frac{9}{10} + \frac{1}{3}$

Evaluate each expression if $a = \frac{2}{3}$ and $b = \frac{7}{12}$.

16. $\frac{1}{5} + a$
17. $a - \frac{1}{2}$
18. $b + \frac{7}{8}$
19. $\frac{7}{8} - a$
20. $a + b$
21. $a - b$

Lesson 5-3

Pages 242–246

Add or subtract. Write in simplest form.

1. $2\frac{1}{3} + 1\frac{1}{3}$
2. $5\frac{2}{7} - 2\frac{3}{7}$
3. $6\frac{3}{8} + 7\frac{1}{8}$
4. $2\frac{3}{4} - 1\frac{1}{4}$
5. $5\frac{1}{2} - 3\frac{1}{4}$
6. $2\frac{2}{3} + 4\frac{1}{9}$
7. $7\frac{4}{5} + 9\frac{3}{10}$
8. $3\frac{3}{4} + 5\frac{5}{8}$
9. $10\frac{2}{3} + 5\frac{6}{7}$
10. $17\frac{2}{9} - 12\frac{1}{3}$
11. $6\frac{5}{12} + 12\frac{5}{12}$
12. $7\frac{1}{4} + 15\frac{5}{6}$
13. $6\frac{1}{8} + 4\frac{2}{3}$
14. $7 - 6\frac{4}{9}$
15. $8\frac{1}{12} + 12\frac{6}{11}$
16. $7\frac{2}{3} + 8\frac{1}{4}$
17. $12\frac{3}{11} + 14\frac{3}{13}$
18. $21\frac{1}{3} + 15\frac{3}{8}$
19. $19\frac{1}{7} + 6\frac{1}{4}$
20. $9\frac{2}{5} - 8\frac{1}{3}$
21. $18\frac{1}{4} - 3\frac{3}{8}$
22. $1\frac{1}{8} + 2\frac{1}{12}$
23. $2\frac{1}{12} - 1\frac{1}{8}$
24. $10 - \frac{2}{3}$

Lesson 5-4

Pages 247–248

Eliminate possibilities to solve each problem.

1. **MEASUREMENT** Guillermo has a 3-gallon cooler with $1\frac{3}{4}$ gallons of juice in it. If he wants the cooler full for his soccer game, how much juice should he add?

   A 4 gallons
   B $3\frac{1}{4}$ gallons
   C $1\frac{1}{4}$ gallons
   D $\frac{1}{4}$ gallon

2. **ELEPHANTS** An elephant in a zoo eats 58 cabbages in a week. About how many cabbages does an elephant eat in one year?

   F 7
   G 700
   H 1,500
   J 3,000

3. **TRAVEL** Mr. Rollins drove 780 miles on a 5-day trip. He rented a car for \$23 per day plus \$0.15 per mile after 500 free miles. About how much did the rental car cost?

   A \$100
   B \$130
   C \$160
   D \$180

Lesson 5-5

Pages 256–257

Multiply. Write in simplest form.

1. $\frac{2}{3} \times \frac{3}{5}$
2. $\frac{1}{6} \times \frac{2}{5}$
3. $\frac{4}{9} \times \frac{3}{7}$
4. $\frac{5}{12} \times \frac{6}{11}$
5. $\frac{3}{8} \times \frac{8}{9}$
6. $\frac{2}{5} \times \frac{5}{8}$
7. $\frac{7}{15} \times \frac{3}{21}$
8. $\frac{5}{6} \times \frac{15}{16}$
9. $\frac{2}{3} \times \frac{3}{13}$
10. $\frac{4}{9} \times \frac{1}{6}$
11. $3 \times \frac{1}{9}$
12. $5 \times \frac{6}{7}$
13. $\frac{3}{5} \times 15$
14. $3\frac{1}{2} \times 4\frac{1}{3}$
15. $\frac{4}{5} \times 2\frac{3}{4}$
16. $6\frac{1}{8} \times 5\frac{1}{7}$
17. $2\frac{2}{3} \times 2\frac{1}{4}$
18. $\frac{7}{8} \times 16$
19. $5\frac{1}{5} \times 2\frac{1}{2}$
20. $7 \times \frac{1}{14}$
21. $22 \times \frac{3}{11}$
22. $8\frac{2}{3} \times 1\frac{1}{2}$
23. $4 \times 6\frac{1}{2}$
24. $\frac{1}{2} \times 10\frac{2}{3}$
25. $\frac{2}{3} \times 21\frac{1}{3}$
26. $\frac{7}{8} \times \frac{8}{7}$
27. $21 \times \frac{1}{2}$
28. $11 \times \frac{1}{4}$

Lesson 5-6

Pages 258–263

Find the multiplicative inverse of each number.

1. $\frac{2}{3}$
2. $\frac{5}{4}$
3. 1
4. 10
5. $\frac{1}{7}$
6. $\frac{9}{16}$
7. $1\frac{1}{3}$
8. $3\frac{3}{4}$
9. $7\frac{3}{8}$
10. $6\frac{2}{5}$
11. $33\frac{1}{3}$
12. $66\frac{2}{3}$

Solve each equation. Check your solution.

13. $\frac{a}{13} = 2$
14. $\frac{8}{9}x = 24$
15. $\frac{3}{8}r = 36$
16. $\frac{3}{4}t = \frac{1}{2}$
17. $16 = \frac{h}{4}$
18. $\frac{m}{8} = 12$
19. $\frac{5}{8}n = 45$
20. $10 = \frac{b}{10}$
21. $\frac{1}{7}x = 7$
22. $5 = \frac{1}{5}y$
23. $\frac{4}{3}m = 28$
24. $\frac{2}{3}z = 20$
25. $\frac{c}{9} = 81$
26. $\frac{m}{9} = 9$
27. $16 = \frac{4}{9}f$
28. $\frac{15}{8}x = 225$

Lesson 5-7

Pages 265–270

Divide. Write in simplest form.

1. $\frac{2}{3} \div \frac{3}{2}$
2. $\frac{3}{5} \div \frac{2}{5}$
3. $\frac{7}{10} \div \frac{3}{8}$
4. $\frac{5}{9} \div \frac{2}{5}$
5. $4 \div \frac{2}{3}$
6. $8 \div \frac{4}{5}$
7. $9 \div \frac{5}{9}$
8. $\frac{2}{7} \div 2$
9. $\frac{1}{14} \div 7$
10. $15 \div \frac{3}{5}$
11. $\frac{9}{14} \div \frac{3}{4}$
12. $\frac{7}{8} \div 10$
13. $16 \div \frac{3}{4}$
14. $\frac{3}{8} \div 2\frac{1}{2}$
15. $5\frac{1}{2} \div 2\frac{1}{2}$
16. $3\frac{1}{4} \div 5\frac{1}{2}$
17. $12\frac{5}{6} \div 2\frac{1}{6}$
18. $7\frac{1}{2} \div 3\frac{1}{2}$

Lesson 6-1

Pages 282–286

LUNCH **Use the survey results to write each ratio as a fraction in simplest form.**

1. fish sticks:macaroni and cheese
2. pizza:macaroni and cheese
3. all votes:macaroni and cheese
4. pizza:all votes
5. other:hamburger

Favorite School Lunch	Votes
Pizza	64
Hamburger	15
Macaroni and Cheese	14
Fish Sticks	4
Other	3

Determine whether the following ratios are equivalent. Explain.

6. 4 out of 6 balloons popped, 8 out of 12 balloons popped
7. 20 out of 25 students agree, 16 out of 30 students agree

Lesson 6-2

Pages 287–292

Find each unit rate. Round to the nearest hundredth if necessary.

1. \$240 for 4 days
2. 250 people in 5 buses
3. 500 miles in 10 hours
4. 18 cups for 24 pounds
5. 32 people in 8 cars
6. \$4.50 for 3 dozen
7. 245 tickets in 5 days
8. 12 classes in 4 semesters
9. 60 people in 4 rows
10. 48 ounces in 3 pounds
11. 20 people in 4 groups
12. 1.5 pounds for \$3.00
13. 45 miles in 60 minutes
14. \$5.50 for 10 disks
15. 360 miles for 12 gallons
16. \$8.50 for 5 yards
17. 24 cups for \$1.20
18. 160 words in 4 minutes
19. \$60 for 5 books
20. \$24 for 6 hours

Lesson 6-3

Pages 293–297

For Exercises 1 and 2, find the rate of change for each table.

1.

Age (yr)	Height (in.)
9	54
10	56
11	58
12	60

2.

Time (h)	Temperature (°C)
0	0
4	3
8	6
12	9

3. **MOVIE RENTALS** The graph shows the cost of renting movies. Use the graph to find the rate of change.

Lesson 6-4

Pages 298–303

Complete.

1. 4,000 lb = ▒ T
2. 5 T = ▒ lb
3. 5 lb = ▒ oz
4. 12,000 lb = ▒ T
5. $\frac{1}{4}$ lb = ▒ oz
6. 12 pt = ▒ c
7. 3 gal = ▒ pt
8. 24 fl oz = ▒ c
9. 8 pt = ▒ c
10. 10 pt = ▒ qt
11. $2\frac{1}{4}$ c = ▒ fl oz
12. 6 lb = ▒ oz
13. 10 gal = ▒ qt
14. 4 qt = ▒ fl oz
15. 4 pt = ▒ c
16. 13,200 ft = ▒ mi
17. 120 oz = ▒ lb
18. $9\frac{1}{4}$ gal = ▒ qt
19. 7,480 yd = ▒ mi
20. $12\frac{1}{2}$ lb = ▒ oz
21. $7\frac{1}{2}$ qt = ▒ pt
22. $3\frac{1}{8}$ c = ▒ fl oz
23. $2\frac{1}{4}$ mi = ▒ ft
24. $3\frac{2}{3}$ T = ▒ lb

Lesson 6-5

Pages 304–309

Complete. Round to the nearest hundredth if necessary.

1. 400 mm = ■ cm
2. 4 km = ■ m
3. 660 cm = ■ m
4. 0.3 km = ■ m
5. 30 mm = ■ cm
6. 84.5 m = ■ km
7. ■ m = 54 cm
8. 18 km = ■ cm
9. ■ mm = 45 cm
10. 4 kg = ■ g
11. 632 mg = ■ g
12. 4,497 g = ■ kg
13. ■ mg = 0.51 kg
14. 0.63 kg = ■ g
15. ■ kg = 563 g
16. 662 m = ■ km
17. 5,283 mL = ■ L
18. 0.24 cm = ■ mm
19. 380 kL = ■ L
20. 10.8 g = ■ mg
21. 83,000 mL = ■ L
22. 56 in. ≈ ■ cm
23. 32.8 ft. ≈ ■ m
24. 609 yd ≈ ■ m
25. 21.78 mi ≈ ■ km
26. 48 lb ≈ ■ g
27. 2.3 T ≈ ■ kg
28. 8.5 c ≈ ■ mL
29. 33 gal ≈ ■ L
30. 1.8 qt ≈ ■ mL

Lesson 6-6

Pages 310–315

Determine if the quantities in each pair of ratios are proportional. Explain.

1. **MONEY** 2 coins for every 3 bills and 6 coins for every 9 bills
2. **SCALE** 3 feet for every 1 in and 15 feet for every 6 in
3. **FAMILY** 2 children for every 1 adult and 8 children for every 3 adults

Solve each proportion.

4. $\frac{u}{72} = \frac{2}{4}$
5. $\frac{12}{m} = \frac{15}{10}$
6. $\frac{36}{90} = \frac{16}{t}$
7. $\frac{g}{32} = \frac{8}{64}$
8. $\frac{5}{14} = \frac{10}{a}$
9. $\frac{k}{18} = \frac{5}{3}$
10. $\frac{15}{w} = \frac{60}{4}$
11. $\frac{81}{90} = \frac{y}{20}$
12. $\frac{45}{8} = \frac{36}{d}$
13. $\frac{125}{v} = \frac{20}{5}$
14. $\frac{4}{5} = \frac{x}{3}$
15. $\frac{45}{75} = \frac{j}{3}$

Lesson 6-7

Pages 318–319

Use the *draw a diagram* strategy to solve the following problems.

1. **TESTS** The scores on a test are found by adding or subtracting points as shown below. If Salazar's score on a 15-question test was 86 points, how many of his answers were correct, incorrect, and blank?

Answer	Points
Correct	+8
Incorrect	−4
No answer	−2

2. **GAMES** Six members of a video game club are having a tournament. In the first round, every player will play a video game against every other player. How many games will be in the first round of the tournament?

3. **FAMILY** At Latrice's family reunion, $\frac{4}{5}$ of the people are 18 years of age or older. Half of the remaining people are under 12 years old. If 20 children are under 12 years old, how many people are at the reunion?

Lesson 6-8

Pages 320–326

On a map, the scale is 1 inch = 50 miles. For each map distance, find the actual distance.

1. 5 inches
2. 12 inches
3. $2\frac{3}{8}$ inches
4. $\frac{4}{5}$ inch
5. $2\frac{5}{6}$ inches
6. 3.25 inches
7. 4.75 inches
8. 5.25 inches

On a scale drawing, the scale is $\frac{1}{2}$ inch = 2 feet. Find the dimensions of each room in the scale drawing.

9. 14 feet by 18 feet
10. 32 feet by 6 feet
11. 3 feet by 5 feet
12. 20 feet by 30 feet

Lesson 6-9

Pages 328–332

Write each percent as a fraction in simplest form.

1. 32%
2. 89%
3. 72%
4. 11%
5. 1%
6. 28%
7. 55%
8. 18.5%
9. 22.75%
10. 25.2%
11. 75.5%
12. 48.25%
13. 6.5%
14. 1.25%
15. 88.9%
16. $52\frac{1}{4}$%
17. 895%
18. 480%
19. 0.78%
20. 0.3%

Write each fraction as a percent. Round to the nearest hundredth if necessary.

21. $\frac{14}{25}$
22. $\frac{28}{50}$
23. $\frac{14}{20}$
24. $\frac{7}{10}$
25. $\frac{17}{17}$
26. $\frac{80}{125}$
27. $\frac{9}{12}$
28. $\frac{4}{6}$
29. $\frac{11}{12}$
30. $\frac{9}{16}$
31. $\frac{8}{9}$
32. $\frac{3}{16}$
33. $\frac{5}{32}$
34. $\frac{1}{16}$
35. $\frac{8}{15}$
36. $\frac{9}{11}$
37. $\frac{1}{250}$
38. $\frac{1}{500}$
39. $12\frac{1}{2}$
40. $18\frac{2}{5}$

Lesson 7-1

Pages 344–348

Find each number. Round to the nearest tenth if necessary.

1. 5% of 40
2. 10% of 120
3. 12% of 150
4. 12.5% of 40
5. 75% of 200
6. 13% of 25.3
7. 250% of 44
8. 0.5% of 13.7
9. 600% of 7
10. 1.5% of $25
11. 81% of 134
12. 43% of 110
13. 61% of 524
14. 100% of 3.5
15. 20% of 58.5
16. 45% of 125.5
17. 23% of 500
18. 80% of 8
19. 90% of 72
20. 32% of 54

Lesson 7-2

Pages 353–354

Find each number. Round to the nearest tenth if necessary.

1. What number is 25% of 280?
2. 38 is what percent of 50?
3. 54 is 25% of what number?
4. 24.5% of what number is 15?
5. What number is 80% of 500?
6. 12% of 120 is what number?
7. Find 68% of 50.
8. What percent of 240 is 32?
9. 99 is what percent of 150?
10. Find 75% of 1.
11. What number is $33\frac{1}{3}\%$ of 66?
12. 50% of 350 is what number?
13. What percent of 450 is 50?
14. What number is $37\frac{1}{2}\%$ of 32?
15. 95% of 40 is what number?
16. Find 30% of 26.
17. 9 is what percent of 30?
18. 52% of what number is 109.2?
19. What number is 65% of 200?
20. What number is 15.5% of 45?

Lesson 7-3

Pages 355–360

Estimate by using fractions.

1. 28% of 48
2. 99% of 65
3. 445% of 20
4. 9% of 81
5. 73% of 240
6. 65.5% of 75
7. 48.2% of 93
8. 39.45% of 51
9. 287% of 122
10. 53% of 80
11. 414% of 72
12. 59% of 105

Estimate by using 10%.

13. 30% of 42
14. 70% of 104
15. 90% of 152
16. 67% of 70
17. 78% of 92
18. 12% of 183
19. 51% of 221
20. 23% of 504
21. 81% of 390
22. 41% of 60
23. 59% of 178
24. 22% of 450

Estimate.

25. 50% of 37
26. 18% of 90
27. 300% of 245
28. 1% of 48
29. 70% of 300
30. 35% of 35
31. 60.5% of 60
32. $5\frac{1}{2}\%$ of 100
33. 40.01% of 16
34. 80% of 62
35. 45% of 119
36. 14.81% of 986

Lesson 7-4

Pages 361–365

Write an equation for each problem. Then solve. Round to the nearest tenth if necessary.

1. Find 45% of 50.
2. 75 is what percent of 300?
3. 16% of what number is 2?
4. 75% of 80 is what number?
5. 5% of what number is 12?
6. Find 60% of 45.
7. 90 is what percent of 95?
8. $28\frac{1}{2}\%$ of 64 is what number?
9. Find 46.5% of 75.
10. What number is 55.5% of 70?
11. 80.5% of what number is 80.5?
12. $66\frac{2}{3}\%$ of what number is 40?
13. Find 122.5% of 80.
14. 250% of what number is 75?

Lesson 7-5

Pages 366–367

Solve each problem using the *reasonable answers* strategy.

1. **SKIING** Benito skied for 13.5 hours and estimated that he spent 30% of his time on the ski lift. Did he spend about 4, 6, or 8 hours on the ski lift?
2. **CLASS TRIP** The class trip at Wilson Middle School costs $145 per student. A fundraiser earns 38% of this cost. Will each student have to pay about $70, $80, or $90?
3. **GAS MILEAGE** Miguel's car gets 38 miles per gallon and has 2.5 gallons of gasoline left in the tank. Can he drive for 85, 95, or 105 more miles before he runs out of gas?
4. **DINING** At a restaurant, the total cost of a meal is $87.50. Nadia wants to leave a 20% tip. Should she leave a total of $95, $105, or $115?

Lesson 7-6

Pages 369–374

Find each percent of change. Round to the nearest whole percent if necessary. State whether the percent of change is an *increase* or *decrease*.

1. 450 centimeters to 675 centimeters
2. 77 million to 200.2 million
3. 500 albums to 100 albums
4. 350 yards to 420 yards
5. 3.25 meters to 2.95 meters
6. $65 to $75
7. 180 dishes to 160 dishes
8. 450 pieces to 445.5 pieces
9. 700 grams 910 grams
10. 55 women to 11 women
11. 412 children to 1,339 children
12. 464 kilograms to 20 kilograms
13. 24 hours to 86 hours
14. 16 minutes to 24 minutes

Lesson 7-7

Pages 375–378

Find the total cost or sale price to the nearest cent.

1. $45 sweater; 6% tax
2. $18.99 CD; 15% discount
3. $199 ring; 10% discount
4. $29 shirt; 7% tax
5. $19 purse; 25% discount
6. $145 coat; 6.25% tax
7. $12 meal; 4.5% tax
8. $899 computer; 20% discount
9. $105 skateboard; $7\frac{1}{2}$% tax
10. $599 TV; 12% discount
11. $12,500 car; $3\frac{3}{4}$% tax
12. $49.95 gloves; $5\frac{1}{4}$% tax

Find the percent of discount to the nearest percent.

13. sneakers: regular price, $72
    sale price, $60
14. dress shirt: regular price, $90
    sale price, $22.50
15. portable game player: regular price, $125
    sale price, $100
16. car: regular price, $25,000
    sale price, $22,000
17. hiking boots: regular price, $139
    sale price, $113.98
18. airline tickets: regular price, $556
    sale price, $500.40
19. CD: regular price, $15
    sale price, $9
20. computer: regular price, $600
    sale price, $450

Lesson 7-8

Pages 379–382

Find the simple interest earned to the nearest cent for each principal, interest rate, and time.

1. \$2,000, 8%, 5 years
2. \$500, 10%, 8 months
3. \$750, 5%, 1 year
4. \$175.50, $6\frac{1}{2}$%, 18 months
5. \$236.20, 9%, 16 months
6. \$89, $7\frac{1}{2}$%, 6 months
7. \$800, 5.75%, 3 years
8. \$225, $1\frac{1}{2}$%, 2 years
9. \$12,000, $4\frac{1}{2}$%, 40 months

Find the simple interest paid to the nearest cent for each loan, interest rate, and time.

10. \$750, 18%, 2 years
11. \$1,500, 19%, 16 months
12. \$300, 9%, 1 year
13. \$4,750, 19.5%, 30 months
14. \$2,345, 17%, 9 months
15. \$689, 12%, 2 years
16. \$390, 18.75%, 15 months
17. \$1,250, 22%, 8 months
18. \$3,240, 18%, 14 months

Lesson 8-1

Pages 395–400

Display each set of data in a line plot. Identify any clusters, gaps, or outliers.

1.

Number of Pets in the Home				
0	1	3	4	0
2	1	0	1	1
10	0	1	5	2

2.

High Temperatures for 18 Days (°F)					
75	81	75	65	76	81
77	80	65	65	80	80
76	85	66	75	80	75

3.

Number of Stories for Buildings in Denver				
56	43	36	42	29
54	42	32	34	
52	40	32	32	

Source: *The World Almanac and Book of Facts*

4.

Ages of Children at Sunny Day Care (years)					
4	1	6	4	5	3
4	5	1	2	5	4
3	2	4	1	3	3

Lesson 8-2

Pages 401–407

Find the mean, median, and mode for each set of data.

1. 1, 5, 9, 1, 2, 6, 8, 2
2. 2, 5, 8, 9, 7, 6, 3, 5, 1, 4
3. 82, 79, 93, 91, 95, 95, 81
4. 117, 103, 108, 120
5. 256, 265, 247, 256
6. 47, 54, 66, 54, 46, 66
7.

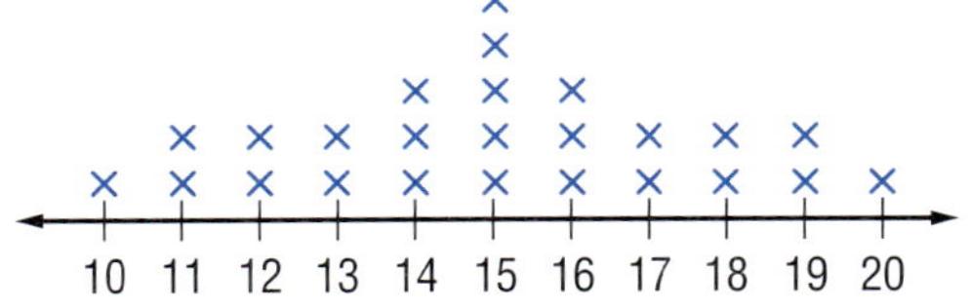

8.

Number of Absences	Tally	Frequency
0	IIII	4
1	~~IIII~~ IIII	9
2	~~IIII~~ I	6
3	~~IIII~~	5

Lesson 8-3

Pages 409–413

Display each set of data in a stem-and-leaf plot.

1. 23, 15, 39, 68, 57, 42, 51, 52, 41, 18, 29
2. 189, 182, 196, 184, 197, 183, 196, 194, 184
3.

Average Monthly High Temperatures in Albany, NY (°F)			
21	46	72	50
24	58	70	40
34	67	61	27

Source: *The World Almanac and Book of Facts*

4.

Super Bowl Winning Scores 1987–2004					
39	55	52	27	34	20
42	20	30	35	23	48
20	37	49	31	34	32

Source: *The World Almanac and Book of Facts*

Lesson 8-4

Pages 414–420

Select the appropriate graph to display each set of data: bar graph or histogram. Then display the data in the appropriate graph.

1.

Longest Snakes	
Snake Name	**Length (ft)**
Royal python	35
Anaconda	28
Indian python	25
Diamond python	21
King cobra	19
Boa constrictor	16

Source: *The Top 10 of Everything*

2.

Least Densely Populated States	
State	**People Per Square Mile**
Alaska	1
Wyoming	5
Montana	6
North Dakota	9
South Dakota	10
New Mexico	15

Source: *The Top 10 of Everything*

3.

Cost of a Movie Ticket at Selected Theaters			
$5.25	$6.50	$3.50	$3.75
$7.50	$9.25	$10.40	$4.75
$10.00	$4.50	$8.75	$7.25
$3.50	$6.70	$4.20	$7.50

4.

Highest Recorded Wind Speeds For Selected U.S. Cities (mph)					
52	55	81	46	73	57
75	54	58	76	46	58
60	91	53	53	51	56
80	60	73	46	49	47

Source: *The World Almanac and Book of Facts*

Lesson 8-5

Pages 424–425

WEATHER For Exercises 1–3, solve by using the graph.

1. In which month is the average high temperature about twice as high as the average low temperature for January?
2. What is the approximate difference between the average high temperature and the average low temperature each month?
3. Predict the high and low temperatures for June based on the data given on the graph.

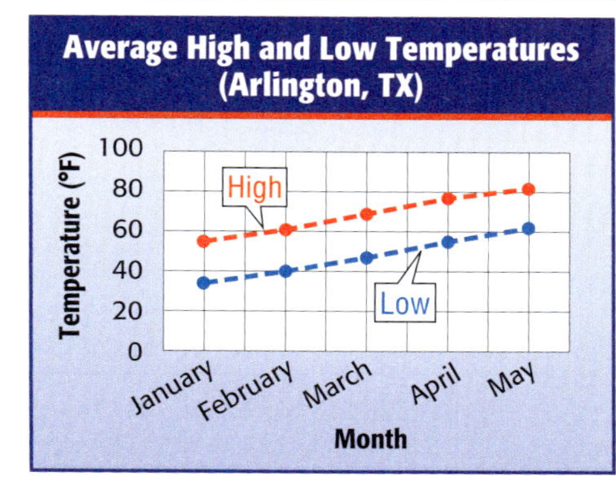

Lesson 8-6

Pages 426–431

For Exercises 1–3, refer to the graph at the right which shows Rachel's quiz scores for six quizzes.

1. Describe the trend in Rachel's quiz scores.
2. If the trend continues, predict Rachel's score on the seventh quiz.
3. If the trend continues, predict Rachel's score on the tenth quiz.

Quiz Scores

Score: 0 1 2 3 4 5 6 7 8 9 10

Quiz: 1 2 3 4 5 6

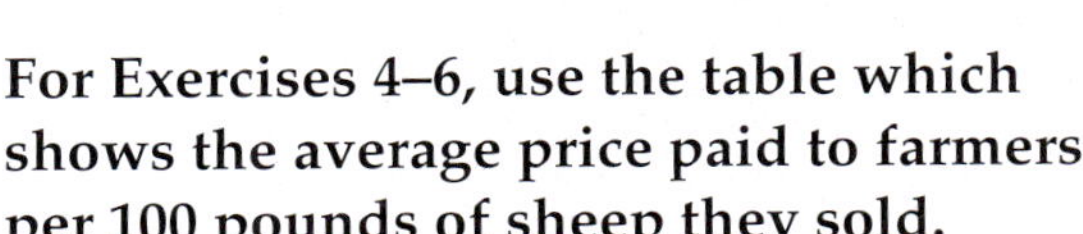

For Exercises 4–6, use the table which shows the average price paid to farmers per 100 pounds of sheep they sold.

4. Make a scatter plot of the data.
5. Describe the relationship, if any, between the two sets of data.
6. Predict the price per 100 pounds for 2010. Explain.

Year	Price Per 100 Pounds ($)
1940	4
1950	12
1960	6
1970	8
1980	21
1990	23
2000	34

Source: *The World Almanac and Book of Facts*

Lesson 8-7

Pages 435–437

1. **SURVEYS** The table shows the results of a survey of students' favorite cookies. Predict how many of the 424 students at Scobey High School prefer chocolate chip cookies.

Cookie	Number
chocolate chip	49
peanut butter	12
oatmeal	10
sugar	8
raisin	3

2. **VACATION** The circle graph shows the results of a survey of teens and where they would prefer to spend a family vacation. Predict how many of 4,000 teens would prefer to go to an amusement park.

Vacation Survey

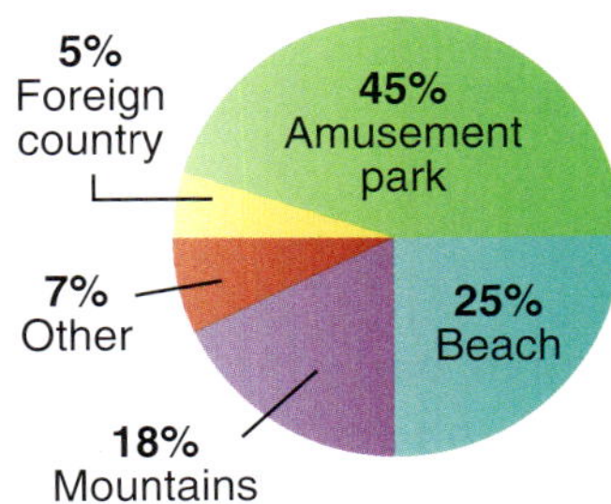

3. **TRAVEL** In 2000, about 29% of the foreign visitors to the U.S. were from Canada. If a particular hotel had 150,000 foreign guests in one year, how many would you predict were from Canada?

Lesson 8-8

Pages 438–443

Determine whether each conclusion is valid. Justify your answer.

1. To determine whether most students participate in after school activities, the principal of Humberson Middle School randomly surveyed 75 students from each grade level. Of these, 34% said they participate in after school activities. The principal concluded that about a third of the students at Humberson Middle School participate in after school activities.
2. To evaluate their product, the manager of an assembly line inspected the first 100 watches produced on Monday. Of these, 2 were defective. The manager concluded that about 2% of all watches produced are defective.
3. A television program asked its viewers to dial one of two phone numbers indicating their preference for one of two brands of shampoo. Of those that responded, 76% said they prefer Brand A. The program concluded that Brand A was the most popular brand of shampoo.

Lesson 8-9

Pages 444–449

Which graph could be misleading? Explain your reasoning.

1. Both graphs show pounds of grapes sold to Westview School in one week.

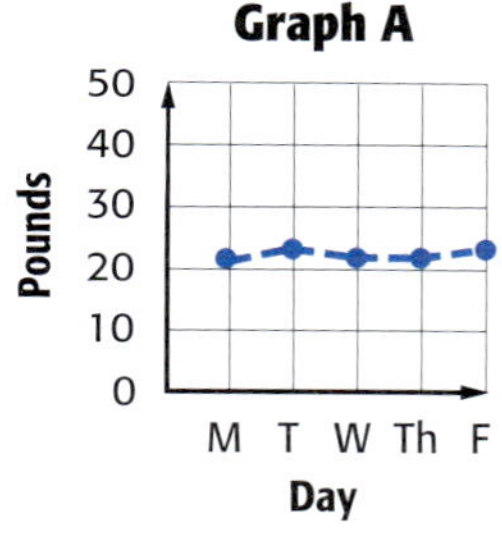

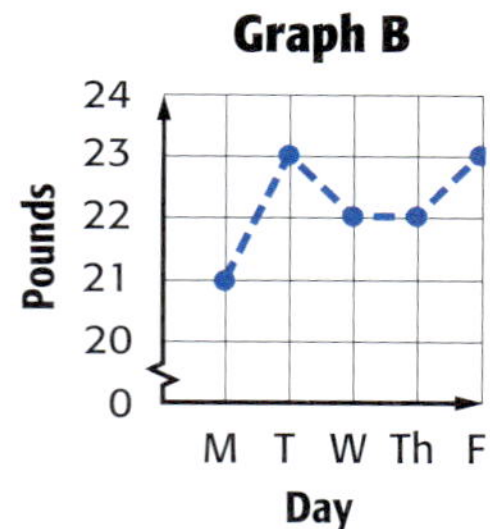

2. Both graphs show commissions made by Mr. Turner for a four-week pay period.

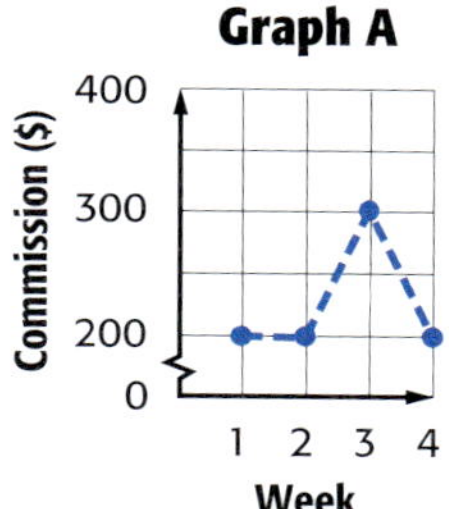

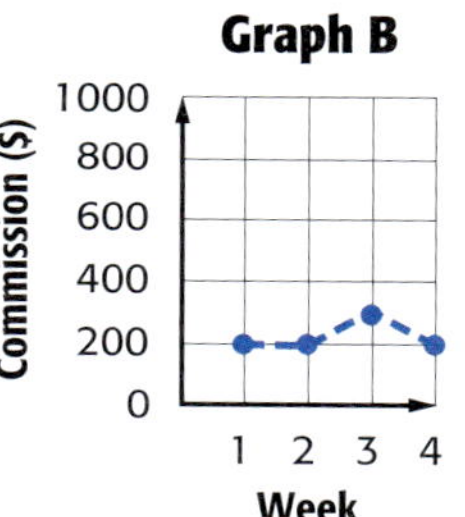

Lesson 9-1

Pages 460–464

Use the spinner at the right to find each probability. Write as a fraction in simplest form.

1. P(even number)
2. P(prime number)
3. P(factor of 12)
4. P(composite number)
5. P(greater than 10)
6. P(neither prime nor composite)

A package of balloons contains 5 green, 3 yellow, 4 red, and 8 pink balloons. Suppose you reach in the package and choose one balloon at random. Find the probability of each event. Write as a fraction in simplest form.

7. P(red balloon)
8. P(yellow balloon)
9. P(pink balloon)
10. P(orange balloon)
11. P(red or yellow balloon)
12. P(*not* green balloon)

Lesson 9-2

Pages 465–470

For each situation, find the sample space using a tree diagram.

1. rolling 2 number cubes
2. choosing an ice cream cone from waffle, plain, or sugar and a flavor of ice cream from chocolate, vanilla, or strawberry
3. making a sandwich from white, wheat, or rye bread, cheddar or Swiss cheese and ham, turkey, or roast beef
4. tossing a penny twice
5. choosing one math class from Algebra and Geometry and one foreign language class from French, Spanish, or Latin

Lesson 9-3

Pages 471–474

Use the Fundamental Counting Principle to find the total number of outcomes in each situation.

1. choosing a local phone number if the exchange is 398 and each of the four remaining digits is different
2. choosing a way to drive from Millville to Westwood if there are 5 roads that lead from Millville to Miamisburg, 3 roads that connect Miamisburg to Hathaway, and 4 highways that connect Hathaway to Westwood
3. tossing a quarter, rolling a number cube, and tossing a dime
4. spinning the spinners shown below

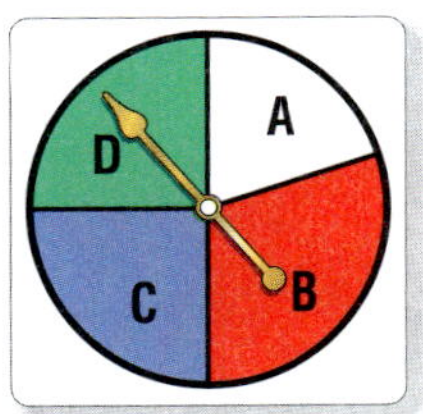

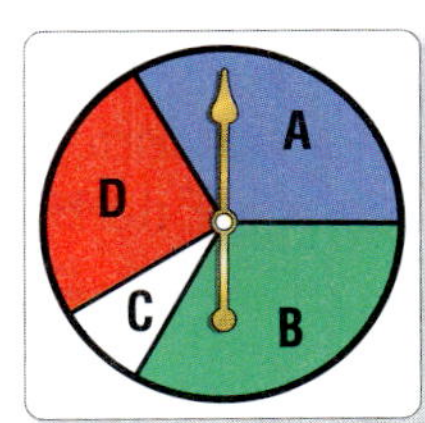

Lesson 9-4

Pages 475–478

1. **RACES** Eight runners are competing in a 100-meter sprint. In how many ways can the gold, silver, and bronze medals be awarded?
2. **LOCKERS** Five-digit locker combinations are assigned using the digits 1–9. In how many ways can the combinations be formed if no digit can be repeated?
3. **SCHEDULES** In how many ways can the classes math, language arts, science, and social studies be ordered on student schedules as the first four classes of their day?
4. **TOYS** At a teddy bear workshop, customers can select from black, brown, golden, white, blue, or pink for their bear's color. If a father randomly selects two bear colors, what is the probability that he will select a white bear for his son and a pink bear for his daughter? The father cannot pick the same color for both bears.
5. **WRITING** If you randomly select three of your last seven writing assignments to submit to an essay contest, what is the probability that you will select your first, fourth, and sixth essays in that order?

Lesson 9-5

Pages 480–483

1. **EXERCISE** How many ways can you choose to exercise three days of a week?
2. **BOOKS** In how many ways can six books be selected from a collection of 12?
3. **REPORTS** In how many ways can you select three report topics from a total of 8 topics?
4. **GROUPS** How many ways can four students be chosen from a class of 26?
5. **ROLLER COASTERS** In how many ways can you ride five out of nine roller coasters if you don't care in what order you ride them?

Lesson 9-6

Pages 484–485

Use the *act it out* strategy to solve each problem.

1. **STAIRS** Lynnette lives on a certain floor of her apartment building. She goes up two flights of stairs to put a load of laundry in a washing machine on that floor. Then she goes down five flights to borrow a book from a friend. Next, she goes up 8 flights to visit another friend who is ill. How many flights up or down does Lynnette now have to go to take her laundry out of the washing machine?
2. **LOGIC PUZZLE** Suppose you are on the west side of a river with a fox, a duck, and a bag of corn. You want to take all three to the other side of the river, but...
   - your boat is only large enough to carry you and either the fox, duck, or bag of corn.
   - you cannot leave the fox alone with the duck.
   - you cannot leave the duck alone with the corn.
   - you cannot leave the corn alone on the east side of the river because some wild birds will eat it.
   - the wild birds are afraid of the fox.
   - you cannot leave the fox, duck, and the corn alone.
   - you can bring something across the river more than once.

   If there is no other way to cross the river, how do you get everything to the other side?

Lesson 9-7

Pages 486–490

The frequency table shows the results of a fair number cube rolled 40 times.

1. Find the experimental probability of rolling a 4.
2. Find the theoretical probability of *not* rolling a 4.
3. Find the theoretical probability of rolling a 2.
4. Find the experimental probability of *not* rolling a 6.
5. Suppose the number cube was rolled 500 times. About how many times would it land on 5?

Face	Frequency
1	5
2	9
3	2
4	8
5	12
6	4

Lesson 9-8

Pages 492–497

1. **COINS** Two evenly balanced nickels are tossed. Find the probability that one head and one tail result.
2. **MONEY** A wallet contains four \$5 bills, two \$10 bills, and eight \$1 bills. A bill is randomly selected. Find *P*(\$5 or \$1).
3. **PROBABILITY** Two chips are selected from a box containing 6 blue chips, 4 red chips, and 3 green chips. The first chip selected is replaced before the second is drawn. Find *P*(red, green).
4. **PROBABILITY** A bag contains 7 blue, 4 orange, 8 red, and 5 purple marbles. Suppose one marble is chosen and not replaced. A second marble is then chosen. Find *P*(purple, red).

Lesson 10-1

Pages 510–513

Classify each angle as *acute, right, obtuse,* or *straight*.

1. 

2.

3. 

4. 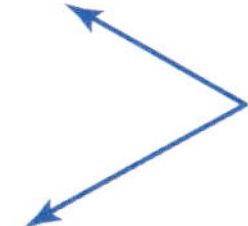

5. Identify a pair of vertical angles in the diagram at the right.

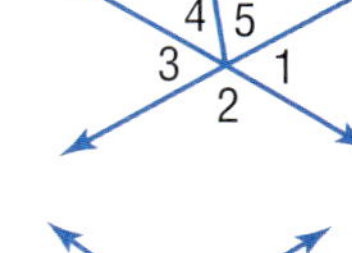

6. Identify a pair of adjacent angles in the diagram at the right.

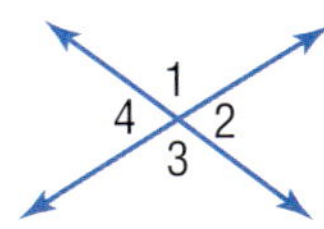

Lesson 10-2

Pages 514–517

Classify each pair of angles as *complementary, supplementary,* or *neither*.

1. 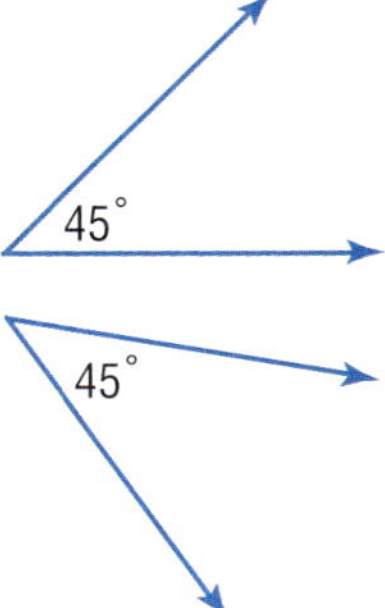

2. 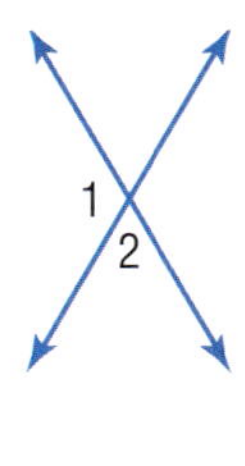

3. 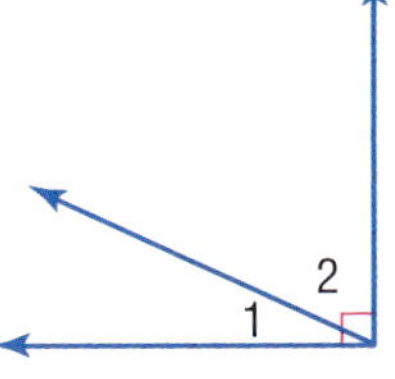

Find the value of x in each figure.

4. 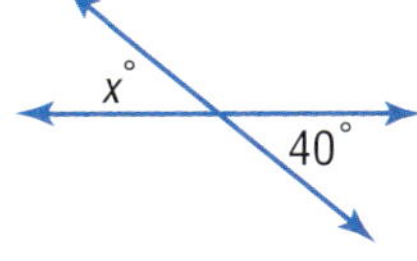

5. 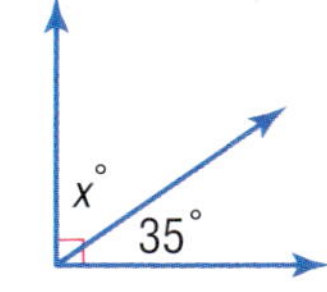

6. 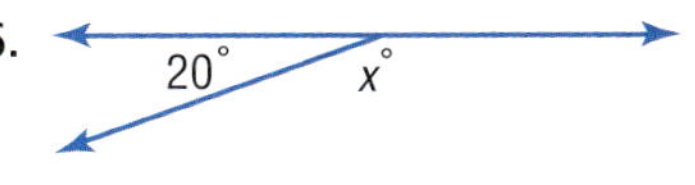

Lesson 10-3

Pages 518–523

Display each set of data in a circle graph.

1.

Car Sales	
Style	**Percent**
sedan	45%
SUV	22%
pickup truck	9%
sports car	13%
compact car	11%

2.

Favorite Flavor of Ice Cream	
Flavor	**Number**
vanilla	11
chocolate	15
strawberry	8
mint chip	5
cookie dough	3

Lesson 10-4

Pages 524–529

Find the value of x.

1. 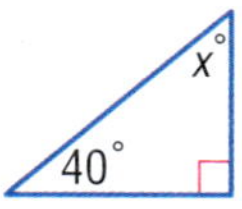

2. 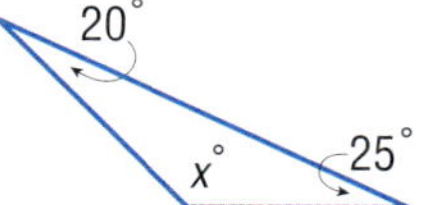

3. 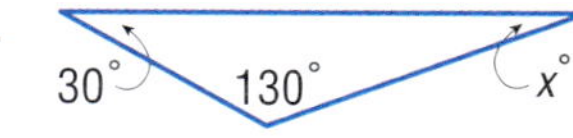

Classify each triangle by its angles and by its sides.

4. 

5. 

6. 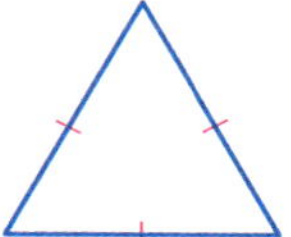

Lesson 10-5

Pages 530–531

Use the *logical reasoning* strategy to solve each problem.

1. **GEOMETRY** Draw several isosceles triangles and measure their angles. What do you notice about the measures of the angles of an isosceles triangle.

2. **BASKETBALL** Placido, Dexter, and Scott play guard, forward, and center on a team, but not necessarily in that order. Placido and the center drove Scott to practice on Saturday. Placido does not play guard. Who is the guard?

Lesson 10-6

Pages 533–539

Classify each quadrilateral using the name that *best* describes it.

1. 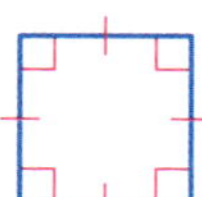

2. 

3. 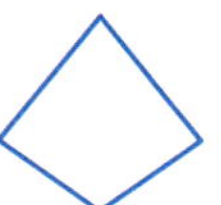

Find the missing angle measure in each quadrilateral.

4. 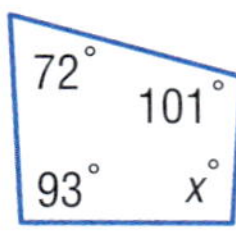

5. 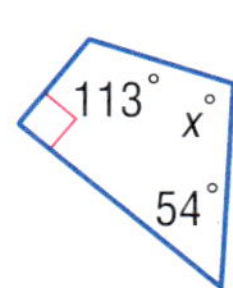

6. 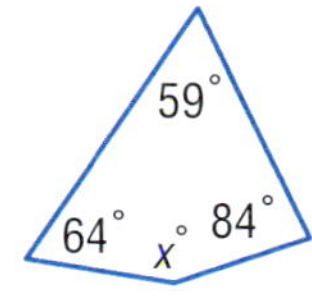

Lesson 10-7

Pages 540–545

Find the value of x in each pair of similar figures.

1. A B E F 8 cm 4 cm D 5 cm C H x G

2. 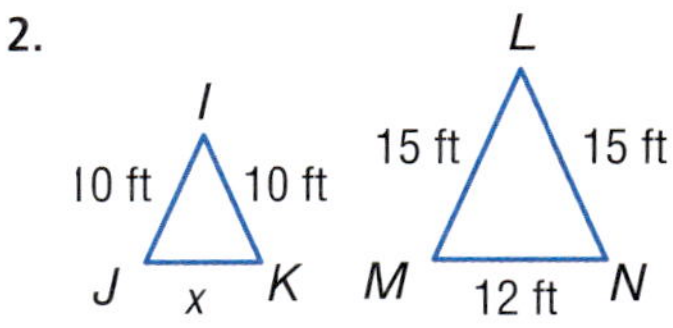

3. 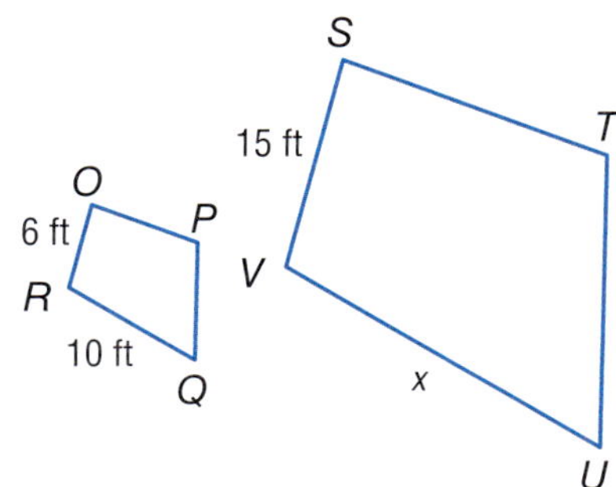

4. 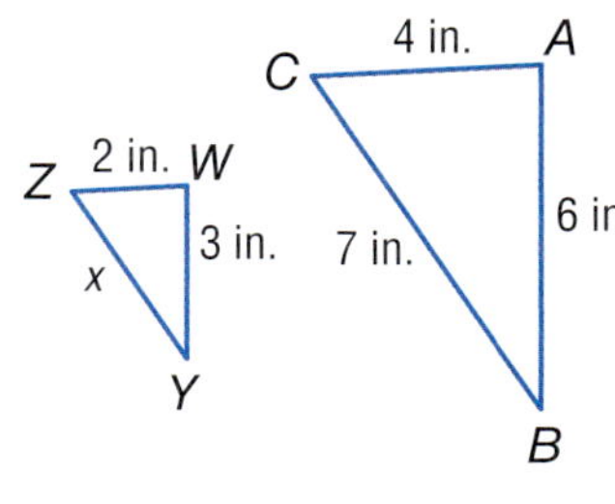

5. 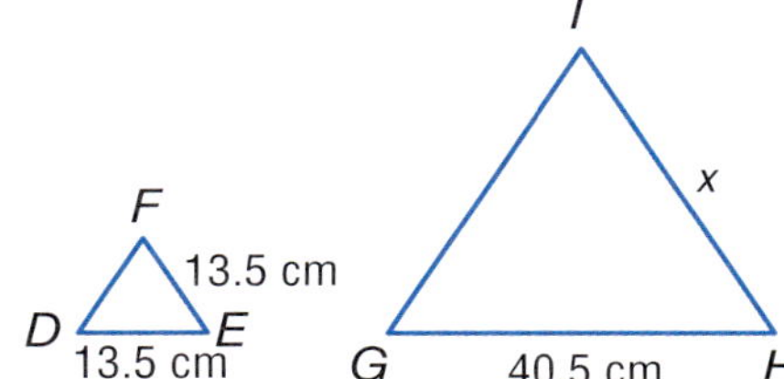

6. 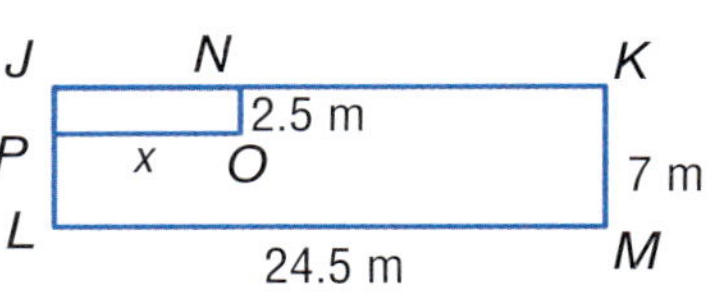

Lesson 10-8

Pages 546–551

Determine whether each figure is a polygon. If it is, classify the polygon and state whether it is regular. If it is *not* a polygon, explain why.

1. 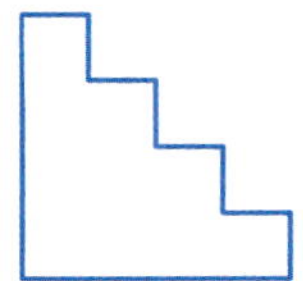

2. 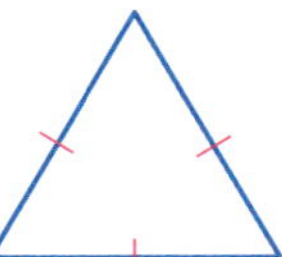

3. 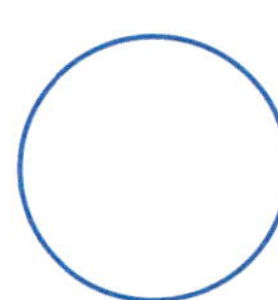

4. 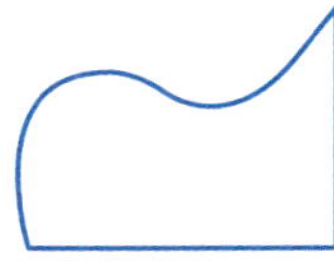

5. 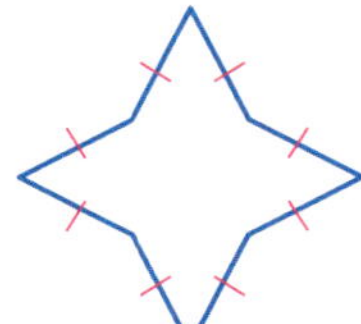

6. 

Find the measure of an angle in each polygon if polygon is regular. Round to the nearest tenth of a degree if necessary.

7. triangle
8. 30-gon
9. 18-gon
10. 14-gon
11. hexagon
12. nonagon
13. 27-gon
14. octagon

Lesson 10-9

Pages 553–557

1. Translate $\triangle ABC$ 2 units right and 1 unit down.

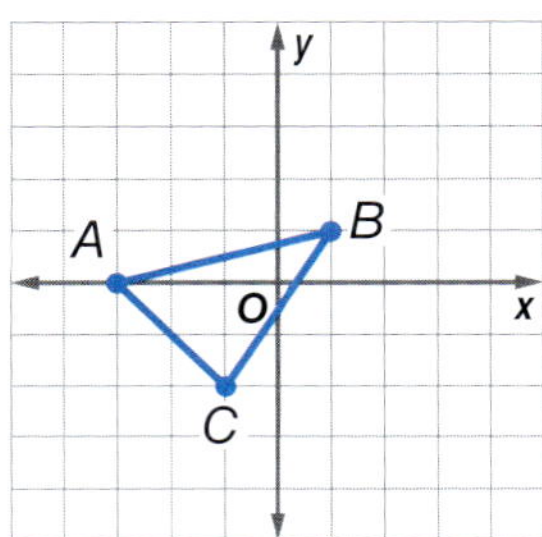

2. Translate quadrilateral *RSTU* 4 units left and 3 units down.

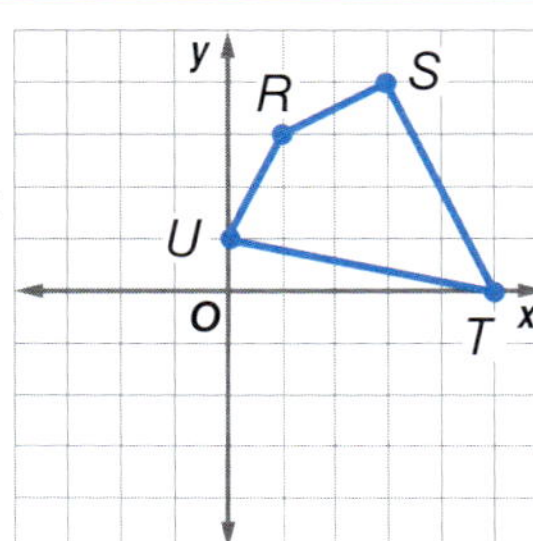

Triangle *TRI* has vertices $T(1, 1)$, $R(4, -2)$, and $I(-2, -1)$. Find the vertices of $T'R'I'$ after each translation. Then graph the figure and its translated image.

3. 2 units right, 1 unit down
4. 5 units left, 1 unit up
5. 3 units right
6. 2 units up

Lesson 10-10

Pages 558–562

Determine whether each figure has line symmetry. Write *yes* or *no*. If so, copy the figure and draw all lines of symmetry.

1. 

2. 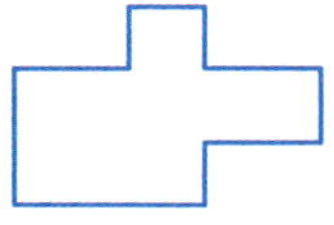

3. 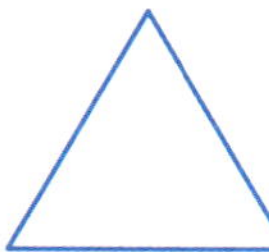

4. 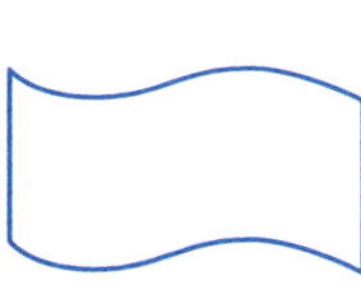

5. 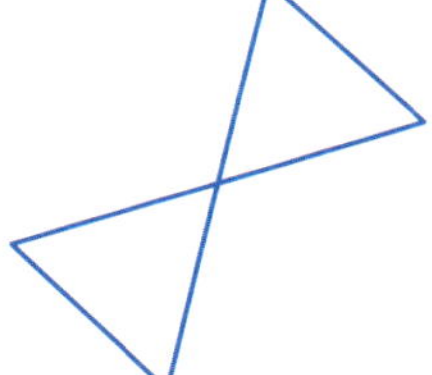

6. 

Graph each figure and its reflection over the x-axis. Then find the coordinates of the vertices of the reflected image.

7. quadrilateral *QUAD* with vertices $Q(-1, 4)$, $U(2, 2)$, $A(1, 1)$, and $D(-2, 2)$
8. triangle $\triangle ABC$ with vertices $A(0, -1)$, $B(4, -3)$, and $C(-4, -5)$

Graph each figure and its reflection over the y-axis. Then find the coordinates of the vertices of the reflected image.

9. parallelogram *PARL* with vertices $P(3, 5)$, $A(5, 4)$, $R(5, 1)$, and $L(3, 2)$
10. pentagon *PENTA* with vertices $P(-1, 3)$, $E(1, 1)$, $N(0, -2)$, $T(-2, -2)$, and $A(-3, 1)$

Lesson 11-1

Pages 570–574

Find the area of each parallelogram. Round to the nearest tenth if necessary.

1. 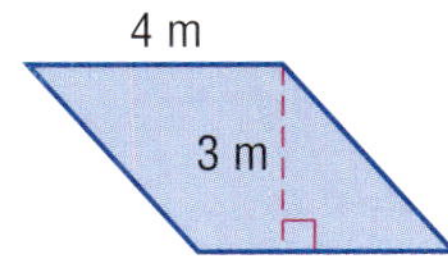

2. 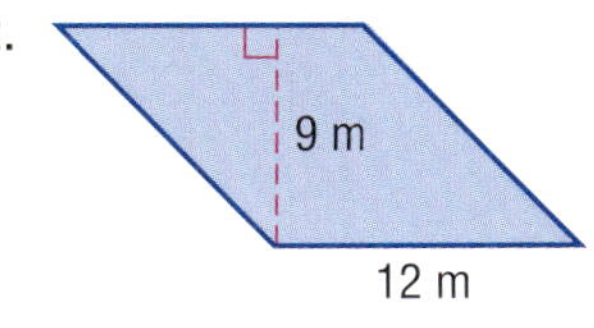

3. 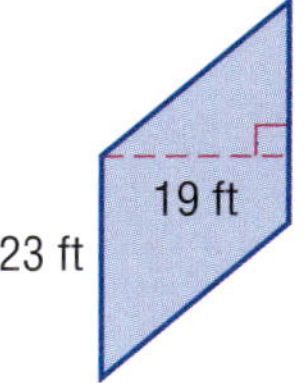

4. base = 19 m
   height = 6 m
5. base = 135 in.
   height = 15 in.
6. base = 8.2 cm
   height = 5.5 cm
7. base = 29.3 m
   height = 10.1 m

Lesson 11-2

Pages 576–580

Find the area of each figure. Round to the nearest tenth if necessary.

1. 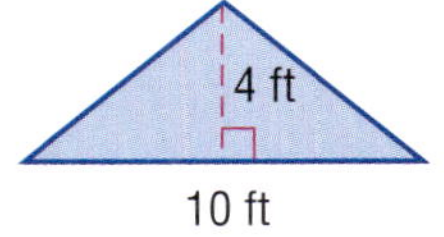

2. 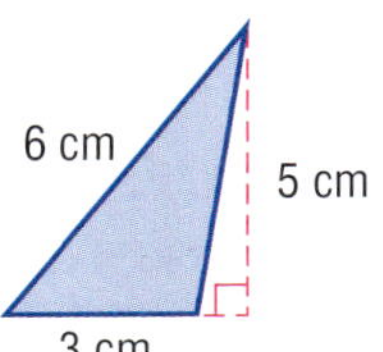

3. 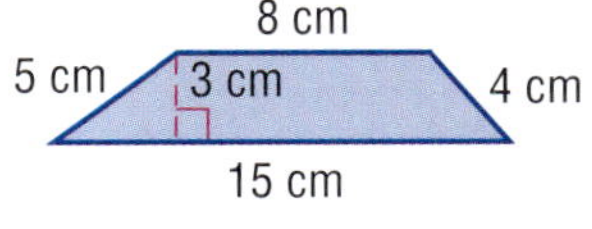

4. triangle: base = 5 in., height = 9 in.
5. trapezoid: bases = 3 cm and 8 cm, height = 12 cm
6. trapezoid: bases = 10 ft and 15 ft, height = 12 ft
7. triangle: base = 12 cm, height = 8 cm
8. trapezoid: bases = 82.6 cm and 72.2 cm, height = 44.5 cm
9. triangle: base = 500.5 ft, height = 254.5 ft

Lesson 11-3

Pages 582–586

Find the circumference of each circle. Use 3.14 or $\frac{22}{7}$ for π. Round to the nearest tenth if necessary.

1. 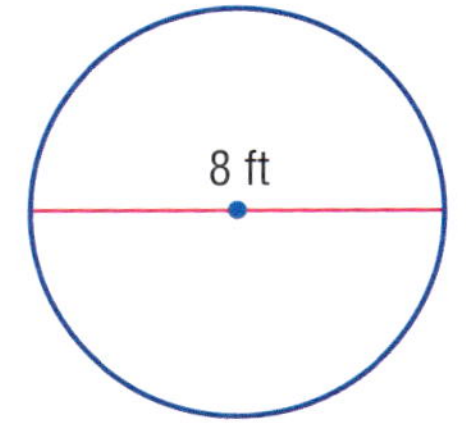

2. 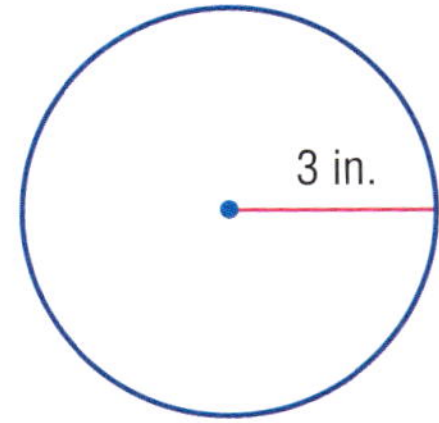

3. 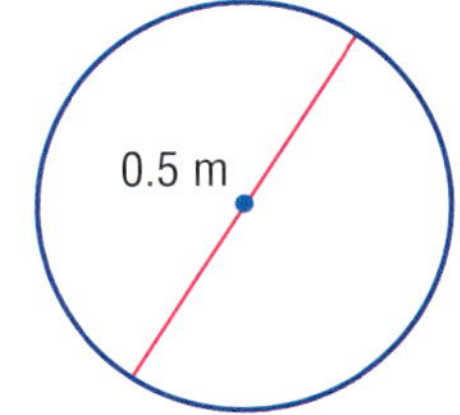

4. 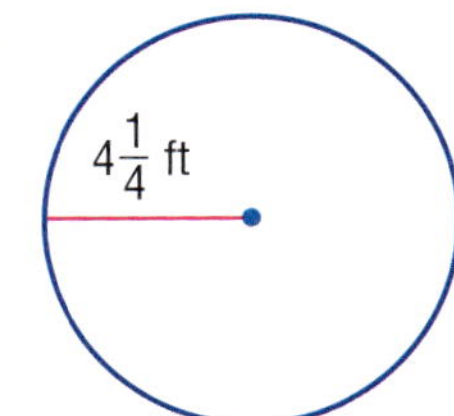

5. $r = 1$ m
6. $d = 2$ yd
7. $d = 5{,}280$ ft
8. $r = 0.5$ cm
9. $d = 6.4$ m
10. $r = 10.7$ km
11. $d = \frac{3}{16}$ in.
12. $r = 5\frac{1}{2}$ mi
13. $d = 42\frac{3}{4}$ ft

Lesson 11-4

Pages 587–591

Find the area of each circle. Round to the nearest tenth.

1. 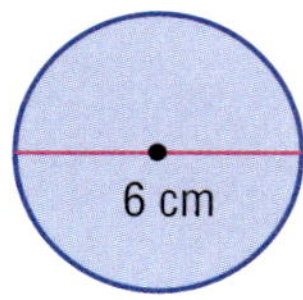

2. 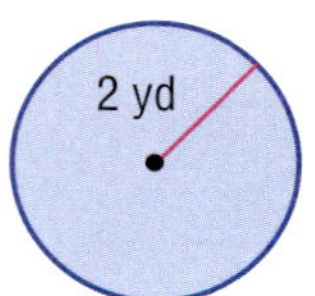

3. 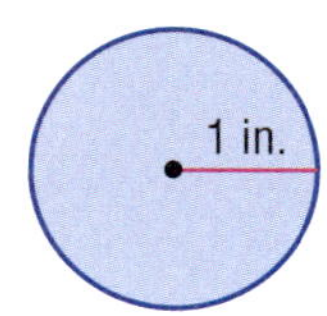

4. radius = 8 in.
5. diameter = 5 ft
6. radius = 24 cm
7. diameter = 2.3 m
8. diameter = 82 ft
9. radius = 68 cm
10. radius = 9.8 mi
11. diameter = 25.6 m
12. diameter = 6.75 in.
13. radius = $1\frac{1}{4}$ ft
14. diameter = $5\frac{2}{3}$ yd
15. diameter = $45\frac{1}{2}$ mi

Lesson 11-5

Pages 592–593

Use the *solve a simpler problem* strategy to solve each problem.

1. **EARNINGS** Cedric makes $51,876 each year. If he is paid once every two weeks and actually takes home about 67% of his wages after taxes, how much does he take home each paycheck? Round to the nearest cent if necessary.

2. **CARS** Jorge plans to decorate the rims on his tires by putting a strip of shiny metal around the outside edge on each rim. The diameter of each tire is 17 inches, and each rim is 2.75 inches from the outside edge of each tire. If he plans to cut the four individual pieces for each tire from the same strip of metal, how long of a strip should he buy? Round to the nearest tenth.

3. **SAVINGS** Erin's aunt invested a total of $1,500 into three different savings accounts. She invested $450 into a savings account with an annual interest rate of 3.25% and $600 into a savings account with an annual interest rate of 4.75%. The third savings account had an annual interest rate of 4.375%. After 3 years, how much money will Erin's aunt have in the three accounts altogether if she made no more additional deposits or withdrawals? Round to the nearest cent.

BIOLOGY For Exercises 4–6, use the following information.
About five quarts of blood are pumped through the average human heart in one minute.

4. At this rate, how many quarts of blood are pumped through the average human heart in one year? (Use 365 days = 1 year)

5. If the average heart beats 72 times per minute, how many quarts of blood are pumped with each beat? Round to the nearest tenth.

6. About how many total gallons of blood are pumped through the average human heart in one week?

7. **LAND** A rectangular plot of land measures 1,450 feet by 850 feet. A contractor wishes to section off a portion of this land to build an apartment complex. If the complex is 425 feet by 550 feet, how many square feet of land will not be sectioned off to build it?

Lesson 11-6

Pages 694–697

Find the area of each figure. Round to the nearest tenth if necessary.

1. 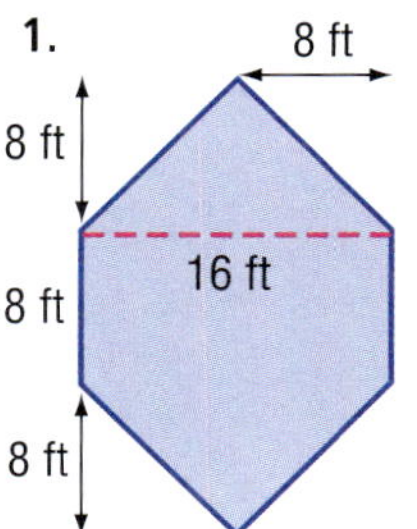

2. 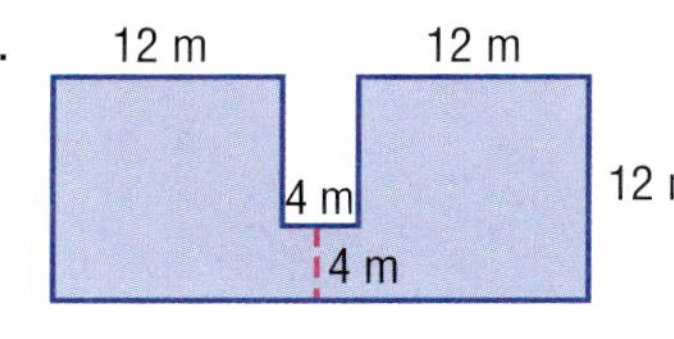

3. 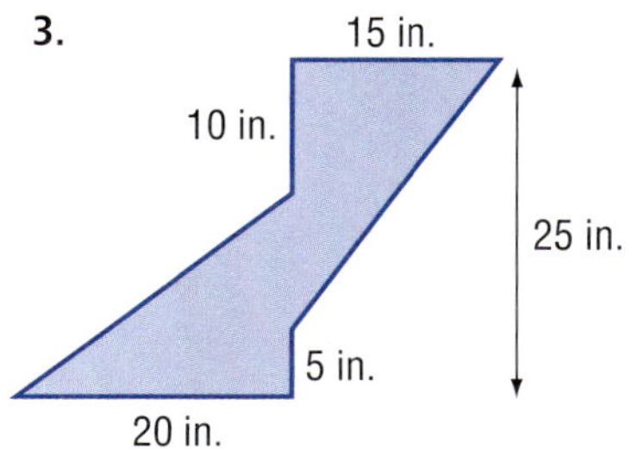

4. 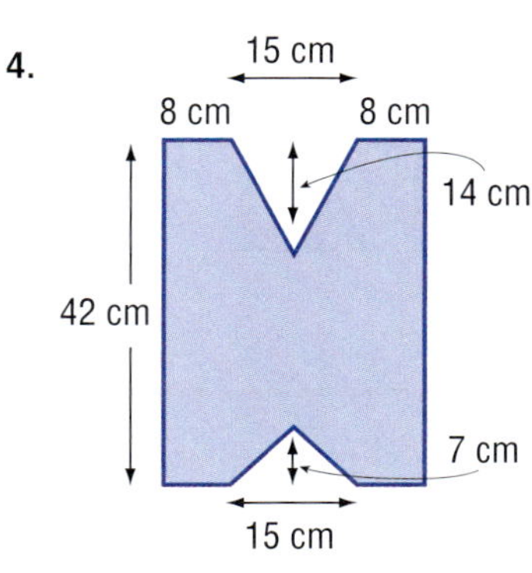

5. 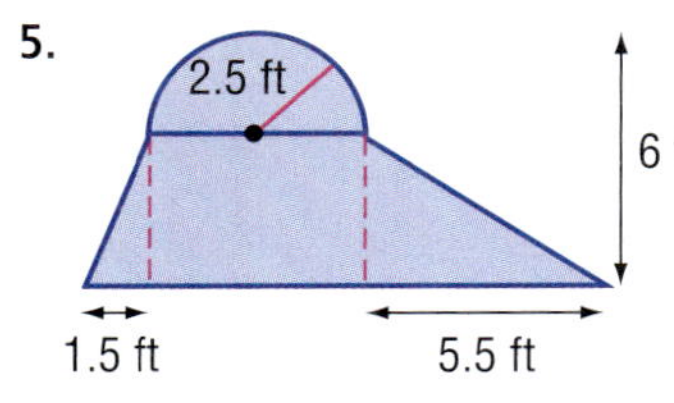

6. 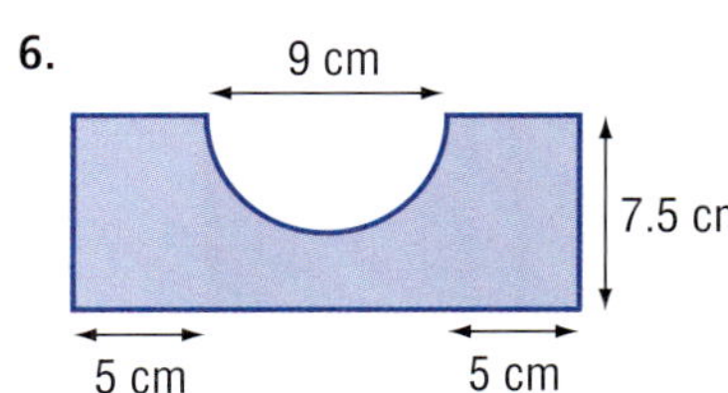

7. 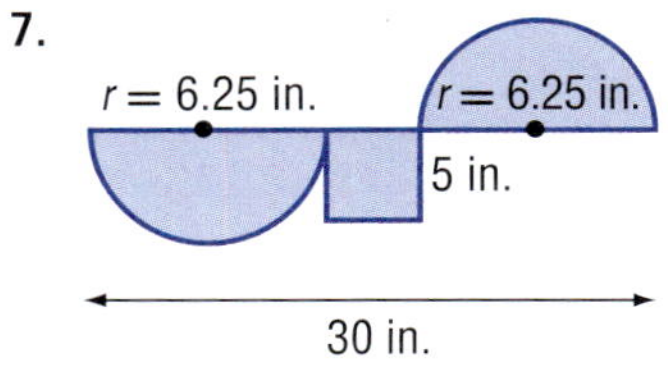

8. 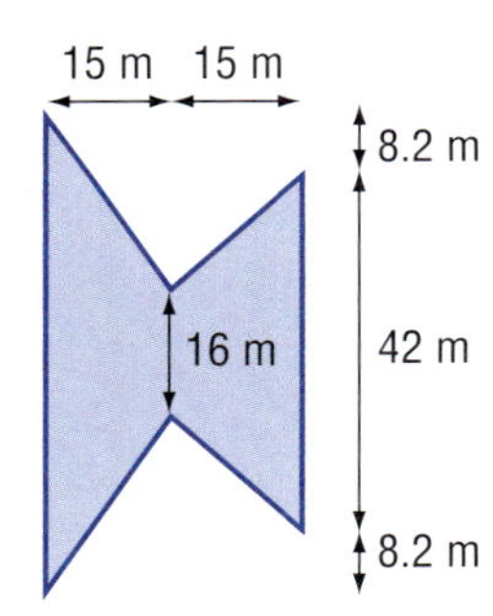

9. 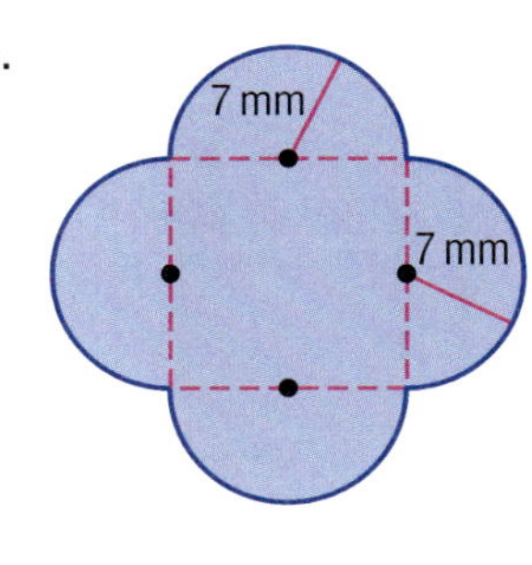

Lesson 11-7

Pages 601–604

For each figure, identify the shape of the base(s). Then classify the figure.

1. 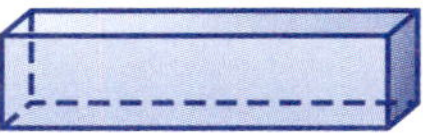

2. 

3. 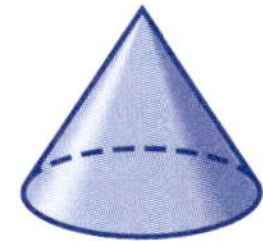

4. 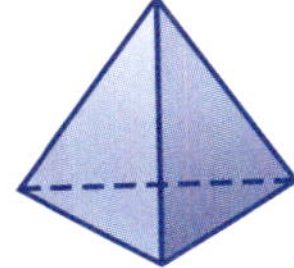

5. 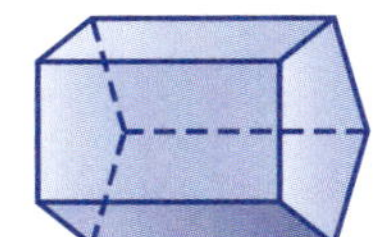

6. 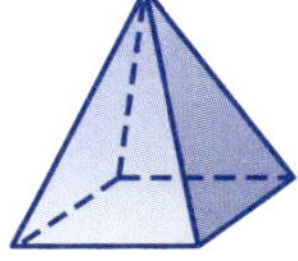

7. **SOUP** Classify the shape of a soup can as a three-dimensional figure.
8. **APPLIANCES** Classify the shape of a microwave oven as a three-dimensional figure.

Lesson 11-8

Pages 606–610

Draw a top, a side, and a front view of each solid.

1. 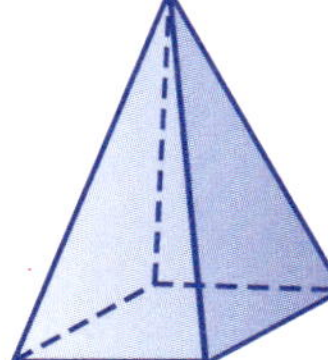

2. 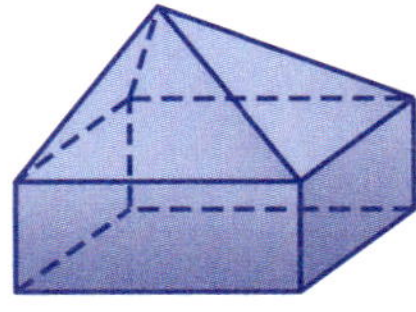

3. 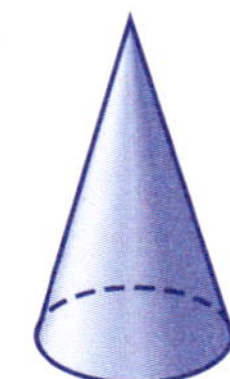

Draw each solid using the top, side, and front views shown. Use isometric dot paper.

4. top 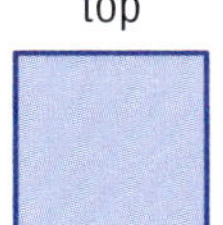 side 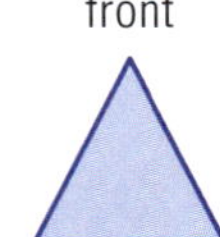 front

5. top 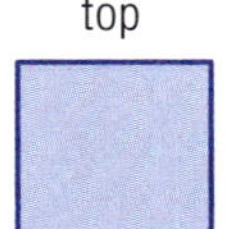 side 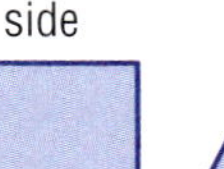 front

Lesson 11-9

Pages 611–616

Find the volume of each prism. Round to the nearest tenth if necessary.

1. 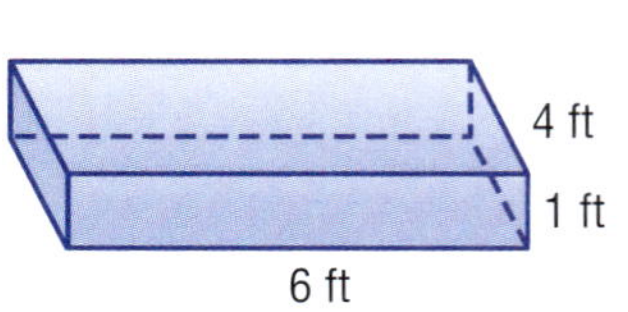

2. 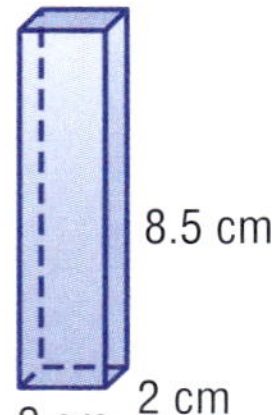

3. 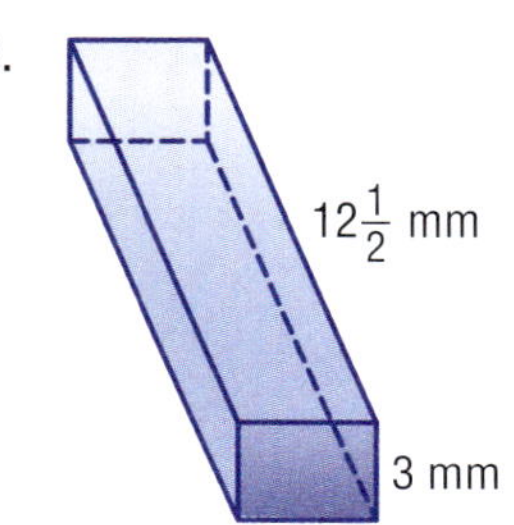

4. 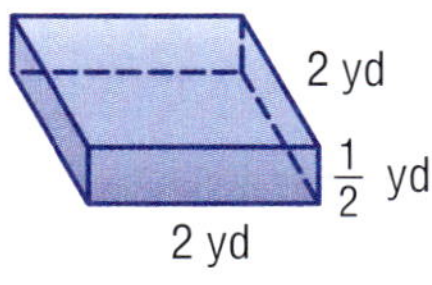

5. 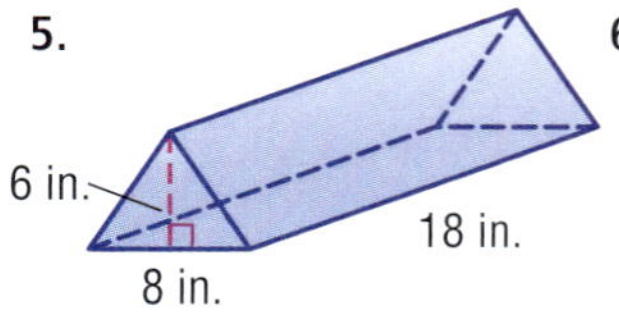

6. 11 m, 5 m, 35 m

7. 12 mm, 5 mm, 8 mm

8. 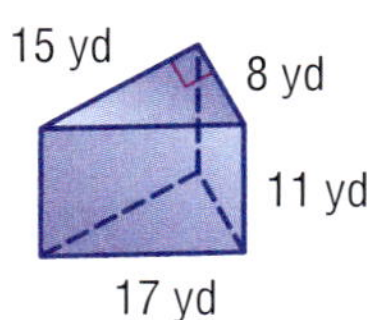

Find the volume of each rectangular prism. Round to the nearest tenth if necessary.

9. length = 3 ft
width = 10 ft
height = 2 ft

10. length = 18 cm
width = 23 cm
height = 15 cm

11. length = 25 mm
width = 32 mm
height = 10 mm

12. length = 1.5 in.
width = 3 in.
height = 6 in.

13. length = 4.5 cm
width = 6.75 cm
height = 2 cm

14. length = 16 mm
width = 0.7 mm
height = 12 mm

15. length = $3\frac{1}{2}$ ft
width = 10 ft
height = 6 ft

16. length = $5\frac{1}{2}$ in.
width = 12 in.
height = $3\frac{3}{8}$ in.

17. Find the volume of a rectangular prism with a length of 3 yards, a width of 5 feet, and a height of 12 feet.

18. Find the volume of a triangular prism whose base has an area of 416 square feet and whose height is 22 feet.

Lesson 11-10

Pages 617–621

Find the volume of each cylinder. Round to the nearest tenth. Use 3.14 for π.

1. 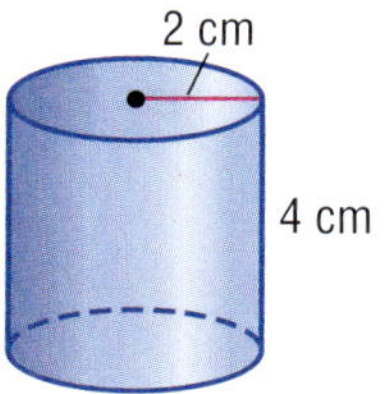

2. 

3. 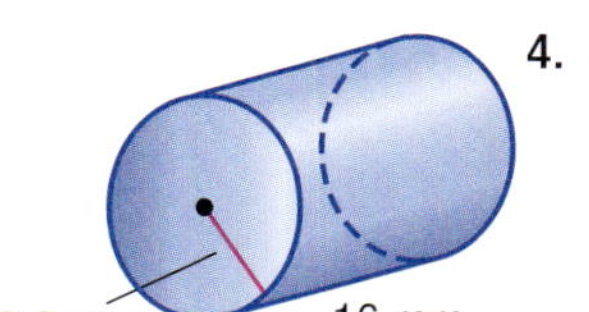

4. 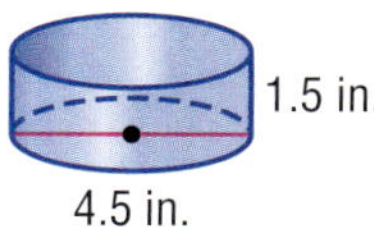

5. radius = 6 in.
height = 3 in.
6. radius = 8 ft
height = 10 ft
7. radius = 6 km
height = 12 km
8. radius = 8.5 cm
height = 3 cm
9. diameter = 16 yd
height = 4.5 yd
10. diameter = 3.5 mm
height = 2.5 mm
11. diameter = 12 m
height = 4.75 m
12. diameter = $\frac{5}{8}$ in.
height = 4 in.
13. diameter = 100 ft
height = 35 ft
14. radius = 40.5 m
height = 65.1 m
15. radius = 0.5 cm
height = 1.6 cm
16. diameter = $8\frac{3}{4}$ in.
height = $5\frac{1}{2}$ in.
17. Find the volume of a cylinder whose diameter is 6 inches and height is 2 feet. Round to the nearest tenth.
18. How tall is a cylinder that has a volume of 2,123 cubic meters and a radius of 13 meters? Round to the nearest tenth.
19. A cylinder has a volume of 310.2 cubic yards and a radius of 2.9 yards. What is the height of the cylinder? Round to the nearest tenth.
20. Find the height of a cylinder whose diameter is 25 centimeters and volume is 8,838 cubic centimeters. Round to the nearest tenth.

Lesson 12-1

Pages 634–637

Estimate each square root to the nearest whole number.

1. $\sqrt{27}$
2. $\sqrt{112}$
3. $\sqrt{249}$
4. $\sqrt{88}$
5. $\sqrt{1,500}$
6. $\sqrt{612}$
7. $\sqrt{340}$
8. $\sqrt{495}$
9. $\sqrt{264}$
10. $\sqrt{350}$
11. $\sqrt{834}$
12. $\sqrt{3,700}$
13. $\sqrt{298}$
14. $\sqrt{101}$
15. $\sqrt{800}$

Graph each square root on a number line.

16. $\sqrt{58}$
17. $\sqrt{750}$
18. $\sqrt{1,200}$
19. $\sqrt{1,000}$
20. $\sqrt{5,900}$
21. $\sqrt{999}$
22. $\sqrt{374}$
23. $\sqrt{512}$
24. $\sqrt{3,750}$
25. $\sqrt{255}$
26. $\sqrt{83}$
27. $\sqrt{845}$
28. $\sqrt{200}$
29. $\sqrt{500}$
30. $\sqrt{10,001}$
31. **ALGEBRA** Evaluate $\sqrt{a - b}$ to the nearest tenth if $a = 16$ and $b = 4$.
32. **ALGEBRA** Estimate the value of $\sqrt{x + y}$ to the nearest whole number if $x = 64$ and $y = 25$.

Lesson 12-2

Pages 638–643

Find the missing measure of each triangle. Round to the nearest tenth if necessary.

1. 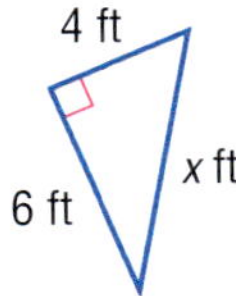

2. 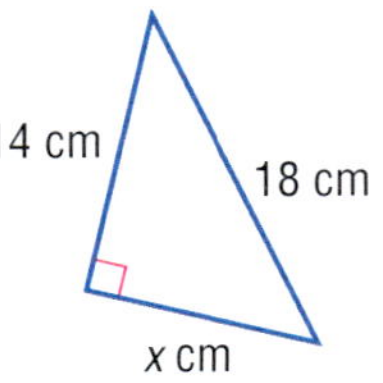

3. 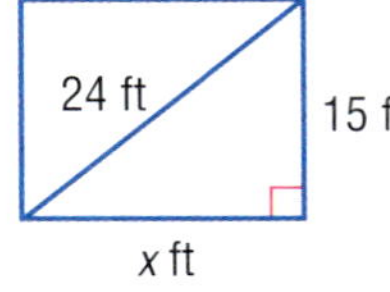

4. $a = 12$ cm, $b = 25$ cm
5. $a = 5$ yd, $c = 10$ yd
6. $b = 12$ mi, $c = 20$ mi
7. $a = 15$ yd, $b = 24$ yd
8. $a = 4$ m, $c = 12$ m
9. $a = 8$ mm, $b = 11$ mm
10. $a = 1$ mi, $c = 3$ mi
11. $a = 5$ yd, $b = 8$ yd
12. $b = 7$ in., $c = 19$ in.
13. $a = 50$ km, $c = 75$ km
14. $b = 82$ ft, $c = 100$ ft
15. $a = 100$ m, $b = 200$ m

Lesson 12-3

Pages 644–645

Use the *make a model* strategy to solve each problem.

1. **ARCHITECTURE** An architect is designing a large skyscraper for a local firm. The skyscraper is to be 1,200 feet tall, 500 feet long, and 400 feet wide. If his model has a scale of 80 feet = 1 inch, find the volume of the model.

2. **STACKING BOXES** Box A has twice the volume of Box B. Box B has a height of 10 centimeters and a length of 5 centimeters. Box A has a width of 20 centimeters, a length of 10 centimeters, and a width of 5 centimeters. What is the width of Box B?

3. **TRAVEL** On Monday, Mara drove 400 miles as part of her journey to see her sister. She drove 60% of this distance on Tuesday. If the distance she drove on Tuesday represents one third of her total journey, how many more miles does she still need to drive?

4. **PIZZA** On Monday, there was a whole pizza in the refrigerator. On Tuesday, Enrico ate $\frac{1}{3}$ of the pizza. On Wednesday, he ate $\frac{1}{3}$ of what was left. On Thursday, he ate $\frac{1}{2}$ of what remained. What fractional part of the pizza is left?

5. **GARDENS** Mr. Blackwell has a circular garden in his backyard. He wants to build a curved brick pathway around the entire garden. The garden has a radius of 18 feet. The distance from the center of the garden to the outside edge of the brick pathway will be 21.5 feet. Find the area of the brick pathway. Round to the nearest tenth.

Lesson 12-4

Pages 647–651

Extra Practice

Find the surface area of each rectangular prism. Round to the nearest tenth if necessary.

1. 4 in., 6 in., 7 in.

2. 15 cm, 4 cm, 4 cm

3. 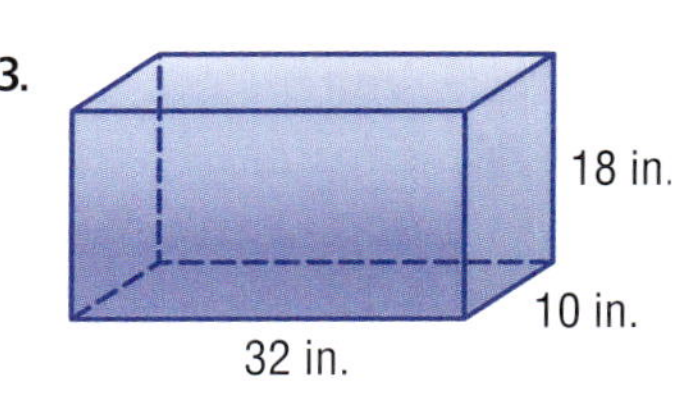

4. 27 yd, 16 yd, 10 yd

5. length = 10 m
width = 6 m
height = 7 m

6. length = 20 mm
width = 15 mm
height = 25 mm

7. length = 16 ft
width = 20 ft
height = 12 ft

8. length = 52 cm
width = 48 cm
height = 45 cm

9. length = 8 ft
width = 6.5 ft
height = 7 ft

10. length = 9.4 m
width = 2 m
height = 5.2 m

11. length = 20.4 cm
width = 15.5 cm
height = 8.8 cm

12. length = 8.5 mi
width = 3 mi
height = 5.8 mi

13. length = $7\frac{1}{4}$ ft
width = 5 ft
height = $6\frac{1}{2}$ ft

14. length = $15\frac{2}{3}$ yd
width = $7\frac{1}{3}$ yd
height = 9 yd

15. length = $4\frac{1}{2}$ in.
width = 10 in.
height = $8\frac{3}{4}$ in.

16. length = 12.2 mm
width = 7.4 mm
height = 7.4 mm

17. Find the surface area of an open-top box with a length of 18 yards, a width of 11 yards, and a height of 14 yards.

18. Find the surface area of a rectangular prism with a length of 1 yard, a width of 7 feet, and a height of 2 yards.

Lesson 12-5

Pages 654–657

Find the surface area of each cylinder. Round to the nearest tenth.

1. 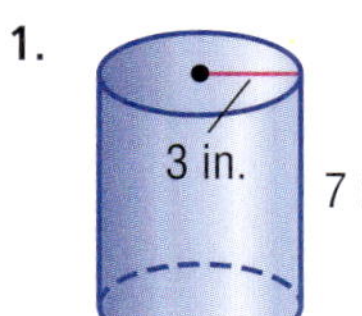

2. 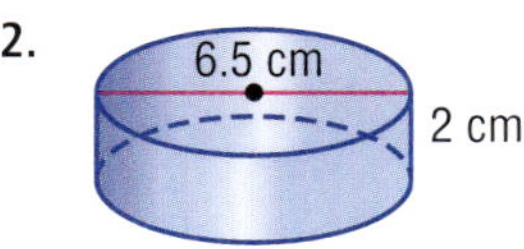

3. 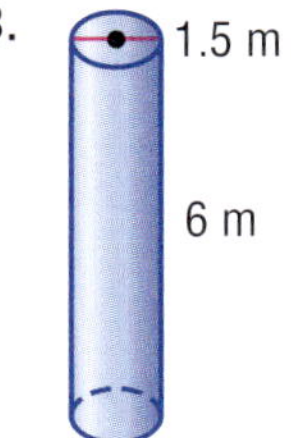

4. 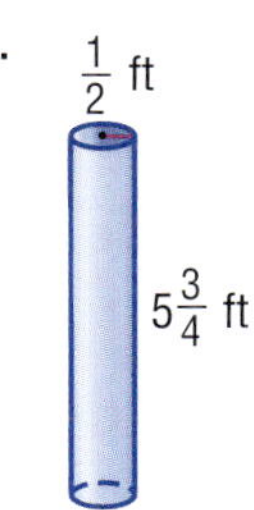

5. height = 6 cm
radius = 3.5 cm

6. height = 16.5 mm
diameter = 18 mm

7. height = 22 yd
radius = 10.5 yd

8. height = 6 ft
radius = 18.5 ft

9. height = 10.2 mi
diameter = 4 mi

10. height = 8.6 cm
diameter = 8.2 cm

11. height = 5.8 km
diameter = 3.6 km

12. height = 32.7 m
radius = 21.5 m

13. height = $2\frac{2}{3}$ yd
diameter = 6 yd

14. height = $12\frac{3}{4}$ ft
radius = $7\frac{1}{4}$ ft

15. height = $5\frac{1}{5}$ mi
radius = $18\frac{1}{3}$ mi

16. height = $5\frac{1}{2}$ in.
diameter = 3 in.

Mixed Problem Solving

Chapter 1 Introduction to Algebra and Functions

Pages 22–77

1. **HISTORY** In 1932, Amelia Earhart flew 2,026 miles in 14 hours 56 minutes. To the nearest mile, what was her speed in miles per minute? (Lesson 1-1)

2. **LIGHT** The speed of light is about 67^3 kilometers per second. How many kilometers per second is this? (Lesson 1-2)

3. **FARMING** Find the length of one side of a square field with an area of 180,625 square feet. (Lesson 1-3)

4. **SALES** A department store is having a back-to-school sale. The table shows the prices of three popular items.

Item	Price ($)
Jeans	37.99
Sweatshirt	19.88
Polo Shirt	22.50

Latonia wants to buy 2 pairs of jeans, 3 sweatshirts, and 1 polo shirt. Write and evaluate a numerical expression that represents the total cost of all three items. (Lesson 1-4)

5. **MONEY** Mateo has $2.58 in coins. If he has quarters, dimes, nickels, and pennies, how many of each coin does he have? Use the *guess and check* strategy. (Lesson 1-5)

6. **FITNESS** You can estimate how fast you walk in miles per hour by evaluating the expression $\frac{n}{30}$, where n is the number of steps you take in one minute. Find your speed in miles per hour if you take 96 steps in one minute. (Lesson 1-6)

7. **BASEBALL** Last year, Scott attended 13 Minnesota Twins baseball games. This year, he attended 24. Solve $13 + n = 24$ to find how many more games he attended this year than last. (Lesson 1-7)

8. **HOT AIR BALLOONS** Miyoki paid $140 for a four-hour hot air balloon ride over the Bridger Mountains. Solve $4h = 140$ to find the cost per hour of the ride. (Lesson 1-7)

ENTERTAINMENT For Exercises 9 and 10, use the following information.
The five members of the Wolff family went to an amusement park. They each purchased an all-day ride pass and a water park pass, as shown below. (Lesson 1-8)

Item	Price ($)
All-Day Ride Pass	14.95
Water Park Pass	6.50

9. Use the Distributive Property to write two different expressions that represent the total cost for the family.

10. Find the total cost of the passes.

11. **NUMBER THEORY** Numbers that can be represented by a square arrangement of dots are called *square numbers*. The first four square numbers are shown below. (Lesson 1-9)

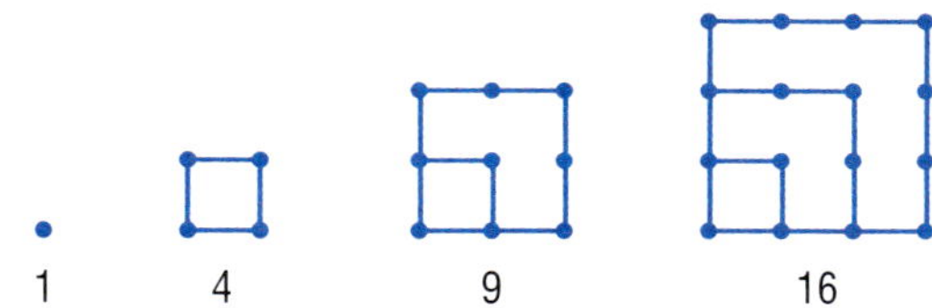

Write a sequence formed by the area of the first eight square numbers.

12. **TIME** Copy and complete the function table showing how many days y there are in various number of weeks x. Then identify the domain and range. (Lesson 1-10)

x	$7x$	y
1		
2		
3		
4		

1. **AIR CONDITIONING** Jacob turned on the air conditioning and the temperature in his apartment decreased 8 degrees. Write an integer to represent the change in temperature. (Lesson 2-1)

EARTH SCIENCE For Exercises 2 and 3, use the table below. It describes the deepest land depressions in the world in feet below sea level.

Depth (ft)			
220	436	511	282
383	505	235	230

Source: *The Top 10 Everything*

2. Write an integer to represent each depth. (Lesson 2-1)

3. Order the integers from greatest depth to least depth. (Lesson 2-2)

ENTERTAINMENT For Exercises 4–8, use the diagram below. It shows the locations of several rides at the Outlook Amusement Park. (Lesson 2-3)

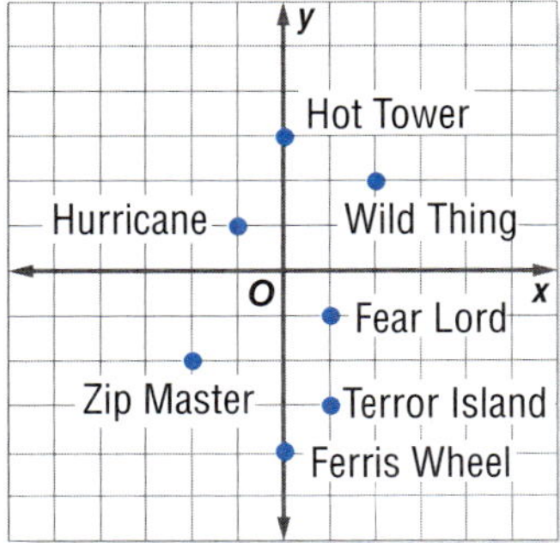

4. Which ride(s) is located in quadrant III?

5. Which ride(s) is located on the y-axis? Name the coordinates.

6. Which ride(s) has coordinates in which the x-coordinates and y-coordinates are equal?

7. In which quadrant is the Hurricane located?

8. A new ride is built with a location on the x-axis and 5 units left of the origin. Name the coordinates of this point.

9. **CAVERNS** Adriana is 52 feet underground touring the Lewis and Clark Caverns. She climbs a ladder up 15 feet. What is her new location? (Lesson 2-4)

10. **RECORDS** The lowest temperature recorded in Verkhoyansk, Russia, was about −90°F. The highest temperature was about 99°F. What is the difference between these temperatures? (Lesson 2-5)

11. **EARTH SCIENCE** The highest and lowest points in California are shown in the table. What is the difference in elevations? (Lesson 2-5)

Location	Elevation
Mount Whitney	14,494 ft above sea level
Death Valley	282 ft below sea level

Source: *The World Almanac of the U.S.A.*

12. **RIDES** A glider ride over the Crazy Mountains has a maximum altitude of 12,000 feet. It is descending at a rate of about 300 feet per minute. At what altitude will the glider be 20 minutes later? (Lesson 2-6)

13. **SPORTS** Every 12 times at bat, Simon hits the ball 3 times. About how many times will he hit the ball after 20 times at bat? 40? 84? Use the *look for a pattern* strategy. (Lesson 2-7)

Times at Bat	Number of Hits
12	3
20	■
40	■
84	■

14. **TEMPERATURE** A temperature of −89°C was recorded in Antarctica. Use the expression $\frac{9C}{5} + 32$, where C is the temperature in degrees Celsius, to find the temperature in degrees Fahrenheit. (Lesson 2-8)

Mixed Problem Solving

Mixed Problem Solving

1. **TOURISM** The Statue of Liberty in New York, New York, and the Eiffel Tower in Paris, France, were designed by the same person. The Statue of Liberty is 152 feet tall. It is 732 feet shorter than the Eiffel Tower, x. Write an equation that models this situation. (Lesson 3-1)

ELECTIONS For Exercises 2 and 3, use the table below and the following information. New York has one more electoral vote than Texas. Pennsylvania has 9 fewer electoral votes than Texas. (Lesson 3-2)

Number of Electoral Votes 2000	
California	54
New York	33
Texas	■
Florida	25
Pennsylvania	23

2. Write two different equations to find the number of electoral votes in Texas, n.
3. Find the number of electoral votes

4. **ROLLER COASTERS** The track length of a popular roller coaster is 5,106 feet. The roller coaster has an average speed of about 2,000 feet per minute. At that speed, how long will it take to travel its length of 5,106 feet? Use the formula $d = rt$. (Lesson 3-3)

5. **NUMBERS** A number is halved. Then three is subtracted from the quotient, and 5 is multiplied by the difference. Finally, 1 is added to the product. If the ending number is 26, what was the beginning number? Use the *work backward* strategy. (Lesson 3-4)

6. **BUSINESS** Carla's Catering charges a $25 fee to serve 15 or fewer people. In addition to that fee, they charge $10 per appetizer. You are having a party for 12 people and can spend a total of $85. How many appetizers can you order from Carla's Catering? (Lesson 3-5)

CHESS For Exercises 7–10, use the chess board below. (Lesson 3-6)

7. What is the perimeter of the chess board?
8. What is the area of the chess board?
9. What is the area of each small square?
10. A travel chess board has half the length and width of the board shown. What is the perimeter and area?

11. **FENCING** Mr. Hernandez will build a fence to enclose a rectangular yard for his horse. If the area of the yard to be enclosed is 1,944 square feet, and the length of the yard is 54 feet, how much fencing is needed? (Lesson 3-6)

12. **GEOMETRY** The formula for the perimeter of a square is $P = 4s$, where P is the perimeter and s is the length of a side. Graph the equation. (Lesson 3-7)

AGES For Exercises 13–16, use the table below. It shows how Jared's age and his sister Emily's age are related. (Lesson 3-7)

Jared's age (yr)	1	2	3	4	5
Emily's age (yr)	7	8	9	10	11

13. Write a verbal expression to describe how the ages are related.
14. Write an equation for the verbal expression. Let x represent Jared's age and y represent Emily's age.
15. Predict how old Emily will be when Jared is 10 years old.
16. Graph the equation.

LAND For Exercises 1–3, use the information below.
A section of land is one mile long and one mile wide. (Lesson 4-1)

1. Write the prime factorization of 5,280.
2. Find the area of the section of land in square feet. (*Hint*: 1 mile = 5,280 feet)
3. Write the prime factorization of the area that you found in Exercise 2.

DECORATIONS For Exercises 4 and 5, use the information below.
Benito is cutting streamers from crepe paper for a party. He has a red roll of crepe paper 144 inches long, a white roll 192 inches long, and a blue roll 360 inches long. (Lesson 4-2)

4. If he wants to have all colors of streamers the same length, what is the longest length that he can cut?
5. If he cuts the longest possible length, how many streamers can he cut?
6. **PRIZES** By reaching into a bag that has the letters A, B, and C, George will select three winners in order. How many possible combinations are there of the people who could win? Use the *make an organized list* strategy. (Lesson 4-3)

OLYMPICS For Exercises 7 and 8, refer to the table below. It shows the medals won by the top three countries in the 2000 Summer Olympics.

Country	Medals		
	Gold	Silver	Bronze
United States	40	24	33
Russia	32	28	28
China	28	16	15

Source: *The World Almanac*

7. Write the number of gold medals that Russia won as a fraction of the total number that Russia won in simplest form. (Lesson 4-4)
8. Write the fraction that you wrote in Exercise 7 as a decimal. (Lesson 4-5)
9. **SPORTS** At Belgrade Intermediate School, 75 out of every 100 students participate in sports. What percent of students do *not* participate in sports? (Lesson 4-6)

ADVERTISING For Exercises 10–13, use the table below. It shows the results of a survey in which teens were asked which types of advertising they pay attention to.

Type of Advertising	Percent of Teens
Television	80%
Magazine	62%
Product in a Movie	48%
Ad in an E-Mail	24%

Source: *E-Poll*

Write each percent as a fraction in simplest form. (Lesson 4-6)

10. television
11. magazine
12. product in a movie
13. ad in an e-mail

GEOMETRY For Exercises 14–16, refer to the grid at the right. (Lesson 4-7)

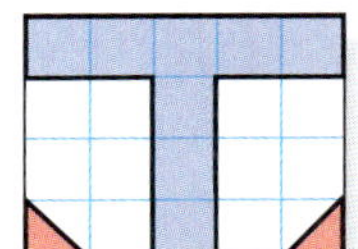

14. Write a decimal and a percent to represent the "T" shaded area.
15. Write a decimal and a percent to represent the area shaded pink.
16. What percent of the grid is *not* shaded?
17. **FLOWERS** Roses can be ordered in bunches of 6 and carnations in bunches of 15. If Ingrid wants to have the same number of roses as carnations for parent night, what is the least number of each flower that she must order? (Lesson 4-8)
18. **WATER** The table at the right shows the fraction of each state that is water. Order the states from least to greatest fraction of water. (Lesson 4-9)

What Part is Water?	
State	Fraction
Alaska	$\frac{3}{41}$
Michigan	$\frac{40}{97}$
Wisconsin	$\frac{1}{6}$

Source: *The World Almanac of the U.S.A*

Mixed Problem Solving

Mixed Problem Solving

1. **MEALS** A box of instant potatoes contains 20 cups of flakes. A family-sized bowl of potatoes uses $3\frac{2}{3}$ cups of the flakes. Estimate how many family-sized bowls can be made from one box. (Lesson 5-1)

2. **BAKING** A recipe calls for $2\frac{1}{3}$ cups of flour. Theo wants to make six batches of this recipe. About how much flour should he have available to use? (Lesson 5-1)

3. **CRAFTS** Kyle bought $\frac{5}{6}$ yard of fabric to make a craft item. He used $\frac{3}{4}$ yard in making the item. How much fabric was left over? (Lesson 5-2)

RAINFALL For Exercises 4 and 5, use the table. It shows the average annual precipitation for three of the driest locations on Earth. (Lesson 5-2)

Location	Precipitation (in.)
Arica, Chile	$\frac{3}{100}$
Iquique, Chile	$\frac{1}{5}$
Callao, Peru	$\frac{12}{25}$

Source: *The Top 10 Everything*

4. How much more rain does Iquique get per year than Arica?

5. How much more annual rain does Callao get than Iquique?

6. **INTERIOR DESIGN** A living room wall is $16\frac{1}{4}$ feet long. A window runs from the floor to the ceiling and has a length along the floor of $6\frac{3}{8}$ feet. How long is the wall without the window? (Lesson 5-3)

7. **HEALTH** The human body is about $\frac{7}{10}$ water. About how much would a person weigh if they had 70 pounds of water weight? Use the *eliminate possibilities* strategy. (Lesson 5-4)

   A 200 pounds
   B 100 pounds
   C 150 pounds
   D 70 pounds

8. **FOOD** The table below shows the carry-out menu for a Benito's Restaurant.

Take-out	Price ($)
Main Dish	5.00
Side Dishes	1.00
Dessert	2.00

A family of four spent $24.00 dollars for a take-home meal. What combination is possible for their meal? Use the *eliminate possibilities* strategy. (Lesson 5-4)

   F 3 main dishes and 2 side dishes
   G 4 main dishes and 3 side dishes
   H 3 main dishes, 3 side dishes, and 3 desserts
   J 4 main dishes and 4 desserts

9. **STARS** The star Sirius is about $8\frac{7}{10}$ light years from Earth. Alpha Centauri is half this distance from Earth. How far is Alpha Centauri from Earth? (Lesson 5-5)

10. **LIFE SCIENCE** Use the table below. It shows the average growth per month of hair and fingernails. Solve $3 = \frac{1}{2}t$ to find how long it takes hair to grow 3 inches. (Lesson 5-6)

Average Monthly Growth	
Hair	$\frac{1}{2}$ in.
Fingernails	$\frac{2}{25}$ in.

11. **SEWING** Jocelyn has nine yards of fabric to make table napkins for a senior citizens' center. She needs $\frac{3}{8}$ yard for each napkin. Use $\frac{3}{8}c = 9$ to find the number of napkins that she can make with this amount of fabric. (Lesson 5-6)

12. **WHALES** During the first year, a baby whale gains about $27\frac{3}{5}$ tons. What is the average weight gain per month? (Lesson 5-7)

1. **SCHOOLS** In a recent year, Oregon had 924 public elementary schools and 264 public high schools. Write a ratio in simplest form comparing the number of public high schools to elementary schools. (Lesson 6-1)

2. **MONTHS** Write a ratio in simplest form comparing the number of months that begin with the letter J to the total number of months in a year. (Lesson 6-1)

3. **EXERCISE** A person jumps rope 14 times in 10 seconds. What is the unit rate in jumps per second? (Lesson 6-2)

4. **FOOD** A 16-ounce box of cereal costs \$3.95. Find the unit price to the nearest cent. (Lesson 6-2)

5. **MARKERS** The table below shows the number of markers per box. Graph the data. Then find the slope of the line. Explain what the slope represents. (Lesson 6-3)

Markers	8	16	24	32
Boxes	1	2	3	4

6. **TEMPERATURE** At 2:00, the temperature is 78°F. At 3:00, the temperature is 81°F. What is the rate of change? (Lesson 6-3)

7. **LIFE SCIENCE** An adult has about 5 quarts of blood. If a person donates 1 pint of blood, how many pints are left? (Lesson 6-4)

8. **COFFEE** In Switzerland, the average amount of coffee consumed per year is 1,089 cups per person. How many pints is this? (Lesson 6-4)

9. **BUILDINGS** A skyscraper is 0.484 kilometers tall. What is the height of the skyscraper in meters? (Lesson 6-5)

10. **WATER** A bottle contains 1,065 milliliters of water. About how many cups of water does the bottle hold? (Lesson 6-5)

11. **PHOTOGRAPHS** Mandy is enlarging a photograph that is 3 inches wide and 4.5 inches long. If she wants the width of the enlargement to be 10 inches, what will be the length? (Lesson 6-6)

12. **TILES** A kitchen is 10 feet long and 8 feet wide. If kitchen floor tiles are $2\frac{1}{2}$ inches by 3 inches, how many tiles are needed for the kitchen? Use the *draw a diagram* strategy. (Lesson 6-7)

13. **MAPS** Washington, D.C., and Baltimore, Maryland, are $2\frac{7}{8}$ inches apart on a map. If the scale is $\frac{1}{2}$ inch : 6 miles, what is the actual distance between the cities? (Lesson 6-8)

14. **MODELS** Ian is making a miniature bed for his daughter's doll house. The actual bed is $6\frac{3}{4}$ feet long. If he uses the scale $\frac{1}{2}$ inch $= 1\frac{1}{2}$ feet, what will be the length of the miniature bed? (Lesson 6-8)

15. **POPULATION** According to the U.S. Census Bureau, 6.6% of all people living in Florida are 10–14 years old. What fraction is this? Write in simplest form. (Lesson 6-9)

COINS For Exercises 16 and 17, use the table below. It shows the fraction of a quarter that is made up of the metals nickel and copper. Write each fraction as a percent. Round to the nearest hundredth if necessary. (Lesson 6-9)

Metal	Fraction of Quarter
Nickel	$\frac{1}{12}$
Copper	$\frac{11}{12}$

16. nickel

17. copper

Mixed Problem Solving

Chapter 7 Applying Percents

Pages 340–391

1. **SEEDS** A packet of beans guarantees that 95% of its 200 seeds will germinate. How many seeds are expected to germinate? (Lesson 7-1)

2. **SKIS** Toshiro spent $520 on new twin-tip skis. This was 40% of the money he earned at his summer job. How much did he earn at his summer job? (Lesson 7-2)

3. **GEOGRAPHY** In Washington, about 5.7% of the total area is water. If the total area of Washington is 70,637 square miles, estimate the number of square miles of water by using 10%. (Lesson 7-3)

4. **GOVERNMENT** Of the 435 members in the U.S. House of Representatives, 53 are from California and 13 are from North Carolina. To the nearest whole percent, what percent of the representatives are from California? from North Carolina? (Lesson 7-4)

FOOD For Exercises 5 and 6, use the graph below. It shows the results of a survey in which 1,200 people were asked how they determine how long food has been in their freezer. (Lesson 7-4)

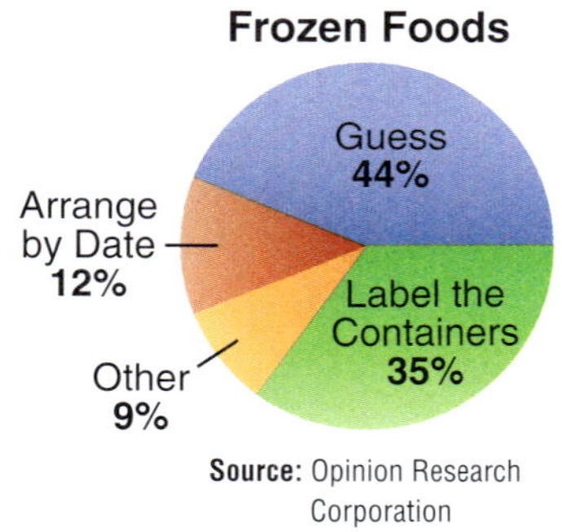

5. How many of the 1,200 surveyed guess to determine how long food has been in their freezer?

6. How many of the 1,200 surveyed label their freezer containers?

7. **DVDs** A store has 1,504 DVDs in stock. The store sold 19.8% of the DVDs last month. About how many DVDs did they sell last month? Use the *reasonable answers* strategy. (Lesson 7-5)

SPORTS For Exercises 8 and 9, use the table below. It shows the number of participants ages 7 to 17 in the sports listed. (Lesson 7-6)

Sport	Number (millions)	
	1990	2000
In-Line Skating	3.6	21.8
Snowboarding	1.5	4.3
Roller Hockey	1.5	2.2
Golf	23.0	26.4

Source: *National Sporting Goods Association*

8. What is the percent of change in in-line skaters 7 to 17 years old from 1990 to 2000? Round to the nearest percent and state whether the percent of change is an *increase* or *decrease*.

9. Find the percent of change from 1990 to 2000 in the number of children and teens who played roller hockey. Round to the nearest percent.

COMPUTERS For Exercises 10 and 11, use the following information.
The Wares want to buy a new computer with a regular price of $1,049. (Lesson 7-7)

10. If the store is offering a 20% discount, what will be the sale price of the computer?

11. If the sales tax on the computer is 5.25%, what will be the total cost with the discount?

BANKING For Exercises 12–15, complete the table below. The interest earned is simple interest. (Lesson 7-8)

	Principal	Rate	Time (yr)	Interest Earned
12.	$1,525.00	5%	$2\frac{1}{2}$	■
13.	$2,250.00	4%	■	$337.50
14.	■	3.5%	4	$498.40
15.	$5,080.00	■	3	$952.50

NUTRITION **For Exercises 1–3, use the data below, that gives the grams of carbohydrates in fifteen different energy bars.**
24, 16, 16, 16, 2, 20, 26, 14, 20, 20, 16, 16, 16, 15, 20

1. Make a line plot of the data. (Lesson 8-1)
2. What is the range of the data? (Lesson 8-1)
3. Identify any clusters, gaps, or outliers and explain what they represent. (Lesson 8-1)

BASKETBALL **For Exercises 4–5, refer to the table below. It shows the number of games played by Michael Jordan each year from 1986–1987 to 2001–2002.**

Number of Games Played							
82	82	81	82	82	80	78	0
17	82	82	82	0	0	0	60

4. Find the mean, median, and mode of the data. (Lesson 8-2)
5. Make a stem-and-leaf plot of the data. (Lesson 8-3)
6. **TOURISTS** The table shows the countries from which the most tourists in the United States came. Make a bar graph of the data. (Lesson 8-4)

Country	Visitors (millions)
Canada	14.6
Mexico	10.3
Japan	5.0
United Kingdom	4.7

7. **LUNCHES** Use the bar graph to determine on what day about twice as many lunches were sold as on Wednesday. (Lesson 8-5)

SWIMMING **For Exercises 8 and 9, refer to the table. It shows the winning Olympic times for the Women's 4 × 100-meter Freestyle Relay in swimming.** (Lesson 8-6)

Year	Time (s)
1976	225
1980	223
1984	224
1988	221
1992	220
1996	219
2000	217

Source: *ESPN Sports Almanac*

8. Make a line graph of the data.
9. Predict the winning time in 2008.
10. **SURVEYS** A survey of randomly selected teens revealed that 68% have a personal cell phone. If there are 1,200 teens at Harrisburg Middle School, about how many have a personal cell phone? (Lesson 8-7)
11. **CATS** To determine what type of cat most customers prefer, the president of a cat food company mailed 250 surveys to cat owners. Of the 185 surveys that were returned, 52% preferred calico cats. The president concluded that about half of cat owners prefer calico cats. Determine whether this conclusion is valid. Justify your answers. (Lesson 8-8)
12. **CELL PHONES** The table shows the number of monthly minutes Mallory used on her cell phone during the past year. She claims that the average number of minutes used is about 324. Explain how this is misleading. (Lesson 8-9)

284	322	286	359	318	294
602	278	292	267	299	285

1. **DENTISTS** A dental hygienist randomly chooses a toothbrush in a drawer containing 17 white, 12 green, and 5 blue toothbrushes. What is the probability that she chooses a green toothbrush? Write as a fraction in simplest form. (Lesson 9-1)

SURVEYS For Exercises 2 and 3, use the table below. It shows the results of a survey in which adults were asked how proud they were to be an American. (Lesson 9-1)

How Proud Are You?	
Response	**Number**
Extremely	650
Very	250
Moderately	60
Little/Not at All	30
No Opinion	10

Source: *Gallup Poll*

2. If one person participating in the survey is chosen at random, what is the probability that the person is extremely patriotic? Write as a fraction in simplest form.

3. If one person participating in the survey is chosen at random, what is the probability that he is *not* moderately patriotic? Write as a fraction in simplest form.

RANCHING For Exercises 4 and 5, use the following information.
For Roger to reach his cattle pasture, he must pass through three consecutive gates. Any of the three gates can be either *open* or *closed*. (Lesson 9-2)

4. Make a tree diagram to show all of the possible positions of the gates.

5. What is the probability that all three gates will be closed when Roger visits this pasture? Write as a fraction.

6. **SKATEBOARDS** World Sports makes skateboards with different deck patterns. You can choose one of four deck lengths and one of six types of wheels. If they have 120 different skateboards, how many deck patterns are there? (Lesson 9-3)

7. **READING** Mr. Steadman plans to read eight children's novels to his second graders during the school year. In how many ways can he arrange the books to be read? (Lesson 9-4)

8. **CRAFTS** Marina has print fabric in pink, blue, magenta, green, yellow, and tan. How many different stuffed bears can she make if each bear has only four different fabrics, and the order of the fabrics is not important? (Lesson 9-5)

9. **TRAVEL** There are four seats in Pedro's car: two in the front and two in the back. If Benny, Carlita, and Juanita are all in the car with Pedro, how many ways can they be seated in the car if Pedro is driving? Use the *act it out* strategy. (Lesson 9-6)

10. **FOOD** The graph shows the results of a survey in which 7th graders at Plentywood Middle School were asked to name their favorite fruit. If a 7th grader at the school is randomly selected, what is the probability that they chose bananas as their favorite? Write as a fraction in simplest form. (Lesson 9-7)

Favorite Fruits

MARBLES For Exercises 11 and 12, refer to the table. (Lesson 9-8)

Color	Number
Red	10
Blue	6
Purple	10
Yellow	4
Green	2

11. What is the probability of randomly selecting one yellow marble and then one purple marble? Assume that the first marble is not replaced.

12. What is the probability of randomly selecting two red marbles? Assume that the first marble is replaced.

ART For Exercises 1 and 2, use the diagram of the Native American artifact.

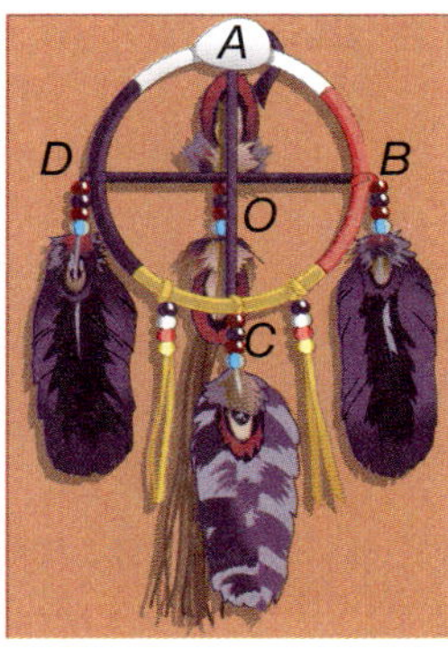

1. Name a right angle and a straight angle. (Lesson 10-1)
2. If $m\angle AOB = 90°$, what is $m\angle DOC$? (Lesson 10-2)

TELEVISION For Exercises 3 and 4, use the survey results shown in the table below. (Lesson 10-3)

Channels Families Watch	
Number	**Percent**
5 or fewer	30%
6–12	33%
13–25	19%
26 or more	14%

3. The fifth category in the survey is *no TV or no opinion*. What percent of the people surveyed were in this category?
4. Make a circle graph of the data.
5. **ART** Victor drew a right triangle so that one of the acute angles measures 55°. Without measuring, describe how Victor can determine the measure of the other acute angle in the triangle. Then find the angle measure. (Lesson 10-4)
6. **GARDENING** Mr. Sanchez has a flower bed with a length of 10 meters and a width of 5 meters. If he can only change the width of the flower bed, describe what he can do to increase the perimeter by 12 meters. Use the *logical reasoning* strategy. (Lesson 10-5)
7. **RUNNING** Four friends are entered in a race. Deirdre finishes directly ahead of Carlos. Mitchell finishes three places ahead of Tramaine and directly ahead of Deirdre. If Tramaine finishes fourth, place the runners in order from first to last. Use logical reasoning. (Lesson 10-5)

For Exercises 8 and 9, use the figure below.

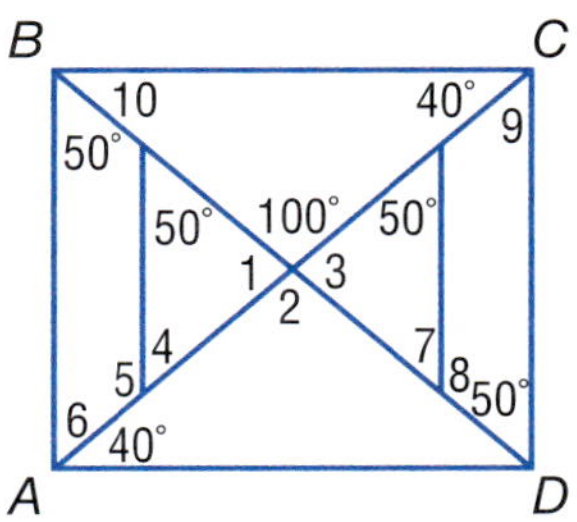

8. Find the measure of each angle numbered from 1–10. (Lesson 10-4)
9. Find the *best* name to classify quadrilateral *ABCD*. Explain your reasoning. (Lesson 10-6)
10. **CRAFTS** Priscilla makes porcelain dolls that are proportional to a real child. If Jody is $4\frac{2}{3}$ feet tall with a 23-inch waist, what should be the waist measure of a doll that is 13 inches tall? Round to the nearest inch. (Lesson 10-7)
11. **ART** Draw a tessellation using two of the polygons listed at the right. Identify the polygons and explain why the tessellation works. (Lesson 10-8)

regular triangles
quadrilaterals
pentagons
hexagons
octagons

For Exercises 12 and 13, use the quadrilateral *MOVE* shown below.

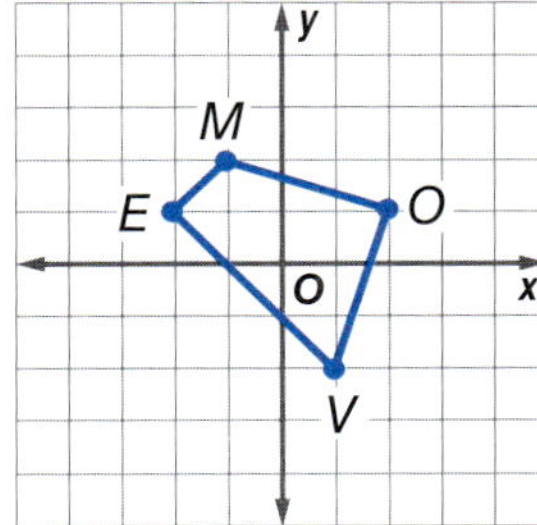

12. Describe the translation that will move *M* to the point at (2, –2). Then graph quadrilateral *M′O′V′E′* using this translation. (Lesson 10-9)
13. Find the coordinates of the vertices of quadrilateral *MOVE* after a reflection over the *y*-axis. Then graph the reflection. (Lesson 10-10)

1. **CRAFTS** A quilt pattern uses 25 parallelogram-shaped pieces of fabric, each with a base of 4 inches and a height of $2\frac{1}{2}$ inches. How much fabric is used to make the 25 pieces? (Lesson 11-1)

2. **FURNITURE** A corner table is in the shape of a right triangle. If the side lengths of the tabletop are 3.5 feet, 3.5 feet, and 4.9 feet, what is the area? Round to the nearest tenth if necessary. (Lesson 11-2)

3. **PUZZLES** Find the area of each small and large shaded triangle. Round to the nearest whole. (Lesson 11-2)

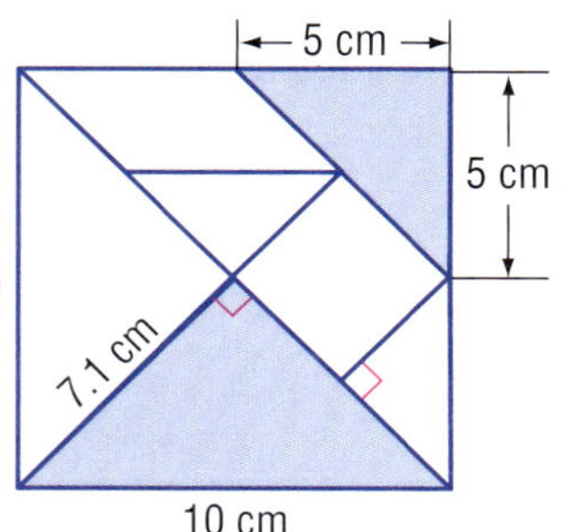

4. **EARTH SCIENCE** Earth has a diameter of 7,926 miles. Use the formula for the circumference of a circle to estimate the circumference of Earth at its equator. (Lesson 11-3)

5. **COOKIES** In New Zealand, a giant circular chocolate chip cookie was baked with a diameter of 81 feet 8 inches. To the nearest square foot, what was the area of the cookie? (Lesson 11-4)

6. **SPORTS PROFIT** A stadium seats 1,001,800 people. 22% of the tickets cost \$134.87 each. 45% of the tickets cost \$67.99 each. The remaining 33% cost only \$35.87 each. About how much revenue is made from one game when each seat is sold out? Use the *solve a simpler problem* strategy. (Lesson 11-5)

7. **LANDSCAPING** Find the area of the flower garden shown in the diagram at the right. Round to the nearest square foot. (Lesson 11-6)

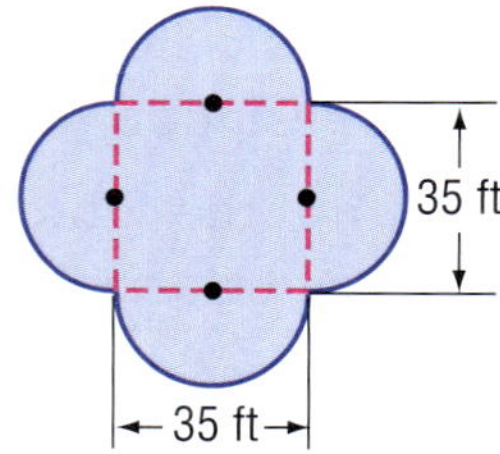

8. **GEOMETRY** A certain three-dimensional figure has four triangular faces and one square face. Classify this figure. (Lesson 11-7)

9. **RECORDS** According to the *Guinness Book of World Records*, the tallest hotel in the world is the 1,053-foot sail-shaped Burj Al Arab in Dubai, United Arab Emirates.

Draw possible sketches of the top, side, and front views of the hotel. (Lesson 11-8)

OCEANS For Exercises 10 and 11, use the following information.
The Atlantic Ocean has an area of about 33,420,000 square miles. Its average depth is 11,730 feet. (Lesson 11-9)

10. To the nearest hundredth, what is the average depth of the Atlantic Ocean in miles? (*Hint*: 1 mi = 5,280 ft)

11. What is the approximate volume of the Atlantic Ocean in cubic miles?

WATER For Exercises 12–13, use the cylinder-shaped water tank. (Lesson 11-10)

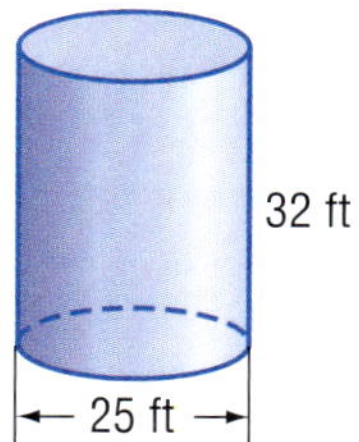

12. Find the volume of the tank. Round to the nearest cubic foot.

13. One cubic foot is approximately 7.48 gallons. Find the approximate volume of the water tank to the nearest gallon.

1. **OMELETS** In Japan, a gigantic omelet was made with an area of 1,383 square feet. If the omelet was a square, what would be its side lengths? Round to the nearest tenth. (Lesson 12-1)

2. **SOFTBALL** A softball diamond is a square measuring 60 feet on each side.

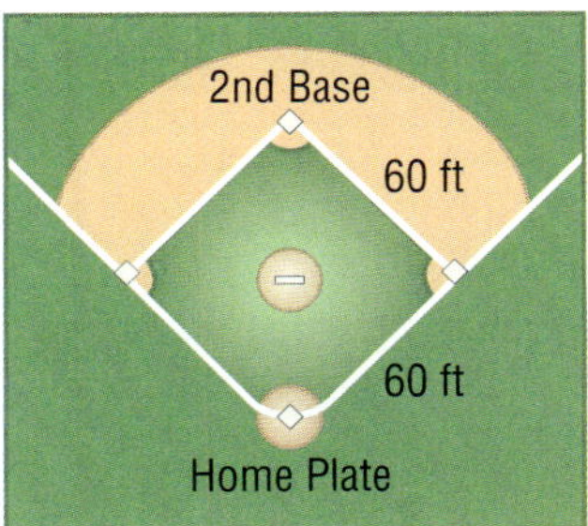

How far does a player on second base throw when she throws from second base to home? Round to the nearest tenth. (Lesson 12-2)

3. **BANDS** Mr. Garcia is planning a band formation at a football game. The diagram shows the dimensions of the field.

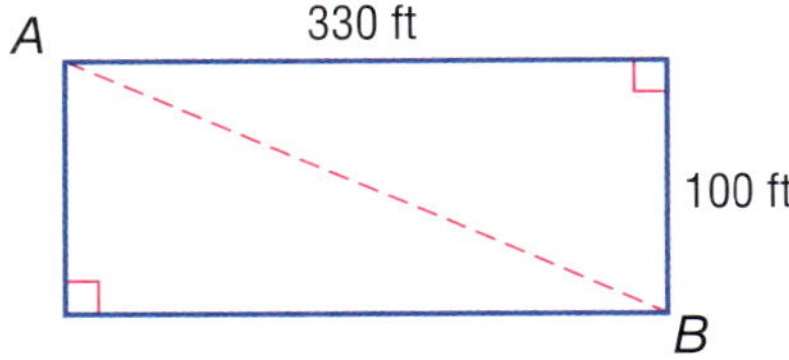

To the nearest foot, what is the distance from A to B? (Lesson 12-2)

4. **GEOMETRY** Two right triangles are side by side such that they form a larger isosceles triangle. If the two right triangles are congruent and each have angle measures of 90°, 45°, and 45°, what type of triangle will the new isosceles triangle be? Use the *make a model* strategy. (Lesson 12-3)

5. **CUBES** A rectangular prism is formed from 48 centimeter cubes such that the height of the prism is one half of the width and one third of the length of the prism. Find the dimensions of the rectangular prism. Use the *make a model* strategy. (Lesson 12-3)

For Exercises 6 and 7, use the following information.
Liz is designing some gift boxes. The small box is 6 inches long, 4 inches wide, and 2.5 inches high. The medium box has dimensions that are each 3 times the dimensions of the small box. (Lesson 12-4)

6. Find the surface area of the small box.

7. What are the dimensions of the medium box? Then find the surface area of the medium box.

STORAGE For Exercises 8–10, use the following information.
The two canisters shown below each have a volume of about 628.3 cubic inches. (Lesson 12-5)

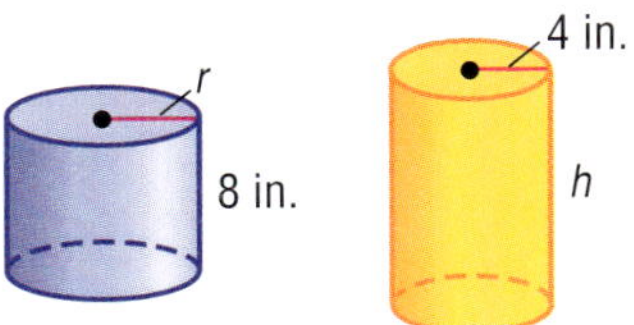

8. What is the radius of the blue canister? Round to the nearest tenth.

9. What is the height of the yellow canister? Round to the nearest tenth.

10. What is the difference between the surface areas of the two canisters?

HATS For Exercises 11–13, use the following information. (Lesson 12-5)
A certain cylinder-shaped hat box has a height of 9 inches and a radius of 5.5 inches. Its lid is also shaped as a cylinder, with a slightly larger diameter so that the lid fits over the box.

11. How many square inches of material are needed to make the hat box, not including the lid? Round to the nearest tenth.

12. If the lid has a height of 3.5 inches and a diameter of 11.8 inches, how many square inches of material are needed to make the lid? Round to the nearest tenth.

13. How many times more material is needed to make the hat box than the lid? Round to the nearest tenth.

Preparing for Standardized Tests

Throughout the school year, you may be required to take several standardized tests, and you may have many questions about them. Here are some answers to help you get ready.

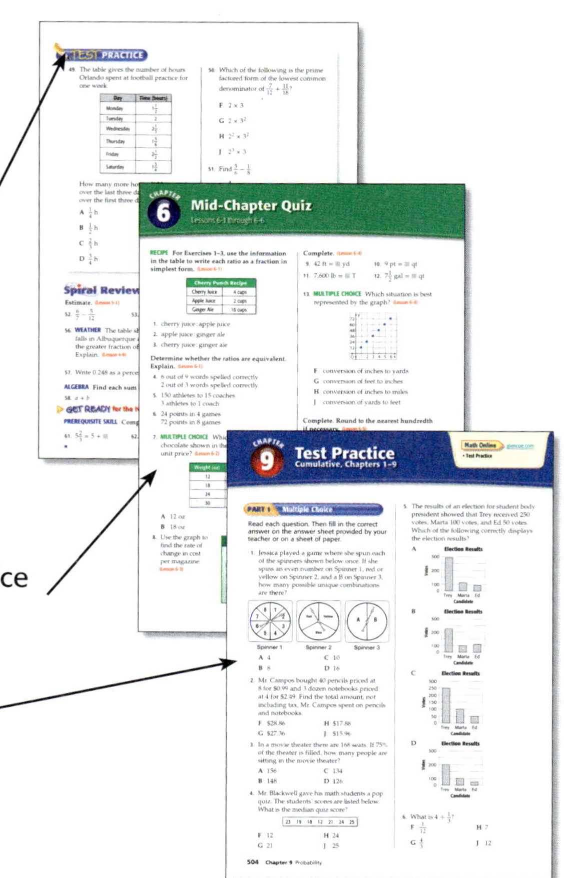

How Should I Study?

The good news is that you've been studying all along—a little bit every day. Here are some of the ways your textbook has been preparing you.

- **Every Day** Each lesson had multiple-choice practice questions.
- **Every Week** The Mid-Chapter Quiz and Practice Test also had several practice questions.
- **Every Month** The Test Practice pages at the end of each chapter had even more questions, including short-response/grid-in and extended-response questions.

Are There Other Ways to Review?

Absolutely! The following pages contain even more practice for standardized tests.

Tips for SUCCESS

Prepare

- Go to bed early the night before the test. You will think more clearly after a good night's rest.
- Become familiar with common formulas and when they should be used.
- Think positively.

During the Test

- Read each problem carefully. Underline key words and think about different ways to solve the problem.
- Watch for key words like *not*. Also look for order words like *least, greatest, first,* and *last*.
- Answer questions you are sure about first. If you do not know the answer to a question, skip it and go back to that question later.
- Check your answer to make sure it is reasonable.
- Make sure that the number of the question on the answer sheet matches the number of the question on which you are working in your test booklet.

Whatever you do...

- Don't try to do it all in your head. If no figure is provided, draw one.
- Don't rush. Try to work at a steady pace.
- Don't give up. Some problems may seem hard to you, but you may be able to figure out what to do if you read each question carefully or try another strategy.

Multiple-Choice Questions

Multiple-choice questions are the most common type of question on standardized tests. These questions are sometimes called *selected-response questions*. You are asked to choose the best answer from four or five possible answers.

Incomplete shading

Too light shading

Correct shading

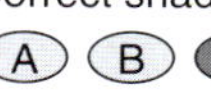

To record a multiple-choice answer, you may be asked to shade in a bubble that is a circle or an oval or just to write the letter of your choice. Always make sure that your shading is dark enough and completely covers the bubble.

The answer to a multiple-choice question may not stand out from the choices. However, you may be able to eliminate some of the choices. Another answer choice might be that the correct answer is not given.

TEST EXAMPLE

Notice that the problem asks for the expression that *cannot* represent the situation.

1 Mrs. Hon's seventh grade students are purchasing stuffed animals to donate to a charity. They bought 3 boxes containing eight animals each and 2 boxes containing twelve animals each. Which expression *cannot* be used to find the total number of animals they bought to give to the charity?

A $8 + 8 + 8 + 12 + 12$

B $3 \times 8 + 2 \times 12$

C $3(8) + 2(12)$

D $5 \times (8 + 12)$

Read the problem carefully and locate the important information. There are 3 boxes that have eight animals, so that is 3×8, or 24 animals. There are 2 boxes of twelve animals, so that is 2×12, or 24 animals. The total number of animals is $24 + 24$, or 48.

You know from reading the problem that you are looking for the expression that *does not* simplify to 48. Simplify each expression to find the answer.

A $8 + 8 + 8 + 12 + 12 = (8 + 8 + 8) + (12 + 12)$
$= 24 + 24$
$= 48$

B $3 \times 8 + 2 \times 12 = 24 + 24$
$= 48$

C $3(8) + 2(12) = 24 + 24$
$= 48$

D $5 \times (8 + 12) = 5 \times 20$
$= 100$

The only expression that *does not* simplify to 48 is D. The correct choice is D.

Some problems are easier to solve if you draw a diagram. If you cannot write in the test booklet, draw a diagram on scratch paper.

STRATEGY

Diagrams
Draw a diagram for the situation.

TEST EXAMPLE

2 On a hiking trip, Grace and Alicia traveled 10 miles south and 4 miles west. If they take the shortest return route, how far will the hike be back to their starting point? Round to the nearest tenth of a mile.

A 6.0 mi **B** 9.2 mi **C** 10.8 mi **D** 14.0 mi

To solve this problem, you need to draw a diagram of the situation. Label the directions and the important information from the problem.

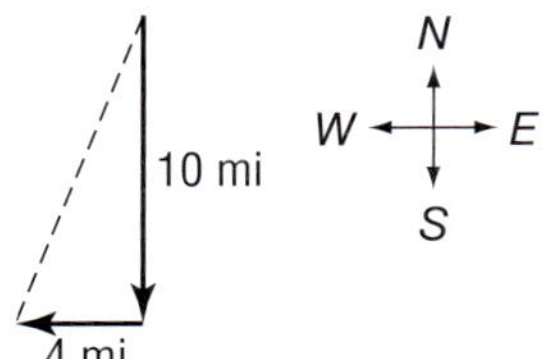

Use the Pythagorean Theorem to find the distance that they will hike back to their starting point.

$c^2 = a^2 + b^2$	Pythagorean Theorem
$c^2 = 4^2 + 10^2$	Replace a with 4 and b with 10.
$c^2 = 16 + 100$	Simplify.
$c^2 = 116$	Add.
$\sqrt{c^2} = \sqrt{116}$	Take the square root of each side.
$c \approx 10.8$	Use a calculator to simplify.

Round the answer to the correct decimal place.

The hike back will be about 10.8 miles. The correct choice is C.

Some problems give you more information than you need to solve the problem. Read the question carefully to determine the information you need.

STRATEGY

Formulas
Use the reference sheet to find the correct formula.

TEST EXAMPLE

3 One of the biggest pieces of cheese ever produced was made in 1866 in Ingersoll, Canada. It weighed 7,300 pounds. It was shaped as a cylinder with a diameter of 7 feet and a height of 3 feet. To the nearest cubic foot, what was the volume of the cheese? Use 3.14 for π.

A 462 ft^3 **B** 143 ft^3 **C** 115 ft^3 **D** 63 ft^3

You need to use the formula for the volume of a cylinder. The diameter is 7 feet, so the radius is $\frac{7}{2}$ or 3.5 feet. The height is 3 feet.

$V = \pi r^2 h$	Volume of a cylinder
$V \approx (3.14)(3.5)^2(3)$	Replace π with 3.14, r with 3.5, and h with 3.
$V \approx 115.395$	Simplify.

The volume of the cheese is about 115 cubic feet. The correct choice is C.

Multiple-Choice Practice

Choose the best answer.

Number and Operations

1. The world's smallest fruit is the fruit of a wolffia plant, which measures about 0.01 inch in length. Another small fruit is the eye of a sewing needle, with a length of 0.20 inch. How many times longer is the eye of a sewing needle fruit than a wolffia fruit?

   A 0.002 **C** 2
   B 0.005 **D** 20

2. The table shows what types of trash fill landfills in the United States. What fraction of the trash in landfills is plastic?

Type of Trash	Percent in Landfills
metal	8%
plastic	24%
food, yard waste	11%
rubber, leather	6%
paper	21%
other trash	30%

Source: *The World Almanac for Kids*

   F $\frac{1}{100}$ **H** $\frac{1}{6}$
   G $\frac{1}{24}$ **J** $\frac{6}{25}$

3. A recent movie earned 317 million dollars in ticket sales. What is this value in scientific notation?

   A 3.17
   B 317×10^6
   C 3.17×10^8
   D 3.17×10^{11}

4. Mercury orbits the sun at 29.75 miles per second. Earth orbits the sun at 18.51 miles per second. How many more miles does Mercury travel in one minute than Earth?

   F 11.24 mi **H** 674.4 mi
   G 269.76 mi **J** 40,464 mi

Algebra

5. The table shows the population growth of a certain bacteria. How many bacteria will there be after 5 hours?

Hours	0	1	2	3	4	5
Number of Bacteria	32	48	72	104	144	?

   A 243 **B** 200 **C** 192 **D** 178

6. Which function rule describes the relationship between distance from home y and hours traveled x?

Time (h)	Distance from Home (mi)
x	y
0	0
1	65
2	130
3	195

   F $65y = x$ **H** $y = x + 65$
   G $y = 65 \div x$ **J** $y = 65x$

7. For a family portrait, a photographer charges a sitting fee and an amount of money per portrait ordered. Which function rule describes the relationship between the total cost y and number of portraits x?

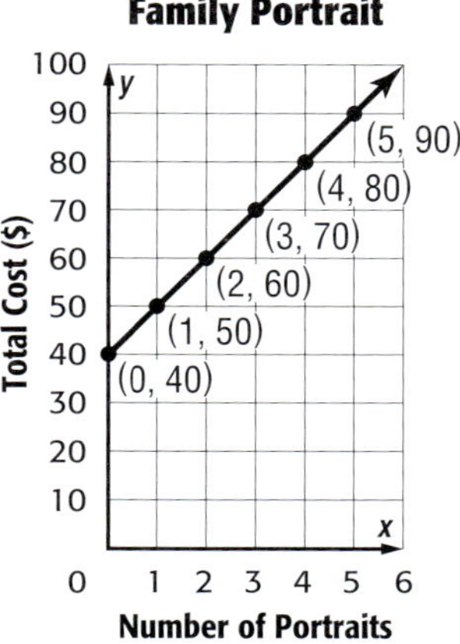

   A $y = 10 + 40x$ **C** $y = 40 + 10x$
   B $y = 40x + 10x$ **D** $y = 10x$

Geometry

8. The three towns on the map form a triangle. Which term *best* describes the angle with vertex at Worthington?

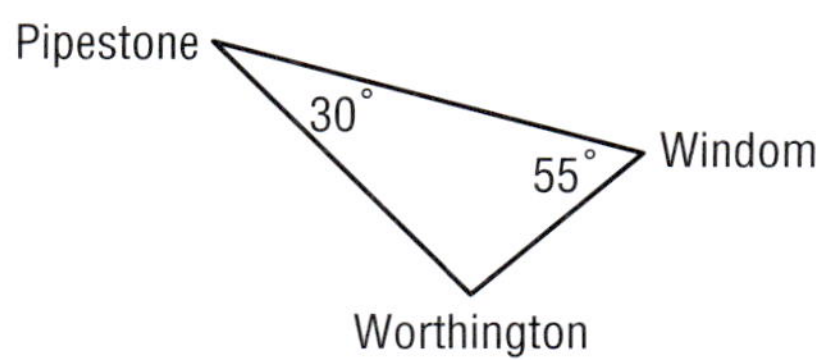

F obtuse **H** acute
G right **J** straight

9. Pedro is using a triangle in a computer graphics design. On a coordinate plane, the vertices of the triangle are $A(-1, 1)$, $B(0, 2)$, and $C(5, -1)$. If Pedro translates the triangle 4 units left and 3 units down, what will be the coordinates of B'?

A $(-1, -4)$ **C** $(4, 5)$
B $(4, -1)$ **D** $(-4, -1)$

10. Jasmine is using this polygon on a poster she is making for the basketball team. Which term *best* describes the polygon?

F quadrilateral **H** hexagon
G decagon **J** heptagon

Measurement

11. Crispy Crackers are packaged in a box that measures 6 inches by 2.5 inches by 10 inches. Which dimensions are of a prism that has the same volume as the Crispy Crackers box?

A 6.5 in. by 2 in. by 10 in.
B 6.25 in. by 3 in. by 8 in.
C 7.25 in. by 2 in. by 9.5 in.
D 4 in. by 7.5 in. by 6 in.

TEST-TAKING TIP

Question 11 Most standardized tests will include any commonly used formulas at the front of the test booklet. Quickly review the list before you begin so that you know what formulas are available.

12. The Crab nebula is a cloud of gas and dust particles in space that is expanding at a rate of 930 miles per second. What is its rate of expansion in miles per hour?

F 22,320 mph **H** 1,339,200 mph
G 55,800 mph **J** 3,348,000 mph

13. Super Toys makes two sizes of building blocks shaped as cubes. The large block has side length four times the length of the small block. What is the ratio of the surface area of the small block to the surface area of the large block?

A 1 to 4 **C** 1 to 16
B 1 to 6 **D** 1 to 32

Data Analysis and Probability

14. The table shows the number of students playing each sport at Wilson Junior High. Find the mean of the data.

Sport	Number of Students
baseball/softball	49
basketball	74
soccer	82
swimming	21
track and field	115
volleyball	25

F 23 **G** 49 **H** 61 **J** 94

15. The spinner is divided into four equal-sized sections. If you spin the spinner 62 times, which is the *best* estimate for the number of times you will land on 2?

A 15 **B** 30 **C** 40 **D** 50

Gridded-Response Questions

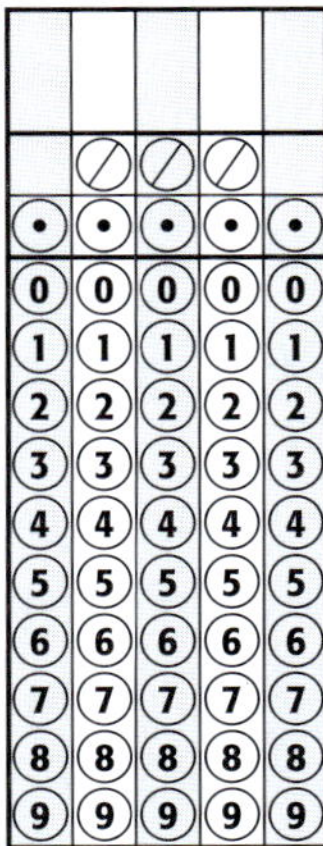

Gridded-response questions are another type of question on standardized tests. These questions are sometimes called *student-produced response* or *grid in*.

For gridded response, you must mark your answer on a grid printed on an answer sheet. The grid contains a row of four or five boxes at the top, two rows of ovals or circles with decimal and fraction symbols, and four or five columns of ovals, numbered 0–9. An example of a grid from an answer sheet is shown.

TEST EXAMPLE

1 Mr. Byrd builds and sells storage buildings. The dimensions of his most popular model are shown in the diagram. What is the volume of the building in cubic feet?

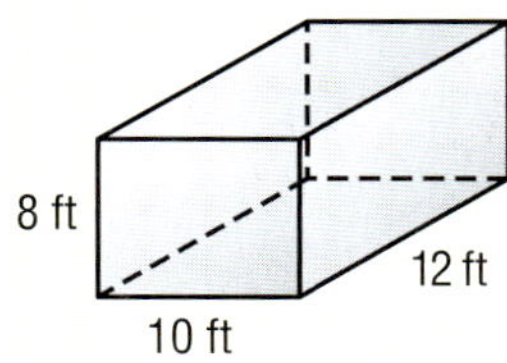

What do you need to find?

You need to find the volume of a rectangular prism. Use the formula and the dimensions given in the diagram.

$V = \ell wh$	Volume of a rectangular prism
$V = 12 \cdot 10 \cdot 8$	Replace ℓ with 12, w with 10, and h with 8.
$V = 960$	Multiply.

The volume is 960 cubic feet.

How do you fill in the grid for the answer?

- Write your answer in the answer boxes.
- Write only one digit or symbol in each answer box.
- Do not write any digits or symbols outside the answer boxes.
- You may write your answer with the first digit in the left answer box, or with the last digit in the right answer box. You may leave blank any boxes you do not need on the right or the left side of your answer.
- Fill in only one bubble for every answer box that you have written in. Be sure not to fill in a bubble under a blank answer box.

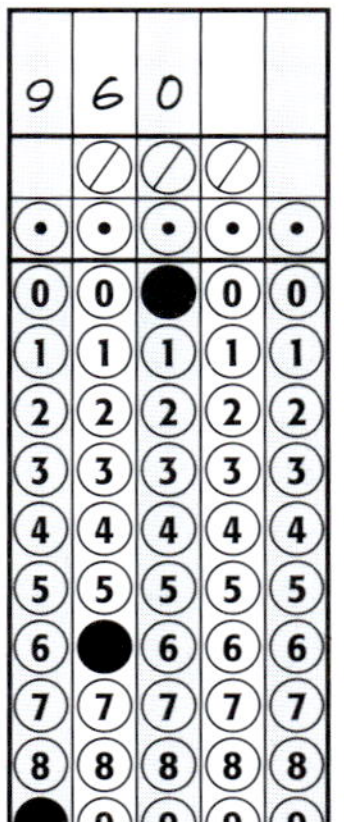

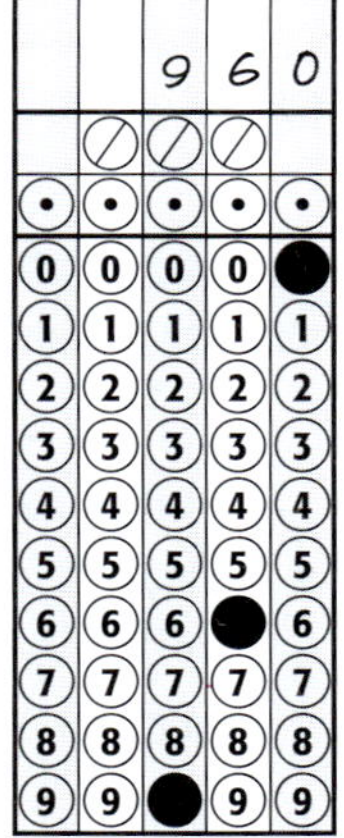

STRATEGY

Formulas Use the reference sheet to find the formula you need.

Many gridded-response questions result in an answer that is a fraction or a decimal. These values can also be filled in on the grid.

TEST EXAMPLE

2 **A prize box contains 12 glitter pencils, 5 fluorescent pens, and 13 mechanical pencils. If Alex randomly selects a prize, what is the probability that he will choose a glitter pencil?**

$$P(\text{glitter pencil}) = \frac{\text{number of favorable outcomes}}{\text{number of possible outcomes}}$$

$$= \frac{12}{12 + 5 + 13} = \frac{12}{30} \text{ or } \frac{2}{5}$$

You can either grid the fraction $\frac{12}{30}$ or $\frac{2}{5}$. You also can rewrite the fraction as a decimal and grid 0.4. Be sure to write the decimal point or fraction bar in the answer box. The following are acceptable answers.

Any equivalent fraction that fits the grid will be counted as correct.

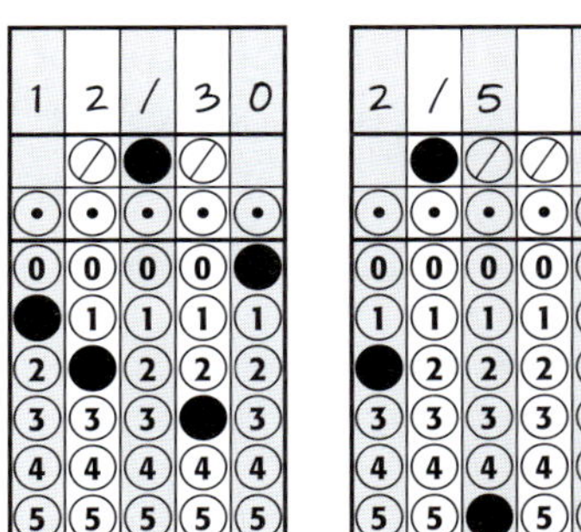

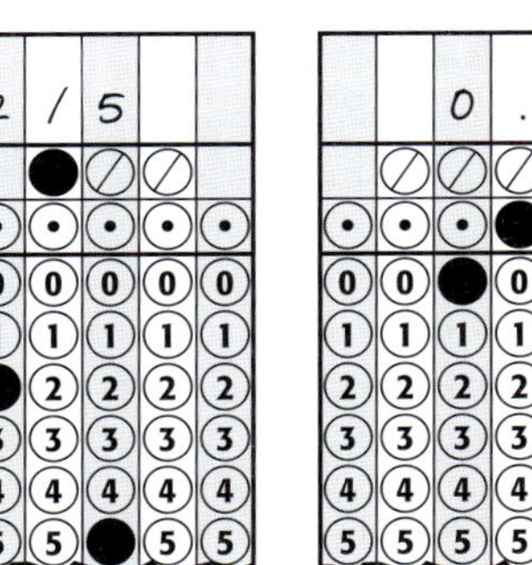

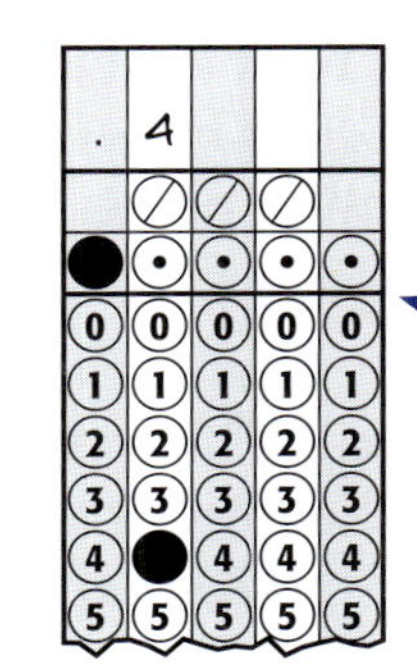

Do not leave a blank answer box in the middle of an answer.

If the answer is a mixed number, change it to an equivalent improper fraction or decimal.

TEST EXAMPLE

3 **A hummingbird measures $2\frac{1}{2}$ inches in length. A sandpiper, measures $4\frac{1}{2}$ inches in length. How many times as long is the sandpiper as the hummingbird?**

Divide the length of the sandpiper by the length of the hummingbird.

$4\frac{1}{2} \div 2\frac{1}{2} = \frac{9}{2} \div \frac{5}{2}$ Rename $2\frac{1}{2}$ as $\frac{5}{2}$.

$= \frac{9}{2} \cdot \frac{2}{5}$ Multiply by the reciprocal of $\frac{5}{2}$, which is $\frac{2}{5}$.

$= \frac{9}{5}$

You can either grid the improper fraction $\frac{9}{5}$, or rewrite it as 1.8 and grid the decimal. Do not enter 14/5, as this will be interpreted as $\frac{14}{5}$.

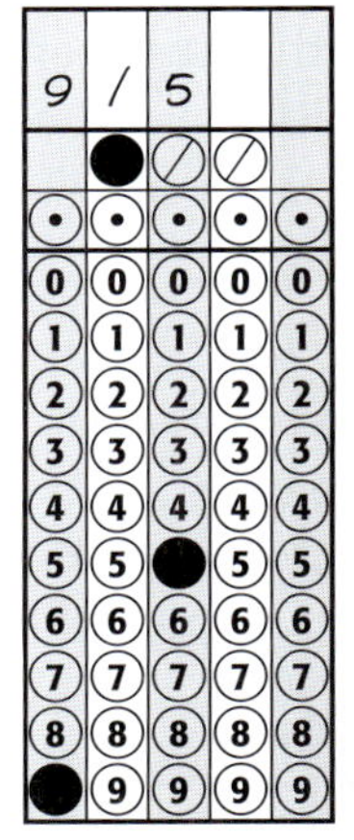

Preparing for Standardized Tests

Gridded-Response Practice

Solve each problem. Then copy and complete a grid like the one shown on page 722.

Number and Operations

1. The seventh-grade class at Willow Creek Middle School is planning a class trip. Each student will need to pay $4.50 for the bus ride, $8.00 for a ticket to the museum, and $5.25 for lunch. If there are 52 students in the class, what will be the total cost in dollars of the trip?

2. The highest point in Louisiana is Driskill Mountain at 585 feet. The lowest point is −8 feet in New Orleans. What is the difference in feet between the highest and lowest elevation points?

3. People in the United States own about 204 million cars. If the number of cars is written in scientific notation, what is the exponent of the 10 in the expression?

4. Ashlee has $5\frac{1}{4}$ cups of cocoa powder. If each batch of chocolate cookies uses $\frac{1}{2}$ cup of cocoa powder, how many batches could she make?

Algebra

5. The number of televisions per 1,000 people in France is 598. The number of televisions per 1,000 people in the United States is 208 greater than the number in France. How many televisions are there in the United States per 1,000 people?

6. The table shows the number of white beads that Carmen uses in each row for a particular pattern in a necklace that she designed. How many white beads will there be in the sixth row?

Row	1	2	3	4	5
Beads	1	2	4	8	16

7. The table shows the cost of renting a booth at the week-long Fall Festival. There is an initial charge for reserving a booth and a fee per day. What is the cost in dollars of renting a booth for the 7 days of the festival?

Days	0	1	2	3
Cost ($)	50	90	130	170

8. The graph shows the cost to rent a power paint sprayer. Let x be the number of hours the sprayer is rented and y be the total cost of the rental. Suppose an equation of the form $y = ax$ represents the data in the graph. What is the value of a?

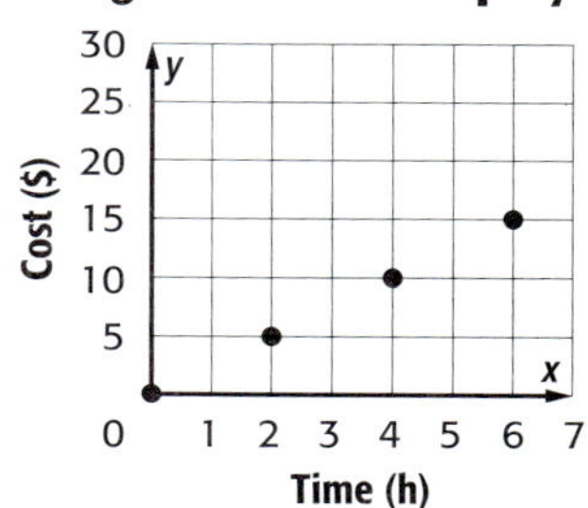

9. The temperature on a January morning is −18°F. The temperature is expected to rise at a rate of 5° each hour for the next several hours. In how many hours will the temperature be 7°F?

Geometry

10. Triangle ABC is similar to triangle XYZ. What is the measure of $\angle Z$ in degrees?

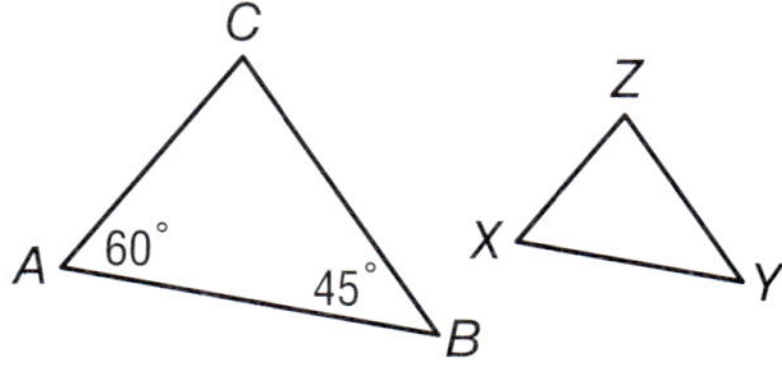

11. Triangle DEF has vertices $D(1, 1)$, $E(4, -2)$, and $F(0, -3)$. Find the y-coordinate of point E after the triangle is reflected over the x-axis.

12. In the diagram, ∠1 and ∠2 are supplementary. Find the measure of ∠3 in degrees.

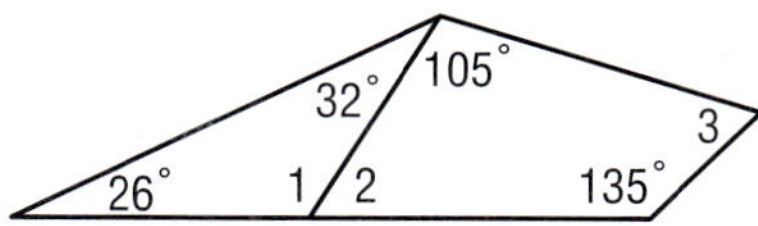

13. Rectangle *B* has width and length 3 times the width and length of Rectangle *A*. As a fraction, what is the ratio of the area of Rectangle *A* to the area of Rectangle *B*?

Measurement

14. In the United States, the average amount of meat eaten per person is 261 pounds per year. If there are 365 days in a year, what is the average number of ounces of meat eaten per day? Round to the nearest ounce.

TEST-TAKING TIP

Question 14 The units of measure given in a question may not be the same as the units of measure asked for in the answer. Check that your solution is in the correct unit.

15. A rectangle has an area of 318 square centimeters and a width of 12 centimeters. What is the length of the rectangle in centimeters?

16. The circle graph shows the results of a survey in Ms. Chen's fifth period math class. What is the exact degree measure of the section of the circle graph representing soccer?

Favorite Sports of Ms. Chen's Students

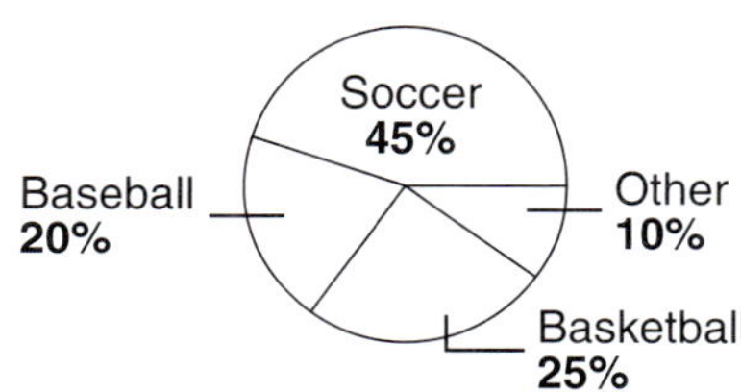

17. One acre of land is 43,560 square feet. How many square yards are in one acre?

18. The Browns plan to paint the top, bottom, and sides of the cylinder-shaped barrel with a waterproof coating. What is the surface area in square feet of the barrel? Round to the nearest square foot.

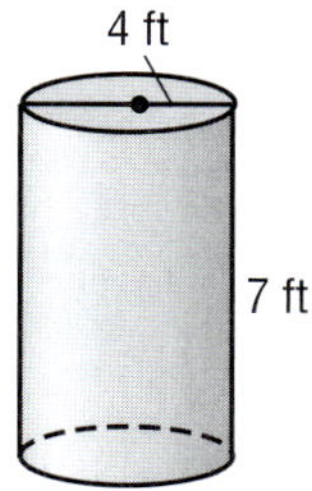

Data Analysis and Probability

19. The table shows the world's highest dams and the countries in which they are located. Find the range of the data.

Country	Height (ft)
Tajikistan	984
Switzerland	935
Georgia	892
Italy	859
Mexico	856

Source: *Scholastic Book of World Records*

20. The table shows the prices in dollars that Mike spent on his college textbooks. What is the mean of the data?

66.00	51.25	50.00	63.00
56.25	9.00	82.00	50.50

21. Kaya has the following scores for the first four tests in her science class: 82%, 95%, 100%, and 90%. She wants the mean of her first five tests to be 93%. What score as a percent must she earn on the fifth test?

22. In a carnival game, the probability of winning is 0.005. As a percent, what is the probability of losing?

23. A beverage cooler contains 6 regular colas, 5 orange drinks, 7 iced teas, and 7 diet colas. James reaches into the cooler and randomly takes two drinks, one after the other. Find the probability that he will choose a regular cola and then an orange drink.

Short-Response Questions

Short-response questions require you to provide a solution to the problem as well as any method, explanation, and/or justification you used to arrive at the solution. These are sometimes called *constructed-response, open-response, open-ended, free-response,* or *student-produced questions.*

The following is a sample **rubric**, or scoring guide.

Credit	Score	Criteria
Full	2	Full credit: The answer is correct and a full explanation is provided that shows each step in arriving at the final answer.
Partial	1	Partial credit: There are two different ways to receive partial credit. • The answer is correct, but the explanation provided is incomplete or incorrect. • The answer is incorrect, but the explanation and method of solving the problem is correct.
None	0	No credit: Either an answer is not provided or the answer does not make sense.

On some standardized tests, no credit is given for a correct answer if your work is not shown.

Preparing for Standardized Tests

TEST EXAMPLE

1 Hanna is deciding between a desktop and a laptop that are on sale. The desktop costs $609.00 with a 10% discount. The laptop costs $725.00 with a 25% discount. There is also a 6.75% sales tax on all purchases. Which computer is less expensive? What will be the total cost of the computer including discount and sales tax?

Full Credit Solution

Since there are two computers to compare, I will first find the discounted price of each computer. I will change each percent to a decimal to make the calculations.

desktop	laptop
$609.00 \times 0.10 = 60.90$	$725.00 \times 0.25 = 181.25$
$609.00 - 60.90 = 548.10$	$725.00 - 181.25 = 543.75$

The laptop is less expensive after the discount.

I still need to find the cost of the laptop computer with tax.

543.75×0.0675 $\quad$ $6.75\% = 0.0675$

$= 36.703125$ $\quad$ Use a calculator.

≈ 36.70

The steps, calculations, and reasoning are clearly stated.

Now I will add the sales tax to the cost of the laptop.

$543.75 + 36.70 = 580.45$

The laptop will cost Hanna $580.45, including sales tax.

STRATEGY

Reread the Problem
Look for the important information in the problem.

Partial Credit Solution

In this sample solution, the calculations are correct and the answer is correct. However, there is no explanation for any of the calculations.

Notice that the student multiplies the discounted price by 1.0675 since the cost is 1 and the tax is 0.0675. So, the total is then 1.0675.

$609.00 \times 0.10 = 60.90$

$609.00 - 60.90 = 548.10$

$548.10 \times 1.0675 = 585.09675$

$725.00 \times 0.25 = 181.25$

$725.00 - 181.25 = 543.75$

$543.75 \times 1.0675 = 580.453125$

The laptop is cheaper for $580.45.

Partial Credit Solution

In this sample solution, the answer is partially incorrect because the student does not add the sales tax.

I will find the discount price for each set.

Desktop: Since the current price is 100% and the discount is 10%, the sale price will be

$100 - 10 = 90\%$ or 0.9.

$609.00 \times 0.9 = 548.10$

Laptop: Since the current price is 100% and the discount is 25%, the sale price will be

$100 - 25 = 75\%$ or 0.75.

$725.00 \times 0.75 = 543.75$

Hanna should get the laptop for $543.75.

The student does not add the cost of the tax.

No Credit Solution

In this sample solution, the student does not understand how to find discounted prices and the sales tax. There are just some calculations using the numbers in the problem.

$609.00 - 10\% = 602.91$

$725.00 - 25\% = 625.00$

$602.91 + 6.75\% = 609.66$

$625.00 + 6.75 = 631.75$

I think Hanna should buy the desktop for $609.66.

Preparing for Standardized Tests

Short-Response Practice

Solve each problem. Show all your work.

Number and Operations

1. A main unit of currency in Egypt is the pound. One U.S. dollar is equal to $3\frac{4}{5}$ pounds. How many pounds are equivalent to $10.00 in the U.S.?

2. The average daytime temperature on Venus is 870°F. The average temperature on Jupiter is −160°F. What is the difference between the average temperatures on Venus and Jupiter?

3. A bag of chocolate candies has a nutrition label stating that each serving contains 20% of the recommended daily amount of fat. A serving has 13 grams of fat. Using this information, what is the total recommended daily amount of fat in grams?

4. The Montana Department of Fish, Wildlife, and Parks raised the price of a tag to catch a paddlefish from $2.50 to $5.00 for residents and from $7.50 to $15.00 for nonresidents. Which percent of increase is greater, the increase for residents or for nonresidents?

5. A recent article in the newspaper said that there were 75 cell phones for every 100 people in Finland. The number of cell phones in Finland was given to be 3,893,000. Estimate the population of Finland using this information.

Algebra

6. Florida has 8,426 miles of shoreline. Alaska has 25,478 more miles of shoreline than Florida. Write and solve an equation to find the number of miles of shoreline for Alaska.

7. Juana is saving money to buy a skateboard that costs $95. She has $25 and plans to save $5 per week. In how many weeks will she have enough money for the skateboard?

8. Tyler delivers televisions for Electronics Depot. The graph shows the amount Tyler charges for delivery based on distance. Name the slope and y-intercept of the graph and describe what they mean in this situation.

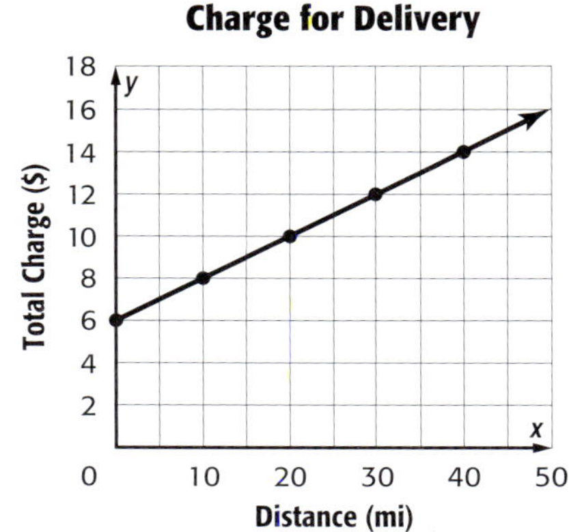

9. Solve $\frac{2}{3}b = \frac{8}{7}$.

Geometry

10. The formula for the area of a trapezoid is $A = \frac{1}{2}h(b_1 + b_2)$. Find the area of the trapezoid.

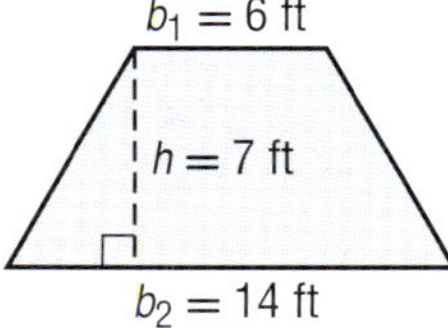

11. Angles MNP and PNO are supplementary. Find $m\angle PNO$.

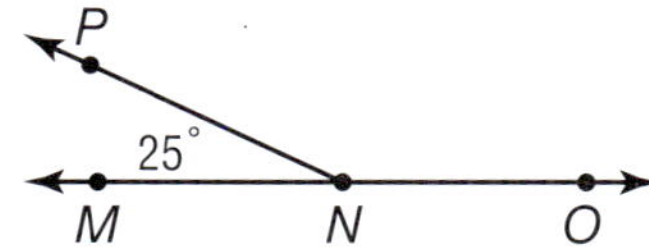

12. What is the value of x?

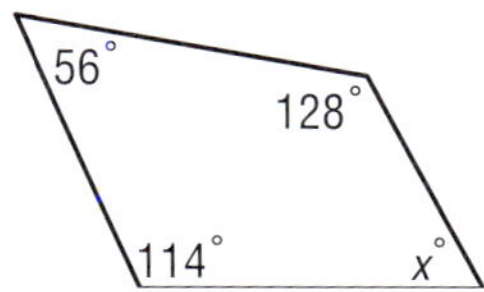

13. Colby is planning to use $\triangle CDE$ for a design by using transformations. He plans to reflect it over the y-axis. Find the coordinates of $\triangle CDE$ after this reflection. Graph the reflected image of the triangle.

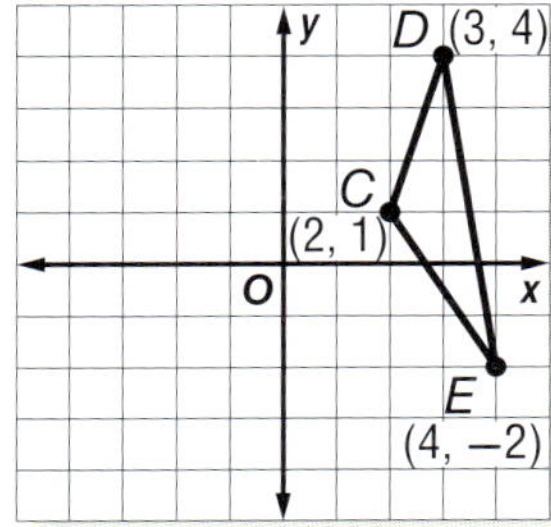

Measurement

14. Diego ran in a 10-kilometer race. What is the distance of this race in meters?

15. What is the surface area of the box?

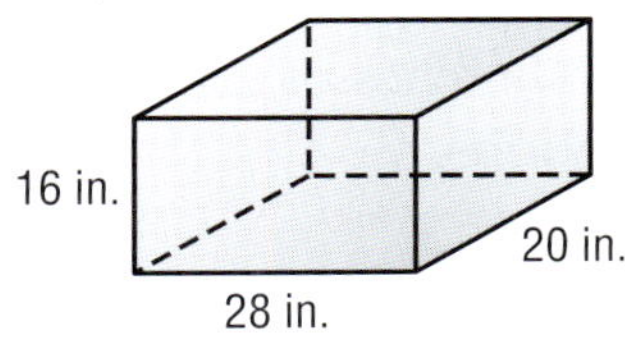

16. A certain aircraft uses 350 gallons of fuel per hour. If the plane used 1,925 gallons of fuel on a flight between two cities, how many hours long was the flight?

17. Curtis is painting the four columns for the set of a school play. What is the surface area that needs to be painted? Assume that the tops and bottoms of the columns do *not* need to be painted.

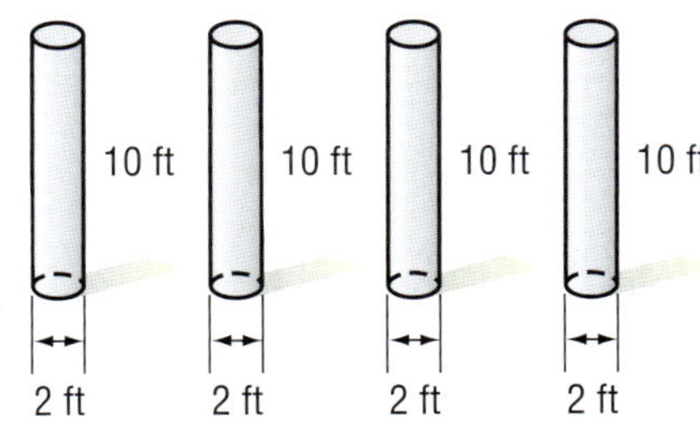

18. The record for women running the Boston Marathon was set in 2002 when Margaret Okayo of Kenya ran the 26.2-mile course in approximately 2 hours and 21 minutes. What was her average speed in miles per hour?

TEST-TAKING TIP

Questions 17 and 18 After finding the solution, always go back and read the problem again to make sure your solution answers what the problem is asking.

Data Analysis and Probability

19. The stem-and-leaf plot shows the scores on the last math test in Mr. Hill's class. What is the range of the data?

Stem	Leaf
9	1 2 3 5 6 9
8	0 2 5 6 6 7 8 8
7	1 2 3 5 7 9 9
6	0 5 8 9 9 *8|2 = 82 points*

20. The table shows the heights of the world's largest flightless birds. Make a bar graph of the data.

Bird	Height (in.)
Ostrich	96
Emu	60
Cassowary	60
Rhea	54
Emperor Penguin	45

21. The table shows the average precipitation in inches for each month in Syracuse, New York. Make a scatter plot of the data. Use the months on the horizontal axis and the precipitation on the vertical axis. Describe the graph.

Month	Precipitation (in.)	Month	Precipitation (in.)
Jan	2.34	July	3.81
Feb	2.15	Aug	3.51
Mar	2.77	Sep	3.79
Apr	3.33	Oct	3.24
May	3.28	Nov	3.72
June	3.79	Dec	3.2

22. Two number cubes each marked with 1, 2, 3, 4, 5, 6 on their faces are rolled. List all the possible outcomes.

Preparing for Standardized Tests

Extended-Response Questions

Extended-response questions are often called *open-ended* or *constructed-response questions*. Most extended-response questions have multiple parts. You must answer all parts to receive full credit.

Extended-response questions are similar to short-response questions in that you must show all of your work in solving the problem and a rubric is used to determine whether you receive full, partial, or no credit. The following is a sample rubric for scoring extended-response questions.

Credit	Score	Criteria
Full	4	Full credit: A correct solution is given that is supported by well-developed, accurate explanations.
Partial	3, 2, 1	Partial credit: A generally correct solution is given that may contain minor flaws in reasoning or computation, or an incomplete solution is given. The more correct the solution, the greater the score.
None	0	No credit: An incorrect solution is given indicating no mathematical understanding of the concept, or no solution is given.

On some standardized tests, no credit is given for a correct answer if your work is not shown.

Make sure that when the problem says to *Show your work*, you show every aspect of your solution including figures, sketches of graphing calculator screens, or the reasoning behind computations.

Preparing for Standardized Tests

TEST EXAMPLE

1 Each fall, the community pool is drained. The pool contains 100,000 gallons of water. The pool has two drains that together drain the pool at a rate of 10,000 gallons per hour.

a. Make a function table for this situation. Let x represent the time in hours the pool drains. Let y represent the gallons of water left in the pool.

b. Make a graph of the data in the function table.

c. Predict how many hours it will take for the pool to drain.

Full Credit Solution

Part a A complete table includes labeled columns.

Every 2 hours there will be 20,000 gallons less water.

Hours (x)	Water Left (y)	(x, y)
2	80,000	(2, 80,000)
4	60,000	(4, 60,000)
6	40,000	(6, 40,000)
8	20,000	(8, 20,000)
10	0	(10, 0)

Part b A complete graph includes a title for the graph, appropriate scales and labels for the axes, and correctly graphed points.

The student gives reasoning in graphing the ordered pairs.

To make a graph, I graphed the ordered pairs from my table and decided to connect them with a line.

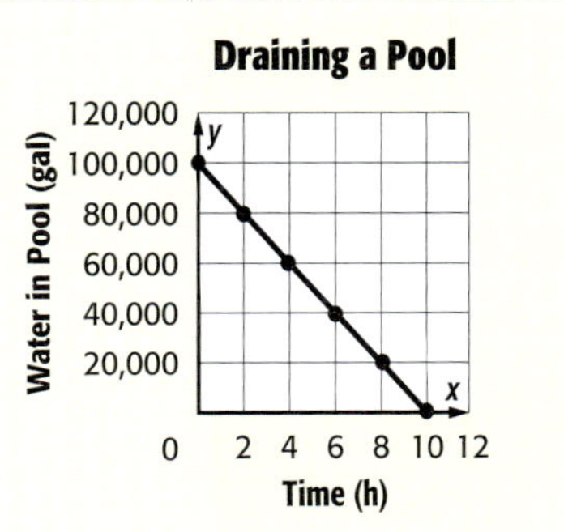

Part c

The pool is drained when the y-value is 0. That is at 10 hours. It will take 10 hours to drain the pool.

Partial Credit Solution

Part a This sample answer has an incomplete table.

1	90,000
2	80,000
3	70,000

Part b Partial credit is given because the points are graphed correctly, but the scale on the y-axis jumps from 0 to 70,000 with no break.

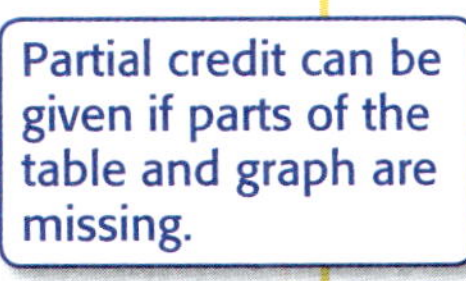

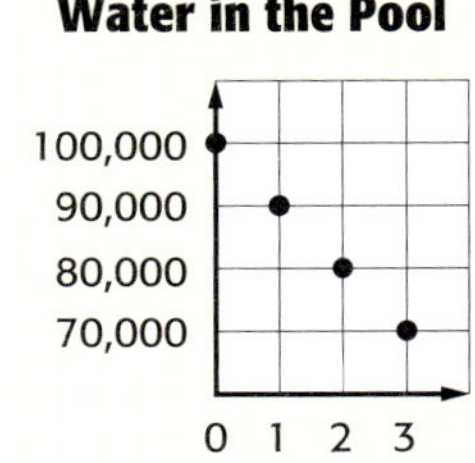

Part c

Full credit is given for Part c.

I wrote a function rule to find how long it will take to drain the pool. I let $y = 0$ to find the number of hours.

$$y = 100{,}000 - 10{,}000x$$

$$0 = 100{,}000 - 10{,}000x$$

$$10{,}000x = 100{,}000$$

$$x = 10$$

It will take 10 hours to drain the pool.

No Credit Solution

If the student demonstrates no understanding of making a table or graph or making a prediction, then no credit is given.

Preparing for Standardized Tests

Extended-Response Practice

Solve each problem. Show all your work.

Number and Operations

1. The table shows the land area and water area of five states.

Land and Water Area of Five States		
State	Land Area (mi^2)	Water Area (mi^2)
Florida	53,937	5991
Colorado	103,729	371
Alaska	570,374	44,856
Iowa	55,875	401
Rhode Island	1,045	186

a. Find the percent of each state that is water. The entire state area is the sum of the land and water areas.

b. Order the states from the state with the least percent water to the greatest percent water.

c. Suppose a state had land and water areas such that the water area was 20% of the total area. Give a possible land and water area, with land area greater than 1,000 square miles, such that this is true.

Algebra

2. The table shows the rental rates for a crane rental service. There is an initial fee to reserve the crane and a daily fee.

Days	Cost	Days	Cost
0	$100	4	$280
1	$145	5	$325
2	$190	6	$370
3	$235		

a. Graph the data. Let x = number of days and y = cost. Connect the points.

b. What is the slope of the line? What does the slope represent?

c. What would be the charge for renting the crane for 10 days?

3. A long-distance phone company charges 40¢ per call plus 4¢ per minute.

a. Write and solve an equation to find the number of minutes used for a call that costs $2.80.

b. Another long-distance company charges 6¢ per minute and no connection fee. What is the cost of a 60-minute call?

c. Which service would charge less for a 90-minute call?

Geometry

4. Ava and Bryn are making rectangular fleece blankets. Ava is making her blanket 40 inches by 60 inches. Bryn says she wants to make her blanket "twice as big."

a. What is the area of Ava's blanket?

b. Bryn makes her blanket such that both the length and width are each twice the length and width of Ava's blanket. What will be the area of Bryn's blanket?

c. What is the ratio of the area of Bryn's blanket in Part b to the area of Ava's blanket in Part a?

d. Ava tells Bryn that a blanket is "twice as big" if the area is twice the area of the other. Give a possible length and width for a blanket twice as big as Ava's using this idea of "twice as big."

5. The map shows five towns and the angle measures for roads connecting them.

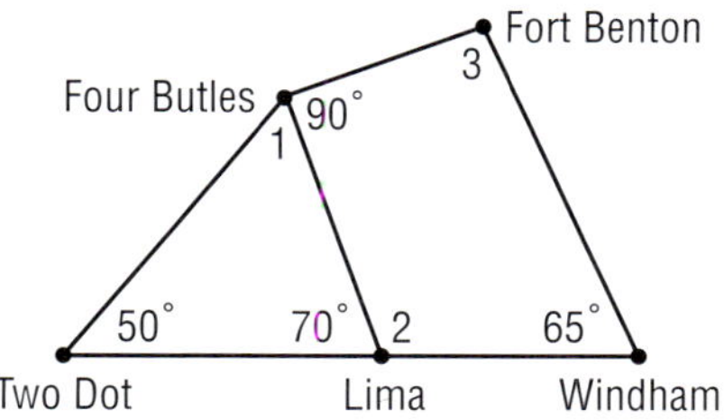

a. Find the measure of ∠1. Explain.

b. Find the measures of ∠2 and ∠3. Explain.

Measurement

6. City planners are considering enlarging the circular manholes in their streets. Currently, the diameter of a manhole cover is 24 inches. The new size being considered is 2 inches greater all the way around.

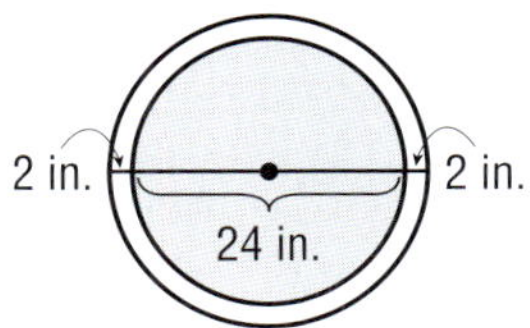

   a. Find the area of a current manhole cover with diameter of 24 inches. Round to the nearest square inch.

   b. Find the area of a new manhole cover. Round to the nearest square inch.

   c. What would be the percent increase in the area of a manhole cover if the new covers are made?

TEST-TAKING TIP

Question 6 Be sure to completely and carefully read the problem before beginning any calculations. If you read too quickly, you may miss a key piece of information.

7. A company that sells beads for craft projects has the two containers shown for packaging the beads.

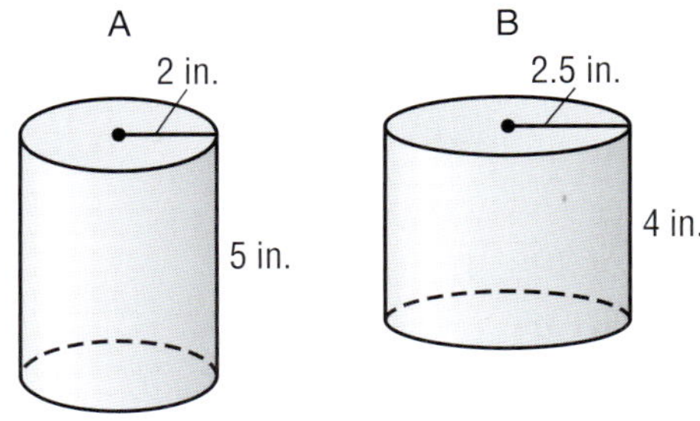

   a. Find the volume of each container. Round to the nearest tenth of a cubic inch.

   b. Find the ratio of the volume of container A to the volume of container B.

   c. The company wants to make a container shaped as a rectangular prism. Find a possible length, width, and height for the container such that its volume is twice the volume of container B.

Data Analysis and Probability

8. The table shows the normal monthly temperatures in degrees Fahrenheit for Honolulu, Hawaii, and Minneapolis, Minnesota.

Month	Honolulu	Minneapolis
Jan	73	13
Feb	73	20
Mar	74	32
Apr	76	47
May	77	59
Jun	80	68
Jul	81	73
Aug	82	71
Sep	82	61
Oct	80	49
Nov	78	33
Dec	75	19

Source: *The World Almanac*

   a. Make a scatter plot of the data for Honolulu. Place the months on the x-axis and the temperatures on the y-axis. Describe the graph.

   b. Make a scatter plot of the data for Minneapolis. Place the months on the x-axis and the temperatures on the y-axis. Describe the graph.

   c. Compare the range for each city's temperature data. Explain a possible reason for the difference in the data.

9. Two 4-sided number cubes are rolled for a game, one white and one black. Each number cube has faces numbered 1 through 4.

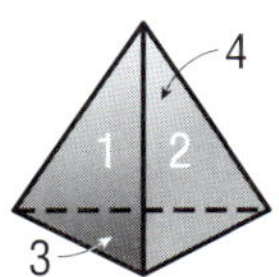

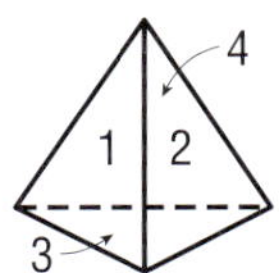

   a. List the sample space for rolling the two number pieces.

   b. What is the theoretical probability that a player will roll a sum of 8?

   c. If you played this game 50 times, how many times would you expect to get a sum of 4?

Preparing for Standardized Tests

Concepts and Skills Bank

 Divisibility Patterns

In $54 \div 6 = 9$, the quotient, 9, is a whole number. So, we say that 54 is **divisible** by 6. You can use the following rules to determine whether a number is by 2, 3, 4, 5, 6, 9, and 10.

A number is divisible by:

- 2 if the ones digit is divisible by 2.
- 3 if the sum of the digits is divisible by 3.
- 4 if the number formed by the last two digits is divisible by 4.
- 5 if the ones digit is 0 or 5.
- 6 if the number is divisible by both 2 and 3.
- 9 if the sum of the digits is divisible by 9.
- 10 if the ones digit is 0.

EXAMPLE Use Divisibility Rules

Determine whether 972 is divisible by 2, 3, 4, 5, 6, 9, or 10.

2: Yes; the ones digit, 2, is divisible by 2.
3: Yes; the sum of the digits, $9 + 7 + 2 = 18$, is divisible by 3.
4: Yes; the number formed by the last two digits, 72, is divisible by 4.
5: No; the ones digit is not 0 or 5.
6: Yes; the number is divisible by 2 and 3.
9: Yes; the sum of the digits, 18, is divisible by 9.
10: No; the ones digit is not 0.

Exercises

Use divisibility rules to determine whether the first number is divisible by the second number.

1. 447; 3
2. 135; 6
3. 240; 4
4. 419; 3
5. 831; 3
6. 4,408; 4
7. 7,110; 5
8. 1,287; 9
9. 2,984; 9
10. 7,026; 6
11. 1,260; 10
12. 8,903; 6

Determine whether each number is divisible by 2, 3, 4, 5, 6, 9, or 10.

13. 712
14. 1,035
15. 8,901
16. 462
17. 270
18. 1,005
19. 32,221
20. 8,340
21. 920
22. 50,319
23. 64,042
24. 3,498

25. **MEASUREMENT** Jordan has 5,280 feet of rope. Can he cut the rope into 9-foot pieces and use all of the rope? Explain.

2 Estimating with Decimals

Estimation can be used to provide quick answers when an exact answer is not necessary. It is also an excellent way to check whether your answer is reasonable. One method of estimating is to use rounding. Round numbers to any place value that makes estimation easier.

EXAMPLES Estimate by Rounding

Estimate by rounding.

1 **23.485 − 9.757**

23.485	→	23	Round to the nearest whole numbers.
− 9.757	→	− 10	
		13	

The difference is about 13.

2 **6.43 + 2.17 + 9.1 + 4.87**

6.43	→	6	
2.17	→	2	Round to the nearest whole numbers.
9.1	→	9	
+ 4.87	→	+ 5	
		22	The sum is about 22.

Another way to estimate sums is to use **clustering**. This strategy is used when all the numbers are close to a common value.

EXAMPLE Estimate by Clustering

3 **Estimate 9.775 + 9.862 + 9.475 + 9.724 by clustering.**

All of the numbers are clustered around 10. There are four numbers.

So, the sum is about 4×10 or 40.

Exercises

Estimate by rounding.

1. 8.56 + 5.34
2. 34.84 − 17.69
3. 6.8 + 2.4
4. 40.79 − 6.8
5. 6.9 + 5.2
6. 23.84 + 12.13
7. 34.3 − 18.9
8. 7.5 + 8.4
9. 65.48 − 9.3
10. 26.3 + 9.7
11. 33.21 − 8.23
12. 67.86 − 24.35
13. 8.99 − 2.6
14. 121.5 + 487.8
15. 32.5 + 81.4

Estimate by clustering.

16. 18.4 + 22.5 + 20.7
17. 56.9 + 63.2 + 59.3 + 61.1
18. 42.3 + 41.5 + 39.8 + 40.4
19. 77.8 + 75.6 + 81.2 + 79.9
20. 239.8 + 242.43 + 236.20 + 240.77
21. 9.9 + 10.0 + 10.3 + 11.1 + 9.8 + 11.2
22. 50.4 + 51.1 + 48.9 + 49.5 + 50.8
23. 100.5 + 97.8 + 101.6 + 100.2 + 99.3

3 Multiplying Decimals

To multiply decimals, multiply as with whole numbers. The product has the same number of decimal places as the sum of the decimal places of the factors. Use estimation to determine whether your answers are reasonable.

EXAMPLES Multiply Decimals

Multiply.

1 **1.3 × 0.9** **Estimate** 1 × 1 = 1

```
  1.3   ← 1 decimal place
× 0.9   ← 1 decimal place
 1.17   ← 2 decimal places
```

The product is reasonable.

2 **0.054 × 1.6** **Estimate** 0 × 2 = 0

```
 0.054  ← 3 decimal places
 × 1.6  ← 1 decimal place
   324
   540
0.0864
```

Annex a zero on the left so the answer has four decimal places. Compare to the estimate.

Exercises

Place the decimal point in each product. Add zeros if necessary.

1. 1.32 × 4 = 528
2. 0.07 × 1.1 = 77
3. 0.4 × 0.7 = 28
4. 1.9 × 0.6 = 114
5. 1.4 × 0.09 = 126
6. 5.48 × 3.6 = 19728
7. 4.5 × 0.34 = 153
8. 0.45 × 0.02 = 9
9. 150.2 × 32.75 = 4919050

Multiply.

10. 0.2 × 6
11. 0.3 × 0.9
12. 0.45 × 0.12
13. 0.0023 × 32
14. 1.5 × 2.7
15. 10.1 × 9
16. 2 × 0.3
17. 6.78 × 1.3
18. 200 × 0.004
19. 0.0023 × 0.35
20. 15.8 × 11
21. 88 × 2.5
22. 33 × 0.03
23. 36 × 0.46
24. 0.003 × 482
25. 1.88 × 1.11
26. 0.6 × 2
27. 38.3 × 29.1
28. 0.7 × 18
29. 8 × 0.3
30. 12.2 × 12.4
31. 380 × 1.25
32. 42 × 0.17
33. 0.4 × 16
34. 0.23 × 0.2
35. 0.44 × 0.5
36. 0.44 × 55
37. 44 × 0.55
38. **JOBS** Antonia earns $10.75 per hour. What are her total weekly earnings if she works 34.5 hours? Round to the nearest cent.

Powers of Ten

You can use a pattern to mentally find the product of any number and a power of 10 that is greater than 1. Count the number of zeros in the power of 10 or use the exponent. Then move the decimal point that number of places to the right.

Decimal Power of 10	Product
19.7×10^1 (or 10)	= 197
19.7×10^2 (or 100)	= 1,970
19.7×10^3 (or 1,000)	= 19,700
19.7×10^4 (or 10,000)	= 197,000

EXAMPLES Use Mental Math to Multiply

Multiply mentally.

1 **12.562×100**

$12.562 \times 100 = 12.562$ — Move the decimal point two places to the right, since 100 has two zeros.

$= 1{,}256.2$

2 **0.59×10^4**

$0.59 \times 10^4 = 0.5900$ — Move the decimal point four places to the right, since the exponent is 4.

$= 5{,}900$

To mentally multiply by a power of ten that is less than 1, count the number of decimal places. Or, if the power is written as a fraction, use the exponent in the denominator. Then move the decimal point that number of places *to the left*.

Decimal Power of 10	Product
$19.7 \times 0.1 \left(\text{or } \frac{1}{10^1}\right)$	= 1.97
$19.7 \times 0.01 \left(\text{or } \frac{1}{10^2}\right)$	= 0.197
$19.7 \times 0.001 \left(\text{or } \frac{1}{10^3}\right)$	= 0.0197

EXAMPLES Use Mental Math to Multiply

Multiply mentally.

3 **10.5×0.01**

$10.5 \times 0.01 = 10.5$ — Move the decimal point two places to the left.

$= 0.105$

4 **$5{,}284 \times 0.00001$**

$5{,}284 \times 0.00001 = 05284$ — Move the decimal point five places to the left.

$= 0.05284$

Exercises

Multiply mentally.

1. 12.53×10
2. 4.6×10^3
3. 78.4×0.01
4. 0.05×100
5. 4.527×100
6. $2.78 \times 1{,}000$
7. 13.58×0.01
8. 5.49×10^3
9. 0.1×0.8
10. 0.925×10
11. 99.44×10^2
12. 0.01×16
13. 1.32×10^3
14. $0.56 \times 10{,}000$
15. 1.4×0.001
16. 11.23×10^5
17. 68.94×0.01
18. 0.8×10^4
19. 28.1×0.01
20. 9.3×10^7
21. $625{,}799 \times 0.0001$

5 Dividing Decimals

To divide two decimals, use the following steps.

- If necessary, change the divisor to a whole number by moving the decimal point to the right. You are multiplying the divisor by a power of ten.
- Move the decimal point in the dividend the same number of places to the right. You are multiplying the dividend by the same power of ten.
- Divide as with whole numbers.

EXAMPLES Divide Decimals

Divide.

1 **25.8 ÷ 2** **Estimate** 26 ÷ 2 = 13

```
   12.9
2)25.8
 - 2
   5
 - 4
   18
 - 18
    0
```

The divisor, 2, is already a whole number, so you do not need to move the decimal point. Divide as with whole numbers. Then place the decimal directly above the decimal point in the dividend.

Compared to the estimate, the quotient, 12.9, is reasonable.

2 **199.68 ÷ 9.6** **Estimate** 200 ÷ 10 = 20

```
       20.8
9.6)199.68
  - 192
      7 68
    - 7 68
         0
```

Move each decimal point one place to the right.

Compare the answer to the estimate.

Exercises

Divide.

1. 0.3)9.81
2. 12)0.12
3. 3.2)5.76
4. 0.22)0.0132
5. 0.04)0.008
6. 3.18)0.636
7. 0.2)8.24
8. 82.3)823
9. 12.02)24.04
10. 0.5)85
11. 74.9)5.992
12. 19.2)4.416
13. 1.9)38.57
14. 13.8)131.1
15. 6.48)259.2
16. 812 ÷ 0.4
17. 0.34 ÷ 0.2
18. 14.4 ÷ 0.12
19. 90.175 ÷ 2.5
20. 39.95 ÷ 799
21. 88.8 ÷ 444
22. 613.8 ÷ 66
23. 2,445.3 ÷ 33
24. 20.24 ÷ 2.3
25. 45 ÷ 0.09
26. 2.475 ÷ 0.03
27. 4.6848 ÷ 0.366
28. 180 ÷ 0.36
29. 97.812 ÷ 1.1
30. 23 ÷ 0.023
31. 1,680.042 ÷ 44.2
32. **OLYMPICS** In the 2000 Olympics, Michael Johnson of the U.S. ran the 400-meter run in 43.84 seconds. To the nearest hundredth, find his speed in meters per second.
33. **SCIENCE** It takes Pluto 247.69 Earth years to revolve once around the Sun. It takes Jupiter 11.86 Earth years to revolve once around the Sun. About how many times longer does it take Pluto than Jupiter to revolve once around the Sun?

Converting Currencies

Countries around the world use different types of currency. By using an exchange rate table, proportions, and a calculator, you can convert from one type of currency to another.

Examine the following exchange rate table. All values in the same column are equivalent to each other.

Exchange Rates					
United States Dollars	1	2.020590	0.999950	1.407465	0.864699
British Pounds	0.494905	1	0.494880	0.696562	0.427944
Canadian Dollars	1.000050	2.020691	1	1.407536	0.864742
Euros	0.710497	1.435623	0.710461	1	0.614366
Australian Dollars	1.156472	2.336756	1.156414	1.627694	1

*Exchange rates as of September 21, 2007

You can use proportions to convert any amount of money from one currency to another.

EXAMPLE

Julian has 16 United States dollars to exchange for euros. How many euros will he receive?

U.S. dollar → (numerator), euros → (denominator)

$$\frac{1}{0.710497} = \frac{16}{x}$$ Set up a proportion.

$$1(x) = 16(0.710497)$$ Cross multiply.

$$x = 11.367952$$ Simplify.

He will receive about 11.37 euros in exchange for 16 United States dollars.

Exercises

Fill in the blanks by converting each currency. Round to the nearest hundredth.

1. 26.41 Canadian dollars = ________ euros
2. 46.82 British pounds = ________ United States dollars
3. 4.7 Australian dollars = ________ euros
4. 285.31 United States dollars = ________ British pounds
5. 567.31 Canadian dollars = ________ Australian dollars
6. 91.67 euros = ________ Canadian dollars
7. 6 Australian dollars = ________ British pounds
8. 37.24 euros = ________ United States dollars
9. 64.28 British pounds = ________ Canadian dollars
10. 74.28 United States dollars = ________ Australian dollars

7 Solving Inequalities

You have already solved one- and two-step equations. You can apply what you learned about equations to solve one- and two-step inequalities. **Inequalities** are sentences that compare quantities that are not equal. The symbols used are $<$, $>$ $\leq$, $\geq$, and $\neq$.

Inequality Symbols

Key Concept

Symbols	$<$	$>$	$\leq$	$\geq$	$\neq$
Words	• less than • fewer than	• greater than • more than	• less than or equal to • no more than • at most	• greater than or equal to • no less than • at least	• not equal to

EXAMPLE Solve a One-Step Inequality

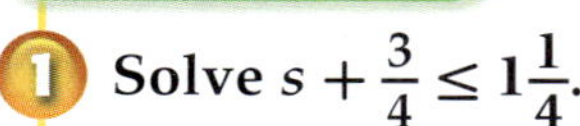

1 **Solve $s + \frac{3}{4} \leq 1\frac{1}{4}$.**

$s + \frac{3}{4} \leq 1\frac{1}{4}$ — Write the inequality.

$s + \frac{3}{4} - \frac{3}{4} \leq 1\frac{1}{4} - \frac{3}{4}$ — Subtract $\frac{3}{4}$ from each side.

$s + \frac{3}{4} - \frac{3}{4} \leq \frac{5}{4} - \frac{3}{4}$ — Change $1\frac{1}{4}$ to an improper fraction, $\frac{5}{4}$.

$s \leq \frac{2}{4}$ or $\frac{1}{2}$ — Subtract.

The solution is $s \leq \frac{1}{2}$.

EXAMPLE Solve a Two-Step Inequality

2 **Solve $7p + 21 \leq 49$.**

$7p + 21 \leq 49$ — Write the inequality.

$7p + 21 - 21 \leq 49 - 21$ — Subtract 21 from each side.

$7p \leq 28$ — Simplify.

$p \leq \frac{28}{7}$ — Divide each side by 7.

$p \leq 4$ — Simplify.

The solution is $p \leq 4$.

Unlike the solution to an equation, the solution $p \leq 4$ reflects a set of numbers. One way to show this is in a number line graph.

EXAMPLE Graph an Inequality

3 **Graph $p \leq 4$.**

Draw a number line and label the integers. Draw a circle at 4. The circle on the graph shows that the numbers up to 4 but not including 4 are included in the solution.

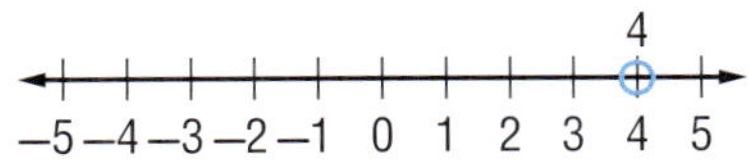

When $\geq$ or $\leq$ is used, the circle on the graph is filled in to show that the number is included in the solution.

Test numbers on either side of 4 to determine the direction of the graph. Draw an arrow pointing in the direction of 2. Use other numbers in this set to check the solution.

4
–5 –4 –3 –2 –1 0 1 2 3 4 5

p	$7p + 21 \leq 49$	Solution
5	$7 \times 5 + 21 \overset{?}{\leq} 49$ $35 + 21 \overset{?}{\leq} 49$ $56 \nleq 49$	No
3	$7 \times 3 + 21 \overset{?}{\leq} 49$ $21 + 21 \leq 49$ $42 \leq 49$	Yes

Exercises

Solve each inequality. Graph each solution on a number line. Round to the nearest tenth if necessary.

1. $2x \geq -14$
2. $30n < 160$
3. $y + 51 \leq 85$
4. $2.5 + 1.5a \leq 7.5$
5. $8.1h + 6.3 \geq 22.5$
6. $0.75g + 23 < 34$
7. $2m + 6.2 \geq 15.6$
8. $3.3(f + 2) > 36.3$
9. $\frac{1}{2}(p + 8) \geq 12$
10. $\frac{1}{3}r - \frac{2}{3} \geq 1$
11. $2n - \frac{1}{5} < 9\frac{4}{5}$
12. $\frac{1}{14}d + \frac{3}{14} \leq \frac{2}{7}$

13. **SAVINGS** Trisha wants to save up to buy a new cell phone that costs less than \$150. She already has \$75 saved. She also makes \$10 a week doing her chores. Write and solve an inequality to find the number of weeks worked that would allow Trisha to buy a new cell phone.

14. **TEXT MESSAGING** Joshua spends \$0.25 every time he sends a text message through his cell phone. Write and solve an inequality that shows the number of text messages he can send with \$3.00.

15. **SPORTS** Allyson spends $7\frac{1}{2}$ hours playing sports each week. Softball takes a total of $3\frac{1}{4}$ hours each week. If she plays sports 4 days a week, write and solve an inequality that shows the average amount of time per day she spends on other sports.

8 Monomials and Polynomials

A **polynominal** is an algebraic expression that includes real numbers and variables. In a polynomial, there are no terms with variables in the denominator and no terms with variables under a radical sign.

polynomial: $2x^2 - 3x + 4$ not a polynomial: $x^2 - \frac{8}{x}$

A specific kind of polynomial is a **monomial**. Since the prefix *mono-* means one, a monomial is a polynomial that contains only one term, like $7x$. Monomials that contain the same variables to the same power are *like terms*.

EXAMPLES Classify Polynomials

Determine whether each expression is a polynomial. Explain your reasoning. If it is a polynomial, state the number of terms in the expression.

1 $3x^3 + 8x + 7$

This is a polynomial because it is the sum of three monomials. There are three terms.

2 $m - \frac{1}{m}$

This is *not* a polynomial because $\frac{1}{m}$ has a variable in the denominator.

EXAMPLE Simplify Polynomials

3 **Find $8x + 7 + 3x + 2$.**

$8x + 7 + 3x + 2$ Write the expression.

$= (8x + 3x) + (7 + 2)$ Group like terms.

$= 11x + 9$ Simplify by combining like terms.

Exercises

Determine whether each expression is a polynomial. Explain your reasoning. If it is a polynomial, state the number of terms in the expression.

1. $\frac{t^2}{5}$
2. $5 + \sqrt{b}$
3. $p^4 + 5p - 2$
4. $-5y^4z$
5. $4a^2 - 2a + \sqrt{90}$
6. $\frac{6}{n^4} + \frac{n^2}{3} - 5$
7. $-8c^5d^3 - 4cd + 3d$
8. $15r^2s^3 - 9r + \sqrt{s}$

Simplify each expression.

9. $12r + 8s + 4r + s$
10. $4a + 5b + 10 + 6a$
11. $7f + 8g + 2f + g$
12. $16x + 12y + 21y + 12x$
13. $5t + 7 + u + 3$
14. $13c + 10d + 4c + 7d$
15. $4j + 6 + 9j + 3$
16. $11p + 12q + 4p + 9q$
17. $15mn + 12m + 4n + 7mn$
18. **GEOMETRY** The sides of a hexagon measure $3x$, $7y$, $6y$, $8x$, y, and $4x$. Write the perimeter of the figure in simplest form.

9 Rotations

A **rotation** occurs when a figure is rotated around a point. A rotation does not change the size or shape of the figure. The rotations shown below are clockwise around the origin.

90° Rotation

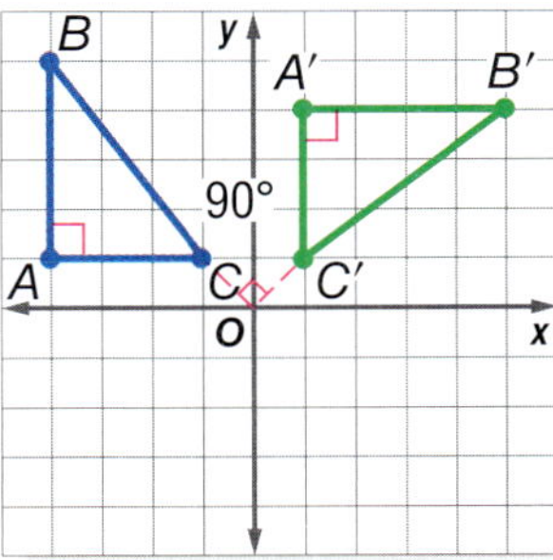

180° Rotation

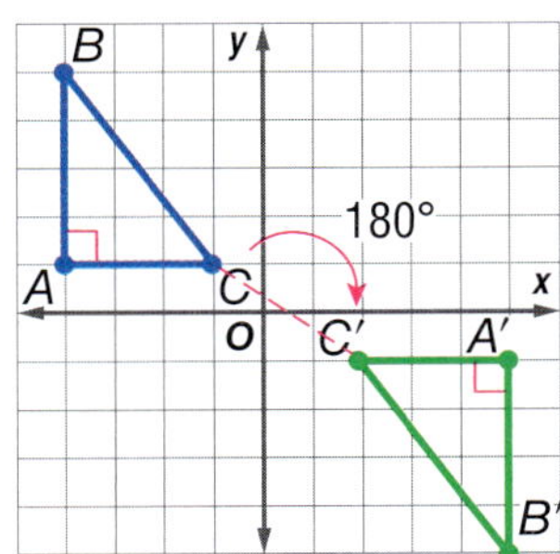

270° Rotation

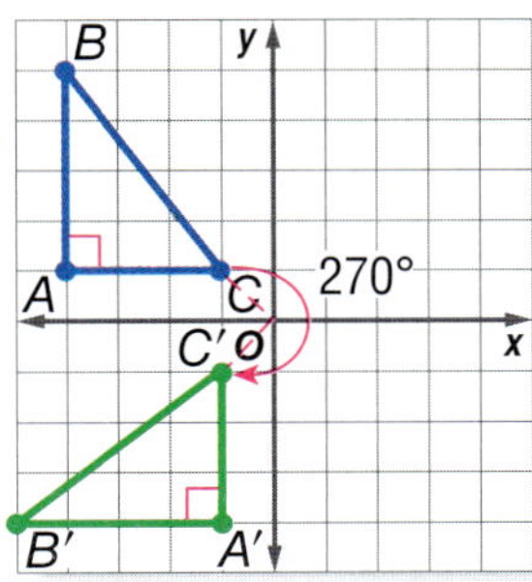

EXAMPLE Rotate a Figure About the Origin

1 **Triangle ABC has vertices $A(-4, 4)$, $B(-1, 2)$, and $C(-3, 1)$. Graph the figure and its rotated image after a clockwise rotation of 90° about the origin. Then give the coordinates of the vertices for $\triangle A'B'C'$.**

STEP 1 Graph $\triangle ABC$ on a coordinate plane.

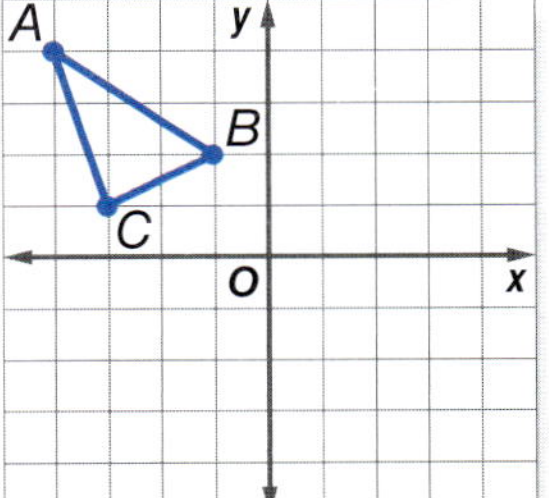

STEP 2 Sketch segment $\overline{BO}$ connecting point B to the origin. Sketch another segment, $\overline{BO}$ so that the angle between point B, O, and B' measures 90° and the segment is congruent to $\overline{BO}$.

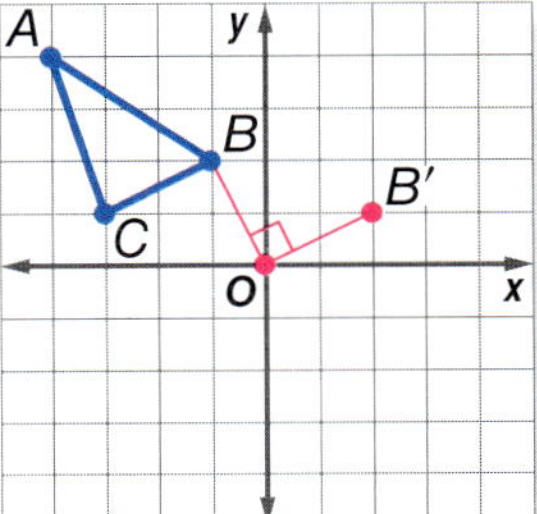

STEP 3 Repeat Step 2 for points A and C. Then connect the vertices to form $\triangle A'B'C'$.

So, the coordinates of the vertices of $\triangle A'B'C'$ are $A'(4, 4)$, $B'(2, 1)$, and $C'(1, 3)$.

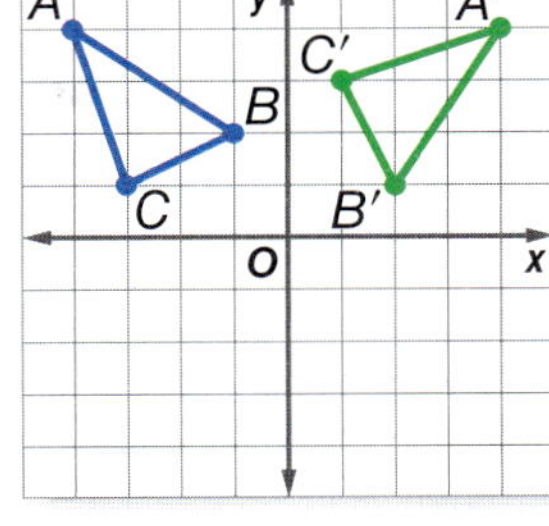

Concepts and Skills Bank

EXAMPLE Rotate a Figure About a Point

2 **Triangle LMN has vertices $L(5, 4)$, $M(5, 7)$, and $N(8, 7)$. Graph the figure and its rotated image after a counterclockwise rotation of 180° about vertex L. Then give the coordinates of the vertices for $\triangle L'M'N'$.**

STEP 1 Graph the original triangle.

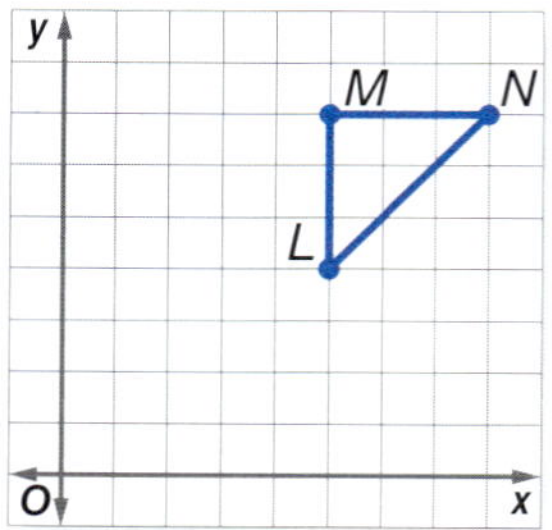

STEP 2 Graph the rotated image.

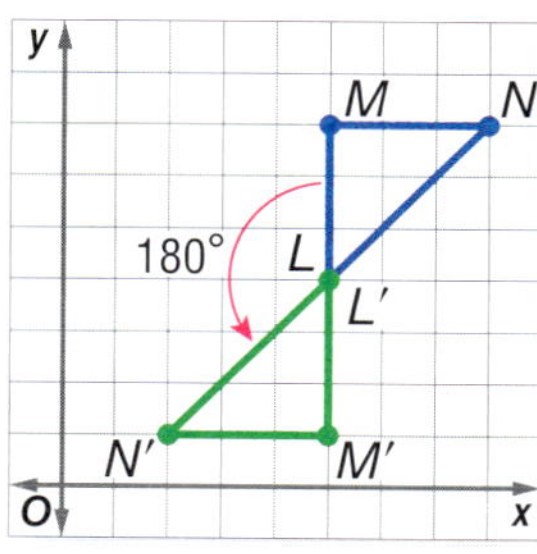

So, the coordinates of the vertices of $\triangle L'M'N'$ are $L'(5, 4)$, $M'(5, 1)$, and $N'(2, 1)$.

Exercises

Graph $\triangle XYZ$ and its rotated image after each rotation. Then give the coordinates of the vertices for $\triangle X'Y'Z'$.

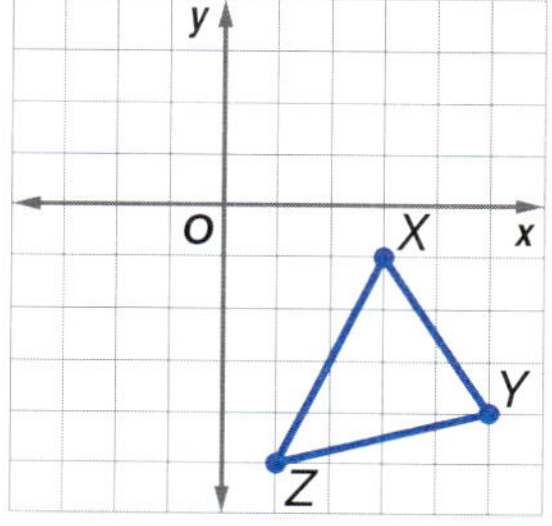

1. 180° clockwise about the origin
2. 270° counterclockwise about vertex X
3. 90° counterclockwise about the origin
4. 270° clockwise about vertex Y
5. 180° counterclockwise about vertex Z
6. 90° clockwise about the origin

Graph quadrilateral $ABCD$ and its rotated image after each rotation. Then give the coordinates of the vertices for quadrilateral $A'B'C'D'$.

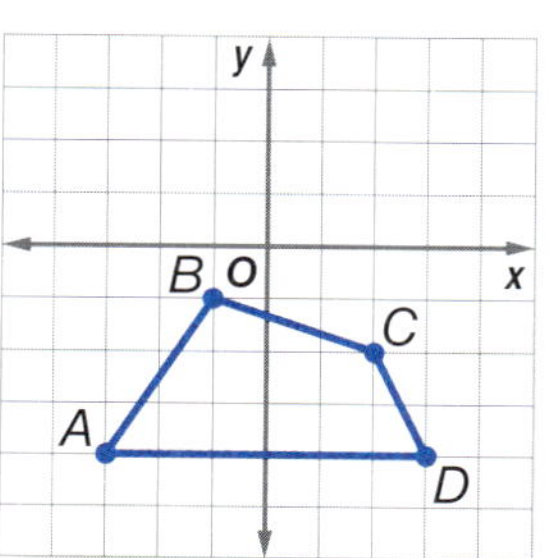

7. 90° counterclockwise about the origin
8. 90° clockwise about vertex A
9. 180° counterclockwise about vertex D
10. 270° clockwise about the origin
11. 90° clockwise about the origin
12. 180° clockwise about vertex B

10 Cross Sections of Three-Dimensional Figures

The intersection of a solid and a plane is called a **cross section** of the solid.

Inequality Symbols

Key Concept

Vertical Slice	Angled Slice	Horizontal Slice
The cross section is a rectangle.	The cross section is an oval.	The cross section is a circle.

EXAMPLE Describe Cross Sections

1 **Draw and describe the shape resulting from a vertical, angled, and horizontal cross section of a square pyramid.**

	Slice	Drawing	Description
Vertical			The cross section is a triangle.
Angled			The cross section is a trapezoid.
Horizontal			The cross section is a square.

Concepts and Skills Bank

Exercises

Draw and describe the shape resulting from each cross section.

1. cone

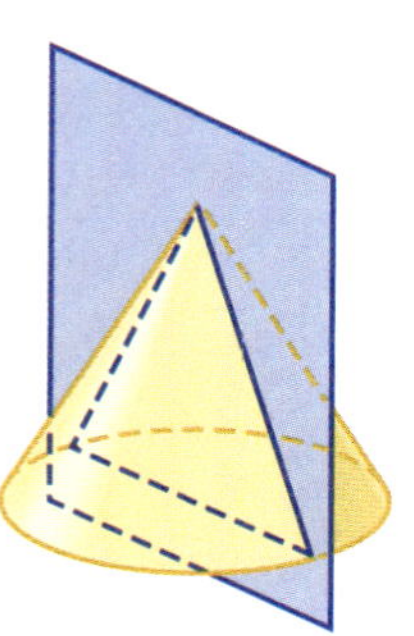

2. triangular pyramid

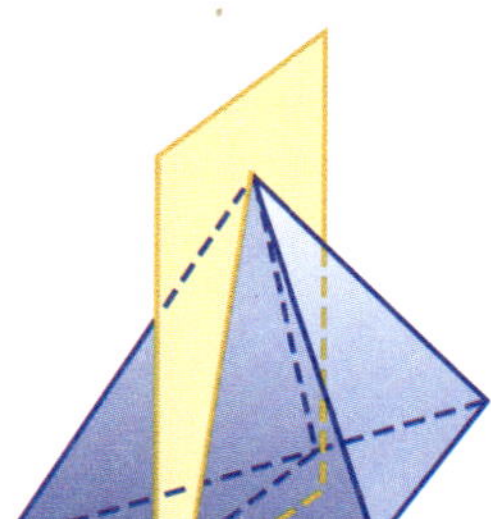

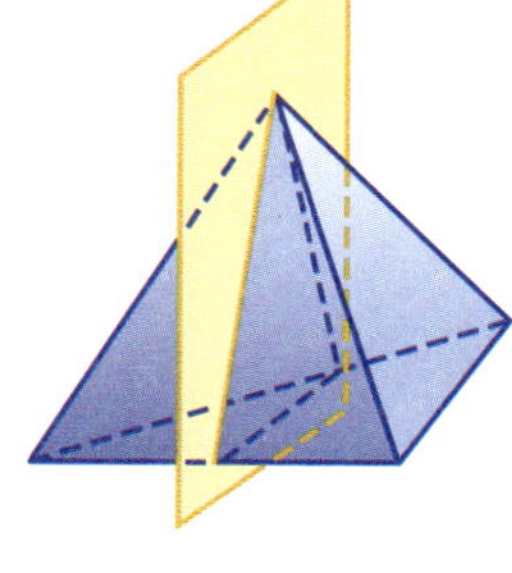

3. rectangular prism

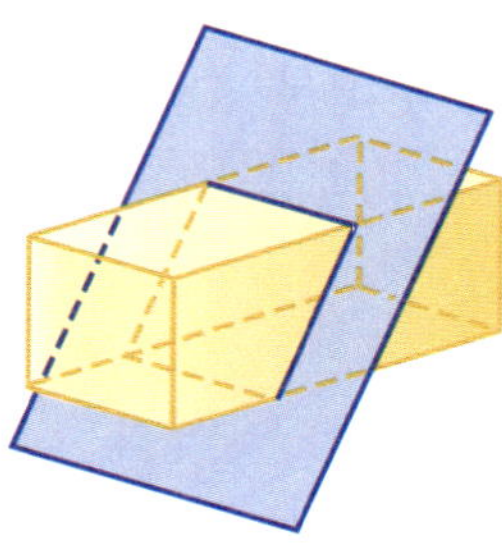

4. cone

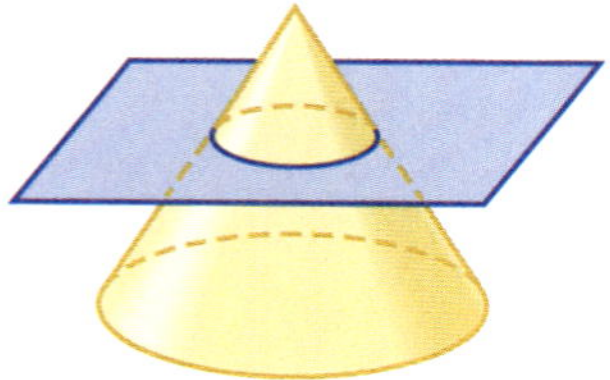

5. rectangular prism

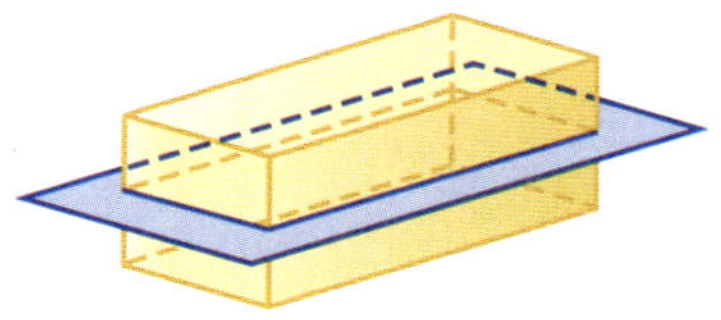

6. cone

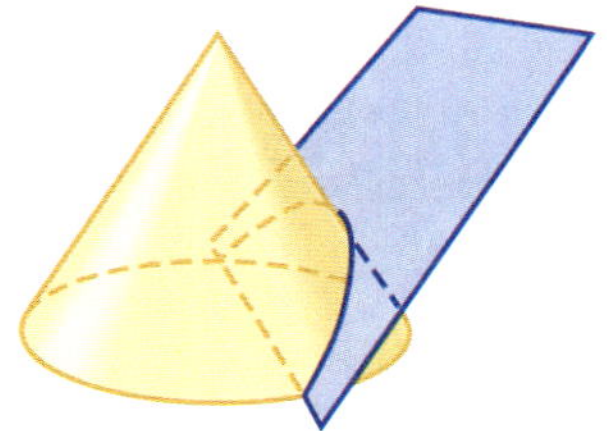

7. triangular pyramid

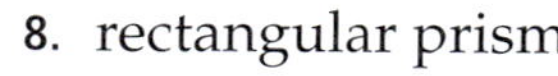

8. rectangular prism

9. triangular prism

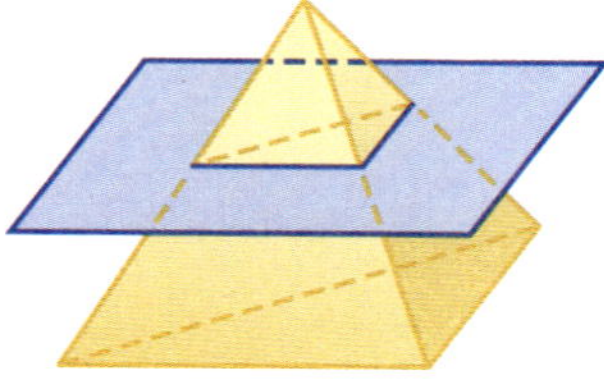

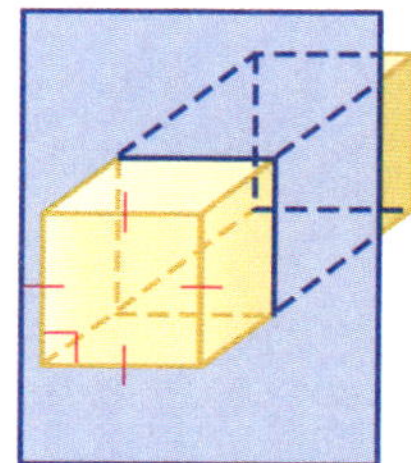

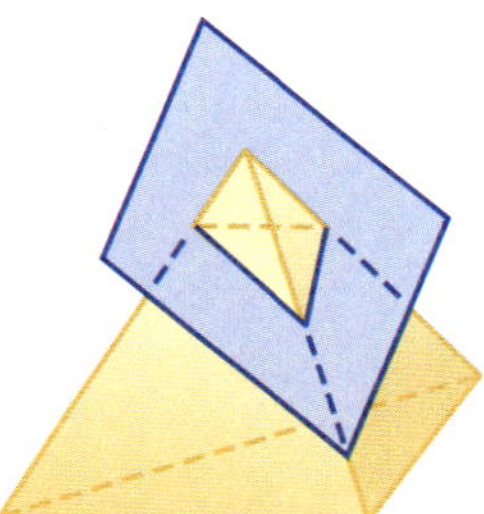

SPORTS For Exercises 10 and 11, use the following information.

A standard basketball is shaped like a sphere.

10. Draw a basketball with a vertical, angled, and horizontal slice.

11. Draw and describe the cross section made by each slice.

SPORTS For Exercises 12 and 13, use the following information.

A soup can is shaped like a cylinder.

12. Draw a soup can with a vertical, angled, and horizontal slice.

13. Draw and describe the cross section made by each slice.

Converting Between Measurement Systems

Dimensional analysis is the process of including units of measurement as factors when you compute. You can use ratios to convert measurements between the two common measurement systems. For example, since 1 in. ≈ 2.54 cm, the ratio $\frac{1\text{ in.}}{2.54\text{ cm}} \approx 1$. So, you can multiply a measurement by this ratio without changing its value.

Conversion Factors for Length	
1 in. ≈ 2.54 cm	1 yd ≈ 0.914 m
1 ft ≈ 0.305 m	1 mi ≈ 1.609 km
Conversion Factors for Capacity and Mass or Weight	
1 fl oz ≈ 29.574 mL	1 qt ≈ 0.946 L
1 pt ≈ 0.473 L	1 gal ≈ 3.785 L
1 oz ≈ 28.35 g	1 lb ≈ 0.454 kg

EXAMPLES Convert Between Systems

1 15 feet to meters

Use 1 ft ≈ 0.305 meters.

$15\text{ ft} \approx 15\text{ ft} \cdot \frac{0.305\text{ m}}{1\text{ ft}}$ — Since 1 ft ≈ 0.305 m, multiply by $\frac{0.305\text{ m}}{1\text{ ft}}$.

$\approx 15\cancel{\text{ft}} \cdot \frac{0.305\text{ m}}{1\cancel{\text{ft}}}$ — Divide out common units, leaving the desired unit, meter.

$\approx 15\text{ ft} \cdot 0.305$ or 4.58 m — Multiply.

So, 15 feet is approximately 4.58 meters.

2 22 kilograms to pounds.

Use 1 lb ≈ 0.454 kg. — Since 1 qt ≈ 0.946 L, multiply by $\frac{1\text{ lb}}{0.454\text{ kg}}$.

$22\text{ kg} \approx 22\text{ kg} \cdot \frac{1\text{ lb}}{0.454\text{ kg}}$ — Divide out common units, leaving the desired unit, pound.

$\approx 22\cancel{\text{kg}} \cdot \frac{1\text{ lb}}{0.454\cancel{\text{kg}}}$

$\approx \frac{22}{0.454}$ or 48.46 pounds. — Divide.

So, 22 kilograms is approximately 48.46 pounds.

Exercises

Complete each conversion. Round to the nearest hundredth.

1. 17 in. ≈ ■ cm
2. 13 L ≈ ■ gal
3. 15 oz ≈ ■ g
4. 12 m ≈ ■ ft
5. 10 L ≈ ■ pt
6. 150 cm ≈ ■ in.
7. 18 fl oz ≈ ■ mL
8. 15 km ≈ ■ mi
9. 8 yd ≈ ■ m
10. 25 mi ≈ ■ km
11. 200 mL ≈ ■ fl oz
12. 12 L ≈ ■ qt
13. 32 ft ≈ ■ m
14. 12 gal ≈ ■ L
15. 575 g ≈ ■ oz
16. 55 lb ≈ ■ kg
17. **ANIMALS** A peregrine falcon can reach a speed of 250 kilometers per hour. How many miles is this per hour?
18. **FOOD** The heaviest apple ever picked weighed about 4 pounds. About how many kilograms did the apple weigh?

12 Volume and Surface Area of Composite Figures

Volume is the measure of space occupied by a three-dimensional figure. The volume of a composite figure can be found by separating the figure into solids whose volumes you know how to find.

EXAMPLE Find the Volume of a Composite Figure

1 Find the volume of the toy house shown at the right.

The toy house is made of one rectangular prism and one triangular prism. Find the volume of each prism.

Rectangular Prism

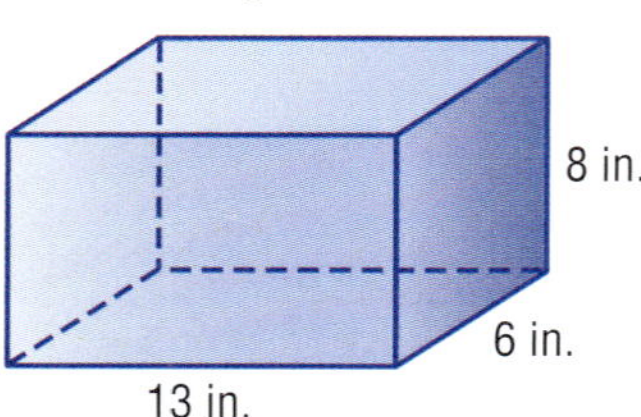

Triangular Prism

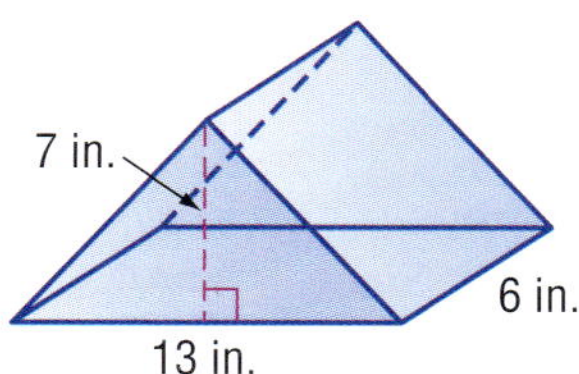

$V = Bh$

$V = (13 \cdot 6)\ 8$ or 624

$V = Bh$

$V = \left(\frac{1}{2} \cdot 13 \cdot 7\right) 6$ or 273

The volume of the toy house is 624 + 273 or 897 cubic inches.

EXAMPLE Find the Surface Area of a Composite Figure

2 Max is painting the mailbox shown. What is the area of the surface that is to be painted? Round to the nearest tenth.

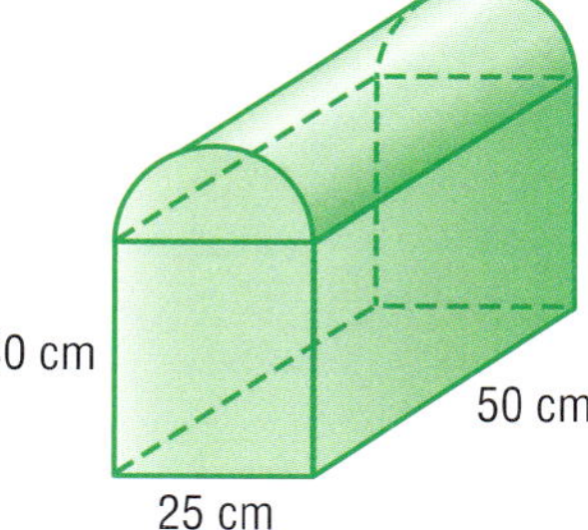

The mailbox is made of one half of one cylinder and one rectangular prism.

Cylinder

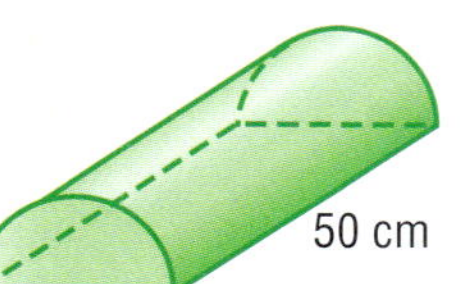

Rectangular Prism

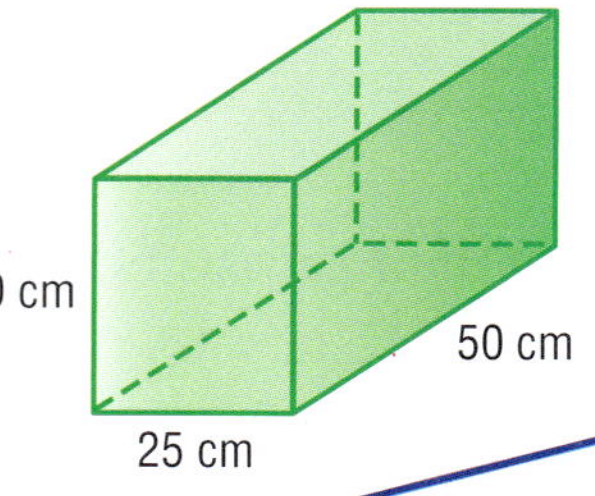

There is only one base needed. The top is covered by the half cylinder.

$S = \frac{2\pi r^2 + 2\pi rh}{2}$

$S = \frac{2\pi(12.5)^2 + 2\pi(12.5)(50)}{2}$

$S \approx 2{,}454.4$

$S = \ell w + 2\ell h + 2wh$

$S = 25 \cdot 50 + 2 \cdot 25 \cdot 30 + 2 \cdot 50$

$S = 5{,}750$

So, the area to be painted is equal to 2,454.4 + 5,750 or 8,204.4 square centimeters.

Exercises

Find the volume of each figure. Round to the nearest tenth if necessary.

1.

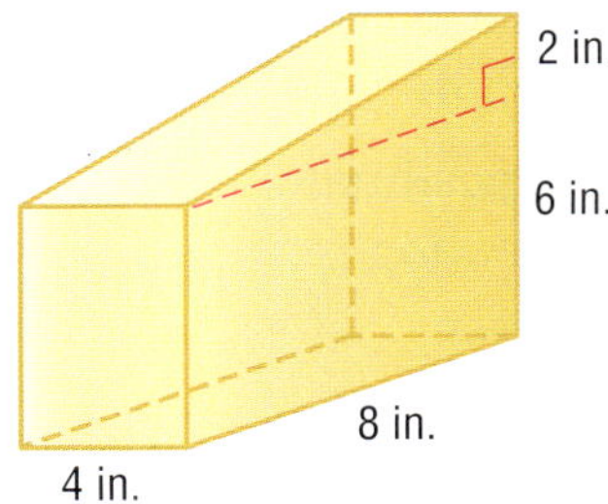

2.

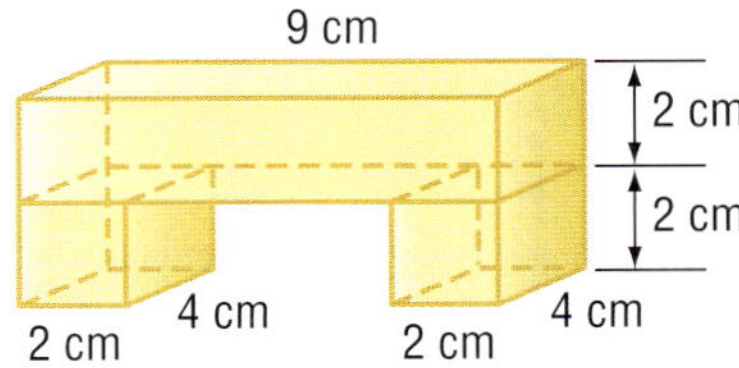

3.

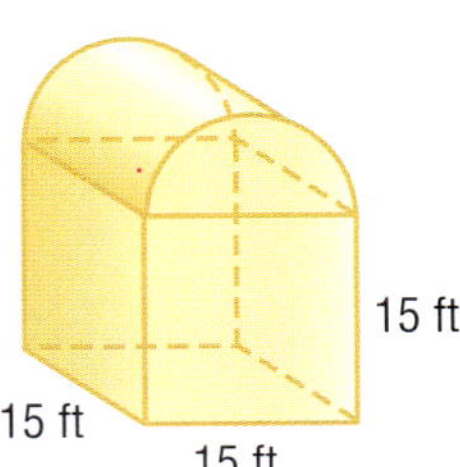

4.

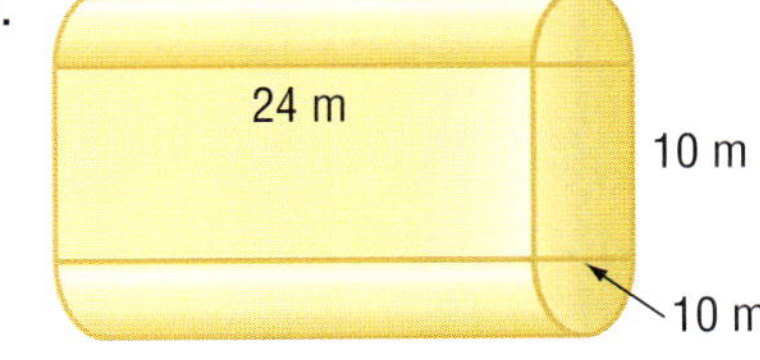

Find the surface area of each figure. Round to the nearest tenth if necessary.

5.

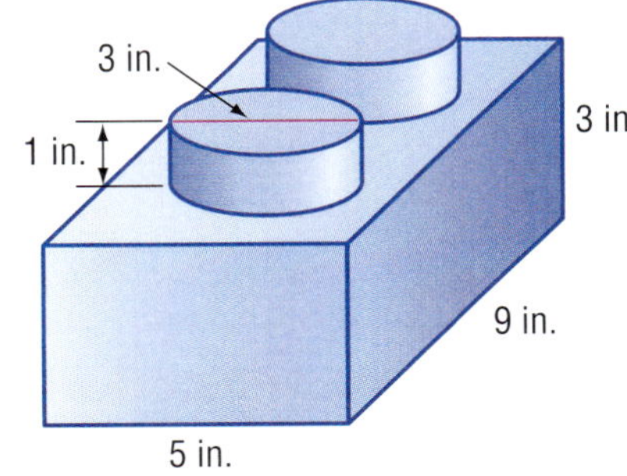

6.

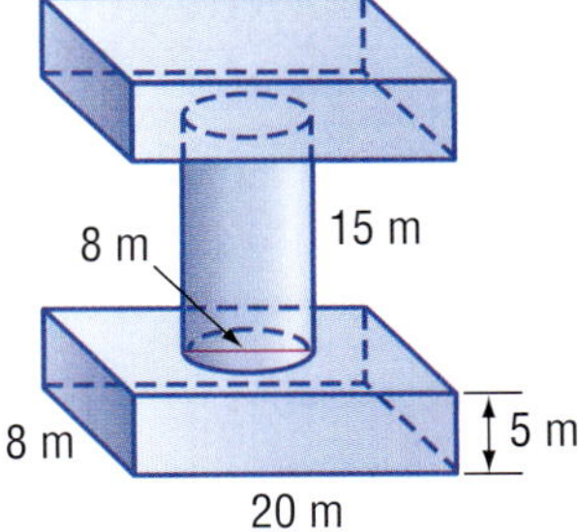

7.

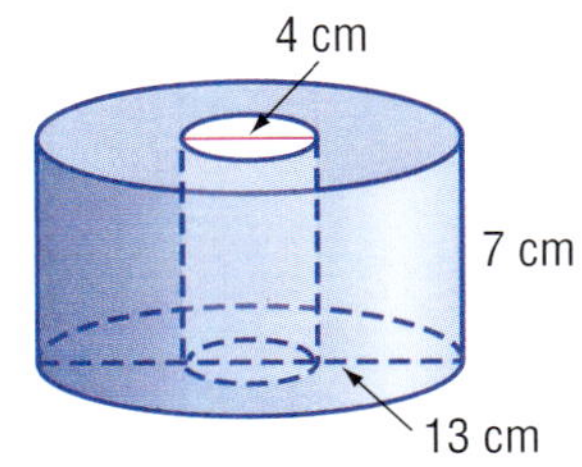

8.

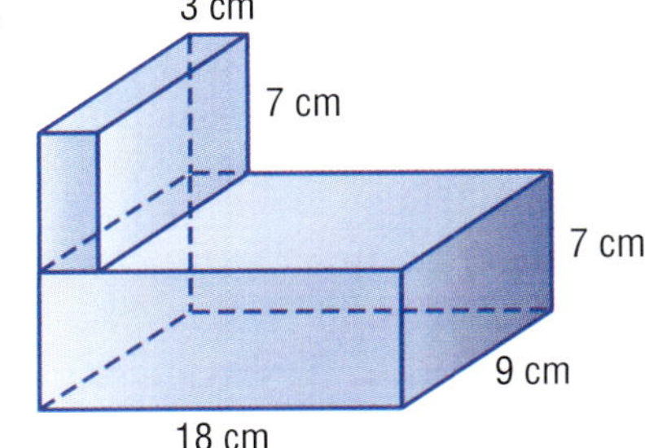

Concepts and Skills Bank

Relative Error and Magnitude

Significant error can occur when estimating or making predictions using large numbers. By comparing estimates to exact calculations, you can identify the amount of error that occurred as a result of rounding or estimating.

The **absolute error** is the magnitude of the difference between the estimate and the actual answer. **Relative error** is the absolute error in estimating a quantity divided by the magnitude of the exact value.

EXAMPLE

Estimate the population increase for New York City from 2003 to 2006. Then find the exact population increase and compare.

New York City	
Year	**Population**
2006	8,214,426
2005	8,143,197
2004	8,104,079
2003	8,085,742

Estimate: 8,200,000 - 8,100,000 = 100,000

Exact: 8,214,426 - 8,085,742 = 128,684

The estimate is much lower than the exact population increase. The absolute error is the difference between the estimate and the exact answer: 128,684 - 100,000, or 28,684 people.

The relative error is $\frac{28{,}684}{128{,}684}$ or approximately 0.22 or 22%.

Exercises

Solve each problem. Compare your estimate to the exact answer by finding the relative error.

1. Find the area of a circle with a radius of 14 centimeters. First calculate the area using 3 as an estimate for π. Then use 3.14 to find the area.

2. Jennifer is planning a wedding reception for 300 guests. The table shows the cost per person for each part of the meal. She needs to know the total approximate cost of the food for the reception.

Cost (per person)	
Appetizer	$2.75
Entrée	$6.75
Beverage	$1.55
Cake	$2.90

3. Antonio is driving 2,452 miles from Albany, New York, to Los Angeles, California. He drives about 68 miles per hour for most of the trip. Antonio estimates how long his trip will take by rounding 68 to 70 and 2,452 to 2,500.

4. As part of their grand opening, a new grocery store decides to give a free gallon of milk to their first 1,500 customers. Normally the milk sells for $3.49 per gallon. How much will the grand-opening special cost the grocery store?

Photo Credits

Cover (t)Created by Michael Trott with Mathematica. From *Graphica 1,* Copyright 1999 Wolfram Media, Inc., (b); Richard Hutchings/Digital Light Source, shot on location courtesy of Busch Gardens/Adventure Island, Tampa Florida; **iv** File Photo; **v** Digital Vision/Getty Images; **vi** Aaron Haupt; **vii** (bl)File Photo, (others) Aaron Haupt; **x-xi** David Frazier/CORBIS; **xii-xiii** Robert Glusic/Photodisc/Getty Images; **xiv-xv** Brand X Pictures/PunchStock; **xvi-xvii** Eastcott Momatiuk/Photodisc/Getty Images; **xviii-xix** Michael Ventura/Alamy Images; **xx-xxi** Kim Karpeles/Alamy Images; **xxii-xxiii** W.A.Hamilton/Alamy; **001** Digital Vision/PunchStock; **003** Reuters/CORBIS; **004** David Frazier/CORBIS; **005** curved-light/Alamy Images; **006** Jonathan Ferrey/Getty Images; **007** Robert Laberge/Getty Images; **008** William Manning/www.williammanning.com/CORBIS; **009** Krista Kennell/ZUMA/CORBIS; **010** Arcaid/CORBIS; **011** Momatiuk-Eastcott/CORBIS; **012** Royalty-Free/CORBIS; **013** PhotoLink/Photodisc/Getty Images; **014** Joe McDonald/Animals Animals; **015** Masterfile; **016** (t)Joel A. Rogers/www.CoasterGallery.com, (b)Daniel Dempster Photography/Alamy Images; **017** (t)Chuck Pefley/Alamy images, (c)Penny Boyd/Alamy Images, (bl)Goodshoot/CORBIS, (br)Marie Read/Animals Animals; **018** (t)Marian Bacon/Animals Animals, (c)Scott Smith/CORBIS, (b)kansastravel.org; **019** (t)Volkmar Wentzel/Getty Images, (cl)John December, (cr)M. Timothy O'Keefe/Alamy Images, (b)Steve Hamblin/Alamy Images; **020-021** JG Photography/Alamy Images; **022** Andre Jenny/Alamy Images; **026** Jose Luis Pelaez, Inc./Blend Images/Getty Images; **032** Stefano Bianchetti/CORBIS; **035** Lawrence Manning/CORBIS; **039** The McGraw-Hill Companies Inc.; **041** (l)Michael Newman/PhotoEdit, (r)David Young-Wolff/PhotoEdit; **042** Kevin Peterson/Photodisc/Getty Images; **045** SW Productions/Photodisc/Getty Images; **049** Photo courtesy of BGSU Photo Services; **052** (l)David Young-Wolff/PhotoEdit, (r)Tony Freeman/PhotoEdit; **054** Tim de Waele/CORBIS; **064** (l)Noel Hendrickson/Digital Vision/Getty Images, (r)Eric and David Hosking/CORBIS; **066** Herbert Kehrer/zefa/CORBIS; **078** SW Productions/Brand X/CORBIS; **080** Chase Jarvis/CORBIS; **090** Kevin Schafer/Photographer's Choice RF/Getty Images; **099** (l)Myrleen Ferguson Cate/PhotoEdit, (r)David Young-Wolff/PhotoEdit; **104** NASA/Photodisc/Getty Images; **106** (l)Cleve Bryant/PhotoEdit, (r)David Young-Wolff/PhotoEdit; **109** Ralph White/CORBIS; **112** John Evans; **116** Lothar Lenz/zefa/CORBIS; **126** Sarah Hadley/Alamy Images; **128** JPL/NASA; **129** Photo by Brad Kuntz; **132** (t)David Siccardi/CORBIS, (bl)Comstock/CORBIS, (br)Dann Tardif/LWA/Blend Images/Getty Images; **137** Stephen Frink/zefa/CORBIS; **139** Eddie Adams/Sygma/CORBIS; **140** Streeter Lecka/Stringer/Getty Images; **143** Jose Luis Pelaez, Inc./Blend Images/Getty Images; **146** (l)Ryan McVay/Photodisc/Getty Images, (r)Comstock/CORBIS; **148** John Evans; **153** John Eder/Stone/Getty Images; **154** Robert Glusic/Photodisc/Getty Images; **160** David Young-Wolff/PhotoEdit; **176-177** Brand X Pictures/PunchStock; **178** Robert Marien/CORBIS; **183** Zigmund Leszczynski/Animals Animals; **184** Mark Duffy/Alamy Images; **185** Raymond K Gehman/National Geographic/Getty Images; **190** Matt Meadows; **193** Jose Luis Pelaez Inc/Blend Images/Getty Images; **195** (l)Seth Kushner/Taxi/Getty Images, (r)Image Source/SuperStock; **198** Comstock/SuperStock; **203** Bäumle Studios/Alamy Images; **208** Steve Bloom/Taxi/Getty Images; **210** (l)RubberBall/SuperStock, (r)RubberBall/SuperStock; **212** Roy Ooms/Masterfile; **216** John Wilkes/SuperStock; **218** United States coin images from the United States Mint; **219** Yiorgos Karahalis/Reuters/CORBIS; **228** Eclipse Studios; **230** Eastcott Momatiuk/Photodisc/Getty Images; **232** Michael Newman/PhotoEdit; **234** Russell Kightley/Photo Researchers; **239** David R. Frazier Photolibrary, Inc./Alamy Images; **240** (l)George Doyle/Stockbyte/Getty Images, (r)Michael Newman/PhotoEdit; **242** Diane Macdonald/Stockbyte/Getty Images; **244** Stockbyte/Getty Images; **248** Getty Images; **254** Garry Black/Masterfile; **256** Rob Lewine/CORBIS; **262** Jeff Greenberg/Alamy Images; **268** Phyllis Greenberg/Animals Animals; **270** (l)Jack Hollingsworth/CORBIS, (r)Barbara Penoyar/Photodisc/Getty Images; **278-279** Christie's Images/CORBIS; **280** Alan Schein/zefa/CORBIS; **283** Brian Snyder/Reuters/CORBIS; **285** (l)Tom Brakefield/CORBIS, (r)Judith Collins/Alamy Images; **286** (l)Donna Day/ImageState, (r)JupiterImages/Thinkstock/Alamy Images; **287** David Young-Wolff/PhotoEdit; **289** Doug Menuez/Photodisc/Getty Images; **290** Ryan McVay/Stone+/Getty Images; **291** Don Emmert/AFP/Getty Images; **295** Thomas Allen/Digital Vision/Getty Images; **298** John Lambert/Brand X/CORBIS; **300** Norbert Wu/Minden Pictures; **305** age fotostock / SuperStock; **307** Lawrence Lawry/Photodisc/Getty Images; **308** (t)Bruce Edwards/America 24-7/Getty Images, (bl)Jonathan Nourok/PhotoEdit, (br)Michael Newman/PhotoEdit; **312** CORBIS; **314** Alley Cat Productions/Brand X/CORBIS; **318** KS Studios; **319** Michael Newman/PhotoEdit; **325** Bilderbuch/Design Pics/CORBIS; **331** Franz Marc Frei/CORBIS; **340** Masterfile; **344** DLILLC/CORBIS; **347** G. Biss/Masterfile; **350** Ingemar Edfalk/Pixonnet.com/Alamy Images; **352** Donna Ikenberry/Animals Animals; **354** Digital Vision/Getty Images; **356** Big Cheese Photo/SuperStock; **358** D. Robert & Lorri Franz/CORBIS; **359** (l)FIRST LIGHT ASSOCIATED PHOTOGRAPHERS, (r)Flying Colours Ltd/Digital Vision/Getty Images; **363** Alaskastock; **366** Adrian Peacock/Digital Vision/Getty Images; **374** (l)RubberBall/ImageState, (r)Barbara Penoyar/Photodisc/Getty Images; **376** Gregor Schuster/Photographer's Choice RF/Getty Images; **380** Don Mason/Blend Images/Getty Images; **392-393** Matthias Kulka/zefa/CORBIS; **394** Michael Ventura/Alamy Images; **399** Harald Sund/Photographer's Choice/Getty Images; **400** (l)MedioImages/Alamy Images, (r)Tony Freeman/PhotoEdit; **406** CORBIS; **410** Barbara Peacock/Taxi/Getty Images; **411** JUPITERIMAGES/Liquid Library Value/Alamy; **413** Brandon D. Cole/CORBIS; **419** Daryl Balfour/The Image Bank/Getty Images; **424** Gabe Palmer/Alamy Images; **431** Bob Daemmrich/Stock Boston; **438** Paul Costello/Getty Images; **441** photocuisine/CORBIS; **446** Andrew J.G. Bell; Eye Ubiquitous/CORBIS; **458** Robert Michael/ CORBIS; **461** Bettmann/ CORBIS; **468** Ariel Skelley/CORBIS; **469** Tom Hauck/Getty Images; **473** O'Brien Productions/CORBIS; **476** Shenval/Alamy Images; **477** Tetra Images/Alamy Images; **481** Doug Menuez/Getty Images; **483** (l)George Doyle/Stockbyte Platinum/Alamy Images, (r)Jose Luis Pelaez Inc/Blend Images/Getty Images; **484** Laura Sifferlin; **488** Zefa RF/Alamy Images; **492** United States coin images from the United States Mint; **506-507** Oberto Gill/Beateworks/CORBIS; **508** Dennis MacDonald/Alamy Images; **510** Kelly-Mooney Photography/CORBIS; **519** Stephen Dalton/Animals Animals; **526** Jeff Greenberg/PhotoEdit; **528** Damir Frkovic/Masterfile; **530** Ryan McVay/Photodisc/Getty Images; **537** (l)Michael Newman/PhotoEdit, (r)Michelle Pedone/zefa/CORBIS; **544** Martin Shields/Alamy Images; **548** (t)Andriy Doriy Textures/Alamy Images, (b)Somos/Veer/Getty Images; **550** (l)Jeff Greenberg/PhotoEdit, (r)Todd Gipstein/National Geographic/Getty Images; **556** Artwork courtesy of Marjorie Rice; **560** Robert Spoenlein/zefa/CORBIS; **561** (t)Jose Fuste Raga/CORBIS, (b)Allen Wallace/Photonica/Getty Images; **570** Kim Karpeles/Alamy Images; **573** Don Farrall/Photodisc/Getty Images; **575** Jules Frazier/Photodisc/Getty Images; **580** Byron Schumaker/Alamy; **583** Getty Images; **584** Iconotec/Alamy Images; **587** (l)BananaStock/PictureQuest/Jupiter Images, (t)Studio Wartenberg/zefa/CORBIS, (cr)Klaus Leidorf/zefa/CORBIS, (r)BananaStock/PunchStock; **590** United States coin images from the United States Mint; **592** (l)MedioImages/CORBIS, (r)Michael Newman/PhotoEdit; **594** Jim Esposito Photography LLC/Photodisc/Getty Images; **604** Judith Collins/Alamy images; **605** (t)C Squared Studios/Photodisc/Getty Images, (c)Glencoe, (b)PhotoLink/Photodisc/Getty Images; **608** Phil Degginger/Alamy Images; **610** Chris Bell/Taxi/Getty Images; **611** (tl)Mark Karrass/CORBIS, (t)Ryan McVay/Photodisc/Getty Images, (b)Lew Robertson/CORBIS; **614** Charles Gupton/CORBIS; **617** Keate/Masterfile; **620** Tony Freeman/PhotoEdit; **621** Duncan Usher/Foto Natura/Minden Pictures; **629** Gregor Schuster/zefa/CORBIS; **634** Horizons Companies; **638** Myrleen Ferguson Cate/PhotoEdit; **641** Steve Bly/Alamy Images; **645** (l)Comstock/SuperStock, (r)Stockbyte/SuperStock; **646** Michael Newman/PhotoEdit; **652** Daly & Newton/Getty Images; **657** W.A.Hamilton/Alamy; **666** Eclipse Studios; **LA0-LA1** Brand X Pictures/Punchstock; **LA2** Charles O'Rear/CORBIS; **LA3** Chris A Crumley/Alamy Images; **LA9** Doug Menuez/Getty Images; **LA13** allOver photography/Alamy Images; **LA14** Brand X Pictures/PunchStock; **LA17** Royalty-Free-CORBIS; **LA18** dbphotos/Alamy Images; **LA21** Merlin D. Tuttle, Bat Conservation International; **LA24** Royalty-Free-CORBIS

Glossary/Glosario

Glossary/Glosario

Math Online A mathematics multilingual glossary is available at glencoe.com.

The glossary includes the following languages.

Arabic	Cantonese	Korean	Tagalog
Bengali	English	Russian	Urdu
Brazilian Portuguese	Haitian Creole	Spanish	Vietnamese
	Hmong		

Cómo usar el glosario en español:

1. Busca el término en inglés que desees encontrar.
2. El término en español, junto con la definición, se encuentran en la columna de la derecha.

English / Español

A

absolute value (p. 81) The distance the number is from zero on a number line.

valor absoluto Distancia a la que se encuentra un número de cero en la recta numérica.

acute angle (p. 511) An angle with a measure greater than 0° and less than 90°.

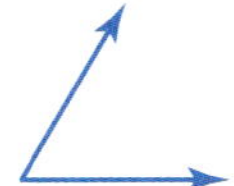

ángulo agudo Ángulo que mide más de 0° y menos de 90°.

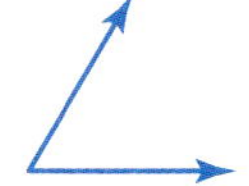

acute triangle (p. 525) A triangle having three acute angles.

triángulo acutángulo Triángulo con tres ángulos agudos.

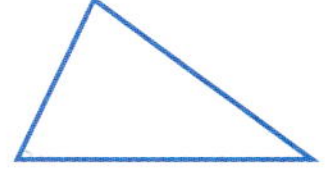

Addition Property of Equality (p. 138) If you add the same number to each side of an equation, the two sides remain equal.

propiedad de adición de la igualdad Si sumas el mismo número a ambos lados de una ecuación, los dos lados permanecen iguales.

additive inverse (p. 96) The opposite of an integer. The sum of an integer and its additive inverse is zero.

inverso aditivo El opuesto de un entero. La suma de un entero y su inverso aditivo es cero.

adjacent angles (p. 511) Angles that have the same vertex, share a common side, and do not overlap.

ángulos adyacentes Ángulos que comparten el mismo vértice y un común lado, pero no se sobreponen.

algebra (p. 44) The branch of mathematics that involves expressions with variables.

álgebra Rama de las matemáticas que involucra expresiones con variables.

algebraic expression (p. 44) A combination of variables, numbers, and at least one operation.

expresión algebraica Combinación de variables, números y por lo menos una operación.

analyze (p. 397) To describe, summarize, and compare data.

analizar Describir, resumir o comparar datos.

angle (p. 510) Two rays with a common endpoint form an angle. The rays and vertex are used to name the angle.

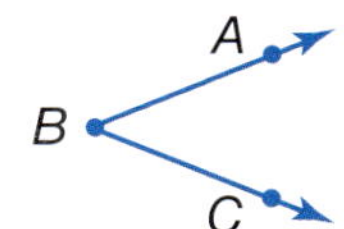

$\angle ABC$, $\angle CBA$, or $\angle B$

ángulo Dos rayos con un extremo común forman un ángulo. Los rayos y el vértice se usan para nombrar el ángulo.

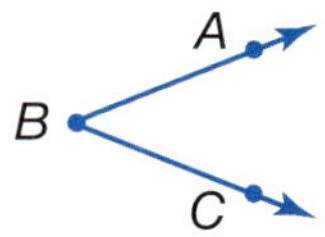

$\angle ABC$, $\angle CBA$ o $\angle B$

area (p. 157) The number of square units needed to cover a surface enclosed by a geometric figure.

área El número de unidades cuadradas necesarias para cubrir una superficie cerrada por una figura geométrica.

arithmetic sequence (p. 57) A sequence in which each term is found by adding the same number to the previous term.

sucesión aritmética Sucesión en que cada término se encuentra sumando el mismo número al término anterior.

Associative Property (p. 54) The way in which three numbers are grouped when they are added or multiplied does not change their sum or product.

propiedad asociativa La manera de agrupar tres números al sumarlos o multiplicarlos no cambia su suma o producto.

average (p. 402) The mean of a set of data.

promedio La media de un conjunto de datos.

B

bar graph (p. 415) A graphic form using bars to make comparisons of statistics.

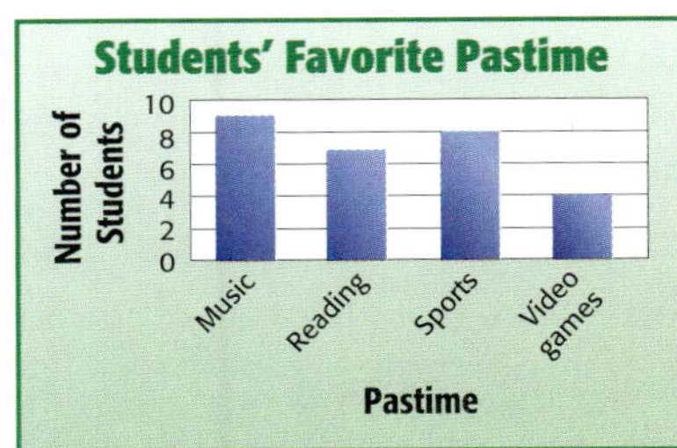

gráfica de barras Forma gráfica que usa barras para hacer comparaciones estadísticas.

bar notation (p. 197) In repeating decimals, the line or bar placed over the digits that repeat. For example, $2.\overline{63}$ indicates that the digits 63 repeat.

notación de barra Línea o barra que se coloca sobre los dígitos que se repiten en decimales periódicos. Por ejemplo, $2.\overline{63}$ indica que los dígitos 63 se repiten.

base (p. 30) In a power, the number used as a factor. In 10^3, the base is 10. That is, $10^3 = 10 \times 10 \times 10$.

base En una potencia, el número usado como factor. En 10^3, la base es 10. Es decir, $10^3 = 10 \times 10 \times 10$.

base (p. 572) The base of a parallelogram or triangle is any side of the figure. The bases of a trapezoid are the parallel sides.

base La base de un paralelogramo o triángulo es el lado de la figura. Las bases de un trapecio son los lados paralelos.

base (p. 603) The top or bottom face of a three-dimensional figure.

base La cara inferior o superior de una figura tridimensional.

biased sample (p. 439) A sample drawn in such a way that one or more parts of the population are favored over others.

muestra sesgada Muestra en que se favorece una o más partes de una población.

center (p. 584) The given point from which all points on a circle or sphere are the same distance.

centro Un punto dado del cual equidistan todos los puntos de un círculo o de una esfera.

circle (p. 584) The set of all points in a plane that are the same distance from a given point called the center.

círculo Conjunto de todos los puntos en un plano que equidistan de un punto dado llamado centro.

circle graph (p. 518) A type of statistical graph used to compare parts of a whole.

Area of Oceans

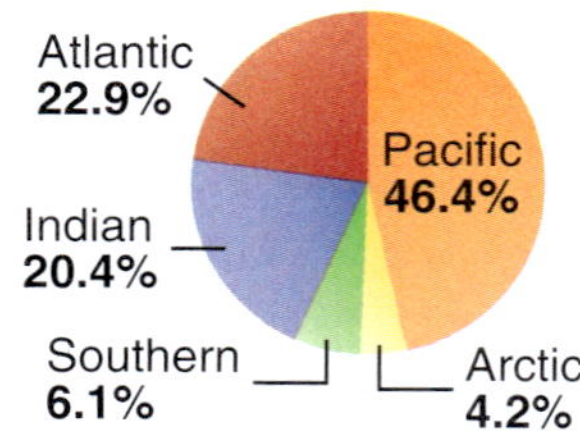

gráfica circular Tipo de gráfica estadística que se usa para comparar las partes de un todo.

Área de superficie de los océanos

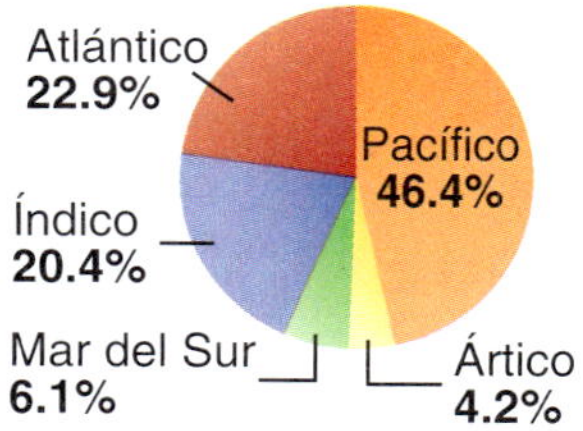

circumference (p. 584) The distance around a circle.

circunferencia La distancia alrededor de un círculo.

cluster (p. 397) Data that are grouped closely together.

agrupamiento Datos estrechamente agrupados.

coefficient (p. 45) The numerical factor of a term that contains a variable.

coeficiente El factor numérico de un término que contiene una variable.

combination (p. 480) An arrangement, or listing, of objects in which order is not important.

combinación Arreglo o lista de objetos donde el orden no es importante.

common denominator (p. 215) A common multiple of the denominators of two or more fractions. 24 is a common denominator for $\frac{1}{3}$, $\frac{5}{8}$, and $\frac{3}{4}$ because 24 is the LCM of 3, 8, and 4.

común denominador El múltiplo común de los denominadores de dos o más fracciones. 24 es un denominador común para $\frac{1}{3}$, $\frac{5}{8}$ y $\frac{3}{4}$ porque 24 es el mcm de 3, 8 y 4.

Commutative Property (p. 54) The order in which two numbers are added or multiplied does not change their sum or product.

propiedad conmutativa El orden en que se suman o multiplican dos números no afecta su suma o producto.

complementary angles (p. 514) Two angles are complementary if the sum of their measures is 90°.

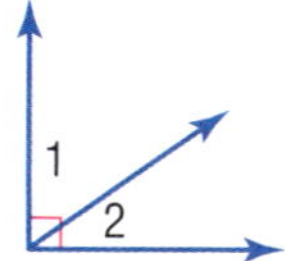

∠1 and ∠2 are complementary angles.

ángulos complementarios Dos ángulos son complementarios si la suma de sus medidas es 90°.

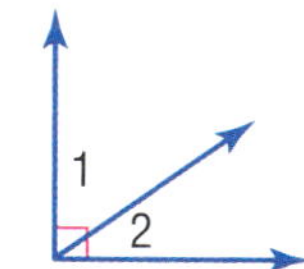

∠1 y ∠2 son complementarios.

complementary events (p. 462) The events of one outcome happening and that outcome not happening are complementary events. The sum of the probabilities of complementary events is 1.

eventos complementarios Se dice de los eventos de un resultado que ocurren y el resultado que no ocurre. La suma de las probabilidades de eventos complementarios es 1.

complex figure (p. 596) A figure made of circles, rectangles, squares, and other two-dimensional figures.

figura compleja Una figura compuesta por círculos, rectángulos, cuadrados y otras dos figuras bidimencionales.

composite number (p. 181) A whole number greater than 1 that has more than two factors.

número compuesto Un número entero mayor que 1 que tiene más de dos factores.

compound event (p. 492) An event consisting of two or more simple events.

evento compuesto Un evento que consiste en dos o más eventos simples.

cone (p. 604) A three-dimensional figure with a curved surface and a circular base.

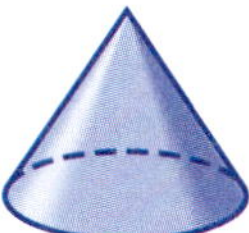

cono Figura tridimensional con una superficie curva y una base circular.

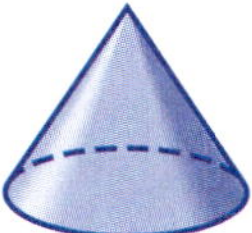

congruent angles (p. 511) Angles that have the same measure.

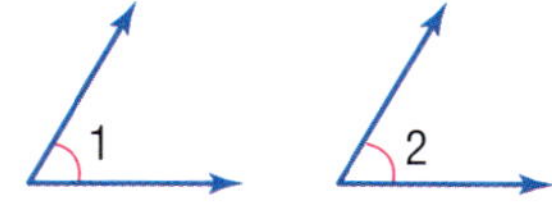

∠1 and ∠2 are congruent angles.

ángulos congruentes Ángulos que tienen la misma medida.

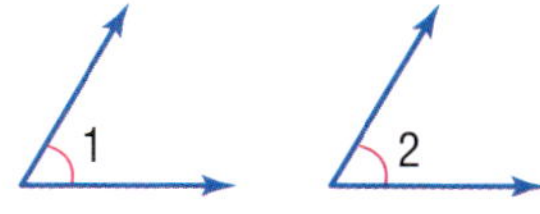

∠1 y ∠2 son congruentes.

congruent figures (p. 554) Figures with equal corresponding sides of equal length and corresponding angles of equal measure.

figuras congruentes Figuras cuyos lados y ángulos correspondientes son iguales.

congruent segments (p. 525) Segments having the same measure.

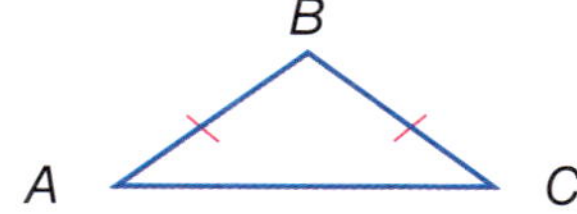

Side $\overline{AB}$ is congruent to side $\overline{BC}$.

segmentos congruentes Segmentos que tienen la misma medida.

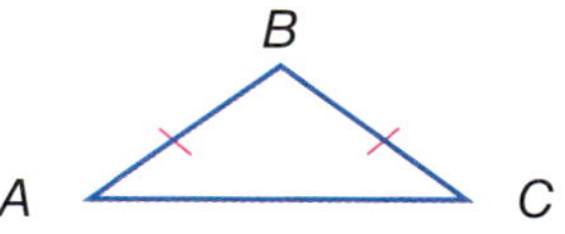

$\overline{AB}$ es congruente a $\overline{BC}$.

convenience sample (p. 439) A sample which includes members of the population that are easily accessed.

muestra de conveniencia Muestra que incluye miembros de una población fácilmente accesibles.

coordinate plane (p. 88) A plane in which a horizontal number line and a vertical number line intersect at their zero points. Also called a coordinate grid.

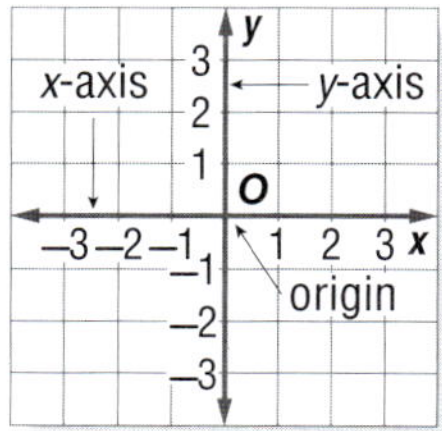

plano de coordenadas Plano en el cual se han trazado dos rectas numéricas, una horizontal y una vertical, que se intersecan en sus puntos cero. También conocido como sistema de coordenadas.

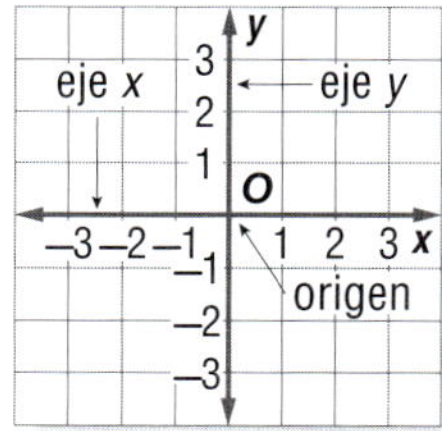

corresponding angles (p. 540) Congruent angles of similar figures.

ángulos correspondientes Ángulos iguales de figuras semejantes.

corresponding sides (p. 540) Congruent or proportional sides of similar figures.

lados correspondientes Lados iguales o proporcionales de figuras semejantes.

counterexample (p. 56) An example showing that a statement is not true.

contraejemplo Ejemplo que demuestra que un enunciado no es verdadero.

cross product (p. 310) In a proportion, a cross product is the product of the numerator of one ratio and the denominator of the other ratio.

productos cruzados En una proporción, un producto cruzado es el producto del numerador de una razón y el denominador de la otra razón.

cubed (p. 30) The product in which a number is a factor three times. Two cubed is 8 because $2 \times 2 \times 2 = 8$.

al cubo El producto de un número por sí mismo, tres veces. Dos al cubo es 8 porque $2 \times 2 \times 2 = 8$.

cylinder (p. 604) A three-dimensional figure with two parallel congruent circular bases.

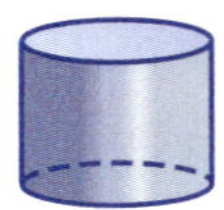

cilindro Figura tridimensional que tiene dos bases circulares congruentes y paralelas.

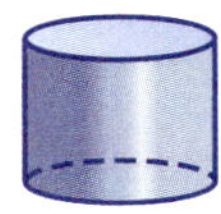

D

data (p. 376) Pieces of information, which are often numerical.

datos Información, la cual a menudo se presenta de manera numérica.

decagon (p. 546) A polygon having ten sides.

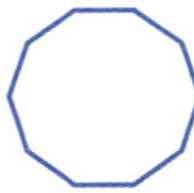

decágono Un polígono con diez lados.

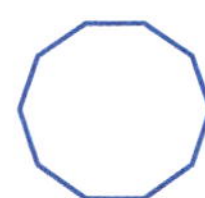

defining the variable (p. 50) Choosing a variable to represent an unknown value in a problem, and using it to write an expression or equation to solve the problem.

definir una variable El elegir una variable para representar un valor desconocido en un problema y usarla para escribir una expresión o ecuación para resolver el problema.

degrees (p. 510) The most common unit of measure for angles. If a circle were divided into 360 equal-sized parts, each part would have an angle measure of 1 degree.

grados La unidad más común para medir ángulos. Si un círculo se divide en 360 partes iguales, cada parte tiene una medida angular de 1 grado.

dependent events (p. 493) Two or more events in which the outcome of one event affects the outcome of the other event(s).

eventos dependientes Dos o más eventos en que el resultado de un evento afecta el resultado de otro u otros eventos.

diameter (p. 584) The distance across a circle through its center.

diámetro La distancia a través de un círculo pasando por el centro.

disjoint events (p. 494) Events that cannot happen at the same time.

eventos disjuntos Eventos que no pueden ocurrir al mismo tiempo.

Distributive Property (p. 53) To multiply a sum by a number, multiply each addend of the sum by the number outside the parentheses.

propiedad distributiva Para multiplicar una suma por un número, multiplica cada sumando de la suma por el número fuera del paréntesis.

Division Property of Equality (p. 142) If you divide each side of an equation by the same nonzero number, the two sides remain equal.

propiedad de igualdad de la división Si divides ambos lados de una ecuación entre el mismo número no nulo, los lados permanecen iguales.

domain (p. 63) The set of input values for a function.

dominio El conjunto de valores de entrada de una función.

E

edge (p. 603) The segment formed by intersecting faces of a three-dimensional figure.

arista Segmento de recta formado por la intersección de las caras en una figura tridimensional.

equation (p. 49) A mathematical sentence that contains an equals sign, =.

ecuación Enunciado matemático que contiene un signo de igualdad, =.

equilateral triangle (p. 525) A triangle having three congruent sides.

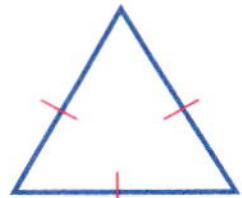

triángulo equilátero Triángulo con tres lados congruentes.

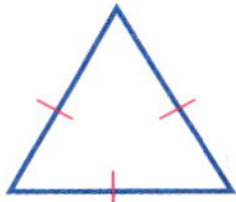

equivalent expressions (p. 53) Expressions that have the same value.

expresiones equivalentes Expresiones que tienen el mismo valor.

equivalent fractions (p. 192) Fractions that have the same value. $\frac{2}{3}$ and $\frac{4}{6}$ are equivalent fractions.

fracciones equivalentes Fracciones que tienen el mismo valor. $\frac{2}{3}$ y $\frac{4}{6}$ son fracciones equivalentes.

equivalent ratios (p. 288) Two ratios that have the same value.

razones equivalentes Dos razones que tienen el mismo valor.

evaluate (p. 31) To find the value of an expression.

evaluar Calcular el valor de una expresión. probabilidad experimental

experimental probability (p. 486) An estimated probability based on the relative frequency of positive outcomes occurring during an experiment.

probabilidad experimental Estimado de una probabilidad que se basa en la frecuencia relativa de los resultados positivos que ocurren durante un experimento.

exponent (p. 30) In a power, the number that tells how many times the base is used as a factor. In 5^3, the exponent is 3. That is, $5^3 = 5 \times 5 \times 5$.

exponente En una potencia, el número que indica las veces que la base se usa como factor. En 5^3, el exponente es 3. Es decir, $5^3 = 5 \times 5 \times 5$.

exponential form (p. 31) Numbers written with exponents.

forma exponencial Números escritos usando exponentes.

 F

face (p. 603) The flat surface of a three-dimensional figure.

cara Superficies planas de una figura tridimensional.

factors (p. 30) Two or more numbers that are multiplied together to form a product.

factores Dos o más números que se multiplican entre sí para formar un producto.

factor tree (p. 182) A diagram showing the prime factorization of a number. The factors branch out from the previous factors until all of the factors are prime numbers.

diagrama de árbol Diagrama que muestra la factorización prima de un número. Los factores se ramifican a partir de los factores previos hasta que todos los factores son números primos.

formula (p. 144) An equation that shows the relationship among certain quantities.

fórmula Ecuación que muestra la relación entre ciertas cantidades.

function (p. 63) A relation in which each element of the input is paired with exactly one element of the output according to a specified rule.

función Relación en que cada elemento de entrada es apareado con un único elemento de salida, según una regla específica.

function rule (p. 63) The operation performed on the input of a function.

regla de función Operación que se efectúa en el valor de entrada.

function table (p. 63) A table used to organize the input numbers, output numbers, and the function rule.

tabla de funciones Tabla que organiza las entradas, la regla y las salidas de una función.

Fundamental Counting Principle (p. 471) Uses multiplication of the number of ways each event in an experiment can occur to find the number of possible outcomes in a sample space.

Principio Fundamental de Contar Este principio usa la multiplicación del número de veces que puede ocurrir cada evento en un experimento para calcular el número de posibles resultados en un espacio muestral.

G

gram (p. 304) A unit of mass in the metric system equivalent to 0.001 kilogram.

gramo Unidad de masa del sistema métrico. Un gramo equivale a 0.001 de kilogramo.

graph (p. 80) The process of placing a point on a number line at its proper location.

graficar Proceso de dibujar o trazar un punto en una recta numérica en su ubicación correcta.

greatest common factor (GCF) (p. 186) The greatest of the common factors of two or more numbers. The GCF of 18 and 24 is 6.

máximo común divisor (MCD) El mayor factor común de dos o más números. El MCD de 18 y 24 es 6.

H

height (p. 572) The length of the segment perpendicular to the base with endpoints on opposite sides. In a triangle, the distance from a base to the opposite vertex.

altura Longitud del segmento perpendicular a la base y con extremos en lados opuestos. En un triángulo, es la distancia desde una base al vértice opuesto.

heptagon (p. 546) A polygon having seven sides.

heptágono Polígono con siete lados.

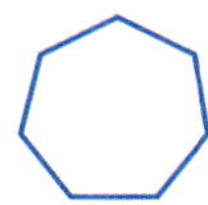

hexagon (p. 546) A polygon having six sides.

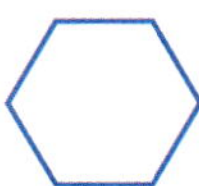

hexágono Polígono con seis lados.

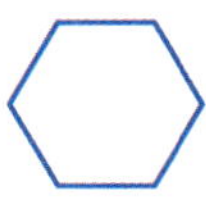

histogram (p. 416) A special kind of bar graph in which the bars are used to represent the frequency of numerical data that have been organized in intervals.

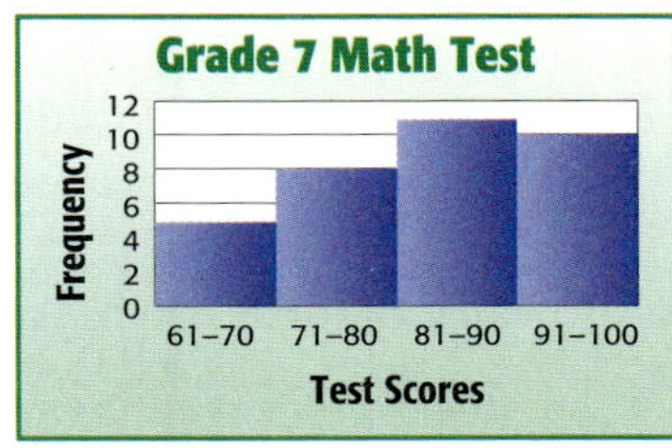

histograma Tipo especial de gráfica de barras que usa barras para representar la frecuencia de los datos numéricos, los cuales han sido organizados en intervalos iguales.

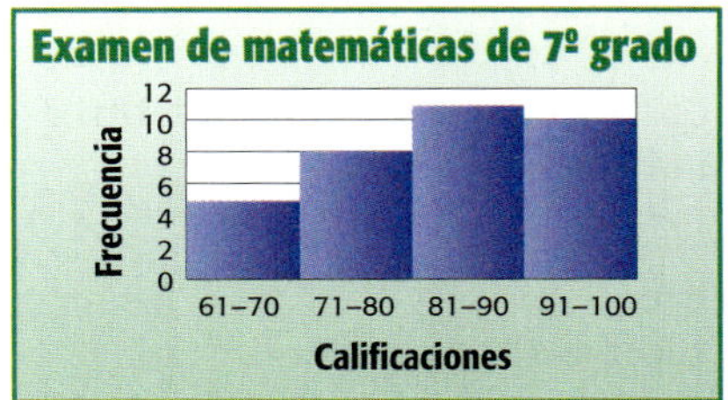

hypotenuse (p. 640) The side opposite the right angle in a right triangle.

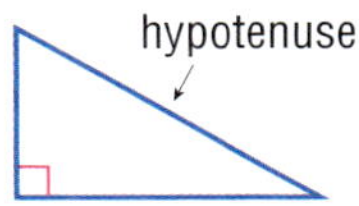

hipotenusa El lado opuesto al ángulo recto en un triángulo rectángulo.

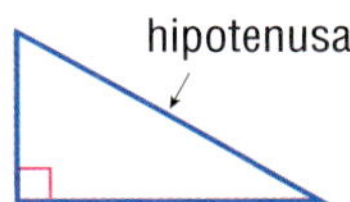

I

Identity Property (p. 54) The sum of an addend and 0 is the addend. The product of a factor and 1 is the factor.

propiedad de identidad La suma de un sumando y 0 es el sumando mismo. El producto de un factor y 1 es el factor mismo.

independent events (p. 492) Two or more events in which the outcome of one event does not affect the outcome of the other event(s).

eventos independientes Dos o más eventos en los cuales el resultado de uno de ellos no afecta el resultado de los otros eventos.

indirect measurement (p. 542) Finding a measurement by using similar triangles and writing a proportion.

medida indirecta Técnica que se usa para calcular una medida a partir de triángulos semejantes y proporciones.

integer (p. 80) Any number from the set $\{\ldots, -4, -3, -2, -1, 0, 1, 2, 3, 4, \ldots\}$

entero Todo número del conjunto $\{\ldots, -4, -3, -2, -1, 0, 1, 2, 3, 4, \ldots\}$

inverse operations (p. 136) Operations that "undo" each other. Addition and subtraction are inverse operations.

operaciones inversas Operaciones que se "anulan" mutuamente. La adición y la sustracción son operaciones inversas.

irrational number (p. 637) A number that cannot be expressed as the quotient of two integers.

número irracional Número que no se puede expresar como el cociente de dos enteros.

isosceles triangle (p. 525) A triangle having at least two congruent sides.

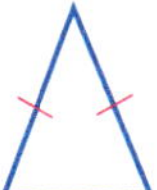

triángulo isósceles Triángulo que tiene por lo menos dos lados congruentes.

K

kilogram (p. 304) The base unit of mass in the metric system equivalent to 1,000 grams.

kilogramo Unidad fundamental de masa del sistema métrico. Un kilogramo equivale a mil gramos.

L

lateral face (p. 603) One side of a three-dimesional figure.

cara lateral Lado de una figura tridimensional.

leaf (p. 410) The second greatest place value of data in a stem-and-leaf plot.

hoja El segundo valor de posición mayor en un diagrama de tallo y hojas.

least common denominator (LCD) (p. 215) The least common multiple of the denominators of two or more fractions.

mínimo común denominador (mcd) El menor múltiplo común de los denominadores de dos o más fracciones.

least common multiple (LCM) (p. 211) The least of the common multiples of two or more numbers. The LCM of 2 and 3 is 6.

mínimo común múltiplo (mcm) El menor múltiplo común de dos o más números. El mcm de 2 y 3 es 6.

leg (p. 640) Either of the two sides that form the right angle of a right triangle.

cateto Cualquiera de los lados que forman el ángulo recto de un triángulo rectángulo.

like fractions (p. 236) Fractions that have the same denominator.

fracciones semejantes Fracciones con el mismo denominador.

line graph (p. 426) A type of statistical graph using lines to show how values change over a period of time.

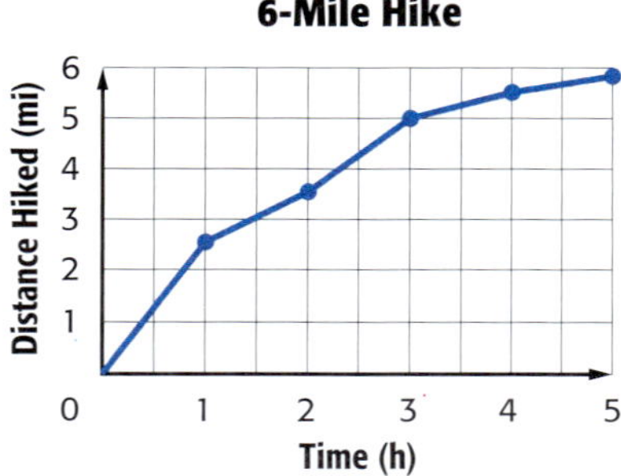

gráfica lineal Tipo de gráfica estadística que usa segmentos de recta para mostrar cómo cambian los valores durante un período de tiempo.

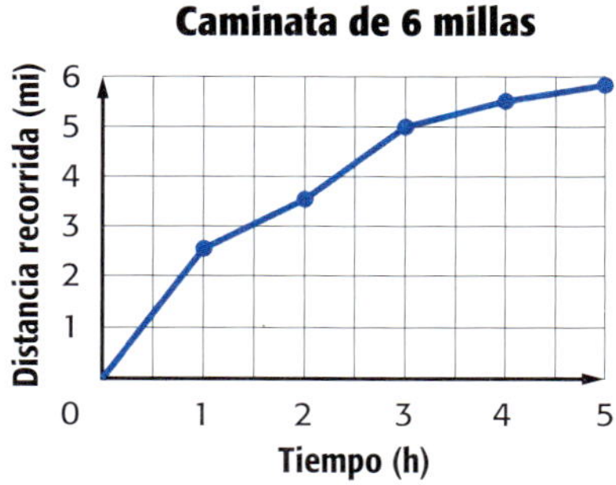

line of reflection (p. 559) The line over which a figure is reflected.

eje de reflexión La línea sobre la cual se refleja una figura.

line of symmetry (p. 558) A line that divides a figure into two halves that are reflections of each other.

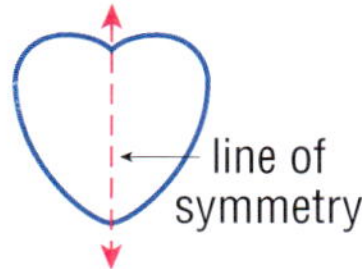

eje de simetría Recta que divide una figura en dos mitades que son reflexiones entre sí.

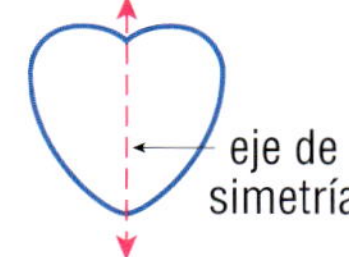

line plot (p. 396) A diagram that shows the frequency of data. An × is placed above a number on a number line each time that number occurs in a set of data.

esquema lineal Grafica que muestra la frecuencia de datos. Se coloca una × sobre la recta numérica, cada vez que el número aparece en un conjunto de datos.

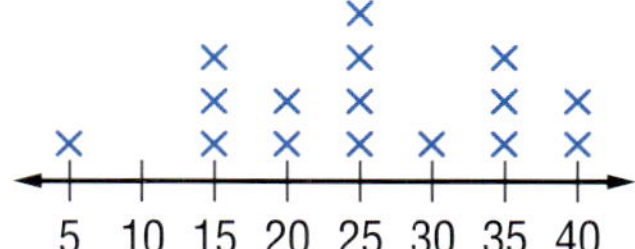

line symmetry (p. 558) Figures that match exactly when folded in half have line symmetry.

simetría lineal Exhiben simetría lineal las figuras que coinciden exactamente al doblarse una sobre otra.

linear equation (p. 164) An equation for which the graph is a straight line.

ecuación lineal Ecuación cuya gráfica es una recta.

liter (p. 304) The base unit of capacity in the metric system. A liter is a little more than a quart.

litro Unidad básica de capacidad del sistema métrico. Un litro es un poco más de un cuarto de galón.

mean (p. 402) The sum of the data divided by the number of items in the data set.

media La suma de los datos dividida entre el número total de artículos en el conjunto de datos.

measures of central tendency (p. 402) Numbers that are used to describe the center of a set of data. These measures include the mean, median, and mode.

medidas de tendencia central Números que se usan para describir el centro de un conjunto de datos. Estas medidas incluyen la media, la mediana y la moda.

median (p. 403) The middle number in a set of data when the data are ordered from least to greatest. If the data has an even number of items, the median is the mean of the two numbers closer to the middle.

mediana El número del medio en un conjunto de datos cuando los datos se ordenan de menor a mayor. Si los datos tienen un número par de artículos, la mediana es la media de los dos números más cercanos al medio.

meter (p. 304) The base unit of length in the metric system.

metro Unidad fundamental de longitud del sistema métrico.

metric system (p. 304) A base-ten system of measurement using the base units: meter for length, kilogram for mass, and liter for capacity.

sistema métrico Sistema de medidas de base diez que usa las unidades fundamentales: metro para longitud, kilogramo para masa y litro para capacidad.

mode (p. 403) The number or numbers that appear most often in a set of data. If there are two or more numbers that occur most often, all of them are modes.

moda El número o números que aparece con más frecuencia en un conjunto de datos. Si hay dos o más números que ocurren con más frecuencia, todosellos son modas.

multiple (p. 211) The product of a number and any whole number.

múltiplo El producto de un número y cualquier número entero.

Multiplication Property of Equality (p. 259) If you multiply each side of an equation by the same nonzero number, the two sides remain equal.

propiedad de multiplicación de la igualdad Si multiplicas ambos lados de una ecuación por el mismo número no nulo, lo lados permanecen iguales.

multiplicative inverse (p. 258) The product of a number and its multiplicative inverse is 1. The multiplicative inverse of $\frac{2}{3}$ is $\frac{3}{2}$.

inverso multiplicativo El producto de un número y su inverso multiplicativo es 1. El inverso multiplicativo de $\frac{2}{3}$ es $\frac{3}{2}$.

N

negative integer (p. 80) An integer that is less than zero.

entero negativo Un entero menor que cero.

net (p. 600) A two-dimensional figure that can be used to build a three-dimensional figure.

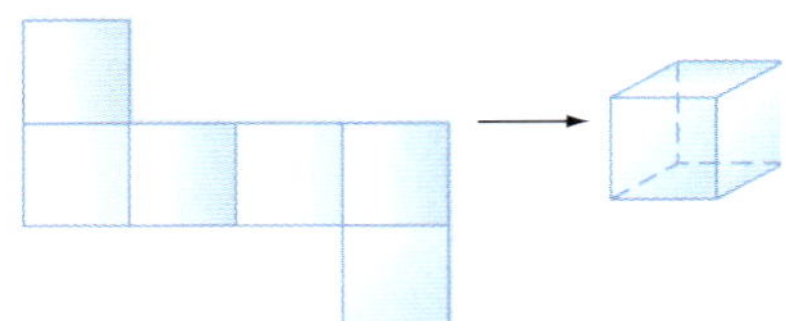

red Figura bidimensional que sirve para hacer una figura tridimensional.

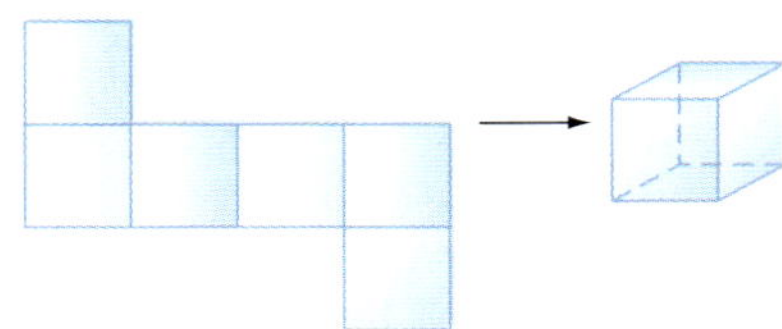

nonagon (p. 546) A polygon having nine sides.

enágono Polígono que tiene nueve lados.

numerical expression (p. 38) A combination of numbers and operations.

expresión numérica Combinación de números y operaciones.

O

obtuse angle (p. 511) Any angle that measures greater than 90° but less than 180°.

ángulo obtuso Cualquier ángulo que mide más de 90° pero menos de 180°.

obtuse triangle (p. 525) A triangle having one obtuse angle.

triángulo obtusángulo Triángulo que tiene un ángulo obtuso.

octagon (p. 546) A polygon having eight sides.

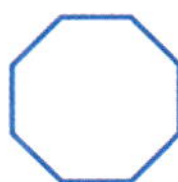

octágono Polígono que tiene ocho lados.

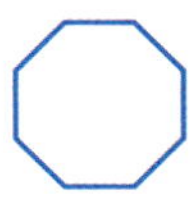

opposites (p. 96) Two integers are opposites if they are represented on the number line by points that are the same distance from zero, but on opposite sides of zero. The sum of two opposites is zero.

opuestos Dos enteros son opuestos si, en la recta numérica, están representados por puntos que equidistan de cero, pero en direcciones opuestas. La suma de dos opuestos es cero.

order of operations (p. 38) The rules to follow when more than one operation is used in a numerical expression.

1. Evaluate the expressions inside grouping symbols
2. Evaluate all powers
3. Multiply and divide in order from left to right.
4. Add and subtract in order from left to right.

orden de operaciones Reglas a seguir cuando se usa más de una operación en una expresión numérica.

1. Primero ejecuta todas las operaciones dentro de los símbolos de agrupamiento
2. Evalúa todas las potencias antes que las otras operaciones.
3. Multiplica y divide en orden de izquierda a derecha.
4. Suma y resta en orden de izquierda a derecha.

ordered pair (p. 88) A pair of numbers used to locate a point in the coordinate plane. An ordered pair is written in the form (x-coordinate, y-coordinate).

par ordenado Par de números que se utiliza para ubicar un punto en un plano de coordenadas. Se escribe de la siguiente forma: (coordenada x, coordenada y).

origin (p. 88) The point at which the x-axis and the y-axis intersect in a coordinate plane.

origen Punto en que el eje x y el eje y se intersecan en un plano de coordenadas.

outcome (p. 460) One possible result of a probability event. For example, 4 is an outcome when a number cube is rolled.

resultado Uno de los resultados posibles de un evento probabilístico. Por ejemplo, 4 es un resultado posible cuando se lanza un dado.

outlier (p. 397) A piece of data that is quite separated from the rest of the data.

valor atípico Dato que se encuentra muy separado del resto de los datos.

P

parallel lines (p. 533) Lines in a plane that do not intersect.

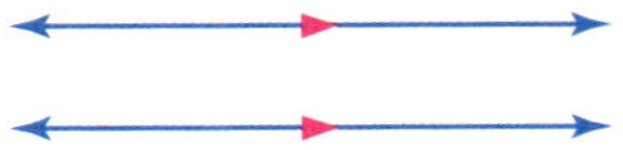

líneas paralelas Rectas situadas en un mismo plano y que no se intersecan.

parallelogram (p. 533) A quadrilateral with opposite sides parallel and opposite sides congruent.

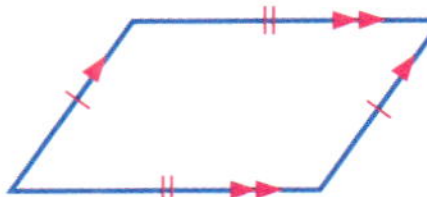

paralelogramo Cuadrilátero cuyos lados opuestos son paralelos y congruentes.

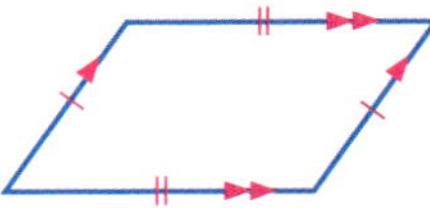

part (p. 350) In a percent proportion, the number that is compared to the whole quantity.

parte En una proporción porcentual, el número que se compara con la cantidad total.

Glossary/Glosario

pentagon (p. 546) A polygon having five sides.

pentágono Polígono que tiene cinco lados.

percent (p. 202) A ratio that compares a number to 100.

por ciento Razón que compara un número con 100.

percent equation (p. 361) An equation that describes the relationship between the part, whole, and percent.
part = percent • whole

ecuación porcentual Ecuación que describe la relación entre la parte, el todo y el por ciento.
parte = por ciento • todo.

percent of change (p. 369) A ratio that compares the change in a quantity to the original amount.

porcentaje de cambio Razón que compara el cambio en una cantidad, con la cantidad original.

percent of decrease (p. 369) A percent of change when the original quantity decreased.

porcentaje de disminución Porcentaje de cambio cuando disminuye la cantidad original.

percent of increase (p. 369) A percent of change when the original quantity increased.

porcentaje de aumento Porcentaje de cambio cuando aumenta la cantidad original.

percent proportion (p. 350) Compares part of a quantity to the whole quantity using a percent.

$$\frac{\text{part}}{\text{whole}} = \frac{\text{percent}}{100}$$

proporción porcentual Comparar partes de una cantidad, a la cantidad entera, usando un porcentaje.

$$\frac{\text{parte}}{\text{todo}} = \frac{\text{porcentaje}}{100}$$

perfect squares (p. 34) Numbers with square roots that are whole numbers. 25 is a perfect square because the square root of 25 is 5.

cuadrados perfectos Números cuya raíz cuadrada es un número entero. 25 es un cuadrado perfecto porque la raíz cuadrada de 25 es 5.

perimeter (p. 156) The distance around a closed geometric figure.

perímetro La distancia alrededor de una figura geométrica cerrada.

permutation (p. 475) An arrangement, or listing, of objects in which order is important.

permutación Arreglo o lista en que el orden es importante.

perpendicular lines (p. 512) Lines that meet to form right angles.

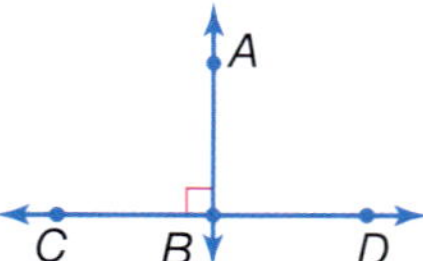

rectas perpendiculares Rectas que al encontrarse forman ángulos rectos.

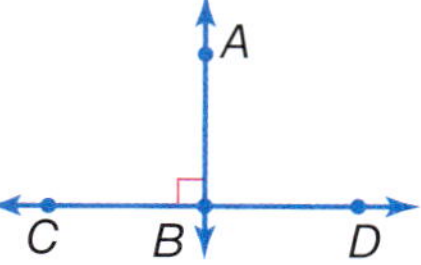

pi (π) (p. 584) The ratio of the circumference of a circle to its diameter. An approximation often used for π is 3.14.

pi (π) Razón entre la circunferencia de un círculo y su diámetro. A menudo, se usa 3.14 como aproximación del valor de π.

polygon (p. 546) A simple closed figure in a plane formed by three or more line segments.

polígono Figura simple cerrada en un plano, formada por tres o más segmentos de recta.

population (p. 434) The entire group of items or individuals from which the samples under consideration are taken.

población El grupo total de individuos o de artículos del cual se toman las muestras bajo estudio.

positive integer (p. 80) An integer that is greater than zero.

entero positivo Un entero mayor que cero.

powers (p. 30) Numbers expressed using exponents. The power 3^2 is read *three to the second power, or three squared.*

potencias Números que se expresan usando exponentes. La potencia 3^2 se lee *tres a la segunda potencia o tres al cuadrado.*

prime factorization (p. 182) Expressing a composite number as a product of prime numbers. For example, the prime factorization of 63 is $3 \times 3 \times 7$.

factorización prima Escritura de un número compuesto como el producto de números primos. La factorización prima de 63 es $3 \times 3 \times 7$.

prime number (p. 181) A whole number greater than 1 that has exactly two factors, 1 and itself.

número primo Número entero mayor que 1 que sólo tiene dos factores, 1 y sí mismo.

principal (p. 379) The amount of money deposited or invested.

capital La cantidad de dinero depositada o invertida.

prism (p. 601) A three-dimensional figure with at least three rectangular lateral faces and top and bottom faces parallel.

prisma Figura tridimensional que tiene por lo menos tres caras laterales rectangulares y caras paralelas superior e inferior.

probability (p. 460) The chance that some event will happen. It is the ratio of the number of ways a certain event can occur to the number of possible outcomes.

probabilidad La posibilidad de que suceda un evento. Es la razón del número de maneras en que puede ocurrir un evento al número total de resultados posibles.

properties (p. 54) Statements that are true for any number or variable.

propiedades Enunciados que se cumplen para cualquier número o variable.

proportion (p. 310) An equation that shows that two ratios are equivalent.

proporción Ecuación que muestra que dos razones son equivalentes.

proportional (p. 310) The relationship between two ratios with a constant rate or ratio.

proporcional Relación entre dos razones con una tasa o razón constante.

protractor (p. 680) An instrument used to measure angles.

transportador Instrumento que sirve para medir ángulos.

pyramid (p. 603) A three-dimensional figure with at least three lateral faces that are triangles and only one base.

pirámide Figura tridimensional que tiene por lo menos tres caras laterales triangulares que son triángulos y una sola base.

Pythagorean Theorem (p. 640) In a right triangle, the square of the length of the hypotenuse is equal to the sum of the squares of the lengths of the legs. $c^2 = a^2 + b^2$

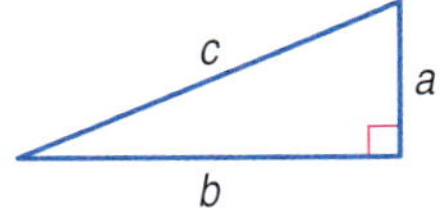

Teorema de Pitágoras En un triángulo rectángulo, el cuadrado de la longitud de la hipotenusa es igual a la suma de los cuadrados de las longitudes de los catetos. $c^2 = a^2 + b^2$

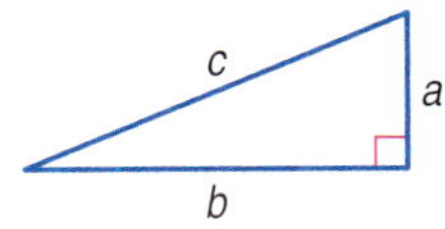

Q

quadrant (p. 88) One of the four regions into which the two perpendicular number lines of the coordinate plane separate the plane.

y-axis
Quadrant II
Quadrant I
O
x-axis
Quadrant III
Quadrant IV

cuadrante Una de las cuatro regiones en que dos rectas numéricas perpendiculares dividen el plano de coordenadas.

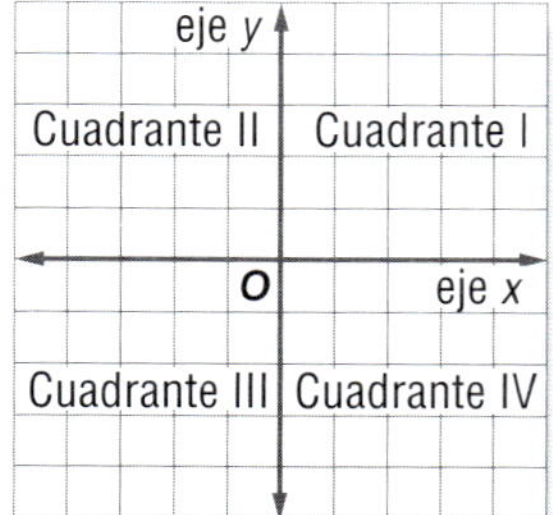

quadrilateral (p. 533) A closed figure having four sides and four angles.

cuadrilátero Figura cerrada que tiene cuatro lados y cuatro ángulos.

R

radical sign (p. 35) The symbol used to indicate a nonnegative square root, $\sqrt{\ }$.

signo radical Símbolo que se usa para indicar una raíz cuadrada no negativa, $\sqrt{\ }$.

radius (p. 584) The distance from the center of a circle to any point on the circle.

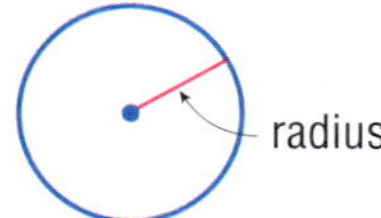

radio Distancia desde el centro de un círculo hasta cualquier punto del mismo.

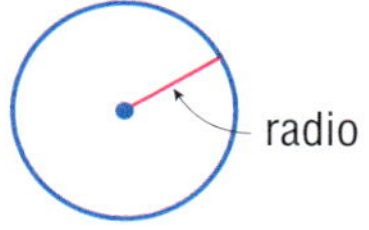

random (p. 461) Outcomes occur at random if each outcome is equally likely to occur.

aleatorio Un resultado ocurre al azar si la posibilidad de ocurrir de cada resultado es equiprobable.

range (p. 63) The set of output values for a function.

rango Conjunto de los valores de salida de una función.

range (p. 397) The difference between the greatest and least numbers in a data set.

rango La diferencia entre el número mayor y el menor en un conjunto de datos.

rate (p. 287) A ratio that compares two quantities with different kinds of units.

tasa Razón que compara dos cantidades que tienen distintas unidades de medida.

rate of change (p. 293) A ratio that shows a change in one quantity with respect to a change in another quantity.

tasa de cambio Razón que representa el cambio en una cantidad con respecto al cambio en otra cantidad.

ratio (p. 202) A comparison of two numbers by division. The ratio of 2 to 3 can be written as 2 out of 3, 2 to 3, 2 : 3, or $\frac{2}{3}$.

razón Comparación de dos números mediante división. La razón de 2 a 3 puede escribirse como 2 de cada 3, 2 a 3, 2:3 ó $\frac{2}{3}$.

rational number (p. 216) A number that can be expressed as a fraction.

número racional Número que puede expresarse como fracción.

reciprocal (p. 258) The multiplicative inverse of a number.

recíproco El inverso multiplicativo de un número.

rectangle (p. 533) A parallelogram having four right angles.

rectángulo Paralelogramo con cuatro ángulos rectos.

rectangular prism (p. 611) A solid figure that has two parallel and congruent bases that are rectangles.

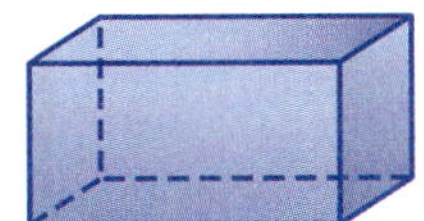

prisma rectangular Figura sólida con dos bases paralelas y congruentes que son rectángulos.

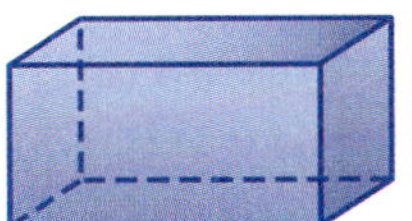

reflection (p. 559) A type of transformation in which a figure is flipped over a line of symmetry.

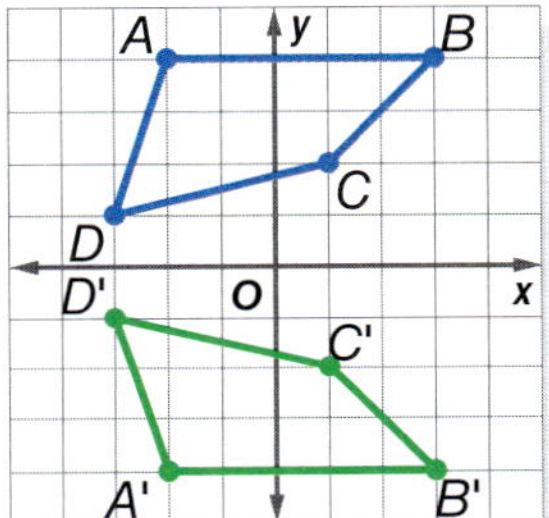

reflexión Tipo de transformación en el que se da vuelta a una figura sobre un eje de simetría.

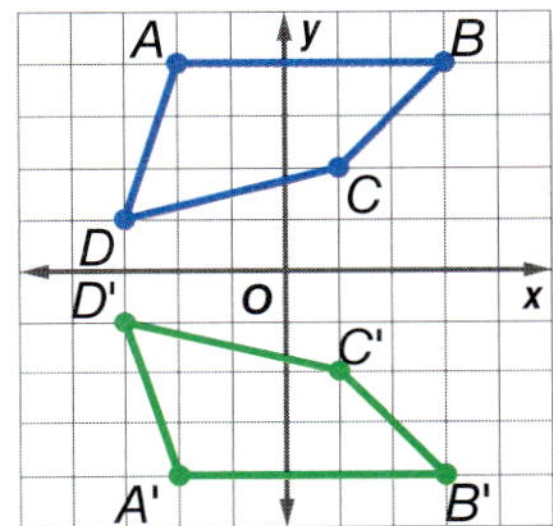

regular polygon (p. 546) A polygon that has all sides congruent and all angles congruent.

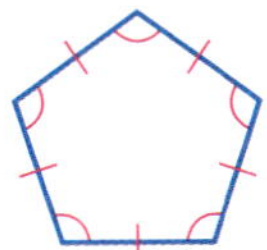

polígono regular Polígono con todos los lados y todos los ángulos congruentes.

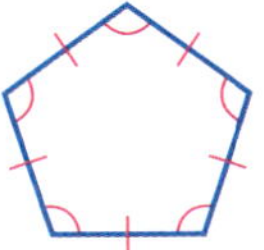

repeating decimals (p. 197) A decimal whose digits repeat in groups of one or more. Examples are 0.181818... and 0.83333... .

decimales periódicos Decimal cuyos dígitos se repiten en grupos de uno o más. Por ejemplo: 0.181818... y 0.83333... .

rhombus (p. 533) A parallelogram having four congruent sides.

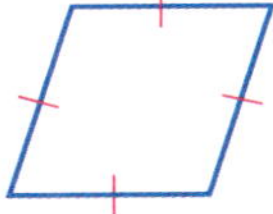

rombo Paralelogramo que tiene cuatro lados congruentes.

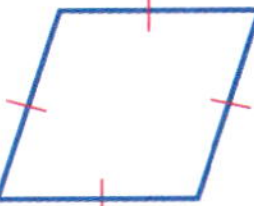

right angle (p. 511) An angle that measures 90°.

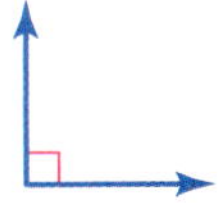

ángulo rect Ángulo que mide exactamente 90°.

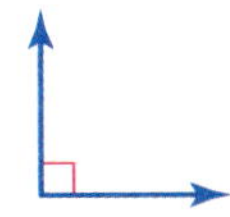

right triangle (p. 525) A triangle having one right angle.

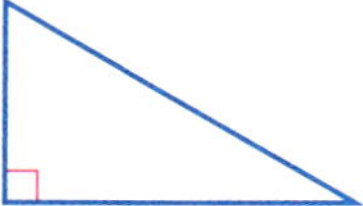

triángulo rectángulo Triángulo que tiene un ángulo recto.

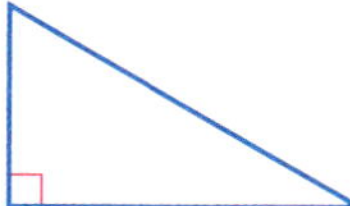

S

sample (p. 438) A randomly selected group chosen for the purpose of collecting data.

muestra Grupo escogido al azar o aleatoriamente que se usa con el propósito de recoger datos.

sample space (p. 465) The set of all possible outcomes of a probability experiment.

espacio muestral Conjunto de todos los resultados posibles de un experimento probabilístico.

sampling (p. 312) A practical method used to survey a representative group.

muestreo Método conveniente que facilita la elección y el estudio de un grupo representativo.

scale (p. 320) On a map, intervals used representing the ratio of distance on the map to the actual distance.

escala En un mapa, los intervalos que se usan para representar la razón de las distancias en el mapa a las distancias verdaderas.

scale drawing (p. 320) A drawing that is similar but either larger or smaller than the actual object.

dibujo a escala Dibujo que es semejante, pero más grande o más pequeño que el objeto real.

scale factor (p. 322) A scale written as a ratio in simplest form.

factor de escala Escala escrita como una tasa en forma reducida.

scale model (p. 320) A model used to represent something that is too large or too small for an actual-size model.

modelo a escala Réplica de un objeto real, el cual es demasiado grande o demasiado pequeño como para construirlo de tamaño natural.

scalene triangle (p. 525) A triangle having no congruent sides.

triángulo escaleno Triángulo sin lados congruentes.

scatter plot (p. 427) In a scatter plot, two sets of related data are plotted as ordered pairs on the same graph.

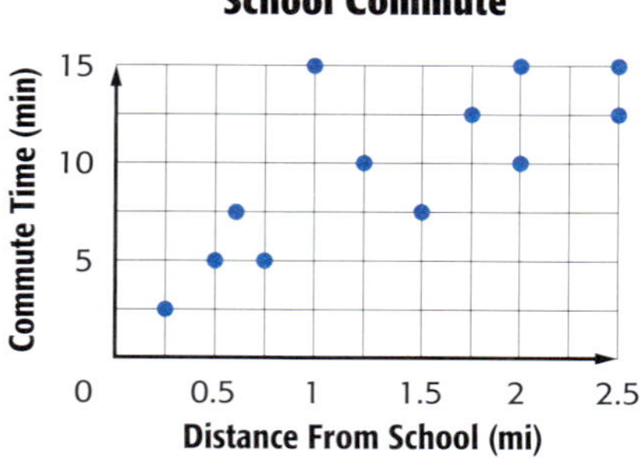

diagrama de dispersión Diagrama en que dos conjuntos de datos relacionados aparecen graficados como pares ordenados en la misma gráfica.

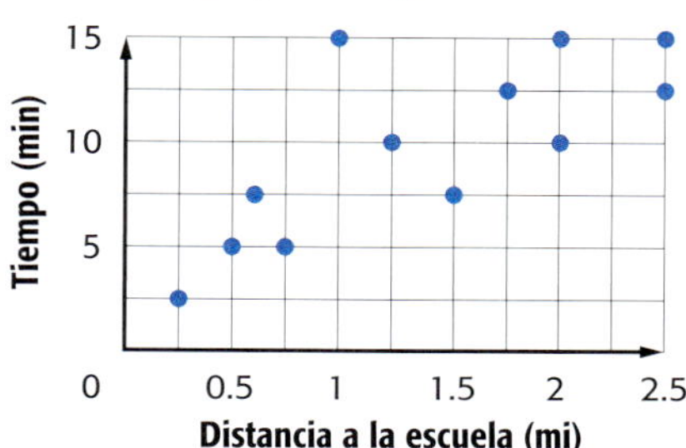

semicircle (p. 696) Half of a circle.

semicírculo Mitad de un círculo con el mismo diámetro.

sequence (p. 57) A list of numbers in a certain order, such as 0, 1, 2, 3, or 2, 4, 6, 8.

sucesión Lista de números en cierto orden, tales como 0, 1, 2, 3 ó 2, 4, 6, 8.

similar figures (p. 540) Figures that have the same shape but not necessarily the same size.

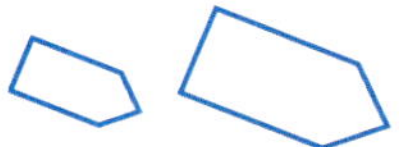

figuras semejantes Figuras que tienen la misma forma, pero no necesariamente el mismo tamaño.

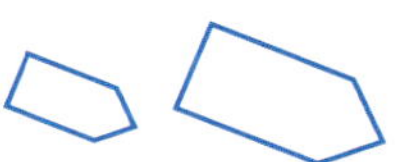

simple event (p. 460) One outcome or a collection of outcomes.

eventos simples Un resultado o una colección de resultados.

simple interest (p. 425) The amount paid or earned for the use of money. The formula for simple interest is $I = prt$.

interés simple Cantidad que se paga o que se gana por el uso del dinero. La fórmula para calcular el interés simple es $I = prt$.

simple random sample (p. 438) A sample where each item or person in the population is as likely to be chosen as any other.

muestra aleatoria simple Muestra de una población que tiene la misma probabilidad de escogerse que cualquier otra.

simplest form (p. 192) A fraction is in simplest form when the GCF of the numerator and the denominator is 1.

forma reducida Una fracción está escrita en forma reducida si el MCD de su numerador y denominador es 1.

simulate (p. 491) A way of acting out or modeling a problem situation.

simulación Manera de modelar o representar un problema.

slope (p. 293) The rate of change between any two points on a line. The ratio of vertical change to horizontal change.

pendiente Razón de cambio entre cualquier par de puntos en una recta. La razón del cambio vertical al cambio horizontal.

solution (p. 49) A value for the variable that makes an equation true. The solution of $12 = x + 7$ is 5.

solución Valor de la variable de una ecuación que hace verdadera la ecuación. La solución de $12 = x + 7$ es 5.

solving an equation (p. 49) The process of finding a solution to an equation.

resolver una ecuación Proceso de encontrar el número o números que satisfagan una ecuación.

sphere (p. 604) A three-dimensional figure in which all points are equal distance from the center.

esfera Figura tridimensional en que todos los puntos están equidistantes del centro.

square (p. 34) The product of a number and itself. 36 is the square of 6.

cuadrado El producto de un número por sí mismo. 36 es el cuadrado de 6.

square (p. 533) A parallelogram having four right angles and four congruent sides.

cuadrado Paralelogramo con cuatro ángulos rectos y cuatro lados congruentes.

square root (p. 35) One of the two equal factors of a number. The square root of 9 is 3.

raíz cuadrada Uno de dos factores iguales de un número. La raíz cuadrada de 9 es 3.

standard form (p. 31) Numbers written without exponents.

forma estándar Números escritos sin exponentes.

statistics (p. 396) The branch of mathematics that deals with collecting, organizing, and interpreting data.

estadística Rama de las matemáticas cuyo objetivo primordial es la recopilación, organización e interpretación de datos.

stem (p. 410) The greatest place value common to all the data values is used for the stem of a stem-and-leaf plot.

tallo El mayor valor de posición común a todos los datos es el que se usa como tallo en un diagrama de tallo y hojas.

stem-and-leaf plot (p. 410) A system used to condense a set of data where the greatest place value of the data forms the stem and the next greatest place value forms the leaves.

diagrama de tallo y hojas Sistema que se usa para condensar un conjunto de datos y en el cual el mayor valor de posición de los datos forma el tallo y el segundo mayor valor de posición de los datos forma las hojas.

straight angle (p. 511) An angle that measures exactly 180°.

ángulo llano Ángulo que mide exactamente 180°.

Subtraction Property of Equality (p. 136) If you subtract the same number from each side of an equation, the two sides remain equal.

propiedad de sustracción de la igualdad Si restas el mismo número de ambos lados de una ecuación, los dos lados permanecen iguales.

supplementary angles (p. 514) Two angles are supplementary if the sum of their measures is 180°.

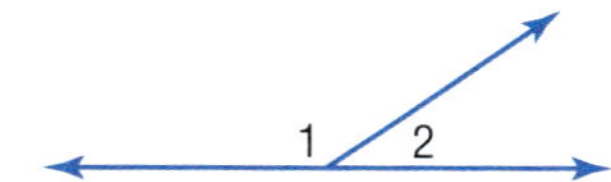

$\angle 1$ and $\angle 2$ are supplementary angles.

ángulos suplementarios Dos ángulos son suplementarios si la suma de sus medidas es 180°.

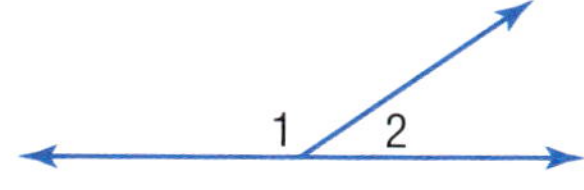

$\angle 1$ y $\angle 2$ son suplementarios.

surface area (p. 649) The sum of the areas of all the surfaces (faces) of a three-dimensional figure.

área de superficie La suma de las áreas de todas las superficies (caras) de una figura tridimensional.

survey (p. 434) A question or set of questions designed to collect data about a specific group of people.

encuesta Pregunta o conjunto de preguntas diseñadas para recoger datos sobre un grupo específico de peronas.

term (p. 57) Each number in a sequence.

término Cada número en una sucesión.

terminating decimals (p. 197) A decimal whose digits end. Every terminating decimal can be written as a fraction with a denominator of 10, 100, 1,000, and so on.

decimales terminales Decimal cuyos dígitos terminan. Todo decimal terminal puede escribirse como una fracción con un denominador de 10, 100, 1,000, etc.

tessellation (p. 548) A repetitive pattern of polygons that fit together with no holes or gaps.

teselado Un patrón repetitivo de polígonos que coinciden perfectamente, sin dejar huecos o espacios.

theoretical probability (p. 486) The ratio of the number of ways an event can occur to the number of possible outcomes.

probabilidad teórica La razón del número de maneras en que puede ocurrir un evento al número total de resultados posibles.

three-dimensional figures (p. 603) A figure with length, width, and depth (or height).

figuras tridimensionales Figuras que poseen largo, ancho y profundidad (o altura).

transformation (p. 553) A movement of a geometric figure.

transformación Movimientos de figuras geométricas.

translation (p. 553) One type of transformation where a geometric figure is slid horizontally, vertically, or both.

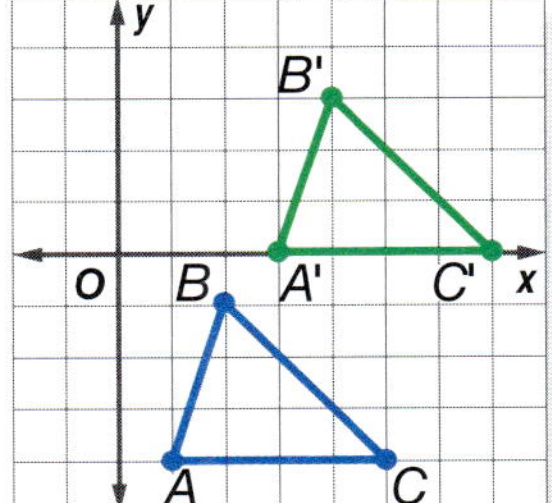

traslación Tipo de transformación en que una figura se desliza horizontal o verticalmente o de ambas maneras.

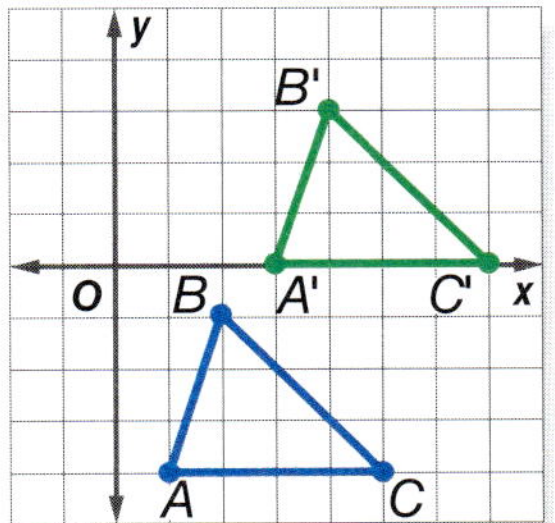

trapezoid (p. 533) A quadrilateral with one pair of parallel sides.

trapecio Cuadrilátero con un único par de lados paralelos.

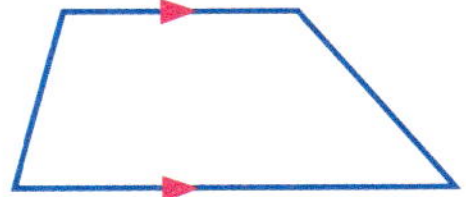

tree diagram (p. 466) A diagram used to show the total number of possible outcomes in a probability experiment.

diagrama de árbol Diagrama que se usa para mostrar el número total de resultados posibles en experimento probabilístico.

triangle (p. 524) A polygon that has three sides and three angles.

triángulo Polígono que posee tres lados y tres ángulos.

triangular prism (p. 615) A prism that has bases that are triangles.

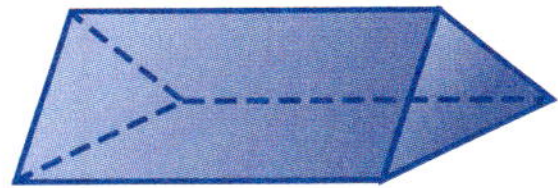

prisma triangular Prisma cuyas bases son triángulos.

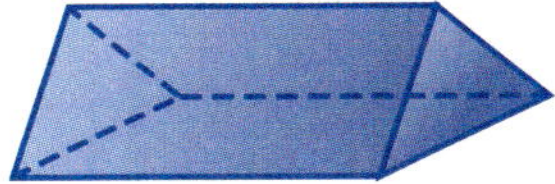

two-step equation (p. 151) An equation having two different operations.

ecuación de dos pasos Ecuación que contiene dos operaciones distintas.

U

unbiased sample (p. 438) A sample representative of the entire population.

muestra no sesgada Muestra que se selecciona de modo que se representativa de la población entera.

unit rate (p. 287) A rate with denominator of 1.

tasa unitaria Una tasa con un denominador de 1.

unit ratio (p. 298) A unit rate where the denominator is one unit.

razón unitaria Tasa unitaria en que el denominador es la unidad.

unlike fractions (p. 237) Fractions with different denominators.

fracciones con distinto denominador Fracciones cuyos denominadores son diferentes.

V

variable (p. 44) A placeholder, usually a letter, used to represent an unspecified value in mathematical expressions or sentences. In $3 + a = 6$, a is a variable.

variable Marcador de posición, por lo general, una letra, que se usa para representar un valor desconocido en expresiones o enunciados matemáticos. En $3 + a = 6$, a es una variable.

Venn diagram (p. 186) A diagram that uses overlapping circles to show how elements among sets of numbers or objects are related.

diagrama de Venn Diagrama que usa círculos para mostrar la relación entre los elementos en un conjunto de números u objetos

vertex (p. 510) A vertex of an angle is the common endpoint of the rays forming the angle.

vértice El vértice de un ángulo es el extremo común de los rayos que lo forman.

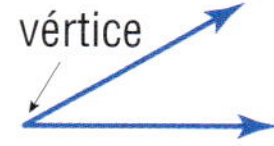

vertex (p. 603) The point where the edges of a three dimensional figure intersect.

vértice Punto donde se intersecan las aristas de una figura tridimensional.

vertical angles (p. 511) Opposite angles formed by the intersection of two lines.

$\angle 1$ and $\angle 2$ are vertical angles.

ángulos opuestos por el vértice Ángulos opuestos que se forman de la intersección de dos rectas.

$\angle 1$ y $\angle 2$ son ángulos opuestos por el vértice.

volume (p. 613) The number of cubic units needed to fill the space occupied by a solid.

volumen Número de unidades cúbicas que se requieren para llenar el espacio que ocupa un sólido.

voluntary response sample (p. 439) A sample which involves only those who want to participate in the sampling.

muestra de respuesta voluntaria Muestra que involucra sólo aquellos que quieren participar en el muestreo.

W

whole (p. 350) In a percent proportion, the number to which the part is being compared.

todo En una proporción porcentual, el número con que se compara la parte.

X

***x*-axis** (p. 88) The horizontal number line in a coordinate plane.

eje *x* La recta numérica horizontal en el plano de coordenadas.

***x*-coordinate** (p. 88) The first number of an ordered pair. It corresponds to a number on the x-axis.

coordenada *x* El primer número de un par ordenado. Corresponde a un número en el eje x.

Y

***y*-axis** (p. 88) The vertical number line in a coordinate plane.

eje *y* La recta numérica vertical en el plano de coordenadas.

***y*-coordinate** (p. 88) The second number of an ordered pair. It corresponds to a number on the y-axis.

coordenada *y* El segundo número de un par ordenado. Corresponde a un número en el eje y.

Z

zero pair (p. 93) The result when one positive counter is paired with one negative counter.

par nulo Resultado que se obtiene cuando una ficha positiva se aparea con una ficha negativa.

Selected Answers

Chapter 1 Introduction to Algebra and Functions

Page 23 ***Chapter 1*** ***Getting Ready***

1. 105.8 **3.** 60.64 **5.** \$72.94 **7.** 2.5 **9.** 6.2 **11.** 29.4 **13.** 10.2 **15.** 5.3 **17.** 4.46

Pages 27–29 ***Lesson 1-1***

1. Sample answer: 4 times; $16,000 \div 4,000 = 4$ **3.** 3,000 **5.** \$763.75

7. 

9. every 45 minutes **11.** 5:10 P.M. **15.** 13 wk **17.** Sample answer: For the school bake sale, Samantha bakes 79 cookies and 42 brownies. If two other students baked the same amount of cookies and brownies, how many items did they bake altogether? **19.** C **21.** 100 **23.** 625

Pages 31–33 ***Lesson 1-2***

1. $9 \cdot 9 \cdot 9$ **3.** $8 \cdot 8 \cdot 8 \cdot 8 \cdot 8$ **5.** 49 **7.** Sample answer: 9,765,625 people **9.** 1^4 **11.** $1 \cdot 1 \cdot 1 \cdot 1 \cdot 1$ **13.** $3 \cdot 3 \cdot 3 \cdot 3 \cdot 3 \cdot 3 \cdot 3 \cdot 3$ **15.** $9 \cdot 9 \cdot 9$ **17.** 64 **19.** 2,401 **21.** 1 **23.** 1,000,000 **25.** 3^2 **27.** 1^8 **29.** $4 \cdot 4 \cdot 4 \cdot 4 \cdot 4$ **31.** 1,296 **33.** 3^3 **35.** $5^4 \cdot 4^3$ **37.** $1^{14}, 17^3, 6^5, 4^{10}$ **39.** $7^2, 5^3, 2^{11}, 4^6$ **41.** $8^2 = 64$ and $4^3 = 64$ **43.** Sample answer: The pattern is that each successive term is $\frac{1}{2}$ of the previous one, so $2^0 = 1$ and $2^{-1} = \frac{1}{2}$. **45.** 7 wins **47.** 4 **49.** 25

Pages 36–37 ***Lesson 1-3***

1. 36 **3.** 289 **5.** 3 **7.** 11 **9.** 24 in. by 24 in. **11.** 1 **13.** 121 **15.** 400 **17.** 1,156 **19.** 4 **21.** 10 **23.** 16 **25.** 25 **27.** 40 ft **29.** 361 **31.** 53,824 mi^2

33. 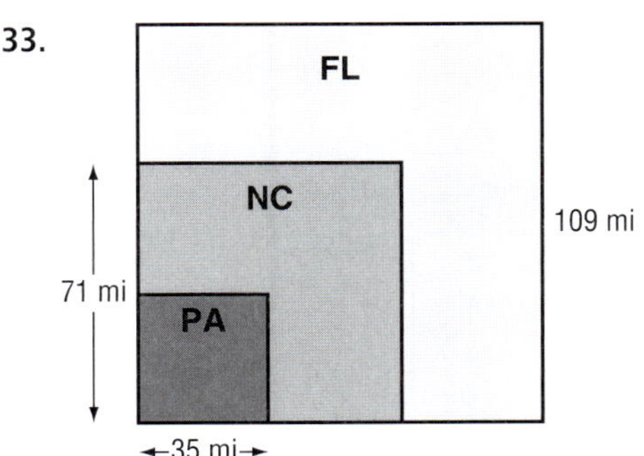

35. 41m^2 greater; The area of a 7 by 7 square has an area of 49 m^2. **37.** Yes; for example, a pen that measures 10 feet by 10 feet has the same perimeter, but its area is 100 square feet, which is greater than 84 square feet. **39.** Sample answer: It is called squaring the number because the area of a square is found by multiplying the two side lengths together. **41.** J **43.** $8 \cdot 8 \cdot 8 \cdot 8 \cdot 8$ **45.** $2 \cdot 2 \cdot 2 \cdot 2 \cdot 2 \cdot 2$ **47.** 21 **49.** 30

Pages 40–41 ***Lesson 1-4***

1. 11; Sample answer: Subtract first since $5 - 2$ is in parentheses. Then add 8. **3.** 11; Sample answer: Multiply 2 by 6 first since multiplication comes before addition or subtraction. Then subtract and add in order from left to right. **5.** 400; Sample answer: Evaluate 10^2 first since it is a power. Then multiply by 4. **7.** 11; Sample answer: Subtract first since $6 - 3$ is in parentheses. Then multiply the difference by 2 and multiply 3 by 4 since multiplication comes before addition or subtraction. Finally, add $17 + 6$ and subtract 12 in order from left to right. **9.** $3(0.05) + 2(0.25) + 2(0.10) + 7(0.01)$; \$0.92 **11.** 3; Sample answer: Add first since $3 + 4$ is in parentheses. Then subtract. **13.** 1; Sample answer: Subtract first since $11 - 2$ is in parentheses. Then divide. **15.** 8; Sample answer: Divide first since division comes before addition or subtraction. Then subtract 1 and add 7 in order from left to right. **17.** 5; Sample answer: Multiply first since multiplication comes before addition or subtraction. Then subtract the product from 118 and add 5. **19.** 30,000; Sample answer: Evaluate 10^4 first since it is a power. Then multiply by 3. **21.** 386; Sample answer: Evaluate 7^2 first since it is a power. Then multiply by 8 since multiplication comes before subtraction. Finally, subtract. **23.** 75; Sample answer: Evaluate 9^2 since it is a power. Then divide 14 by 7 and multiply the quotient by 3 since multiplication and division occur from left to right. Finally, subtract. **25.** 22; Sample answer: Add first since $6 + 5$ is in parentheses. Then subtract 6 from 8 since $8 – 6$ is in parentheses. Finally, multiply. **27.** 23; Sample answer: Add first since $4 + 7$ is in parentheses. Then multiply the sum by 3. Next, multiply 5 by 4 and divide the product by 2 since multiplication and division occur in order from left to right. Finally, subtract. **29.** \$3.25 **31.** 19; Sample answer: Evaluate 3^3 first since it is a power. Then add 8. Next subtract 6 from 10 since $10 – 6$ is in parentheses. Then square the difference since the power is 2. Finally subtract 16 from 35. **33.** 64; Sample answer: Subtract first since $4 - 3.2$ is in parentheses. Multiply 7 by 9 next since multiplication occurs from left to right. Then subtract 0.8 from the product, 63, and add 1.8 since addition and subtraction occur from left to right. **35.** Peggy; the first step is to do the division $24 \div 6$. Phoung incorrectly multiplied 6 and 2 first. **37.** Yes; For example, a pen that measures 10 feet by 10 feet has the same perimeter, but its area is 100 square feet, which is greater than 84 square feet. **39.** H **41.** 8 **43.** 28 **45.** 968

Pages 42–43 ***Lesson 1-5***

1. Sample answer: You need to keep track of what numbers you have already guessed, so that you do not make the same guess twice. You also need to know what numbers produce answers that are too large or too small, so you can make better guesses. **3.** 125 adult tickets and 250 student tickets **5.** birthday, holiday, vacation **7.** The circumference of Earth is 24,900 miles long at the Equator. **9.** 512 and 1,024 **11.** 324.8 in. of snow. **13.** 2, 3, 6

Pages 46–47 Lesson 1-6

1. 10 **3.** 2 **5.** 32 **7.** 22 **9.** 7 **11.** 3 **13.** 4 **15.** 7 **17.** 5 **19.** 12 **21.** 48 **23.** 4 **25.** 18 **27.** 36 **29.** 5 **31.** 4 quarts **33.** 5.1 **35.** $19.99d + 0.17m$ **37.** 64 ft **39.** Sample answer: $5x - 37$ if $x = 8$ **41.** Sample answer: Sometimes; $x - 3$ and $y - 3$ represent the same value only when $x = y$ **43.** G **45.** 28 **47.** 56 **49.** 19 **51.** false

Pages 51–52 Lesson 1-7

1. 3 **3.** 54 **5.** $2.25 **7.** 7 **9.** 28 **11.** 46 **13.** 33 **15.** 64 **17.** 7 **19.** 11 **21.** m = the number of miles Derrick walked on Monday; $m + 2.5 = 6.3$; 3.8 mi **23.** 5.4 **25.** 4.4 **27.** 1.2 **29.** $\$1.75 + c = \$6.25$; $c = \$4.50$ **31.** Antonio; $105 - 35 = 70$ is a true statement. $35 - 35 \neq 70$ **33.** A **35.** J **37.** 31 **39.** 19 **41.** 28 **43.** 150

Pages 55–56 Lesson 1-8

1. $7(4) + 7(3)$; 49 **3.** $3(9 + 6)$; 45 **5.** $4(12 + 5)$; $68; Sample answer: The expression $12 + 5$ represents the cost of one ticket and one hot dog. The expression $4(12 + 5)$ represents the cost of four tickets and four hot dogs. Since $4 \times 12 = 48$ and $4 \times 5 = 20$, find $48 + 20$, or 68, to find the total cost of four tickets and four hot dogs. **7.** Sample answer: Rewrite $44 + (23 + 16)$ as $44 + (16 + 23)$ using the Commutative Property of Addition. Rewrite $44 + (16 + 23)$ as $(44 + 16) + 23$ using the Associative Property of Addition. Find $44 + 16$, or 60, mentally. Then find $60 + 23$, or 83, mentally. **9.** $2(6) + 2(7)$; 26 **11.** $4(3 + 8)$; 44 **13.** Sample answer: Rewrite $(8 + 27) + 52$ as $(27 + 8) + 52$ using the Commutative Property of Addition. Rewrite $(27 + 8) + 52$ as $27 + (8 + 52)$ using the Associative Property of Addition. Find $8 + 52$, or 60, mentally. Then find $60 + 27$, or 87, mentally. **15.** Sample answer: Rewrite $91 + (15 + 9)$ as $91 + (9 + 15)$ using the Commutative Property of Addition. Rewrite $91 + (9 + 15)$ as $(91 + 9) + 15$ using the Associative Property of Addition. Find $91 + 9$, or 100, mentally. Then find $100 + 15$, or 115, mentally. **17.** Sample answer: Rewrite $(4 \cdot 18) \cdot 25$ as $(18 \cdot 4) \cdot 25$ using the Commutative Property of Multiplication. Rewrite $(18 \cdot 4) \cdot 25$ as $18 \cdot (4 \cdot 25)$ using the Associative Property of Multiplication. Find $4 \cdot 25$, or 100, mentally. Then find $100 \cdot 18$, or 1,800, mentally. **19.** Sample answer: Rewrite $15 \cdot (8 \cdot 2)$ as $15 \cdot (2 \cdot 8)$ using the Commutative Property of Multiplication. Rewrite $15 \cdot (2 \cdot 8)$ as $(15 \cdot 2) \cdot 8$ using the Associative Property of Multiplication. Find $15 \cdot 2$, or 30, mentally. Then find $30 \cdot 8$, or 240, mentally. **21.** Sample answer: Rewrite $5 \cdot (30 \cdot 12)$ as $5 \cdot (12 \cdot 30)$ using the Commutative Property of Multiplication. Rewrite $5 \cdot (12 \cdot 30)$ as $(5 \cdot 12) \cdot 30$ using the Associative Property of Multiplication. Find $5 \cdot 12$, or 60, mentally. Then find $60 \cdot 30$, or 1,800, mentally. **23.** $5(20 + 7)$; 135 million **25.** $7(9 - 3)$; 42 **27.** $9(7 - 3)$; 36 **29.** $y + 5$ **31.** $32b$ **33.** $2x + 6$ **35.** $6c + 6$ **37.** $55 + 184 = 184 + 55$ **39.** Sample answer: $(5 + z) + 9 = 5 + (z + 9)$ **41.** Sample answer: Since $24 \div (12 \div 2) = 4$ and $(24 \div 12) \div 2 = 1$, $24 \div (12 \div 2) \neq (24 \div 12) \div 2$. **43.** B **45.** 11.3 **47.** 75 yr **49.** 10 **51.** 4.6

Pages 59–61 Lesson 1-9

1. 9 is added to each term; 36, 45, 54 **3.** 0.1 is added to each term; 1.4, 1.5, 1.6 **5.** $3n$; 36 in. **7.** 6 is added to each term; 25, 31, 37 **9.** 12 is added to each term; 67, 79, 91 **11.** 5 is added to each term; 53, 58, 63 **13.** 0.8 is added to each term; 5.6, 6.4, 7.2 **15.** 1.5 is added to each term; 10.5, 12.0, 13.5 **17.** 4 is added to each term; 20.6, 24.6, 28.6 **19.** $7n$; 42 laps **21.** 25 is added to each term; 120, 145, 170 **23.** 256, 1,024, 4,096 **25.** 324, 972, 2,916 **27.** 1,200 **29.** 4,950 **31.** The Fibonacci sequence is 1, 1, 2, 3, 5, 8, 13, ... In this sequence, each term after the second term is the sum of the two terms before it. Fibonacci numbers occur in many areas of nature, including pine cones, shell spirals, and branching plants. **33.** + 2, + 4, + 6, + 8, ...; 30, 42, 56 **35.** Sample answer: paper/pencil; Write the equation that represents this situation, $15n$. Since 2 years = 24 months, evaluate the expression when n is 24. $15(24) = 360$. So, after 2 years, $360 will be saved. **37.** D **39.** 48; Sample answer: Rewrite $(23 + 18) + 7$ as $(18 + 23) + 7$ using the Communicative Property of Addition. Rewrite $(18 + 23) + 7$ as $18 + (23 + 7)$ using the Associative Property of Addition. Find $23 + 7$, or 30, mentally. Then find $18 + 30$, or 48, mentally. **41.** 29 **43.** 20 **45.** 8 **47.** 3

Pages 65–67 Lesson 1-10

1.

x	3x	y
1	3 • 1	3
2	3 • 2	6
3	3 • 3	9
4	3 • 4	12

; domain: {1, 2, 3, 4}; range: {3, 6, 9, 12}

3.

x	8x	y
1	8 • 1	8
2	8 • 2	16
3	8 • 3	24
4	8 • 4	32

; domain: {1, 2, 3, 4}; range: {8, 16, 24, 32}

5. 693 mi; Sample answer: Replace h with 3 in the equation $m = 231h$ to find the distance in miles the race car travels in 3 hours.

7.

x	6x	y
1	6 • 1	6
2	6 • 2	12
3	6 • 3	18
4	6 • 4	24

; domain: {1, 2, 3, 4}; range: {6, 12, 18, 24}

9.

x	$25x$	y
1	25 • 1	25
2	25 • 2	50
3	25 • 3	75
4	25 • 4	100

; domain: {1, 2, 3, 4}; range: {25, 50, 75, 100}

11. $c = 40m$ **13.** $t = 35m$

15.

x	$x - 1$	y
1	1 − 1	0
2	2 − 1	1
3	3 − 1	2
4	4 − 1	3

; domain: {1, 2, 3, 4}; range: {0, 1, 2, 3}

17.

x	$x + 0.25$	y
0	0 + 0.25	0.25
1	1 + 0.25	1.25
2	2 + 0.25	2.25
3	3 + 0.25	3.25

; domain: {0, 1, 2, 3}; range: {0.25, 1.25, 2.25, 3.25}

19.

Width (units)	$6w$	Area (sq units)
2	6 • 2	12
3	6 • 3	18
4	6 • 4	24
5	6 • 5	30

21. $m = 8s$ **23.** 480 mi; 1,140 mi; Sample answer: Replace s with 60 in the equation $m = 8s$ and in the equation $m = 19s$ to find the number of miles Jupiter travels in 1 minute the number of miles Earth travels in 1 minute, respectively. **25.** $y = 3x$ **27.** Sample answer: Sam charges $3 for each dog that he walks. In the equation $y = 3x$, x represents the number of dogs and y represents the total amount of money earned. **29.** C **31.** 63, 72, 81 **33.** (12)4 +(4)4; 64 **35.** 10(6 − 5); 10 **37.** 7 **39.** 7

Pages 70–74 Chapter 1 Study Guide and Review

1. false, equivalent expressions **3.** false, domain **5.** true **7.** false, square **9.** 60 ft **11.** 3 • 3 • 3 • 3 **13.** 5 **15.** 5 • 5 • 5 • 5 **17.** 40,353,607 **19.** 324 **21.** 100 **23.** 8 **25.** 169 **27.** 18 **29.** 25 **31.** 33 **33.** 36 ÷ 4 + 12 ÷ 3; 13 **35.** 22 **37.** 5 **39.** 48 **41.** 8 **43.** 108 **45.** $9 + x = 15$; 6 tickets **47.** 68; Sample answer: Rewrite 14 + (38 + 16) as 14 + (16 + 38) using the Commutative Property of Addition. Rewrite 14 + (16 + 38) as (14 + 16) + 38 using the Associative Property of Addition. Find 14 + 16, or 30, mentally. Then find 30 + 38, or 68, mentally. **49.** $2(15 + 12); $54; Sample answer: The expression 15 + 12 represents the total number of roses Wesley sold. The expression $2(15 + 12) represents the total amount of money Wesley earned. Since $2 × 15 = $30 and $2 × 12 = $24, find $30 + $24, or $54, to find the total amount Wesley earned. **51.** Each term is found by adding 0.8 to the previous term; 6.6, 7.4, 8.2 **53.** 4.50n$

55.

x	$4x$	y
5	4(5)	20
6	4(6)	24
7	4(7)	28
8	4(8)	32

; domain: {5, 6, 7, 8}; range: {20, 24, 28, 32}

Chapter 2 Integers

Page 79 Chapter 2 Getting Ready

1. < **3.** < **5.** Garrett **7.** 20 **9.** 9 **11.** 216 **13.** 29 **15.** 1,900 mi

Pages 82–83 Lesson 2-1

1. −11 **3.** 16 **5.** −15

7. –10–8–6–4–2 0 2 4 6 8 10

9. 8 **11.** 9 **13.** −53 **15.** −2 **17.** 12 **19.** −7

21. –3–2–1 0 1

23.

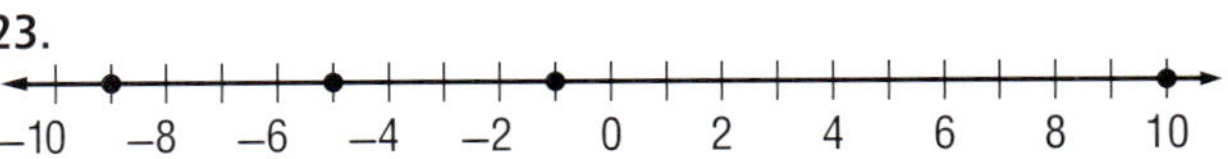

25. 10 **27.** 2 **29.** 14 **31.** 25 **33.** 5 **35.** 17 positive charges: 17; 25 negative charges: −25 **37.** false; 0 **39.** C

41.

x	$x - 4$	y
4	4 − 4	0
5	5 − 4	1
6	6 − 4	2
7	7 − 4	3

; domain: {4, 5, 6, 7}; range: {0, 1, 2, 3}.

43.

x	$5x + 1$	y
1	5 • 1 + 1	6
2	5 • 2 + 1	11
3	5 • 3 + 1	16
4	5 • 4 + 1	21

; domain: {1, 2, 3, 4}; range: {6, 11, 16, 21}

45. > **47.** >

Pages 85–87 Lesson 2-2

1. > **3.** > **5.** {−18, −16, −10, 12, 19} **7.** < **9.** > **11.** > **13.** < **15.** {−8, −5, −3, 6, 11} **17.** {−7, −6, −4, 1, 3, 5} **19.** Sunlight, Twilight, Midnight, Abyssal, Hadal **21.** < **23.** < **25.** −5, −2, 5, 10, 20 **27.** 5° with a 10-mile-per-hour wind **29.** true **31.** true **33.** −1 **35.** C **37.** −9 **39.** $r = 6t$

41–44. 10 8 6 4 2 0 −2 −4 −6 −8 −10

Pages 90–92 **Lesson 2-3**

1. (−2, −4), III **3.** (0, 3), y-axis

5–8.

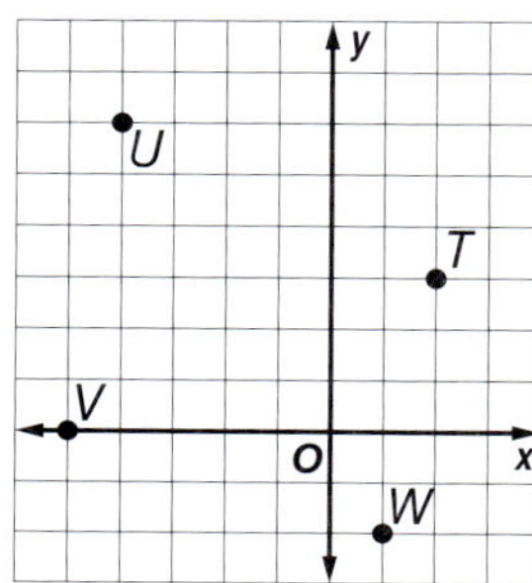

9. Sea Cliffs
11. (−2, 2), II
13. (−5, 0), x-axis
15. (2, −2), IV
17. (−4, −1), III
19. (2, 2), I
21. (0, 4); y-axis

23–34.

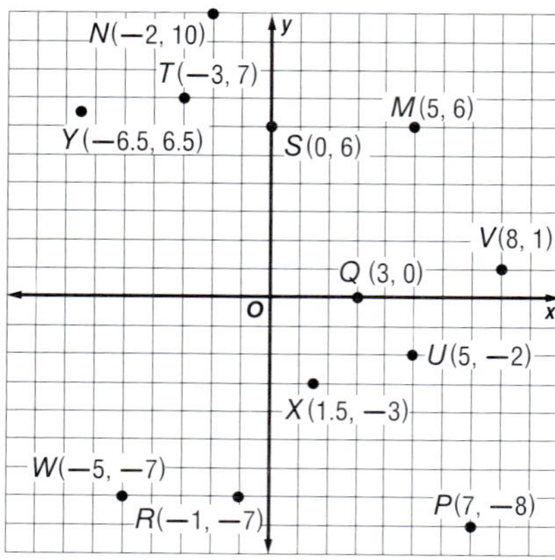

35. Africa **37.** South America

39–41.

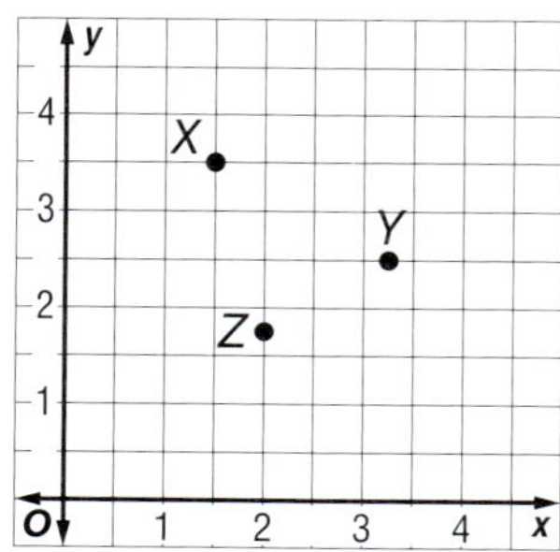

43. Sample answer: Rene Descarte is often credited with inventing the coordinate plane and so the coordinate plane is sometimes called the Cartesian plane, in his honor. The myth is that while a child, Descarte lay in bed one day watching a fly crawling around on the ceiling. In wondering how to tell someone else where the fly was, he realized that he could describe its position by its distance from the walls of the room. **45.** Sample answer: Sometimes; both (0, −2) and (0, 2) lie on the y-axis.

47. Sample answer: Using the graphic, you can see that an ordered pair such as (−5, −4) is in Quadrant III.

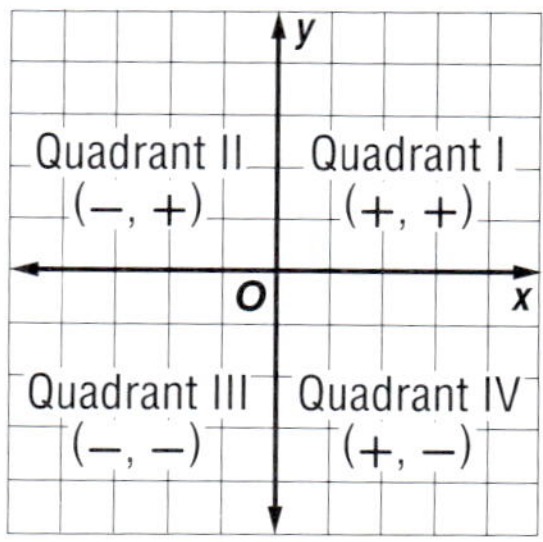

49. Sample answer: Point A is 1 unit to the right and 2 units down from the origin, in quadrant IV. Point B is 2 units to the left and 1 unit up from the origin, in quadrant II. **51.** G **53.** > **55.** < **57.** 41 mi **59.** 1,326 **61.** 11,737

Pages 98–99 **Lesson 2-4**

1. −14 **3.** 7 **5.** −4 **7.** 0 **9.** −\$25 + \$18; −\$7; Camilia still owes her brother \$7. **11.** −25 **13.** 28 **15.** −6 **17.** −13 **19.** −2 **21.** 2 **23.** 0 **25.** 22 **27.** −19 **29.** 60 + (−60); 0; The pelican is now at sea level. **31.** −5 + (−15) + 12; The team has lost a total of 8 yards. **33.** 4 **35.** −3 **39.** a **41.** m + (−15) **43.** Sample answer: Look at the signs. If the numbers being added are both positive, the sum is positive. If the numbers being added are both negative, the sum is negative. If the numbers being added have different signs, subtract their absolute values and give the sum the sign of the number with the greatest absolute value. If the numbers being added are opposites, the sum is zero. **45.** B **47.** (−2, 4); 11 **49.** (−3, −1); 111 **51.** −8, −4, −3, 0, 1, 4, 6 **53.** 103 **55.** 3,109

Pages 105–106 **Lesson 2-5**

1. −3 **3.** −12 **5.** 24 **7.** −2 **9.** −21 **11.** 22 **13.** −10 **15.** −14 **17.** 23 **19.** 31 **21.** −14 **23.** −30 **25.** 104 **27.** 6 **29.** 0 **31.** 0 **33.** 15 **35.** 11 **37.** 8,757 ft **39.** 5,066 ft **41.** −31 **43.** 23 **45.** Mei; Alicia did not add the additive inverse of −18. **47.** Sample answer: To subtract an integer, add its additive inverse. **49.** J **51.** −11 **53.** −14 **55.** 8 **57.** −33 **59.** −24

Pages 109–111 **Lesson 2-6**

1. −60 **3.** −28 **5.** 45 **7.** 64 **9.** −12 **11.** 100(−3) = −300; Tamera's investment is now worth \$300 less than it was before the price of the stock dropped. **13.** 70 **15.** −220 **17.** −70 **19.** −50 **21.** 80 **23.** −125 **25.** 81 **27.** −45 **29.** 49 **31.** −24 **33.** 24 **35.** 64 **37.** −160 **39.** 5(−650) = −3,250; Ethan burns 3,250 Calories each week. **41.** −243 **43.** 88

47. Sample answer: new triangle $A'B'C'$ is on the other side of the origin (in quadrant III) from original triangle ABC (which is in Quadrant I).

49. Sample answer: −6 × 3 = −18 **51.** Sample answer: 1; (−1)(−1) = 1. Since there are 50 ÷ 2 = 25 pairs of (−1) factors, $(-1)^{50} = 1^{25}$. One raised to any power is still 1. **53.** Sample answer: The product of three integers is positive when exactly two integers are negative or all three integers are positive. **55.** J **57.** 8 **59.** −21 **61.** −6 **63.** −9 **65.** 18 + x = 51; x = 33

Pages 112–113 Lesson 2-7

1. Sample answer: Use the look for a pattern strategy when there is a data table, a series of numbers, or a geometric pattern as part of the problem. **3.** Sample answer: Amanda has $2 in change in her bank. If she adds $0.50 each week for 7 weeks, how much money will be in her bank? $5.50 **5.** 8 months **7.** Sample answer: 3 quarters, 2 nickels, and 1 penny **9.** 2 letters and 10 postcards **11.** 8,914,113 **13.** 84 cm

Pages 116–118 Lesson 2-8

1. −4 **3.** −6 **5.** 5 **7.** −3 **9.** −48.3°C **11.** −7 **13.** −9 **15.** 10 **17.** −7 **19.** −9 **21.** 9 **23.** 5 **25.** −12 **27.** −3 **29.** 2 **31.** −1 **33.** −10°F **35.** 8 **37.** 1 **39.** −53 ft **41.** −32 ÷ (−4) has a positive quotient; the others have negative quotients **43.** −20, −10, −5, −4, −2, −1, 1, 2, 4, 5, 10, 20 **45.** A **47.**

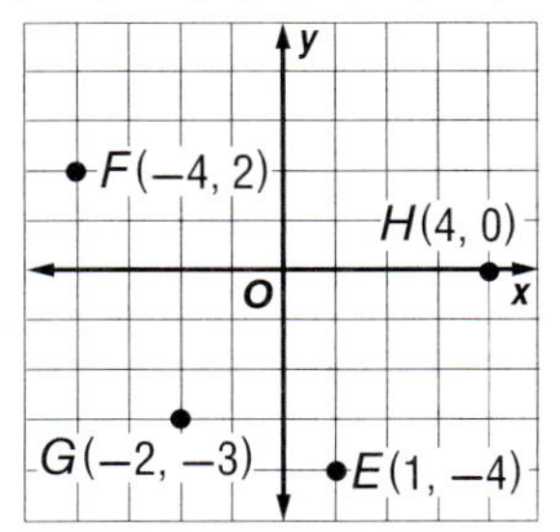

49. 60 **51.** 81 **53.** −10 **55.** 30

Pages 119–122 Chapter 2 Study Guide and Review

1. false, negative **3.** false, opposite **5.** false, y-coordinate **7.** true **9.** false, positive **11.** 350 ft **13.** −12° **15.** 32 **17.** −48 mL **19.** > **21.** < **23.** < **25.** {−32, −23, −21, 14, 19, 25} **27.** −10, −6, −5, 0, 2, 5, 10, 12, 20, 25 **28–31.**

33. 2 **35.** −5 **37.** 123 ft **39.** −3 **41.** 4 **43.** −12 **45.** 35 **47.** 28 **49.** −35 **51.** 17,280 **53.** 576 ft **55.** −3 **57.** 9

Chapter 3 Algebra: Linear Equations and Functions

Page 127 Chapter 3 Getting Ready

1. 4 **3.** −11 **5.**

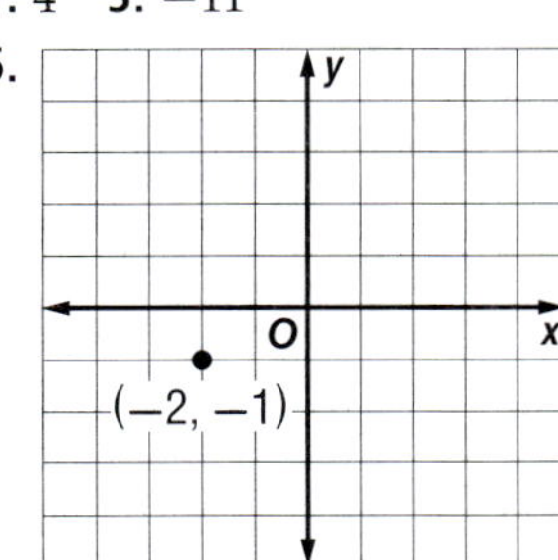

7. −8 **9.** 4 **11.** −11 **13.** 14 **15.** 2 **17.** −2

Pages 131–133 Lesson 3-1

1. $n + 8$ **3.** $n - 9 = 24$ **5.** $2m = 18$ **7.** $x - 1 = 34.3$ **9.** $15 + t$ **11.** $n - 10$ **13.** $8r$ **15.** $\frac{a}{3}$ **17.** $n + 4 = -8$ **19.** $5d = -20$ **21.** $h - 10 = 26$ **23.** $c + 3.5 = 5.5$ **25.** the length is 4 times the width **27.** the width is 5 less than the length **29.** $2b + 2$ **31.** $3(a - 43)$ **33.** $13k^2$ **35.** American toad **37.** 3 less than a number is 6. **39.** $x + 2$; $x - 2$ **41.** C **43.** −7 **45.** 15 **47.** 25 **49.** 49 **51.** Plan A **53.** −11 **55.** −8

Pages 139–141 Lesson 3-2

1. 2 **3.** −2 **5.** $d + 120 = 364$; 244 ft **7.** 5 **9.** 7 **11.** 7 **13.** −3 **15.** −9 **17.** 17 **19.** 7 **21.** $7 = w + 2$; 5 **23.** $15 = t - 3$; 18 years old **25.** 61 **27.** −5 **29.** −12 **31.** 18.4 **33.** 6.4 **35.** −0.68 **37.** $d - 5 = 18$; $23 **39.** $35 + 45 + x = 180$; 100° **41.** $1 - 1 + s = -5$; −5 **43.** $s - 65 = 13$; 78 mph **45.** $n - 13 = 163$; 176 ft **47.** The value of y decreases by 2. **49.** C **51.** $p + 180$ **53.** 46 pages **55.** 2.6 **57.** 1.52

Pages 144–146 Lesson 3-3

1. 3 **3.** −3 **5.** 8 h **7.** 7 **9.** −3 **11.** 7 **13.** −9 **15.** 4 **17.** −8 **19.** $15w = 300$; 20 weeks **21.** $3h$ **23.** 23 **25.** 18 **27.** 4.7 **29.** Sample answer: Evelyn Ashford has the faster average speed. Her race is half the distance as Sanya Richards, and it took her less than half the time as Sanya Richards to complete the race. **31.** $20.88h = 145$; $h \approx 6.94$ **33.** Steve; the variable is multiplied by −6. To solve for x, you need to divide each side of the equation by the entire coefficient, −6. **35.** Sample answer: Billie has twice as many cards as Tyree. If Billie has 16 cards, how many does Tyree have? **37.** Sample answer: If it takes a scuba diver 4 seconds to swim 8 meters below the surface of the water, what is the rate of descent? **39.** 8 **41.** 5 **43.** $-3y$

45.

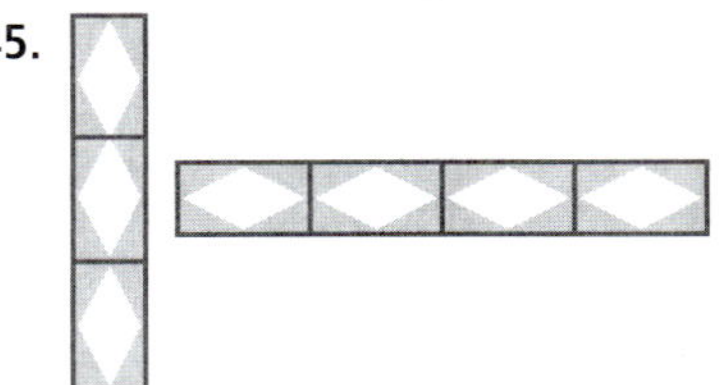

Pages 148–149 Lesson 3-4

1. When you are given the final result and asked to find an earlier amount. **3.** Sample answer: In the first four games, Hannah scored a total of 83 points. In the fourth game she scored 19 points. In game three, she scored 27 points and in the second game she scored 22 points. How many points did she score in the first game? To solve, first subtract 19 from 83, which is 64. Then subtract 27 from 64 to get 37. Finally, subtract 22 from 37. So, Hannah scored 15 points in her first game. **5.** 4 **7.** 19,200 tennis balls **9.** Brie is 14 years old. **11.**

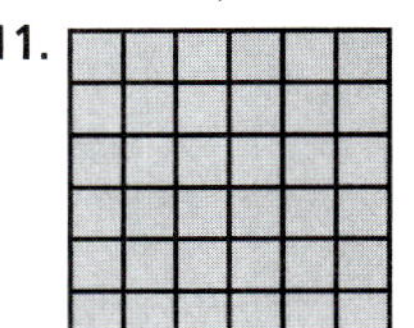

13. Raquels's car gets 1,774,074 more inches per gallon than an aircraft carrier. **15.** 1-$10 bill, 2-$5 bills, and 7-$1 bills

Pages 153–155 Lesson 3-5

1. 2 **3.** 3 **5.** 3 **7.** $14c + 23 = 65$; 3 CDs **9.** 3 **11.** −4 **13.** 4 **15.** 9 **17.** 8 **19.** 11 **21.** $2c + 10 = 14$;

2 cups **23.** 2.25 **25.** 2.1 **27.** 28 **29.** $8 + 47.6d = 960$; 20 days **31.** 92.2°F **33.** $\frac{1}{2}(20x) - 18 = 200$; $x = 21.8$; They must sell at least 22 subscriptions. **35.** Sample answer: A flower shop charges $2 for each flower in a vase and $5 for the vase. How many flowers can you place in a vase if you have $15 to spend? **37.** G **39.** 7 **41.** 41 **43.** 213 ft **45.** 14 **47.** 16

Pages 158–161 ***Lesson 3-6***

1. 18 yd **3.** 7 in. **5.** 26.25 ft^2 **7.** 36 ft **9.** 14.8 mm **11.** 11 ft **13.** 18 in. **15.** 78 ft^2 **17.** 183.6 m^2 **19.** 6.5 in^2 **21.** 5 squares **23.** $\ell = 33$ ft **25.** 3,200 yd^2 **27.** perimeter; 4 mi **29.** area; 13 ft **31.** 270 m^2

35. 9;

1 yd, 1 yd, 3 ft, 3 ft

1 yd^2 = 9 ft^2

37. 144;

1 ft, 1 ft, 12 in., 12 in.

1 ft^2 = 144 in^2

39. When the width of a rectangle is doubled, the perimeter becomes $2\ell + 4w$ and the area becomes $2\ell w$, or in other words, the area is doubled. **41.** $P = 2(3w + 1) + 2w$ or $P = 8w + 2$ **43.** A **45.** −2 **47.** 3.5 **49.** $5x = 11.25$; $2.25 **51.** −27 **53.** 11 years old

55. **57.**

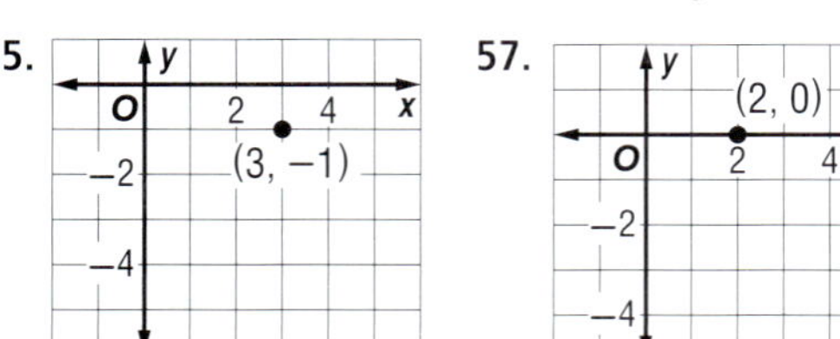

Pages 166–167 ***Lesson 3-7***

1.

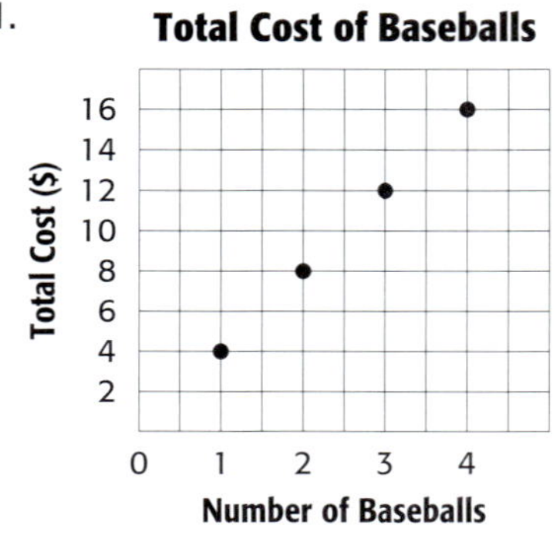

3.

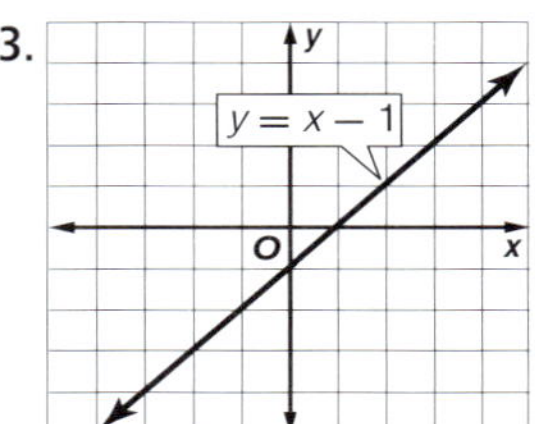

5.

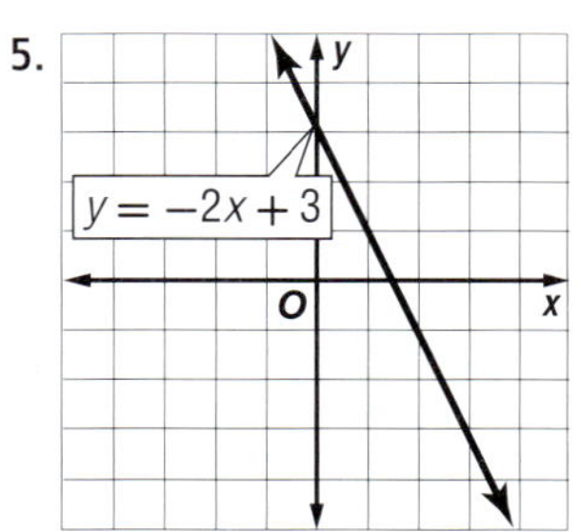

7.

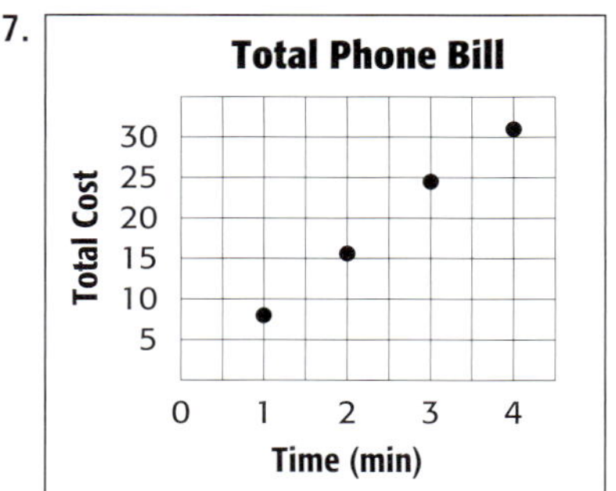

9. **11.**

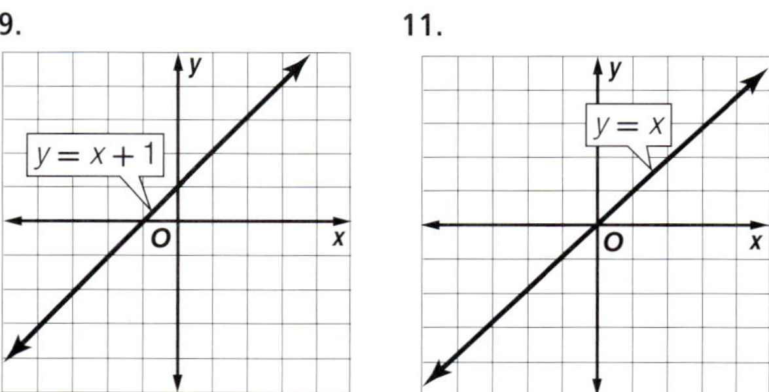

13. **15.**

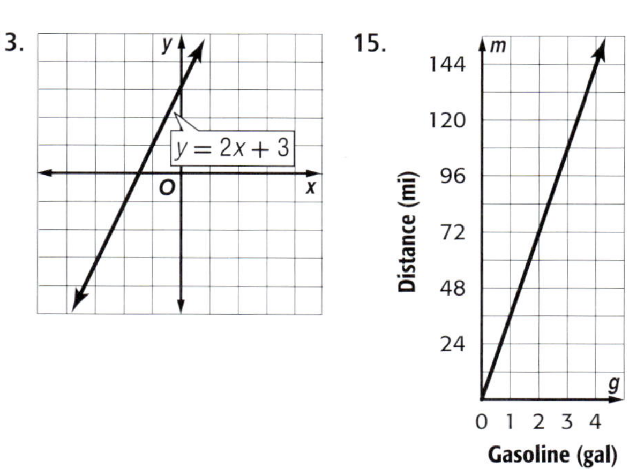

17.

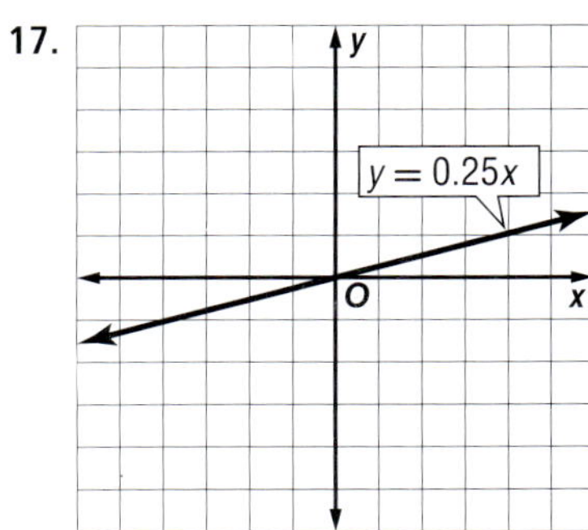

19.

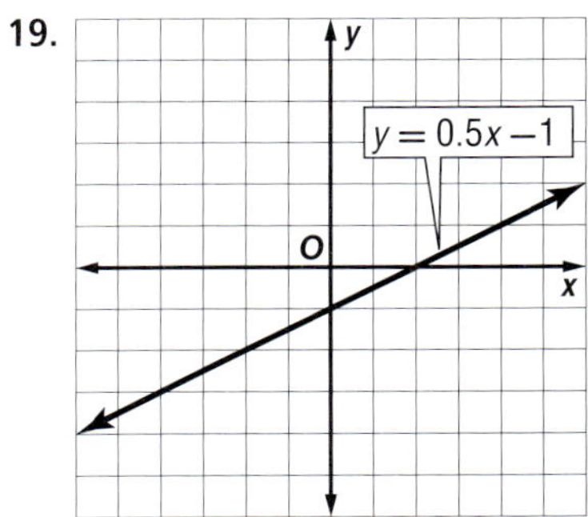

23.

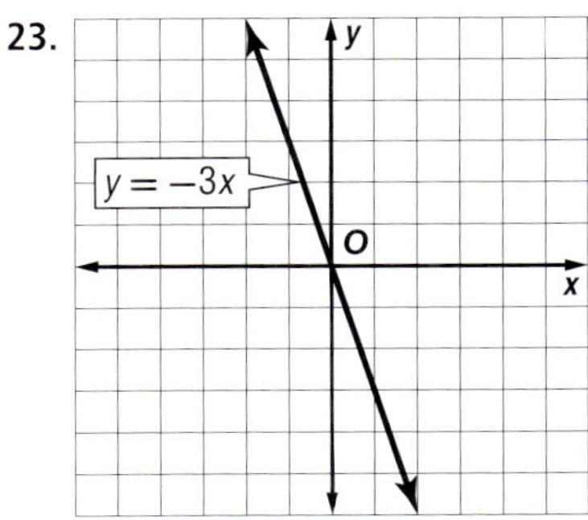

25. C **27.** –3 **29.** 4 **31.** 15

Pages 169–172 ***Chapter 3*** ***Study Guide and Review***

1. true **3.** true **5.** true **7.** False; subtract 3 from each. **9.** true **11.** false; perimeter **13.** $x + 5$ **15.** $2a$ **17.** $n - 4 = 19$ **19.** $f + \$8.75$ **21.** –6 **23.** 23 **25.** 37 **27.** 4 **29.** –9 **31.** $14w = 98$; 7 weeks **33.** \$146.70 **35.** 4 **37.** –2 **39.** 5 **41.** 53.4 in.; 142.82 in^2 **43.** 7 mi **45.** 16 yd **47.** 12 ft

49.

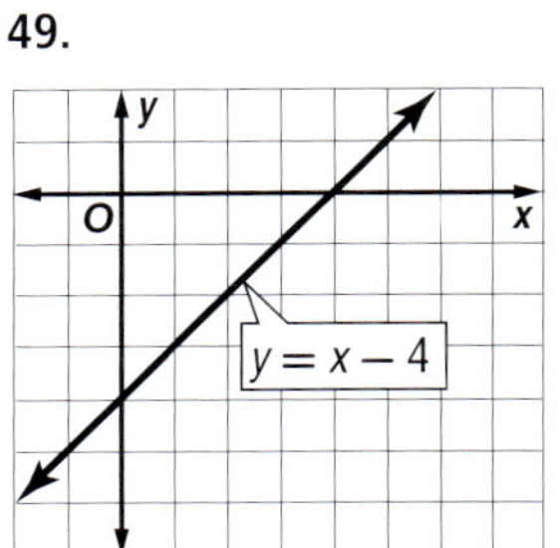

51.

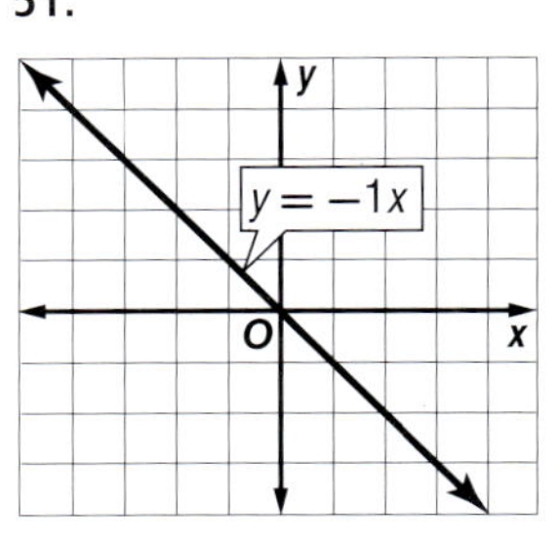

53.

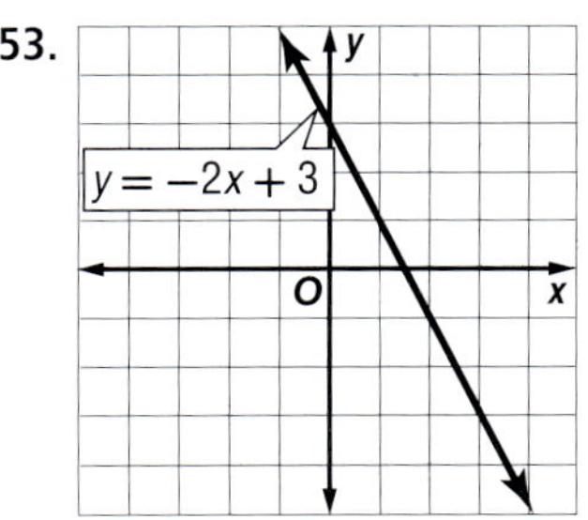

55. $y = 9x$

Chapter 4 Fractions, Decimals, and Percents

Page 179 ***Chapter 4*** ***Getting Ready***

1. 0.61 **3.** 0.33 **5.** Kirsten **7.** 2, 3, 6 **9.** Yes; the sum of the digits, 6, is divisible by 3. **11.** 6 **13.** 0.75 **15.** $5 \times 5 \times 5 \times 5 \times 5$ **17.** $9 \times 9 \times 9 \times 9$

Pages 183–184 ***Lesson 4-1***

1. prime **3.** prime **5.** 2×17 **7.** $2^2 \times 3$ **9.** $2 \cdot 2 \cdot 2 \cdot 2 \cdot x \cdot x$ **11.** composite **13.** prime **15.** composite **17.** prime **19.** $2^5 \times 3$ **21.** $3^2 \times 11$ **23.** $2 \times 3 \times 5 \times 7$ **25.** $2 \times 3^2 \times 7$ **27.** $2 \cdot 5^2$ **29.** $3 \cdot 5 \cdot m \cdot n$ **31.** $2 \cdot 17 \cdot j \cdot k \cdot m$ **33.** $2 \cdot 2 \cdot 13 \cdot g \cdot h \cdot h$ **35.** 7 **37.** 5^2 **39.** $2 \times 5^2 \times 29$ **41.** prime **43.** 81: 9×9, 3×27; 225: 9×25, 5×45; 441: 9×49; 7×63 **45.** 36 **47.** If $n = 1$, $2n$ is a prime number. If $n > 1$, $2n$ is a composite number with at least three factors. **49.** H **51.** 36 ft; 65 ft^2 **53.** –4 **55.** 0 **57.** 2, 5, 10 **59.** 3, 9

Pages 188–189 ***Lesson 4-2***

1. 6 **3.** 10 **5.** 4 **7.** 9 **9.** 6 **11.** 5 **13.** 24 **15.** 8 **17.** 6 **19.** 7 **21.** 8 students **23.** 6 care packages **25.** 25¢ **27.** $6a$ **29.** $5y$ **31.** Sample answer: 24 and 36 **33.** Sample answer: 60 and 90 **35.** Sample answer: The first prism is 8 in. high, 3 in. long, and 4 in. wide. The second prism is 8 in. high, 6 in. long, and 5 in. wide. The third prism is 8 in. high, 5 in. long, and 5 in. wide. **37.** always **39.** Sample answer: 4 and 12 are factors of 24. The greatest common factor of 4, 12, and 24 is 4. **41.** G

43.

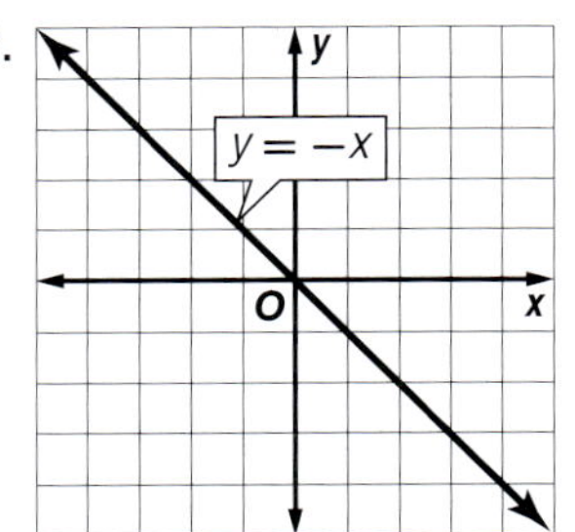

Selected Answers

45. (graph of $y = 2x - 1$)

47. 20 songs

Pages 190–191 Lesson 4-3

1. Sample answer: By making an organized list, you can show all the possible pizza combinations. Count the number of pizzas to determine the answer. **3.** 6 outfits **5.** 6 ways **7.** 27, 29 **9.** Paul: 9; Angelina: 5; Bret: 9; Jill: 1 **11.** 7 in. **13.** 0.5m

Pages 194–195 Lesson 4-4

1. $\frac{1}{3}$ **3.** $\frac{2}{5}$ **5.** $\frac{2}{3}$ **7.** $\frac{5}{7}$ **9.** $\frac{7}{10}$ **11.** $\frac{4}{7}$ **13.** $\frac{6}{7}$ **15.** 1 **17.** $\frac{5}{6}$ **19.** $\frac{5}{7}$ **21.** $\frac{2}{5}$ **23.** $\frac{1}{5}$ **25.** $\frac{3}{4}$ **27.** $\frac{1}{3}$ **31.** No, because both the numerator and denominator can be divided by 2. **33.** Sample answer: A fraction is in simplest form if the GCF of the numerator and denominator is 1. **35.** F **37.** 9 **39.** 5 **41.** 0.5 **43.** 0.7

Pages 199–200 Lesson 4-5

1. 0.4 **3.** 7.5 **5.** 0.125 **7.** $0.\overline{5}$ **9.** $\frac{11}{50}$ **11.** $4\frac{3}{5}$ **13.** 0.8 **15.** 4.16 **17.** 0.3125 **19.** 0.66 **21.** 5.875 **23.** $0.\overline{4}$ **25.** $0.\overline{16}$ **27.** $5.\overline{3}$ **29.** $\frac{1}{5}$ **31.** $\frac{11}{20}$ **33.** $5\frac{24}{25}$ **35.** $30\frac{1}{2}$ cm **39.** $\frac{22}{3}$ **41.** $\frac{-16}{5}$ **43.** Felisa; Sample answer: Felisa's batting average is about 0.286. Harmony's batting average is about 0.263. 0.286 > 0.263, so Felisa's average is better than Harmony's. **45.** Sample answer: $3\frac{1}{7} \approx 3.14286\ldots$ and $3\frac{10}{71} \approx 3.14085$; Since $3.1415927\ldots$ is between $3\frac{1}{7}$ and $3\frac{10}{71}$, Archimedes was correct. **47.** B **49.** $\frac{5}{12}$ **51.** $\frac{2}{7}$ **53.** 9 pizzas **55.** $\frac{3}{9}$ or $\frac{1}{3}$ **57.** $\frac{4}{12}$ or $\frac{1}{3}$

Pages 204–205 Lesson 4-6

1. 57% **3.** 25% **5.** 85% **7.** $\frac{9}{10}$ **9.** $\frac{11}{50}$ **11.** 42% **13.** 99.9% **15.** $66\frac{2}{3}$% **17.** 80% **19.** 26% **21.** 60% **23.** 100% **25.** 30% **27.** $\frac{3}{10}$ **29.** $\frac{22}{25}$ **31.** $\frac{13}{100}$ **33.** 3 **35.** < **37.** = **39.** > **41.** 64% **43.** 5%; the other ratios equal 25% **45.** C **47.** $\frac{3}{5}$ **49.** $2\frac{4}{5}$ **51.** 3 **53.** 4 **55.** 71 **57.** 0.791

Pages 208–210 Lesson 4-7

1. 0.68 **3.** 0.276 **5.** 9% **7.** 73% **9.** 0.27 **11.** 0.06 **13.** 0.185 **15.** 0.022 **17.** 0.277 **19.** 0.3025 **21.** 0.686 **23.** 70% **25.** 580% **27.** 95% **29.** 17% **31.** 67.5% **33.** 1.2% **35.** 34.7% **37.** 33.9% **39.** < **41.** > **43.** < **45.** 0.01389; 0.04167; 0.02083; 0.05; 0.03125 **47.** 1.2 ft **49.** Sample answer: 0.25, $\frac{1}{4}$, 25% **51.** 37.5% **53.** 3.125% **55.** D **57.** 72% **59.** 3.1% **61.** −125 **63.** $2 \times 5 \times 5$ **65.** $2 \times 2 \times 19$

Pages 213–214 Lesson 4-8

1. 28 **3.** 60 **5.** 60 **7.** 2020 **9.** 72 **11.** 72 **13.** 315 **15.** 72 **17.** 420 **19.** 144 **21.** 6:00 P.M. **23.** 50¢ **25.** Sample answer: 5, 7 **27.** Sample answer: 10, 35 **29.** 4 packages of juice boxes and 5 packages of oatmeal snack bars **31.** $2^2 \cdot 3 \cdot 5$, or 60 **33.** Sample answer: 3, 10, 15 **35.** C **37.** 0.55 **39.** 0.0025 **41.** $\frac{17}{25}$ **43.** $2s + 7$ **45.** <

Pages 218–220 Lesson 4-9

1. > **3.** < **5.** Eliot; 3 out of 4 has an average of 0.75; 7 out of 11 has an average of 0.64 **7.** C **9.** < **11.** = **13.** < **15.** > **17.** > **19.** < **21.** > **23.** = **25.** Jim; $\frac{10}{16} > \frac{4}{15}$ **27.** $\frac{8}{10}$, 0.805, 81% **29.** −1.4, −1.25, $-1\frac{1}{25}$ **31.** 3.47, $3\frac{4}{7}$, $3\frac{3}{5}$ **33.** > **35.** < **37.** 6c, $6\frac{1}{3}$c, 6.5c **39.** $\frac{1}{5}$g, 1.5g, 5g **41.** Eastern Chipmunk **43.** Bustos: 0.346; Kretschman: 0.333; Nuveman: 0.313; Watley: 0.400; Watley **45.** 0.08; 0.08 equals 8% and the other ratios equal 80%. **47.** Sample answer: Gwen needs $\frac{2}{5}$ yard of fabric and $\frac{3}{8}$ yard of ribbon to make a pillow. Which item does she need more, fabric or ribbon? Answer: fabric **49.** H **51.** 42 **53.** 48 **55.** 0.0625 **57.** 18 **59.** 4 **61.** 12

Pages 221–224 Chapter 4 Study Guide and Review

1. false; division **3.** true **5.** false; least common multiple **7.** true **9.** 2^7 **11.** 5×19 **13.** $65 = 5 \cdot 13$ **15.** 6 **17.** 21 **19.** $12 **21.** 15 different plans **23.** $\frac{7}{12}$ **25.** $\frac{2}{9}$ **27.** $\frac{1}{2}$ **29.** 0.75 **31.** $0.\overline{5}$ **33.** 6.4 **35.** $\frac{7}{10}$ **37.** $\frac{1}{20}$ **39.** $\frac{27}{50}$ **41.** $5.1\overline{3}$ min **43.** 44% **45.** 40% **47.** $\frac{19}{20}$ **49.** $\frac{4}{25}$ **51.** 0.48 **53.** 0.125 **55.** 61% **57.** 19% **59.** 0.12 **61.** 8 **63.** 24 **65.** 120 **67.** < **69.** > **71.** English

Chapter 5 Applying Fractions

Page 229 Chapter 5 Getting Ready

1. 35 **3.** 30 **5.** 21.6 **7.** 0.83 **9.** 4 **11.** $2\frac{6}{5}$ **13.** $5\frac{5}{4}$ **15.** $\frac{5}{3}$ or $1\frac{2}{3}$ c

Pages 233–235 Lesson 5-1

1–41. Sample answers are given. **1.** $8 + 2 = 10$ **3.** $6 \times 3 = 18$ **5.** $0 + \frac{1}{2} = \frac{1}{2}$ **7.** $\frac{1}{2} \times 1 = \frac{1}{2}$ **9.** $\frac{1}{4} \cdot 16 = 4$ **11.** $\frac{2}{3}$ of $6 \approx 4$ft **13.** $1 + 6 = 7$ **15.** $4 - 2 = 2$ **17.** $2 \cdot 3 = 6$ **19.** $9 \div 3 = 3$ **21.** $\frac{1}{2} + \frac{1}{2} = 1$ **23.** $1 - \frac{1}{2} = \frac{1}{2}$ **25.** $\frac{1}{2} \cdot 1 = \frac{1}{2}$ **27.** $0 \div 1 = 0$ **29.** 16 + 1 or 17 in. **31.** $\frac{1}{6} \times 36 = 6$ **33.** $25 \div 5 = 5$ **35.** $24 \div 2 = 12$ **37.** 39 **39.** 24 **41.** $\frac{1}{2} \times 200$ or 100

43. Sample answer: $\frac{1}{4} \times 60$ inches or 15 inches **45.** Sample answer: $\frac{11}{12}$ and $\frac{7}{15}$; $\frac{11}{12} - \frac{7}{15} \approx 1 - \frac{1}{2}$ or $\frac{1}{2}$ and $\frac{11}{12} \cdot \frac{7}{15} \approx 1 \cdot \frac{1}{2}$ or $\frac{1}{2}$ **47.** Estimation; Dion doesn't need an exact answer. Sample answer: $3\frac{1}{4} + 1\frac{2}{3} + 1\frac{2}{3}$ is about halfway between 6 and 7 cups. Since this is more than 6 cups, Dion cannot use this bowl to mix the ingredients. **49.** 38 cups **51.** > **53.** < **55.** 5 pkg. of necklaces and 3 pkg. of bracelets **57.** 37.5% **59.** 1.9% **61.** 10 **63.** 15

Pages 238–241 ***Lesson 5-2***

1. $\frac{2}{3}$ **3.** $\frac{1}{4}$ **5.** $\frac{13}{24}$ **7.** $\frac{1}{4}$ **9.** addition; Sample answer: To find how much smaller the total height of the photo is now, add $\frac{5}{16}$ and $\frac{3}{8}$; $\frac{11}{16}$ in. **11.** $\frac{4}{7}$ **13.** $\frac{2}{3}$ **15.** $\frac{2}{3}$ **17.** $1\frac{13}{24}$ **19.** $\frac{4}{9}$ **21.** $\frac{14}{45}$ **23.** addition; Sample answer: To find the smallest width to make the shelf, add $\frac{4}{5}$ and $\frac{3}{4}$; $1\frac{11}{20}$ ft **25.** subtraction; Sample answer: To find how much more turkey Makayla bought, subtract $\frac{1}{4}$ from $\frac{5}{8}$; $\frac{3}{8}$ **27.** $\frac{23}{28}$ **29.** $\frac{7}{12}$ **31.** $1\frac{1}{4}$ **33.** $2\frac{2}{3}$ **35.** $\frac{2}{15}$ **37.** $1\frac{1}{4}$ **39.** $\frac{1}{12}$ **41.** $\frac{2}{3} - \left(\frac{1}{6} + \frac{1}{4}\right) = \frac{1}{4}$ **43.** $\frac{3}{4}$ **45.** Sample answer: The sum of two unit fractions $\frac{1}{a}$ and $\frac{1}{b}$, where a and b are not 0, is $\frac{a+b}{ab}$.

$\frac{1}{a} + \frac{1}{b} = \frac{1 \cdot b}{a \cdot b} + \frac{1 \cdot a}{b \cdot a}$	Rename each fraction using the LCD, *ab*.
$= \frac{b}{ab} + \frac{a}{ab}$	Simplify.
$= \frac{b+a}{ab}$	Add the numerators.
$= \frac{a+b}{ab}$	Commutative Property

So, $\frac{1}{99} + \frac{1}{100} = \frac{99 + 100}{99 \cdot 100}$ or $\frac{199}{9{,}900}$ **47.** Lourdes; Meagan did not rename the fractions using the LCD. **49.** A **51.** D **53.** Sample answer: $4 + 4 = 8$ **55.** Sample answer: $6 \cdot 3 = 18$ **57.** 24.8% **59.** −5 **61.** $\frac{2}{3}$ **63.** 5

Pages 244–246 ***Lesson 5-3***

1. $9\frac{6}{7}$ **3.** $4\frac{2}{3}$ **5.** $1\frac{1}{2}$ **7.** $4\frac{5}{8}$ **9.** $3\frac{3}{20}$ gal **11.** $7\frac{5}{7}$ **13.** $2\frac{1}{7}$ **15.** $7\frac{5}{12}$ **17.** $18\frac{17}{24}$ **19.** $3\frac{1}{2}$ **21.** $2\frac{11}{20}$ **23.** $5\frac{7}{8}$ **25.** $7\frac{1}{6}$ **27.** addition; Sample answer: To find the length of the necklace, add $7\frac{1}{4}$ in. and $10\frac{5}{8}$ in.; $17\frac{7}{8}$ in. **29.** subtraction; Sample answer: To find how many inches Alameda had cut, subtract $6\frac{1}{2}$ from $9\frac{3}{4}$; $3\frac{1}{4}$ in. **31.** $15\frac{1}{4}$ **33.** $1\frac{3}{4}$ **35.** $7\frac{1}{8}$ yd **37.** Estimation; You do not need an exact answer; Less than; $7 + 1 < 2 + 7$ **39.** Sample answer: Since the garden is a rectangle, the length of one side added to the length of the other side would equal half the length of the perimeter. If one side of the garden is $2\frac{5}{12}$ ft long, find 6 ft $- 2\frac{5}{12}$ ft, or $3\frac{7}{12}$ ft. **41.** H **43.** Sample answer: $1 \div 1 = 1$ **45.** Sample answer: $9 \times 7 = 63$ **47.** 15 ft

Pages 248–249 ***Lesson 5-4***

1. Sample answer: Use estimation, look for a pattern, work backward. **3.** Sample answer: A fishbowl holds $1\frac{1}{2}$ gallons of water. If there is $\frac{1}{3}$ gallon of water in the bowl, how many more gallons are needed to fill the bowl; $\frac{2}{3}$ gallons, $1\frac{1}{6}$ gallons, or $2\frac{1}{6}$ gallons. Answer: $\frac{2}{3}$ gallon is not enough because that would make exactly 1 gallon of water in the tank. $2\frac{1}{6}$ gallons is too much, since the tank only holds $1\frac{1}{2}$ gallons. The answer is $1\frac{1}{6}$ gallons. **5.** J **7.** $\frac{5}{8}$ in.

9.

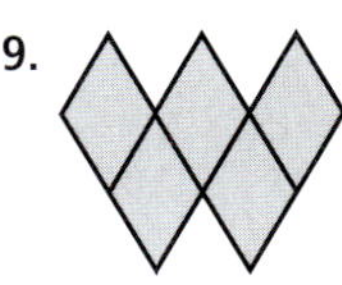

11. $\frac{1}{49}$ inch **13.** $\frac{4}{15}$

Pages 255–257 ***Lesson 5-5***

1. $\frac{2}{9}$ **3.** $\frac{2}{3}$ **5.** $1\frac{1}{2}$ **7.** 32 pounds **9.** $\frac{4}{15}$ **11.** $4\frac{4}{5}$ **13.** $\frac{1}{9}$ **15.** $\frac{1}{20}$ **17.** $\frac{3}{8}$ **19.** $\frac{3}{4}$ **21.** $\frac{3}{16}$ **23.** 14 c **25.** $1\frac{9}{16}$ **27.** 30 **29.** $31\frac{1}{3}$ **31.** 20 **33.** $7\frac{1}{20}$ mi **35.** $\frac{8}{21}$ **37.** $\frac{11}{48}$ **39.** $16\frac{1}{3}$ yd; $10\frac{5}{6}$ yd^2 **41.** one pint **43.** one centimeter **45.** $15\frac{3}{4}$ **47.** $28\frac{3}{4}$ **49.** broccoli: $1\frac{7}{8}$ c, pasta: $5\frac{5}{8}$ c, salad dressing: 1 c, cheese: 2 c; Multiply each amount by $1\frac{1}{2}$. **51.** $\frac{2}{5} \times \frac{3}{5}$; $\frac{6}{25}$; Sample answer: The model shows that $\frac{3}{5}$ of the rectangle is 15 sections out of 25 sections. Since $\frac{2}{5}$ of 15 sections is six sections, $\frac{2}{5}$ of $\frac{3}{5}$ is $\frac{6}{25}$. **53.** Always; Sample answer: Improper fractions are always greater than 1. **55.** Sample answer: The model shows that $\frac{3}{4}$ of one rectangle is 3 sections out of 4 sections shaded since 2 sets of rectangles with 3 sections out of 4 sections is $\frac{6}{4}$, 2 of $\frac{3}{4}$ is $\frac{6}{4}$, or $1\frac{1}{2}$. **57.** H **59.** $2\frac{1}{10}$ in. **61.** > **63.** $4.95 + 0.6x = 22.95$; 300 min **65.** 3

Pages 261–263 ***Lesson 5-6***

1. $\frac{5}{8}$ **3.** $\frac{5}{29}$ **5.** 32 **7.** 20.5 **9.** $\frac{4}{5}$ **11.** 32 **13.** $\frac{6}{5}$ or $1\frac{1}{5}$ **15.** $\frac{6}{1}$ or 6 **17.** $\frac{1}{3}$ **19.** $\frac{8}{41}$ **21.** 36 **23.** 14.4 **25.** 2.88 **27.** $\frac{6}{5}$ **29.** $\frac{20}{21}$ **31.** $6\frac{2}{3}$ **33.** 195 mi **35.** −75 **37.** 41.4 **39.** $1\frac{1}{2}$ **41.** x = elevation change of the Wild Cave Tour; $140 = \frac{7}{15}x$; 300ft **43.** x = number of servings; $\frac{3}{4}x = 16\frac{1}{2}$; 22 servings **45.** x = the person's age; $\frac{1}{3}x = 26$; 78 years old

47. 20; Sample answer: By solving $8 = \frac{m}{4}$, you find that $m = 32$. So, replace m with 32 to find $32 - 12 = 20$. **49.** Sample answer: Multiply each side by 2. Then divide each side by $(b_1 + b_2)$. So, $\frac{2A}{b_1 + b_2} = h$. **51.** A **53.** $\frac{1}{6}$ **55.** $\frac{2}{5}$ **57.** $3\frac{5}{12}$ c **59.** 0.08 **61.** 1.23 **63.** −1 **65.** −8 **67.** Sample answer: $18 \div 3 = 6$ **69.** Sample answer: $0 \div 1 = 0$

Pages 267–270 Lesson 5-7

1. $\frac{3}{8}$ **3.** $3\frac{1}{2}$ **5.** $\frac{1}{15}$ **7.** $1\frac{1}{5}$ **9.** 56 segments **11.** $\frac{7}{16}$ **13.** $1\frac{1}{3}$ **15.** 12 **17.** $\frac{2}{3}$ **19.** 12 **21.** $\frac{4}{15}$ **23.** $\frac{2}{3}$ **25.** $2\frac{17}{20}$ **27.** $7\frac{4}{5}$ **29.** 36 **31.** $3\frac{34}{35}$

33. $1\frac{1}{4}$;

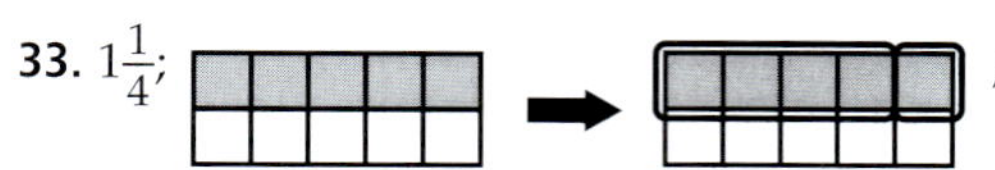

;

35. $2\frac{3}{4}$;

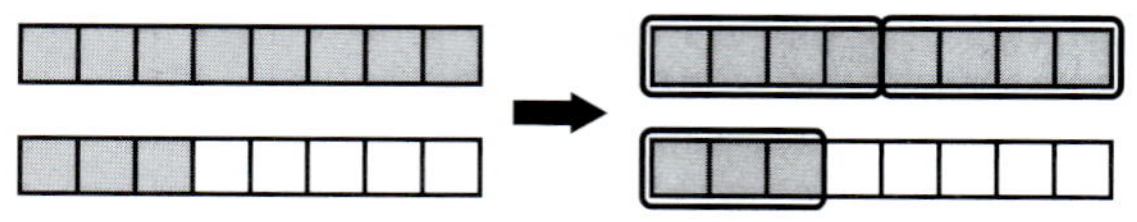

37. 25 **39.** $\frac{1}{22}$ **41.** $\frac{3}{11}$ **43.** 4 **45.** $7\frac{9}{10}$ times as many **47.** 6:30 P.M.; Sample answer: $105 \div 35 = 3$, The storm will travel 105 miles in 3 sets of $\frac{1}{2}$ hour, or $1\frac{1}{2}$ hours. Adding $1\frac{1}{2}$ hours to 5:00 P.M. will make it 6:30 P.M. **49.** Sample answer; You could use paper and pencil; $\frac{3}{4}$ of what number is $1\frac{1}{2}$? $1\frac{1}{2}$ feet $\div \frac{3}{4} = \frac{3}{2}$ feet $\cdot \frac{4}{3} = 2$ feet. **51.** Yes. If the first proper fraction is larger than the second proper fraction then the resulting quotient will be a whole number or mixed number. **53.** H **55.** $\frac{13}{4}$ or $3\frac{1}{4}$ **57.** $\frac{4}{21}$ **59.** 4.5 ft

Pages 271–274 Chapter 5 Study Guide and Review

1. numerators **3.** reciprocal **5.** unlike **7.** $1\frac{11}{7}$ **9.** 3 **11.** reciprocal **13.** Sample answer: $3 \div 1 = 3$ **15.** Sample answer: $1 \times 0 = 0$ **17.** Sample answer: $\frac{1}{2} \times 26 = 13$ **19.** Sample answer: 19×10 or about 190 ft^2 **21.** $\frac{1}{6}$ **23.** $\frac{2}{3}$ **25.** $\frac{5}{24}$ **27.** $\frac{5}{8}$ in. **29.** $9\frac{11}{15}$ **31.** $10\frac{1}{7}$ **33.** $2\frac{4}{15}$ **35.** $15\frac{1}{8}$ **37.** $7\frac{11}{12}$ h **39.** G **41.** $\frac{5}{27}$ **43.** $2\frac{3}{5}$ **45.** $9\frac{3}{8}$ **47.** $\frac{12}{7}$ or $1\frac{5}{7}$ **49.** $\frac{3}{10}$ **51.** 15 **53.** 0.75 **55.** $\frac{7}{10}$ **57.** $3\frac{3}{10}$ **59.** $1\frac{21}{22}$ **61.** 54

Chapter 6 Ratios and Proportions

Page 281 Chapter 6 Getting Ready

1. 48.1 **3.** 7.4 **5.** $\frac{1}{5}$ **7.** $\frac{19}{23}$ **9.** $\frac{39}{50}$ **11.** $\frac{3}{50}$ **13.** 450 **15.** 2,200

Pages 284–286 Lesson 6-1

1. $\frac{2}{15}$ **3.** $\frac{1}{51}$ **5.** yes. $\frac{12}{20} = \frac{3}{5}$ and $\frac{6}{10} = \frac{3}{5}$ **7.** no; Sample answer: $\frac{2 \text{ boxes}}{\$5} \neq \frac{6 \text{ boxes}}{\$20}$, since $2 \cdot 3 = 6$, but $5 \cdot 3 \neq 20$ **9.** $\frac{3}{2}$ **11.** $\frac{1}{3}$ **13.** $\frac{2}{5}$ **15.** $\frac{21}{1{,}600}$ **17.** $\frac{21}{32}$ **19.** yes; $\frac{4}{16} = \frac{1}{4}$ and $\frac{10}{40} = \frac{1}{4}$, so $\frac{4}{16} = \frac{10}{40}$ **21.** no; $\frac{8}{6} = \frac{4}{3}$ and $\frac{12}{10} = \frac{6}{5}$, so $\frac{8}{6} \neq \frac{12}{10}$ **23.** no; Sample answer: $\frac{12 \text{ in.}}{3 \text{ in.}} = \frac{4}{1}$ and $\frac{6 \text{ in.}}{1 \text{ in.}} = \frac{6}{1}$, so $\frac{12 \text{ in.}}{3 \text{ in.}} \neq \frac{6 \text{ in.}}{1 \text{ in.}}$ **25.** no; $\frac{71}{42} \neq \frac{16}{9}$ **27.** 9 lb **29.** yes; $\frac{330}{396} = \frac{5}{6}$; **31.** Areas A and C; both ratios simplify to a growth-to-removal ratio of $\frac{11}{30}$. **33.** 80; Sample answer: $440 + 80 = 520$; $\frac{520}{1{,}200} = \frac{13}{30}$ which is the same ratio as area B **35.** 2,400; The denominator of the ratios increases by 1. $\frac{20}{40} = \frac{1}{2}$, $\frac{40}{120} = \frac{1}{3}$, $\frac{120}{480} = \frac{1}{4}$ **37.** B **39.** $\frac{6}{7}$ **41.** $1\frac{2}{3}$ **43.** $5\frac{2}{3}$ **45.** 4.9 **47.** $0.31

Pages 289–292 Lesson 6-2

1. 6 mi per gal **3.** $0.50 per lb **5.** C **7.** 60 mi/h **9.** 30.4 people per class **11.** 3.5 m/s **13.** $0.14/oz **15.** about $0.50 per pair **17.** Susanna; 1.78 m/s > 1.66 m/s > 1.23 m/s **19.** Soft drinks A and B have about 3 grams of sodium per ounce and Soft drink C has about 6 grams per ounce. **21.** 510 words **23.** Sample answer: about 60 **25.** 182.7 **27.** 38¢ per lb; $1.89 ÷ 5 ≈ $1.90 ÷ 5 or $0.38 **29.** 3 c **31.** about 1 h 29 min 49 s **33.** The bear's heart beats 120 times in 2 minutes when it is active. **35.** the bear's heart rate in beats per minute **37.** when it is active; Sample answer: The active line increases faster than the hibernating line when read from left to right. **41.** Always; every rate is a ratio, because it is a comparison of two quantities by division. **43.** Sample answer: a; $\frac{30 \text{ ft}}{2 \text{ min}} = 15$ ft/min, $\frac{40 \text{ ft}}{2 \text{ min}} = 20$ ft/min **45.** C **47.** $\frac{2}{9}$ **49.** $\frac{9}{14}$ **51.** 8 subs **53.** $\frac{1}{2}$ **55.** $\frac{1}{4}$

Pages 295–297 Lesson 6-3

1. 1.5°F every hour **3.** slope: $\frac{8}{1}$ or 8; There are 8 packs of fruit snacks in each box.

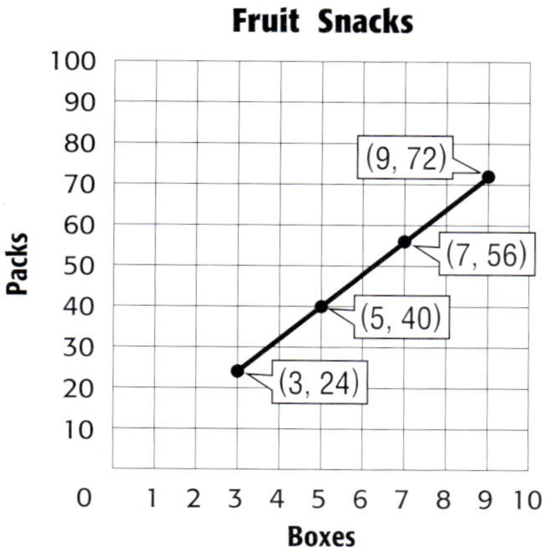

5. \$9 per h **7.** \$9 per shirt **9.** 0.45mi/min

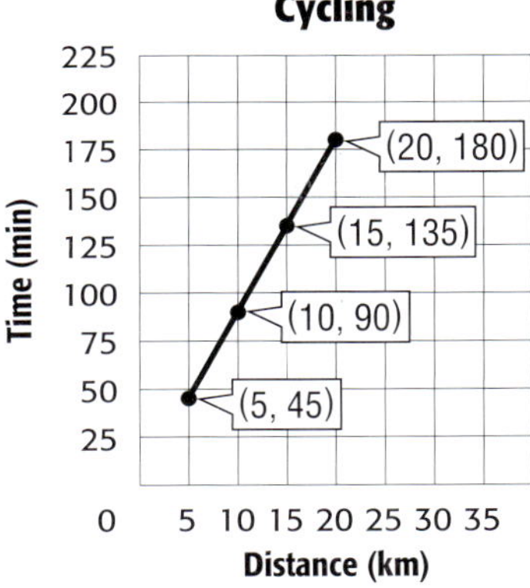

11. $\frac{1}{6}$ inch per minute

13.

Length of Poster (ft)	Ribbon Needed (in.)
3	18
6	36
9	54
12	72

15. A **17.** \$11.90 **19.** $\frac{18}{1}$ **21.** 50 **23.** 6.5

Pages 301–303 ***Lesson 6-4***

1. 48 **3.** 52 **5.** 3 **7.** $7\frac{1}{2}$ **9.** 0.0075 mi/s **11.** $4\frac{1}{2}$ **13.** 16 **15.** 24 **17.** 6,600 **19.** $6\frac{1}{2}$ **21.** 6,750 **23.** 3,520 ft **25.** $17\frac{1}{2}$ qt **27.** 1,056,000 ft/h **29.** No; 15 in. + $4\frac{1}{2}$ in. + $6\frac{3}{4}$ in. = $26\frac{1}{4}$ in. and $26\frac{1}{4} \div 12 = 2\frac{3}{16}$. So, it snowed a total of $2\frac{3}{16}$ ft or about 2 ft, not $2\frac{1}{2}$ ft. **31.** $\frac{1}{2}$ **33.** about $8\frac{1}{2}$ mi **35.** $\frac{1}{4}$ **37.** 3 gal; Sample answer: the graph increases by 1 gallon for every 4 quarts. **39.** < **41.** = **43.** 720 in^2; Square feet mean a unit of feet × feet. To divide out each unit, you must multiply by two conversion factors that have feet in the denominator and inches in the numerator.
$5\text{ ft}^2 \cdot \frac{12\text{ in.}}{1\text{ ft}} \cdot \frac{12\text{ in.}}{1\text{ ft}} = 720\text{ in}^2$ **45.** G **47.** \$9 per h **49.** 8 ft **51.** $2v$ **53.** 118.9 **55.** 142.127

Pages 307–309 ***Lesson 6-5***

1. 370 **3.** 1.46 **5.** 8.52 **7.** 128.17 **9.** about 5,333.33 ft **11.** 0.98 **13.** 3.0 **15.** 0.08 **17.** 130,500 **19.** 106.17 **21.** 36.01 **23.** 15.75 **25.** 0.51 kg **27.** about 35,420 meters per hour **29.** 16,582.42 **31.** 403,704 **33.** 0.06 L, 660 mL, 6.6 kL **35.** 130 cm, 2650 mm, 5 m **37.** 50 cm **39.** Jake; Gerardo divided 3.25 by 1,000; he should have multiplied. **41.** about 621,118.01 mi **43.** There are a greater number of smaller units. **45.** H

47. slope: $\frac{12}{1}$ or 12; There are 12 inches in 1 foot.

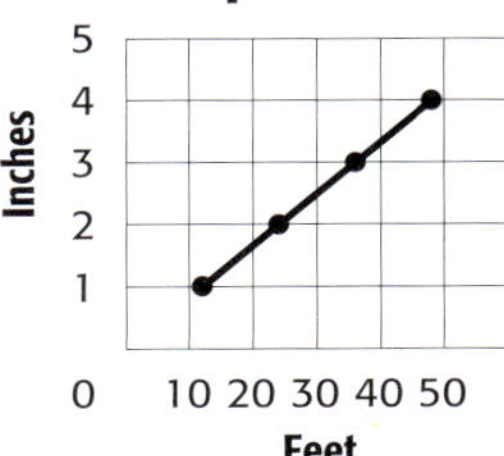

49. $6\frac{1}{5}$ **51.** $5\frac{19}{20}$ **53.** 10 **55.** 3.2

Pages 313–315 ***Lesson 6-6***

1. No; sample answer: $\frac{10\text{ children}}{2\text{ adults}} = \frac{5\text{ children}}{1\text{ adult}}$ and $\frac{12\text{ children}}{3\text{ adults}} = \frac{4\text{ children}}{1\text{ adult}}$. The unit rates are not equal. **3.** Yes; sample answer: The cross products of the ratios $\frac{8}{21}$ and $\frac{12}{31.5}$, 8 × 31.5 and 21 × 12, are both equal to 252. **5.** 15 **7.** 29.4 **9.** 20 **11.** \$8.33 **13.** No; sample answer: The cross products of the ratios $\frac{20}{6}$ and $\frac{16}{5}$, 20 × 5 or 100 and 6 × 16 or 96, are not equal. **15.** Yes; sample answer: The cross products of the ratios $\frac{16}{200}$ and $\frac{28}{350}$, 16 × 350 and 200 × 28, are both equal to 5,600. **17.** No; sample answer: The cross products of the ratios $\frac{1.4\text{ T}}{18\text{ days}}$ and $\frac{10.5\text{ T}}{60\text{ days}}$, 1.4 × 60 or 84 and 18 × 10.5 or 189, are not equal. **19.** No; $\frac{45\text{ min}}{25\text{ pages}} = \frac{1.8\text{ min}}{1\text{ page}}$ and $\frac{60\text{ min}}{30\text{ pages}} = \frac{2\text{ min}}{1\text{ page}}$. These rates are not equivalent. **21.** 15 **23.** 3 **25.** 1.5 **27.** 63 **29.** 2.4 **31.** 13.5 **33.** 4.2 lb **35.** 1.6 oz **37.** (3, 15) represents 3 pizzas cost \$15. (5, 25) represents 5 pizzas cost \$25. Yes, as the number of pizzas increases by 1, the cost increases by \$5. **39.** 5, with delivery fee; 5 no delivery fee; the slope represents the cost per pizza **41.** \$19.50 **43.** $\frac{325}{13} = \frac{100}{x}$; 4 **45.** \$5.70 for 6 lb; Sample answer: This ratio has a unit rate of 0.95/lb, while all of the other ratios have a unit rate of \$0.90/lb.**47.** Sample answer: Mental math; \$10 is 4 times more than \$2.50, so the number of ears is 4 times more than a dozen, which is 4 dozen or 48 ears of corn. **49.** B **51.** about 2.27 kg **53.** 56 **55.** $20\frac{9}{16}$ **57.** $17\frac{5}{32}$

Pages 318–319 ***Lesson 6-7***

1. $\frac{3}{4}$ feet

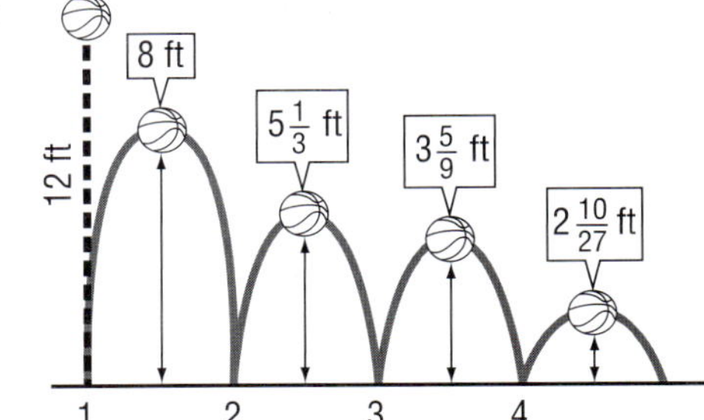

Selected Answers

3. 30 miles **5.** 125 minutes **7.** 28 games **9.** Mary, Isabela, Anna, Pilar

Pages 323–326 Lesson 6-8

1. 50 km **3.** 130 km **5.** 14 feet **7.** $16\frac{2}{3}$ in. **9.** $\frac{1}{48}$ **11.** $\frac{1}{63,360}$ **13.** 81 mi **15.** 40 mi **17.** 12 ft by 9 ft **19.** $11\frac{3}{5}$ in.; $\frac{1}{90}$ **21.** 6 in.; $\frac{1}{720}$ **23.** 26 mi **25.** $\frac{1}{3}$; about 6.33 feet **29.** $\frac{5,000}{1}$ **31a.** A; 0.5 cm is larger than 1 mm. If 0.5 cm on the model is equal to 1 mm on the actual figure, then model A must be larger than the actual figure. **31b.** B; 1.5 mm is smaller than 4 cm. If 1.5 mm on the model is equal to 4 cm on the actual figure, then model B must be smaller than the actual figure. **31c.** C; 0.25 cm is equal to 2.5 mm. If 0.25 cm is equal to 2.5 mm on the actual figure, then model C must be the same size as the actual figure. **33.** Sample answer: Using the scale given on the map, look at the distance between the two cities on the map and then estimate the actual distance based on the distance given in the scale. **35.** F **37.** 200 people **39.** 15 **41.** Sample answer: 7 + 9 + 10 + 12 + 7 or 45 mi **43.** 24 **45.** 30 **47.** 60 **49.** $\frac{13}{30}$ **51.** $\frac{7}{8}$

Pages 331–332 Lesson 6-9

1. $\frac{27}{100}$ **3.** $\frac{3}{40}$ **5.** $\frac{5}{8}$ **7.** 0.16% **9.** 11.11% **11.** $\frac{5}{8}$ **13.** 0.13% **15.** $\frac{1}{3}$ **17.** $\frac{15}{16}$ **19.** $\frac{1}{1000}$ **21.** 555% **23.** 375% **25.** 96.67% **27.** 71.43% **29.** 0.13% **31.** 0.42% **33.** 140% **35.** $<$ **37.** $>$ **39.** $\frac{1}{2}$%, $\frac{2}{5}$, 0.48, 0.5 **43.** Less than; $\frac{26}{125}$ = 20.8% **45.** Sample answer: Since a percent is a ratio that compares a number to 100, 80% is the ratio $\frac{80}{100}$. The ratio $\frac{80}{100}$ can be read as eighty-hundredths or written as a decimal, 0.80 or 0.8. The ratio $\frac{80}{100}$ also simplifies to $\frac{4}{5}$ if you divide the numerator and denominator by the same number, 20. **47.** G **49.** 2 **51.** $\frac{9}{20}$ **53.** $1\frac{3}{4}$

Pages 333–336 Chapter 6 Study Guide and Review

1. ratio **3.** rate **5.** scale drawing **7.** scale factor **9.** unit rate **11.** $\frac{4}{3}$ **13.** $\frac{2}{3}$ **15.** no; $\frac{18}{24} = \frac{3}{4}$, $\frac{5}{20} = \frac{1}{4}$, and $\frac{3}{4} \neq \frac{1}{4}$ **17.** 90 mi per day

19.

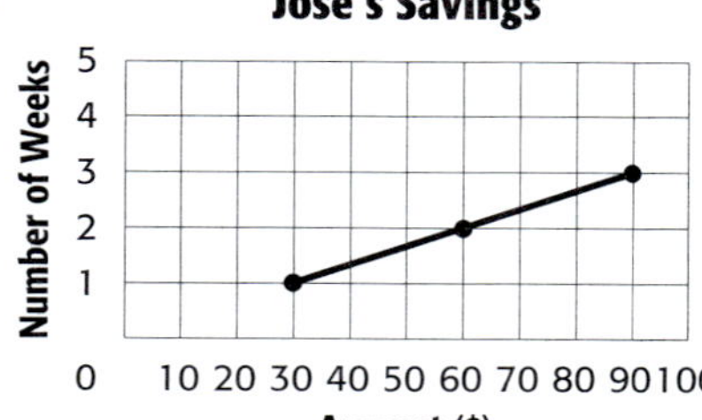

slope: $\frac{30}{1}$ or 30; José saved $30 every week. **21.** 24 **23.** $4\frac{1}{2}$ **25.** 50 bushels **27.** 51,528.96

29. 18.43 **31.** about 345 lb **33.** 54 **35.** 9 **37.** $2\frac{1}{3}$ **39.** 27 feet **41.** 24 mi **43.** $\frac{11}{40}$ **45.** $\frac{181}{400}$ **47.** 91.67%

Chapter 7 Applying Percents

Page 341 Chapter 7 Getting Ready

1. 48 **3.** 1,512 **5.** $54.75 **7.** 0.34 **9.** 0.75 **11.** 75 **13.** 38.9 **15.** 0.17 **17.** 1.57 **19.** 0.075

Pages 346–348 Lesson 7-1

1. 4 **3.** 110.5 **5.** 23 **7.** $3.25 **9.** $194.40 **11.** 45.9 **13.** 14.7 **15.** 17.5 **17.** 62.5 **19.** $290 **21.** 3.5 **23.** 97.8 **25.** 92.5 **27.** about 19.5 million **29.** 3.3 **31.** 990 **33.** 520 **35.** 0.24 **37.** $9.75 **39.** $297 **41.** about 316 **43.** Sample answer: 53% of 60 → 50% × 60 or $\frac{1}{2}$ × 60 = 30 **45.** Sample answer: 75% of 19 → 75% × 20 or $\frac{3}{4}$ × 20 = 15 **47.** 80 **49.** Sample answer: 24% × 250 or 60 people prefer cherries. So, 250 − 60 or 190 people did not prefer cherries. **51.** 15 **53.** Sample answer: Determine the number of questions answered correctly on a test and find how much to tip a restaurant server. **55.** Less than the original number; you are subtracting 10% of a greater number. **57.** C **59.** 71% **61.** $\frac{3}{5}$ **63.** $\frac{17}{24}$ **65.** 1267.81

Pages 353–354 Lesson 7-2

1. 36% **3.** 0.7 **5.** 75 **7.** 3 c **9.** 7.5% **11.** 8.6 **13.** 375 **15.** 24 **17.** 40% **19.** 4.1 **21.** 192 **23.** 0.2% **25.** $8 **27.** about 3.4% **29.** about 6,378 km **31.** 20% of 500, 20% of 100, 5% of 100; If the percent is the same but the base is greater, then the part is greater. If the base is the same but the percent is greater, then the part is greater. **33.** B **35.** 30 **37.** 2.75 **39.** 3 **41.** 30 **43.** 18

Pages 357–360 Lesson 7-3

1. 5; $\frac{1}{2} \cdot 10 = 5$; $0.1 \cdot 10 = 1$ and $5 \cdot 1 = 5$ **3.** 24; $\frac{2}{5} \cdot 60 = 24$; $0.1 \cdot 60 = 6$ and $4 \cdot 6 = 24$ **5.** $(1 \cdot 70) + \left(\frac{1}{2} \cdot 70\right) = 105$ **7.** about $50; $\frac{1}{4} \cdot \$200 = \$50$; $0.1 \cdot 200 = 20$ and $2.5 \cdot 20 = \$50$ **9.** about 160,000 acres; $0.1 \cdot 20,000,000 = 200,000$ and $\frac{4}{5}$ of 200,000 = 160,000 **11.** 18; $\frac{1}{5} \cdot 90 = 18$; $0.1 \cdot 90 = 9$ and $2 \cdot 9 = 18$ **13.** 135; $\frac{3}{4} \cdot 180 = 135$; $0.1 \cdot 180 = 18$ and $7.5 \cdot 18 = 135$ **15.** 90; $\frac{9}{10} \cdot 100 = 90$; $0.1 \cdot 100 = 10$ and $9 \cdot 10 = 90$ **17.** 36; $\frac{3}{10} \cdot 120 = 36$; $0.1 \cdot 120 = 12$ and $3 \cdot 12 = 36$ **19.** 90; $\frac{3}{5} \cdot 150 = 90$; $0.1 \cdot 150 = 15$ and $6 \cdot 15 = 90$ **21.** 168; $\frac{7}{10} \cdot 240 = 168$; $0.1 \cdot 240 = 24$ and $7 \cdot 24 = 168$ **23.** about 12 muscles; $\frac{3}{10} \cdot 40 = 12$ **25.** $(2 \cdot 300) + \left(\frac{1}{4} \cdot 300\right) = 675$ **27.** $0.01 \cdot 200 = 2$ and $\frac{3}{4} \cdot 2 = 1.5$ **29.** $0.01 \cdot 70 = 0.7$ **31.** about 2,700 birds; $0.01 \cdot 450,000 = 4,500$ and $\frac{3}{5} \cdot 4,500 = 2,700$ **33.** $\frac{1}{2} \cdot 80 = 40$ **35.** $\frac{1}{10} \cdot 240 = 24$ **37.** $1 \cdot 45 = 45$ **39.** about 3 hours; Method 1: $\frac{1}{3} \cdot 24 = 8$ and $\frac{1}{5} \cdot 24 \approx 5$;

$8 - 5 = 3$ **41.** 1,200 **43.** Sample answer: about 400,000 people; $.08 \cdot 5{,}000{,}000 = 400{,}000$ **45.** 3.6 ounces **47.** Sample answer: Find 1% of \$800, then multiply by $\frac{3}{8}$. **49.** Sometimes; sample answer: one estimate for 37% of 60 is $\frac{2}{5} \times 60 = 24$. This is greater than the actual answer because $\frac{2}{5}$ is greater than 37%. Another estimate is $\frac{1}{3} \times 60 = 20$. This is less than the actual answer because $\frac{1}{3}$ is less than 37%. **51.** B **53.** D **55.** 64.8 **57.** 157.1 **59.** Sample answer: $1 + 0 = 1$ **61.** Sample answer: $1 - \frac{1}{2} = \frac{1}{2}$ **63.** 50 **65.** 357.1 **67.** 0.7 **69.** 0.75

Pages 363–365 Lesson 7-4

1. $p = 88 \cdot 300$; 264 **3.** $75 = n \cdot 150$; 50% **5.** $3 = 0.12 \cdot w$; 25 **7.** 39 loaves **9.** $p = 0.39 \cdot 65$; 25.4 **11.** $p = 0.53 \cdot 470$; 249.1 **13.** $26 = n \cdot 96$; 27.1% **15.** $30 = n \cdot 64$; 46.9% **17.** $84 = 0.75 \cdot w$; 112 **19.** $64 = 0.8 \cdot w$; 80 **21.** 4,400 games **23.** 1 **25.** $p = 0.004 \cdot 82.1$; 0.3 **27.** $230 = n \cdot 200$; 115% **29.** about 42% **31.** about 27% **33.** Sample answer: 30 is 125% of what number?; 24 **35.** Sample answer: It may be easier if the percent and the base are known because after writing the percent as a decimal or fraction, the only step is to multiply. When using the percent proportion, you must first find the cross products and then divide. **37.** H **39.** \$1.95 **41.** 170.73% **43.** 37 yr

Pages 366–367 Lesson 7-5

1. Sample answer: Look for a rule or pattern in the data or number facts, estimation, guess and check, make an organized list, or work backward. **3.** Sample answer; $\$10 \cdot 12 = \$120$ **5.** 500; $60\% \cdot 830 \approx 500$ **7.** 2 quarters, 1 dime, 4 nickels, and 3 pennies **9.** \$30 **11.** \$3.50 **13.** $15 \cdot 18 + 18 \cdot 20 = 630$ ft^3. Then convert 630 ft^3 to square yards; $630 \div (3 \cdot 3) = 70$ yd^2

Pages 372–374 Lesson 7-6

1. 20% decrease **3.** 19% increase **5.** C **7.** 40% increase **9.** 71% decrease **11.** 25% decrease **13.** 5% decrease **15.** 13% increase **17.** 38% decrease **19.** 2% increase **21.** 75% decrease **23.** 150% increase **25.** 400% **29.** about \$31 billion **31.** 23% **33.** 2005 to 2006; 50% **35.** The \$60 sound system since 10 is a greater part of 60 than of 90. **37.** No; after a 10% increase, the quantity is greater then the original quantity. Decreasing a larger number by the same percent results in a greater change. **39.** D **41.** Sample answer: $0.5 \cdot 800$ or 400 students **43.** $n = 0.21 \cdot 62$; 13.0 **45.** 0.065 **47.** 0.0825

Pages 377–378 Lesson 7-7

1. \$3.10 **3.** \$1,338.75 **5.** \$98.90 **7.** \$1,605 **9.** \$4.90 **11.** \$7.99 **13.** \$96.26 **15.** \$7.50 **17.** \$180.00 **19.** \$35.79 **21.** \$333.60 **23.** \$25 **25.** \$50, \$25; The percent of discount is 50%. All of the other pairs have a discount of 25%. **27.** C **29.** C **31.** 9% decrease **33.** about 500×0.7 or 350 mi **35.** $\frac{1}{18}$

Pages 381–382 Lesson 7-8

1. \$38.40 **3.** \$5.80 **5.** \$1,417.50 **7.** \$1,219.00 **9.** \$21.38 **11.** \$123.75 **13.** \$45.31 **15.** \$14.06 **17.** \$1,353.13 **19.** \$116.25 **21.** Yes, he would have \$5.208. **23.** \$825.60, \$852.02, \$879.28 **25.** C **27.** \$21.39 **29.** 37% decrease **31.** $1\frac{1}{5}$ **33.** $2\frac{2}{15}$

Pages 384–388 Chapter 7 Study Guide and Review

1. true **3.** true **5.** false; 10% **7.** true **9.** false; original **11.** 39 **13.** 135 **15.** 14 games **17.** 0.3 **19.** \$27.49 **21.** Sample answer: 40; $\frac{1}{3} \cdot 120 = 40$ **23.** Sample answer: 20; $\frac{1}{5} \cdot 100 = 20$ **25.** Sample answer: 360; $0.1 \cdot 400 = 40$; $9 \cdot 40 = 360$ **27.** $32 = p \cdot 50$; 64% **29.** $n = 42 \cdot 300$; 126 **31.** $108 = 0.12 \cdot w$; 900 **33.** 333 **35.** Sample answer: $\$700 \times 0.4 = \$280$ **37.** 93% increase **39.** 10% increase **41.** \$26.75 **43.** \$8,440 **45.** 14% **47.** \$3.51 **49.** \$1,500 **51.** \$101.25 **53.** \$311.85

Chapter 8 Statistics: Analyzing Data

Page 395 Chapter 8 Getting Ready

1. 95.89, 96.02, 96.2 **3.** 22, 22.012, 22.02 **5.** 74.7, 74.67, 74.65 **7.** 3.340, 3.304, 3.04 **9.** 2.32

Pages 398–401 Lesson 8-1

1.

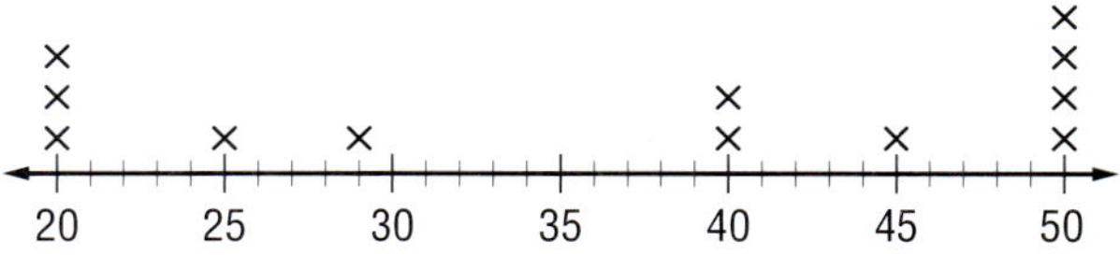

3. clusters: 6–12; gaps: 12–20; outlier: 20; range: 20 − 4, or 16 **5.** 1 or 2 glasses per day **7.** 5 glasses

9.

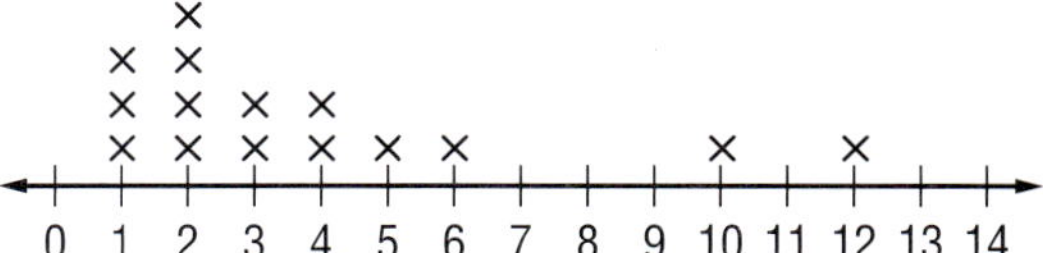

11.

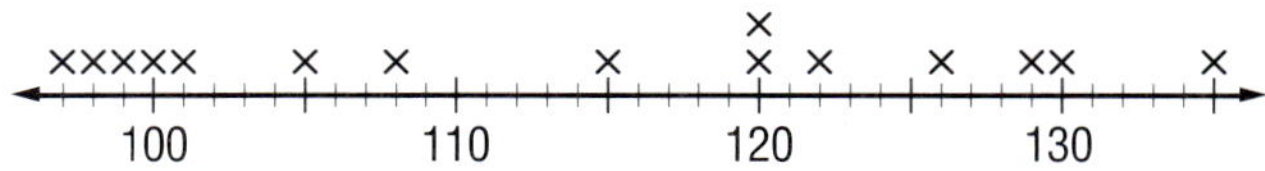

13. 34° **15.** Sample answer: cluster 104°F–122°F; gaps 100°F–104°F, 122°F–125°F, 125°F–128°F, and 128°F–134°F; outliers 100°F and 134°F **17.** 36 − 10 or 26 **19.** 15 **21.** Sometimes; the range will only change if the new data value lies above or below the greatest and least points, respectively, of the original data set. **23.** 10 **25.** about 72% **27.** Sample answer: range 28; cluster 1–19; gap 19–29; outlier 29

Selected Answers

29. **The House of Representatives, Southwestern States**

Sample answer: The data are more clustered between 4 and 25 with a range of 35 and a gap from 25 to 39. Most frequently occurring is 7, 8, and 9. 39 is an outlier. **31.** Sample answer: The range of a data set excluding the outlier(s) is a lesser value than the range of the same data set including the outlier(s). This is because any outliers will lie below and above the least and greatest values, respectively, of the data set and the range will change to include these values. **33.** Sample answer: A frequency table shows the number of times data occur by using tally marks. A line plot shows the number of times data occur by using ×s. A frequency table usually shows intervals of data and is useful when a summary is needed. A line plot shows individual data points and is useful when you need to see how all the data points are spread out. **35.** C **37.** $60 **39.** $4.46 **41.** 47 **43.** 12.6

Pages 405–408 ***Lesson 8-2***

1. 52.3; 57; 59 **3.** 26.5, 25.5, 23, and 25 **5.** Sample answer: Either the mean, median, or mode could be used to represent the data. The mean is slightly less than most of the data items, and therefore is a less accurate description of the data. **7.** 87; 90; 80 and 93 **9.** $12; $9; $6 **11.** 46, 45, 44 **13.** Sample answer: The mean, 15.6, is higher than most of the data. The median, 1, or mode, 1, best represents the data. **15.** $3.50, $3.50, $3.50 **17.** Always; Sample answer: Any value that is added which is greater than the maximum value, 23, will increase the average, or mean, of the values. **19.** Sometimes; Sample answer: The mean of the data set is currently 14.5. If a value that is greater than 14.5 is added, the mean will increase. If a value that is less than 14.5 is added, the mean will decrease. If a value that is exactly 14.5 is added, the mean will remain unchanged. **21.** Sample answer: A length of 960 inches is much greater than the other pieces of data. So, if this piece of data is added, the mean will increase. **23.** 10 points; Sample answer: The sum of the points for the first thirteen games is 158. In order for the average number of points to be 12, the total number of points for fourteen games would need to be 12 × 14 or 168. So, 168 – 158 or 10 points need to be scored during the last game. **25.** Sample answer: 4, 5, 2, 2, 3, 3, 1, 0, 1, 2, 4, 68, 5; the mean, 7.7, is not the best representation since it is greater than all the data items except one. **27.** Sometimes; if there is an odd number of items, the median is the middle number. If there is an even number of items, the median is the mean of the two middle numbers. **29.** Mean; a mode must be a member of the data set, and it is impossible to have 2.59 family members. **31.** H

33. **High Temperatures for July in Kentucky**

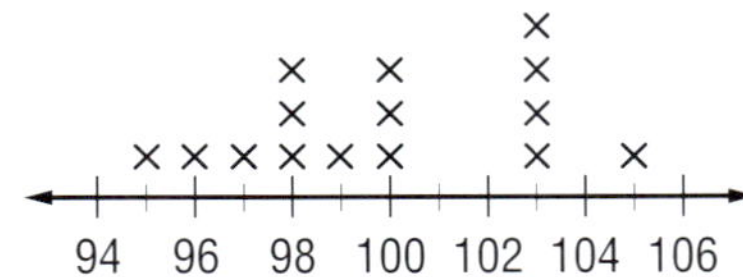

35. $10.43 **37.** Commutative (×) **39.** ones **41.** tenths

Pages 412–414 ***Lesson 8-3***

1. **Height of Trees(ft)**

Stem	Leaf
0	8 8
1	0 2 5 5 6 8
2	0 5

2|0 = 20 ft

3. 5 **5.** mean

7. **Low Temperatures (°F)**

Stem	Leaf
1	3 3 5
2	0 4 8
3	0 1 2 2 5 6 8 8 8

1|3 = 13°F

9. **School Play Attendance**

Stem	Leaf
22	5 7 9
23	0
24	3 6
25	
26	7 9 9
27	8 8 8

26|7 = 267 people

11. 4; 1 **13.** $45 **15.** mean **17.** 26 **19.** Sample answer: Yes; Thirty-six of the 56 signers were 30–49 years. Since 36 out of 56 is greater than half, you can say that the majority of the signers were 30–49 years old.

21. **Average Length (ft) of Crocodiles**

Stem	Leaf
6	3
7	
8	1
9	8 8
10	
11	4
12	
13	6
14	
15	
16	0 3 3 3 3
17	
18	
19	5

13|6 = 13.6 ft

Sample answer: A reasonable length for an average crocodile is about 16 feet.

23. Diana; three out of the six or 50% of the pieces of ribbon are 20–30 inches in length.

25. **Fiber in Cereal (g)**

Stem	Leaf
0	0 1 1 1 1 1 1 1
	2 3 3 3 4 5 5
	0|1 = 1 gram

0 1 2 3 4 5

Both representations show the frequency of data occurring. The line plot gives a good picture of the spread of the data. The stem-and-leaf plot shows individual grams of fiber as in the line plot, as well as intervals. See students' favorites and reasons. **27.** C **29.** 48.7; 50; 55

31.

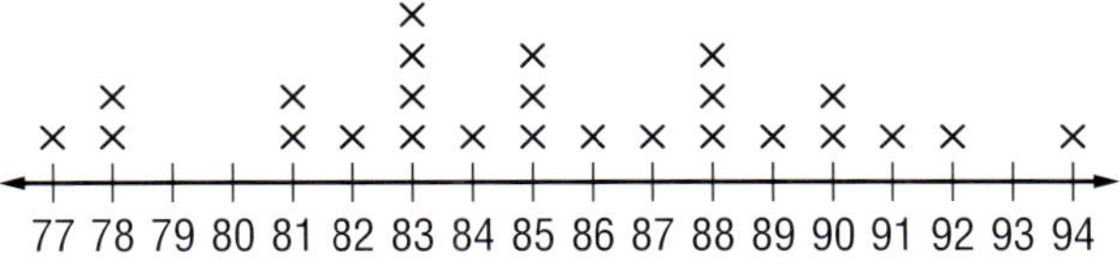

33. $\frac{3}{8}$ **35.** Sample answer: 20; 20–120

Pages 418–421 ***Lesson 8-4***

1. histogram

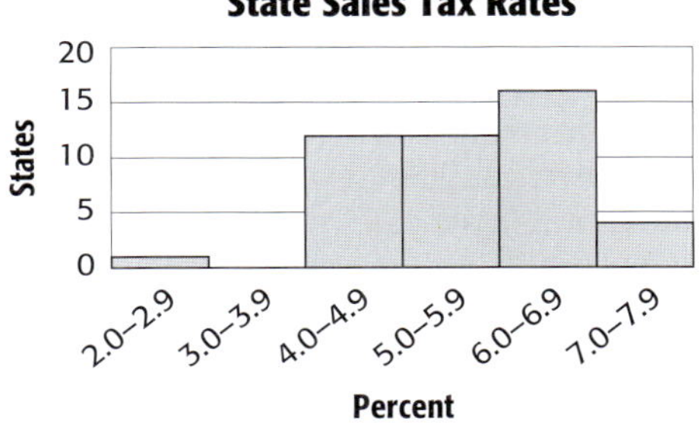

3. health

5. bar graph

Most Threatened Reptiles

Number of Species

40 35 30 25 20 15 10 5 0

Australia China Indonesia U.S. India

Country

7. histogram

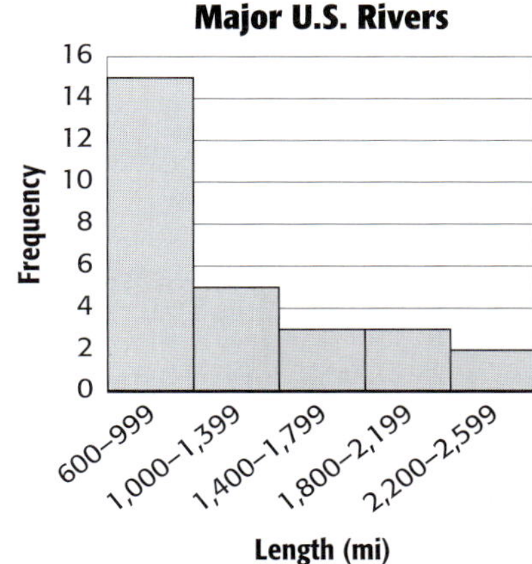

9. 13 students **11.** The 60–69 interval is three times larger than the 70–79 interval. **13.** 43 **15.** Sample answer: The number of zoos with 0.0–0.9 million visitors is about 4 times the number of zoos with 3.0–3.9 million visitors. **17.** a **19.** b **21.** about 15.8% **23.** Sample answer: It is easier to compare two sets of data. **25.** tennis **27.** Yes, 20% of girls prefer basketball and 35% of boys prefer basketball. **29.** Sample answer: Each interval represents a portion of the data set. The number of items in each interval is indicated by the frequency, typically shown along the vertical scale. By adding the frequencies for each interval, you can determine the number of values in the data set. **31.** C

33. **Number of Wins**

Stem	Leaf
1	5 7 9
2	3 5 6
3	0 1 2 6
4	0 0 1 3 4 5 6 7 7
5	0 0 0 1 2 3 3 5 6 6
	5|3 = 53 wins

35. Mental math; the numbers are easy to computer mentally. Sample answer: $\frac{1}{5}$ of \$50 is \$10 and \$50 − \$10 = \$40. So, he will need an additional \$40.

Pages 424–425 ***Lesson 8-5***

1. Sample answer: Graphs provide a visual representation of a situation involving comparisons. A graphical model can sometimes show conclusively what is often difficult to interpret from looking at lists alone.

3.

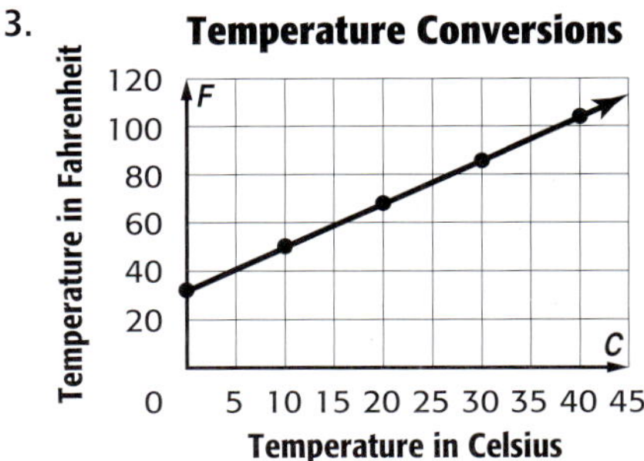

Selected Answers

5. Taylor 7. Wednesday 9. 27, 29 11. 2

Pages 428–431 **Lesson 8-6**

1. Sample answer: The graph shows a positive relationship. That is, as the years pass, the population increases. 3. about 155–160 people 5. about 400 7. about 95 min 9. Sample answer: As sleep decreases, the math test score decreases.

11. 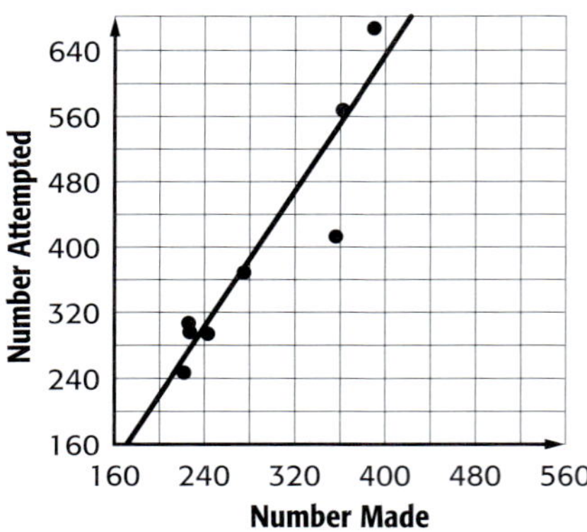

13. There is a positive relationship. That is, as the number of attempts increases, the number of free throws made increases. 15. about $55,000 17. Sample answer: Both lines have a positive trend. The population of Phoenix, Arizona, is now more than San Diego, California. 19. mode; the other three are ways to display data. 21. Graphs often show trends over time. If you continue the pattern, you can use it to make a prediction. 23. J

25. 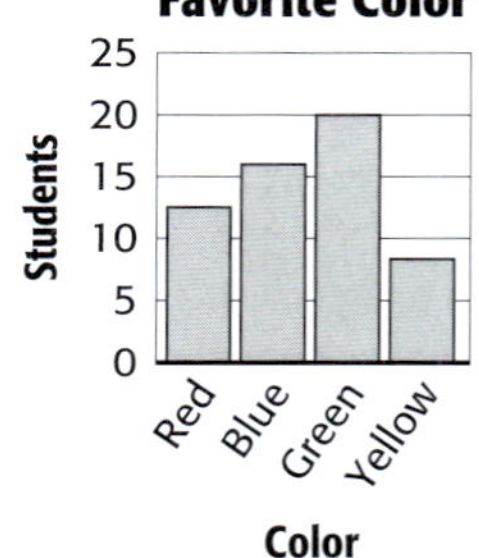

27. 83°; 83°

Pages 435–437 **Lesson 8-7**

1. 19,800 3. about 59 5. 1,419 people 7. 62,280 teens 9. b. 11. a. 13. about 38 people 15. about 1,040 19. D 21. B 23. It takes Dale a little bit longer to run each successive mile of the 5-mile run. 25. −24 27. 54 29. $\frac{3}{10}$ or 0.3 31. $\frac{9}{2}$ or 4.5

Pages 440–443 **Lesson 8-8**

1. The conclusion is invalid. This is a biased sample, since people in other states might have more umbrellas than those in Arizona. The sample is a convenience sample since all the people are from the same state. 3. This is an unbiased random survey, so the sample is valid; about 102 students. 5. The conclusion is invalid. This is a biased, convenience sample. 7. The conclusion is valid. This is an unbiased random sample. 9. The conclusion is invalid. This is a biased, convenience sample. 11. This is an unbiased random sample, so the results are valid; about 132 boxes. 13. This sample is a voluntary response sample. Therefore, no valid conclusion can be made. 15. about 443 17. Sample answer: This is an unbiased random sample. The time a student spends on the Internet during this week may not be typical of other weeks. 19. Sample answer: This is a convenience sample. The softball team may not represent the entire student population. 21. Not necessarily; Sample answer: Because you may be surveying different people in each sample, you may get different results. 23. Sample answer: If the entire population is too large to survey, it will be less time-consuming and easier to use a sample. 25. Yes; Sample answer: Every 10th person at a basketball game is asked whether they prefer basketball or baseball. This survey is a convenience sample because people attending a basketball game probably prefer basketball. 27. C 29. about 292 students 31. $58.44 33. $\frac{5}{8}$ 35. true

Pages 447–449 **Lesson 8-9**

1. Graph B; From the length of the bars, it appears that it appears that Cy Young had about 3 times as many wins as Jim Galvin. However, Jim Galvin had 365 wins and Cy Young had 511 wins. So, the conclusion is not valid. 3. Sample answer: The mean is 8,638 and the median is 8,941. Since the median is greater than the mean, use the median to emphasize the average length. 5. The sample is a biased convenience sample. Mr. Kessler's first period class may not be representative of all his students. The display is biased because the data used to create the display came from a biased sample. 7. The median or the mode because they are much closer in value to most of the pieces of data. 9. The sample is a biased convenience sample. The first 100 batteries produced may not be representative of all the batteries produced. The display is biased because the data used to create the display came from a biased sample.

11. 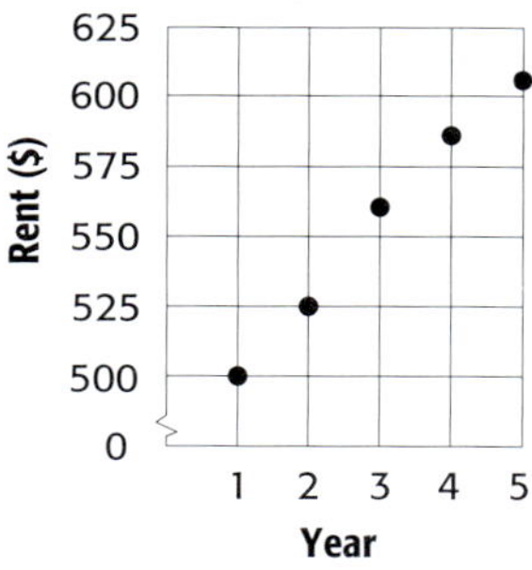

13. Sample answer: Outliers may distort measures of central tendency; data shown in graphs may be exaggerated or minimized by manipulating scales and intervals. 15. G 17. about 391 teens

Pages 450–454 Chapter 8 Study Guide and Review

1. true **3.** true **5.** false; outlier **7.** true

9.

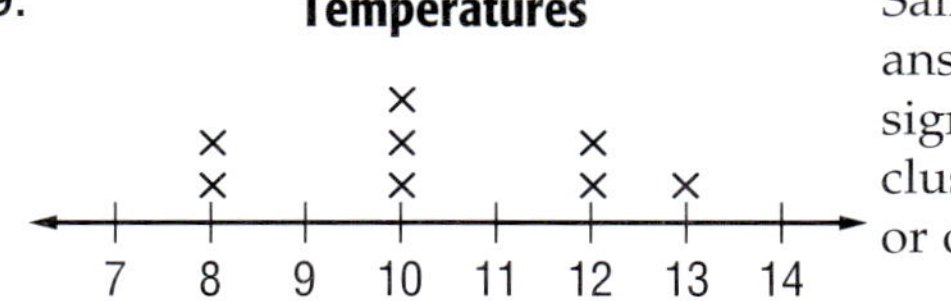

Sample answer: no significant clusters, gaps, or outliers.

11.

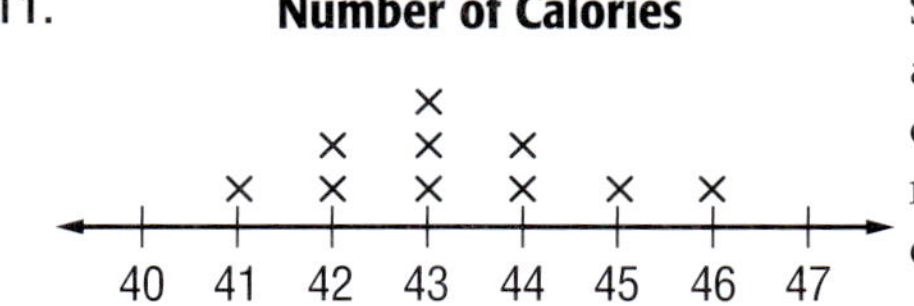

Sample answer: cluster 42–44; no gaps or outliers.

13. 84.3°; 86°; none

15. **Hours Worked**

Stem	Leaf
2	1 3 6 9
3	1 2 7 8
4	6
5	4

3|2 = 32 hours

17. **Birthdates**

Stem	Leaf
0	3 5 7 9
1	0 1 2 4 6 8
2	1 4

1|2 = 12

19. 10.75 million **21.** *Crazy Horse* **23.** Sample answer: The graph shows a positive relationship. That is, as the number of people in a family increases, the number of telephone calls per week increases. **25.** about 208 **27.** 162 teens **29.** The conclusion is valid. This is an unbiased random sample. **31.** The graph does not include the hot summer months or the cold winter months, which could have higher electricity bills.

Chapter 9 Probability

Page 459 Chapter 9 Getting Ready

1. 105 **3.** 52 **5.** 160 **7.** 210 **9.** 360 **11.** 5,040 **13.** \$315 **15.** $\frac{1}{6}$ **17.** $\frac{1}{3}$ **19.** 5 **21.** 4

Pages 462–464 Lesson 9-1

1. $\frac{1}{8}$ **3.** $\frac{1}{8}$ **5.** $\frac{3}{5}$ **7.** $\frac{23}{30}$ **9.** 1 **11.** $\frac{1}{20}$ **13.** $\frac{3}{10}$ **15.** $\frac{19}{20}$ **17.** $\frac{5}{8}$ **19.** $\frac{7}{20}$ **21.** 1 **23.** $\frac{3}{4}$ **25.** 60% **27.** $\frac{14}{33}$

29. Sample answer: The complementary event is the chance of no rain. Its probability is 63% **31a.** 1; Sample answer: Since 2032 is a leap year, there will be 29 days in February, making this event certain to happen; **31b.** 0; Sample answer: Since 2058 is not a leap year, there will only be 28 days in February, making this event impossible to happen. **33.** 0.33, 0.44 are probabilities that are not complementary because $0.33 + 0.44 \neq 1$. The other sets of probability are complementary. **35.** C **37.** There are no labels on the vertical scale. **39.** $\frac{1}{3}$ **41.** $\frac{1}{2}$ **43.** $\frac{9}{16}$

Pages 467–470 Lesson 9-2

1. Sample answer:

	Outcomes					
	1	**2**	**3**	**4**	**5**	**6**
1	1, 1	1, 2	1, 3	1, 4	1, 5	1, 6
2	2, 1	2, 2	2, 3	2, 4	2, 5	2, 6
3	3, 1	3, 2	3, 3	3, 4	3, 5	3, 6
4	4, 1	4, 2	4, 3	4, 4	4, 5	4, 6
5	5, 1	5, 2	5, 3	5, 4	5, 5	5, 6
6	6, 1	6, 2	6, 3	6, 4	6, 5	6, 6

3. C **5.** Sample answer:

Shape	Number	Sample Space
heads	1	heads, 1
	2	heads, 2
	3	heads, 3
	4	heads, 4
	5	heads, 5
tails	1	tails, 1
	2	tails, 2
	3	tails, 3
	4	tails, 4
	5	tails, 5

7. Sample answer:

Coin	Number Cube	Sample Space
H	1	H, 1
	2	H, 2
	3	H, 3
	4	H, 4
	5	H, 5
	6	H, 6
T	1	T, 1
	2	T, 2
	3	T, 3
	4	T, 4
	5	T, 5
	6	T, 6

9. Sample answer:

Color	Speeds	Sample Space
purple	10	purple, 10-speed
	18	purple, 18-speed
	21	purple, 21-speed
	24	purple, 24-speed
green	10	green, 10-speed
	18	green, 18-speed
	21	green, 21-speed
	24	green, 24-speed
black	10	black, 10-speed
	18	black, 18-speed
	21	black, 21-speed
	24	black, 24-speed
silver	10	silver, 10-speed
	18	silver, 18-speed
	21	silver, 21-speed
	24	silver, 24-speed

11. Sample answer:

Outcomes		
Short Sleeve	Gray	Small
Short Sleeve	Gray	Medium
Short Sleeve	Gray	Large
Short Sleeve	White	Small
Short Sleeve	White	Medium
Short Sleeve	White	Large
Long Sleeve	Gray	Small
Long Sleeve	Gray	Medium
Long Sleeve	Gray	Large
Long Sleeve	White	Small
Long Sleeve	White	Medium
Long Sleeve	White	Large

13. Sample answer:

Quarter Dime Nickel Sample Space

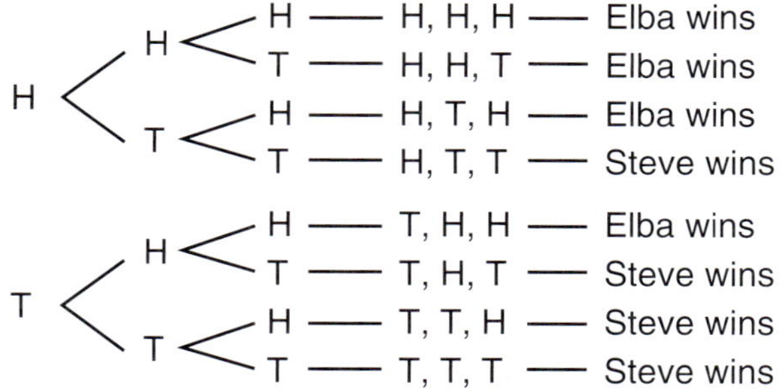

There are 8 equally likely outcomes with 4 favoring Elba. So, the probability that Elba wins is $\frac{1}{2}$. **15.** $\frac{1}{8}$ **17.** $\frac{3}{8}$ **19.** $\frac{1}{8}$ **21.** 16 **25.** Sample answer: Mei can draw a model of the situation using a tree diagram to show the sample space. Then she can determine the probability. The probability of guessing correctly is $\frac{1}{4}$.

Right/ Wrong	Right/ Wrong	Sample Space
R	R	R, R
	W	R, W
W	R	W, R
	W	W, W

27. Sample game: Each player tosses a coin 10 times. If it comes up heads, player 1 receives 1 point. If it comes up tails, player 2 receives 1 point. The player with the most points at the end of 20 tosses wins. **29.** $\frac{2}{5}$ **31.** $\frac{13}{20}$ **33.** $\frac{3}{10}$ **35.** The cost is increasing over time. In about a year's time, the cost has more than tripled. **37.** $3,876 **39.** 15.6 **41.** 154 **43.** 460

Pages 472–474 ***Lesson 9-3***

1. 8 **3.** 24 **5.** 12 **7.** 84 **9.** 24 **11.** 6 possible routes; $\frac{1}{6}$ **13.** 7,776 **15.** No; the number of selections is 32 • 11 or 352, which is less than 365. **17.** 2; 4; 8; 2^n; Sample answer: I used a pattern to determine the number of outcomes for n coins. One coin: 2^1 outcomes, two coins: 2 • 2 or 2^2 outcomes, three coins: 2 • 2 • 2 or 2^3 outcomes, n coins: 2^n outcomes. **19.** Sample answer: When there are multiple events, the Fundamental Counting Principle is a much faster method of obtaining the total number of outcomes than drawing a tree diagram. The Fundamental Counting Principle also saves paper space and can often be done mentally. When you need to see what the specific outcomes are, make a tree diagram since the Fundamental Counting Principle only gives the number of outcomes. **21.** 6 **23.** $\frac{1}{2}$ **25.** $\frac{1}{5}$, 0.22, 27%, 20.1 **27.** 6 **29.** 120

Pages 476–478 ***Lesson 9-4***

1. 5,040 **3.** $\frac{1}{20}$ **5.** 24 **7.** 720 **9.** $\frac{1}{90}$ **11.** $\frac{1}{12}$ **13.** Sample answer: Calculator; An exact answer is required. 24 × 23 × 22 × 21 = 255,024 **15.** $\frac{1}{4}$ **17.** Sample answer: The number of ways you can order 3 books on a shelf is 3 • 2 • 1 or 6. **19.** H

21.

Meat	Cheese	Outcomes
turkey	cheddar	turkey, cheddar
	Swiss	turkey, Swiss
ham	cheddar	ham, cheddar
	Swiss	ham, Swiss
salami	cheddar	salami, cheddar
	Swiss	salami, Swiss

23. $1\frac{13}{15}$ **25.** $4\frac{11}{48}$ **27.** 56 **29.** 3

Pages 482–483 ***Lesson 9-5***

1. 21 ways **3.** 6 **5.** 210 **7.** 924 **9.** $\frac{1}{20}$ **11.** 10; $\frac{1}{10}$ **13.** permutation; 90 **15.** 15 **17.** The number of ways you can choose three CDs from a collection of ten CDs is 120 ways. **19.** H **21.** 72 **23.** Sample answer: $\frac{1}{2} - 0 = \frac{1}{2}$ **25.** $\frac{1}{5}$

Pages 484–485 ***Lesson 9-6***

1. Sample answer: Results would vary slightly. **3.** No; Sample answer: the experiment produces about 1–2 correct answers, so using a spinner with 4 sections is not a good way to answer a 5-question multiple-choice quiz. **5.** 30 **7.** 65 is a reasonable answer because 40% of 160 is 64. **9.** No, the 6th row should have the numbers 1, 5, 10, 10, 5, 1. **11.** No; Sample answer: the experiment produces about 2–3 correct answers, so using a number cube is not a good way to answer a 5-question true-false quiz. **13.** $195

Pages 488–490 ***Lesson 9-7***

1. $\frac{14}{25}$ **3.** The experimental probability, $\frac{14}{25}$ or 56%, is close to its theoretical probability of $\frac{1}{2}$ or 50%. **5.** 22 people **7.** $\frac{9}{10}$; the experimental probability, $\frac{9}{10}$ or 90%, is close to its theoretical probability of $\frac{5}{6}$, or about 83% **9.** $\frac{3}{35}$ **11.** 134 **13.** $\frac{6}{25}$, $\frac{13}{50}$ **15.** $\frac{13}{25}$ **17.** No; The experimental probability that a mother will receive jewelry is $\frac{17}{100}$. Out of 750 mothers that receive gifts, only about 128 can expect to receive jewelry not 250. **19.** Yes; Sample answer: If there are 40 unsharpened pencils in the box, then there are twice as many unsharpened pencils as there are sharpened pencils. If there are five sharpened pencils in the sample that was taken out, then there should be ten unsharpened pencils which would give a total of 15 pencils in the sample, which was the size of the sample. It is important to note that this was only one sample. To be sure that the sample represents the population, other samples should be taken and compared to the first sample. **21.** B **23.** 6 **25.** 60% **27.** 55% **29.** 78%

Pages 495–497 ***Lesson 9-8***

1. $\frac{1}{30}$ **3.** $\frac{1}{10}$ **5.** $\frac{2}{9}$ **7.** $\frac{1}{90}$ **9.** $\frac{2}{3}$ **11.** $\frac{1}{2}$ **13.** $\frac{1}{6}$ **15.** $\frac{3}{25}$ **17.** 0 **19.** $\frac{3}{16}$ **21.** $\frac{15}{92}$ **23.** $\frac{3}{7}$ **25.** $\frac{4}{7}$ **27.** $\frac{3}{20}$ **29.** $\frac{1}{10}$ **31.** $\frac{1}{1,024}$ **33.** 21%

35.

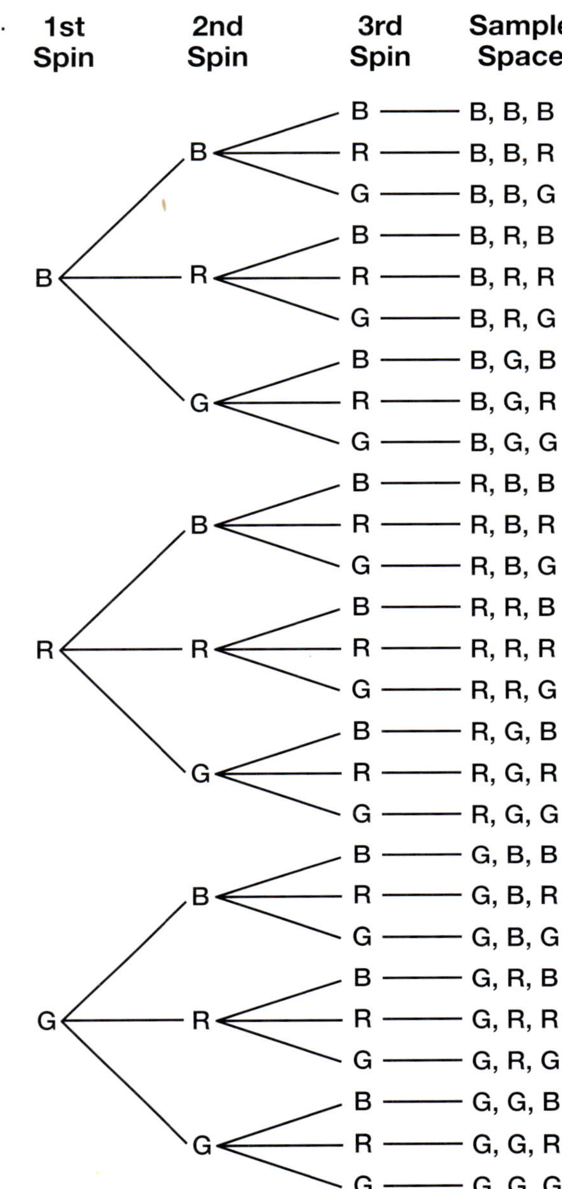

37. These events are dependent, not independent. Selecting one book and not returning it to the shelf limits your choices for the next pick to 2 books, not 3, as on the first pick. **39.** G **41.** 6 **43.** −48 **45.** 80

Pages 498–502 ***Chapter 9*** ***Study Guide and Review***

1. true **3.** false; probability **5.** false; independent events **7.** false; disjoint **9.** $\frac{1}{6}$ **11.** $\frac{13}{18}$ **13.** 8%

Selected Answers

15.

Outcomes	
Pepperoni	Water
Pepperoni	Milk
Pepperoni	Juice
Mushroom	Water
Mushroom	Milk
Mushroom	Juice
Cheese	Water
Cheese	Milk
Cheese	Juice

17. 36 **19.** $\frac{1}{12}$ **21.** 40,320 **23.** 105 **25.** 364 **27.** No; Sample answer: the experiment produces about 3 correct answers, so tossing a coin is not a good way to answer a 6-question true-false quiz. **29.** 8 **31.** $\frac{5}{16}$ **33.** $\frac{9}{32}$ **35.** $\frac{23}{32}$ **37.** $\frac{3}{64}$; $\frac{1}{20}$ **39.** $\frac{1}{16}$; $\frac{7}{120}$ **41.** $\frac{1}{3}$

Chapter 10 Geometry: Polygons

Page 509 Chapter 10 Getting Ready

1. 306 **3.** 0.15 **5.** 0.11 **7.** 44 **9.** 105 **11.** 14 **13.** 36

Pages 512–513 Lesson 10-1

1. $\angle MNP$, $\angle PNM$, $\angle N$, $\angle 1$; obtuse **3.** $\angle 1$ and $\angle 3$; Sample answer: Since $\angle 1$ and $\angle 3$ are opposite angles formed by the intersection of two lines, they are vertical angles. **5.** $\angle DEF$, $\angle FED$, $\angle E$, $\angle 5$; right **7.** $\angle MNP$, $\angle PNM$, $\angle N$, $\angle 7$; straight **9.** $\angle RTS$, $\angle STR$, $\angle T$, $\angle 9$; acute **11.** neither **13.** adjacent **15.** vertical **17.** $\angle 1$ and $\angle 2$; Sample answer: Since $\angle 1$ and $\angle 2$ share a common vertex, a common side, and do not overlap, they are adjacent angles.
19. True; Sample answer:

1

2

21. A **23.** $\frac{1}{24}$ **25.** $\frac{5}{24}$ **27.** 46 **29.** 54

Pages 516–517 Lesson 10-2

1. supplementary **3.** 135 **5.** supplementary **7.** supplementary **9.** neither **11.** 65° **13.** 137° **15.** Sample answer: $\angle CGK$, $\angle KGJ$ **17.** adjacent; adjacent; vertical **19.** $m\angle 1 = 180° - m\angle 2$; $m\angle 3 = 180° - m\angle 2$; Sample answer: $m\angle 1$ and $m\angle 3$ both equal the same expression. **21.** $m\angle E = 39°$, $m\angle F = 51°$ **23.** B **25.** $\angle P$, $\angle I$, $\angle RPQ$, $\angle QPR$; acute **27.** 223.2 **29.** 0.12

Pages 520–523 Lesson 10-3

1. **Blood Types in U.S.**

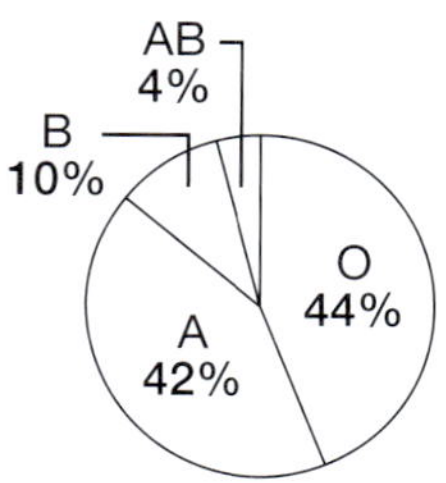

3. blue

5. **U.S. Steel Roller Coasters**

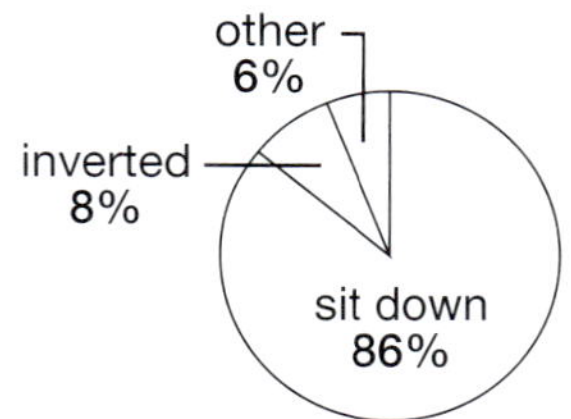

7. Endangered Species in U.S.

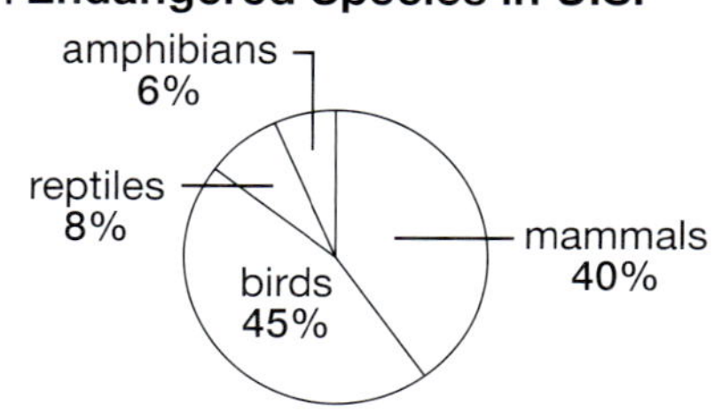

9. paper **11.** 48 million tons **13.** about 12 million
15. 15
17. bar graph

Birthplaces of Presidents

Number of Presidents

8
4
0

Virginia
Ohio
Massachusetts
New York
Texas

State

19. **Sizes of U.S Great Lakes**

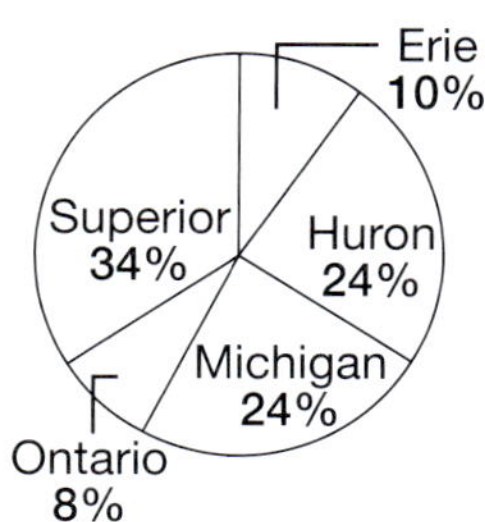

21. Lake Ontario is one third the size of Lake Michigan. **23.** No; a 50% increase in 126 students is 189, and 189 is not equal to 366. So, it is not reasonable to say that 50% more students said they could make a difference. Since 300% of 126 is 378, it is reasonable to say that 300% more students said they could make a difference than those who said they cannot make a difference. **25.** 12.5%; English is half of the circle. Since Science is half of English, Science is half of 50% or 25%. Math is half of Science, which is half of 25% or 12.5%. **27.** Sample answer: No; the sum of the percents is greater than 100. The people surveyed must have been able to choose more than one fruit juice. **29.** Sample answer: ∠1 and ∠3 **31.** 68 **33.** 101

Pages 527–529 ***Lesson 10-4***

1. 44 **3.** 45 **5.** C **7.** right, scalene

9.

11. 118 **13.** 27 **15.** 90 **17.** 53° **19.** acute, equilateral **21.** obtuse, isosceles **23.** obtuse, isosceles **25.** right

27.

29.

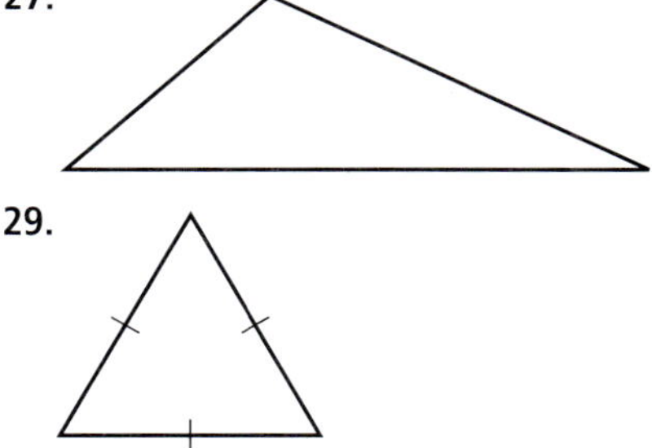

31. 79.5 **33.** 79.2 **35.** 21.3 **37.** 80° **39.** 60 **41.** 77.5

43.

Sample answer: All of the angles are acute and there are no congruent sides. **45.** Never; Sample answer: The sum of the three angles in a triangle is 180°. If a triangle has two obtuse angles, the sum of these two angles, not including the third angle, would already be greater than 180°. **47.** B **49.** about 101° **51.** supplementary **53.** about $9

Pages 530–531 ***Lesson 10-5***

1. Sample answer: They used inductive reasoning because they made a rule after seeing four examples. **3.** See students' work; none of the angles are congruent. **5.** Julio: mango, Rashanda: banana, Perry: orange. **7.** $3.75 **9.** 196 sq units **11.** 3 packs **13.** Sample answer: addition and division; Find the score that when added to the others, the total sum divided by the number of scores, 5, is equal to 82. The answer is 79.

Pages 535–538 ***Lesson 10-6***

1. rectangle **3.** parallelogram **5.** 120° **7.** 64° **9.** square **11.** quadrilateral **13.** trapezoid **15.** 56° **17.** 67° **19.** 90° **21.** 116° **23.** Bricks A, B, and D are rectangles and brick C is a square. **25.** 129.1° **27.** 131.8° **29.** trapezoids, squares, scalene triangles, equilateral triangles **31.** right isosceles triangles, squares, trapezoids **33.** No; a quadrilateral with three right angles will have both pairs of opposite sides parallel. So, it cannot be a trapezoid. **35.** 45 **37.** 80 **39.** Property B states that there are 4 right angles; Sample answer: A rectangle has 4 right angles in addition to property A. So, property B must state that there are 4 right angles. **41.** Never; Sample answer: A trapezoid has only one pair of parallel sides. A parallelogram has 2 pairs of parallel sides. **43.** Sometimes; Sample answer; A rhombus is only a square if all 4 angles are right angles. **45.** Since a square has all the properties of a rectangle and a rhombus, the diagonals of a square must be congruent and perpendicular. Nothing can be concluded about the diagonals of a parallelogram unless more information is provided. If a quadrilateral is a parallelogram, it is not necessarily a rectangle or a rhombus. So, it would not necessarily have the properties of a rectangle or a rhombus. **47.** J **49.** Neva: hamster, Sophie: turtle, Seth: dog **51.** right, scalene **53.** 720 **55.** $3.45 **57.** 3 **59.** 7

Pages 543–545 ***Lesson 10-7***

1. rectangle *PQRS* **3.** 45 mm **5.** triangle *CAB* **7.** 25 mi **9.** 7.2 in. **11.** 6 ft **13.** 12 m **15.** 1,207 feet **17.** 120 m **19.** 1:16 **21.** B **23.** C **25.** trapezoid **27.** 69° **29.** 90 **31.** 120

Pages 549–551 ***Lesson 10-8***

1. decagon; not regular **3.** hexagon; regular **5.** 128.6° **7.** not a polygon; the figure is not simple **9.** isosceles right triangle; not regular **11.** hexagon; not regular **13.** 144° **15.** 90° **17.** No; the figure is a decagon. Each angle of a decagon measures 144°; since 144° does not divided evenly into 360°, a decagon cannot make a tessellation. **19.** hexagon and triangle **21.** octagon and square **23.** $36\frac{1}{4}$ yd **25.** No; the stop sign is an octagon in shape. An octagon cannot make a tessellation. So, there will be some steel that is wasted after the nine signs are cut from the sheet. **27.** trapezoid

29. square **31.** pentagon hexagon

the Pentagon section of honeycomb

33. Sample answer; A copy of the parallelogram can fit next to it since 45° + 135° = 180° and above or below it since 135° + 45° = 180°. **35.** B **37.** trapezoid **39.** 1.5 m per s **41.** $3\frac{1}{6}$ **43.** $4\frac{37}{40}$

44–47.

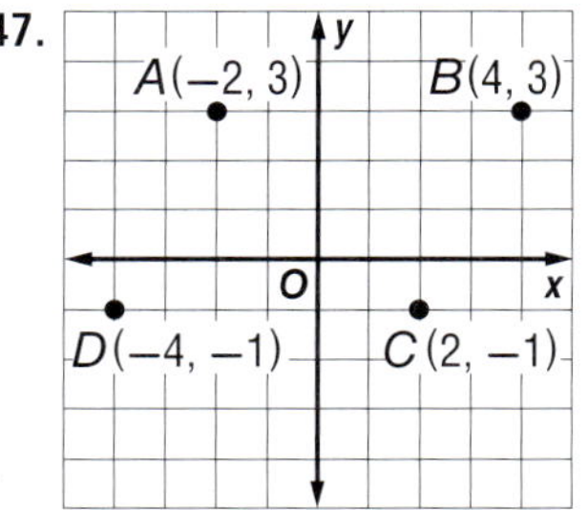

Pages 555–557 **Lesson 10-9**

1.

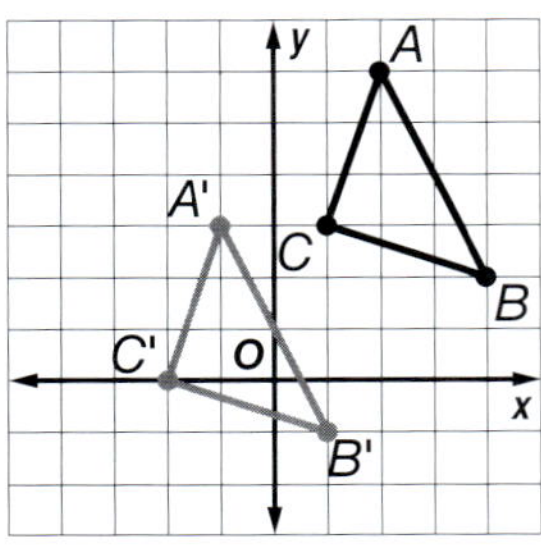

3. $D'(7, 0)$, $E'(4, -2)$, $F'(8, 4)$, $G'(12, -3)$

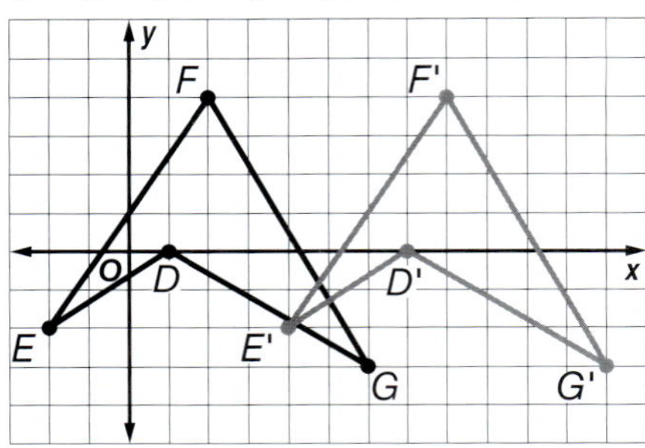

5.

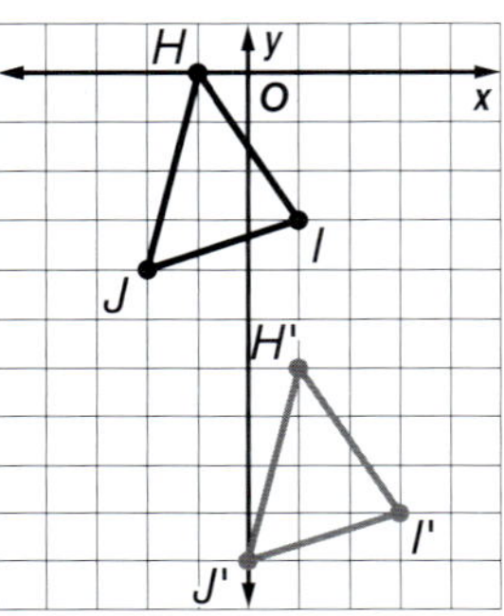

7. $P'(6, 5)$, $Q'(11, 3)$, $R'(3, 11)$

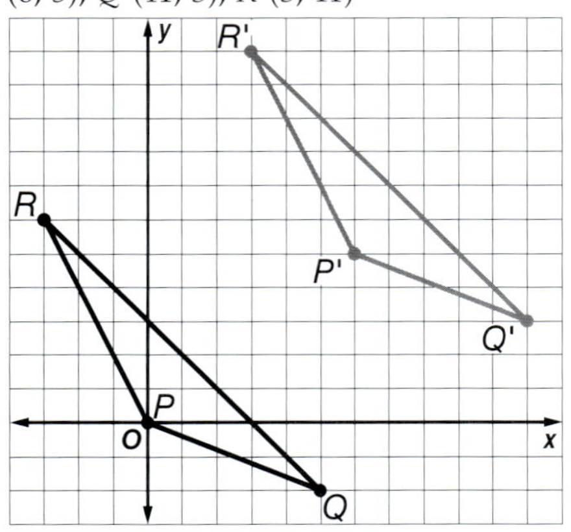

9. $P'(-3, 0)$, $Q'(2, -2)$, $R'(-6, 6)$

11. 3 units right and 1 unit up, (3, 1)

13.

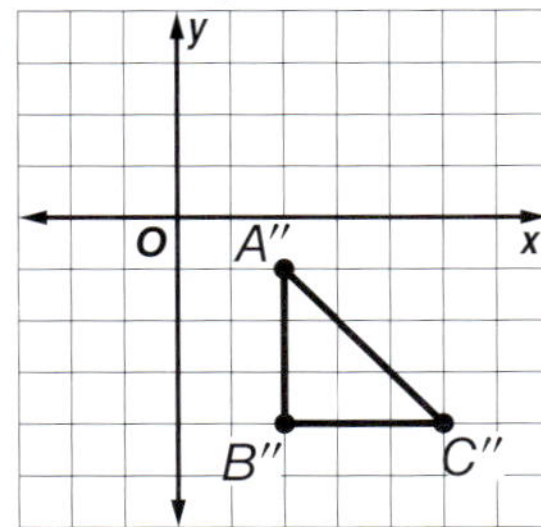

15. Sample answer: There are two main images, the small fish and the large fish. The fish are translated to different parts of the picture. These translations allow for the tessellation of the fish.

17. $F'\left(8\frac{1}{2}, 2\frac{1}{2}\right)$, $G'\left(4\frac{1}{2}, \frac{1}{2}\right)$, $H'\left(2\frac{1}{2}, 1\frac{1}{2}\right)$

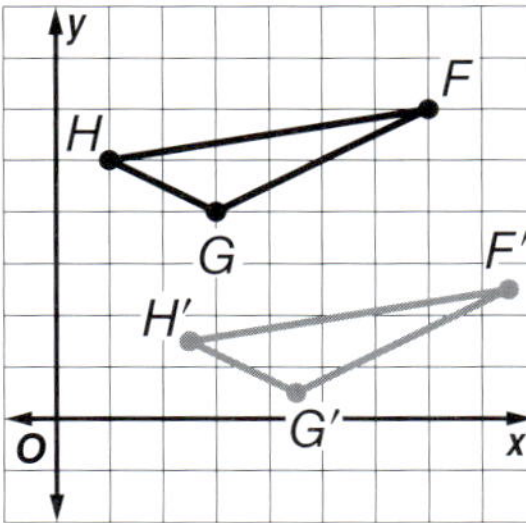

19. 5 units left and 3 units down; $(-5, -3)$ 21. 5 units right and 4 units up; (5, 4) 23. Transformation A is not a translation; the others are translations. 25. B 27. octagon 29. $2 \times 4 \times 3$ or 24 dinners 31. The range would be 62 instead of 55. 33. The range would be 8 instead of 6. 35. Sample answer: 0.567 37. Sample answer: 1.026 39. no 41. yes

Pages 560–562 **Lesson 10-10**

1. no 3. yes 5. $A'(5, -8)$, $B'(1, -2)$, and $C'(6, -4)$

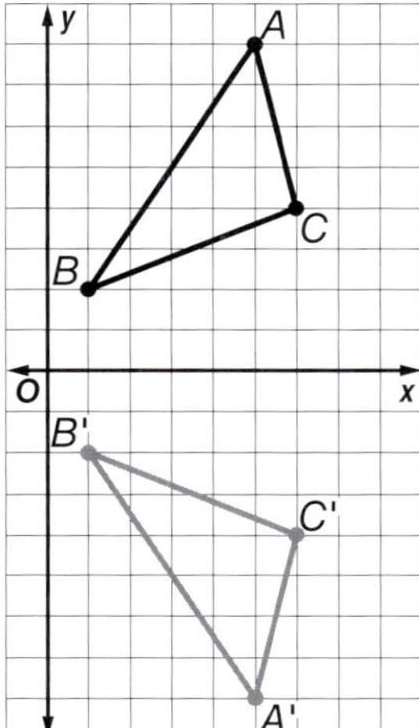

7. $Q'(-2, -5)$, $R'(-4, -5)$, and $S'(-2, 3)$

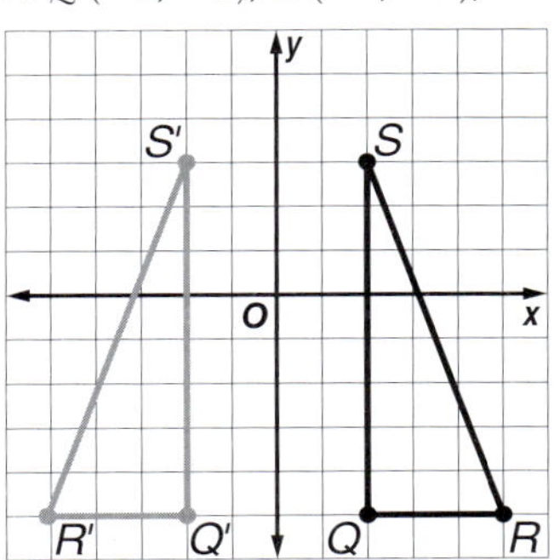

9. yes

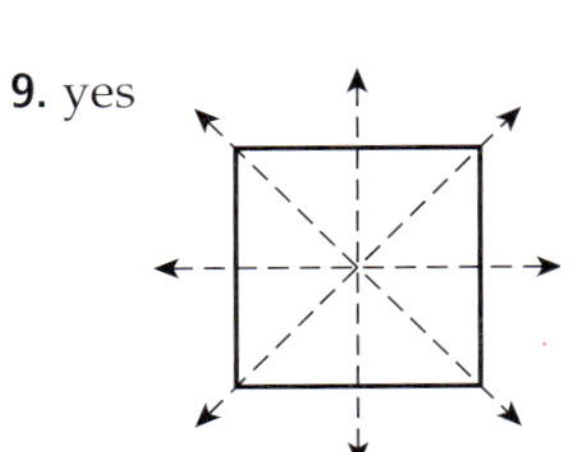

11. yes

13. yes

15. $T'(-6, 1)$, $U'(-2, 3)$, and $V'(5, 4)$

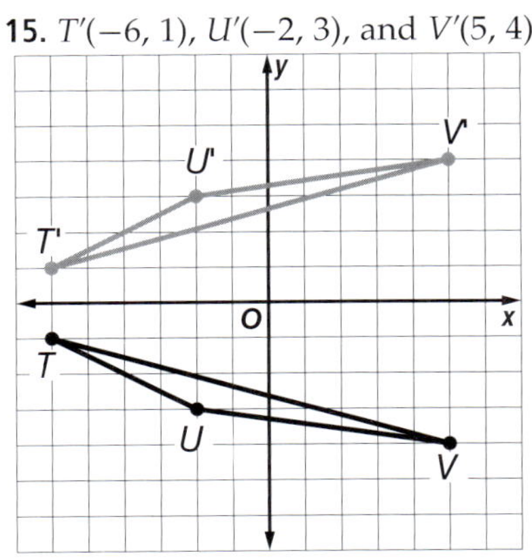

17. $A'(2, -4)$, $B'(-2, -4)$, $C'(2, -8)$, $D'(-2, -8)$

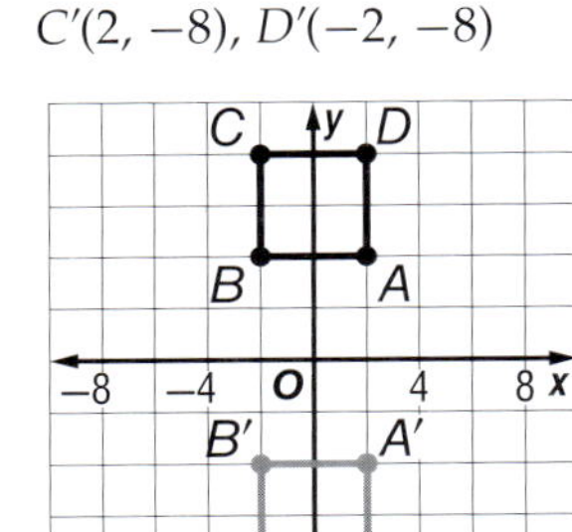

19. $R'(5, 3)$, $S'(4, -2)$, $T'(2, 3)$

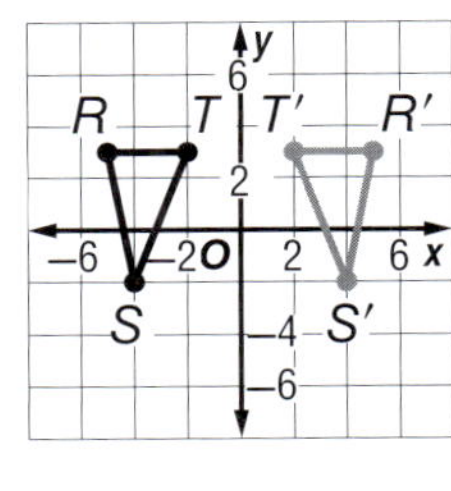

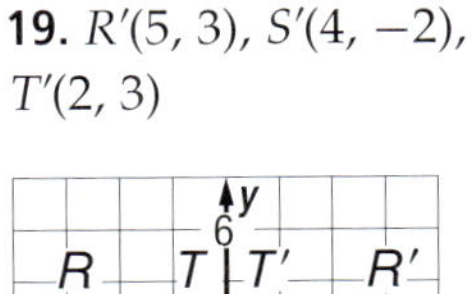

21. $H'(1, 3)$, $I'(1, -1)$, $J'(-2, -2)$, and $K'(-2, 2)$

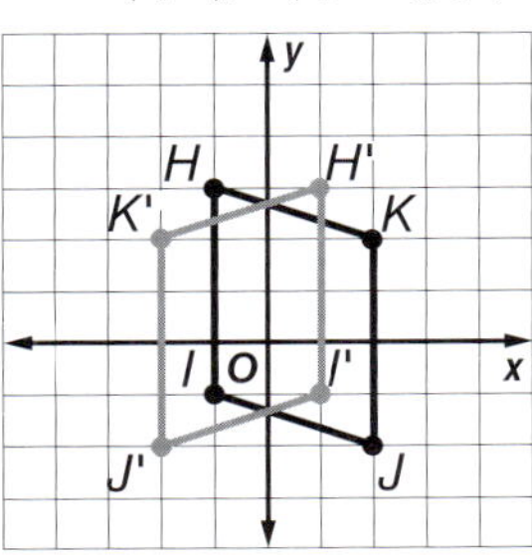

23. There is a line of symmetry vertically down the center of the picture. **25.** 1 **27.** figures *A* and *C* **29.** Sample answer; A reflection over the *y*-axis followed by a reflection over the *x*-axis.

31.

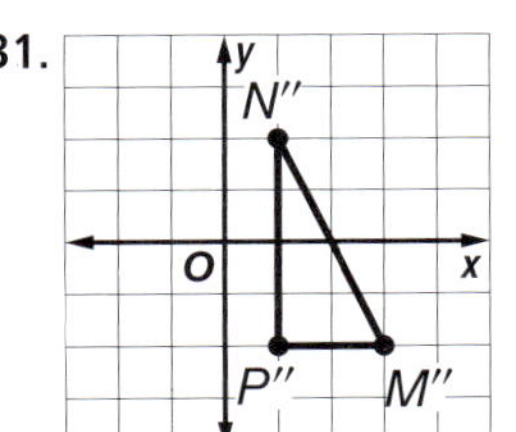

33. *x*-axis **35.** *y*-axis **37.** $J''(7, -4)$, $K''(-7, -1)$, and $L''(-2, 2)$ **39.** C

41. $F'(1, 6)$, $G'(3, 4)$, $H'(2, 1)$

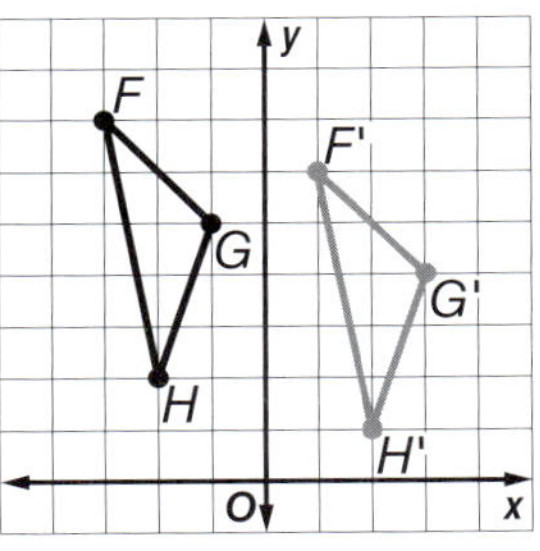

43. Sample answer: $\frac{1}{2} + 8 = 8\frac{1}{2}$ **45.** Sample answer: $12 \div 6 = 2$

Pages 563–566 Chapter 10 Study Guide and Review

1. false; supplementary angles **3.** false; acute angle **5.** false; $(-2, 1)$ **7.** $\angle 1$ and $\angle 4$; Sample answer: Since $\angle 1$ and $\angle 4$ are opposite angles formed by the intersection of two lines, they are vertical **9.** neither

11.

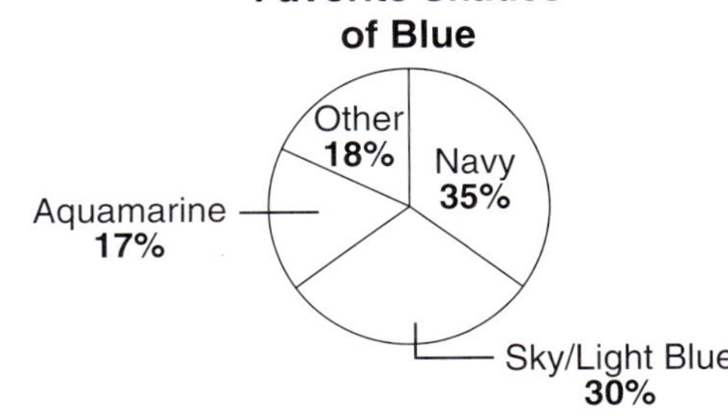

13. 45 **15.** right, isosceles **17.** parallelogram **19.** 10 cm **21.** 8m **23.** nonagon; regular

Selected Answers

25. $P'(-2, 1)$, $Q'(-8, 0)$, and $R'(-7, 9)$

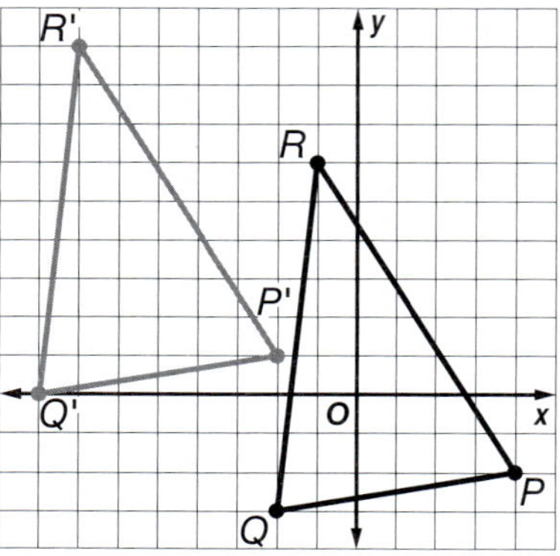

27. $P'(1, -2)$, $Q'(-5, -3)$, and $R'(-4, 6)$

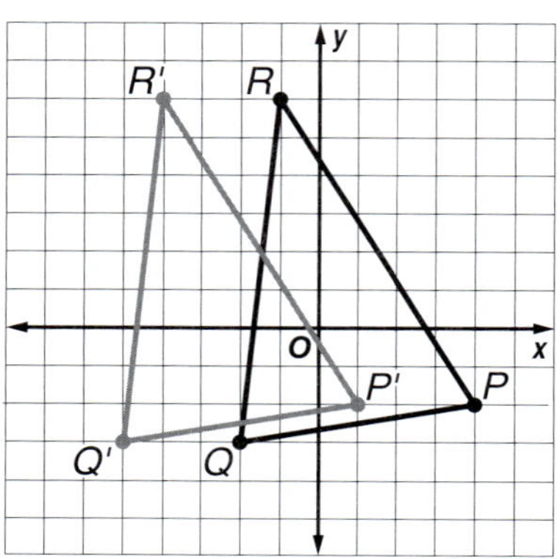

29. $R'(-1, -3)$, $S'(2, -6)$, and $T'(6, -1)$

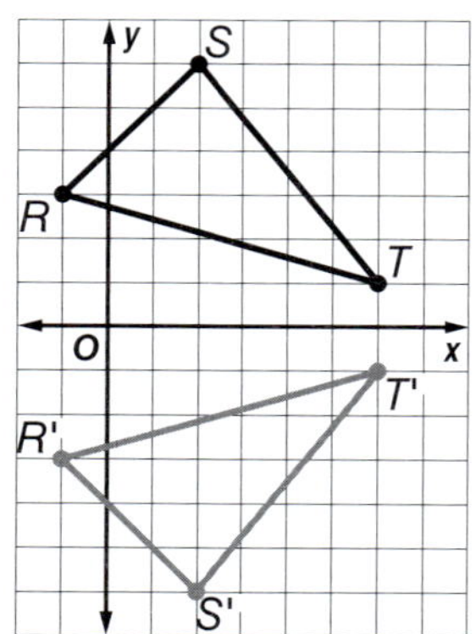

31. $E'(4, -2)$, $F'(-2, -2)$, $G'(-2, 5)$, $H'(4, -5)$

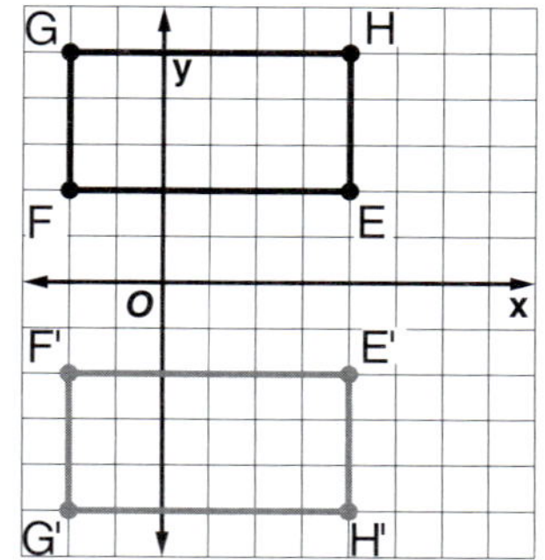

Chapter 11 Measurement: Two- and Three-Dimensional Figures

Page 571 Chapter 11 Getting Ready

1. 136 **3.** 1,248 **5.** 77 **7.** \$41.67 **9.** 121 **11.** 36 **13.** 12.6 **15.** 31.4 **17.** 254.5

Pages 574–576 Lesson 11-1

1. 135 cm^2 **3.** 17.5 in^2 **5.** 32 in^2 **7.** 60 cm^2 **9.** 0.2 cm^2 **11.** 49.5 yd^2 **13.** 190.625 m^2 **15.** 525 mm^2 **17.** 216 in^2 or 1.5 ft^2 **19.** 972 in^2 or 0.8 yd^2 **21.** 42,000 mi^2 **23.** 15 in. **25.** $11\frac{2}{3}$ ft^2 **27.** False; if the base and height are each doubled, then the area is $2b \cdot 2h = 4bh$, or 4 times greater. **29.** D **31.** $A'(2, 5)$, $B'(1, 2)$, $C'(4, 1)$

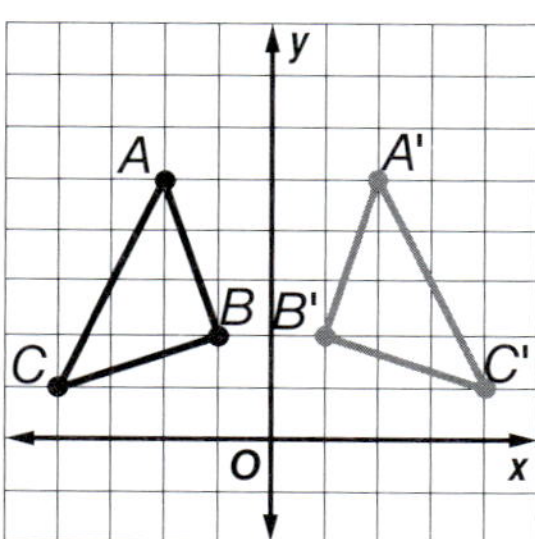

33. Sample answer: The sum of the measures of an octagon is 1,080°. Each angle measure is 1,080° ÷ 8 or 135°. Since 135 does not go into 360 evenly, an octagon does not tessellate the plane. **35.** 84 **37.** 19.5

Pages 580–582 Lesson 11-2

1. 6 in^2 **3.** 90.4 ft^2 **5.** 147 in^2 **7.** 4.5 cm^2 **9.** 183.7 in^2 **11.** about 95,000 mi^2 **13.** 125 ft **15.** Sample answer: 10 cm^2 **17.** Sample answer: 7 ft^2

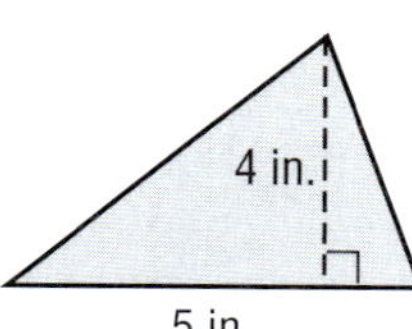

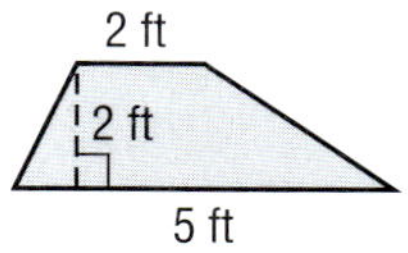

19. 6,500 ft^2 **21.** Sample answer: the ratio of the area is the square of the ratio of the bases. **23.** The area of a triangle is half the area of a parallelogram with the same base and height, because two of these triangles make up the parallelogram. **25.** 11,000 ft^2 **27.** $J'(-1, 4)$, $K'(1, -1)$, $L'(3, 2)$

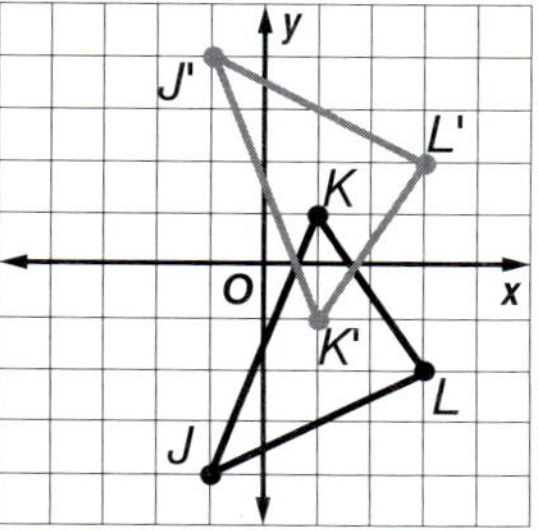

29. 25% **31.** 156.3 **33.** 91.1 **35.** 72.4

Pages 586–588 **Lesson 11-3**

1. 31.4 ft **3.** 44 m **5.** 67.2 cm **7.** 50.2 ft **9.** 22.6 cm **11.** 66 ft **13.** 33 in. **15.** 33.9 km **17.** $38\frac{1}{2}$ mi **19.** $28\frac{2}{7}$ in. **21.** 94.2 ft **23.** 11.0 in. **29.** 8.0 ft **31.** 4.8 yd **33.** Sample answer: Using the circumference formula, you find that the unicycle travels 3.14 • 10 • 2 or 62.8 inches on one revolution. So, in 5 revolutions, it will travel 62.8 • 5 or 314 inches. To change into feet, divide 314 by 12. So, the unicycle will travel $26\frac{1}{6}$ feet in 5 revolutions. **37.** Elsa; Logan incorrectly applied the formula that uses the diameter. **39.** Both will be doubled. If the value of x is doubled, the diameter will be $2x$ instead of x. The circumference will increase from $2\pi x$ to $2\pi(2x)$ to $4\pi x$. **41.** C **43.** B **45.** 3.7 ft^2 **47.** $\frac{15}{27}$ or $\frac{5}{9}$ **49.** 153.9 **51.** 63.6

Pages 591–593 **Lesson 11-4**

1. 78.5 cm^2 **3.** 201.1 m^2 **5.** B **7.** 28.3 in^2 **9.** 227.0 cm^2 **11.** 32.2 mm^2 **13.** 124.7 cm^2 **15.** 44.2 ft^2 **17.** 338.2 yd^2 **19.** 2,827.4 ft^2 **21.** Sample answer: $3 \cdot 6^2 = 108$ ft^2 **23.** 32; 60 **25.** about 50.3 cm^2 **27.** 29.0 m^2 **29.** 52,276.1 km^2 • 0.1 = 1,582.9 yd^2 **31.** 62.8 m^2 **33.** 103.5 cm^2 **35.** Sample answer: If the radius of a circular garden is 6 feet, how much room is there for gardening? about 113.1 ft^2 **37.** J **39.** 50.2 yd **41.** 120 in^2 **43.** 100.1 m^2 **45.** 113.04 **47.** 150.5

Pages 594–595 **Lesson 11-5**

1. Sample answer: Finding the areas of the separate geometric figures and then adding is easier than trying to find the area of the irregular figure as a whole.
3. Sample answer: Find the area of the wall below to determine how much paint to buy. To solve, find the area of the triangle and the area of the rectangle, then add. The answer is 77 ft^2.

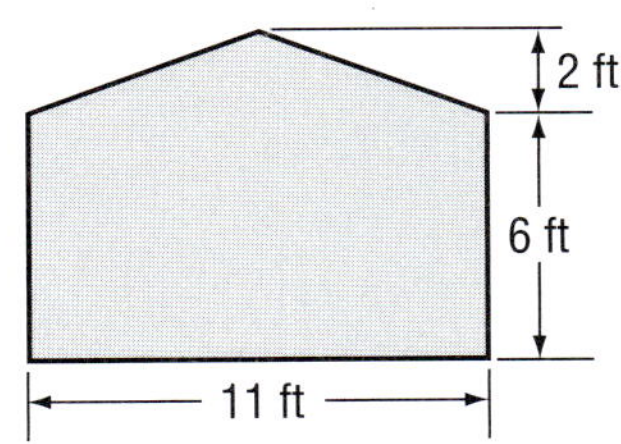

5. Sample answer: Asia, 17,251,712.4 mi^2; Africa, 11,616,153.02; N. America, 9,488,441.82 mi^2; S. America, 6,900,684.96 m^2; Antarctica, 5,118,008.012 mi^2; Europe, 3,852,882.436 mi^2; Australia/Oceania, 3,047,802,524 mi^2 **7.** B **9.** 175.84 ft^2

Pages 597–599 **Lesson 11-6**

1. 112 m^2 **3.** 145 m^2 **5.** 195 ft^2 **7.** 58.6 in^2 **9.** 257.1 mm^2 **11.** 66.2 yd^2 **13.** approximately 847.2 ft^2 **15.** 196.1 in^2 **17.** $x^2 + \frac{1}{2}(6x)$ or $x^2 + 3x$
19. 467.4 ÷ 350 ≈ 1.34; Since only whole gallons of paint can be purchased, you will need 2 gallons of paint. At \$20 each, the cost will be 2 • \$20 or \$40.
21. Sample answer: Add the areas of a small rectangle and a trapezoid. Area of a rectangle: 3 × 1 = 3; Area of trapezoid: $\left(\frac{1}{2} \times 6.5\,(4 + 5)\right) = 29.25$; 3 + 29.25 = 32.25. So, an approximate area is 32.25 = 2,400 or 77,400 mi^2.
23. B **25.** Sample answer: about 30% of \$500 or \$150
27. 452.2 in^2

29.  **31.**

Pages 605–606 **Lesson 11-7**

1. square; square pyramid **3.** circle; cylinder **5.** triangle; triangular pyramid **7.** rectangle; rectangular pyramid **9.** cone **11.** trapezoid; trapezoidal prism **13.** octagon; octagonal prism **15.** triangular prism and rectangular prism **17.** rectangular prism **19.** Sample answer: A cone has only one base that is a circle. A pyramid also has only one base, but its base is a polygon. They both have only one vertex. A cone does not have any lateral faces and a pyramid has at least three lateral faces. **21.** F **23.** 102.0 m^2 **25.** 53° **27.** square **29.** circle

Pages 610–612 **Lesson 11-8**

1. top side

front

3. top side front

5. top side front

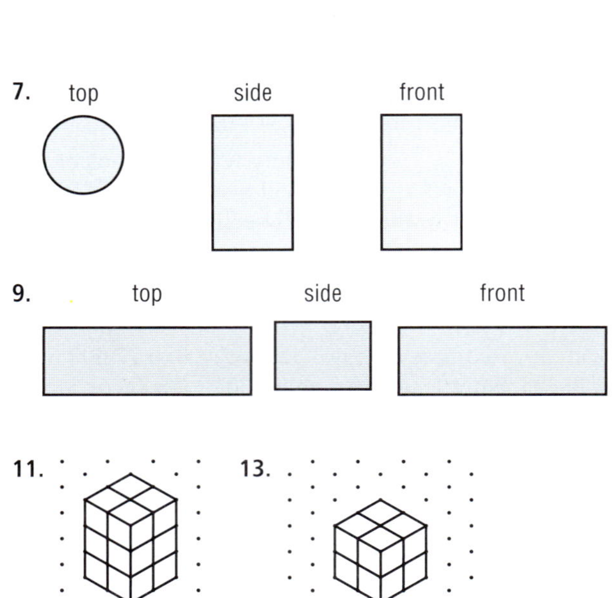

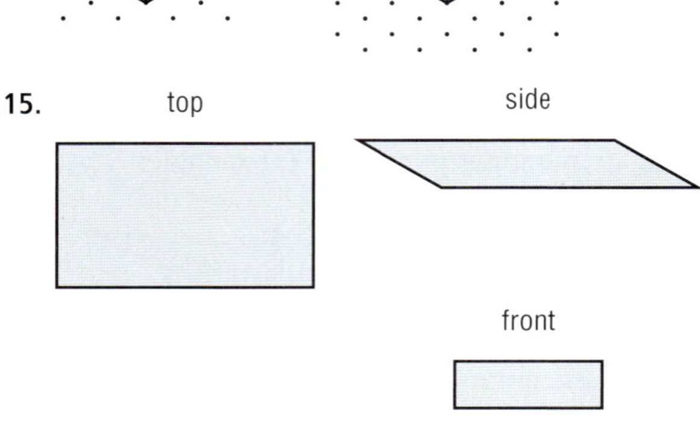

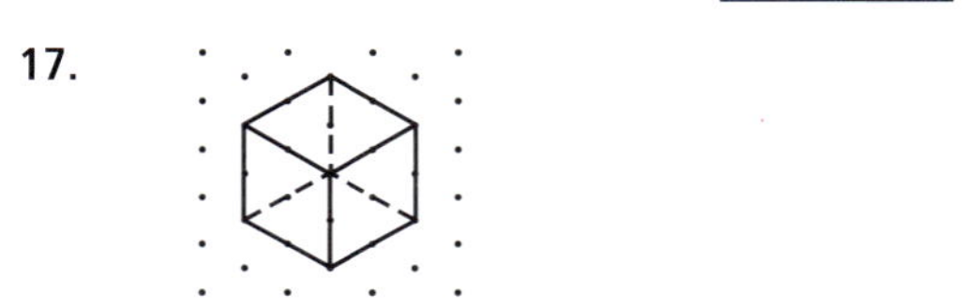

19. Sample answer:

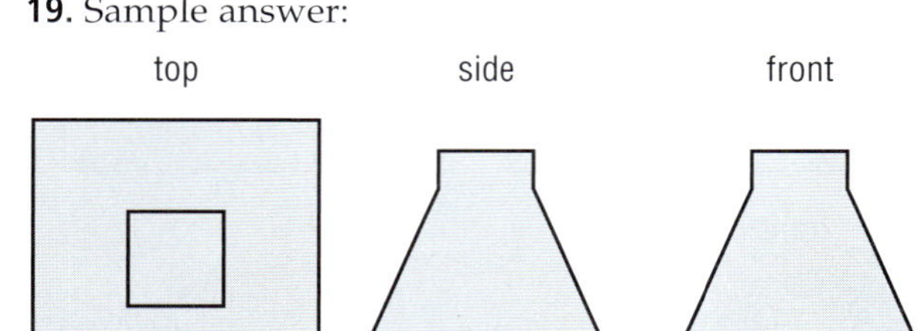

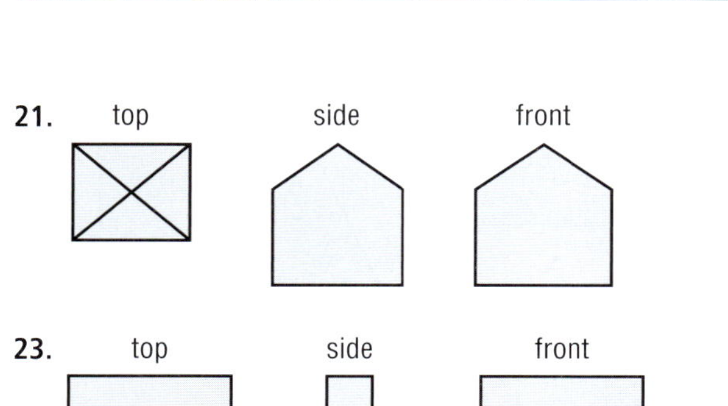

25. Sample answer:

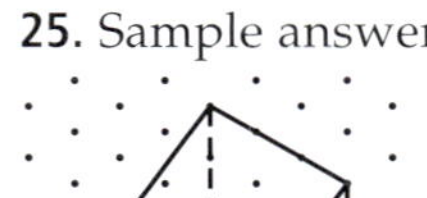

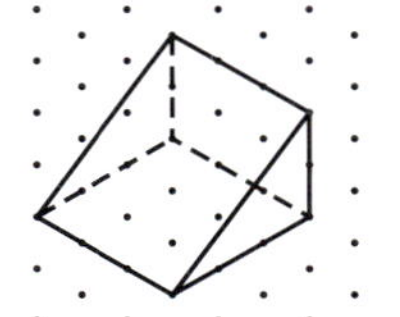

29. B **31.** sphere **33.** 96 ft^2 **35.** 112.8 in^2 **37.** \$77.39 **39.** 22 **41.** 68

Pages 616–618 ***Lesson 11-9***

1. 220 in^3 **3.** 63 yd^3 **5.** 37.5 ft^3 < 63 ft^3; second cabinet **7.** 90 ft^3 **9.** 236.3 cm^3 **11.** 108 m^3 **13.** 20.4 mm^3 **15.** 40 ft^3 > 36 ft^3, so too much was bought **17.** $166\frac{1}{4}$ yd^3 **19.** 2,157,165 ft^3 **21.** 306.52 = 19.4*h*; 15.8 *m* **23.** Sample answer: 5 × 4 × 2 or 40 ft^3 **25.** 6 ft **27.** No; the area of Prism A is 80 in^2, and the area of Prism B is 640 in^2, which is eight times greater. **29.** D

31.

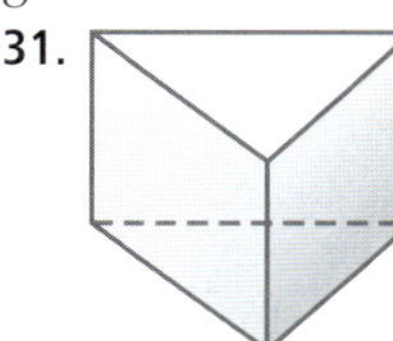

33. rectangle; rectangular prism **35.** 50 mph **37.** Sample answer: $5 \cdot 3^2$ or 45 **39.** Sample answer: $3 \cdot 2^2 \cdot 2$ or 24

Pages 620–623 ***Lesson 11-10***

1. 141.4 in^3 **3.** 617.7 ft^3 **5.** about 603.2 cm^3 **7.** 4,071.5 ft^3 **9.** 2,770.9 yd^3 **11.** 35.6 m^3 **13.** 103.4 m^3 **15.** 288.6 in^3 **17.** about 226.2 in^3 **19.** 124,642.7 m^3 **21.** d. **23.** a. **25.** 2,375 cm^3 **27.** 8 in. **29.** The volume is 8 times greater than the previous cylinder.
31. Sample answer:

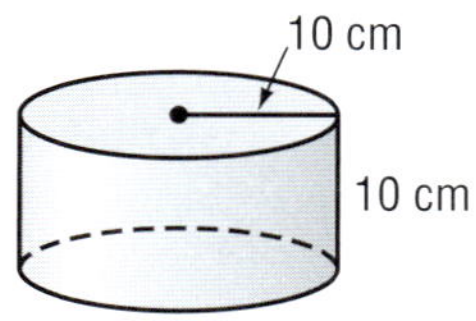

33. 1 to 4 **35.** D **37.** 152.9 m^3
39. Sample answer:

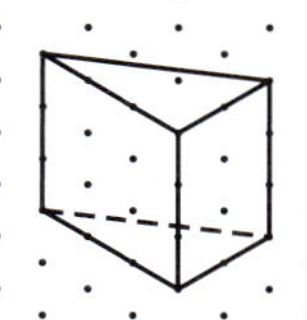

41. $\frac{1}{4}$ **43.** $\frac{5}{12}$

Pages 626–630 ***Chapter 11*** ***Study Guide and Review***

1. rectangular prism **3.** trapezoid **5.** cylinder **7.** circle **9.** 2,520 in^2 **11.** 36 ft^2 **13.** 527.3 yd^2 **15.** 75.4 in. **17.** $26\frac{2}{5}$ ft **19.** 29.8 ft **21.** 1,520.5 cm^2 **23.** 800 cakes **25.** \$105 **27.** 67.8 yd^2 **29.** triangle; triangular prism **31.** cylinder **33.** rectangular pyramid

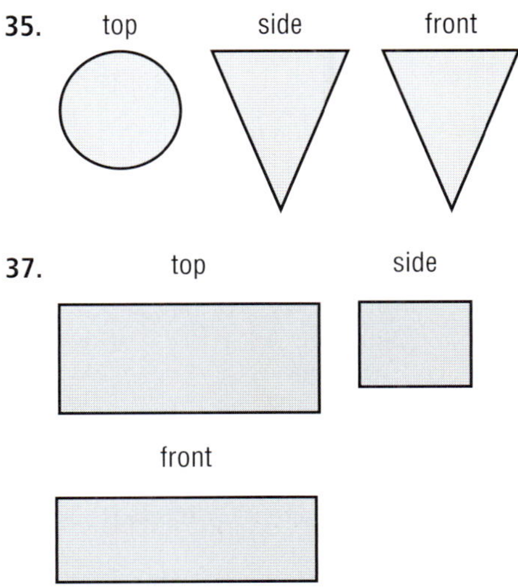

39. 639.6 in^3 **41.** 1,330 ft^3 **43.** 3,728.7 mm^3 **45.** 942 $in.^3$

Chapter 12 Geometry and Measurement

Page 635 Chapter 12 Getting Ready

1. 16 **3.** 169 **5.** 89 **7.** 225 **9.** 130 yr **11.** 226 **13.** 42.1 **15.** 527.8

Pages 637–639 Lesson 12-1

1. 6 **3.** 9 **5.** 2.6 **7.** 7.1 **9.** 10 ft **11.** 4 **13.** 8 **15.** 11 **17.** 20 **19.** 2.8 **21.** 9.4 **23.** 23.9 **25.** 52.9 **27.** 6 **29.** 50 **31.** 81 **33.** 0.7 **35.** 1.7 **37.** 3.8 **39.** 3.17 cm **43.** Sample answer: 17, 18, 19 **45.** 2 **47.** 5 **49.** It cannot be written as a fraction. **51.** G **53.** 28.3 in^3 **55.** acute **57.** obtuse **59.** 74 **61.** 16

Pages 643–645 Lesson 12-2

1. 26 mm **3.** 18.5 cm **5.** 4.0 ft **7.** 16.1 m **9.** 14.1 m **11.** 5.4 ft **13.** 2.8 yd **15.** 25 in. **17.** 5.6 mi **19.** 72.1 in. **21.** Sample answer: The plank will not fit horizontally or vertically. However, the diagonal of the doorway measures about 18 feet. So, the plank will fit through the doorway if you tilt it diagonally. **23.** about 10.4 in. **27.** G **29.** 1,413 in^3 **31.** 0.08 **33.** 2.65

Pages 646–647 Lesson 12-3

1. Sample answer: making a model helps you see what is happening in the problem to help solve it. **3.** 8 cars and 4 motorcycles **5.** 47 in. **7.** $5\frac{1}{3}$ min **9.** Sample answer: The boxes could be arranged on the shelf 4 boxes wide and 5 boxes deep. **11.** $125\frac{7}{16}$ ft^2 **13.** 6 DVDs

Pages 651–653 Lesson 12-4

1. 108 ft^2 **3.** Yes; the surface area of the box is 252 in^2. The surface area of the paper is 288 in^2. Since 252 in^2 < 288 in^2, she has enough paper. **5.** 314 cm^2 **7.** 833.1 mm^2 **9.** 125.4 in^2 or $124\frac{3}{8}$ in^2 **11.** 234 in^2 **13.** 243.8 ft^2 **15.** 64.5 in^2 **17.** $s = 6x^2$ **19.** Sample answer: Not all sides of the rectangular prism will be painted. The top will not be painted. The number of square feet to be painted is (18)(12) + 2(18)(6) + 2(12)(6). **21.** Surface area measures the area of the faces, and area is measured in square units. **23.** G **25.** 12.4 ft **27.** 804.2 ft^2 **29.** 145.3 yd^2

Pages 657–659 Lesson 12-5

1. 88.0 mm^2 **3.** about 471.2 m^2 **5.** 1,215.8 m^2 **7.** 272.0 mm^2 **9.** 1,120.0 in^2 or $1{,}119\frac{44}{45}$ in^2 **11.** 61.3 cm^2 **13.** Sample answer: $2 \cdot 3 \cdot 4^2 + 2 \cdot 3 \cdot 4 \cdot 4$ or 192 m^2 **15.** 205.0 in^2 **17.** No; the surface area of the side of the cylinder will double, but the area of the bases will not. **19.** A cylinder with radius 6 cm and height 3 cm has a greater surface area than a cylinder with height 6 cm and radius 3 cm; Sample answer: The first cylinder has a surface area of 339.3 cm^2 while the second cylinder has a surface area of 169.6 cm^2. **21.** G **23.** 112 cm^2 **25.** 12.8 in. **27.** 7.2 cm

Pages 660–662 Chapter 12 Study Guide and Review

1. false; right triangle **3.** true **5.** true **7.** false; positive and negative **9.** false; cylinder **11.** 2 **13.** 7 **15.** 4 **17.** 7.8 **19.** 21.1 **21.** 11 ft **23.** 26.7 in. **25.** 29.8 ft **27.** 875 in^2 **29.** 202 yd^2 **31.** 43 ft^2 **33.** 2,261.9 in^2

Index

Index

Index

N

P

Index

Index

Index

Index

Symbols

Number and Operations

$+$	plus or positive
$-$	minus or negative
$a \cdot b$, $a \times b$, ab or $a(b)$	a times b
$\div$	divided by
$\pm$	plus or minus
$=$	is equal to
$\neq$	is not equal to
$>$	is greater than
$<$	is less than
$\geq$	is greater than or equal to
$\leq$	is less than or equal to
$\approx$	is approximately equal to
%	percent
$a:b$	the ratio of a to b, or $\frac{a}{b}$
$0.7\overline{5}$	repeating decimal 0.75555...

Algebra and Functions

$-a$	opposite or additive inverse of a
a^n	a to the nth power
a^{-n}	$\frac{1}{a^n}$
$\|x\|$	absolute value of x
$\sqrt{x}$	principal (positive) square root of x
$f(n)$	function, f of n

Geometry and Measurement

$\cong$	is congruent to
$\sim$	is similar to
$\circ$	degree(s)
$\overleftrightarrow{AB}$	line AB
$\overrightarrow{AB}$	ray AB
$\overline{AB}$	line segment AB
AB	length of $\overline{AB}$
∟	right angle
$\perp$	is perpendicular to
$\parallel$	is parallel to
$\angle A$	angle A
$m\angle A$	measure of angle A
$\triangle ABC$	triangle ABC
(a, b)	ordered pair with x-coordinate a and y-coordinate b
O	origin
π	pi $\left(\text{approximately } 3.14 \text{ or } \frac{22}{7}\right)$

Probability and Statistics

$P(A)$	probability of event A

Formulas

Perimeter	square	$P = 4s$
	rectangle	$P = 2\ell + 2w$ or $P = 2(\ell + w)$
Circumference	circle	$C = 2\pi r$ or $C = \pi d$
Area	square	$A = s^2$
	rectangle	$A = \ell w$
	parallelogram	$A = bh$
	triangle	$A = \frac{1}{2}bh$
	trapezoid	$A = \frac{1}{2}h(b_1 + b_2)$
	circle	$A = \pi r^2$
Surface Area	cube	$S = 6s^2$
	rectangular prism	$S = 2\ell w + 2\ell h + 2wh$
	cylinder	$S = 2\pi rh + 2\pi r^2$
Volume	cube	$V = s^3$
	prism	$V = \ell wh$ or Bh
	cylinder	$V = \pi r^2 h$ or Bh
	pyramid	$V = \frac{1}{3}Bh$
	cone	$V = \frac{1}{3}\pi r^2 h$ or $\frac{1}{3}Bh$
Pythagorean Theorem	right triangle	$a^2 + b^2 = c^2$
Temperature	Fahrenheit to Celsius	$C = \frac{5}{9}(F - 32)$
	Celsius to Fahrenheit	$F = \frac{9}{5}C + 32$

Measurement Conversions

Length	1 kilometer (km) = 1,000 meters (m) 1 meter = 100 centimeters (cm) 1 centimeter = 10 millimeters (mm)	1 foot (ft) = 12 inches (in.) 1 yard (yd) = 3 feet or 36 inches 1 mile (mi) = 1,760 yards or 5,280 feet
Volume and Capacity	1 liter (L) = 1,000 milliliters (mL) 1 kiloliter (kL) = 1,000 liters	1 cup (c) = 8 fluid ounces (fl oz) 1 pint (pt) = 2 cups 1 quart (qt) = 2 pints 1 gallon (gal) = 4 quarts
Weight and Mass	1 kilogram (kg) = 1,000 grams (g) 1 gram = 1,000 milligrams (mg) 1 metric ton = 1,000 kilograms	1 pound (lb) = 16 ounces (oz) 1 ton (T) = 2,000 pounds
Time	1 minute (min) = 60 seconds (s) 1 hour (h) = 60 minutes 1 day (d) = 24 hours	1 week (wk) = 7 days 1 year (yr) = 12 months (mo) or 52 weeks or 365 days 1 leap year = 366 days
Metric to Customary	1 meter ≈ 39.37 inches 1 kilometer ≈ 0.62 mile 1 centimeter ≈ 0.39 inch	1 kilogram ≈ 2.2 pounds 1 gram ≈ 0.035 ounce 1 liter ≈ 1.057 quarts